W9-ATD-116

LET'S GO

■ THE RESOURCE FOR THE INDEPENDENT TRAVELER

"The guides are aimed not only at young budget travelers but at the indepedent traveler; a sort of streetwise cookbook for traveling alone."

—The New York Times

"Unbeatable; good sight-seeing advice; up-to-date info on restaurants, hotels, and inns; a commitment to money-saving travel; and a wry style that brightens nearly every page."

—The Washington Post

"Lighthearted and sophisticated, informative and fun to read. [Let's Go] helps the novice traveler navigate like a knowledgeable old hand."

—Atlanta Journal-Constitution

"A world-wise traveling companion—always ready with friendly advice and helpful hints, all sprinkled with a bit of wit."

—The Philadelphia Inquirer

■ THE BEST TRAVEL BARGAINS IN YOUR PRICE RANGE

"All the dirt, dirt cheap."

—People

"Anything you need to know about budget traveling is detailed in this book."

—The Chicago Sun-Times

"Let's Go follows the creed that you don't have to toss your life's savings to the wind to travel—unless you want to."

—The Salt Lake Tribune

■ REAL ADVICE FOR REAL EXPERIENCES

"The writers seem to have experienced every rooster-packed bus and lunar-surfaced mattress about which they write."

—The New York Times

"A guide should tell you what to expect from a destination. Here Let's Go shines."

—The Chicago Tribune

"[Let's Go's] devoted updaters really walk the walk (and thumb the ride, and trek the trail). Learn how to fish, haggle, find work—anywhere."

—Food & Wine

LET'S GO PUBLICATIONS

TRAVEL GUIDES

Alaska 1st edition **NEW TITLE**
Australia 2004
Austria & Switzerland 2004
Brazil 1st edition **NEW TITLE**
Britain & Ireland 2004
California 2004
Central America 8th edition
Chile 1st edition
China 4th edition
Costa Rica 1st edition
Eastern Europe 2004
Egypt 2nd edition
Europe 2004
France 2004
Germany 2004
Greece 2004
Hawaii 2004
India & Nepal 8th edition
Ireland 2004
Israel 4th edition
Italy 2004
Japan 1st edition **NEW TITLE**
Mexico 20th edition
Middle East 4th edition
New Zealand 6th edition
Pacific Northwest 1st edition **NEW TITLE**
Peru, Ecuador & Bolivia 3rd edition
Puerto Rico 1st edition **NEW TITLE**
South Africa 5th edition
Southeast Asia 8th edition
Southwest USA 3rd edition
Spain & Portugal 2004
Thailand 1st edition
Turkey 5th edition
USA 2004
Western Europe 2004

CITY GUIDES

Amsterdam 3rd edition
Barcelona 3rd edition
Boston 4th edition
London 2004
New York City 2004
Paris 2004
Rome 12th edition
San Francisco 4th edition
Washington, D.C. 13th edition

MAP GUIDES

Amsterdam
Berlin
Boston
Chicago
Dublin
Florence
Hong Kong
London
Los Angeles
Madrid
New Orleans
New York City
Paris
Prague
Rome
San Francisco
Seattle
Sydney
Venice
Washington, D.C.

COMING SOON:
Road Trip USA

AUSTRALIA
2004

AMELIA LESTER EDITOR
TOR KREVER ASSOCIATE EDITOR
ERIN PROBST ASSOCIATE EDITOR

RESEARCHER-WRITERS
TIMMY BOULEY
AMY CAIN
SARA A. CLARK
JANE A. LINDHOLM
SCOTT ROY
SHAWN SNYDER
JOSHUA J. VANDIVER
MARC A. WALLENSTEIN
KEVIN YIP

CHRISTINE C. YOKOYAMA MAP EDITOR
JESSE REID ANDREWS MANAGING EDITOR

ST. MARTIN'S PRESS ✹ NEW YORK

HELPING LET'S GO If you want to share your discoveries, suggestions, or corrections, please drop us a line. We read every piece of correspondence, whether a postcard, a 10-page email, or a coconut. **Address mail to:**

> **Let's Go: Australia**
> **67 Mount Auburn Street**
> **Cambridge, MA 02138**
> **USA**

Visit Let's Go at **http://www.letsgo.com,** or send email to:

> **feedback@letsgo.com**
> **Subject: "Let's Go: Australia"**

In addition to the invaluable travel advice our readers share with us, many are kind enough to offer their services as researchers or editors. Unfortunately, our charter enables us to employ only currently enrolled Harvard students.

Maps by David Lindroth copyright © 2004 by St. Martin's Press.

Distributed outside the USA and Canada by Macmillan.

ISBN: 0-312-31977-0

First edition
10 9 8 7 6 5 4 3 2 1

Let's Go: Australia is written by Let's Go Publications, 67 Mount Auburn Street, Cambridge, MA 02138 USA.

Let's Go® and the LG logo are trademarks of Let's Go, Inc.
Printed in the USA.

HOW TO USE THIS BOOK

ORGANIZATION. Australia has six states and two territories. Each chapter of this book corresponds to a state or territory of Australia and begins with information on that region or state's capital city. The chapters are listed in alphabetical order. The black tabs on the side of the book should help you navigate your way through.

PRICE RANGES & RANKINGS. Our researchers list establishments in order of value, with the best listed first. Look out for great value establishments with Big Splurge and Hidden Deal features. Our absolute favorites are denoted by the Let's Go thumbs-up (📖). Since the best value does not always mean the cheapest price, we have incorporated a system of price ranges in the guide. Symbols are based on the lowest cost for one person, excluding special deals or prices. Many accommodations in Australia offer a range of lodging all in one locale. Read listings carefully, as accommodations listed as ❶ may offer higher-range options as well. Sydney has accommodation and food price diversity charts to aid in planning. The table below outlines our price diversity scheme, listed in Australian dollars.

AUSTRALIA	❶	❷	❸	❹	❺
ACCOMMODATIONS	under $15	$16-25	$26-40	$41-60	over $60
FOOD	under $10	$11-15	$16-20	$21-25	over $25

PHONE CODES & TELEPHONE NUMBERS. Area codes for each city or town appear opposite the name of the city or town and are denoted by the ☎ icon. Phone numbers in text are also preceded by the ☎ icon.

PLANNING YOUR ITINERARY. For a rough idea of where to go and how much time you'll need, check out our Things to Do and Suggested Itineraries in the Discover section (p. 5), as well as temperature charts in the Appendix (p. 748). The Great Outdoors (p. 72) will help you make the most of Australia's stunningly diverse natural landscape. For longer stays, Alternatives to Tourism (p. 62) has lots of ideas on volunteering, studying, and working your way around Australia.

GETTING AROUND. Public transportation options are listed in tables for major hubs; for all other cities and towns, "(duration, price)" is noted after each destination listing. Due to the sheer distances involved in travel within Australia, most travelers find that a car is essential for getting around. Essentials (p. 52) has information on renting and buying cars, as well as insurance options. The Great Outdoors (p. 80) has important safety information for outback driving.

AUSTRALIA EXPLAINED. Learn about Australia's history and culture in Life and Times (p. 9) and talk like a local with a 'Strine glossary in the Appendix (p. 746). There's information on Australian flora and fauna in the Great Outdoors (p. 72). And you can get informed about Australian politics (p. 100) and indigenous history (p. 22) with our in-depth scholarly articles. Also look out for In Recent News features, scattered throughout the book.

A NOTE TO OUR READERS The information for this book was gathered by *Let's Go* researchers from May through August of 2003. Each listing is based on one researcher's opinion, formed during his or her visit at a particular time. Those traveling at other times may have different experiences since prices, dates, hours, and conditions are always subject to change. You are urged to check the facts presented in this book beforehand to avoid inconvenience and surprises.

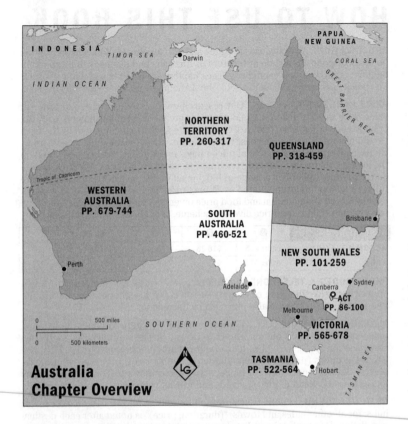

Australia
Chapter Overview

INDONESIA
TIMOR SEA
INDIAN OCEAN
Darwin
PAPUA NEW GUINEA
CORAL SEA
GREAT BARRIER REEF

NORTHERN TERRITORY
PP. 260-317

QUEENSLAND
PP. 318-459

Tropic of Capricorn

WESTERN AUSTRALIA
PP. 679-744

SOUTH AUSTRALIA
PP. 460-521

Brisbane

Perth

NEW SOUTH WALES
PP. 101-259

Adelaide
Canberra
Sydney
ACT
PP. 86-100

Melbourne

0   500 miles
0   500 kilometers

SOUTHERN OCEAN

VICTORIA
PP. 565-678

TASMANIA
PP. 522-564
Hobart

TASMAN SEA

MAP LEGEND

■	Point of Interest	∧	Cave	℞	Pharmacy	Beach
	Accommodations		Church		Police	Park
▲	Camping		Consulate	✉	Post Office	Building
	Food	⚓	Ferry Landing	▲	Ranger Station	Water
★	Nightlife	❀	Garden		Restrooms	4WD Road
	Shopping		Golf Course		Shipwreck	Ferry Line
	Winery	✚	Hospital		Synagogue	Pedestrian Zone
	Adult Entertainment		Internet Café	☎	Telephone Office	Railroad
✈	Airport		Library		Theater	State Boundary
$	Bank		Lighthouse	ⓘ	Tourist Office	Unsealed Road
	Beach	▲▲	Mountain		Train Station	Walking Trail
	Bus Station		Museum	∬	Waterfall	The Let's Go compass always points NORTH.

CONTENTS

MAPS

RESEARCHER-WRITERS

Timmy Bouley *Northern Queensland*

We have no doubt that Timmy was a great explorer of exotic lands in a past life. A true adventurer right down to his sun-bleached roots, Mr. Bouley braved the wild waters of far north Queensland with a seemingly never-ending supply of good humor and grace. Ever modest, Timmy may attribute his daring river-crossings to a trusty snorkel-equipped 4WD, but we know better. Paul Hogan, move over: here's a genuine Crocodile Dundee.

Amy Cain *Sydney & Surrounds*

Busting out of the office to try her moves on the dance floor down under, the former editor of *Let's Go: Europe* taught the Aussies how to bump and grind. Between befriending drag queens and leaping from planes, Amy produced copy to make even the most pedantic of editors rejoice. Now tackling a career in architecture with equal tenacity, Amy's future is as sparkling as Sydney Harbour on a sunny day.

Sara A. Clark *Southern Queensland*

We're not sure whether Sara was more charmed by the Sunshine Coast or the Sunshine Coast was more charmed by Sara. One thing's certain: Sara's boots were made for walking—all over Queensland. Whether staving off dingoes on Fraser Island, braving the local brew in Bundaberg, or raving alongside globe-trotting millionaires at Surfers Paradise, this veteran researcher of *Let's Go: California* is truly one in a million.

Jane A. Lindholm *South Australia & the Great Ocean Road*

Sleeping outdoors en route, Jane awoke to find a mouse making a nest in her hair. Undeterred by such intrusions from furry foes, however, this aspiring anthropologist soldiered on. With *Let's Go* experience including work on the guides to *Central America*, *Mexico*, *Spain & Portugal*, and the first edition of *Chile*, Jane surprised no one with an innate ability to negotiate both the Oondatta track and free jacuzzi jaunts producing flawless copy all the while.

Scott Roy *Northern Territory & the Kimberley*

After his triumphant conquest of the wild west for last year's edition of *Let's Go: Australia*, Scott came back hungry for more Antipodean adventuring. This time his penchant for wide open spaces led Scott to the vast red center, where a temperamental laptop did little to hinder his pursuit of meticulous coverage. Ever evasive of tired tourist traps, this avid evolutionary biologist sought out the authentic Outback with nary a hairy moment along the way.

Shawn Snyder *New South Wales & Canberra*

Following a stint on America's west coast for *Let's Go: San Francisco*, Shawn embraced Australia's east coast in one of his legendary bear hugs and won the heart of even the most rugged of locals with his perpetual good humor and warmth. Guitar and smile permanently in tow, Shawn demonstrated an astonishing eye for local color and significant details—traits which will serve him well in his next career as a folk-inspired singer-songwriter.

Joshua J. Vandiver   *Central & Southern Western Australia*

Anyone who says renaissance men are a myth has obviously never encountered the ever-versatile Josh. This Colorado-bred classics scholar was impressed by both the wildflowers and wind-swept terrain of Australia's far western reaches. Back in the office, we were continually amazed with Josh's ability to go beyond the basic service of a researcher-writer to diligently dig for local legends and ripping yarns.

Marc A. Wallenstein   *Victoria & Arnhem Land*

Is there any end to Marc's talents? While in Australia, Marc not only produced innovative copy for *Let's Go*, but also pursued an independent photography project as well as tutored for the School of the Air. This former researcher for *Italy 2000* and *Hawaii 2003* and editor for *Italy 2001* is now hitting the books at the University of Chicago Law School, but with his chronic case of the travel bug, we suspect Marc's passport won't lie dormant for long.

Kevin Yip   *Tasmania & Southeastern Victoria*

With a bevy of Let's Go work to his credit—as a researcher for *USA* and *California*, editor for *USA 2001*, and countless hours logged as new media manager—Kevin was undaunted by Tasmania's wilderness and Victoria's chilly climes. Thriving on open spaces and fresh air, Kevin upped the ante on outdoors coverage while waxing lyrical on the joys of meat pies. Australia's southernmost regions were a match made in heaven for this gourmand outdoorsman.

CONTRIBUTING WRITERS

Andrew Leigh is a Ph.D. student at the John F. Kennedy School of Government at Harvard University. He has served as a policy advisor to the Australian senate and is the co-editor of *The Prince's New Clothes: Why do Australians Dislike Their Politicians?*

Tim Rowse works in the History Program, Research School of Social Sciences at the Australian National University. His publications on Australian history include studies of colonial policy in Central Australia and a biography of H.C. Coombs.

ABOUT LET'S GO

GUIDES FOR THE INDEPENDENT TRAVELER

Budget travel is more than a vacation. At *Let's Go*, we see every trip as the chance of a lifetime. If your dream is to grab a knapsack and a machete and forge through the jungles of Brazil, we can take you there. Or, if you'd rather enjoy the Riviera sun at a beachside cafe, we'll set you a table. If you know what you're doing, you can have any experience you want—whether it's camping among lions or sampling Tuscan desserts—without maxing out your credit card. We'll show you just how far your coins can go, and prove that the greatest limitation on your adventure is not your wallet, but your imagination. That said, we understand that you may want the occasional indulgence after a week of hostels and kebab stands, so we've added "Big Splurges" to let you know which establishments are worth those extra euros, as well as price ranges to help you quickly determine whether an accommodation or restaurant will break the bank. While we may have diversified, our emphasis will always be on finding the best values for your budget, giving you all the info you need to spend six days in London or six months in Tasmania.

BEYOND THE TOURIST EXPERIENCE

We write for travelers who know there's more to a vacation than riding double-deckers with tourists. Our researchers give you the heads-up on both world-renowned and lesser-known attractions, on the best local eats and the hottest nightclub beats. In our travels, we talk to everybody; we provide a snapshot of real life in the places you visit with our sidebars on topics like regional cuisine, local festivals, and hot political issues. We've opened our pages to respected writers and scholars to show you their take on a given destination, and turned to lifelong residents to learn the little things that make their city worth calling home. And we've even given you Alternatives to Tourism—ideas for how to give back to local communities through responsible travel and volunteering.

OVER FORTY YEARS OF WISDOM

When we started, way back in 1960, Let's Go consisted of a small group of well-traveled friends who compiled their budget travel tips into a 20-page packet for students on charter flights to Europe. Since then, we've expanded to suit all kinds of travelers, now publishing guides to six continents, including our newest guides: *Let's Go: Japan* and *Let's Go: Brazil*. Our guides are still annually researched and written entirely by students on shoe-string budgets, adventurous travelers who know that train strikes, stolen luggage, food poisoning, and marriage proposals are all part of a day's work. Even as you read this, work on next year's editions is well underway. Whether you're reading one of our new titles, like *Let's Go: Puerto Rico* or *Let's Go Adventure Guide: Alaska*, or our original best-seller, *Let's Go: Europe*, you'll find the same spirit of adventure that has made *Let's Go* the guide of choice for travelers the world over since 1960.

GETTING IN TOUCH

The best discoveries are often those you make yourself; on the road, when you find something worth sharing, please drop us a line. We're Let's Go Publications, 67 Mt. Auburn St., Cambridge, MA 02138, USA (feedback@letsgo.com).

For more info, visit our website: www.letsgo.com.

ACKNOWLEDGMENTS

Australia Thanks: World's best RWs, our tireless ME Jesse, Christine, Team USA, Prod, Nitin, Matt, Michael & Jill Lester, Vicki Miller.

Amelia Thanks: Tor, for your complete competence and courage under fire; Erin, for your amazing dedication and unfailing positive attitude; Jesse, for your guidance and support; Jeremy, Mac and Kristin, for an incredible summer in the office; Dunia and Tabby, for big late night convos; Emma, for a good tan and a great time; Ashley, for lattes and sympathy; Julia, for being my bestest friend; and my parents, for absolutely everything.

Tor Thanks: Amelia, for we all try, but she succeeds; Erin, here's looking at you kid; Clay, for showing that the problems of Team AUS didn't amount to a hill of beans; Christina, for the beginning of a beautiful friendship; Jeremy, a drunkard and a citizen of the world; Mac, for letting me win at roulette; Kristin, who remembers every detail; and Jim, who, somehow, just because he despises me, is the only one I trust. We'll always have Australia.

Erin Thanks: Amelia, for leadership, vision, and grace; Tor, for format wizardry, organization, and laughs; USA, for their bid in the custody battle; my Bostonians, for making every moment count; Haggo, for rocking my world; Lyons Ave., for Bob, Laur, and Ike; and my family, for being the reason this smile will never fade.

Christine Thanks: Amelia, Tor, and Erin for quick and efficient edits; my roommates for listening to me complain and worrying about me; and my mom, dad, and brother for always being supportive and for everything in general.

LET'S GO

Editor
Amelia Lester
Associate Editors
Tor Krever, Erin Probst
Map Editor
Christine C. Yokoyama
Managing Editor
Jesse Reid Andrews
Typesetter
Ankur Ghosh

Publishing Director
Julie A. Stephens
Editor-in-Chief
Jeffrey Dubner
Production Manager
Dusty Lewis
Cartography Manager
Nathaniel Brooks
Design Manager
Caleb Beyers
Editorial Managers
Lauren Bonner, Ariel Fox,
Matthew K. Hudson, Emma Nothmann,
Joanna Shawn Brigid O'Leary,
Sarah Robinson
Financial Manager
Suzanne Siu
Marketing & Publicity Managers
Megan Brumagim, Nitin Shah
Personnel Manager
Jesse Reid Andrews
Researcher Manager
Jennifer O'Brien
Web Manager
Jesse Tov
Web Content Director
Abigail Burger
Production Associates
Thomas Bechtold, Jeffrey Hoffman Yip
IT Directors
Travis Good, E. Peyton Sherwood
Financial Assistant
R. Kirkie Maswoswe
Associate Web Manager
Robert Dubbin
Office Coordinators
Abigail Burger, Angelina L. Fryer,
Liz Glynn

Director of Advertising Sales
Daniel Ramsey
Senior Advertising Associates
Sara Barnett, Daniella Boston
Advertising Artwork Editor
Julia Davidson, Sandy Liu
President
Abhishek Gupta
General Manager
Robert B. Rombauer
Assistant General Manager
Anne E. Chisholm

INDONESIA

TIMOR SEA

●Darwin

Melville
Island

Bathurst
Island

ARNHEM
LAND

Katherine●

INDIAN OCEAN

Wyndham● Kununurra
[1]

THE KIMBERLEY

96

87

Derby●
Broome● Fitzroy
Crossing
[1]

Halls Creek●

[1]

NORTH
TERR

GREAT SANDY DESERT

●Port
Hedland

Karratha●
PILBARA

Lake
Mackay

Onslow●
[1]
HAMMERSLEY RANGE

95

~Alice Springs

Ningaloo
Reef
Exmouth● Tom Price

Newman●

MACDONNELL

Coral Bay●

GIBSON DESERT

Uluru [4]
(Ayers Rock)

WESTERN
AUSTRALIA

●Carnarvon

Shark Bay

Denham●

GREAT VICTORIA DESERT

87

SOUTH

Kalbarri●
[1]

Mt. Magnet●

95

Geraldton●

Kalgoorlie-
●Boulder

NULLARBOR PLAIN
[1]

●Ceduna

Lancelin●

94

Norseman●

Whyalla

Fremantle● ●Perth
[1]

94

[1]

GREAT AUSTRALIAN BIGHT

Bunbury●

Esperance●

Augusta●

●Albany

SOUTHERN OCEAN

Australia

0   200 miles

0   200 kilometers

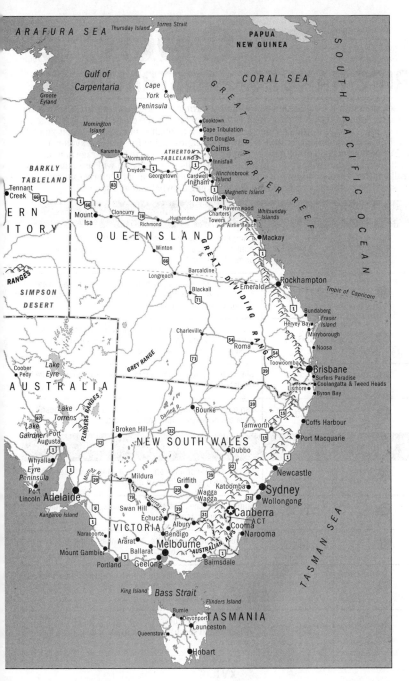

PRICE RANGES>>AUSTRALIA

Our researchers rank establishments by value, starting with the best; our favorites get the *Let's Go* thumbs-up (📛). Since the best value is not always the cheapest price, we have a system of price ranges for quick reference, based on a rough expectation of what you will spend. For **accommodations,** it's based off the cheapest price for a solo traveler for one night. For **restaurants** and other dining establishments, we estimate the average amount that you will spend in that restaurant. The table below tells you what you will *typically* find in Australia at the corresponding price range; keep in mind that a particularly expensive ice cream stand may still only be marked a ❶ depending on what you will spend.

ACCOMMODATIONS	RANGE	WHAT YOU'RE LIKELY TO FIND
❶	$0-15	Camping and dorm rooms or dorm-style rooms. Expect bunk beds and a communal bath; you may have to provide or rent towels and sheets.
❷	$16-25	Upper-end hostels or small hotels. You may have a private bathroom, or there may be a sink in your room and communal shower in the hall.
❸	$26-40	A small room with a private bath. Should have decent amenities, such as phone and TV. Breakfast may be included in the price of the room.
❹	$41-60	Similar to 3, but may have more amenities or be in a more touristed area.
❺	$60+	Large hotels or upscale chains. If it's a 5 and it doesn't have the perks you want, you've paid too much.
FOOD	**RANGE**	**WHAT YOU'RE LIKELY TO FIND**
❶	$1-10	Mostly street-corner stands, pizza places, or fast-food joints. Rarely ever a sit-down meal.
❷	$11-15	Some sandwiches and take-out options, but also quite a few sit-down restaurants.
❸	$16-20	Entrees are more expensive, but chances are, you're paying for decor and ambience.
❹	$21-25	As in 3, the higher prices are probably related to better service, but in these restaurants, the food will tend to be a little fancier or more elaborate.
❺	$26+	If you're not getting delicious food with great service in a well-appointed space, you're paying for nothing more than hype.

DISCOVER
AUSTRALIA

People have been arriving awestruck to this far-flung island at the edge of the earth for over 40,000 years. Australia's diverse population testifies to the fact that, time after time, the strange and fantastic landscape made the long journey all worthwhile. Even for today's visitors, the island-continent retains a magical, dream-like quality, unlike anywhere else on earth. It offers astonishingly varied yet consistently stunning natural terrain, exotic animal and plant life forged from Mother Nature's wildest imaginings, and shimmering hyper-modern cosmopolitan oases populated by denizens entirely genuine in their mantra of "no worries." Where else are you presented a choice among world-class wine-tasting, getting dangerously close to a salt-water croc, fashioning yourself a didge, snorkeling in vast expanses of ancient coral reef, and dancing the night away at the largest club in the Southern Hemisphere? What other continent offers the bustling metropolis of Sydney on the same platter as the vastness of the Outback, the rainforests of Cape York, and the colored sands of Fraser Island? The locals have discovered this ancient continent's secret, and so will you: it's not a dream, it's Australia.

FACTS & FIGURES

CAPITAL: Canberra.

HUMAN POPULATION: 19.9 million.

KANGAROO POPULATION: 40 million.

WEST-TO-EAST DISTANCE: 4000km.

NUMBER OF ABORIGINAL LANGUAGES: Over 500.

PERCENT IN SIZE LARGER THAN BRITAIN: 3152%.

NUMBER OF BEACHES: Over 7,000.

AMOUNT OF FOLIAGE KOALAS MUST EAT DAILY: 9kg (about 20 lb.).

JARS OF VEGEMITE CONSUMED PER YEAR: 22 million.

MOST VALIANT ATTEMPT TO SAVE SHEEP: World's longest fence (5,531km) keeps Queensland's dingoes in the north away from sheep in the south.

NUMBER OF PLANT SPECIES: 25,000 (Europe supports only 17,000).

AUSTRALIANS WHO FOLLOW THE JEDI FAITH: 70,509 (2001 Census).

ANNUAL BEER CONSUMPTION, PER AUSTRALIAN: 94L.

WHEN TO GO

Australia is huge, so when to travel depends on where you want to go and what you want to do. Crowds and prices of everything from flights to hostel bunks tend to be directly proportional to the quality of the weather.

In the south, the **seasons** of the temperate climate zone are reversed from those in the Northern Hemisphere. Summer lasts from December to February, autumn from March to May, winter from June to August, and spring from September to November. In general, Australian winters are mild, comparable to the southern U.S. or southern Europe, but while snow is infrequent except in the mountains, in winter, it's generally too cold to have much fun at the beach. In the south, peak season falls roughly between November and April.

The north, however, is an entirely different story—many people forget that over one-third of Australia is in the sweltering tropics. Seasons here are defined by wildly varying precipitation rather than generally constant temperatures. During **The Wet** (November to April), heavy downpours and violent storms plague Australia, especially on the north coast. During **The Dry** (May to October), sections of Australia away from the temperate zone endure drought. Traveling in the Wet is not recommended for the faint of heart; the heavy rains, washing out unsealed roads, make driving a challenge in non-urban areas.

Diving on the Great Barrier Reef is seasonal as well; January and February are rainy months, and the water is clearest between April and October. The toxic **box jellyfish** is most common around the northeast coast between October and April.

Ski season in New South Wales, Victoria, and Tasmania runs from late June to September, and the famous wildflowers of Western Australia bloom from September to December. For help planning when and where to go, read below, and see the chart of **temperature and rainfall** (p. 748) and the list of major **holidays and festivals** (p. 19).

THINGS TO DO

THE OUTBACK

Geographically contained by the continent's more developed coasts, Australia's outback seems like the most infinite place on earth. Every year, both travelers and Aussies take on the *never never*, looking for adventure or serious solitude. During the Dry season, the **Kimberley** (p. 730) opens to those brave souls who dare to rumble along the rough but stunning **Gibb River Road** (p. 736). In the Northern Territory, **Kakadu National Park** (p. 262) is a gateway to another world of thundering waterfalls, snapping crocs, and mystical beauty. Perhaps capturing the essence of the outback most completely is the Aboriginal homeland **Arnhem Land** (p. 296). In Australia's Red Centre, imposing **Uluru (Ayers Rock)** (p. 314) and its cousin **Kata Tjuta** (p. 313) keep a dignified watch over the rest of the outback. Down into South Australia, **Coober Pedy** (p. 511) playfully affirms the Down Under mentality—scorching temperatures force residents to carve their homes underground. The **Nullarbor** (p. 519), as its name suggests, is a vast stretch of empty plain. For travelers who don't make it out of the east, Queensland's outback mining towns (p. 453) and New South Wales's **Broken Hill** (p. 254) are on the fringe but offer a taste of what lies within.

THE OUTDOORS

Australia has a national park around every corner, preserving all types of terrain—from rainforest to desert, from mountain to coast. The Northern Territory has the best national parks. The itinerary-topping **Uluru** (**Ayers Rock**; p. 314) and timeless **Kakadu** (p. 272) ensure the other (some say better) Territory parks stay more pristine and untrammeled. The **Macdonnell Ranges** (p. 307) have some of the continent's best hiking; just next door is the spectacular **Kings Canyon** (p. 312). Up the track, the write-home-to-mum lookouts of **Nitmiluk** (**Katherine Gorge**; p. 288) are equaled by the spectacular waterfalls of **Litchfield** (p. 282). In Queensland, lush rainforest complements the nearby reef from the tip of **Cape York** (p. 450) all the way down to **Eungella** (p. 399). In New South Wales, the **Blue Mountains** (p. 150) attract avid abseilers, and in winter, **Kosciuszko** (p. 237) becomes a haven for skiers. There's also a number of beautiful North Coast hinterland parks, such as **Mt. Warning** (p. 212), which offer bushwalks for all skill levels. **Wilsons Promontory** (p. 663) is a gorgeous stretch of southern coast. Tasmania is Australia's hiking mecca; the **Overland Track** (p. 544) is among the best bushwalks in the world. South Australia's **Flinders Ranges** (p. 501) cater to the truly hardcore, while Western Australia showcases marine life, including the whales and dolphins that call **Bunbury** (p. 697) and **Monkey Mia** (p. 720) home.

MARINE LIFE

Whether you're a seasoned scuba diver or a determined beginner, you probably have "see the Great Barrier Reef" on your list of things to do in your lifetime. And for good reason—off the coast of Queensland, the 2000km reef system encompasses hundreds of islands and cays and thousands of smaller coral reefs, making the reefs accessible to everyone. Most choose to venture out from **Cairns** (p. 425), the main gateway to the reef. Further south, on the reef's doorstep, the sunken *S.S. Yongala* near **Townsville** (p. 410) is among the best wreck dives in the world. **Airlie Beach** (p. 401) draws backpackers ready to leave the bars for the thrill of the reefs. And though the Great Barrier Reef is quintessential, most coasts have good diving spots as well. In New South Wales, the diving in **Batemans Bay** (p. 231) and **Coffs Harbour** (p. 192) is spectacular and highly accessible. In South Australia, **Innes National Park** (p. 500) yields access to the Southern Ocean's depths. In Western Australia, giant whale sharks patrol **Ningaloo Reef** in Exmouth (p. 723), making for an exhilarating dive.

TOP TEN LIST

TOP 10 BIG THINGS

Australia is a big country full of big things; no road trip would be complete without a few of these structures. Here are our favorites in height order.

1. Big Prawn, Ballina (p. 198). The garish hue and steely gaze of the 20m shrimp has jolted many a driver on the NSW North Coast.

2. Big Pineapple, Nambour (p. 372). 16m of pineapple makes for one big fruit salad.

3. Big Murray Cod, Swan Hill (p. 648). The 15m fish is so popular it has been encased in wire to keep admirers at a distance.

4. Big Guitar, Tamworth (p. 222). Country music is immortalized in the 12m golden guitar shimmering on the parched landscape.

5. Big Galah, Kimbah (p. 519). The 8m pink bird marks Australia's halfway point.

6. Big Ned Kelly, Glenrowan (p. 655). The 6m bushranger folk-hero arrests passing vehicles with his haunting garb and gun aloft.

7. Big Cassowary, Mission Beach (p. 421). A flightless bird-*cum*-roundabout.

8. Big Banana, Coffs Harbour (p. 192). The 5m structure houses a banana cultivation museum. Entry to the exhibit, banana, and feelings of inadequacy free.

9. Big Sundial, Singleton (p. 169). An appropriately huge sundial for a land drenched in light.

10. Big Macadamia, Nambour (p. 372). Australia's biggest nut.

The cheapest diving certification courses can be found in Queensland at **Hervey Bay** (p. 373), **Bundaberg** (p. 384), and **Magnetic Island** (p. 415). For additional diving information, see **The Great Barrier Reef** (p. 318).

ABORIGINAL CULTURE

Aborigines traditionally see a strong connection between the earth and its inhabitants. During the "Dreaming," spirits are believed to have carved the canyons and gorges and come to life as animals and trees. In New South Wales, **Mungo National Park** (p. 259) records the earliest Aboriginal presence. Sacred regions and timeless rock art sites can be found from **Tasmania** (p. 522) to **Kakadu National Park** (p. 272) in the Northern Territory's Top End. Though lore in a glitzier, commercialized form has become popular among tourists, **Tjapukai** (p. 425) near Cairns, **Brambuk Living Cultural Centre** (p. 627) in Grampians National Park, and **Warradjan Aboriginal Cultural Centre** (p. 272) in Kakadu National Park attempt to present accurate representations of "Dreaming" stories and European interaction with Aborigines. Modern Aboriginal art can be found in small galleries in many larger cities, but the **National Gallery of Australia** in Canberra (p. 94) has the continent's best collection.

CITY SIGHTS

Australia's cosmopolitan meccas are enticing enough to lure travelers away from the rugged beauty of the Outback. Multicultural **Sydney** (p. 104) lives a laid-back lifestyle while enjoying the excitement of a global center. **Melbourne** (p. 567) offers style and genteel grandeur—incredible nightlife, a thriving cafe society, and a bustling budget food scene. Smooth as the jazz in its clubs, **Brisbane** (p. 322) eases coastal backpackers into urban culture. Charming and historic **Hobart** (p. 524) is Tasmania's civilized outpost. The antithesis of a tourist trap, **Adelaide** (p. 462) lives at a slower pace. Farther from the east, **Perth** (p. 679) and **Darwin** (p. 263) have relaxed coastal stretches and hopping nightlife on the *never never's* other edge.

■ LET'S GO PICKS

BEST VIEW: Sparkling **Sydney Harbour, NSW** (p. 131) from the top of the Harbour Bridge, or the pristine **Franklin River, TAS** (p. 547) in a white-water raft.

BEST PLACE TO SHOUT YOURSELF SILLY: An Aussie Rules game at the **Melbourne Cricket Ground, VIC** (p. 590), or by testing the astounding acoustics of **Jenolan Caves, NSW** (p. 165).

BEST PLACE TO GET A BITE: The land of wine and honey in **Mudgee, NSW** (p. 247), or with a shark at Scuba World, in **Maroochy, QLD** (p. 362).

BEST UNDERGROUND SCENE: Underground city **Coober Pedy, SA** (p. 511), or the mosh pits of the **Adelaide Fringe Festival, SA** (p. 473).

BEST PLACE FOR DREAMING: Under the stars along the **Gibb River Road, WA** (p. 736), or in the Aboriginal art galleries of **Kakadu National Park, NT** (p. 272).

MOST UNDERRATED: South Coast, NSW (p. 223) or **Tasmania** (p. 522).

BEST PLACE TO PONDER YOUR INSIGNIFICANCE: The surreal emptiness of the **Nullarbor Plain, SA** (p. 519), or the thumping dance floor of Metro, **Melbourne, VIC** (p. 567).

BEST PLACE TO GET WRECKED: At the best wreck dive in the world, the *S.S. Yongala*, off **Townsville, QLD** (p. 410), or for free in the wine vineyards of the **Hunter Valley, NSW** (p. 166).

BEST DRIVE: The winding seaside cliffs of the **Great Ocean Road, VIC** (p. 611), or off your very own plot of astroturf in the **Outback, SA** (p. 509).

BEST SPOT TO GO TROPPO: The untamed beauty of far north Queensland's **Iron Range NP, QLD** (p. 452), or the classy hedonism of Sydney's **Darling Harbour, NSW** (p. 143).

SUGGESTED ITINERARIES

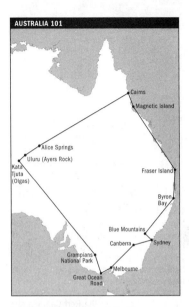

AUSTRALIA 101 (6 WEEKS)

This trip will give you a taste of everything Australia has to offer: pristine, untamed wilderness, exciting urban centers, awe-inspiring outback landscapes, and achingly beautiful stretches of seemingly endless coastline. Begin the tour in cosmopolitan **Sydney** (p. 104), then head west for some abseiling and sightseeing in the World Heritage listed **Blue Mountains** (p. 150). Head up the north coast through countless sleepy coastal hamlets before having your aura read in beautiful **Byron Bay** (p. 150). Hop into Queensland to the ever-shifting sand dunes of **Fraser Island** (p. 378). Dive the Great Barrier Reef from **Magnetic Island** (p. 415) before heading farther north to **Cairns** (p. 425). Spend a few days snorkeling or check out the magical rainforest en route to catching a flight to the Northern Territory's laid-back **Alice Springs** (p. 300). From this famous Outback town, it's just a short trip to the most famous of Australian icons: experience the wonder of **Kakadu National Park** (p. 272), **Uluru (Ayers**

Rock; p. 313), and **Kata Tjuta (the Olgas;** p. 315). Then get set to head down south to the world's most breathtaking road trip along the **Great Ocean Road** (p. 611) and break for another natural high atop the jagged peaks of **Grampians National Park** (p. 627). It's time for some urban energy in **Melbourne** (p. 567), Australia's cultural heart, before observing Aussie politics in action in **Canberra** (p. 86), just a few hours' drive from Sydney.

EAST COAST WALKABOUT (6 WEEKS)

The quintessential backpacker route, promising sun, surf and shouts galore. Start in **Melbourne** (p. 567) before setting forth to coo at the adorable penguins on **Phillip Island** (p. 605). Next explore the uncharted wilderness of Tasmania on the stunning **Overland Track** (p. 544). Catch up on some much-needed R&R in charming **Devonport** (p. 548) then embark on another world-renowned bushwalking track on the mainland at **Wilson's Promontory** (p. 663) on Victoria's south coast. Hit the ski-slopes of **Snowy River National Park** (p. 673) and then marvel at Australia's bush capital, **Canberra** (p. 86). Party on the beach in **Sydney** (p. 104), before touring the beautiful **Blue Mountains** (p. 150) and the vineyards of the **Hunter Valley** (p. 166). Grab a coldie with your mates in **Coffs Harbour** (p. 192) and head to **Byron Bay** (p. 200) for surfing and relaxation. **Surfers Paradise** (p. 349) is a non-stop party, but never fear, for you can nurse that hangover at **Brisbane's** (p. 322) smoky jazz clubs or the gorgeous beaches of **Fraser** (p. 378) and **Great Keppel Islands** (p. 393). After recuperating from a big night in **Airlie Beach** (p. 401), go scuba diving or sail to the **Whitsunday Islands** (p. 406). **Townsville** (p. 410) and **Magnetic Island** (p. 415) promise sunshine and great diving. Bounce over to the sparkling white sands of **Mission Beach** (p. 421) and then **Cairns** (p. 425) puts it all together with unlimited diving and adventure opportunities, along with hearty backpacker nightlife. Those with extra time can daytrip to the rainforests,

DISCOVER

roads, and reef of nearby **Port Douglas** (p. 439) and **Cape Tribulation** (p. 444).

EAST COAST WALKABOUT

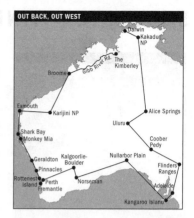

OUT BACK, OUT WEST

OUT BACK, OUT WEST (6-7 WEEKS)

Not for the faint of heart, this itinerary will have you well acquainted with dusty outback roads and large open spaces. Base yourself in the Northern Territory's tropical backpacker playground of **Darwin** (p. 263), from where you can reach the breathtaking landscape and Aboriginal art of **Kakadu** (p. 272). Head down to the Red Centre's surprisingly cosmopolitan **Alice Springs** (p. 300) and make the pilgrimage to **Uluru** (**Ayers Rock;** p. 300), a site sacred to Aboriginal cultures and local tourism alike. Descend into the curious subterranean opal town of **Coober Pedy** (p. 511). Resurface for the dusty hills and majestic peaks of the **Flinders Ranges** (p. 501) and then head south to **Adelaide** (p. 462) and the caves and happy creatures of **Kangaroo Island** (p. 481). Cross the legendary **Nullabor Plain** (p. 519) to enjoy historic **Norseman** (p. 715) and the iconic mining town of **Kalgoorlie** (p. 712). Watch bustling **Perth** (p. 681) emerge from nothingness and soak up the history of **Fremantle** (p. 688), then bike around beautiful **Rottnest Island** (p. 694). Daytrip out to the eerie limestone pillars rising from the dunes at the **Pinnacles** (p. 717). Heading north, learn to windsurf in **Geraldton** (p. 718) and frolic with the dolphins of **Monkey Mia** (p. 720) in Western Australia's only World Heritage Area, **Shark Bay** (p. 720). Dive into the ocean off of **Exmouth** (p. 723), then swim in the plunge pools within the red gorges of **Karijini National Park** (p. 727). The wayward tourist destination of **Broome** (p. 730) entices backpackers with pristine beaches and serves as a gateway to the indescribable wilderness adventure that is **The Kimberley** (p. 730), starting from the incomparable **Gibb River Road** (p. 736).

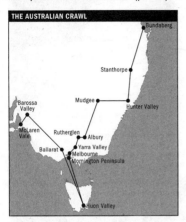

THE AUSTRALIAN CRAWL

AUSTRALIAN CRAWL (3-4 WEEKS)

Here's a journey that will take you to legendary Outback drinking holes, famous drinking epicenters, and plenty of top-notch vineyards—think of it as the world's longest, and classiest, pub crawl. Begin in the home of Australia's favorite rum, **Bundaberg** (p. 384), near Brisbane. Make some money fruit-picking to pay for all those drinks you'll be knocking back then head to **Stanthorpe** (p. 359), where over thirty famous Granite Belt wineries await. Sample the world's best Shiraz in the picturesque **Hunter Valley** and then enjoy more tastings at the foothills of the Great Diving Range in **Mudgee** (p. 247). Indulge in the goofy kitsch of the Ettamogah Pub outside **Albury** (p. 242) before sampling a Muscat in temperate **Rutherglen** (p. 655). The **Yarra Valley** (p. 603) is famous for its Pinot Noir varieties, while nearby **Melbourne** offers a non-stop bar-hopping scene year-round. The beautiful **Mornington Peninsula** (p. 608) is dotted with a plethora of wineries, as is Tasmania's **Huon Valley** (p. 536), where the cool climate nurtures a number of superb vineyards tucked away from the tourist hub-bub. Back on the mainland, **Ballarat** (p. 635) is fast gaining a reputation for its delectable Chardonnays. We've saved the best for last, though, with rounds in the **Barossa Valley** (p. 488) and **McLaren Vale** (p. 476), where visiting the abundance of world-renowned wineries will require Bacchanalian endurance.

(Continued on next page)

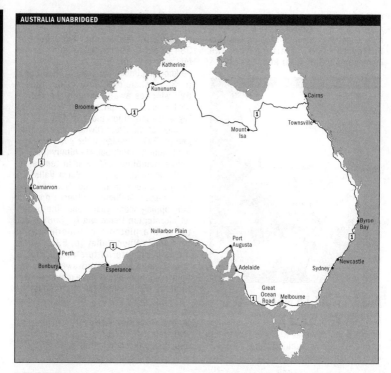

AUSTRALIA UNABRIDGED (UP TO A LIFETIME)

Highway 1 conveniently circles everyone's favorite country-continent, providing an epic itinerary catering to only the truly hardcore. Begin your odyssey among the creature comforts of **Sydney** (p. 104). Gear up, 'cos it's gonna be a long ride. Surf your way up the NSW coast, through the quintessentially Aussie sea-side city of **Newcastle** (p. 171) and effortlessly hip **Byron Bay** (p. 200) then hit the diving mecca of **Townsville** (p. 410). Make a detour to **Cairns** (p. 425) for a quick skydive or parasail. Heading west, let a miner show you how it's done in **Mount Isa** (p. 457), then head toward **Katherine** (p. 286) to take a dip in the hot springs before

the oasis of **Kununurra** (p. 741), in the eastern **Kimberley** (p. 730). Indian Ocean surf and outdoor cafes greet you upon your arrival in **Broome** (p. 730). After rounding the country's well-worn west, pausing to make some quick cash on the plantations of **Carnarvon** (p. 721), tour the parks and pubs of mellow **Perth** (p. 681); soldier on to **Bunbury** (p. 697) to frolic with the dolphins. Take a deep breath in **Esperance** (p. 709) then traverse the vast emptiness of the **Nullarbor Plain** (p. 519). **Port Augusta** (p. 501) will nurse you back to animation, while the culinary capital of **Adelaide** (p. 462) will put some meat on those well-traveled bones. Pause for some photo-ops along the amazing **Great Ocean Road** (p. 611), then it's back to the big smoke in **Melbourne** (p. 567). Good on ya, mate.

LIFE & TIMES

HISTORY

ABORIGINAL AUSTRALIA

THE PEOPLE. By some estimates, **Aborigines** have inhabited the island continent for as long as 100,000 years and had settled across most of the continent by 30,000 years ago. Archaeologists have unveiled evidence of ancient art, complex burial practices, and Stone Age boomerangs. Estimates of the Aboriginal population of Australia just prior to European colonization vary widely, from 300,000 to over one million. Aborigines were **hunters and gatherers,** migrating seasonally in search of food and increasing the land's productivity by setting controlled fires.

COMMUNITY LIFE. The Aborigines formed groups largely based on territorial claims. While language did not determine any groups' boundaries, it has been estimated that more than 200 languages, with up to 600 dialect groups, were spoken. Within their tribes, Aborigines divided into even smaller groups made up of two or three different families. In place of a system of private land ownership, an unwritten charter tied together a particular group and the territory they covered in their travels. The relationship between these caretakers and the land was considered one of reciprocal responsibility. Along with strong ties to the land, there was a strong cultural emphasis on personal relationships, namely those bonds formed through kinship, marriage, and ceremony.

BELIEF SYSTEMS. Although historically Aboriginal people across Australia belonged to separate groups with their own legends, countries, customs and ceremonies, they generally shared similar religious beliefs. Aborigines believe the world was created during **the Dreaming,** or Creation Time, a mythological period of time when the acts and deeds of powerful ancestral beings shaped the land and populated it with humans, animals, and plants. The **spirit ancestors** gave Aboriginal people their laws and customs and are the source of the songs, dances, designs and rituals that are the basis of Aboriginal religious expression. There are three categories of sacred land in Aboriginal culture: ceremonial sites, *djang* (Dreaming), and *djang andjamun* (Sacred Dreaming). Ceremonial sites are now used for burials, rites of passage, and other events. At *djang* sites, a creator passed through, took shape, or entered or exited the Earth, leaving the site safe to visit. *Djang andjamun* sites, however, where the ancestor still lingers, are considered spiritual hazard zones. Laws prohibit entry to the latter group of sites. Because features of these areas are linked to the ancestors, they are considered sacred sites rather than inherited possessions.

EUROPEAN SETTLEMENT

COLONIZATION

EXPLORATION. **Chinese** explorers were among the first non-Aborigines to arrive, and **Dutch** explorers included a misshapen Australia on 16th-century maps, leaving a memorial at **Shark Bay** (p. 720) in 1616. In 1642, **Abel Tasman,** a Dutch explorer, sailed south to chart the rest of Australia—a "new" southern island which came to be known as Tasmania. Though he explored Australia's coast, a settlement was never established. In 1770, the English captain **James Cook,** in his ship *Endeavour*, explored the eastern coast of what would become Australia. Cook and his crew of astronomers and scientists discovered and named **Botany Bay** (p. 147), and returned to England with stories of strange animals and plants.

THE FIRST FLEET. The motives for the British colonization of Australia have been a matter of debate. The traditional explanation is that Britain needed to solve its prison overcrowding problem, while another explanation suggests that the English hoped to establish a base for a global navy with plentiful natural resources and an available work force, particularly prisoners. In any case, the prisons in London were full, and on May 13, 1787, the 11-ship **First Fleet** left from England. Led by **Arthur Phillip,** appointed to command the fleet by British Home Secretary **Lord Sydney,** the fleet arrived with about 730 convicts in Botany Bay after a grueling eight-month voyage. After local resources were deemed insufficient, Commander Phillip headed north to Port Jackson. The English flag was raised on January 26, on the spot where **Sydney** (p. 107) stands today.

THE CONVICT ERA

BEGINNINGS. Upon arrival in Australia, the convicts and their guards faced a strange and inhospitable land. The colony saw little success: half the workforce was occupied guarding the other half; livestock escaped into the bush; relations with Aborigines deteriorated; and most subsequent supply ships were wrecked. The convicts themselves were mainly petty criminals from the slums of London with no agricultural experience. The seeds and cuttings that the fleet had so carefully carried across the sea failed in the local climate. Captain Phillip's grand plans for 200-foot-wide streets had to be scrapped; no mill or team of cattle would be available for another eight years.

ABORIGINAL INTERACTION. When the British landed in Australia and claimed the land for the Crown, they did so under a doctrine of **terra nullius** (empty land), which meant either that there were no people on the continent, or that inhabitants were mere occupants rather than landowners. Under common law, this conveniently gave the British free rein to take what land they wished, without the hassle of treaties or agreements. Many Aborigines were displaced, if not eradicated; European settlement destroyed watering holes, displaced communities, and brought numerous diseases. Many Aboriginal children were kidnapped and forced into assimilation programs, a practice not officially ended until the twentieth century. The history of Aboriginal and white interaction in Tasmania, where the Aborigines had remained isolated for thousands of years, is particularly atrocious; genocide of the Aboriginal population caused their near-complete disappearance within 70 years of contact.

EXPANSION

FREE SETTLERS. After the appointment of Governor Macquarie in 1809, convicts who had served for seven years were allowed to start their lives again as free citizens. England also encouraged free settler migration with land grants and offered inexpensive passage for young single women. Since upkeep of the convicts was an increasingly onerous economic burden, the Crown began to heed protests of free settlers against continued convict deportation to Australia and in 1868, the last convict ship arrived. Approximately 165,00 convicts had been sent to Australia.

PROSPERITY. Wool was Australia's major export and by 1845, sheep farming was the most profitable business in the country. The discovery of gold in 1851 triggered a **gold rush,** attracting wealth and immigrants, and increasing the population two-fold in the decade following to over 1.1 million. Competition for gold inevitably led to conflict, and the 1854 **Eureka Stockade Rebellion** marked Australia's closest brush with civil war. Miners in Ballarat, Victoria (p. 635), formed a collective and built a stockade, in protest of the government's licensing fees for miners. Government forces crushed the uprising in a 15-minute clash that cost about two dozen miners their lives.

TWENTIETH CENTURY

UNIFICATION

FEDERATION. Before the formation of a central government, each of Australia's six individual colonies had little to do with each other and instead communicated directly with London. The **Commonwealth of Australia** was founded on January 1, 1901. Federation had been a difficult process for Australia; the new constitution was only ratified after a decade of debate among the colonies. The six states of Australia are New South Wales, Victoria, Queensland, South Australia, Western Australia, and Tasmania. The Northern Territory and the Australian Capital Territory are self-governing territories that do not have state status.

SUFFRAGE. In 1902, Australia became the second country in the world, after New Zealand, to grant federal **suffrage to women.** In 1921, Western Australia's **Edith Dircksey Cowan** became the first female in an Australian state parliament.

RACE. When convicts stopped arriving, Europeans encouraged the immigration of Chinese laborers. However, race-based immigration restrictions were soon adopted, especially when **Chinese immigrants** started working the goldfields. By 1888, the "Chinese question" had emerged onto center stage, and a Queensland journal coined the rallying cry **"White Australia."** In 1896, immigration restrictions were extended to include all non-whites. With federation came the **Immigration Restriction Act of 1901,** which required immigrants to pass a 50-word dictation test in any European language chosen at the discretion of the immigration officers. Not surprisingly, most Chinese immigrants failed this highly dubious test.

WORLD WAR

THE GREAT WAR. At the outset of **World War I,** Australia's prime minister declared support for the mother country, saying: "Our duty is quite clear—to gird up our loins and remember that we are Britons." About 330,000 Australians were sent into battle and 60,000 lost their lives. 165,000 more soldiers were wounded—a shocking percentage of the country's relatively small population. The single worst day of battle was April 25, 1915, when 2000 members of the **Australian and New Zealand Army Corps** (ANZAC) were killed at **Gallipoli,** Turkey, initiating a campaign that eventually took 8500 Australian lives and forced evacuation of the troops. Australia celebrates **Anzac Day** (April 25) each year to remember their heroism and loss.

WORLD WAR II. A generation later, The Royal Australian Air Force reiterated its commitment to Great Britain and its allies in **World War II,** and Australian troops enjoyed victories at Tobruk and El-Alamein in North Africa. After the Japanese attack on Hawaii's Pearl Harbor (Dec. 7, 1941) and the fall of British-protected Singapore (Feb. 15, 1942), Australian citizens became increasingly concerned about safety on their own shores. On February 19, 1942, **Darwin,** the capital of the Northern Territory, suffered the first of many bombings by the Japanese. The US, engaged in the Pacific theater, became a closer ally to Australia than more distant Britain. About 30,000 Australian soldiers were lost over the course of the war.

AFTER 1945

POST-WAR BOOM. The 50s were a time of relative peace and prosperity for Australia, marked by rapid immigration. In fact, the population nearly doubled in the thirty years following the end of the war, growing from seven million in 1945 to 13.5 million. Immigrants came first from southern Europe, and then later from Asia with the abolition of the White Australia policy in 1965.

POWERFUL FRIENDS. Australia has gradually moved its foreign policy allegiances away from the "Mother Country" of Britain to the United States. Australian-American relations were formalized in 1951 with the signing of the Australia-New Zealand-United States **(ANZUS)** pact. Consequently, when the United States became embroiled in the **Vietnam** conflict, Australians were conscripted to serve, touching off a slowly gathering storm of anti-war protest. Successive Labor governments in the 1990s promoted Australian interests in Asia. Together with a large influx of Asian immigrants in the last twenty years, Australia's place in **Asia** is increasingly important, both economically and culturally.

TODAY

Australia may not hit headlines internationally with any great frequency, but no traveler should arrive in the country without brushing up briefly on Australia's recent events of interest.

REFUGEES. In August 2001, the Norwegian freighter *Tampa*, carrying 460 refugees (largely Afghan), was denied entrance to the country by conservative Liberal Party Prime Minister John Howard. Thanks in large part to his hard-line stance against asylum seekers, Howard managed a surprise election win later in the year, revealing a **strong anti-refugee sentiment** among many Australian voters. More recently, demonstrations at Woomera Detention Centre in South Australia and refugee protests (some involving arson) at Western Australia's Curtin Detention Centre, have brought refugee conditions to national attention.

TERRORISM. The largest terrorist attack since September 11, 2001, the bombing of a nightclub in **Bali's** heavily touristed beach district in October 2002 had a grim significance for Australia. Bali is a popular destination for many Australian tourists, and about half of the 200 victims of the attack were Australian. The bombing was widely seen as a proxy attack on Australia, an active member of the US-led coalition to depose the Iraqi Hussein regime. Although 1500 troops were committed to the war in **Iraq,** the issue divided the nation and massive peace rallies were held in all capital cities.

ABORIGINAL RECONCILIATION. The landmark **Stolen Generations** report, which documented the removal of young children from their Aboriginal mothers as state policy until as late as 1969, heightened community awareness of structural and historical Aboriginal inequality in Australia. The **Native Title Act** of 1993 set out to devise a means of compensating Aborigines whose land claim had been lost. Despite this, the issue of Aboriginal land rights remains a contentious one in Australia, as farmers, miners, and conservatives remain strongly opposed to any return of land. While progress has stalled under Howard, a grass-roots movement for Aboriginal reconciliation has swelled in reaction to the Liberal government's stance on the issue.

PEOPLE

The Commonwealth of Australia is home to 19.8 million people, 1% of whom are indigenous Australians. Immigration has defined the Australian narrative, with over a quarter of the population born overseas. A formal immigration policy began after WWII out of a simple need to fill the sparsely populated landmass. This first wave of immigrants came primarily from Europe, the US, Turkey, and the USSR. In recent years, increasing numbers of migrants have arrived from Asia. Asians now account for about 7% of the Australian population. **Multiculturalism** as a planned government project of cultural diversity is today regarded as a cornerstone of the Australian national identity.

Australia's population density is 2.5 people per square kilometer. In comparison, the US averages 28.2 people per square kilometer, and the UK a whopping 243.6. Eighty-five percent of Australians live in urban areas, and the suburbs are still growing. The vast majority live on or relatively near the coasts, particularly the east coast—some theories point to the vast, inhospitable desert in the center of the country as the reason for this coastal population concentration.

English (See **'Strine,** p. 746 for some quirks of Australian English) is Australia's only national language, spoken in 85% of Australian homes. The religious composition of the population generally reflects immigrant backgrounds. Just over 75% of Australians declare themselves **Christians; non-Christian** religions comprise 11%. The rest (about 15%) reject organized religion.

CULTURE

FOOD & DRINK

Though Australian cuisine has traditionally been regarded as uninspiring, it has been remarkably successful at adding layers of flavor with each wave of immigration. European and Middle Eastern arrivals spiced up the Australian menu in the post WWII boom. Japanese, Thai, Malay, Vietnamese and Chinese restaurants are now also abundant, particularly in cosmopolitan urban centers. An emerging **Modern Australian** cuisine involves the use of high-quality fare indigenous to Australia prepared in a fusion of Asian styles.

Breakfast, or **"brekkie"**, is usually not eaten out, and most restaurants don't open until noon except in the larger cities. The infamous **Vegemite,** a yeast by-product of the beer-brewing process, is scraped thinly on toast for a quintessential Aussie breakfast. The evening meal of **"tea"** is the largest meal of the day. Beware of ordering only an **"entree,"** an appetizer in Australia. **Tipping** in Australian restaurants or pubs is rare and never expected. **Vegetarians** shouldn't go hungry despite Australia's meat-hungry reputation.

AUSTRALIAN CUISINE

FRUIT & VEGETABLES. The Australian continent boasts a cornucopia of fruit varieties; tropical north Queensland supports fruit industries that other western countries can only fantasize about having. Travelers from fruit-deprived countries will salivate at such exotic tropical offerings as custard apples, lychees, passionfruit, star fruit, coconuts, quandong, and pineapples, as well as bountiful colder-climate offerings such as pears, apples, and various berries. Locally-grown vegetables recall a variety of world cuisines and are also readily accessible for the even the most frugal gourmand.

MEAT & SEAFOOD. Generally cheap and high-quality. Though Australian beef is export-ready, world-class fare, the meat-pie may contain meat of more dubious origin. Its doughy shell is often doused in tomato sauce (a ketchup-like concoction) to disguise the taste. Veal and lamb are popular and available at uncommonly low prices. Unsurprisingly, seafood is a favorite on this island-continent, with regional specialities including king prawns (shrimp), Balmain Bugs (a type of lobster), and Barramundi (a freshwater fish).

BUSH TUCKER. Coastal Aborigines have eaten crayfish, **yabbies** (freshwater shrimp), and fish for centuries. **Witchetty grubs** (ghost moth larvae) are the most well known of the bush foods that make some first-timers twinge. Australia has recently discovered a taste for its "exotic" indigenous food, and with "bush tucker" (indigenous bush foods) as the new urban catch phrase, menus are increasingly inclined to incorporate Aboriginal wild foods like bunya nuts, Kakadu plums, and wild rosella flowers with specialty meats such as kangaroo filet, crocodile meat, Northern Territory buffalo, and wild magpie geese eggs.

CHEAP EATS. Australia offers plenty of ways to eat well on a budget. Self-catering is a cinch, since most budget accommodations offer kitchen facilities and fresh produce is very cheap. Enjoying a steak in the great outdoors is easy, since public barbecues are available at most parks, beaches and campsites. If you want someone else to do the cooking, your best bet for an inexpensive midday meal out is a pub **counter lunch,** which usually entails generous portions of "meat and two veg." **Fish 'n' chips** is another hearty Aussie institution, and is available at any **takeaway** (takeout restaurant). The fish is fried, battered, and served with British-style chips (thick french fries). Finally, make like the locals do and check out an Australian-style bakery, which even in the smallest country-towns offer breads baked with cheese, onion and other savory additions, sandwich-ready **rolls** (like hamburger buns) and true-blue treats like the **lamington** (a coconut-covered chunk of pound cake dipped in chocolate) or **pavlova** (a giant meringue).

DRINKING

COFFEE. Ordering "just coffee" is nearly impossible in Australia. Though they are a long way from Italy, Australia's major cities harbor a cappucino culture that can deliver caffeine into your bloodstream in an infinite number of ways. If you need help ordering, see **Cool Beans,** p. 745. **Tea,** often affectionately referred to as a **cuppa,** is also very popular. For the sweet-toothed fan of cafe culture, try an **iced chocolate,** a frothy and creamy concoction of ice-cream, cream and syrup.

BEER. Australia produces some of the world's best brews, and Australians consume them readily. The best place to share a coldie with your mates is the omnipresent Aussie **pub.** Traditional payment etiquette is the **shout,** in which drinking mates alternate rounds. If the beach is more your style, throw a **slab** (24 containers) in the **Esky** (ice chest). For more beer terminology and information on the types of beer available, consult **Terms of Embeerment,** p. 745.

WINE. Australian **wines** rival the best wines in the world. Overseas export started soon after the first vineyards began to produce wine in the early 1800s, and the industry has gained renown after a post-WWII influx of European talent. The **Hunter Valley** (p. 166), the **Barossa** and **Clare Valleys** (p. 488), the **Swan** and **Margaret Rivers** (p. 698), and the **Derwent** and **Tamar Valleys** (p. 539) possess some of the best Aussie vineyards. Many cafes and low-end restaurants advertise that they are **BYO,** or "bring your own." Though typically not licensed to serve alcohol, these establishments permit patrons to furnish their own bottle of wine with the meal and charge only a small **corkage fee,** if anything.

CUSTOMS & ETIQUETTE

TABOOS. While it's generally difficult to offend an Australian, it's a good idea to avoid making public pronouncements on **sensitive topics,** such as race relations, refugees, or US-led involvement in the Middle East. Extending your **middle finger** at someone (otherwise known as "giving the finger") is considered very rude and might get you into trouble.

PUBLIC BEHAVIOR. Australians are known for their friendly informality, and most people are on a first-name basis immediately. This lack of pretension also renders rank largely irrelevant. There's no need to tip; in fact, the Australians' very disregard for authority and rank can even render tipping offensive. When eating, most people find loud **chewing, burping, and talking with a full mouth** rude. **Littering** in this environmentally conscious society is not taken lightly.

WHAT TO WEAR. For women, almost anything is acceptable as long as it covers the essential parts—tube tops, halters, and tank tops are all common. For men, pants or shorts are the norm. **Cossies/swimmers/togs** (affectionate terms for Australia's favorite garment, the swimsuit) are usually appropriate only at the beach.

SPORTS & RECREATION

Sport is an essential part of national identity. You can't walk into a pub without a sports event from somewhere in the country on TV. In winter, Western Australia, South Australia, and Victoria catch **footy fever** for **Australian Rules Football,** while New South Wales and Queensland traditionally follow **rugby league** and **rugby union.** In summer, **cricket** is the spectator sport of choice across the nation. Star sporting figures enjoy hero status. Tune in to H. G. Nelson and Roy Slaven's Sunday afternoon Triple-J radio show *This Sporting Life* for a taste of Aussie sport culture, or check out the ridiculously popular *Footy Show,* on television's Channel 9.

CRICKET

The uninitiated may have trouble making sense of a sport where people can "bowl a maiden over of five flippers and a googly," but visitors won't be able to avoid the enthusiasm. Two teams of 11 players face off in a contest that can last anywhere from an afternoon to five days. Each summer, **international cricket** overshadows the national competition. Not just a scrimmage, a "test match" is the most lengthy and serious form of international cricket. In 1877, Australia's cricket team headed to England for its first international test against the mother country, emerging victorious. The Australians, as a shocked English reporter wrote, had "taken off with the ashes" of English cricket. Ever since then, British and Australian Test teams have been in noble contest for **"the Ashes"** (the trophy is a small, symbolic urn). In December and January, international teams arrive for a **full tour,** consisting of five test matches, one each in Melbourne, Sydney, Perth, Adelaide, and Brisbane. The five-day tests, accompanied by smaller one-day matches, are over by February, just in time for the country to turn its attention to national cricket and the **Sheffield Shield** finals in March.

AUSTRALIAN RULES FOOTBALL

In Victoria, South Australia, and Western Australia, the **Australian Football League (AFL)** teams fill the winter void that the end of the cricket season leaves. Played on cricket ovals, the game was originally designed to keep cricket players in shape in the off-season. The **AFL grand final,** in September, is a marvelous spectacle at the home of Australian sport, the **Melbourne Cricket Ground** (p. 590).

RUGBY

According to legend, **rugby** was born one glorious day in 1823 when one inspired (or perhaps frustrated) student in Rugby, England, picked up a soccer ball and ran it into the goal. Since then, rugby has evolved (or devolved) into an intricately punishing game with two variants: **rugby union** involving 15-man teams, and **rugby league** with 13-man teams. Despite the international reputation of the national union team, the **Wallabies,** rugby union sometimes carries a muted following. Since the Wallabies defeated France to win the World Cup in 1999, though, rugby union has grown in popularity. Matches such as the **Super 12** tournament and **Tri-nation** series (Australia, South Africa, and New Zealand) often pack stadiums and pubs. Part of the Tri-nation series, the **Bledisloe Cup** perpetuates a healthy animosity toward Australia's fellow Antipodeans, New Zealand.

Rugby league attracts a larger following, especially in New South Wales and Queensland. The national league competition culminates in September's **National Rugby League (NRL) final.** The only match that comes close to the intensity or popularity of the NRL final is June's **State of Origin** series, when Queensland takes on New South Wales. Both games promise a mix of blood, mud, and lots of drinking.

OTHER SPORTS

While the Australian team hasn't entered the World Cup since 1974, **soccer** is widely played, and Australia's **National Soccer League** has a fierce fanbase. Melbourne hosts one of **tennis's** Grand Slam events, the **Australian Open,** each January. Grassy tennis courts, bowling greens, and golf courses pepper the cities coast-to-coast. Most towns also have a horse racing track, and on the first Tuesday in November, the entire country stops to watch the prestigious **Melbourne Cup** horse race, where fashionable and outlandish attire sometimes appears more important than the competition. On Boxing Day, even as the Melbourne Cricket Test gets underway, half of Australia's amateur sailing community fills Sydney Harbour with billowing white sails to begin the **Sydney-to-Hobart yacht race,** the highlight in a full calendar of water sports. Australia is famous for its **surfing,** which for some is a competitive sport in addition to a great way to spend a summer morning.

THE ARTS

Australia is a young nation still seeking a balance in its national arts between distinctively Australian and more universal themes. Historically, European influences shaped the work of non-Aboriginal Australian artists and writers. Today, Australian artists work in a variety of styles, reflecting the nation's diffuse identity and search for coherence amid cosmopolitanism.

LITERATURE

THE DREAMING. The literature of indigenous Australians comprises over 50,000 years of **oral tradition** and is intertwined with Aboriginal conceptions of spirituality. The Dreaming involve legends of creation set in a mythological time where the landscape is endowed with mythic and symbolic status. Narratives of the Dreaming represent a complex network of beliefs, practices and customs that define Aboriginal spiritual beliefs and, specifically, their unique affinity with the land.

BUSH BALLADS. Often garishly exaggerated convict narratives gave way to accounts of pioneer life imbued with a novel spirit of nationalism. Possibly the first uniquely Australian literature was the bush ballad, a form of poetry that celebrated the working man and the superiority of bush to urban life. The most famous of these ballads is **AB Banjo Paterson's** *Waltzing Matilda*, often thought of as the unofficial Australian national anthem. **Henry Lawson** celebrated bush life in both poetry and short story form. Stories like *The Drover's Wife* provided a popular mythology of the life on the land for what was already a heavily urbanized society.

EARLY NOVELISTS. Early colonial novels tended to focus on the convict experience, seen both in the first Australian novel, **Henry Savory's** *Quintus Servinton*, as well as perhaps the first real Australian classic, **Marcus Clarke's** *For the Term of His Natural Life*. In the early twentieth century two women writers highlighted the changing face of the newly independent nation. Early feminist **Miles Franklin's** *My Brilliant Career* is a portrait of an independent and strong-willed woman seeking emancipation, while another woman writer, **Henry Handel Richardson,** documented an immigrant family's history in *The Fortunes of Richard Mahoney*.

CONTEMPORARY FICTION. Since World War II, Australian literature has adopted a more outward-looking voice. *Voss*, by Nobel Prize winner **Patrick White,** is both uniquely Australian in its depiction of the bleak emptiness of the center and universal in its treatment of individual isolation. **Thomas Keneally** writes with a strong social conscience, such as in *The Chant of Jimmie Blacksmith*, a gut-wrenching portrayal of domestic, turn of the century race relations, or Holocaust epic *Schindler's Ark*, later made into the film *Schindler's List*. Two-time Booker-prize winner **Peter Carey** is best known for his dark satire *Oscar and Lucinda* and more recently, *The True History of the Kelly Gang*, an imaginative account of outlaw and Australian folk hero Ned Kelly. **David Malouf's** work explores the relation between cultural centers and peripheries in the immigrant experience, with his background as a poet emerging in novels like *Remembering Babylon*. Australia's unofficial poet laureate, **Les Murray,** celebrates the anti-authoritarian with his "larrakin" characters, while **Judith Wright** carves a niche for a female poetic voice.

POPULAR MUSIC

ROCK 'N' ROLL. Popular music in Australia began in the late 50s, epitomized by rocker **Johnny O'Keefe** whose sound, inspired by the unique musical blend emerging from the US, took the country by storm. The British explosion in the 60s also caused an Australian ripple effect, with **The Easybeats** scoring big internationally with their infectious tune, "Friday on My Mind." The wholesome acoustic sounds of **The Seekers** led the folk bandwagon.

PUB ROCK. In the late 70s, **AC/DC** hit the charts with blues-influenced heavy metal grown out of pub culture. **The Skyhooks, Cold Chisel,** and **Australian Crawl** gained local fame and influence with Aussie-themed hits that refused to simply emulate sounds from across the seas. In the 80s, politically aware pub-rock bands like **Midnight Oil** became famous for their energetic and enthusiastic live shows. **Men at Work** broke into the American music scene and paved the way for superbands like **INXS** in the late 80s and beyond.

INDIGENOUS SOUNDS. After the success of Arnhem land group **Yothu Yindi** in the 90s, who blended dance music and rock in politically conscious hits like "Treaty," indigenous music is now seen as commercially viable. Other similarly politicized Aboriginal "bush rock" artists are the **Coloured Stones,** the **Warrumpi Band,** and country-influenced **Archie Roach,** who sings of his background as a **"stolen child."** Indigenous pop artists in the charts recently include **Shakaya** and **Christine Anu.**

LATEST HITS. Purveyors of pure pop internationally include **Natalie Imbruglia, Savage Garden,** and pint-sized Aussie icon **Kylie Minogue,** while rock is represented with such bands as **silverchair** and **The Vines. Nick Cave and the Bad Seeds** carry a

AUSSIE STARS Australian movie stars with recent international success include: **Geoffrey Rush** (*Shine, Shakespeare in Love, Quills, The Tailor of Panama*), **Cate Blanchett** (*Elizabeth, The Shipping News,* the *Lord of the Rings* series), **Nicole Kidman** (*Moulin Rouge!, The Hours*), **Russell Crowe,** born a Kiwi but raised an Aussie (*Gladiator, A Beautiful Mind*), **Guy Pierce** (*Memento*), **Heath Ledger** (*10 Things I Hate About You, A Knight's Tale*), **Hugh Jackman** (*X-Men, Kate and Leopold, X-Men 2*), **Toni Collette** (*About a Boy, The Sixth Sense*), **Adam Garcia** (*Coyote Ugly, Bootmen*), **Mel Gibson** (*Signs, Braveheart, The Patriot*), and **Rose Byrne** (*Obsessed*).

fair-sized European following, while country artist **Kasey Chambers** is popular in the US. Australia's nation-wide youth radio station, **Triple J** (www.triplej.net.au), plays contemporary local music and actively promotes new acts.

VISUAL ARTS

ABORIGINAL ART. The origins of Aboriginal art are not exclusively artistic but also educational, spiritual, and functional. Australia's most well-known Aboriginal artist **Albert Namatjira** depicted Western-style landscapes in the early twentieth century. While traditionally restricted in the public consciousness to "bark paintings," Aboriginal art is now celebrated in its many forms, including mural art, body painting, and rock painting.

AUSTRALIAN IMPRESSIONISTS. The **Heidelberg School** of Australian impressionists, led by **Arthur Streeton,** depicted distinctively Australian landscapes, usually on plein-air canvases. **Tom Roberts,** for example, found inspiration in the red, dry, dusty land of the cattle station, while **Frederick McCubbin** drew on the thin forests of smoky green gum trees.

CONTEMPORARY ARTISTS. Possibly the most famous work of Australian painting is **Sidney Nolan's** Ned Kelly series, which tells the story of the folk hero's exploits, final capture, and execution. Other artists in the last half-century to have found a distinctively Australian idiom include the acclaimed but controversial **Brett Whitely,** abstract artist **John Colburn, Russell Drysdale,** and **Arthur Boyd,** who depicts popular figures of Australian legend.

FILM

SILENT ERA. Given the national love of a good yarn, its little wonder that Australia also boasts one of the world's most prolific and innovative film industries—the world's first feature film, *The Story of the Kelly Gang* (1906), was an Australian production. Australian directors during the silent period pioneered the field, with classic productions such as *The Sentimental Bloke* and *For the Term of His Natural Life* receiving international attention.

POST-WAR & NEW-WAVE. Despite these auspicious beginnings, it was difficult for Australian films with their inevitably miniscule budgets to compete with overseas blockbusters. It wasn't until the post-WWII economic boom, which meant foreign financial backing for Australian films, that further strides were made. Films like *The Shiralee,* a joint British-Australian production about a fancy-free wanderer, spurred questions about whether local productions should aspire for a national or more universal perspective. Australian film didn't emerge from this crisis of confidence until the 1970s, when generous government support ushered in the "New Wave" of films like the eerie *Picnic at Hanging Rock* and Boer War epic *Breaker Morant.*

BOX-OFFICE BLITZ. After the critical successes of the 70s, the 80s brought Australian films into commercial favor at the box office, both at home and abroad, with hits like *Mad Max* and *Crocodile Dundee*. Films of the 1990s were personal, Australia-specific, and ultra-quirky—seen in intriguing character studies like *Muriel's Wedding* and *Shine*. Recent productions, such as Baz Luhrmann's *Moulin Rouge!* and Phillip Noyce's *Rabbit Proof Fence* demonstrate the multiplicity of themes and styles present in contemporary Australian film.

HOLIDAYS & FESTIVALS

Major regional festivals are also included within the state capitals. Banks, museums and other public buildings are often closed or operate with reduced hours during these times. School holidays differ between regions, but as a general rule, tourism peaks when school is out of session. **Summer holidays** for primary and secondary schools run from mid-December through January. There is a shorter set of **winter holidays** which run from the end of June through early July. Virtually every Australian town boasts a festival of some sort during the year, so we've listed only a few of the major ones to whet the appetite. More specific festival listings can be found by region throughout.

2004 DATE	HOLIDAY	DESCRIPTION
Jan. 1	New Year's Day	National public holiday
Jan. 16-26	Telstra Country Music Festival (Tamworth, NSW)	Over 2500 performances and golden guitars galore in Australia's country music capital (www.tamworth.nsw.gov.au)
Jan. 26	Australia Day	National day to commemorate the arrival of the First Fleet in 1788, with festivities centered in Sydney (www.australia-day.com.au)
Feb. 8-Mar. 1	Sydney Gay & Lesbian Mardi Gras	Famous display of pride that culminates in a spectacular street parade (www.mardigras.com.au)
Feb. 20-Mar. 14	Adelaide Fringe Festival	The largest independent alternative festival in Australia; held biannually to showcase cutting edge artists (www.adelaide-fringe.com.au)
Mar. 18-21	Australian Surf Lifesaving Championships	Gruelling ironman and ironwoman contests as well as the world's biggest surf party (www.slsa.asn.au)
Apr. 9	Good Friday	National public holiday
Apr. 12	Easter Monday	National public holiday
Apr. 25	Anzac Day	National commemoration that marks the anniversary of WWI ANZAC troops in Gallipoli (www.anzacday.org.au)
June 14	Queen's Birthday	National public holiday
Mid Jul. to early Aug.	Melbourne International Film Festival	Once a year, buffs, stars and critics flock to this exhibition of world film (www.melbournefilmfestival.com.au)
Nov. 2	Melbourne Cup	The horse race that stops the nation (www.melbourne-cup.com)
Dec. 27	Christmas Day/ Boxing Day Holiday	National public holiday

ADDITIONAL RESOURCES

GENERAL HISTORY

The Fatal Shore: The Epic of Australia's Founding, by Robert Hughes (1988). A vast and entertaining tableau of Australia's early history that looks at the effects of the transportation system on both colonists and Aboriginals.

A Short History of Australia, by Manning Clark (1987). A considerably condensed version of Clark's six-volume history that was voted the most influential work of Australian non-fiction in a recent poll.

Damned Whores and God's Police: the Colonization of Women in Australia, by Anne Summers (1975). A landmark work that details the treatment of women from the colonial era to contemporary times in Australian society.

Prehistory of Australia, by John Mulvaney and Johan Kamminga (1999). Offers a detailed account of the development of Aboriginal culture over the course of the last 40,000 years, from the continent's initial colonization to current issues of Aboriginal control over archaeological fieldwork.

FICTION & NON-FICTION

My Brother Jack, by George Johnston (1964). This highly moving and deeply felt story is laden with historical details from some of the most eventful years in Australia's development as a nation.

My Place, by Sally Morgan (1987). Morgan, who discovered her Aboriginal ancestry in her teens, tells a personal story of modern indigenous culture spanning 3 generations.

A Fortunate Life, by A.B. Facey (1981). An autobiographical novel about the quintessential "Aussie battler." Facey, who received no formal education, provides a personal account of early rural settlement with honesty and humor.

Cloudstreet, by Tim Winton (1991). A fragmented and poignant evocation of Perth suburban life in a rich Australian idiom.

The Harp in the South, by Ruth Park (1948). A nostalgic portrait of a working-class Irish family in olden-days Sydney by a popular Australian literary icon.

FILM

Gallipoli, dir. Peter Weir (1981). The WWI battle of Gallipoli has become a defining moment of Australian nationhood. Even as the futility of war is exposed, enduring Australian qualities of stoicism and mateship are celebrated.

The Adventures of Priscilla, Queen of the Desert, dir. Stephan Elliott (1994). A drag-queen road-trip that showcases both stunning outback scenery and fabulous frocks in a flick more camp than a tent-site.

The Castle, dir. Rob Sitch (1997). A blue-collar family from Melbourne's red-roofed suburbia takes on the system, and wins. Irreverent, egalitarian and fiercely Australian.

The Tracker, dir. Rolf de Heer (2002). This unique visual essay set against the grim landscape of the Red Center artfully and sensitively dramatizes the brutal treatment of Aborigines at the turn of the century.

TRAVEL BOOKS

The Songlines, by Bruce Chatwin (1987). Outback travel story based on the "dreaming-tracks" or "songlines" of Aboriginal Australia. Combines history, science, and philosophy.

Sydney, by Jan Morris (1992). Impressionistic, elegant account of Australia's greatest city which provides a portrait of modern Sydney illuminated through historical details.

Tracks: A Woman's Solo Trek Across 1,700 Miles of Australian Outback, by Robyn Davidson (1995). Armed with four camels and accompanied by a National Geographic photographer, Robyn Davidson crosses the desert and lives to tell the tale.

The Confessions of a Beachcomber, by E.J. Banfield (2001). Following Thoreau's example, Banfield ditches a stressful life and heads for the sun and sand of Dunk Island.

From Oppression to Reconciliation

In acquiring the Australian landmass in 1788, the British acted upon two assumptions that had served their interests well in North America. First, though the native peoples (dubbed "Australian Aborigines") evidently had "customs," these did not amount to a system of law and government, which would entitle them to indigenous sovereignty. Second, they roamed the land, hunting and gathering, and did not grow crops; therefore, the land was not their "property." Aborigines, who had previously occupied the continent for 50,000 years, suffered greatly under the British colonists. Investors in the wool industry rapidly dispersed flocks over their hunting grounds. When Aborigines killed these animals, the colonists responded with force ranging from imprisonment to summary execution. When Aborigines attempted trade (including men offering the sexual hospitality of their women), colonists often did not honor reciprocity. Australia's pastoral and mining frontiers were very often marked by greed, racism, misunderstanding and suspicion. Lacking fire-arms, horses, and fortifications, Aborigines were at a military disadvantage. These "frontier" conditions could be found in Australia as recently as the eve of WWII. The last known (unpunished) mass killing of Aborigines was in 1928, near Alice Springs. Twenty thousand slain is a reasonable estimate of the Aboriginal toll over the 140-year war of invasion, about 10 times the known toll on colonists. It is likely that disease was an even greater killer. There were three waves of smallpox—around 1789, 1830, and the late 1860s—against which Aborigines had neither immunity nor systems of care. Influenza, measles and venereal diseases also did great damage.

Aborigines who survived the killings and the diseases faced colonial authorities who were not sure what to do about them. The first wave of Christian missionaries had found them difficult to convert. Pastoralists began cautiously to employ them. "Half-castes"—children of (usually) white men and black women—would be absorbed into the wider population if they were trained in useful occupations.

Aborigines tried to maintain and adapt their communal life. They sought land security, requesting to learn the colonists' agriculture, as well as education and health services. However, Aborigines' efforts to be part of cities and rural communities were hindered by popular prejudice and restrictive laws. Aborigines found that their extended kinship networks were often their only source of emotional and material security. Where land security and services were granted, it was usually poorly funded and badly supervised. One form of "help" is now recalled with particular shame by most Australians. From 1897, state after state removed children from Aboriginal parents, reasoning that it was the state's duty to "rescue" younger Aboriginals from their cultural milieu. The emotional pain of these "Stolen Generations" got a respectful public hearing in Australia from 1997; the practice of racially-motivated removal had ceased by the 1970s.

Despite this ill treatment, some Aborigines developed sufficient loyalty to "King and Country" to enlist for the first and second world wars. After WWII, the Australian government began to dismantle discriminatory legal and institutional devices. Aborigines who had "risen" to white standards were now rewarded with "assimilation." This policy's most important benefit was admission to the social security system, for economic change was destroying the rural job market. However, assimilation required Aborigines to renounce their claims to land and to comply with prejudicial views of their heritage. The remote Aborigines, and many Aborigines with longer exposure to colonial authority, refused "assimilation," instead proposing the alternative policy of "self-determination."

Since the 1970s, Australian governments have acknowledged Aboriginal title to about one fifth of the continent. Some land-based industries enable Aboriginal pride and modest prosperity; but most Aborigines must find their opportunities in towns and cities. There, old prejudices compete with new understandings, sincere regrets about the past, and more or less helpful affirmations of the worth of "Aboriginality." Disproportionately unemployed, imprisoned, and afflicted by physical and emotional disorders, Aboriginal Australians still find that the colonial past weighs heavily. But a communal sense of being a "surviving" people remains strong.

Tim Rowse works in the History Program, Research School of Social Sciences at the Australian National University. His publications on Australian history include studies of colonial policy in Central Australia and a biography of H.C. Coombs.

ESSENTIALS

FACTS FOR THE TRAVELER

ENTRANCE REQUIREMENTS.
Passports (p. 23). Required of all visitors.
Visas (p. 24). Required of all visitors except holders of Australian and New Zealand passports.
Working Visa (p. 24). Required of all foreigners planning to work in Australia.
Inoculations (p. 32). Only necessary for those who come from or have just visited yellow fever-infected areas.
Driving Permit (p. 55). Recommended; required for most car rental agencies.

EMBASSIES & CONSULATES

AUSTRALIAN CONSULAR SERVICES ABROAD

Canada: High Commission, 50 O'Connor St. #710, **Ottawa,** ON K1P 6L2 (☎613-236-0841; fax 236-4376; www.ahc-ottawa.org).

Ireland: Fitzwilton House, 2nd Fl., Wilton Terr., **Dublin** 2 (☎01 6645 300; fax 661 3576; www.australianembassy.ie).

New Zealand: High Commission, 72-78 Hobson St., P.O. Box 4036, **Wellington** (☎04 473 6411; fax 498 7135; www.australia.org.nz). Consulate, Union House, 186-194 Quay St., Private Bag 92023, **Auckland** (☎09 921 8800; fax 921 8820).

South Africa: High Commission, 292 Orient St., Arcadia, **Pretoria** 0083; Private Bag X150, Pretoria 0001 (☎012 342 3740; fax 342 4222; www.australia.co.za).

United Kingdom: High Commission, Australia House, The Strand, **London** WC2B 4LA (☎171 379 4334; fax 465 8217; www.australia.org.uk). Consulate, Melrose House, 69 George St., **Edinburgh** EH2 2JG (☎131 624 3333; fax 240 5333).

United States: Visa requests should go to Washington, D.C. or Los Angeles. Embassy, 1601 Massachusetts Ave. NW, **Washington, D.C.** 20036-2273 (☎202-797-3000; fax 797-3168; www.austemb.org). Consulate, 150 E. 42nd St., 33rd fl., **New York,** NY 10017-5612 (☎212-351-6600; fax 351-6601). Consulate, 2049 Century Park E, 19th fl., **Los Angeles,** CA 90067-3121 (visas ☎310-229-4840; general 229-4800).

CONSULAR SERVICES IN AUSTRALIA

Canada: High Commission, Commonwealth Ave., **Canberra** ACT 2600 (☎02 6270 4000; fax 6273 3285). Consulate, Level 5, Quay West Building, 111 Harrington St., **Sydney** NSW 2000 (☎02 9364 3000; fax 9364 3098). Consulate, 267 St. George's Terr., **Perth** WA 6000 (☎08 9322 7930; fax 9261 7706).

Ireland: Embassy, 20 Arkana St., Yarralumla, **Canberra** ACT 2600 (☎02 6273 3022; fax 6273 3741). Consulate, Aberdeen St., P.O. Box 20, **Perth** WA 6865 (☎/fax 09 9385 8247). Consulate, Level 30, 400 George St., **Sydney** NSW 2000 (☎02 9231 6999; fax 9231 6254).

New Zealand: High Commission, Commonwealth Ave., **Canberra** ACT 2600 (☎02 6270 4211; fax 6273 3194). Consulate, Level 10, 55 Hunter St., GPO Box 365, **Sydney** NSW 2001 (passport ☎02 9223 0222; visa 9223 0144; fax 9221 7836).

South Africa: High Commission, State Circle, Yarralumla, **Canberra** ACT 2600 (☎ 02 6273 2424; fax 6273 3543).

United Kingdom: High Commission, Commonwealth Ave., Yarralumla, **Canberra** ACT 2600 (☎ 02 6270 6666; fax 6273 3236). Consulate, 17th fl., 90 Collins St., **Melbourne** VIC 3000 (☎ 03 9650 4155; fax 9650 3699). Consulate, Level 26, Allendale Sq., 77 St. George's Terr., **Perth** WA 6000 (☎ 08 9224 4700; fax 9224 4720). Consulate, Level 16, The Gateway, 1 Macquarie Pl., **Sydney** NSW 2000 (☎ 02 9247 7521; fax 9251 6201).

United States: Embassy, Moonah Pl., Yarralumla, **Canberra** ACT 2600 (☎ 02 6214 5600; fax 6214 5970). Consulate, Level 59, MLC Ctr., 19-29 Martin Pl., **Sydney** NSW 2000 (☎ 02 9373 9200; fax 9373 9184). Consulate, 553 St. Kilda Rd., **Melbourne** VIC 3004 (☎ 03 9526 5900; fax 9525 0769). Consulate, 13th floor, 16 St. George's Terr., **Perth** WA 6000 (☎ 08 9202 1224; fax 9231 9444).

TOURIST OFFICES

The government-sponsored **Australian Tourist Commission (ATC)** promotes tourism internationally, distributing literature and sponsoring helplines. The ATC carries books, magazines, and fact sheets for backpackers, younger people, disabled travelers, and others with special concerns. More info is on www.australia.com and www.atc.net.au, or you can contact these office affiliates:

Australia (Head Office): Level 4, 80 William St., **Wolloomooloo** NSW 2011; GPO Box 2721, **Sydney** NSW 1006 (☎ 02 9360 1111; fax 9331 6469).

New Zealand: Level 13, 44-48 Emily Pl., P.O. Box 1666, **Auckland** 1 (☎ 09 915 2826 or 0800 65 03 03; fax 307 3117).

United Kingdom: Gemini House, 10-18 Putney Hill, **London** SW15 6AA (☎ 20 8780 2229; fax 8780 1496).

US/Canada: 2049 Century Park E, Ste. 1920, **Los Angeles,** CA 90067 (☎ 310-229-4870 or 800-333-4305; fax 310-552-1215).

DOCUMENTS & FORMALITIES

PASSPORTS

REQUIREMENTS. Citizens of Canada, Ireland, New Zealand, South Africa, the UK, and the US need valid passports to enter Australia and to re-enter home countries. Be aware that travelers whose passports are scheduled to expire within 6 months may be refused entry. Returning home with an expired passport is illegal.

NEW PASSPORTS. Citizens of Canada, Ireland, New Zealand, the UK, and the US can apply for a passport at any post office, passport office, or court of law. Citizens of South Africa can apply for a passport at any office of Home Affairs. Any new passport or renewal applications must be filed well in advance of the departure date, though most passport offices offer rush services for a very steep fee. Citizens living abroad who need a passport or renewal should contact the nearest passport office of their home country.

PASSPORT MAINTENANCE. See **Identification** (p. 24), and make sure to keep copies of your passport handy as described. If you lose your passport, immediately notify the local police and the nearest embassy or consulate of your home government. To expedite its replacement, you will need to know its information and show ID and proof of citizenship. In some cases, a replacement may take weeks to process, and it may be valid only for a limited time. Visas stamped in your old pass-

> **US PASSPORTS.** Since April 8, 2002, US embassies and consulates no longer issue American passports abroad. Applying for a passport in a foreign consulate now takes longer because it needs to be printed in the US. In the case of lost or stolen passports, consulates will only issue temporary passports, which cannot be extended. For more info about lost and stolen passports, see the Australian US Embassy website (www.usembassy-australia.state.gov/consular/pptlost.html).

port will be hard to verify; in Australia, you must visit a regional office of the Department of Immigration and Multicultural and Indigenous Affairs, and you may incur a fee. In an emergency, ask for immediate emergency traveling papers that will permit you to re-enter your home country.

VISAS & ETA

Australia requires all visitors except Australian citizens and New Zealand passport holders to have a visa. You can obtain an **Electronic Travel Authority (ETA)** while purchasing your ticket at a travel agency, at the airport ticket counter, or over the Internet (www.eta.immi.gov.au). Quick and simple, the fully electronic ETA replaces a standard visa. It allows multiple visits within a one-year period provided that no trip lasts longer than three months. To extend a visit over three months, contact the nearest office of the Department of Immigration and Multicultural and Indigenous Affairs in Australia before the end of your three-month stay period. There is no provision for obtaining a further ETA when you are in Australia. For more info, contact the nearest Australian Tourist Commission branch (see p. 23). Standard visas (US$40) may be obtained from the nearest Australian high commission, embassy, or consulate. If you register in person, it will take two days to process; allow 21 working days by mail. Rates on extending your ETA or visa depend on length of stay and type of visa; an application to extend a standard visa is AUS$150. Contact the Department of Immigration and Multicultural and Indigenous Affairs at their inquiries line (☎ 13 18 81) before your stay period expires. Otherwise, contact an Australian consulate or embassy (see p. 22).

US citizens can take advantage of the **Center for International Business and Travel** (**CIBT**; ☎ 800-929-2428; customerservice@cibt.com), which secures visas for travel to most countries for a variable service charge. Between 8:30am and 8pm EST Monday through Friday, email will be returned within two hours.

Be sure to double-check on entrance requirements at the nearest embassy or consulate of Australia for up-to-date info before departure. US citizens can also consult www.pueblo.gsa.gov/cic_text/travel/foreign/foreignentryreqs.html.

IDENTIFICATION

Always carry two or more forms of identification on your person, including at least one photo ID; a passport combined with a driver's license or birth certificate is usually adequate. Be sure to separate your forms of ID in case of theft or loss, and keep photocopies of them in your luggage and at home. Before leaving, copy any visas and the page of your passport with your photo. Consulates also recommend that you carry an expired passport or an official copy of your birth certificate in your baggage, separate from other documents.

STUDENT, YOUTH, & TEACHER IDENTIFICATION. The **International Student Identity Card (ISIC),** the most widely accepted form of student ID, provides discounts on sights, accommodations, food, and transport (typically around 10%); access to a 24hr. emergency helpline (in North America ☎ 877-370-ISIC, elsewhere US collect +1 715-345-0505); and insurance benefits for US cardholders (see **Insurance**, p. 35). The ISIC is preferable to the ID of a specific university or other institution because it is more likely to be recognized and honored abroad. Applicants must be degree-seeking students of a secondary or post-secondary school and must be of at least 12 years of age. Because of the proliferation of fake ISICs, some services (particularly airlines) require additional proof of student identity, such as a school ID or a letter attesting to your student status.

For travelers who are under 26 but not students, the **International Youth Travel Card (IYTC)** offers many of the same benefits as the ISIC. The **International Teacher Identity Card (ITIC)** offers teachers the same insurance coverage as the ISIC as well as similar but limited discounts. Each of these identity cards costs US$22 or equivalent. Many student travel agencies (see p. 47) issue the cards. For a listing of issuing agencies, or for more information, contact the **International Student Travel Confederation (ISTC)**, Herengracht 479, 1017 BS Amsterdam, Netherlands (☎ +31 20 421 28 00; fax 421 28 10; www.istc.org).

DISCOUNTS. "Concessions" is the Australian catch-all phrase for discounts always given to specific groups, most often students and senior citizens. However, it may be limited to holders of specific Australian concession cards. "Pensioners" are Australian senior citizens, and discounts for pensioners may not apply to non-Australians who otherwise fit the bill. Student discounts often require that you show an ID and may only apply to Australian university students, or even to university students within the particular state. Discounts on accommodations are regularly given to VIP, YHA, ISIC, or NOMADS card holders.

CUSTOMS

As an island nation, geographically isolated Australia has managed to avoid some of the pests and diseases that plague other countries. But burgeoning tourism has increased the risk of contamination from imported goods, and the Customs Bureau takes the need to protect Australia's shores seriously. Articles not automatically forbidden but subject to a **quarantine inspection** may include camping equipment, live animals, food, animal products, plants, plant products, and protected wildlife. Don't risk large fines or hassles when entering Australia—throw out questionable items in the big customs bins as you leave the plane, and declare anything about which you have the slightest suspicion. The beagles in orange smocks know their stuff, and they *will* find you out. If you must bring your **pets** with you, contact the **Australian Quarantine and Inspections Service,** Edmund Barton Building, Kings Avenue, Barton ACT 2600 (☎ 02 6272 3933; animal-imp@aqis.gov.au) to obtain a permit. Pick up *Customs Information for Travellers* at an Australian consulate or any travel agency for more info. Australia expressly forbids the entry of drugs, steroids, and weapons.

Visitors over 18 may bring into Australia up to 1125mL alcohol and 250 cigarettes (or 250g tobacco) **duty-free.** For other goods, whether or not intended as gifts, the allowance is AUS$400 (over 18) or AUS$200 (under 18). Upon returning home, you must declare articles acquired abroad and pay a **duty** on the value of articles that exceeds the allowance established by your country's customs service. Goods bought at **duty-free** shops abroad are not exempt from duty tax at your return; you must declare these items as well. "Duty-free" merely means that you need not pay a tax in the country of purchase. On the bright side, Australia recently implemented a **Tourist Refund Scheme** (TRS) that refunds the **Goods and Services Tax** (GST) on items bought in Australia (see **Tipping and Taxes,** p. 29). For more information on customs requirements, contact the following:

Australia: Australian Customs Service (in Australia ☎ 1300 363 263, elsewhere ☎ 02 6275 6666; www.customs.gov.au).

Canada: Canadian Customs and Revenue Agency, 2265 St. Laurent Blvd., Ottawa, ON K1G 4K3 (☎ 800 461 9999, elsewhere ☎ 204 983 3500; www.ccra-adrc.gc.ca).

Ireland: Customs Information Office, Irish Life Ctr., Lower Abbey St., Dublin 1 (☎ 01 878 8811; fax 878 0836; ceadmin@revenue.iol.ie; www.revenue.ie).

New Zealand: New Zealand Customhouse, 17-21 Whitmore St., Box 2218, Wellington (☎ 04 473 6099, general 09 300 5399 or 0800 428 786; fax 04 473 7370; www.customs.govt.nz).

South Africa: Customs and Excise, P.O. Box 13802, Tramshed, Pretoria 0001 (☎ 012 334 6400; fax 328 6478; www.sars.gov.za).

United Kingdom: Her Majesty's Customs and Excise, Passenger Enquiry Team, Wayfarer House, Great South West Rd., Feltham, Middlesex TW14 8NP (☎ 020 8910 3744; National Advice Service: 0845 010 9000; www.hmce.gov.uk).

United States: US Customs Service, 1300 Pennsylvania Ave. NW, Washington, D.C. 20229 (☎ 202-927-1000; fax 354-1010; www.customs.gov).

MONEY

CURRENCY. *Let's Go: Australia* lists all prices in Australian Dollars unless otherwise noted in the text.

In cities, credit cards are widely accepted; in rural areas, consider carrying more cash. Personal checks are seldom accepted, and even traveler's checks may not be accepted in some locations.

CURRENCY & EXCHANGE

AUSTRALIAN DOLLARS	
US$1 = AUS$1.52	AUS$1= US$0.66
CDN$1 = AUS$1.09	AUS$1= CDN$0.92
UK£1 = AUS$2.44	AUS$1= UK£0.41
NZ$1 = AUS$0.89	AUS$1= NZ$1.12
ZAR1 = AUS$0.21	AUS$1= ZAR4.81
EUR€ = AUS$1.72	AUS$1= EUR€0.58

The Australian currency comes in dollars ($) and cents (¢). Notes come in $5, $10, $20, $50, and $100 denominations, and coins in 5¢, 10¢, 20¢, 50¢, $1, and $2 denominations. The chart above is based on August 2003 exchange rates between local currency and US dollars (US$), Canadian dollars (CDN$), British pounds (UK£), New Zealand dollars (NZ$), South African Rand (ZAR), and European Union euros (EUR€). Check a large newspaper or the currency calculator on our website (www.letsgo.com) for the latest exchange rates.

As a general rule, it's much cheaper to convert money in Australia than it is to convert it in your home country. However, it's a good idea to bring enough Australian dollars to last for the first 24-72 hours of a trip to avoid being penniless after banking hours or on a holiday. In the US, **International Currency Express** (☎ 888-278-6628; www.foreignmoney.com) will deliver foreign currency for over 120 countries or traveler's checks to your home overnight (US$15) or second-day (US$12) at competitive exchange rates.

Watch out for commission rates, and check newspapers for the standard rate of exchange. When changing money abroad, try to go only to banks or *bureaux de change* that have at most a 5% margin between their buy and sell prices. The largest and most widespread banks in Australia are ANZ, Commonwealth, National, and Westpac. Since you lose money with every transaction, **convert large sums** (unless the currency is depreciating rapidly, which is not likely to be the case in Australia in the near future), **but no more than you'll need**. In fact, using an ATM (see p. 46) or a credit card (see p. 27) often gets you the best possible rates.

When you use traveler's checks or bills in your home currency, carry some in small denominations (the equivalent of US$50 or less) for times when you are forced to exchange money at disadvantageous rates, but bring a range of denominations, since charges may be levied per check cashed. Store your money in a variety of forms; ideally, you will at any given time be carrying some cash, some traveler's checks, and an ATM card and/or credit card (see p. 27).

TRAVELER'S CHECKS

Traveler's checks are one of the safest and least troublesome means of carrying funds, since they can be refunded if stolen or lost. Several agencies and banks sell them, usually for face value plus a small commission. Sometimes you can even escape the commission; for instance, members of the American Automobile Association and some banks and credit unions can get American Express checks commission-free (see **International Driving Permits,** p. 55). Each traveler's check agency provides refunds if checks are lost or stolen, and many provide additional services like toll-free refund hotlines, emergency message services, and stolen credit card assistance. The most recognized brands are listed below.

While traveling, keep check receipts and a record of which ones you've cashed (separate from the checks themselves). Leave a list of check numbers with someone at home. Never countersign checks until you're ready to cash them, and when you do cash them, always have your passport with you. If your checks are lost or stolen, immediately contact one of your agency's refund centers to be reimbursed; they may require a police report verifying the loss. Less touristed, rural areas may not have refund centers at all, so you might have to wait to be reimbursed.

American Express: Checks available with commission at select banks and all AmEx offices. US residents can also purchase checks by phone (☎888-887-8986) or online (www.aexp.com). AAA (see p. 55) offers commission-free checks to its members. Checks available in US, Australian, British, Canadian, Japanese, and Euro currencies. *Cheques for Two* can be signed by either of 2 people traveling together. For purchase locations or more information, contact AmEx's service centers: in the US and Canada ☎800-221-7282; in the UK 0800 521 313; in Australia 800 25 19 02; in New Zealand 0800 441 068; elsewhere US collect +1 801-964-6665.

Visa: Checks available (generally with commission) at banks worldwide. For the location of the nearest office, call Visa's service centers: In the US ☎800-227-6811; in the UK 0800 89 50 78; elsewhere UK collect +44 020 7937 8091. Checks available in US, British, Canadian, Japanese, and Euro currencies.

Travelex/Thomas Cook: In the US and Canada ☎800-287-7362; in the UK 0800 62 21 01; elsewhere UK collect +44 1733 31 89 50.

CREDIT & DEBIT CARDS

Credit cards are generally accepted by all but the smallest businesses in Australia. Where they are accepted, credit cards often offer superior exchange rates—up to 5% better than the retail rate used by banks and other currency exchange estab-

ESSENTIALS

lishments—but some credit cards will then charge you a special fee for the service, so be sure to check beforehand. Credit cards may also offer traveler services such as insurance or emergency help; credit cards are also sometimes required to reserve rental cars or rooms at accommodations. **MasterCard** and **Visa** are the most welcomed cards; **American Express** cards work at some ATMs and major airports, and of course at American Express offices.

ATM CARDS

ATM cards are widespread in Australia. Depending on the system that your home bank uses, you can most likely access your personal bank account from abroad. ATMs get the same wholesale exchange rate as credit cards get, but banks or card issuers often place a limit on the amount of money you can withdraw per day (around US$500). Most importantly, computerized withdrawal networks sometimes fail. There is typically also a surcharge of US$1-5 per withdrawal. Be sure to memorize your PIN code in numeric form since machines often don't have letters on their keys. Also, if your PIN is longer than four digits, ask your bank whether you need a new number.

ELECTRONIC BANKING

The two major international money networks are **Cirrus** (US ☎ 800-424-7787) and **PLUS** (US ☎ 800-843-7587). To locate ATMs around the world, call the above numbers or consult www.mastercard.com/cardholderservices/atm or http://visaatm.infonow.net/bin/findNow?CLIENT_ID=VISA. **Cirrus** is the most widespread ATM network in Australia; **PLUS** is almost as frequent, and **Visa,** though probably third best, is still fairly common. **MasterCard** and **American Express** are found less often and **NYCE** not at all. Though ATMs are increasingly prevalent in smaller towns and rural areas, they are scarce in northern Western Australia and more remote interior areas.

Visa TravelMoney (for emergency assistance in Australia ☎ 0800 450 346) is a system allowing Visa cardholders to access money from any ATM with a Visa sticker on it; these are quite common throughout the country. You deposit an amount of money in your account before you travel (plus a small administration fee), after which you can withdraw up to that sum. These cards, which give you the same favorable exchange rate for withdrawals as a regular Visa card, are especially useful if you plan to travel through many countries. Check with your local bank or AAA chapter to see if it issues TravelMoney cards.

EFTPOS

Electronic Funds Transfer at Point Of Sale (EFTPOS) is an extremely common way for Australians to pay for goods. ATM cards (from Australian banks only) swiped at the register double as debit cards, withdrawing money directly from your bank account. What's more, most establishments offer EFTPOS with a **cashback** option, cutting down on the number of transactions you must perform and thereby saving you time and per-transaction bank fees. EFTPOS is useful for travelers because it means they can carry less cash and not have to worry about credit card bills, so if you'll be in Australia for a while, it might make sense to open an Australian bank account. A permanent Australian address and two or three forms of identification are required to open an account—your home driver's license and your passport are the most sure-fire bets—and you can expect a routine check on your credit history. Bringing along bank statements from home for the last three months can expedite the process enormously; accounts can be ready in as little as an hour. Banks accept cash or traveler's checks as initial deposits.

GETTING MONEY FROM HOME

If you run out of money while traveling, the easiest and cheapest solution is to have someone back home make a deposit to your credit card or ATM card. Failing that, consider one of the following options.

WIRING MONEY

It is possible to arrange a **bank money transfer,** which means asking a bank back home to wire money to a bank in Australia. This is the cheapest way to transfer cash, but it's also the slowest, usually taking several days or more. Note that some banks may only release your funds in local currency, potentially sticking you with a poor exchange rate; inquire about this in advance. Money transfer services like **Western Union** are faster and more convenient than bank transfers, but also much pricier. Western Union has many locations worldwide. (To find one, visit www.westernunion.com, or call in Australia ☎800 501 500, in the US ☎800-325-6000, in Canada ☎800-235-0000, in the UK ☎0800 83 38 33, in New Zealand ☎800 27 0000, or in South Africa ☎0860 100031.) Money transfer services are also available at **American Express** and **Thomas Cook** offices.

US STATE DEPARTMENT (US CITIZENS ONLY)

In dire emergencies only, the US State Department will forward money within hours to the nearest consular office, which will then disburse it according to instructions for a US$15 fee. To use this service, contact the Overseas Citizens Service division of the US State Department (☎202-647-5225; nights, Sundays, and holidays ☎202-647-4000).

TIPPING & TAXES

In Australia, tipping is not required at restaurants, bars, taxis, or hotels—service workers do not rely on tips for income. Tips are occasionally left at pricier restaurants, when the service is exceptionally attentive. In this case, 10% is more than a sufficient amount. Taxes are always already included in the bill, so only pay the price that is advertised.

The New Tax System of 2000 provides for a **10% Goods and Services Tax (GST).** Some goods such as basic foods and medicines are not subject to this tax. However, the System also implemented a **Tourist Refund Scheme (TRS)** whereby tourists may be entitled to a refund of the GST and of the **Wine Equalisation Tax (WET)** on purchases of goods bought from Australian retailers. The refund is only good for GST or WET paid on purchases of $300 or more. Travelers can claim the refund from customs officers when departing Australia by presenting tax receipts from retailers along with a valid passport and proof of travel at TRS booths in the international airports or cruise terminals. For more information on the TRS, see the Australian Customs Service web page (www.customs.gov.au).

SAFETY & SECURITY

Although Australia is a relatively safe country, it is always important to keep personal safety in mind. Tourists are particularly vulnerable to crime because thieves assume that they are carrying large amounts of cash and are sometimes more easily disoriented than locals are.

 EMERGENCY NUMBER. Throughout Australia, dial ☎000.

PERSONAL SAFETY

EXPLORING

To avoid unwanted attention, try to blend in as much as possible. Familiarize yourself with your surroundings before setting out, and carry yourself with confidence. Check maps in shops and restaurants rather than on the street. If you are traveling alone, be sure someone at home knows your itinerary, and never admit that you're traveling alone.

At night, stick to busy, well-lit streets and avoid dark alleyways. If you feel uncomfortable, leave as quickly and directly as you can. Find out about unsafe areas tourist offices, the manager of your hotel or hostel, or a local whom you trust. You may want to carry a **whistle** to scare off attackers or attract attention. For **emergency medical help, police, or fire, dial ☎000** anywhere in Australia.

SELF DEFENSE

There is no sure-fire way to avoid all the threatening situations you might encounter, but a good self-defense course will give you concrete ways to react to unwanted advances. **Impact, Prepare, and Model Mugging** can refer you to local self-defense courses in the US (☎800-345-5425; www.impactsafety.org). Workshops (2-3hr.) start at US$50; full courses (20hr.) run US$350-500.

DRIVING

If you are using a **car,** learn local driving signals and wear a seatbelt. Children under 40 lbs. should ride only in a specially-designed carseat, available for a small fee from most car rental agencies. Study route maps before you hit the road, and if you plan on spending a lot of time driving, consider bringing spare parts. If your car breaks down, wait for the police to assist you. For long drives in desolate areas, invest in a cellular phone and a roadside assistance program. Be sure to park your vehicle in a garage or well traveled area, and use a steering wheel locking device in larger cities. **Sleeping in your car** is one of the most dangerous ways to get your rest. For info on the perils of **hitchhiking,** see p. 56. Also see **Driving in the Outback** (p. 79) for more info on driving in Australia.

TERRORISM

Australia has been at a heightened level of alert for possible terrorist attacks since the attacks on the United States on 11 September, 2001. An up-do-date assessment of the terrorism threat can be found at **National Security Australia's** website (www.nationalsecurity.gov.au). Travelers can also call the National Security Hotline (☎1-800-123-400). The box on **travel advisories** below refers to offices and webpages that provide the most updated list of your home government's warnings about travel.

FINANCIAL SECURITY

PROTECTING YOUR VALUABLES. There are a few steps you can take to minimize the financial risk associated with traveling. First, **bring as little with you as possible.** Second, buy a few combination **padlocks** to secure your belongings either in your pack or in a hostel or train-station locker. Third, **carry as little cash as possible.** Keep your traveler's checks and ATM/credit cards in a **money belt** along with your passport and ID cards. Fourth, **keep a small cash reserve separate from your primary stash.** This should be about US$50 (US$ is best) stored in the depths of your pack, along with your traveler's check numbers and important photocopies.

! TRAVEL ADVISORIES. The following national government offices provide extensive country information and international travel advisories by telephone, by fax, or via the web:

Australian Department of Foreign Affairs and Trade: ☎ 1300 555 135; faxback service 02 6261 1299; www.dfat.gov.au.

Canadian Department of Foreign Affairs and International Trade (DFAIT): In Canada and the US call ☎ 800-267-6788, elsewhere call +1 613-944-4000; www.dfait-maeci.gc.ca. Call for their free booklet, *Bon Voyage...But.*

New Zealand Ministry of Foreign Affairs: ☎ 04 439 8000; fax 494 8506; www.mft.govt.nz/travel/index.html.

United Kingdom Foreign and Commonwealth Office: ☎ 020 7008 0232; fax 7008 0155; www.fco.gov.uk.

US Department of State: ☎ 202-647-5225; faxback service 202-647-3000; http://travel.state.gov. For their free *A Safe Trip Abroad,* call 202-512-1800.

ESSENTIALS

PICKPOCKETS

Never let your passport and your bags out of your sight. Beware of **pickpockets** in city crowds, especially on public transportation. Also, be alert in public telephone booths. If you must say your calling card number, do so very quietly; if you punch it in, make sure no one can look over your shoulder.

ACCOMMODATIONS & TRANSPORTATION

Never leave your belongings unattended; crime occurs in even the most demure-looking hostel or hotel. Bring a **padlock** for hostel lockers, and don't ever store valuables in any locker.

Be particularly careful on **buses** and **trains;** horror stories abound about determined thieves who wait for travelers to fall asleep before striking. Always carry your backpack in front of you where you can see it. When traveling with others, sleep in alternating shifts. When alone, use good judgement in selecting a train compartment; never stay in an empty one, and use a secure lock to secure your pack to the luggage rack. Try to sleep on top bunks with your luggage stored above you (if not in bed with you), and keep important documents and other valuables on your person. If traveling by **car,** don't leave valuables (such as radios or luggage) in it while you are away.

DRUGS & ALCOHOL

Australia has quite strict drug laws. There is currently a debate over whether or not to legalize marijuana, but for now it remains illegal. Australia does not differentiate between illicit substances; all are illegal to possess in any quantity. If you carry **prescription drugs,** take a copy of the prescription with you.

There are very strict **drunk-driving** (or "drink-driving," as Aussies say) laws in effect all over the country, and most states operate frequent random breath-testing. The maximum legal blood-alcohol limit for drivers is .05%. For drivers under 21 or drivers under 25 who have had their license for less than three years, the maximum blood-alcohol limit is 0%. You must be 18 or older in order to purchase alcohol or consume it in public.

Smoking is prohibited in most enclosed buildings and on most public transportation in Australia; remember that this rule also includes domestic and international flights. Furthermore, in some Australian states smoking is also prohibited in restaurants and bars.

HEALTH

Common sense is the simplest prescription for good health while you are traveling. Drink plenty of fluids to prevent dehydration and constipation in the bright Australian sun, and always wear sturdy, broken-in shoes and clean socks. In the event of a serious illness or emergency, call ☎**000 from any phone** to connect to police, an ambulance, or the fire department.

BEFORE YOU GO

In your **passport,** write the names of any people you wish to be contacted in case of a medical emergency, and list any allergies or medical conditions. Matching a prescription to a foreign equivalent is not always easy, safe, or possible, so carry up-to-date, legible prescriptions or a statement from your doctor stating the medication's trade name, manufacturer, chemical name, and dosage. While traveling, be sure to keep all medication with you in your carry-on luggage. For tips on packing a basic **first-aid kit** and other health essentials, see p. 32.

IMMUNIZATIONS

INOCULATION REQUIREMENTS. Vaccinations are not required unless you have visited a yellow fever-infected country or zone within six days prior to arrival. See www.health.gov.au/pubhlth/strateg/communic/factsheets/yellow.htm for more information.

Travelers over two years old should make sure that the following vaccines are up to date: MMR (for measles, mumps, and rubella); DTaP or Td (for diptheria, tetanus, and pertussis); OPV (for polio); HbCV (for haemophilus influenza B); and HBV (for hepatitus B). For recommendations on immunizations and prophylaxis, consult the CDC (see below) in the US or the equivalent in your home country, and check with a doctor for guidance.

USEFUL ORGANIZATIONS & PUBLICATIONS

The US **Centers for Disease Control and Prevention** (**CDC;** ☎877-FYI-TRIP; fax 888-232-3299; www.cdc.gov/travel) maintains an international travelers' hotline and an informative website. The CDC's comprehensive booklet, *Health Information for International Travel*, an annual rundown of disease, immunization, and general health advice, is free online; paper copies are US$25 via the Public Health Foundation (☎877-252-1200). Consult the appropriate government agency of your home country for consular information sheets on health, entry requirements, and other issues for various countries (see the listings in the box on **Travel Advisories,** p. 31). For info on health and other travel warnings, call the **Overseas Citizens Services** (☎202-647-5225; after-hours 647-4000), or contact a passport agency, embassy, or consulate abroad. US citizens can send a self-addressed, stamped envelope to the Overseas Citizens Services, Bureau of Consular Affairs, #4811, US Department of State, Washington, D.C. 20520. For info on medical evacuation services and travel insurance firms, see the US government's website (http://travel.state.gov/medical.html) or that of the **British Foreign and Commonwealth Office** (www.fco.gov.uk).

For detailed information on travel health, including a country-by-country overview of diseases, try the **International Travel Health Guide** (US$24.95; www.travmed.com). For general health info, contact the **American Red Cross** (☎800-564-1234; www.redcross.org).

MEDICAL ASSISTANCE ON THE ROAD

If you are concerned about obtaining medical assistance while traveling, you may wish to employ special support services. The *MedPass* from **GlobalCare, Inc.,** 6875 Shiloh Rd. East, Alpharetta, GA 30005, USA (☎ 800-860-1111; fax 678-341-1800; www.globalems.com), provides 24hr. international medical assistance, support, and medical evacuation resources. The **International Association for Medical Assistance to Travelers** (**IAMAT;** US ☎ 716-754-4883, Canada ☎ 519-836-0102, New Zealand ☎ 03-352-4630; www.cybermall.co.nz/NZ/IAMAT) has free membership, lists English-speaking doctors worldwide, and offers detailed info on immunization requirements and sanitation. If your regular **insurance** policy does not cover travel abroad, you may wish to purchase additional coverage (see p. 35)

ONCE IN AUSTRALIA

ENVIRONMENTAL HAZARDS

Heat exhaustion & dehydration: Heat exhaustion leads to nausea, excessive thirst, headaches, and dizziness. Avoid it by drinking plenty of fluids, eating salty foods (e.g. crackers), and abstaining from dehydrating beverages (e.g. alcohol and caffeinated drinks). Continuous heat stress can eventually lead to heatstroke, characterized by a rising temperature, severe headache, delirium and cessation of sweating. Victims should be cooled off with wet towels and taken to a doctor.

Sunburn: Apply sunscreen liberally and often to avoid burns and lower the risk of skin cancer. If you are planning on spending time near water, in the desert, or in the snow, you are especially at risk of getting burned, even through clouds. If you get sunburned, drink more fluids than usual and apply an aloe-based lotion. Severe sunburns can lead to sun poisoning, a condition that affects the entire body, causing fever, chills, nausea, and vomiting. Sun poisoning should always be treated by a doctor.

INSECT-BORNE DISEASES

Many diseases are transmitted by insects—mainly mosquitoes, fleas, ticks, and lice. Be aware of insects in wet or forested areas (such as northern Queensland and Kakadu, NT), especially while hiking and camping. Wear long pants and long sleeves, tuck your pants into your socks, and buy a mosquito net. Use insect repellents such as DEET, and soak or spray your gear with permethrin (licensed in the US for use on clothing). **Ticks**—responsible for Lyme and other diseases—can be particularly dangerous in rural and forested regions. While walking, pause periodically to brush off ticks from exposed parts of your body using a fine-toothed comb. Do not attempt to remove ticks by burning them. Natural repellents can be useful; taking vitamin B-12 pills regularly can make you smelly to insects, as can garlic pills. Calamine lotion or topical cortisones (like Cortaid) may stop insect bites from itching, as can a bath with a half-cup of baking soda or oatmeal.

The following insect-borne diseases occur in parts of Australia; consult the **Communicable Diseases Network Australia** (http://www.health.gov.au/pubhlth/cdi/cdihtml.htm) for a more complete list.

Dengue fever: An "urban viral infection" transmitted by *Aedes* mosquitoes, which bite during the day rather than at night. Causing periodic epidemics in parts of northern Queensland and the Torres Strait Islands, dengue fever is often indicated by a rash 3-4 days after the onset of fever. Early symptoms include chills, high fever, headaches, swollen lymph nodes and muscle aches. If you experience these symptoms, see a doctor, drink plenty of liquids, and take fever-reducing medication such as acetaminophen (Tylenol). *Never take aspirin to treat dengue fever.*

Murray Valley encephalitis (MVE): A rare viral infection of the central nervous system, transmitted by mosquitoes, and found primarily in northern Western Australia, Queensland, and the Northern Territory. Symptoms include headache, fever, stupor, neck stiffness, confusion, paralysis, and coma.

Ross River & Barmah Forest Virus (epidemic polyarthritis): A disease transmitted by mosquitoes occurring primarily in coastal areas of Australia. Symptoms include fever, rash, joint pain and lethargy. Full recovery can take up to several months.

OTHER HEALTH CONCERNS

AIDS, HIV, & STDS

For detailed information on **Acquired Immune Deficiency Syndrome (AIDS)** in Australia, call the **US Centers for Disease Control's** 24hr. hotline at ☎800-342-2437, or contact the **Joint United Nations Programme on HIV/AIDS (UNAIDS)**, 20, ave. Appia, CH-1211 Geneva 27, Switzerland (☎+41 22 791 3666; fax 22 791 4187). Australia only requires HIV testing of applicants for permanent residence.

Sexually transmitted diseases (STDs) such as gonorrhea, chlamydia, genital warts, syphilis, and herpes are easier to catch than HIV and can be just as deadly. **Hepatitis** B and C can also be transmitted sexually. Though condoms may protect you from some STDs, oral or even tactile contact can lead to transmission. If you think you may have contracted an STD, see a doctor immediately.

WOMEN'S HEALTH

Women travelers may be vulnerable to **urinary tract** and **bladder infections,** common and uncomfortable bacterial diseases that cause a burning sensation and painful (sometimes frequent) urination. Over-the-counter medicines can sometimes alleviate symptoms, but if they persist, see a doctor.

Vaginal yeast infections may flare up in hot and humid climates. Wearing loosely fitting trousers or a skirt and cotton underwear will help, as will over-the-counter remedies like Monostat or Gynelotrimin. **Tampons** and **pads** are sometimes hard to find when traveling, especially in less populated areas, so it may be advisable to take supplies along. **Reliable contraceptive devices** may also be difficult to find. Women on the pill should bring enough to allow for extended stays.

INSURANCE

Travel insurance generally covers four basic areas: medical/health problems, property loss, trip cancellation/interruption, and emergency evacuation. Although your regular insurance policies may well extend to travel-related accidents, you may consider purchasing travel insurance if the cost of potential trip cancellation/interruption is greater than you can absorb. Prices for travel insurance purchased separately generally run about US$50 per week for full coverage, while trip cancellation/interruption may be purchased separately at a rate of about US$5.50 per US$100 of coverage.

Medical insurance (especially university policies) often covers costs incurred abroad; check with your provider. **US Medicare** does not cover foreign travel. **Canadians** are protected by their home province's health insurance plan for up to 90 days after leaving the country; check with the provincial Ministry of Health or Health Plan Headquarters for details. **Homeowners' insurance** (or your family's coverage) often covers theft during travel and loss of travel documents (passport, plane ticket, railpass, etc.) up to US$500.

ISIC and ITIC (see p. 24) provide basic insurance benefits, including US$100 per day of in-hospital sickness for up to 60 days, US$3000 of accident-related medical reimbursement, and US$25,000 for emergency medical transport. Cardholders have access to a toll-free 24hr. helpline (run by the insurance provider **TravelGuard**) for medical, legal, and financial emergencies overseas (US and Canada ☎ 877-370-4742, elsewhere US collect +1-715-345-0505). **American Express** (US ☎ 800-528-4800) grants most cardholders automatic car rental insurance (collision and theft, but not liability) and ground travel accident coverage of US$100,000 on flight purchases made with the card.

PACKING

Pack light: lay out only what you absolutely need, then take half the clothes and twice the money. The less you have, the less you have to lose (or store, or carry on your back). Save any extra space left for souvenirs or for items that you might pick up along the way in your travels.

LUGGAGE. Toting a suitcase or trunk is fine if you plan to stay in one or two cities in Australia and explore from there, but not a great idea if you plan to move around frequently. If you plan to cover any extended part of your itinerary by foot, a sturdy **frame backpack** is absolutely unbeatable. (For the basics on buying a pack, see p. 78.) A small backpack or courier bag may be useful as a daypack for sightseeing expeditions.

CLOTHING. No matter if it's the Wet or the Dry, it's always a good idea to bring a **warm jacket** or wool sweater, a **rain jacket** (Gore-Tex® is both waterproof and breathable), sturdy shoes or **hiking boots,** and **thick socks. Flip-flops** or waterproof sandals are crucial for grubby hostel showers. You may also want to add one outfit beyond the jeans and t-shirt uniform, and maybe a nicer pair of shoes if you plan to do any clubbing in the bigger cities.

SLEEPSACKS. Many hostels require that you either provide your own linen or rent sheets from them. You can save cash by making your own sleepsack: simply fold a full-size sheet in half the long way, then sew it closed along the long side and along one of the short sides. Keep in mind that some of the bigger hostels in larger cities prohibit sleeping bags.

CONVERTERS & ADAPTERS. In Australia, electricity is 220-240V AC, 50Hz, enough to fry North American appliances, calibrated for 110V. Hardware stores sell adapters (to change the shape of the plug) and converters (to change the voltage). Don't make the mistake of using only an adapter without a converter, unless instructions state otherwise.

FIRST-AID KIT. For a basic first-aid kit, pack: bandages, pain reliever, antibiotic cream, a thermometer, a Swiss Army knife, tweezers, moleskin, decongestant, motion-sickness remedy, diarrhea or upset-stomach medication (Pepto Bismol or Imodium), an antihistamine, sunscreen, insect repellent, and burn ointment.

FILM. Film and developing are widely available. Less serious photographers may want to bring a **disposable camera** or two rather than an expensive permanent one. Despite disclaimers, airport security X-rays *can* fog film, so buy a lead-lined pouch at a camera store or ask security to hand-inspect it. Always pack film in your carry-on luggage, since higher-intensity X-rays are used on checked luggage.

OTHER USEFUL ITEMS. For safety purposes, you should bring a **money belt** and small **padlock.** Basic **outdoors equipment** (plastic water bottle, compass, waterproof matches, pocketknife, sunglasses, sunscreen, hat) may also prove useful. **Quick**

repairs of torn garments can be done on the road with a needle and thread; also consider bringing electrical tape for patching tears. If you want to do laundry by hand, bring detergent, a small rubber ball to stop up the sink, and string for a makeshift clothes line. **Other things** you're liable to forget: an umbrella, sealable **plastic bags** (for damp clothes, soap, food, shampoo, and other spillables), an **alarm clock,** safety pins, a flashlight, earplugs, garbage bags, and a small **calculator.**

IMPORTANT DOCUMENTS. Don't forget your passport, traveler's checks, ATM and/or credit cards, adequate ID, and photocopies of all of the aforementioned in case these documents are lost or stolen (see p. 24).

ACCOMMODATIONS

HOSTELS

> **A HOSTELER'S BILL OF RIGHTS.** There are certain standard fea-
> tures that we do not include in our hostel listings. Unless we state otherwise,
> you can expect that every hostel has no lockout, no curfew, a kitchen, free hot
> showers, and no key deposit.

Hostels are generally dorm-style accommodations, often in single-sex rooms with bunk beds, although many hostels also offer private rooms for families and couples. Some have kitchens and utensils for your use, bike rentals, storage areas, transportation to airports and train stations, breakfast, organized tours, and laundry facilities. There can be drawbacks: hostels may close during certain daytime "lockout" hours, have a curfew, don't accept reservations, or impose a maximum stay. Bring your own **padlock** for your storage locker. Many hostels allow guests to leave valuables in a safe at the front desk. In Australia, a bed in a hostel will average around AUS$15-20. A **VIP** membership card offered by **VIP Backpackers** (www.backpackers.com.au) gets discounts at many hostels. *Let's Go* designates these hostels with a VIP at the end of the listing. The two most common hostel chains in Australia are YHA and NOMADS (see below). A list of many hostels, regardless of affiliation, can be found at www.hostels.com.

HOSTELLING INTERNATIONAL

Joining the youth hostel association in your own country (listed below) automatically grants you membership privileges in **Hostelling International (HI),** a federation of national hosteling associations. The Australian branch of HI, **YHA Australia,** has hostels and agencies throughout Australia that are typically less expensive than private hostels. Many accept reservations via the **International Booking Network** (Australia ☎02 9261 1111, Canada ☎800-663-5777, England and Wales ☎1629 58 14 18, Northern Ireland ☎1232 32 47 33, Republic of Ireland ☎01 830 1766, NZ ☎03 379 9808, Scotland ☎8701 55 32 55, US ☎800-909-4776, all international reservations ☎202-783-6161; www.hostelbooking.com). HI's umbrella organization's web page (www.iyhf.org) lists the websites and phone numbers of all national associations.

Most HI hostels also honor **guest memberships**—you'll get a blank card with space for six validation stamps. Each night you'll pay a nonmember supplement (one-sixth the membership fee) and earn one guest stamp; get six stamps, and you're a member. Most student travel agencies (see p. 47) sell HI cards, as do all of the national hosteling organizations listed below. All prices listed below are valid for **one-year memberships** unless otherwise noted.

> **BOOKING HOSTELS ONLINE** One of the cheapest and easiest ways to ensure a bed for a night is by reserving online. Our website features the **Hostelworld** booking engine; access it at **www.letsgo.com/resources/accommodations.** Hostelworld offers bargain accommodations everywhere from Argentina to Zimbabwe with no added commission.

YHA Australia, Level 3, 10 Mallett St., Camperdown NSW 2050 (☎02 9565 1699; fax 9565 1325; www.yha.com). AUS$52, under 18 AUS$16.

Hostelling International-Canada (HI-C), 205 Catherine St. #400, Ottawa, ON K2P 1C3 (☎613-237-7884; fax 237-7868; www.hihostels.ca). CDN$35, under 18 free.

An Óige (Irish Youth Hostel Association), 61 Mountjoy St., Dublin 7 (☎01 830 4555; fax 830 5808; www.irelandyha.org). €25, under 18 €10.50.

Youth Hostels Association of New Zealand (YHANZ), 116 Moorhouse Ave., Level 1, P.O. Box 436, Christchurch (☎03 379 9970; fax 365 4476; www.stayyha.com). NZ$40, under 17 free.

Hostels Association of South Africa, 73 St. George's House, 3rd fl., Cape Town 8000 (☎021 424 2511; fax 424 4119; www.hisa.org.za). R70, under 18 R40.

Scottish Youth Hostels Association (SYHA), 7 Glebe Crescent, Stirling FK8 2JA (☎01786 89 14 00; fax 89 13 33; www.syha.org.uk). UK£6.

Youth Hostels Association (England and Wales), Trevelyan House, Dimple Rd., Matlock, Derbyshire DE4 3YH, UK (☎0870 870 8808; fax 01727 84 41 26; www.yha.org.uk). UK£13, under 18 UK£6.50.

Hostelling International Northern Ireland (HINI), 22 Donegal Rd., Belfast BT12 5JN (☎02890 31 54 35; fax 43 96 99; www.hini.org.uk). UK£10, under 18 UK£6.

Hostelling International-American Youth Hostels (HI-AYH), 733 15th St. NW, #840, Washington, D.C. 20005 (☎202-783-6161; fax 783-6171; www.hiayh.org). US$25, under 18 free.

NOMADS

Another large hosteling chain in Australia is **NOMADS Backpackers** (www.nomadsworld.com). Though it has only about one third as many locations as YHA, with about 50 hostels nationwide, the services and amenities are similar. You don't have to be a member to stay at a NOMADS hostel. The NOMADS Adventure Card (AUS$29) offers discount international calling, cheaper rates at many Internet cafes, and either $1 off per night or seventh night free at NOMADS hostels. Bookings can be made through the website or calling hostels direct. The NOMADS Adventure Card and Travel Guide (AUS$29) offers discount international calling and internet access, either $1 off per night or seventh night free, and various other backpacker discounts. NOMADS also offer Arrival Packages into all Australian gateways, that organize accommodations and activities for the first few days of a trip. Bookings are via the website.

HOTELS

While **hotels** in large cities are similar to those in the rest of the world, "hotels" in rural Australia, particularly in Victoria and New South Wales, are often simple furnished rooms above local pubs. Some resemble fancy Victorian-era lodging with grand staircases, high ceilings, and wrap-around verandas. Others have been converted to long-term worker housing, and are thus less conducive to brief overnight stays. Singles in these hotels usually cost AUS$15-30. This generally includes a

ESSENTIALS

towel, a shared bathroom, and a private bedroom. The pubs downstairs can be noisy. **Motels** in Australia are mid-range accommodations with parking. Quality and price varies, but most motel rooms will include ensuite, TV, and fridge.

BED & BREAKFASTS

A cozy alternative to impersonal hotel rooms, B&Bs are private homes with rooms available to travelers. Hosts will sometimes go out of their way to be accommodating by giving personalized tours or offering home-cooked meals. On the other hand, many B&Bs do not provide phones, TVs, or private bathrooms. Rooms in B&Bs generally cost AUS$40-80 for a single and AUS$60-100 for a double but are more expensive in touristed areas. A Check out **BABS** (www.babs.com.au) for a list of Australian B&Bs.

UNIVERSITY DORMS

Many colleges and universities open their residence halls to travelers when school is not in session; some do so even during term-time. Getting a room may take a couple of phone calls and require advanced planning, but rates tend to be low, and many offer free local calls and internet access.

Typical university holidays include most of September and the summer break from late November to late February. Easter break lasts for two weeks, while winter break encompasses the first two weeks of July. No one policy covers all institutions. Contact the universities directly; demand is high, so book ahead.

CAMPERS & RVS

Caravanning is popular in Australia, where many campgrounds double as caravan parks, consisting of both tent sites and powered sites for caravans. On-site caravans (also called on-site vans) are a frequent feature at caravan parks and are anchored permanently to the site and rented out. "Cabins" at caravan parks are often analogous to an on-site van, with a toilet inside.

In Australia there is a distinction drawn between **caravans** and **campervans (RVs).** The former is pulled as a trailer, while the latter has its own cab. Renting a caravan or campervan is expensive, but cheaper than renting a car and staying in hotels. The convenience of bringing along your own bedroom, bathroom, and kitchen makes caravanning an attractive option, especially for older travelers and families traveling with children.

It's not difficult to arrange a campervan rental for your trip to Australia, although you should definitely start gathering information several months before your departure. Rates vary widely by region, season (December through February are the most expensive), and type of van. It pays to contact several different companies to compare vehicles and prices. **Maui Rentals** (☎03 8379 8891; fax 9687 4844; www.maui-rentals.com) and **Britz Campervan Rentals and Tours** (☎03 8379 8890; fax 9687 4844; www.britz.com) rents RVs in Australia. Check out **Family Parks of Australia** (www.fpa.org.au) for a list of caravan and cabin parks across Australia belonging to their chain.

CAMPING

If your travels will be taking you to Australia when the weather is agreeable, camping is by far the cheapest way to spend the night. The ubiquitous caravan parks found throughout the country offer basic camping sites without power for campers; in addition, some hostels have basic camping facilities or at the least allow guests to pitch their tents in the front or back yard. Unpowered campsites can vary in price from free to up to AUS$20 per night for a prime spot during Christmas holidays; most powered sites go for about AUS$3-5 more. Caravan parks also offer unpowered sites, and some hostels either have camping facilities or will allow guests to pitch tents in the yard. See **Camping & Bushwalking** (p. 76) for more information about camping outdoors.

KEEPING IN TOUCH

BY MAIL

SENDING MAIL HOME FROM AUSTRALIA

Airmail is the best way to send mail home from Australia. **Aerogrammes,** printed sheets that fold into envelopes and travel via airmail, are available at all post offices. Write "par avion" or "air mail" on the front. Most post offices will charge exorbitant fees or simply refuse to send aerogrammes with enclosures. **Surface mail** is by far the cheapest and slowest way to send mail. It takes one to three months to cross the Atlantic and two to four to cross the Pacific—good for items you won't need to see for a while. The **Australia Post** website (www.auspost.com) has a postage calculator for international deliveries. These are standard rates for mail from Australia to:

Canada: Allow 5-7 days for regular airmail. Postcards/aerogrammes cost AUS$1. Letters up to 50g cost $1.65; packages up to 0.5kg $12, up to 2kg $42.

Ireland: Allow 4-5 days for regular airmail. Postcards/aerogrammes cost AUS$1. Letters up to 50g cost $1.65; packages up to 0.5kg $14, up to 2kg $50.

New Zealand: Allow 3-4 days for regular airmail. Postcards/aerogrammes cost AUS$1. Letters up to 50g cost $1.10; packages up to 0.5kg $8, up to 2kg $26.

UK: Allow 4-5 days for regular airmail. Postcards/aerogrammes cost AUS$1. Letters up to 50g cost $1.65; packages up to 0.5kg $14, up to 2kg $50.

US: Allow 4-6 days for regular airmail. Postcards/aerogrammes cost AUS$1. Letters up to 50g cost $1.65; packages up to 0.5kg $12, up to 2kg $42.

SENDING MAIL TO AUSTRALIA

Mark envelopes "air mail" or "par avion" or your letter or postcard will never arrive in Australia. In addition to the standard postage system—whose rates are listed by country of origin below—**Federal Express** (Australia ☎ 13 26 10, US and Canada ☎ 800-247-4747, New Zealand ☎ 0800 73 33 39, UK ☎ 0800 12 38 00; www.fedex.com) handles express mail services from the above countries to Australia; they can get a letter from New York to Sydney in three business days for US$35.70, and London to Sydney for UK£32.

Canada: www.canadapost.ca. Allow 4-10 days for regular airmail to Australia. Postcards and letters up to 30g cost CDN$1.25; packages up to 0.5kg CDN$10.00, up to 2kg CDN$38.55.

Ireland: www.letterpost.ie. Allow 5-7 days for regular airmail to Australia. Postcards and letters up to 25g cost €0.57. Add €3.60 for Swiftpost International (1 day faster); packages up to 0.5kg €5, up to 2kg €20.

New Zealand: www.nzpost.co.nz. Allow approximately 7 days for regular airmail to Australia. Postcards NZ$1.50. Letters up to 20g cost NZ$1.50-2.50; small parcels up to 0.5kg NZ$8, up to 2kg NZ$20.21.

UK: www.royalmail.com. Allow approximately 5 days for airmail to Australia. Letters up to 20g cost UK£0.68; packages up to 0.5kg UK£5.21, up to 2kg UK£20.21.

US: www.usps.gov. Allow 4-10 days for regular airmail to Australia. Postcards/aerogrammes cost US$0.70; letters under 1 oz. US$0.80; packages under 1 lb. cost US$14.50. **US Global Priority Mail** delivers small/large flat-rate envelopes to Australia in 4 business days for US$5/$9.

RECEIVING MAIL IN AUSTRALIA

There are several ways to arrange pick-up of letters or postcards sent to you by friends and relatives while you are abroad in Australia and beyond. Mail can be sent fairly reliably via **Poste Restante** (known as General Delivery in the United States) to almost any city or town in Australia that has a general post office. Your correspondents should address *Poste Restante* letters like so:

Croc O'DOYLE
C/- Poste Restante
[City] [STATE] [Postcode]

Mail addressed in this manner will go to a special desk in the central post office of the town indicated, unless the writer specifies a post office by exact street address (which we list in the **Practical Information** section of most towns in this guide). It's best to use the largest post office, since mail may be sent there regardless. Bring passport (or other photo ID) for pick-up.

ESSENTIALS

BY TELEPHONE

CALLING HOME FROM AUSTRALIA

A **calling card** is probably your cheapest bet. You can frequently call collect without even possessing a company's calling card just by calling their access number and following the instructions. See the **Inside Back Cover** of this book for calling card access numbers in Australia.

Let's Go has recently formed a partnership with ekit.com to provide a calling card that offers a number of services, including email and voice messaging services. For more information, visit www.letsgo.ekit.com.

You can usually make **direct international calls** from pay phones in Australia. Prepaid phone cards and occasionally major credit cards can be used for direct international calls as well, but they are almost always less cost-efficient. Although incredibly convenient, in-room hotel calls will invariably include an arbitrary and sky-high surcharge.

The expensive alternative to dialing direct or using a calling card is using an international operator to place a **collect call;** sometimes in an emergency, though, this is the only way to reach home.

CALLING WITHIN AUSTRALIA

Public phones are easy to find nearly everywhere you go in Australia. Some phone booths in Australia are coin-operated, some are phone-card operated, and some accept either coins or phone cards. Local calls made from phone booths cost $0.40 and are untimed. Public phones (often small blue- or orange-colored boxes) can also sometimes be found in select bars and hotels; note that local calls placed on

ESSENTIALS

PLACING INTERNATIONAL CALLS. To call Australia from home or to call home from Australia, dial:

1. **International dialing prefix.** To dial out of: **Australia,** dial 0011; **Canada** or the **US,** 011; **Ireland, New Zealand,** or the **UK,** 00; **South Africa,** 09.
2. **Country code** of the country you want to call. To call **Australia,** dial 61; **Canada** or the **US,** 1; **Ireland,** 353; **New Zealand,** 64; **South Africa,** 27; the **UK,** 44;
3. **City/area code.** *Let's Go* lists the city/area codes for cities and towns in Australia opposite the city or town name, next to a ☎. If the first digit is a zero (e.g., 02 for Sydney), omit the zero when calling from abroad (e.g., dial 2 from Canada to reach Sydney).
4. **Local number.**

these often cost $0.50. **Long-distance calls** within Australia use STD (Subscriber Trunk Dialing) services. You must first dial an **area code** (listed next to town names in this guides) before the eight-digit number.

Australia has two main telecommunications companies: **Optus** and **Telstra.** Prepaid phone cards that you can insert into phone-card operated public phones carry a certain amount of phone time depending on the card's listed denomination. Another kind of prepaid phone card has a toll-free access number and a personal identification number (PIN). Instead of inserting the card into the phone, you call the access number and follow the directions on the card. These cards can be used to make international as well as domestic calls and usually have better rates than those offered by Optus and Telstra. A few public phones in Australia (mostly those located at airports, in and around city centers, and at major hotels) will even allow you to charge a phone call to your **credit card.**

For local and national **directory assistance** in Australia, you can call toll-free ☎ 1223 from any phone; for international assistance dial ☎ 1225 instead. Six-digit phone numbers beginning with **13** are information numbers that can be dialed from anywhere in Australia for the same price as a local call. Numbers beginning with **1300** operate similarly. Numbers beginning **1800 or 0800** are **toll-free** and can be dialed as such from public phones.

Mobile phones are quite common in urban parts of Australia. Mobile phone numbers are either nine or 10 digits long and always begin with one of two codes; nine-digit mobile phone numbers always begin with 01, while all ten-digit mobile numbers begin with 04. Usually the caller picks up the charges when calling a mobile phone, and charges run about AUS$0.80 per minute.

EMAIL & INTERNET

Internet cafes are commonplace in most every decent-sized city in Australia. In most major cities, internet shops will have booths offering discounted international calling as well. Access to the Internet ranges from as low as **free** to as high as $8 per hour. Coin-operated Internet kiosks are an expensive (usually $2 per 10min.) yet common option in cities and increasingly more hostels. In addition, virtually all public libraries now offer free access to the web, though sometimes you are restricted from checking email or must make a prior reservation with the library before being allowed access to their computers. *Let's Go* lists Internet access options in the **Practical Information** section of towns and cities in this guide. Other Internet access points in Australia can be found at www.gnomon.com.au/publications/netaccess.

TIME ZONES

Time zones in Australia can be a bit confusing for travelers, especially when only certain states across the continent observe Daylight Saving Time (which happens every year from late October to late March). This means that Australia's times zones follow state borders both vertically and horizontally. Greenwich Mean Time (GMT), also known as Universal Standard Time (UST), is not affected by **Daylight Saving Time (DST),** providing a standard to calculate differences in time zones. In the table that appears below, the rows on the left represent where you are. The columns across the top represent where you wish to know the time. To calculate the time in a different zone, simply add or subtract the difference in hours between the two places. For example, if it is noon in GMT, then it is 10pm in Victoria. Remember that the date is affected in some cases—Australia is ahead of the Western Hemisphere, so Monday evening in New York is Tuesday morning in Sydney. All regions that observe DST have an asterisk. Therefore, during DST, if you start in a row with an asterisk, you must subtract one hour. If you end in a column with an asterisk, you must add one hour. For example, if it is noon in GMT during DST, then it is 11pm in Victoria. South Australia, Victoria, New South Wales, and the Australia Capital Territory start DST on the last Sunday in October, while Tasmania begins its observation on the first Sunday of October. All states end DST on the last Sunday in March.

London is 1 hour ahead of GMT from the last Sunday in March to the last Sunday in October due to DST. **New York City** is normally 5 hours behind GMT. However, from the first Sunday in April to the last Sunday in October, NYC is only 4 hours behind GMT due to DST.

TIME ZONES	GMT	WA	NT	SA*	QLD	ACT, NSW, TAS, VIC*
Greenwich Mean Time (GMT)		+8	+9.5	+9.5	+10	+10
Western Australia (WA)	-8		+1.5	+1.5	+2	+2
Northern Territory (NT)	-9.5	-1.5		0	+0.5	+0.5
Southern Australia* (SA)	-9.5	-1.5	0		+0.5	+0.5
Queensland (QLD)	-10	-2	-0.5	-0.5		0
ACT, NSW, Tasmania, Victoria*	-10	-2	-0.5	-0.5	0	

GETTING TO AUSTRALIA

Your plane ticket will most likely be your biggest expenditure when traveling to Australia. When it comes to airfares, a little effort can save you a bundle. The key to finding affordable fares is to hunt around, be flexible, and ask persistently about discounts of all types. Students, seniors, and travelers under 26 years of age should never pay full price for a ticket.

AIRFARES

Airfares to Australia peak between December and February; holiday periods also tend to be expensive. The cheapest times to travel to Australia are between September and November. Midweek (meaning mornings on Monday through Thursday) flights that are round-trip (return) run US$40-50 cheaper than weekend flights, but they are generally more crowded and less likely to permit frequent-flier upgrades. Traveling with an "open return" ticket can be pricier than fixing a return date when buying the ticket. Round-trip flights are by far the cheapest; "open-jaw" (arriving in and departing from different cities, e.g. Los Angeles-Sydney and Mel-

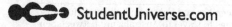

bourne-Sydney) tickets tend to be pricier. Patching one-way flights together is the most expensive way to travel. Flights between Australia's regional hubs—Sydney, Brisbane, Melbourne—will tend to be cheaper.

If Australia is only one stop on a more extensive globe-hop, consider a round-the-world (RTW) ticket. Tickets usually include at least 5 stops and are valid for about a year; prices range US$1200-5000. Try **Northwest Airlines/KLM** (US ☎ 800-447-4747; www.nwa.com) or **Star Alliance,** a consortium of 22 airlines including United Airlines (US ☎ 800-241-6522; www.staralliance.com).

The privilege of spending 24 hours or more on a plane doesn't come cheap. Full-price round-trip **fares** to Australia from the US or Canada (depending upon which coast of each continent you are heading to and from) can be US$900-2000; from the UK, ₤500-1100; from New Zealand, NZ$400-700.

BUDGET & STUDENT TRAVEL AGENCIES

While knowledgeable agents specializing in flights to Australia can make your life easy and help you save, they may not spend the time to find you the lowest possible fare—they get paid on commission. Travelers holding **ISIC and IYTC cards** (see p. 24) qualify for big discounts from student travel agencies.

CTS Travel, 30 Rathbone Place, **London,** UK W1T 1GQ (☎0207 290 0630; ctsinfo@ctstravel.co.uk).

STA Travel, 7890 S. Hardy Dr., Ste. 110, **Tempe,** AZ 85284, USA (24hr. reservations and info ☎800-781-4040; www.sta-travel.com). A student and youth travel organization with over 150 offices worldwide (check their website for a listing of all their offices). Ticket booking, travel insurance, railpasses, and more.

Travel CUTS (Canadian Universities Travel Services Limited), 187 College St., **Toronto,** ON M5T 1P7 (☎416-979-2406; fax 979-8167; www.travelcuts.com). Travel CUTS has some 60 offices across Canada. Also in the UK, 685 Richmond St. Suite 102, **London** ON N6A 5M1 (☎519 675 1005).

USIT World (www.usitworld.com). Over 50 **USIT campus** branches in the UK, including 52 Grosvenor Gardens, **London** SW1W 0AG (☎0870 240 10 10); **Manchester** (☎0161 200 3278); and **Edinburgh** (☎0131 668 3303). Nearly 20 **usit NOW** offices in Ireland, including 19-21 Aston Quay, O'Connell Bridge, **Dublin** 2 (☎01 602 1600; www.usit-now.ie), and **Belfast** (☎02 890 327 111; www.usitnow.com).

COMMERCIAL AIRLINES

Commercial airlines' lowest regular offer is the **APEX** (Advance Purchase Excursion) fare, which provides confirmed reservations and allows "open-jaw" tickets. Generally, reservations must be made seven to 21 days ahead of departure, with seven- to 14-day minimum-stay and up to 90-day maximum-stay restrictions. These fares carry hefty cancellation and change penalties (fees rise in high season). Book peak-season APEX fares early; by October you may have a hard time getting your desired departure date. Use **Microsoft Expedia** (msn.expedia.com) or **Travelocity** (www.travelocity.com) to get an idea of the lowest published fares, then use the resources outlined here to try to beat them.

Popular carriers to Australia include **Air New Zealand** (www.airnew-zealand.co.nz), **British Airways** (www.britishairways.com), **Cathay Pacific** (www.cathaypacific.com), **South African Airlines** (www.saa.co.za), and **United Airways** (www.united.com), most of which have daily nonstop flights from Los Angeles to Sydney. **Qantas** (www.qantas.com.au) is Australia's main airline and has the most international connections.

Don't be left out...
Get your travel on.
The International
Student Identity Card
International Student Identity Card
Carte d'étudiant internationale / Carné internacional de estudiante
STUDENT
Studies at / Étudiant à / Est. de Enseñanza
University of Student Travel
Name / Nom / Nombre
CHIN, S
Born / Né(e) le / Nacido/a el
23/06/1982
Validity / Validité / Validez
09/2003 - 12/2004
UNESCO
ISIC
S 000 123 456 789
$22 is all it takes to save hundreds.
Accepted worldwide for awesome discounts!
The International Student Identity Card (ISIC) is a great way to take advantage of discounts and benefits such as airfare, accommodations, transportation, attractions, theme parks, hotels, theaters, car rentals and more!
visit www.ISICus.com to find out about discounts and the benefits of carrying your ISIC.
ISIC
Call or visit STA Travel online to find the nearest issuing office and purchase your card today:
www.ISICus.com
(800) 474.8214

enough already...
Get a room.

Book your next hotel with the people who know what you want.

✈ **FLIGHT PLANNING ON THE INTERNET.** Many airline sites offer special last-minute deals on the Web. Other sites do the legwork and compile the deals for you—try www.bestfares.com, www.flights.com, www.hotdeals.com, www.onetravel.com, and www.travelzoo.com.

StudentUniverse (www.studentuniverse.com), **STA** (www.sta-travel.com), and **Orbitz.com** provide quotes on student tickets, while **Expedia** (www.expedia.com) and **Travelocity** (www.travelocity.com) offer full travel services. **Priceline** (www.priceline.com) allows you to specify a price, and obligates you to buy any ticket that meets or beats it; be prepared for inconvenient hours and odd routes. **Skyauction** (www.skyauction.com) allows you to bid on both last-minute and advance-purchase tickets.

An indispensable resource on the Internet is the *Air Traveler's Handbook* (www.cs.cmu.edu/afs/cs/user/mkant/Public/Travel/airfare.html), a comprehensive listing of links to everything you need to know before you board a plane.

Just one last note—to protect yourself, make sure that the site you use has a secure server before handing over any credit card details. Happy hunting!

GETTING AROUND

BY PLANE

Because Australia is so large, many travelers, even those on a budget, take a domestic flight at some point while touring the country. Oz Experience (p. 52) and Qantas offer an **Air-Bus Pass** with which travelers can fly one-way, and bus back (or vice versa) around Australia. Passes are valid for six months with unlimited stops; all dates can be changed. **Flight Centre** (www.flightcentre.com.au) offers a plethora of Internet-only deals, including group rates.

Qantas: Reservations ☎ 13 13 13 in Australia, 800-227-4500 in the U.S. and Canada, 0845 7 747 767 in the UK; www.qantas.com.au. Qantas "boomerang passes" allow travelers to change flight dates free of charge on domestic flights; cities can be changed for $50. For international travelers (with the exception of New Zealanders and Fijians, who are not eligible), a boomerang pass may be the best domestic flight option (min. 2 flights, max. 10). One-way passes within zones are US$160, between zones starts at US$190. The first two segments must be purchased before arriving in Australia.

Regional Express (Rex): Reservations ☎ 13 17 13; www.regionalexpress.com. Formed from the acquisition and merger of Kendell and Hazelton Airlines in August, 2002. Offers service to much of South Australia, New South Wales, Victoria, and Tasmania.

VirginBlue: Reservations ☎ 13 67 89 in Australia, 7 3295 2296 outside Australia; www.virginblue.com.au. Service between all coastal cities.

BY TRAIN

The **Austrail Pass** (www.train-ticket.net/austral/austrail.htm) allows unlimited travel over consecutive days within a given period (14 days AUS$660, 21 days $860, 30 days $1035). The **Austrail Flexipass** allows you to purchase eight (US$559), 15 (AUS$862), 22 ($1210), or 29 ($1569) traveling days to be used over a six-month period. Both passes are only available to non-Australians and must be bought overseas. **Rail Australia** (www.railaustralia.com.au) has agents in the US (☎ 1 310 643 0044 ext. 420), Canada (☎ 416-322-1034), New Zealand (☎ 08 008 1060), South

Africa (☎021 419 9382), Japan (☎03 3818 5671, and the UK (☎87075 150 00). The **East Coast Discovery Pass** allows unlimited stops in one direction on the Eastern Seaboard within six months (Sydney-Cairns AUS$312, Melbourne-Cairns $393). For information on more passes, go to www.railpage.org.au/pass.html.

Each state runs its own rail service, and transfers between services may require a bus trip to the next station. For reservations and ticketing from the US, call ☎800 423 2880. Wheelchair access on interstate trains can be poor, as the corridors are often too narrow. Some but not all larger stations provide collapsible wheelchairs. The main rail companies are:

Countrylink (☎ 13 22 32; www.countrylink.nsw.gov.au), based in New South Wales. Ages 4-15 and ISIC/concession card holders 50% discount.

V/Line (☎ 13 61 96; www.vline.vic.gov.au) in Victoria. Off-peak fares up to 30% discount. Children and concessions 50% discount on interstate travel.

Queensland Rail (☎ 13 22 32; www.qr.com.au) in Queensland. The cheapest and fastest way to travel Queensland's coast. Students 50% discount.

Westrail (☎ 13 10 53; www.wagr.wa.gov.au) in Western Australia. Pensioners, seniors, and children 50% discount.

Great Southern Railways (☎ 13 21 47; www.gsr.com.au) in South Australia and the Northern Territory. Consists of the *Indian Pacific*, the *Overland*, and *The Ghan*. Students and backpackers 50% discount, children and pensioners 55%.

BY BUS

Buses cover more of the rural landscape of Australia than do trains. Buses run regularly to major cities, but journeys off the beaten track may require a wait of a few days. It may be more cost efficient to buy a kilometer or multi-day pass if you are planning on doing a large amount of travel by bus. **Contiki Travel** (☎ 1-888-CONTIKI; www.contiki.com), offers comprehensive tour packages that include accommodations, transportation and some meals. They run 3- to 26-day tours starting at $335.

MCCAFFERTY'S/GREYHOUND

While Greyhound (☎ 13 20 30; www.greyhound.com.au) was recently acquired by McCafferty's (☎ 13 14 99; www.mccaffertys.com.au), the two lines generally operate under the single name of Greyhound and almost always honor each other's tickets and passes.

Greyhound's 7- to 21-day passes allow you to travel on any route within 30 to 60 days, depending on the length of your pass; days of travel do not have to be consecutive. These passes cost from AUS$672. The **Aussie Explorer Pass** allows you to predetermine a route and take up to 12 months to get there, while an **Aussie Kilometer Pass** lets you choose a number of kilometers to be used on any Greyhound route (minimum 2000km, AUS$289). Most of these passes can be used to take **Greyhound Pioneer Tours,** offering combinations of tours for National Parks and highlights of Central Australia, Western Australia, and the Top End.

McCafferty's **Travel Australia** passes are valid for anywhere from six to 12 months (up to AUS$1116), and let travelers ride with unlimited stops one way along any of seven predetermined routes. A 10% discount is available for international students, pensioners, and backpacker card holders; the discount is 15% if the purchase is made outside of Australia. McCafferty's also offers an **Australian Roamer** pass, which allows long-distance travelers to pay by the kilometer (2000km AUS$239, 10,000km AUS$915); the Roamer pass is available only to backpacker card and ISIC card holders. Non-Australians can also get the **Discover Australia Day Pass,** but it must be purchased before arrival in Australia. The pass allows for unlimited travel on the McCafferty's network of buses for an allotted time; you can choose between 7 (AUS$693) and 30 (AUS$1643) days worth of travel, to be redeemed within a range of 30 to 60 days.

OZ EXPERIENCE

This popular bus company offers backpacker packages with a lot of flexibility and charismatic drivers who double as tour guides. The packages must be purchased for predetermined routes (cheaper if bought outside of Australia), and travelers can usually take up to six months to finish with unlimited stopovers. Be prepared for a younger, party-ready crowd. (☎ 02 9213 1766 or 1300 30 00 28; www.ozexperi-ence.com. YHA discount 5%.)

BY CAR

Some regions of Australia are virtually inaccessible without a car and in many sparsely populated areas public transportation options are simply inadequate. The public highways in Australia are very well-maintained and span the circumference of the country. One of the major dilemmas of traveling in Australia off highways is that the road system can be basic and often poorly maintained. To travel on most outback roads and in many national parks, you will often need a **four-wheel-drive (4WD)**, which unfortunately can double the cost of renting or buying. Shopping around well ahead of time is advisable.

RENTING

Although the cost of renting a car can be prohibitive for an individual traveler, rentals can become cost-efficient when traveling with a group.

RENTAL AGENCIES

You can generally make reservations before you leave by calling their offices in your home country. However, occasionally the price and availability information they give doesn't jive with what the local offices in Australia will tell you. Try checking with both numbers to get the best price and most accurate information. Australia numbers and web addresses are listed below:

Avis (☎ 02 9353 9000, nationwide 13 63 33; www.avis.com).

Britz (☎ 800 331 454; www.britz.com) offers super saver 4WD discounts; rents to under 25 with no surcharge.

Budget (☎ 03 9915 3322, nationwide ☎ 1300 36 28 48; www.budget.com.au).

Delta Europcar (☎ 03 9330 6160; www.deltaeuropcar.com.au).

Hertz (☎ 03 9698 2555, nationwide ☎ 13 30 39; www.hertz.com).

Thrifty (☎ 1300 36 72 27; www.thrifty.com.au).

To rent a car from most establishments, you need to be at least 21 years old. Some agencies require renters to be 25, and most charge those aged 21-24 an additional insurance fee (around AUS$15-25 per day). Policies and prices vary greatly. Small local operations occasionally rent to people under 21, but be sure to ask about the insurance coverage and deductible, and always read the fine print.

COSTS & INSURANCE

Rental car prices in Australia start at around AUS$45 a day from national compa-nies and AUS$30 from local agencies. Expect to pay more for larger cars and for 4WD vehicles. Cars with **automatic transmission** can cost up to AUS$15 a day more than standard manuals (stick shift), and in Western Australia, Northern Territory,

and more remote areas of the eastern states, automatic transmission is hard to find at all, even from the major national and international agencies. It is virtually impossible to find an automatic 4WD.

Many rental packages offer unlimited kilometers, while others offer 100-600km per day with a surcharge of approximately AUS25¢ per kilometer after that. Return the car with a full tank of petrol to avoid high fuel charges at the end. Be sure to ask whether the price includes **insurance** against theft and collision. Remember that if you are driving a conventional vehicle on an **unsealed road** (Australian for unpaved) in a rental car, you are almost never covered by insurance; ask about this before leaving the rental agency.

Check with your credit card company to see if cars rented on an **American Express** or **Visa/MasterCard Gold or Platinum** credit card in Australia still carry the automatic insurance that they would in some other countries. Insurance plans almost always come with an **excess** (or deductible) of around AUS$1000 for conventional vehicles. Younger drivers and those renting 4WD should be prepared to assume an excess up to around AUS$2500. This means you pay for all damages up to that sum, unless they are the fault of another vehicle. The excess you will be quoted applies to collisions with other vehicles. Collisions with non-vehicles, such as trees or kangaroos ("single-vehicle collisions"), will cost you even more. The excess can often be reduced or waived entirely if you pay an additional charge, between AUS$5-30 per day.

National chains often allow you to arrange one-way rentals, where you will be picking up your vehicle in one city and dropping it off in another. However, there is usually a minimum hire period for these types of rentals, and sometimes there is an extra drop-off charge of several hundred dollars. Inquire at individual agencies about their policies for such one-way rentals.

ESSENTIALS

BUYING & SELLING USED CARS

Buying used cars and then reselling them is popular among long-term travelers or those too young to rent. Automotive independence costs around AUS$1600-5000. However, used car dealers have been known to rip off foreigners, especially backpackers. Research prices, or ask a trustworthy Aussie about reasonable prices; some people recommend bringing a local along when purchasing the car. Buying from a private owner or fellow traveler is often a cheaper alternative. In many cities, hundreds of private sellers rent space at used car lots, as buyers stroll around and haggle. Hostel or university bulletin boards are another good bet. In Sydney, check the *Weekly Trading Post* on Thursdays for used car advertisements and the *Daily Telegraph Mirror* and *Sydney Morning Herald* on Saturdays. When selling a car back, consider the high tourist season for the region you're in. Vehicles are also easier to sell if they are registered in the state where they are being sold—new owners need to register the car, and some states don't allow registration transfer by mail. If you buy a car privately, check the registration papers against the license of the person who is selling the car.

WHAT TO LOOK FOR

Before buying a used car, check with the local branch of the AAA, as states have varying requirements for a transfer of ownership, and local organizations can advise you on how to get your money's worth. The NRMA in New South Wales publishes *International Tourists Car Buying Advice* and *Worry-free Guide to Buying a Car*. In Victoria, all cars are required to carry a Road Worthiness Certificate. Local auto clubs also do mechanical inspections (NRMA inspections ☎ 13 11 22 or 612 8836 8631).

BEFORE YOU BUY

When buying a car, call the **Register of Encumbered Vehicles** or check online at www.revs.nsw.gov.au to confirm that a vehicle is unencumbered—that it has not been reported as stolen and has no outstanding financial obligations nor traffic warrants. Nationwide ☎ 1800 424 988 or 02 9633 6333. You'll need to provide the registration-, engine-, and VIN/chassis-numbers of the vehicle. In New South Wales, a car must have a pink inspection certificate to guarantee that it is roadworthy. It is valid for 20 days and available at most service stations.

REGISTRATION

Within two weeks after purchase, you'll need to **register** the car in your name at the Motor Vehicle Registry. Although requirements vary between states, re-registration costs about AUS$15, and must be completed within about two weeks. The local automobile organization can always help.

INSURANCE AT A GLANCE. Here is a run-down of the different options you have for insuring your car:

Third-party personal injury insurance (a.k.a. green slip): automatically included with every registered vehicle. Covers any person who may be injured except the driver at fault; does not cover damage or repairs to cars or property.

Third-party property damage insurance: covers cost of repair to other people's cars or property if you're responsible for an accident.

Full comprehensive insurance: covers damage to all vehicles.

International Insurance Certificate: proof of liability insurance, required of all rented, leased, and borrowed cars.

INTERNATIONAL DRIVING PERMITS

If you plan to drive a car while in Australia, your home country's driver's license will suffice. If your home country's driver's license is not printed in English, you must have an English translation with you. After driving in the same state for three months, you must have an International Driving Permit (IDP). Your IDP, valid for one year, must be issued in your own country before you depart; AAA affiliates cannot issue IDPs valid in their own country. You must be 18+ to receive the IDP. A valid driver's license from your home country must always accompany the IDP. An application for an IDP usually needs to include one or two photos, a current local license, an additional form of identification, and a fee. To apply, contact the national or local branch of your home country's Automobile Association.

Canada: www. caa.ca/e/travel/id/idp.shtml. Permits CDN$13.

Ireland: www.aaireland.ie/travel/id_permit.htm. Permits €5.08.

New Zealand: www.nzaa.co.nz/cg/MainMenu. Permits NZ$12.

South Africa: www.aasa.co.za. Permits ZAR45.

UK: www.theaa.co.uk/motoringandtravel/idp/. Permits UK£4.

US: www.aaa.com/aaa/240/sne/travel/idpc.html. Permits US$10.

ON THE ROAD

Australians drive on the **left side** of the road. In unmarked intersections, a driver must yield to vehicles entering the intersection from the right. In some big cities, right turns often must take place from the farthest left lane, after the light has already turned red—keep your eyes peeled for signs to that effect. By law, **seat belts** must be worn at all times by all persons riding in the vehicle. Children under 40 lb. should ride only in a special kind of carseat, available for a small fee at most car rental agencies. The speed limit in most cities is 60kph (35mph) and on highways 100 or 110kph (62 or 68mph). Radar guns are often used to patrol well-traveled roads; sly speed cameras nab offenders on less populated paths. **Petrol (gasoline)** prices vary by state, but average about AUS$0.80-1 per liter in cities and AUS$0.90-1.05 per liter in outlying areas.

PRECAUTIONS

When traveling in the summer or in the outback, bring substantial amounts of water (a suggested 5L of **water** per person per day) for drinking and for the radiator. For long outback drives, travelers should register with police before beginning the trek, and again upon arrival at the destination. Check with the local automobile club for details. In the north, **four-wheel-drive (4WD)** is essential for seeing the parks, particularly in the Wet, when dirt roads turn to mud. If you have a breakdown, **stay with your car;** if you wander off, it's less likely that trackers will find you. See **Driving in the Outback** (p. 79) for more information.

ASSISTANCE

The **Australian Automobile Association (AAA)** is the national umbrella organization for all of the local automobile organizations. You won't often see it called the AAA, though; in most states, the local organization is called the **Royal Automobile Club (RAC).** In New South Wales and the ACT, it's the **National Royal Motorist Association (NRMA).** In the Northern Territory, it's the **Automobile Association of the Northern Territory (AANT).** Services—from breakdown assistance to map provision—are similar to those offered by automobile associations in other countries. Most overseas organizations have reciprocal membership with AAA (including AAA in the US; AA and RAC in the UK; NZAA in New Zealand; AASA in South Africa). Bring proof of your membership to Australia, and you'll be able to use AAA facilities free of charge. **AAA roadside assistance** can be reached at ☎ 13 11 11, as well as at 08 8941 0611 in the Northern Territory. It's possible to join AAA through any state's auto-motible organization. *Let's Go* lists the location of the state organization in the introduction to each state.

BY BICYCLE

Australia has many **bike tracks** to attract cyclers. Much of the country is flat, and road bikers can travel long distances without needing to huff and puff excessively. In theory, bicycles can go on **buses and trains,** but most major bus companies require you to disassemble your bike and pay a flat AUS$15 fee. You may not be allowed to bring your bike into train compartments. Safe and secure cycling requires a quality helmet and lock. A good **helmet** costs about AUS$40—much cheaper than critical head surgery. Helmets are required by law in Australia. Travel with good **maps** from the state Automobile Associations.

The **Bicycle Federation of Australia (BFA),** PO Box 1109, Civic Square ACT 2608 (☎ 612 6249 6761; www.bfa.asn.au), is a nonprofit bicycle advocacy group. The BFA publishes *Australian Cyclist* magazine and has a list of regional bicycling organizations on its web page.

BY THUMB

⬛!   **LET'S GO DOES NOT RECOMMEND HITCHHIKING.** *Let's Go* strongly urges you to seriously consider the risks before you choose to hitch. We do not recommend hitching as a safe means of transportation, and none of the information printed here is intended to do so.

Given the infrequency of public transportation to several popular destinations, travelers often need to find other ways to get where they're going. Hostels frequently have message boards where those seeking rides and those seeking to share the cost of gas can meet up. On the east coast, backpacker traffic moves from Sydney to Brisbane (and possibly as far north as Cairns; see p. 425).

Standing on the side of the highway with your thumb out is much more dangerous than making a new friend at your hostel. Safety issues are always imperative, even when you're traveling with another person. **Hitching** (Australian for hitchhiking) means risking assault, sexual harassment, and unsafe driving, all while entrusting your life to anyone who happens to stop beside you on the road. If you're a woman traveling alone, don't hitch. A man and a woman are a safer combination; two men will have a harder time finding a ride, as drivers also must be careful. Avoid getting in the back of a two-door car (there is little chance of escape if in trouble), and never let go of your backpack. Hitchhiking at night can be particularly dangerous. Don't accept a ride that you are not entirely comfortable with. If you ever feel threatened, insist on being let off, but keep in mind that the vast distances between towns on some stretches of highway increase your chance of being left literally in the middle of nowhere.

If you do decide to hitch, choose a spot on the side of the road with ample space for a car to pull over, where traffic is not moving too quickly. The roadways on the edges of town are more suitable for hitchhiking, as people have not yet accelerated to highway speed. Those who decide to hitchhike dress nicely and keep their backpack in full view, as it tells drivers that they are a backpacker and justifies their reason for hitching. A sign with the destination you are headed for, marked in large letters, can also help.

SPECIFIC CONCERNS

WOMEN TRAVELERS

It is generally safe for women to travel alone in Australia. However, women exploring on their own inevitably face some additional safety concerns while traveling, but it's easy to be adventurous without taking undue risks. If you are concerned about traveling on your own as a woman, consider staying in either hostels that offer single rooms that can be locked from the inside or in religious organizations that are either single sex or have rooms set aside for women only. Communal showers in some hostels are safer than others; always be sure to check the facilities before settling in. Stick to centrally located accommodations and avoid solitary late-night treks or metro rides at all times.

Always remember to carry extra money with you for a phone call, bus, or taxi, preferably kept somewhere secure and separate from your regular stash of funds. **Hitchhiking** is never safe for solo women, or even for two women who are traveling together. For general information, contact Australia's **Women's Electoral Lobby**, PO Box 191, Civic Square ACT 2608; (☎02 6247 6679; www.wel.org.au).

TRAVELING ALONE

There are many benefits to traveling alone, including independence and greater interaction with locals. On the other hand, any solo traveler is a more vulnerable target of harassment and street theft. As a lone traveler, try not to stand out as a tourist, look confident, and be especially careful in deserted or very crowded areas. If questioned, never admit that you are traveling alone. Maintain regular contact with someone at home who knows your itinerary. For more tips, pick up *Traveling Solo* by Eleanor Berman (Globe Pequot Press; US$17) or subscribe to **Connecting: Solo Travel Network,** 689 Park Road, Unit 6, Gibsons, BC V0N 1V7, Canada (☎604-886-9099; www.cstn.org; membership US$35). **Travel Companion Exchange,** P.O. Box 833, Amityville, NY 11701, USA (☎631-454-0880; www.whytravelalone.com; US$48), will link solo travelers with companions.

OLDER TRAVELERS

Senior citizens are eligible for a wide range of discounts on transportation, museums, movies, theaters, concerts, restaurants, and accommodations. If you don't see a senior citizen price listed, ask, and you may be delightfully surprised. The books *No Problem! Worldwise Tips for Mature Adventurers*, by Janice Kenyon (Orca Book Publishers; US$16) and *Unbelievably Good Deals and Great Adventures That You Absolutely Can't Get Unless You're Over 50*, by Joan Rattner Heilman (NTC/Contemporary Publishing; US$15) are both excellent resources. For more information, contact one of the following organizations:

Elderhostel, 11 Ave. de Lafayette, Boston, MA 02111, USA (☎877-426-8056; www.elderhostel.org). Organizes 1- to 4-week "educational adventures" in Australia on varied subjects for those 55+.

The Mature Traveler, P.O. Box 1543, Wildomar, CA 92595, USA (☎909 461 9598; www.thematuretraveler.com). Deals, discounts, and travel packages for the 50+ traveler. Subscription $30.

Walking the World, P.O. Box 1186, Fort Collins, CO 80522, USA (☎800-340-9255; www.walkingtheworld.com), organizes trips for 50+ travelers to Australia.

BISEXUAL, GAY, & LESBIAN TRAVELERS

The profile of bisexual, gay, and lesbian community in Australia has risen in recent years, most notably in the popularity of the **gay and lesbian Mardi Gras** in Sydney each year, which is now the largest gay and lesbian gathering in the world (see p. 141). Though pockets of discrimination exist everywhere, the east coast is especially gay-friendly—Sydney ranks in the most gay-friendly cities on earth. The further into the interior you get, the more homophobia you are likely to encounter. Homosexual acts are now legal in every state except Tasmania.

Gay and Lesbian Tourism Australia (GALTA) is a nonprofit nationwide network of tourism industry professionals who are dedicated to the welfare and satisfaction of gay and lesbian travelers to, from, and within Australia. They can be reached at ☎ 08 8379 7498 or on the web at www.galta.com.au. Listed below are contact organizations, mail-order bookstores, and publishers that offer materials addressing some specific concerns. Although not specific to Australia, **Out and About** (www.outandabout.com) offers a bi-weekly newsletter addressing travel concerns and a comprehensive site addressing gay travel concerns.

 FURTHER READING: BISEXUAL, GAY, & LESBIAN.
Odysseus: The International Gay Travel Planner (17th Edition). Odysseus Enterprises (US$31).
Ferrari Guides' Gay Travel A to Z, Ferrari Guides' Men's Travel in Your Pocket, and *Ferrari Guides' Inn Places.* Ferrari Publications (US$16-20). Purchase the guides online at www.ferrariguides.com.
The Gay Vacation Guide: The Best Trips and How to Plan Them, Mark Chesnut. Citadel Press (US$15).

TRAVELERS WITH DISABILITIES

Travelers with disabilities should inform airlines and hotels of their disabilities when making arrangements for travel; some time may be needed to prepare special accommodations. Call ahead to restaurants, hotels, parks, and other facilities to find out about the existence of ramps, the widths of doors, the dimensions of elevators, etc. **Guide dog owners** should inquire as to the quarantine policies of each destination country. At the very least, they will need to provide a certificate of immunization against rabies. After the 2000 Sydney Olympics and Paralympics, many locations in Australia (particularly the east) became wheelchair-accessible, and budget options for the disabled are increasingly available. The following organizations provide information or publications that might be of assistance:

National Information Communication Network (NICAN), P.O. Box 407, Curtin ACT 2605 (☎ 02 6285 3713; fax 6285 3714; www.nican.com.au). National database of accommodations, recreation, tourism, sport and arts for the disabled.

Australian Quadriplegic Association, Letterbox 40 184 Bourke Rd., Alexandria NSW 2015 (☎ 02 9661 8855; fax 02 9661 9598; www.aqa.com.au). Network of community services for individuals with spinal cord injuries.

Accessibility.com.au, provides information about accessible opportunities in Sydney.

Wheelabout Van Rental, 86 Mallawa Drive, Palm Beach QLD 4221 (☎ 02 4367 0900; fax 4365 5840; www.wheelabout.com). Wheelchair-accessible van rentals and sales.

Mobility International USA (MIUSA), P.O. Box 10767, Eugene, OR 97440, USA (☎ 541 343 1284, voice and TDD; www.miusa.org). Sells *A World of Options: A Guide to International Educational Exchange, Community Service, and Travel for Persons with Disabilities* (US$35).

Society for Accessible Travel and Hospitality (SATH), 347 5th Ave., #610, New York, NY 10016, USA (☎ 212-447-7284; www.sath.org). An advocacy group that publishes free online travel information and the travel magazine *OPEN WORLD* (US$18, free for members). Annual membership US$45, students and seniors US$30.

MINORITY TRAVELERS

Some would classify most white Australians as racist in their attitudes toward the **Aborigines,** and this assessment may not be unfounded. Black travelers and some travelers of color may be likely to get a few stares in smaller towns, and may encounter some hostility in more remote outback areas, but will probably not be discriminated against in major cities across the country. As is the case in most parts of the world, cities tend to be more tolerant than more far-flung and less populated destinations; however, this should in no way dissuade travelers from venturing off the beaten track.

TRAVELERS WITH CHILDREN

Family vacations almost always require that you slow down your pace, and absolutely necessitate that you plan ahead, both before you depart and once you're on the road. If you will be renting a car while traveling in Australia, make sure that the rental company provides a car seat for younger children, as these are required by law for children of a certain age. Always be sure that your child is carrying some form of **basic identification** in case of an emergency or in case he or she gets separated from you or lost. Finding a private place for **breast feeding** is often a problem while traveling, so be sure to plan accordingly. For more information, consult one of the following books:

Backpacking with Babies and Small Children, Goldie Silverman. Wilderness Press (US$12).

How to take Great Trips with Your Kids, Sanford and Jane Portnoy. Harvard Common Press (US$5).

Have Kid, Will Travel: 101 Survival Strategies for Vacationing With Babies and Young Children, Claire and Lucille Tristram. Andrews McMeel Publishing (US$9).

Adventuring with Children: An Inspirational Guide to World Travel and the Outdoors, Nan Jeffrey. Avalon House Publishing (US$15).

Trouble Free Travel with Children, Vicki Lansky. Book Peddlers (US$9).

DIETARY CONCERNS

Despite the prevalence of hearty meat pies in Australia, **vegetarians** and **vegans** should have little problem finding suitable cuisine anywhere in the country. *Let's Go* notes restaurants with vegetarian selections in city listings. For more information, visit the online home of the **Australian Vegetarian Society** at www.veg-soc.org. For a vegetarian shopping guide and restaurant listings, consult *The Vegetarian Traveler: Where to Stay If You're Vegetarian, Vegan, Environmentally Sensitive,* by Jed and Susan Civic (US$16).

Travelers who keep **kosher** should contact synagogues in larger cities for information on kosher restaurants and lists of Jewish institutions throughout Australia. If your observance is strict, you may have to prepare your own food while on the road. A good resource is the *Jewish Travel Guide,* by Michael Zaidner (Vallentine Mitchell; US$17).

OTHER RESOURCES

Let's Go tries to cover all aspects of budget travel, but we can't put *everything* in our guides. Listed below are resources that can serve as jumping off points for your own research.

TRAVEL PUBLISHERS & BOOKSTORES

Hunter Publishing, PO Box 746, Walpole, MA 02081, USA (☎617-269-0700; www.hunterpublishing.com). Has an extensive catalog of travel guides and diving and adventure travel books.

Rand McNally, P.O. Box 7600, Chicago, IL 60680, USA (☎800 275 7263; www.randmcnally.com), publishes road atlases.

Adventurous Traveler Bookstore, P.O. Box 2221, Williston, VT 05495, USA (☎800-282-3963; www.adventuroustraveler.com).

Travel Books & Language Center, Inc., 4437 Wisconsin Ave. NW, Washington, D.C. 20016, USA (☎800-220-2665; www.bookweb.org/bookstore/travelbks). Over 60,000 titles from around the world.

UBD, P.O. Box 1530, Macquarie Park NSW 2113 (☎02 9857 3700; fax 9888 9074; www.ubd.com.au). Incredibly helpful street directories and motoring atlases.

THE WORLD WIDE WEB

Almost every aspect of budget travel (with the most notable exception, of course, being experience) is accessible via the web. Listed here are some budget travel sites to start off your surfing; other relevant web sites are listed throughout the book. Because website turnover is high, use search engines (such as www.google.com) to strike out on your own.

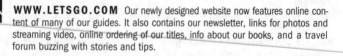

WWW.LETSGO.COM Our newly designed website now features online content of many of our guides. It also contains our newsletter, links for photos and streaming video, online ordering of our titles, info about our books, and a travel forum buzzing with stories and tips.

THE ART OF BUDGET TRAVEL

How to See the World: www.artoftravel.com. A compendium of great travel tips, from cheap flights to self defense to interacting with local culture.

Travel Library: www.travel-library.com. A fantastic set of links for general information and personal travelogues.

Lycos: http://travel.lycos.com. Features broad general introductions to cities and regions throughout Australia, accompanied by links to applicable histories and news asn well as local tourism sites.

INFORMATION ON AUSTRALIA

Atevo Travel: www.atevo.com/guides/destinations. Detailed introductions, travel tips, and suggested itineraries.

Australia Tourist Commission: www.australia.com. Information about Australia and travel including climate, economy, health, and safety concerns.

Australian Tourism Net: www.atn.com.au. Has tons of service listings and Oz facts.

Australian Whitepages: www.whitepages.com.au. If you ever need a phone number or address in Australia, this is the place to go.

Central Intelligence Agency (CIA) World Factbook: www.odci.gov/cia/publications/factbook/docs/notesanddefs.html. Tons of vital statistics on Australia, including information on geography, government, economy, and people.

Embassy of Australia: www.austemb.org. Facts about Australia and travel information related to Australian law and politics.

PlanetRider: www.planetrider.com. A subjective list of links to the "best" websites covering the culture and tourist attractions of Australia.

TravelPage: www.travelpage.com. Links to official tourist office sites in Australia.

World Travel Guide: www.travel-guides.com/navigate/world.asp. Helpful practical info.

ESSENTIALS

ALTERNATIVES TO TOURISM

When we started out in 1961, about 1.7 million people in the world were traveling internationally each year; in 2002, over 4.8 million trips were made to Australia alone. The dramatic rise in tourism has created an interdependence between the economy, environment, and culture of Australia and the tourists it hosts. **Sustainable travel** seeks to counteract the negative impact of our journeys.

Two rising trends in sustainable travel are ecotourism and community-based tourism. **Ecotourism** focuses on the conservation of natural habitats and using them to build up the economy without exploitation or overdevelopment. To find tours and products backed by a commitment to ecological sustainability and quality ecotourism experiences, look for recognition from the **Nature and Ecotourism Accreditation Program (NEAP)** or visit Ecotourism Australia's website at www.ecotourism-australia.info.

Community-based tourism aims to channel tourist dollars into the local economy by emphasizing tours and cultural programs that are run by members of the host community and that often benefit disadvantaged groups. Individually, you can contribute to this effort by buying locally made products and choosing independent restaurants and accommodations operated by locals instead of larger chains.

Those looking to **volunteer** in the efforts to resolve these issues have many options. In Australia, you can participate in an enormously diverse range of projects from dune preservation to koala rescue. Involvement varies depending on your particular issue; however, it may occur on an infrequent basis over the course of your journey or as the main component of your trip. Later in this section, we recommend organizations that can help you find the opportunities that best suit your interests, whether you're looking to pitch in for a day or a year.

There are a number of other ways that you can integrate yourself with the communities you visit. **Studying** at a college is an extremely popular option in Australia, where 16% of higher education students are from overseas. Many travelers also structure their trips by the work that they can do along the way—either odd jobs as they go, or full-time stints in cities where they plan to stay for some time. See **Working** for information about job opportunities and important legal requirements.

For more information about sustainable tourism, www.worldsurface.com features photos and personal stories of volunteer experiences. Another useful site is www.sustainabletravel.org. For those who seek more active involvement, Earthwatch International, Operation Crossroads Africa, and Habitat for Humanity offer fulfilling volunteer opportunities all over the world.

VOLUNTEERING

Combining volunteering with travel is one of the most fulfilling ways to experience a new culture. In Australia, travelers looking to do their part will find a number of options. Environmental conservation is by far the most popular choice. Check out www.afconline.org.au for details from the Australian Conservation Foundation. Other popular issues include coastal care and animal rescue.

A NEW PHILOSOPHY OF TRAVEL

We at *Let's Go* have watched the growth of the 'ignorant tourist' stereotype with dismay, knowing that the majority of travelers care passionately about the state of the communities and environments they explore—but also knowing that even conscientious tourists can inadvertently damage natural wonders, rich cultures, and impoverished communities. We believe the philosophy of **sustainable travel** is among the most important travel tips we could impart to our readers, to help guide fellow backpackers and on-the-road philanthropists. By staying aware of the needs and troubles of local communities, today's travelers can be a powerful force in preserving and restoring this fragile world.

Working against the negative consequences of irresponsible tourism is much simpler than it might seem; it is often self-awareness, rather than self-sacrifice, that makes the biggest difference. Simply by trying to spend responsibly and conserve local resources, all travelers can positively impact the places they visit. Let's Go has partnered with **BEST** (**Business Enterprises for Sustainable Travel,** an affiliate of the Conference Board; see www.sustainabletravel.org), which recognizes businesses that operate based on the principles of sustainable travel. Below, they provide advice on how ordinary visitors can practice this philosophy in their daily travels, no matter where they are.

TIPS FOR CIVIC TRAVEL: HOW TO MAKE A DIFFERENCE

Travel by train when feasible. Rail travel requires only half the energy per passenger mile that planes do. On average, each of the 40,000 daily domestic air flights releases more than 1700 pounds of greenhouse gas emissions.

Use public mass transportation whenever possible; outside of cities, take advantage of group taxis or vans. Bicycles are an attractive way of seeing a community firsthand. And enjoy walking—purchase good maps of your destination and ask about on-foot touring opportunities.

When renting a car, ask whether fuel-efficient vehicles are available. Honda and Toyota produce cars that use hybrid engines powered by electricity and gasoline, thus reducing emissions of carbon dioxide. Ford Motor Company plans to introduce a hybrid fuel model by the end of 2004.

Reduce, reuse, recycle—use electronic tickets, recycle papers and bottles wherever possible, and avoid using containers made of styrofoam. Refillable water bottles and rechargable batteries both efficiently conserve expendable resources.

Be thoughtful in your purchases. Take care not to buy souvenir objects made from trees in old-growth or endangered forests, such as teak, or items made from endangered species, like ivory or tortoise jewelry. Ask whether products are made from renewable resources.

Buy from local enterprises, such as casual street vendors. In developing countries and low-income neighborhoods, many people depend on the "informal economy" to make a living.

Be on-the-road-philanthropists. If you are inspired by the natural environment of a destination or enriched by its culture, join in preserving their integrity by making a charitable contribution to a local organization.

Spread the word. Upon your return home, tell friends and colleagues about places to visit that will benefit greatly from their tourist dollars, and reward sustainable enterprises by recommending their services. Travelers can not only introduce friends to particular vendors but also to local causes and charities that they might choose to support when they travel.

> **!**
>
> **VOLUNTEERING TIPS.** Before handing your money over to any volunteer or study program, make sure you know exactly what you're getting into. It's a good idea to get the name of **previous participants** and ask them about their experience, as some programs sound much better on paper than in reality. The **questions** below are a good place to start:
>
> –Will you be the only person in the program? If not, what are other participants like? How old are they? How much will you be expected to interact with them?
>
> –Is room and board included? If so, what is the arrangement? Will you be expected to share a room? A bathroom? What are the meals like? Do they fit any dietary restrictions?
>
> –Is transportation included? Are there any additional expenses?
>
> –How much free time will you have? Will you be able to travel around?
>
> –What kind of safety network is set up? Will you still be covered by your home insurance? Does the program have an emergency plan?

Most people who volunteer in Australia do so on a short-term basis, at organizations that make use of drop-in or once-a-week volunteers. These can be found in virtually every city. The best way to find opportunities that match your interests and schedule is to check local or national volunteer centers before you depart.

More intensive volunteer services will take care of logistical details for you and frequently provide a group environment and support system; however, potential do-gooders beware: many volunteer services charge a fee to participate in the program and to do work. These fees can be surprisingly hefty (although they frequently cover airfare and most, if not all, living expenses). Do research on a program before committing—talk to people who have previously participated and find out exactly what you're getting into, as living and working conditions can vary greatly. Different volunteer programs are geared toward different ages and levels of experience, so make sure that you are not taking on too much or too little. Above all, being well-informed and having realistic expectations will ensure that you enjoy the experience.

GENERAL VOLUNTEER ORGANIZATIONS

Amizade, Ltd., 367 S. Graham St., Pittsburgh, PA 15232, USA (☎888-973-4443; fax 412-648-1492; www.amizade.org). Volunteers spend two weeks in an Aboriginal community, working to promote culture and provide opportunities for economic self-sufficiency. Must be 18+. $1800 program fee, $350 deposit required.

Elderhostel, Inc., 11 Avenue de Lafayette, Boston, MA 02111-1746, USA (☎877-426-8056; fax 877-426-2166; www.elderhostel.org). Seniors age 55 and over can experience Australia through 2-5 week learning tours. Costs $4500-7500, including international airfare, but not domestic connections.

Habitat for Humanity International, 121 Habitat St., Americus, GA 31709, USA (☎229-924-6935 x2551; www.habitat.org/intl). Offers volunteer opportunities in Australia to live and build houses in a host community. Short-term program costs range from US$1200-4000.

International Volunteers for Peace (IVP), 499 Elizabeth St., Surry Hills NSW 2010 (☎(02) 9699 1129; www.ivp.org.au). Arranges placement in Australian community work camps for those 18+. Membership $35. If you are not in Australia, contact **Service Civil International (SCI),** IVP's affiliate, in your home country (www.sciint.org).

Involvement Volunteers, P.O. Box 218, Port Melbourne VIC 3207 (☎03 9646 5504; www.volunteering.org.au). Offers volunteering options in Australia ranging from social service, research, education, conservation, and farmwork. Registration fee AUS$242.

Volunteers for Peace, 1034 Tiffany Rd., Belmont., VT 05730, USA (☎802-259-2759; www.vfp.org). Affiliated, but not synonymous, with IVP (above). Arranges placement in work camps in Australia. Membership required for registration. Annual *International Workcamp Directory* US$20. Programs average US$200-500 for 2-3 weeks

VOLUNTEER OPPORTUNITIES BY ISSUE

LAND MANAGEMENT

This century, nearly 3000 natural habitats are predicted to disappear from Australia forever, taking more than 1500 species with them. Much of this can be attributed to the destruction of native bushlands, forests, savannah woodlands, native grasslands and the draining of wetlands. Several organizations have mobilized to stop this tragedy. To find out how you can help, contact one listed below.

Landcare Australia, P.O. Box 5666, West Chatswood, NSW 1515. (☎02 9412 1040; www.landcareaustralia.com.au). Landcare Australia works to raise funds and awareness about environmental issues. It also operates as an umbrella organization for Bushcare and Coastcare Australia. Contact regional headquarters to learn how you can help.

Bushcare Australia, National Resource Management Branch, Environment Australia, G.P.O. Box 787, Canberra, ACT 2601 (☎02 6274 1111; www.ea.gov.au/landbushcare/). In a country where only 20% of native bush remains, Bushcare's goal is to reverse the long-term decline of native vegetation. Volunteers can join groups or work individually.

Conservation Volunteers Australia, P.O. Box 423, Ballarat VIC 3353 (☎03 5333 1483 or nationwide ☎1800 032 501; www.conservationvolunteers.com.au). Offers travel volunteer packages (AUS$23 per day) that include service opportunity as well as accommodations, meals, and project-related transport.

Earthwatch, 3 Clocktower Pl., Suite 100, Box 75, Maynard, MA 01754, USA (☎800-776-0188 or 978-461-0081; www.earthwatch.org). Arranges 1- to 3-week programs in Australia to promote conservation of natural resources. Fees vary based on program location and duration, costs average $1800 plus airfare.

COASTAL PRESERVATION

With 25,760km of coastline, Australian beaches are second to none. Unfortunately, these national treasures are feeling the strain of increased development. In Australia, where 70% of the population lives within 100km of the coast, there is much to be done to protect coastal regions.

Coastcare Australia, Marine and Water Division, Environment Australia, G.P.O. Box 787, Canberra, ACT 2601. (☎1800 803 772; www.ea.gov.au/coasts/coastcare/). Volunteers build access paths, remove weeds, fence dunes, and educate visitors about the fragility of coastal ecosystems. Join one of the 2,000 groups in Australia.

Shell Coastal Volunteers, Conservation Volunteers Australia, 41 Tribune Street, South Brisbane, QLD 4101. (☎03 5221 0300; www.conservationvolunteers.com.au/shell/index.htm). In a joint effort between Shell Coastal Volunteers and Conservation Volunteers Australia, participants confront issues such as pollution, threats to marine biodiversity, and habitat degradation. The program undertakes about 100 urban and regional projects every year along Australia's coastline.

ANIMAL RESCUE

Australian Koala Foundation, With an estimated 80% of their original habitat destroyed, Australia's koalas are seriously threatened. The AKF works to save their natural habitat. Volunteers can participate in a 2-week field trip, working with researchers and staff in the field. Expect to pay about $2500.

STUDYING ABROAD

Study abroad programs range from informal cultural courses to college-level classes, often for credit. In order to choose a program that best fits your needs, you will want to research all you can before making your decision—determine costs and duration, as well as what kind of students participate in the program and what sort of accommodations are provided. Dorm life provides a better opportunity to mingle with fellow students, but there is less of a chance to experience the local scene. If you live with a family, there is potential to build lifelong friendships with natives and to experience day-to-day life in greater depth, but conditions can vary greatly from family to family.

A good resource for finding programs that cater to your particular interests is www.studyabroad.com, which has links to various semester abroad programs based on a variety of criteria, including desired location and focus of study. Another useful site is the Australian government's website, www.studyinaustralia.gov.au, which contains comprehensive information about requirements, programs, and fees. The following is a list of organizations that can help place students in programs in Australia.

PROGRAMS BY COUNTRY

IN AUSTRALIA

Association of Commonwealth Universities (ACU), John Foster House, 36 Gordon Sq., London WC1H OPF, UK (☎+44 020 7380 6700; www.acu.ac.uk). Publishes information about Commonwealth universities including Australian National University, University of Sydney, University of Melbourne, and all state universities.

DP Education Australia, 1 Geils Court, Deakin, ACT 2600 (☎02 6285 8222; www.idp.com). DP is an independent organization that offers information about Australian institutions, access to IDP counsellors, and a free application and enrollment processing service.

International Student Exchange Australia, Unit 16, 172 Redland Bay Rd., Capalaba, QLD 4157 (☎07 3390 3838; fax 07 3390 3446; www.i-s-e.com.au). Arranges voluntary work experience, individual homestays, and high school exchange programs (1-4 terms, AUD$3000-13,000) for a AUD$100 application fee.

IN CANADA

University of Alberta, 172 HUB International, Edmonton, AB T6G 2E2, (☎780 492 2692, www.international.ualberta.ca/epdb/unprotected.html. Coordinates exchanges with 4 Australian universities.

McGill University, Student Exchanges and Study Abroad, James Administration Annex, McGill University, 845 Sherbrokke Street West, Montreal, Quebec, Canada H3A 2T5, (☎514 398 8342; fax 398 8342; www.mcgill.ca/student-records/exchanges). McGill has an extensive exchange program with universities in Queensland, New South Wales, and Western Australia.

IN THE UK

Prospects.ac.uk, CSU, Prospects House, Booth Street East, Manchester, M13 9EP, UK (☎44 (0) 161 277 5200, www.prospects.ac.uk/cms/ShowPage/Home_page/ Explore_working_and_studying_abroad). Details various opportunities for postgraduate study in Australia. The website provides a useful timetable for those navigating the application process.

IN THE US

American Institute for Foreign Study, College Division, River Plaza, 9 West Broad St., Stamford, CT 06902, USA (☎800-727-2437, ext. 5163; www.aifsabroad.com). Organizes programs for high school and college study in universities in Oz.

Arcadia University for Education Abroad, 450 S. Easton Rd., Glenside, PA 19038, USA (☎866-927-2234; www.arcadia.edu/cea). Operates programs in Australia. Costs range from $2200 (summer) to $29,000 (full-year).

Central College Abroad, Office of International Education, 812 University, Pella, IA, 50219, USA (☎800-831-3629 or 641-628-5284; www.central.edu/abroad). Offers internships, as well as summer-, semester-, and year-long programs in Australia. US$25 application fee.

International Association for the Exchange of Students for Technical Experience (IAESTE), 10400 Little Patuxent Pkwy. Suite 250, Columbia, MD 21044-3519, USA (☎410-997-2200; www.aipt.org). 8- to 12-week programs in Australia for college students who have completed 2 years of technical study. US$25 application fee.

Institute for the International Education of Students (IES), 33 N. LaSalle St., 15th fl., Chicago, IL 60602, USA (☎800-995-2300; www.IESabroad.org). Offers year-long, semester, and summer programs for university study in Adelaide and Melbourne. Internship opportunities. US$50 application fee. Scholarships available.

School for International Training, College Semester Abroad, Admissions, Kipling Rd., P.O. Box 676, Brattleboro, VT 05302, USA (☎800-336-1616 or 802-257-7751; www.sit.edu). Semester- and year-long programs in Australia run US$10,600-13,700. Also runs the **Experiment in International Living** (☎800-345-2929; fax 802-258-3428; www.usexperiment.org), 3- to 5-week summer programs that offer high-school students cross-cultural homestays, community service, and ecological adventure and cost US$1900-5000.

Council on International Educational Exchange (CIEE), 633 3rd Ave., 20th fl., New York, NY 10017-6706 USA (☎800-407-8839; www.ciee.org/study) sponsors university study in Sydney, Melbourne, Perth, and Wollongong.

AUSTRALIAN UNIVERSITIES

Applying directly through Australian schools can be much cheaper than an outside university program, though it can be hard to receive academic credit (and sometimes housing). Services that connect foreigners to study abroad programs are listed below. For a more complete list of schools and services, check out www.studyabroadlinks.com/search/Australia. Another good resource for finding programs that cater to your particular interests is www.studyabroad.com, which has links to various semester abroad programs based on a variety of criteria, including desired location and focus of study. Listed below are several of Australia's universities which sponsor their own international study programs.

University of New South Wales, Level 16 Matthews Building, UNSW Kensington, Sydney NSW (☎02 9385 3179; www.studyabroad.unsw.edu.au). UNSW, aside from semester offerings, hosts several 6-week study programs during the Northern Hemisphere sum-

VISA INFORMATION

See the Department of Immigration and Multicultural and Indigenous Affairs website (www.immi.gov.au) to apply for visas. The following visas are required for temporary work and study in Australia.

Working Holiday Visa. For 18-30 year old citizens of Canada, China, Denmark, Germany, Ireland, Japan, Korea, Malta, the Netherlands, Norway, Sweden, and the UK. Valid for 12 months. Requirements include application and US $84 fee, valid passport, and proof of medical coverage and adequate funds.

Special Program Visa. For 18-30 year old United States citizens. Allows up to 4 months of temporary work with an approved exchange program. Requirements include application and US$84 fee, valid passport, flight itinerary, proof of funds, and letter from employment program (see p. 69 for eligible programs).

Student Visa. All student visas require application and US$158 fee, valid passport, and Electronic Confirmation of Enrollment (eCoE)/Acceptance Advice Form from Australian institution. Students enrolling for over 12 months need a signed medical report. Citizens of the US, Sweden, and Norway visiting for 12 months or less can get a visa online at www.immi.gov.au/e_visa/index.htm.

mer for undergraduates, graduate students, and adults looking to study abroad in Australia. Subjects include Australian history, Outback art, biogeography, conservation, and mass media, among others.

University of Sydney, Services Building G12, The University of Sydney, NSW 2006 (☎ 02 9351 3699; www.usyd.edu.au/io/studyabroad/index.html). The university's Study Abroad offers an opportunity to study in Australia's most famous city. Applicants should be enrolled in a university and have a GPA of a 3.0 or higher. Tuition is approximately $7,500 per semester.

University of Melbourne, International Centre, University of Melbourne, VIC 3010 (☎ 03 0344 4505; www.unimelb.edu.au/international/index1.html). Exchange students can choose from a variety of courses while experiencing the sophistication of Melbourne. Expect to pay about $8,500 per semester.

Australian National University, International Education Office, Australian National University, Canberra, ACT 0200 (☎ 02 6125 4643; www.anu.edu.au/ieo/ivsp/index_int.html). Situated in the Aussie capital, ANU boasts a multicultural community with over 1,400 international students. Tuition varies.

WORKING

Working in Australia is a great way to experience Aussie culture while funding further travels. But before signing on, be sure you're legal. Obtaining working permits can be difficult, especially for U.S. citizens. See the box on p. 68 for specific **visa requirements** to work in Australia. If you plan to work in Australia, you should apply for a **tax file number (TFN)** from the Australian Taxation Office (www.ato.gov.au). Without a TFN, you may be taxed at a higher rate than necessary. You also may consider opening a **bank account,** which is easier to do within Australia than before arriving.

Though most work programs and employers in Australia hire travelers carrying a 12-month Working Holiday Visa, United States citizens must obtain a **Special Program Visa** in order to work in Australia. This Special Program Visa is valid for up to 4 months and only applies to the organizations listed below (which also all accept **Working Holiday Visas**).

LONG-TERM WORK

If you're planning on spending a substantial amount of time (more than three months) working in Oz, search for a job well in advance. International placement agencies are often the easiest way to find employment abroad. Try Council Exchanges at www.councilexchanges.org. Be wary of advertisements or companies that claim the ability to get you a job abroad for a fee—often times the same listings are available online or in newspapers, or even out of date. It's best, if going through an organization, to use one that's somewhat reputable. A few agencies to look into are listed.

Council Exchanges, 633 Third Ave., New York, NY 10017 USA (☎888-268-6345; http://councilexchanges.org). The US$475 program fee includes document assistance, overseas and emergency aid, arrival orientation, and one night free accommodation; fee does not include visa application fee and mandatory US$40/month insurance cost.

International Exchange Programs, P.O. Box 4096, Sydney NSW 2001 (☎02 9299 0400; www.iep-australia.com). Helps organize working holidays; arranges visas, bank accounts, and tax file numbers; forwards mail; and helps find jobs and accommodations. For application and fees, contact the partner organization in your home country.

Visitoz, Springfield Farm, Goomeri QLD 4601 (☎07 4168 6106; www.visitoz.org). Arranges jobs, English language instruction, farm holidays, and agricultural training. Job options range from pubs and hostels to domestic work to teaching in the outback. Farm and station work requires introductory agricultural courses at a Visitoz training farm.

Work Experience Down Under, 2330 Marinship Way, Suite 250, Sausalito, CA 94965 USA (☎800-999-2267 or 415-339-2728; www.ccusa.com). The US$750 cost includes visa processing, work and travel insurance, and two nights accommodation.

INTERNSHIPS & WORK EXPERIENCES

For the career-minded traveler, professional experience in Australia is a great way to get ahead while getting away. When looking into your options, be sure to differentiate between internships and work experience. In Australia, internships are usually only found in the media sector and even then are scarce and extremely competitive. Although unpaid, work experience is a more laid-back option usually involving a few weeks of unstructured time on-the-job. Whatever you decide, be sure to secure **workplace insurance**, as most Australian employers won't take you on without it. The most economical way to plan your experience is to organize a placement on your own; however, this can be difficult for someone without connections. Listed below are several internship placement programs that will take care of the leg-work.

Australian National Internships Program (ANIP), Sir Roland Wilson Building, No. 120, Australian National University, Canberra, ACT 0200. (☎ 02 6125 8540; www.anu.edu.au/anip/index.htm). Arranges internships in public policy for college students from Australia or abroad. In addition to on-the-job experience, interns learn interview techniques and hone their computer skills. Cost falls between $3400-5200.

Australearn, 12050 N. Pecos St., #320, Westminster, CO 80234, USA. (☎ 1800 980 0033; www.australearn.org/Programs/Internship/). US-based company that coordinates with Global Internship Services. Opportunities exist to work in a variety of fields. Expect to pay US$3000-4500.

Australia Internships, Level 3, 80 Stamford Rd., Indooroopilly, QLD 4068 (☎ 07 3720 2244; www.interships.com.au). Organizes internships lasting from 1 month to a year in fields ranging from accounting to forestry. Cost ($1,190-3,000) includes placement, assistance with the visa process, and counseling support services.

SHORT-TERM WORK

Traveling for long periods of time can get expensive; many travelers try their hand at odd jobs for a few weeks to make extra cash. Seasonal fruit-picking is a widespread and popular option in Australia. Climatic diversity across the continent ensures that picking jobs are available year-round, and the popularity of the work has created a sort of fruit-picking subculture. Many hostels in picking areas cater specifically to workers, offering transportation to worksites and other such amenities. In cities and highly touristed areas, hostels often contain employment boards and sometimes even employment services to help lodgers find temporary work. One popular option is to work several hours a day at a hostel in exchange for free or discounted room and/or board. Most often, these short-term jobs are found by word of mouth, or simply by talking to the owner of a hostel or restaurant. Due to the high turnover in the tourism industry there are always establishments eager for help, even if only temporary.

STATE	LOCATION	SEASON	WORK AVAILABLE
Queensland	Inland on NSW border; Warwick	*Summer*	Stone and orchard fruits; grapes
	Central Coast	*May-December*	Fruit and vegetables
	Northern Coast	*May - November*	Sugar cane, bananas, tobacco
	Bundaberg, Childers	*Year-round*	Fruit and vegetables
New South Wales	Bathurst, Dubbo, Orange	*Summer*	Orchard and other fruits, cotton, onions, asparagus
	North Coast	*Year-round*	Bananas
South Australia	Barossa Valley	*February-April*	Grapes
	The Riverland	*Year-round*	Citrus, soft fruits
Western Australia	Southwest	*October-June*	Grapes and orchard fruits, prawn
	West coast	*March-November*	Crayfish, prawn, and scallop fishing and processing
	Northeast	*May-October*	Fruit and vegetables
Victoria	Central northern areas	*Summer*	Orchard fruits, tomatoes, tobacco, grapes, and soft fruits
Tasmania	Anywhere	*Summer*	Orchard and soft fruits, grapes

While word of mouth is generally an effective method of finding work, many employers join networks that connect workers to jobs nationwide. These services usually charge a membership fee, but often their websites alone can be helpful. The following resources provide information and access to job networks.

Employment National, (Harvest Hotline ☎ 1300 720 126; www.employmentnational.com.au, click on "Go Harvest"). Features a "Go Harvest" jobs board with up-to-date harvesting opportunities.

Workabout Australia, 8 White St., Dubbo NSW 2830 (☎ 02 6884 7777; www.workaboutaustralia.com.au). Joining the club costs $27.50, but the website offers a list of employment vacancies by state, including employers' contact information. Also sells *Workabout Australia*, a book containing seasonal and casual employment info by state.

WorldWide Workers, 234 Sussex St., Sydney NSW 2000 (☎ 02 8268 6001; www.worldwideworkers.com). Also locations in Melbourne and Cairns. $99 club membership includes 6 month membership in WorldWideWorkers, 12-month membership in World-

WidePickers, travel and social discounts, free Internet access at store locations, and access to job network with opportunities in labor, hospitality, sales, fruit-picking, nursing, accounting, and clerical work.

Willing Workers on Organic Farms (WWOOF), Buchan VIC 3885 (☎03 5155 0218; www.wwoof.com.au). Exchange your labor for food, accommodation, and local culture. There can be stipulations on minimum stays and work expected from a WWOOFer, but each site has its own expectations. Membership (AUS$45 or AUS$50 for two people) includes a guide to hosts in Australia and can be purchased from many outlets throughout Australia (see www.wwoof.com.au/agents.html).

ECOTOURISM

Those concerned with combining travel and environmental responsibility should consider ecotourism. Emphasizing the importance of sustainability and cultural understanding, ecotourism seeks to support local communities and conserve natural areas. In Australia, where ecological preservation and Aboriginal issues are pressing concerns, environmental consciousness has evolved into a rich industry. To find tours or products backed by a commitment to ecological sustainability and quality ecotourism experiences, look for recognition from the Nature and Ecotourism Accreditation Program (NEAP) or visit Ecotourism Australia's website at www.ecotourism-australia.info. Guides certified by NEAP's Ecoguide Program meet the industry's standards for competency.

FURTHER READING ON ALTERNATIVES TO TOURISM

Alternatives to the Peace Corps: A directory of third world and U.S. Volunteer Opportunities, by Joan Powell. Food First Books, 2000 (US$10).

How to Get a Job in Europe, by Sanborn and Matherly. Surrey Books, 1999 ($US22).

How to Live Your Dream of Volunteering Oversees, by Collins, DeZerega, and Heckscher. Penguin Books, 2002 (US$17).

International Directory of Voluntary Work, by Whetter and Pybus. Peterson's Guides and Vacation Work, 2000 (US$16).

International Jobs, by Kocher and Segal. Perseus Books, 1999 (US$18).

Overseas Summer Jobs 2002, by Collier and Woodworth. Peterson's Guides and Vacation Work, 2002 (US$18).

Work Abroad: The Complete Guide to Finding a Job Overseas, by Hubbs, Griffith, and Nolting. Transitions Abroad Publishing, 2000 ($16).

Work Your Way Around the World, by Susan Griffith. Worldview Publishing Services, 2001 (US$18).

Invest Yourself: The Catalogue of Volunteer Opportunities, published by the Commission on Voluntary Service and Action (☎718-638-8487).

THE GREAT OUTDOORS

ENVIRONMENT

Australia's environment is both amazingly diverse and unique. The continent's isolation from the rest of the planet for millions of years has allowed a distinctive array of species to evolve, with some of the most peculiar plants and animals in the world now inhabiting the country.

The continent's inevitable contact with the outside, however, has presented an enormous challenge, upsetting Australia's delicate ecology; it is estimated that over thirteen species of mammals and birds have already become extinct since European settlement. In recent years, environmental policy has begun to recognize the importance of protecting Australia's precious biodiversity.

FLORA

TREES

Dominating forests from coast to coast, the **eucalypts,** also known as **gum trees,** amaze biologists with their successful adaptation to diverse environments, taking on many different shapes and sizes across the continent. The majestic **karri** soars to over 50m in ancient stands along well-watered valleys, while the **mallee** gum tends to grow in stunted copses across scrubland. The characteristically bulging trunk and splayed branches of the **boab** mark the horizon, particularly in the arid **Kimberley** of Western Australia (p. 730).

In the drier areas of the southeast, a common species of the **acacia** tree known as the **golden wattle** is distinguished by its fragrant blooms, which also happen to be Australia's national flower. Perhaps the most unusual—and most rare—tree is the **Wollemi pine.** The pine was discovered only a few years ago by scientists who had previously thought that the species was extinct (see **Wollemi National Park,** p. 163). Other trees common to the bush and coastal thickets include **banksias, tea trees,** and **grevillias.** Feathery and almost pine-like in appearance, **casuarinas** also exist in multiple habitats. In temperate, rain-fed stretches of Victoria and Tasmania, valleys of tall, dinosaur-era **tree ferns** are dwarfed by towering **mountain ash,** the tallest flowering plant in nature.

Most of Australia's large tree species have trunks that are lighter in color than their leaves, and the leaves themselves usually grow high above the ground. The effect created is quite different than that of European and North American forests and wooded areas. Here **bushwalkers** find themselves surrounded by white and gray in place of brown and green.

The **mangrove,** found along parts of Australia's tropical coasts, has adapted readily to its unfavorable environment, its stilt-like trunks clinging tenaciously to the briny mud of alluvial swamps. Australia also has wide expanses of land with few if any trees. The arid outback is dominated by dense tufts of **spinifex** grasses. Another common plant is the **saltbush,** a hearty shrub pivotal in converting harsh habitats to livestock pastures.

FLOWERS

In more fertile areas, wildflowers are abundant. Western Australia is home to **swamp bottlebrush, kangaroo paw,** and **Ashby's banksia,** along with nearly 10,000 other species. Yellow and pink **everlastings** cover fields across the country, while rare **spider orchids** hidden in the forests reveal themselves only to the most dogged of investigators. The **Sturt pea** adds a distinctive splash of red and black to the inland deserts of South Australia and Western Australia. Elsewhere, **orchids** and **begonias** provide extra visual garnish.

LAND ANIMALS

MAMMALS

Marsupials, which bear immature young and nurse them in a pouch, had few mammalian competitors on the Australian continent and consequently flourished, filling various ecological niches. Perhaps the best known marsupial, **kangaroos** can grow up to 3m (10 ft.) long, nose to tail, and are capable of propelling themselves nearly 9m (30 ft.) in a single bound. The kangaroo's smaller, look-alike cousin, the **wallaby,** is another common sight in the outback. Australia's other best loved marsupial, the **koala,** lives on and among the leaves of certain eucalypt trees. Sleeping 18 of every 24 hours, koalas exist on a diet comprised exclusively of eucalyptus leaves. Other native marsupials include **wombats** (a rare, rotund, and profoundly cuddly burrowing creature), **possums, bandicoots,** and **quolls.**

Giant marsupials once roamed the landscape of prehistoric Australia. Now extinct, these megafauna included towering relatives of kangaroos called diprotodons. The megafauna died off soon after the arrival of humans. The **thylacine,** or **Tasmanian tiger,** is a more recent loss. Resembling a large wolf with stripes, the predator was driven to the edge of extinction by competition with dingoes, then hunted by white settlers who feared for livestock. One infamous marsupial carnivore has survived, however. Fierce in temperament, **Tasmanian devils** are nocturnal scavengers, known to hunt small prey and kill livestock with their powerful jaws.

Two families of **monotremes,** or egg-laying mammals, call Australia home. **Echidnas** are small porcupine-like ant-eaters with protruding snouts. The **platypus** sports a melange of zoological features: the bill of a duck, the fur of an otter, the tail of a beaver, and webbed claws. So outrageous did this anatomy seem to colonists that early British naturalists refused to consider stuffed specimens real.

REPTILES

The most fearsome reptiles, saltwater crocodiles **(salties)** actually live in both brine and freshwater and grow to lengths of 7m. Freshwater crocodiles **(freshies)** are found only in freshwater and, unless provoked, generally present little danger to humans. Crocodiles are found only in the tropical north of Australia. In addition to crocodiles, Australia's reptiles include **goannas** (large lizards growing up to 3 or 4 metres long) and a wide array of **snakes,** many of them poisonous, including the **taipan, smooth snake, tiger snake, brown snake,** and **death adder**.

BIRDS

Outshining Australia's mammals in vividness of color is the continent's tremendous diversity of **birds.** The **emu** is related to other flightless birds such as the African ostrich and the extinct moa of New Zealand. Flightless hordes of **little** (or **fairy**) **penguins** can be spotted at sites on the south coast, where they wade ashore each night (a great place to see fairy penguins is at **Phillip Island** near Melbourne; p. 605). Australia's flight-endowed birds include noisy flocks of **galahs,** colorful **rainbow**

lorikeets, and large **cassowaries.** Songs and poems have immortalized the unmistakable laugh of the **kookaburra,** a common barbecue guest from the kingfisher family. All of these native Australian animals can be seen, and many handled, at open-air zoos such as **Healesville Sanctuary** (p. 602) in Victoria and **Western Plains Zoo** (p. 248) in regional NSW.

INTRODUCED SPECIES

Humans have been responsible for the introduction of animals to Australia since prehistoric times, and many of these introduced species are now considered pests. The **dingo,** a lithe, wild canine with a vicious bite but no bark, crossed the Timor Sea with ancestors of Aboriginal populations several thousand years ago. The creatures mainly hunt small, wild prey, but may also menace livestock. Although dingoes pose little threat to adults, they are can injure and even kill small children. Accidental introductions such as European **rats** and **cane toads** present serious threats to native fauna as well. The massive overpopulation of **rabbits,** purportedly introduced to Australia to provide practice targets for marksmen, has become one of Australia's gravest wildlife problems. **Foxes** also present a serious problem to wildlife, particularly in Tasmania.

With ranches across the continent, domesticated **cattle** and **sheep** have always been of tremendous economic importance in Australia since European settlement. Vast tracts of land have been converted to pasture to support the meat industry, creating a dramatic impact on the landscape and national ecological balance. The farming of non-native **honeybees** has also become a growing part of the economy.

SEA ANIMALS

Fur seals, elephant seals, and **sea lions** populate Australia's southern shores during summer breeding seasons. **Kangaroo Island** (p. 481) is a particularly good place to get up close to sea lions in their natural habitat. **Dolphins** are another common sight on Australia's coasts. The best places to see and even swim with dolphins are **Monkey Mia** on Shark Bay (p. 720) and **Sorrento** on Port Phillip Bay (p. 607). **Humpback Whales** also frequent the waters off Australia's eastern coast, on show in **Hervey Bay** (p. 373) between July and November.

GREAT BARRIER REEF

The Great Barrier Reef is one of Australia's biggest tourist draws and a diving wonderland (see **The Great Barrier Reef,** p. 319). The longest coral formation in the world, it is actually a series of many reefs that stretches more than 2000km along the eastern coast of Queensland from the Tropic of Capricorn to Papua New Guinea. Although adult **coral polyps** are sedentary, corals belong to the animal kingdom. Thus, the Great Barrier Reef is the only community of animals visible to the eye from space. Beware of national marine park rules against removing living creatures from the sea and **fines up to $500** for removing any piece of a coral reef.

CORAL

Hard corals come in hues ranging from purple to emerald to red, and are mostly categorized as either branched, boulder, or plate coral. The fast-growing **branched coral** is named for its appearance; its most common varieties are the thin, brittle **needle coral,** the antler-like **stag coral,** and **finger coral. Boulder coral** is sturdier and slower-growing, including the **honey-comb, golfball,** and **brain boulders. Plate corals,** such as **sheet** and **table corals,** are named for their shapes. The reefs that make up the Great Barrier Reef take a number of different forms. Closest to the shore are **patch reefs,** comprising patches of hard and soft coral. Farther out from shore are

DANGEROUS WILDLIFE. If bitten or stung, it is best to take the offending creature to the hospital with you (if you are not in danger of being bitten or stung again) so that doctors can administer the correct anti-venom. The following list contains some dangerous creatures found in Australia.

Box jellyfish: Large with multiple trailing tentacles. *Warnings to stay out of the water should be strictly observed.* If you're stung, your chances of surviving are virtually zero; the pain alone causes immediate shock. Box jellyfish that have washed up on shore are still dangerous, so walking barefoot at the water's edge is discouraged. Box jellyfish inhabit the waters on the Top End Oct.-Apr., and the northern shores on the west and east coasts Nov.-Apr. Douse jellyfish stings in vinegar. Calamine lotion and antihistamines help to relieve pain. Beware also the **stonefish** and **blue-ringed octopus.**

Cassowaries: Large flightless birds characterized by brown crests and dagger-like claws, found mainly in Queensland. Have been known to attack during mating season, in winter.

Crocodiles: "Salties" are found in fresh and saltwater; they are hard to see and attack without provocation. Heed local warning signs; don't swim or paddle in streams, lakes, the ocean, or other natural waterways, and keep kids away from the water's edge. **"Freshies,"** the saltie's freshwater counterpart, will not attack unless provoked but are also hard to see.

Dingoes: Pose little threat to adults; can injure or even kill children. Pack away all food and keep fish and bait off the ground.

Sharks: Lifeguards at heavily visited beaches generally keep a good look out—don't swim outside the red and yellow flagged areas.

Snakes: Most species are scared enough of humans that they will slide away at the sound of footsteps. If cornered, though, a few might attack in self-defense. Wear boots and long pants when walking through the wilderness, and never approach, attempt to step over, or try to kill a snake. Instead, walk around it at a safe distance. If bitten, tightly wrap the wounded area and work the bandage down to the tip of the limb and back up to the next joint to help slow the spread of venom. If possible, keep the infected area immobile, and seek medical attention immediately. Do not try to suck out the venom or clean the bite. Don't panic—most snake bites can be treated effectively.

Spiders: The **funnel-web** (found in eastern Australia including Tasmania), which is oval-shaped with brown or gray markings, and the **redback** (common throughout Australia, particularly in urban areas), so-called due to its red-striped back, are among the most dangerous.

Stinging insects: Bull-ants, wasps, bees, and bush-ticks may hurt a lot, but they are not life-threatening. If allergic to bee stings or other insect bites, carry your own epinephrine kit. Calamine lotion provides some relief from stings and bites; ice reduces swelling. Check for lumps on your skin to remove bush-ticks.

GREAT OUTDOORS

fringe reefs. Their arrangement in circular patterns deeply entrenched in the sea floor means that they frequently fill with silt, clouding visibility for divers. The far outer reef is made up of 710km of **ribbon reef.**

FISH

The reef also houses a spectacular variety of fish, from the enormous **potato cod** to the **fusaleres,** a family of fish that change color at night. The **parrotfish** eats bits of coral by cracking it in its beak-like mouth, and at night envelops itself in a protective mucus sac. If you're diving, taking a **briefing course** on marine life is an excellent way to familiarize yourself with what you'll see. While it's impossible to memorize every species, many shops sell **fish identification cards** that you can take down with you. A few terms to know: the **wrasse** is a long, slender, cigar-like fish; **angel** and **surgeon fish** have similar oblong shapes, but the surgeon has a razor-sharp barb close to its tail; the **butterfly** and **bat fish** are round, but the latter is larger and has a black stripe across the eye. Despite Australia's reputation for **sharks,** only gray **reef sharks** (and the very occasional **tiger shark**) are seen around the reef and are typically harmless if left unprovoked. Besides fish, the reef houses **turtles, giant clams, dolphins,** and **whales,** as well as **echinoderms:** sea cucumbers, sea stars, feather stars, and brittle stars.

WHERE TO GO

NATIONAL PARKS

A major source of pride for Australians—and a highlight for many visitors—is the number and variety of national parks across the continent. From the jagged ranges of the far northwest to the scrub plains of the Red Centre to the great sandy beaches of the east coast and the mountains of the southwest, Australia offers a dramatically changing landscape, much of which, thanks to government protection, is accessible to campers, climbers, and bushwalkers of all levels.

Most national parks require visitor fees; day passes are usually around $10 per vehicle, while Parks Passes allow you to make unlimited visits to selected parks within a given period. Some parks require camping permits (usually an additional $5) which can be obtained from the local ranger station. The list below contains contact information for each state's parks service, most of whom provide free publications on state and national protected areas. For direct links to individual parks across Australia, visit www.ea.gov.au/pa/contacts.html.

New South Wales National Parks Centre, 43 Bridge St., Hurstville NSW 2220 (☎02 9585 6444; www.nationalparks.nsw.gov.au).

Northern Territory Visitors Centre, 22 Cavenagh St., Darwin NT 0800 (☎08 8941 2167; www.northernterritory.com).

Queensland Parks and Wildlife Service, 160 Ann St., Brisbane QLD 4002 (☎07 3227 7111; www.epa.qld.gov.au).

Nature Foundation South Australia, 32 Holden St., Hindmarsh SA 5007 (☎1300 366 191; www.naturefoundationsa.asn.au).

Tasmania Parks & Wildlife Service, GPO Box 44, Hobart, TAS 7001 (☎1300 368 550; www.parks.tas.gov.au).

Parks Victoria, Level 10, 535 Bourke St., Melbourne VIC 3000 (☎03 8627 4699; www.parkweb.vic.gov.au).

Conservation and Land Management, Western Australia, Locked Bag 104, Bentley Delivery Ctr. 6983 (head office ☎08 9442 0300, general inquiries 9334 0333; www.calm.wa.gov.au).

CAMPING & BUSHWALKING

Camping and bushwalking (hiking) are the best ways to experience Australia's unspoiled wilderness. Some of the finest bushwalking tracks can be found in the southeast. In Victoria, **Wilsons Promontory** (p. 663), the southernmost point on the

Australian mainland, and the rugged mountains of the **Grampians** (p. 627), are among the state's most popular tourist destinations. In New South Wales, the World Heritage-listed **Blue Mountains** (p. 150), the alpine **Snowy Mountains** (p. 233), and the **Warrumbungle Ranges** (p. 252), where the bush meets the outback, have some amazing terrain and breathtaking views. In Queensland, walk through spectacular rainforests in the **Atherton Tablelands** (p. 436) or trek along remarkable sandstone cliffs rich with Aboriginal rock art in **Carnarvon Gorge** (p. 393). In the **Stirling Ranges** (p. 705) in Western Australia, you can walk among ancient giant eucalypts, while the **Flinders Ranges** (p. 501) in South Australia and **Freycinet National Park** in Tasmania offer spectacular views and exciting hikes. The vastness of the Australia Outback can be fully appreciated in the expanses of the Red Centre at **Watarrka** (p. 312) and **Uluru-Kata Tjuta National Parks** (p. 313), and the unspoiled wilderness of **Litchfield** (p. 282), **Nitmiluk** (p. 288), and **Kakadu National Parks** (p. 272) reveal the unique charm of the Top End.

For the more adventurous, Australia has its share of longer treks. The 220km **Larapinta Trail** (p. 307) in the Red Centre, winds from Alice Springs into the West MacDonnell ranges. In Western Australia, the **Bibulman Track** (p. 708) runs 964km from Perth to Albany on the south coast. Perhaps Australia's most famous trail, the **Overland Track** (p. 544) connects Cradle Mountain and Lake St. Clair through 80km of World Heritage wilderness in Tasmania.

Australian Bushwalking & Camping (www.galactic.net.au/bushwalking) offers a list of walks and parks in Australia, along with valuable tips and links to national parks. Another excellent general resource for travelers planning on camping or spending time in the outdoors is the **Great Outdoor Recreation Pages** (www.gorp.com). For information on ecotourism opportunities, please refer to the section in our **Alternatives to Tourism** chapter (p. 71).

OUTDOORS ESSENTIALS

EQUIPMENT

WHAT TO BUY...

Good camping equipment is both sturdy and light. Camping equipment is generally more expensive in Australia, New Zealand, and the UK than in North America.

Sleeping Bag: Most sleeping bags are rated by season ("summer" means 30-40°F at night; "four-season" or "winter" often means below 0°F). Prices range US$80-210 for a summer synthetic to US$250-300 for a good down winter bag. **Sleeping bag pads** include foam pads (US$10-30), air mattresses (US$15-50), and Therm-A-Rest self-inflating pads (US$45-120). Bring a **stuff sack** lined with a plastic bag to store your sleeping bag and keep it dry.

Tent: The best tents are free-standing (with their own frames and suspension systems), set up quickly, and only require staking in high winds. Low-profile dome tents are the best all-around. Good 2-person tents start at US$90, 4-person at US$300. Seal the seams of your tent with waterproofer, and make sure it has a rain fly. Other tent accessories include a **battery-operated lantern,** a **plastic groundcloth,** and a **nylon tarp.**

Backpack: Internal-frame packs mold better to your back, keep a lower center of gravity, and flex adequately to allow you to hike difficult trails. **External-frame packs** are more comfortable for long hikes over even terrain, as they keep weight higher and distribute it more evenly. Make sure your pack has a strong, padded hip-belt to transfer weight to your legs. Any serious backpacking requires a pack of at least 4000 in^3

(16,000cc), plus 500in³ for sleeping bags in internal-frame packs. Sturdy backpacks cost anywhere from US$125-420—this is one area in which it doesn't pay to economize. Fill up any pack with something heavy and walk around the store with it to get a sense of how it distributes weight before buying it. Either buy a **waterproof backpack cover,** or store all of your belongings in plastic bags inside your pack.

Boots: Be sure to wear hiking boots with good **ankle support** which are appropriate for the terrain you plan to hike. They should fit snugly and comfortably over 1-2 pairs of wool socks and thin liner socks. Break in boots over several weeks first in order to spare yourself painful and debilitating blisters. Waterproof your boots with waterproofing treatment before leaving on a hike.

Other Necessities: Synthetic layers, like those made of polypropylene, and a **pile jacket** will keep you warm even when wet. A **"space blanket"** will help you to retain your body heat and doubles as a groundcloth (US$5-15). Plastic **water bottles** are virtually shatter- and leak-proof. Bring **water-purification tablets** for when you can't boil water. In Australia, fires are only permitted in designated fireplaces; to cook elsewhere you'll need a **camp stove** (the classic Coleman starts at US$40) and a propane-filled **fuel bottle** to operate it. Also, don't forget a **first-aid kit, pocketknife, insect repellent, calamine lotion,** and **waterproof matches** or a **lighter**.

...& WHERE TO BUY IT

The mail-order/online companies listed below offer lower prices than many retail stores, but a visit to a local camping or outdoors store will give you a good sense of the look and weight of certain items.

Campmor, 28 Parkway, P.O. Box 700, Upper Saddle River, NJ 07458, USA (☎888-226-7667; www.campmor.com).

Discount Camping, 880 Main North Rd., Pooraka, SA 5095, Australia (☎08 8262 3399; www.discountcamping.com.au).

Eastern Mountain Sports (EMS), 1 Vose Farm Rd., Peterborough, NH 03458, USA (☎888-463-6367; www.ems.com).

L.L. Bean, Freeport, ME 04033 (US and Canada ☎800-441-5713, UK ☎0800 891 297; www.llbean.com).

Mountain Designs, 51 Bishop St., Kelvin Grove, QLD 4059, Australia (☎07 3856 2344; www.mountaindesigns.com).

Recreational Equipment, Inc. (REI), Sumner, WA 98352, USA (US and Canada ☎800-426-4840, elsewhere 253-891-2500; www.rei.com).

YHA Adventure Shop, 19 High St., Staines, Middlesex, TW18 4QY, UK (☎1784 458625; www.yhaadventure.com).

WILDERNESS SAFETY

Stay warm, stay dry, and stay hydrated. The vast majority of life-threatening wilderness situations can be avoided by following this simple advice. Prepare yourself for an emergency, however, by always packing **raingear,** a **hat and mittens,** a **first-aid kit,** a **reflector,** a **whistle, high energy food,** and extra **water.** On a longer trip, you should carry a **compass** and a detailed **topographical map** of the area where you are hiking. Dress in warm layers of **synthetic materials** designed for the outdoors, or **wool.** Pile fleece jackets and Gore-Tex® raingear are excellent choices. Never rely on **cotton** for warmth, as it is useless when wet. Make sure to check all equipment for any defects before setting out. Check **weather forecasts** and pay attention to the skies when hiking, since weather patterns can change suddenly. Whenever possible, *let someone know when and where you are going hiking*—either a friend, your hostel, a park ranger, or a local hiking organization. **National Parks and Wildlife Service (NPWS)** offices at the entrance to many larger parks often offer registration services. Do not ever attempt a hike beyond your ability—you may very well be endangering your life.

Take enough **water** with you when exploring outdoors; the average person requires at least 1.5L per day. Avoid alcohol and coffee, which cause dehydration. **Sunglasses, sunscreen**, and a **hat** are essential sun protection. **Light-colored clothing** also helps reflect the sun's rays. Although at times uncomfortable, wearing a sweaty shirt prevents dehydration more effectively than going shirtless. Total fire bans are common in many parts of the country. Make sure you check on this before going hiking, as some walks are sometimes closed due to fire dangers. See **Environmental Hazards** for info on outdoor ailments and basic medical concerns. For information on **dangerous wildlife**, see p. 75.

USEFUL PUBLICATIONS & RESOURCES

A variety of publishing companies offer hiking guidebooks to meet the educational needs of novice or expert. For information about camping and hiking, write or call the publishers listed below to receive a free catalog. Aside from those listed below, other publications about camping and hiking are available from the **NSW National Parks and Wildlife Service Head Office,** 43 Bridge St., Hurstville NSW 2220 (☎02 9585 6444; fax 9585 6555; www.nationalparks.nsw.gov.au; open M-F 8:30am-5pm). **Australia Outdoor Connection** (www.flinders.com.au/home.htm), sponsored by Flinders Camping in Adelaide, provides camping, hiking, and environmental information and links. For **topographical maps of Australia,** contact the **Geoscience Australia** (☎02 6201 4201 or 1800 80 01 73; www.ga.gov.au), or write to P.O. Box 2, Belconnen ACT 2616.

Automobile Association, Contact Ctr., Car Ellison House, William Armstrong Dr., Newcastle-upon-Tyne, UK NE4 7YA. (☎0870 600 0371; www.theaa.co.uk).

Sierra Club Books, 85 Second St., 2nd fl., San Francisco, CA 94105 (☎415-977-5500; www.sierraclub.org/books). Publishes general resource books on hiking, camping, and women interested in the outdoors.

The Mountaineers Books, 1001 SW Klickitat Way #201, Seattle, WA 98134 (☎800-553-4453; www.mountaineersbooks.org). Over 600 titles on hiking, biking, mountaineering, natural history, and conservation.

DRIVING IN THE OUTBACK

Driving is the most convenient way of getting around outback Australia, but be prepared for some long roadtrips. Outside of major urban areas, public transport is limited, and a car may be the only way to visit many sights. Certain roads should not be attempted unless you have a **4WD** vehicle and some national parks are inaccessible without one.

BEFORE YOU GO

If you're using a 4WD and you've never driven one before, it may be worth taking a short introductory lesson; many rental companies offer half- and full-day lessons. Make sure you have **recent, accurate maps**; regional topographic maps are useful. Also, always inquire locally to find out about the condition of roads and tracks.

GREAT OUTDOORS

SUPPLIES FOR YOUR VEHICLE

Ideally, your vehicle will be equipped with either a long-range fuel tank or two fuel tanks; if it isn't, bring at least one full tank's worth of **extra fuel** in fuel safe containers. Use a **metal safety can** and secure it down in your trunk so that it does not slosh around while you drive. Plastic cans are cheaper, but they are also more apt to spill, which creates both noxious fumes and a fire hazard.

There is a lost of dust on some roads, and it may be necessary to carry extra **windshield washer fluid.** It is also important to carry at least two spare tires and a full set of tools. One of the simplest ways to get yourself stalled out in the midst of nowhere is to overlook your **battery;** if it is at all old or corroded, get a new one before heading out. Some travelers carry an additional charged battery in the trunk of their car in case of battery failure, but remember that battery acid is highly corrosive, and that a spare battery should be stored very carefully in static-resistant, absorbent packaging.

In order to make minor repairs on your car, or to keep it moving after a problem, you will need to carry several tools, including a **wrench,** a **flashlight,** a few good **screwdrivers** with both Phillips and flat-head ends (these should range in size from small to large, and should be long enough to reach down into concealed engine spaces), and a couple different kinds of **pliers** (one for gripping larger items and a narrower needle-nosed pair of pliers for reaching into tight spaces).

Other vital items include extra oil, extra coolant, a jack, a tire iron, a full-sized spare tire, extra gasoline, extra clean water, a tire pressure gauge, road flares, a knife, hose sealant, a first-aid kit, jumper cables, fan belts, extra windshield washer fluid, plastic sheeting, string or rope, a larger tow rope, duct tape, an ice scraper, rags, a funnel, a spray bottle filled with glass cleaner, a compass, matches, and blankets and food. The uses of many of these items are described below. Even if you don't have a tow hitch, or are traveling alone, carry a **tow rope.** Having one on hand will make it easier for others who find you to help get you out of your jam.

PERSONAL SUPPLIES

Supplies are often few and far between on the road, so self-sufficiency is a must. Water is the most important supply; you should carry at least 5L of water per person per day. Also bring ample amounts of food. You'll need light clothing to help you brave the midday sun, sturdy boots for any hiking you do, and warm clothing for the chilly nights, when the temperature, in some parts of the country, can fall below freezing. In case of emergency, bring a first-aid kit and a fire extinguisher. Also, consider bringing an Electronic Position Indicator Radio Beacon (EPIRB) or a satellite phone, as cellular telephones do not work in remote areas.

ON THE ROAD

If ever your vehicle breaks down, it is generally best to stay with it; it is likely that you will eventually be discovered by another passer-by. Putting up your hood is a universal signal of distress. It is customary to wave at passing motorists. If you decide to stop, give passing cars a thumbs-up to let them know you're okay, and slow down as you pass other cars that have stopped to look for the thumbs-up.

Speed is by far the number-one cause of accidents, so *slow down*. Don't drive at night, while tired, or after drinking. Listen to your impulses; *if you feel tired, then rest*. Being on the road for long periods of time may lead to you lose track of your speed. Road conditions change quickly, and there isn't always a lot of signage to warn you about what is ahead, especially on 4WD-only tracks. You'll need to be alert to catch these changes. For your safety and the safety of others, it is best to run your **headlights** at all times while driving.

TIRES

MAINTENANCE. The best defense against tire problems is good maintenance. Look on the tires, on the inside of your driver's side door, or in your vehicle's owner's manual for the appropriate pressure to which your tires should be inflated. You can use a **tire pressure gauge** to determine the actual pressure of your tires. Overinflation and underinflation are both dangerous and can contribute to tire failure. You should check the pressure periodically throughout your trip. Since hot temperatures will give you inaccurate readings, check the pressure after your tires have cooled down from driving.

RUPTURES. The first sign of a tire rupture will probably involve a change in the way the vehicle feels while you are driving. You might notice that the car doesn't turn as easily, or it might feel a bit more wobbly than usual. Pull over to a safe place at the first sign of trouble; make sure that you stop somewhere off the road, away from blind corners, and on level ground. You will feel a **tire blowout** (or tread separation) right away. The car will suddenly become much more difficult to steer, especially on turns, and you may be tugged forcefully in a particular direction.

To handle a tire blowout, *do not slam on the brakes*, even though this may be your first instinct. A blown tire (especially a blown front tire) will reduce your braking capability, and slamming on the brakes will just send you in an uncontrolled skid. Grip the wheel firmly while you take your foot off of the gas, steering only enough to keep the vehicle in a straight line or away from obstructions. Let the vehicle slowly come to a complete stop.

CHANGING A TIRE. Make sure your vehicle is parked securely on level ground with the emergency (hand) brake applied. Turn on your emergency flashers to alert other vehicles that you are stalled on the side of the road. At night, it may be helpful to light a couple **road flares,** especially if your vehicle is not entirely off of the road. Place the jack on smooth ground and locate the place underneath the vehicle where the jack will do its lifting.

Remove the hubcaps and loosen the lugnuts. Loosen one lugnut until it spins freely. Then loosen the lugnut diagonally opposite from it. The third lugnut you loosen should be next to the first. The fourth will be diagonally opposite the third.

Use the jack to carefully raise up your vehicle far enough for your tire to rotate freely. Once the vehicle is raised, remove the loosened lugnuts and then carefully remove the tire. Take the spare tire and align its holes with the tire studs on the wheel hub. If you can't see the tire's air valve facing you, the tire is probably on backwards. Once the spare tire is resting against the wheel hub, replace the lugnuts in the same order you removed them, and tighten then down with your fingers. Slowly lower down your vehicle, remove the jack, and use the tire iron to tighten the lugnuts. Drive slowly at first to make sure that the tire is on correctly. Gradually increase your speed, and make your way down to the next service station to *buy another spare.*

If you suffer a tire blowout, it is possible that the blown tire will pull various material into your wheel well, or will tear off the protective plastic cover on your car's struts. If this happens, you will need to remove any material that scrapes against the new tire, or prevents it from spinning without difficulty.

OVERHEATING

PRECAUTIONS. Take several gallons of **clean water** with you. The water should be clean and sterile to prevent damage to your radiator. It is possible to use impure stream or lake water to top off your radiator, though you'll need to have the radiator flushed afterwards. You should also carry additional **coolant** along with you.

GREAT OUTDOORS

Coolant needs to be mixed with water after being poured into the radiator. On a hot day, you can help prevent overheating by turning off your air conditioning system. If your vehicle has a temperature gauge, check it frequently. If not, stop periodically and check for signs of overheating—any sort of boiling noise coming from under your hood is a strong indicator that you need to let the vehicle cool down for a while. Turning the heater on full blast will help cool the engine.

SOLUTIONS. If your car overheats, pull off the road and turn the heater on full force to cool the engine. If radiator fluid is steaming or bubbling, turn off the car for 30min. or more. If not, run the car in neutral at about 1500 r.p.m. for a few minutes, allowing the coolant to circulate. *Never pour water over the engine and never try to lift an extremely hot hood.* If you need to open your radiator cap, always wait 45min. or more until the coolant inside the radiator loses its heat— otherwise, you may be spattered with boiling coolant. Even after waiting, you may still be spattered with warm coolant, so stand to the side. Remember that 'topping off' your radiator does not mean filling it completely. Pour a small amount of water and coolant in (equal amounts of each) and wait for it to work its way into the system and raise the reservoir. Continue to do so until the radiator is filled to the level indicated by the reservoir or your vehicle's manual. Coolant leaks are sometimes just the product of overheating pressure, which forces coolant out of the gaps between the hoses and their connections to the radiator. If this happens to you, allowing the vehicle and coolant to cool down may be enough. If not, or if there are other holes in the hose, it helps to have **hose sealant** on hand with you. Treat the use of sealant as a short-term solution; get the vehicle to a service station as soon as possible. Drive slowly and keep your heater on to avoid stressing the seal.

OIL

Some areas of Australia can be incredibly dusty. This means you will need to **change your oil** and your **oil filter** more frequently than you normally would. Most service stations offer oil changes, though the prices may rise in remote areas. You should check your oil level every few days by taking your vehicle's dipstick and sliding it into the engine's oil level test tube. To get an accurate measurement, wipe it off first and then plunge it in and out of the tube, checking the actual level against the level recommended on the dipstick or in your vehicle's manual. Test the level after your vehicle has been at rest for at least several minutes. If your level is low, add more oil. Your owner's manual will outline appropriate grades of motor oil for your particular vehicle. Check these against the oil you pour into your engine—a motor oil's grade is usually indicated right on its packaging.

HOSES & BELTS

Hoses and **belts** are extremely important to monitor for wear and damage. Even very small problems with vacuum hoses, for instance, will prevent your vehicle from starting. **Fan belts** are notorious for snapping on travelers in the direst places. It is worthwhile to carry along a few extra fan belts, but it is even better to get failing belts replaced. Replace the fan belt if it looks loose, cracked, or if it is glazed or shiny (signs that it is at risk of cracking). In an emergency, **pantyhose** can serve as a very temporary substitute for a fan belt, enough to help you hobble back to a garage at low speed. Other items you should have inspected both before your journey and after hard driving include your **air filter, brake fluid, transmission fluid, fuel filter, PCV breather filter** (which filters out gases from engine combustion and protects your oil system), **automatic transmission filter, spark plugs,** and your **distributor cap and rotor.** It is cheaper to replace all of these items than it is to fix a single potential catastrophe caused by ignoring any one of them.

HAZARDS

The signs along the road come in all shapes and sizes, but they all mean one thing to a driver: *slow down*. All road signs refer to possible obstructions, both to driving and to visibility.

KANGAROOS. A common hazard on Australian roads is animals, in particular kangaroos. Signs alerting you to the presence of kangaroos are common along large highways, but less frequent on smaller roads. Dusk and dawn are particularly dangerous times. **Kangaroos are a serious danger to drivers** and may jump in front of or into the side of cars, causing significant damage. Never assume that an animal will get out of your way.

UNSEALED ROADS. Unsealed roads dominate rural Australia, ranging from smooth, hard-packed sand to an eroded mixture of mud, sand, and stones. Locals are a good source of information on the road conditions in the immediate vicinity. When driving on unsealed roads, call regional tourist boards ahead of time for **road conditions,** especially in the north, as the Wet sometimes makes roads impassible for months after the rains stop. Furthermore, you should allow at least twice as much time as you would for travel on paved roads. One can skid on gravel almost as badly as on ice. Loose gravel may feel comfortable at high speeds if you are traveling in a straight line, but as soon as you attempt to turn or brake, you will realize why it is unwise to take things too quickly.

SKIDS. If you find yourself in a skid, *do not apply the brakes*. This will only make things worse, and may cause your vehicle to roll over and start skidding on its top. Instead, at the beginning of a skid, ease off of both the brake and gas. The most important thing to do is to control the steering wheel. Grip the wheel firmly with both hands, but do not steer against the skid. If you are skidding to the right, then take the wheel and firmly turn it to the right. *Steer into the skid.* Don't fling the wheel or slam it to the right, but instead use your grip to direct the wheel gently toward the direction of the skid. Once you feel the vehicle straightening out, carefully tug the wheel back toward a straightened position. At this point, you may need to press down on the gas pedal a bit to push the vehicle onto its new course.

STREAM CROSSINGS. On some northern roads, **stream crossings** are not bridged, meaning you will need to **ford** them. Before fording, scout the area as extensively as you can. Wade into the water and **check the conditions of the bottom**, removing any logs. *Do not wade in if there is a risk of crocodiles in*

FROM THE ROAD

'ROOS IN THE DARK

It's hard to believe that excitement abounds in a land as barren as the Australian outback, where miles of pavement melt into the horizon and dry low-lying shrub dots the landscape. Yet, anyone who has hopped behind the wheel knows there is plenty of adventure hidden within the seeming monotony. Steve Fitzgerald, a driver for Heritage Trucking Co. in Bundaberg, QLD, is well-versed in the challenges of Outback driving. He say, "a lot of people come in and expect driving in the outback to be like city-driving, and it just isn't."

The most obvious dangers are the notorious kangaroos and the very thing Steve drives: 50m road trains. These vehicles weigh up to 150 tons and have as many as 84 wheels and three different trailers. Because of this, they are a menace on the two-lane carved through the outback.

Steve says that the best way to deal with them is to back off. "Pebbles can do quite a number on windshields and [car hoods] if you get too close to a road train. Best bet to stay back, that way they can see you and you won't end up with a shattered windshield," he says.

And as for the 'roos? Stay off the road at sunrise and sunset, when they're the most active. Or, says Steve, "use the road trains. He'll clear all the skippys right out of your path, and you won't have to worry about a thing."

—Sara Clark

the area. Feel for silt that could catch your wheels. Look for sharp, protruding rocks and entangling weeds. Choose your exit point on the other side of the stream and inspect that area for the same problems. Take a stick or a ruler and find out how deep the deepest part of the crossing is. Compare this to your vehicle; if it rises very far above the undercarriage, or if the water is especially violent, you may want to turn back around. Be especially cautious during or after rain.

If you decide to ford the stream, ford it relatively quickly to avoid becoming stuck in the streambed. Start driving toward the stream from a few dozen meters down the road and enter it in full motion, not stopping until after the crossing is finished. If you are stuck in the middle of a stream during or after rain, remember that the water levels may rise very quickly, and that it doesn't take all that much depth to lift your vehicle up and send it down river. If you experience a punctured tire while fording a stream, your best option might be to keep on driving until you can get to flat, level ground on the other side. Throwing it into reverse might be all right if you've just entered the stream, but otherwise, it could just bog you down.

ADVENTURE ACTIVITIES

WATER

If you don't mind getting wet, then Australia is the place for adventure. The country offers unparalleled **surfing, scuba diving** and **kayaking** and **whitewater rafting** conditions. **Waterskiing** is also popular in the southeast, while **windsurfing** and **sailing** are particularly prevalent in the **Whitsunday Islands** (p. 396). Rental equipment is available from most resorts.

SWIMMING

Many of Australia's **beaches** are patrolled by lifeguards, especially during the summer months. Patrolled beaches will be clearly marked with yellow and red striped flags that designate areas safe for swimming. Make sure you swim only between these flags. **Undertows** or **"rips"** are not uncommon. *If you get caught in a rip, don't try to swim against it, but rather swim parallel to the shore until out of the rip and only then swim back to shore.* Make sure you **check with locals** about conditions if you are going to swim at an unpatrolled beach.

SURFING

Australia's beaches offer pristine conditions for surfing, whether you're learning or an expert. On the east coast, the waves at **Surfers Paradise** (p. 349) are perfect for beginners, while **Coolangatta** (p. 346) is the place for pros. **Byron Bay** (p. 200) and **Newcastle** (p. 171) are among the country's most popular spots, whereas **Lennox Head** (p. 199) is home to one of the longest right-hand breaks in the world. On the southern coast, Victoria's **Bells Beach** in Torquay (p. 614) hosts the annual Rip Curl Classic. **Yallingup** (p. 700), in the southwest, is also popular, as is Bruny Island's **Cloudy Bay** (p. 537).

SCUBA DIVING & SNORKELING

Some of the best scuba diving conditions in the world are found in Australia. The marine wonderland that is **Great Barrier Reef** (p. 319) lies along the northeastern coast of Australia. Bases for reef access include **Cairns** (p. 425), **Port Douglas** (p. 439), and **Airlie Beach** (p. 401). In New South Wales, the diving in **Batemans Bay** (p. 231) is pristine, while in Western Australia, giant whale sharks patrol **Ningaloo Reef** near **Exmouth** (p. 723). For beginners, most dive operators offer **introductory dives** with a trained guide. Eventually you will want to get certified. The most common certification is with the Professional Association of Diving Instructors (PADI) and the cheapest courses in Queensland can be found at **Hervey Bay** (p. 373), **Bundaberg** (p. 384), and **Magnetic Island** (p. 415), although courses are generally even cheaper in less touristed areas. A **diving medical** exam is required for certified dives and certification courses. These are usually cheapest in diving hotspots such as **Cairns** and **Airlie Beach** and cost about $60. A cheap alternative to diving is **snorkeling**. All you need is a **mask, snorkel**, and **fins**, which are available at most hostels and resorts for free or a small fee.

KAYAKING & RAFTING

Whitewater enthusiasts can tackle rapids on Australia's rivers while passing through spectacular and often remote wilderness. The **Franklin River** (p. 547) in Tasmania is popular for whitewater kayaking and rafting. **Sea-kayaking** is an increasingly popular activity, with more stable boats and calmer waters than its river equivalent. Sea-kayakers have the freedom to explore remote and pristine coastal wilderness that is often inaccessible by car or foot. Opportunities are widespread, particularly in the **Whitsunday Islands** (p. 406) in Queensland.

LAND

From **mountain biking** to **skiing,** Australia's interior abounds with opportunities for the thrill-seeking adventurer. **Horseback riding** is available in almost all rural areas, while **camel riding** is found in the **Red Centre** (p. 299) and **Broome** (p. 730). Major **rock climbing** and **abseiling** areas include the **Grampians** (p. 627) and the **Blue Mountains** (p. 160). Use common sense when it comes to any activity and make sure you have the correct and adequate equipment.

CYCLING & MOUNTAIN BIKING

Towns are spread thinner the farther inland you move, so if you're cycling between cities, be prepared for long days in the saddle. Bike shops may be scarce in rural areas, so take your own equipment for repairs. Mountain biking is growing in popularity; of particular note are trails on **Mount Buller** (p. 653) in Victoria, and **Thredbo** in NSW (p. 240).

SKIING & SNOWBOARDING

The best snowfields are in the southeast. **Mount Buller** (p. 653) and the **High Country** (p. 658) in Victoria, and the **Snowy Mountains** (p. 233) in New South Wales are the largest and most developed ski areas in the country. Downhill skiing and snowboarding are not the only options; cross-country is also popular. The peak ski season is in July and August. All equipment is available for rental in the snowfields.

ORGANIZED ADVENTURE TRIPS

Organized adventure tours offer another way of exploring the wild. Activities include hiking, biking, skiing, canoeing, kayaking, rafting, and climbing. Tourism bureaus can often suggest trails, and outfitters; other good sources for information are stores and organizations that specialize in camping and outdoor equipment. Companies such as **Adventure Tours Australia** (☎ 08 8309 2277 or ☎ 1300 654 604; www.adventuretours.com.au) and the award-winning **Adventure Company Australia** (☎ 07 4051 4777; www.adventures.com.au) provide educational programs on ecology and Aboriginal culture in addition to adventure activities.

GREAT OUTDOORS

AUSTRALIAN CAPITAL TERRITORY

Carved out of New South Wales in 1908, the Australian Capital Territory, or ACT, was a geographic and political compromise between the cities of Sydney and Melbourne in the competition to host the capital of a newly federated Australia. Although it is not a fully qualified state, the center of the territory—Canberra—is the political heart of the entire country. Home to commuters and suburban shopping areas, neatly designed satellite towns creep outward from Canberra into the wilds of the bush. The ACT's fusion of a cosmopolitan center and outlying natural refuges promises visitors a truly capital look at high culture and government, all at an easygoing pace.

ACT

CANBERRA ☎ 02

For a city that is home to 320,000 people and the government of an entire continent, Canberra's streets are, for the most part, amazingly quiet. Wide avenues, huge tracts of green spaces, and sleek modern architecture offer a utopian vision of a metropolis, yet the city feels empty, as if the city planner expected a lot more people to show up. Canberra houses a myriad of beautifully planned, state-of-the-art tourist attractions—everything from space centers to dinosaur museums—but there is a shortage of tourists to see any of it.

This unique city was designed by one Walter Burley Griffin, student of famed architect Frank Lloyd Wright. The marvel is that Canberra is an entirely planned urban space, built from mere farm land. Its subsequent symmetry, therefore, comes off as somehow eerie, but also inspiring; from certain spots in the city, it is completely apparent that you're standing in the middle of carefully calculated geometric perfection. The American architect's proposal was selected from a pool of 137 competitors before construction began in 1913. Parliament first convened in Canberra fourteen years later, in 1927.

AUSTRALIAN CAPITAL TERRITORY HIGHLIGHTS

QUESTION TIME. Don't miss the political antics that ensue when the Parliamentary floor is opened to lively debate. (p. 93)

NATIONAL MUSEUM OF AUSTRALIA. Learn about the history of the nation through moving and fancifully themed permanent exhibits. (p. 95)

NATIONAL GALLERY OF AUSTRALIA. Peruse this massive gallery of Australian and International art, contemporary and ancient—for free. (p. 94)

AUSTRALIAN WAR MEMORIAL. The striking monument-lined Anzac Parade on approach sets the tone for this humble and moving memorial. (p. 96)

✈ INTERCITY TRANSPORTATION

BY PLANE

Located in Pialligo, 7km east of the city center, the **Canberra International Airport** is an easy ride by car. From Commonwealth Ave., take Parkes Way east past the roundabout at Kings Ave. The name of the road changes first to Morshead Dr., then to Pialligo Ave., en route. On weekdays, **Deane's Buslines** (☎6299 3722; http://deansbuslines.com.au) operates the **Air Liner,** a shuttle service that transports passengers between the airport and the City Interchange (20min.; 14 per day; $5 oneway, $9 return). For weekend transit, a **taxi** (☎13 22 27) is your best bet. ($17 oneway from the city center.) The airport only handles domestic flights to four cities; all international travel requires a stop in Sydney. **Virgin Blue Airlines** (☎13 67 89; www.virginblue.com.au) is a new major player in the Canberra travel market, offering competitive service and low prices to: **Adelaide** (3 per day, from $104 one way); **Brisbane** (2hr., 3 per day, from $124); **Melbourne** (1hr., 2 per day, from $84); and **Sydney** (50min., 2 per day, $66). **Qantas** (☎13 13 13; www.qantas.com.au), connects Canberra to: **Adelaide** (1½hr., 2-4 per day, from $106 one way); **Brisbane** (2hr., 5 per day, from $128 one way); **Melbourne** (1hr., 12 per day, from $89 one way); and **Sydney** (50min., 25 per day, from $71 one way). To get the best fares, book at least 14 days in advance and check for special deals on the Internet.

BY TRAIN

The **Canberra Railway Station,** on the corner of Wentworth Ave. and Mildura St. in Kingston, 6km from the city center, is on ACTION bus route #39 (bus to Civic 25min., at least 1 per hr.), 80, 83, and 84. Alternatively, a taxi ride from the station to the city will cost $12-14. The station houses little more than a **Countrylink** office. (☎13 22 32. Open M-Sa 6:20am-5:30pm, Su 10:30am-5:30pm.) **Trains** leave for **Brisbane** (24hr., 1 per day, $128.70) via **Sydney** (4hr., 3 per day, $47). Discounts for advanced bookings: 7-14 day 40%, 15+ day 50%. Student discount is 50%.

BY BUS

Intercity **buses** converge at **Jolimont Tourist Centre,** 65-67 Northbourne Ave., just north of Alinga St. in Civic. (Open daily 6am-10:30pm; in winter 5am-10:30pm.) Self-service coin lockers cost $6-11 per day. The McCafferty's/Greyhound ticketing office stores bags for the day ($2 per piece of luggage if traveling with the company, $4 otherwise). Several bus companies, both major domestic airlines, and Countrylink have desks in the building.

    McCafferty's/Greyhound (☎13 14 99 or 13 20 30) provides **bus** service to: **Adelaide** (17hr., 1 per day, $127); **Albury** (5-6hr., 4 per day, $34); **Goulburn** (1hr., 2-3 per day, $24); **Griffith** (6hr., 1 per day, $48); **Gundagai** (1¾hr., 3 per day, $27); **Melbourne** (8-10hr., 4 per day, $62); **Parramatta** (3½hr., 3 per day, $35); **Sydney** (3-4hr., 10 per day, $35); and **Wagga Wagga** (3hr., 2 per day, $34). From June to October buses run to: the snowfields at **Cooma** (1½hr., 2 per day, $37); **Perisher Blue** via the **Skitube** (3hr., 2 per day, $53); and **Thredbo** (3½hr., 2 per day, $54). **Murrays** (☎13 22 51) also runs to: **Batemans Bay** (2½hr., 1 per day, $24); **Goulburn** (1¼hr., 1 per day, $19); **Narooma** (4¼hr., 1-2 per day, $36.25); **Sydney** (4hr., 3-5 per day, $35); **Wollongong** (3½hr., 1 per day, $30.80). Murrays also has ski-season service to: **Cooma** (1¼hr., 1 per day, $34); **Jindabyne** (3¼hr., 1 per day, $34); **Perisher Blue** (3hr., 1 per day, $34); and **Thredbo** (3hr., 1per day, $41). Murrays offers great deals on **ski packages,** which include return transport, lift tickets, ski rental, and park entrance from $119. **Transborder Express** (☎6241 0033) runs to **Yass** (1hr., 1-4 per day, $13); **Countrylink** has an office at Jolimont (open M-F 7am-5pm) and runs **coaches** to: **Bega** (3½hr., 1 per day, $33);

ACT

Cooma (1¼hr., 1 per day, $16.50); **Goulburn** (1¼hr., 3 per day, $13.20); **Melbourne** (8½hr., 1 per day, $90); and **Wollongong** via **Moss Vale** (4hr., 1 per day, $37). Discounts for advanced bookings.

BY CAR

The **NRMA automobile club,** 92 Northbourne Ave., is the place to turn for road service or car problems. (☎ 13 21 32. Open M-F 9:30am-5pm.) For 24hr. **emergency road service,** call ☎ 13 11 11. **Avis,** 17 Lonsdale St. (☎ 6249 6088; open M-F 8am-6pm, Sa 8am-2pm, Su 8am-noon); **Budget** (☎ 1300 362 848; open M-F 8am-5pm, Sa 8am-noon), on the corner of Mort and Girraween St.; **Delta Europcar,** 74 Northbourne Ave. (☎ 13 13 90; www.deltaeuropcar.com.au; open M-F 8am-6pm, Sa 8am-4pm, Su 9am-1pm); **Hertz,** 32 Mort St. (☎ 6257 4877; open M-F 8am-6pm, Sa 8am-3pm, Su 9am-3pm); and **Thrifty,** 29 Lonsdale St. (☎ 6247 7422; open M-F 8am-5:30pm, Sa-Su 8am-5pm) all have offices in Braddon and at the airport. Local outfit **Value Rent-a-Car,** in the Rydges Capital Hill Hotel on Canberra Ave. and National Circuit, offers some of the cheapest rates, starting from $39 per day and $225 weekly. (☎ 1800 629 561. Open M-F 8am-6pm, Sa-Su for pick-up and drop-off only.)

◪ ORIENTATION

Lake Burley Griffin, formed by the damming of the Molonglo River, splits Canberra in two; on each side is a central hill with concentric roads leading outwards. **Commonwealth Avenue** spans the lake to connect these points. To the north of the lake is **Vernon Circle,** marking the center of Canberra and the southern edge of the area known as **Civic.** Civic serves as the city's social center and bus interchange. Restaurants, shops, and nightclubs crowd the pedestrian mall known as **City Walk** in the area between Northbourne Ave., Akuna St., Bunda St., and London Circuit. Immediately north of Vernon Circle, Commonwealth Ave. becomes Northbourne Ave. To the south of the lake is **State Circle** and the governmental part of the capital. Within State Circle, **Capital Hill's** huge four-pronged flagpole reaches up from the new Parliament House. One corner of the area known as **Parliamentary Triangle** encloses most of the city's museums and government-related attractions. Commonwealth Ave., Kings Ave., and Parkes Way form the three sides of the triangle.

The key to understanding the city plan is the system of roundabouts, the multiple concentric streets ("circuits"), and the wheel-spoke offshoots. If you drive, a good map is absolutely essential. Roundabouts are well marked, but signs often refer to districts rather than to streets. The railway station and an assortment of budget lodging are to be found in **Kingston,** southeast of Capital Hill, which, along with neighboring **Manuka** (MAHN-ah-ka), is home to a slew of trendy restaurants and nightspots. The embassies populate **Yarralumla,** west of Capital Hill. **Dickson,** northeast of Civic via Northbourne Ave. and Antill St., has clusters of reasonably priced restaurants with a Chinatown feel.

◪ LOCAL TRANSPORTATION

The primary hub for Canberra's public transit system, **ACTION** bus service (☎ 13 17 10; www.action.act.gov.au), centers on the city bus interchange, located at the junction of East Row, Alinga St., and Mort St. Full maps and timetables for all routes are available, free of charge, at the ACTION information office, next to the Civic Library on East Row, between Alinga St. and London Circuit. Route maps are also clearly posted near the passenger shelters at the city bus interchange. Relevant timetables are posted at individual bus stops. Buses generally run M-Sa 6am-12:30am and Su 7am-8:15pm, though some routes have more limited hours.

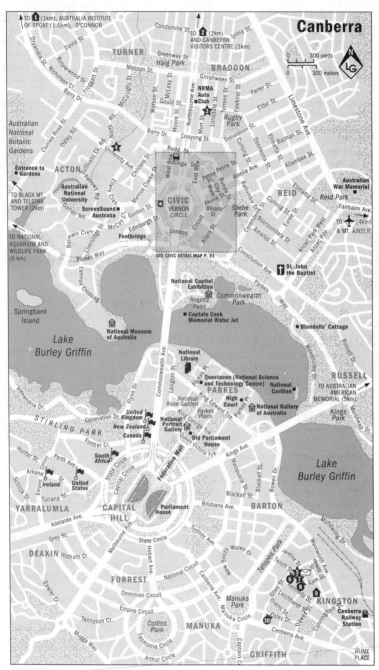

Canberra

TO ■1 (1km), AUSTRALIA INSTITUTE
OF SPORT (1.5km), O'CONNOR

TO ■2 (2km)
AND CANBERRA
VISITORS CENTRE (1km)

0   300 yards
0   300 meters

Condamine St.   plma St.

David St.

TURNER   Greenway St.
Haig Park   BRADDON

Dryandra St.   Masson St.   Girrahween St.

Bolgerwood St.   Nicholson Cr.   McLeay St.   Farrer St.

Froggatt St.   Watson St.   NRMA   Torrens St.   Fawkner St.   Elder St.   Limestone Ave.
Barry Dr.   Gould St.   Auto
Club   Lonsdale St.   Rugby   Donaldson St.
Currie Ross St.   Moore St.   Park
Daley Rd.   North Rd.   Cooyong St.   Currong St.   Batman St.

Australian
National   McCaughy St.   Barry Dr.   Rudd St.   Ainslie Ave.   Doonkuna St.   Allambee St.
Botanic
Gardens   Ballinga St.   Elimatta St.   REID

University Ave.   Childers St.   East Row   Petrie Petrie St.   Ballumbir St.   Boorroondara St.   Reid Park   Australian
War Memorial

Entrance to   ACTON   West Row   Pl.   City   Currong St.   Fairbairn Ave.
■ Gardens   Marcus Clarke St.   Bunda St.   Euree St.
Sullivans Ck. Rd.   Akuna St.   Glebe   Coorabonda St.   Anzac Park West
Australian   Elouy Cres.   CIVIC   Park   Anzac Pde.   TO ■ (4km)
National   VERNON   Bloar St.   & MT. AINSLIE
TO BLACK MT.   University   C Gordon St.   CIRCLE   Amaroo St.
AND TELSTRA   Garran Rd.   McCoy   Ballumbir   Allara St.
TOWER (2km)   ScreenSound   Edinburgh Ave.   London   Circuit   Constitution Ave.
Australia   Bateman Cres.   Footbridge   St. John
Liversidge St.   Parkes Way   the Baptist

TO NATIONAL
AQUARIUM AND   SEE CIVIC DETAIL MAP P. 91
WILDLIFE PARK
(6km)   Lennox Crossing   National Capitol
Exhibition   Parkes

Springbank   National Capitol   Commonwealth   Way
Island   Exhibition   Park

Regatta   Commonwealth
Point   Park

Lake   ■ Captain Cook   ■ Blundells' Cottage
Burley Griffin   National Museum   Memorial Water Jet
of Australia

National   Wendouree Dr.   Russell Dr.
Library

RUSSELL
Commonwealth Ave.   Parkes Pl.   ■ Questacon (National Science   National
Langton St.   and Technology Centre)   Carillon   TO AUSTRALIAN
AMERICAN
Flynn Dr.   King Edward Tce.   High   MEMORIAL (5km)
National   Court   National Gallery
Rose Garden   King George Tce.   of Australia   Kings
Alexandria Dr.   United   Parkes Pl.   Park
STIRLING PARK   Kingdom   National   Queen Victoria Tce.
Coronation Dr.   Portrait   Old Parliament   Lake
New Zealand   Gallery   House   Burley Griffin
Hunter St.   Canada   Federation Mall   Kings Ave.
Perth Ave.   Forster Cr.   Macquarie St.   Blackall St.   Bowen Dr.
Arkana St.   South   Queen Victoria Tce.
Schlick St.   Ireland   Africa   State Circle   Blackall St.
Empire Circuit   United   Brisbane Ave.   BARTON
Turrana St.   States   Capital Circle   Parliament
House   Mundaring Dr.

YARRALUMLA   CAPITAL   Sydney Ave.
HILL
Adelaide Ave.   State Circle   Telopea Park   Wentworth Ave.
Grey St.   Melbourne Ave.   Hobart Ave.   Jardine St.   Tench St.
DEAKIN   Hotham Cr.   National Circuit   Canberra Ave.   Eyre St.   Hume
Gawler Cr.   Dominion Circuit   South Wales Cr.   ■5   ■ KINGSTON
FORREST   Manuka   ■6 ■7   Giles   ■9
Empire Circuit   Park   ■8   Leichhardt St.
Tennyson Cr.   Manuka Circle   Ovens St.   Oxley St.   Dawes   Canberra Railway
Collins   ■10   Cunningham   Station
Park   MANUKA   Canberra Ave.
Mugga Way   Tasmania Circle   Captain C   HUME
Arthur Circle   GRIFFITH   PLACE

ACT

ACTION has recently converted to a "one fare, anywhere" flat rate policy. $2.40 will buy you a single ticket, valid for a single trip; ask for a **transfer ticket** from the bus driver, which is good for one hour. A **full-day ticket** is $6, but you'll get the most for your money with a **Shopper's Off-Peak Daily ticket** ($3.50), valid weekdays 9am-4:30pm and after 6pm, and all day weekends and public holidays. **Fare-saver tickets** ($21, student at an Aussie institution $10.50) are available for ten rides. Purchase tickets on the bus or at most news agencies.

Though considerably more expensive than an ACTION off-peak daily ticket, City Sightseeing's less logistically complex **Canberra Tour** makes 15 stops at major tourist attractions. The ticket is valid for 24hr. with unlimited stops. Tickets can be purchased on the bus, in most hotels, or at the visitors center. (☎0500 505 012. $25.) **Canberra Cabs** (☎13 22 27) covers the city and suburbs 24hr. a day. A couple of **guided tours** are available as well. **Pilot Guides** (☎6231 0961) leads tours of Canberra attractions ($25), the surrounding bush ($25), and daytrips to Kosciusko ($85) and Wadbilliga National Park ($85). **Go Bush Tours** (☎6231 3023; www.gobushtours.com.au) leads tours of Canberra's natural surrounds.

Thanks to a superb system of **bicycle paths,** the capital can also be covered easily on a bike. A ride along the shores of Lake Burley Griffin is an excellent way to take in Parliamentary Triangle without having to find parking. Many hostels rent bikes for around $15 dollars a day. Alternatively, **Row 'n' Ride** (☎6228 1264), at Canberra South Motor Park on Canberra Ave., offers mountain bikes at $30 half-day, $39 full-day, including free delivery and pick-up to your hotel.

⁊ PRACTICAL INFORMATION

TOURIST & FINANCIAL SERVICES

Tourist Offices: Canberra and Region Visitors Centre, 330 Northbourne Ave. (☎6205 0044, accommodations booking 1800 100 660; www.visitcanberra.com.au), about 3km north of Vernon Circle. Take bus #51, 52, 56, or 80. Open M-F 9am-5:30pm, Sa-Su 9am-4pm. Wheelchair-accessible. Smaller occasionally volunteer-staffed **Canberra Tourism Booth,** inside Jolimont Tourist Centre, is 2 blocks from the city bus interchange. Open M-F 9am-5pm, Sa-Su 11am-3pm.

Budget Travel: STA Travel, 13 Garema Pl. (☎6247 8633), on the corner of City Walk. Open M-Th 9am-5pm, F 9am-7pm, Sa 10am-2pm.

Embassies: Unless specified, all locations listed below are located in Yarralumla. To get there, take bus route #31, 32, or 84. **Canada** (☎6270 4000; fax 6273 3285), on Commonwealth Ave. south of the lake. Open for consular services M-F 8:30am-12:30pm and 1-4:30pm. **Ireland,** 20 Arkana St. (☎6273 3022; fax 6273 3741). Open M-F 9:30am-12:45pm and 2-4pm. **New Zealand** (☎6270 4211; fax 6273 3194), on Commonwealth Ave. south of the lake. Open M-F 8:45am-5pm. For other consular services, contact the consulate in Sydney (☎02 8256 2000; fax 9221 7836). **South Africa** (☎6273 2424; fax 6273 3543), on the corner of State Circle and Rhodes Pl. Open M-F 8:30am-5pm. The consular section is open M-F 8:30am-1pm. **United Kingdom** (☎6270 6666, emergency 6285 6171; fax 6270 6606), on Commonwealth Ave. Open M-F 9am-5pm. Consular services located at 39 Brindlebellah Circuit at the Canberra Airport. Open M-F 9am-3pm. **United States,** 21 Moonah Pl. (☎6214 5600, emergency 6214 5900). Open M-F 8am-5pm. For routine consular services, contact the consulate in Sydney (☎02 9373 9200).

Currency Exchange: TravelX (☎6247 9984), Canberra Centre shopping mall, Bunda St., corner of Petrie Plaza, offers a flat fee of $7.50 or 2% on checks and currency exchange. Open M-F 9am-5pm, Sa 9:30am-12:30pm.

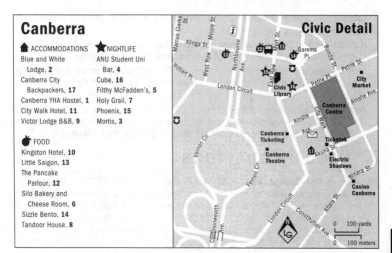

Canberra

Civic Detail

🏠 ACCOMMODATIONS   ⭐ NIGHTLIFE
Blue and White   ANU Student Uni
   Lodge, **2**   Bar, **4**
Canberra City   Cube, **16**
   Backpackers, **17**   Filthy McFadden's, **5**
Canberra YHA Hostel, **1**   Holy Grail, **7**
City Walk Hotel, **11**   Phoenix, **15**
Victor Lodge B&B, **9**   Mortis, **3**

🍎 FOOD
Kingston Hotel, **10**
Little Saigon, **13**
The Pancake
   Parlour, **12**
Silo Bakery and
   Cheese Room, **6**
Sizzle Bento, **14**
Tandoor House, **8**

LOCAL SERVICES

Library: Civic Library (☎ 6205 9000; www.act.gov.au/library), on East Row between Alinga St. and London Circuit. One of 9 branches within the ACT. Open M-Th 10am-5:30pm, F 10am-7pm, Sa 9:30am-5pm. See **National Library of Australia,** p. 94.

Ticket Agencies: Ticketek, GIO building, 11 Akuna St., Civic (☎ 6219 6666; www.ticketek.com). Tickets to sport and music events and **Royal Theatre.** Open M-F 9am-5pm, Sa 9am-noon. **Canberra Ticketing** (☎ 6257 1077), in Civic Square London Circuit, covers the **Canberra Theatre, Playhouse, Courtyard Studio,** and **Erindale.** Open M-Sa 9am-5:30pm, later on the nights of shows.

Travel Books and Maps: Map World (☎ 6230 4097), inside the Jolimont Tourist Centre. Open M-F 9am-5:30pm, Sa 9am-3pm.

Public Markets: Gorman House Markets (☎ 6281 3140), on Ainslie Ave. between Currong and Doonkuma St., vend crafts, clothing, and miscellany. Open Sa 10am-4pm. The **Old Bus Depot Markets,** 49 Wentworth Ave., Kingston (☎ 6292 8391), feature many food and arts-and-crafts stalls, as well as live entertainment. Open Su 10am-4pm.

MEDIA & PUBLICATIONS.
Newspapers: The main newspaper is the *Canberra Times* ($1.10), but also look out for *The Chronicle,* a local suburban newspaper.
Entertainment: *bma* (bands music action) is Canberra's free, alternative, entertainment bimonthly. *Times Out,* released on Thursdays in the Canberra Times, also has a list of entertainment options.
Radio: Easy Listening, 106.3FM; Rock, Triple J 101.5FM; News, 1440AM.

EMERGENCY & COMMUNICATIONS

Emergency: ☎ 000.

Police: ☎ 1 1444. On London Circuit opposite University Ave., Civic

Crisis Lines: Drug and Alcohol Crisis Line: ☎ 6205 4545; 24hr. **Poison Info Centre:** ☎ 13 11 26; 24hr. **Gay/Lesbian Info and Counseling Service:** ☎ 6247 2726; daily 6-10pm, after-hours recording. **Women's Info and Referral Centre:** ☎ 6205 1075; M-F 9am-5pm.

A C T

Late-Night Pharmacy: O'Connor Capital Chemist, 9 Sargood St. (☎6248 7050), in the O'Connor Shopping Ctr. Open daily 9am-11pm.

Hospital/Medical Services: Canberra Hospital on Yama Dr., Garren. ☎6244 2222, emergency 6244 2611. Follow signs to Woden southwest from Capital Hill.

Internet Access: Cheap access is not common. The **ACT Library Service** (see **Local Services,** p. 91) offers free 1hr. sessions; book ahead. **Go Internet Cafe,** 16 Gareema Place (☎6247 2355) charges $6 per hr. and is open daily 9am-late.

Post Office: General Post Office (GPO), 53-73 Alinga St. (☎13 13 18). Open M-F 8:30am-5:30pm. **Australia Post** at Civic Square, outside Canberra Centre mall, on Bunda St., has counter service. Open M-F 8:45am-5:15pm. **Postal Code:** 2601.

⚓ ACCOMMODATIONS

▨ **Canberra City Backpackers,** 7 Akuna St., Civic (☎1800 300 488). This centrally located swanky hostel-hotel puts travelers within easy reach of downtown cafes, shops, and nightlife. Multiple kitchens and common areas, rooftop BBQ, small gym, heated pool, pool tables, laundry ($3), Internet ($3.50 per 30min.), bike rentals ($16), security cameras, in-room lockers ($10 deposit), TVs with free movies available, and bar in the basement. 24hr. reception. Dorms $26; singles $55; twins $70; doubles with bath $80; family rooms from $95. VIP/ISIC. ❸

▨ **Canberra YHA Hostel,** 191 Dryandra St., O'Connor (☎6248 9155). Bus #35 travels to and from the city interchange, stopping directly out front. By car, follow Northbourne Ave. north from the city center. Turn left on Macarthur Ave., go 2km, then turn right on Dryandra. Situated away from the urban jungle on the eastern edge of a Canberra nature park, 3.5km northwest of the city center, this pleasant, family-friendly hostel is impeccably clean and has a wonderfully helpful staff. Multiple kitchens, free daily shuttles to the city upon request, free pick-up and drop-off from bus and train stations upon arrangement, TV/pool room, great movie selection, bike rental ($15), small store, laundry ($3), and Internet ($2 per 20min.). Key deposit $10. Reception 7am-10pm. 10-bed dorms $23.50, YHA $20; 4-bed $25.50/$22. Doubles $59.50/$56; ensuite twins $67.50/$64; family rooms $90.50/$87. ❷

▨ **Victor Lodge Bed and Breakfast,** 29 Dawes St., Kingston (☎6295 7777; www.victor-lodge.com.au), 6 km south of the city center, 5min. walk from the train station. Free pick-up in Civic at Jolimont Tourist Centre by arrangement. Bus #38 or 39 from the city bus interchange stops 2 blocks away on Eyre St. Within biking distance of Parliamentary Triangle, this quiet lodge/hostel is only a block from the shops and restaurants of Kingston. Kitchen, TV, laundry, Internet ($1 per 7min.), bike hire ($15), and free all-you-can-eat continental breakfast (7:30-9am). Also has information on job opportunities. Key deposit $10. Linens included. Reception 7:30am-9:30pm. Dorms $25; twins and doubles $65, weekly $390; 3-share rooms $27 per person. Ensuite in motel next door $89 single, $95 double. VIP. ❷

City Walk Hotel (☎6257 0124 or 1800 600 124), located at 2 Mort St., in the center of Civic, just off City Walk offers backpacker accommodation. Not particularly social, as its main function is as a hotel, but central, comfortable and clean. Laundry ($2). Guest lounge with TV and video. Kitchen. Bike rental $16. Free linen, free luggage storage. Dorms $22-24; singles $45, ensuite $70; doubles/twins $60/$80; family ensuite from $105. NOMADS. ❷

Blue and White Lodge, 524 Northbourne Ave., Downer, and **Canberran Lodge,** 528 Northbourne Ave., Downer (both ☎6248 0498). It's hard to differentiate between the two B&Bs, both owned by the same people. Each guesthouse offers TV, fridge, and kettle in a large, clean, floral-smelling room. Some rooms have verandas; most are ensuite. Breakfast included. Reception 7am-9pm. Singles $77; doubles $93.50. ❺

◘ FOOD

In a city populated by government officials, cheap food isn't easy to find. Inexpensive cafes near the city bus interchange, along with the food court at Canberra Centre (☎6247 5611), a three-story mall with main entrances off either City Walk or Bunda St., between Petrie Plaza and Akuna St., provide welcome exceptions. On Bunda St., opposite the Canberra Centre, the **City Market** complex packs in fruit stands, butcher shops, and prepared food stalls. You'll also find a vast Supabarn **supermarket.** (☎6257 4055. Open M-F 8am-10pm, Sa-Su 8am-9pm.) **Kingston** has over 30 restaurants of all varieties around its main commercial block, and nearby **Manuka** is a similar dining hotspot with a number of posh options. **Dickson**, north of city center, is a miniature Chinatown with lots of cheap food options.

CIVIC

Little Saigon Restaurant, (☎6230 5003) on Alinga St. in the Novotel, Civic. Popular Vietnamese restaurant has traditional food at tantalizing prices. Mains average $13. Lunch box deal (menu item plus rice) $5. Open daily 10am-3pm and 5-10:30pm. ❷

Sizzle Bento, Unit 3 Garema Place, Civic (☎6262 6022). Sticking with the Asian theme, Sizzle serves up cheap Japanese dishes ($5-10) and circulates sushi samples ($2-4) on a rotating train. Sushi/Japanese combo plates are a bargain at $10. Open daily 10am-9pm. Cash only. ❷

The Pancake Parlour, 121 Alinga St., Civic (☎6247 2982), downstairs. Despite its slightly franchised feel, late night munchies and early-morning cravings are easily satisfied, whether you opt for fruit pancakes (around $11) or more standard steak and fish fare ($14-20). YHA discount 10%. Daily breakfast specials 7-9am and early bird dinner specials 5-7pm. Open Su-Th 7am-10:30pm, F-Sa 7am-1am. ❷

KINGSTON

▨ **Silo Bakery and Cheese Room,** 36 Giles St., Kingston (☎6260 6060). Known by locals as the best bakery in Canberra. Although only offering a few dishes each day, Silo creates delicate and intense appetizers and mains that feature their quality imported cheeses, freshly made breads, and other authentic ingredients. Mains $13-20. Open Tu-Sa for breakfast and lunch. ❸

Tandoor House, 39 Kennedy St., Kingston (☎6295 7318). Sit back and savor subtly spiced Indian curries, vindaloos, and masalas ($12-16). Vegetarian options galore. Open daily 5:30-11pm, M-Sa also noon-2:30pm. ❷

Kingston Hotel, 73 Canberra Ave, on the corner of Giles St. (☎6295 0123), sells massive steaks at absurdly low prices ($10-14) and lets you cook them yourself on the communal grill. Salad and sides included. Kitchen-prepared mains range from $6-14. Open daily noon-3pm and 6-10pm. Cash only. ❶

◙ SIGHTS

PARLIAMENTARY TRIANGLE

A showpiece of grand architecture and cultural attractions, Canberra's Parliamentary Triangle is the center of the capital. The triangle is bordered by Commonwealth Ave., Kings Ave., and, across the lake, Parkes Way.

▨ **PARLIAMENT HOUSE.** The focal point of the triangle, Parliament House takes the ideal of unifying architecture and landscape to a new level. The building is actually built *into* Capital Hill so that two sides jut out of the earth, leaving the grassy hilltop on its roof undisturbed and open to the public via an internal lift.

A C T

The design intentionally places the people above Parliament. Perched on this landmark is a four-pronged stainless steel flagpole visible from nearly every part of Canberra. Inside the building, free guided tours give an overview of the building's unique features, its significant symbolism, and the workings of the government housed inside. Self-guided audio tours are available in multiple languages. A video on the building's construction plays hourly. Visitors can observe both houses in action from viewing galleries. The House of Representatives, which meets more often than the Senate, allows advance bookings. The televised **Question Time** provides some viewer-friendly acrimony. Every day when the House and the Senate are sitting, the floor is opened up at 2pm for on-the-spot questioning of the Prime Minister and other ministers. Though question time is political banter at its finest, the chambers can be visited at any time when Parliament is in session. *(Take Bus #34 from Civic. ☎ 6277 5399, reservations 6277 4889; www.aph.gov.au/house. Open daily 9am-5pm, as late as 11pm when either chamber is in session. Free. Wheelchair-accessible. Tours 45-50min., depart every 30min., daily 9am-4pm. Self-guided audio tours $2. House and Senate sit M-Th in approximately 2-week blocks, for a total of 20 weeks a year, except during recess in Jan. and July.)*

OLD PARLIAMENT HOUSE & NATIONAL PORTRAIT GALLERY. This building, aligned with the front of Parliament House, was Australia's seat of government from 1927 until 1988, when the current Parliament House was completed. It is now a political history museum and home to the impressive ⬛**National Portrait Gallery,** which features portraits of famous Australians and alternating exhibits. *(Take Bus #34 from Civic. ☎ 6270 8222, gallery 6270 8236. Daily "Behind the Scene" tours of Old Parliament House every 45min. 9:30am-3:15pm. Tours of the Portrait Gallery daily 11:30am and 2:30pm. Open daily 9am-5pm. $2, concessions $1, families $5. Wheelchair-accessible.)*

⬛**NATIONAL GALLERY OF AUSTRALIA.** The third side of the Parliamentary Triangle is comprised of the four large modern buildings on Parkes Pl., just off King Edward Terr. On the southeastern end, nearest Kings Ave., the National Gallery displays an extensive Australian art collection, Aboriginal works spanning more than 30,000 years of indigenous culture, and a commendable contemporary collection. Keep your eyes open for a few big-name French Impressionists. The surrounding sculpture garden is free and open 24hr. *(☎ 6240 6502, info 6240 6501; www.nga.gov.au. Take Bus #34 from Civic. Open daily 10am-5pm. 1hr. guided tours daily 11am and 2pm. Aboriginal art tour Th and Su 11am. Free. Self-guided audio tours in multiple languages are also free; separate fees for special exhibits $10-18. Wheelchair-accessible.)*

QUESTACON (NATIONAL SCIENCE & TECHNOLOGY CENTRE). Despite its guise as a children's museum, Questacon's interactive and state-of-the-art exhibits will captivate any inquisitive mind. Gain insight into indigenous knowledge as you interact with tribal elders on video screens, discover how the earth works and even experience an earthquake, or learn the science behind theme parks by freefalling 6m and riding a rollercoaster simulator. This and much more awaits for hours of fun with your inner kid. *(☎ 1800 020 603; www.questacon.edu.au. On King Edward Terrace. $11, concession $7, child $6, family $32. Open daily 9am-5pm.)*

HIGH COURT OF AUSTRALIA. Next door to the National Gallery, Australia's highest court is encased in a seven-story wall of seemingly impregnable glass and steel. When court is in session—two weeks every month—visitors may watch proceedings from public galleries in the courtrooms. *(Take Bus #34 from Civic. ☎ 6270 6811. Open M-F 9:45am-4:30pm. Free. Wheelchair-accessible.)*

NATIONAL LIBRARY OF AUSTRALIA. The nation's largest library (six million volumes) is the final stop on Parkes Way. Open for research and visitation, it houses copies of Australian publications on over 200km of shelving. The library also features alternating exhibits on Australian topics. Free **Internet** and printing is available for research, but not email. *(Take Bus #34 from Civic. ☎6262 1111, exhibition schedule 6262 1156; www.nla.gov.au. Free tours Tu and Th 12:30pm. Open M-Th 9am-9pm, F-Sa 9am-5pm, Su 1:30-5pm. Wheelchair-accessible.)*

LAKE BURLEY GRIFFIN. The last two attractions in the Parliamentary Triangle are actually located in the middle of the lake. The **Captain Cook Memorial Jet** blows a six-ton column of water to heights of up to 147m to commemorate Captain James Cook's arrival at the east coast of Australia. The bell tower of the **National Carillon** is located on Aspen Island at the other end of the lake's central basin. A gift from Britain on Canberra's 50th birthday in 1963, the Carillon, one of the largest musical instruments in the world, is rung several times a week. Small tours can also be arranged and are particularly recommended for the musically inclined. *(For info on either the Jet or the Carillon, contact the National Capital Authority ☎6271 2888; concert schedule www.nationalcapital.gov.au/visiting/carillon.htm.)*

OTHER GOVERNMENT BUILDINGS. West of Capital Hill, on the south side of the lake, Yarralumla is peppered with embassies of over 70 nations, displaying a multicultural melange of architecture (take bus route #31, 32, or 84). **The Lodge,** home to the Australian Prime Minister, is on the corner of Adelaide Ave. and National Circuit, but hecklers be warned—it's closed to the public. (Take bus route #34 or 39) Farther down Adelaide Ave., at the **Royal Australian Mint,** on Denison St. in Deakin, you can watch coins being minted. Push a button to "press your own" dollar coin—for $2. *(Take bus #30, 31, or 32. ☎6202 6819; www.ramint.gov.au. Open M-F 9am-4pm, Sa-Su 10am-4pm; coin production M-F 9am-noon and 1-4pm. 45min. tours available upon request. Free. Wheelchair-accessible.)*

NORTH OF THE LAKE

■ **NATIONAL MUSEUM OF AUSTRALIA.** Opened in 2001, this architecturally wondrous attraction, just a short trip from the city center, recounts the history of the nation's land and the stories of its people in profoundly moving and often truly poetic ways. Five permanent exhibits range from a glance at Australian history through the nation's expressions and symbols, and a glimpse into the lives of ordinary and extraordinary Australians, categorized by human emotions. Multimedia components are state of the art, including *Circa*, a futuristic rotating theater which poignantly introduces visitors to the museum's three themes of Land, Nation, and People. Rotating exhibits are also impressive. Various daily

IN RECENT NEWS

CAPITAL CATASTROPHE

Canberra is one of the few capital cities in the world where residents who live within a few minutes of the city center can keep horses or cattle studs just blocks from their homes. Known Australia-wide as "the bush capital" because much of the city resembles Australia's rural outback, Canberra's suburban regions are divided by large undeveloped tracts of land. The climate is hot and dry, and like much of the outback, the region must deal with periodic bush fire in the summer months.

During the weekend of January 18-20, 2003, this occasional inconvenience became a major catastrophe when a fire of unprecedented scale and intensity swept through the city. The worst natural disaster in the history of the Australian Capital Territory (ACT), the blaze killed five people, destroyed more than 400 houses, and left more than a quarter of the city full of black smoke and without electrical power for more than a week. Even the world-famous Australian Emergency Forces were overwhelmed by the sheer size of the fire. The Chief Minister of ACT estimates that fully controlling the blaze would have required a team of firefighters and engine-pumps nearly ten times the size of Canberra's current division. Had a sudden cold front not helped tame the fire, the entire city could have been destroyed.

tours are a great way to take in the museum. *(Take bus #34 from Civic. ☎ 6208 5000 or 1800 026 132. Open daily 9am-5pm. Free; fees for special exhibitions. Tours $7.50, children $5, families $20, and students $5.50.)*

■ AUSTRALIAN WAR MEMORIAL. The popular crucifix-shaped memorial, with a museum inside containing artifacts, photos, and depictions of wartime life by Australian artists, makes a moving and expansive tribute (meriting an entire day's exploration). The Hall of Memory holds the tomb of an unknown Australian soldier beneath a handmade mosaic dome. Lining Anzac (Australian New Zealand Army Corps) Parade on the way up to the memorial is a series of profound and striking memorial sculptures commemorating the Australians and New Zealanders who served in all major military conflicts. *(Anzac Pde., on bus route #33 from Civic. ☎ 6243 4211. Tours daily; call for times. Open daily 10am-5pm. Free. Wheelchair-accessible.)*

SCREENSOUND AUSTRALIA. Formerly the **National Screen and Sound Archive,** Screensound is one of Canberra's least-known but most enjoyable attractions. The bonanza of sight-and-sound relics of Australian radio, film, and television ranges from the 19th century to today. *(On McCoy Circuit in Acton. Take bus #34 to Liversidge St. ☎ 6248 2000. Open M-F 9am-5pm, Sa-Su 10am-5pm. Free for permanent exhibit. Changing gallery has various fees. Wheelchair-accessible from Liversidge entrance.)*

AUSTRALIAN NATIONAL BOTANIC GARDENS. Designed in the 1950s and opened to the public in 1970, the park is a living monument to the vast and unique biodiversity of the nation. Planting groups highlight the diversity within Australian species, as in the Eucalypt Lawn, and ecosystems, as in the Mallee and Rainforest Gully. A 40-60min. walk will take you through the gardens, and the athletically inclined can continue on to the Black Mountain Summit Walk (a 2.7km steep path to Telstra Tower), accessible from the garden path. The Visitors Centre is chock full of up-to-date information, from bird sightings to what's in bloom, and also houses changing exhibitions. *(Take bus #34 to Daley Rd.; walk 20min. toward the lake along Clunies Ross Rd. ☎ 6250 9540. www.anbg.gov.au/anbg. Free guided walks daily 11am and 2pm. Open daily 9am-5pm. Visitors Centre open 9:30am-4:30pm. Free.)*

AUSTRALIAN INSTITUTE OF SPORT (AIS). Tours led by resident athletes take regular humans through the world of the aerobically superhuman, offering a chance to see athletes in training and a stop at the hands-on Sportex exhibit where you can try your hand at rowing, golfing, wheelchair basketball, simulated ski runs, and rock climbing. There's also a pool and several tennis courts. *(On Leverrier Crescent just northwest of O'Connor. Take bus #80 from Civic. ☎ 6214 1010. Open M-F 8:30am-5pm, Sa-Su 10am-4pm. Tours daily at 10, 11:30am and 1, 2:30pm; $12, children $6, families $33. Outdoor Tennis Courts $10 per hr. Pool $4; swim cap mandatory.)*

NATIONAL ZOO & AQUARIUM. Unless you're a kid (or have one), you may have trouble justifying the long trip out, as there is no direct public transport. Features a 90min. *Animal Action Tour* (from $40, children from $29; includes full-day admission) and a 2-hour hand feed *Zooventure Tour* (from $95, children from $45). The seven-hectare sanctuary for native fauna does have some redeeming features, though these unique up close and personal animal opportunities are a bit of a splurge. *(About 3½km from the city. From Parkes Way, heading out of the city to the west, Lady Denman Dr. branches south toward the zoo at Scrivener Dam. ☎ 6287 8400. Open daily 9am-5pm. $18.50, children $10.50, students $15.50, families $55.50.)*

LOOKOUTS

A stop at one of the city's lookouts can give you a general idea of what's in store on a sightseeing tour. On a hill in Commonwealth Park at Regatta Point, on the north shore of Lake Burley Griffin, the **National Capital Exhibition** is a great place to start your explorations and learn the somewhat fascinating story of Canberra, providing a panorama of Canberra with a ten-minute film and displays on the planning and growth of the city. They also offer brochures for various self-guided walking tours of the city. (☎6257 1068; www.nationalcapital.gov.au. Open daily 9am-5pm. Free. Wheelchair-accessible.)

Farther back from the city's center, Mt. Ainslie and Black Mountain offer broader views of the city and are—for the energetic—within walking distance. North of Lake Burley Griffin and east of the city center, **Mt. Ainslie** rises 845m above the lake, the Parliamentary Triangle, and the Australian War Memorial, providing the classic postcard view down Anzac Pde. To reach the summit by car, turn right onto Fairbairn Ave. from the Memorial end of Anzac Pde., to Mt. Ainslie Dr. Hiking trails lead to the top from directly behind the War Memorial. Two lookout points above the city on **Black Mountain** are a vigorous walk away. The first, on Black Mountain Dr., accessible by taking Barry Dr. to Clunies Ross St. and heading left, faces southeast and takes in the Parliamentary Triangle and Lake Burley Griffin. The second viewpoint faces north toward the surrounding countryside and the **Australian Institute of Sport** (see p. 96). From the peak of Black Mountain, **Telstra Tower** climbs 195m to ensure viewers an unobstructed gaze in every direction. Exhibits in the tower catalogue the history of Australian telecommunications. (☎6248 1991 or 1800 806 718. Open daily 9am-10pm. $3.30.) A Black Mountain Summit Walk can also be accessed from the Botanical Gardens.

Another option for those hoping to see Canberra's geometric symmetry from above is in a sunrise **hot-air balloon** flight with Balloon Aloft. (☎6285 1540, www.balloon.canberra.net.au. Weekday Flight $180, children under 12 $120. Weekend deluxe flight $235/$150.)

⚑ ENTERTAINMENT

Casino Canberra, 21 Binara St., for the gambler tired of mere pokies, can help you strike it rich or leave you stranded with empty pockets in the nation's capital. (☎6257 7074. Open daily noon-6am.) In addition to the usual first-run cinemas, Canberra is home to several funky art-house alternatives, including **Electric Shadows,** on Akuna St. near City Walk. (☎6247 5060. $13.50, students $8.50; before 5pm $8.50/$7. W $7 all day.) Housing several venues in varying shapes and sizes, the **Canberra Theatre** on London Circuit is the best place to start looking for live entertainment. Register for the free Under 27 Club and take advantage of great savings on tickets. (☎6257 1077. $30-70, ages 18-27 available for most performances, $23-25.) Canberra's calendar is packed with minor **festivals,** but a few annual events temporarily transform the city. Easter weekend (Apr. 9-12, 2004) brings the **National Folk Festival** (☎6249 7755; www.folkfestival.asn.au), with music, dance, poetry, and art exhibitions. For 18 days in March, the **Celebrate Canberra Festival** (www.celebratecanberra.com) brings artistic displays, food showcases, a hot-air balloon fiesta, and Canberra Day festivities. **The Floriade** (mid-September to mid-October) paints the shores of Lake Burley Griffin with thousands of springtime blooms and relieves the city of all accommodations; book ahead. (☎6205 0044; www.floriadeaustralia.com.)

⚞ NIGHTLIFE

Canberra's after-hours scene is surprisingly vibrant. The city's substantial student population supports a solid range of bars and clubs, while relaxed licensing allows boozing to continue until 4am. Most places claim to close "late," meaning midnight on slow nights and until whenever people stop partying on busier nights.

A C T

CIVIC

Phoenix, 21 East Row (☎6247 1606). This bohemian bar is watering hole to a motley crew of artists, intellectuals, and down to earth folk. The mix of people matches the mismatched tables, chairs, and couches, and the collaged conglomeration of pictures, pots, and instruments that adorn the walls. Frequent live music. Open daily noon-late.

Mortis, 1/34 Mort St. (☎0405 102 132), a 5min. walk from City Walk. Perhaps a pinch posh, this morbidly themed bar is worth an examination. Just be sure they don't examine you as you enter through the morgue doors, into the hospital waiting room foyer, and up to metallic autopsy table bar (with blood drains to boot). The owner's own X-rays hang on the wall and a digital timer above the bar counts down to his death. Th-Sa nights DJs spin from the hospital bed booth. Open daily 4pm-late.

Cube, 33 Petrie Plaza., Civic (☎6257 1110). A gay/lesbian friendly club. The dance floor grooves, especially on F-Sa nights. Open W-Th 8pm-2am, F-Sa 8pm-5am.

ANU Student Uni Bar (☎6249 0786; www.anuunion.com.au), in the student union building, near the corner of North Rd. and University Ave., Acton. A popular student hangout and the cheapest pub in Canberra, hosting some of the biggest names in music. Check *bma* (see p. 91) or the website for a comprehensive gig listing. Open M-F noon-late, Sa 4pm-late, except during uni holidays.

KINGSTON

Filthy McFadden's (☎6239 5303), in the far corner of Green Square at the intersection of Jardine and Eyre St., Kingston. Frequented by loyal backpackers and regulars, "Filthy's" epitomizes the Irish country pub. The latest open spot in Kingston. Pints of Guinness will set you back $6.20, but you can bring in pizza from the shop around the corner. Largest whiskey collection in the southern hemisphere (200+). Live music Sa nights. No cover. Open daily noon-late.

Holy Grail (☎6295 6071), in Green Square at the intersection of Jardine and Eyre St. This small and trendy restaurant and bar turns into a packed nightclub F-Sa nights, with live cover bands and DJs. Cover $5. Open daily 9am-late. Also sports a larger, younger location in Civic, which pulls in popular live music acts.

▶ DAYTRIPS FROM CANBERRA

CANBERRA DEEP SPACE COMMUNICATION COMPLEX. One of the most powerful antenna centers in the world, the Communication Complex will awe novices and serious space cadets alike. The 70m radio dish tracks signals from spacecraft across the solar system. The Canberra Space Centre has displays on the history of space exploration. (Off Paddy's River Rd., 40km southwest of Civic. ☎6201 7880; www.cdscc.nasa.gov. Open daily 9am-5pm, and till 6pm in summer. Free.)

NAMADGI NATIONAL PARK. The expansive Namadgi National Park is the western border of Tidbinbilla Nature Reserve and fills almost all of the southern arm of the ACT with preserved alpine wilderness traversed by only one major paved route, the Naas/Bobayan Rd. Though the park has walking tracks for all experience levels, it is most famous for its untrammeled recesses accessible only to serious hikers. **Campsites ❶** at Orroral River and Mt. Clear, each with parking nearby, have firewood, untreated water, and toilets. The **Namadgi Visitors Centre,** on the Naas/Bobayan Rd. 3km south of **Tharwa,** sells maps and has info about Aboriginal rock painting and camping options. (☎6207 2900; namadginationalpark@act.gov.au. Park open 24hr, daily, except on days of total fire ban or heavy snow when it may be closed. Sites $3.30 per person. Register at Visitors Centre. Open M-F 9am-4pm, Sa-Su 9am-4:30pm.)

LANYON HOMESTEAD. Built in the 1800s, the buildings at Lanyon Homestead survey Canberra's European architectural history, from the days of convict labor through Federation. An Aboriginal canoe tree gives evidence of earlier habitation at the same site. Lanyon's greatest draw may be the **Nolan Gallery,** which has many of Sidney Nolan's paintings of bushranger Ned Kelly. (Tharwa Dr., 30km south of Canberra. Homestead ☎6237 5136, gallery 6237 5192. Open Tu-Su 10am-4pm. Homestead buildings $7, students and children $4, and families $15, including gallery $8/$5/$18.50. Wheelchair-accessible.)

NATIONAL DINOSAUR MUSEUM. The privately-run museum includes over 300 fossils, ten full-sized dinosaur skeletons, and three reconstructions. (Barton Hwy. at the corner of Gold Creek Rd. Follow Northbourne until the turn-off to Barton Hwy. Take bus #51 or 52. ☎6230 2655; www.nationaldinosaurmuseum.com.au. Open daily 10am-5pm. $9.50, students $7.40, children $6.50, families $30.)

ACT

Australian Politics 1983-2003

Australian politics is dominated by the Australian Labor Party (a social democratic party much like the British Labour Party or American Democrats), and a coalition of two conservative parties, the Liberal Party and the National Party. At a federal level, politics has been relatively static for the past two decades, with the Labor Party governing from 1983-1996, and the Coalition governing since 1996.

When Labor won office in 1983, its Prime Minister was Bob Hawke, a charismatic former trade union official. While studying at Oxford, Hawke won himself a place in the Guinness Book of Records by drinking 1.4 liters of beer in 12 seconds. In September 1983, when Australia broke the US's 132-year dominance over the America's Cup Yacht Race, Hawke proclaimed that any boss who fired a worker for taking the day off was a "bum." Unsurprisingly, he connected well with ordinary Australians.

During the 1980s, the Hawke Government implemented several major economic reforms. It floated the Australian dollar, dramatically reduced tariff barriers, and privatized Qantas airlines. In 1991, Paul Keating, a lover of Gustav Mahler and antique French clocks, decided to challenge Hawke for leadership. Keating won a ballot among federal Labor Party politicians and became Prime Minister. The beginning of Keating's five-year term was spent trying to pull Australia out of the early 1990s recession, which peaked with unemployment at 11%. As the economy began to recover, he moved on to other reforms. Keating began strengthening economic ties with Asia and asking Australians to admit responsibility for the brutal way in which their ancestors had treated the Aboriginal people.

In 1996, John Howard came through for the Coalition, trouncing Keating in a bitterly fought election. Recognizing that Keating's policies on Asia and indigenous Australians had made many voters uneasy, Howard promised that his new government would make the nation "relaxed and comfortable." When Pauline Hanson, a redheaded fishmonger who had been newly elected as an independent, began speaking of the need to reduce Asian immigration and criticizing Aboriginal welfare, Howard was slow to condemn her views. In 1998, Hanson's party, One Nation, won a raft of seats in the Queensland state election. Amid constant infighting, financial irregularities, and the lack of a coherent set of policies, the One Nation party has now slid into irrelevance, but not without powerfully affecting the race debate in Australia.

In 2000, Australia switched to a Goods and Services Tax, a European-style value-added tax. The transition was unpopular, and in the lead-up to the 2001 election, it was widely expected that Howard would be defeated by the Labor Party, then led by Kim Beazley. But in August 2001, a Norwegian container ship, the *Tampa*, carrying 453 asylum-seekers picked up when their boat sank, was turned back from Australian waters. Labor opposed broad-based legislation to restrict refugee entry, and was painted as soft on refugees. Labor was trounced in the November 2001 election and after the poll, Simon Crean replaced Kim Beazley as leader of the Labor Party.

In the past few years, the political scene has been marked by debates over university funding, refugee policy, and the war in Iraq (Labor opposed the government's decision to send troops without a UN mandate). Labor has also experienced some infighting—in June 2003, Kim Beazley unsuccessfully challenged Simon Crean for leadership of the party. But the party's chances should not be underestimated—although it is out of power at the federal level, Labor has been in government in all six states and two territories since 2001.

Despite the limitations of a three-year election cycle, Australian governments have managed to bring about a number of important reforms over the past two decades. Its healthcare system provides universal coverage to all Australians. Its social security system is better able to handle upcoming demographic changes than the US or European system. And thanks to a swag of reforms, its economy has been one of the best-performing in the OECD. But major challenges remain to be confronted. Australia's unemployment rate is unacceptably high, inequality is rapidly rising, and educational attainment is inadequate for a twenty-first century workforce.

Andrew Leigh is a Ph.D. student at the John F. Kennedy School of Government at Harvard University. He has served as a policy advisor to the Australian Senate and is the co-editor of The Prince's New Clothes: Why do Australians Dislike Their Politicians?

NEW SOUTH WALES

From a historical perspective, there's no disputing that New South Wales is Australia's premier state. It was here that British convicts lived through the first bitter years of colonization, dreaming of what might lie beyond the impassable Blue Mountains, and here that explorers first broke through the Great Dividing Range, opening the interior of the country for settlement and ensuring the stability of the colony. In the central plains and on the rich land of the Riverina, Merino wool and agricultural success provided the state with its first glimpses of prosperity. Then, in 1851, prospectors struck gold just west of the mountains, and Australia's history changed forever. No longer the desolate prison of exiled convicts, New South Wales became a place that promised a new life and a chance to strike it rich. Although the gold rush days are long gone, New South Wales has continued to grow. Today, it's the most populous state and—thanks largely to Sydney—the diverse and sophisticated center of modern Australia.

The country's biggest and flashiest city, Sydney sits midway along the coast. North and south of Sydney, sandy beaches string together in an almost unbroken chain. The trip up the coast is the ultimate backpacker party, with the large coastal towns of Port Macquarie and Coffs Harbour whetting appetites for the full-on delights that await in counter-culture infused Byron Bay. The south coast is colder but refreshingly far less crowded and every bit as beautiful. Directly west of Sydney's suburban reaches, the Blue Mountains encompass some of the state's favorite getaways and separate the coastal strip from the expansive Central West and outback regions. The New England Plateau, along the Great Dividing Range north of the wineries of the Hunter Valley, achieves an unusually lush and high-altitude setting for a cozy collection of small Australian towns and stunning national parks. Just below the carved-out enclave of the Australian Capital Territory, the Snowy Mountains offer winter skiing and superb summer hiking.

The attractions of New South Wales are as varied as the terrain. Whether it's the cosmopolitan buzz of Sydney, the challenging bushwalks of the Blue Mountains, the laid-back surf culture of Byron, or the post-apocalyptic simplicity of the outback, visitors find plenty to write home about.

HIGHLIGHTS OF NEW SOUTH WALES

SYDNEY. 'Quite possibly the world's most beautiful city. (p. 104.)

BLUE MOUNTAINS. Escape urban life in the great outdoors of the Blue Mountains. Venture to the Three Sisters outcropping at Echo Point or go on a walkabout. (p. 150.)

HUNTER VALLEY. Tour the vineyards and taste the fine red and white wines of the Hunter Valley. (p. 166.)

WARRUMBUNGLE NATIONAL PARK. Jagged spires and rambling peaks mark the dramatic juncture of the state's lush east and barren west. (p. 252.)

THREDBO. Fly down the long runs on Thredbo's black diamond slopes. (p. 240.)

NIMBIN. Inhale the counterculture and wily ways of Nimbin. (p. 208.)

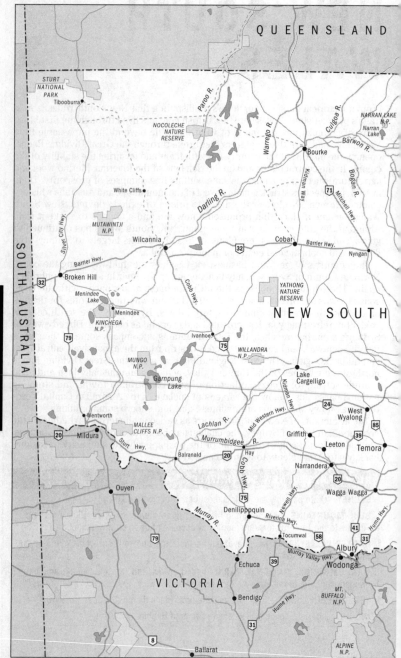

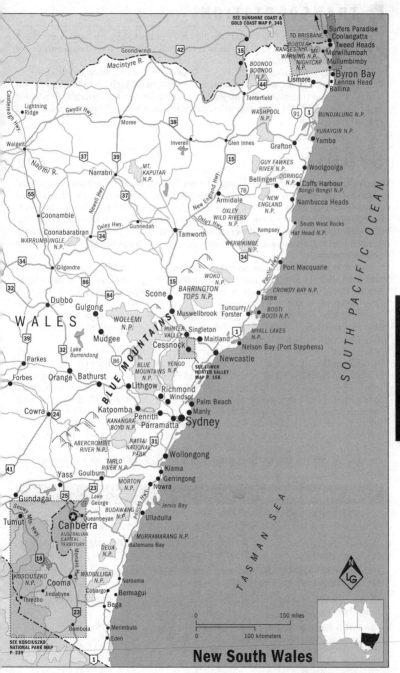

SEE SUNSHINE COAST & GOLD COAST MAP P. 346

Surfers Paradise
Coolangatta
Tweed Heads
TO BRISBANE
BORDER
RANGES N.P. MT.
WARNING N.P.
NIGHTCAP N.P.
Murwillumbah
Mullumbimby
Byron Bay
Lennox Head
Ballina
Lismore

Goondiwindi

Macintyre R.

42
15
BOONOO BOONOO N.P.
44

Tenterfield

Lightning Ridge
Gwydir Hwy.

Moree

WASHPOOL N.P.
91 1 BUNDJALUNG N.P.

Castlereagh Hwy.

Walgett

Naomi R.

37
39
38
Inverell
Glen Innes
Grafton
YURAYGIR N.P.
Yamba

55
Narrabri
MT. KAPUTAR N.P.
37
GUY FAWKES RIVER N.P.
Woolgoolga
DORRIGO N.P.
Coffs Harbour
Bongil Bongil N.P.

Bellingen
78
NEW ENGLAND N.P.
Nambucca Heads

Coonamble

New England Hwy.

Armidale
OXLEY WILD RIVERS N.P.

Coonabarabran
34
WARRUMBUNGLE N.P.
Gunnedah
Oxley Hwy.
Oxley Hwy.
Tamworth
Kempsey
South West Rocks
Hat Head N.P.

WERRIKIMBE N.P.
34

34
Gilgandra

32
Dubbo
Gulgong

WALES

WOKO N.P.
BARRINGTON TOPS N.P.
Port Macquarie

Pacific Hwy.

CROWDY BAY N.P.

86
84
15
Scone
Taree
BOOTI BOOTI N.P.
Tuncurry/ Forster

39
Mudgee

WOLLEMI N.P.
Muswellbrook
Singleton
1
MYALL LAKES N.P.

Parkes
32
Lake Burrendong
86
HUNTER VALLEY
Cessnock
Maitland
Nelson Bay (Port Stephens)
YENGO N.P.
Newcastle

Forbes
Orange
Bathurst
BLUE MOUNTAINS N.P.
SEE LOWER HUNTER VALLEY MAP P. 168

Lithgow
Richmond
Windsor
Palm Beach

Cowra
24
Katoomba
KANANGRA BOYD N.P.
Penrith
Parramatta
Manly
Sydney

ABERCROMBIE RIVER N.P.
NATTAI NATIONAL PARK
31
Wollongong

TARLO RIVER N.P.

41
Yass
Goulburn
MORTON N.P.
Kiama
Gerringong
Nowra

Gundagai
25
Lake George

23
Princes Hwy.
Jervis Bay

Tumut
BUDAWANG N.P.
Queanbeyan
Ulladulla
Canberra
AUSTRALIAN CAPITAL TERRITORY

MURRAMARANG N.P.

Snowy Mtns. Hwy.

DEUA N.P.
Batemans Bay

18
Monaro Hwy.

KOSCIUSZKO N.P.
WADBILLIGA N.P.
Narooma
Cobargo
Bermagui

Cooma
Jindabyne
Thredbo
23
Bega

Bombala
Merimbula
Eden

SEE KOSCIUSZKO NATIONAL PARK MAP P. 239
1

SOUTH PACIFIC OCEAN

TASMAN SEA

0   100 miles
0   100 kilometers

New South Wales

⌐ TRANSPORTATION

The cities and towns of New South Wales are connected by the state's excellent **public transportation** system; the system is especially good in the coastal part of the state. For timetables or route information for all bus, rail, and ferry systems both within Sydney and throughout NSW, call **CityRail** (☎ 13 15 00; www.cityrail.info) or **Countrylink** (☎ 13 22 32; www.countrylink.nsw.gov.au), which provides New South Wales' sole rail transport. The major bus companies are **McCafferty's/Greyhound** (☎ 13 14 99 or 13 20 30; www.mccaffertys.com.au or www.greyhound.com.au) and **Premier** (☎ 13 34 10).

SYDNEY ☎ 02

Australia's unofficial capital, cosmopolitan Sydney blends liveliness and loveliness like only one of the world's greatest cities can. As the country's international gateway and the home of one-fifth of the national population, Sydney is undoubtedly Australia's major urban center. After the building boom brought on by the 2000 Olympic Games, the city certainly looks the part; indeed, in its futuristic financial center, an elevated train even snakes through the district's tangled mass of skyscrapers.

Like many major cities the world over, Sydney's personality is much more liberal than the rest of the country. Its substantial gay population is out and about, setting the tone for what's hot in nightlife, and the annual Gay & Lesbian Mardi Gras celebration attracts enormous crowds of all persuasions from around the globe. Sydney also refuses to be culturally contained, as the wide range of available cuisines makes clear. The city houses a diverse Asian population, and the bustling Chinatown district is growing quickly.

For all of Sydney's urban bustle, however, it is refreshingly in tune with nature. Its outdoor beauty is expansive, concentrated most remarkably in its famous harbor, where the First Fleet of colonists and convicts landed in 1788. Today, the iconic Opera House and Harbour Bridge define Sydney's skyline and draw visitors to the boat-filled water's edge for gorgeous ferry rides. The city's obsession with the water also comes through in its heavy beach culture, epitomized by glamorous Bondi Beach and the more secluded Northern Beaches above the harbor. Many travelers use Sydney as a springboard for the rest of the continent—but after dining by the waterfront, raging at the clubs, relaxing at the beach, and marveling at the taste of vibrant Australian culture, you'll be ready to relocate Sydney-side for the long haul.

HIGHLIGHTS OF SYDNEY

SYDNEY OPERA HOUSE. Defining the Sydney skyline, the Opera House is not to be missed. You can see the stunning Concert Hall by tour or performance only. (p. 131)

MANLY. Take the ferry to this friendly surfing suburb for grand coastal walks and a glimpse of the utopia that is the Northern Beaches. (p. 136)

ROYAL BOTANIC GARDENS. Sydney's Eden has spectacular views of Sydney Harbour at Mrs. Macquarie's Point. (p. 133)

KINGS CROSS. You haven't seen the city until you've experienced its 24-hour neon den of sin. (p. 131)

DARLING HARBOUR. The stunning Powerhouse Museum and Sydney Aquarium explain why it's so touristy. (p. 134)

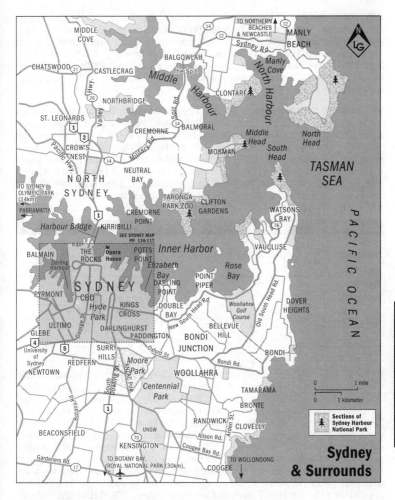

Sydney & Surrounds

SEE SYDNEY MAP PP. 116-117

NEW SOUTH WALES

✈ INTERCITY TRANSPORTATION

BY PLANE. Sydney's **Kingsford-Smith Airport**, 10km southwest of the Central Business District, serves most major international carriers. **Qantas** (☎13 13 13) and **Virgin Blue** (☎13 67 89) cover most domestic destinations. For security reasons, locker storage is not available; however, **Tempo baggage store** holds bags for $8.75 apiece per 24hr. period. The **Sydney Airport Information** kiosk, on the arrivals level in the international terminal, offers a booking service and free calls to area youth hostels. (☎9667 6058. Open daily from 5:30am until after the last flight lands.) Transportation into the city is available directly outside the terminal. **Airport Link** (☎13 15 00; www.airportlink.com.au) is part of the underground CityRail network, which runs trains Su-Th 5am-12:35am and F-Sa until 2am along the green East

Hills line to the City Circle, including Circular Quay (15min.; every 10min.; $11, $14-16 return.) **Kingsford-Smith Transport (KST),** one of several airport shuttle companies, runs buses to city and inner suburb accommodations. (☎9666 9988; www.kst.com.au. Daily every 20min. 5am-10pm. $8 one-way, $13 return.) Many hostels offer free pick-up. A **taxi** to the city center costs about $20 from the domestic terminal and $25 from the international area; the drive takes 20-45min., depending on traffic.

BY TRAIN. Countrylink trains (☎13 22 32) depart from the **Central Railway Station** above Eddy Ave. Branch offices at **Town Hall Station, Bondi Junction Station,** and on **Alfred St.** at Circular Quay also sell tickets. Tickets come in 3 classes: economy seat, first-class seat, and first-class sleeper. Booking by phone 2 weeks in advance saves 50%, 1 week saves 40%. ISIC cardholders also get a 50% discount. **Great Southern** (☎13 21 41) tickets come in 3 classes that vary greatly in price: Red Kangaroo seat, Red Kangaroo sleeper, and Gold Kangaroo sleeper. Return fares for all trips are double the price of one-way. The following table lists information for trains running from Sydney to:

DESTINATION	COMPANY	DURATION	DAYS	PRICE
Adelaide	Great Southern	25hr.	M, Th	$176
Alice Springs	Great Southern	45hr.	Su, W	$390
Brisbane	Countrylink	14½-15hr.	2 per day	$110
Byron Bay	Countrylink	12½hr.	2 per day	$98
Canberra	Countrylink	4hr.	3 per day	$47
Coffs Harbour	Countrylink	8hr.	3 per day	$79
Melbourne	Countrylink	10½hr.	2 per day	$110
Surfers Paradise	Countrylink	14-15hr.	2 per day	$105
Perth	Great Southern	3 days	M, Th	$459

BY BUS. Fifteen bus companies operate from the **Sydney Coach Terminal,** Central Station, on the corner of Eddy Ave. at Pitt St. (☎9281 9366. Open daily 6am-10:30pm.) Luggage storage is available ($6-11 per day). Because special rates and concessions vary, consult a travel agent for the lowest rate on any given itinerary. The major national company, **McCafferty's/Greyhound** (☎13 14 99 or 13 20 30; www.mccaffertys.com.au or www.greyhound.com.au) generally offers more frequent trips to major destinations than the smaller regional carriers, but their rates are often not the best. Check online for their special deals. Their Aussie Explorer Pass allows travelers to make unlimited stops in one direction along a pre-set route; the "Mini Travelers" route, which runs along the east coast, is especially popular (☎13 20 30; Mini Travelers $299 from Sydney, ISIC/YHA/VIP/NOMADS $269). The table below refers to McCafferty's/Greyhound. The following table lists information for buses running from Sydney to:

DESTINATION	DURATION	TIMES	PRICE
Adelaide (via Canberra)	24hr.	2 per day	$127
Alice Springs (via Adelaide)	40hr.	2 per day	$294
Brisbane	17hr.	6 per day	$94
Byron Bay	13hr.	4 per day	$94
Cairns (via Brisbane)	2½ days	6 per day	$285
Canberra	4¾hr.	11 per day	$35
Coffs Harbour	9hr.	5 per day	$78
Darwin (via Alice Springs)	3½ days	2 per day	$498

DESTINATION	DURATION	TIMES	PRICE
Melbourne	12hr.	5 per day	$65
Mt. Isa (via Brisbane)	3½ days	2 per day	$244
Perth (via Adelaide)	2½ days	1 per day	$397
Surfers Paradise	15hr.	5 per day	$94

◢ ORIENTATION

NEIGHBORHOODS AT A GLANCE

NEIGHBORHOOD	FEATURES	LOCAL BUS ROUTES
Bondi Beach	Home to most of Sydney's celebrity types.	380, 382, L82
Central Business District (CBD)	Includes Martin Place, Chinatown, Paddy's Market.	380, 394
Circular Quay	Sydney Opera House and the wharves for all Sydney Harbour ferries.	380, 394
Coogee Beach	Bondi's rival; youthful energy and a vibrant nightlife.	314, 372, 373, 374
Darling Harbour	Sydney Aquarium and Powerhouse Museum. Touristy, with swanky nightlife scene.	Short walk from Town Hall or monorail
Darlinghurst & Paddington	Hip neighborhood for young, fashionable, creative types; hot gay nightlife.	380, 394
Glebe	Cafes, pubs, and bookstores; influenced by neighboring student population.	431, 432, 433, 434
Kings Cross	Seedy center of Sydney backpacker culture, with hostels, cafes, and strip shows.	380, 394
Manly	Friendly holiday resort area with great beaches and surfing.	151, 190/155, 247/144
Mosman	Taronga Park Zoo, other parks and gardens.	151, 190, 247
Newtown	Bohemian; vintage clothing, used books.	423
North Sydney	Tree-lined financial district; upmarket cafes abound.	151
The Rocks	Historic neighborhood, upscale boutiques.	380, 394, 423
Surry Hills	Artsy cafes and clothing stores.	394, 380, 373
Vaucluse/Rose Bay	Historic, upscale homes and Euro-style shopping.	325

NEIGHBORHOOD OVERVIEW

The Sydney metropolitan area is immense. The city seems to be contained only by the forces of nature, with **Ku-Ring-Gai Chase National Park** to the north, the **Blue Mountains** to the west, **Royal National Park** to the south, and the **Pacific Ocean, Tasman Sea,** and **Sydney Harbour** to the east. Much of this area, however, is made up of largely quiet, residential outer suburbs.

Unlike its metropolitan area, Sydney's actual center is manageably sized. The walk to Circular Quay along Pitt St. takes only 30min. from Central Station and only 15min. from Kings Cross. Outside the city center but still within the city proper are the inner suburbs—really big neighborhoods such as Glebe and Surry Hills that each have a distinctive feel. For a bird's eye view of it all, ascend **Centrepoint Tower** (see p. 132).

CITY CENTER. Sydney's most famous sights lie on Sydney Harbour at **Sydney Cove,** directly north of the city center. On the Cove and at the southern end of the **Sydney Harbour Bridge** is **The Rocks,** a historic neighborhood with upscale boutiques. Drivers entering the city center from the north can use the **Harbour Bridge** or the **Harbour Tunnel,** which emerges in the **Central Business District (CBD)** east of the Cove (southbound toll only, $3). Though less scenic, the tunnel is a more convenient route for anyone heading into the eastern suburbs. The **Sydney Opera House** is located prominently on Bennelong Point, east of the Cove. For the best views of the Harbour Bridge and Opera House, take a stroll via **Mrs. Macquaries Road** through the Royal Botanic Gardens to **Mrs. Macquaries Point,** the tip of the peninsula that forms the northeast corner of the Botanic Gardens; or take a ferry ride from the wharves at **Circular Quay.**

Sydney proper, or the **city center,** is bounded by Circular Quay to the north, **Central Station** to the south, **Darling Harbour** to the west, and the green expanse of the **Royal Botanic Gardens, the Domain,** and **Hyde Park** to the east. **George Street** and **Pitt Street** are major avenues that run from Circular Quay straight through the **CBD** to Central Station in the south. Street numbers begin at the water and increase proceeding from The Rocks to the 800s near Central Station. **Martin Place,** a pedestrian mall spanning the five blocks between George and Macquarie St., is the heart of the CBD, and contains the sprawling **Pitt Street Mall,** which is composed of numerous shopping centers. Farther south in the CBD, the next major center of activity is **Town Hall,** on Druitt St. between George and Kent St. Between Town Hall and Central Station is Sydney's rapidly growing **Chinatown,** radiating from the intersection of Hay, Sussex, and George St. This area is home to the famous weekend-discount **Paddy's Market. Redfern,** the area directly south of Central Station, *may be unsafe at night.*

INNER SUBURBS. Many tiny municipalities (or neighborhoods) known as the inner suburbs compose the rest of Sydney's central urban area. Despite their proximity to one another, the suburbs maintain distinct characters and special attractions. Many areas overlap, and some are known by more than one name. West of the city center, **Pyrmont** covers the point of land between Darling Harbour and Blackwattle Bay. The waterside here is also called **Darling Harbour** and is serviced by the Sydney Monorail. South of Pyrmont, **Ultimo** approaches the west side of Central Station stretching to the Chinatown area. **Glebe,** southwest of Ultimo and just north of the **University of Sydney,** benefits from the presence of students in all the usual ways: casual cafes, cheap food, crowded pubs, and well-supplied bookstores. Glebe Point Rd. is the center of activity in this village-like district and home to a number of hostels. **Newtown,** just south of the university, is a bohemian neighborhood with a city feel, and is centered around the main second-hand shopping and cheap dining artery of King St.

The infamous red-light suburb of **Kings Cross,** east of the CBD at the far end of William St., once reigned (and continues to, albeit half-heartedly) as the center of Sydney backpacker culture. Hostels and small restaurants line Victoria St., while busy nightclubs and pubs are packed in along Bayswater Rd. Travelers should watch as belongings while in the Cross and avoid walking alone at night, especially solo female backpackers.

To the south of Kings Cross, **Victoria Street** goes chic with the city's coolest cafes lining the way to trendy **Darlinghurst.** Along with gritty **Surry Hills** to the south and ritzy **Paddington** to the east, Darlinghurst is home for young, creative types. Sydney's nightlife revolves around the outrageous clubs on gay-friendly **Oxford Street,** the main road through Darlinghurst, Paddington, and Woollahra to the east. Just south of the army's stately Victoria Barracks, **Moore Park** and **Centennial Park** to the east form the city's largest swath of greenery and house some of Sydney's major athletic facilities, including the **Sydney Football Stadium** and the **Cricket Ground.**

FAR EAST & SOUTHERN BEACHES. Outside of these central areas, surroundings get less urban. East of Paddington and above Centennial Park, **Woollahra's** terrace houses provide a pleasant change of scenery. To the north, **Double Bay** and **Rose Bay** are Sydney's most exclusive residential areas and the location of Sydney's elegant resort shopping areas. **Bondi Junction** (BOND-eye), south of Woollahra, is the last stop on CityRail's eastern line. Ten minutes east by bus or train is the famous **Bondi Beach,** model of many a surf movie and home to some of Sydney's A-list. Farther south, the beaches of **Tamarama, Bronte,** and **Clovelly** offer less crowded sand for families and quieter sunbathers. **Coogee Beach** lies farthest south and rivals Bondi with its popular beachlife and young residents. Sample all the beaches in between by taking the hour-long **Bondi to Coogee coastal walk.**

NORTH SHORE. Crossing the Harbour Bridge takes you to Sydney's North Shore. **North Sydney,** which includes suburbs like Kirribilli, Neutral Bay, Cremorne, and Mosman, was originally settled by wealthy merchants and its upper-crust heritage gleams through today. Tourist attractions on the Lower North Shore are essentially limited to **Taronga Park Zoo** in Mosman, although the harborside beaches and walks are charming. The popular surf-side **Northern beaches** begin at **Manly.** Accessible by a lovely ferry ride, Manly is good for both surfers and families, and a good base for the rest of the surf beaches, which run north all the way to **Palm Beach.**

⫼ LOCAL TRANSPORTATION

Sydney's well-oiled public transportation machine makes for simple traveling within the city limits. The **Sydney Transit Authority (STA)** is comprised of **Sydney Buses, CityRail Trains,** and **Sydney Ferries;** the network stops just about anywhere. For information or route advice on any part of the STA system, call ☎ 13 15 00. Check out the various passes, frequently cheaper than paying individual fares. For $13.40 per day, the **DayTripper** grants unlimited use of Sydney ferries, local buses, and central CityRail lines. The **TravelPass** for the four central zones includes unlimited seven-day access to buses, trains, and ferries for $30. The **Sydney Pass** includes unlimited bus, train, and ferry use within the basic TravelPass zone, return Airport Link service, access to the Sydney, Bondi, and Parramatta Explorer buses, and passage on Sydney Harbour cruises and the high-speed ferries to Manly and Parramatta. (3-day pass $90, ages 4-15 $45, families $225; 5-day pass $120/$60/$300; 7-day pass $140/$70/$350.)

BY BUS. Buses don't automatically stop at bus stops; hail them from the sidewalk as you would a taxi. Fares range from $1.50 to $4.70 (ages 4-15 half-price, seniors $1.10-3; ask for student concessions). You must pay the fare when boarding. Color-coded **TravelTen** passes cover 10 trips at a significant discount and can be purchased from most news agencies. (Blue TravelTen for 10 trips from $11.30, children $5.60.) The **Bus Tripper** ($9.70, children $5.60; bus and ferry $13.40/$6.70) covers one full day of bus travel. Most buses run between 5am and 11:30pm, but there is 24hr. service between the city center and central locales.

In addition to local commuter bus service, the Sydney Transport Authority operates two sightseeing buses, the **Sydney Explorer** and the **Bondi Explorer,** which allow passengers to get on and off at major attractions along designated routes. The Sydney Explorer covers sights between Sydney Harbour and Central Station, moving as far east as Woolloomooloo Bay and as far west as Darling Harbour, originating in Circular Quay every 20min. between 8:40am and 5:20pm. The Bondi Explorer service visits the eastern bays and southern beaches down to Coogee, departing from Circular Quay every 30min. between 8:45am and 4:15pm. The Explorer services are expensive but can be an excellent way to do concentrated touring. ($30 for a 1-day pass for either route, ages 4-15 $15, families $75; tickets combining both routes over 2 non-consecutive days $50/$25/$125. Purchase tickets on a bus at any stop along the route.) Start early to make the most of your money.

A **bus information kiosk** labeled Transit Shop is located at the corner of Alfred and Loftus St., between McDonald's and Circular Quay. (Open M-F 7am-7pm, Sa-Su 8:30am-5pm). The STA info line (☎ 13 15 00) also has schedule details.

BY SUBWAY & TRAIN. Sydney's **CityRail** underground train system (Su-Th 5am-12:35am, F-Sa 5am-2am) runs from Bondi Junction in the east to the most distant corners of the suburban sprawl in the north, west, and south. Service is fast, frequent, and easy to navigate. CityRail's lowest one-way fare is $2.60, but most trips cost a little more. Return fares are double the one-way price weekdays before 9am. At all other times, the purchase of a round-trip "off-peak" ticket gets you a sizeable discount. The combined **TravelPass** is generally a bargain for regular train users. (Good for 1 week beginning on day of validation; Red Pass for city center and beaches $30.) The **train information office** is at Circular Quay (open daily 9am-4:30pm), as well as at Central Station (☎ 8202 2000. Open daily 6:30am-9:30pm).

Both the **Monorail** and **Light Rail** (☎ 9285 5600; www.metromonorail.com.au), operated by the same company, provide futuristic methods of transportation. Riding above the city bustle is a nice change if you are traveling directly and don't mind the slightly heftier fee. The **Monorail** links the City Centre with Darling Harbour and Chinatown. (Every 3-5min. M-Th 7am-10pm, F-Sa 7am-midnight, Su 8am-10pm. $4, seniors $2.20, under 6 free; day passes with unlimited transport $8, families $20.) The somewhat more practical **Light Rail** connects Chinatown, Darling Harbour, Glebe, Star City, and Ultimo. (Daily every 10-15min. 6am-midnight; every 30min. midnight-6am. $2.50-4.80, seniors and ages 4-15 $1.30-3.50; unlimited day pass $8, families $24. Signal the driver from designated stopping areas.)

BY FERRY. STA green and gold ferries (www.sydneyferries.nsw.gov.au) offer a magnificent view of the harbor. Ferries embark from the **Circular Quay** wharves between the Opera House and the Harbour Bridge (daily 5am-midnight; check the timetables for schedules). Short one-way trips in the harbor cost $4.30; a FerryTen pass for the same area costs $26.50 and works much like the TravelTen bus pass. The fare for the high-speed **JetCat** to Manly is $6.70 (FerryTen pass $55.80). The STA's fastest commuter ferry services its most distant port: take the RiverCat to Parramatta for $6.40, or FerryTen for $45.10. Children ages 4-15 ride for half-price.

STA has several **Sydney Ferries Harbour Cruises:** the Morning Cruise (1hr.; daily 10:30am; $15, ages 4-16 $7.50, families $37.50); the Afternoon Cruise (2½hr.; M-F 1pm, Sa-Su 12:30pm; $22/$11/$55); and the after-dark Evening Harbour Cruise (1½hr.; M-Sa 8pm; $19/$9.50/$47.50). Posher private ships, such as Captain Cook, Matilda, and Majestic Cruises, have slightly more comprehensive themed harbor cruises. Browse along East Circular Quay for the lowest fare; fares typically range from $20 to $40, and ships depart from mid-morning to evening. The **ferry information office** is opposite Wharf 4. (☎ 9207 3170. Open M-F 7am-6pm, Sa-Su 8am-6pm.)

BY CAR. All major **car rental** companies have desks in Kingsford-Smith Airport, and most appear again on William St. near Kings Cross. The big names include: **Avis,** 200 William St. (☎ 13 63 33 or 9357 2000); **Budget,** 93 William St. (☎ 13 27 27 or 8255 9600); **Hertz** (☎ 13 30 39 or 9360 6621), corner of William and Riley St.; and **Thrifty,** 75 William St. (☎ 8374 6172 or 1300 367 227). All rental cars starting around $55 per day, with surcharges for 21- to 25-year-olds. In general, local and regional outfits offer much better prices than the big companies, but fewer locations translates to more difficult interstate travel and drop-off. **Bayswater Car Rental,** 180 William St., at corner of Dowling, Kings Cross, charges $10 per day for a week or longer (☎ 9360 3622; www.bayswatercarrental.com.au. Open M-F 8am-6pm; Sa 8am-noon.) All companies offer reduced long-term rental rates, and most offer free pick-up from the airport or Central Station.

Hostel notice-boards overflow with fliers for privately owned cars, campers, and motorcycles **selling** for as little as several hundred dollars. When purchasing a car this way, it's a good idea to make sure it's registered to the seller so the registration can be transferred. For more information on car sales, see **Buying and Selling Used Cars,** p. 54. **Kings Cross Backpackers Car Market,** Level 2, Kings Cross Carpark, on the corner of Ward Ave. and Elizabeth Bay Rd., brings buyers and sellers together. They offer third-party insurance for travelers (see **Insurance at a Glance,** p. 54) and their knowledgeable staff has valuable information on registration and other matters for car-buyers. (☎9358 5000 or 1800 808 188; www.carmarket.com.au. Open daily 9am-5pm. Weekly charge for sellers from $40. Required vehicle inspection from $27.50.) **Travellers Auto Barn,** 177 William St., offers guaranteed buy-back agreements on cars over $3000. Minimum buy-back rates are 30-50% of purchase price, depending on the length of time you take the car. Cheaper cars are also available but do not come with warranties and buy-back guarantees, whereas purchases over $3000 include 5000km engine warranties and free NRMA Service membership. (☎9360 1500. Open M-Sa 9am-6pm, Su 10:30am-3pm.)

The city branch of the **National Royal Motorist Association (NRMA),** 74-76 King St., around the corner from the corporate headquarters on George St., is a comprehensive driver's resource. Anyone planning on doing extensive driving should consider joining—benefits include roadside and accident assistance, knowledgeable staff, accurate maps, and emergency passenger transport and accommodation. (☎13 21 32. Open daily 7am-10pm. $99 first-time annual membership, $46 renewal or if a member of an international agency.)

BY TAXI. Taxis can be hailed from virtually any street. Initial fare is $2.55 ($1.25 surcharge with call-in request), plus $1.32 per km. Companies include: **Taxis Combined** (☎8332 8888); **Legion Cabs** (☎13 14 51); **Silver Service** (☎13 31 00); **Premier Taxi** (☎13 10 17); and **RSL Cabs** (☎13 22 11).

BY BICYCLE. For taking in lots of scenery at a manageable pace, cycling is an option; by complementing cycling with ferries and trains, it's possible to tour Sydney Harbour and the northern and eastern beaches in a single day, or even venture out to Royal or Ku-Ring-Gai Chase National Park. **Bicycle NSW,** Level 2, 209 Castlereagh St., organizes weekly rides and advises where to rent bikes. (☎9283 5200. Membership annual dues $69.) For a coastal ride, visit **Manly Cycle Centre,** 36 Pittwater Rd., at Denison St. in Manly. (☎9977 1189. Open M-W and F 9am-6pm, Th 9am-7pm, Su 10am-5pm. $12 per hr., $18 per 2hr., full-day $25.)

🔢 PRACTICAL INFORMATION

TOURIST & TRAVEL INFORMATION

Tourist Office: Sydney Visitors Centre, 106 George St. (☎9240 8786 or 1800 067 676; www.sydneyvisitorcentre.com), in the white historic sailors' building in the Rocks. Heaps of brochures, as well as booking services for accommodations, tours, and harbor cruises. Open daily 9am-6pm.

Travel Offices: Sydney is riddled with travel offices, including:

■**Travellers Contact Point,** Level 7, 428 George St. (☎9221 8744; fax 9221 3746; sydney@travellers.com.au), between King and Market St. Free 30min. **Internet** access. Mail forwarding and holding in Australia $50 per year. Employment board with recruiting officers for travelers with work visas. Open M-F 9am-6pm, Sa 10am-4pm.

Student Uni Travel, Level 8, 92 Pitt St. (☎9232 8444; www.sut.com.au), near Martin Pl. Free 15min. email and **Internet** access. Mail forwarding. Luggage storage $1 per day. Job agency and visa assistance. Open M-F 9am-6pm, Sa 10am-5pm.

NEW SOUTH WALES

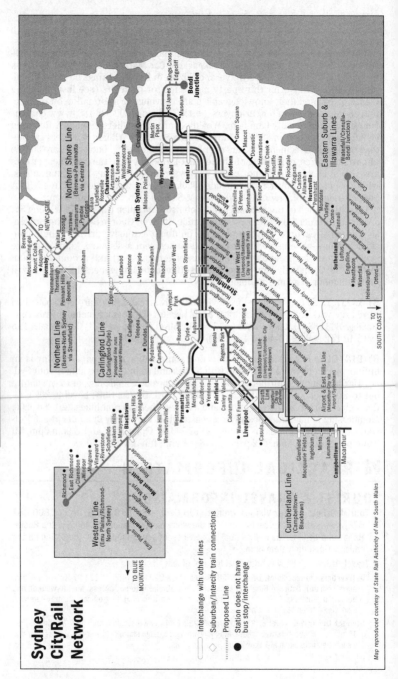

Sydney CityRail Network

Interchange with other lines

Suburban/Intercity train connections

Proposed Line

Station does not have bus stop/interchange

TO BLUE MOUNTAINS

Map reproduced courtesy of State Rail Authority of New South Wales

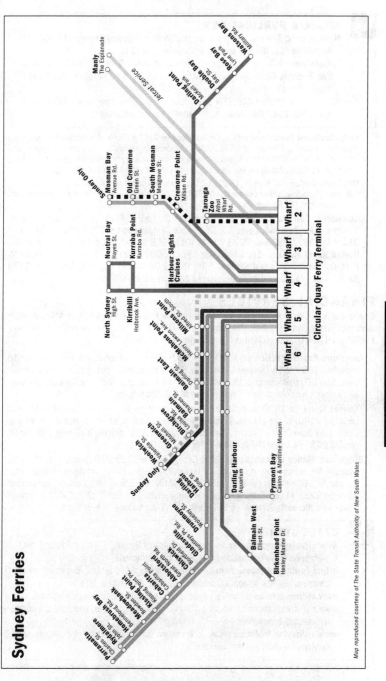

Sydney Ferries

Map reproduced courtesy of The State Transit Authority of New South Wales

NEW SOUTH WALES

MEDIA & PUBLICATIONS

Newspapers: The main papers are the *Sydney Morning Herald* ($1.20), *The Australian* ($1.20) and tabloid *Daily Telegraph* ($1).

Entertainment: The *Metro* section of Friday's *Sydney Morning Herald,* as well as free weeklies *Beat, Sydney City Hub, Streetpress,* and *Revolver* (find them in music stores).

Radio: Rock, Triple J 105.7FM and Triple M 104.9FM; Pop, Nova 969 96.9FM and 2DAY 104.1FM; News, ABC 630AM; Tourist Info, 88FM.

Australian Travel Specialists, Jetty 6, Circular Quay (☎9247 5151) and in Harbourside Shopping Centre, in Darling Harbour (☎9555 2700). Comprehensive info on trips around Sydney and beyond. Also books chauffeured Harley-Davidson tours, ranging from a Harbour tour (1hr., $110) to a tour of the Hunter Valley and Blue Mountains (8hr., $380). Open daily 9am-9pm.

YHA Travel Center, 422 Kent St. (☎9261 1111; www.yha.com.au), behind Town Hall. Also at 11 Rawson Pl., below Sydney Central YHA (☎9281 9444). Open M-W and F 9am-5pm, Th 9am-6pm, Sa 10am-2pm (11 Rawson Pl. also open Sa until 4pm and Su 2-6pm).

Consulates: Canada, Level 5, 111 Harrington St. (☎9364 3000). Open M-F 8:30am-4:30pm. **New Zealand,** Level 10, 55 Hunter St. (passport ☎9223 0222, visa 9223 0144; fax 9221 7836 or 9223 0166). Open M-F 9am-12:30pm and 1:30-5:00pm. **United Kingdom,** Level 16, 1 Macquarie Pl. (☎9247 7521; fax 9251 1201). Open M-F 10am-4:30pm. **United States,** 59th fl., 19-29 Martin Pl., MLC Centre (☎9373 9200). Open M-F 8am-12:30pm; phones answered 8am-4:30pm.

FINANCIAL SERVICES

Banks such as Commonwealth and National pack the CBD, and their **ATMs** usually accept Cirrus, MasterCard, Plus, and Visa. Banks and exchange offices are normally open M-Th 9am-4pm and F until 5pm, and include:

American Express Office (☎1300 139 060). Dozens of locations around the city, including 105 Pitt St. Traveler's checks cashed and currency changed with no commission; $13.20 minimum or 1.1% commission to buy checks. Mail held for card and traveler's check holders up to a month. Open M-F 8:30am-5pm.

Thomas Cook (☎1800 801 002). Several locations in the international terminal (☎9317 2100) of the airport. $7 charge on traveler's checks and currency exchanges. Open daily 5am-9:30 or 10pm. There are dozens of other offices, including 175 Pitt St. (☎9231 2877). Open M-F 8:45am-5:15pm, Sa 10am-1pm.

Singapore Money Exchange, 304-308 George St. (☎9223 6361), opposite Wynyard Station. No commission on US or UK traveler's checks. Other locations include: 401 Sussex St., Chinatown (☎9281 0663); on Eddy Ave., Shop #10 by the Greyhound office (☎9281 4118); Darling Harbour's Harbourside Mall (☎9212 7124); Centrepoint Tower's Castlereagh St. level (☎9223 9222). All open daily 9am-5:30pm.

CYBER-SYDNEY

www.cityofsydney.nsw.gov.au The homepage of Sydney. Visitor guide and information on services provided by the local government.

http://sydney.citysearch.com.au A comprehensive business directory, entertainment listings, shopping, restaurants, and gay/lesbian info.

www.sydney.com.au Sydney's sights, accommodations, and transportation.

www.eatstreetsatnight.com.au Listings of restaurants open late into the night for late-night munchies.

www.sydneyforchildren.com.au Information on a wide range of activities and services for children and families.

LOCAL SERVICES

Bookstores: Dymocks Booksellers, 424 George St. (☎1800 688 319; www.dymocks.com.au). Open M-W 9am-6:30pm, Th 9am-9pm, F 9am-6:30pm, Sa-Su 9am-5:30pm. Australia's largest bookstore has franchise locations all over the CBD.

Library: Sydney City Library, Town Hall House, 456 Kent St. (☎9265 9470), at the corner of Kent and Druitt St. Open M-F 8am-7pm, Sa 9am-noon. **Internet** $2 per hr. The **State Library of New South Wales** (☎9273 1414), next to the Parliament House on Macquarie St., houses galleries and research facilities, but does not lend books. Open M-F 9am-9pm, Sa-Su 11am-5pm.

Ticket Agencies: Ticketek (☎9266 4800; www.ticketek.com.au), has offices in retail stores and an information kiosk at 195 Elizabeth St. Full-price advance booking for music, theater, sports, and selected museums. Phone lines open for purchases by credit card M-Sa 9am-9pm and Su 9am-8pm. **Ticketmaster** (☎13 61 00; www.ticketmaster7.com), covers many concert and theatrical venues. Phones answered M-Sa 9am-9pm, Su 9am-5pm.

EMERGENCY & COMMUNICATIONS

Emergency: ☎000 anywhere in Australia for police, ambulance, or fire assistance.

Police: 570 George St. (☎9265 6595). Kings Cross police station, 1-15 Elizabeth Bay Rd. (☎8356 0099), on Fitzroy Gardens.

Crisis Lines: Alcohol and Drug Information Service, ☎9361 8000; 24 hr. **Rape Crisis Centre** ☎9819 6565; 24 hr. **HIV/AIDS Information Line** ☎9332 4000; M-F 8am-7pm, Sa 10am-6pm. **Suicide prevention** ☎9331 2000. **Gay & Lesbian Counselling Service** ☎9207 2800 or 1800 805 379; daily 8:30-10:30pm.

Late-Night Pharmacy: Crest Hotel Pharmacy, 91-93 Darlinghurst Rd., Kings Cross (☎9358 1822), four doors left of the rail station. Open 8am-midnight. **Wu's Pharmacy,** 629 George St., Chinatown (☎9211 1805). Open M-Sa 9am-9pm, Su 9am-7pm.

Medical Services: Sydney Hospital (☎9382 7111 or 9382 7009), on Macquarie St. opposite the Martin Pl. station. **Sydney Medical Centre,** 580 George St. (☎9261 9261), in the Pavilion Plaza. Consultation fee $45-65. Open daily 7am-9pm. **Contraceptive Services,** Level 3, 195 Macquarie St. (☎9221 1933). Consultation fee $35. Open M-F 8:30am-1pm.

Internet Access: Internet cafes abound, especially on George St. near Chinatown and the Sydney YHA, and in Kings Cross. Common charges in the city center are $3-4 per hr., but rates fluctuate. **Global Gossip** (☎9212 1466) charges $3.95 per hr., and their shops are franchised across the city. Hours vary by location. Their main store is at 770 George St., near Sydney Central YHA. Open daily 8am-1am. They also offer postboxes and mail-forwarding ($10 per month).

Telephones: Public payphones abound in Sydney; local calls cost 40¢, though calling mobile phones can be found easily. For international calls, invest in a cheap **calling card,** which can be easily found in Chinatown and at convenience stores in the CBD. **Apple** brand calling cards have particularly good rates. Calls to the US and UK cost 5¢ per minute all day, and there is no connection fee. **Global Gossip** (see above) offers super-cheap rates for calls placed noon-6pm (2.9¢ per minute to the US and UK, plus a 59¢ connection fee). **Directory Assistance:** ☎1223.

Post Office: Sydney General Post Office (GPO), 1 Martin Pl. (☎9244 3710), corner of George St. Open M-F 8:15am-5:30pm, Sa 10am-2pm. Poste Restante available at 310 George St., inside Hunter Connection across from Wynyard Station. They will hold mail for up to a month. Enter up the ramp with the "Hunter Connection" sign and go up the escalator and then the stairs. Open M-F 8:15am-5:30pm. Many hostels will also hold mail for up to a month. **Postal code:** 2000.

NEW SOUTH WALES

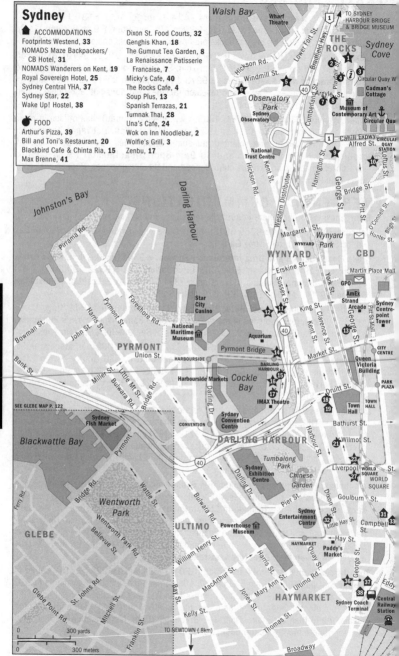

Sydney

ACCOMMODATIONS
Footprints Westend, **33**
NOMADS Maze Backpackers/
  CB Hotel, **31**
NOMADS Wanderers on Kent, **19**
Royal Sovereign Hotel, **25**
Sydney Central YHA, **37**
Sydney Star, **22**
Wake Up! Hostel, **38**

FOOD
Arthur's Pizza, **39**
Bill and Toni's Restaurant, **20**
Blackbird Cafe & Chinta Ria, **15**
Max Brenne, **41**

Dixon St. Food Courts, **32**
Genghis Khan, **18**
The Gumnut Tea Garden, **8**
La Renaissance Patisserie
  Francaise, **7**
Micky's Cafe, **40**
The Rocks Cafe, **4**
Soup Plus, **13**
Spanish Terrazas, **21**
Tumnak Thai, **28**
Una's Cafe, **24**
Wok on Inn Noodlebar, **2**
Wolfie's Grill, **3**
Zenbu, **17**

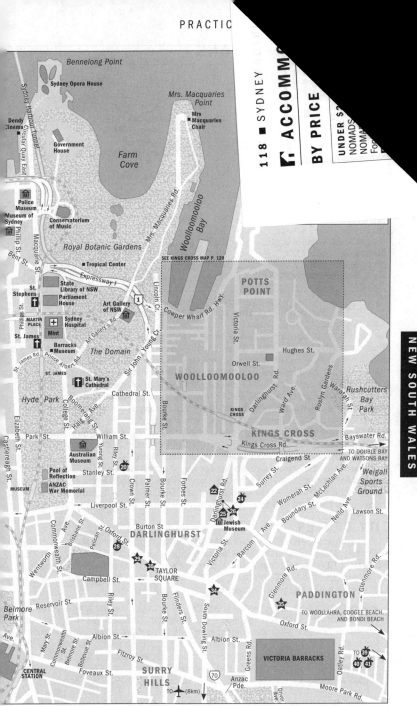

UNDER $3
NOMADS
NOMA
Fo

Bennelong Point

Sydney Opera House

Mrs. Macquaries
Point

Mrs
■ Macquaries
Chair

Dendy
Cinema

Sydney Harbour Tunnel

Circular Quay East

Government
House

Farm
Cove

Police
Museum
Museum of
Sydney

Phillip St.

Bent St.

Conservatorium
of Music

Woolloomooloo Bay

Royal Botanic Gardens

Mrs. Macquaries Rd.

SEE KINGS CROSS MAP P. 120

POTTS
POINT

■ Tropical Center

Expressway I

Lincoln Cr.

Cowper Wharf Rd. Hwy.

Victoria St.

St.
Stephens

State
Library of NSW

Parliament
House

Macquarie St.

Phillip St.

Art Gallery Rd.

Art Gallery
of NSW

Hughes St.

Roslyn Gardens

Rushcutters
Bay
Park

MARTIN
PLACE

Sydney
Hospital

Mint

Orwell St.

WOOLLOOMOOLOO

St. James

Barracks
Museum

Prince Albert Rd.

The Domain

Darlinghurst Rd.

Ward Ave.

Roslyn St.

Ward Ave.

ST. JAMES

St. Mary's
Cathedral

Cathedral St.

KINGS
CROSS

Bayswater Rd.

James St.

Hyde Park

Boomerang Ave.

College St.

Haig Ave.

Bourke St.

KINGS CROSS

Kings Cross Rd.

TO DOUBLE BAY
AND WATSONS BAY

Park St.

William St.

Craigend St.

Surrey St.

Womerah Ave.

McLachlan Ave.

Weigall
Sports
Ground

Elizabeth St.

Castlereagh St.

Australian
Museum

Yurong St.

Riley St.

Crown St.

Palmer St.

Bourke St.

Forbes St.

Darlinghurst Rd.

22

24

Boundary St.

Neild Ave.

Lawson St.

MUSEUM

Pool of
Reflection

ANZAC
War Memorial

Stanley St.

20

Liverpool St.

Burton St.

DARLINGHURST

25

26

Jewish
Museum

Barcom Ave.

Glenmore Rd.

Commonwealth Ave.

Brisbane St.

Pelican St.

Oxford St.

28

Victoria St.

Glenmore Rd.

PADDINGTON

Wentworth Ave.

29

30

TAYLOR
SQUARE

Campbell St.

Riley St.

Bourke St.

Flinders St.

South Dowling St.

34

35

TO WOOLLAHRA, COOGEE BEACH,
AND BONDI BEACH

Belmore
Park

Reservoir St.

Oxford St.

Glenmore Rd.

Albion St.

Greens Rd.

Albion St.

Ave.

Mary St.

Commonwealth St.

Bellevue St.

Bellevue St.

Fitzroy St.

Foveaux St.

SURRY
HILLS

70

Anzac
Pde.

VICTORIA BARRACKS

Oatley Rd.

TO 39

40 41

CENTRAL
STATION

TO ✈ (8km)

Driver Ave.

Moore Park Rd.

5 (❷)		$26-40 (❸)	
Wanderers on Kent (119)	CC	Sydney Central YHA (118)	CC
DS Maze Backpackers (119)	CC	Wake up! Hostel (119)	CC
tprints Westend (119)	CC	▨ Wattle House (123)	GL
▨ Original Backpackers (119)	KC	Alishan International Guest House (123)	GL
▨ The Pink House (119)	KC	Glebe Point YHA (123)	GL
The V Backpackers (120)	KC	▨ Collaroy Beach YHA (123)	NB
Blue Parrot Backpackers (120)	KC		
Sydney Central Backpackers (121)	KC	**$41-60 (❹)**	
Noah's Bondi Beach (121)	BB	Sydney Star Accommodation (121)	DA
Indy's Bondi Beach Backpackers (121)	BB	Royal Sovereign Hotel (121)	DA
The Biltmore Private Hotel (122)	BB		
Coogee Beach Wizard of Oz (122)	CB	**OVER $60 (❺)**	
▨ Manly Bunkhouse (123)	NB	O'Malley's Hotel (120)	KC
Manly Beach Resort (124)	NB	Bondi Beachside Inn (122)	BB
Manly Backpackers Beachside (124)	NB	Verona Guest House (123)	GL
		Manly Lodge (124)	NB

BB Bondi Beach **CC** City Center **CB** Coogee Beach
DA Darlinghurst **GL** Glebe **KC** Kings Cross **NB** Northern Beaches

The city center is an obvious choice because of its prime location and abundance of accommodations. The huge hostels near Central Station are more like hotels with dorm rooms—which usually means their facilities are excellent but atmosphere sterile. Well-located, traveler-friendly, and party-ready, Kings Cross is another established backpacker mecca, and the high concentration of steadily improving hostels ensures that beds are almost always available. However, the omnipresence of prostitutes and strip clubs make many travelers uncomfortable. If you do opt to stay in the Cross, be sure you feel comfortable with your hostel's security measures before letting your valuables out of sight. Good suburban bets include Coogee Beach and Glebe, which both offer many laid-back backpacker accommodations in proximity to cafes and student nightlife.

Unless stated otherwise, hostels accept major credit cards, have 24hr. access, no linen fee, and a 10am check out. Laundry, when available, is generally $3 per wash. Most dorm beds increase in price by a few dollars ($2-5) during peak season (Nov.-Feb.). The most expensive time to travel is during late December and April.

CITY CENTER

These backpacker-friendly accommodations, located primarily in the CBD close to Central Station and other main transportation lines, can't be beat for location. While the CBD is not Sydney's most charming area, it is its most convenient: it's steps from the food of Chinatown and the shopping of the CBD, and about a 10min. walk to the sights of Circular Quay and The Rocks.

Sydney Central YHA, 11 Rawson Pl. (☎9281 9111; sydneycentral@yhansw.org.au), near the corner of Pitt St. and Rawson Pl. Visible from Central Station's Pitt St. exit. Incredible facilities: pool, sauna, game room, employment and travel desks, TV rooms, Internet ($2 per 30min.), parking ($12 per night), multiple kitchens, bar and cafe. Its size is amazing but alienating. No sleeping bags allowed. Lockers $2-5. Linen free. Laundry $4.40. No key deposit. 14-day max. stay. Reception 24hr. Check-in from noon. Check-out 10am. Dorms $28-34, twins $81, ensuite doubles $91. YHA discount $3. ❸

Wake up! Hostel, 509 Pitt St. (☎9288 7888; www.wakeup.com.au), opposite Central Station. Just one year old, this pristine hostel has a sleek, modern feel and rooms with high ceilings. Each brightly painted floor has a different geographic theme and color. Subterranean cafe and bar, Internet access ($3.95 per hr.), travel desk, and a funky raised-TV lounging area. Laundry $6. Reception 24hr. 10-bed dorms $27; 8-bed $28; 6-bed $30; 4-bed $32. Weekly 10-bed $175; 8-bed $182; 6-bed $196; 4-bed $210. $210. Twins and doubles $85, ensuite $95. ❸

NOMADS Wanderers on Kent, 477 Kent St. (☎9267 7718 or 1800 424 444; www.wanderersonkent.com.au), between Druitt and Bathurst St., a block from Town Hall. Close to Darling Harbour, the heart of the CBD, and Chinatown. In addition to being the best-located, this hostel is one of the most secure as well. Clean rooms and 340 beds, friendly staff, and many facilities: basic TV and pool rooms, helpful employment and travel desks, tanning booth ($4 per 3min.), Internet ($5 per 45min). Attached **Transit Underground Bar and Cafe** is social and has cheap meals ($4.50-8). No sleeping bags. Lockers $2-8 per day. Linen deposit $20. Laundry $6. Key deposit $10. 28-day max. stay. Free airport shuttle with 2-night stay. Reception 24hr. Dorms $24-32.50; twins and doubles $84. NOMADS $1 discount. 5th or 7th night free. ❷

NOMADS Maze Backpackers/CB Hotel, 417 Pitt St. (☎9211 5115; www.nomadsworld.com), 3 blocks from Central Station walking toward Circular Quay. Close to Chinatown and good city center nightlife. The 475 beds and newly-renovated common areas are basic, but the super-friendly staff creates a welcoming social atmosphere. Planned activities such as free wine and cheese F 8pm, as well as pub crawls and yoga sessions. Employment desk, TV and pool rooms. Lockers $4 per day. Laundry $6. Free airport transfer. Reception 24hr. Apr.-Nov. 4- to 6- bed dorms $19-23; singles $49; twins and doubles $55. ❷

Footprints Westend, 412 Pitt St. (☎9211 4588 or 1800 013 186; www.footprintswestend.com.au), opposite NOMADS Maze Backpackers/CB Hotel. Balances its simple, small rooms with daily planned activities. Job board. Free airport pick-up with 2-night stay. Breakfast included. Lockers $5 per day. Laundry $6. Reception 24hr. Check-out 10am. Ensuite dorms $21-28; twins $69; doubles $76, ensuite $85. ❷

KINGS CROSS

If you decide to take up residence in the Cross, expect good nightlife, lots of backpacking company, and seedy streets. Some accommodations here can be pretty run-down, but plenty of clean, well-maintained rooms exist. Victoria St. locations are rather stately as hostels go. **CityRail** runs from Martin Pl. in the city to Kings Cross Station. **Buses** run from Circular Quay (#324, 325, or 327) and Chatswood (#200) to the Cross as well.

▨ Original Backpackers, 160-162 Victoria St. (☎9356 3232; www.originalbackpackers.com.au). State-of-the-art kitchen, TV lounge, dining area, and courtyard with arched doorways, plants, and fountains make for the loveliest and most spacious hostel common area in the Cross. Cable TV, Internet ($5 for 45min.), a safe for valuables, and laundry ($5.20). Luggage storage free first day, $2 per day after. Every room has a TV and fridge; some boast baths, kitchens, and balconies at no extra cost. Key deposit $20. Reception 24hr. Check-out 10am. Dorms $21-23; singles $45; twins and doubles $65. Weekly $126-138/$270/$390. ❷

▨ The Pink House, 6-8 Barncleuth Sq. (☎9358 1689 or 1800 806 385; www.pinkhouse.com.au), off Ward Ave. Unlike most other Kings Cross hostels, the Pink House feels like a house—a big, fun, light-pink house. Plentiful group activities (daytrips, pub outings, skydiving, soccer) promote a family atmosphere. Brick kitchen next to a BBQ terrace. All rooms have TVs, couches, and sturdy wooden beds; most have decorative fireplaces and large mirrors. Luggage storage $5 per week, $15 per month. Laundry $5.

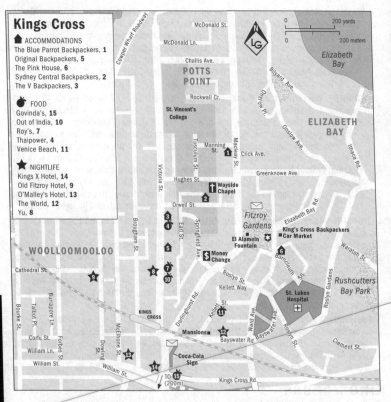

Kings Cross

🛏 ACCOMMODATIONS
The Blue Parrot Backpackers, **1**
Original Backpackers, **5**
The Pink House, **6**
Sydney Central Backpackers, **2**
The V Backpackers, **3**

🍎 FOOD
Govinda's, **15**
Out of India, **10**
Roy's, **7**
Thaipower, **4**
Venice Beach, **11**

★ NIGHTLIFE
Kings X Hotel, **14**
Old Fitzroy Hotel, **9**
O'Malley's Hotel, **13**
The World, **12**
Yu, **8**

Free Internet (max. 20min.) Book ahead. Reception 8:30am-9pm. Breakfast included. Dorms $20-22; twins and doubles $50-55; triples $69. Discounts for long-term stays. VIP/YHA discount $1 per night. Weekly $120-130/$300-330/$405. ❷

The V Backpackers, 144 Victoria St. (☎9357 4733 or 1800 667 255). A tight-knit hostel with one of the swankiest common rooms in the city. Comes with pool table, free Internet down the road, free BBQ M and F, and (most importantly) free beer. Travel desk downstairs. Free airport or city pick-up. Free safe at reception. Luggage storage $2. Laundry $4. Reception 7:30am-8pm. 4-bed dorms $24-25; twins and doubles $55-65. Weekly $140-150/$330-360. ❷

Blue Parrot Backpackers, 87 Macleay St. (☎9356 4888 or 1800 252 299). Darlinghurst Rd. turns into Macleay St. past Fitzroy Gardens. A recent addition to the Kings Cross scene, this very blue hostel comes small and sweet, with a great outdoor terrace, TV lounge with fireplace, and bright kitchen. Spacious lockers in rooms. Dorms $22-25; twins and doubles $55-60. ❷

O'Malley's Hotel, 228 William St. (☎9357 2211), above the popular pub. Entrance is to the left of the pub's doors. The 15 elegantly furnished rooms with TV and fridge are not as loud as you would expect from the location. Breakfast included. Check-out 10am. Reception M-F 8am-5pm, Sa-Su 9am-midnight. Doubles $66, with kitchen and bath $88; triples $88. ❺

Sydney Central Backpackers, 16 Orwell St. (☎9358 6600 or 1800 440 202; www.sydneybackpackers.com.au). Sydney Central features clean bedrooms with animal caricatures on the doors. The rooftop patio has a great eating area and views of the city and opera house. Free pickup from airport or Central Station. Lockers in rooms. Laundry $4. Key deposit $20, blanket deposit $10. Reception 7am-9pm. Dorms $21; twins and doubles $55. 7th night free. VIP discount $1. ❷

DARLINGHURST

Many of the old-school Aussie pubs in and around the greater Darlinghurst area double as hotels for travelers, and generally have a few reasonably priced rooms to let.

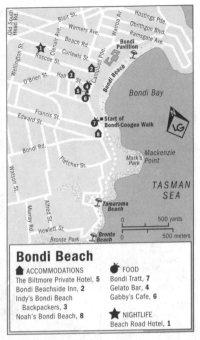

Bondi Beach

🏠 ACCOMMODATIONS
The Biltmore Private Hotel, **5**
Bondi Beachside Inn, **2**
Indy's Bondi Beach
  Backpackers, **3**
Noah's Bondi Beach, **8**

🍴 FOOD
Bondi Tratt, **7**
Gelato Bar, **4**
Gabby's Cafe, **6**

⭐ NIGHTLIFE
Beach Road Hotel, **1**

Sydney Star Accommodation, 275 Darlinghurst Rd. (☎9232 4455 or 1800 13 44 55), opposite Darlo Bar on the corner of Liverpool St. A very quiet hotel ideal for longer stays. Each room comes equipped with a TV, fridge, and microwaves; there is also a common kitchen downstairs. Reception noon-5pm. Singles $50-55; twins and doubles $55-65; deluxe suite (fits 4) $80-85. Weekly $200-250/$280-340/$450-480. ❹

Royal Sovereign Hotel, above Darlo Bar on the corner of Liverpool St. (☎9331 3672; www.darlobar.com.au). The 19 pea-green rooms with TV and fridge are all doubles. Reception at Darlo Bar. Level 1 rooms directly above the bar $55-66; Level 2 rooms with A/C $66-77. ❹

BONDI BEACH

Take bus #380, 382, or L82 from Circular Quay via Oxford St., or drive east along Oxford St.; it's stop 12 on the Bondi Explorer. **CityRail** runs to Bondi Jctn., where a bus runs to the waterfront. The oceanfront **Campbell Parade** is the main street; its addresses begin at the southern part of town and increase as you go downhill.

Noah's Bondi Beach, 2 Campbell Pde. (☎9365 7100, reservations 1800 226 662), perched at the top of the beach's southernmost end. Bondi's biggest and best hostel has two rooftops' worth of great views and BBQ. Free surf and boogie board use. Pool table, TV. Breakfast included. Dinner in connected bar/restaurant $5-12. Female-only ensuite dorm available. Laundry $4. Key deposit $20. Reception 24hr. Dorms $20-25; twins and doubles $50; beachside doubles $55. Weekly $150/$300/$330. VIP. ❷

Indy's Bondi Beach Backpackers, 35A Hall St. (☎8300 8802 or 1800 110 971; www.indysbackpackers.com.au). 1½ blocks inland from Campbell Pde. Extensive surfboard exchange program. TV, Nintendo 64, and video library. Free use of bikes, inline skates, wetsuits, and boards. Breakfast included. Laundry $4. Internet $2 per 30min. Key deposit $25. Reception 8am-10pm. Less social location at 252 Campbell Pde. Large dorms $19; doubles at 252 Campbell Pde. $49. Weekly $133/$299. VIP. ❷

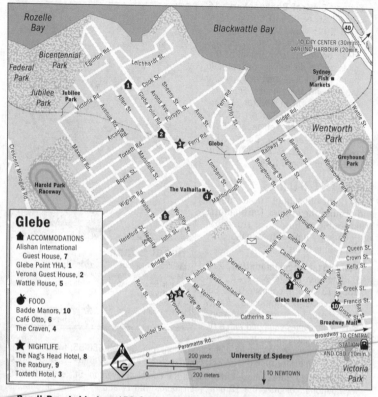

Rozelle Bay

Blackwattle Bay

TO CITY CENTER (30min.)
DARLING HARBOUR (20min.)

Bicentennial Park

Federal Park

Jubilee Park

Sydney Fish Markets

Wentworth Park

Greyhound Park

Harold Park Raceway

The Valhalla ■

Glebe

🏠 ACCOMMODATIONS
Alishan International
  Guest House, 7
Glebe Point YHA, 1
Verona Guest House, 2
Wattle House, 5

🍎 FOOD
Badde Manors, 10
Café Otto, 6
The Craven, 4

⭐ NIGHTLIFE
The Nag's Head Hotel, 8
The Roxbury, 9
Toxteth Hotel, 3

Glebe Market ■

Broadway Mall ■

Broadway TO CENTRAL
STATION
AND CBD (10min.)

University of Sydney

TO NEWTOWN

Victoria Park

200 yards

200 meters

Bondi Beachside Inn, 152 Campbell Pde. (☎9130 5311; www.bondiinn.com.au), entrance around the corner from Hungry Jack's on Roscoe St. Seven stories of hotel-like rooms over the beach; ideal for families or couples. Rooms have kitchenette, TV, balcony, and phone. No laundry. Parking. Reception 24hr. Oceanview singles and doubles $110-120. Discounts for stays of over one week. Wheelchair-accessible. ❺

The Biltmore Private Hotel, 110 Campbell Pde. (☎9130 4660 or 1800 684 660). This "private hotel" close to the beach is actually a hostel, with airsprayed paintings and average facilities. Laundry $4. Key deposit $20. Reception 7:30am-12:30pm and 2:30-7:30pm. Dorms $18-22; singles and twins $40-45; doubles $49; triples $66. Weekly $85-130/$250-270/$299/$420. ❷

COOGEE BEACH

Take bus #373 or 374 from Circular Quay, #372 from Central Station, or #314 from Bondi Junction.

Coogee Beach Wizard of Oz, 172 Coogee Bay Rd. (☎9315 7876 or 1800 013 460; www.wizardofoz.com.au), at the 2nd set of traffic lights. Hardwood floors, spacious dorms, and lots of open common space allow for relaxation and socializing. Free Th BBQs in summer. Free pick-up. No smoking. Laundry $6. Key deposit $20. Reception 8am-noon and 5-7pm. Check-out 9:30am. Dorms $23; singles $50; doubles $55. Weekly $129/$298/$350. VIP. ❷

GLEBE

To get to Glebe Point Rd., your main artery for all Glebian antics, take bus #431, 432, 433, or 434. Or, from Central Station, follow George St., and then Broadway, west 15min. to Victoria Park and turn right onto Glebe Point Rd.

Wattle House, 44 Hereford St. (☎9552 4997; www.wattlehouse.com.au), a 5min. walk from Glebe Point Rd. A hostel with a B&B feel, this is Sydney's smallest—and one of its nicest—backpackers. Restored Victorian decor includes brick kitchen and manicured garden. Plush bean bags fill the small TV room, where guests actually get to know each other. Laundry $6. 2-week max. stay. Book way ahead. Reception 9am-noon; reservations 8am-8pm. 4-bed dorms from $27; doubles and twins $70-80. ❸

Alishan International Guest House, 100 Glebe Point Rd. (☎9566 4048; www.alishan.com.au). Classy, 3-star Victorian house, with an open common area surrounded by a terrace. Private rooms have TVs and fridges; dorms have wooden beds. Parking available. Key deposit $10. Laundry $6. Internet $3 per hr. Reception 8am-10:30pm. Dorms $27-33; ensuite singles $88-99; ensuite doubles $99-115; ensuite family room for 4 $154, each extra person $16. Wheelchair-accessible room available. ❸

Glebe Point YHA, 262-264 Glebe Point Rd. (☎9692 8418; glebe@yhansw.org.au). Guests hang out on the large roof for BBQs and in the basement common spaces. Spacious kitchen and dining area. Sinks in rooms. Bus service to the airport $11. No sleeping bags allowed. Luggage storage free for returning guests. Laundry $5. Key deposit $10. Internet $1 per 15min. Reception 7am-10:45pm. Dorms $28-32; twins and doubles $68. Weekly dorms $154. YHA discount $3.50. ❸

Verona Guest House, 224 Glebe Point Rd. (☎9660 8975; www.verona-guesthouse.com). This bright Victorian manor has gleaming hardwood floors and elegant furniture in every room, not to mention A/C and private bathrooms. Hot breakfast included. Free laundry. Reception 24hr; call first. Singles $125; doubles $145. 3-night stay singles $110, doubles $130. ❺

MANLY & THE NORTHERN BEACHES

Lively, surfside Manly has a good range of accommodations and is the best base for exploring Sydney's beautiful Northern Beaches. To get to Manly from Circular Quay, take the **ferry** (30min.; M-F 6am-11:45pm, Sa 8am-11:45pm, Su 8am-11pm; $5.40) or **Jetcat** (15min; M-F 6-9:25am and 4:20-8:30pm, Sa 6:10am-3:36pm, Su 7:10am-3:36pm; $6.70). See **Local Transportation,** p. 110.

Manly Bunkhouse, 35 Pine St. (☎9976 0472 or 1800 657 122; www.bunkhouse.com.au). From the ferry, cross the Esplanade to Belgrave St., which becomes Pittwater St., then turn left onto Pine St. (10min.). This small and quiet hostel is one of the best-kept in Manly; each 4-bed dorm has its own kitchenette, bathroom, TV, heater, lockers, and closet space. Free wharf pick-up. Key deposit $20. Reception M-F 8:30am-1pm and 4-8pm, Sa-Su 9am-noon and 6-7pm. Dorms $22-25; twins $55-65. Weekly $130-150/$350-400. VIP. ❷

Sydney Beachouse/Collaroy Beach YHA, 4 Collaroy St. (☎9981 1177; www.sydneybeachouse.com.au). This spectacular hostel located just across the street from the beach makes it worthwhile to use smaller Collaroy as a base for exploring the Northern Beaches. To get to Collaroy, take bus #L90 or L88 from Railway Square or Wynyard Station (Carrington St. side). Alternatively, take the ferry to Manly and catch bus #151, 155, or 156. The modern, social hostel has free surfboards, snorkeling gear, skateboards, and bikes. Outdoor pool. Free luggage storage. Laundry $4. Key and cutlery deposit $20. Reception 8am-8pm. Dorms $26; doubles $64, ensuite $84; ensuite family rooms for 5 $104. YHA. ❸

NEW SOUTH WALES

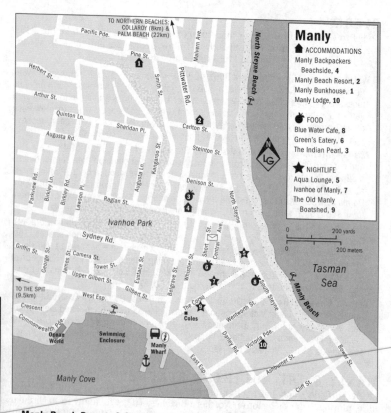

Manly

🏠 ACCOMMODATIONS
Manly Backpackers
  Beachside, **4**
Manly Beach Resort, **2**
Manly Bunkhouse, **1**
Manly Lodge, **10**

🍎 FOOD
Blue Water Cafe, **8**
Green's Eatery, **6**
The Indian Pearl, **3**

⭐ NIGHTLIFE
Aqua Lounge, **5**
Ivanhoe of Manly, **7**
The Old Manly
  Boatshed, **9**

Manly Beach Resort, 6 Carlton St. (☎9977 4188; www.manlyview.com.au). From the ferry, walk 10min. down Belgrave St., which becomes Pittwater St., and turn right onto Carlton St. The Manly Beach Resort features neat, large backpacker dorms with lockers and motel rooms. Free pick-up from the wharf 9am-noon when available. Dining/TV room, pool for motel guests. Laundry $3.20. Key deposit $20. Reception 24hr. Continental breakfast included. Dorms $20-24; doubles $45-55; triples $150. Weekly dorms $120-150; doubles $300-350. VIP $1 discount. Motel rooms: singles $95-115; twins $120-140; single studios $140-160; family rooms $195-215. Advance motel room bookings require $100 deposit. ❷

Manly Lodge, 22 Victoria Pde. (☎9977 8655). Small but luxurious ensuite rooms all have A/C, TV, VCR, and kitchenettes. Sauna and spa. Laundry $6. Continental breakfast included. Reception 7am-10pm. Doubles $120-144, deluxe with hot tub $135-155. Extra person $35, under age 10 $20. ❺

Manly Backpackers Beachside, 28 Raglan St. (☎9977 3411; www.manlybackpackers.com.au). From the ferry, cross the Esplanade to Belgrave St., which becomes Pittwater St., and turn right onto Raglan St. Despite the blank, narrow hallways, the hostel manages to have an open, friendly atmosphere. Large TV room/kitchen. Safe for valuables at reception. Free body boards. Laundry $6. Key deposit $30. Reception M-F 9am-1pm and 4-7pm, Sa-Su 9am-2pm. Dorms $22-25; twins and doubles $50-65. Weekly $119-161/$315-420. VIP. ❷

◘ FOOD

BY TYPE

AFRICAN		Cafe Otto (129)	GL ❸
◪ Kilimanjaro African Eatery (129)	NT ❷	Arthur's Pizza (128)	PA ❸
ASIAN		**INDIAN**	
Ghenghis Khan (127)	CC ❷	Govinda's (127)	KC ❸
Chinatown food courts (126)	CC ❷	Out of India (128)	KC ❸
Zenbu (126)	CC ❸	The Indian Pearl (130)	NB ❸
Chinta Ria: Temple of Love (127)	CC ❸	Mehrey Da Dhaba (128)	SH ❷
Tumnak Thai (128)	DA ❶		
Wok on Inn Noodlebar (127)	RO ❷	**LATE-NIGHT**	
Hana Haru (128)	SH ❸	Blackbird Cafe (126)	CC ❸
		Roy's (127)	KC ❶
BREKKY		◪ Soup Plus (126)	CC ❹
Gabby's Cafe (129)	BB ❷	Arthur's Pizza (128)	PA ❸
Cozzi Cafe (129)	CB ❷	The Rocks Cafe (127)	RO ❸
The Craven (129)	GL ❶		
Blue Water Cafe (130)	NB ❸	**MOD OZ**	
Micky's (128)	PA ❷	Bondi Tratt (129)	BB ❸
The Rocks Cafe (127)	RO ❸	Gelato Bar (129)	BB ❸
		Coogee Cafe (129	CB ❷
DESSERT		The Craven (129)	GL ❶
Gelato Bar (129)	BB ❸	Blue Water Cafe (130)	NB ❸
Max Brenner (128)	PA ❶	The Peasant's Feast (130)	NT ❷
La Renaissance (127)	RO ❷	Wolfie's Grill (127)	RO ❺
◪ The Gumnut Tea Garden (127)	RO ❷		
		VEGETARIAN	
EUROPEAN		Cozzi Cafe (129)	CB ❷
Spanish Terrazas (126)	CC ❸	Badde Manors (129)	GL ❶
◪ Soup Plus (126)	CC ❹	Govinda's (127)	KC ❸
◪ Una's Cafe and Restaurant (128)	DA ❶	◪ Green's Eatery (130)	NB ❶
Bill & Toni's Restaurant (128)	DA ❷	Green Gourmet (130)	NT ❷

BB Bondi Beach **CC** City Center **CB** Coogee Beach **DA** Darlinghurst **GL** Glebe **KC** Kings Cross **NB** Northern Beaches **NT** Newtown **PA** Paddington **RO** The Rocks **SH** Surrey Hills

NEW SOUTH WALES

Sydney's multicultural makeup shows through in its excellent food for any budget. **Asian** options, most notably small sushi shops and Thai cuisine, are particularly abundant all over the city. The CBD is packed with quick, cheap options. Slightly south, a tiny Spanish quarter provides classier, pricier meals while Chinatown's numerous restaurants are always frenetic.

Just east of the city center, the Oxford St. social artery that runs from Surry Hills in the south, is lined with ethnic restaurants. A (very) **Little Italy** is located on Stanley St., between Crown and Riley St., in Darlinghurst. For a larger selection of authentic Italian eats, head out to **Norton Street** in the western suburb of Leichardt. Continuing east through Darlinghurst, the strip of restaurants on Oxford St. near St. Vincent's Hospital (at Victoria St.) are a mix of Euro-style cafes and Asian restaurants. Victoria St. runs north from Oxford St. at the hospital into the land of high **cappuccino chic** before depositing the last of its cafe class amid the hostels of Kings Cross. In the Cross, Darlinghurst Rd. and Bayswater Rd. offer **late-night cheap bites** and fast-food chains.

As usual, a large student population means good, **cheap cafes** and restaurants on both Glebe Point Rd. in Glebe and King St. in Newtown. Blues Point Rd. on McMahons Point, Fitzroy St. in Kirribilli, and Military Rd. through Neutral Bay and Mos-

THE INSIDER'S CITY

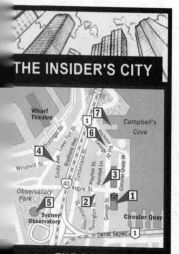

THE ROCKS

In Sydney's historic tourist center, it's all about the eclectic.

1 The **Museum of Contemporary Art** has an excellent Aboriginal art collection (☎9252 4033).

2 Enjoy free live music with your scones at the **Gumnut Tea Garden** (☎9247 9591).

3 Indulge your inner child at the **Toy Museum** (☎9251 9793).

4 A local favorite since back in 1845, **The Hero of Waterloo Pub** offers live Irish music (☎9252 4553).

5 Enjoy some little gardens and big views at the **Sydney Observatory** (☎9217 0485).

6 With something to accommodate all tastes, the **Rocks Market** serves all your local art-and-craft, homewares, and collectible needs.

7 Splurge on a romantic candlelit dinner with some amazing harbor views at **Wolfie's Grill** (☎9241 5577).

man lead the North Shore's stylish and affordable offerings, with well-loved local cafes as well as a plethora of ethnic-inspired **family-focussed eateries.** At most **coastal cafes** in Manly and Balmoral in the north and Bondi and Coogee in the south, $6-7 buys a large cooked breakfast and an excuse to appreciate the view over the morning paper. Though the neighborhoods vary in their offerings, none disappoint. Unless otherwise noted, major credit cards are accepted everywhere in the many malls of the city center. The CBD is rife with quick lunch stops for the professional masses working in the skyscrapers. Sandwiches, meat pies, and focaccia run $2.50-6 at sandwich counters throughout these blocks. Slightly south, away from Circular Quay, the feeding frenzy of **Chinatown** lurks west of Central Station, especially along **Dixon Street Plaza.**

CITY CENTER

🍴 **Soup Plus,** 383 George St. (☎9299 7728), between King St. and Market St., opposite the Strand Arcade in the CBD. With a $28 cover on F-Sa nights, this smoky jazz bar is an expensive option, but per-dollar value is unbeatable. The price covers entertainment and a 2-course dinner; mains include moussaka, lasagna, and stuffed pumpkin. Cover M-Th $5-8 from 7:30pm. ❹

Zenbu (☎9211 9888), on Southern Promenade, in the IMAX Complex of Darling Harbour. This date-ready restaurant has many candles and a menu of Japanese fusion cuisine, the "usual in an unusual way," including tasty saki-tails ($9) and an extensive sushi bar. Mains like the tuna with green tea noodles run $15-20, but that includes complementary 5min. head and neck massages given right at your table. Open M-F noon-10:30pm, Sa-Su noon-11pm. ❸

Chinatown food courts, along Dixon St., all boast cheap meals ($5-9): **Dixon House Food Court,** 80 Dixon St., downstairs, at Little Hay St. (open daily 10:30am-8:30pm); **Sussex House Food Court,** 60 Dixon St., (open daily 10:30am-9:30pm); and **Harbour Plaza Eating World,** at the corner of Dixon and Goulburn St. (open daily 10am-10pm; no credit cards). ❷

Blackbird Cafe (☎9283 7385), Cockle Bay Wharf, in Darling Harbour. Very trendy eatery with a great lounging atmosphere and view of the harbor. Diverse selection of pizza ($7-17), as well as breakfast ($4-13) and delicious desserts ($7.50). Open daily 8am-late. ❸

Spanish Terrazas, 541 Kent St. (☎9283 3046). Affordable tapas ($6-9) and paella ($32-35 for 2) in the pricey Spanish Quarter. Wash it all down with a pitcher of sangria while you enjoy the live Latin music F-Sa. Open for lunch M-F noon-3pm, for dinner M-Th 5:30-10pm, F-Sa 5:30pm-11pm. ❸

Chinta Ria: Temple of Love (☎9264 3211), Roof Terr. Level 2, Cockle Bay Wharf, in Darling Harbour. A fantastic spot for soaking in the trendy wharf neighborhood among stunning Malaysian decor. Yummy, if expensive, Malaysian fare $12-28. Open daily noon-2:30pm and 6-11pm (10pm on Su). No reservations. ❸

Genghis Khan, 469 Kent St. (☎9264 3863). Diners concoct their own Mongolian BBQ from a limited selection of meats and vegetables, and watch as a chef cooks it in an enclosed central grill. Lunch $11.50, dinner $14.50; all-you-can-eat $16.20/$18.90. Open for lunch M-F noon-3pm; dinner Su-W 6-10pm, Th-Sa 6-10:30pm. ❷

THE ROCKS

The Rocks has some of Sydney's most tourist-targeted eating. Should you desire, you may pay dearly for an evening dining at the harbor's edge, but even the budget traveler will find splendor. Plenty of the food is still cheap, and many restaurants have good views of The Rocks and Sydney Harbour.

■ **The Gumnut Tea Garden,** 28 Harrington St. (☎9247 9591). Tucked away on the corner of Harrington and Argyle St., the Gumnut charms customers with assorted cakes and puddings all day ($3-8), as well as tasty breakfasts ($6-10, until 11:30am) and lunches ($12-16). The front room is lit by a fireplace and the leafy garden terrace has live music F 7-9pm and Su noon-3:30pm. Open daily 8am-10pm. ❷

Wolfie's Grill, 17-21 West Circular Quay (☎9241 5577). Two levels of elegant candlelit dining for lovers of Australian prime beef and fresh seafood. Supremely good eating and priceless harbor views make up for the steep prices (grill items $27-40). Open daily 11:30am-10pm. ❺

The Rocks Cafe, 99 George St. (☎9247 3089). An extensive selection of breakfasts ($10), lunches ($15-22), and dinners ($15-22). Eat outdoors on the terrace across the street. Open daily 8am-midnight. ❸

La Renaissance Patisserie Francaise, 47 Argyle St. (☎9241 4878). All the tempting confections are made on the premises, and can be eaten in the courtyard out back. Truffles $1.50-1.80 each; tiramisu $4.80. Open daily 8:30am-6pm. ❷

Wok on Inn Noodlebar (☎9247 8554), in the Rocks Square, on Playfair St., facing The Rocks Centre. Despite Wok on Inn's name, there's only outdoor seating here. Noodle and rice dishes ($8-13) are cooked in your choice of Chinese, Malay, and Thai styles. Open daily 11:30am-10pm. ❷

KINGS CROSS

Govinda's, 112 Darlinghurst Rd. (☎9380 5155; www.govindas.com.au). A unique restaurant and cinema. $19 covers a mostly Indian, wholly vegetarian, all-you-can-eat buffet, and a current (usually artsy) movie in the moody, upstairs theater. Reservations strongly suggested. Dinner only $16; movie only $9.90. Open daily 6-10:30pm. ❸

Venice Beach, 3 Kellett St. (☎9326 9928), at the bend in Kellett St. A long, narrow restaurant with funky red walls, fireplaces, and a heated outdoor terrace. The chef's specials are a poach fillet with savory sauce ($16.90) and New York steak with mushroom sauce ($15.90). Open daily 6pm-late. ❷

Thaipower, 146 Victoria St. (☎8354 0434). Design your own noodle dish ($9-13.50) or stick to Thai favorites like garlic and pepper beef ($10) or fresh basil vegetables and tofu ($9). Lunch specials offered noon-4pm bring everything on the menu down to $7-9. BYO. Open daily noon-10:30pm. ❶

Roy's, 176 Victoria St. (☎9357 3579). Huge portions and terrace seating make Roy's a popular place for a sandwich ($8-9) or meal ($12-20). Su roast dinner, W pasta night comes with wine for $14.50 after 6pm. Open Su-F 7am-10pm, Sa 7am-midnight. ❶

Out of India, 178 Victoria St. (☎9357 7055). The only place for lovers of Indian food has free wine with eat-in meals, $10 takeaway only specials, a $10 "Thali Meal" with entree and main (5-7pm), and a "Special Banquet" deal ($20 per person). The chef's specialty is a spinach *palakwala* dish ($14-18). BYO. Open daily 11:30am-2pm and 5-11:30pm. ❸

DARLINGHURST

The suburbs of East Sydney have some of the city's best dining, particularly along Oxford St. and Stanley St. Oxford St. addresses start at the street's origin on Hyde Park, but confusingly begin again at the intersection with Victoria and South Dowling St., the dividing line between Darlinghurst and Paddington.

⧉ **Una's Cafe and Restaurant,** 340 Victoria St., Darlinghurst (☎9360 6885). Austrian food in a delightful wood and brick enclave, with cafe seating on the street. The locals have been coming here for over 30 years; you can (and inevitably will) wait for your table in the bar upstairs. Vienna schnitzel ($14.50) and bratwurst ($11.90). Daily special $13.50-16.50. Open daily 7:30am-10:30pm. Licensed. No credit cards. ❶

Bill & Toni's Restaurant, 74 Stanley St. (☎9360 4702), between King St. and Crown St., E. Sydney. Huge pasta entrees $8. For the hungrier, mains include schnitzel and casseroles. Full meal with orange punch $18. Takeaway sandwiches at the cafe downstairs $3-5. Open daily noon-2:30pm and 6-10:30pm. BYO. No credit cards. ❷

Tumnak Thai, 101 Oxford St. (☎9331 3364). Paper parasols hang from the ceiling in this modest but delicious Thai restaurant. Many vegetarian options ($10.50), as well as a not-to-be-missed lunch special, where mains cost $6.50-10 instead of the usual $10-15.50. Open M-F noon-3pm and 6-11pm, Sa-Su 6-11pm. ❶

PADDINGTON

Max Brenner, 447 Oxford St. (☎9357 5055). Enough chocolate to overwhelm the most diehard cacao bean fanatic. Try a chocolate cocktail ($4.50) with a pastry or fudge ($6-10). Popular strawberry fondue plate $7. Mobbed on the weekends. Open M-F 11:30am-6pm, Sa-Su 10am-6pm. ❶

Arthur's Pizza, 260 Oxford St. (☎9331 1779). Hits the spot with gourmet options like lamb sausage and double-smoked ham. Be prepared for one-hour waits in peak hours. Pizzas from $15-24, family size $28. Open M-F 5pm-midnight, F-Sa noon-midnight. ❸

Micky's Cafe, 268 Oxford St. (☎9361 5157). This dimly-lit bistro offers every combination under the sun: stir-fry, burgers, burritos, cheesecakes, pasta, and chicken satay. Meals from $13-23; burgers $14. Open Su-Th 9am-midnight, F-Sa 9am-1am. ❷

SURRY HILLS

Tucked beneath Oxford St. east of Central Station, the former industrial wasteland of Surry Hills is now a pleasant residential area. It's home to student-artist types, working-class old-timers, and recent immigrants—a diversity well-reflected in the range of ethnic restaurants that line Crown St. At night, reach Surry Hills by walking down Crown St. from Oxford St. instead of coming from Central Station.

Mehrey Da Dhaba Indian Street Restaurant, 466 Cleveland St. (☎9319 6260). Mehrey Da, the oldest *dhaba* in Sydney, has a storied tradition of serving up inexpensive and filling East Indian food. Whole tandoori chicken $10. Vegetarian meals from $6-10; meat dishes $10-18. *Naan* or *roti* $1.20. Open Su-Tu 5:30-10:30pm, W-F noon-3pm and 5:30-11pm, F-Sa noon-3am. BYO. No credit cards. ❷

Hana Haru, 660 Crown St. (☎9699 3999). Japanese and Korean, with teriyaki ($14.50-17), huge sushi/sashimi plates ($35.50-42), and grill-your-own BBQ ($16-24). The adventurous should try a spicy hot pot ($14.50-16.50). Open daily 5:30-11pm. ❸

BONDI BEACH

Campbell Parade is lined with trendy cafes facing the beach, while perpendicular **Hall Street** has cheaper eats.

Bondi Tratt, 34b Campbell Pde. (☎9365 4303). Its outdoor terrace high on Campbell Pde. provides excellent people-watching and beach views. Mostly Italian with occasional mod-Oz twists like kangaroo fillet. Entrees $11.50; pasta and pizza $13.50; mains from $18.50. BYO. Open daily 7am-10pm. ❸

Gabby's Cafe, 94 Campbell Pde. (☎9130 3788). Gabby's has served its all-day filling breakfasts ($6) for more than 20 years. Soup special $6; sandwiches $11. Open daily 7am-4pm. No credit cards. ❶

Gelato Bar, 140 Campbell Pde. (☎9130 4033 or 9130 3211). You won't be able to resist the delectable display of cakes and tortes ($5-6.50). Gelato Bar also serves a wide variety of chicken and steak dishes ($19.50-22.50), as well as basic sandwiches ($11-13). Takeaway available. Open Su-F 8am-11pm, Sa 8am-midnight. ❸

COOGEE BEACH

Coogee Bay Road provides small cafes and seafood eateries with dinner specials.

Cozzi Cafe, 233 Coogee Bay Rd. (☎9665 6111). The Cozzi has wraps ($7.50), salads ($12.50), and an extensive selection of more complex lunch specials ($11-16). Dinner specials 6-8pm $10-12. Open daily 7am-10pm. ❷

Coogee Cafe, 221 Coogee Bay Rd. (☎9665 5779). This nautical-themed restaurant with small fireplace serves standard mains (fish 'n chips $13.50), as well as cheap early-bird dinner specials for $10. Open daily 8am-10pm. ❷

GLEBE

Glebe Point Road is packed with small bohemian cafes, bakeries, and supermarkets. It's one-stop shopping for all meals cheap, tasty, and Thai, Indian, or Italian (or some interesting combination thereof).

Badde Manors, 37 Glebe Point Rd. (☎9660 3797), at the corner of Francis St. It's the one with plastic angels on the roof. An artsy-grungy vegetarian cafe with gourmet coffee, fresh sorbet, and smoothies. Tofu or lentil burger $9. Delicious daily soup specials $7.50. Dessert cakes $6.50 (try the raved-about sticky date pudding). Open M-Th 7:30am-midnight, F-Sa 7:30am-1am, Su 9am-midnight. No credit cards. ❶

Cafe Otto, 79 Glebe Point Rd. (☎9552 1519). High ceilings, old-fashioned furnace, and heated outdoor courtyard. Everything from popular pastas ($12.50-22) and pizza ($8-20) to meat dishes like calves liver ($16). Separate kids menu $10. Happy Hour 4-7pm; schooners $2.20, cocktails $8. Open Su-Th 9am-11pm, F-Sa 9am-midnight. ❸

The Craven, 166 Glebe Point Rd. (☎9552 2255), next to The Valhalla. A popular spot with outdoor seating for a big hot breakfast ($8-12). Also serves pastas ($11) and a wide-range of blackboard specials, from Mediterranean lamb to T-bone steak ($16). Open daily 7:30am-10:30pm. No credit cards. ❶

NEWTOWN

King St. bisects Newtown and provides backpacker-style cheap eats, from Indian and Thai takeaways to filling espresso-shop breakfast deals. Newtown is a very young and bohemian place—cheap and tasty options are endless.

🏠 **Kilimanjaro African Eatery,** 280 King St. (☎9557 4565), opposite Dendy Cinema. Recreates the flavors of African nations with meals cooked in glazed clay pots and served in a simple dark-wood setting. Filling mains like tangy *yassa* chicken from $10. Appetizers and sides $6. Delicious ginger or flower drink $1.50. BYO. Open daily noon-late. ❷

HE HIDDEN DEAL

SYLVIA'S PIE SHOP

From the road, Sylvia's Uppercrust Pie Shop looks less like a building and more like a mass of yellow banners and green letters with the same message: that their shop has the best pies in NSW. Coming from such a tiny shop—there is room only for 8 people, including outdoor seating—it's a claim that seems easy enough to dismiss.

Except that it's true. And, on weekends, the daunting line of patrons spilling out of the building all the way down the block attests to it. Sylvia's has the awards to back its claims: the shop was the winner of both the 2002 and 2001 Great Aussie Pie Competition held in Melbourne—a very special title in a land that has adopted the pie as its national food. For 17 years, ever since owner Sylvia McGrigor first opened shop, the staff has begun baking at 2am to produce delicious pies with multicultural twists. There's the beef and burgundy pie (a gold medal winner), as well as a range of award-winning curry pies. Just like the shop, which hasn't expanded despite its local fame, the prices of the pies haven't grown too much. The cheapest pies, like the dahl lentil, begin at $4, and prices go up to just $5.50 or the meatiest of pies.

Sylvia's Uppercrust Pie Shop, 1003 Pittwater Rd., just past the intersection with Anzac Rd. ☎9971 5182. Open daily 7am-5pm. ❶

The Peasant's Feast, 121a King St. (☎9516 5998). The restaurant that reforms skeptics of organic food. Delicious, affordable gourmet dishes like kangaroo fillet ($23.50) and octopus and chilled noodle salad ($14.50). BYO. Open M-F for lunch noon-2pm, for dinner daily 6pm-late. ❷

Green Gourmet, 115-117 King St. (☎9519 5123; www.greengourmet.com). A veritable cornucopia of Asian-inspired vegan cuisine awaits inside Green Gourmet. Try a pair of delicious Kumera Ginger Purses (a hearty sweet potato pastry with ginger and vegetable filling, $3) or the Lion King's Clay Pot ($15). Open Su-Th noon-3pm and 6-10pm, F-Sa noon-3pm and 6-11pm. When you're in the area, be sure to check out the neighboring **Vegan's Choice Grocery,** 113 King St. (☎9519 7646). ❷

MANLY & THE NORTHERN BEACHES

In and around Manly, fashionable open-terraced cafes line the beachfront on **South Steyne.** Cheaper eats, including several fast-food chains, can be found on **The Corso.** This buzzing pedestrian mall connects the beachfront to the harbor, and also splits Steyne St. into North and South. Of the beaches further north, **Palm Beach** has the most eating options, with plenty of trendy oceanfront cafes. The listings below are all in Manly. Coles **supermarket** is near the intersection of The Corso and Whistler St. (☎9977 3811. Open daily 6am-midnight.)

Green's Eatery, 1-3 Sydney Rd. (☎9977 1904), on the pedestrian stretch of Sydney Rd. near the ocean. Sunny, vegetarian cafe serves amazingly hearty meals, with rice and interesting vegetable combos for $4-8. Roll-ups $4.70-5.20; salads $3-7. Open daily 8am-7pm. No credit cards. ❶

The Indian Pearl, 26-28 Pittwater Rd. (☎9977 2890), located north of the town center, near the intersection of Pittwater Rd. and Denison St. Meltingly good curry and tandoori dishes include chicken, lamb, and beef ($13-14). The chef's speciality is a tropically flavored Goan fish curry ($15). Takeaway 10% discount. BYO wine only. Free delivery. Live music F-Sa. Open Tu-Su 5:30-11pm. ❸

Blue Water Cafe, 28 South Steyne (☎9976 2051), just below the Corso. One of many trendy oceanfront cafes lining the waterfront South Steyne, Blue Water serves a variety of dependable dishes at a decent price, from fish 'n' chips to Thai-influenced salmon. Entrees $13-15, mains $14-25. 10% surcharge on Su. Open daily 7:30am-10:30pm. ❸

◎ SIGHTS

The main sights of Sydney are truly the city's two **harbors** (Sydney Harbour near Circular Quay and Darling Harbour) and the **green spaces** of the Royal Botanical Gardens, Hyde Park, and the Domain. Each of these merits a day of strolling and perusal. Sydney's neighborhoods do not have specific "sights" per se—their attraction lies in their local nooks. Find adrenaline-fixes and pulse-quickeners in **Activities** (see p. 137) and the best spots for retail-therapy in **Shopping** (see p. 137).

SYDNEY HARBOUR

■**SYDNEY OPERA HOUSE.** Built to look like a fleet of sails full of wind, the Opera House defines all harbor views of Sydney. Designed by Danish architect Jørn Utzon, Sydney's pride and joy took 14 years to construct—a decade longer than originally planned. A saga of bureaucracy and broken budgets characterized the construction, eventually leading the architect to leave the project. Finally opened in 1973, the Opera House has recovered from a rocky start by starring in thousands of tourist photographs daily and hosting operas, ballets, classical concerts, plays, and films—eventually coming to symbolize Sydney itself. The ■**Concert Hall,** which holds a massive pipe organ that took a decade to build, is stunning. *(On Bennelong Point, opposite the base of the Harbour Bridge. ☎9250 7250; www.sydneyoperahouse.com. For box office info, see **Entertainment,** p. 139. 1hr. tours every 30min. daily 9am-5pm. $17, ISIC $10.60, families $41.45.)*

■**SYDNEY HARBOUR BRIDGE.** Spanning the harbor, the arching steel latticework of the massive Harbour Bridge has been a visual symbol of the city, and the best place to get a look at the Harbour and the cityscape, since its opening in 1932. Pedestrians can enter the bridge walkway from a set of stairs on Cumberland St. above Argyle St. in The Rocks. At the bridge's southern pylon, there is an entry on the walkway which leads up to solid photo-ops. The **Harbour Bridge Exhibition** inside the pylon tells the baffling story of the bridge's construction. *(☎9247 7833 for more info. Open daily 10am-5pm. Lookout and museum $5, children $3, families $12.)* For high adventure, **Bridgeclimb** will take you up to the summit for a gut-wrenching view of the city and harbor. Only mildly strenuous and hyper-safe, this offers maximum bragging potential with minimum stress—though it will noticeably lighten your wallet. All potential climbers must first take a Breathalyzer test, so don't hit the pubs beforehand. *(5 Cumberland St. From Argyle St., go all the way up the Argyle Stairs before the bridge at the "bel mundo" sign; turn right onto Cumberland St. ☎8274 7777; www.bridgeclimb.com. Open daily 7am-4:30pm. 3hr. climbs every 10min. Day climbs M-F $145, ages 12-16 $125; Sa-Su $175/$125. Twilight climbs daily $175/$125. Night climbs M-Th and Su $145/$100, $175/$125.)*

CIRCULAR QUAY. Between Dawes Point and Bennelong Point is the departure point for both the city ferry system and numerous private cruise companies. The Quay (KEY) is always a lively hub of tourist activity, with street performers, souvenir shops, and easy access to many major sights. It's also a prime place for those sun-worshippers who find that the concrete jungle of the CBD blocks their rays.

SYDNEY HARBOUR CRUISES. Ferry cruises are a great way to take in the harbor. In addition to Sydney Ferries (see p. 110), **Australian Travel Specialists** books one- to three-hour Harbour cruises from Circular Quay and Darling Harbour. *(Jetty 6, Circular Quay. ☎9247 5151 or 1800 355 537. Depart 9:30am-8pm. From $19.)*

SYDNEY HARBOUR ISLANDS. The **Sydney Harbour National Park** preserves four Harbour islands, several south shore beaches, a few green patches on the northern headlands, and North and South Head. Guided visits to the islands must be booked ahead through the park's info center. *(Info center in Cadman's Cottage, 110 George St., in The Rocks. ☎9247 5033. Open M-F 9:30am-4:30pm, Sa-Su 10am-4:30pm.)* The two most popular tours are the Fort Denison Heritage Tour, which explores the history of the island off Mrs. Macquaries Point *(M-F 11:30am, Sa-Su also 2:30pm; $22)* and the creepy Quarantine Station Ghost Tour, which takes visitors by lantern light to a hospital, cemetery, isolation ward, and mortuary *(W and F-Sa 7:30pm, $22-27.50; no children allowed).* On **Fort Denison Island,** once known as Pinchgut Island, the early colony's most troublesome convicts were isolated on the exposed rock with a diet consisting of only bread and water. On **Goat Island,** near East Balmain, the sandstone gunpowder station and barracks were the site of cruel punishments for the convicts who built them. *(Both islands accessible by guided tour only.)* **Shark Island** (named for its shape), near Rose Bay, and **Clark Island,** near Darling Point, are lovely picnic areas. **Rodd Island,** in Iron Cove near Birkenhead Point, has a colonial-style hall. *(All 3 islands open daily 9am-sunset.)*

THE ROCKS & NORTHERN CITY CENTER

At the southern base of the Harbour Bridge, The Rocks is the touristy site of the original Sydney Town settlement, where living spaces were, at one time, literally chiseled out of the face of the shoreline rock. Built up slowly during the lean years of the colony's founding, the area remained rough-and-tumble into the 1900s. In the 70s, when plans to raze the slums which had grown up here were revealed, a movement to preserve the area began. Street performers and live bands now liven up the Rocks Market (every Sa-Su; see **Shopping,** p. 137). The **Sydney Visitors Centre** and the **Rocks Walking Company** share the white, three-story Sailors' Home at 106 George St. The former has info on local attractions, and the latter conducts informative walking tours of The Rocks. (Visitors Centre ☎9240 8786 or 1800 067 676. Open daily 9am-6pm. Walking Co. ☎9247 6678. 90min. tours depart M-F 10:30am, 12:30, and 2:30pm; Sa-Su 11:30am and 2pm. $16, ages 10-16 and seniors $10.70, under 10 free.)

■**ROYAL BOTANIC GARDENS.** The city center's greenery is concentrated in landscaped plants, flowers, and trees filling 30 edenic hectares around Farm Cove. Daily guided walks begin at a Visitors Centre, in the southeast corner of the park near Art Gallery Rd. Within the gardens, attractions such as the Aboriginal plant trail and the formal rose garden are free, but the **Tropical Centre** greenhouses charge admission. *(Open daily 10am-4pm. $2.20, ISIC $1.10, families $5.50.)* **Government House,** in the northwest corner of the Gardens, served as the home of the governor of New South Wales as recently as 1996. *(☎9931 5222. Grounds open daily 10am-4pm; house tours every 30min. F-Su 10:30am-3pm. Free.)* On the eastern headland of Farm Cove, the Botanic Gardens end at **Mrs. Macquaries Chair.** The chair, which looks like a simple bench carved in the stone, is now a classic Sydney photo-op—though turning the camera around, so that it faces the gorgeous view of the harbor, makes more sense. *(☎9231 8125; www.rbgsyd.nsw.gov.au. Open daily 9:30am-5pm. Gardens open 7am to sunset. Free. 90min. guided walks daily 10:30am; 1hr. lunchtime walks M-F 1pm.)*

MUSEUM OF CONTEMPORARY ART (MCA). The main entrance is on Circular Quay West; entering on George St. puts you on Level 2. Three floors of intriguing, contemporary artwork, with exciting temporary exhibits. *(140 George St. ☎9252 4033. Open daily 10am-5pm. Free.)*

JUSTICE & POLICE MUSEUM. A small but perfectly formed museum dedicated to trends in Sydney crime over the last 150 years, including gruesome murders such as the "Pajama Girl" and "Shark Arm" cases. Includes an old courtroom and prisoner holding cells. On the corner of Albert and Phillip St. *(☎9252 1144; www.hht.nsw.gov.au. Open Sa-Su 10am-5pm. $7, ISIC $3, family $7.)*

MUSEUM OF SYDNEY. You'll have to love history to appreciate the meticulous attention paid to Sydney's social past through artifacts and stylish high-tech multimedia. (*37 Phillip St., at the corner of Bridge St.* ☎*9251 5988; www.hht.net.au. Open daily 9:30am-5pm. $7, ISIC $3, families $17.)*

CITY CENTER

▨ **SYDNEY CENTREPOINT TOWER.** Rising 325m above sea level (and containing four floors of shopping mall), the tower affords a stunning panoramic view of the city and surroundings. The 40-second ride to the top of Australia's highest building is steep in grade and price, so don't waste the trip on a cloudy day. When the sky is clear, views extend as far as the Blue Mountains to the west, the New South Wales central coast to the north, and Wollongong to the south. **Sydney Tower Restaurant ❺**, the city's only revolving restaurant, spins on the second-highest floor. (*100 Market St.* ☎*9223 0933; www.sydneyskytour.com.au. Open Su-F 9am-10:30pm, Sa 9am-11:30pm. $20, ISIC $16, families $55. Restaurant reservations* ☎*8223 3800. Buffet lunch $40, dinner $50. Fixed price menu also available.)*

ART GALLERY OF NEW SOUTH WALES. Sydney's major art museum has a captivating, fresh display of modern art. Its strength lies in its contemporary Australian works, including its extensive Aboriginal and Torres Strait Islander gallery, as well as in its new Asian wing. Bonnard, Picasso, and other big names are also represented. (*Northeast corner of the Domain, on Art Gallery Rd.* ☎*9225 1744; www.artgallery.nsw.gov.au. Open daily 10am-5pm. Free.)*

QUEEN VICTORIA BUILDING. An imposing statue of Queen Victoria guards the main entrance to this lavish building. The Romanesque edifice was constructed in 1898 as a home for the plebeian city markets, but recent renovations have brought in four floors of ritzy shopping venues. Fortunately, a stroll in the fantastically tiled and carpeted interior still doesn't cost a cent. (*455 George St.* ☎*9265 6855; www.qvb.com.au. Open M-W and F-Sa 9am-6pm, Th 9am-9pm, Su 11am-5pm. Guided tours M-Sa 11:30am and 2:30pm, Su noon and 2:30pm; $8.)*

TOWN HALL. Sydney's age ensures that architecture in the center is far from uniformly modern. The Italian Renaissance-style Town Hall was built in the prosperity of the late 1800s. The building is important today as a performance venue. (*483 George St.* ☎*9265 9007. Open daily 9am-5pm. Free.)*

HYDE PARK. Between Elizabeth and College St. at the eastern edge of the city center, Hyde Park was set aside in 1810 by Governor Lachlan Macquarie and is still Sydney's most structured public green space, complete with fountains and stately trees. A buzzing urban oasis during the day, the park warrants some caution for those strolling at night. In the southern half, below Park St., the Art Deco-style **ANZAC Memorial** commemorates the service of the Australian and New Zealand Army Corps in WWI, as well as all Australians who have fought in war. (☎*9267 7668. Open M-Tu and Th-Su 9am-5pm, W 1-5pm.)* To the park's east sits the Neo-Gothic **St. Mary's Cathedral.** The structure was first erected in 1833, burned to the ground in 1865, and completed again in 1928. The originally-planned two Gothic towers on the southern end were constructed in 2000. An exhibit placed awkwardly in the crypt gives an informative account of the cathedral's place in a modern city. (☎*9220 0400. Crypt open daily 10am-4pm. Admission $5, photography permit $2. Tours Su noon after mass or by arrangement.)*

AUSTRALIAN MUSEUM. The creatively titled museum houses a unique mix of natural and indigenous cultural history. Stuffed recreations of prehistoric Australian "megafauna" cast shadows over popular Aussie animals such as the koala and kangaroo. Though the science exhibits are fun for kids, the museum is fascinating

THE INSIDER'S CITY

SYDNEY OLYMPIC PARK

The impressively huge Homebush Bay Olympic Site, 14km west of the city center along the Parramatta River, is where most events of the 2000 Games took place. To get to Homebush Bay, take a CityRail train to "Olympic Park Station." Contact the Sydney Olympic Park Visitors Centre for information on tours and to book facilities (☎9714 7888; www.sydneyolympicpark.com.au).

1 Take a tour or catch a rugby match at **Telstra Stadium.** With 80,000 seats, it's the largest Olympic Stadium to date.

2 Stop to swim a few laps at the **Aquatic Centre,** arguably the site's best facility, made famous by the 38 Olympic and 15 world records broken in it at the 2000 Games.

3 Dry off with a round of tennis (watching or playing) at the sprawling **Tennis Centre.**

4 End your tour with a picnic and a hike at the 100-hectare **Bicentennial Park.**

for all ages. Free Internet in the "Search and Discover" wing. (6 College St., on the east side of Hyde Park. ☎9320 6000; www.amonline.net.au. Open daily 9:30am-5pm. $8, ages 5-15 $3, under 5 free, families $19. Special and temporary exhibits cost extra, up to $7.)

THE DOMAIN. Between the buildings on Macquarie St. and the Art Gallery, the grassy expanse of the Domain stretches east along the south edge of the Royal Botanic Gardens. Concerts fill the area during January's **Sydney Festival** (see p. 141). During the rest of the year, the park is most popular for picnics and informal footy games, as well as the Sunday-morning **Speakers' Corner,** a low-key version of London's traditional weekly public speaking in the park.

BARRACKS MUSEUM. A small, unusual display of artifacts from the days of convict immigration is housed in this eerie building, once a barracks, women's immigration depot, and asylum. Visitors can lie in convicts' hammocks and search for convict ancestors on a computer database. (In Queens Sq., on Macquarie St. ☎9223 8922; www.hht.net.au. Open daily 9:30am-5pm. $7, students with ID $3, families $17.)

SYDNEY HOSPITAL & NSW PARLIAMENT HOUSE. The 3-building complex of the Parliament House, Hospital, and Royal Mint, was once the Rum Hospital. The 1814 hospital building is a landmark of colonial architecture; the central section is still the main medical center. Visitors are welcome into the **NSW Parliament House,** the Rum Hospital's former north wing. Access to public viewing galleries granted during parliamentary sessions and free tours. (Parliament faces Macquarie St. between Martin Pl. and Hunter St. ☎9230 3444. Open M-F 9:30am-4pm. Free admission. Book ahead for tours when Parliament is not in session or for Parliamentary session viewing.)

DARLING HARBOUR

The site of several events of the XXVII Olympiad, Darling Harbour, on the west side of the city center, is a popular tourist stop reminiscent of Disneyland, with immaculate brick walkways, trams, squealing children, and opportunities to spend money. The concentration of tourist attractions in this small area makes it a perfect outing for afternoon sightseeing and a popular spot for families. On foot, Darling Harbour is five minutes from Town Hall Station. Follow George St. toward Circular Quay, then turn left on Market St. to Pyrmont Bridge. Bus #888 approaches Darling Harbour from Circular Quay by way of Town Hall, and ferries run from Circular Quay to the Aquarium steps. For transport as tourist-oriented as the destination, hop on the **monorail** from Pitt St., at Park or Market St. in the CBD.

⊠ SYDNEY AQUARIUM. Over 11,000 marine animals from Australia's many aquatic regions inhabit the tanks on the pier at Darling Harbour's eastern shore. If you need more evidence that Australia has the weirdest fauna on earth, stop at the mudskipper containment where these freaks of the fish world display their ability to live out of water by absorbing moisture from the air. More conventional attractions include the recently-opened Great Barrier Reef exhibit, a penguin pool, a seal pool, and a small touching pool. The underwater Oceanariums, three plexiglass walking tunnels below street level featuring huge enclosures of fish, sharks, and stingrays, help justify the pricey admission. (On Aquarium Pier. ☎ 9262 2300; www.sydneyaquarium.com.au. Open daily 9am-10pm; last entry 9pm. Seal sanctuary closes at sunset. $23, ages 3-15 $11, under 3 free, families of 5 $49.)

⊠ POWERHOUSE MUSEUM. Give yourself plenty of time for this gigantic museum, which explores the breadth of a vague, potentially boundless topic: human ingenuity. Exhibits, interactive displays, and demos focus on technology and applied science. (500 Harris St., just south of Darling Harbour between Ultimo and Haymarket St. ☎ 9217 0444; www.phm.gov.au. Open daily 10am-5pm. $10, students $3, ages 5-15 $3, under 5 free, families $23.)

CHINESE GARDEN. This serene garden was a bicentennial gift to New South Wales from her sister province in Guangdong, China. The delicately manicured plot in traditional southern Chinese style provides a sheltered break from the hubbub of the city. You can dress up as an emperor or empress for free at the **Chinese Royalty Costume Shop,** though permission to take photos costs $10. (On the corner of Harbour and Pier St. ☎ 9281 6863. Open daily 10am-4:30pm; teahouse open noon-4:30pm. $4.50, ages 4-15 $2, families $10.)

STAR CITY CASINO. A twinkling $1.2 billion complex entices the punters 24/7 with lucky seven restaurants, seven bars, a nightclub, plastic trees, an indoor waterfall, 5-star hotel, and an endless (okay, a mere 145,000 square meters) gaming room with 1500 poker machines and 160 gaming tables. The casino, in existence since 1997, can be accessed by light rail or shuttle bus to the casino or monorail to Harbourside. (80 Pyrmont St., Pyrmont. ☎ 9777 9000. Open daily 24hrs.)

INNER EAST

The suburbs just east of the city center are some of Sydney's most vibrant areas for shopping, eating, and meandering. Although Kings Cross tends to be a bit seedy, the neighborhood is not without a certain vibrance and charm to travelers. Oxford St. slides through Surry Hills, Darlinghurst, and Paddington with a seemingly endless array of cafes, boutiques, and hip houseware outlets. Sydney's sizeable gay community inhabits much of this strip, especially Darlinghurst. Buses #378, 380, and 382 run the length of Oxford St., connecting the city center to the eastern suburbs.

SYDNEY JEWISH MUSEUM. Designed around a staircase in the shape of the star of David, this museum is a modest but moving exhibition of Australia's Jewish heritage and the horrors of the Holocaust. It's run entirely by volunteers, many of whom are Holocaust survivors who work as informative guides to the museum's seven levels (148 Darlinghurst Rd., at the corner of Burton St. ☎ 9360 7999. Open Su-Th 10am-4pm, F 10am-2pm. $10, children $6, families $22.)

MOORE PARK. South of Paddington, Moore Park contains the **Sydney Football Stadium** and the city's major **cricket oval** (see **Sports and Recreation,** p. 15). For a tour of the Stadium and a small museum of Aussie sports history, call **Sportspace.** (☎ 9380 0383. Tours M-F 10am and 1pm on non-game days. $19.50, concessions $13.)

NEW SOUTH WALES

NORTH SHORE

The Lower North Shore, between Sydney Harbour and Middle Harbour, is primarily home to wealthy Sydneysiders. Its residential neighborhoods and upscale boutiques are lovely but don't draw many travelers—with the exception of Mosman, which holds Taronga Park Zoo. The popular Northern Beaches start in the lively surfing suburb of Manly after the Spit Bridge, which crosses Middle Harbour, and run up the coast to Palm Beach.

MOSMAN & MIDDLE HARBOUR. Mosman is best known for the **Taronga Park Zoo**, at the end of Bradley's Head Rd., where the animals enjoy amazing views of Sydney Harbour thanks to the zoo's hilltop position. The impressive collection contains animals from all over Australia and the world; the photo opportunities with the koalas and giraffes are especially popular. Admission includes an enclosed chair-lift safari ride, often considered the best part of a visit. To reach the zoo, take a 12min. ferry ride from Circular Quay, an attraction by itself. (☎9969 2777; www.zoo.nsw.gov.au. Open daily 9am-5pm. $25, students $17.50; families $65. A Zoopass, purchased at Circular Quay, covers admission, ferry, and bus; $28.40, child $14.30. Parking $10.)

Near Mosman, the boat-filled Middle Harbour is particularly beautiful around the **Spit Bridge,** which has several seafood restaurants and kayak rental stores. The picturesque **Balmoral Beach** is popular with North Shore families.

MANLY. It seems fitting that there's no train access to Manly, since the gorgeous **ferry ride** from Circular Quay sets the tone for the oceanside suburb, whose major sights and activities are all water-related. The 30min. ride goes by the Opera House and Kirribilli House, the Prime Minister's Sydney residence, and ends at Manly Wharf. The **Visitors Centre** (☎9977 1088; open M-F 9am-5pm, Sa-Su 10am-4pm) is in front of the wharf near the enclosed swimming area of **Manly Cove.** The cove is the starting point of the famous **Manly to Spit walk.** The 9.5km walk (3hr.) offers uncluttered harbor coastline, sandy beaches, national park, and bayside homes. From the Spit Bridge, bus #144 and 143 return to Manly and run to Sydney.

Oceanworld, on the West Esplanade at Manly Cove, is very modest compared to the Sydney Aquarium, but has a shark tunnel where you can dive, as well as a show about Australia's dangerous animals 3 times a day. (☎9949 2644. Open daily 10am-5:30pm. $16, concessions $11, children $8; families $25-40. Admission reduced 15% after 3:30pm. Shark feeding M, W, F 11pm. 30min. Xtreme shark dive $195 for uncertified divers, $150 certified; includes admission.) **The Corso,** a pedestrian street lined with cheap cafes and fast food joints, can take you from the cove and wharf area to the popular surfing area of **Manly Beach.** Off the Corso is the pedestrian part of **Sydney Road,** which turns into an arts and crafts marketplace on the weekends.

NORTHERN BEACHES. A string of popular surfing beaches line the Pacific Ocean above Manly. Most are also suitable for families because they have beach pools or areas with calm water. **Dee Why Beach** is about 4km north of Manly, just below surf-friendly **Collaroy Beach** and **Narrabean Beach.** Crowds flock to **Newport Beach,** as well as to stunning **Avalon Beach,** chosen as the set for "Baywatch" until locals balked. Northernmost **Palm Beach,** the gem of the Northern beaches, acts as the set of the popular Aussie soapie "Home and Away." There is no train access to the Northern Beaches. To get there, take the Northern Beach express bus L88 or L90 from the city; change at Warringah Mall for Manly services. Bus #183, 187, 188, 189, 190, and 151 originate at Wynyard Station (Carrington St. side), and will also get you there. Or, take a ferry to Manly, and catch bus #151, 155, or 157. The website www.sydneybeaches.com.au provides useful info.

⚫ ACTIVITIES

WATER SPORTS

SAILING. On any sunny day, white sails can be seen clipping across the waters. **East Sail Sailing School,** at d'Albora Marina on Rushcutters Bay, caters to all experience levels and offers intimate courses and trips. (Follow William St. until it merges with Bayswater Rd., then turn left on Beach Rd. ☎9327 1166; www.east-sail.com.au. 2½hr. yacht trips depart daily 10am; 2-12 passengers. $89, includes morning tea. Full intro sailing course from $425.) **Sydney by Sail** runs intro sailing lessons from the National Maritime Museum. (☎9280 1110; www.sydneyby-sail.com. 8-12 person max. 3hr. harbor sail to Port Jackson $120. Full intro course $450. Book ahead.)

SURFING. While **Bondi** is Sydney's famous surfing beach, **Manly** and the more secluded **Northern Beaches** (including Freshwater, Curl Curl, Dee Why, Collaroy, Narrabeen, Newport, and Avalon) are better options. The **Manly Surf School,** at the North Steyne Surf Club at Manly Beach and at the Lifeguard Pavilion in Palm Beach, gives lessons to surfers of all skill levels. (☎9977 6977; www.manlysurf-school.com. Open for lessons Oct.-Apr. M-F 9-11am, 11am-1pm, and 4-6pm, Sa-Su 9-11am, 11:30am-1:30pm, and 2-4pm; May-Sept. M-F 11am-1pm, Sa-Su 9-11am, 11:30am-1:30pm, and 2-4pm. One lesson $50; 5-day $160; 10-day $250. Private lessons $80 per hr.; prices include wetsuit and board. Bookings essential.) In Manly, **Aloha Surf,** 44 Pittwater Rd., rents boards and wetsuits. (☎9977 3777. Open M-W and F-Sa 9am-6:30pm, Th 9am-8pm, Su 9am-6pm. Short and long boards half-day $20, full-day $40; bodyboards $20.) **Bondi Surf Co.,** 72-76 Campbell Pde., rents surfboards and bodyboards with wetsuits. (☎9365 0870. Open daily 9am-6pm. 2hr. $25, full-day $50. Credit card or passport required.)

BEACHES. World-class beaches are an integral part of Sydney. Most beaches are packed during the summer, though the Northern beaches are more secluded and offer great surfing.

BEACH	FEATURES	TAKE BUS
SOUTH		
Bondi	"A-list" beach. Surfing makes the postcards.	380, 382, L82
Tamarama	"Glamarama" is just beneath Bondi. Strong undertow.	380, 382, L82
Bronte	Quiet, family beach with strong undertow.	378
Coogee	Bondi's young rival, often just as packed. Good ocean pools.	372, 373, X73, X74
Maroubra	Locals' beach gaining in popularity. Great surf.	375, 377, 395, 396, X75
NORTH		
Balmoral	Quiet, elegant harbor beach is good for kids.	233, 238
Manly	Relaxed, popular beach with fantastic surfing.	144, 143, or Manly ferry
Collaroy	Attracts families and surfers, with sand running to Narrabeen.	187-190, E83-89, L88
Avalon	Beautiful spot almost chosen as set of "Baywatch."	188, 190, L88, L90, E88
Palm Beach	Glam set of TV soap "Home and Away."	190, L90

JETBOATING & DIVING. Several jetboat companies take poncho-clad passengers on adventure rides in Darling and Sydney Harbours. Come for the exhilarating ride rather than gorgeous harbor views; the boat will be spinning, turning, and braking too fast for you to notice them. **Sydney Jet,** located in Cockle Bay Wharf, Darling Harbour, is one of the cheapest options. (☎9982 4000. 40min. "Jet Thrill" ride departs daily every hr. from 10am; $55, children under 14 $35. 55min. "Adventure Thrill" ride departs Sa-Su 10 and 11am; $70/$50. For a more leisurely, pictur-esque ride, see **Harbour Cruises** (p. 131). **ProDive** has excellent advice on local diving spots, gear, and certification courses. (CBD: 478 George St. ☎9264 6177 or 1800 820 820. Manly: 169 Pittwater Rd. ☎9977 5966. Coogee: 27 Alfreda St. ☎9665 6333. Open M-W and F-Su 9am-5:30pm, Th 9am-6pm, until 8pm for George St. location. 4-day courses from $248; trips and courses for other Australian locations can be arranged. Double-dive boat and gear $169; just gear $109.)

FISHING & WHALE-WATCHING. A number of charter boats run guided deep-sea **fishing** trips; groups get cheaper rates. **Whale watching season** is from June-July and Sept.-Oct. **Halicat**, 410 Elizabeth St., Surry Hills., has both fishing and whale watch-ing tours for up to 23 people running from Rose Bay and Cremorne. (☎9280 3043. Trips depart 6:30am and return mid-afternoon. Reef fishing $110. Sport fishing trips (these go farther out and find bigger fish) $200. Whale watching 3½hr. week-end trips $60, seniors and students $50, children $40.) **Zane Grey** offers similar rates. (☎9565 4949 or 0412 225 201. Trips depart 7am and return mid-afternoon. Reef fishing $110; sport fishing $240.) Award-winning **Broadbill** runs a smaller operation (their boat holds six) at competitive prices from Sans Souci Wharf. (☎9534 2378. Trips depart 7am and return 5-6pm. Sport fishing $170-200.)

SCENIC WALKS

SYDNEY'S BEST CITY & COASTAL WALKS

Opera House to Mrs. Maquaries Point. This 20min. stroll along the edge of the lush Royal Botanic Gardens gives one of the best views of the Opera House and the boat-filled harbor at Farm Cove.

Across the Harbour Bridge. You can cross the Harbour Bridge for free by foot, beginning in The Rocks near Argyle St. Once across the bridge in Kirribilli, walk downhill on Broughton St. for a spectacular harbor view.

Hyde Park to Darling Harbour. A 15min. walk down Market St. from either end will take you through the heart of the city, and right by the Centrepoint Tower, Pitt Street Mall, Strand Arcade, Queen Victoria Building, and numerous designer shops.

Oxford Street to King's Cross. Beginning at the southeastern edge of Hyde Park, walk down proudly gay Oxford St., and turn onto Darlinghurst Rd. You'll see chic outdoor cafes and, once across William St., will land right in the seedy, pumping heart of King's Cross.

Bondi to Coogee. This 1hr. coastal stroll will take you along cliffs and through a cemetery for good views of Sydney's best Southern Beaches (see below).

Manly to Spit. This slightly strenuous 3hr. coastal walk will give you a taste of bushland and the Northern Beaches (see below).

Mosman to Cremorne Wharf. A picturesque 40min. walk along the harbor fore-shore between two ferry wharves. Bring your cossies—the world's prettiest har-borside pool is en route, and open to the public year-round.

WALKING TOURS. Walking tours of The Rocks depart from the Visitors Centre, 106 George St. (☎9247 6678; see p. 111.) Additionally, **Unseen Sydney** conducts 1½hr. evening walking tours entitled "History, Convicts, and Murder Most Foul," which include a complimentary drink from the historic Hero of Waterloo's cellar. (☎9907 8057. Tu and Th-Sa 6:30pm. $20, students $16.) The **Original Sydney Walking Tours** runs five different tours delving into the sensational past of The Rocks and Kings Cross. (☎0413 139 162. $16, students $12.)

AIR ADVENTURES

SKYDIVING. Skydiving in Australia is cheaper than anywhere else. **Sydney Skydivers,** 77 Wentworth Ave., takes tandem divers on a half-day trip to Sydney's highest skydive. (☎9280 4355; www.sydneyskydivers.com.au. From $275.) **Simply Skydive Australia** offers similar services, with dives up to 13,000 ft. (☎9970 5037. From $275.)

SCENIC FLIGHTS. For aerial views of Sydney without having to plummet towards it, a couple places offer scenic flights around Sydney and environs. **Sydney Air Scenic Flights** runs from the Bankstown Airport. (☎9790 0628. Sydney Harbour or Blue Mountains 1hr. $335 for 5 people.) **Dakota National Air** also operates out of the Bankstown airport. (☎9791 9900 or 1800 246 747; www.dakota-air.com. Sa night 1hr. Sydney Harbour "Lights Flight" with champagne supper $159. Su morning 45min. "Scenic Coastal" flight from Palm Beach to Bondi $120.

🔲 ENTERTAINMENT

MUSIC & THEATER

The iconic **Sydney Opera House** is the lynchpin of Sydney's creative culture and its primary venue. With five stages (described below), the Opera House nimbly hosts a variety of the city's artistic endeavors. (Box office for all venues ☎9250 7777; www.sydneyoperahouse.com.au. Open M-Sa 9am-8:30pm, Su 2hr. prior to show only for ticket pick-up. Doors close at showtime. Student rush ticket policy differs from company to company; contact each one for information.)

- **Concert Hall.** The 2679-seat Concert Hall, the most majestic of the Opera House's stages, is the primary venue for symphony, chamber, and orchestral music performances. **Sydney Symphony Orchestra** (☎9334 4644; www.symphony.org.au) and the innovative **Australian Chamber Orchestra** (☎9357 4111; www.aco.com.au) perform here throughout the year. Call for ticket info.

- **Opera Theatre.** The excellent **Opera Australia** (☎9699 1099, tickets 9319 1088; www.opera-australia.org) performs here. Reserved seats range from $83-180 and sell out fast, even though there are 1547 of them. Partial-view seats (the seats block the stage) start at $43. Standing room and listening-only are $33 and are available only over-the-counter from 9am the morning of the performance; limit 2 per person. Leftover tickets are sometimes sold 30min. before showtime on performance night as student rush tickets for $33 (ISIC required). Doors close promptly at showtime—be sure to arrive on time. The **Australian Ballet Company** (☎1300 36 97 41; www.australianballet.com.au) and the **Sydney Dance Company** (☎9221 4811; www.sydneydance.com.au) share the same theater space. Call for ticket prices and info.

- **Drama Theatre.** This theater seats 544 frequently stars the **Sydney Theatre Company** (☎9250 1777; www.sydtheatreco.com/~exstce). Theater seats 544. Advance seating from $50, standing room tickets $25 available 1hr. prior to show, student rush tickets from $15 available 30min. prior to show.

- **Playhouse Theatre.** A traditional round-stage forum with 398 seats. Contact the **Bell Shakespeare Company** (☎9241 2722; bellshakespeare@orangemail.com.au) for information on which of Will's classics they might be presenting.

- **Studio Stage.** This catch-all, transformable stage seats 318 and exhibits less traditional Opera House offerings, including cabaret shows and contemporary performances.

Sydney's daily **live music** scene consists largely of local cover bands casting their pearls for free before pub crowds. The *Metro* section of the Friday *Sydney Morning Herald* and free weeklies such as *Beat* and *Sydney City Hub* contain listings for upcoming shows, along with info on art showings, movies, theater, and DJ appearances city-wide. Major concerts are held in the **Sydney Entertainment Centre,** on Harbour St., Haymarket (☎9320 4200; www.sydentcent.com.au; box office open M-F 9am-5pm, Sa 10am-1pm); the **Hordern Pavilion,** in Moore Park; and the **Enmore Theatre,** 130 Enmore Rd., Newtown (☎9550 3666). The *Metro* section of the Friday *Sydney Morning Herald* and free weeklies like *Beat* and *Sydney City Hub* have listings, along with info on art showings, movies, theater, and DJ appearances city-wide.

SPECTATOR SPORTS

Like Australians everywhere, Sydneysiders are sports mega-fans. All events below sell tickets through **Ticketek** (☎9266 4800; www.ticketek.com.au) and are played in stadiums in Moore Park, accessible by bus #349, 373, 393, and 395. The main number for all the stadiums is at the Cricket Ground. (☎1300 724 737; www.sydney-cricketground.com.au.) See **Sports,** p. 15.

Cricket. To some, the cricketers are men wearing white straw hats and sweater vests; to others, they're gods. Decide for yourself at the **Sydney Cricket Ground,** on Moore Park Rd. Tickets $10-40, depending upon the game.

Rugby League. The **Sydney Football Stadium,** on the corner of Driver Ave. and Moore Park Rd., is home to the **Sydney City Roosters.** It draws rowdy, fiercely loyal fans throughout the winter season and in Sept. for the Telstra Premiership. Tickets $17-25. Children receive discounts.

Australian Rules Football. This head-crushing, uniquely Aussie game is also held at the Sydney Football Stadium. Root for the home team: the not-so-delicate **Sydney Swans.** Tickets cost more and are harder to get than rugby tickets ($20-60).

CINEMAS

Sydney's film scene contains a variety of independent movie houses, as well as mainstream cinemas showing American schlockbusters. Tuesdays are often **bargain day**—tickets are half price. The rest of the week, prices hover around $13-14 and $10-11 for children. Call **Movieline** (☎13 27 00) for showtimes at all cinemas. For info on the **Sydney Film Festival,** see p. 141.

Dendy Cinemas, 2 East Circular Quay (☎9247 3800; www.dendy.com.au); 19 Martin Pl. (☎9233 8166), 261-263 King St., Newtown (☎9550 5699). All locations show quality films of artsy ilk. Open daily noon-9pm; bar closes at midnight.

Govinda's, 112 Darlinghurst Rd., (☎9360 7853) Darlinghurst. Shows 2 well-acclaimed contemporary films per day in a cushion-filled lounge, and throws in an all-you-can eat vegetarian buffet (see **Food,** p. 125).

Valhalla, 166 Glebe Point Rd., (☎9552 2456 or 9660 8050), Glebe. Possibly the best independent cinema in the city. Valhalla's got two theaters and a busy schedule. Hosts the **International Animation Festival** in mid-July and sometimes has concerts.

Panasonic IMAX Cinema (☎9281 3300), Southern Promenade, Darling Harbour. The eight-story-high movie screen is the largest in the world. A different film is shown every hour. Open daily 10am-10pm.

Hoyts Centre, 505-525 George St. (☎9273 7431). The largest mainstream cinema, located midway between Chinatown and the CBD.

SHOPPING

Sydneysiders love to shop, and the city's numerous department stores, designer boutiques, factory outlets, and vintage stores make it easy for them. Fittingly, Sydney's commercial heart, the **CBD**, is also its shopping epicenter. Designer names like Chanel, Versace, and Louis Vuitton line **Castlereagh Street,** while department stores like **David Jones,** on Market and Castlereagh St., and **Grace Bros,** 436 George St., link to the **Pitt Street Mall** (see **Malls** below). **The Rocks** holds small, upscale boutiques on Argyle and George St. geared toward tourists, as well as a weekend market (see Markets below). **Paddington** has pricey boutiques on Oxford St., while mellow **Newtown** has the best selection of secondhand clothing stores along King St. **Leichhardt,** Sydney's Little Italy, has fine Italian shoes and clothing on Norton St. Shopaholics should pick up a free copy of *Sydney Shopping: The Official Guide* from The Rocks' Visitors Centre.

MALLS. Sydney's hardest-to-miss shopping spot is **Pitt Street Mall,** several pedestrian-only blocks on Pitt St. lined with shopping complexes like **Mid City Centre, Westfield Centrepoint, Skygarden,** and **Sydney Central Plaza.** For high-end shopping in elegant, old-world style, head to the ornate **Strand Arcade** and **Queen Victoria Building** (see p. 133). Both these shopping arcades feature upmarket Australian designer boutiques, ranging from the hypercolored Ken Done in the QVB to high fashion labels like Bettina Liano, Alannah Hill, and Third Millennium in the Strand. In Darling Harbour, **Harbourside** has Australian homewares; in Haymarket, **Market City** holds factory outlets and the famous Paddy's Market (see below).

MARKETS. Sydney's year-round weekend markets tend to specialize in arts, crafts, and souvenirs. **Paddington Markets,** 395 Oxford St., is Sydney's best known and liveliest market, featuring entertainment, food, and a variety of clothing and crafts. (Open Sa 10am-4pm.) **Paddy's Markets,** under Market City in Haymarket, is legendary and as old as the city itself. The goods on sale here are always cheap but only sometimes of good quality. (Open Th 10am-6pm, F-Su 9am-4:30pm.) **The Rocks Market,** at the north end of George St. under the bridge, is more touristy and upmarket, with antiques, jewelry, and collectibles, as well as street performers and live musicians. (Open rain or shine Sa-Su 10am-5pm.) **Sydney Opera House Markets,** at Bennelong Point at Circular Quay, is more spread-out but just as touristy. (Open Su 9am-5pm.) The hip **Bondi Beach Market,** at Bondi Beach Public School on Campbell Pde., features locally made arts and crafts. (Open Su 10am-4pm, weather permitting.) **Glebe Markets,** at Glebe Public School, on the corner of Glebe Point Rd. and Derby Pl., sells new and second-hand crafts and amazing clothes by talented young designers. (Sa 10am-4pm, weather permitting.)

⚡ FESTIVALS

Sydney Festival, throughout Jan. (☎8248 6500; www.sydneyfestival.org.au). Features arts and entertainment events. Check the *Daily Telegraph* for details on free concerts in The Domain, street theater in The Rocks, and fireworks in Darling Harbour.

Tropfest, last Su in Feb. (☎9368 0434; www.tropfest.com.au). World's largest short film festival screens in The Domain, Royal Botanic Gardens, and cafes along Victoria St.

Gay and Lesbian Mardi Gras, Mar. (☎9557 4332; www.mardigras.com.au). This huge international event is always rip-roaring, no-holds-barred good time. The festival climaxes on its final day with a parade attended annually by over 500,000 people and a gala party at the RAS Show Ground in Moore Park. Though the party is restricted and the guest list fills up way, way ahead of time, travelers can get on the list by becoming "International Members of Mardi Gras" well in advance. Intl. Membership $60, tickets around $110, concession $55.

Royal Agricultural Society's Easter Show, Apr. (☎9704 1111; www.eastershow.com.au). Held at Sydney Olympic Park. The carnival atmosphere and rides make it fun even for those with no interest in farming.

Sydney Film Festival, mid-June (☎9660 3844; www.sydfilm-fest.com.au). The ornate State Theatre, 49 Market St., between George and Pitt St., and Dendy Opera Quays showcase documentaries, retrospectives, and art films from around the world. The festival tours Australia throughout the year.

City to Surf Run, Aug. (☎9282 3606). Draws 50,000 contestants for a semi-serious 14km trot from Park St to Bondi Beach. Some are world-class runners; others treat the race as a lengthy pub crawl. Entries ($25) are accepted up to race day.

Manly Jazz Festival, Oct. (☎9977 1088). Australia's biggest jazz festival, featuring all types of national and international artists.

Bondi Beach Party, Dec. 25 each year. Bondi sets the pace for debauchery all along the coast as people from around the world gather for a foot-stomping Christmas party.

Sydney-to-Hobart Yacht Race, Dec. 26 each year. Brings the city's hungover attention back to civilized entertainment.

▚ NIGHTLIFE

Whether they're out on the town dancing or huddling around a pub TV for the latest sports telecast, many Sydneysiders hit the pub and club scene up to four or five times per week. Different neighborhoods have distinctly different scenes, and the scenes vary from night to night. The dress code tends to be "smart casual" in the clubs, meaning no shorts or sandals, and trendy sneakers only.

The city center of Sydney is a bit more upscale and exclusive, particularly in the suit-filled CBD and the trendy Darling Harbour. The Rocks is more laid-back, although still pricey. Bars in Kings Cross attract a sizeable straight male contingent which quickly spills over from the strip joints into the pubs and dance clubs. Backpackers round out the mix in this neighborhood, giving several spots an international feel. **Gay and lesbian** Sydney struts its stuff on Oxford St., Sydney's hottest nightspot—in Darlinghurst and Paddington, as well as in Newtown. Some establishments are specifically gay or lesbian and many others are mixed. Because the gay clubs provide much of the city's best dance music, flocks of young, beautiful clubbers of all persuasions fill any extra space on the vibrant, vampy dance floors. Taylor Square, at the intersection of Oxford, Flinders, and Bourke St., is the heart of this district. For more casual pub crawling, wander on Bourke and Flinders St. in Surry Hills. Large **student populations** in Glebe and Newtown make for a younger crowd and cheaper drinks on special nights at pubs here. Manly holds up the North Shore's end of the nightlife equation, with a range of options for the more chill party-goer.

The bible of the Sydney clubber is *3-D World* (www.threedworld.com.au), a free Tuesday publication that can be found in hostels, music stores, and trendy clothing stores. Look for the free *Streetpress* or *The Revolver*, which highlight the weekly hotspots for shaking your groove thang; *Drum Media* covers music. *Sx News* (www.sxnews.com.au) and *Sydney Star Observer* (www.sonet.com.au) focus on the gay community.

CITY CENTER

▨ **Three Wise Monkeys,** 555 George St. (☎9283 5855), at the corner of George St. and Liverpool St. Twenty-somethings pack 3 intimate, red-swathed levels of bars. Daily live music on the top level starting at 10pm. Schooners $4.30. No cover. Open Su-Th 10am-3am, F-Sa until 4am.

▨ **The Basement,** 29 Reiby Pl. (☎9251 2797). Arguably the hottest live music venue in the CBD, with acts ranging from jazz to rock. Schooners $5.50. Cover ranges from $10 to $50 for the most exclusive acts. Open daily noon-3pm for lunch and 7:30pm-late.

Jackson's on George, 176 George St. (☎9247 2727), near Circular Quay. Four swanky levels hold 6 bars, as well as a dance club, games, and restaurant. "Stik" drinks ($9) pack a punch with fresh fruit, ice, and spirits. Happy Hour F-Sa 5-7pm. Schooners $4. Cover F-Sa $10 after 10pm. Open M-Th 9am-late, F 9am-6am, Sa-Su 10am-6am.

Cheers Sports Bar, 561 George St. (☎9261 8313), at the corner of George St. and Liverpool St., near Three Wise Monkeys. When a game's on, this usually chill sports bar gets rowdy. A mixture of backpackers and locals hits the relaxed dance club downstairs. Schooners $4.10. No cover. Open Su-Th 10am-5:30am, Sa-Su until 6am.

Scubar, 4 Rawson Pl. (☎9212 4244; www.scubar.com.au), in the YHA basement, 1min. from Central Station walking toward George St. Pool competitions, big screen cable TVs, and the ever-popular M night hermit crab racing bring backpackers over from next door in droves. Not really a place to meet Sydneysiders, but a mecca for international travelers. Open M-F noon-late, Sa-Su 5pm-late.

DARLING HARBOUR

If you thought Darling Harbour was just a touristy playground with sharks, come back at night. When the sun goes down, family-oriented Darling Harbour gets surprisingly ready to party.

🔲 Slip Inn, 111 Sussex St. (☎9299 2199). A refreshing break from the pretentiousness of venues like Tank and Cargo. Slip Inn's bar area includes a ground-level bar and pool area, chill courtyard, and downstairs sandbar. Schooners $3.80, cocktails $12. Its underground streetwear-only nightclub, Chinese Laundry, plays hard techno trance on "Technical" F and forward-thinking house on "Good Vibrations" Sa. Club cover F $12; Sa $5 before 10pm, $18 after. Open M-Th 11am-midnight, F 11am-4pm, Sa 6pm-2am.

Home, 101 Cockle Bay Wharf (☎9266 0600). This UK-inspired nightclub hit Sydney with a vengeance. The scene is ultra-trendy and very happening—be prepared for huge lines to get in. The cover charge is steep, but it remains a popular place. F-Sa 4 dance floors and 15 DJs have the place grinding with everything from disco to break-beat 11pm-7am. Cover $25.

Cargo Bar, 52-60 The Promenade, King St. Wharf (☎9262 1777), at the corner of King St. and Lime St. Crowds of smartly dressed people flock to the lower level of Cargo Bar, where an outdoor terrace next to the harbor and instrumental house music await them. Later on, the upstairs level is exclusively for a few select trendy people. Schooners $3.90-5.40, cocktails $14. Open M-Th noon-midnight, F-Sa noon-5am.

Pontoon Bar, 201 Sussex St., The Promenade, Cockle Bay Wharf (☎9267 7099), right at the bridge. The entire bar is an open terrace right on the harbor. Slightly more casual than Cargo, with a younger, rowdier crowd. Schmitties $3-5, cocktails $13-14. Open Su-Th noon-1am, F-Sa noon-4am.

THE ROCKS

🔲 The Observer Hotel, 69 George St. (☎9252 4169). A mixed crowd packs this popular pub in the heart of The Rocks. Good live music starting daily at 8pm, as well as pokies, a bistro, and courtyard. Schooners $3.70, F-Sa $4.70. Open M-W and F 10am-11:30pm, Th until midnight, F-Sa until 2:30am, Apr.-Aug. open starting at 11am.

The Lord Nelson, 19 Kent St. (☎9251 4044), at Argyle St. Nautical flags drape from sturdy wooden beams in this colonial building. Sydney's oldest hotel and pub shelters a young crowd. A very chill place for an after-work pint from one of Sydney's only microbreweries. Try the award-winning Old Admiral (pints $6). Open daily 11am-11pm.

The Hero of Waterloo, 81 Lower Fort St. (☎9252 4553). Since 1845, this pub has been a local favorite; its underground tunnels were once used for rum smuggling. Live Irish and folk music daily starting around 7pm. Open M-Sa 10am-11pm, Su 10am-10pm.

IN RECENT NEWS

CLEANING UP KINGS XXX

Infamous Darlinghurst Rd. is always buzzing with partying backpackers, blinking sex shop signs, and the hubbub of late-night traffic. But now it's buzzing with something new: word of Sydney City Council's policy designed to "discourage the continuation of the area as a red-light district," according to the *Sydney Morning Herald*. In June 2003, the Council passed a policy that prohibits the opening of any more sex industry businesses in Kings Cross, meaning that the area won't be getting any new brothels, strip clubs, or adult shops. Although the policy can't make existing sex businesses shut down, it sends a message that the new Council is trying to clean up the area.

In addition to the sex industry policy, the Council allotted $14 million to making Darlinghurst Rd. more pedestrian-friendly with changes such as wider footpaths, more trees, better street lighting, and improved signage. Stephen Carnell of the Kings Cross Partnership said the Council's actions are designed to create more positive street traffic through the area, which should lure in a variety of new businesses. However, he emphasized that the Council's changes won't kill the character of the Cross, which has been lively and rebellious since its beginnings as a bohemian artists' community. "What's important is the spirit in a place," he said. "That's something the Council can't change."

KINGS CROSS

It may have sketchy streets, but King's Cross is a 24-hour buzz of activity (of all sorts), and nightlife is its specialty. The bars are crammed with backpackers and locals alike. Be sure to use caution late at night.

Old Fitzroy Hotel, 129 Dowling St. (☎9356 3848), on the corner of Cathedral St. From William St., walk down McElhone St. (*not* Dowling St.), take your 1st left at Reid Ave. and you'll see it. A neighborhood pub comfortably sequestered from the more hectic Cross. The cozy downstairs bar has a fireplace and mellow music, while the upstairs level holds a younger crowd and feels like an apartment with its several nooks. Pool $2 per game. Also connected to a Malaysian restaurant ❶ (laksa under $10) and a theater ($30 for dinner, beer, and play). Frequent discounts through local hostels. Schooners $3.60. Happy Hour M 5:30-7:30pm and Th 6-9pm. Tu free pool. Open M-F 11am-midnight, Sa noon-midnight, Su 3-10pm.

The World, 24 Bayswater Rd. (☎9357 7700). This former brothel keeps the sex theme going with red moodlighting and vintage Playboy and Playgirl posters in the bathrooms ($5). Daily Happy Hours make the World go 'round and 'round (schooners $2.50 6-7pm), as do the teapots full of shots ($15). W free pool; F classic house; Sa house; live DJs every night. Open M-Th noon-3am, F-Su noon-6am.

Yu, 171 Victoria St. (☎9358 6511), in the black and silver building with a tiny "soho" sign, across from Out of India. Also known as Soho, though that technically refers to the posh upstairs bar, Yu nightclub has a delicious mix of classic and modern hip-hop and soul with irreverent breaks. Full of cuties of all makes and models. Dress to look too cool to care about impressing anyone, and you'll be sure to dazzle on the dance-floor. Cover F $15, Sa $20, Su $10. Open F-Su 10pm-6am.

King's X Hotel, 248 William St. (☎9358 3377), opposite the Coca-Cola sign. What it lacks in atmosphere, the King's X makes up for with a central location—at the heart of all the action and a good place for an alcoholic refuel. Happy Hour schooners $2.50, house spirits $3 (daily 6-7pm and 11pm-midnight). Small drag shows and DJs on Sa. Open daily noon-3am.

DARLINGHURST

Darlo Bar, 306 Liverpool St. (☎9331 3672), on the corner of Darlinghurst Rd. The cool version of your grandma's living room, this chill retro lounge attracts a mixed crowd that boozes to a tune slightly cheaper than the usual. Schooners $3.80. Rooms available upstairs (see **Accommodations** p. 118). Open M-Sa 10am-midnight, Su noon-10pm.

The Stonewall, 175 Oxford St. (☎9360 1963). A very happening gay bar with buff bartenders and lots of live entertainment (Tu karaoke, Th go-go dancers, F-Sa drag shows). DJs spin funkier dance music, while patrons downstairs lip-sync to cookie-cutter pop. Happy Hour schooners $3 daily until 7pm. Open Su-Th 11am-5am, F-Sa 11am-6am.

The Colombian Hotel, 117-123 Oxford St. (☎9360 2157), at the corner of Crown St. The casual but trendy upstairs level has brown leather sofas for lounging while sipping cocktails ($12). Male-oriented, but popular with lesbians as well. Schooners before 10pm $3.20, after 10pm $4.50. Open Su-W 10am-3am, Th-Sa 10am-4am.

PADDINGTON

Though it's right next to the boisterous nightlife of Darlinghurst, Paddington is much tamer. If you make it further out on Oxford St. before the sun rises, hit these nightspots.

Durty Nelly's, 9-11 Glenmore Rd. (☎9360 4467), off Oxford St. at Gipps St. Though wedged in on a street of frou-frou shops, Nelly takes her Guinness very seriously; those in the know claim hers is the best around (schooners $4.50). Even on weekends when it's packed, the dark wood decor and jovial staff create a relaxing refuge from the nearby Oxford St. melee. Open M-Sa 11am-midnight, Su noon-10pm.

Grand Pacific Blue Room (☎9331 7108), on the corner of Oxford and S Dowling St. A big stairwell leads to the red and black restaurant, club, and bar, which has live acoustic performances and DJs spinning underground hip-hop, '80s, and funky house (W-Su). Shed the backpack for a night to join a young and dressy Paddo crowd. Cover F-Sa $10. Open W-Sa 6:30pm-3am, Su 6:30pm-1am.

SURRY HILLS

Crown St., the main drag of Surry Hills, is wide-awake at night and easily accessible from Oxford St, which it intersects in Darlinghurst.

Trinity Bar, 505 Crown St. (☎9319 6802), at the corner of Devonshire St., Surry Hills. A 5min. walk from Oxford St., the Trinity Bar is a hopping Irish sports bar with a terrace and, oddly enough, jam-packed bookshelves. The mixed, mostly local crowd, however, is too busy socializing to read. Schooners $3.80. Open M-Th 11am-midnight, F-Sa 11am-2am, Su noon-midnight.

Obar, 156 Devonshire St., Surry Hills (☎9319 6881). A laidback, lounge-y feel for sexy young things. Come with friends, discard them on the couches, and then leave with a few brand-new ones. Open M-Th 11am-midnight, F-Sa 11am-3am, Su noon-10pm.

BONDI & COOGEE BEACH

Bondi's nightlife, like its beach, is more glamorous than its southern rival. But Coogee Beach—with its younger, less pretentious, and more energetic options— ultimately knows how to party better.

Coogee Bay Hotel (☎9665 0000; www.coogeebayhotel.com.au), on the corner of Coogee Bay Rd. and Arden St., in **Coogee Beach.** Backpackers and UNSW students swarm to the cheap drinks. Multiple bars, beer garden, and a nightclub with no cover. **Selina's Entertainment Centre,** in the hotel, is one of Sydney's more popular concert venues and gets international acts. Schooners $3.80. Happy Hour M-Sa 9am-6pm. Open Su-W 9am-midnight, Th-Sa 9am-3am or later.

The Palace, 169 Dolphin St., (☎9664 2900), at the corner of Dolphin St. and Arden St. in **Coogee Beach.** The Palace features a full three levels of nighttime craziness: the ground-floor Beach Bar is your standard sports bar (open M-Th 11am-1am, F-Sa until 3am, Su until midnight). The Mid-Palace danceclub, popular with a well-dressed younger crowd, blasts Top 40 dance music and R&B (open Su 8pm-midnight, W-Th

8pm-1am, F-Sa 9pm-3am; Sa cover $5 after 10pm). The top-level Aquarium Bar features a much more casual mixed crowd and live entertainment (open M-F 5pm-midnight, Sa-Su noon-midnight).

Beach Road Hotel, 71 Beach Rd. (☎9130 7247), in **Bondi Beach.** A staple of Bondi nightlife. The ground-level sports bar holds a slightly older crowd, while upstairs draws uni students and young travelers to its live bands and pool tables. Lower level open M-Tu 10am-11:30pm, W-F 10am-1:30am, Sa noon-1:30am, Su 10am-9:30pm. Upper level open M-W noon-midnight, Th-Sa until 1am, Su until 10pm.

GLEBE

The Nag's Head Hotel, 162 St. John's Rd. (☎9660 1591), at the corner of Lodge St. A relaxed Irish-style pub with a rooftop terrace and lots of rugby pride. Within stumbling distance of the Forest Lodge Hotel. Schooners $3.65. W Uni night with $8.50 jugs, 4 spirits for $14. Open M-Sa 9am-midnight, Su noon-midnight.

The Roxbury, 182 St. Johns Rd., Glebe (☎9692 0822). A stylish yet unpretentious lounge bar with upbeat live music and a carpeted dance floor. No cover, except for special events. Schooners $3.60, cocktails $10. Open daily 11am-midnight.

Toxteth Hotel, 345 Glebe Point Rd. (☎9660 2370), at Ferry Rd. Lively and usually packed with young students and backpackers from the nearby Glebe Village and YHA. Schooners of VB $3.90. Th and Sa free movies in the courtyard 8:30pm. Happy Hour Su-Th 4-6pm; pints of Stella $3.90. Open M-Sa 11am-1am, Su 11am-midnight.

NEWTOWN

Kuletos Cocktail Bar, 157 King St. (☎9519 6369). Deliciously fruity liqueurs go down smooth during Kuletos' Happy Hour (M-Sa 6-7:30pm and Th 9:30-10:30pm), with 2-for-1 cocktails ($10-14.50). The Toblerone ($12), an essence of everyone's favorite pointy chocolate, and the Red Corvette ($11) are by far the best. Schooners $3.70. Open M-W 4pm-late, Th-Sa 4pm-3am.

Marlborough Hotel, 145 King St. (☎9519 1222). The Marly is the place to be after Happy Hour at Kuletos for pokies, casual boozin', and some decent local musical talent. Th-F DJ; Sa band night. Schooners $3.50. Open M-Sa 10am-3am, Su noon-midnight.

Imperial Hotel, 35 Erskineville Rd., (☎9519 9899) Erskineville. Take a train to "Erskineville," turn left onto Erskineville Rd. and keep going for 2min. The costumes at the outrageous weekend drag shows make the trip well worthwhile. The crowd is straight, gay, lesbian, and huge by showtime. Schooners of VB $3.90. M free pool; Happy Hour 2:30-9pm. Shows Th 10, 11pm, and midnight; F-Sa also at 1am. Th-Sa dance music until 7am. Cover $5 from 4:30pm. Open M-Tu 2:30pm-midnight, W 2:30pm-3am, Th 2:30pm-4am, F-Sa 1pm-6am, Su 1pm-midnight.

NORTH SHORE

The North Shore is somewhat quieter than the city center, but it still knows how to party. Manly keeps it lively at night with fashionable bars and clubs.

Oaks Hotel, 118 Military Rd., (☎9953 5515) at the intersection of Ben Boyd Rd., in Neutral Bay. A huge old oak tree dominates the immensely popular outdoor beer garden, providing shade in the day and a lit-up centerpiece for yuppie gatherings at night. Several other bars attract a diverse but uniformly cool clientele, with a younger crowd in the Tramway Bar and both suits and sports fans in the Garden Palace Bar. Open Th 10am-1:30am, F noon-1:30am, Su-W and Sa 10am-midnight.

The Old Manly Boatshed, 40 The Corso (☎9977 4443; www.manlyboatshed.com.au), in Manly. A cozy, subterranean pub with live music most weeknights. M comedy. Open daily 6pm-3am.

Ivanhoe of Manly, 27 The Corso (☎9976 3955), opposite the fountain, in Manly. A popular nightspot with 3 different levels. The ground-level lobby bar has live bands W-Sa (open Su-Tu 9am-midnight, W-Th until 1am, F-Sa until 3am). Downstairs, Oliver's Nightclub spins techno and trance (open daily noon-5am; Sa cover $10), while the dressier Arriba Cocktail Lounge upstairs plays house music (open F-Sa 5pm-3am).

Aqua Lounge, 42 North Steyne St. (☎9977 2300), near The Corso, in Manly. A sleek restaurant by day, the Aqua Lounge is a packed bar with a row of daiquiri machines by night. Comfy purple couches and a fireplace upstairs and hordes of smartly dressed clubbers downstairs. Club open Th-Sa 9:30pm-3am; bar open M-F 11am-3am, Sa 9am-3am, Su 11am-midnight. Cover $5 F-Sa after 10pm.

▶ DAYTRIPS FROM SYDNEY

Sydney's attractions are not just limited to the city proper. The surrounding hills and valleys, consisting largely of natural parks with a wide range of plant and animal life, contain a sampling of the greater natural beauty for which the continent is known. If your stay in Oz is confined to Sydney, these daytrips will offer a sampling of the rest of the continent.

ROYAL NATIONAL PARK. Just 30km south of Sydney's city center, the Royal National Park is an accessible yet glorious escape from city life. "The Royal," Australia's oldest national park and the world's second-oldest (after the United States's Yellowstone), consists of over 16,000 hectares of beach, heath, rainforest, and woodland. The range of activities available in the park is as diverse as its habitats—bushwalkers, birdwatchers, swimmers, and surfers all find favorite getaways in different corners of the park. Across the Princes Hwy. on the west side of the park, the smaller, often-forgotten **Heathcote National Park** offers a further 2000 hectares of heathland for those aching to lose themselves in green. **Escape Sydney Ecotours** (www.escapecotours.com.au) takes travelers from several pick-up locations in Sydney to the highlights of the park. Tours range from the half-day whale-watching trek (May-Aug. only; $40, includes transport and park entry) to the 2-day coast walk tour ($240, includes transport, park entry, and accommodation). To get there by **car,** turn off the Princes Hwy. at either Farnell Ave., south of Loftus, or at McKell Ave. at Waterfall ($10 park fee for cars). CityRail **trains** (☎13 15 00) also run from Sydney to both Engadine and Heathcote stations ($4.40). A **ferry** from Cronulla will get you to the park at Bundeena (☎9523 2990).

BOTANY BAY NATIONAL PARK. Lying on both sides of the entrance to Botany Bay, this national park is a unique combination of natural and cultural heritage. The Solander Track, which takes you past stunning sandstone cliffs, is one of the most beautiful walks in the park and contains remnants of the vegetation that Captain Cook's botanist first studied when they landed here in 1770. The Cape Baily Coast walk takes you along the heath-covered coast past many of the historic sites related to Cook's first contact with the Aboriginal people. The La Perouse Museum documents the park's history as the place where famed French explorer le Comte de La Perouse arrived within a week of the British First Fleet in 1788. The NPWS-run Bare Island Fort Tour digs through the bizarre history of the military fort set up in 1885 when British colonists feared an invasion by the Russians (☎9247 5033; 1hr.; meets at the entrance to the fort; Sa-Su 12:30pm and 2:30pm; $7.70, children $5.50, families $22). By car, drive to the end of Anzac Parade to reach La Perouse in the northern part of the park. To get to the park's southern end, take Rocky Point Rd. off the Princes Hwy., then Captain Cook Dr. ($6 park fee for cars.) Bus #394 from Circular Quay also runs to La Perouse, and bus #987 arrives at Captain Cook Dr. from Cronulla Station.

NEAR SYDNEY

PARRAMATTA
☎02

In April 1788, Governor Phillip led an expedition to discover what lay upriver from the new settlement of Sydney, and as a result, Australia's second town was established. Steeped in history, Parramatta is a bustling, modern extension of the city, attracting Sydneysiders with its heritage walks, upscale dining, and scenic one-hour cruises on the RiverCat pontoon (1 per hr. from Wharf 2; $5.50).

Parramatta has several buildings from the early days of colonization, including the **Old Government House,** in Parramatta Park at the town's west end. The oldest public building in Australia is perfectly preserved to display how the governor's household lived. (☎9635 8149. Open M-F 10am-4pm, Sa-Su 10:30am-4pm. $7, concessions $5; with Experiment Farm $10/$7.) On the opposite side of town along the Harris Park Heritage Walk, **Elizabeth Farm,** 70 Alice St., in Rosehill, was home to John and Elizabeth Macarthur, founders of the Australian merino wool industry. (☎9635 9488. Open daily 10am-5pm. $7, concessions $3, families $17.) In 1789, the colonial government made its first land grant to convict James Ruse at the **Experiment Farm Cottage** site, 9 Ruse St., in Harris Park. (☎9635 5655. Open Tu-F 10:30am-3:30pm, Sa-Su 11:30am-3:30pm. $5.50, concessions $4, families $14.)

Although many sights lie along specific walking routes (available from the tourist office), the **Paramatta Explorer** is a good option for weekend sightseeing. It stops at the RiverCat terminal, the Visitors Centre, historic sights, and the largest **Westfield Mall** in NSW. (☎13 15 00. Runs Sa-Su every 30min. 10am-4pm. $10, children $5.) Locally, **Church Street** is known as "Eat Street" for its many fine dining options. **Encore at Riverside ❸,** 353 Church St., opposite the tourist office, is a popular spot that serves inventive salads (king prawn and mango with lime mayonnaise $16) and traditional but tasty mains for $17-26. (☎9630 2150. Open daily 10am-late.)

Parramatta is 20min. from Sydney along Parramatta Rd. Before reaching Parramatta, the road becomes the M4 Tollway at Strathfield, the most direct route to the Blue Mountains. Both **trains** and **ferries** make the trip from Sydney. The RiverCat pontoon (see above) is much more enchanting than the 30min. train ride ($4). **CityRail** also runs to: Blackheath ($10.80); Katoomba ($9.80); Lithgow ($13); and Penrith ($4.40). The **Parramatta Visitors Centre,** 346 Church St., is within the Parramatta Heritage Centre. (☎8839 3311; www.parracity.nsw.gov.au. Open M-F 10am-5pm, Sa-Su 10am-4pm.) Parramatta's accommodations scene does not cater to budget travelers, but Sydney is close enough to allow commuting.

PENRITH
☎02

The urban center of Penrith sits as the base of the Blue Mountains, 35km west of Parramatta along the Great Western Hwy. (Hwy. 44) or the M4 Motorway, just on the edge of Sydney's sphere of suburban influence. Though it's small compared to Sydney, Penrith has the gritty feel of a city, particularly along its commercial heart, **High Street.** Running through the western half of town, the placid **Nepean River** brings a touch of beauty to the plain landscape. The **Nepean Belle** paddlewheel riverboat floats through the Nepean Gorge in **Blue Mountains National Park.** (☎4733 1274. Departs Tench Reserve Park, off Tench Ave., with morning, afternoon, and dinner cruises. Shortest cruise 90min. $18.) For a view of the Nepean River from up high, follow Mulgoa Rd. south toward Wallacia to see the **Rock Lookout.** From Mulgoa Rd., turn right onto Fairlight Rd., then right onto the unsealed road when it ends. Just across the river in Emu Plains, the **Penrith Regional Gallery & The Lewers Bequest,** 86 River Rd., showcases contemporary Australian sculptures and gorgeous gardens. (☎4735 1100. Open daily 10am-5pm. Free.)

CityRail trains (ticket office at railway; open M-F 5am-9pm, Sa 5:45am-8:30pm, Su 6:45am-8:30pm) run to: Blackheath (1½hr., 15-21 per day, $8); Katoomba (1hr., 15-21 per day, $6); Lithgow (2hr., 12-14 per day, $10.20); Parramatta (30min., 23-34 per day, $4.40); and Sydney (1hr., 23-33 per day, $6.60). The **Penrith Valley Visitors Centre,** on Mulgoa Rd., in the carpark of Panthers World of Entertainment Complex, provides useful info on Penrith, including a weekly *What's On* guide. (☎4732 7671; www.penrithvalley.com.au. Open daily 9am-4:30pm.)

Explorers Lodge ❸, 111 Station St., at Union Rd., is Penrith's backpacker accommodation. Its rooms are spacious with extra-long beds. (☎4731 3616; www.explorerslodge.com. Linen included. Reception 9am-9pm. Flexible check-in time. Checkout 11am. 6-bed dorms $27.50, weekly $165; singles $44/$264; twins and doubles $66/$330.) **Nepean River Caravan Park ❷,** on MacKellar St., in Emu Plains, is a short but slightly tricky drive over the river (or a 400m walk from the rail station). It provides campsites and cabins, along with a kitchen, pool, games room, and TV lounge. (☎4735 4425. Reception M-F 8am-7pm, Sa-Su 8-11am and 4-6pm. Linen $10. Sites for 2 $18, powered $22.50; dorms $25; ensuite cabins for two $75-90.)

KU-RING-GAI CHASE NATIONAL PARK

The second oldest national park in NSW (after the Royal National Park, founded 1879), Ku-Ring-Gai Chase covers some 15,000 hectares of the lands traditionally owned by the Guringai Aboriginal people. Today, the rugged park, popular with Sydneysiders, draws over two million visitors a year who come for the peace and quiet, the numerous Aboriginal rock engravings, and the bright wildflowers that bloom in early August.

It's much easier to access the park with a car, since public transportation will only get you to the park's entrances. Ku-Ring-Gai Chase is split in two by access roads. **Ku-Ring-Gai Chase Road** from the Pacific Hwy. and **Bobbin Head Road** from Turramurra provide access to the southwest area of the park, while **West Head Road** runs through the eastern section. From Sydney, you can reach the Bobbin Head Rd. entrance by first taking the **train** to Turramurra (35min., $3.80) and then catching bus #577 of **Shorelink Bus Company** (☎9457 8888 or 13 15 00; www.shorelink.com.au. 15min.; M-Sa every hr., Su every 2hr.; $3) from North Turramurra Station to just outside the park gates. A three-hour hike then brings you to the Kalkari Visitors Centre. Another option is to take **bus** L90 or L85, which run from Circular Quay in Sydney (1½hr.) to Church Point, where it's possible to catch a **ferry** (☎9999 3492 or 0408 296 997; $4.50 one-way, $7.50 return) or **water taxi** (Pink Water Taxi ☎9634 4791, urgent 0428 238 190; www.pinkwatertaxi.au.com; max. 6 passengers; available 24hr.; $14 one-way) across Broken Bay to Halls Wharf, with free and direct hiking access to the park.

Palm Beach Ferry Service (☎9918 2747) departs from Palm Beach (accessible from Sydney by bus L90) and stops at The Basin (see below), the park's sole camping area (8 per day, $9 return). **Palm Cruises** (☎9997 4815) runs scenic cruises from Palm Beach to Bobbin Head (departs daily 11am, returns 3:30pm; $32) and stops at Patonga along the way (at least 1 per day; $13).

The Bobbin Head area in the southwest is home to the main **Kalkari Visitors Centre,** on Ku-Ring-Gai Chase Rd., 3km inside the park gates. The Center distributes free hiking maps, conducts guided walks and tours, and offers educational information on the park's wildlife. (☎9457 9853. Open daily 9am-5pm.) One kilometer further, the **Bobbin Head Information Centre,** inside the Wildlife Shop at the bottom of the hill, also distributes info about the park. (☎9472 8949. Open daily 10am-4pm.) General inquiries can be made to **The Rocks Visitors Centre** (☎1300 361 967 or 9253 4600; www.npws.nsw.gov.au) in Sydney.

NEW SOUTH WALES

The only place you can camp in Ku-Ring-Gai Chase National Park is at **The Basin ❶**. You can get there on foot along The Basin Track, by car on West Head Rd., or by the hourly ferry from Palm Beach ($9 return). Campsites have cold showers, toilets, gas BBQs, and a public phone, but all supplies other than bait and drinks must be carried in. Vehicles staying overnight require a day pass ($10). Bookings are required and must be arranged through the NPWS 24hr. automated reservation service; your call will be returned within 3 days. (☎9974 1011. Max. 8 per site. Sites Sept.-Apr. $9 per person, $4.50 per child; May-Aug. $7.50/$4.)

Certainly the most refreshing and remote hostel in the greater Sydney area, the friendly **Pittwater YHA Hostel ❷** is set among lush greenery in a lofty, terraced perch over Pittwater. The open, outdoorsy hostel provides a secluded retreat without TV or radio. You'll need to bring your own food (the only grocery store is a ferry-ride away) as well as a flashlight. To get there, follow a confusing path 15min. uphill from Halls Wharf, accessible by ferry from Church Point ($4.50 single, $7.50 return). To reach Church Point, drive along Pittwater Rd., or take bus #156 from Manly (1hr.), bus E86 from Wynyard (1¼hr.), or bus L85 or L90 from Sydney. (☎9999 5748; fax 9999 5749. Kayak hire $15 for 1hr, $25 for 3hr. Linen $2. No laundry. Bookings required. Reception 8-11am and 5-8pm. Dorms $25.50; twins $65. YHA discount $3.50 per person.)

Ku-Ring-Gai Chase has **bushwalks** for any level of expertise. The **Discovery Walk** (20min.; wheelchair-accessible) just outside the Kalkari Visitors Centre is a quick, easy way to spot a few kangaroos, emus, and some native plant life. An easily accessible bushwalk (10km) begins at the Bobbin Head Rd. entrance to the park and follows the **Sphinx-Warrimoo Track** (6.5km) to Bobbin Head. The hike can be made into a circuit by taking the Bobbin Head Track (3.5km) back to the park entrance. The bushwalk passes through mangroves, along a creek, and near an Aboriginal engraving site. The **Basin Bay Track** and **America Track** (3.5km) at West Head are both moderately difficult hikes which incorporate stunning Aboriginal engraving sites, accessible by West Head Rd. Rock engravings in the park depict mythical beings and whales up to 8m long. For the best views of the Hawkesbury River as it feeds into Broken Bay, proceed north along West Head Rd. until you reach the ◼West Head Lookout.

BLUE MOUNTAINS

The gorgeous Blue Mountains region is Sydney's favorite escape, a tourist wonderland just outside the city where it's still possible to get away from it all. Although a variety of adventure activities such as abseiling and canyon rafting have become popular in recent years, the major attractions of the Blue Mountains remain the excellent hiking trails and lookouts. The remarkable blue color of the hazy valleys and ridges in this area results from sunlight filtering through the eucalyptus oil in the air. From lookout points all along canyon edges, the earth falls away to endless blue foliage speckled with white bark and bordered by distant sandstone cliffs. Whether you want to take a dip in a towering waterfall, hike through serene rainforest and Aboriginal ceremonial grounds, abseil into a deep canyon, or enjoy jaw-dropping panoramic views, your passion will be satiated here.

Because the so-called mountains are actually a series of canyons separated by several high plateaus, colonial explorers found impassable cliffs at the edges of the valleys instead of hills. Although several Aboriginal groups had been traveling the mountains for thousands of years, white explorers struggled for decades with the crossing until finally asking the indigenous tribes for help in 1813. Today, the mountains are an easy getaway for Sydneysiders and the first stop on most backpacker trips out of Sydney. The short trip inland grants summertime visitors a

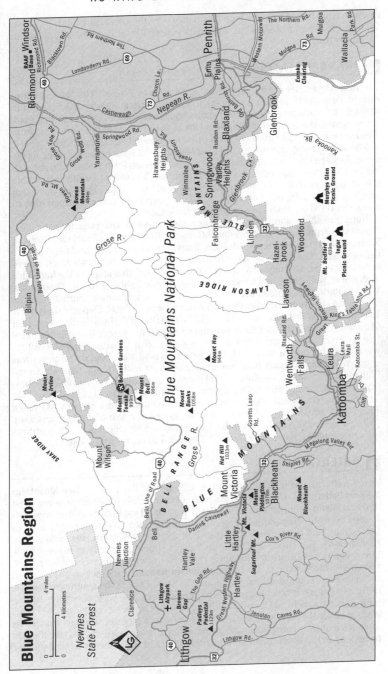

Blue Mountains Region

Newnes State Forest

NEW SOUTH WALES

Blue Mountains National Park

Ku-ring-gai Chase National Park

RAAF Windsor Base
Richmond
Richmond Rd.
Blacktown Rd.
The Northern Rd.
Londonderry Rd.
69
Penrith
Emu Plains
Western Motorway
The Northern Rd.
Mulgoa
Wallacia
Park Rd.
73
Mulgoa Rd.
Emoka Clearing
Grose Vale Rd.
Grose Wold Rd.
Bowen Mt. Rd.
Yarramundi
Springwood Rd.
Castlereagh
Nepean R.
73
Church La.
Rd.
Old Bathurst Rd.
Blaxland
Rusden Rd.
Springwood
Valley Heights
Glenbrook
Glenbrook Ck.
Kanooka Bk.
Bowen Mountain 484m
Hawkesbury Heights
Hawkesbury Rd.
Winmalee
BLUE MOUNTAINS
Falconbridge
Murphys Glen Picnic Ground
Grose R.
Linden
32
Woodford
Mt. Bedford 639m
Ingar Picnic Ground
40
Bells Line of Road
Hazelbrook
LAWSON RIDGE
Lawson
Great Western Highway
King's Tableland Rd.
Bilpin
Blaxland Rd.
Mount Hay 944m
Wentworth Falls
Leura
Leura Mall
Katoomba St.
Mount Irvine
Botanic Gardens
Mount Tomah 999m
Mount Bell 996m
Mount Banks 1068m
Goretts Leap Rd.
Katoomba
Cliff Dr.
SHAY RIDGE
Mount Wilson
Grose R.
BELL RANGE
Hat Hill 1033m
Megalong Valley Rd.
Shipley Rd.
32
Bells Line of Road
BLUE MOUNTAINS
40
Bell
Mount Victoria
Mount Piddington 1076m
Blackheath
Mount Blackheath
Newnes Junction
Darling Causeway
Little Hartley
Mt. Victoria
Cox's River Rd.
Clarence
Hartley Vale
The Gap Rd.
Hartley
Sugarloaf Mt.
Lithgow Airpark
Browns Gap
Great Western Highway
Jenolan Caves Rd.
40
Padleys Pedestal 1124m
Lithgow Rd.
Lithgow
32

0 4 miles
0 4 kilometers

LG

reprieve from the oppressive heat that hangs over the coast. In winter, the crisp sunny days, occasional snowfall, and Yulefest festivities (Christmas in July; see p. 141) draw travelers.

▐ TRANSPORTATION

The Blue Mountains are an easy 1½hr. drive west of Sydney. The M4 Motorway runs to Penrith ($2.20 toll) and meets the **Great Western Highway,** the main route through the mountains. All service centers and attractions lie on or near this road. Alternatively, the northern route, **Bells Line of Road** (see p. 162), roams west from Windsor, northeast of Parramatta and provides a more beautiful passage.

  CityRail trains stop throughout the Blue Mountains at most of the towns along the Great Western Hwy., offering the least expensive option for travelers who are willing to walk sizable distances from rail stations and bus stops to trailheads. Within the towns, most distances are walkable, and local bus companies cover those that aren't (for bus info, see **Katoomba,** p. 153). There is **no public transportation** to Kanangra-Boyd National Park or Wollemi National Park.

  There are three above-par companies running **small bus tours** into the Blue Mountains from Sydney. **Wonderbus** offers an "Eco-tour" that includes stops at Euroka Campground, Wentworth Falls, Katoomba's Echo Point, and Blackheath's Govetts Leap. The aim is to allow time for wilderness bushwalks with an experienced driver-guide. They also have a "Discovery tour" that stops at the highlights of the Blue Mountains, and also goes to the Olympic sights and to the Featherdale Wildlife Park. Participants who wish to adopt a more leisurely touring pace can opt for an overnight stay in the mountains. (☎9555 9800. Departs daily from 7:30am, returns 7pm. Eco-tour $70, ISIC/NOMADS/VIP/YHA $65; discovery tour $100/$95.) The **OzTrails** tour takes you and up to 13 other people to the highlights of the region, and includes morning tea and lunch. (☎9387 8390; www.oztrails.com.au. $83, including Scenic World $95. Departs 8am, returns 6pm.) **Wildframe Ecotours** provides similar services and offers a trip into Grand Canyon, a tremendous rainforest-filled gorge in Blackheath. (☎0500 505 056. Day-trip $76, concessions $68; with 1 night at the Katoomba YHA $114, 2 nights $134.) Several companies run **large-bus tours** to the mountains from Sydney. **AAT Kings,** Jetty 6, on Circular Quay, offers a basic tour, as well as a tour of the Jenolan Caves. (24hr. ☎9518 6095. Basic tour $99, concessions $94; Departs 8:45am, returns 5:45pm. Jenolan Caves tour $117/$112. Departs 8:40am, returns 6:45pm.)

✦ ORIENTATION

Three national parks divide the wild stretches of the region. **Blue Mountains National Park** (see p. 160), the largest and most accessible of the three, spans most of the Jamison Valley (south of the Great Western Hwy. between Glenbrook and Katoomba), the Megalong Valley (south of the Great Western Hwy., west of Katoomba), and the Grose Valley (north of the Great Western Hwy. and east of Blackheath). The Grose and Jamison Valleys appeal primarily to hikers, while horseback riders favor the Megalong Valley (for more information on horseback riding, see **Blackheath,** p. 158). **Kanangra-Boyd National Park** (see p. 164), tucked between two sections of Blue Mountains National Park in the southwest reaches of the mountains, is reserved for skilled bushwalkers. The park, accessible by partially paved roads from Oberon and from Jenolan Caves, has only one 2WD road. **Wollemi National Park** (see p. 163) contains the state's largest preserved wilderness area. It's a place so unspoiled and untrafficked that a species of pine tree thought to be long extinct was found here in 1994, alive and well. Access to Wollemi, the

Katoomba & Leura

🏠 ACCOMMODATIONS
Blue Mountains Backpackers, 1
Blue Mountains Katoomba YHA, 9
Katoomba Falls Caravan Park, 10
Mountain Escapes Lodge, 11
Number 14, 4

🍴 FOOD
Blues Cafe, 6
Food Co-op, 7
Parakeet Cafe, 8

⭐ NIGHTLIFE
Carrington Hotel, 5
Gearin Hotel, 2
TrisElies, 3

NEW SOUTH WALES

southern edge of which abuts the north side of **Bells Line of Road,** is possible at Bilpin and at several points north of the central Blue Mountains.

The national parks of the Blue Mountains region are administered by different branches of the **National Parks and Wildlife Services (NPWS).** If you are planning to bushcamp or even to drive into these parks, contact the appropriate NPWS office (see specific park listings below) a few days in advance to ensure that roads are drivable and that no bushfire bans are in place. It is also recommended that you leave a bushwalk plan filed with the appropriate NPWS office before you go.

KATOOMBA ☎ 02

A main gateway to the Blue Mountains National Park, Katoomba (pop. 9000) offers excellent hiking, climbing, and biking opportunities in a very convenient rail-accessible location. The result is an outdoor enthusiast's dream. Though Katoomba is touristy, the town retains a distinctly alternative flavor, replete with vegetarian eateries, secondhand clothing stores, and dreadlocks galore. The image most widely associated with the Blue Mountains is that of the Three Sisters, a trio of towering stone outcroppings jutting out into the Jamison Valley, silently holding vigil over the dark blue-green valley below. One of the most accessible places to marvel at the formation is Echo Point, at the south end of Katoomba.

▐ TRANSPORTATION

Trains: Katoomba Railway Station (☎4782 1902) is on Main St., at the north end of Katoomba St. **CityRail** (☎13 15 00) trains and **Countrylink** (☎13 22 32) trains and buses run to: **Bathurst** (2hr., 7 per day, $12.80); **Blackheath** (13min., 17-23 per day, $2.80); **Dubbo** (5hr., 1 per day, $51.70); **Glenbrook** (50min., 18-28 per day, $5.20); **Lithgow** (45min., 12-15 per day, $6); **Mt. Victoria** (20min., 12-15 per day, $3.40); **Orange** (3hr., 1 per day, $28.60); **Parramatta** (1½hr., 20-29 per day, $9.80); **Penrith** (1hr., 19-26 per day, $6); **Sydney** (2hr., 20-29 per day, $11.40); and **Zig Zag Railway** (45min., 2 per day, $5.20); make sure you request this stop with the guard at the rear of the train; see p. 163. **Mountainlink** (☎4782 3333) runs to **Leura** ($3), **Blackheath** ($5), and **Mt. Victoria** ($5.30).

Buses: Greyhound McCafferty's (☎13 20 30) runs from opposite the Gearin Hotel, 273 Great Western Hwy., to: **Adelaide** (21½hr., 1 per day, $133); **Bathurst** (2hr., 1 per day, $32); **Broken Hill** (14hr., 1 per day, $133); **Dubbo** (4¾hr., 1 per day, $58); **Lithgow** (40min., 1 per day, $15); **Orange** (3hr., 1 per day, $35).

Local and Park Transportation: The public **Blue Mountains Bus Company** (☎4782 4213) runs between Katoomba and Wentworth Station, with stops at Woodford, near Echo Point, the Edge Cinema, Leura Mall, the Valley of the Waters trailhead, Scenic World, and Wentworth Falls. $0.80-6; unlimited day-pass $12. Regular service M-F approx. 7:30am-6pm, Sa-Su 7:30am-3pm. For day-touring at your own pace, the **Blue Mountains Explorer Bus** (☎4782 4807) runs a 27-stop circuit allowing passengers to get on and off as often as they choose. $25, ISIC $22, children $12.50. Buses run daily every hour (and every 30min. along the clifftop) 9:30am-5:15pm. Timetables for both services are available at the Blue Mountains Tourism Authority on Echo Point. All pick-up stops opposite the Carrington Hotel on Main St. **Mountainlink Trolley Tours** (☎1800 801 577) runs the cheapest bus tours in the area, with all-day access and unlimited stops for just $12, stopping throughout the Leura and Katoomba areas.

Taxis: Katoomba Cabs (☎4782 1311) picks up 24hr. anywhere between Wentworth Falls and Mt. Victoria. Initial fare $4, plus $1.07 per km.

Automobile Clubs: NRMA (road service ☎13 11 11).

Bike Rental: Cycletech, 182 Katoomba St. (☎4782 2800). Mountain bikes half-day $28, full-day $50. Helmets, locks, and repair kits included. YHA/backpacker discount 10%. Open Tu-F 9am-5:30pm, Sa 9am-5pm, Su 9am-4pm.

▐ PRACTICAL INFORMATION

Katoomba sits just south of the Great Western Hwy., 2km west of Leura and 109km from Sydney. The town's main drag, **Katoomba Street,** runs south from the Katoomba Railway Station through town toward Echo Point. **Main Street,** where much of the nightlife and adventure tour offices are located, runs along the top of town by the rail station, and changes names to Bathurst Rd. and Gang Gang Rd. Near the bottom of town, Echo Point Rd. brings visitors to the Blue Mountains' most famous sight, the Three Sisters.

Tourist Office: Blue Mountains Tourism (☎1300 653 408; fax 4739 6787; www.blue-mountainstourism.org.au), at the end of Echo Point Rd., on Echo Point. Take Lurline St. south and veer left onto Echo Rd. Open daily 9am-5pm. For hiking advice from park rangers, try the **NPWS Blue Mountain Heritage Center** in Blackheath (see p. 158).

Work Opportunities: Backpackers can usually quite easily find hospitality-related work in the Blue Mountains region; check with hostels about hiring. **Quindalup Permaculture Farm and Education Centre** (☎6355 5800), located 60km northeast of Katoomba in

Portland, hires farm workers. Seasonal, temporary fruit-picking work is often available at the **Fruit Shack** (contact Michael ☎0417 655 984; fruitshack@hotmail.com), in Leeton, near Narrandera.

Hospital: Blue Mountains District Anzac Memorial Hospital (☎4780 6000), on the Great Western Hwy., 1km east of the railway station.

Internet Access: Blue Elephant Thai Kitchen, 6 Katoomba St. (☎4782 6896), near the back of the restaurant. $1 per 10min., $5 per hr. Open daily 10:30am-10pm.

Post Office (☎13 13 18), on Pioneer Pl., opposite Coles. Open M-F 9am-5pm. **Postal Code:** 2780.

ACCOMMODATIONS

Katoomba provides a range of accommodations for travelers on any budget, but is especially backpacker-friendly. Although beds here are plentiful, so are the vacationers that swamp the town November through April and on winter weekends. Advance bookings are highly recommended, especially on school holidays and long weekends.

▨ **Blue Mountains Katoomba YHA,** 207 Katoomba St. (☎4782 1416; bluemountains@yhansw.org.au), a 10min. walk downhill from the train station. Spacious kitchen, dining area, huge common area with fireplace, pool table, Internet ($2 per 30min.), TV/video lounge, activity-planning room, outside terrace, laundry, lockers, and ample parking. Helpful staff provides heaps of info. Linen included. Reception 7am-10pm. Dorms $22.50-26.50; doubles $69, ensuite $77; family rooms $112. YHA discount $3.50 per person. ❷

▨ **Number 14,** 14 Lovel St. (☎4782 7104; www.bluemts.com.au/no14), the small yellow house 5min. from the train station via Gang Gang St. If the outstanding kitchen, the sunny side-porch, and the comfortable furnishings don't convince you to stay in this small home-away-from-home, the quiet and friendly atmosphere will. Reception 8am-noon and 4:30-9:30pm. Dorms $20-22; twins and doubles $55-59; ensuite doubles $60-65. ❷

Blue Mountains Backpackers, 190 Bathurst Rd. (☎4782 4226; kac@kacadventures.com.au), a 5min. walk west of the station. Fun, friendly, mellow, and aimed at a young crowd. Small kitchen, dining area with TV/video, common room, outdoor spa, and BBQ/patio. Free luggage storage. Linen $1; laundry $6; key deposit $10. Reception 9am-noon and 5-8pm. Occasionally closes Tu-Th in winter. Sites $12 per person, dorms $19; twins and doubles $48-54. Weekly $63/$112/$336. VIP/YHA. ❶

YULEFEST

Most Australians have given up dreaming of a white Christmas. December 25 comes in the middle of summer, when temperatures even in the shade can be as high as 40°C. Accordingly, the typical Aussie Christmas is spent gathering around the barbie, downing some coldies, and lounging on the beach, usually in that order. It's not a rough life, but it's a far cry from the northern hemisphere's traditions of eating roast ham in front of a roaring fire.

Enter "Yulefest," which began some 23 years ago when a particularly biting Blue Mountains winter reminded a group of Irish visitors of their own crisp Christmas weather back home. They requested a traditional Christmas dinner at their guesthouse, the Mountain Heritage Country House Resort, and the Christmas celebration soon became established as an annual event. Hotels and restaurants across the Blue Mountains quickly hopped onto the Yulefest bandwagon and today it is widely celebrated from June to August. Most businesses celebrate in some way, whether it's sprinkling tinsel on the trees or serving a full Christmas dinner. Some accommodations even offer special family-oriented accommodation packages during Yulefest.

Mountain Escapes Lodge, 77 Darley St. (☎ 1800 357 577; www.bluemts.com.au/escapes), a 15min. walk from the train station and a 5min. walk to Echo Point. Colorful walls, abundant windows, and wood floors add to the homey feel of this converted house. TV/video, kitchen, BBQ, laundry, and off-street parking. Linen and continental breakfast included. Reception 24hr. Dorms $25; doubles with veranda $65. ❷

Katoomba Falls Caravan Park (☎ 4782 1835), on Katoomba Falls Rd., south of town via Katoomba St. Well-positioned for bushwalks and Scenic World. Toilets, hot showers, indoor BBQ, laundry, and children's playground. No linen. Key deposit $20. Reception 8am-7pm. Sites for 2 $22, families $26; powered for 2 $26.40, families $30; ensuite cabins for 2 $81, extra adult $11, extra child $6. ❷

🍴 FOOD

You can't go wrong finding food on Katoomba St., which is packed with delicious cafes, takeaways, and nicer restaurants serving a variety of cuisines and many vegetarian options. One of several popular cafes clustered at the top of the hill near the train station, the **Blues Cafe** ❶, 55-57 Katoomba St., prepares excellent, high-class cuisine for dine-in or takeaway. (☎ 4782 2347. Mains $9.50-14.50. YHA discount 10%. Open daily 9am-5pm.) Further downhill, **Parakeet Cafe** ❶, 195b Katoomba St., prepares delicious focaccia ($9.50) and cheaper sandwiches. (☎ 4782 1815. Open M-F 8am-8pm, Sa-Su until 9:30pm. YHA discount.) The **Food Co-Op,** on Hapenny Ln. off Katoomba St. (pedestrian access only), behind the post office, sells organic foods in bulk. (Open M-W and F 9am-5:30pm, Th 9am-6:30pm, Sa 9am-5pm. YHA discount 10%.) Coles **supermarket** is next to K-Mart on Parke St. (Open daily 6am-midnight.)

🎵🎭 ENTERTAINMENT & NIGHTLIFE

The **Edge Maxvision Cinema,** 225 Great Western Hwy., a 5min. walk from the rail station, projects *The Edge,* a 38min. film on the Blue Mountains, onto a six-story screen. The movie, which focuses on the fragile ecosystem of the Blue Mountains, takes viewers to several places that cannot be accessed by visitors, including the secret grove where the recently-discovered Wollemi pine species grows. The cinema also shows other giant-format films and recent feature films. (☎ 4782 8900. *The Edge:* 6 shows daily 10:20, 11:05am, 12:10, 1:30, 2:15, and 5:30pm. $13.50, concessions $11.50, YHA, seniors, and children $8.50. Other films: M and W-Su $10.50/$9.50/$8, Tu $8.) Outdoor **markets** run year-round in the Blue Mountains region. In Katoomba, they are held on the 1st and 4th Saturday of each month at the Civic; Leura, on the 1st Sunday of each month at the public school on the Great Western; in Mt. Victoria, on the 2nd Sunday of each month at Imperial Park in the town center, on the 3rd Sunday of each month at the public school on the Great Western in Springwood, and on the 2nd Saturday of each month on Macquarie Rd.

The **Gearin Hotel,** 273 Great Western Hwy., filled with a local crowd, tends to be smokier and rougher around the edges than other nightspots. On Wednesdays, the Gearin hosts a popular Jam Night for local bands. (☎ 4782 4395. Open daily 8am-3am.) Katoomba's nightlife revolves around the area by the rail station. The historic **Carrington Hotel,** 15-47 Katoomba St., contains two bars: a small, mellow piano bar with live music Th-Su at the top of Katoomba St. (open daily noon-midnight), and a large pub with an upstairs nightclub and DJs Th-Sa on Main St. (☎ 4782 1111. Pub open daily 9:30am-2am. Nightclub open Th-Sa until 4am; cover $5.) **TrisElies,** 287 Bathurst Rd., next to the rail station, is Katoomba's coolest nightclub, and draws a younger crowd with big-name DJs F night. By day, it's a Mexican restaurant decorated with nude artwork. (☎ 4782 4026; www.triselies.com.au. Nightclub open Th-Sa 9pm-3am, Su until midnight. Cover F up to $20, Sa $7.)

☘ LOOKOUTS, WALKS, & ACTIVITIES

ECHO POINT. Nearly everyone who visits the Blue Mountains ventures out to Echo Point, at the southernmost tip of Katoomba, to take in the geological grandeur of the **Three Sisters.** According to Aboriginal legend, the Three Sisters are more than just pretty rocks; they are beautiful maidens trapped since the Dreamtime in stone pillars. After sunset, strategically placed floodlights lend a surreal brilliance to these three golden dames (dusk-10:30pm). There are numerous short trails and dramatic overlooks in the Echo Point area, but if you're up for a longer, more demanding circuit, descend the steep and taxing 860-step **Giant Stairway Walk** (2½hr) down the back of the Three Sisters and connect up with the **Federal Pass Trail.** At the trail junction, turn right and follow Federal Pass as it snakes its way through the Jamison Valley and past the base of **Katoomba Falls,** and the beautiful, free-standing pillar known as **Orphan Rock.** Just beyond the base of Orphan Rock are two ways out of the valley. You can either hike the seemingly endless **Furber Steps** and ascend through overhanging sandstone and clay rock formations, past the spray of waterfalls, and through rainforest foliage; you can buy a ticket for the adrenaline rush of the mechanized **Scenic Railway** (see below) or walk ten minutes along the boardwalk to the sleek, steady **Sceniscender** (see below). From the top of the canyon, it's possible to return to Echo Point via the **Prince Henry Cliff Walk.**

SCENIC WORLD. At the corner of Violet St. and Cliff Dr., this touristy transportation hub offers three unique perspectives on the Blue Mountains region. The **Scenic Railway,** the world's steepest inclined passenger-railway, is an attraction in its own right. Originally designed for hauling unappreciative chunks of coal, its almost vertical 52° pitch now thrills white-knuckled tourists and hikers during its very short trip in or out of the depths of the Jamison Valley (one-way $8, return $16). The large, transparent **Sceniscender** cable car smoothly travels from clifftop to valley floor and vice versa, offering passengers a more tranquil and relaxing view of the Jamison Valley than the Scenic Railway (one-way $8, return $16). Both the Scenic Railway and the Sceniscender link up with popular hikes around Echo Point (see above). The **Scenic Skyway** is a cable gondola suspended high over the Katoomba Falls Gorge. Though you only travel out and back, the views looking down are tremendous (return only; $10). The Skyway will be closed for renovation from Apr.-Nov. 2004. (☎4782 2699; www.scenicworld.com.au. Open daily 9am-5pm. Trips depart approx. every 10min. 9am-4:50pm.)

NARROW NECK PLATEAU. Jutting out and separating the Jamison Valley and the Megalong Valley, the Narrow Neck Plateau offers short and long **walks,** excellent **mountain biking,** panoramic views, and spectacular sunsets. To reach the plateau by car, follow Cliff Dr. west out of Katoomba. Just past the Landslide Lookout, turn right onto the gravel **Glen Raphael Drive.** You can drive about 1.5km along Narrow Neck up to a locked gate, but the next 7km is for walkers or bicyclists only. One kilometer after the Cliff Dr. turn-off is the trailhead for the **Golden Stairs.** This track runs down the cliff face and intersects the Federal Pass track. To get to the Scenic Railway (1½hr. one-way), turn left at the bottom of the stairs. To get to **Ruined Castle** (5-6hr. return), a distinctive rock formation reminiscent of crumbling turrets, turn right at the bottom and follow the path to the Ruined Castle turn-off on the right. At the Ruined Castle, a short climb to the top yields views straight across the valley to distant parts of the Blue Mountains and Kanangra-Boyd National Parks. On the return from Ruined Castle, some walkers avoid going back up the Golden Stairs and continue east instead to the Scenic Railway (see above). If you do this, add another hour to your itinerary.

TOURS. Several companies in Katoomba, many clustered at the top of Katoomba St. across from the rail station, organize adventure trips throughout the Blue Mountains. The price for activities from guided **bushwalking** to **abseiling** to **canyoning** is similar across companies.

High 'n' Wild Mountain Adventures, 3/5 Katoomba St. (☎4782 6224; www.high-n-wild.com.au). Abseiling course half-day $79, full-day $125; rock climbing course $135/$149; Mountain bike tours $99/$149; year-round canyoning courses from $135. Winter ice-climbing courses by demand. Student and backpacker discount $10. Open daily 8:30am-5:30pm.

Katoomba Adventure Centre, 1 Katoomba St. (☎1800 624 226). Offers standard packages for abseiling (half-day $75, full-day $129), as well as rock climbing and canyoning. Rafting from $130; summer only. Open daily 9am-6pm.

Blue Mountains Adventure Company, 84a Bathurst Rd. (☎4782 1271; www.bmac.com.au), opposite the rail station. Offers abseiling (full-day $119), canyoning ($145), rock climbing ($155), and mountain biking on both Anderson's and Oaks Fire Trails ($149).

Australian School of Mountaineering, 166 Katoomba St. (☎4782 2014; www.asmguides.com.au), inside the Paddy Pallin outdoor shop. Offers both introductory and advanced technical courses from 1-10 days. All-day abseiling trip with lunch $119. YHA discount $10. Open daily 9am-5:30pm.

Blue Mountains Walkabout (☎0408 443 822). Evan, who is part-Darug, takes groups on a challenging 8hr. bushwalk to Aboriginal ceremonial and living spaces, with ochre body painting, sample bush tucker, and boomerang lessons along the way. Begins at Faulconbridge rail station, ends at Springwood rail station. Tours leave daily in summer; call for times and book in advance. $95.

Tread Lightly Eco-Tours, (☎4788 1229; www.treadlightly.com.au). One of the few tour operators in Australia with national Advanced Ecotourism accreditation, focuses on the ecology, flora and fauna, history, and Aboriginal culture of the Blue Mountains. Wilderness walks from $25; Grand Canyon walk from $75; "Rocks to Rainforest" 4WD from $85. YHA discount 10%.

BLACKHEATH

☎02

Blackheath's location makes it a natural choice as a Blue Mountains gateway, though its services are more limited than Katoomba's. To the northeast, the beautiful Grose Valley offers many of the area's best lookouts and most challenging walks. To the south, Megalong Valley is a popular spot for horseback riding.

🖥🚆 TRANSPORTATION & PRACTICAL INFORMATION. The Great Western Hwy. snakes 11km west and north from Katoomba to the town of Blackheath on the way to Mt. Victoria and Lithgow. **Mountainlink** runs buses from Katoomba to Mt. Victoria by way of Blackheath and comes as close as possible to the town's major trailheads. (☎4782 3333. Service M-F 7:30am-6pm, Sa 6:30am-4:30pm; from $4.80.) **CityRail** train service connects Blackheath to: Glenbrook (1hr., 15-22 per day, $6); Katoomba (11min., 15-23 per day, $2.80); Lithgow (30min., 12 per day, $5.20); Parramatta (2hr., 15-20 per day, $10.20); Penrith (1¼hr., 15-20 per day, $8); and Sydney (2½hr., 15-20 per day, $12.80). Hikers, keep in mind that Blackheath Station is 3km from the trailhead at Govetts Leap.

Regional tourist information falls under the auspices of **Blue Mountains Tourism**, at Echo Point, Katoomba (☎1300 653 408). Questions concerning Blue Mountains National Park, Wollemi National Park, and Kanangra-Boyd National Park are best handled by the NPWS-run **Blue Mountains Heritage Centre**, at the roundabout near the end of Govetts Leap Rd. Staffed by knowledgeable park officials, the center also has exhibits, detailed trail guides ($2-4), and refreshments. (☎4787 8877. Open daily 9am-4:30pm.)

🏠🏕 ACCOMMODATIONS & FOOD. The **New Ivanhoe Hotel ❸**, at the corner of the Great Western Hwy. and Govetts Leap Rd., has clean, tasteful rooms. (☎4787 8158. Light breakfast included. Reception at bar Su-Th 6am-midnight, F-Sa 6am-2am. Twins and doubles $66, ensuite family room $88.) **Blackheath Caravan Park ❶**, on Prince Edward St. off Govetts Leap Rd., opposite Memorial Park, has toilets, showers, and BBQ. (☎4787 8101. Key deposit $10. Reception 8am-7pm. Sites $9 per person, powered $12; cabins for 2 $42, ensuite $58.) There are two **NPWS camping areas ❶** accessible from Blackheath: **Perrys Lookdown,** 8km from the Great Western Hwy. at the end of the mostly unpaved Hat Hill Rd. (5 walk-in sites; 1-night stay only), and **Acacia Flat,** on the floor of the Grose Valley, a hefty four-hour hike from Govetts Leap and a two- to three-hour hike from Perrys Lookdown. Both sites are free and lack facilities other than pit toilets. Campfires are not permitted. Water from Govetts Creek is available at Acacia Flat, but it must be treated. There is no reliable water source at Perrys Lookdown. If small Blackheath is too big for you, head 7km west on the Great Western Hwy. to **Mt. Victoria,** a quiet village that serves as an alternate Blue Mountains base. It has several historic buildings, including **Manor House,** on Montgomery St., built in 1876. The **Victoria and Albert Guesthouse ❺**, 19 Station St., is a beautiful restored B&B home with a pool, spa, and sauna. (☎4787 1241; victoria.albert@ourguest.com.au. Reception 8am-9pm. Twins and doubles $110-120, ensuite $120-140.)

🥾 HIKES & LOOKOUTS. Walks in the Blackheath area vary widely in length and level of difficulty. The **Fairfax Heritage Track** (30min. one-way) is wheelchair-accessible and leads to the **Govetts Leap,** one of the most magnificent lookouts in Blue Mountains National Park. From Govetts Leap, the moderate **Pulpit Rock Track** (3hr. return) follows the cliff line north for spectacular views along the way of Horseshoe Falls and a 280° view of the Grose Valley from the Pulpit Rock lookout. The **Cliff Top Walk** travels the other direction to **Evans Lookout** (2½hr. return) past the wispy **Govetts Leap Falls,** a thin stream that takes nearly ten seconds to tumble all the way into the valley below. The moderate **Grand Canyon Walking Track** (5km; 3-4hr. circuit) is undoubtedly one of the most popular hikes in all the Blue Mountains. You can start at either **Neates Glen** or **Evans Lookout,** but if you need to park a car, leave it at the Grand Canyon Loop Carpark, along the Evans Lookout Rd. On a misty day or after a rainstorm, the steps leading from there can be slippery; be cautious and consider beginning at Evans. The circuit passes through sandstone cliffs, wet rainforest, and exposed heathland. Anthropologists speculate that the Grand Canyon was probably a route long used by Aboriginal people to gain access to the deposits of chert (a quartzite rock used in cutting tools) at the base of Beauchamp Falls. Archaeological evidence suggests that Aborigines occupied the Grand Canyon at least 12,000 years ago. Six kilometers north of Blackheath along the Great Western Hwy. is **Hat Hill Road,** a mostly dirt route that bumps and bounces to an excellent lookout and a popular trailhead for the **Blue Gum Forest.** Near the end of the road, the turn-off leading to the parking area for **Anvil Rock** and the magical features of the misnamed **Wind Eroded Cave** (the feature is the result of water) is well worth the side trip.

The scenic drive into the **Megalong Valley** begins on Shipley Rd., across the Great Western Hwy. from Govett's Leap Rd. Cross the railroad tracks from the highway and take an immediate left onto Station St., following it until it turns right to become Shipley Rd. Megalong Rd. is a left turn from Shipley Rd., leading down to a picturesque farmland area that contrasts nicely with the surrounding wilderness.

In the valley, outfitters supply horses or conduct guided **trail rides. Werriberri Trail Rides** is 10km along Megalong Rd. near Werriberri Lodge. (☎4787 9171. Open daily 9am-3:30pm; reservations 7:30am-4pm. 30min. $22; 3hr. $78. 2-9 day rides by request.) The **Megalong Australian Heritage Centre,** a bit farther south on Megalong Rd., also has guided rides, as well as unguided outings, livestock lassoing shows, and 4WD bush trips on their 2000 acres. (☎4787 8688; www.megalong.cc. Open daily 7:30am-6pm. Horse rides daily 10am-4pm. 3hr. ride $82, full-day $135; unguided $40 per hr. 4WD $22-25 per hr.)

BLUE MOUNTAINS NATIONAL PARK

The largest and most touristed of the Blue Mountain region national parks, the Blue Mountains National Park is one of eight protected areas making up the World Heritage site collectively known as the Greater Blue Mountains Area. This World Heritage status was awarded only three years ago.

BLUE MOUNTAINS AT A GLANCE	
AREA: 208,756 hectares.	**GATEWAYS:** Glenbrook (p. 160), Katoomba (p. 153), Blackheath (p. 158).
FEATURES: Govetts Leap (Blackheath), Three Sisters (Katoomba), Wentworth Falls.	**CAMPING:** Minimum impact camping allowed; see individual regions.
HIGHLIGHTS: Over 140km bushwalking trails, horseback riding, canyoning, and riding the world's steepest railway.	**FEES:** Vehicles $6 (Glenbrook only).

⊞⊠ ORIENTATION & PRACTICAL INFORMATION

Blue Mountains National Park lies between Kanangra-Boyd National Park to the south and Wollemi National Park to the north. Two east-west highways partition the park into three sections: the section north of the **Bells Line of Road,** the section south of the **Great Western Highway,** and the small section between the two highways. Three gateway towns lie along the Great Western Hwy. from east to west, **Glenbrook** (p. 160), **Katoomba** (p. 153), and **Blackheath** (p. 158).

Blue Mountains Tourism operates offices in Glenbrook and Katoomba (☎1300 653 408; www.bluemountainstourism.org.au. Glenbrook open M-F 9am-5pm, Sa-Su 8:30am-4:30pm and Katoomba open daily 9am-5pm). The NPWS-run **Blue Mountains Heritage Centre,** at the roundabout near the end of Govetts Leap Rd. in Blackheath, handles questions regarding the national parks. (☎4787 8877. Open daily 9am-4:30pm.)

⊠ BLUE MOUNTAINS: A TOWN BY TOWN GUIDE

ALONG THE GREAT WESTERN HIGHWAY
Leaving Sydney, the Great Western Hwy. passes Penrith just before the entrance to the Blue Mountains National Park. It extends to Lithgow, passing Katoomba (p. 153) and Blackheath (p. 158) on its way through the park.

GLENBROOK. Glenbrook is a gateway town just north of the easternmost entrance to the park. From the highway, take Ross St. until it ends, turn left on Burfitt Pde. (later named Bruce Rd.), and follow it to the park. The walking track to **Red Hands Cave** starts at the national park's entrance station and runs an easy 8km circuit through patches of open forest, leading ultimately to a gallery of **hand**

stencils attributed to the Darug Aborigines. Along the way to the cave, the trail passes the turn-off for **Jellybean Pool**, a popular swimming hole near the park's entrance. You can reduce the length of the hike to a mere 300m stroll (one-way) if you drive to the Red Hands carpark and begin there.

The **Tourist Information Centre**, off the Great Western Hwy., is a convenient place to pick up maps and info of the Blue Mountains before heading farther into the region. (☎4739 6266. Open daily 8:30am-4:30pm.) Four kilometers beyond the Bruce Rd. entrance, over mostly paved roads, is the **Euroka Campground ❶**. The site has pit toilets and BBQ plates, but no water. Kangaroos congregate at dawn and dusk. The park entrance is locked in the evenings (summer 7pm-8:30am; winter 6pm-8:30am); campers are advised to bring ample firewood, food, and drinking water. Call the **NPWS** in Richmond to book ahead. (☎4588 5247. Open M-F 9am-5pm. Sites $5, children $3.) Bushcamping is free.

BLAXLAND. At **Blaxland**, roughly 4km west of Glenbrook, Layton Ave. turns off onto a pleasant 2km detour towards **Lennox Bridge**, the **oldest bridge** on the Australian mainland. West of Blaxland (and the towns of Warrimoo, Valley Heights, and Springwood) lies **Faulconbridge**, site of the National Trust-owned **Norman Lindsay Gallery**, at 14 Norman Lindsay Crescent. The gallery displays a large collection of works focusing on the female form by the multitalented artist who once inhabited the house. To get to the gallery by car from Sydney, turn right off the Great Western Hwy. onto Grose Rd., in Falconbridge, and follow the well-posted signs. (☎4751 1067. Open daily 10am-4pm. $8, ISIC $6. Public transportation to the site is limited to a **taxi** ($8) from the Springwood Railway Station.

WOODFORD. Woodford, about 15km east of Katoomba on the Great Western Hwy., is the start of a popular **mountain biking** trail. The **Woodford Oaks Fire Trail** is a 27km, mostly downhill track that leads to Glenbrook. Woodford also serves as a turn-off to a few popular campgrounds. A left off the highway onto Park Rd., a left onto Railway Pde., and a right onto Bedford Rd., lead to the **Murphys Glen Campground ❶**, 10km south of Woodford. Located within a forest of eucalypts, turpentines, and angophoras, the campground has pit toilets but lacks drinking water.

WENTWORTH FALLS. The town of **Wentworth Falls**, 14km beyond Woodford, is renowned for its picturesque waterfall walks and foliage diversity—more varieties of plants exist in the Blue Mountains than in all of Europe. To find the trailhead at the **Wentworth Falls Picnic Area**, turn off the Great Western Hwy. onto Falls Rd. and continue to the end of the road. From this area, several viewpoints are within easy reach. The 15min. walk to **Princes Rock** gives the best views with the least effort. It ends at a lookout with views of Wentworth Falls, Kings Tableland, and Mt. Solitary. The 30min. walk to **Rocket Point Lookout** wanders through open heathland and has views into the Jamison Valley. To find the trailhead at the **Conservation Hut**, turn off the highway at either Falls Rd. or Valley Rd., turn right onto Fletcher St., and continue straight to the parking area.

For an ambitious and stunning loop hike, begin at the hut off Fletcher St. and follow the **Valley of the Waters Track** to **Empress Lookout**, head down the metal stairs, then follow the trail along the Valley of Waters Creek. Take the Wentworth Pass through the valley to Slacks Stairs, where the steep steps take you up to Wentworth Falls and the **Wentworth Falls Picnic Area**. From the carpark, you can head back to the hut via the **Shortcut Track** (5hr. circuit) or the **Undercliff-Overcliff Track** (6-7hr. circuit). Spectacular scenery and lush hanging swamps will reward the extra effort. **National Pass**, an alternate route through the valley between Empress Lookout and Slacks Stairs, is closed until mid-2004; check with the NPWS for info on its re-opening. On starry nights, visit the **Kings Tableland Observatory**, 55 Hordern

Rd. A local astronomer extraordinaire shows you constellations, globular clusters, and distant planets. (☎4757 2954. Open daily 7-9pm; Daylight Savings 8-11pm. 2hr. $10, children $8, families $28.)

To reach the **Ingar Campground ❶**, drive west past Woodford (and the towns of Hazelbrook, Lawson, and Bullburra), turn left off the highway onto Tableland Rd., travel 2km, turn left at Queen Elizabeth Dr., and proceed 11km along an unpaved road to Ingar. The campground has pit toilets but lacks drinking water and cooking facilities. (No permits required. Free.) Nearby, a small pond and creek make the spot popular for picnics and camping.

LEURA. The pleasant and affluent town of Leura (pop. 8500), 5km west of Wentworth Falls and adjacent to Katoomba, offers shops, cafes, and galleries along its central street, Leura Mall. **Everglades Gardens,** 37 Everglades St., is a lush example of the former floral cultivation for which the town is known. Designed by Dutch master gardener Paul Sorensen, this 5.2ha estate in the Jamison Valley is now owned and run by the National Trust. (☎4784 1938. Open daily Sept.-Feb. 10am-5pm; Mar.-Aug. 10am-4pm. $6, YHA $4.) Near the gardens, Fitzroy St. intersects Everglades Rd. and leads east to Watkins Rd., which soon turns into Sublime Point Rd. and ends at the breathtaking overlook at **Sublime Point,** a great spot for watching the sunrise. For travelers continuing west toward Katoomba, the 8km **Cliff Drive,** beginning at Gordon Rd. near the south end of Leura Mall, provides a scenic escape from the highway, passing many lookouts and several trailheads. In Katoomba, Cliff Dr. turns into Echo Point Rd. The helpful staff at the **Visitor Information Centre,** 208 The Mall, book accommodations, offer Internet ($2 per 15min.), and arrange guided tours (☎4784 2222; tourist@pnc.com.au. Open daily 9am-5pm.)

ALONG THE BELLS LINE OF ROAD

This 87km drive runs north of the Great Western Hwy. through the Blue Mountains National Park and just below Wollemi National Park. It connects with the Great Western Hwy. in the town of Lithgow (its left endpoint), and runs east to Windsor.

BILPIN. The town of Bilpin, 5km west of Kurrajong Heights, has several active orchards and roadside fruit stands that sell fresh-picked produce most of the year.

MT. TOMAH BOTANIC GARDEN. A few kilometers west of Berambing, Mt. Tomah Botanic Garden is the cool-climate and high-altitude plant collection of Sydney's Royal Botanic Garden. With the exception of the formal terrace garden, the plants (including 13 Wollemi pines) thrive on the rich volcanic soil and grow in naturalistic arrangements. The garden's best moments are in spring (Sept.-Oct.), when the large collection of rhododendrons and other flowers bloom, and in autumn (Apr.-May), when the deciduous forests change their colors. Free tours depart the Visitors Centre during the week. (☎4567 2154; open daily Apr.-Sept. 10am-4pm; Oct.-Mar. 10am-5pm. $4.40, children $2.20, families $8.80.)

MT. WILSON. People come from far and wide to see the formal, European-style gardens and unspoiled rainforest of the small town of Mt. Wilson, 8km north of Bells Line of Road, between Mt. Tomah and Bell. For a sample of the fern-laden rainforest, turn right onto Queens Ave. off the main road through town and proceed about 500m until you reach a park area on the left. From there, follow signs to a moderate 45min. **Waterfall Trek** (with steep steps) that leads to the base of two small waterfalls. Three gardens in and around town stay open throughout the year: **Sefton Cottage,** on Church Ln. (☎4756 2034; open daily 10am-6pm; $3); **Merry Garth,** on Davies Ln., 500m from Mt. Irvine Rd. (☎4756 2121; open daily 9am-6pm; $3); and **Lindfield Park,** on Mt. Irvine Rd., 6km northeast of Mt. Wilson (☎4756 2148. Open daily 10am-dark; $3).

ZIG ZAG RAILWAY. The **Zig Zag Railway,** 10km east of Lithgow at Clarence, is a functional train operating on a piece of the 1869 track that first made regular travel possible across the Blue Mountains and down into the Lithgow Valley. (☎6353 1795. 1½hr. tours depart daily at 11am, 1, and 3pm. $18 return, concessions $15, ages 5-18 $9.) By request, **CityRail** trains from Sydney's Central Station stop near the bottom of the track ($13).

LITHGOW. The Great Western Hwy. and Bells Line of Road meet on the west side of the Blue Mountains at Lithgow, a medium-sized, semi-industrial town at the end of the Sydney's CityRail train line. The town provides a good base from which to explore nearby wilderness areas such as Wollemi National Park to the north and the Jenolan Caves and Kanangra-Boyd National Park to the south. The highest lookout in the Blue Mountains (1130m) is indisputably worth the five minute detour along the **Hassans Walls Link** drive. **Blackfellows Hands Reserve,** 24km north of Lithgow, off Wolgen Rd. to Newnes, was a meeting place for Aboriginal tribes, and paintings adorn the walls of the cave. The 4WD-access **Gardens of Stone National Park,** 30km north of Lithgow, features pagoda-like formations from millions of years of erosion. The spectacular granite formations of **Evans Crown Nature Reserve** (☎6354 8155), 32km west of Lithgow, make for a climbers' playground.

The **Visitor Information Centre,** 1 Cooerwull Rd. off the Great Western Hwy., just past the intersection with Main St., can book accommodations and provide maps and info on Wollemi National Park. (☎6353 1859; fax 6353 1851; www.tourism.lithgow.com. Open daily 9am-5pm.) Several hotels line Main St., but the **Grand Central Hotel ❷,** 69 Main St., is the pick of the litter with its spacious singles, TV lounge, **pub,** and adjacent **bistro.** Take a left out of the train station and walk two blocks. (☎6351 3050. Bistro open M-Sa noon-2pm and 6-9pm. Singles $25; continental breakfast included.) The **Blue Bird Cafe ❶,** 118 Main St., prepares basic sandwiches ($3-7), various fried dishes, and tasty milkshakes. (☎6352 4211. Open daily 6:30am-7pm.) The Food For Less **grocery store** is on Railway Pde. (☎6352 2011. Open M-Sa 7am-7pm, Su 7am-6pm.)

WOLLEMI NATIONAL PARK

Covering 4875km², Wollemi (WOOL-em-eye) National Park is the second largest park in New South Wales. It extends north of Blue Mountains National Park all the way to the Hunter and Goulburn River valleys. Because 2WD access is extremely lim-

FROM THE ROAD

OVER THE TOP

If everyone else jumped off a cliff, would I? Yes, as it turns out. After six people in my introductory abseiling group disappeared down the first of several cliffs, it was my turn to go over the edge.

Back in Sydney, I had heard of abseiling, but the concept remained a vague one. I envisioned rocks and rope, though I couldn't be sure since it did have sailing in the name.

Standing with my back facing the edge of an 80m cliff about to lean back, take the first step down, and put a lot of trust into the harness awkwardly fastened around my waist and thighs, it became very clear to me that abseiling had nothing to do with boats. Or sea level, for that matter. It felt like I was about to willingly walk off a cliff, which was exactly the case.

What ended up being important wasn't abseiling skill or experience, but rather having a sense of humor and openness. On the last cliff, which had an overhang, our feet could no longer touch the rock so we had to fully trust the rope and dangle 50m in the air. For the first time, I turned away from the rock and looked around me. I was hanging freely in the middle of the gorgeous Megalong Valley: suspended in the still, silent air, the effect was simply breathtaking.

—Amy Cain

ited, the park still has many pockets of undiscovered land. One such area yielded an amazing find in 1994, when scientists found a species of pine tree known previously only through the fossil record. Only around 40 adult **Wollemi Pine** trees have been found in three remote locations in the region, but these few trees provide a view to the past that has already helped researchers retrace evolutionary steps back to the era of dinosaurs. The location of the grove is a closely-guarded secret, and scientists studying the trees must have their instruments sterilized to avoid introducing disease to the grove.

The southernmost entrance point to the park is at Bilpin on Bells Line of Road. In this corner of the park, also accessible from Putty Rd. north of Windsor, the **Colo River** slices the landscape along the 30km Colo Gorge. The picturesque, car-accessible **camping area** at **Wheeny Creek ❶** lies near good walking tracks and swimming holes. Entrance and campgrounds are free. Additional information is available at the **NPWS** office, 370 Windsor Rd., in Richmond. (☎4588 5247. Open M-F 9:30am-12:30pm and 1:30-5pm.) The NPWS office in Mudgee (☎6372 7199; mudgee@npws.nsw.gov.au; open M-F 9am-5pm) services the northwest section of the park and can give info about camping in **Dunns Swamp ❶**, 25km east of Rylstone. (No toilets or water. $3, children $2.) Farther west, a 37km unsealed road from Lithgow takes starry-eyed observers within 1.5km of **Glow Worm Tunnel,** an abandoned railway tunnel housing hundreds of tiny bioluminescent worms. There are no marked trails in the northern section of Wollemi National Park.

KANANGRA-BOYD NATIONAL PARK

Southwest of the Blue Mountains National Park, Kanangra-Boyd National Park stuns visitors with stark wilderness punctuated by rivers and creeks, still-developing caves, and the dramatic sandstone cliffs that mark the edges of the Boyd Plateau. The park's remote location and rugged terrain attracts experienced bushwalkers looking for some serious solitude.

The park is nonetheless worthwhile for the casual visitors who follow its only 2WD access, the unpaved Kanangra Walls Rd., across the **Boyd Plateau** to the famous lookouts at **Kanangra Walls.** Use caution when driving; accidents from speeding are common on the unsealed roads dense with wildlife. From the east via Mt. Victoria, drive to Jenolan Caves off the Great Western Hwy. (see p. 160). From there, a 5km stretch of dirt road will lead to the park and the junction with Kanangra Walls Rd., turn left at the intersection, and the Kanangra Walls carpark is another 26km farther. From the west, drive to the town of **Oberon** and follow the unpaved Jenolan Caves Rd. south to the junction with Kanangra Walls Rd. Turn right to reach the lookouts.

The **NPWS** office, 38 Ross St., Oberon (northeast of the park), has details on the park's longer tracks. Be sure to call before visiting or you may find the branch unattended. Cave exploration permits must be obtained at least four weeks in advance. (☎6336 1972. Open M-F 9am-4:30pm.)

The **Boyd River Campground ❶**, on Kanangra Walls Rd. 6km before Kanangra Walls, has the park's only car-accessible camping. There are pit toilets and fireplaces. Bring your own wood or a camp stove. Water is available from the Boyd River but it should be treated before consumption. Camping is free, but park fees apply ($6 per vehicle per day). Most bushwalks in the park are not signposted, with the exception of these three **scenic walks,** which begin at the Kanangra Walls carpark. **Lookout Walk** (20min. return) is a wheelchair-accessible path leading to two viewpoints. The first gazes out across the Kanangra Creek gorge towards **Mt. Cloudmaker,** and the other peers into the ravines at the head of the eight-tiered, 400m **Kanangra Falls.** The **Waterfall Walk** (20min. one-way with steep return) leads from the second lookout to the deep pool at the bottom of **Kalang Falls.** The moderate **Plateau Walk** (2-3hr.) branches off from the Lookout Walk between the parking lot and the first lookout, descending briefly from the plateau before ascending to Kanangra Tops for views of Kanangra Walls. Along the way to the Tops, **Dance Floor Cave** contains indented floors and other signs of old-time recreation in the park. A water container placed in the cave in 1940 catches pure, drinkable water dripping down from the cave ceiling. Longer walks are available in the park as well, like the three- or four-day **hike** from Kanangra Walls to Katoomba via Mt. Stormbreaker, Mt. Cloudmaker, the Wild Dog Mountains, and the Narrow Neck Plateau. These longer, more intensive walks must always be planned in advance with help from the NPWS.

JENOLAN CAVES

The amazing limestone and crystal formations of Jenolan (Je-NO-lan) Caves have intrigued visitors since they were opened to the public in 1838. Any of the caves are stunning just to look at, and several adventure tours (see below) offer visitors to chance to explore further. The caves, which are 46km south of the Great Western Hwy. from Hartley, on the northwestern edge of Kanangra-Boyd National park, can be reached by bus from Katoomba (see p. 153). Nine different areas within the massive cave system, overseen by the **Jenolan Caves Reserve Trust**, at the Jenolan Caves turn-off, have **guided tours**. (☎ 6359 3311; www.jenolancaves.org.au. Ticket office open daily in summer 9am-5pm; in winter 9am-4:30pm. M-F 11 tours per day, Sa-Su 25; $15-22. YHA discount 10%.)

Lucas Cave (1½hr., $15) displays a broad range of features and is generally considered the best place to start exploring the Jenolan Caves, but the large crowds can seriously detract from the experience. Cello concerts are given once a month in this cave; call ahead for dates. ($33, children $20; includes admission.) **Orient Cave** (1½hr., $22) and **Imperial Cave** (1hr., $15) both have a more tolerable flow of visitors as well as several eye-catching stalactites and stalagmites. The **Temple of Baal** (1½hr., $22) and the **River Cave** (2hr., $28) are also exciting options for spelunkers hoping to escape some of the bigger tourist crowds. **Orient Cave** and **Chifley Cave** (1hr., $15) are two of the few caves that are partially wheelchair-accessible.

Adventure tours, run by the Trust, take small groups of people who want to get down and dirty through some of the cave system's less accessible areas. These trips involve moderate to strenuous climbing, some crawling, and a healthy dose of darkness. The most popular adventure tour is the one that runs to the so-called **Plughole** (2½hr., $55; departs daily at 1:15pm). Spelunkers heading to the Plughole must be at least ten years old; those venturing into **Aladdin Cave** (3hr., $61; departs 9am last Su every month) must be at least 12 years of age, and those exploring **Mammoth Cave** (6hr., $155; runs 1st Sa every month) must be at least 16. The Trust also offers theme tours such as ghost tours and off-track adventures, complete with miner's lights and overalls (2hr., from $28). For those not wanting to head underground, well-defined pathways amble along the surface and lead to **Carlotta Arch,** the **Devils Coachhouse, McKeown's Valley,** and the **Blue Lake.**

Overnight **camping ❶** is available at Jenolan Caves. Each site has a fireplace, and the campground has a shared amenities block (sites $11). Serious outdoor enthusiasts might want to head off for two to three days of hiking along the original dirt roadway that once connected Katoomba and Jenolan Caves back in the late 1800s. Today there is the **Six Foot Track,** a 42km trail that runs from the Jenolan Caves to Nellies Glen Rd. off the Great Western Hwy., at the western end of Katoomba. The trail, which takes 3 days to complete, is quite steep in places, and hikers must bring their own water. Overnight **camping ❶** is available at four primitive sites along the way. One-way transfers to Katoomba are available from Jenolan Caves ($47, children $32).

NEW SOUTH WALES

HUNTER VALLEY

Located within just a few hours' drive of Sydney and known for its famous world-wide wine exports, the Hunter Valley is a popular holiday destination for international travelers and Sydneysiders alike. Over 100 wineries take advantage of the region's warm, dry climate and sandy loam creek soils. Many guesthouses and B&Bs dot the landscape to cater to the mostly weekend tourist onslaught. Though only 8-10% of all Australian wines are made from Hunter Valley fruit, local vintages claim more than their share of national wine trophies and medals. Chief among the varieties produced in the area are the peppery red **Shiraz** and the citrusy white **Semillon**. The area can be cheaply explored via free wine tastings, a hired car, and a designated driver. Most of the vineyards are clustered around **Pokolbin** in the lower Hunter Valley at the base of the Brokenback Mountains, but several notable labels are situated in the upper Hunter, centered around the small town of **Denman.**

▐ ▀ ▚ TRANSPORTATION & TOURS

The best time to visit wine country is mid-week, when the number of people is fewer and the prices of tours and accommodations are lower. **Countrylink** (☎ 13 22 32) departs daily from Sydney to Scone (4½hr., $47.30) via Muswellbrook (3½hr., $41.80). **Keans Travel Express** departs from Bay 14 in Sydney Central Station's coach terminal (☎ 6543 1322 or 1800 043 339; M-Th 3pm, F 3 and 6pm, Sa-Su 6:40pm) en route to: Cessnock (2¼hr., $30); Singleton (2¾hr., $35); Muswellbrook (3½hr., $38.50); and Scone (3¾hr., $37.50). **Rover Coaches,** 231 Vincent St., in Cessnock, runs a bus from Sydney Central Station to Cessnock and the Visitor Information Centre. (☎ 4990 1699 or 1800 801 012; www.rovercoaches.com.au. Departs 7:30am. $30, ISIC $20.). A bus also directly connects Cessnock and Newcastle (1¼hr., M-Sa 4-6 per day, $10.60). On Sundays, take the bus to Maitland (45min., 5 per day, $7) and then catch the **CityRail** train to Newcastle (50min., 5 per day, $4.40). **Bicycle rental** is available from **Hunter Valley Cycling,** in the Hunter Valley Garden complex (☎ 4998 6633), as well as **Grapemobile Bicycle Hire** in Pokolbin, at the corner of McDonalds Rd. and Palmers Ln. (☎ 4991 2339. Half-day $25, full-day $35.) The general guideline for drivers is that 5 tastings (20mL each) equals one standard drink. If you're not on a tour and your Bacchanalian revelries have gotten the best of you, **Cessnock Radio Cabs** (☎ 4990 1111) can get you home safely.

Unless you have a car to get you to the individual wineries, and a responsible designated driver who can resist all the tempting free tastings, you'll need to book a tour. If you're starting in Newcastle or Maitland, the standard 10- to 20-person tour generally lasts from 9am to 5pm (10am-4pm from Cessnock) and visits four to five wineries. The **Vineyard Shuttle Service** lets passengers suggest wineries rather than following a strict itinerary. (☎ 4993 7779 or 4991 3655. M-F $33, Sa-Su $35-40; with evening restaurant transfer add $10.) **Shadows** visits both boutiques and large, commercial wineries. Book ahead to arrange door-to-door transfers for Newcastle and surrounding addresses. (☎ 4990 7002. $40, with lunch $60.) **Hunter Vineyard Tours** (☎ 4991 1659) picks up from Cessnock ($45, with lunch $65), Newcastle, and Maitland (both $50/$70). **Trekabout** creates a more intimate setting by limiting tours to 12. (☎ 4990 8277. M-F half-day $28, daily full-day $44.) **Horse-drawn carriage tours** generally start at $45 and are available through **Paxton Brown** (☎ 4998 7362) on Deasys Rd.; and **Pokolbin Horse Coaches,** on McDonald's Rd. (☎ 4998 7305).

Several tour companies offer daytrips from Sydney. **Wonderbus** runs 20-person groups straight to the Hunter Valley, and also offers a trip to Port Stephens in the morning for a dolphin-watching excursion followed by a half-day wine tour in the Hunter Valley. (☎ 9555 9800. Departs 7am, returns 7:30pm. $165, ISIC/backpackers

$150; includes lunch.) **Oz Trails** caters to groups up to 14 and visits the valley via the Hawkesbury River for morning tea and lunch. (☎9387 8390. pick-up 8am, drop-off 6:30pm. $100, without tea and lunch $89.)

WINERIES

Most wineries are open for free tastings and occasional tours daily 10am-5pm (some 9:30am-4:30pm), although some of the smaller ones are only open on weekends. Of the over 100 wineries, the largest are **McGuigan's, Lindemans, Tyrrell's, Drayton's, Rothbury Estate, Wyndham Estate,** and **McWilliams-Mount Pleasant Estate.** Smaller boutiques, such as **Ivanhoe, Pokolbin Estate, Rothvale,** and **Sobel's,** only sell their wines on their private premises. While not as glitzy, they are generally more relaxed. Check with Hunter Valley Wine Country Tourism about free tours of individual wineries. Wine prices vary widely but typically start around $15 per bottle.

LOWER HUNTER VALLEY   ☎02

Most visitors to the Hunter stay in the very accessible lower valley, whose wineries are concentrated in the Pokolbin and Rothbury shires, just north of the town of **Cessnock.** Travelers who use Cessnock as a base to explore the wineries can save money by staying at one of the town's numerous budget accommodations, but Cessnock lacks the charm that impels many to visit the Hunter in the first place.

ORIENTATION & PRACTICAL INFORMATION. Those traveling by car should follow signs on the F3 Freeway (Sydney-Newcastle) to Cessnock, which is approximately two hours from Sydney and 20min. from Newcastle. **Hunter Valley Wine Country Tourism,** on Annandale Rd., 6km north of Cessnock toward Branxton, will book vineyard tours and accommodations, and has a daily specials board with cheaper standby rates at guesthouses and B&Bs. The free *Hunter Valley Wine Country Visitors Guide* has an indispensable map, as well as info on wineries, cellar doors, attractions, restaurants, and accommodations. (☎4990 4477; www.winecountry.com.au. Open M-Sa 9am-5pm, Su 9am-4pm.) **Maitland,** 30min. east of Cessnock, is a historic town by the Hunter River filled with craft and antique galleries. Maitland's **Visitor Information Centre** is in Ministers Park, near the junction of High St. and the New England Hwy. (☎4931 2800; www.hunterrivercountry.com.au. Open daily 9am-5pm.)

ACCOMMODATIONS & FOOD. The **Hunter Valley Accommodation Centre ❷,** 210 Allandale Rd., about a 10min. drive north of Cessnock, has basic, clean motel and backpacker accommodations in a very convenient location. Ask about discounts on skydiving next door. (☎4991 4222. Pool and BBQ. Continental breakfast included on weekends for motel guests. Heated dorms $25; motel ensuite doubles with TV Su-Th $66, F-Sa $99; family rooms that sleep up to 13 from $66-99 for 2, extra person $17-20. Wheelchair-accessible.) **Harrigan's Irish Pub ❺,** on Broke Rd. next to Hunter Valley Gardens, has been voted best pub accommodation in NSW. Its 4-star ensuite rooms wrap around its lively pub (see below), and have TVs, fridges, and balconies. There's also a heated pool. (☎4998 7819 or 1800 800 522. Doubles Su-Th $155, F-Sa $410; 4-person suite $184/$518.) Pubstays are also available in Cessnock. **Wentworth Hotel ❹,** on Vincent St., is one of the nicer ones. (☎4990 1364; www.wentworthhotelcessnock.com.au. Continental breakfast included. Doubles $95.) The **Hill Top Country Guest House ❹,** 81 Talga Rd., in Rothbury, is a 15min. drive from the Visitors Centre via Lovedale Rd. and offers horseback riding, a pool, billiards, and a gorgeous view of the surrounding countryside. (☎4930 7111; www.hilltopguesthouse.com.au. Twins and kings with shared bath Su-Th $88, F-Sa $165; ensuite twins and doubles $110/$186; spa suite $154/$240.

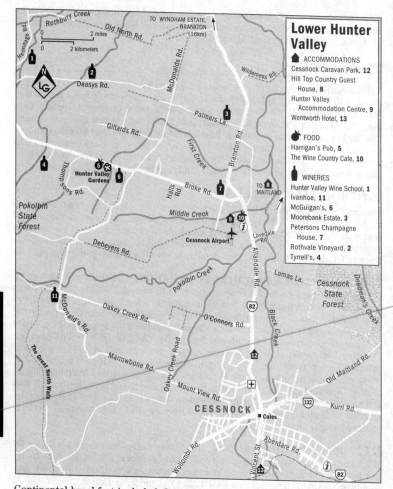

Lower Hunter Valley

🏠 ACCOMMODATIONS
Cessnock Caravan Park, **12**
Hill Top Country Guest
House, **8**
Hunter Valley
Accommodation Centre, **9**
Wentworth Hotel, **13**

🍴 FOOD
Harrigan's Pub, **5**
The Wine Country Cafe, **10**

🍷 WINERIES
Hunter Valley Wine School, **1**
Ivanhoe, **11**
McGuigan's, **6**
Moorebank Estate, **3**
Petersons Champagne
House, **7**
Rothvale Vineyard, **2**
Tyrrell's, **4**

Continental breakfast included. 2-night min. on weekends, but negotiable.) The **Cessnock Caravan Park ❶,** on Allandale Rd., 3km north of the town center on the main tourist route, has a pool, BBQ, and a wheelchair-accessible cabin. (☎ 4990 5819. Sites for 2 $18-20; on-site caravans for 2 $50-65.)

There are few cheap options for eating out in the Hunter Valley. **The Wine Country Cafe ❶,** adjoining the Hunter Valley Wine Country Tourism office on Allandale Rd., offers delicious gourmet sandwiches ($7.50-12.50), hot drinks ($3-5), and sweet treats. (☎ 4990 9208. Open daily 9am-5pm.) Many vineyards have restaurants and cafes. Both Woolworths and Coles **supermarkets** lie near Cooper and Darwin St. in Cessnock. **⧫Harrington's Irish Pub,** in addition to its accommodation and bistro with cook-your-own steaks and wood-fired pizzas ($16-22), is the center of night-life in the lower Hunter Valley. Weekend nights are packed with a mixed crowd partying to popular funk, while Su night has a 16-20 person jam session. (Bistro open daily 7:30am-10:30pm. Pub open Su-W 7:30am-11:30pm, Th-Sa 7:30am-2am.)

◙ ▧ **SIGHTS & ACTIVITIES.** The **Hunter Valley Gardens,** on the corner of Broke and McDonald Rd., is a touristy shopping complex that also contains 25 hectares of stunning, formally sculpted gardens with 12 different themes. (☎ 4998 7600; www.hvg.com.au. Open daily 10am-5pm. $12, children $7, families $38.) The mind-boggling views are well worth the cost at the **Hunter Valley Skydiving Centre,** 210 Allandale Rd. (☎ 9790 5867). **Balloon Aloft** (☎ 4938 1955), **Cloud Nine** (☎ 9686 7777), and **Hunter Valley Ballooning** (☎ 1800 818 191) all have sunrise hot air balloon flights lasting roughly one hour. ($250-290; usually includes a champagne breakfast.) Hill Top Country Guest House (see **Accommodations**) conducts nighttime **4WD wildlife tours** ($20, children $10), as well as 1½hr. **horseback rides** ($45) and canoeing trips down the Hunter River ($35).

▧ **WINERIES.** The vineyards of the lower Hunter are situated along a tangle of rural roads, the free map from Hunter Valley Wine Country Tourism is the best way to navigate. Even so, the entire area is well-signposted, and large billboard maps are located at major intersections. A good place to start is the Hunter Resort, where the **Hunter Valley Wine School** gives lessons in the art of wine tasting. The tour of their Hermitage Road Cellar finishes with an evaluation of three whites and three reds. (☎ 4998 7777. Daily 9-11am. $25. Book ahead.) In addition to free tastings, **Tyrrell's** (☎ 4993 7000), on Broke Rd., gives free one-hour tours (M-Sa 1:30pm) revealing the wine-making process of the 145-year-old family-run business. **McGuigan's** (☎ 4998 7402; www.mcguiganwines.com.au), on McDonalds Rd., is the valley's busiest winery. Daily tours ($2) depart at noon. A cheese shop next door has free tastings. **Wyndham Estate** (☎ 4938 3444), on Dalwood Rd., is the oldest winery in Australia, first planting vines in 1828. Today, it has a huge historic tasting room, and gives free tours at 11am. **Petersons Champagne House** (☎ 4998 7881; www.petersonhouse.com.au), at the corner of Broke and Branxton Rd., is the only place in New South Wales strictly devoted to the bubbly brew, and also has an interesting selection of sparkling red wines.

Of the smaller boutique wineries in the lower valley, **Rothvale** (☎ 4998 7290), on Deasys Rd., consistently receives high praise. Groups can arrange for a 1½hr. wine education session ($15). Another notable boutique, **Ivanhoe** (☎ 4998 7325), on Marrowbone Rd., is owned and operated by a member of the distinguished wine-making Drayton family. The vineyard produces "big, gutsy reds" and a deliciously sweet and fruity dessert wine. In addition to wine, **Moorebank Estate** (☎ 4998 7610; www.moorebankvineyard.com.au), on Palmers Ln., gives tastings of its famous spicy grape sauce. (Open Su-Tu and F-Sa.)

UPPER HUNTER VALLEY ☎ 02

A few towns well northwest of Cessnock are great bases from which to explore the Upper Hunter Valley vineyards.

SINGLETON. This small town (pop. 12,500) is in between the lower and upper Hunter on the New England Hwy., though it's a bit of a drive to either one. It's notable mostly for its massive sundial, which is the world's largest. The **Visitors Information Centre,** 39 George St., on the New England Hwy., can provide info about accommodations. (☎ 1800 449 888. Open daily 9am-5pm.)

MUSWELLBROOK. On the New England Hwy., Muswellbrook (MUSCLE-brook) is closest to the action. The small town (pop. 12,000) has an abundance of historical buildings, many of them visible on the 4.5km **Muswellbrook Heritage walk** beginning at the Old Tea House on Bridge St. (New England Hwy.). The highway is also the site of a living **Vietnam Memorial,** a grove of 519 trees that represent each of the

NEW SOUTH WALES

Australian casualties in the conflict. The **Tourist Office,** 87 Hill St., just off Bridge St., shares a building with the Upper Hunter Wine Centre, which gives free tastings of wines from the region. (☎6541 4050; www.muswellbrook.org.au. Open daily 9:30am-5pm.) **Horse Stud Tours,** run by the owner of the Upper Hunter Wine Centre, takes travelers to the valley's famous horse studs ($75 per stud). **Eatons Hotel ❷,** 188 Bridge St., has basic rooms in an 1830s building. (☎6543 2403. Reception and pub open M-Th 10am-midnight, F-Sa 10am-1:30am, Su 10am-10pm. Singles $25; twins and doubles $35; triples $45.) **Pinaroo Leisure Park ❶** is 3km south on the New England Hwy. (☎6543 3905. Pool, laundry, BBQ, and social room. Sites for 2 $14, powered $18; cabins $50-65.)

SCONE. A more charming alternative for upper Hunter Valley accommodations is Scone, 26km north on the New England Hwy., a small but pretty town which prides itself on being the horse capital of Australia. The distinction is owed to the annual, two-week-long Scone Horse Festival in mid-May, which culminates in two days of thoroughbred racing for the Scone Cup. The race course is five minutes from the town center. The **Scone Visitor Information Centre** is at the corner of Kelly St. (New England Hwy.) and Susan St., in front of the train station. (☎6545 1526; www.horsecapital.com.au. **Internet** $2.50 per 30min. Open daily 9am-5pm.) The peaceful and remote **Scone YHA ❷,** 1151 Segenhoe Rd., is a converted country schoolhouse surrounded by horse stud farms and has a kitchen, BBQ, warm fireplace, and friendly hosts. Take Gundy Rd. 9km from the southern end of town. (☎/fax 6545 2072. Dorms $25, YHA $21.50; twins and soubles $46.50/$43.) The **Highway Caravan Park ❶,** 248 New England Hwy., is a place to pitch a tent, albeit next to the humming of road noise. (☎/fax 6545 1078. Sites for 2 $12.10, powered $16.50; ensuite caravans $36.30.)

WINERIES OF THE UPPER HUNTER VALLEY. The upper Hunter Valley has fewer wineries, is more spread out, and has less tourists than the lower Hunter, but its wines are fabulous and the countryside is beautiful. Pick up the *Vineyards of the Upper Hunter Valley* brochure with listings and a map from any area tourist centers. The well-marked trail starts off the New England Hwy. a few kilometers north of Muswellbrook. Unfortunately, no tour groups operate here, so you need your own car. All the wineries can easily be visited in one day, but be sure to keep tabs on how much wine you're drinking. **Rosemount Estate** (☎6549 6400), on Rosemount Rd., in Denman, is the largest vineyard and has an extraordinary variety of wines, ranging from a light Sauvignon Blanc to a peppery Cabernet Sauvignon. Since it exports 70% of its 2.5 million cases, you may be familiar with this label from home. **Arrowfield** (☎6576 4041), on the Golden Hwy. in Jerrys Plains, prides itself on producing affordable wines. **Cruickshank Callatoota Estate,** 2656 Wybong Rd., specializes in Cabernet Sauvignon and Cabernet Franc wines. **James Estate,** 951 Bylong Valley Way (☎6547 5168), in Sandy Hollow, produces a delicious Shiraz.

CENTRAL COAST

Known widely as the Holiday Coast, the mid-New South Wales coast is too often passed over by international tourists eager to reach the bright lights and holiday hot spots farther north. The region's slightly slower pace of life exists somewhere pleasantly in between the rat race of the big city and the permanent-vacation attitude of the north coast. Thriving coastal cities like Newcastle and Port Macquarie draw locals for good reason, offering ample opportunities to sunbathe, water-ski, or hang ten, as well as offering easy access to nearby national parks.

NEWCASTLE ☎02

Newcastle (pop. 265,000), originally a colony to which the most troublesome convicts were sent and once dubbed "Sydney's Siberia", is a city with a complex. As the world's largest coal exporter, Newcastle ships out over one and a half million tons each week, giving it a historical reputation as a smokestack-ridden industrial metropolis. But as the second-largest city in NSW, Newcastle is industriously changing its industrial image, balancing its coal exports with a newfound sense of laid-back cool. In addition to high-adrenaline surfing, a spectacular view of the Pacific seemingly at the end of every street, and easy access to the nearby Hunter Valley wineries and wetland reserves, Newcastle is home to a vibrant, creative, and international uni student crowd as well as a flourishing live music scene.

▄ TRANSPORTATION

Trains: Newcastle Railway Station (☎ 13 15 00), on the corner of Scott St. and Watt St. **CityRail trains** chug often to Sydney (averages 2½hr., at least 1 per hr. 2:45am-11:15pm, $17). The main transfer station for **CountryLink** (☎ 13 22 32, between 6am-10pm) access to the northern coast is **Broadmeadow,** a 5min. train ride on CityRail. From Broadmeadow, Countrylink runs to: **Brisbane** (12hr., 2 per day, $98); **Coffs Harbour** (6-7hr., 3 per day, $66); and **Surfers Paradise** (12hr., 2 per day, $98). Luggage storage at the station is $1.50 per day (cloak room open daily 8am-5pm). Broadmeadow station open daily 6am-7:15pm; ticket machines after hours. Broadmeadow CountryLink office open 8am-5:30pm; Newcastle office open 9am-5pm. Discounts for booking one or two weeks in advance. ISIC holders get half fare on CountryLink.

Buses: The bus depot abuts the wharf side of the railway station. Several bus lines including **McCafferty's/Greyhound** (☎ 13 14 99 or 13 20 30; www.mccaffertys.com.au or www.greyhound.com.au) zip to: **Sydney** (3½hr.; at least 5 per day; $29, with ISIC $26); **Brisbane** (14½hr., 4 per day, $82/$74); **Byron Bay** (10hr., 2 per day, $81/$73); **Cairns** (through Brisbane, 42½hr., 4 per day, $279/$247; **Coffs Harbour** (7hr., 3 per day, $56/$50); **Port Macquarie** (4hr., 2 per day, $48/$38); Surfers Paradise (12hr., 3 per day, $82/$74); and **Taree** (3hr., 2 per day, $41/$37). **Rover Coaches** (☎ 4990 1699) goes to Cessnock, which is a gateway for the Hunter Valley vineyards (1¼hr.; M-F 6 per day; $10.60, children $5.30). **Port Stephens Coaches** (☎ 4982 2940; www.psbuses.nelsonbay.com) shuttles to Port Stephens (about 1½hr.; M-F 11 per day, Sa-Su 5 per day; up to $10.60, backpackers and students $5.30; the Bay Rover Pack includes roundtrip ticket and travel within and between Port Stephens' townships, $22/$11). The depot has no ticket offices, so tickets should be purchased in advance from a Newcastle travel agency or online; the CountryLink office in the train station (9am-5pm) also sells bus tickets.

Public Transportation: City buses (☎ 13 15 00) run along Hunter St. every few minutes during the day, less frequently at night; some run as late as 3:30am. Tickets allow unlimited travel (1hr. ticket $2.50).

Ferries: Passenger ferries (☎ 13 15 00) depart from the tip of the wharf, just west of the train station, and cross the river north to **Stockton** (3min.). The ferry leaves at least once every 30min. Operates M-Sa 5:15am-12:05am, Su and holidays 8:30am-10:05pm. Tickets $1.80, purchase onboard.

Taxis: Newcastle Taxi Services (☎ 4979 3000).

Car and Motorcycle Rental: Thrifty Car Rental, 113 Parry St. (☎ 4961 1141; www.thrifty.com.au), rents from $44 per day (under 25 $11 surcharge). Get a $10 discount voucher from the tourist office. **Budget,** 107 Tudor St., Hamilton (☎ 4913 2727; www.budget.com.au), has comparable rates. Check both websites for online specials.

NEW SOUTH WALES

✦ ORIENTATION

Hunter Street, at the heart of the city, is Newcastle's commercial district and runs parallel to the wharf. On the eastern end of the main drag, atop a peninsular hill, lies **Fort Scratchley,** a number of hostels and seaside bars, and the emerald-green **Foreshore Park. Queen's Wharf** runs the distance of the city, starting with the Convict Lumberyard on east Scott St., next to the train station and near the shore. Follow the wharf west and look for the perpendicular (north-south) **Darby Street** to find Newcastle's hip happenings. For another dose of hip, a significant trek further west away from the shore will get you to **Beaumont Street** in Hamilton; the bus might be a better option. Westward, Hunter St. leads to a split in the highway; the New England Hwy. heads west toward the **Hunter Valley** wineries (see p. 223) and the Pacific Hwy. climbs north up the coast. Take a ferry from Newcastle's town center to cross the river to **Stockton,** though the quiet residential neighborhood doesn't offer much in the way of tourist options.

🛈 PRACTICAL INFORMATION

Tourist Office: 361 Hunter St. (☎4974 2999 or ☎1800 654 558; www.visitnewcastle.com.au). From the train station, take a right onto Scott St. and continue as Scott merges onto Hunter St. Walk past Darby St. and the office will be on your left after a couple of blocks (right before the Civic Theatre). Free maps of Newcastle and the Macquarie area; free accommodation location service and tour bookings. **Internet** $3.75 per 30min. Open M-F 9am-5pm, Sa-Su 9:30am-4:30pm.

Library: (☎4974 5300), in the Newcastle Memorial Cultural Centre on Laman St., next to the Newcastle Art Gallery at the corner of Darby St. **Internet** free for non-email sites, email $3 for 30min. Call ☎4974 5340 to book ahead. Open M-F 9:30am-8pm, Sa 9:30am-2pm.

Surf Shop: Pacific Dreams, 7 Darby St. (☎4926 3355; www.pacificdreams.com.au) rents boogie boards and short boards from $20 per day, $100 per week; long boards $30/$160. Open M-W 9am-5:30pm, Th 9am-8pm, F 9am-5:30pm, Sa 9am-4pm, Su 10am-3pm. Credit card and driver's license required. **Avago Sports** (☎0404 278 072), also rents sporting equipment (bikes, bodyboards, surfboards for short term or long term hire) and delivers to wherever you're at. Inquire about YHA discounts. Also see **Backpackers by the Beach,** p. 172.

Police: (☎4929 0999), on the corner of Church and Watt St.

Internet Access: Backpackers by the Beach has speedy computers for only $4 per hr. (see p. 172). **Newcastle Regional Museum,** 787 Hunter St., has 3 free terminals, although they're slow and often have a wait. Also see public **library** and **tourist office** above.

Post Office: (☎13 13 18), on the corner of Scott and Market St. Open M-F 8:30am-5pm. **Postal Code:** 2300.

♞ ACCOMMODATIONS

With tourism on the rise, budget accommodations have flourished in Newcastle. Other than the listings below, pub rooms abound (in summer from $40; in winter from $30). Book ahead in peak periods.

■ **Backpackers by the Beach (NOMADS),** 34-36 Hunter St. (☎4926 3472, www.backpackersbythebeach.com.au). Less than a 5min. walk north of the train station, this hostel occupies its own yellow corner of Hunter and Pacific St. Small but modern dorms, with heaps of bright light and high ceilings. Single sex dorms. Unbeatable location close

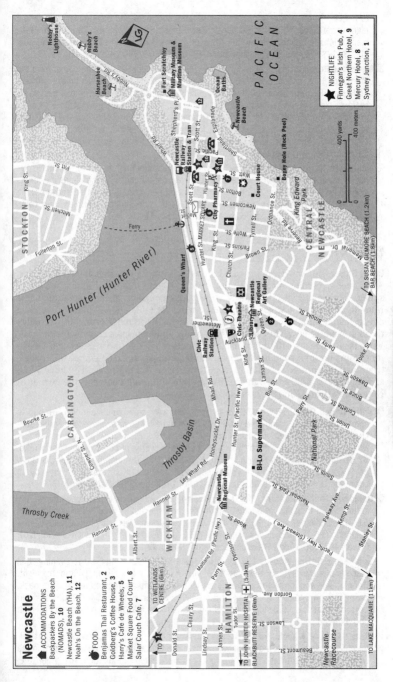

Newcastle

▲ ACCOMMODATIONS
Backpackers By the Beach
(NOMADS), **10**
Newcastle Beach (YHA), **11**
Noah's On the Beach, **12**

● FOOD
Benjamas Thai Restaurant, **2**
Goldberg's Coffee House, **3**
Harry's Cafe de Wheels, **5**
Market Square Food Court, **6**
Salar Couch Cafe, **7**

★ NIGHTLIFE
Finnegan's Irish Pub, **4**
Great Northern Hotel, **9**
Mercury Hotel, **8**
Sydney Junction, **1**

PACIFIC OCEAN

Port Hunter (Hunter River)

Throsby Basin

Throsby Creek

STOCKTON

CARRINGTON

WICKHAM

HAMILTON

CENTRAL NEWCASTLE

NEW SOUTH WALES

Nobby's Lighthouse
Nobby's Beach
Horseshoe Beach
Fort Scratchley
Military Museum & Maritime Museum
Ocean Baths
Newcastle Beach
Bogey Hole (Rock Pool)

Nobby's Rd.
Wharf Rd.
Shepherd's Pl.
Scott St.
Pacific St.
Esplanade
Shortland
King Edward Park

Newcastle Railway Station & Tram
City Pharmacy
Market St.
Hunter St.
MARKET SQUARE
Queen's Wharf
Civic Railway Station
Newcastle Regional Museum
Bi-Lo Supermarket

Ferry

Pitt St.
King St.
Mitchell St.
Fullerton St.

Bourke St.
Cowper St. N.
Albert St.
Hannell St.
Lee Wharf Rd.
Honeysuckle Dr.
Wood St.
Denison St.
Parry St.
Maitland Rd. (Pacific Hwy.)
Pacific Hwy. (Stewart Ave.)

Scott St.
Watt St.
Bolton St.
Newcomen St.
Wolfe St.
Perkins St.
Church St.
Brown St.
Tyrrell St.
Ordnance St.
Reserve Rd.
Memorial Dr.
Brooks St.
Darby St.
Tooke St.
Dawson St.
Corlette St.
Bruce St.
Laman St.
Bull St.
Parry St.
Union St.
Smith St.
National Park St.
Parkway Ave.
Kemp St.
Stanley St.

Newcomen St.
Hunter St.
King St.
Auckland St.
Merewether St.
Civic Theatre
Library
Newcastle Regional Art Gallery
Court House

Hunter St. (Pacific Hwy.)
Wharf Rd.
Hannell St.

National Park

Newcastle Racecourse

Gordon Ave.
Lawson St.
Beaumont St.
James St.
Tudor St.
Lindsay St.
Cleary St.
Donald St.

TO WETLANDS CENTRE (6km)
TO SUSAN GILMORE BEACH (1.2km)
BAR BEACH (1.8km)
TO JOHN HUNTER HOSPITAL; BLACKBUTT RESERVE (6km)
TO LAKE MACQUARIE (11km)
[5.3km]

400 yards
400 meters

to beaches, transportation, and the wharf. Free surfboard and bike loans, linen, and F night pizza. Speedy Internet $4 per hr. Key deposit $15. Reception 7am-11pm. Make reservations in advance during the summer. Dorms $22, weekly $126; twins and doubles $51/$322. Same rates year round. ISIC/NOMADS/VIP/YHA/discount $3. ❷

■ **Newcastle Beach (YHA),** 30 Pacific St. (☎4925 3544). Just around the corner from the breaking surf and local train station lies this crown jewel of hostels in a breezy, bricked, and retro-flavored remodeled heritage building. This hostel offers cavernous accommodations, clean facilities, and a common area reminiscent of a country club with a TV, pool table, and fireplaces for chilly winter months. Winery tour $35. Kitchen. Free dinner at Finnegan's for YHA backpackers Su, M, and Tu. Internet $2 per 30min. Linen free. Laundry $6. Reception 7am-10:30pm. Book ahead in summer. Dorms $26-50, YHA $20-22; twins and doubles $62/$58. ❷

Noah's on the Beach (☎4929 5181; www.noahsonthebeach.com.au), on the Esplanade. A big, standard hotel with stunning views of the Pacific. All motel-pristine rooms come with A/C and heat, TV, data ports, mini-fridges, bars, and coffee and tea. Free parking, laundry services. Reception 24hr. Harborside singles, doubles, and twins $130; oceanview singles, doubles, and twins $150. ❺

◖ FOOD

Darby Street is by far the best place in town to hunt for eateries. **Hunter Street** has $5-6 lunch specials, but stick to the Pacific St. end if you're looking for atmosphere. Though a 25-30min. walk southwest of city center, over 80 restaurants line Hamilton's **Beaumont Street,** a popular hangout for students and home to bustling cheap restaurants favored by Newcastle's lunching number-crunchers. Monday through Wednesday nights in Newcastle bring dinner specials at many restaurants. Various specials are offered for backpackers through their hostels, as well. Cheap food-court options can also be found at **Market Square,** in the center of a pedestrian mall on Hunter St. running from Newcomen to Perkins St. The huge Bi-Lo **supermarket** (☎4926 4494), in the Marketown shopping center at the corner of National Park and King St., is open 24hr., 7 days a week.

■ **Salar Couch Cafe,** 54 Watt St. (☎4927 5329; www.salarcouchcafe.cjb). Draped in comfortable colors, a good old-fashioned candle-in-a-bottle and mismatched-table-and-chair kind of place—with a touch of the exotic. Enjoy Peruvian- and Bolivian-inspired fare while perusing the book-lined "boudoir," a socks-only area of comfortable floor pillows. $7.50 lunch specials and lavish brekkie $4.50-13; 10% YHA member discount. Soon to be 100% organic, with lots of veggie and vegan options. Kept toasty in winter by an open fire. Open Su and Th-Sa 11am-late, Tu-W 11am-5pm. No credit cards. ❶

■ **Benjamas Thai Restaurant,** 100 Darby St. (☎4926 1229). Pastel decor, sparkling table settings, and magnificent menus. Sundry seafood specialties (squid $15, king prawns $14-16, whole fish $20), all Thai-style and incorporating local catches. Great vegetarian menu ($5-13) and oodles of noodles ($11-16). Weekday $7.90 lunch special. BYO. Open daily 5:30-10pm, W-F also 11:30am-2:30pm. ❷

Goldberg's Coffee House, 137 Darby St. (☎4929 3122). Early in the evening, this place is where everybody meets up for dinner or drinks before heading out for the night. Dark interior with hardwood and a classy soundtrack and an impressive patio out back. Swing in for a late cup of coffee ($2.50-3.50) or a glass of wine ($4.40) to scope and be scoped at this Euro-style coffeehouse. Varied and reasonably priced menu; lunch and dinner dishes $8-20. Open daily 7am-midnight. ❶

Harry's Cafe de Wheels, (☎4926 2165) on Wharf Rd., opposite Scratchley's. What better place to sample a famous Australian meat pie than the oldest takeaway joint in the whole nation? And what's more, it's now at its new waterfront location. The "Tiger" presents brave souls with a thick, hearty pie smothered in mushy peas, mashed potatoes, and steaming gravy ($4.50). A quick and historic snack or light meal only $2.50-4.50. Open daily 9am-late. ●

🔘🔘 SIGHTS & ACTIVITIES

Though the ornate convict-built **heritage buildings** and the towering **cathedral** in the city center are architecturally impressive, visitors don't flock to Newcastle for Victorian balconies. They come instead to enjoy the quintessential laid-back Australian coastal lifestyle, replete with all the creature comforts of a major urban center. Newcastle's a place to bide your time, with plenty of ocean-front parks, the sound of crashing waves on the rocky shore and the hardcore surf.

⬛ NEWCASTLE'S TRAM. The famous tram offers a delightful, informative city overview and tells of the devastation that resulted from a freak earthquake in 1989. The ride is a great way to get a quick feel for the city's sights, from the historic architecture to whales breaching off the coastline. (☎ 4963 7954, 45min., *Departs from Newcastle Railway Station M-F every hr. 10am-1:45pm, Sa-Su 10am-2pm; extra ride 3pm on school holidays. $10, children $6.)*

FORT SCRATCHLEY. Climb the hill for one of the best views in the city. Play around on the cannons and explore the underground tunnel system for $2.50. Scratchley is the only fort in Australia to have engaged the enemy in a maritime attack but has been an inactive military site since the 1970s and now houses the Military Museum and, next door, the Maritime Museum. Jumbly Boat Gallery just outside the walls has a big pile of boats. *(Military Museum ☎ 4929 3066 open Sa-Su noon-4pm. Free. Maritime Museum ☎ 4929 2588. Open Tu-F 10am-4pm, Sa-Su noon-4pm. Free.)*

BEACHES. Newcastle's shore is lined with white sand beaches, tidal pools, and landscaped parks. At the tip of Nobby's Head peninsula is a walkable seawall, and **Nobby's Lighthouse,** surrounded by **Nobby's Beach,** a terrific surfing spot. Walking clockwise around the peninsula from Nobby's leads to a surf pavilion, then to the **Ocean Baths,** a public saltwater pool below; keep walking to find its predecessor **Bogey Hole,** a convict-built ocean bath at the edge of the manicured **King Edward Park.** Farther along, you'll see a cliffside walk leading to the **Susan Gilmore nude beach;** farther still is the large **Bar Beach,** popular with surfers. To tackle all the beaches, follow the **Bather's Way** coastal walk from Nobbys to Mereweather.

BLACKBUTT RESERVE. A 182-hectare tree sanctuary with five walking trails over 20km and many animals along the way. There's a koala enclosure as well as kangaroo and emu reserves. If you're lucky, you can pet a koala (Sa-Su 2:30pm). Bring your own picnic food; no food is available. *(Catch bus #232 or 363 in the city center for 45min. to Lookout Rd. and follow signs down the hill. ☎ 4957 6436; www.ncc.nsw.gov.au. Open daily 7am-5pm, Daylight Savings 7am-7pm; wildlife exhibits 9am-5pm. Free.)*

WETLANDS CENTRE. Founded in 1985 to provide sanctuary to birds and reptiles, these "rehabilitated wetlands" also offer respite to city-weary humans with walking paths and a creek for canoeing. Monthly events such as breakfast with the birds, twilight treks, and canoeing safari. Check website in advance for details. *(Take the City Train to Sandgate, in the suburb of Shortland, and then walk 10min. on Sandgate Rd. ☎ 4951 6466; www.wetlands.org.au. Canoe rental: 2-person, 2hr., $7.50; 3-person, 2hr., $9.90.) Open M-F 9am-3pm, Sa-Su 9am-5pm. $4.50, ISIC $3, families $9.)*

FESTIVALS. Surfest rides into town in late February for a two-week international surfing spectacular, drawing crowds from all of Oz. The **Newcastle Jazz Festival** plays out in late August at City Hall. The **King Street Fair** is a city-wide carnival in early December. **Newcastle Maritime Festival's** boat races and watersports are the last week of January. The **This is Not Art Festival** (☎4927 0470) brings together Newcastle's young media-makers, musicians, artists, writers, and troublemakers for five days of creative energy at the end of September and early October.

🎵 📷 ENTERTAINMENT & NIGHTLIFE

Newcastle is fast becoming one of Australia's major musical hubs. *The Post*, a free Newcastle newspaper, publishes a guide to the week's live music around the area each Wednesday. For up-to-date info, peruse the free local guide *TE (That's Entertainment)* at the tourist office. Wednesday night is "uni night" all around town; keep your eyes open for special events and offers.

The Great Northern Hotel (☎4927 5728), on the southeast corner of Watt St. and Scott St., is the latest uni party spot and was recently reopened after renovations. Open M until 10am, Tu and Th until midnight, W and F-Sa until 3:30 or 4am.

Sydney Junction Hotel, 8 Beaumont St. (☎4961 2537) is a super-slick establishment with a packed line-up. Features rock bands Th-Su and is swamped F and Sa nights with live music in the back room and a DJ up front.

The Mercury Hotel, 23 Watt St. (☎4926 1119), is the most convincingly trendy dance club in town; Sydney and overseas DJs shipped in on Sa nights. $5 cover F-Sa. Open W and F-Sa until 3am. $5 cover F-Sa.

Finnegan's Irish Pub (☎4926 4777), on Darby and King St., is a bit more hearty, home-spun, and down to earth, and a great place to catch rugby and footy games. Happy Hour 5-7pm. Live music M and Th-Sa and a DJ W and F-Sa. YHA free meals Su, M, Tu. Open Su-Th 10:30am-midnight, F-Sa until 3am.

PORT STEPHENS BAY   ☎02

North of Newcastle, Port Stephens is a region comprised of a placid, secluded bay, sleepy rural townships, beautiful blue-green water and **Tomaree National Park.** Most of the region's activities, restaurants, and facilities are in Nelson Bay. Anna Bay and Shoal Bay offer beautiful and somewhat isolated beaches. During the summer, surfing beaches and luxury resorts draw backpackers and families alike, clogging central shopping areas with traffic. The ocean beyond the surf also attracts visitors of the aquatic kind. Bottlenose dolphins are visible year-round in the harbor and are quite cheeky—they'll come right up and tag along with the daily dolphin cruises. The whale-watching season runs from June to October, after which the giants head north to warmer waters in order to breed.

📠 **TRANSPORTATION. Port Stephens Coaches** (☎4982 2940 or 1800 045 949; www.psbuses.nelsonbay.com) shuttles to Port Stephens (1½hr.; M-F 11 per day, Sa-Su 5 4 per day; up to $10.60 depending on which township, backpackers and students $5.30; the Bay Rover Pack includes roundtrip ticket and travel within and between Port Stephens' townships, $22/$11). The main stop in Nelson Bay is at the Bi-Lo **supermarket** on Stockton St. **Local buses** run hourly on weekdays, every two hours on Saturday and Sunday ($3; 1-day unlimited travel $11). It may be more convenient to rent a car from Newcastle to avoid being stranded in one township for a few hours. The **Port Stephens Ferry Service** (☎0412 682 117) makes three trips daily to **Tea Garden,** a fishing village across the water from Nelson Bay (8:30am, noon, and 3:30pm; $17, children $9, families $40). **Shoal Bay Bike Hire,** 63 Shoal Bay Rd., near the YHA, is a cheap bike option. (☎0249 8141 21. From $7 per hour, $55 per week. Open M and W-Su 9am-5pm in winter, around 8am-7pm in the summer. Closed Tuesdays, except school holidays.) For a **taxi,** call ☎4984 6699.

Port Stephens

🏠 ACCOMMODATIONS
Malaleuca Backpackers, **5**
Samurai Beach Bungalows, **4**
Shoal Bay Holiday Park, **1**
Shoal Bay YHA, **2**

🍎 FOOD
Game Fish Club, **3**
Greek Village Restaurant, **7**
Incredible Edibles, **8**
Terrace Café, **6**

⚡ 🔧 ORIENTATION & PRACTICAL INFORMATION. Nelson Bay Road leads from Newcastle to the Port Stephens area's four residential townships. The road forks onto **Gan Gan Road,** which leads to the seaside **Anna Bay,** home to **Stockton Bight,** the largest sand dune area in the southern hemisphere, and close to the popular surfing destination of **One Mile Beach,** known simply as "The Big Beach" to locals. Gan Gan and Nelson Bay Rd. rejoin en route to three other townships: **Nelson Bay** (the largest), **Shoal Bay,** and the rural **Fingal Bay.** The marina, shopping complex, and cafes are on **Victoria Parade** and **Stockton Street** in Nelson Bay. The **tourist office,** on Victoria Pde. by the wharf, arranges bookings for local attractions. (☎ 4981 1579 or 1800 808 900; www.portstephens.org.au. Open daily 9am-5pm.) The **Salamander Shopping Centre,** a 5min. bus ride west from Nelson Bay, is home to the Tomaree public **library,** where you can access the **Internet.** (☎ 4982 0670. Open M, W, F 10am-6pm, Tu and Th 10am-8pm, Sa 9:30am-2pm. Access free; email $2.75 per 30min. Book ahead for both.) **Terrace Cafe** also offers Internet in a convenient shopping arcade on Victoria Pde. overlooking the tourist office. (☎ 4981 0450. Open 8am-4pm in the summer, 7:30am-9pm in the winter. $2 per 15min.)

🏠 ACCOMMODATIONS. Samurai Beach Bungalows Backpackers ❷, on Robert Connell Cir., reached by Frost Rd. off Nelson Bay Rd., just outside Anna Bay, is located among dense bushland. They have a volleyball court, outdoor kitchen, TV, pool

GIVING BACK

PEPPERS ANCHORAGE

Port Stephens has always been lauded for its pristine, uncrowded beaches and wildlife preserves with an abundance of koalas. Now, visitors looking to explore the region's natural wonders while minimizing their impact on the environment can visit **Peppers Anchorage.** Overlooking Port Stephens Bay, the resort is just a few miles away from a national park with hiking trails and beaches and the spectacular Stockton beach sand dunes. Stretching 30km along the seaside coast, some of the dunes are as high as ten stories. Tony Burrell leads horseback and quad-bike tours through the dunes. He also councils Peppers Anchorage guests on safeguarding the environment and leaving no traces of their time in the dunes. Another tour operator, Dieter Hartmann, offers group rides (up to 24 people) on a "Bushmobile," a vehicle he designed himself by re-engineering a military transport vehicle. Mr. Hartmann is a self-educated expert on sustainable living—after coming from Germany where he worked as an engineer, he spent several years living entirely unassisted with several friends in a nearby cabin.

Peppers Anchorage, Corlette Point Rd. (☎4984 2555). For more info, see www.peppers.com.au.

table, pet snake, free surfboards, boogie boards, and a campfire at night. (☎4982 1921; www.ports-tephens.org.au/samurai. Linen included. Bike rentals $12 per day; free for those staying 3 or more days. Laundry $3. Reception 8:30am-10:30pm. 5-bunk dorms with shared bath $20; family room with TV and bar fridge $69. Rates higher in the summer; book ahead. ISIC/VIP/YHA.) To get to **Malaleuca Backpackers ❷,** 33 Eucalyptus Drive, turn right at the Anna Bay Roundabout, head down Gan Gan Road, and turn left onto Eucalyptus Dr. Difficult to access without a car, Malaleuca nonetheless offers comfortable cabins, camping, and car sites in a bushland setting. (☎0427 200 950. Laundry $2. Sites $12.50 per person, $10 in winter; cabins $25 per person per night, $20 in winter. Book 2-3 months in advance in the summer time and Easter holiday. VIP.) **Shoal Bay Holiday Park ❷** is on Shoal Bay Rd. on the way to Fingal Bay, within earshot of the ocean. There is a new kitchen, two common TV areas, rec room with ping-pong tables, and tennis court. (☎4981 1427 or 1800 600 200. Laundry $2.50. Reception 8:15am-6pm. Powered tent and caravan sites for 2 $19-39, additional adult $8; ensuite caravan sites $29-49; budget bungalows for 2 $39-79, additional adult $10. Discount for 7-night stay.) **Shoal Bay YHA ❸,** 59-61 Shoal Bay Beachfront Rd., is in the Shoal Bay Motel, across from the beach and a 15min. walk west of the Tomaree trails. Rooms have TV, fridge, heat, and A/C. There is also a kitchen, TV lounge, sauna, and BBQ. (☎4981 0982. $20 key deposit includes linen rental. Laundry machines $6. Reception 7:45am-10pm. Dorms $30, YHA $20; private rooms $36/$30.)

◘ FOOD. Nelson Bay—the Port Stephens hub—is the best place to find cheap food, particularly on Magnus and Donald St., parallel to Victoria Pde. For a generous breakfast around $9, try the **Terrace Cafe Restaurant,** Shop 13 in Nelson Towers (☎4981 0450), the shopping arcade overlooking the tourist office. Lunch ($9) and summer dinner ($12) are served as well. (Open daily 8am-4pm in winter, 7:30am-9pm in summer. Cash only). Upstairs on the corner of Stockton and Victoria Pde. is the **Greek Village Restaurant ❸,** 19 Stockton St. Bring along a bottle of wine and enjoy a romantic evening of Greek cuisine. (☎4984 3388. Mains $20. Open Su and W-Sa 6pm-late.) For a scrumptious sandwich ($5-6.20), swing by **Incredible Edibles,** Shop 6 Donald St. (☎4981 4511; open daily 8am-4pm, in winter M-Sa 8am-4pm). Trusty **supermarket** Bi-Lo has locations on the corner of Stockton and Donald St. (☎4981 1666) and in the Salamander Shopping Centre, which also offers a Woolworths supermarket and a number of fast-food joints. In

Shoal Bay, stop by the **Game Fish Club,** 57 Shoal Bay Rd. (☎4981 1459), for a $4.90 daily lunch special. (Open daily for lunch noon-2:30pm, dinner 6-9pm, and breakfast on Su 9-11am).

◑◕ **SIGHTS & ACTIVITIES.** You've probably seen sport-utility-vehicle ads on TV and wondered if anyone really drives off-road like that. Now's your chance to find out. The fun-loving folks at Port Stephens Visitors Centre (☎4981 1579) will let you buy a day pass for $5 so you and your 4WD can go play on **Stockton Bight,** the biggest sand dune in the Southern Hemisphere (about 30km long and 2km wide, the 2500-year-old dunes are said to move inland 5 to 12 meters every year); passes are also available at the Mobil station in Anna Bay. Follow signs to Anna Bay from Nelson Bay Rd.; the Mobil is past the beach access sign. For renting or participating in more organized group-duning, try a 1½hr. trip with **6-Wheeler Bushmobile Dune Adventure** and conquer the deserts for just $20 per person. (☎0500 55 00 66; www.bushmobile.com.au.) **▧Sand Safaris** offers a pricey but worthwhile adventure activity. For $99 a head, you get two hours on your very own ATV and an award-winning guided trip at 40kph over dunes nearly 100m high. (☎4965 0215 or 0418 209 747; www.sandsafaris.com.au. 4-5 trips daily; pick-up from Newcastle Airport.) For a tamer sand activity, join **Sahara Trails** on spectacular 2hr. dune and beach horse rides and 1hr. beginners bush rides starting at $35 per hr. (☎4981 9077; www.saharatrails.com. Open daily. Bookings required.)

Whale watching and **dolphin cruise boats** depart five times per day in the summer (winter trips are weather-permitting). The cheapest of the lot is the large **Tamboi Queen,** which cruises the harbor for sightings of the over 150 dolphins that live there year-round. (☎4981 1959. 3 trips daily, 10:30am, 12:30pm, and 2pm. 1½hr. dolphin cruise $15 adult, $13 concession, $39 family, children under 4 free). On the ocean side, try **Moonshadow Cruises** (☎4984 9388) for whale watching trips, departing from d'Albora Marina. **Blue Water Sea Kayaking** (☎4981 5177 or 0409 408 618; www.seakayaking.com.au) offers trips starting at $25 for adults, but does not operate June-August. Book a high-speed jet **boat ride** with **X-Jet** at the tourist office or call ☎4997 2555 (20min. adult $40, concessions $30). **Anna Bay Surf School** (☎4981 9919), inside the kiosk at the southern end of One Mile Beach, will start you surfing in only 2hr. They also hire equipment. (Group lesson is $40 a person, $35 for backpackers. Open 7 days, 9am-5pm, subject to seasonal variation.)

For less action and more cuddling, stop off at **Oakvale Farm and Fauna World,** 2828 Nelson Bay Rd., on your way to or from Nelson Bay to pet or feed a koala or kangaroo. (☎4982 6222; www.oakvalefarm.com.au. Open daily 10am-5pm, except Christmas; feeding times 11am and 2pm; $11 adults, $6.50 children.)

For a few second-to-none views of Port Stephens Bay's rippling blue-green waters, stark headlands, and the far-away expanse of the South Pacific horizon, take the 1½hr. walk to the summit of **Tomaree Head** at the end of Shoal Bay. The Gan Gan Hill Lookout, off Stockton Rd. before entering the Nelson Bay area., also offers a panoramic perspective (without the hike) from Stockton in the south to the Myall Lakes in the North. You can find opportunities for **surfing** and **nude bathing** on the Anna Bay shore; inquire at the Port Stephens tourist office in Nelson Bay for information.

GREAT LAKES

This underrated region is home to some of the most spectacular scenery on the coast. The beautiful beaches are ripe for scuba exploration, and a host of little-known national parks offer ample opportunities for seclusion, as well as the perfect opportunity to spot some unique Australian wildlife.

FORSTER
☎02

Situated on twin isthmuses, the small towns of Forster (FOS-ter) and Tuncurry, the most urban locales in the popular Great Lakes region, are favorite holiday spots for NSW families. Blessed with a temperate climate and near endless stretches of empty beaches, the Forster area makes for a pleasant stop on the way to Sydney or Byron Bay and the most comfortable spot from which to explore the Great Lakes region.

TRANSPORTATION & PRACTICAL INFORMATION. From the south via the Pacific Hwy., take the Failford Rd. exit east and then **The Lakes Way** south. For a more scenic route, The Lakes Way turn-off heads east right after Buladelah, and Forster is one hour down the road. From the north, The Lakes Way turn-off is east at Rainbow Flat, and Forster is a 15min. drive. Tuncurry is on the northern side of The Lakes Way bridge, before you cross into Forster; but most activity is in Forster itself. **King Brother's Great Lakes Coaches** (☎4983 1560 or 1800 043 263) connects to Bluey's Beach (M-F 3 per day, Sa-Su 2 per day; $9.40, concessions $4.70) and Sydney (5½hr.; 1-2 per day; $45, concessions $31) via Newcastle (3hr.; 3 per day M-F, 2 per day Sa-Su; $29, concessions $24). **Eggins Comfort Coaches** (☎6552 2700) goes to Taree (1hr.; 2-4 per day M-Sa; $10, 50% student and YHA discounts). The **Forster Visitors Centre** (the central **Great Lakes Visitors Centre**), on Little St. by the wharf, is the **coach terminal** and a booking agency. Tickets can also be bought on the bus. (☎6554 8799 or 1800 802 692. Open daily 9am-5pm.) As the main Great Lakes Visitors Centre, this is the place to gather information on the whole area, including Booti Booti. Be sure to pick up a map of the area, since much of its charm lies in pottering around the many tiny secluded beaches off main roads. The **police station** is on Lake and West St. (☎6555 1299), and the **post office** is on the corner of Wallis Ln. and Beach St. in the center of Forster. **Postal Code:** 2428.

ACCOMMODATIONS & FOOD. The owners of the **Dolphin Lodge ❷**, 43 Head St., treat their guests to surf and boogie boards, a kitchen, and a TV lounge with cable and videos, all just a block from the beach and four blocks from town. They offer pre-arranged pick-up at the bus stops in Nabiac on the Pacific Hwy., bike rentals, and Internet access. (☎6555 8155; dolphin_lodge@hotmail.com. Internet $2 per 20min. $10 key deposit. Dorms $22; singles $36; ensuite doubles $25 per person. YHA.) **Smugglers' Cove Holiday Village ❷**, 45 The Lakes Way, has top-notch (and loosely pirate-themed) facilities, including a pool, mini-golf, a kitchen, and $10 per hr. canoe hire. (☎6554 6666. Sites $15-33, powered $21-40; economy cabins $46-90, ensuite $58-190; ranges refer to off-peak and peak seasons.) The tourist office can provide you with a list of budget motel clones around the area.

For food, Wharf St., in Forster Town Centre, has small food **markets** and restaurants serving burgers, pizza, and fresh seafood. A scattering of restaurants in Town Centre offer diverse international fare, but are fairly pricey. For a bit of a splurge, try the cosmopolitan **Casa del Mundo ❸**, 8 Little St. (☎6554 5906), off Town Centre, a tapas bar and restaurant which carries of the fusion of Spanish and world cuisine with considerable aplomb. (Small tapas $3.50-12.50, big tapas $11-17, international dishes $18-25; open Tu-Sa 5pm-late in the winter, closed only on Su in the summer.) **The Wharf Bar and Grill ❶**, 32 Wharf St. (☎6555 7200), transforms into a groovy nightclub Friday from 10:30pm-2:30pm.

SIGHTS & ACTIVITIES. Tobwabba, 10 Breckenridge St., means "place of clay" to the Worimi Aborigines who welcome visitors to this studio and art gallery. The beautiful prints and canvasses are a unique souvenir alternative to the ubiquitous stuffed kangaroos and koalas. (☎6554 5755; www.tobwabba.com.au. Open M-

Sa 9am-5pm.) At the south of **Forster Beach,** on West St. off Head St., there's a gas BBQ, a saltwater swimming pool, and a beach. To explore more beaches, take the **Bicentennial Walk** from Forster Beach to Pebbly Beach, then up to Bennet's Head; rock pools and dolphin-spotting opportunities fall along the way.

Near Forster, **Clarendon Forest Retreat** offers **horseback riding.** (☎ 6554 3162. Starting at $45.) Boat and tackle rental sheds line the shore. Climb aboard the **Joy-C** for a deep sea fishing cruise, $80, or a 1½-2hr. swim with dolphins cruise, $30. (☎ 6554 6321 for bookings.) **Forster's Dive School,** at Fisherman's Wharf opposite the post office, runs a variety of trips, including a **swim with dolphins** cruise ($50, non-swim $30, 10% Dolphin Lodge YHA discount) and a dive with gray nurse sharks near Seal Rock. (☎ 6554 7478. Rates vary; two dives with equipment $135.) For other fishing or diving options, consult the Visitors Centre. **Pacific Palms Kayak Tours** offer fully guided tours departing from different locations around the area. (For booking ☎ 6554 0079; www.ppkayaktours.com.au. $27.50 for a sunset paddle.)

NEAR FORSTER

MYALL LAKES NATIONAL PARK. Ecotourists will be in heaven in the Myall Lakes National Park among over 10,000 hectares of lakes, 40km of beaches, and walking tracks traversing coastal rainforest, heath, and paperbark swamp. With only two major vehicular access points ($6 vehicle entry fee per day)—one from the south through Tea Gardens and the other from the north at Bulahdelah—the area provides endless opportunities for undisturbed recreation and relaxation. Coming from the south, turn off Pacific Hwy. at Myall Way and head all the way down until you hit Mungo Brush Road. The northern entrance, however, is the more popular option and is accessible through **Bulahdelah** (meeting of the waters), 83km north of Newcastle. The **Bulahdelah Visitors Centre** (☎ 4997 4981), at the corner of Pacific Hwy. and Crawford St., serves as the park's only "interpretive center." The **Visitors Centre** informs on various ways of accessing and enjoying the park. (Visitors Centre open daily 10am-4pm, except Christmas. $6 vehicle entry fee per day.) From Bulahdelah, take the Lakes Rd. (not to be confused with The Lakes Way), a one-lane partly-paved road with an absurd 100kph speed limit. Beware of cars, caravans, and boat tugs barreling along. *Let's Go* and the Visitors Centre alike do not recommend traveling at full speed.

Lakes Rd. finishes at **Bombah Point,** a center of activity for both Myall Lakes and Bombah Broadwater. Here, the **Myall Shores Ecotourism Resort ❷** (☎ 4997 4495; www.myallshores.com.au) office, in the green building on the right before the ferry crossing, distributes maps and some supplies, rents canoes ($14 per hr.) and outboards ($40 per 2hr.), and also sells **petrol.** The **campground's** facilities include BBQs, laundry, a store, and a restaurant. (Sites $11-26, powered $13-30; prices vary by season.) A **toll ferry** carries vehicles over to the Mungo Brush area of the park. (5 min., every 30min. 8am-6pm, $3.) The paved **Mungo Brush Road** extends 25km along the coast to the park's southern edge. The lake side of the road has various entrances to the usually-crowded **Mungo Brush campgrounds ❶** which have toilets, BBQs, and access to the shallow lake, but no water. (NPWS office ☎ 6591 0300. Sites for 2 $10, not including $6 daily vehicle fee. First come first served. Pay a ranger if one comes by, or use the honesty box.) On the Bulahdelah side of the park the secluded **Yagon park campsite** on the ocean headland is accessible via Seal Rocks Rd. (turn-off is after Bungwahl on The Lakes Way). Travel all the way down Seal Rocks Rd. for a cliff-perched lighthouse and luminous views.

BOOTI BOOTI NATIONAL PARK. Booti Booti means "place of plentiful native hunting." While the park does not allow hunting, it does offer one of the largest stands of coastal rainforest in New South Wales, extensive coastal wetlands and heath communities, and palm forest along the edge of Wallis Lake. Follow The Lakes Way south of Forster along the coastline of Elizabeth Beach. Wallis Lake, the forest between the road and beach, and the hinterland on the road's other side make up **Booti Booti National Park** (NPWS Office ☎6591 0300; greatlakesarea@npws.nsw.gov.au). **Biking** from Forster to the park's beaches is the best way to go (at least an hour each way). Bike hire is available from the Dolphin Lodge YHA (see above; $10 per 4hr., $16 per day; guests/members $12). **Cape Hawke** is a climb by bike but provides both a spectacular view from the newly-built tower and access to a significant part of NSW's coastal rainforest. **Tiona Park ❷**, 15min. south of Forster, rents sites on both the lake and beach sides of the road. (☎6554 0291. Sites $18; cabins $38-67.) A one-hour walk around the lake through cabbage tree palms and eucalyptus leads you to the ocean and **Elizabeth Beach** (see below). You can camp with less clutter at **The Ruins Camping Area ❶** by the soft white sand of **Seven-Mile Beach,** next to a mangrove forest. (BBQ, toilets, and showers. Pay camping fees in slots at the entrance to camping area; $7.50 per person per night.) The **Information Centre** at Booti Booti is also at the camping site (☎6591 0300. Open M-F 8:30am-4:30pm.)

PACIFIC PALMS & NEARBY BEACHES. Approximately 20min. along The Lakes Way south of Forster, a sign appears for Bluey's Beach. Boomerang Dr. passes several beaches and continues through the small town of Pacific Palms before rejoining The Lakes Way a few kilometers south. **Elizabeth Beach** is the first turn-off on the left. Patrolled by pelicans and lifeguards, the waves usually die down in summer, making the safe surf ideal for swimmers. Right next door is **Shelly's Beach,** a calm secluded stretch with clothing-optional bathing, reached by a short walk through the foresty area next to Elizabeth Beach. **Boomerang Beach,** home of many avid **surfers,** is just a couple minutes farther. From here, Boomerang Dr. loops through **Pacific Palms,** which has a small strip of shops selling junk food, sundries, surf gear, and magazines. At the strip's end is the **Info Centre.** (☎6554 0123. Open daily 9am-4pm.) A bit farther on, you can camp in style at the **Oasis Caravan Park ❷**, with petrol, a market, and a small pool on premises. (☎6554 0488. Reception 8am-8pm; in summer open later. Sites $16-25; cabins $75-130.)

Pacific Palms is also home to the 6500-hectare **Wallingat National Park,** which adjoins the Wallis Lake system. About 4km south of the southern end of Boomerang Dr. along The Lakes Way is the turn-off for a dirt road that takes you to the **Sandbar and Bushland Parks.** Travel all the way to reach the **Sandbar and Bushland Caravan Park ❶**, a wilderness site on **Smith's Lake.** (☎6554 4095. Sites $9-30; cabins without bath $45-95; ensuite cabins $55-110; prices vary seasonally.) Take a left off the main dirt road to reach **Celito Beach.** The 300m boardwalk leads through dry littoral forest to a fabulous beach for surfers and sunbathers alike.

NORTH COAST

The far north coast of New South Wales may well be a well-trodden route, but it has by no means been trampled by all the attention from sun-seeking Sydneysiders and raging backpackers alike. Offering a seemingly never-ending stretch of bush and beach, the north coast boasts impressive tourist amenities that regions farther south lack. There's plenty of accommodations to suit every budget at virtually every beachside town, as well as a burgeoning adventure sports industry.

TAREE   ☎02

Taree, on the Manning River off the Pacific Hwy. (200km south of Coffs Harbour, 83km south of Port Macquarie, 30km north of Forster, and 310km north of Sydney), is a small but convenient base to explore nearby beaches, state parks, and forests. The many budget hotels, motels, and caravan parks in Taree and surrounding areas also make it a convenient stop on long road trips. Taree's growing B&B and "country retreat" industry, particularly in nearby Wingham, provides plenty of opportunities for a more lengthy and luxurious getaway.

Taree's main street, **Victoria Street,** conveniently feeds directly to the Pacific Hwy. Most shops, food, and bus stations are on Victoria St. or the streets between Pulteney and Macquarie St. **Countrylink** (☎ 13 22 32), **McCafferty's/Greyhound** (☎ 13 14 99 or 13 20 30), **Premier** (☎ 13 34 10), **Eggins Comfort Coaches** (☎ 6552 2700), and **Great Lakes Coaches** (☎ 1800 043 263) run **buses** to: Brisbane (10-11hr., 7 per day, $54-66); Byron Bay (7½hr., 6 per day, $54-65); Coffs Harbour (3½hr., 7 per day, $37-40); Forster (1hr.; 2-4 per day; $10, YHA $5); Port Macquarie (1½hr., 6 per day, $26-35); Sydney (5-6hr., 10 per day, $44-59). The **Manning Valley Visitors Information Centre** on Manning River Dr., 4km north of town, is on the left, just past the Big Oyster car dealership (☎ 1800 801 522 or 6592 5444. Open daily 9am-5pm. Public holidays and winter weekends 9am-4pm). The **post office** is on Albert St. (parallel to Manning River Dr.), near the corner of Manning St.

Accommodations are cheap and plentiful, and the hotels in town all offer backpacker rates. **Exchange Hotel ❷,** on the corner of Victoria and Manning St., offers basic but clean rooms. (☎ 6552 1160. Reception at bar 10am-late. Singles $25; doubles $35.) Motel after indistinguishable motel line Manning River Dr. with singles starting at $50 and doubles at $60. **Twilight Caravan Park ❶,** 3km south of the town center on Manning River Dr., has laundry ($3), BBQ, and kitchen facilities. (☎ 0500 854 448; twilight@tsn.cc. Linen $1.20 per item. Powered sites for 2 $20; caravans for 2 $35-42; cabins $40-60, ensuite $50-80.) Those looking to camp might also consider trekking to one of the nearby national parks rather than staying in town.

Beaches near Taree are gorgeous and inviting, but have unexpected currents, so swim only where patrolled. The closest is **Old Bar Beach** in the little village of Old Bar, a 15min. drive southeast from the town center on Old Bar Rd. **Badger's Beachouse ❸** (☎ 6557 4224), David Street, Old Bar Beach, is a spunky new hostel (the only one in the area) with a multi-colored "vibrant 70s feel." ($30; twin/double $50; family room $80; cheaper for longer stays.) **Wallabi Point,** to the south, offers great surfing and **Saltwater** offers a swimming lagoon. Farther south, **Hallidays Point** includes the well-known **Diamond Beach** and **Black Head Beach** and offers **camping.** A 40min. drive to the north is **Crowdy Head,** site of a lighthouse lookout.

FROM TAREE TO PORT MACQUARIE

There are two alternate routes from Taree to Port Macquarie, each with its own charm. Beach bums are advised to stick to Pacific Hwy. and stopover in Crowdy Bay. Joy-riding daytrippers, however, can take the circuitous and scenic 99km Tourist Drive 8, circling inland before meeting up again with the Pacific Hwy.

CROWDY BAY NATIONAL PARK. Crowdy Bay, 45min. north of Taree off Pacific Hwy., is home to some of the area's most popular beaches, bushwalks, picnic areas, and a healthy supply of kangaroos. The park supposedly derives its name from Captain Cook's passing observation that the headland was crowded with Aborigines. Coralville Rd., at Moorland on the Pacific Hwy., leads into the southern entrance of the park. Wild eastern grey kangaroos live at all three of the camping sites: **Diamond Head, Indian Head,** and **Kylie's Rest Area.** There are septic toilets and cold showers at Diamond Head; all other sites have pit toilets. (For info, contact NPWS ☎ 6586 8300; portmacquarie@npws.nsw.gov.au.) Whereas groups of **kangaroos** hop within feet of astounded visitors and **whales** can be spotted off the headlands, it often takes an expert to spot more elusive **koalas** at Indian Head and Kylie's Hut. There are three reasonably tame **bushwalks** in the park which pass through delicate habitats stunted from exposure to wind and subject to harsh salt

NEW SOUTH WALES

sprays. The shortest walk is along the base of the cliff of the headland, accessible from Diamond Head at low tide. During low tide, the **Cliff Base Walk** passes rock pools abounding with marine life. The longer **Diamond Head Loop Track** (4.8km) links Diamond Head and Indian Head, while a third, short track goes from Kylie's Hut to the beach at Crowdy Bay. Visitors must bring their own fresh water into the park. The roads are 2WD-accessible dirt tracks. (Daily vehicle fee $6; camping fee $5 per person per night, children $3.)

TOURIST DRIVE 8 & BULGA STATE FOREST. A 99km scenic route linking Taree to Wauchope and Port Macquarie (25km rough unsealed, but 2WD suitable if driven cautiously), passes through Wingham and up to Elands, before continuing through the lush Comboyne countrysides known as the Emerald Heartland, then on to Oxley Highway and Port Macquarie or back onto the Pacific Hwy. The most spectacular sight of Tourist Drive 8 is **Ellenborough Falls** in Elands, an hour's drive from Taree. Created by a fault line 30 million years ago, it's one of the largest drops in the southern hemisphere (200m). There are multiple walking tracks, the most difficult of which leads to the bottom of the gorge.

Continue past Ellenborough Falls and divert from the Tourist Drive to explore the **Bulga State Forests,** which are actually four separate forests: the Bulga, Doyles River, Dingo, and Knorrit. The Bulga is home to **Tirrill Creek Flora Reserve,** with walking trails, picnic areas, and the **Blue Knob Lookout,** from which even Taree is sometimes visible. **Maxwells Flat,** with toilet and BBQ facilities, has camping.

Returning back to the Tourist Drive, **Comboyne Road** also gives access to the **Boorganna Nature Reserve.** For a meal on the mooove, stop off at the **The Udder Cow Cafe** in Comboyne (☎ 6550 4188; www.uddercow.com.au; open daily), to savor one last bite of country before heading back to the coast.

PORT MACQUARIE ☎ 02

Travelers often make the sad mistake of bypassing Port Macquarie (ma-KWAR-ie; pop. 40,000), once a lock-up for Sydney's worst offenders. Today, this pristine port town draws nature enthusiasts and offers the country's largest urban koala population. The mouth of the Hastings River meets the Pacific in Port Macquarie, providing a potpourri of water sports and adventure activities.

☐ TRANSPORTATION

Major bus lines including **McCafferty's/Greyhound** (☎ 13 14 99 or 13 20 30) and **Premier** (☎ 13 34 10) each pass through town three times a day in both directions. Check to make sure your bus stops at Hayward St. rather than out on the highway. Car rental outlets include: **Budget** (☎ 13 27 27), at the corner of Gordon and Hollingsworth St.; **Hertz,** 102 Gordon St. (☎ 6583 6599); and **Thrifty** (☎ 6584 2122), at the corner of Horton and Hayward St.

✦ ⚡ ORIENTATION & PRACTICAL INFORMATION

Port Macquarie's town center is bordered to the north by the **Hastings River** and to the west by a bridged section of Kooloonbung Creek. **Horton Street** is the main commercial drag, and the area in the surrounding two-block radius comprises the central business district. Perpendicular to Horton St., and running along the river to the Marina, is **Clarence Street,** along which you'll find numerous restaurants and cafes. The well-organized **Visitors Centre** is at the corner of Clarence and Hay St. (☎ 6581 8000 or 1300 303 155. Open M-F 8:30am-5pm, Sa-Su 9am-4pm.) The **police** station (24hr. ☎ 6583 0199) is on the corner of Hay St. and Sunset Pde. **Banks** with

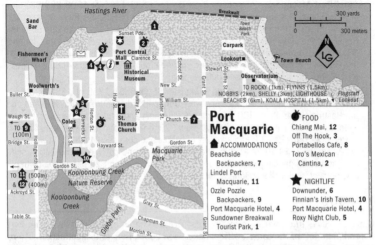

ATMs are on both sides of Horton St. between Clarence and William St. The **library,** on the corner of Grant and Gordon St., has **Internet** (☎6581 8723; open M-F 9:30am-6pm, Sa 9am-noon; $4 per hr., bookings essential), as does the **Port Surf Hub,** 57 Clarence St. right across from the Visitors Center (☎6584 4744; open Su-W 9am-6pm, Th-Sa 9am-7pm, and in summer 9am-9pm; $2 initial access fee, then $4 per hour). The **post office** is on the corner of Clarence and Horton St. **Postal Code:** 2444.

■ ACCOMMODATIONS

Port Macquarie has a range of good budget options, and most offer a weekly discount. During peak season (summer, school holidays, and Easter), when motels and caravan parks sometimes double their prices, booking ahead is essential.

Ozzie Pozzie Backpackers (NOMADS), 36 Waugh St. (☎6583 8133 or 1800 620 020; ozziepozzie@bigpond.com), off Gore St. between Buller and Bridge St. Friendly owners go beyond the call of duty with an impressive and updated activities board and personalized activity recommendations. Bright rooms (with lockers) open onto a cozy, colorful inner courtyard complete with hammocks. Free dinner Tu, Th, and daily breakfast included. Free use of bikes, boogie boards, and video collection (with deposits). Well equipped kitchen, laundry ($4), Internet ($1 per 15min), TV lounge, and dart board. Free pick-up from bus stop. Check-in hours flexible. Dorms from $22; twins and doubles from $50; 1 ensuite double from $55. Slightly higher during peak season, discounts for longer stays. ISIC/NOMADS/VIP/YHA. ❷

Beachside Backpackers (YHA), 40 Church St. (☎6583 5512 or 1800 880 008; portmacqyha@hotmail.com). The closest hostel to the beaches and a 5min. walk from the town center. Clean and friendly. Free use of bikes, boogie boards, and fishing rods. F night feast $5. Common area lights-out 11pm. Free pick-up from bus stop. Laundry $4, Internet $2 per 20min., TV, and free videos. Reception 24 hr. as needed. Dorms from $23, YHA $22; twins from $55/$50; family rooms from $60/$65. YHA. ❷

Port Macquarie Hotel (☎6583 1011), at the corner of Horton and Clarence St. In the middle of downtown, only a half-block from the beach, the old-style Port Macquarie Hotel is outfitted in Art Deco design. Basic singles from $33, ensuite with TV $55; doubles $50/$66. ❸

Lindel Port Macquarie, 2 Hastings River Dr. (☎ 6583 1791 or 1800 688 882; lindel@midcoast.com.au), on the heavily-trafficked corner of Hastings River Dr. and Gordon St., 10min. from the town center. The closest backpackers to the bus terminal. Small and friendly. Pool, BBQ, satellite-TV room, social veranda porch, billiards, laundry $3, kitchen, and free pick-up. Free use of boogie boards and fishing gear. Limited parking. Quiet time at 11pm, but kitchen and common room remain open 24hr. Key deposit $10. Dorms from $18; twins and doubles from $40. VIP. ❷

Sundowner Breakwall Tourist Park, 1 Munster St. (☎6583 2755 or 1800 636 452; www.sundownerholidays.com) A huge waterfront park adjacent to the Town Beach and the Hastings River. Pool, BBQ, free Internet at office, and kitchen for backpackers. No linen. Book ahead in summer. Sites off-peak $20, holidays and long weekends $23-34; powered $23-50/$25-37; and a variety of cabins and cottages $110-120 in winter (all prices are for 2; $9.50 for additional person). Cabins and cottages $250-270 in summer (additional people included). Dorm-style accommodation $22 per person (with pillow, blanket, and locker included). ❷

▐ FOOD

Clarence St. is lined with a number of affordable cafes and takeaways. The **Port Central Mall,** left of the tourist office, has a food court, deli, and **supermarket.** There is also a Woolworths on Buller St. and a Coles around the corner on Short St.

▓ **Portabellos Cafe and BYO Restaurant,** 124 Horton St. (☎6584 1171), prepares handmade dishes using regional foods. Try a mouth-watering sandwich, focaccia or wrap ($5-9) for lunch, or savor one of the innovative salads or pastas ($8-15) for dinner, followed by one of their fantastic desserts. Choose between bright indoor or sunny patio dining. Open Tu-W 8am-5pm, Th-Sa 8am-late. ❷

Off the Hook (☎6584 1146), on Horton St., off the town green. The best bet for fresh seafood takeaway. Your choice of fish is freshly cooked while you wait. Fish 'n' chips from $4.50 (or try a healthier gourmet grill option for 55 cents more). Open daily 10:30am-8pm. Cash only. ❶

Toro's Mexican Cantina (☎6583 4340), on Murray St. between Sunset Pde. and Clarence St. Serves up filling burritos and enchiladas ($12-15), and yummy, if inauthentic, desserts. Open 5pm-late. BYO. ❷

Chiang Mai, 153 Gordon St. (☎6583 1766) Within walking distance of the hostels, Chiang offers cheap and tasty Thai takeaway and eat-in dining (mains $8-12, seafood $12.60-14.80). Open M, W-Su 5-9:30 pm. ❶

◉ SIGHTS

KOALAS

Like koalas? The Port Macquarie area has the biggest urban population in the country. The secret to spotting them in the wild is to look through the trees rather than at individual forks. The town also provides a home for two of the best koala facilities in New South Wales. At one of Australia's few **Koala Hospitals,** there are usually four or more injured or sick koalas on site. *(20min. from the town center on Lord St. ☎6584 1522. Feedings daily at 8am and 3pm. Gold coin donation requested.)* At the ▓**Billabong Koala Breeding Centre,** you can pet and feed koalas, wallabies, and kangaroos on the landscaped grounds. This is an unparalleled opportunity to interact with Australia's best-loved marsupial. *(61 Billabong Dr., west of the intersection of the Oxley and Pacific Hwy. 10km from Port Macquarie. ☎6585 1060. Feedings 10:30am, 1:30, and 3:30pm. $9.50, backpackers $7.50, children $6.)*

BEACHES

Starting at the **Lighthouse Beach** lookout at the end of Lighthouse Rd. south of town, follow the **beach and headland walk,** an 8km track (2-3hr.) back to Port Macquarie past all eight area beaches. Hostels are usually willing to drop you off at the lookout. From the viewpoint, retrace your steps back up Lighthouse Rd. (5-10min.) to the sign for **Miners Beach** (a nude beach). The forest path leads to the beach and then continues up along the cliffs. North of Harry's Lookout is **Shelly Beach,** home to huge goannas and a perfect picnic spot, complete with BBQ area and family-friendly calm waters. Next in line is **Nobby's Beach,** immediately north of Nobby's Hill (the obelisk here stands in memory of those who died swimming in the dangerous blowhole—don't even think about trying). After Nobby's, you'll find **Flynns Beach** (popular with surfers), **Rocky Beach,** and **Oxley Beach.** The walking track ends at **Town Beach.** From the headlands overlooking Town Beach, you can see **North Beach** and across the inlet to the **Hasting River.** Lighthouse, Flynns, and Town Beaches are patrolled during summer.

PARKS

The **Sea Acres Rainforest Centre,** at Shelly's Beach, preserves the largest and southernmost stretch of coastal rainforest in the country. A 1.3km raised boardwalk circles through a portion of the 72-hectare reserve and allows glimpses of brush turkeys and flying foxes. You can explore on your own, but illuminating guided walks, led by volunteers, head out roughly every 45min. The last tour leaves at 3pm. The **Visitors Centre** has a 20min. film and ecological display. (☎6582 3355. Open daily 9am-4:30pm. $10 entrance). At the end of Horton St. is one of several entrances to **Kooloonbung Creek Nature Reserve,** a 52-hectare conservation area of peaceful bushland. Several kilometers of footpaths wind through mangroves and rainforest. At the northern tip of North Beach is **Point Plomer** and **Limeburner Creek Nature Reserve,** the site of Aboriginal artifacts and the **Big Hill walking track.** A vehicle ferry runs across the river from Settlement Point in Settlement City (free for pedestrians and bikers, $2.50 for cars). The 16km coastal Pt. Plommer Road up to the Point is unsealed and rough but bikeable. For a 2WD-safe unsealed road, take Maria River Rd. instead. **Campsites ❶** are available at Melaleuca near Big Hill and Barries Bay at Point Plomer. The campgrounds provide toilets and cold showers. Bring drinking water. (☎6583 8805. Sites for 2 $10; extra adult $5, extra child age 5-15 $3. Check-in at campground kiosk daily 8am-4pm. First come, first serve.)

ⓐ ACTIVITIES

BY LAND. Aussie adventurer Greg leads **Port Macquarie Camel Safaris.** Caravan along Lighthouse Beach and perhaps spot a wild koala. pick-up in the camel car can be arranged. (☎6583 7650. 30min., $20, children $15; 1hr. $35/$25. Book 1hr. tours at least a day in advance.) **Bicycles** can be rented from **Graham Seers Cyclery** (Port Marina, Park St.; ☎6583 2333; $6.60 per hr., $22 per day, $55 per week), but most hostels loan bikes as well. **Macquarie Mountain Tours** visits four nearby **vineyards** for free tastings. (☎6582 3065; www.atotaladventure.com.au. Th, Sa, and Su afternoons. $29.) **Cassegrain Winery,** the oldest of the four, has free tastings (Corner of Fernbank Creek Rd. and Pacific Hwy. ☎6582 8320. Daily 9am-5pm.)

BY WATER. Port Macquarie Sea Kayak takes paddlers out in 2-person boats to play in the creek, river, and ocean. (☎0409 776 566. Tours daily 10am-2pm. 2hr. $30; includes morning tea or snack.) **Port Macquaire Kayak Adventures** offers sea and surf kayaking. (☎0419 733 202. $35 per person, $25 backpacker rate. Daily 8:30am, includes breakfast.) Built in 1949, *The Pelican* is the second oldest wooden boat still in service, operating on the Hastings River. You don't travel fast, but you do cruise in style. (☎0418 652 171. Departs from Berth 7, Town Wharf. 2¼hr. Explorer cruise M and F 10am and 1pm, $21, children $11. BBQ cruise Tu-Th 10am-3pm, $41, children $21. 10% backpacker discount.) **Port Venture** has the largest boat. (☎6583 3058. 2hr. tea and dolphin cruise Tu and Th-Su 10am and 2pm; $20, backpackers $15. 4-5hr. BBQ cruise W 10am; $37, backpackers $33.) **Port Macquarie Cruise Adventures** offers similar trips. (☎6582 5009 or 1300 555 890. 2hr. tea and dolphin-spotting cruise daily 10am and 2pm; $20. 3½hr. oyster farm lunch cruise Th 11am; $35. 5½hr. Everglades lunch cruise Tu 9:30am; $55; 5hr. Timbertown Heritage Village cruise W and Su 10am; $45.)

BY AIR. Coastal Skydivers offers backpacker-friendly prices for tandem skydiving. (☎6584 3655. 3000m jumps $290, backpackers $270.) **High Adventure Air Park** offers a variety of tandem flights. (☎6556 5265. 30min. hang gliding $175; 30min. paragliding $165; 30min. motorized microlight (a tiny motorized plane) $140.) **Port Water Sports** offers **parasailing** September through April (☎0412 234 509; Berth 17 Town Wharf. $65.) To see the night sky with your feet safely planted, visit the **Observatorium** (☎6583 1933), situated in Rotary Park, corner of Stewart and Lord St. $5 entry W and Su nights (7:30pm; Daylight Savings 8:15pm) to view the southern hemisphere's stars and constellations through a telescope.

⚡ NIGHTLIFE

The local watering hole is the **Port Macquarie Hotel,** on the corner of Clarence and Horton St. (☎6583 1011. Open Su-Tu 10am-midnight, W-Th 10am-1:30am, F-Sa 10am-3am. Live music F-Sa. Karaoke Su and W). Look for the **Roxy Night Club** on William St. between Horton and Short St. (☎6583 5466. Cover F-Sa after 11pm.) **Downunder** (☎6583 4018), on Short St., next to the Coles supermarket, has W karaoke and live music on weekends. **Finnian's Irish Tavern** (☎6583 4646), on the corner of Gordon and Horton St., attracts a slightly older crowd. F-Sa nights live music, Th trivia.

SOUTH WEST ROCKS ☎02

Because South West Rocks is ~~way~~ off the typical backpacker trail and is a tough place to get to without a car, it is often bypassed in the frenetic rush to travel up and down the coast to more mainstream destinations. Although the lack of nightlife might be a drawback, you can easily fill your days with spectacular scuba diving, leisurely bushwalks, and quiet beaches. Surreal, serene, and secluded seascapes make it a perfect place for a romantic weekend (or perhaps retirement).

The turn-off for South West Rocks and **Hat Head National Park,** off the Pacific Hwy., is about 10km north of Kempsey. After crossing the Macleay River and Spencers Creek, the twisting rural route becomes Gregory St. To visit the national park and the **Smoky Cape Lighthouse,** turn right onto Arakoon Rd., drive 6km, and then turn right onto Lighthouse Rd. To find the **Tourist Information Centre,** housed in the old Boatman's Cottage, drive to the end of Gregory St. and turn left on Ocean St. The volunteer staff there knows the area's trails and beaches inside-out. (☎6566 7099. Open daily 10am-4pm.) **Cavanagh's Coaches** has **buses** departing from Kempsey (☎6562 7800; 30min., 2 per day, $8 each way).

Next door to the tourist office, **Horseshoe Bay Beach Park ❷** is just paces from a surf and swim beach. (☎6566 6370. Powered sites $23, in winter $21; vans $47/$40; cabins $68/$65. Call ahead for reservations in summer. Christmas/New Years holiday reservations should be made more than a year in advance.) **Lighthouse Bed and Breakfast ❺,** Lighthouse Rd., Arakoon, is a heritage-listed, fully restored lighthouse keeper's home with two beautifully appointed bedrooms; guests are pampered with four-poster beds, three-course breakfasts on the lawn, and sweeping vistas of the beach and ocean far below. There are also two self-contained cottages that were originally assistant lighthouse keeper's homes, both of which sleep six. (☎6566 6301; www.smokycapelighthouse.com. Main house singles $110; doubles $165; includes 3-course breakfast. Cottages for 2 nights $363-484; weekly $671-1474 depending on season; no 2-night rentals Apr., Sept.-Oct., and Dec.-Jan.) **Arakoon State Recreation Area,** a five- to ten-minute drive from the town center (around the bay, on Philip Dr.), features **campsites ❷** at the **Trial Bay Gaol.** The sites are cheap and right next to the seriously spectacular Front Beach. (☎6566 6168. Toilets, water, coin-operated hot showers. Powered sites for two $20-27.)

A surprisingly full spectrum of dining options (in both cuisine and price range) are available in South West Rocks. Some of the best is served up at the award- winning ⬛**Geppy's Seaside Restaurant ❸**, on the corner of Livingstone St. and Memorial Ave. The gregarious Geppy will delight your palate with modern but authentic Italian cuisine. Geppy's speciality, live mud crab, is worth the $50 price tag. (Entrees from $6.50, mains from $19. ☎6566 6196. Open daily 6pm-late.)

The best **surfing** waves break northwest of the tourist office at **Back Beach. Wave Wear,** on the corner of Prince Wales Ave. and Livingstone St., rents boogie boards for $15 per day. (☎6566 5177. Open daily 9am-5pm.) Sunbathers will enjoy **Front Beach,** which surrounds Trial Bay, a warm-water swimming hole. To see what's under the waves, visit Fish Rock Cave, considered one of the ten best dives in Australia. Contact the **Fish Rock Dive Centre,** 328 Gregory St. Though their prices are higher than elsewhere, courses range from beginner to instructor and the center offers technical expertise in rebreathers, nitrox blending, and underwater photography. (☎6566 6614; www.fishrock.com.au. 4-5 day open water course with on-site accommodation $525; double boat-dive $80, including 2nd cylinder; full set of gear $40.) **South West Rocks Dive Centre,** Shop 5, Gregory St., also takes divers out to Fish Rock Cave and offers certification classes for similar prices. (☎6566 6474; www.southwestrocksdive.com.au. Double boat-dive $90, including gear hire $140. Open daily 7:30am-5pm. Book in advance.)

NAMBUCCA HEADS ☎02

For the traveler in need of a break from relentless tourist attractions and constant activities, peaceful Nambucca Heads (nam-BUH-kuh; pop. 6,500) provides a welcome respite—though with the loss of its only hostel, Nambucca is no longer as convenient for backpackers. The town's allure lies with the charming Nambucca River, which winds lazily through lush hills on its way to the Pacific, as well as the area's dazzling beaches.

⏚ TRANSPORTATION. The **railway station** is a few kilometers out of town. From Mann St., bear right at the roundabout to Railway Rd. **Countrylink** (☎13 22 32) goes to Coffs Harbour (40min., 3 per day, $5.30). **King Bros** (☎6652 2744 or 1300 555 611) runs **buses** to Coffs Harbour. (1hr., 5 per day, $6.30.) **McCafferty's/Greyhound** (☎13 14 99 or 13 20 30) and **Premier** (☎13 34 10) stop multiple times daily on their Sydney-Brisbane route. **Radio Cabs** (☎6568 6855) run 24hr.

◪◪ ORIENTATION & PRACTICAL INFORMATION. Heading north, the Pacific Hwy. splits off to the right and joins the multiple-personality **Riverside Drive,** the main road in Nambucca Heads. As Riverside Dr. climbs the hill at the RSL club, it becomes **Fraser Street;** at the town center, it becomes **Bowra Street;** on the way back out to the Pacific Hwy., it's **Mann Street;** and then **Old Coast Road.** To get to the beaches, follow Ridge St. until it forks upon leaving town. Liston St. to the left, leads to the **Headland** and **Surf Beach.** Parkes St. to the right, leads to **Shelly Beach.**

Use caution when driving in Nambucca Heads—the roads are like roller coasters, and it's often hard to see past the crest of the next hill. For general information, visit the brand-new **Nambucca Valley Visitor Information Centre**, at the intersection of the Pacific Hwy. and Riverside Dr. (☎6568 6954; www.nambuccatourism.com. Open daily 9am-5pm.) The **bus stop** for travelers heading north and south from Nambucca Heads is also at the info center. On the other side of the highway, is an IGA **supermarket** and a movie theater. A Woolworths supermarket is located off Bowra St., up the hill from the RSL Club. For a cheap **Internet** fix, head to the **Nambucca Heads Public Library** (☎6568 6906), on Ridge St. (Internet $2 per hr; Open M-Th 9:30am-12:30pm and 2pm-5:30pm, F 9:30am-5:30pm). **Commonwealth Bank** and the **post office** are on Bowra St. **Postal Code:** 2448.

⚐ ACCOMMODATIONS. Nambucca and the surrounding townships of Bowraville, Scotts Head, and Valla Beach are chock-a-block with accommodations situated near the beaches or along the Pacific Hwy. near the tourist office. To get to **Beilby's Beach House ❹,** 1 Ocean St., take Ridge St. toward the beaches, turn left on Liston St., and follow the signs. This romantic guesthouse with private verandas, hardwood floors, and a large pool is ideal for families, couples, and hostel-weary backpackers. Less than a 5min. walk to the beach, it has free bikes, surfboards, and boogie boards, kitchen, Internet ($6 per hr.), laundry, and off-street parking. Call to arrange for pick-up. (☎6568 6466; www.beilbys.com.au. Breakfast included. Twins and doubles from $50; ensuite doubles from $60; ensuite queen from $70; ensuite double with connecting twin from $80. Rates are cheaper for 3 or more nights. **White Albatross Holiday Centre ❷,** at the ocean end of Wellington Dr., next to the V-Wall Tavern, is a sprawling caravan park with a gorgeous setting near a swimming lagoon and the Nambucca River. There are picnic and BBQ areas, a camp kitchen, laundry, game room, and convenience store. (☎6568 6468; www.white-albatross.com.au. Linen $5.50. Sites from $20, on-site vans from $27.50; flats and homes from $50. All prices for two people; extra adult from $11, extra child $5.50. Call ahead during summer.)

⧉⧉ FOOD & ENTERTAINMENT. Bowra St. has an assortment of quick, cheap food possibilities. **⚑The Bookshop and Internet Cafe ❶,** on the corner of Bowra and Ridge St., is the perfect place to trade in your old books and have a delicious lunch. The cafe serves mouth-watering sandwiches ($6-9) and unusual juices ($4.50), including spinach, celery, and watermelon. (☎6568 5855. Open daily in the summer 9am-5pm, and in the winter 8:30am-4:30pm. Internet $9 per hr.) For an upscale meal at a moderate price, try **Spices Cafe ❸,** 58 Ridge St., for a caesar salad ($8.50), spring rolls ($10.50), or fresh seafood ($9.50-19), and great ambience. (☎6568 8877. Open daily for dinner.) The **V-Wall Tavern ❶,** at the mouth of the Nambucca River on Wellington Dr., has unbeatable views, televised sports, and an active night scene, with disco on Saturdays. (☎6568 6344. Open daily 10am-midnight. Meals from $7.50) The **White Albatross Kiosk ❶,** the holiday park's takeaway and general store, is adjacent to the tavern and has the cheapest prices. (☎6568 9160. Open daily 7:30am-7:30pm.)

◰◱ SIGHTS & ACTIVITIES. Nambucca is full of delightful and spontaneous artwork. Don't miss the **mosaic wall** in front of the police station on Bowra St., a glittering 3-D 60m-long sea serpent scene made completely of broken crockery and a toilet. Many of the town's lampposts are painted with colorful underwater scenes. Hundreds of rocks along the breakwater **V-Wall,** named for its shape, are painted with dates and rhyming ditties from years of tourists, honeymooners, and families. It's one of the few places where graffiti artists are welcomed and even provided with an outdoor gallery; travelers are encouraged to contribute.

There are **walks** of varying difficulty throughout the beach and bush areas of Nambucca, some of which pass by the gorgeous **Rotary, Captain Cook,** and **Lions Lookouts.** For more structured exploring, **Kyeewa Bushwalkers,** a volunteer-based group, organizes a variety of free walks on Wednesdays, Saturdays, and Sundays. Visit the info center or check online (www.here.com.au/kyeewa) for an updated schedule. For some surfing action, try out **Surf Beach.**

BELLINGEN   ☎ 02

Bellingen (pop. 2,600), is a laid-back country town situated cozily on the banks of the Bellinger River, 30min. from the World Heritage-listed **Dorrigo National Park** (see p. 192) and roughly halfway between Coffs Harbour and Nambucca Heads. Running parallel to the Bellinger River, **Hyde Street** cuts right through the center of town. Travel east to reach Urunga and Coffs Harbour or drive west to explore the rainforests of Dorrigo National Park and streets of Armidale. Buses stop at Hyde and Church St. **King Bros** (☎ 1300 555 611) services Coffs Harbour (1hr., 3 per day, $5.80) and Nambucca Heads (1hr., M-F 2 per day, $5.80). **Keans** (☎ 1800 043 339) travels to: Port Macquarie (3hr., M, W, F 1 per day; $31) via Coffs Harbour (45min., $17) and Nambucca Heads (1hr., $21); and Tamworth (5hr.; M, W, F 1 per day; $54) via Armidale (3hr., $29). ISIC discounts. **Traveland,** 42 Hyde St. (☎ 6655 2055), books seats on various bus services. Local travel is easily accomplished through **Bellingen Taxi** (☎ 6655 9995). The **Bellingen Shire Tourist Information Centre** (☎ 6655 5711) is located on Pacific Hwy., in the small town of Urunga. Open M-Sa 9am-5pm, Su 10am-2pm. The **library,** in the park across from the post office, has **Internet.** (☎ 6655 1744. $2 per hour. Preferable to book ahead. Open Tu-W 10:30am-5:30pm, Th-F 10:30am-12:30pm and 1:30-5:30pm.)

Winner of the 2001 and 2002 NSW Tourism Board award for "Best Budget Accommodation," ⊠**Bellingen Backpackers (YHA) ❶,** 2 Short St., can't help but impress with its huge verandas, awesome tree-fort, and terraced sites that overlook the Bellinger River. Turn off Hyde St. at the driveway for the Lodge 214 Gallery Cafe on the north end of town. The lounge/kitchen has oversized floor pillows, musical instruments and a TV. The super-friendly owners and staff pick up guests from the Urunga train or bus stations and arrange group daytrips to Dorrigo National Park ($15). Bike rentals ($5), laundry ($4), and Internet are available. (☎ 6655 1116; backpack@bellingenyha.com.au) Sites for two $14; dorms $24; twins and doubles $58. YHA discount $2.) The delicious, fresh, and organic **Cool Creek Cafe ❷,** 5 Church St., plays host to local and national musicians. Call or check the website for events. (☎ 6655 1886; www.coolcreekcafe.com.au. Open M, Th-F 5-10pm, Sa-Su 11am-3pm and 5-10pm; holidays and festivals daily 11am-10pm. Lunch from $7.50, dinner $13-24.) The **Lodge 241 Gallery Cafe ❸,** 117-121 Hyde St., on the western edge of town, combines panoramic views, displays of local art, and generous portions of freshly prepared dishes to great effect. (☎ 6655 2470. Open Su-Th 8am-5pm, F-Sa 8am-late. Brekkie and lunch $8-12. Dinner $12-24.)

Even if you're not in the market for a "didge" and have no idea how to circular breathe, **Heartland Didgeridoos,** 25 Hyde St., opposite the Shell Service Station, has an outstanding collection of homemade instruments good enough for galactic travel (in October 2002 a Heartland didgeridoo headed into space with an American astronaut). The owners are incredible musicians and offer lessons. If you're sticking around town for a couple days, consider making your own didge under Heartland tutelage. (☎ 6655 9881; www.heartdidg.com. Open M-F 9am-5pm, Sa 10am-2pm. Didgeridoos from $100. Lessons $15 per 30min., $20 per hr. Make your own from $150.) Just across the Bellinger River on Hammond St., behind the Bellingen Caravan Park, is the entrance to **Bellingen Island,** a year-round home to an active colony of "flying foxes," or **fruit bats,** which have a one-meter wingspan. A forest trail loops through the surprisingly open understory for excellent views.

DORRIGO NATIONAL PARK

Begin your exploration of Dorrigo National Park, part of the World Heritage-listed "Central Eastern Rainforest Reserves of Australia," at the **Rainforest Centre,** complete with a cafe and educational audio-visual displays. Keep your eyes open; red-necked **pademelons** (they look like mini-wallabies) and brush turkeys often hop through the picnic area. (☎6657 2309. Open daily 9am-5pm.) Allow 35min. to drive from Bellingen (29km east) or one hour from Coffs Harbour (64km east). Dorrigo is pure lush rainforest, with sections of multi-layered canopy and wet eucalypt forest. When the rain makes things sloppy (not usually a problem on the fully sealed trails), the **leeches** have a field day. Pick them off, or buy some personal insect repellent from the Centre. Do *not* rub them with salt—this is bad for the rainforest. The 75m-long **Skywalk** extends out and over the steep slope behind the Rainforest Centre up in the tree canopy, 21m above the forest floor. For a more relaxed (or less vertigo-inducing) stroll, try the **Walk with the Birds** (2.5km; 45min. return). On the **Wonga Walk** (6.6 km; 2½hr. return), you'll soak your shoes as you journey past waterfalls. Take the trail only as far as Crystal Shower Falls for a chance to walk behind a waterfall (3.3km; 1hr. return). Drive the well-maintained, gravel **Dome Road** from the Rainforest Centre to the **Never Never Picnic Area** (10km; 5km sealed, 5km unsealed; safe for 2WD) for several hiking tracks. 1km up the road from the Centre is the **Glade Picnic Area**, where many of the walking tracks lead. From the park, follow Megan Rd. through the town of Dorrigo to visit the spectacular **Dangar Falls** lookout. A sealed pathway leads from the viewpoint to the base of the falls if you want to go for a swim. Numerous picnic areas and varied walks and attractions make this a good day excursion. If you do decide to stay the night, however, **Gracemere Grange ❷**, 325 Dome Road, (☎6657 2630; helenp@omcs.com.au), just 2km from Dorrigo National Park, offers B&B-style accommodation for backpacker price at $20 a head.

COFFS HARBOUR ☎02

Situated along the coast backed by the hills of the Great Dividing Range and covered in lush banana plantations, Coffs Harbour (pop. 60,000) is a popular spot for partyers, scuba divers, and adrenaline junkies. The town is also known for its proximity to Solitary Islands National Marine Park. Coffs' rapid expansion in the past decade has come partly at the expense of its coastal charm, but the town's tight-knit hostelling community, as well as its reputation as action-sport capital of NSW, make Coffs Harbour a worthwhile stop.

▐ TRANSPORTATION

Trains: The **railway station** is at the end of Angus McLeod St. by the jetty. From Harbour Dr., turn right on Camperdown St. and take your first left. **Countrylink** (☎13 22 32) goes to: Brisbane (6-7hr., 2 per day, $71.50); Byron Bay (4hr., 1 direct per day, $30.80); Nambucca Heads (2hr., 3 per day, $5.30); and Sydney (9hr., 3 per day, $79.20). Discounts of up to 40% for booking more than 1 week ahead, 50% for more than 2 weeks.

Buses: The long-distance bus stop is off the Pacific Hwy., on the corner of Elizabeth and McLean St. **McCafferty's/Greyhound** (☎13 14 99 or 13 20 30) go to: Byron Bay (5hr., 4 per day, $53); Brisbane (7hr., 5 per day, $56); Newcastle (6½hr., 4 per day, $56); Port Macquarie (2½hr., 4 per day, $36); and Sydney (9hr., 5 per day, $78). ISIC/VIP/YHA 10% discount. **Premier** (☎13 34 10) go to: Byron Bay (4hr., 3 per day, $53); Brisbane (7hr., 3 per day, $52); Newcastle (6½hr., 2 per day, $50); Port Macquarie (2½hr., 2 per day, $41); and Sydney (9hr., 3 per day, $57). ISIC/VIP/YHA 15% discount. **King Bros** (☎1300 555 611) runs locally to Bellingen (1hr., M-F 3 per day, 1

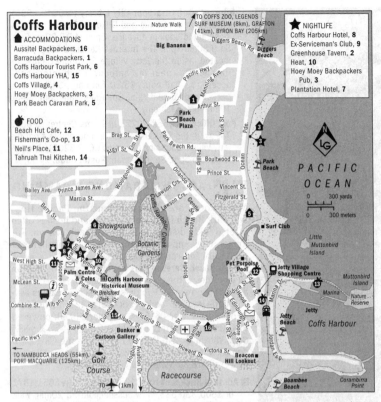

Coffs Harbour

▲ ACCOMMODATIONS
Aussitel Backpackers, **16**
Barracuda Backpackers, **1**
Coffs Harbour Tourist Park, **6**
Coffs Harbour YHA, **15**
Coffs Village, **4**
Hoey Moey Backpackers, **3**
Park Beach Caravan Park, **5**

🍴 FOOD
Beach Hut Cafe, **12**
Fisherman's Co-op, **13**
Neil's Place, **11**
Tahruah Thai Kitchen, **14**

★ NIGHTLIFE
Coffs Harbour Hotel, **8**
Ex-Serviceman's Club, **9**
Greenhouse Tavern, **2**
Heat, **10**
Hoey Moey Backpackers
Pub, **3**
Plantation Hotel, **7**

---- Nature Walk

TO COFFS ZOO, LEGENDS
SURF MUSEUM (8km), GRAFTON
(41km), BYRON BAY (205km)

PACIFIC OCEAN

NEW SOUTH WALES

---

service Sa, \$5.80) and Nambucca Heads (1hr., M-F 4 per day, 1 service Sa, \$6.30). **Keans** (☎ 1800 043 339) travels once per Tu, Th, and Su to: Armidale (4hr., \$29.50); Dorrigo (1½hr., \$17); and Tamworth (5hr., \$56.50). Return trips once per M, W, and F. ISIC discount.

Car Rental: Coffs Harbour Rent-A-Car (☎ 6652 5022), at the Shell Service Station, on the corner of Pacific Hwy. and Marcia St., rents from around \$44 per day. National companies such as **Budget** (☎ 13 27 27), **Thrifty** (☎ 6652 8622) and **Delta Europcar** (☎ 13 13 90) are also available.

Taxi: Coffs District Taxi Network (☎ 131 008).

✴🔋 ORIENTATION & PRACTICAL INFORMATION

As it passes through the city of Coffs Harbour, the long Pacific Hwy. takes on two new names: **Grafton Street** and **Woolgoolga Road.** Three large shopping centers divide the part of the town most important to travelers and locals: the **Palms Centre** on Vernon St. in the center of town, the **Jetty Village Shopping Centre** on Harbour St. near the water, and the **Park Beach Plaza** on the Pacific Hwy. in the northern part of town. The NPWS **Muttonbird Island Nature Reserve** is accessible by walking along the breakwater boardwalk at the end of Marina Dr. The city can be difficult to maneuver without a car, but hostels will often provide rides to attractions that are more than a 15min. walk away.

THE BIG SPLURGE

BUSH TURKEY

You've gazed at them in wildlife reserves, seen them on the Australian coat of arms, and heard they taste like beef. If you're a curious carnivore dreaming of sampling some indigenous Aussie meats, it's time to throw caution to the wind and pay a visit to Bush Turkey. Pauline Andree uses French and Asian methods and ingredients to cook native catches. Dishes include BBQ crocodile with vegetable and noodle stir fry ($26) and kangaroo mignonettes, wrapped in bacon, beetroot confit, and red wine sauce ($22.50). When seasonally available, emu ($26) and camel fillet ($24.50) also find their way onto the menu.

For the provincial palate that thinks adventurous dining is a spectator sport, more mainstream options abound, from fettuccine to fresh fish. Vegetarians are more than welcome, as well, but Bush Turkey didn't win its arsenal of NSW Tourism and Speciality Restaurant accolades for its salads—as wonderful as they are. For a uniquely Australian dining experience, Bush Turkey is well worth the expenditure. And you'll get to discover whether 'roo really does taste like beef.

Bush Turkey, 382 Harbour Dr. ☎ 6651 1544; www.bushturkey.com.au). Three-course meal $29.50. Open in summer M-Sa 6-9pm; in winter Tu-Sa 6-9pm. ❺

Internet: Coffs Harbour City Library (☎ 6648 4900), on the corner of Coffs and Duke St. Free 30min. sessions; try to book in advance. Open M-F 9:30am-6pm, Sa 9:30am-3pm. **The Internet Room** (☎ 6651 9155) located inside the Jetty Village Shopping Centre, on Harbour Dr., near the harbour, offers broadband access. $3 half hour, $5.50 full hour, $4/hr. backpacker and student rate. Open M-F 9am-5pm, Sa-Su 10am-4pm. Cash only.

Post Office: (☎ 6652 2022), in Palms Centre; (☎ 6652 7499), in the Park Beach Plaza, and across from the Jetty Village Shopping Centre (☎ 6652 3200). Open M-F 8:30am-5pm, Sa 9am-noon. **Postal Code:** 2450.

ACCOMMODATIONS & CAMPING

Many motels are clustered along the Pacific Hwy. and Park Beach Rd. Caravan parks and hostels often offer weekly discounts in the off-peak season. For longer stays and larger groups, book apartments at the Visitor Information Centre.

Park Beach Caravan Park ❷, near the Surf Club on Ocean Pde., is the closest to the beach. (☎ 6648 4888. Sites $16, powered $19; on-site vans $35; cabins $44-68.) **Coffs Harbour Tourist Park** ❷ is at 123 Pacific Hwy. (☎ 6652 1694. Sites $16.50, summer $19.80, powered $18.80/$22.20; variety of cabins from $44-77/$58-88.) **Coffs Village** ❶, 215 Pacific Hwy., is in the Clog Barn complex. (☎ 6652 4633; www.clogbiz.com. All sites powered $18-25; variety of cabins $50-92.)

🛏 **Aussitel Backpackers,** 312 Harbour Dr. (☎ 6651 1871 or 1800 330 335; www.aussitel.com), a 20min. walk from the town center; 10min. walk from the beach. Social, clean, intimate, and resource-full. The busy open kitchen/lounge area offers Internet ($2 per 20min), TV, and fireplace in winter. Further spruced up by BBQ, pinball machine, darts, foosball, heated pool, luggage storage, and laundry ($2.40 a machine), as well as free boogie boards, wetsuits, bikes, and canoes. Some diving charters and specialty courses are offered by owner, Mark, and a partnership with Jetty Dive Centre allows for cheaper accommodation while getting your PADI certification; free pick-up and drop-off. Scheduled social events nightly. Dorms $22, in winter $20. 3-night winter special $54; twins and doubles from $45. VIP/NOMADS/YHA. ❷

Coffs Harbour YHA, 110 Albany St. (☎/fax 6652 6462; coffsyha@ozemail.com.au), a 10min. walk from the town center; 20min. walk from the beach. This laid-back 2-story feels like a beach house. A chalkboard downstairs lists local activities. Kitchen, snack shop, common area, TV, Internet ($2 per 20min), laundry ($2 per machine), and pool. Billiards, ping-pong, and basketball on the laid-back patio. Use of mountain bikes, boogie boards, surfboards, golf clubs, and tennis rackets for $10 (taken out of a $50 deposit). $10 key and linen deposit. Free pick-up and drop-off. Bus runs to the beaches twice daily (10am and 3pm) and on request to local attractions. M, W, F BBQ nights. Breakfast $4-8. Reception from around 7am-11pm (changes slightly with the seasons). Dorms $22; twins and doubles from $50; family rooms for 4-6 from $70. ❷

Barracuda Backpackers (NOMADS), 19 Arthur St. (☎ 6651 3514 or 1800 111 514; www.backpackers.coffs.tv), a 2min. walk from the Park Beach Plaza; 5min. walk from the beach. Each 4- and 6-bunk dorm has linen, lockers, fan, and a small fridge. Internet ($5 per hr), laundry ($3 per machine), BBQ, pool table, swimming pool, and spa. Free use of fishing gear, cricket bats, boogie boards, and surfboards. Free pick-up and drop-off (schedule in advance) and courtesy half hour orientation van tour of town on request. Frequent organized activities (pub nights and hostel-chill nights), and rides to local sights (rainforests, headlands, beaches). Reception 6am-10pm. Dorms from $20; twins from $48; doubles from $50, ensuite from $55. NOMADS/ISIC/VIP/YHA. ❷

Hoey Moey Backpackers (☎ 6651 7966 or 1800 683 322; hoey@hoeymoey.com.au), on Ocean Pde., at the end of Park Beach Rd. A 10min. walk from the Park Beach Plaza; 1min. walk to the beach. Hoey Moey, slang for "Hotel Motel," is a backpackers, motel, and pub all rolled into one. The rowdy pub has weekly bands, a beer garden, and meals starting at $5.50. Kitchen and BBQ. Free surfboards and boogie boards. Bikes ($5 per day). All rooms have bath, TV, and small fridge. Free linen. Free pick-up and drop-off. Shuttle to town available. Internet and laundry. M, free pizza and pool comp for all Coffs backpackers; W, free pizza and DJ by the pool. Reception 6am-11:30am and 1:30pm-7:30pm. Check in at the pub after hours. Key deposit $10. Hostel-style dorms $20; doubles $48. Motel singles $42. VIP/ISIC/NOMADS/YHA. ❷

▸ FOOD

Across from the Jetty Village Shopping Centre, on Harbour Dr. near the harbor, is a row of diverse and popular restaurants. The **Palms Centre Mall, Park Beach Plaza,** and **Jetty Village Shopping Centre** each have **supermarkets.** The Hoey Moey Hotel and Plantation Hotel (see **Nightlife,** p. 156) have cheap pub meals.

Tahruah Thai Kitchen ❷, 366 Harbour Dr. (☎ 6651 5992). A local favorite with mains from $11. Open daily 6-10pm.

The Fisherman's Co-op ❶, (☎ 6652 2811), at the end of Marina Dr. by the breakwater boardwalk. Serves hot seafood straight off the boat, with fish 'n' chips $6. Fresh fish counter open daily 9am-6pm; cooked counter open daily 10am-early evening.

Beach Hut Cafe ❶ (☎ 6651 6944), on Orlando St., just up from Pet Porpoise Pool. Bountiful brekkie served all day, from $6-10. Open daily 8am-3pm; dinner served Sept.-Mar. daily 6-9pm.

Neil's Place ❶, 40 Moonee St. (☎ 6652 5922). Offers a variety of vegetarian options. Open M-F 7:30am-5pm.

Rainforest Restaurant and Bar ❶ (☎ 6651 5488), in the Greenhouse Tavern. A more upscale menu, including fresh seafood, steaks, salads, and pasta, at reasonable prices. An extensive menu, with hamburgers $9, salads $9-14.50, entrees $7-13, and mains $13-19. Open daily for lunch noon-2pm, and dinner 6-8:30.

◉ SIGHTS

The Coffs Harbour **jetty,** built in 1890, was the center of a busy marine industry at the start of the 20th century. Commercial fishing boats continue to take refuge in the protected harbor, but the area's emphasis has shifted to recreation in recent

years. The jetty foreshore has BBQ facilities and is an easy walk from **Jetty Beach.**
The breakwater boardwalk, near the marina, connects the mainland to **Muttonbird
Island** (named after the wedge-tailed shearwaters that nest there), a terrific lookout for spotting **whales.** The island was sacred to the region's Aborigines, whose
adolescent males would swim out to the island for several weeks of initiation into
manhood. The occasionally patrolled **Park Beach** and the beach immediately north
of the marina are also popular hang-outs but have dangerous currents.

The **Botanic Gardens,** one block north at the corner of Harbour Dr. and Hardacre
St., display colorful native and exotic plants and endangered species. (☎6648 4188.
Open daily 9am-5pm. Donation requested.) The 4km-long **Coffs Creek Walk** connects Rotary Park, at the intersection of Gordon and Coffs St. in the city center,
and the Coffs Creek inlet, near Orlando St., and also has a detour to the gardens.
You can make the hike a 10km circuit by following the 6km-long **Coffs Creek Habitat Walk** that follows the northern bank of the creek.

At the **Pet Porpoise Pool (Oceanarium),** on Orlando St. by Coffs Creek, dolphins
and seals perform tricks daily at 10:30am and 2:15pm in the Sea Circus. (☎6652
2164. Open daily 9am-5pm. $17, backpackers and students $13, children $8, fami-
lies $52.) The **Coffs Zoo,** 12km north of Coffs along the Pacific Hwy. past Moonee
Beach, offers daily presentations on koalas at 11am and 3pm, wombats at 10:30am,
and echidnas at 10:45am. (☎6656 1330. Open daily 8:30am-4pm, later during holidays. $16, Aussitel and YHA discount $10.80, children $8, families $40.)

Big Banana, on the Pacific Hwy. 4km north, is quintessential kitsch. Zoom
around the plantation on a monorail and learn more than you need to know about
banana cultivation ($12), try your luck at ice-skating ($12), indoor snow tubing
($15 per 30min.) or tobogganing (5 rides $15), or just gawk at the giant banana out
front. (☎6652 4355. Open daily 9am-4pm. Admission to shops and banana free.)

🔊 ACTIVITIES

There's no shortage of activities in Coffs (adrenaline, adventure, or otherwise) and
the variety is ever-increasing. Hostels can offer good rates, but don't hesitate to
call companies and ask about commission-free fun. The Visitor Information Centre does bookings, as well. Or go through the convenient **Coffs Central** online for all
your info and booking needs (☎6651 3185 or 1800 629 797; www.coffscen-
tral.com). Some companies may offer cheaper rates during the winter months.

WHITEWATER RAFTING & JET SKIING. The **Nymboida River,** two hours west of
Coffs, is the most popular place to raft. The rapids, mostly grade 3 to 4 with some
grade 5 sections, pass through dense rainforest. Award-winning **Wildwater Adventures,** 754 Pacific Hwy. (☎6653 3500), 7km south of Coffs, and **WOW Rafting Professionals** (☎6654 4066 or 1800 640 330) lead one- and multi-day trips down the
Nymboida, complete with BBQ dinner. (Wildwater: full-day $153, 2-day with camp-
ing $312, 4-day with camping $525; WOW: Full-day $153, 2-day with camping $325,
4-day with camping $560.) The **Goolang River,** a man-made kayaking course, is a
steady grade 3, but depending on season and weather conditions, the Goolang isn't
always flowing. **Liquid Assets Adventure Tours,** the pioneers of surf-rafting, runs
unbeatable whitewater rafting on the Goolang, as well as the slightly tamer, but
still adrenaline-charged wave-riding sea-kayak and rafting tours. (☎6658 0850.
Half-day $80. 3hr. sea kayaking $35; 3hr. surf-rafting $40; combo kayak and surf-
rafting $50; or go for the "big day out" pack of kayaking, surf-rafting, and whitewa-
ter $135. Meals included with all tours). **Rapid Rafting** also plunges down the Gool-
ang. (☎6652 1741 or 1800 629 797. Full-day $125, half-day $80.) **Coffs Water Sports**
on Park Beach, offers jet skiing. (☎0418 665 656. Single-seat jet ski 15min. $45;
30min. $75, 1hr. $135, double-seat 15min. $55, 30min. $95, 1hr. $165.)

SURFING. With the sand as its chalkboard, **East Coast Surf School** has a remarkable success rate with novices. Classes for advanced surfers are also available. Call to arrange pick-up from hostels. (☎6651 5515. One 2hr. group lesson $40 per person, five 2hr. group lessons $160 per person; 2hr. private group lesson $45; 1hr. private lesson $50.) **Liquid Assets** (see above) also offers "learn to surf" classes ($40 for 3hr. and breakfast). Most hostels provide surfboards and boogie boards for trying out the waves on your own. The best **surfing** is at **Diggers Beach** (patrolled only during school holidays), north of Macauleys Headland, accessible off the Pacific Hwy. From the Big Banana, turn onto Diggers Beach Rd. and follow it to the end. **The Gallows Beach,** down at the Jetty, also offers good surf. To learn about surfing without getting your feet wet, visit ex-surfing champ Scott Dillon's **Legend Surf Museum** (☎6653 6536), on Gaudron's Rd. in Korora, about 2km north of Coffs Harbour on the Pacific Hwy. $5, children $2. Open daily 10am-4pm.

FISHING & WHALE WATCHING. The fishing boats **Adriatic III** (☎6651 1277) and **Cougar Cat 12** (☎6651 6715) will set you up with bait, line, and tackle. (Half-day reef fishing $70; game fishing by appointment.) Whales swim north past Coffs from June to July and again from September to November. The catamaran ▧**Pacific Explorer** (☎6652 7225 or 0418 663 815) and the **Spirit of Coffs Harbour II** (☎6650 0155) lead whale-watching cruises. (At the Marina. 2-2½hr. Pacific: $49, backpackers $45, children $35, family $150. **Spirit:** $49, children $30, family $140.)

◪ DIVING OFF THE SOLITARY ISLANDS

Solitary Islands Marine Reserve stretches 70km from Coffs Harbour to the Sandon River and encompasses nearly 100,000 hectares. It is composed of at least 19 protected beaches, headlands, creeks, and rocky islands. Because of the unique mixing of warmer, tropical waters from the north and cooler, temperate waters from the south, the area has some of the most diverse marine life on the coast. Species common to the Great Barrier Reef mingle with species typically found near Tasmania. The marine park is well-respected as one of Australia's top diving spots. Visibility is often better during the winter, but the water gets chilly. Luckily, you can swim with harmless gray nurse sharks year-round. Contact the **NSW Fisheries and Marine Parks Office,** 32 Marina Dr., for more info. (☎6652 3977; www.mpa.nsw.gov.au. Open M-F 8:30am-5pm.)

▧ **Jetty Dive Centre,** 298 Harbour Dr. (☎6651 1611). The 4-day PADI course, including all boat-dives, costs $195 for backpackers staying at any Coffs hostel, min. 6 people. Double boat-dive with gear from $115; single intro-dive $109, double intro-dive $137. Snorkeling charters $45. Open daily 9am-5pm. Cheap accommodations through Aussitel Backpackers if you're taking your PADI course.

Aussitel Backpackers (see p. 194) runs charter dives two times a week off the hostel boat to see and swim with the gray nurse sharks (two dives $115), and also offers an array of advanced specialty courses starting from $100.

♪ ▧ ENTERTAINMENT & NIGHTLIFE

Coffs nightlife, focused around Grafton St., isn't quite as pumping as the daytime scene, but finding the party crowd isn't too difficult; hostels sometimes organize nights out for their guests. Most pubs have cover bands or DJs on weekends. Friday is the youthful night in town, while Saturdays tend to pull in an older crowd. **Coffs Harbour Hotel,** at the corner of Grafton and W. High St. pours the best drink in town—$5.50 pints of Guinness. (☎6652 3817. Entertainment nightly. M DJ, Tu live music, W-Th karaoke, Th-Su DJ and live bands; Irish Night first F of every month.)

Some of the cheapest drinks are found at the state-subsidized **Ex-Serviceman's Club** (☎ 6652 3888), on the corner of Grafton and Vernon St. You need a passport or laminated driver's license to get in. Friday nights are the most happening, but non-members must arrive before 10:30pm. Many people start their evenings at the club before hitting up other spots. **Hoey Moey Backpackers Pub** (☎ 6652 3833), on Ocean Pde., has hard rock a few nights a week, a pool competition with free pizza Monday nights, and free pizza and DJ on Wednesday nights. Hoey caters to a biker crowd on weekends. The **Plantation Hotel** (☎ 6652 3855), on Grafton St., half a block north of the Coffs Hotel, has a relaxed sports bar and live music on weekends with an occasional cover. The **Greenhouse Tavern** (☎ 6651 5488), on the Pacific Hwy. across from the Park Beach Plaza, has two bars and various live music weekly. Greenhouse also ships in topless lingerie waitresses from the gold coast every Wednesday night. For dance clubs, check out the boisterous backpacker scene at **Heat** (☎ 6652 6426), in the City Centre Mall.

WOOLGOOLGA
☎ 02

On its edges, Woolgoolga (20km north of Coffs Harbour) is an intriguing coastal town. It is flanked to the south by a strikingly white Indian temple, **Guru Nanak Sikh Gurdwara,** indicative of a thriving Punjabi Sikh community, and to the north by a mini-replica of the Taj Mahal, complete with large artificial elephants in the front lawn. If you leave the Pacific Hwy., and continue to the town center, however, the Indian influence fades and the beautiful coastline takes center-stage. The views are fantastic from the **Woolgoolga Headland** of the **Solitary Islands Marine Reserve** (see p. 197), an aquatic sanctuary with marine biodiversity approaching that of the Great Barrier Reef. Dolphin and whale sightings are common May-Oct. From the headland, the surfing- and fishing-friendly **Back Beach** stretches to the south and the pristine, patrolled **Front Beach** extends to the north. To stroll in the rainforest, go to the roundabout on the Pacific Hwy. near the elephants and exit onto Pullen St. Drive 3km, veer left at the fork, then continue another 1km until a locked gate.

Ryans buses (☎ 6652 3201) run to Coffs Harbour (40min.; M-F 5-7 per day, Sa 2 per day; $8.70) and Grafton (1½hr., M-F 2 per day, $17.70). The **Tourist Information Centre** is at the corner of Boundary Rd. and Beach St., the main drag. (☎ 6654 8080. Open M-F 9:30am-4pm, Sa 9:30am-1pm, Su 11am-1:30pm.) **Internet** is at Access.Net, 166 River St. (☎ 6654 9999. Open M-F 9am-6pm, Sa 10am-4pm. $2 per 20min.)

To sleep in the bush—or near it, anyway—turn left at the town center onto Wharf St. and drive 1km to the end of the road where you'll find the peaceful **Lakeside Holiday Park ❶,** with direct access to the beach and a lake. (☎ 6654 1210. Sites for 2 $15-20; powered $17-23; cabins $46-63.) To sleep in the middle of town, look for a spot at **Sunset Caravan Park ❷,** also right on the beach. (☎ 6654 1499. Sites for 2 $16-23, powered $19-28; 5-person cabins $45-83.) The ornate but weary-looking **Raj Mahal ❷** restaurant, behind the imposing elephant structures, has terrific traditional Indian cuisine. (☎ 6654 1149. Open daily 5:30pm-late; also Tu-Su noon-3pm. Meals $9-16.) Though not in Woolgoolga, **Coffs Harbour Dive Centre,** 15min. north of Coffs Harbour, conducts trips to both the north and south Solitary Islands. (☎ 6654 2860. Double boat-dive $88, full-gear hire $44; 4-day PADI certification course $399; 2hr. snorkeling $50.)

BALLINA
☎ 02

Technically an island, Ballina (pop. 18,750) is a peaceful port and beach town 2½ hours north of Coffs and 30min. south of Byron Bay. Getting around is surprisingly easy considering the extensive network of **bike paths** linking Ballina and Lennox Head; pick up a *Bike Safe* booklet and map from the Visitors Centre. **Lighthouse Beach** and **Pat Morton Lookout** are two great vantage points for whale watching. The

68-hectare reserve at **Angels Beach,** in East Ballina, features playful dolphins, dune ecology, and ocean invertebrates. **Flat Rock** has fantastic surfing and an incredible array of marine life occupying three distinct intertidal zones, home to sea anemones, sea stars, octopi, and neptune's necklace.

McCafferty's/Greyhound (☎ 13 14 99 or 13 20 30) and **Premier** (☎ 13 34 10) stop in Ballina on their Sydney-Brisbane runs. The long-distance **bus stop** at the **Transit Centre** is a good 4km from town center, in a large complex known as **The Big Prawn** for the enormous pink fiberglass shrimp nailed to its roof; tickets can be purchased inside the restaurant. **Ballina Taxi Service** (☎ 6686 9999) will take you into town for $10-12. Regional bus companies stop in town at the Tamar St. bus zone. **Blanch's Bus Company** (☎ 6686 2144) travels daily to **Lennox Head** (20min., 7 per day, $5.20) and **Byron Bay** (50min., 7 per day, $8.20).

The **Visitor Information Centre,** on the eastern edge of town at the corner of Las Balsa Plaza and **River Street** (the main drag), has details on area and regional activities. (☎ 6686 3484; www.discoverballina.com. Open M-F 9am-5pm, Sa-Su 9am-4pm.) Woolworths **supermarket** is at 72 River St. Another is in the Ballina Fair Shopping Centre on Kerr St., and a Coles is directly across the street. **Internet** is at the **Ballina Ice Creamery Internet Cafe,** 178 River St. (☎ 6686 5783. Open daily in summer 8:30am-9pm; in winter 9:30am-6pm. $6 per hr.) The **post office** is on the corner of Tamar and Moon St. (☎ 13 13 18. Open M-F 9am-5pm.) **Postal Code:** 2478.

The ⚑**Ballina Travelers Lodge (YHA) ❷**, 36-38 Tamar St., is a motel and hostel combo. Go one block up Norton St. from the tourist office, then turn left. The friendly owners keep the lodge quiet and meticulously clean. The YHA part of the complex has four basic rooms, a separate communal kitchen/TV area, BBQ, and laundry. The larger motel rooms have TVs and lots of amenities. There's a small saltwater pool, bikes (for a nominal fee), limited fishing gear, and free boogie boards. (☎ 6686 6737. Courtesy pick-up from the Transit Centre by arrangement. Dorms from $20; twins and doubles from $24 per person. Motel rooms $70-105. The **Ballina Central Caravan Park ❷**, 1 River St., is just north of the info center. (☎ 6686 2220. Open daily 7am-7pm. Sites $16-20, powered $18-22; cabins $38-72).

Paddy McGinty's ❶, 56 River St., is the local Irish pub and serves counter lunches and dinners. (☎ 6686 2135. Burgers from $9.50. Mains $12-20. Open daily noon-3pm and 6-9pm. Bar open later.) Delicious deli food awaits at **Sasha's Gourmet Eatery ❶**, in the Wigmore Arcade off River St. Takeaway selections such as pasta salads, quiches, and fancy sandwiches ($4-7) make for perfect picnic fare. (☎ 6681 1118. Open M-F 8am-5pm, Sa 8am-1pm.)

Ballina Ocean Tours offers 2½-3hr. dolphin and whale-watching tours at 9am and 1pm (☎ 6680 7006. $55). Learn to surf or perfect your technique with **Summerland Surf School.** (☎ 6682 4393. Private 1½hr. lessons in Ballina $100, 2 on 1 $50, 3 on 1 $40, group class $30, in Evans Head $50/$40/$35/$30.) **MV Bennelong** conducts cruises along the Richmond River. (☎ 6688 8266. 2hr. $16.) For self-guided exploring, **Jack Ransom Cycles,** 16 Cherry St., just off River St., rents bikes. (☎ 6686 3485. Half-day $12; full-day $18, plus $50 deposit.) Swing by the **Ballina Naval and Maritime Museum (☎** 6681 1002), on the corner of North St. and Regatta Ave., just down from the Info Centre, to see the 1973 Las Balsas Trans Pacific Expedition Raft, a genuine article that made it all the way across the ocean to Aussie shores.

LENNOX HEAD   ☎ 02

Lennox Head (pop. 2300) between Ballina and Byron Bay (about 15 minutes from each), is consistently lauded as the serene and tranquil alternative to Byron Bay. It may not figure on the typical backpacker's agenda, but Lennox Head provides an opportunity for the savvy traveler to step back from all the hype and hedonism of Byron and beyond.

NEW SOUTH WALES

The Coast Road, off the Pacific Hwy., runs between Ballina and Byron and passes through Lennox Head. The town center is accessible by taking the roundabout to coastal Ballina St., which becomes Pacific Pde. and runs along **Seven Mile Beach,** prime dolphin-spotting territory. **Lennox Point,** 2km south, is an excellent but crowded surf area. **Blanch's Coaches** (☎ 6686 2144) run through Lennox Head a few times daily to Byron Bay and Ballina; the bus stop is on Ballina St. near the town center, but you can also flag buses down along Pacific Pde. ($5.20).

ATMs, food stores, eateries, the **post office,** and the local pub are clustered within one minute's walk of each other at the southern end of Ballina St. The family-owned and operated ▨**Lennox Head Beach House YHA ❷,** 3 Ross St., is north of the town center, just off Pacific Pde. and a short walk from Lake Ainsworth. The intimate beachouse has free surfboards, boogie boards, bicycles, and fishing rods; unlimited use of windsurfers is just $5 and lessons are free. Aspiring gourmands can help themselves in the herb garden and dine in the open courtyard. On Thursdays, enjoy a 10 minute massage in the "natural healing center." Bedrooms are small but tidy. Between September and December, hostel guests are offered a special $75 deal for tandem hang gliding off Lennox Pt. through **Flightzone** (☎ 6687 7636. Internet $1 per 10min. 4-bed dorms $26; doubles $56. Ask about weekly rates. YHA.) **Lake Ainsworth Caravan Park ❷** is across Ross St. next to the lake. (☎ 6687 7249. Sites $16-20, powered $18-22; cabins $38-70.)

Lennox Head Pizza and Pasta ❶, Shop 2, 56 Ballina St (☎ 6687 7080), serves up heaping helpings of homemade comfort food. Pizzas range $6.50-21.50 and pastas start at $11. (Open Su-Th 5-9pm, F-Sa 5-10pm. Cash only.) You can sit back and watch the town go by at **Cafe de Mer ❷,** 1/70 Ballina St. (☎ 6687 7132), which offers coffee, cakes and light meals. (Open daily 8:30am-5pm. Cash only.)

Lennox is renowned for its excellent surf—**Lennox Point,** 2km south of town, has one of the longest right hand surf breaks in the world, and from June to August is rated one of the top 10 international surfing areas. Tamer surfing spots are found all along Seven Mile Beach. **All Above Board,** 68 Ballina St. (☎ 6687 7522), rents surfboards (half-day $15, full-day $20), and body boards ($10/$15). They also rent snorkel sets for $8. An age-old **Aboriginal Bora Ring** is two blocks from the hostel and caravan park at the end of Ross St. Forty meters around, the indented area was a spiritual spot for ancient coming-of-age ceremonies.

BYRON BAY ☎ 02

The "come for a day, stay for a week" coastal malaise that infects a wandering traveler on the Holiday Coast of Australia peaks in Byron Bay, one of the most popular stops on the Sydney-to-Cairns route. With Byron's excellent family and surfing beaches and refreshing lack of high-rises and mass consumerism, it's not hard to see why. While Byron feeds its happy, muesli-eating masses with palm readings, massage classes, and bead shops, it's more than just commercialized karma. The relaxed, rejuvenating coastal town with a famously "alternative" attitude is nirvana for a host of diverse devotees: aged hippies, dreadlocked backpackers, bleached surfers, young families, businessmen, and yoga gurus.

▛ TRANSPORTATION

Trains: Countrylink (☎ 13 22 32) runs to: **Brisbane** (5hr., 1 per day, $28); **Coffs Harbour** (4hr., 3 per day, $45); **Surfers Paradise** (4½hr., 1 per day, $17); and **Sydney** (13hr., 2 per day, $102).

Buses: Among **McCafferty's/Greyhound** (☎ 13 14 99 or 13 20 30), **Kirkland's** (☎ 1300 367 077), **Blanch's Coaches** (☎ 6686 2144), and **Premier** (☎ 13 34 10), buses run to: **Ballina** (50min., 5 per day, $8); **Brisbane** (4hr., at least 10 per day, $35); **Coffs Har-**

bour (4-5hr., 8 per day, $53); **Lennox Head** (20min., 3-7 per day, $5); **Lismore** (1hr., 2-4 per day, $12); **Murwillumbah** (1hr., 2-6 per day, $13); **Port Macquarie** (6-7hr., 4 per day, $68); **Surfers Paradise** (2hr., at least 6 per day, $29); and **Sydney** (11-13hr., 8 per day, $93). McCafferty's/Greyhound offers 10% discounts for backpackers. Buses depart from the **Bus Depot** in the center of town. Tickets can be purchased at **Peterpan Adventures** (see Practical Info, p. 201.)

Car Rental: Earth Car Rentals, 18 Fletcher St. (☎6685 7472 or 6680 9708). **JetSet Travel,** at the corner of Marvell and Jonson St., hires small, manual cars from $49 per day (☎6685 6554; bustop@bigpond.net.au).

Tours: 🖼 **Jim's Alternative Tours** (☎6685 7720; www.jimsalternativetours.com) offers a great 9hr. trip (with synchronized CD soundtrack) through Nimbin, Minyan Falls and Night-cap National Park, with a stop at Paul Recher's Fruit Spirit Botanical Gardens (reforested with 350 different varieties of exotic fruit from around the world). Named Backpackers "Party Tour of the Year 2001" by The International Party Guide. $30. **Grasshoppers Eco-Explorer Tours** (☎0500 881 881; www.rockhoppers.com.au) offers an all-day trip to subtropical rainforest, waterfalls, koala- and platypus-sighting spots, and Nimbin (and the Sunday markets, as well). Daily tours 10am-6pm. $30; includes BBQ lunch.

✈🛈 ORIENTATION & PRACTICAL INFORMATION

Byron is not on the Pacific Hwy., but is accessible from it through nearby Bangalow (15km away). From Bangalow, **Bangalow Road** enters Byron Bay from the south. Turn off a roundabout onto **Browning Street,** which leads to **Jonson Street,** the southern boundary of the city center. **Lawson Street** is to the north of town, running at times along **Main Beach.** Be careful of your belongings while on the beach. To the east, Lawson St. becomes **Lighthouse Road,** running past Clarkes Beach, The Pass surfing spot, Wategos Beach, the lighthouse, and the Cape Byron lookout. To the west, Lawson becomes **Shirley Street** and curves off to **Belongil Beach.** Farther west it becomes **Ewingsdale Road** and passes the **Arts and Industrial Estate** before reaching the Pacific Hwy. (Byron can also be accessed from the Pacific Hwy. on the end through Ewingsdale, 6km away.)

Tourist Office: Byron Visitors Centre, 80 Jonson St. (☎6680 9271 or 6680 8558; info@visitbyronbay.com.au), at the bus station. Friendly staff books local adventure activities and separate accommodations desk helps you book. Open daily 9am-5pm.

Budget Travel: Most hostels have travel desks which will book trips and local activities. At **Peterpan Adventures,** 87 Jonson St. (☎6880 8926 or 1800 252 459; www.peter-pans.com), the friendly staff does the same (and will book most local activities for free). Purchase a $20 Gold Card for discounts on trips, activities, and accommodations up and down the coast. Open daily 9am-9pm.

Currency Exchange: Banks on Jonson St. are open M-Th 9:30am-4pm, F 9:30am-5pm. Other **ATMs** are across the street from the tourist office. **Byron Foreign Exchange Shop** 4 Central Arcade, Byron St. (☎6685 7787), advertises the lowest fees and best rates.

Taxis: Byron Bay Taxis (☎6685 5008). 24hr. Wheelchair access available.

Police: (☎6685 9499), on the corner of Butler and Shirley St.

Internet: Internet cafes line the streets of backpacker-ready Byron Bay. **Peterpan Adventures** offers the cheapest in town at $2 per hour (**Budget Travel,** above; open daily 9am-9pm). **Global Gossip,** 84 Jonson St. (☎6680 9140), at the bus stop, is open late. $4.50 per hr. Open daily 9am-10pm in winter, 9am-midnight in summer. Some Internet shops pass out vouchers on the street for free to cheaper-than-average access. Most activity-booking offices also offer free Internet access with bookings.

Post Office: 61 Jonson St. (☎13 13 18). Open M-F 9am-5pm. **Postal Code:** 2481.

ACCOMMODATIONS

In summer, especially around Christmas, Byron floods with thousands of tourists; everything gets packed, and some accommodation prices go up as much as two-fold. The best advice is to book early, but demand is so high that some hostels don't even accept reservations in summer. Many would-be Byron dwellers make do in Ballina (see p. 198) or Lennox Head (see p. 199), 20 and 10 minutes south, respectively. Sleeping in cars and on the beach is strictly prohibited.

Aquarius Backpackers Resort, 16 Lawson St. (☎6685 7663 or 1800 028 909; www.aquarius-backpack.com.au), at the corner of Middleton St., 2 blocks off Jonson St. Formerly a luxury resort, many of the spacious rooms have 2 levels, porches, and fridges; all have beautiful rosewood beds. Poolside bar with Happy Hour, nightly meals, fully licensed travel desk, parking, kitchen, and cafe where guests receive discounts (all-you-can-eat pancakes $5). Free boogie boards and shuttle bus. Free pick-up and drop-off. Linen $1, blanket deposit $10. Laundry $4. Key deposit $10. Internet $4 per hr. Reception 7am-10pm. Check-in 24hr. Ensuite dorms $18-30. Doubles $55-65; self-contained motel units, 2 with spa, $120-220. 3- and 7-day discounts. ❷

Arts Factory Backpackers Lodge (☎6685 7709; www.artsfactory.com.au), on Gordon St. Cross the railroad tracks behind the bus stop and take a right on Burns St. to Gordon St. A 10min. walk to town; 10min. walk to beach. Sprawling 5-acre grounds with "funky abodes" ranging from teepees ($25) to island bungalows ($27) on a lake. Amid nature, so bring bug repellent. Free daily activities include didgeridoo lessons (make your own for $150), yoga, fire-twirling, massage classes, and drum workshops. Volleyball courts, pool, sauna, laundry ($4), Internet ($3 per 30min.), bikes ($15 per day), large shop, cinema, and day spa. Live music Sa nights. Surfboard ($15) and bodyboard ($5) hire. Weekly talent shows W and $10 BBQ W and F. Cafe open for breakfast and lunch, restaurant open for dinner. Reception 7am-noon and 4-9pm. 24 hour check-in. Free pick-up and drop-off. Sites $9-14; dorms $22-27; twins and doubles $55-130; 3- and 5-night and winter discounts. VIP/YHA. ❶

Backpackers Inn on the Beach, 29 Shirley St. (☎6685 8231; www.byron-bay.com/backpackersinn). Follow Jonson St., veer left onto Lawson St., cross the railroad tracks, and continue on Shirley St. to the corner of Milton St. A 5-10min. walk to town. The only hostel in Byron with direct beach access. Large and social. Loft kitchen, volleyball, heated pool, BBQ, game room, pool table, free bus shuttle, cable TV, free linen, and Internet ($6 per hr.). Free luggage storage, bikes, and boogie boards. Small cafe sells food like veggie burgers and chicken sandwiches for under $6. BBQ Sa night and Sangria Night W, both with live entertainment. Reception 8am-8pm. Reserve 1 week ahead. Dorms $23-26; doubles $30-34 per person. Rates drop $1 nightly after 3 days, another $1 after one week. VIP/ISIC/YHA discounts. Wheelchair-accessible. ❷

J's Bay Hostel, 7 Carlyle St. (☎6685 8853 or 1800 678 195; www.jsbay.com.au). Clean, colorful, and cozy, J's has one of the best all-you-can-eat-and-drink BBQ deals with live music Th ($6). Billiards and picnic tables in an upstairs covered pavilion, very large kitchen, heated pool, and secure parking. Family-friendly. Free linen. Free use of bikes and boogie boards. 300m to beach, 200m to bus stop. Laundry $5. Reception 8am-9pm. Book 1 week ahead. Dorms $25-28; twins and doubles $59-75; ensuite doubles $68-88; separate family room $75-90. YHA. ❸

Cape Byron Hostel, (☎6685 8788 or 1800 652 627; www.capebyronhostel.com.au), on the corner of Middleton and Byron St. From the bus stop, go 2 blocks down Byron St. and take a left on Middleton. Pinball machines, TV/VCR, a pool table, and video games in the living room. Upstairs deck and eating area overlooks a heated pool bordered by lush palm trees. $9 BBQ Tu and F. Free bikes ($50 deposit) and boogie boards ($20 deposit). Family-friendly. Free pick-up and drop-off. Free parking. Laundry $4. Internet

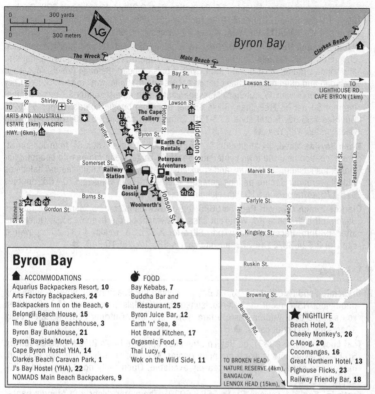

Byron Bay

▲ ACCOMMODATIONS
Aquarius Backpackers Resort, **10**
Arts Factory Backpackers, **24**
Backpackers Inn on the Beach, **6**
Belongil Beach House, **15**
The Blue Iguana Beachhouse, **3**
Byron Bay Bunkhouse, **21**
Byron Bayside Motel, **19**
Cape Byron Hostel YHA, **14**
Clarkes Beach Caravan Park, **1**
J's Bay Hostel (YHA), **22**
NOMADS Main Beach Backpackers, **9**

🍎 FOOD
Bay Kebabs, **7**
Buddha Bar and
  Restaurant, **25**
Byron Juice Bar, **12**
Earth 'n' Sea, **8**
Hot Bread Kitchen, **17**
Orgasmic Food, **5**
Thai Lucy, **4**
Wok on the Wild Side, **11**

★ NIGHTLIFE
Beach Hotel, **2**
Cheeky Monkey's, **26**
C-Moog, **20**
Cocomangas, **16**
Great Northern Hotel, **13**
Pighouse Flicks, **23**
Railway Friendly Bar, **18**

$1 per 15 min. $4 per hr. Lockers $4 per day. Reception 6:45am-10pm. YHA travel office open 9am-5pm. Dorms $20-30; twins and doubles $60-90; ensuite doubles $70-110. YHA. ❷

The Blue Iguana Beachhouse, 14 Bay St. (☎6685 5298), opposite the beach and Surf Club, on the corner of Bay and Fletcher St. Relax in an intimate beachhouse near the town center. Sundeck and screened front porch with couches and TV. Free bodyboards and surfboards. Small food kiosk. Off-street parking. Reception 9am-noon and 4-9pm. Book 1 week ahead. Free linen. Ensuite dorms $26; doubles from $65. 7th night free. No credit cards. ❸

Byron Bay Bunkhouse, 1 Carlyle St. (☎6685 8311 or 1800 241 600; www.byronbay-bunkhouse.com.au), opposite the Jonson St. Woolworths. Crowded and loud, but with nightly $4 dinners that can be eaten on the candle-lit terrace. Live entertainment and BBQ W. Pancake breakfast included. Free linen and boogie boards. Booking office. Laundry $4. Free Internet 1hr. per day. Key deposit $15. Reception 7:30am-10pm. Dorms $20-26; doubles $58-65; ensuite $65-75. Weekly rates available. ❷

NOMADS Main Beach Backpackers (☎6685 8695 or 1800 150 233), at the corner of Lawson and Fletcher St. Take a right on Lawson from the beach end of Jonson St. High ceilings, wood paneling, fireplace, rooftop deck with outdoor pool table overlooking Lawson St., patio, saltwater pool, secured parking, and a common room with TV and another pool table. Bedrooms have individual lockers. BBQ twice a week in summer, once a week in winter. Laundry $4. Reception 8am-9:30pm. Key deposit $20. Book at least 1 week ahead. Dorms $19-26; doubles $50-90. Winter and multiple night discounts. ISIC/NOMADS/VIP/YHA. Wheelchair-accessible. ❷

Belongil Beach House (☎6685 7868; www.belongilbeachouse.com, info@belongilbeachouse.com) on Kendall St., 2km south of town, turn off Pacific Hwy. onto Kendall St., and follow around. A bit distant from Byron's pulsing heart, Belongil Beach House is a secluded and quiet retreat. Direct beach access and a 15min. walk to town center. Cozy common room with TV. Kitchen. Massage center and cafe. Laundry $3 per machine, Internet $4 per hr. Free linen. Bikes $5 per day. Free boogie boards. Dorms $18-28. Doubles $55-65. Motel style $75-130. 2 bedroom cottages $160-180. 3-day and weekly rates. VIP/YHA. ❷

Byron Bayside Motel, 14 Middleton St. (☎6685 6004). Take Byron St. from Jonson St. Great location near the town center and beaches. Large, clean rooms with beautiful furniture, full kitchen, TV, laundry, and sparkling private bathroom; many feature balconies with flowerbeds. Secure parking garage locked 9pm-7am. Singles $70-165; doubles $75-175, extra person $15. Wheelchair-accessible. ❺

Clarkes Beach Caravan Park (☎6685 6496; www.bshp.com.au/clarkes), on Clarkes Beach, off Lighthouse Rd. Well-kept sites, a few right on the beach's edge. Quiet time after 9:30pm. Reception 7am-7pm. Sites for 2 $22-36, weekly $132-252; powered sites for 2 $24-39/$144-273; ensuite cabins $85-120/$510-840. ❷

◪ FOOD

◪ Orgasmic Food (☎6680 7778), on Bay Ln. behind the Beach Hotel. Word is spreading throughout NSW about the self-proclaimed "best falafels in Australia" ($6.50). When you sample their Middle Eastern fare, you'll see why. Outdoor seating. Open daily 10am-late. No credit cards. ❶

Thai Lucy (☎6680 8083), on Bay Ln., the alley opposite Hog's Breath Cafe on Jonson St. Every savory bite is worth the price (mains $12-18), as well as the wait to get in. Indoor and outdoor seating. Takeaway available. Open daily noon-3pm and 5:30-10pm. BYO. ❷

Earth 'n' Sea, 11 Lawson St. (☎6685 6029). The surfer decor and friendly banter between waiters make this long-running, family-friendly joint a great place to unwind. It caters to "pastaholics," hitting a nerve with anyone who wants a hearty helping of carbo-goodness. Try their original "Beethoven" pizza, a surprisingly delicious combo of prawns, banana, and pineapple. Pastas from $11, 20 different pizza pies from $16-32. Delivery available. Open daily 5:30-9pm; also in summer for lunch and later hours. ❸

Bay Kebabs (☎6685 5596), at the corner of Jonson and Lawson St. Try the traditional *doner* (lamb and beef; $5.90), or the highly addictive marinated chicken ($6.90). Meal deal ($6) gets you a sizable kebab and a drink. Open daily 10am-late. Cash only. ❶

Wok on the Wild Side, 18 Jonson St. (☎6685 6220). Choose from 5 different noodles and 9 choices of meat and vegetarian options to make your own pasta stir-fry in Malay, Chinese, or Thai sauces. Large portions at $10-14 make this a great dinner option, though there's a $5-7 breakfast as well. Open daily 7am-10pm. No credit cards. ❷

Buddha Bar and Restaurant (☎6685 5833), at the Arts Factory. Classy, bistro style dining. Large steak, chicken, and pasta dishes ($10-17), served in a harmonious setting. Candles cast flickering shadows on the lofty ceiling; long wooden tables are surrounded by stone statues, sculptures, and a splashing waterfall. Happy Hour 5-6pm. Open M-Sa 4pm-midnight, Su 4pm-10pm. ❷

Byron Juice Bar, 20 Jonson St. (☎6680 7780), fixes up fresh juices ($4.40) and smoothies ($4.90), as well as wheatgrass and herbal shots ($2-3) for health nuts. Open daily 8am-6pm. Cash only. ❶

Hot Bread Kitchen, 50 Jonson St. (☎6685 6825), across from the Great Northern Hotel. This bakery satiates the munchies with delectable breads ($2) and pastries ($3) 24 hours a day. Cash only. ❶

👁 SIGHTS

Built in 1901, the **Byron Bay Lighthouse,** at the end of Lighthouse Rd., is Cape Byron's crowning glory: the most powerful lighthouse and the easternmost point in all of Australia. Its steadily rotating beam pierces through 40km of darkness every night. The last lighthouse keeper left in 1988, long after the lighthouse became fully automated. The keepers' cottages are still standing, however; one is a small museum, and the other is available for private holiday rental. (Grounds open daily 8am-seasonal. Tours during school holidays. Contact Cape Byron Trust ☎6685 5955 for rental information.) A boardwalk leads to the lighthouse, a one-hour walk passing along Main Beach to Clarks Beach and **Captain Cook Lookout.** From here, a walking circuit follows the beach to **The Pass** and winds up a steep gradient past Wategos Beach to the **Headland Lookout,** an excellent place for spotting dolphins and whales. The lighthouse is just a short distance farther; the track then heads through forest back to **Captain Cook Lookout.**

Byron's artistic community is flourishing; the best example is **The Cape Gallery,** 2 Lawson St., which exhibits primarily local artists and a fine pottery collection. (☎6685 7659; www.capegallery.com.au. Open daily in summer 10am-6pm; in winter 10am-5pm.) **Gondwana Gifts,** 7-9 Byron St., has Aboriginal art and free weekly didgeridoo and fire-twirling lessons. (☎6685 8866; info@ozarts.net. Open M-F 10am-5pm, Sa 10am-4pm.) West of town, the **Arts and Industrial Estate,** off Ewingsdale Rd. (called Shirley Rd. in town), is home to a number of stores hawking industrial glass and metals, paintings, sculptures, crafts, and shoes. Colin Heaney **blows glass** at 6 Acacia St. (☎6685 7044. Gallery open M-F 9am-5pm, Sa-Su 10am-4pm; glass-blowing M-Th 9am-4pm, F 9am-2:30pm.)

🏃 ACTIVITIES

For those who wish to sharpen their skills beyond the first stumbling day, many activities offer lengthier packages that can extend beyond a week. Nearly all have free accommodation pick-up/drop-off. The Byron Bay Visitors Centre books activities, as does Peter Pan and many hostels.

SURFING

Boards slung over their shoulders, herds of bleach-blonde surfers trudge dutifully to Byron's beaches every morning at sunrise. Surf schools entice novices by providing all equipment and soliciting through hostels; most have a stand-up guarantee. Byron has excellent surfing spots all around the bay, so no matter the wind conditions there are always good waves somewhere. Just off Main Beach, **The Wreck** is known for waves that break close to the beach. Working down the shore toward the lighthouse, **The Pass** promises long, challenging rides, but can be dangerous because of overcrowding, sharp rocks, and boats. The water off **Wategos Beach,** close to The Pass, is best for longer surfboards, since the waves are slow and rolling. Again, the rocks can be dangerous. **Cosy Corner,** on the other side of the headland from Wategos, has great northern-wind surfing. **Belongil Beach,** to the north of Main Beach, is long and sandy with clothing optional sections. **Broken Head Nature Reserve,** 4km south of Byron on the Coast Rd., has verdant rainforest growing right down to its magnificent beaches. Take the track from Broken Head Caravan Park along the clifftop to **King's Beach,** or enjoy a swim at **Broken Head Beach** or **Whites Beach.**

■ **Black Dog Surfing,** in Shop 8, next to Woolworths, Jonson St. (☎ 6680 9828, after hours 0411 029 893; www.blackdogsurfing.com) 3hr. lesson $45; 3- and 5-day courses and private lessons available. Surfboards full-day $30, weekly $120. Wetsuits $10/$40; boogie boards $15/$60.

Byron Bay Surf School (☎ 1800 707 274; www.byronbaysurfschool.com). The original surf school in the area. 4hr. lesson $45, 3-day course $110, 5-day course $150. All-female lessons available.

Byron Surf (☎ 6685 7536) on the corner of Lawson and Fletcher St., rents surfboards $8 per hr., $20 per 4hr., and $120 per week and wetsuits $5 per day. ($600 board deposit, cash or visa. $100 wetsuit deposit).

Byron Bay Kiteboarding (☎ 1300 888 938; www.byronbaykiteboarding.com). If you've got the money and the time, try the newest craze in watersports. Half-day group lesson $150; 2 hour private lesson $200.

Two companies offer **multi-day surf trips** to get an extended taste of the surfing lifestyle up and down the coast.

A Real Surf Journey (☎ 1800 828 888; www.arealsurfjourney.com), run through Black Dog, takes a 3-day trip from Byron north to Noosa every M and F and hits the best surf breaks along the coast. For all experience levels. Camping or cabin accommodations. All food provided (including vegetarian). Free return. $288.

Surfaris (☎ 1800 634 951) offers similar 5 or 6 day surf trips between Sydney and Byron (850km of coast). Departs M from Sydney, Su from Byron. Free return. $499.

DIVING

Most diving is done at **Julian Rocks Marine Park,** 2.5km off Main Beach, widely considered one of the best dive sites in Australia. Julian Rocks has both warm and cold currents and is home to 500 species of fish, including the occasional grey nurse shark. Required medical clearances cost $50. Dive certification courses can go up by $70-100 or more during the summer.

Sundive (☎ 6685 7755), on Middleton St. next to the Cape Byron YHA. Has an on-site pool and offers many types of dives. Courses usually start Tu and F, but certification courses over two weekends are sometimes offered. 4-day PADI certification $325-395. Intro dives $130, day dives $65-75, additional trips $55; snorkeling $45.

Byron Bay Dive Centre, 9 Marvel St. (☎ 6685 8333 or 1800 243 483; www.byronbaydivecentre.com.au), between Middleton and Fletcher St. 4-day SSI or PADI certification courses start M and Th $450, winter $350; intro dives $130-150, day dives $75, additional trips $55; snorkeling $45. Seasonal whale watching trips $45.

KAYAKING & RAFTING

Byron Bay Sea Kayaking (☎ 6685 8044). 3½hr. trips around the Cape via Little Wategos beach, incl. morning tea. $45.

Dolphin Kayaking (☎ 6685 8044). Half-day guided tour of Byron's marine life, taking guests right up to a school of local dolphins or whales in season. Summer trips 9am and 2pm; winter 11am. $40.

OUT OF THE SKY

Byron Air Charter (☎ 6684 2753). For the non-adventurer who still wants to catch a glimpse. Scenic flights over Cape Byron and Mt. Warning starting at $40 per seat.

Skylimit (☎ 6684 3711). Motorized ultralight tours from $80. 1½hr. trip to view Mt. Warning $290. Half hour lighthouse trip $150. Tandem hang gliding $145.

Flightzone Hanggliding School (☎ 6685 8768 or 0408 441 742). 30min. tandem flights $110. 10-day certification course $1500. Cash only.

Byron Airwaves (☎6629 0354 or 0427 615 950). Tandem hang gliding flights $110. Ten-day course, $100 per day. Cash only.

Skydive Cape Byron (☎6685 5990 or 1800 666 770; www.skydive-cape-byron.com). Coastal tandem skydiving directly over Cape Byron with tandem instructors from $260. Backpacker and student specials available.

Byron Bay Skydiving Centre (☎6684 1323). Dives $223-388 for dives 8000-14,000 feet over Cape Byron.

MASSAGES

Samadhi Flotation Centre (☎6685 6905, www.byronbay.com/samadhisatbyron), on Jonson St., opposite Woolworths. Massages and great-value massage classes ($100 for a 2-day course). Open daily 10am-6pm. Book ahead. 1hr. massage $70, backpackers 10-20% off.

Relax Haven (☎6685 8304), at the rear of Belongil Beachhouse on Childe St., 2km from town. Much smaller, but offers great value. Open daily 10am-8pm. 1hr. float and 1hr. massage $50.

Osho's House Healing Centre, 1/30 Carlyle St. (☎6685 6792 or 0407 299 258; www.byron-bay.com/oshoshouse), also offers a massage and float special ($40 1hr., $60 2hr.), as well as an array of other techniques.

OTHER ACTIVITIES

Rockhoppers, 87 Jonson St. (☎0500 881 881; www.rockhoppers.com.au). across from the bus stop. Package deals combine trips and can save you money if you're planning several adventures. All equipment and food included, with vegetarian options. Mt. Warning sunrise trip with champagne breakfast at the top $59; departs 2:30am. Full-day mountain biking $79. "Extreme Triple Challenge" includes abseiling and caving; full-day $119. Learn-to-wakeboard (like snowboarding off a skiboat) ski trips $129.

Byron Bay Bicycles, 93 Jonson St. (☎6685 6067). Half-day $13.20, full-day $28.60, weekly $93.50. $50 security deposit.

Pegasus Park Equestrian Centre (☎6687 1446), 15min. west of Byron. Leads horseback rides and canoe trips along Byron Creek ($45 per hr., $65 per 2hr.) and along the beach ($65 per hr., $85 per 2hr.). Beach rides not offered weekends or holidays. Ask about backpacker rates. Cash only.

Seahorses (☎6680 8155), 20min. west of Byron, 1½hr. forest horseback ride. $55.

▣ ♫ NIGHTLIFE & ENTERTAINMENT

Cheeky Monkey's (☎6685 5886), on the corner of Jonson and Kingsley St. Caters pointedly to backpackers, who dance on the tables and stir up a raucous party. While the nightly routine might get old fast (for some, at least), it's no doubt worth an indulgent peek. Themed nights and frequent backpacker specials. Dinner from $5 ($2 on F). Happy Hour 3pm, 6pm, and 10:30pm. Open M-Sa Noon-3am, Su Noon-Midnight. $5 cover after 10:30pm. If you're too tired to talk, the Cheeky Monkey Party Van scans the streets nightly to whisk you away.

C-Moog (☎6680 7022; www.c-moog.com.au), on Jonson St., in the Woolworths plaza. This new underground dance club offers less hype and more music, pulling in big time international DJs, who do their thang on the 4300 watt sound system. $5-10 cover charge. Open W-Sa 9pm-3am. Backpacker nights W featuring drum and bass.

Cocomangas, 32 Jonson St. (☎6685 8493). Calmer, smaller dance floor and affordable drinks. Try the tasty Jam Jar, a mix of juices, gin, Malibu rum, and triple sec for $3.50. M '70s night; Tu 90s and 2000 mix; Th R&B; W 1 free drink for the first 75 women. Cover $3-5; no cover before 10pm, in winter before midnight. Open M-Sa until 3am.

Beyond the backpacker partying listed below, Byron has a thriving live music scene. The town gets jam-packed every year for two major music festivals, which pull in well-known international acts as well as Australia-based performers: **The Blues and Roots Music Festival** (☎665 8310) the third weekend in April and **Splendour in the Grass** (www.splendourinthegrass.com) the third weekend in July. Buy tickets and book accommodation far in advance. **A Taste of Byron** (☎0419 170 407) is a popular one week food festival, the third week in September. Check out the weekly entertainment magazine *Echo* for gig information (on the streets or online at www.echo.net.au every Tu morning).

Beach Hotel (☎6685 6402), on Jonson St., overlooking the beach. A local favorite with a garden bar and huge patio. Large indoor stage hosts both local and nationally recognized bands. Live music Th-Su. DJs Su. No cover. Open until around 1am.

Great Northern Hotel, on the corner of Jonson and Byron St. (☎6685 6454). An incredible venue for live music, 7 nights a week, from contemporary folk to rock and punk. Concerts range in price, but there are frequent freebies. Open M-Sa until 2:30am, Su until midnight. Cash only.

Railway Friendly Bar, on Jonson St, right next to the Railway Station (☎6680 9009). An amazing array of live music every night of the week (6:30am-9:30pm) pulls in a rather large spectrum of people and ages. A great early evening option to jam out and drink up before heading elsewhere.

Byron also offers a number of alternative entertainment options.

Pighouse Flicks (☎6685 5828), at the Piggery on Gordon St. by the Arts Factory. Shows classics, arthouse, foreign, and mainstream films in a funky lounge-like theater, 3 times nightly M-F, 4 times Sa-Su. Opens around 5pm. 4 shows Sa $11, students $9. Movie-and-dinner deal with nearby vegetarian restaurant $13.90 or $15.90.

Aborignal Culture Show at the **Buddha Bar and Restaurant** (☎6685 5833), every M night, is both entertaining and educational. $15, or dinner included for $20 (vegetarian options). Dinner served 6pm-7:30pm. Show starts at 8:30pm.

NIMBIN ☎02

A popular daytrip from Byron (about 1½hr. away), Nimbin is an experience you shouldn't forget, though maybe you will—it's Australia's cannabis capital. Galleries and psychedelic streetscape facades attest that the area's artistic talents are as rich as the soil. Since thousands of university students descended on Nimbin Village (pop. 800) for the 1973 Aquarius Festival, Australia's answer to America's Woodstock, the community has retained an image as Australia's alternative/hippie hub. But alternative does not simply refer to the town's infamous relaxed attitude toward drugs; Nimbin's residents also passionately support an array of other liberal causes, including environmentalism, animal rights, and a return to natural living (these constitute a flourishing and inspiring side of Nimbin, unexplored by the average in-and-out visitor). More than 350 shared communities, some open to the public, are sheltered by the volcanic valley around the town. WWOOF (see **Volunteering**, p. 62) has a strong presence here, with many area farms accepting travelers for farmstays and organic farming opportunities. Residents' lives are closely intertwined with the land and its fruits, most of which are legal.

⊟⊠ TRANSPORTATION & PRACTICAL INFORMATION. The Nimbin **Shuttle Bus** (☎6680 9189) is the only direct public transportation to the village from Byron. It departs M-Sa from Byron Bay at 11:30am, returning at 5:30pm ($25, one-way $14). Runs Sunday Market trips, as well. For visitors who just want a glimpse of the spectacle, Byron-based **Jim's Alternative Tours** stops in town for an hour or two as part of a day-long trip including the area's national parks (☎6685 7720; trips M-F 9:30am-6pm; $30), as does **Grasshoppers Eco-Explorer Tours** (☎0500 881 881; www.rockhoppers.com.au; $30). A new bus service is now offered from Brisbane ($28), Surfers ($20), and Murwillumbah ($10), as well, through **Queensland Scenic Tours** (☎3211 3155). Buses depart Tu, F, and Su. Inquire at Nimbin Connexion about an attached cheap accommodation and transport package.)

Nimbin's commercial district and center is on **Cullen Street,** between the police station and the corner hotel—you can't miss the vivid murals, wild storefront displays, and thin wisps of smoke. **The Nimbin Connexion,** 80 Cullen St., at the north end of town, has info on local activities, national parks, regional WWOOFing opportunities, WWOOF membership, and serves as a booking agency for buses and trains; it also has a gift shop, foreign currency exchange, and the cheapest **Internet** in town for $4.50 per hour. (☎6689 1764. Open daily 10am-5:30pm.) The **police** station is on the south end of Cullen St., as is the **hospital,** 35 Cullen St. (☎6689 1400). The **post office** is at 43 Cullen St. (Open M-F 9am-5pm, Sa 9am-noon.) **Postal Code:** 2480.

▪▪ ACCOMMODATIONS & FOOD. Although many visitors to Nimbin come for just the day, there are a number of accommodation options for those who wish to stay longer. **◪Nimbin Rox YHA ❷,** 74 Thorburn St., is worth the 20min. walk from town for its breathtaking views, landscaped gardens (with tropical fruits), and intimate family guest house feel, not to mention its pool, art workshops, cooking classes ($15), massages ($35), yoga, eco-conscious, partially solar-heated facilities, weekly rainforest and swimming hole trips, and nighttime wildlife walks in their 30 acre backyard. Internet $4.50 an hour, laundry $3. Take a left onto Thorburn from Cullen St., just across a green creek; the hostel is up an unpaved driveway through a horse pasture. (☎6689 0022; www.nimbinroxhostel.com. Dorms $20-22; doubles and twins $48; 2-person cabins $55; 5-person teepee $15-18 per person. YHA.) For the funkier traveler, **◪Rainbow Retreat ❶,** 75 Thorburn St., right across the way from the YHA, has a brightly colored VW ($30), gypsy wagon, mushroom bungalow, and love shack with floor futon (each $40), in addition to more standard accommodations and camping sites. Free linen, kitchen, and also an open-aired cafe and common rooms with large TV and countless musical instruments. (☎6689 1262; Free bus from Byron M, W, and F 2pm. Sites $8 per person; dorms $15; doubles $40. Cash only). **Nimbin Backpackers at Granny's Farm ❶** is a 10min. walk from the center north on Cullen St.; turn left before the bridge. The creekside lodge has two pools, showers, a large kitchen and TV room, BBQs, nightly outdoor fires, free-roaming horses, and platypi wading in the creek. (☎6689 1333. Laundry $4. Sites $10 per person; dorms $20; doubles $28. VIP.) **The Nimbin Hotel ❶,** 53 Cullen St. (☎6689 1246), has recently renovated and redecorated dorm-style accommodations. ($15 if more than one person, $20 for solo traveler; $10 key deposit.) Nimbin eateries, like everything else, are all along Cullen St. The **Rainbow Cafe ❶,** 64A Cullen St., was the first alternative cafe in Nimbin, with sandwiches ($6.50), fresh juices ($4), vegetarian options (of course), and a sunny garden patio out back. (☎6689 1997. Open daily 8am-5pm. Cash only). **Aquarius Cafe ❶,** 45 Cullen St., grills tofu burgers and meat kebabs for around $6 and has homemade cakes for $3.50. (☎6689 1698. Open daily 6am-5pm. Cash only.) A nearby **grocery** store, the Nimbin Emporium, 58 Cullen St., sells health and bulk foods and rents videos. (☎6689 1205. Open M-Sa 8:30am-7:30pm, Su 8:30am-6:30pm.) **Bush Theatre/ Picture Factory ❷,** just outside the village center on Cullen, has put together a $13.50 movie/meal deal with wine. (☎6689 1111. Open Su, Tu-W, F-Sa. Current and art-house movies $7.50. Cash only.)

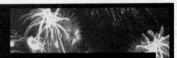

NO WORK, ALL PLAY

MARDI GRASS

Though walking the center of Nimbin any time of the year gives new meaning to the phrase "main drag," reefer-induced revelry reaches its peak the first weekend in May, when Nimbin hosts its annual Mardi Grass Cannabis Law Reform Rally. In 1988, a few public demonstrations and political events centered on the cause of marijuana legalization were staged to coincide with the Aquarius Festival, a celebration of counter-culture on a broader level. The 1993 rally culminated with 1000 dancing, chanting pot smokers brandishing a massive joint with the words "Let It Grow" inscribed in four foot tall letters outside the makeshift Nimbin Hemp Embassy.

The following year, Mardi Grass became an official event and since then, numbers have been growing exponentially. Events include the Hemp Olympics, where contestants battle it out in everything from a bong-throwing competition to a joint-rolling contest. The **Cannabis Cup** lets lucky judges test local growers' products in categories including aroma, size, and effect. Celebration aside, the gathering is a serious protest to rally for cannabis reform. It may seem like a party, but protesters say the real party will begin only once political change is effected. Once this lofty goal is reached, Mardi Grass will become a Hemp Harvest Festival, celebrating newly legal, local produce.

SIGHTS & FESTIVALS. The odd ◪**Nimbin Museum,** 62 Cullen St., across from the HEMP Embassy, redefines creativity and historical interpretation. Its drug-induced strangeness is ingenious and oddly beautiful. The rooms relate the founders' version of regional history through myriad murals, chaotic collages, stimulating quotes, countless thingamabobs and trinkets, with proportionate coverage of all three major historical periods: the first room is about Aborigines, the second about European settlers, and the next five about the hippies. (☎6689 1123. $2 donation. Open 9am-dark.) The **HEMP (Help End Marijuana Prohibition) Party,** which must be one hell of a party, has its base at the **Hemp Embassy,** 51 Cullen St. In the spirit of Aussie big things, come here to at least to gawk at the famously massive joint. (☎6689 1842; www.nimbinaustralia.com/hemp. Open daily 9am-6pm.) The attached **Hemp Bar** offers "refreshments." (☎6689 1842; www.nimbinhempbar.com).

To see a bit beyond Nimbin's drug culture, swing by **Nimbin Artists Gallery,** 49 Cullen St., which displays solely the work of local artists. (☎6689 1444. Open daily 10am-4pm.) A vibrant music scene abounds, as well, in Nimbin's cafes, pubs, parks, and streets. The **Rainbow Power Company,** a 10min. walk from the city center down Cullen St. to Alternative Way, on the right, is a remarkable achievement in solar and wind energy production; they even sell their excess generated power to the electricity grid for general consumption. (☎6689 1430; www.rpc.com.au. Open M-F 9am-5pm, Sa 9am-noon. Group tours by advance arrangement; 1hr., $2 per head or minimum of $33.) For a hands-on look at earth-conscious living, trek to **Djanbung Gardens Permaculture Centre,** 74 Cecil St. Take a left onto Cecil St. at the southern end of Cullen; the Djanbung Gardens are just after Neem Rd. A resource center offers insights and workshops on organic gardening, permaculture design, village and community development, among other similar topics. Ask about accommodations for long-term workshop and class stays. (☎6689 1755; www.earthwise.org.au. Guided tours of the garden Tu and Th 10:30am, $10. In-depth farm tour Sa 11am, other times by appointment, $15. Open Tu-Sa 10am-4pm.) Beyond Djanbung lies Jarlanbah, a 55 acre community which lives by the permaculture (permanent agriculture) code. If you are interested in exploring both Rainbow Power and Djanbung—two places many locals feel represent the true spirit of Nimbin— use the ◪**Nimbin Shuttle** (☎6689 1764) offers its own insightful guided tour. (M-F from 2pm-4pm. $5 or free for those catching the shuttle from Byron.)

NIGHTCAP NATIONAL PARK

An 8000-hectare park with the highest rainfall in the state and containing the southern rim of the 20-million-year-old **Mt. Warning** volcano crater, Nightcap has two main areas: **Mt. Nardi**, 12km out of Nimbin, and the **Terania Creek/Protestors Falls** area (named so for being the site of one of the first successful anti-logging protest), 15km out of **The Channon** (20km from Nimbin). Mt. Nardi, one of the highest peaks, is accessible on sealed roads and has BBQ and picnic facilities. The viewing platform has info on the walk to nearby **Mt. Matheson** (1.5km) and **Pholi's Walk** (2km), with a lookout to the **Tweed Valley.**

Gravel Terania Creek Rd. leads to Protestor's Falls in the Terania Creek basin and to a picnic area with BBQ, toilets, wood, and shelter. **Camping ❶** is limited to one night. The track to Protestor's Falls (1.4km return) passes **Waterfall Creek** on the way. **Tuntable Falls** in the Tuntable Falls commune is a 120m waterfall (from the parking lot, 3-4hr. return). From Nimbin, the turn-off is 6km down Sibley St., then another 6km. The **Nimbin Rocks,** an Aboriginal sacred site, are another way out of town, toward Lismore. **Hanging Rock Falls** is just 25min. from Nimbin near Wadeville. The natural swimming hole, bordered by basalt columns, is perfect for picnics.

WHIAN WHIAN & MULLUMBIMBY ☎02

Surrounded by Nightcap National Park, the **Whian Whian State Forest** (WHY-an WHY-an) is another rainforest and waterfall showcase, easily accessible from Dunoon, Mullumbimby, or some of the small villages around Lismore. One of the best ways to see the park is by following the **Whian Whian Forest Drive** (30km; 2hr.). Traveling roughly east to west, the first highlight along the drive is the view of **Minyon Falls**. A bit farther along, a short detour to the right onto **Peates Mountain Road** leads to **Rummery Park** (200m), a popular picnic and camping spot, and **Peates Mountain Lookout** (3.5km). The lookout is a 5 to 10min. walk from the road. Beyond the junction with Peates Mountain Rd., the Forest Drive continues through logged areas replanted with blackbutt trees, the **Gibbergunyah Roadside Reserve** (a 40m strip of unlogged forest), and the **Big Scrub Flora Reserve.** The drive ends near the **Rocky Creek Dam,** a favorite family picnic stop.

Mullumbimby (MUH-lum-BIM-bee; pop. 2700), the self-proclaimed "Biggest Little Town in Australia," isn't quite big enough to have its own tourist office. It is, however, a convenient stopping place when travelling to **Whian Whian** or the **Border Ranges National Park.** Mullumbimby has a string of motels on Dalley St. The **Mullumbimby Motel ❹**, 121 Dalley St., is popular and nicely landscaped. (☎6684 2387. Singles $50-70; twins and doubles $60-80.) **Brunswick Valley Coaches** (☎6680 1566) runs to Brunswick Heads (15min., 4 per day, $4.80), the transfer point for **Kirkland's** (☎1300 367 077), serving Byron Bay (30min., 4 per day M-F, $9).

MURWILLUMBAH ☎02

Located in a mountain valley (read: former volcanic floor) halfway between Byron Bay (about 1hr. north) and Tweed Heads, Murwillumbah (mur-wuh-LUM-buh) is a small country town bisected by the **Tweed River** (which turns a dark mud-color after it rains). To get to Murwillumbah, turn off the Pacific Highway onto Tweed Valley Way. There are several national parks near Murwillumbah including **Springbrook, Lamington** (both deceptively far, full-day trips from Murwillumbah, due to circuitous roads around the mountain range), **Mebbin, Border Ranges, Nightcap, Mt. Jerusalem, Mooball, Wollumbin**, and **Mt. Warning** (see **Mt. Warning and Border Ranges,** p. 212). Approaching Murwillumbah from the east on the Tweed Valley Way, the ancient volcanic plug that forms Mt. Warning dominates the skyline. Though the majority of town lies west of the Tweed River, you'll find Tweed Valley Way, the tourist office, and the **railway station** on its east bank.

Southbound **buses** stop at the railway station on the Pacific Hwy.; northbound buses stop outside the tourist info center. **McCafferty's/Greyhound** and **Premier** stop on their Sydney/Brisbane route. **Kirkland's** (☎ 1300 367 077) buses run to Brisbane (2¼hr.; 2 per day M-F, 1 per day Sa-Su; $23); Byron Bay (1hr.; 2 per day M-F, 1 per day Sa-Su, $14.20); and Surfers Paradise (1¼ hr.; 2 per day M-F, 1 per day Sa-Su; $16.20). In **Budd Park,** at the corner of Tweed Valley Way and Alma St., is the **Tourist Information Centre,** in the **World Heritage Rainforest Centre,** which has fascinating displays and videos about the area's volcanic past, and other natural and cultural wonders. (☎ 6672 1340 or 1800 674 414; www.tweedcoolangatta.com.au. Open M-Sa 9am-4:30pm, Su 9:30am-4pm.) To reach the town center, cross the Tweed River on the **Alma Street** bridge. Alma St. crosses Commercial Rd. and becomes **Wollumbin Street.** A Coles **supermarket** is in the Sunnyside Shopping Center at the end of the block. Parallel to Wollumbin St. one block north is **Main Street** (also called Murwillumbah St.). An abundance of cafes and eateries line Main St. and spill over onto Commercial Rd. The choice is yours as to type of cuisine, but for split opinions, consider **Riverside Pizza Cafe ❶,** 6 Commercial Rd., ☎ 6672 1935, which has a handful of Thai offerings ($7-11) alongside its Italian origins, including tasty pizzas from $9-17.50. (Open daily 5pm-9:30pm. Cash only.) **Internet** is at **Precise PCs,** 13 Commercial Rd. (☎ 6672 8300. $5 per hr. Open M-F 9am-5pm, Sa 9am-noon.)

The ▨**Mt. Warning/Murwillumbah YHA ❷,** 1 Tumbulgum Rd., is a well-kept, colorfully painted lodge. From the info center, cross the Alma St. bridge, turn right on Commercial Rd., and follow the river about 100m. The lodge, originally a sea captain's house, sits on the riverbank with a fabulous deck directly facing Mt. Warning and offers free use of inner tubes and a canoe for paddling in the river. There's also a small pontoon moored to the riverbank that sports comfy hammocks and serves as a swimming platform. (☎ 6672 3763. Kitchen, laundry ($7-9), separate TV lounge. M, W, F trips to Mt. Warning, ice cream nightly at 9pm. Bike rental $5 per day, $50 deposit. Reception 8-10am and 5-10pm. Dorms $23; twins and doubles, including the "penthouse," $25 per person.) The **Hotel Murwillumbah ❶,** 17 Wharf St., offers cheap pubstays on the newly-renovated, clean, and backpacker-friendly second floor. Meals downstairs are $5. (☎ 6672 1139; www.murwillumbahhotel.com.au. Dorms $15; twins and doubles $50.)

MT. WARNING & BORDER RANGES ☎ 02

From a distance, the stony spire of **Mt. Warning** greatly resembles a gigantic thumb extending towards the heavens. Named by Captain Cook in 1770 in an effort to warn mariners of dangerous offshore reefs and known to the area's Aboriginal people as *Wollumbin* (meaning "cloud catcher"), **Mt. Warning National Park** attracts hikers and geology enthusiasts alike. Formerly a shield volcano at twice the height, most of the ancient lava flows have eroded away, leaving behind an enormous bowl-shaped landform known as a **caldera**—the largest in the Southern Hemisphere. The prominent spire in the middle of the caldera represents the volcano's erosion-resistant central chamber. The summit of Mt. Warning is the first place on the continent to greet the dawn. The climb to the peak offers a fantastic 360° view of the coast and surrounding forest, but in summer the view is sometimes blocked by clouds. The **Summit Track** (8.8km return; 4-5hr.) is moderately strenuous; the last segment is a vertical rock scramble with a necessary chain handrail. Watching the sunrise is spectacular, especially during the Dry (June-Nov.). You'll need a flashlight for the climb—although the abundance of glowbugs is magical, they don't provide an abundance of light. If you'd prefer a daylight hike, make sure to set out early enough, so as not to be stuck on the mountain top once the sun goes down. Bring your own water and keep in mind the only toilets are at the start of the walk. To reach the Summit Track from Murwillumbah, take Kyogle

Rd. 12km west, turn on Mt. Warning Rd., and go about 6km to Breakfast Creek. *Let's Go* does not recommend hitchhiking, but it is a popular way to get from town to the mountain. Camping on Mt. Warning is not allowed. The nearest hostel is the **Murwillumbah YHA** (see **Murwillumbah,** p. 211). The **Mount Warning Caravan Park ❶,** on Mt. Warning Road, 2km from the junction with Kyogle Rd, also makes a great base for exploring the mountain. (☎6679 5120. TV room, pool, BBQ, and a few friendly wallabies. Camp kitchen. Reception 8am-5pm. Sites for 2 $16, powered $19; caravans for 2 $35; budget cabins $46, ensuite $68.)

If you find Mt. Warning too touristed, the gorgeous **Border Ranges National Park** is an ideal getaway ($6 vehicle entry fee). It takes some work to get there, but intrepid travelers will be rewarded with the shade of a lush canopy and a great vantage point for viewing the volcano region. Take the Kyogle Rd. west from Murwillumbah for 44km (5.2km past the turn-off to Nimbin marks the start of the signposted **Tweed Range Scenic Drive** (60km; 4-5hr.); the Barker Vale turn-off leads 15km along gravel road to the park entrance. The drive exits the park at **Wiangaree,** 13km from Kyogle and 66km from Murwillumbah. The first picnic area in the park is **Bar Mountain,** with a lovely beech glade. Less than 1km farther is the even more remarkable **Blackbutts** picnic area, with striking views of Mt. Warning and the basin. If your daytripping stops not for picnics, travel 8km north for a similar view from **Pinnacle Lookout.** To reach the **Forest Tops ❶** camping area, travel 4km past the lookout, turn left at the junction, go another 4km, and turn left again ($3.50 per person). If you turn right instead of left at this last junction, you'll wind up at the **Brindle Creek** picnic area, the departure point for the **Brindle Creek Walk** (10km return; 3-4hr.), a track that winds among rainforests and waterfalls and ends at the **Antarctic Beech** picnic area, home to 2000-year-old trees. For a shorter scenic trip, turn off Kyogle Rd. at Doon Doon Rd., 1km past Uki Village, and head to **Cram's Farm Picnic Area,** a delightful spot on the lake. Travel farther down Doon Doon Rd., turn right at Doon Doon Hall, and follow the road down to its dead end to catch a glimpse of **Doughboy,** a smaller, but nonetheless impressive, volcanic plug.

LISMORE ☎02

Lismore (pop. 43.000) is the largest town in the North Coast area. Wide, tree-lined boulevards, brick sidewalks, and well-preserved buildings give the town the charm of a slower era, while students at nearby Southern Cross University bring a certain youthful vibrance. A legacy of environmental protection stems naturally from Lismore's surroundings: three World Heritage-listed rainforests and the volcanic remains of Mt. Warning National Park. The disproportionately high number of rainbows (due to the position of local valleys) earn the area the nickname "Rainbow Region." Refreshingly normal, Lismore is one of the few places where you can walk through the business district without feeling like a tourist.

 TRANSPORTATION. The **railway station** is on Union St., across the river. **Countrylink** (☎13 22 32) hugs the overnight rails to Sydney (12hr., 1 per day, $98). The new **Transit Centre** (☎6621 8620) is on the corner of Molesworth and Magellan St. **Kirkland's** (☎1300 367 077) runs **buses** to: Brisbane (4½hr., 4 per day M-F, 2 per day Sa-Su, $33) via Byron Bay (1hr., $13.20) and Surfers Paradise (3hr., $31), and other smaller regional centers. Local operator **Marsh's** (☎6689 1220) services Nimbin (45min., M-F 3 per day, $7.50). **McCafferty's/Greyhound** (☎13 20 30) run once per day to Brisbane (5½hr., $39) and Sydney (11½hr., overnight, $92) and **Premier** (☎13 34 10) does the same route slightly cheaper (Brisbane $34; Sydney $81). The best way to get around is to rent a car. Options include **Hertz,** 49 Dawson St. (☎13 30 39), and **Thrifty,** 147 Woodlark St. (☎1300 367 227). For a **taxi,** call ☎13 10 08.

NEW SOUTH WALES

▦ ⁊ ORIENTATION & PRACTICAL INFORMATION. In the hinterlands west of Ballina, Lismore lies off the Bruxner Hwy. (called **Ballina Street** in town) just east of the **Wilson** (or **Richmond**) **River.** Approaching the river from the east, Ballina St. crosses Dawson, Keen, and Molesworth St., the busiest part of town. Perpendicular to these streets in the town center are small Conway and Magellan St. and the main thoroughfare **Woodlark Street,** accessible from the Dawson St. roundabout and leading across the river to Bridge St. and Nimbin. At the corner of Molesworth and Ballina St., the **Lismore Visitor Information Centre** has a small indoor tropical rainforest and social history exhibit. (☎ 6622 0122; www.liscity.nsw.gov.au. Exhibit $1. Open M-F 9:30am-4pm, Sa-Su 10am-3pm.) Other services include: **ATMs** everywhere; **police** (☎ 6623 1599) on Molesworth St.; **Internet** at the Visitors Centre ($1.50 per 10min, $3 per 30min, $5 per hr) and at **Lismore Internet Services,** 172 Molesworth St. (☎ 6622 7766; open M-F 9am-5pm; $5.50 per hr.; **Lismore Base Hospital,** 60 Uralba St (☎ 6621 8000); **post office** on Conway St. (☎ 6622 1855. Open M-F 8:30am-5pm.) **Postal Code:** 2480.

⊓⊏ ACCOMMODATIONS & FOOD. Currendina Lodge/Lismore Backpackers ❷, 14 Ewing St., has neat rooms, TV lounge, kitchen, a shaded porch, and off-street parking. From the info center, go left on Ballina St., cross Keen St., and turn left on Dawson St. Ewing is the 2nd right off Dawson. (☎ 6621 6118; currendi@nor.com.au. Laundry $3. Reception 8am-10pm. Dorms $22, weekly $110; singles $30/$125; doubles $45/$165. No credit cards.) **Lismore City Motor Inn ❹,** 129 Magellan St., on the corner of Dawson St., features comfy ensuite motel-style rooms with TV, fridge, and A/C. (☎ 6621 4455. Pool and laundry $4. Reception 7:30am-9pm. Singles $55-72; twins $68-78 and doubles $65-75; extra person $10.) The **Lismore Palms Caravan Park ❶** is at 42 Brunswick St. and offers basic rooms with kitchen and laundry access.

The demand by uni students for cheap vegetarian eats has resulted in some terrifically funky eateries. The cheapest **supermarket** in town is Woolworths on Keen St., with a back entrance on Carrington St. (Open M-Sa 7am-10pm, Su 9am-6pm.) Many pubs offer cheap lunch and dinner meals. No cows are served at vegan **▨20,000 Cows ❷,** 58 Bridge St., which serves up fresh pasta, Indian, and Middle Eastern food (mains $6.50-19) to patrons reclining on comfy sofas. (☎ 6622 2517. Open W-Su from 6pm. Cash only.) **Dr. Juice Bar ❶,** 142 Keen St., is another popular vegetarian/vegan student haunt. The doctor prescribes marvelous fresh smoothies, veggie burgers, and wildly popular tofu cheesecake, all for less than $7. (☎ 6622 4440. Open M-F 8:30am-4pm. Cash only.) The indoor deck, outdoor patio, and beautiful stained glass make **Caddies Coffee ❷,** 20 Carrington St., a sure shot, with gourmet sandwiches, pasta, and focaccia from $2.75. (☎ 6621 7709. Open M-F 7:30am-6pm, Sa 8am-1:30pm.)

◉ SIGHTS. For a breath of fresh air, there are many parks nearby. **Rotary Park,** at Uralba St., in the center of town, is a hoop pine and giant fig rainforest restoration project with an easy boardwalk through its six hectares. Visit the **Nimbin Candle Factory,** in the Bush Theatre Building (☎ 6689 1010), to watch the local artists craft colorful handmade candles. The fabulous **Richmond River Historical Society,** 165 Molesworth St., in the Municipal Building houses a natural-history room with preserved baby crocs and mummified tropical birds as well as a hallway displaying Aboriginal boomerangs. (☎ 6621 9993. Open M-Th 10am-4pm. $2.) The **Boatharbour Nature Reserve,** 6km northeast of Lismore on Bangalow Rd., sports 17 hectares of rainforest trees, the remnants of the "Big Scrub Forest," and a large bat colony. The original 75,000 hectares of lowland forest throughout northern New South Wales have been almost completely deforested. **Tucki Tucki Nature Reserve,** which doubles as a koala sanctuary, is 15min. from Lismore on Wyrallah Rd. For a guaranteed glimpse of the snuggly fur-balls, visit the **Koala Care and Research Centre** (☎6622 1233) on Rifle Range Rd. (next to Southern Cross University) for their Saturday morning tours (9:30am). For those seeking additional Lismorian koala spotting territory, inquire at the Visitors Centre. Lismore's water supply comes from the **Rocky Creek Dam** (30min. from Lismore, between Nightcap NP and Whian Whian), home to a waterfront boardwalk along a platypus lagoon.

NEW ENGLAND

The **New England Highway** is a north-south route that takes you the 566km between Brisbane and Newcastle through different terrain than the coastal drive. At its northern reach, beyond Tenterfield, the road begins the climb over the Dividing Range into Tamworth, Armidale and New England proper. From there, the highway diverges with two national park-laden tourist routes: the north-coast bound **Waterfall Way,** and later, the south-bound **Oxley Highway,** which ventures coastward from Bendemeer to meet Port Macquarie at the coast. Both Waterfall Way and the Oxley comprise a stretch of raw and remote national parks that are nothing short of spectacular and both well worth re-routing an itinerary. The New England Hwy., meanwhile, continues through Scone's horse stud farms and Muswellbrook's coal mines, past Singleton's army base, then traverses the Hunter Valley, cruising slightly west of Maitland, before turning east to its coastal conclusion.

TENTERFIELD & NEARBY PARKS   ☎02

It was in Tenterfield in 1889 that Sir Henry Parkes cried out, "One People. One Destiny," in a now-famous speech that foresaw Australia's federation. Although it clings to its history with preserved buildings and the Sir Henry Parkes Festival—a celebration of nationhood and community achievements—travelers today know Tenterfield as a base for exploring nearby national parks.

Tenterfield is 150km from Lismore, 370km from Brisbane, and 95km from Glen Innes. As the northernmost town on the highway, Tenterfield is known as the Gateway to New England. Its **Visitors Centre**, on the corner of Rouse and Miles St. (☎6736 1082; www.tenterfield.com), follows suit, with info available on all New England destinations. (Open M-F 9am-5pm, Sa-Su 9am-4pm.) The Tenterfield incarnation (and origin) of the New England Hwy. is **Rouse Street,** and is lined with shops, restaurants, pubs, ATMs, a **post office** (postal code: 2372), and a large grouping of motels to the south. The **police station** (☎6736 1144) is on Molesworth St. **McCafferty's/Greyhound** (☎13 20 30) stops in Tenterfield once a day in both directions on its Melbourne to Brisbane route, and runs to Sydney once daily ($74). **Kirkland's** (☎1300 367 077) runs from Ballina to Lismore ($11.10), then connects on to Tenterfield ($26.80). **Crisp's Coaches** (☎07 4661 8333) runs to and from Brisbane daily ($40). Buses stop at various points on Rouse St.; call for specific details.

For cheap accommodation, the **Tenterfield Lodge Caravan Park ❸**, 2 Manners St., (☎6736 1477), houses a hostel with a friendly host who goes out of her way to help travelers find farmstays. Call in advance for free pick-up from the bus station. (Sites for 2: unpowered $15.50, powered $17; caravans $24 for one person, $28 for 2 people; cabins $35/$38, extra person $4; ensuite cabins $45/$50, extra person $4. Backpacker accommodations $21, twin/double $44, family $60. VIP.)

For car-driving travelers, 3 unsealed kilometers north of Bald Rock National Park on Mt. Lindesay Rd., is a 650 acre gem: the ⬛**Bald Rock Bush Retreat ❷,** which includes a backpacker guest house (☎4686 1227. $22; up to 8 people; min. 4 people or $88 per night; BYO sleeping bags), luxurious ensuite waterfront cabin ($137.50; min. 2 nights), and guestrooms ($82.50; 2 people—cash only). The retreat is recently responsible for the **Exodus Festival,** a week long summer trance party and music extravaganza which pulls in international DJs and combines Aboriginal stylings with typical rave fare. Regrettably, the festival is only pseudo-annual and will not be held in 2004, but in its stead, four pumping weekend parties will be thrown during the summer months. The bizarre juxtaposition of trance in the bush is guaranteed to be worth the trip. (www.happypeopleproductions.com.) From brekkie to burgers, **Cafe New England ❶**, 164 Rouse St., offers the ultimate in cheap and hearty food. Everything on the menu is priced between $5-10. (☎6736 1114. Open M-Tu and Th 7:30am-7:30pm, W 9am-3pm, F-Sa 7:30am-8pm, Su 8am-7pm.)

To explore the town's history on foot, pick up a **heritage walk** brochure from the Visitors Centre. Tenterfield lies near three national parks ($6 NPWS entry fee applies); a great map ($8) is available at the Visitors Centre or the **NPWS**, 68 Church St., in Glen Innes. (☎6732 5133. Open M-F 8:30am-4:30pm.) **Boonoo Boonoo National Park** (BUN-ner BER-noo) is 27km north; take Rouse St. north, turn right on Naas St., then quickly bear left on Mt. Lindesay Rd. The next 27km to the park entrance is sealed. On the way to Boonoo Boonoo, history buffs might want to take a look at the remains of Tenterfield's **WWII tank traps,** off Mt. Lindesay Rd. These traps constituted part of the Brisbane Line, Australia's second line of defense in case the northern part of the country fell into enemy hands. Tenterfield was a major strategic center; during the war, up to 10,000 troops were camped in the area. From the entrance of Boonoo Boonoo, 14km of gravel leads to the stunning, carved-granite **Boonoo Boonoo Gorge and Falls,** the park hub and overnight **camping ❶** area (no water; $5). There is a swimming hole surrounded by wildflowers and grasses upstream from the falls. For a less touristy look at a giant rock monolith, skip Ayers Rock and head to **Bald Rock National Park,** which showcases the largest exposed granite rock in Australia. To reach it, head down Mt. Lindesay Rd. for 29km to a road that runs 5km to the park's camping and picnic areas (sealed all the way). The **Burgoona Walk** (5km return) is the less steep and the more scenic (showing off large rock formations along the way) of two hiking routes to the 1277m summit that provides amazing views of the McPherson Ranges. Another route heads straight up the face of the rock (just follow the white dotted trail; about a 1hr. return). **Girraween National Park** (see p. 324) is just west of Bald Rock but is located in Queensland, 9km down a paved road 11km north of Wallangara on the New England Hwy. **Tenterfield Tours** (☎6736 1864) runs tours of the area's wineries, heritage, Aboriginal culture, and national parks. Tours depart daily at 10:15am. Call for details and bookings.

GLEN INNES ☎02

Glen Innes (pop. 10,000), 7hr. from Sydney, 4½hr. from Brisbane, and 1hr. from both Armidale and Tenterfield on the New England Hwy., has a Celtic heritage and constantly finds cause to celebrate it. A full slate of annual festivals complements the changing seasons. Glen Innes's most striking monument is a collection of vertical megalithic **Standing Stones** overlooking the town and valley, an homage to an ancient Celtic form of timekeeping which rest on **Martins Lookout**, 1km east of the Visitors Centre on Meade St. (Gwydir Hwy.).

The main commercial street in town is **Grey Street,** parallel to and one block west of the **New England Highway** (called **Church Street** as it runs through town). The **Gwydir Highway,** known in town as **Meade Street** and **Ferguson Street,** runs west 65km to Inverell and east 160km to Grafton and the Pacific Hwy. **Countrylink** (☎13 22 32) has **bus** service to Sydney (9¾hr., 1 per day, $87) and also has direct services to nearby towns. **McCafferty's/Greyhound** (☎13 14 99 or 13 20 30) send buses to: Brisbane (5hr., 2 per day, $65), and Sydney (9hr., 1 per day, $74), and other smaller regional centers. Buses stop at various local service stations; contact individual companies for details. Call **taxis** at ☎6732 1300.

The **Visitors Centre,** 152 Church St., is near the intersection of the New England and Gwydir Hwys. (☎6732 2397; www.gleninnestourism.com.au. Open M-F 9am-5pm, Sa-Su and public holidays 9am-3pm.) Grey St. is home to several **banks** with **ATMs, supermarkets,** pubstays, basic eateries, and a **library** with free **Internet.** (☎6732 2302. Open M-F 10am-5pm.) An impressive array of 160 years of local history awaits at the **"Land of the Beardies" History House Museum** (☎6732 1035), located in the historic hospital building on the corner of West Ave. and Ferguson St. ("Beardies" refers to the two facial-haired former convicts who originally settled the area). Of particular note is a rare Japanese map of Australia in a WWII-themed room. (Open M-F 9am-5pm, Sa-Su 2pm-5pm. $4, children $1.) **Fossicking** (for gems, that is) and **fishing** are both extraordinarily popular, with prolific opportunities both in and around Glen Innes. Inquire at the Visitors Centre for details.

Cheap rooms are available at the **pubs ❷** on Grey St. (singles $20-25; twins and doubles $35-40), and motels line the New England Hwy. More charming stays, however, are found a bit west of town. **Bullock Mountain Homestead ❸,** on Bullock Mountain Rd., is a horse homestead with bunkstyle accommodations. A three day package includes accommodation, meals, and one hour horseback riding a day—basic riding instruction and horsemanship provided ($210). Guests come for horseriding, bushwalking, fossicking, and plain old vegging out. Arrange for free pick-up from bus stop in town or call for directions. Free laundry facilities. (☎6732 1599. $20, double $40. VIP.) Bullock Mountain Homestead also runs a variety of splurge-worthy **horseback riding,** including the ever popular **pub crawl on horseback** (from $295 for one weekend to a $1285 5-day trip; meals and accommodation included.) For a different sort of experience, head to **Three Waters Au Naturel Rural Naturist Retreat ❶,** (15km northwest of Glen Innes, also on Bullock Mountain) to unwind and undress on 420 hectares of secluded country, with permanent flowing water on three sides. $8 per day unpowered campsites line the river, and access to homestead showers, toilets, laundry, and gas BBQ is available. Free accommodation and meals for backpackers willing to do a bit of work around the property. Au Naturel offers the same activities as Bullock Mountain Homestead (fossicking $6, horseback riding $25 per hour, and free bushwalking), just with your clothes off. (☎6732 4863; www.gleninnes.com/3waters. No credit cards.)

ARMIDALE
☎02

The town of **Armidale** (pop. 22,5000) has two claims to fame: it has four distinct seasons and it is the highest city in Australia (elevation 980m). The **University of New England** is the oldest regional university in Australia, and its nearby campus, brings energy and business to a healthy number of pubs. The town is also conveniently positioned at the start of Waterfall Way (see p. 218), making it a great base from which to explore the varied and magnificent countryside.

Armidale's main drag is **Beardy Street.** The **Visitors Centre,** 82 Marsh St., is attached to the bus terminal. (☎6772 4655 or 1800 627 736; armvisit@bigpond.net.au. Open M-F 9am-5pm, Sa 9am-4pm, Su 10am-4pm.) **McCafferty's/Greyhound** (☎13 14 99 or 13 20 30) runs to Sydney (10hr., 1 per day, $74) and Brisbane (7hr., 1 per day, $68). **Countrylink** (☎13 22 32) provides limited train service south to Sydney (8hr., daily 9am, $79.20).

One block south on Marsh St. (from the Visitors Centre) marks the start of the **Beardy Street Mall,** Armidale's outdoor cluster of shops and cafes. **New England Travel Centre,** 188 Beardy Mall, is helpful for booking trips, buses, and trains in the area. (☎6772 1722; www.newengland.tvl.com.au. Open M-F 9am-5pm, Sa 9am-noon.) For a **taxi,** call ☎13 10 08 or 6766 1111. The Armidale **NPWS office** (☎6776 0000), at 85-87 Faulkner St., has info on area parks. (Open M-F 8:30am-4:30pm.) The cheapest and fastest (broadband) **Internet** access in town is at **Armidale Com-**

(Continued on next page)

puters, 100 Jessie St. (☎6771 2712. Open M-F 9am-5pm, Sa 9am-12:30pm. $4.40 per hr.) A Coles **supermarket** is on the corner of Marsh St. and Beardy St., across from the Visitors Centre. **ATMs** are available on Beardy St., between Marsh and Dangar St., the **police station** (☎6771 0699) is on the corner of Moore and Faulkner St.; the **post office** is on the corner of Beardy and Faulkner St. **Postal Code:** 2350.

The **Pembroke Caravan Park ❶,** 39 Waterfall Way (also known as Grafton Rd. and Barney St. in town), is 2km east of town and has an adjoining **YHA hostel ❷** with a huge recreation room and TV lounge area. Tennis courts and a solar heated pool are also on the premises. (☎6772 6470 or 1800 355 578; www.pembroke.com.au. Free linen. Kitchen attached to dorms. Laundry. Reception 7:30am-6pm. Sites $15; dorms $24, YHA $20; cabins $50-78.) **Tattersall's Hotel ❸,** 174 Beardy St. Mall, is a central pubstay with small, quiet rooms. (☎6772 2247. Breakfast included. Singles $28; doubles $44; extra person $11.) A large number of motels abound as well.

Rumours on the Mall ❶ (☎6772 3084) serves up tasty and thrifty breakfast and lunches ($5-11.50. Open M-F 8am-5pm, and Sa-Su 8am-2pm. Cash only). A slightly more expensive option is to be found at **Newie's ❷,** on the corner of Beardy and Dangar St. Gourmet mains run from $13.50-24.50 and include adventurous options like kangaroo and crocodile fillet grills. Lighter and less exotic lunch fare $6.50-16. (☎6772 7622. Open daily for lunch noon-2pm and dinner 6pm-9pm.)

To sample the uni-infused pub scene, particularly buzzing on Th-Sa nights, stop by Newie's later in the evening, or head to **The Wiklow** (☎6772 2421; on the corner of Marsh and Djmaresque St.) or **The Club Hotel** (☎6772 3833; further up on Marsh St. before the McDonald's). Most feature live bands or DJs.

The Tourist Centre provides a free two-hour **heritage tour** of Armidale daily; call to book. Following Marsh St. south and uphill to the corner of Kentucky St. leads to the much-praised ◪**New England Regional Art Museum,** which features the works of classic Aussie painters as well as traveling exhibits. (☎6772 5255. Open Tu-Su 10:30am-5pm. Free.) To the left of the museum is the **Aboriginal Cultural Centre & Keeping Place.** (☎6771 1249. Open M-F 9:30am-4pm. Free.)

NATIONAL PARKS EAST OF ARMIDALE

WATERFALL WAY

Waterfall Way (Rte. 78) runs east-west between Armidale and the north coast of New South Wales. Along the way, the aptly-named tourist route passes four excellent national parks with accessible campgrounds, several tiny hamlets, and the charming town of Bellingen (see p. 191). The 169km route is worth the trip, but be cautious on the often steep highway. In addition to the parks below, the **Ebor Falls**, approximately 4km east of Cathedral Rock, 42km west of Dorrigo, and 600m off the highway, are an excellent photo-op. A 600m walk from the carpark leads to a scintillating lookout. **Waterfall Way Tours** (☎6772 2018) runs to the national parks (see Armidale, p. 217). **Gumnuts Wilderness Adventures** (☎6775 3990) also offers a variety of tour packages.

OXLEY WILD RIVERS NATIONAL PARK. World Heritage-listed Oxley is an extensive park of rough, rocky terrain with a network of gorges, campsites, bushwalks, and appropriately wild rivers. Useful pamphlets with photos and maps can help you choose a site to camp or picnic; contact the Armidale **NPWS** (☎6776 0000; armidale@npws.nsw.gov) or **Armidale Visitors Centre** (☎1800 627 736; armvisit@big-pond.net.au). **Point Macquarie** (☎6586 8300), **Dorrigo** (☎6657 2309), and **Walcha** (☎6777 1400) **NPWS offices** all have info, as well, depending on the direction from which you are approaching. For info on **Apsley** and **Tia Gorges** at the more remote western end of the park, see p. 220. $6 NPWS visitor fee applies.

Dangars Gorge with the 120m Dangars Falls as the centerpiece, is an easy 22km trip from Armidale. Take Dangarsleigh Rd. (Kentucky St.) from Armidale for about 11km, then go left at the Perrott's War Memorial; 10km of gravel leads to the gorge. The rest area there is equipped with BBQ, firewood, and pit toilets and is the trailhead for a series of walks ranging from the Gorge Lookout path (100m) to 10-14km half-day treks. Make your first left after passing the grid into the park for **campgrounds ❶** ($3). **Gara Gorge**, also a popular daytrip from Armidale, is the site of Australia's first public hydro-electric scheme, built in 1894. Follow Castledoyle Rd., which leaves Waterfall Way just east of Armidale; it's only an 18km trip (about 5km of gravel as you approach the gorge). The **Threlfall Walk** (an easy 5km) circles around the edge of the gorge, surveying the leftover sites from the historic engineering scheme. **Long Point** is a secluded wilderness area in an open eucalypt forest adjacent to a rare dry rainforest—a natural wonder bestowed with World Heritage status. The turn-off for Long Point appears 40km east of Armidale along Waterfall Way. A 7km stretch of sealed track passes through Hillgrove, where a left turn skips onto a dirt track that reaches the park 20km below. The attached **campsite ❶** has pit toilets, picnic tables, and fresh water. It is also the trailhead for the excellent **Chandler Walk** (5km; 2-2½hr.), which leads through a grove

(Continued from previous page)

In the Australian spirit of affectionately teasing Americans, let's deconstruct the word *seppo*, an Australian jibe for "American." *Seppo* is an abbreviation of *septic*, originally part of the full phrase *septic tank*, *tank* rhyming, of course, with *Yank*, or American. Easy enough? To discern rhyming slang, simply try to use your *loaf* (of bread)—that is, your head. Chances are you won't hear rhyming slang around *steak and kidney* (Sydney), but if you do encounter it in smaller towns, what follows is a pre-emptive practice run, infused with plenty of authentic Aussie blokiness:

When in a small town *rubbity-dub* (pub), if the *pig's ear* (beer) makes you crave some grub, you might want to order a *dog's eye* (meat pie) with a splash of *dead horse* (tomato sauce). Just don't forget to pay your *jack and jill* (restaurant bill) or rather your *goose's neck* (check, alternatively *Gregory Peck*). After having a *captain* (a *captain cook*, or look) around the place in efforts to *optic nerve* (perve, the 'Strine equivalent for ogling) a *charlie* (a *Charlie Wheeler*, pronounced Wheela, rhyming with *sheila*, which is 'Strine for girl), you'll end up feeling you've had a little too much *pot of good cheer* (an alternative rhyme for beer); in fact, about a *country cousin* (dozen) of schooners, to be precise. Get it? Got it? Good.

of mosses, vines, and yellow-spotted Hillgrove Gums, found only in this area. A tremendous lookout along the walk surveys the valley and Chandler River.

The **Wollomombi Falls** gorge is severely sublime and the surrounding forest rugged and dry. Turn-off 40km east of Armidale onto a 2km bitumen road leading to the Falls. The strenuous **Chandler River Track** (5.6km; 4hr.), which drops 800m, starts here (the same 800m must be traversed upwards on the return trip). Alternatively, the moderately strenuous **Wollomombi Walk** (2km return) takes you around the rim of the gorge, giving access to a series of lookouts. Want to catch a glimpse without a workout? One 700m path and another 200m path will take you from the carpark to respective lookouts. There is a free **bushcamping** site near the entrance to the gorge area with a gas BBQ.

NEW ENGLAND NATIONAL PARK. New England National Park, also World Heritage-listed (for its range of cool temperate to warm subtropical rainforest), offers some fabulous bushwalking trails. Its densely vegetated basalt cliffs were formed 18 million years ago by the Ebor volcano. The park gets chilly in summer and downright cold in winter. Near the entrance, 85km from Armidale and 75km from Dorrigo, is the **Thungutti Campground ❶** ($5). Nearby begin the Wright's **Lookout Walk** (2½hr.) and **Cascades Walk** (3½hr.). Most people skip these outskirts to head for the **Point Lookout Picnic Area,** the park's hub, with toilets, fire pits, and ample parking. Point Lookout Rd. heads up to the area; about 11km is gravel and 2.5km of it is sealed. Point Lookout marks the start of nine walks ranging from 5min. to 3½hr., all of which can be linked for nearly a full day of walking. **The Point Lookout,** a vertical escarpment rising 1564m from sea level, surveys dense forest often shrouded in mist. **Eagles Nest Track** (2hr.) passes straight down and along the steep cliffside. It takes ingenuity to negotiate the rocky areas through moss-covered beeches, snow gum woodland, and water sprays that turn to icicles in winter. The difficult **Lyrebird Walk** links with the Eagles Nest Track and can be made a 2km (1hr.) route or a 7km (3½hr.) circuit. The NPWS also rents three cabins within the park; **The Residence ❺** ($60-70; sleeps 10) and **The Chalet ❹** ($50-60) are both fully self contained (all you need to bring are blankets, pillows, and linens); **Tom's Cabin ❸** ($35-40), on the other hand, is a basic unadorned, electricity-less camper's cabin. Minimum stay is 2 nights, maximum is 7 nights. Contact the Dorrigo **NPWS** office for bookings, which can be made up to six months in advance (☎ 6657 2309).

CATHEDRAL NATIONAL PARK. About 3km past the New England NP turn-off is the entrance for **Cathedral National Park,** where 8km of gravel will lead you to the Barokee Rest Area. While its waterfall-less nature belies its spot on Waterfall Way, the park's granite boulders and eucaluypt forests are impressive nonetheless. The **Warrigal Track** (1km; 30min. return) is an easy stroll showcasing some of the boulders. The **Cathedral Rock Track** (5.8km; 2½hr. return) runs into a short walking route (400m) to the top of Cathedral Rock, which has deep crevices and can be slippery. Your agility is rewarded, however, with expansive views of the park. **Camping ❶** is available at the Barokee Rest Area ($3 adult, $2 children).

OXLEY HIGHWAY NATIONAL PARKS

APSLEY & TIA GORGES. The highlights of the southwestern end of **Oxley Wild Rivers National Park** (see p. 220) are the must-see waterfalls of the Apsley and Tia Gorges, which are most easily accessed from the Oxley Hwy. The larger part of the park is usually accessed from Waterfall Way, closer to Armidale (see p. 217). About 83km south from Armidale and 20km east of Walcha is the turn-off for the **Apsley Gorge,** 1km off the highway. This mighty gorge will take your breath away, even when the Dry season reduces the falls to a trickle. At the far end of the car-park is a stairway leading partway into the gorge with a good view of the falls. Swimming in the pool above the falls is permitted at your own risk. Beware of swift currents and sometimes-submerged boulders. The **Oxley Walk** (2km; 45min.) takes you around the rim of the gorge and across a bridge over the Apsley River. Camping and fresh water are available at what is one of the areas most scenic camping spots. Nineteen kilometers south of the Apsley Falls entrance is a 5km unsealed turn-off which takes you to the small picnic and camping area of **Tia Falls.** A nearby walk shows off the **Tia Gorge.** (Both camping sites are $3 per person, per night. The $6 national park entrance fee also applies for both spots.)

Small and rather unexciting, **Walcha** is still a useful jumping-off point for Apsley and Tia Gorges and the rest of Oxley Wild Rivers National Park. You'll find the **Tourist Information Centre** in the Fenwicke House Bed and Breakfast on the Oxley Hwy. (☎6777 2713; open daily 8am-5pm), and the **NPWS outpost** at 188 W. North St. (from the only roundabout in Walcha, turn north onto Darby St., then left (at the showground) onto North St. (☎6777 1400; open M-F 8:30am-4:30pm). The **Commercial Hotel ❸**, on Meridian St. off the highway, has food and rooms. (☎6777 2551. Singles $40, doubles $60, twins $70.)

WERRIKIMBE NATIONAL PARK. Remoteness has preserved the rugged wilderness of Werrikimbe National Park, though it is accessible by 2WD. This is a camper's paradise (and as luck would have it, camping is free here), gleefully veering from the paths into the depths of temperate and subtropical rainforest, eucalypt forest, and snow gum woodlands. District managers in Walcha (☎6777 1400) or Port Macquarie (☎6586 8300) have extensive information on expeditions beyond the western section of the park. Look closely for the sign for Werrikimbe National Park and Mooraback Rd., which appears 55km east of Walcha along the Oxley Hwy. The first 15km of this track isn't too bad, but the twisting, climbing, and loose gravel may wear on conventional vehicles. Inside the park, the tracks to the campground and visitor facilities are maintained to a 2WD standard (any further travel into the park will require a 4WD). You can go either left a few kilometers to Mooraback Rest Area or right to Cobcroft's Rest Area, both trail-head facilities with carpark, picnic tables, and toilets (Mooraback also has campsites). **Mooraback** is set amid snow gum woodlands and by the Mooraback Creek. Walks meander along the creek and deeper into the forest. The rest area at **Cobcroft** is set in open eucalypt forest with a few tree ferns for seasoning. The **Carrabeen Walk** (1hr. return) passes through an adjacent warm temperate rainforest. Longer walks into the Werrikimbe Wilderness Area are possible, but you should consult the NPWS office first.

Three spots are accessible from the Oxley Hwy. on the eastern side of the park, along Forbes River Road or Hastings Forest Way (note that these are more conveniently reached from Pt. Macquarie): **Grass Tree Rest Area, Brushy Mountain Camping Area,** and **Plateau Beech Camping Area**. All three are trailheads for walks of varying lengths. Of particular note, the vivid passage from Plateau Beech Camping Area crosses through gullies of Antarctic beeches with gnarled, web-like bases that take on outstanding shapes, before heading on to King Fern Falls and Filmy Ferns Cascades (about 1½hr. return). The eastern and western sides of the park are linked within by the 4WD-only **Racecourse Trail.**

Fifteen kilometers further down the Oxley Hwy. from Werrikimbe (and 65km east of Walcha), is the gleefully named **Cottan-bimbang National Park.** The park's main feature is the **Myrtle Scrub Scenic Drive,** a looping 15km 2WD dry weather track which stops off at a picnic ground on Cells River, adjacent to a magnificent timber bridge (with massive logs up to 4ft. in diameter).

TAMWORTH
☎ 02

Tamworth (pop. 38,000) annually hosts the **Country Music Festival,** which brings famous crooners and hordes of people to town (Jan. 16-26, 2004; www.country.com.au). The country spirit is otherwise maintained by gallon-hatted city slickers and tie-in tourist attractions such as a giant golden guitar and a concrete slab with handprints of country artists.

TRANSPORTATION. The **train station,** at the corner of Brisbane and Marius St., has a Travel Centre that books trains. (☎6766 2357. Open M-F 8:30am-5:30pm, Sa 8:30am-noon.) **Countrylink** (☎13 22 32) runs express trains to Sydney (6hr., 1 per day, $71.50). All buses run from the **coach terminal** in the Visitors Centre. **McCafferty's/Greyhound** (☎13 14 99 or 13 20 30) travels to: Brisbane (10hr.; daily 10:05pm, also Tu, Th, Sa-Su 6:50am; $68); Coonabarabran (2hr.; Su-M, W, F 8:50pm; $71); and Sydney (8hr., daily 5am, $66). **Kean's Travel Express** (☎6543 1322) goes to Port Macquarie (8hr.; M, W, F; $71); and Scone (2½hr.; Tu and Th, $19). **Budget** (☎13 27 27), **Avis** (☎6760 7404), and **Thrifty** (☎6765 3699), have locations in town. Ring **Tamworth Radio Cabs** for a taxi (☎13 10 08 or 6766 1111).

PRACTICAL INFORMATION. Tamworth is 412km north of Sydney on the New England Hwy. (which, coming from Armidale, enters the town from the east and departs south) and is a convenient rest stop on a journey to Brisbane (578km). The town center lies along **Brisbane Street,** which crosses the Peel River, becoming **Bridge Street** in West Tamworth. The **Visitors Centre** is at the corner of Peel and Murray St. (☎6755 4300; www.tamworth.nsw.gov.au. Open daily 9am-5pm.) Banks and **ATMs** are all along Peel St. **Police** (☎6768 2999) are located at 40 Fitzroy St, and the **post office** (☎ 6755 5988) is at 406 Peel St., on the corner of Fitzroy St. **Postal Code:** 2340. The **library,** 203 Marius St., has free **Internet.** (☎6755 4460. Open M-Th 10am-7pm, F 10am-6pm, Sa 9am-2pm. Advisable to book ahead.)

ACCOMMODATIONS & FOOD. Most rooms for January's Country Music Festival are booked up to a year in advance; throughout the rest of the year, beds are plentiful. **Tamworth Hotel ❸,** 147 Marius St., also opposite the train station, is the most upscale pubstay. The downstairs **restaurant ❶** has breakfast deals from $6-9. (☎6766 2923. Singles $35.) **Paradise Caravan Park ❶,** next to the Visitors Centre along the creek on Peel St., has grills and a playground. (☎/fax 6766 3120. Linen $5 per single, $7 per double; laundry $4.40. Key deposit $5. Reception 7am-7pm. Sites for two $14, powered $19; budget cabins for two $44; cabins with A/C, kitchen, and TV $55. Off-season 7th night free.)

Each end of Peel St. is marked by locally beloved cafes. The **Inland Cafe ❷,** 407 Peel St., serves up gourmet mains like grilled tiger prawns and goat cheese ($15). (☎6761 2882. Open M-W and F-Sa 7am-6pm, Th 7am-11pm, and Su 8am-4pm.) The **Old Vic Cafe ❷,** 261 Peel St., frequented by a relaxed local clientele, fixes up gourmet mains in the same vein (average $14), as well as Turkish bread sandwiches ($9-10), freshly squeezed juices ($4) and its own homemade sauces and vinaigrettes. (☎6766 3435. Open M-F 8am-5pm, Sa 8am-4pm, Su 9am-noon. BYO.) **Deepka ❷,** 23 Brisbane St., cooks up classic Indian dishes ($12-17.50), including a fiery beef vindaloo. (☎6766 1771. Open for dinner daily 5:30pm-late, M-F for lunch noon-2pm.) Coles **supermarket** is at 436-444 Peel St. in the K-Mart shopping plaza. (Open M-Sa 6am-midnight, and Su 8am-8pm.)

SIGHTS & ACTIVITIES. You don't have to be a country music fan to enjoy Tamworth—you just need a high tolerance for kitsch. The turn-off for **The Golden Guitar Complex,** south of town on the New England Hwy., is marked by, predictably enough, a gaudy 12m golden guitar. A realistic "Gallery of Stars" **wax museum**

dresses 22 replicas in the donated clothes of the stars themselves, including Slim Dusty. In an odd juxtaposition, a gem and mineral display shares the complex. (☎6765 2688; www.big.goldenguitar.com.au. Open daily 9am-5pm. $8, children $4, families $18.) The popular **Hands of Fame Cornerstone** is on New England Hwy. (Brisbane St.) at Kable Ave. This cement memorial holds the imprints of country music celebrities. Also check out **Joe Macguires' Noses of Fame,** 148 Peel St. (☎6766 2114), a 15min. walk west of town at Joe Macguires Pub, for a more comical tribute to country and a chat with the locals at the bar. For real devotees, the **Australian Country Music Foundation,** 93 Brisbane St., is an archive with a small museum (☎6766 9696; open M-Sa 10am-2pm; $5.50, concessions $3.30, family $13.20), and the newly-opened **Walk A Country Mile Interpretive Centre** at the Visitors Centre takes you interactively through the history of country music in Australia. Bring out your inner cowboy or cowgirl at one of the **"Jackaroo and Jillaroo schools"** in the Tamworth area, with crash courses on how to ride horses, train dogs, milk cows, lasso, operate farm equipment, and muster cattle from the saddle. Certificates and help finding jobs are given upon completion. **▓Leconfield** runs a highly recommended school about an hour out of Tamworth. If you're lucky, they'll even let you castrate a baby lamb the old fashioned way—with your teeth. (☎6769 4328; www.leconfield.com. 5-day course from $440, begins M. Includes food and accommodation. Free Tamworth pick-up at YHA.) **Dag Sheep Station** in Nundle runs a similar, shorter three-day course for $373 (☎6769 3234; www.thedag.com.au; begins W and Su. Includes food and accommodation).

▐▌▐▌ ENTERTAINMENT & NIGHTLIFE. Tamworth is indeed a country town, and nightlife has a very local flavor. Local teens cruise the streets on weekend nights, but their older siblings fill the pubs most nights. Most establishments close after 2am, but the standard 1 or 1:30am curfews mean that if you want to stay later, be in the door by that time. The **West Diggers Club,** on Kable Ave., off Brisbane St., has good country music lineups on the weekend (☎6766 4661). Check out *The Gig Guide* in Thursday's *Leader,* Tamworth's local paper, for details and other venues. The **Imperial Pub,** on the corner of Marius and Brisbane St., draws a younger crowd resistant to their country music heritage. (☎6766 2613. Live (mainly rock) music Th-Sa (and sometimes Su). Curfew 1:30am. Closes 2:30am, F-Sa 3am.)

SOUTH COAST

While the path from Sydney up the North Coast has been well-worn by hordes of backpackers, the South Coast is only beginning to be discovered as a travel destination. Local residents proudly proclaim that it's one of Australia's best-kept secrets, and city-weary visitors will be inclined to agree. The region's beaches, just as good for surfing as up north, are far less crowded and only minutes from lush dairy land and rainforests. The Princes Hwy., south of Sydney, is the string that links the pearls of the South Coast like Kiama, Jervis Bay, and Narooma.

WOLLONGONG ☎02

About 80km down the coast from Sydney, Wollongong is the gateway to the scenic Shoalhaven. As the third-largest metropolitan area in NSW, Wollongong is anxious to push its cosmopolitan city appeal, but it's still essentially a small university beach-side town—which translates to boisterous nightlife and great surfing beaches. While its foundations lie in industry, the 'Gong's stunning natural surroundings can't help but promote an outdoorsy lifestyle. In addition to world-class surfing, there are adrenaline-pumping activities in nearby Stanwell Park, as well as great views of the towering Illawarra Escarpment.

🖅🔁 TRANSPORTATION & PRACTICAL INFORMATION. CityRail trains (☎13 15 00) stop at Wollongong City Station on Station St. and run to: Bomaderry, near Nowra (1½hr., 4-10 per day, $8); Kiama (45min., 11-16 per day, $5.20); and Sydney (1½hr., 12-28 per day, $9). **Premier buses** (☎13 34 10) run to: Batemans Bay (3-3¾hr., 2-3 per day, $33); Bermagui (6hr., 1 per day, $45); Melbourne (15hr., 1 per day, $69); Narooma (4½-5¼hr., 2-3 per day, $44); Sydney (1½-2hr., 1-3 per day, $13); and Ulladulla (2¾hr., 2-3 per day, $26). **Murrays** (☎13 22 51) runs to Canberra (3½hr., 1 per day, $31). The Princes Hwy. leads directly into Wollongong, becoming **Flinders Street** just north of the city center and merging into **Keira Street** downtown. Pedestrian **Crown Street Mall** between Keira and Kembla St. is the city's commercial heart. **ATMs** are abundant here. **Tourism Wollongong,** 93 Crown St., is on the corner of Crown and Kembla St. (☎4227 5545 or 1800 240 737; www.tourism-wollongong.com.au. Open M-F 9am-5pm, Sa 9am-4pm, Su 10am-4pm.) **Network Cafe** has **Internet** access. (☎4228 8686. Open M-W 10am-6pm, Th 10am-10pm, F 10am-midnight, Sa 9:30am-midnight, Su 10am-5pm. $6 per hr.) The **post office** is at 110-116 Crown St., in the pedestrian mall. (☎13 13 18. Open M-F 6am-5:30pm, Sa 6am-noon, Su 6-11am.) **Postal Code:** 2500.

🛏 ACCOMMODATIONS Keiraleagh House ❷, 60 Kembla St., between Market and Smith St., is Wollongong's cheapest and friendliest option, though the building and straw-covered backyard show their age. (☎4228 6765; backpack@primus.com.au. Laundry, kitchen, and TV living room. Key deposit $10. Bunks $17; singles $25, ensuite $35; doubles $45; family rooms $50-60.) The simple rooms in the **Hotel Illawarra ❸,** on the corner of Market and Keira St., are not as swanky as the nightclub downstairs, but they're easy to crawl home to after an evening of your favorite schooners. (☎4229 5411; fax 4229 5140. 1st-floor singles $45, 2nd-floor $35; doubles $75.) **Wollongong Surf Leisure Resort ❷,** on Pioneer Rd. in Fairy Meadow, is the nearest campground, 4.5km north of downtown and a 20min. walk from Fairy Meadow CityRail station. By car from Wollongong, go north on Corrimal St. to Stuart Park to George Hanley Dr. at the roundabout and turn right when it ends, then turn right onto Pioneer Rd. (☎4283 6999. Laundry, pool, spa, and indoor tennis courts. Bicycle hire $5 per 1hr. Reception M-Sa 8am-9pm, Su 8am-6pm. Sites for two $16.50, powered $20. Family-style cabins from $75.)

🍽🔖 FOOD & NIGHTLIFE The restaurants lining Keira St., Corrimal St., and lower Crown St. cover an astonishing variety of Asian cuisines with main dishes from $9-12. Wollongong also has many Indian and Italian restaurants. The affordable and popular **Food World Gourmet Cafe ❶,** 148 Keira St., serves tasty Chinese dishes from $6.50-9.20. (☎4225 9655. Open Su-W 11am-8pm, Th-Sa 11:30am-9pm.) At North Beach, trendy **Stingray,** 1-5 Bourke St., opposite the Novotel at the corner of Cliffe St., serves dishes with exotic twists, like Moroccan lamb strudel ($15.50) and pizza ($11-16) topped with exotic flavors like Chinese duck. (☎4225 7701. Open M 8am-5pm, Tu-Su 8am-late.) Woolworths **supermarket** is on the corner of Kembla and Burelli St. (☎4228 8066. Open M-Sa 7:30am-midnight, Su 8am-10pm.) The **Hotel Illawarra** (see **Accommodations,** p. 224) draws a 20-something crowd in the early evening for cocktails and conversation. On Saturdays, when the backroom is opened, DJs rule the dance-floor. (☎4229 5411. Open M-F 10am-2am, Sa until 4am, Su until midnight.) Another favorite night spot, the **Bourbon Street Night Club,** 150 Keira St., often has party-goers lined up as early as 8pm, eager to join the in-crowd. (Open W-Sa 8pm-3am.) The **Glasshouse Tavern,** 90 Crown St. (☎4226 4305), between Kembla and Corrimal St., is oriented toward a young crowd trying to impress each other, especially on its extremely popular W Uni Night and on week-

Wollongong

🏠 **ACCOMMODATIONS**
Hotel Illawarra, **6**
Keiraleagh House, **5**
Wollongong Surf Leisure
  Resort, **1**

🍴 **FOOD**
Food World Gourmet Cafe, **3**
Stingray, **2**

⭐ **NIGHTLIFE**
Bourbon Street Night Club, **4**
Glasshouse Tavern, **7**
Oxford Tavern, **8**

ends, when its back room is also a dance club (cover $10). At the **Oxford Tavern,** 47 Crown St., there's live music W-Sa, including many up-and-coming rock bands. (☎ 4228 3892. Open Su-Tu and Th 10am-11pm, W and F-Sa 10am-3am.)

🔲🔲 **SIGHTS & ACTIVITIES.** Like most of the South Coast, Wollongong's best features are outdoors. **Wollongong Harbour** is the city's most scenic spot. The small convict-created cove shelters sailboats and the local fishing fleet. The old lighthouse, visible from the beach, adds an air of old-time charm. Visitors and residents enjoy a beautiful walking and cycling path following the harbour's edge that leads up to **North Beach,** a popular spot for surfing. Wollongong's other popular surfing beach is **City Beach,** in the southern part of the city, just a few blocks from the tourist office. If you want to break into the surfing scene or just refine your technique, **Pines Surfriders School** can help. (☎ 0500 824 860. $45 per hr., students $35.) In addition to surfing, adventure options like skydiving and hang gliding abound in Wollongong. At Stuart Park in North Beach, **Skydive the Beach** has scenic tandem skydiving for $275-310, as well as an accelerated freefall course. (☎ 4225 8444. Book ahead.) Near Wollongong, **Stanwell Park** offers even more adventure sport (see **Northern Scenic Drive,** p. 226). Back indoors, the **Wollongong City Gallery,** on the corner of Kembla and Burelli St., creatively displays regional, Aboriginal, and contemporary art. (☎ 4228 7500. Open Tu-F 10am-5pm, Sa-Su noon-4pm. Free.)

NEAR WOLLONGONG

NORTHERN SCENIC DRIVE

The winding Bulli Pass road twists and turns inland to the Southern Fwy., 12km north of Wollongong, and leads to a magnificent panoramic view of the area. Down at sea level, Wollongong's biggest attractions await at Bulli Point (also know as Sandion Point Headland) and, farther north, Austinmer Beach. Beach bums flock to Bulli or Thirroul for some of the area's best surfing. For those without a car, CityRail runs from Wollongong ($2). For several months in 1922, English writer D.H. Lawrence resided in Thirroul between Bulli and Austinmer, and described the area in his novel *Kangaroo*. The home is privately owned and inaccessible to the public, but the beach is open for strolling and literary speculation. North of Bulli Pass, Lawrence Hargrave Dr. winds along the coast, providing tantalizing glimpses of the shore below before reaching the lookout at Bald Hill, north of Stanwell Park, considered by many to be the best view on this stretch of coast. You can get an even better view of Stanwell Park up in the air; both **HangglideOz** (☎0417 939 200) and **Sydney Hang Gliding Centre** (☎4294 4294) have tandem hang gliding starting at $165.

ILLAWARA ESCARPMENT

The Illawarra Escarpment defines Wollongong's inland border. The nearest peak, Mt. Keira, is a short drive from town on Mt. Keira Rd. Take bus #39 to get within 8km of Mt. Keira's peak. Bushwalking trails lead to fantastic views at the top. The Cockatoo Run, a scenic mountain railway, stops at Wollongong City Station and offers day-long excursions over the escarpment into the highlands at Robertson and back. (☎1300 653 801; www.3801limited.com.au. Operates W and Su 1 per day most of the year; departs Wollongong 10:55am, returns 4:35pm. Bookings required in summer. $40, children $30, families $110.)

KIAMA   ☎02

Lovely Kiama (KAI-amma), whose name appropriately means "sound of the sea," is known for its geyser-like Blowhole. Under the right conditions, when the wind is high and the waves surge from the southeast, water washing into a sea cave is forced noisily upward through a hole in the rocks to heights of 20-35m. Even if the wind and waves don't comply, Kiama is well worth the stop for its craggy cliffs, turbulent surf, and friendly, small-town feel.

From the **CityRail** station, on Bong Bong St., just west of Blowhole Pt., **trains** (☎13 15 00) run to: Bomaderry/Nowra (30min., 10-15 per day, $4.40); Sydney (2hr., 12-16 per day, $13); and Wollongong (45min., 13-17 per day, $5.20). From the Bombo Railway Station, **Premier buses** (☎13 34 10) run to: Batemans Bay (2½-3¼hr., 2-3 per day, $33); Bega (5-5½hr., 2-3 per day, $48); Bermagui (5¼hr., 1 per day, $45); Melbourne (15hr., 1 per day, $69); Narooma (4-4¼hr., 2-3 per day, $44); Nowra (40min., 2-3 per day, $13); Sydney (2½hr., 2-3 per day, $19); Ulladulla (2¼hr., 2-3 per day, $25); and Wollongong (35min., 2-3 per day, $13). The **Visitors Centre** is on Blowhole Pt. (☎4232 3322 or 1300 654 262; www.kiama.com.au. Open daily 9am-5pm.) **Internet** is available in the Kiama **Library,** 7 Railway Pde. (☎4233 1133. Bookings required. Open M and W-F 9:30am-5:30pm, Tu 9:30am-8pm, Sa 9:30am-2pm. Browsing free; email $2.50 per 30min.) The pink **post office** is at 24 Terralong St. (☎13 13 13. Open M-F 9am-5pm.) **Postal Code:** 2533.

The **Grand Hotel ❸,** 49 Manning St., around the corner from the CityRail Station, has simple rooms above its pub. (☎4232 1037. Singles $30; doubles and twins $60.) Next door, the small **Kiama Backpackers Hostel ❷,** 31 Bong Bong St., feels like an old university dormitory. (☎/fax 4233 1881. TV, kitchen. Internet $5 per hr. Key deposit $10. Dorms $20; singles $25; twins and doubles $49.) The **Blowhole Point Holiday Park ❷** reveals picturesque views of the harbor. (☎ 4232 2707. Sites for two $26; caravans and motor homes $50-80.) Locals recommend the fish 'n chips ($6.50) at the **Kiama Harbour Takeaway ❶,** right on the harbor below the Blowhole Point Holiday Park. (☎ 4232 1138. Open daily 10:30am-6:30pm, later during summer.) In addition to selling books, the intimate **Coffee Table Bookshop ❶,** 2/3 Railway Pde., at the corner of Terralong St., serves an assortment of sandwiches and crepes for $7-10. (☎ 4233 1060. Open M-Sa 9am-5pm, Su 10am-4pm.)

Every visitor to Kiama should visit the **Blowhole** for an impressive show. At **Marsden Head,** at the end of Tingira Crescent, near the Endeavour Lookout, the **Little Blowhole** erupts when the ocean swell comes from the opposite direction. It's worth the extra trip if its big brother proves to be a disappointment. For swimming, check out either the **natural rock pool** on the northern side of Blowhole Point or the deeper rock pool, north of Kiama Harbour at Pheasant Point. To the north of Pheasant Point, experienced **surfers** brave the riptides at **Bombo Beach.** Slightly north of Bombo Beach, just around the next headland, sightseers will discover the striking rock formation known as **Cathedral Rock.** Surfers refer to this same area as the **Boneyard;** despite the menacing nickname, it's a popular spot for catching waves. Less experienced surfers and swimmers should head south to popular **Surf Beach,** where waters are patrolled. For those who get tired of just idly gazing out across the ocean, **Kiama Charter Service** (☎ 4237 8496), **Kiama Harbour Game and Reef Fishing Charter** (☎ 4232 1725), and **Signa Charter** can send you out on the deep sea for some sport fishing. (☎ 4233 1020). Their fishing expeditions generally last 7-8hrs. and cost $70-80, including bait and gear.

NOWRA & BOMADERRY   ☎ 02

Every sign along the Princes Hwy. directs you to Nowra. Smaller sibling Bomaderry lies immediately north and marks the end of the rail line. Together, they are the residential and administrative centers of the Shoalhaven. Nowra is often used as a base for exploring greener, more scenic areas like Kangaroo Valley and.

CityRail's (☎ 13 15 00) last stop is in Bomaderry on Railway St. **Trains** run to: Kiama (30min., 12-15 per day, $4.40); Sydney (2¾hr., 12-15 per day, $15); and Wollongong (1½-2hr., 9 per day, $8.50). **Premier buses** (☎ 13 34 10) run to: Batemans Bay (1¾hr., 2-3 per day, $21); Bega (4¼hr., 2-3 per day, $37); Bermagui (4hr., 1 per day, $34); Kiama (40min., 2-3 per day, $13); Melbourne (13½hr., 1 per day, $66); Narooma (2¾hr., 2-3 per day, $32); Sydney (3-3¼hr., 2-3 per day, $19); Ulladulla (1hr., 2-3 per day, $14); and Wollongong (1¼hr., 2-3 per day, $13). **Kennedy's Coaches** (☎ 4421 7596 or 0411 232 101) services Fitzroy Falls (1hr., 1 per day, $12) and Kangaroo Valley (30min.-1hr., 2 per day, $8). The **police station** (☎ 4421 9699) is on Kinghorn St. The **post office** (☎ 4421 3155) is at 59 Junction St. (Open M-F 9am-5pm, Sa 9am-noon.) **Postal Code:** 2541. The **Shoalhaven Visitors Centre** lies on the corner of Princes Hwy. and Pleasant Way, south of the bridge to Nowra, on the left. (☎ 4421 0778 or 1300 662 808; www.shoalhaven.nsw.gov.au. Open daily 9am-4:30pm.) The **National Parks and Wildlife Service,** 55 Graham St., Nowra, has info on parks in the area. (☎ 4423 2170. Open M-F 8:30am-5pm.) The **Nowra Public Library,** on Berry St., has **Internet.** (☎ 4429 3705. Browsing free; email $2 per hr.) For ideas about what to do in Nowra and throughout the South Coast, visit www.nowrabackpackers.com.

Due to its proximity to Kangaroo Valley and Jervis Bay, many choose to stay in Nowra when exploring the area. The cozy, bungalow-style **M&M's Guesthouse ❷,** 1A Scenic Dr., on the right off Bridge Rd. just across the bridge into Nowra, has a backpackers building and an adjacent motel. (☎ 4422 8006; www.mmguesthouse.com. Laundry, TV, fireplace, and kitchen. Reception 8am-10pm. Dorms $22;

motel singles $50, doubles $60.) For camping sites next to a wildlife park, head for **Nowra Animal Park ❶.** From Bomaderry, take a right on Illaroo Rd., just before the grey metal bridge to Nowra; follow McMahon's Rd. left from the roundabout, and take a left at the first stop sign onto Rock Hill Rd. The owner can also direct travelers to local rock climbing sites. (☎/fax 4421 3949. Toilets and hot showers. Reception 8am-5pm. Sites $5.50 per person; powered $8.) Campers get discounts to the nearby 16-acre wildlife park, which has wombats, koalas, and kangaroos. ($10, campers $7.50; children $5/$4; families $26.)

Most area climbers recommend **Thompson's Point,** on the southern shore of the Shoalhaven river and find PC, Grotto, and South Central to be challenging. Climbers must supply their own gear. **The Gym** (☎ 4421 0587), at the corner of McMahons and Illaroo Rd., offers indoor rock climbing and takes climbers to climb outdoors in North Nowra. **Skydive Nowra** (☎ 0500 885 556) offers tandem skydives ($380 with video) and freefall courses ($420). Book in advance.

KANGAROO VALLEY

More than a place to spot kangaroos, tiny Kangaroo Valley (pop. 280) is best for canoe trips down the Kangaroo and Shoalhaven Rivers. It has the pleasant feel of a remote, rural area, which makes it popular for camping retreats, and its main street, Moss Vale Rd., is dotted with arts-and-crafts shops. At the northwest end of town, the **Hampden Bridge** spans the Kangaroo River. Built in 1898, it is Australia's oldest suspension bridge. With two locations on the north side of the bridge, **Kangaroo Valley Safaris,** 2210 Moss Vale Rd., organizes beginner-intermediate canoe camping trips to Kangaroo River and Shoal Haven, including a 25km overnight canoe trip. A shuttle picks up from the rail station. (☎ 4465 1502. Open daily 7am-7pm. Canoes $45 per day, kayaks $25-55 per day, sea kayaks $65 per day, tents $30 per day.) At the northern entrance of **Morton National Park,** 20km from Kangaroo Valley on Moss Vale Rd., **Fitzroy Falls** greets visitors. Run by the NPWS, the **Fitzroy Falls Visitors Centre** has maps for bushwalking trails. (☎ 4887 7270. Open daily 9am-5:30pm.) By car, avoid the steep, winding Kangaroo Valley Rd. leading west from Berry and opt for Moss Vale Rd., which leads northwest from Bomaderry, off the Princes Hwy. Caution should still be used on Moss Vale Rd., which is still narrow and winding; check road conditions ahead of time for both routes.

Tourist info is available at **News Agents,** next to the post office. (☎ 4465 1150; www.kangaroovalley.net. Open daily 6am-7pm.) The **Bendeela Picnic Area ❶,** 7km outside town, provides free **camping,** toilets, BBQ, and water. Reach it by driving north of town and turning left on Bendeela Rd., following signs to the entrance. **Prior's buses** (☎ 1800 816 234) run daily except Saturday to: Batemans Bay (2¼hr., $20); Narooma (4hr., $26); Parramatta (3hr., $20); and Ulladulla (1½hr., $15).

JERVIS BAY   ☎ 02

The jewel of the South Coast, Jervis Bay is a serene body of water surrounded by strikingly white beaches and magnificent national parks. It teems with marine life and contains underwater rock formations that make for some of the best diving in Australia outside of the Great Barrier Reef. To take in the bay, stop at any of the surrounding towns and wander down to the water's edge.

Underwater, Jervis Bay is an exquisite natural meeting place for tropical marine life from the north and a variety of southern species not found in the Great Barrier Reef. Divers rave about the massive archways and rock shelves; spots such as Cathedral Cave and Smuggler's Cave are perfect for **cave diving.** The Arch, Stoney Creek Reef, and the Ten Fathom Dropoff are known for deep diving. **Steamers Beach Seal Colony** is great for open-water dives and snorkeling. Despite chillier waters, visibility is best from April to early August. **Pro-Dive,** 64 Owen St. (☎4441 5255), takes certified divers on 2 dives for a day ($130, including gear). They also offer a 4-day PADI course ($385). **Jervis Bay Sea Sports,** 47 Owen St. (☎4441 5012), offers slightly more expensive services. For those content to enjoy marine life from a drier vantage point, **Dolphin Watch Cruises,** 50 Owen St. (☎1800 246 010), and **Dolphin Explorer Cruises,** 62 Owen St. (☎4441 5455 or 1800 444 330), offer 2½hr. dolphin cruises daily at 12:30 and 1pm ($25, ISIC $20-22) and 3hr. whale watching trips ($40) during peak whale migrations (June-Nov.). If you just want to paddle around, **Jervis Bay Kayak Company,** Shop 7b in Campbell Ct., off the Wool Rd. in Vincentia, allows you to work your arms in style. The tour cost includes transport, snack, and park user fees. (☎4443 3858. Rentals $66-85 per day; half-day guided tours $85; full-day tours $115.)

HUSKISSON. Twenty-four kilometers southeast of Nowra along the coast of Jervis Bay lies Huskisson (nicknamed Husky). **Nowra Coaches** (☎4423 5244) goes to Huskisson (35min., 2-4 per day, $10) and Jervis Bay Village in Booderee National Park (1¼hr.; Tu and F; $9). For tourist info, visit the antiques-filled **Huskisson Trading Post** on the corner of Tomerong and Dent St. (☎4441 5241. Open daily 9:30am-5pm.) **Leisure Haven Caravan Park ❷,** 1.5km outside of town along Currambene Creek on Woollamia Rd., provides sites with free hot showers and laundry, and has BBQs, TVs, and a kitchen. (☎4441 5046. Key deposit $20. Reception 8am-6pm. Sites for two $20-30, powered $25-35. Cabins for two $55-80. Seventh night free.) **The Husky Pub ❸,** on Owen St. overlooking the Bay, is the town's pubstay. The rooms are basic and have shared toilets, and are right above the popular late-night spot in Jervis Bay. (☎4441 5001; www.thehuskypub.com.au. Bar and reception 11am-11pm. Singles $30; twins and doubles $55.) On the way out of Huskisson, heading toward Booderee National Park through **Vincentia,** many beautiful beaches lie hidden down side streets just off the main road. Almost any street will lead to a scenic bit of coast. Especially beautiful are **Greenfields Beach** and **Hyams Beach,** said to have the world's whitest sand.

BOODEREE NATIONAL PARK. On the southern end of the bay, **Booderee National Park,** which is under joint Aboriginal management, covers over 6000 hectares of land that contain gorgeous beaches. The **Botanic Gardens** has numerous walks, a rainforest gully, many native plants and birds. (☎4442 1122. Open M-F 8am-4pm, Sa-Su 10am-5pm. Free.) You'll also have to enter the park to reach many of Jervis Bay's most beautiful beaches. Locals rave about the beach at **Green Patch,** often a good place to see rainbow lorikeets and eastern gray kangaroos and a popular snorkeling spot. ◙**Murrays Beach,** staggering in its beauty, is a great place to take a dip. Deep in the woods near Murray's Beach, the historic **Ruined Lighthouse** is now just a heap of stones. At **Steamers Beach,** you can snorkel among a seal colony. The **Visitors Centre,** just beyond the park entry gates, accepts campsite bookings and can provide maps to the various hiking tracks. (☎4443 0977. Open daily 9am-4pm. $10 per car per day.) The park also has three **camping** areas: **Greenpatch ❷,** on Jervis Bay (hot showers, toilets, and water; sites $14-20); **Cave Beach ❶,** near Wreck Bay to the south (cold showers, no electricity; max. 5 people; sites $9-11); **Bristol Point ❷** is intended for larger groups and has toilets, hot showers, fireplaces, and very large sites. (Sites $69, peak $87.)

ULLADULLA   ☎02

Moving south through the Shoalhaven, the next major service center is the small town of Ulladulla (uh-luh-DUH-luh; pop. 12,000), given its name back in 1828 because it was thought to sound like its original Aboriginal name, *Woolahderrah*.

Outdoorsy Ulladulla has plenty of diving, surfing, and fishing. Off the coast between Jervis Bay and Ulladulla Harbour are shipwrecks for divers to explore, including the famous 1870 wreck of the *Walter Hood*. Still, the best-known and most beautiful draw is the Pigeon House Bushwalk.

Premier buses (☎ 13 34 10) stop at the Marlin Hotel (southbound) and the Traveland Travel Agency (northbound) on route to: Batemans Bay (45min., 2-3 per day, $11); Bermagui (3hr., 1 per day, $25); Kiama (2hr., 2-3 per day, $14); Melbourne (12½hr., 1 per day, $66); Narooma (1¾hr., 2-3 per day, $20); Nowra (1hr., 2-3 per day, $14); Sydney (5hr., 2-3 per day, $27); and Wollongong (3hr., 2-3 per day, $25). The **Visitors Centre** is on the Princes Hwy. (☎ 4455 1269. Open M-F 10am-5pm, Sa-Su 9am-5pm.) **Internet** is available there and at the adjacent **library**. (Open M-F 10am-6pm, Sa 9am-2pm. Browsing free; email $1.10 per 30min.) The **police station** (☎ 4454 2542) is on the corner of Princes Hwy. and North St.

The local hostel, ▇**South Coast Backpackers ❷**, 63 Princes Hwy., between Narrawallee and North St., is a small, impeccably neat operation with beautiful hardwood floors, brightly-colored walls, parking lot, and a great sundeck and hammock area. (☎ 4454 0500. Key deposit $10. Dorms $20; twins; and doubles $45. VIP discount.) For a total indulgence of the senses, check into the award-winning ▇**Ulladulla Guest House ❺**, 39 Burrill St., just down South St. off the Princes Hwy. In addition to phenomenal pampering (free champagne and fruit upon arrival), the guest house is also a fabulous art gallery and contains a renowned French restaurant. (☎ 4455 1796; www.guesthouse.com.au. Rooms start at $188; occasionally rates reduced to $99 for same-day standby.) At the end of South St., **Ulladulla Headland Tourist Park ❶** has camping space, though the site area slopes slightly. (☎ 4455 2457 or 1300 733 021. Showers, toilets, laundry, BBQ, and pool. Sites $15 per person, powered $11-16; cabins $100-165, off-peak $45-90.)

Bushwalkers generally stop in Ulladulla for the **Pigeon House Walk,** a 5km hike with some ladder climbing, which has knock-out views at the top. (Allow 3-4hr. Turn off the Princes Hwy. onto Wheelbarrow Rd. 3km south of Burrill Lake. The trailhead is 27km farther on unsealed road at a picnic area.) **One Track for All** is a gentle 2km trail dotted with hand-carved stumps, statues, and logs depicting the Aboriginal and post-settlement history of the land. The trail, which winds about the North Head cliffs near Ulladulla Harbour, affords several staggering ocean lookouts. (Turn off Princes Hwy. onto North St., across from the Police Station, take a left onto Burrill St., then a right onto Dolphin St. The trailhead is at the end of Dolphin St. Wheelchair-accessible.) The people at the **Ulladulla Dive Shop,** 150 Princes Hwy., at the corner of Deering St., offer seasoned advice on **reef diving** in the area, and can take you out themselves. (☎ 4455 5303. Open Nov.-Apr. daily 7am-6pm; May-Oct. M-F 9am-5pm, Sa-Su 8am-5pm. Gear $55 per day; intro dives $85.) The **Ulladulla Dive and Adventure Centre,** 211 Princes Hwy., at the southern end of Ulladulla near Dolphin Point, gives diving, snorkeling, canoe, and kayak lessons. (☎ 4455 3029. Open M-Tu and Th-Sa 8:30am-5:30pm, Su 8:30am-5pm.) Nearby **Lakes Burrill** and **Conjola** have nice **swimming** beaches, and **Mollymook Beach,** just north of town, is good for **surfing** and dolphin-spotting.

MURRAMARANG NATIONAL PARK

With expansive views of the Pacific and tame kangaroos all over, the coastline in the Murramarang National Park makes a great detour from the highway and a superb spot to check out the 'roo beach bums and parrots who congregate on the grass next to ▇**Pebbly Beach.** A number of worthy campgrounds and caravan parks are speckled throughout the park, but tent **camping ❶** sites are cheapest at the Pebbly Beach camping area, which has even more kangaroos than the beach itself. (☎ 4478 6006. Sites $5 per person; cabins for two $77.) At the southernmost point in the Shoalhaven half of Murramarang National Park, **Durras North** looks onto Durras Lake and a beautiful windswept ocean beach. Pick up a brochure for a self-guided bushwalk from the tourist office in Batemans Bay. The ⬛**Murramarang Beach Resort ❶**, on Durras Rd. off the Princes Hwy., is a luxurious campsite with "presidential" cabin suites costing upwards of $234. (☎4478 6355; www.murramarangresort.com. Reception Sept.-Mar. Su-Th 8am-midnight, F-Sa 8am-1am; Apr.-Aug. Su-Th 8am-10pm, F-Sa 8am-midnight. All powered sites $15-25 for 2 people; standard bungalows for two $59-73, ensuite $74-91.)

BATEMANS BAY ☎02

Situated south of the junction at the mouth of Clyde River, the town begins where the Kings Hwy. from Canberra (152km inland) meets the Princes Hwy. at the coast. Though you won't see any threatening fins from shore, dozens of grey nurse sharks—comprising one of Australia's largest colonies—circle the islands offshore, making Batemans Bay a popular dive spot. Or, if you're not easily impressed by zombie-eyed fauna, join the dozens of other backpackers who migrate to this laid-back fishing village for its proximity to the 'roos and parrots at Murramarang National Park.

🚍 **TRANSPORTATION & PRACTICAL INFORMATION. Buses** leave from outside the Promenade Plaza on Orient St. **Premier** (☎13 34 10) goes to: Bega (2½-3½hr., 2-3 per day, $22); Bermagui (2½hr., 1 per day, $18); Kiama (3hr., 2-3 per day, $33); Melbourne (12hr., 1 per day, $59); Narooma (1-1¾hr., 2-3 per day, $14); Nowra (2hr., 2-3 per day, $21); Sydney (5½hr., 2-3 per day, $35); Ulladulla (45min., 2-3 per day, $11); and Wollongong (3½hr., 2-3 per day, $33). **Murrays** (☎13 22 57) offers a 10% YHA discount and goes to Canberra (2½hr., 1-2 per day, $24). The staff at **Batemans Bay Tourist Information Centre,** on Princes Hwy. at Beach Rd., will book your accommodations in town at no charge as well as supply you with a stack of brochures and suggestions. (☎4472 6900 or 1800 802 528; fax 4472 8822. Open daily 9am-5pm.) The **police station** is at 28 Orient St. (☎4472 0044). The **post office** is on Orient St., adjacent to the bus stop. (Open M-F 9am-5pm.) **Postal Code:** 2536.

🏠 **ACCOMMODATIONS & FOOD.** Copious motels fringe Orient St. and Beach Rd.; rooms usually start at $60-70 in winter. The **Batemans Bay Backpackers (YHA) ❷**, inside a caravan park on the corner of Old Princes Hwy. and South St., off the new Princes Hwy., offers tidy facilities as well as daily trips to Pebbly Beach ($11) and Mogo ($5) when there is enough interest. The hostel rents bikes ($12 per day) and lends boogie boards. (☎4472 4972; www.shadywillows.com.au. Laundry, kitchen, TV, and pool. Call to arrange pick-up from the bus stop in town. Dorms $23, YHA $19; twins and doubles $62/$58.) Small and friendly, **Beach Road Backpackers ❷**, 92 Beach Rd., is a flat 1km walk from town. (☎4472 3644; fax 4472 7208. Trips to Pebbly Beach $15. TV, kitchen, free pick-up and drop-off at bus stop. Bike hire $7.50 per day. Dorms $19; doubles $40. VIP.) Fish 'n' chips seems to be the town's favorite meal; try **The Boat Shed ❶**, next to the bus stop on Orient St., with a back porch overlooking the waterfront, for eat-in or takeaway seafood. (☎4472 4052. Open in summer daily 9am-8pm; in winter M-W 9am-4pm, Th-Su 9am-7pm.)

📷 **SIGHTS & ACTIVITIES.** The 1880 wreck of the Lady Darling is considered a fantastic dive and is suitable for all levels of diving and snorkeling. Other dives include the Burrawarra Wall, the Maze, and, for scoping the nurse sharks, Montague Island. The **Dive Shop,** 33 Orient St., can be your link to the water world. (☎4472 9930. Single boat dive $38; double $66; full equipment hire $50-88.) The compact **Opal and Shell Museum,** 142 Beach Rd., owned and operated by a veteran opal miner, showcases an extensive display of opals and shells from Australia and around the world; for those interested in buying a token opal, prices are much more affordable here than in larger cities. (☎ 4472 7248. Open M and W-Su 10am-6pm. Closed Aug. $1.50, families $3.) Buy or rent a surfboard at **Kaffir Surfboards.** (☎ 4472 3933. Single fin $25; 3-fin thrusters $35.)

To indulge in a spot of bushwalking, join the locals from **Batemans Bay Bushwalkers** ($2). Contact Len Tompkins (☎ 4472 3113) or ask the tourist office for a schedule. Traveling south on the coastal road, Malua Bay and Broulee have good **surf. U-Canoe** has canoe and kayak hire. (☎ 4474 3348; www.sci.net.au/ucanoe. $30 per day for 1 person, $40 for 2, $50 for 3; includes pick-up and delivery.)

NAROOMA   ☎ 02

With several parks and protected natural areas nearby, the town of Narooma is a good basecamp for outdoor exploration. **Premier Motor Service** (☎ 13 34 10) stops in Narooma and goes to: Batemans Bay (1hr., 2-3 per day, $14); Bega (1½hr., 2-3 per day, $15); Kiama (4-5hr., 2-3 per day, $44); Melbourne (11hr., 1 per day, $53); Nowra (3-3½hr., 2-3 per day, $32); Sydney (6½-7½hr., 2-3 per day, $46); Ulladulla (2-2½hr., 2-3 per day, $20); and Wollongong (4¾-5½hr., 2-3 per day, $44). **Murrays** (☎ 13 22 51) runs from Narooma Plaza to Canberra (4½hr., 1-2 per day, $36.25). The **Narooma Visitors Centre,** on Princes Hwy., handles advance bookings for some campgrounds and tours. (☎ 4476 2881. Open daily 9am-5pm.) The **NPWS** office is a block away on the corner of Princes Hwy. and Field St. (☎ 4476 2888. Open M-F 8:30am-4:30pm.) The **post office** is just up the hill on Princes Hwy. (☎ 4476 2049. Open M-F 9am-5pm.) **Postal Code:** 2546.

The **Bluewater Lodge (YHA) ❷,** 8 Princes Hwy., is clean and comfortable. The knowledgeable and gracious owner has lived in the area his whole life. (☎ 4476 4440; naroomayha@narooma.com. Breakfast included. Laundry, kitchen, TV. Bikes and canoes $6 per day. Internet $5 per hr. Reception May-Aug. 8am-noon and 3-9pm; Sept.-Apr. 8am-9pm. Dorms $24, YHA $21, children $15; twins $24; family rooms $55-65.) **Easts Narooma Shores Holiday Park ❷** is off the Princes Hwy. just after the bridge into town. (☎ 4476 2046. Reception 8am-8pm. Sites for 2 $18-28, powered $20-30.) **Narooma Golf Club and Surfbeach Resort ❷,** on Ballingala St., has fine views of the water and good facilities. (☎ 4476 2522. Reception 8:30am-5:30pm. Sites for 2 $20-27, powered $24-32.)

Only 7km offshore, fur seals, crested terns, and some 10,000 pairs of fairy penguins inhabit the ◪**Montague Island Nature Reserve.** The island, of volcanic origin, was used by Aborigines for food and ceremony for over 4500 years. In 1770, Captain Cook was the first European to discover the island; years later settlers introduced goats and rabbits to Montague for shipwreck victims. When the lighthouse was built, horses and cows (and grasses to feed them) continued a gradual destruction of the island's original habitat. Today, National Parks and Wildlife Service (NPWS) is working hard to preserve the island's amazing range of wildlife by restoring the natural habitat and managing the *kykuya* grass, which has choked much of the original vegetation, making it difficult for fairy penguins and other birds to nest. The reserve is only accessible through official NPWS-sanctioned tours; watch for whales on your trip out to the island. (3½hr.; 1-2 per day; $69, families $198; 90 people allowed per day.) Book through NPWS or the Visitors Centre (see below). **Eurobodalla National Park** (☎ 4476 2888), a popular 2WD-accessible destination, protects a 30km stretch of coastline, from Moruya Head in the north to Tilba Tilba Lake in the south. Featuring, among other things, lush spotted gum forest, this park has one **campground ❶** at Congo ($5 per person), near the town of **Moruya.** On Wagonga Head, off Bar Rock Rd., ocean waves, coastal winds, and a bit of chiseling have left one rock, known as **Australia Rock,** with a hole, amazingly enough, in the shape of Australia, minus a bit of the Cape York peninsula. The resemblance is uncanny. **Glasshouse Rocks,** another locally famous rock formation, lies at the south end of Narooma Beach. Depending on the winds, **surfers** will head out to Handkerchief, Bar, Carter's, or Josh's Beaches.

SNOWY MOUNTAINS

While skiers and snowboarders make the Snowies their playground during the winter, the warmer months attract swarms of hikers to Australia's highest mountains. Kosciuszko National Park, home of **Mount Kosciuszko** (2228m), Australia's highest peak, covers most of this area. The Snowy Mountains Hwy. and the Alpine Way ramble past the boulder-strewn countryside where the skiing industry is king, though compared to other mountain ranges around the world, the runs are shorter and less challenging. Conditions on each mountain vary wildly: **Thredbo** is a black diamond paradise with challenging advanced slopes; **Perisher,** despite its ominous-sounding name, is a favorite of hikers and draws large crowds; and **Mt. Selwyn** offers unbeatable deals and family-friendly easier slopes.

COOMA
☎ 02

The self-proclaimed "Capital of the Snowy Mountains," the town of Cooma links the national capital at Canberra and the coast with the mountains. Because of its peripheral location on the eastern edge of the substantial Snowy Mountains region, Cooma is far enough from the price-inflated snowfields to permit bargain accommodation and reasonable rental rates during the ski season for those willing to make the commute. Cooma is also at a fork in the road, providing access to both Mt. Selwyn and Perisher/Thredbo.

◨◪ TRANSPORTATION & PRACTICAL INFORMATION. Cooma's main drag is **Sharp Street,** flanked on either side by Massie St. and Commissioner St. **Buses** come through frequently during ski season, but service is severely curtailed the rest of the year. **Countrylink** (☎ 13 22 32) runs to Canberra (1½-2hr., 1 per day, $16.50), where you can connect with a train to Sydney ($66 total from Cooma); Jindabyne (50min., 1 per day, $19.80) and Thredbo (1¾hr., 1 per day in winter only, $30.80). **McCafferty's/Greyhound** (☎ 13 20 30) run to: Canberra (1½-2hr., 1-2 per day, $37); Sydney (6hr., 1-2 per day, $77); Jindabyne (50min., 2 per day, $24); and Thredbo (1¾hr., 2 per day, $29), with more limited service in the summer. **Murray's** (☎ 13 22 51) services the mountains once a day during ski season, as well. **Snowliner Coaches,** 120 Sharp St. (☎ 6452 1584), services Jindabyne (50min.; M-F 2 per day; $13.20, correct change required). **Harvey World Travel,** 114 Sharp St., opposite the Visitors Center, arranges reservations. (☎ 6452 4677. Open M-F 9am-5pm, Sa 9am-noon.) **Hertz** (☎ 13 30 39 or 6457 2160) and **Thrifty** (☎ 6452 5300 or 1800 552 008) have locations in Cooma.

The **Cooma Visitors Centre,** 119 Sharp St., is in the center of town. (☎ 6450 1742 or 1800 636 525; fax 6450 1798. Open daily mid-Oct. to May 9am-5pm, June to mid-Oct. 8am-5pm.) You can book accommodations through the Visitors Centre, but beware: some hotel owners will charge extra if you use this service. There is **Internet access** available at the Visitors Centre (see above; $3 per 30min.) or at **Percy's News Agency,** 158 Sharp St. (☎ 6452 2880. Open M-F 6am-6pm, Sa 6am-3pm, Su 6am-2pm. $3 per 30min.) The **police station** is on Massie St., just up the street from the post office. The **post office,** on the corner of Massie St. and Vale St., is open M-F 9am-5pm. **Postal Code:** 2630.

⌐⌐ ACCOMMODATIONS & FOOD. The **Cooma Bunkhouse Backpackers ❷,** 30 Soho St., on the corner of Commissioner St., has great year-round hostel accommodation. Every room is equipped with a private bathroom, kitchen, and TV. Breakfast $7. (☎6452 2983; www.bunkhousemotel.com.au. Reception 24hr. Heated dorms $20; singles in adjacent motel $35-40; doubles $44-55; family rooms from $65-75. VIP.) The pricier **White Manor Motel ❺,** 252 Sharp St., has rooms with color TV, A/C, heat, and electric blankets. (☎6452 1152; www.whitemanor.com. Reception 7am-10:30pm. Ensuite singles in winter $70-105, in summer $63-68; doubles $68-105/$70; family units available from $130/$92-98.) Hotel pubstays range from $20-30; the newly renovated **Alpine Hotel ❸,** 170 Sharp St., while at the upper range, is the classiest. (☎6452 1466. Singles $30, twins/doubles $50, 4-person ensuite $90.) On Sharp St., 1.6km west of the town center, **Snowtels Caravan Park ❶** provides a kitchen, laundry, and BBQ. (☎6452 1828; fax 6452 7192. Sites $15, powered $20; caravans $35-55; ensuite cabins $45-90.)

⎐Organic Vibes ❶, 82A Sharp St., is a beacon of hope to road-weary travelers surviving on fish 'n' chips and meat pies. The mother-daughter team sells organic produce, gluten and wheat-free pastas, and fresh juices ($4-5). Try the dried mangoes or the homemade lunch specials ($4-9) or simply stock up on snacks for ski-induced munchies. (☎/fax 6452 6566. Open M-F 9am-5:30pm, Sa 9am-noon.) **Grumpy's Diner ❶,** across from the Visitors Centre on Sharp St., has traveler-friendly staff, tummy-friendly meals, and some of the best coffee in town. Focaccia, sandwiches, and filling veggie options run $6-10. (☎6452 1002. Open M-F 7am-4pm, Sa-Su 7am-2:30pm. Cash only.) For a swankier a la carte meal, **Elevation ❹** in the Alpine Hotel, 170 Sharp St., specializes in modern Australian, with steak, seafood, and vegetarian options. Mains $20-24, entrees $8-12. (☎6452 1466. Open Tu-Sa from 6:30pm.) Purchase **groceries** at Woolworths, on the corner of Vale and Massie St. as well as at 228 Sharp St. (Open daily 7am-10pm.)

⛷ SKIING. Because the ski resorts of Thredbo, Perisher, and Mt. Selwyn lie within 100km of Cooma, **rental shops** clutter the town's street, with flashing signs advertising "round-the-clock" rentals. Rates are slightly cheaper than those closer to the mountains. Skis, poles, and boot rentals run about $30 the first day and $10-15 per day thereafter; snowboard and boot rental cost about $45 for the first day; clothing rental is around $20 for the first day, $5 per day thereafter; and snowchains run $20 a day, and $10 thereafter. The Visitors Center (see p. 233) has brochures with 10-15% discount coupons.

JINDABYNE ☎02

On the scenic shores of man-made **Lake Jindabyne,** Jindy acts as a satellite ski town during ski season, with the corresponding services and high seasonal prices. After the ski season, when prices drop significantly (as does tourist influx), bushwalkers stop through while exploring the vast Kosciuszko National Park.

▐ TRANSPORTATION

During the busy ski season, **Jindabyne Coaches** (☎6457 2117 or 0411 020 680) runs four shuttles to the Skitube ($15 return). From there, it's possible to catch a train up to **Perisher Blue** ($31 return, children $18). Transport into Jindabyne from the northeast passes through Cooma (see p. 233). **McCafferty's/Greyhound** (☎13 20 30) operates limited service in the winter and summer, as does **Countrylink** (☎13 22 32). Snow and ski packages are a popular option. **Oz Snow Adventures** (☎1800 851 101; www.ozsnowadventures.com.au) offers trips from Sydney and Canberra starting at $219, including accommodation, transportation, meals, and national park fees. **Murrays** (☎ 13 22 51) offers daytrip skiing and snowboarding packages from Canberra from $119. (Includes return bus, park entry, lift ticket, and equipment hire.) There are also **taxis** (☎ 13 10 08).

▊ PRACTICAL INFORMATION

The **Snowy Region Visitors Centre,** on Kosciuszko Rd. in the center of town, combines a NPWS office and a tourist center. They have tons of info and also sell entry into the National Park. (☎ 6450 5600; fax 6456 1249. Road conditions ☎ 6450 5551, snow reports 6450 5553, weather 6450 5550. Open daily in winter 8am-5:30pm, in summer 8:30am-5pm.) To get to Perisher by car, follow Kosciuszko Rd. (2WD vehicles *must* carry snowchains). Alternatively follow the **Alpine Way** to the Skitube station (23km from town), which services the Perisher Blue resorts. The Alpine Way then continues 22km farther on to **Thredbo** (chains might be required in extreme weather). From Thredbo, the Alpine Way extends through the mountains to **Khancoban,** a full-service town on the western edge of Kosciuszko National Park. 2WD cars traveling to Khancoban are *required* to carry **snow chains** and caution should, of course, be exercised in adverse conditions. The **Shell station** at the Perisher/Thredbo junction, outside of Jindabyne, rents snow chains for $30 and has a drop-off program with the Khancoban's Shell station. Other service stations offer similar programs.

    Job opportunities are everywhere in Jindabyne (mainly hospitality and ski-related work); many of the skiers and snowboarders who worship the Australian snow shrines of Thredbo and Perisher arrive in Jindabyne without work or housing and find work both through postings and word of mouth. Three great places to look are outside the IGA **supermarket** in Nuggets Crossing shopping center, in the windows of **Snowy River Continental Butchery** in Snowy Mountains Plaza, and at the **Snowy Region Visitors Centre. Snowy Mountain Backpackers** (see below) and **Leading Edge Video,** Lakeview Plaza on Snowy River Ave., both have **Internet** for $10 per hr. (☎ 6456 2665; open Su-Th 9:30am-9pm, F-Sa 9:30am-9:30pm). **ATMs** can be found in Nuggets Crossing Shopping Centre. The **police station** (☎ 6456 2244) is on Thredbo Terr. And the **post office** (☎ 6456 2394) is on the corner of Gippsland St. and Snow River Ave. **Postal Code**: 2627.

▊ ACCOMMODATIONS

Even in the height of ski madness, affordable accommodation in Jindabyne does exist, but availability may be a problem. Be sure to book well in advance. ◪**Snowy Mountain Backpackers ❸,** 7 Gippsland St., behind the Nuggets Crossing shopping center, combines an unbeatable location with new facilities, laundry, Internet, and kitchen. **Cafe SuSu** (see below) and a massage center are also on the premises. (☎ 6456 1500 or 1800 333 468; backpackers@snowy.net.au. Key deposit $10. Reception June-Oct. 8am-8pm; Nov.-May 9am-6pm. Bunks $25-40; doubles $50-100. VIP. Wheelchair-accessible.) The **Jindy Inn ❹,** 18 Clyde St., has private ensuite rooms with TVs and fridges. There's a well-equipped kitchen downstairs and a nice adjoining restaurant. During ski season the inn functions more as a B&B. Bookings are essential and single-night stays are rare, especially on weekends. (☎ 6456 1957; fax 6456 2057. Breakfast included during winter. Twin-share in winter $45-105, in summer from $55.) **Mad Mooses Guest House ❺,** 21 Monyang St., on the corner of Gippsland St., is just a 5min. walk up Gippsland St. from the post office, and offers 2-share ($90-150) and 4-share ($360-480) B&B-style accommodations. (☎ 6456 1108; www.madmooses.com.) **Jindabyne Holiday Park ❶** is in the center of town on

N E W S O U T H W A L E S

a choice stretch of Lake Jindabyne shoreline. (☎6456 2249. Laundry ($2.20 per machine) and camp kitchen. Key deposit $20. Ski-and-boot rental from $32; snowboard-and-boot from $45. Sites for 2 $15-22, powered $16-18; extra person $5-10. On-site caravans Oct.-June from $35, July-Aug. from $75.) The **Station Resort ❺** is in a self-contained village a short 6km south of Jindabyne, at the corner of Barry Way and Dalgety Rd., and is popular for cheap lodging with little hassle. Bars, restaurants, and bus services are all on the premises, and the Resort is responsible for Jindy's biggest parties. (☎6456 2895 or 1300 369 9090. TV and small fridge in rooms. Laundry and Internet available. Reception 24hr. During ski season, F-Sa 2 nights (for 2 people) including breakfast and 2-day lift tickets in Perisher $389 per person; Su-F 5 nights (for 2 people) including 5-day lift tickets $579 per person; other packages vary.)

🚺 FOOD

Cheap food is hard to come by. Preparing a flavorful range of traditional grub and some multicultural dishes, **Cafe SuSu,** 8 Gippsland St., part of the Snowy Mountain Backpackers, has decent prices (most meals $8-12) and a relaxed, funky interior. (☎6456 1503. Open daily June-Oct. 7am-9pm; Nov.-May M-F 10am-9pm, Su brunch 8am-2pm.) **Wrap A Go-Go ❷,** in Lakeview Plaza on Snowy River Ave., features spicy Mexican meals and tasty wraps. (☎6457 1887. Open daily noon-9pm; in summer closed M. Mains around $12-15.) **Mountain Munchees ❶,** 10a in Nuggets Crossing, serves up cheap comfort food, with brekkie averaging $3.50-6 and sandwiches from $4-7. (☎6457 2255. Open daily 6am-5pm. Cash only.) An IGA **supermarket** is also in Nuggets Crossing.

🔼 ACTIVITIES

The experts at **Wilderness Sports,** in Nuggets Crossing, hire equipment—including snowshoes, telemark and cross-country skis, and snowcamping gear—and organize cross-country skiing, back-country snowboarding, snowshoe, and alpine touring adventures from $70 per day in the Thredbo area. (☎6456 2966; www.wildernesssports.com.au. Open daily June-Oct. 8am-6pm, Nov.-May M-Tu and Th-Sa 9am-5pm. Prices generally depend upon group size.) Their **Snowsport Adventure Centre** in Perisher Valley also offers a myriad of rentals, as well as courses on activities such as snowcamping and rock climbing. (☎6457 6955. Open daily 9am-4pm. Snowshoe hire $25-35 per day; half-day abseiling $69; full-day Mt. Kosciuszko tour $129, includes lunch.) **Paddy Pallin,** next to the Shell station at the Perisher-Thredbo junction, offers similar services as well as mountaineering courses and **mountain bike rental.** (☎6456 2922 or 1800 623 459. 4-day intro to mountaineering course Jul.-Sept. $975; mountain bike tours in summer: half-day beginner cruise or half-day advanced slog $59, child 10-15 $49; full-day Mt. Kosciuszko champagne ride $99/$89. Min. 4 people for bookings. Mountain bike and helmet $16 per hour, $36 half-day, $50 full-day.)

Rapid Descents Whitewater Rafting, based out of Canberra, organizes thrill-ride rafting down the Murray River in spring and summer. Book in advance. (☎6076 9111; www.rapiddescents.com.au.) **Pender Lea Trail Rides** (☎ 64572 442) offers horseback riding trips.

Snowline Caravan Park, at the Kosciuszko/Thredbo Road Junction, offers **boat hire** (☎6456 2180 or 1800 248 148; www.snowline.com.au. Fishing boats $35 for first 2 hours, $10 per hour thereafter, $80 for the day, $100 deposit; paddle boats and aqua bikes $10 per half hour; canoes $15 for first hour, $5 for each additional hour, $40 deposit; and water skiing, all equipment provided, $30 per person).

Those with bigger budgets can try **Snowy Helicopters** (☎0402 11 00 33; www.snowyhelicopters.com.au), which is based at the Jindabyne Airport and runs scenic flights over the mountains starting at $50 per person.

NIGHTLIFE

Nightlife roars in Jindy throughout most of the snow season, fueled mainly by those who work on the mountains. As Wednesday is payday at all ski-related spots in the area, things really go off that night—with the same intensity as the weekend, if not greater. Crowds of locals swarm to the **Banjo Paterson Inn,** 1 Kosciuszko Rd., (☎6456 2372), which houses three full bars within its walls and features DJs and live bands many nights of the week. (Bars open daily till late. Nightclub W and F-Sa till 3am. No cover.) The place reaches capacity quickly, though, so err on the early side. **Lake Jindabyne Hotel,** on Kosciuszko offers a quieter drink, a handful of pool tables, and live cover bands Sa nights. (☎6456 2203. Open M-Sa 10am-late, Su 10am-midnight.) The **Station Resort** throws the biggest parties and pulls in the biggest named DJs throughout the season; you won't be able to miss the brochures and posters around town.

KOSCIUSZKO NATIONAL PARK

Named after the heroic Polish nationalist, Thadeus Kosciuszko (kaw-zee-AW-sko), Kosciuszko National Park contains Australia's **tallest mountains,** several stunning **wilderness areas,** and NSW's premier **ski fields.** While the park may forever be associated with ski resorts, outdoor enthusiasts appreciate the year-round beauty of **Yarrongobilly Caves** and the wildflower-strewn alpine walks in summer that lead to the rooftop of Australia.

Numerous **hiking tracks** and **camping** areas are available throughout the park. Bush camping is free in Kosciuzko National Park, so long as you pay your $15 entry free. Popular, well signposted spots along the Alpine Way include Geehi, Tom Groggin, and Leatherbarrel Creek. There's an entry fee for Kosciuszko ($15 per car per 24hr.), though motorists passing through non-stop on Alpine Way are exempt. During ski season (June 1-Oct. 10), snow chains must be carried by 2WD vehicles. The Shell stations along the Alpine Way, Khancoban, and Jindabyne, allow one-way chain rental and drop-off ($30). Trail maps, camping information, guide books, and park stickers can be obtained at the **Snowy Region Visitors Centre** in Jindabyne (see p. 234), the entrance stations on Alpine Way, and Kosciuszko Rd on the way to Perisher Blue (stickers only), or the **NPWS office** at the corner of Scott and Mitchell Ave. in Khancoban. (☎6076 9373. Open daily 8:30am-4pm.)

KOSCIUSZKO NATIONAL PARK AT A GLANCE

AREA: 6494km^2 or 690,000 hectares.

HEIGHTS: Mount Kosciuszko: 2228m. Mount Selwyn: 1520m.

FEATURES: Australia's tallest mountain, for which the park is named; the Snowy River; Yarrongobilly Caves; Mount Selwyn.

HIGHLIGHTS: Skiing some of Australia's best slopes; camping and hiking during the warmer months.

GATEWAYS: Cooma and Jindabyne.

CAMPING: Free, although a few privately-run sites charge various fees.

FEES: $15 per day vehicle fee, though motorists passing through non-stop on Alpine Way are exempt.

SKI SEASON: Approximately June to October 10.

⚠ MOUNTAINS

SKI SLOPE OVERVIEW

Cross-country skiing is always free on the following slopes.

SKI SLOPE	THE LOWDOWN	FEATURES	PRICES
PERISHER BLUE	Australia's premier resort, with Perisher Valley, Blue Cow, Smiggins, and Guthega alpine villages.	7 peaks, 51 lifts, and over 95 trails.	$80 per day, under 14 $44; night skiing (Tu, Sa) $17/$11. Lift pass and lesson $108/$72. First timer $61/$61.
SELWYN SNOWFIELDS	Lacks the difficulty of other mountains in the park, but has 45 hectares of marked trails.	Beginner runs as well as a few expert runs; draws families.	$61 per day, under 15 $30.50. Lift pass and lesson $78/$52.
THREDBO	Home to Australia's longest slopes. Outdoor activities abound year-round.	12 lifts and a majority of intermediate runs.	$80 per day, under age 15 $44; night ski (Tu and Sa) free with valid lift pass. Lift pass and lesson $107/$72. First timer $80/$58.

PERISHER BLUE

New South Wales's premier ski resort, Perisher Blue (☎ 1300 655 822; www.perisherblue.com.au), is actually four resorts in one. One single lift ticket buys entry to the interconnected slopes of all the resorts, leading down to the **Perisher Valley, Blue Cow, Smiggins,** and **Guthega** alpine villages. Surprisingly, access between the seven peaks is relatively easy. Situated above the natural snow line, with a slightly higher elevation than its competitors, Perisher offers some of the best snow around. **Zali's Run,** named after Zali Steggall, the female Australian World Cup skier, is a popular intermediate slope. **Kamikaze** and **Double Trouble** will put snowbunnies to the test. All **lift tickets** include unlimited use of the Perisher-Blue Cow segment of the Skitube. Purchase tickets at Bullocks Flat or at the **Perisher Blue Jindabyne Ticket Office** in the Nuggets Crossing shopping center. (☎ 6456 1659. Open daily in winter 7am-7pm.) **Murrays** (☎ 13 22 51) offers daytrip skiing and snowboarding packages from Canberra from $119. (Includes return bus, park entry, lift ticket, and equipment hire.)

Perisher is not a full-service village and has neither budget accommodation nor overnight parking available for visitors. To get there by car, follow Kosciuszko Rd. (2WD are required to have snow chains on this road). On busy days, the Perisher Valley day lot fills up quickly and is often entirely inaccessible due to road conditions, but the **Skitube** (☎ 6456 2010) is an all-weather train that makes the 8km journey into the Perisher Valley Alpine Village from **Bullocks Flat,** located along the Alpine Way ($31 return, $18 children). You can either start your adventures in the Village or keep riding the Skitube halfway up the mountain to the Blue Cow terminal. There, chairlifts take more advanced skiers and boarders to the blue and black runs atop **Guthega Peak** and **Mount Blue Cow.** To get to the Skitube station at Bullocks Flat, take **Jindabyne Coaches** (☎ 6457 2117), which runs shuttles from **Jindabyne** (4 per day, $15 return). **Summit Coaches** also runs to the Skitube twice a day (☎ 1800 608 008; $35 return). By **car,** drive along the Alpine Way from Jindabyne until you reach the station; there's plenty of parking. Once at the Perisher Station, follow your nose to the Bullocks Flat platform, on the lower level, to **Lil' Orbits Donuts ❶** (☎ 6457 5655), where you can grab a dozen cinnamon mini-donuts for $3. If donuts aren't enough, **Gingers ❶** (☎ 6457 5558), on the main floor, serves up cheese and tomato melts for $4.

NEW SOUTH WALES

Kosciuszko National Park

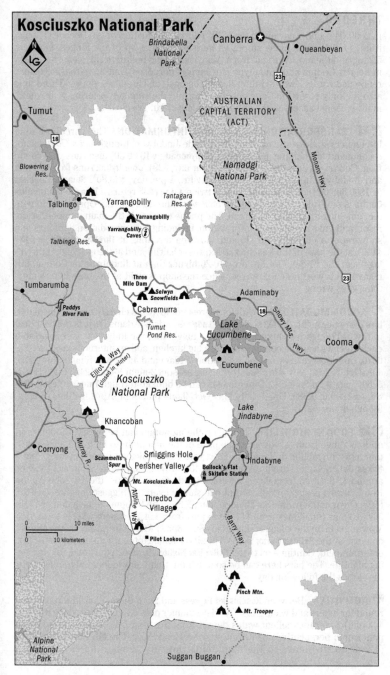

THREDBO

In 2000, Thredbo was named the NSW Tourist Destination of the Decade. Though it does not have as many slopes as Perisher, it does sport the longest slope, at 5.9km, and the most vertical drops. Many skiers and boarders eat, sleep, and party in nearby Cooma and Jindabyne (for budget purposes), but an extensive resort, renowned for its own nightlife, lies at the base of Thredbo's slopes. Thredbo is also the only resort that doesn't shut down in the summer, offering year-round, multi-seasonal access to the natural wonders of Mt. Kosciuszko.

TRANSPORTATION & PRACTICAL INFORMATION. The Thredbo-bound hitchhikers stand at the roundabout outside Jindabyne, though *Let's Go* does not recommend hitchhiking. **McCafferty's/Greyhound** (☎13 20 30) also runs year round from Cooma via Jindabyne (1½hr., 1-2 per day, $29). **Countrylink** runs from Cooma and Jindabyne in the winter months (1½hr., 1 per day, $30.80). **Summit Coaches** (☎1800 608 008) runs from Jindabyne twice a day ($35 return). **Thredbo Information Centre** is on Friday Dr. (☎ 1800 020 589; www.thredbo.com.au. Open daily in winter 8am-6pm, in summer 9am-5pm. The phone number is the main number for the resort and links to extensive information, including accommodation bookings and snow reports.) Charges for ski and snowboard rentals at **Thredbo Sports** (☎6459 4100), at the base of the Kosciuszko Express chairlift, and at the east end of the village near the Friday Flat lift, are $10-20 higher than in Jindabyne or Cooma, but many find it worth the extra cost, since the shop is right at the base in case anything goes wrong.

ACCOMMODATIONS. With its nearest competitors charging hundreds of dollars more per night, the ▓**Thredbo YHA Lodge ❸**, 8 Jack Adams Path, is the best deal in town. Though less luxurious than its neighbors, the lodge has a comfortable chalet feel with ample common space, a big kitchen, and an Internet kiosk. (☎6457 6376; thredbo@yhansw.org.au. Reception 7-10am and 4:30-9pm. Singles June $26; July-Oct. $52-62; Nov.-May $22. During ski season, 2-night F-Sa $124; 5-night Su-Th $260; 7-night Su-Sa $384.) Other lodges can be booked through **Thredbo Resort Centre.** (☎1800 020 589. Open daily May-Oct. 9am-6pm; Sept.-April. 8-10am, 3-9pm, though hours can vary.)

FOOD & NIGHTLIFE. Eating on the mountain can be pricey, though food options range from takeaway at the base of the mountain to high-end, classy restaurants with million dollar views. Start your day or take your lunch break at **Snowflakes Bakery ❶**, in Thredbo Village. (☎6457 7157. Pies, pastries, and sandwiches around $3-6. Open from 6am.) **Alfresco Pizzeria ❸**, just below the Thredbo Alpine Hotel, serves pastas and pizza that will satisfy even the biggest appetite. (☎6457 6327. Open in the winter Su-Th noon-9pm, F-Sa noon-9:30pm; in the summer W-Su 5:30-8:30pm. Small pies from $11, large pies from $14.) A **supermarket** is located in Mowamba Pl. in the village. (Open daily 8am-8pm.) After a tiring day on the slopes, collapse at the **Schuss Barm,** in the Thredbo Alpine Hotel, for an afternoon of live entertainment. Continue on to the **Keller Bar Nightclub,** also in the hotel, for riproaring nightlife. The bars here can be so much fun that many skiers fail to make it to the slopes the following day.

ACTIVITIES. Between **Kosciuszko Express** and **Snow Gums,** chairlifts runs year-round for hikers and wanderers. (All-day summer pass $21. Operates daily 8:30am-4:30pm.) Several excellent walks depart from the top of the chairlift, leading to panoramic perspectives of Kosciuszko National Park. The **Mt. Kosciuszko Walk** (12km return) leads to the mountain's summit, though the easy walk to

Kosciuszko Lookout (4km return) also provides sweeping views. Another option is the **Dead Horse Gap and Thredbo River Track** (10km), which ends in the village. Free maps of all trails are available throughout Thredbo.

A $110 splurge will get you a guided trip to the top of Mt. Kosciuszko at sunrise in the summer. The helpful **Thredbo Activities Booking Desk** (☎ 6459 4100) arranges adventure activities during the summer, including horseriding, abseiling, mountain biking, and rafting, through various other companies. Thredbo is perhaps best known for its steep downhill Mountain Bike tracks, particularly its infamous 4.2km Cannonball Run.

BEYOND THE SKI RESORTS

SELWYN SNOWFIELDS

Along the Snowy Mountains Hwy., halfway between Cooma and Tumut (TOO-mut), the **Selwyn Snowfields** offers beginner and budget skiing. (☎ 6454 9488; www.selwynsnow.com.au.) Primarily a family resort, Selwyn has a small number of trails, minimal amenities, and only a couple advanced runs. Many snowboarders are said to learn on the other mountains, then venture to Selwyn so that they can look good. Elevation at the base is 1492m, and the summit is only 122m higher. When natural snowfall is scarce, Mt. Selwyn relies on its 80% snowmaking coverage. **Lift tickets** are inexpensive. ($61 per day, under 15 $30.50. Over 65 and under 6 free. Lift pass and lesson $78/$52). Forty-five hectares of marked trails and no lift fee make **cross-country skiing** another attractive option. Park entry is $15. (Cross-country skiing is free on all mountains with the park entry fee).

Equipment hire for alpine or cross-country skis and snowboards is pretty reasonable on the mountain. (Skis, boots, and poles half-day $30, full-day $37; snowboards and boots $38/$46.) Skiing or snowboarding can be arranged in a 1½hr. lift and lesson package ($80, under 15 $54; includes full-day lift ticket). **Toboggans** are available for $9 per day ($22.50 will get you ten rides at *Snowtube* or $19.50 covers toboggan and two hour lift ticket at *Toboggan*.) There is no accommodation or Visitors Centre at Mt. Selwyn, but Cooma (see p. 233) is an hour away with both.

YARRANGOBILLY CAVES

Hidden near a valley floor in the beautiful northern scrub wilderness of the Kosciuszko National Park, the Yarrangobilly Caves attract curious visitors and hardcore spelunkers alike. The **Yarrangobilly River,** off the Snowy Mountains Hwy. 77km south of Tumut and 109km northwest of Cooma, runs through a 12km long stretch of limestone, riddled with caves. The caves are a well-signposted 6½km from the highway, downhill on a windy unsealed road. There is a $3 per car site fee for the Yarrangobilly Caves precinct. Only **South Glory Cave** is open for a **self-guided tour** (45min.), but you'll need a token from the Visitors Centre to explore beyond the unusual "glory arch" entrance. (Open daily 9:30am-4:30pm. $9, children $5.50, families $22.) The remaining caves are open to **guided tours.** (1-1½hr. daily 11am, 1, and 3pm; other times with advance scheduling. $11, children $8, families $33.) **Jill-abenan Cave** is the only **wheelchair-accessible** cave. Its stalactites and stalagmites amid crystal-lined nooks are spectacular. **Jersey Cave** and **North Glory Cave** contain equally stellar sights. After wandering around underground, head to the surface and try a short bushwalk on a maintained trail, or take a load off in the 27°C (81°F) **thermal pools** near the river, a 700m steep downhill walk from the carpark (free). The **NPWS Visitors Centre** at the site is an essential first stop. (☎ 6454 9597. Open daily 9:30am-5pm. $3 car site fee.)

RIVERINA

Dry, brown, and mostly flat, the Riverina's terrain is not naturally suited for farming. Heavy irrigation, however, has turned the land into a fertile plain. Two rivers supply water to the region: the Murrumbidgee, which starts as a trickle in the Snowy Mountains, and the Murray. While the area is not a prime sightseeing destination, the Riverina attracts many budget travelers seeking seasonal farm or fruit-picking work (see **Alternatives to Tourism,** p. 62) or those looking to experience some authentic small-town Australian charm.

ALBURY   ☎02

Spanning the Murray River, which marks the border between New South Wales and Victoria, the Albury-Wodonga metropolitan area (pop. 90,000) belongs to both states. Split by the Hume Hwy., the town breaks the transit between Sydney and Melbourne and provides an excellent base for daytrips to nearby wineries, alpine retreats, and the neighboring Riverina. The preponderance of quality budget accommodations and cheap eats makes Albury the most backpacker-friendly place to stop along the Hume, and the small town is just large enough to house a surprisingly comprehensive array of shops and services.

▐▆ TRANSPORTATION

Trains: Countrylink Travel Centre, in the railway station, books Countrylink and V/Line transport. (☎6041 9555. Open M-F 9am-5pm.) **Countrylink** (☎13 22 32) trains run to: **Goulburn** (5hr., 2 per day, $66); **Melbourne** (3hr., 2 per day, $56.10); **Sydney** (7½hr., 2 per day, $85.80); **Wagga Wagga** (1¼hr., 2 per day, $22); **Wangaratta** (45min., 2 per day, $13.20); and **Yass** (4hr., 2 per day, $47.30).

Buses: V/Line (☎13 61 96) services destinations in Victoria far more frequently and cheaply; they run buses to: **Echuca** (3-4hr., 1-2 per day, $23.70); **Melbourne** (3-3½hr., 4-6 per day, $44); **Mildura** (10hr.; M, W, Th, Sa mornings; $62); **Wangaratta** (45min., 4-6 per day, $11); **Rutherglen** (40min.; M, W, Th, Sa mornings; $7); and **Swan Hill** (5½-7hr., 1-2 per day, $39.10). **McCafferty's/Greyhound** (☎13 20 30) runs from the corner of Ebden St. and Wodonga Pl. to: **Adelaide** (16½hr., 3 per day, $118); **Brisbane** (26½hr., 5 per day, $141); **Canberra** (5hr., 4 per day, $34); **Melbourne** (4½hr., 5 per day, $41); **Sydney** (9½hr., 5 per day, $48); and **Wangaratta** (45min., 2 per day, $24).

▟█ ▐ ORIENTATION & PRACTICAL INFORMATION

The **Hume Highway** (Hwy. 31) from Sydney enters Albury from the northeast, runs through town, and then turns sharply west to bypass Wodonga. The **Murray Valley Highway** (Hwy. 16) runs along the Victorian side and enters Wodonga from the southeast, running through town before uniting with the Hume Hwy. Along the river on the New South Wales side, the **Riverina Highway** (Hwy. 58) runs west to Corowa. Albury's main street, **Dean Street,** runs east to west from the railroad tracks and is crossed by (east to west) **Young,** Macauley, David, Olive, Kiewa, and Townsend St. **Smollett Street** runs parallel to Dean St. one block south.

Tourist Office: Gateway Visitors Information Centre (☎1300 796 222; fax 6051 3759) is located in the Gateway Village between Albury and Wodonga, just south of the Murray on the Hume Hwy. A bus goes back and forth between Albury (Dean St.) and Wodonga (High St.), passing by the info center every 30min. Open daily 9am-5pm.

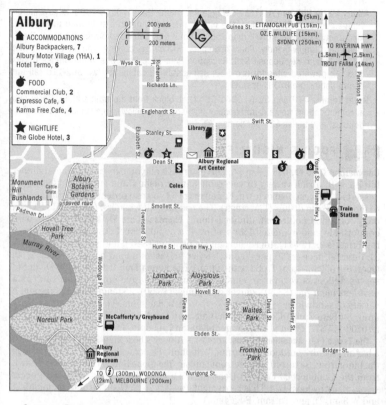

Albury

↟ ACCOMMODATIONS
Albury Backpackers, **7**
Albury Motor Village (YHA), **1**
Hotel Termo, **6**

🍴 FOOD
Commercial Club, **2**
Expresso Cafe, **5**
Karma Free Cafe, **4**

★ NIGHTLIFE
The Globe Hotel, **3**

Currency Exchange: Several banks and 24hr. **ATMs** line Dean St. Bank hours M-Th 9:30am-4pm and F 9:30am-5pm.

Police: 539-543 Olive St. (☎6023 9299), near Swift St.

Internet Access: Albury City Library (☎6041 6633), in the city block behind the Regional Art Centre, has 2 terminals. Free for research, but email costs $2.75 per 30min. Book ahead. Open M-F 9am-7pm, Sa 9am-2pm. **Cyberheaven** (☎6023 4320), across from the post office on Kiewa St., has more terminals. ($5.50 per 30min., $8.80 per hr. Open M-F 9am-6pm, Sa 10am-2pm.)

Post Office: (☎6051 3633), at the corner of Dean and Kiewa St. Open M-F 9am-5pm. Poste Restante. **Postal Code:** 2640.

🏠 ACCOMMODATIONS

🏨 Albury Backpackers, 452 David St. (☎6041 1822; www.alburybackpackers.com.au). Just south of Smollett St. Recently renovated, this comfy hostel has laundry facilities, kitchen, dining hut, and mosaic-tiled hall bath. Laid-back travelers join town pub crawls, varied regional daytrips, and renowned canoe trips run by the affable owner. Linens included. Internet $5 per hr. Check-out 11am. Dorms $17; twins and doubles $38. Wheelchair-accessible. ❷

Albury Motor Village (YHA), 372 Wagga Rd., Hume Hwy (☎6040 2999; albury@motor-village.com.au), 5km north of the city center in Lavington just beyond Kaylock Rd. McCafferty's/Greyhound will drop you off here; $10 cab ride from train station. Quiet, clean, and family-friendly. Pool, kitchenette, TV lounge, parking, and laundry. Internet $2 per 20min. Key deposit $10. Reception 8am-8pm. Book ahead in summer. Dorms $18.50; powered sites for two $20; self-contained cabins for two $62-110 (all but deluxe cabins are BYO linens). ❷

Hotel Termo, 47 Dean St. (☎6041 3544), 1 block from the train station. Basic pub accommodations upstairs and popular nightspot (see below). Linens included. Singles, doubles, and triples $22 per person. ❷

🏠🍴 FOOD & NIGHTLIFE

Commercial Club ❷, 618 Dean St., serves an $11 all-you-can-eat lunch and dinner buffett with a rich variety of vegetables, meat dishes, and surprisingly gourmet desserts—the best deal in town. For an extra $2 you can order a plate from a menu of more upscale dishes (like steak). The casino is downstairs. (☎6021 1133. Open daily for lunch noon-2pm, dinner 6-9pm.) **Expresso Cafe ❶,** 449c Dean St., with comfortable indoor and outdoor seating, is a popular local destination that serves full breakfasts ($9-11), focaccias and sandwiches ($4-7), and great coffee ($2.50-3). Internet access ($6 per 30min., $8 per hr.) is an added bonus. (☎6023 4730. Open Su-W 9am-4pm, Th-Sa 9am-10pm.) The **Karma Free Cafe ❶,** 440b Dean St., serves delicious vegetarian cuisine, including creative concoctions such as a meatless meat pie ($3.50), ginger dumplings ($3.50), a steam bun ($2.50), and a variety of sandwiches. (☎6041 1856. Open M-W 8am-5pm, Th 8am-7:30pm, F 8am-5pm, Sa 8am-2pm.) Coles **supermarket** is in the West End Plaza on Kiewa St. (☎0260 415 377. Open M-Sa 7am-midnight, Su 7am-8pm.)

   The Termo (see **Accommodations,** above) is Albury's best nightspot. It houses both a bar and an airy outdoor biergarten. W hiphop, Th acoustic guitar, F live music in the biergarten, Sa top 40, Su electronic music. **The Globe Hotel** is a few streets down from the Commercial Club on Dean St. It's a good live music venue with occasional visits by local DJs; Th is retro night. (☎6021 2622. Open Su until midnight, M and W 3am, Tu and Th 1am, F-Sa 4am.)

👁🏔 SIGHTS & OUTDOOR ACTIVITIES

The ⬛**Murray River** is by far the main attraction in Albury, and on hot summer afternoons, most of the town takes to the water. The river lazily meanders its way through cattle pastureland and green wooded terrain alike. David, the owner of the Albury Backpackers (see **Accommodations,** above) runs not-to-be-missed canoe and kayak trips (half-day Murray trip $20, 1-day $26, 2-day $59). No stop in Albury is complete without at least a jump in the river. A good spot for a dip is just south of the botanic gardens in Noreuil Park, though it is popular among families with young (and often loud) children.

   On Wodonga Pl. between Smollett and Dean St., the **Albury Botanic Gardens** (☎6023 8241) have diverse arboreal displays and plenty of grassy picnic space. To take in a sweeping view of the region, climb to the top of the **Monument Hill Bushlands** and gaze out onto Albury-Wodonga from the base of the Art Deco obelisk Albury War Memorial. Walk uphill from Dean St. or follow the street up and around the back of the hill. On the Riverina Hwy. 14km east of Albury, the **Hume Weir Trout Farm** raises rainbow trout for commercial and recreational purposes. You can catch trout (rod and bait free, fish caught $10 per kg) and sample smoked trout. (☎6026 4334. Open daily 9am-5pm. $6, students $5, children $3.50.)

⚡ DAYTRIP: ETTAMOGAH PUB

Just 15km north of Albury along the Hume Hwy., the goofy humor of the **Ettamogah Pub** caters to gawking tourists by satirizing and stereotyping all things Aussie. The late cartoonist Ken Maynard had been drawing the place for the *Australia Post* for years before someone decided to actually construct it. The amusement-park-style village is composed of eye-popping, off-kilter buildings decorated with a running stream of witticisms. The centerpiece is the hilariously constructed and fully operational Ettamogah Pub itself, capped with a vintage Fosters beer truck on the roof and a crashed airplane next door. (☎ 6026 2366. Pub open M-Th 10am-9pm, F-Su 10:30am-10pm. Bistro open F-Sa 6-9pm.) The **Ettamogah Winery** predates the pub but is now part of the complex, and features free tastings and wine sales. Next door is a restaurant and souvenir shop. (Open daily 9am-4pm.) There's no admission to tour the site, and signs will clearly direct you from the highway.

oz.e.wildlife, formerly the Ettamogah Sanctuary, allows visitors to hand-feed kangaroos and wallabies and get close to penguins and koalas. A parade (daily 11am, 1, and 3pm) will ensure you get your money's worth. (☎ 6040 3677. Open daily 9am-5pm. $10, concessions $8, children $5, families $25, under 4 free.)

WAGGA WAGGA   ☎ 02

The largest inland city in New South Wales, Wagga Wagga (WAH-guh; pop. 58,000) derives its name from the local Aboriginal tribe, for whom repetition implied plurality. *Wagga* means crow; hence, *wagga wagga* means a place of many crows.

Baylis Street is the town's main drag, becoming **Fitzmaurice Street** once it crosses the bridge over Wollundry Lagoon. The bus stop is at the railway station, on the south end of Station Pl. **Countrylink** (☎ 13 22 32) and **Fearnes Coaches** (☎ 1800 029 918 or 6921 2316) operates **bus** and **train** service to Gundagai (1hr., 2 per day, $27); and Sydney (8½hr., 2 per day, $48). The **Visitors Centre** is at 183 Tarcutta St. (☎ 6926 9621; www.tourismwaggawagga.com.au. Open daily 8:30am-5pm.) A **post office** is in the Wagga Wagga Marketplace on Forsyth St. and Baylis St. (Open M-F 8:30am-5pm.) **Postal Code:** 2650.

For inexpensive accommodations, try the **Wagga Wagga Guesthouse ❷,** 149 Gurwood St., a popular spot with seasonal workers because of its amenities: kitchen, TV, laundry, lockers, Internet, and wheelchair accessibility. (☎ 6931 8702. Singles and dorm beds $25; doubles $45; weekly rates available.) **Billy's Cafe ❶,** 35 Gurwood St., serves popular breakfasts for $10 and under. (Open daily 6am-3:30pm). For good, cheap food, try the **Bridge Tavern ❶,** 188 Fitzmaurice St. (Mains $6.60-11.95. ☎ 6921 2222. Open M-Sa 10am-late, Su 10am-10pm). A Woolworths **supermarket** is directly across from Billy's Cafe on Gurwood St. (Open daily 7am-10pm.)

The attractive **Botanic Gardens,** with an entrance near the intersection of Urana and Macleay St., are arranged across nine hectares. Pathways wind pleasantly among the trees. (☎ 6925 4065. Open daily 7:30am-dusk. Discovery Centre with information about local flora and fauna open Su and Th-Sa 10am-4pm. Free.) The **Wiradjuri Walking Track** meanders for 30km, covering many of the town's natural highlights. The trail runs through the Botanic Gardens, along the Murrumidgee River, and past Lake Albert to many panoramic views of the region.

For fun on the river, check out **Murrumbidgee River Cruises** (☎ 6925 8700). Cruises take passengers to see nearby islands and inform them of the history and natural wonders of the region. (Depart M and W-Su 2pm. Adults $12, concessions $10, children $6. Call ahead to book.) You can hire canoes from **Action Outdoors,** 140 Hammond Ave. (☎ 6931 8681. One-day canoe hire $40; pick-up and drop-off programs available for multi-day hire. Open M-F 9:30am-5:30pm, Sa 9am-1pm.) In the summertime, **Wagga Beach,** at Cabriata Park, is a popular spot.

CENTRAL WEST

The cities and towns of the Central West lie between the rugged plateaus of the Blue Mountains and the stark dryness of outback New South Wales. Surrounded by miles of rolling hills and abundant agriculture, most are regarded as stopovers between grander destinations. For the traveler who's looking to stray from the typical tourist routes, however, these towns conjure a charm all their own. Even with a short stay in this region, you'll notice an extraordinary degree of hospitality from locals who have chosen to live a less hectic life.

BATHURST   ☎02

Bathurst (pop. 30,900) features wide avenues and large, ornate lampposts, suggesting it was once slated for greatness. However, it is actually a formerly unadorned route on the southwest corner of town that has brought the city notoriety. Originally built in 1938 as a scenic drive, the 6km loop road up Mt. Panorama and back down doubles as a public road and the track for the annual touring car races for **V-8 Supercars** and the **24-hour Race,** held in early October and mid-November, respectively. During these events, over 150,000 people descend upon the usually low-profile town.

▐▌ TRANSPORTATION & PRACTICAL INFORMATION. Bathurst is 101km

west of Katoomba on the Great Western Hwy. **Trains** and **buses** leave the **Railway Station** at the corner of Keppel and Havannah St. **Countrylink** (☎ 13 22 32) goes to: Cowra (1½hr.; M, W, F-Sa 1 per day; $19); Dubbo (3hr., 3 per day, $35); Forbes and Parkes (3½hr., M-Sa 1 per day, $33); Katoomba (2hr., 2 per day, $19); Lithgow (1-1¼hr., 3-7 per day, $13); Orange (1hr., 1-2 per day, $24); Parramatta and Penrith (3hr., 2 per day, $28-31); and Sydney (4hr., 2 per day, $38). **McCafferty's/Greyhound** (☎ 13 14 99 or 13 20 30) runs to: Dubbo (3hr., 1 per day M, W, F $50); Katoomba (2hr., 1 per day Tu, Th, Sa $32); Lithgow (1hr., 1 per day Tu and Th-F $32); Parramatta (2½hr., 1 per day Tu-W, F $32); Penrith (3½hr., 1 per day Tu, Th, Sa, $32); and Sydney (3½-4½hr., M, W, F, 1 per day, $32). The **Bathurst Visitor Information Centre,** on Kendall Ave., has brochures, advice, and free maps. (☎6332 1444 or 1800 681 000. Open daily 9am-5pm.) The **police station** (☎6332 8699) is on Rankin St., between Russell and Howick St. **ATMs** abound on William and Howick St. **Internet** is to be found at the **library** at 70-78 Keppel St. (☎6332 2130. Open M-F 10am-6pm, Sa 10am-5pm, Su 11am-2pm.) And the **post office,** 230 Howick St., is between George and William St. (☎6339 4813. Open M-F 9am-5pm.) **Postal Code:** 2795.

▐▌ ACCOMMODATIONS & FOOD. Rates for all accommodations skyrocket

during the races faster than the cars themselves. Bathurst has a few pubstays downtown; the nicest and cheapest (a refreshingly uncommon combination when it comes to pubstays) is by far the backpacker-friendly **Commercial Hotel ❶,** 135 George St., which also serves up cheap traditional Aussie pub food ($5-12) in its **restaurant ❶** downstairs. (☎6331 2712; www.commercialhotel.com.au; single $25, double $44.) Outside of town, the **Bathurst Explorer's Hotel ❹,** 357 Stewart St., offers rooms with TV, fridge, heat, A/C, and a $12 dinner coupon for area restaurants. (☎6331 2966 or 1800 047 907. Reception 7am-9pm. Singles $62; twins and doubles $74, extra person $10. $6 weekend surcharge.) **East's Bathurst Holiday Park ❷** is on Sydney Rd. (the Great Western Hwy.), 4km east of town. (☎6331 8286 or 1800 669 911. Showers, laundry, BBQ, and TV room. Reception 8am-6pm. Sites for 2 $18, powered $21; cabins $53, ensuite $65-105.) **Ziegler's Cafe ❷,** 52 Keppel St., has a wide range of healthy salads and grilled veggie dishes and less healthy burgers.

(☎6332 1565. Lunches $10-20, dinners $12-22. BYO. Open M-F 10am-9pm, Sa 9am-9pm, Su 10am-3pm.) A Coles **supermarket** is at 47 William St. (☎6332 9566. Open M-Sa 6am-midnight, Su 8am-8pm.)

⬛ **SIGHTS.** A trip to Bathurst would be incomplete without a spin round the ▓**Mt. Panorama circuit head,** southwest on William St. until it becomes Panorama Ave. As you twist your way up and down the steep hills, you'll gain an appreciation for the pros who do it in excess of 200kph. Don't let the banner ads and tire piles seduce you; local police patrol the area frequently, looking for drivers who edge above the 60kph speed limit. The recently expanded **National Motor Racing Museum,** near the starting line, keeps the thrill of the race alive year-round. (☎6332 1872. Open daily 9am-4:30pm. $7, concessions $5, families $16.) To slow the pace down take the **self-drive heritage tour;** alternatively (if you did get a ticket and your car was impounded), there's a **historic walking tour,** as well. Pick up the information for both from the Visitor Centre.

If you're not in for the long haul but still want to feel a bit cultured, heritage highlights include: The **courthouse** on Russell St., which was considered so grand when it was built in 1880 that residents of the town thought there must have been a mistake when it was put in Bathurst. Rumors circulated that the building had been meant for a more prominent colony in India or Africa, as the massive railings encircling the building would easily have kept elephants out. (Open M-F 9am-5pm, but hours vary when in use.) The **Chifley Home,** 10 Busby St. (☎6332 1444), abode of Australia's prime minister from 1945-49, Ben Chifley, is so stark, simple, and unpretentious that it serves as a fading glimmer of hope in the potential humility of politicians. (Open M, Sa-Su 11am-3pm; $5, children $3.) Don't miss the **Abercrombie Caves,** part of the Jenolan Caves Trust, 70km south of Bathurst via Trunkey Creek. The majestic Grand Arch is the largest limestone archway in the southern hemisphere. (☎6368 8603; www.jenolancaves.org.au. Open daily 9am-4pm. Self-guided archway tour $12, children $8. Guided tour on weekends 2pm; $15, children $10.) **Fossicking** is popular in the area and its surrounds. **Bathurst Goldfields,** 428 Conrod Straight on Mt. Panorama is a reconstructed mining area that allows you to try your hand panning for gold as the company pans for the tourist dollar (☎6332 2022; $10.20). For something more authentic, head out to surrounding villages such as **Sofala** (45km north of Bathurst), one of Australia's oldest surviving gold mining towns, eerily preserved from its olden days and still in full operation.

MUDGEE ☎02

A land of wine and honey cradled in the foothills of the Great Dividing Range, Mudgee (from the Aboriginal for "nest in the hills"; pop. 18,000) has over 20 vineyards and a lot of small town charm, but not much else to offer the sight-seeing set. Still, the locals who love it proudly proclaim that Mudgee is "tasting better each year," a claim confirmed by even a short, tipsy visit.

Mudgee is a 3½hr. drive from Sydney on Hwy. 86 (Castlereagh Hwy.), between Lithgow (159km) and Dubbo (109km). **Countrylink** (☎13 22 32) connects by **coach** to Mudgee and runs one to two times per day to: Coonabarabran (3hr., $33); Lithgow (2½hr., $24); and Sydney (5hr., $49). Book at **Harvey World Travel,** in National Centre on Church St, across from the Bi-Lo supermarket. (☎6372 6077. Open M-F 8:30am-5:30pm, Sa 8:30am-noon.) The **railway station** is on the corner of Church and Inglis St. (and also houses a small gallery of local art), but Countrylink coaches stop at the Visitors Centre. For **taxis,** call ☎13 10 08. The **Mudgee Visitors Centre,** 84 Market St., is armed with maps and advice. (☎6372 1020 or 1800 816 304. Open M-F 9am-5pm, Sa 9am-3:30pm, Su 9:30am-2pm.) The **NPWS office,** 160 Church St., administers the northwest section of Wollemi National Park (☎6372 7199;

mudgee@npws.nsw.gov.au. Open M-F 9am-5pm. See p. 164.) **Police** (☎6372 8599) are located at 90-94 Market St. **Banks** and **ATMs** are to be found on Church St. And **free Internet** is available at the **library** at 64 Market St. (☎6374 0441; Open M-F 10am-6pm, Sa 9:30am-12:30pm, preferable to book in advance). A **post office** (☎6378 2021) is on the corner of Market and Perry St. **Postal Code:** 2850.

Pubstay accommodations are the most readily available in town. **The Woolpack Hotel ❷,** 67 Market St. is down the street from the Visitors Centre, near the corner of Church St. A friendly and colorful cast of characters frequents the downstairs pub. (☎6372 1908. Reception 7am-midnight at bar. Singles and doubles $20 per person; $25 includes dinner). The **Mudgee Riverside Caravan and Tourist Park ❶,** 22 Short St., behind the Visitors Centre, has showers and laundry. (☎6372 2531; www.mudgeeriverside.com.au. Linen $10. Laundry $2. Reception 8am-8pm. Sites for 2 $16, powered $18; ensuite cabins with A/C $55-67.)

🍴**Red Heifer Grill and Carvery ❸,** 1 Church St., inside the Lawson Park Hotel, is a great spot for good grub—grill your own steak dinner ($16-18) and enjoy it with a bottle of local wine (from $10). Mains (also $16-18) come with all-you-can-eat salad bar for only $5 extra. (☎6372 2183. Open daily for lunch noon-2:30pm, dinner 6-9pm.) Stop in at **Melon Tree ❶,** 75 Church St. (☎6372 4005), to grab a gourmet sandwich snack ($4.50-6) or pick up a picnic pack for your day at the wineries. Brekkie for under $10 might also help to pad your stomach before you set out. (Open M-F 8am-6pm, Sa 8am-close. Cash only.) A Bi-Lo **supermarket** is on Church St., in the Town Centre shopping plaza. (Open M-Sa 7am-10pm, Su 8am-8pm).

Mudgee's selling point is its victual offerings, ranging from small, communal vineyards to large, self-sufficient **wineries.** There are many vineyards in the area; consult the tourist office for extensive information on which will most suit your palate. Travelers passing through in September will find the streets hopping with the **Mudgee Wine Festival,** but your glass can be filled with Mudgee's renowned reds year round. If you want to do the wine-tasting circuit but also wish to avoid running afoul of stringent drink-driving laws, try **Mudgee Transit Wine Tours** (☎6372 0091 or 1800 779 997; half-day leaves at 1pm $30, full-day leaves at 10am $55.) **Biking** is also an option, and **Mudgee Riverside Caravan and Tourist Park** has rentals. ($5 per hr., $15 per half-day, $20 per full-day.) Picking vineyards might be hard with over 20 to choose from, but a few stand out. **Poet's Corner Wine Cellar,** a conglomeration of Craigmoor, Montrose, and Poet's Corner labels, is located at the home of Mudgee's oldest vineyard (circa 1858) and has been making tawny Rummy Port for 70 years. A classy restaurant is also on the premises. To reach the winery, bike or drive 7km northwest of Mudgee on Henry Lawson Dr., then turn onto Craigmoor Rd. (☎6372 2208. Open M-Sa 10am-4:30pm, Su 10am-4pm.) **Huntington Estate Wines,** 8km from town past the airport on Cassilis Rd., has an array of reds for sample on a free self-guided tour. (☎6373 3825. Open M-F 9am-5pm, Sa 10am-5pm, Su 10am-3pm.) **Botobolar,** 89 Botobolar Rd., 16km northeast of town, is Australia's oldest organic vineyard and offers daily tastings. (☎6373 3840. Open M-Sa 10am-5pm, Su 10am-3pm.)

DUBBO ☎02

The hub of the Central West region, Dubbo is a bustling, blue-collar service city. In the midst of the populous town's buzzing center, it's possible to forget how close you are to the Outback, but a drive after dark in any direction (not recommended) will reveal just how isolated you really are. Dubbo is sprinkled with things to do and places to see, but the city's headline attraction is the Western Plains Zoo. No visit to the central west would be complete without a stop at this amazingly well-developed massive menagerie.

TRANSPORTATION. Countrylink (☎ 13 22 32) **trains** and **buses** depart from the **railway station** on Talbragar St. to: Albury (7hr.; Su, Tu, Th 1 per day; $71.50); Broken Hill (8½hr, 1 per day, $86); Forbes (2hr.; Su, Tu, Th 1 per day, $19); Melbourne (10½hr.; Su, Tu, and Th 1 per day, $98); Orange (2hr., 1 per day, $22); Sydney (7-11hr., 1 per day, $66); and Wagga Wagga (5½hr.; Su, Tu, Th 1 per day, $47.30). The Shell Station at the intersection of the Newell and Mitchell Hwy. is the drop-off point for coaches. **McCafferty's/Greyhound** (☎ 13 14 99 or 13 20 30) services: Adelaide (15hr., 2 per day, $119); Brisbane (11½-14hr., 3 per day, $113-159 depending on route); Broken Hill (8hr., 1 per day, $119); Coonabarabran (2hr., 2 per day, $47); Bathurst (2¾hr, 1 per day, $50); and Melbourne (11½-13hr., 3 per day, $119-178 depending on route). All tickets can be booked online, over the phone, or at the railway station. (Open M-F 8am-5pm, Sa-Su 8-9:30am and 10:30am-2pm.) **Rendell Coaches** (☎ 1800 023 328 or 6884 4199) runs to and from Sydney daily except Tu, departing Dubbo at 7am (6½hr, $50). Drop-off in Dubbo frequently occurs in the wee hours of the morning as coaches ramble on to farther destinations. To reach accommodations once in Dubbo, rely on 24hr. **taxis** (☎ 6882 1911 or 13 10 08). **Darrell Wheeler Cycles**, 25 Bultje St., hires bikes for $15 per day. (☎ 6882 9899. Open M-F 8:30am-5:30pm, Sa 8:30am-1pm.) Bike trails cross town, run alongside the Macquarie River, and head out to the zoo.

ORIENTATION & PRACTICAL INFORMATION. Dubbo sits at the intersection of the **Newell Highway,** which runs between Melbourne (856km) and Brisbane (895km), and the **Mitchell Highway,** which leads from Sydney (414km) to points west. The town's sprawling layout could make life difficult for the carless, although major sights are clustered around the zoo or the town center. **Talbragar Street** runs east-west, parallel to the two major highways that sandwich the town. The intersection of Talbragar and **Macquarie Street** marks the town center, with most of the action, including **banks, ATMs,** and **pharmacies** on Macquarie St.

The **Dubbo Visitors Centre,** on the corner of Erskine and Macquarie St. (Newell Hwy.) in the northwest corner of the small downtown area, has maps of biking trails and books river cruises. (☎ 6884 1422; www.dubbotourism.com.au. Open daily 9am-5pm.) The **police station** (☎ 6881 3222) is on Brisbane St. across from the Grape Vine Cafe. Find **Internet** at the **Dubbo Regional Library,** on the southwest corner of Macquarie and Talbragar St. ($5.50 per hr.; open M-F 10am-6pm, Sa 10am-3pm, Su noon-4pm), or the **Grape Vine** cafe ($2.50 per 30min.; see **Food,** p. 249). A Woolworths **supermarket** (open M-Sa 7am-10pm, Su 8am-8pm) is in the **Riverdale Shopping Centre.** The **post office** is on Talbragar St. between Brisbane and Macquarie St. **Postal Code:** 2830.

ACCOMMODATIONS & FOOD. Plenty of hotels cluster near and around Talbragar St. in the city center, with singles from $20; motels in the area generally run $50-80 for a single and $60-90 for a double. The cheapest beds are at the **Dubbo YHA Hostel ❷,** 87 Brisbane St., near the corner of the Newell Hwy. The talking pet cockatoo and verandas off every room add flavor to the peaceful hostel, as do nightly fire-side gatherings to watch sports on the telly and occasional trips to the owners' farm. (☎ 6882 0922; yhadubbo@highway.com.au. Washer $3, no dryer. Internet $3 per hr. Bikes $7 per day. Reception 7:30am-10:30pm. Dorms $22, YHA $20; twins and doubles $42/$40; family rooms $53.) The upscale **Amaroo Hotel ❸,** 83 Macquarie St., is in the middle of town. (☎ 6882 3533. Breakfast included. Singles $59; doubles $80.) The **Dubbo City Caravan Park ❶,** on Whylandra St. just before it becomes the Newell Hwy., has beautiful shaded sites overlooking the Macquarie River. (☎ 6882 4820; dccp@dubbo.nsw.gov.au. Bikes $15 per day, $10 per half-day. Linen $12. Laundry $3. Reception 7:30am-7:30pm. Check-in 1pm. Curfew 10pm.

Sites from $14, powered $19; caravans $29; cabins from $43, ensuite $50. $10 surcharge on cabins during school holidays.)

Sandwich shops and bakeries are plentiful in the city center, but cheap restaurants are few and far between. For the best coffee concoctions, pastries, and light meals, seek out the **Grape Vine Cafe ❶**, 144 Brisbane St. (☎6884 7354. Lunch $8-15. Internet $2.50 per 30min. Open M-Sa 8:30am-10:30pm, Su 9am-4pm.) For more exotic flavorings, **Darbar ❶**, 215 Macquarie St. (☎6884 4338), does tasty traditional Indian dishes, with mains around $14.50. (Open nightly 6-10pm.) There are **local markets** at the showground on Wingewarra St. every 2nd and 4th Saturday of the month. (Open 2nd Sa 9am-1pm with crafts, produce, and bric-a-brac; 4th Sa 8am-noon with fresh produce, cheese, and flowers.)

◪ SIGHTS. Dubbo's premier tourist attraction is the **◪Western Plains Zoo,** on Obley Rd., 4km south of the city center off the Newell Hwy. In addition to Australian native species, the zoo houses Bengal tigers, black rhinoceroses, and Australia's only **African elephants;** exhibits are arranged by continent around a paved track suitable for driving or biking with BBQ and picnic areas along the way. Many of the animals wander unrestrained through loose enclosures. Don't miss the nursery for injured and orphaned animals; the sight of infant joeys snuggling together under baby blankets is priceless. On weekends, and Wednesdays and Fridays during school holidays, 6:45am zoo walks provide a behind-the-scenes look at the animals for an additional $3. (☎6882 5888; www.zoo.nsw.gov.au. Open daily 9am-5pm; last entry 3:30pm. 2-day pass $25, students $17.50, ages 4-16 $13.50. 4hr. bike rental $13 plus license or credit card imprint deposit.) **Macquarie River Cruises** offers trips on one of the biggest riverboats in outback New South Wales. Some trips stop for tea or lunch at Dundullimal Homestead (the oldest timber slab house in Australia, built in 1842) before a hay ride and trip down the river. (One-hour cruise leaves 1:30pm: $16, ages 4-16 $8. Two-hour lunch cruise leaves 12:45pm: $25, ages 4-16 $12.50. Book through the Visitors Centre.) Still, the river is as easily seen from the **walking and bike tracks** which run alongside it. **Dundullimal Homestead,** on Obley Rd., two minutes past the zoo, can be visited on its own without cruise. The property is part of Australia's National Trust and features period furniture. (☎6884 9984. $6, children $3, family $15.)

COONABARABRAN   ☎02

From the salt of the earth to the star speckled sky (which, on a clear night, looks as though salt had been spilled across it), Coonabarabran (coon-a-BAR-a-bran, Aboriginal for "an inquisitive person"; pop. 3000) embodies all that is good about laid-back, friendly, and slightly isolated country life. Thanks to its relative proximity to major urban areas (Sydney and Brisbane are only a day's drive) and plethora of clear night skies, the town draws countless visitors and proudly sports the title "Astronomy Capital of Australia."

◪◪ TRANSPORTATION & PRACTICAL INFORMATION. Coonabarabran lies 159km northeast of Dubbo on the Newell Hwy., and 120km south of Narrabri. It's accessible from the northeast through Gunnedah (105km away) on the Oxley Hwy., which joins the Newell and enters from the north. **Countrylink** (☎13 22 32) runs **buses** from the Visitors Centre to Lithgow, which connect with the train to Sydney (8hr., Su-F 1 per day, $81.40). **McCafferty's/Greyhound** (☎13 14 99 or 13 20 30) leave from the Caltex Service Station outside of town, once a day to Melbourne (12-15 hr., $121) and Brisbane (9hr., $101). **Harvey World Travel,** 79 John St. (☎6842 1566), makes transport bookings for a $5 service fee.

The main drag is **John Street** (the Newell Hwy.), home to several motels and crossed by **Dalgarno, Cassilis,** and **Edwards Street.** Warrumbungle National Park and the observatories are both west of town. The **Visitors Centre** is at the south end of town on the Newell Hwy. It has a display on Australian megafauna, including the skeleton of a 33,000-year-old giant diprotodon, the largest marsupial ever to roam the earth. (☎6842 1441 or 1800 242 881; www.coonabarabran.com. Open daily 9am-5pm.) Other services include: **NPWS office,** 30 Timor St. (☎6842 1311), with info on Warrumbungle National Park; 24hr. **ATMs** on John St.; **Internet** at the **library** on John St. (☎6842 1093) and across the street at the **Community Technology Center,** 71 John St. (☎6842 2920), both open M-F 9am-5pm and both for $5.50 per hr, so take your pick; and a **post office,** 71a John St., in the center of town. (☎6842 1198. Open M-F 9am-5pm.) **Postal Code:** 2357.

⌂◖ ACCOMMODATIONS & FOOD. Book ahead for accommodations during school holidays. The **Imperial Hotel ❷,** at the corner of John and Dalgarno St., is over a pub with thin walls and floors through which the cries (and crying) of pokies-players downstairs can be heard. (☎6842 1023. Reception 8:30am-11pm. Check-out 9am. Singles $22, with breakfast $29; ensuite doubles $41/$55; extra person in family room $12, in unit $15.) The other two pubstays are smaller but similar. Slightly more expensive motel options line John St. At **John Oxley Caravan Park ❶,** 1km north of town on the Oxley Hwy., the affable hosts tend a shop, playground, and gas grill. (☎6842 1635. Reception in summer 8am-8pm; in winter 8am-7pm. Linen $11. Sites for 2 $12, powered $16; on-site vans for 2 $29; ensuite cabins for 2 $43-48; large family ensuite cabins $53-60.) A number of **B&Bs** and **farmstays** are also available in Coonabarabran and within the Warrumbungle area, with singles starting at $60; ask at the Visitors Centre.

The **Golden Sea Dragon Restaurant ❷,** next to the Visitors Centre at 8 John St., features a golden Buddha and instrumental Bette Midler but serves fantastic Chinese fare. (☎6842 2388. 2-course traveler's special $12. Open daily noon-2:30pm; also Sa-Su 5-10 or 11pm.) The **Jolly Cauli Coffee Shop ❶,** 30 John St., has reasonable prices and **Internet.** (☎6842 2021. Open M-F 8am-5pm, Sa 9am-1pm. Sandwiches $6. Devonshire tea (read: tea and scone) $5.80. Internet $6 per hr—no credit cards.) The IGA **supermarket** is on Dalgarno St. (open M-W 8:15am-6:30pm, Th 8:15am-7:30pm, F 8:15am-7pm, Sa 8:15am-4:30pm, Su 8:45am-2pm), as is a new BI-LO (open M-W, F 8am-7pm, Th 8am-9pm, Sa 8am-5pm, Su 9am-5pm).

◐ SIGHTS. The highlight of Coonabarabran is the ▨**Skywatch Night and Day Observatory,** 2km from town on the road to Warrumbungle National Park. The effusive staff guides nightly viewing sessions that clarify the jumbled stars. A loosely astronomically themed mini golf course is also on the premises. (☎6842 3303; www.skywatchobservatory.com. Open daily 2-5pm (except Feb.). Night session daily Nov.-Jan. 9 and 10pm; Feb. 9pm; Mar. 8:30 and 9:30pm; Apr.-Sept. 7 and 8pm; Oct. 7:30 and 8:30pm. Display only or astro golf $8, students and children $6, families $24; display and nightshow $14/$9/$38. Preferable to book in advance, by phone or online.) Australia's largest optical telescope (with a lens 3.9m in diameter) resides at **Siding Spring Observatory,** 28km from Coonabarabran on the road to Warrumbungle National Park, and is recently credited with the discovery of a new extrasolar planet resembling Jupiter. The observatory's Visitors Centre offers an interactive, multimedia window onto the work of the resident astronomers but no public viewing of the night sky. You'll learn about groundbreaking research here, but you'll have more laughs at Skywatch. (☎6842 6211. Special group tours by arrangement. Open daily 9:30am-4pm. $5.50, concessions $3.50.) The impressive **sandstone caves,** hollowed out by wind and water erosion, are within the **Pilliga**

Nature Reserve. They are tricky to locate and are not accessible between September and December due to the protected breeding of an endangered bird species. For the geologically inclined nature enthusiast, however, the Visitors Centre can provide specific directions the rest of the year. If you're carless in Coonabarabran, a new company leads **4WD tours** of the region and its attractions, including the natural wonders of the Warrumbungles. (☎6843 4494 or 0428 599 588; http://insideaustralia.com.au. Half- to extended day tours $70-160, children under 12 $50-110, standby rate $45-100.) **Ukerbarley Tours,** meanwhile, focuses on local Aboriginal history and culture and visits nearby sites of cultural significance. (☎6843 4446; judd@tpg.com.au. Half-day backpacker tours $40 per person, min. 3, max. 10; full-day tours $110 per person, min. 2. No credit cards.)

WARRUMBUNGLE NATIONAL PARK ☎02

At the juncture of the lush east and the barren west, the jagged spires and rambling peaks of the Warrumbungle Mountains are the result of volcanic activity millions of years ago. Softer sandstone worn away under hardened lava rock has left unusual shapes slicing into the sky above the forested hills. Kangaroos and wallabies have long called the area home, while hikers, rock-climbers, and campers have discovered its splendor more recently.

A 75km **scenic drive** (approximately 7km unsealed) branches off from the Newell Hwy. 39km north of Gilgandra and runs through the park, circling back to the highway at Coonabarabran. There is no public transport to the park. The park entry fee can be paid at the **Warrumbungle National Park Visitors Centre,** on the park road 33km west of Coonabarabran. They also have free bush camping and rock climbing permits; climbing is not permitted on Breadknife. (☎6825 4364. Open daily 9am-4pm; outside drop-box for after hours fees. Entry $6 per car; pedestrians free.) The **NPWS** (☎6842 1311) has a district office at 30 Timor St., Coonabarabran.

Of the park's serviced **camping ❶** areas, only four are open to individual travelers. **Camp Blackman** is car-accessible and has toilets, rainwater, showers, and a pay phone (unpowered sites $5 per adult, $3 per child; powered sites $7.50/$4). **Camp Wambelong** and **Guneemooroo** are both car-accessible and have unpowered sites and toilets, but no shower ($5/$3). **Wambelong** is right off the main park road and **Guneemooroo** (place of snakes) is reached by an unsealed road from **Tooraweenah. Camp Pincham** lies a short walk from the nearest carpark and has unpowered sites and toilets, but also no shower ($3/$2). Firewood cannot be collected in the park, so bring your own supplies or pack a fuel stove. Pets are not allowed either. Contact the **Visitors Centre** at the park for information on free bushcamping sites or campsites for large groups.

NARRABRI ☎02

Equidistant from Sydney and Brisbane (560km) and 120km north of Coonabarabran on the Newell Hwy., Narrabri (NEHR-uh-BRYE, meaning "forked waters"; pop. 7900) is a wheat and cotton-growing center that has three major attractions: the six-dish Australia Telescope complex, the brand-new Cotton Centre, and the beautifully rugged scenery of Mt. Kaputar National Park.

▛▞ TRANSPORTATION & PRACTICAL INFORMATION. Countrylink (☎13 22 32) **trains** run to Sydney (8hr., daily 1 per day, $79.20) from the train station at the east end of Bowen St., four blocks from Maitland St. **McCafferty's/Greyhound** (☎13 14 99 or 13 20 30) **buses** depart from the corner of Bowen and Maitland St., two blocks south of the **post office.** They leave for Brisbane (8hr., 1 per day, $71) and Melbourne (14-16hr., 1 per day, $136) via Coonabarabran (1¼hr., 2 per day, $55) and Dubbo (4hr., 2 per day, $70). Tickets can be booked through **Harvey World**

Travel, 60 Maitland St., for a $5 service fee. (☎6792 2555. Open M-F 8am-5:30pm, Sa 8:30-11:30am.) **Thrifty,** 39 Maitland St. (☎6792 3610) and **Budget,** 121 Barwan St. (☎13 27 27), rent cars. The main drag is **Maitland Street,** which runs parallel to Tibbereena one street farther from the creek. The **Narrabri Visitors Centre** is opposite Lloyd St. on the Newell Hwy. (Tibbereena St.), which veers north in town along Narrabri Creek. (☎6792 3583 or 1800 659 931. Open M-F 9am-5pm, Sa-Su 9am-noon.) The **NPWS** office, Level 1, 100 Maitland St., offers info about outdoor activities. (Enter around the corner on Dewhurst St. and go up the stairs. ☎6792 7300. Open M-F 8:30am-4:30pm.) The **post office** is at 140 Maitland St., at the corner of Dewhurst St. (☎6799 5999. Open M-F 9am-5pm.) **Postal Code:** 2390.

⚑⚑ ACCOMMODATIONS & CAMPING. Many of the pubs along the central three-block stretch of Maitland St. offer inexpensive accommodation, and there are a number of motels on the highway leading into town. Camping is also a great option (see **Sights,** below). The **Commercial Hotel ❷,** 170 Maitland St., has fairly sizeable rooms with shared bathrooms. (☎6792 2132. Singles $20, twins and doubles $35. Cash only.) The cheapest motel and camping are both at the **Narrabri Motel and Caravan Park ❶,** 52 Cooma Rd., on the Newell Hwy. toward Coonabarabran. (☎6792 2593. Pool, grill, and free linen. Sites for two $12, powered $16; singles $45; doubles $53; basic, backpacker friendly cabins $30 for 2 people, $2 extra person; ensuite cabins $45-53; luxury motel rooms for 2 $95, extra person $10.) Woolworths **supermarket** is on the corner of Lloyd and Maitland St. (Open M-F 7am-10pm, Sa 7am-9pm, Su 8am-8pm.)

Bark Hut Camping Area ❶ is 14km inside the park, and **Dawsons Spring Camping Area ❶** is 21km inside near the Mt. Kaputar summit. Both have hot showers, toilets, electricity, and BBQs (sites $3, children $2); be sure to bring your own firewood. The two **cabins ❺** at Dawsons Spring, each with four beds, a full kitchen, and a shower, are a great deal for families or groups. (Book well in advance at NPWS office ☎6792 7300. $60; 2 night min.)

⚡ OUTDOOR ACTIVITIES. Narrabri's newest tourist attraction is the **Australian Cotton Centre,** located next to the Visitors Centre on the Newell Hwy. (☎6792 6443; www.australiancottoncentre.com.au. Open daily 8:30am-4:30pm. $7, concession $6.30, children $5.50.) Surprisingly spiffy interactive exhibits (including a 3-D theaterette and a "kill the pests before they kill your crop" game) will teach you all you ever wanted to know about what the shirt on your back is made from. Signs on the Newell Hwy. heading toward Coonabarabran lead to the **Australia Telescope,** 24km west of Narrabri, a set of six large radio dishes that comprise the largest, most powerful telescope array in the Southern Hemisphere. While viewing the universe through these monstrous magnifiers isn't open to the public, the Visitors Centre has a helpful staff, and its videos and displays are fun and simplified into layman's terms. (☎6790 4070. Open daily 8am-4pm; staffed M-F. Free.) East of Narrabri, the peaks of the **Nandewar Range** beckon travelers to leave the paved road behind (either by hiking or unsealed driving) and scale the summit of **Mount Kaputar,** whose views encompass one-tenth of New South Wales. The entrance to the central section of **Mount Kaputar National Park** lies 31km east of Narrabri heading south on Maitland St. and Old Gunnedah Rd. The park's most famous attraction is **Sawn Rocks,** an amazing basalt rock formation, in the northern section accessible from the Newell Hwy. north of Narrabri (30min. drive northeast, 15min. walk from the parking lot). The eerie pipe-organ geometry is best seen from down in the creek bed. There is an excellent pamphlet available from the NPWS office in Narrabri with hiking info on 13 tracks of varying difficulties, including Mt. Kaputar, Sawn Rocks, and **Waa Gorge** ($3.50). The roads to and within the park are mostly unsealed and unstable after rain; call the NPWS office (☎6792 7300) for updates.

OUTBACK NEW SOUTH WALES

The empty stretches of northwest New South Wales are sparsely populated, difficult to reach, and largely untouched by the typical traveler. Those who do venture into these arid lands are rewarded with the satisfaction of being able to say to typical traveler friends Sydneyside, "Yes, I have been Back O' Bourke. I know what life looks like after the road ends."

BOURKE   ☎02

On a blistering hot day, Bourke (BURK) can be eerily quiet. Haze covering the unusually wide, naked streets distorts distance. Bourke is a study in racial division of the sort that is often hidden beneath the surface of Australian society. At one end of Oxley St., the main drag, white office workers stroll past the immaculately restored Federation-style courthouse, post office, and banks. At the other end, Aboriginal kids in worn clothing loiter beside the pub, convenience store, and public housing office. That shouldn't scare you away; visiting Bourke is an important experience in many ways. Once an important inland port town, Bourke is rich with history, and acts as both symbolic (as per the idiom "Back o' Bourke") and real gateway to the Outback.

Bourke lies on the Mitchell Hwy. (Hwy. 71), 367km northwest of Dubbo and 142km south of the Queensland-NSW border. The Mitchell Hwy. becomes Anson St. through town; Richard St. branches off to the north and runs all the way to the Darling River. Oxley St. runs off Richard St. to the left, and should be avoided at night. Mitchell St. crosses Richard St. a half block from Oxley St. The **Tourist Information Centre,** on Anson St., a block west of Richard St., can suggest farms for **year-round work.** (☎6872 1222; tourinfo@lisp.com.au. Open daily 9am-5pm.) The **library,** 46 Mitchell St., has **Internet.** (☎6872 2751. $2.50 per hr. Open M-F 9am-5pm, Sa 9:30am-12:30pm.)

Port of Bourke Hotel ❸, 32 Mitchell St., has large rooms with hardwood floors, shared baths, A/C, and heaters; many have balconies. (☎6872 2544; pobh@bigpond.com. Singles $38; doubles $59; family rooms $59, ensuite $85.) For a real "Outback" experience, contact **Comeroo Camel Station ❺,** in the red desert of Comeroo, where you can bushcamp, take a camel safari, or stay in cottages. A 4WD is necessary to reach the 100,000-acre family-run station. (☎/fax 6874 7735. Cottages with full board and activities $100 per person.) A **supermarket** is on the corner of Warraweena and Darling St. (☎6872 2613. Open daily 8am-8pm.)

The all-purpose guide *Back o' Bourke Mud Map Tours,* free at the tourist office, details trips beyond the town borders, up to several thousand kilometers into the Outback. Trips include **Mt. Oxley's** eagles and **Gundabooka National Park's** Aboriginal rock art (NPWS ☎6872 2744). The manly **Darling River Run,** billed as "The Last of the Great 4WD Adventures," is a 439km route tracing the Darling to its junction with the Murray at Wentworth and passes famous bush pubs, camping spots, and fishing holes.

BROKEN HILL   ☎08

Broken Hill sits at the extreme western end of New South Wales, right on the edge of nowhere. In 1883, Charles Rasp, a German-born boundary rider, discovered that the misshapen hill known locally as the "hog's back" was in fact the biggest lode of silver-lead ore in the world (though he thought it was tin until he sent a bit of it off to an assayer's office). Rasp and his associates attracted thousands of people, transforming seemingly worthless scrubland into a booming expanse almost overnight. As with Victoria's Goldfield boom towns, Broken Hill's burgeoning tourism

Broken Hill
City Center

♠ ACCOMMODATIONS
Mario's Palace Hotel, 2
The Tourist Lodge (YHA), 1
West Darling Motor Hotel, 4

♦ FOOD
Cafe Alfresco, 5
Oceania, 6
Ruby's Coffee Lounge, 3

board hopes to lure visitors with the area's rich history. Local mining continues to this day on the same giant lode of silver, zinc, and lead discovered by Rasp. However, as the last operational mine is expected to shut its shafts in 2010, the town's other markets now quietly vie for the position of leading industry. At the same time, the city supports a thriving art scene that has century-old roots in miners' "naive art," attracting a broadening international renown. This odd conjunction of commercialism, contemporary artistry, and a history of gritty labor has imbued Broken Hill with a character all its own.

▐ TRANSPORTATION

Trains: The train station (☎8087 1400) is on Crystal St. near the intersection with Chloride St. **Great Southern** (☎13 21 47) runs the *Indian-Pacific* to Sydney (16½hr.; Su and W 4:30pm; $102, ISIC $61.50) and Perth (48hr., Tu and F 9:20am, $345/$174) via Adelaide (6½hr., Tu and F 9:30am, $61/$32). Great Southern also runs the *Ghan* to Alice Springs (27hr.; Su 5:50am; $250/$125) via Adelaide (6¼hr., M 5:55am, $59/$30). **Countrylink** (☎13 22 32) trains go to Sydney (16¼hr.; daily 1-2 per day; $121.50/$61.50; booked 15 days in advance $61.50/$32).

Buses: The bus depot (☎8087 2735; open M-F 9am-4pm) is just outside the Visitors Centre, at the corner of Blende and Bromide St. **McCafferty's/Greyhound** (☎13 14 99 or 13 20 30) goes to: Melbourne (17hr.; $143.50, ISIC $129) via Adelaide (7hr., daily 10:30am, $84.50/$78.80); other destinations are accessible via Dubbo (9hr.; daily 3:35pm; $121.50/$109), including Sydney (16hr., $132/$119.50) and Brisbane (24hr., $184.20/$166).

Local Buses: Murton's Citybus runs 4 routes throughout greater Broken Hill M-F 8am-5:30pm and Sa roughly 9am-noon. Timetable available at the Visitors Centre.

Taxi: Yellow Radio Cabs (☎13 10 08).

Car Rental: Sundry around-town rentals can go as low as $58 per day. **Thrifty,** 190 Argent St. (☎8088 1928), and **Hertz** (☎8087 2719) at the Visitors Centre.

Bike Rental: The **YHA Tourist Lodge** (☎8088 2086) hires bikes for $15 per day.

NEW SOUTH WALES

> **TIME WARP.** Broken Hill uses the **phone code** of South Australia (☎08) and its **time zone,** Central Standard Time (CST), 30min. behind the rest of NSW.

◼ ▐ ORIENTATION & PRACTICAL INFORMATION

Rather than use the points of the compass, Broken Hill's streets are aligned with the line of lode upon which the mining city has long depended. Most shops and services congregate in the walkable rectangle bounded by **Bromide** (W), **Mica** (N), **Iodide** (E), and **Crystal** (S) St. Cutting west-to-east, one block above Crystal St., Argent St. is the main thoroughfare, with most of the food and lodging. Several outlying attractions require motorized transport, but rental cars are extremely expensive. Organized tours are a reasonable option for seeing the sights.

Tourist Office: Broken Hill Visitors Centre (☎8087 6077; www.murrayoutback.org.au), on the corner of Blende and Bromide St. From the railway station, turn left onto Crystal and walk 2 blocks west, then turn right onto Bromide; the office is 2 blocks down on the left. Tune in to 88FM for a recorded replay of the town's history. Open daily 8:30am-5pm.

Tours: Eight tour operators offer similarly priced daytrips to **Silverton** ($39-70), the **Living Desert Sculptures** ($20-25), and multi-day outback safaris. Though pricey, the tours are the best option for lone risk-averse travelers and those without their own vehicle. Book through the tourist office.

National Parks Information: New South Wales National Parks and Wildlife Service (NPWS), 183 Argent St. (☎8080 3200; fax 8080 3201). Open M-F 9am-5pm

Bank: ANZ, 357 Argent St. (☎13 13 14), is right next to **Commonwealth,** 338-340 Argent St. (☎13 22 21). Both open M-Th 9:30am-4pm, F 9:30am-5pm. 24hr. **ATMs.**

Library: Broken Hill Library (☎8088 3317), on Blende St. Free **Internet access.** Open M-W 10am-8pm, Th-F 10am-6pm, Sa 10am-1pm, Su 1-5pm.

Police: 252 Argent St. (☎8087 0299).

Internet Access: Slow but free at the library (see above). **Unihope—The Net Centre,** on Oxide St. between Chapple and Williams St., located in a church building, has many computers and great rates. (☎8087 8506. Internet $3.30 per hr. Open M-F 10am-6pm, Sa 10am-4pm.)

Post Office: 260 Argent St. (☎8087 7071). Open M-F 9am-5pm. Poste Restante available; pick-up at the window around side of building. **Postal Code:** 2880.

▐ ACCOMMODATIONS

If everything is full, try a pubstay on Argent St. Campers have also been known to set up in the dry creekbed near the Pinnacles Mine, southwest of town.

◼ **Mario's Palace Hotel,** 227 Argent St. (☎8088 1699). What the rooms lack in value, they more than compensate for in character. Foyer, corridor, and lounge walls beam with waterfall murals painted by a local Aborigine. One wildly-decorated 6-person bedroom was featured in *Priscilla, Queen of the Desert.* All rooms have fridge, TV, A/C, heat, and electric blankets. Reception 7am-late. Key deposit $10. Singles $32, ensuite $48; doubles $45/$67; *Priscilla* room $95-160. ❸

The Tourist Lodge (YHA), 100 Argent St. (☎8088 2086; mcrae@pcpro.net.au). This hostel has a swimming pool to beat the desert heat. A/C and heat cost $6 extra. The Visitors Centre and bus depot are at the back door. Kitchen with TV, common room with ping-pong table, and laundry. Reception 7:30am-noon and 3-9pm. Key deposit $10. Dorms and twins $22; singles $28-34; doubles $44-50. $4 YHA discount. ❷

West Darling Motor Hotel, 400 Argent St. (☎8087 2691, www.westdarling.hotel.com.au), on the corner of Oxide St. Plain, neat rooms, some with fridge and veranda, all with A/C, heat, and washbasin. TV lounge, parking, and continental breakfast. Reception open M-Sa 11am-midnight, Su 11am-10pm. Singles $28; twins and doubles $55, ensuite $60; families $55-88. Weekly $168/$330/$360/$396-528. ❸

🍴 FOOD

Broken Hill's numerous hotels, service clubs, and takeaways, most on or near Argent St., offer a fair amount of cheap chow. **Cafe Alfresco ❷,** on the corner of Argent and Oxide St., serves up big portions of quality pasta ($13-16). The funky pizzas (from $11) are decent, but order at least a medium if you're at all hungry. (☎8087 5599. Open 8am-11:30pm or midnight.) To beat the heat, try a fruit smoothie ($3.50) at **Ruby's Coffee Lounge ❶,** 393 Argent St. (☎8087 1188. Open M-F 8am-4pm.) **Oceania ❶,** 423 Argent St., has an $8.20 all-you-can-eat Chinese buffet. (☎8088 4539. Open daily 5-9:30pm.) **Schinella's Food and Liquor,** on Argent St. across from the YHA hostel, has a solid variety of **groceries.** (Open M-Sa 8:30am-6pm, Su 9am-1pm.)

🔆 SIGHTS

▨ DELPRAT'S MINE TOUR. Gain insight into the city's rugged history with a tour of the original Broken Hill Proprietary mine. The fascinating two-hour trip—conducted 130m underground—features equipment demonstrations and an insightful comparison of the mining labor system through time, with former miners-*cum*-annotative tour guides. Don your miner's hat and marvel at how they did it with only a candle 100 years ago. *(The BHP mine site is on the Broken Hill. Follow the sealed road off Iodide St. just past the train tracks, or walk 10-15min. ☎8088 1604. Tours M-F 10:30am, Sa 2pm; during school holidays daily 10:30am and 2pm. $34, concessions $30, children $26, families from $80; book ahead during school holidays.)*

LINE OF LODE VISITORS CENTRE. The pinnacle of Broken Hill's tourism movement, on the pinnacle of the hill itself. This shiny new complex runs daily Heritage Hill surface tours of the South Mine as well as special night tours throughout the week. Just outside, the **Miners' Memorial** pays homage to the hundreds of individuals who have died mining the Lode from the 1850s to the present. The Centre also contains a macabre touchscreen database of fallen miners, as well as a cafe with panoramic views of the city. *(The entire complex is on Broken Hill's highest point, a short drive or 5-10min. walk past Delprat's up the hill. ☎8088 1318; www.lineoflodebrokenhill.org.au. Tours 3½hr.; M-F 2-5:30pm, Sa 1:30-5pm; $28, concessions $24, under 16 $10, families $60. Sunset BBQ tour Su 3:30-8pm; $39/$35/$15/$87; book ahead. Miners' Memorial $2.50, concessions $2, under 16 free. Open daily 9am-10pm.)*

BUSHY WHITE'S MINING MUSEUM. Former miner Bushy White and his wife Betty teach the history of Broken Hill mining through creative dioramas and demonstrations. Over 250 original mineral art works by White depict mining equipment and techniques as well as landscapes and assorted Australiana. *(1 Allendale St., off of Brookfield Ave., about 2km west of the city center. ☎8087 2878. Tours upon request. Open daily 9am-5pm. $4, families $10. Wheelchair-accessible.)*

ROYAL FLYING DOCTOR SERVICE. A museum and film detail the history of this noble institution, which provides health care to outback residents living across 90% of the Australian continent. *(At the Broken Hill Airport. ☎8080 1717. Open M-F 9am-5pm, Sa-Su 11am-4pm. 1hr. session $5.50, concessions $4.40, children $2.20, families $15.)*

SCHOOL OF THE AIR. The School of the Air provides remote education for distant schoolchildren. Visitors can observe the lessons being broadcast on weekdays, but must book at the tourist office the day before and be seated by 8:20am (demerits for tardiness). The proceedings give an authentic insight into the quirks of bush and Outback life. *(On Lane St., 2 blocks east of Iodide St. $3.30, children $2.20.)*

LIVING DESERT RESERVE. In 1993, the Broken Hill Sculpture Symposium commissioned a group of local and international sculptors to create sandstone works atop a hill. The masterful pieces blend Aboriginal with modern and international influences and are best viewed at sunrise and sunset, when the light plays upon the colors. A 1½hr. walking trail loops from the sculpture site past gullies, ledges, and plenty of outback critters. *(Head north 8km along the northern segment of Kaolin St. From Argent St., turn left onto Bromide, left onto Williams, then right onto Kaolin St. You can drive all the way up the hill by obtaining a gate key from the tourist office for $6 with a $10 deposit, but the 15min. hike from a nearby carpark is more fun and free.)*

BROKEN HILL CITY ART GALLERY. Although small, this carefully assembled collection showcases both excellent local and 20th-century Australian painting. The signature piece, *Silver Tree*, is a delicately wrought arboreal centerpiece commissioned by Charles Rasp for the 1882 Melbourne Exhibition. *(At the corner of Blende and Chloride St. ☎8088 5491. Open M 1-4pm, W-Th 10am-5pm, F 8:30am-5pm, Sa 10am-5pm, Su 10am-4pm. $2, concessions $1, families $5.)* Across Chloride St., the **Silver City Art Centre** houses **The Big Picture.** Local artist Peter Andrew Anderson created the largest canvas painting in the world, measuring 100m long and 12m high. The wraparound work depicts the greater Broken Hill Outback. The gallery also includes an active silver workshop. *(☎8088 6166. Gallery free; admission to The Big Picture $5.)*

SILVERTON

Silverton makes Broken Hill, 25km to the south, look like a metropolis. The 1876 discovery of silver, zinc, and lead ore at Thackaringa brought Silverton into existence. Prospectors arrived in droves, and the population peaked at around 3000 in 1885. Unfortunately for Silverton, most of the ore was gone by this point, just as Broken Hill's lode was revealing its precious potential. This combination of circumstances rendered Silverton a ghost town, today home to fewer than 60. Silverton has featured in numerous films, including the classic *Mad Max II*. But don't let fear of post-nuclear desert mutants keep you away from Silverton; it is an experience like no other.

Silverton's handful of buildings ranges from old brick ruins that have stood abandoned since the 1800s to some good art galleries specializing in outback naturalism. The main social activity 'round these parts is getting sloshed, making the legendary **Silverton Hotel ❶** the most important building in town. Filled to the rafters with a huge diversity of beer cans and signs emblazoned with naughty sayings, the hotel serves simple food and drink until 8 or 9pm and has ensuite cabin-style accommodations with fridge. (☎8088 5313. Singles $33; doubles $44.) **Penrose Park ❶**, a five-minute walk north of town, offers powered and unpowered sites with toilet blocks, livable 6- to 8-person bunkhouses with kitchen, A/C, BBQ, and fridge, and six tennis courts free for day use but $4 at night. Also houses a display of Mad Max **"action cars"** used in the film. (☎8088 5307. BYO linen. Sites $5 per person or $12 per family, powered $7/$14; bunkhouses $30-40.) The **Silverton Camel Farm,** on the road from Broken Hill, grants rides on the temperamental humped beasts. (☎8088 5316. $5 per 15min.; $25 per hr.; 2hr. sunset safari $50; day rides including BBQ lunch $100.)

MUNGO NATIONAL PARK

Fascinating **Mungo National Park** lies 110km northeast of Mildura on the **Arumpo-Ivanhoe Road.** Ages ago, before the pyramids at Giza were even a twinkle in the eye of world history, hunter-gatherer communities flourished on the banks of Lake Mungo, in the extreme southwest corner of present-day New South Wales. Forty thousand years and 1600 Aboriginal generations later, life continues at one of the oldest continually inhabited sites in the world. Today, the lake is dry (and has been for 15,000 years), and Mungo has undergone some spectacular weathering. Sand dunes on the edges of the lake bed have been sculpted into strange, otherworldly landforms by erosion, accelerated over the course of the past hundred years by settlers' unwitting introduction of harmful foreign species: grazing sheep and foraging rabbits. Known as the **Walls of China,** their erosion has revealed countless fossils and artifacts, including **Mungo Three,** a skeleton of a human male that is, at an estimated 40,000 years, the oldest remaining *Homo sapiens* relic in the world. (The skeleton was buried again in a secret location so that it wouldn't be plundered.) The colored layers of sand clearly demarcate periods of water change up to 120,000 years ago. The archaeological information uncovered here has earned the **Willandra Lakes** region status as a **World Heritage Site.**

Roads to and within Mungo National Park are unsealed and subject to weather conditions; call ahead to the **NPWS** (☎03 5021 8900). In addition, visitors are advised to carry their own food, drinking water, and petrol. The park's **Visitors Centre** offers info on the park's history, visitor rules and regulations, and the incredible 70km **self-guided drive tour** that allows visitors to see the diverse wonders of the park at their own pace. This is also the place to pay vehicle fees ($6 per vehicle per day). Camping facilities are available at the **Main Camp ❶** (near the park entrance) and at **Belah Camp ❶** (farther into the park along the drive tour). Both sites have toilets and tables, but wood fires are only allowed at the Main Camp—be warned that in the winter months, you're going to want a campfire. (Both sites $3, children $2, plus vehicle fees.) The old, unheated **Shearers Quarters ❷,** next to the Visitors Centre, have been converted into basic bunk accommodations and provide access to the kitchen next door. (Book ahead with the Lower Darling Area Office in Buronga ☎5021 8900. Bunks $16.50, children $5.50.) The **Mungo Lodge ❺,** on the park road just before the park entrance, has heated ensuite cabins. (☎5029 7297. Reception 8am-6pm. Book ahead. Singles $78; doubles $88.)

NEW SOUTH WALES

NORTHERN
TERRITORY

Against the backdrop of a pastel sky, silver eucalyptus trees contort their limbs into ghost-like curves as cockatoos squawk noisily from branches. Sparse foliage and palm trees break the otherwise dry woodland. The thick smoke of a bush fire bruises the horizon. A well-worn 4WD rumbles down an endless road toward a fiery sunset, bellowing pumpkin-colored dust behind its growling motor. The mud-caked license plate says "Northern Territory: Outback Australia." And if it's Outback Australia you're after, you've come to the right place.

The Northern Territory (NT) stretches into the country's most extreme regions. In its 1.3 million km² area, the 200,000 inhabitants could enjoy 6½km² of land apiece. Instead, nearly 60% choose to settle in the cities of Darwin in the tropical Top End or Alice Springs in the desert-like Red Centre. The rest scatter among three or four substantially sized towns such as Katherine or Tennant Creek or upon the cattle stations and Aboriginal homelands that lend droplets of human life to the vast outback. The stretches between such outposts can be a day's drive, giving rise to the notion that most of the NT is simply empty. The wonderfully wide-open spaces, however, truly reveal the Australian landscape at its best.

Traveling through the NT is getting easier as the tourism infrastructure keeps building. Kakadu and Litchfield National Park in the Top End and Uluru and the MacDonnells in the Red Centre are accessible once the vast distances between them are overcome. While being a tourist in the NT is certainly more adventurous than participating in the overcrowded beach culture of the east coast, it is most rewarding (and highly recommended) to stay for longer than a whirlwind tour of the NT's greatest hits.

NORTHERN TERRITORY HIGHLIGHTS

MINDIL BEACH MARKET. Experience Darwin at its best as crafts, culture, and delicious food come out in festive form to greet the Top End twilight. (p. 268)

TWIN FALLS. Hike across white sand then swim in croc territory to reach this tropical earthly paradise in Kakadu National Park. (p. 281)

ABORIGINAL ART. Visit some of Australia's best-preserved rock art galleries in remote Arnhem Land. (p. 291)

DEVIL'S MARBLES. Ponder the origin of these stunning rock formations. (p. 299)

ULURU. The rock never disappoints. (p. 313)

VALLEY OF THE WINDS. Free your mind in Kata Tjuta National Park. (p. 315)

⌐ TRANSPORTATION

The NT's vast expanses make transportation a significant issue. Darwin, Alice Springs, and Yulara (Ayers Rock Resort) are most commonly reached by air. Smaller planes often fly to smaller destinations, but prices are high. There is as yet **no train system** traversing the Territory, except from Alice heading south to Adelaide, but one is in the works. **McCafferty's/Greyhound** (☎ 13 14 99 or 13 20 30) **buses**

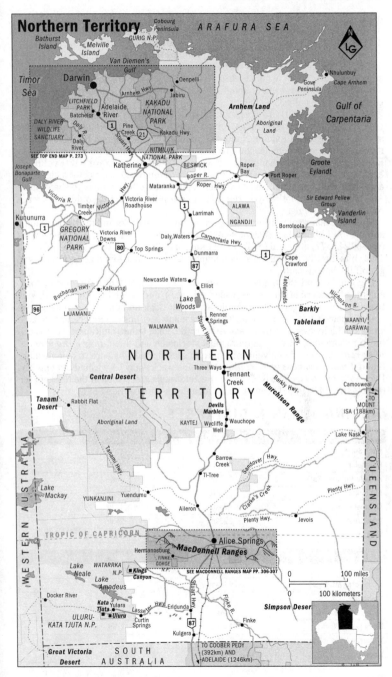

Northern Territory

Cobourg Peninsula

ARAFURA SEA

GURIG N.P.

Bathurst Island

Melville Island

Van Diemen's Gulf

Timor Sea

Darwin

Oenpelli

Arnhem Hwy.

Jabiru

LITCHFIELD PARK

Adelaide River

Batchelor

KAKADU NATIONAL PARK

Pine Creek

Kakadu Hwy.

DALY RIVER WILDLIFE SANCTUARY

Daly R.

Stuart Hwy.

21

NITMILUK NATIONAL PARK

Daly River

SEE TOP END MAP P. 273

Katherine

BESWICK

Nhulunbuy

Gove Peninsula

Cape Arnhem

Arnhem Land

Aboriginal Land

Gulf of Carpentaria

Joseph Bonaparte Gulf

Victoria R.

Roper R.

Mataranka

Roper Bay

Roper Hwy.

Port Roper

Groote Eylandt

Kununurra

Timber Creek

Victoria River Roadhouse

Victoria Hwy.

1

Larrimah

ALAWA

NGANDJI

Borroloola

Sir Edward Pellew Group

Vanderlin Island

GREGORY NATIONAL PARK

Victoria River Downs

80

Top Springs

Daly Waters

Carpentaria Hwy.

Dunmarra

87

Cape Crawford

1

Buchanan Hwy.

Kalkuringi

Newcastle Waters

Elliot

Tablelands

Nicholson R.

96

LAJAMANU

Lake Woods

Renner Springs

Barkly Tableland

WAANYI/ GARAWA

WALMANPA

Stuart Hwy.

N O R T H E R N

Central Desert

Three Ways

Tennant Creek

Barkly Hwy.

Murchison Range

Camooweal

TO MOUNT ISA (188km)

T E R R I T O R Y

Tanami Desert

Rabbit Flat

Aboriginal Land

Devils Marbles

KAYTEJ

Wauchope

Wycliffe Well

Lake Nash

Tanami Hwy.

YUNKANJINI

Lake Mackay

Yuendumu

Barrow Creek

Ti-Tree

Sandover Hwy.

Clarke's Creek

Plenty Hwy.

Aileron

Plenty Hwy.

Jervois

TROPIC OF CAPRICORN

Alice Springs

Hermannsburg

MacDonnell Ranges

FINKE GORGE

Lake Neale

WATARRKA N.P.

King's Canyon

SEE MACDONNELL RANGES MAP PP. 306-307

Docker River

Lake Amadeus

Kata Tjuta

Yulara

Lasseter Hwy.

Erldunda

Simpson Desert

ULURU-KATA TJUTA N.P.

Uluru

Curtin Springs

Stuart Hwy.

87

Finke R.

Finke

Kulgera

Great Victoria Desert

SOUTH AUSTRALIA

TO COOBER PEDY (392km) AND ADELAIDE (1246km)

WESTERN AUSTRALIA

QUEENSLAND

0   100 miles

0   100 kilometers

NORTHERN TERRITORY

offer service to most major tourist centers but not to the farther reaches of the national parks. **Renting a car** is the best way to retain freedom and flexibility, but it's also the most expensive, and you must be at least 21. There are many national chains that have offices all over the NT; **Territory-Thrifty Car Rental** (☎ 1800 891 125) and **Budget** (☎ 13 27 27) are the cheapest but limit kilometers (100km per day, each additional km 25-32¢), whereas **Britz** (☎ 1800 331 454) offers unlimited kilometers and rents 4WD to customers under 25. Each company does one-way rentals, but charges a fee, usually $300-400.

Major tourist centers are accessible by sealed or gravel roads. You'll need a 4WD only to venture onto dirt tracks; however, this is necessary to see many of the spectacular sights of Kakadu National Park and the MacDonnell Ranges. Furthermore, conventional vehicles are not insured for any accident on unsealed roads. Rental companies determine their own restrictions, even for 4WD vehicles; explain your itinerary before you rent. If going to remote areas, ask for a **high-clearance 4WD** with **two petrol tanks;** trendier vehicles are often too low to the ground. Also, make sure the 4WD you rent is not so top-heavy that it could flip over in rough terrain driving.

There are many safari tours that operate in national parks and the bush, running about $100-130 per day. **Wilderness 4WD Adventures** (☎ 1800 808 288) or **Gondwana** (☎ 1800 242 177) are good for Top End tours, and **Wayoutback Desert Safaris** (☎ 8953 4304) hits the Uluru area. These companies center around small groups and try to get off the beaten path.

If going beyond the highways, make sure to bring lots of extra water, food, emergency materials (tire, tools, rope, jack, etc.), and check in with a friend, Visitors Centre, or ranger station. Avoid driving at dusk and dawn, when **kangaroos** and **wild camels** loiter in the road. There are many sections of unfenced ranch land along the highways; beware of **wandering cattle. Road trains** (multi-part trucks) can be up to 50m long, often generating dust storms behind them. *It is dangerous to pass road trains.* When venturing onto unsealed roads, be sure to call ahead to find out **road conditions** (☎ 1800 246 199); some tracks may be washed out entirely. For **weather reports,** call ☎ 8982 3826. The **Automobile Association of the Northern Territory** (**AANT;** ☎ 8941 0611) can provide valuable assistance.

DRIVING TIMES & DISTANCES

FROM DARWIN TO:	KILOMETERS	APPROX. TIME
Alice Springs	1491km	15hr.
Batchelor	98km	1¼hr.
Kakadu National Park	257km	3hr.
Katherine	314km	3½hr.
Litchfield National Park	129km	1½hr.
Pine Creek	226km	2½hr.
Tennant Creek	986km	10hr.

FROM ALICE SPRINGS TO:	KILOMETERS	APPROX. TIME
Darwin	1491km	15hr.
Kata Tjuta (Mt. Olga)	500km	5¼hr.
Katherine	1177km	12hr.
Tennant Creek	504km	5hr.
Uluru (Ayers Rock)	461km	4¾hr.
Watarrka (King's Canyon)	331km	4hr.
Yulara	444km	4½hr.

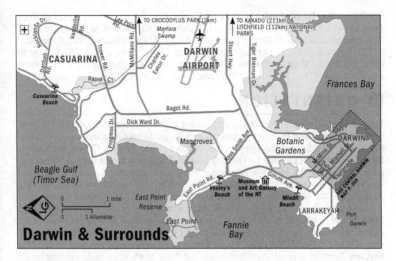

Darwin & Surrounds

DARWIN ☎ 08

Anywhere else in the world it would be just another small city, but Darwin (pop. 80,000) is not anywhere else—it is the gateway to the splendor of the Top End. Compared to the wonders at its doorstep, the capital of the Northern Territory is a pit stop, but its location makes it an oasis. From its incessant sunshine and azure beaches to its thumping nightlife, Darwin offers an escape from the limitless expanses of outback that surround it. As in other extreme northern parts of Australia, seasons here are divided only into the **Wet** monsoonal season (Nov.-May) and the desert-like **Dry** season (Jun.-Oct.). In the Dry, central Darwin is awash in beer, noise, and backpacker midriffs. Torrents of twenty-something visitors flood the sidewalks, slogging to and fro between the bars along the strip.

But Darwin has not always been so footloose. Two years of intense Japanese bombing reduced the city to rubble during WWII. The city rebuilt, only to be cruelly decimated a second time by Cyclone Tracey on Christmas Eve, 1974. With true Territorian grit, Darwin started from scratch once again, creating the convenient city center, manicured parks, and breezy outdoor malls of today. Darwin can provide a shot in the arm of whatever you've been missing in the outback, be it museums, refined cuisine, or a rip roaring party.

⚐ INTERCITY TRANSPORTATION

BY PLANE. Darwin International Airport (☎8920 1850) is about 10km northeast of the city center on McMillans Rd.; from the city center, take a left on Bagot Rd. off the Stuart Hwy. Both **Qantas,** 16 Bennett St. (☎13 13 13), and **Virgin Blue** (☎13 67 89), at the airport, fly to destinations within Australia. Various airlines offer service to Southeast Asia, Singapore, and Bali. Other airline offices include **Royal Brunei Airlines,** 22 Cavenagh St. (☎8941 0966); **Merpati Nusantara,** 6 Knuckey St. (☎1800 624 932); and the Territory-carrier **Airnorth** (☎8945 2866), at the airport. For transport between the city and the airport, the **Darwin Airport Shuttle** is your best bet. (☎8981 5066 or 1800 358 945. $7.50 one-way, return $14.) Many accommodations will reimburse patrons for the ride. **Taxis** (☎13 10 08) run to the airport for $20.

BY BUS. The **Transit Centre** is at 67-69 Mitchell St., between Peel and Nuttall St. (☎8941 0911. Open daily 6am-7:45pm.) **McCafferty's/Greyhound** (☎13 14 99 or 13 20 30) runs to: Adelaide (39hr., 1-2 per day, $371); Alice Springs (20hr., 2 per day, $194); Broome (24hr., 1 per day, $260); Cairns (41hr., 1 per day, $402); Katherine (4hr., 3 per day, $52); Melbourne (51hr., 1 per day, $430); Sydney via Alice Springs and Adelaide (67hr., 1 per day, $488); and Tennant Creek (12hr., 2 per day, $137).

■ ORIENTATION

Darwin is on a peninsula, with the city center in the southeastern corner. The tree-lined **Esplanade** and the rocky **Lameroo Beach** run along the western edge of the peninsula. The hub of the backpacker district is the Transit Centre on **Mitchell Street,** which runs parallel to The Esplanade. The **Smith Street Mall,** a pedestrian zone occupying the block between Knuckey and Bennett St., is home to many shops and services and runs parallel to Mitchell St. at the southern end of the city. At the tip of the peninsula, **Stokes Hill** and the **Wharf** area hold several sights.

Moving northeast out of downtown, **Daly Street** eventually becomes the **Stuart Highway** and heads out to the airport. Smith St. and Mitchell St. both continue north of the city center for 500m before converging with Gilruth Ave. at **Lambell Terrace,** which leads to the **MGM Casino, Mindil Beach,** and the **Museum and Art Gallery of the Northern Territory.** Gilruth Ave. becomes **East Point Road,** eventually leading to the **East Point Reserve,** 6km from the city center.

■ LOCAL TRANSPORTATION

Buses: Darwinbus (☎8924 7666) runs to suburbs and beaches along the major thoroughfares. Terminal is between Harry Chan Ave. and Bennett St. just south of the Smith St. Mall, with stops along Mitchell and Cavenagh St. Fares $1.40-2.40. **Tourcards** allow unlimited travel for 1 day ($5, concessions $2.50) or 1 week ($25, concessions $12.50). **Territory Shuttle** (☎8928 1155) will take you anywhere downtown for $2.

Taxis: Darwin Radio Taxis (☎13 10 08). $1.25 per km.

Car Rental: Rental companies abound but demand can outstrip availability in the Dry, so book ahead. Sedans start around $50 per day and small 4WDs from $90 per day, including 100km per day and $0.23-0.33 per extra km. Damage liability can usually be reduced at an additional rate of $15-45 per day. Large chains include: **Avis,** 145 Stuart Hwy. (☎8981 9922); **Budget,** 3 Daly St. (☎8981 9800), at the corner of Doctors Gully Rd.; **Hertz** (☎8941 0944), at the corner of Smith and Daly St.; and **Territory Rent-a-Car,** 64 Stuart Hwy. (☎8981 4796). For short distances, **Port** (☎8981 8441), at Fisherman's Wharf, and **Europcar,** 77 Cavenagh St. (☎13 13 90) offer rates from $39 per day and charge per km, while unlimited km are available at **Britz,** 44-66 Stuart Hwy. (☎8981 2081), and **Advance/Nifty,** 86 Mitchell St. (☎8981 2999). The minimum age for rental is 21 at Britz and **Apollo** (☎8981 4796), on McMinn St.; the rest usually require renters to be at least 25. Most major chains offer 4WD options, and Britz rents 4WD with sleeper compartments ideal for long treks into the bush.

Buying and Selling Used Cars: The **Travelers Car Market** (☎0418 600 830), at Peel and Mitchell St., caters to backpackers. Sellers pay $40 per week to cram into the lot, but buyers browse for free. Cars sell fastest May-Oct. Open daily 8am-4:30pm. Also check bulletin boards at hostels and Internet shops. Registration requirements vary for each state. Also, see **Buying and Selling Used Cars,** p. 54.

Automobile Club: The **Auto Association of the Northern Territory (AANT),** 79-81 Smith St. (☎8981 3837). Open M-F 9am-5pm.

Bike Rental: Available through most hostels ($5 per hr., $20 per day) or at **Kakadu Dreams,** 52 Mitchell St. (☎1800 813 266) for $5 per hr., $16 per day.

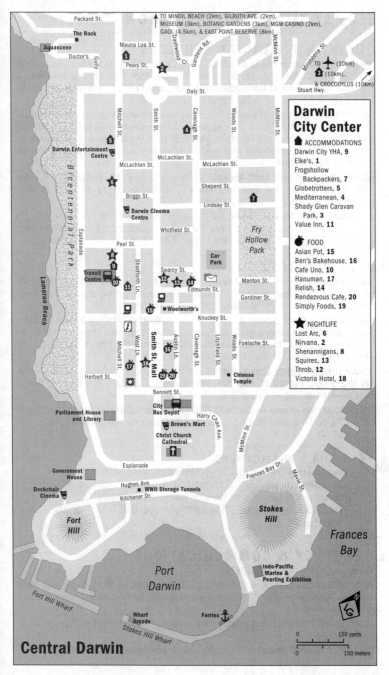

TO MINDIL BEACH (2km), GILRUTH AVE. (2km), MUSEUM (3km), BOTANIC GARDENS (3km), MGM CASINO (2km), GAOL (4.5km), & EAST POINT RESERVE (8km)

Packard St.

The Rock

Aquascene

Doctor's

Gully

Mauna Loa St.

Peary St.

Dashwood Cr.

Gardens Rd.

McMinn St.

Daly St.

Mirambeena St.

TO ✈ (10km)

3 (10km),

& CROCODYLUS (10km)

Stuart Hwy.

Mitchell St.

Smith St.

Cavenagh St.

Woods St.

McMinn St.

Darwin City Center

🏠 ACCOMMODATIONS
Darwin City YHA, **9**
Elke's, **1**
Frogshollow Backpackers, **7**
Globetrotters, **5**
Mediterranean, **4**
Shady Glen Caravan Park, **3**
Value Inn, **11**

Darwin Entertainment Centre

McLachlan St.

McLachlan St.

McLachlan St.

Sheperd St.

Briggs St.

Lindsay St.

7

Darwin Cinema Centre

Whitfield St.

Fry Hollow Park

Peel St.

Car Park

🍴 FOOD
Asian Pot, **15**
Ben's Bakehouse, **16**
Cafe Uno, **10**
Hanuman, **17**
Relish, **14**
Rendezvous Cafe, **20**
Simply Foods, **19**

Bicentennial Park

Esplanade

8

9

Transit Centre

10

Shadforth Ln.

Searcy St.

11

12

13

14

Edmunds St.

Manton St.

Gardiner St.

15

Woolworth's

Knuckey St.

⭐ NIGHTLIFE
Lost Arc, **6**
Nirvana, **2**
Shenannigans, **8**
Squires, **13**
Throb, **12**
Victoria Hotel, **18**

ℹ️

Lameroo Beach

Mitchell St.

West Ln.

Smith St. Mall

Austin Ln.

Cavenagh St.

Litchfield St.

Woods St.

Foelsche St.

17

18

19

20

Herbert St.

Chinese Temple

Bennett St.

City Bus Depot

Parliament House and Library

Brown's Mart

Harry Chan Ave.

Christ Church Cathedral

✝️

Government House

Esplanade

McMinn St.

Deckchair Cinema

Hughes Ave.

WWII Storage Tunnels

Kitchener Dr.

Frances Bay Dr.

Mavie St.

Stokes Hill

Fort Hill

Frances Bay

Port Darwin

Indo-Pacific Marine & Pearling Exhibition

Fort Hill Wharf

Wharf Arcade

Stokes Hill Wharf

Ferries ⚓

0   150 yards

0   150 meters

Central Darwin

◪ PRACTICAL INFORMATION

TOURIST & FINANCIAL SERVICES

Tourist Office: Tourism Top End (☎8936 2499), at the corner of Mitchell and Knuckey St. Open M-F 8:30am-5pm, Sa 9am-3pm, Su 10am-3pm. Main office of the **Parks & Wildlife Commission of the Northern Territory** (☎8999 5511; www.nt.gov.au/pawis) is in Palmerston, but info can be found at the tourist office.

Travel Offices: Tours can be booked from many locations on Mitchell St. or the Smith St. Mall. **STA** (☎8941 2955), in the Casuarina shopping center, sells ISIC ($16.50) and VIP ($34) cards. Open M-F 9am-5pm, Sa 10am-4pm. **Flight Centre,** 24 Cavenagh St. (☎13 16 00), guarantees to beat any quoted current airfare price. Open M-F 9am-5:30pm, Sa 9am-4pm.

Currency Exchange: Bank South Australia, 13 Knuckey St. (☎13 13 76). Open M-Th 9:30am-4pm, F 9:30am-5pm. **ANZ Bank** (☎13 13 14), on Knuckey St. by the Smith St. Mall. Open M-Th 9:30am-4pm, F 9:30am-5pm.

American Express: Travellers World, 27 Cavenagh St. (☎8981 4699), holds mail (no packages) for 30 days for card or Traveler's Cheque holders. Address mail "ATTN: Client Mail, GPO Box 3728, Darwin NT 0801." Open M-F 8:30am-5pm, Sa 9am-noon.

LOCAL SERVICES

Backpacking Supplies: NT General Store, 42 Cavenagh St. (☎8981 8242), at Edmunds St., has everything you need for the outdoors and a large selection of good maps. Open M-W 8:30am-5:30pm, Th-F 8:30am-6pm, Sa 8:30am-1pm.

Book Exchange: Dusty Jackets, 30 Cavenagh St. (☎8981 6772), has a great selection which exceeds the usual backpacker pop-fiction bookstore fare. Open M-F 10:30am-4:30pm, Sa 9am-noon. **Read Back Book Exchange** (☎8981 8885), Darwin Plaza off Smith St. Mall. Open M-F 9am-5:30pm, Sa-Su 9am-3pm.

Library: Northern Territory Library (☎8999 7410), in the Parliament building at the corner of Mitchell and Bennett St. Open M-F 10am-6pm, Sa-Su 1-5pm. Free Internet, though not intended for long email sessions.

Gym: Holiday Inn Fitness Centre (☎8980 0800), in the Holiday Inn Hotel on the Esplanade. The best-equipped gym in Darwin city. Free for guests, non-guests $8 per hr., students $5.50.

◤ MEDIA & PUBLICATIONS

Newspapers: *NT News* (90¢) daily; *Darwin Sun* on Wednesday.
Entertainment: *The Top End Visitors' Guide* monthly; *Arts Darwin* monthly; Entertainment section of *NT News* on Wednesday and Friday.
Radio: Rock, Triple J 103.3FM and HOT-100 101.1FM; News, ABC 105.7FM; Tourist info, 88FM.

EMERGENCY & COMMUNICATIONS

Emergency: ☎000 or 1800 019 116.

Hospital: Darwin Private Hospital (☎8920 6011, after hours 8920 6055) and **Royal Doctors Hospital** (☎8922 8888), are near each other, north of Darwin near Casuarina on Rocklands St.

Police: (☎8927 8888), in the Mitchell Centre, corner of Mitchell and Knuckey St. Open daily 8am-11pm.

Crisis Lines: NT AIDS Council ☎1800 880 899; **Sexual Assault** ☎8922 7156.

Internet Access: Didjworld Internet Shop, 60 Smith St. (☎8953 7979), in the Harry Chan Arcade, which charges $5.40 per hr. (7-10pm $4.50 per hr.) and has a fast connection. Open M-Sa 9am-10pm, Su 10am-8pm.

Post Office: General Post Office Darwin, 48 Cavenagh St. (☎13 13 18), at Edmunds St. Poste Restante held 30 days. Open M-F 8:30am-5pm, Sa 9am-noon. **Postal Code:** 0800.

ACCOMMODATIONS

Many of Darwin's hostels and budget accommodations are clumped around the Transit Centre on Mitchell St.; their offerings are pretty standard. High-end accommodations sit along the Esplanade, although most are overpriced. For better prices (and often nicer facilities), try the spots along Smith and Cavenagh St. Book ahead in the Dry; try to bargain in the Wet.

Camping options in central Darwin are sadly quite limited. Camping or sleeping in cars is strictly forbidden around the Mindil Beach area. The **Shady Glen Caravan Park ❶** is closest to the city, about 10km from central Darwin at the intersection of the Stuart Hwy. and Farrell Crescent. Patrons here are treated to pool, kitchen, BBQ, and laundry. (☎8984 3330. Unpowered sites $10.50 per person; powered sites $24 for 2 people.)

Darwin City YHA, 69 Mitchell St. (☎8981 3995), next to the Transit Centre. Large, clean, and efficient—the most liveable of Darwin's downtown hostels. International crowd and competent staff. Large lockers in every room, A/C, pool, kitchen, dining area, Internet ($8 per hr.), sun deck, 2 TV rooms, and luggage storage ($2 per day). All-you-can-eat BBQ F $5. Free airport shuttle. Linen and key deposit $15. Laundry $4.20. Reception 24hr. Dorms $21.50-23.50; singles and doubles $57. YHA discount $3.50 per person. Sometimes cheaper rooms in the Wet. VIP/YHA. ❷

Frogshollow Backpackers, 27 Lindsay St. (☎8941 2600 or 1800 068 686; www.frogs-hollow.com.au), at Woods St., 10min. from the Transit Centre. Exceptional facilities under overhanging palm trees. Friendliest hostel staff in Darwin. Airport shuttle reimbursed for 2-night stay or longer. Lockers, luggage storage and safe, pool, spa, laundry, spacious kitchen, TV room, and Internet ($7 per hr.). Breakfast included. Key, linen, and cutlery deposit $20. Reception 6am-9pm. Most rooms have A/C. Dorms $21; twins and doubles $50, ensuite $60. VIP/YHA. ❷

Elke's, 112 Mitchell St. (☎8981 8399), has large outdoor spaces and pool graced by lush greenery. Not too far out of downtown, but a much more relaxed feel. 4-share dorms $20; twins and doubles $54. VIP/YHA. ❷

Globetrotters, 97 Mitchell St. (☎8981 5385). A party hostel and pub together in one place. Madness ensues around the clock and around the big-screen TV. Rooms are somewhat crowded with 6-8 beds. Pool, tiny kitchen, and laundry. Key and linen deposit $20. Dorms $22 in the Dry, $16 in the Wet; twins and doubles $58/$50. NOMADS/VIP/YHA. ❷

Mediterranean, 81 Cavenagh St. (☎8981 7771 or 1800 357 760). Though not much to look at from the outside, on the inside the Mediterranean offer spacious ensuite rooms with huge sitting areas, full kitchens, chilly A/C, and satellite TV. Parking, swimming pool, and on-site tours desk. Rooms from $160 in the Dry, $130 in the Wet. Wheelchair-accessible. ❺

Value Inn, 50 Mitchell St. (☎8981 4733), across from the Transit Centre. The most centrally located motel in all of Darwin features modest, modern, clean, and simple ensuite rooms, all equipped with TV, fridge, and A/C. Pool. Reception 10am-11pm. Book ahead. $50 deposit. Rooms from $79 for 1-3 people in the Dry, $59 in the Wet. Wheelchair-accessible. ❺

🗋 FOOD

Darwin has no shortage of places to eat, though good, low-cost options are hard to find. The food stalls inside the **Transit Centre** serve decent food at reasonable prices. **Mindil Beach market** (see **Sights,** p. 268) offers a sprawl of trucks and stalls with delicious pan-Asian food ($6-10). The **Parap market** is smaller and more mellow but popular with locals. Take bus #4 to Parap Shopping Plaza. (Open Sa 8am-2pm.) The **Victoria Hotel** (see **Nightlife,** p. 271) and **Globetrotters** (see **Accommodations,** p. 267) often lure backpackers with heaping plates of food for around $5. Woolworths **supermarket** is at the corner of Knuckey and Smith St. (Open M-Sa 6:30am-midnight, Su 8am-10pm.)

Rendezvous Cafe, Star Village (☎8981 9231), at Smith St. Mall. Tucked into an arcade at the south end of Smith St. is one of the city's better curry places. Mains $10-16. Open for lunch M-F 10:30am-2:30pm, Sa 9am-2pm; for dinner Th-Sa 5:30pm-9pm. ❷

Asian Pot (☎8941 9833), corner of Smith and Knuckley St. Shop 6 in arcade. Some of the best affordable Asian food. Noodle and rice dishes from different countries for $8-9. The laksa ($6) is excellent. Open M-Sa 10am-4pm. ❶

Cafe Uno, 69 Mitchell St. (☎8942 2500), next to the Transit Centre. While it serves everything from gourmet pizzas ($13-16) to huge burgers ($10-13.50), Cafe Uno's specialty is breakfast. Try any of their fabulous egg breakfasts served with thick-cut toast ($9) while soaking up the sun in their outdoor cafe seating. Open daily 7am-late. ❷

Relish, 35 Cavenagh St. (☎8941 1900), across from the General Store. The best sandwich joint in town. Devour one of their wild creations or invent your own for $6. Try it toasted on focaccia bread, one of their melt-in-your-mouth rolls, or wrapped and ready to go as a beach snack. Lots of vegetarian options. Open M-F 6:30am-5pm. ❶

Ben's Bakehouse, Shop 4, Anthony Plaza (☎8981 1561), at Smith St. Mall. Tempting pies, pastries, and other sinful delights, and it's all baked fresh daily. Don't miss their hot pumpkin rolls ($2). Open M-F 9am-6pm, Sa-Su 9am-2:30pm. ❶

Simply Foods (☎8981 4765), Star Village at the Smith St. Mall. Escape the heavy sauces and fried foods with a light salad or sandwich packed with fresh, healthy ingredients ($4-6). Open M-F 9am-3pm. ❶

Hanuman, 28 Mitchell St. (☎8941 3500). The perfect place to indulge in some of Darwin's famous Asian cuisine. Elegant but relaxed. Enjoy Thai, Indian, and Nonya dishes in the purple interior. Mains $17-27. Open M-F noon-2:30pm and daily 6:30pm-late. ❹

🗺 SIGHTS

For many visitors, Darwin is merely a pit stop for a pint and a party before heading out to the vast natural wonderland beyond. However, the city itself boasts a handful of interesting sights scattered around its periphery. Many of the sights are a long walk or moderate bike ride from the city center. The underutilized bus system in Darwin is also an option. The **Tour Tub** rounds up passengers at major accommodations and at the corner of Smith and Knuckey St. and herds them to ten popular sights from Stokes Hill Wharf to East Point Reserve. (☎8981 5233. Operates daily 9am-4pm. Full-day pass $25. Half-day pass valid 1-4pm $15.)

▓ **MINDIL BEACH SUNSET MARKET.** This collection of arts, crafts, and food stalls highlights the creativity and cosmopolitanism of Darwin's populace, too often buried by the backpacker-courting travel agencies and bars downtown. As the sun blushes over the waves, musicians entertain the mingling, munching crowds while booths hawk crocodile skulls, saris, and laksa. (*Open May-Oct. Th 5-9pm, also June-Sept. Su 4-9pm.*)

MUSEUM & ART GALLERY OF THE NORTHERN TERRITORY. A wonderful introduction to the history, art, and biology of the NT. An extensive gallery traces the development of Aboriginal art from some of the earliest known rock painting on the planet to its current kaleidoscope of styles. Pictures and a short film reveal the devastation wreaked on the city by Cyclone Tracey. Neon-lit exhibits investigate the history of life in Darwin, from ancestral megafauna to the ecosystems of the area today. Nearby, but less thrilling, is the **Fannie Bay Gaol,** with self-guided tours through the facility which served as Darwin's main jail from 1883-1979. *(Museum is along the shore toward Vestey's Beach; turn left on Conacher St. off East Point Rd. Gaol is 1km further up the road on the right.* ☎*8999 8201. Open M-F 9am-5pm, Sa-Su 10am-5pm. Free. Wheelchair-accessible.)*

MINDIL BEACH & VESTEY'S BEACH. Prime locales for soaking up rays are north of the city, just off Gilruth Ave. Mindil Beach is on the left behind the casino, and Vestey's Beach is just north of the museum. Box jellyfish warnings (see **Dangerous Wildlife,** p. 75) apply from October to March, but stings have been recorded all months of the year. *(Heading away from downtown, take Smith St. past Daly St. and turn right onto Gilruth Ave. at the traffic circle. 30min. walk, or catch bus #4 or 6.)*

AQUASCENE. True, $6 may seem a bit steep to feed bread to fish. However, the throng of tourists that line up are seldom disappointed by the equally impressive throng of fish that arrive with each high tide. Wade into the teeming waters or watch from the concrete bleachers. *(28 Doctors Gully Rd. North off Daly St.* ☎*8981 7837. Call ahead for the feeding schedule. $6, under 15 $3.60.)*

PARKS. The area around Darwin is full of tranquil parks. Just north of Daly St., the shaded paths of the **Botanic Gardens** wind through a series of Australian ecosystems: rainforest, mangroves, and dunes. The hearty gardens survived cyclones in 1897, 1937, and 1974. *(Entrances on Geranium St. off the Stuart Hwy., and just past Mindil Beach on the opposite side of Gilruth Ave. Wheelchair-accessible.)* The **East Point Reserve,** on the peninsula to the north of Mindil and Vestey's Beach, beckons with picnic areas and the croc-and-jelly-free swimming of Lake Alexander. Wallabies are often spotted, especially in the evening. *(Access from East Point Rd. A 45min. bike ride from city. No bus service.)* Walking trails, picnic areas, and views of Darwin Harbour lie in wait at **Charles Darwin National Park.** *(Bennett St. eastbound becomes Tiger Brennan Dr. Follow this for 5km to the park entrance.* ☎*8947 2305. Open daily 7am-7pm.)*

CROCODYLUS PARK. This research and education center holds lions, rheas, iguanas, and other assorted critters in addition to the featured reptiles. Sure, you might encounter crocs in the wild, but they probably won't let you hold them and pose for a picture. *(Take local bus #5, then walk 10min. Shuttle available from city at* ☎*8981 3300. $35, families $90; prices include park entry.* ☎*8947 2510. Open daily 9am-5pm. Feedings and tours 10am, noon, and 2pm. $22, concessions $18, ages 4-15 $11.)*

OTHER MUSEUMS & EXHIBITS. At the **East Point Military Museum,** photos and a video display the decimation caused by the Japanese bombing of Darwin Harbour in 1942. *(East Point Rd. at East Point Reserve. It's a 7min. drive or 45min. bike ride from downtown.* ☎*8981 9702. Open daily 9:30am-5pm. $10, seniors $8, children $5, families $28.)* The **Australian Aviation Heritage Centre's** collection of old aircraft is crowned by an old American B-52 bomber. *(10km from Darwin on the Stuart Hwy., served by bus #8.* ☎*8947 2145. Open daily 9am-5pm. $11, students $7.50, children $6, families $28.)* **Indo-Pacific Marine** features one of three self-sustained man-made coral reef systems in the world. No feeding, no filters. All that has been added in 14 years is rainwater. *(On Stokes Hill Wharf.* ☎*8981 1294. Open in the Dry daily 10am-5pm; in the Wet M-Sa 9am-1pm, Su 10am-5pm. $16, concessions $14, under 14 $6, families $38. Free talks every 30min.)*

NORTHERN TERRITORY

◪ ACTIVITIES

Scuba diving in Darwin Harbour is possible, though opportunities are limited. **Cullen Bay Dive** offers guidance, gear, and certification. (☎8981 3049. $80 for 2 dives, $160 with gear; certification courses $400-600.) Back on land, **biking** is a convenient way to explore Darwin. A 45min. bike path extends from Darwin City to East Point Reserve (see p. 269).

Darwin also has a selection of gravity-defying adventures. At **The Rock**, on Doctors Gully Rd. next to Aquascene, climbing connoisseurs can tackle a variety of wall climbs in the old tanker. (☎8941 0747. Unlimited-length sessions $11; harness rental $3; boot rental $3.) Go **skydiving** from 10,000 ft. with **Pete's Parachuting.** (☎1800 641 114. Tandem $299.) **Parasailing** with **Odyssey Adventures** provides breathtaking aerial views. Sunset flights run from June to September; book ahead. (☎0418 891 998. Single $75; tandem $60 per person.)

♫ ENTERTAINMENT

You can quickly blow your bus fare at the underwhelming 24hr. **MGM Grand Casino** (☎1800 891 118). The ■**Deckchair Cinema**, on a beautiful spot overlooking the ocean, has a mixed program ranging from blockbusters to artsy lesser-known films. Enjoy a beer while you sit on canvas benches under the stars. (In the Wharf Precinct below Parliament House, near Fort Hill. ☎8981 0700. Open in the Dry only. Su and W-Sa 7:30pm, occasional shows F-Sa around 9:30pm. $12, concessions $10.) The **Darwin Entertainment Centre,** 93 Mitchell St., between Peel and Daly St., puts on a variety of theatrical productions. Call the box office for same-day 50% discounts and free shows. (☎8981 1222. Open M-F 10am-5:30pm.) **Brown's Mart,** 12 Smith St. (☎8981 5522), near Bennett St., hosts productions in one of Darwin's oldest buildings. The **Botanic Gardens Amphitheatre** has open-air theater in the midst of the lush gardens.

◪ FESTIVALS

Darwin celebrates the Dry with a number of festivals. The **Darwin Beer Can Regatta,** held off Mindil Beach in early August, is decidedly not dry. Teams of devout beer-chuggers use their empties to make vessels and race them across the harbor. The **Darwin Cup Carnival** begins in July and ends with Cup Day in August (along with the Territory's Picnic Day). On the second Sunday in June, the Greek population of Darwin stages the **Glenti Festival,** a musical and culinary celebration of heritage, on the Esplanade. **Australian Football League** games occur every weekend in the Dry. Ask the tourist office for a schedule. As the Dry dwindles, Darwin goes for broke with the 17-day **Festival of Darwin** in mid-August.

■ NIGHTLIFE

Central Darwin is alive every night, pulsating with party-starved backpacking refugees from the surrounding outback. Pubs and clubs advertise aggressively, even accosting you by the hostel pool. Darwin city law requires late-night clubs to charge a cover, but they're generally only a modest sum. Some don't start charging a cover until midnight, making it possible to dodge the fee with some planning.

■ **Lost Arc,** 89 Mitchell St. (☎8942 3300). The most reliable party in town is found with the *beautiful* crowd at this funky joint. Extraordinary people-watching from the plush sidewalk couches. Live music usually Su-Tu. Open Su-Th 4pm-4am, F-Sa 4pm-2am. Next door, the much-hyped (and rightly so) **Discovery** showcases talent from local DJs to the occasional international superstar (the Violent Femmes played here in 2003). Cover $6-8. Open F-Sa 9pm-4am.

Throb, 64 Smith St. (☎8942 3435). Escape the top 20 blues and break it down at one of Darwin's hippest clubs. This gay and lesbian nightclub is not as raunchy as its name might suggest; the crowd is stylish and chill. Funky pool tables, friendly staff, and by far the best music in town. Sa drag shows at midnight. Cover $5. Open Th-Sa 10pm-4am.

The Victoria Hotel, 27 Smith St. Mall (☎8981 4011). The lines out the door welcome you to the most sexually charged outback-meets-blitzed-backpacker scene. **Settlers** pub downstairs serves beer in a rustic atmosphere. Live music nightly. Open M-F 10am-4am, Sa 11am-4am, Su 4pm-4am. Upstairs, **Banjo's** pool tables draw backpackers early in the night, then the music begins and the place starts to jump. Cover $6 after midnight. Open M-F 4pm-4am, Sa-Su 7pm-4am.

Nirvana (☎8981 2025), on Smith St. near Peary St. Technically not a bar, this upscale Southeast Asian restaurant hosts quality musical entertainment for the price of a drink and some munchies. The law won't let them serve you a drink without food; they won't let you stay without ordering something, so eat and drink up. Try a frozen Japanese Slipper for $9. Tu open jam session. Th-Sa jazz. Open Tu-Sa 9am-2am.

Shenannigans, 69 Mitchell St. (☎8981 2100). Your standard loud and happy Irish pub, always packed to the gills with boisterous and primarily male merry-mak-

(Continued from previous page)

Part of the difficulty in understanding why reconciliation still feels a long way off is that the very concept of a "united Australia" means different things to different communities. The world of sports, a central element to the life and culture of most Australians, is one area where this difference is most apparent. With the help of organizations like the Council for Reconciliation, attempts have been made to use sport as a cultural unifier, giving Aboriginal and non-Aboriginal people a common ground on which to relate and interact. But despite some success in the area of professional sports, making positive use of the highly active local sports network in Australia has proved more difficult. The integration of community sports teams and leagues was one of the Council's goals, yet sports leagues within Aboriginal communities have resisted all attempts to integrate teams. For Aboriginal people, sport is not only recreation, it is a cultural event. Integrated teams and the standards of play imposed by participating against outside teams favor recreation over the cultural side of the competition. For Aboriginal communities, a "united Australia" is one in which respect, not common experience, serves as the unifier. Yet, without this kind of integration, the communities remain separated, true communication is rare, and the future of reconciliation remains uncertain.

ers. Occasional live music draws several locals into what is normally an entirely back-packers crowd. M karaoke. Tu trivia night. Happy Hour F 4:30-6:30pm. Open M-Sa 10am-2am, Su noon-2am.

Squires, 3 Edmund St. (☎8981 9761), off Smith St. behind Woolworths. Away from the backpacking hordes, locals know the place to go for a no-frills beer and a game of pool. Free BBQ W-F 5-7pm. Th $6 jugs. F $3 schooners. Happy Hour M-F 12:30-1:30pm and 5-6pm. Open M-Sa 11am-4am, Su 5pm-4am. Next door is **Time,** Darwin's original dance club. Cover $6. Open F-Sa 10pm-4am.

TOP END

A lush tropical crown atop a vast arid interior, the winterless Top End enjoys per-petually warm weather. In the Dry, backpack-toting pilgrims descend on Darwin and use this island of civilization as a base to explore the region's prime natural wonders—Kakadu, Litchfield, and Nitmiluk National Parks. The trickle of travel-ers who brave the Top End during the Wet are rewarded by the region at its most dramatic. Biblical rains flatten the red landscape, followed by outbursts of velvet green vegetation. Eternal summer has its drawbacks, however; be prepared also for broiling heat and plagues of mosquitoes.

ARNHEM HIGHWAY: TOP END WETLANDS

Intersecting the Stuart Hwy. 33km southeast of Darwin, the **Arnhem Highway** glides for 120km through the **Adelaide** and **Mary River Wetlands** before hitting **Kakadu National Park.** During the Dry, these wetlands are a lush sanctuary for birds and crocs; during the Wet, much of the area floods. A wide variety of birds fre-quent the **Fogg Dam Conservation Reserve,** 25km east of the junction of the Stuart and Arnhem Hwy. and 10km north on an access road.

KAKADU NATIONAL PARK

While the attractions of Kakadu National Park are beautiful and fascinating in their own right, what makes Kakadu truly special is the diversity and density of the wonders packed within its borders. Its biological diversity alone is astounding: it boasts six distinct ecosystems with 64 mammal, 100 reptile, 200 ant, and 1000 fly species, as well as one-third of all bird species found in Australia. Alongside this natural diversity stands the world's most extensive and perhaps oldest rock art galleries, some of which date back tens of thousands of years. Geologically, it incorporates the four Alligator river systems, the low-lying floodplains of the west, and the proud stone escarpments of the east, with their panoramic views and pounding waterfalls. In the Wet, lush greenery covers the whole of the park, the sky fills with lightning and rainfalls soak the landscape. In the Dry, rainfall ceases almost entirely and the lush fields of the Wet become cracked flat expanses. The dominant color in the Dry is the burnt cinnamon of the dirt. The early Dry is also the time in which park rangers continue the ancient traditions of the Aborigines in burning sections of the park for conservation purposes.

Intimately intertwined with this awe-inspiring landscape is the living legacy of the Aboriginal community that resides in Kakadu. Aboriginal people have inhab-ited this land for an estimated 50,000 years. Today's Aboriginal population in Kakadu has dwindled from the original European estimate of 2000 to a mere 300. The number of clans has likewise decreased from 20 to 12, and of the dozen lan-guages once spoken here, only three remain active. The language of *Gagudju*, spoken here a century ago, lives on in the park's name. Aboriginal people are active in the management and conservation of the park, and about 30% of

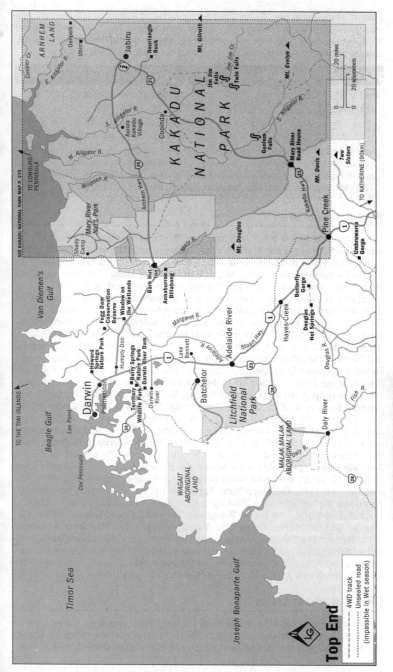

Top End

4WD track
Unsealed road
(impassible in Wet season)

Kakadu's employees are of Aboriginal descent. Half of Kakadu is still owned by its traditional Aboriginal owners, who leased their land to the National Parks and Wildlife Service in 1978. Cultural sensitivity is a primary goal throughout the park, and the most sacred Aboriginal Dreaming sights remain off-limits to visitors.

KAKADU AT A GLANCE	
AREA: 19,804 sq. km.	**GATEWAYS:** Darwin (see p. 263) and Pine Creek (see p. 285).
FEATURES: Stone country, floodplains of the Alligator River System, township of Jaribu, Jim Jim and Twin Falls.	**CAMPING:** From free bushcamping to commercial campgrounds (see p. 277).
HIGHLIGHTS: Galleries of Aboriginal rock art, walks through grasslands and to sunset lookout points, riverboat cruises, 4WD treks to waterfalls and plunge pools.	**FEES:** $16.25 park entrance fee. Fees are required for Yellow Water River Cruise, Guluyambi East Alligator Cruise, and day tours of Jim Jim and Twin Falls.

■ ORIENTATION

Kakadu National Park is roughly rectangular. The two entries into the park are the **Arnhem Highway** in the north, which runs east-west, and the **Kakadu Highway** in the south, which runs northeast-southwest. These two fully paved roads converge in the park's northeastern interior near the township of **Jabiru** (JAB-ber-roo). They remain open year-round, except during the most severe floods in the Wet.

Kakadu is divided into seven regions. The **South Alligator Region** is east of Kakadu's north gate, 120km east of the junction between the Arnhem and Stuart Hwy. It is marked by the flood plains that sprawl around the mighty South Alligator River and includes the Aurora Kakadu Resort, 77km from the park entrance. After another 39km, the Arnhem Hwy. enters the **East Alligator Region** and arrives at Ubirr Rd., the 36km turn-off to **Ubirr**, a rock art site and lookout. The Kakadu Hostel and Border Store are near Ubirr. The junction of the Arnhem and Kakadu Hwy. is about 1km past Ubirr Rd. in the **Jabiru Region.** Just 2km from this junction, tidy **Jabiru** (pop. 2000) is the primary town in Kakadu, with the Kakadu Lodge and Caravan Park, post office, and a grocery store. The **Bowali Visitors Centre** is 5km from Jabiru on the Kakadu Hwy. Kakadu's most impressive sights cluster around Jabiru, making the town a useful base for exploration. The remaining four regions are accessed from the Kakadu Hwy. The turn-off for the **Nourlangie Region** is 21km from Jabiru; a 12km paved road leads to Nourlangie Rock. The turn-off for the **Jim Jim/Twin Falls Region** is 20km farther on the Kakadu Hwy. This 4WD-only road (impassable in the Wet) runs 60km to the Jim Jim Falls camping area and 10km more to Twin Falls. The **Yellow Water Region** is much easier to reach (just 9km farther down the highway). The Warradjan Aboriginal Cultural Centre and Gagudju Cooinda Lodge are in the Yellow Water area. The south gate of Kakadu is 99km farther on the Kakadu Hwy. through the **Mary River Region,** and **Pine Creek** is another 59km farther. The three regions in the center of the park, **Jabiru, Nourlangie,** and **Yellow Water,** are all close together and contain most of the sights, accommodations and services in the park. A copy of the invaluable *Kakadu National Park Visitor Guide and Map* is provided with each park entry ticket.

▐ TRANSPORTATION

Armed with the *Kakadu National Park Visitor Guide and Map*, the most ideal way to do Kakadu is in your own car. A 4WD is by far the most convenient, allowing for a more personal and off-the-beaten-path experience. Renting a 4WD, how-

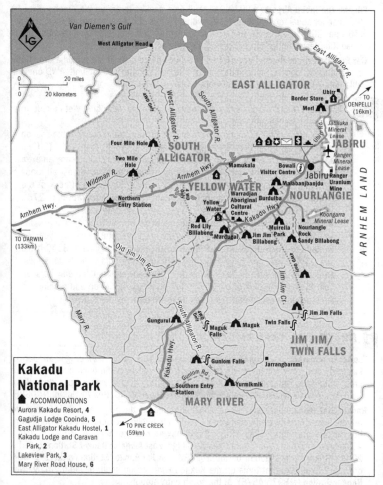

Kakadu National Park

🏕 ACCOMMODATIONS
Aurora Kakadu Resort, **4**
Gagudja Lodge Cooinda, **5**
East Alligator Kakadu Hostel, **1**
Kakadu Lodge and Caravan
  Park, **2**
Lakeview Park, **3**
Mary River Road House, **6**

NORTHERN TERRITORY

ever, is expensive, and rental companies might not even allow access to certain sights even if the roads are open; check with them before you book. A 2WD will get you to the top tourist destinations in the Dry, except Jim Jim and Twin Falls.

Daytours from Darwin with **McCafferty's/Greyhound** can be expanded to three or more days. Conductors double as knowledgeable, witty tour guides, although the visit compresses the sights without exploring the park's more rugged, remote gems. You have the option of connecting with tours of the rivers and Jim Jim/Twin Falls. (☎ 13 14 99 or 13 20 30. $90, not including park entry fee.) Plenty of **tour companies** offer packages, and almost all 4WD operations work out of Darwin. **Wilderness 4WD Adventures** specializes in tours with biology-savvy guides geared toward fit nature-lovers. (☎ 1800 808 288. 3- to 5-day $440-625.) **Northern Territories Adventure Tours** also offers 4WD safaris. (☎ 1800 654 603. Camping 2- to 5-day $320-675; 3-day "safari in style" with hotel accommodation $775.)

Flights: The Jabiru Airport (☎8979 2411), 6.5km east of Jabiru on the Arnhem Hwy., is the base for aerial tours of Kakadu. **Kakadu Air** offers bird's-eye **scenic flights** of Kakadu ($85 per 30min., $135 per hr.). Flights during the Wet are popular since many roads close. Courtesy shuttles run between the airport and Jabiru.

Car Rental: Territory Rent-a-Car (☎0418 858 601) has a desk in the Gagudja Croc Hotel on Flinders St., Jabiru. Small sedans from $90 per day with 100km limit. 4WD unavailable. Many people rent cars out of Darwin (see p. 263).

> **WHEN TO GO.** Locals say they have a hard time describing Wet Kakadu to Dry season visitors, and vice versa.
>
> **The Dry,** from April to October, is the most convenient and comfortable season to visit for most travelers. Dry highs average 30°C (86°F), lows 17°C (59°F), and the humidity is low. It can get cold at night; travelers should carry an extra layer and repellent to ward off mosquitoes. During the Dry, almost all roads are open except for a few unpaved ones early in the season. Check at the Bowali Visitors Centre for road openings (see **Practical Information,** p. 276). Most camping, accommodations, and attractions operate in the Dry.
>
> **The Wet** dramatically alters the landscape of Kakadu with its monsoon rains and floods. Locals insist that the Wet is the most beautiful time of the year, as the land teems with foliage and flowers. Still, the humidity, heat (35°C highs and 25°C lows), and bugs make the land harder to enjoy. The famous falls, particularly Jim Jim and Twin, are at their most powerful but can only be seen from the air. One plus of the Wet is that boat cruises are up and running, as the Ubirr drive becomes a river (see **East Alligator** sights, p. 280).

■ PRACTICAL INFORMATION

Tourist Information: The **Bowali Visitors Centre** (☎8938 1120; www.ea.gov.au/parks/kakadu), 2km south of Jabiru on the Kakadu Hwy., gives a thorough overview of the park. During the Dry, rangers give free daily talks and guided walks. Open daily 8am–5pm. Wheelchair-accessible. Reach the **Park Manager** at P.O. Box 71, Jabiru NT 0886.

Ranger Stations: Ranger stations can relay information to the police and clinic from more remote areas, but the stations are only open to the public sporadically (daily 8am-4pm, but rangers are often called away). **South Alligator Ranger Station** (☎8979 0194), 40km west of Jabiru near Aurora Kakadu Village. **East Alligator Ranger Station** (☎8979 2291), 36km north of Jabiru on the Ubirr Rd. **Jim Jim Ranger Station** (☎8979 2038), down a 2.5km road that turns off the Kakadu Hwy., 45km south of Jabiru. **Mary River Ranger Station** (☎8975 4578), at the south entry station.

Auto Services: Diesel and unleaded **fuel stations** are at the Aurora Kakadu Village, Jabiru, Cooinda, the Border Store near Ubirr, and the Mary River Roadhouse at the south entrance. **Jabiru's Mobil Station** (☎8979 2001) has **auto repair.** Open daily 7am-8pm.

Potable Water: At Bowali, Jabiru, Cooinda, and Aurora Kakadu Village. *Rangers recommend boiling water from any other source, including the campgrounds listed below.*

Swimming: The safest places to swim in Kakadu are the lodge pools and the mighty Olympic-size **Jabiru Pool.** (☎8979 2127. Open daily 9am-7pm. $3.50.)

Banks: Westpac Bank (☎8979 2432), at Jabiru Plaza, has currency exchange and a 24hr. **ATM.** Open M-Th 9:30am-4pm, F 9:30am-5pm. Cooinda Lodge, near Yellow Water, has **EFTPOS** only.

Police: Jabiru Police, 10 Tasman Crescent (**Emergency** ☎000 or 8979 2122), across the street from Jabiru Plaza at the end of Flinders St.

Internet Access: Library (☎8979 2097), at Jabiru Plaza. Open Tu-W 10am-4pm, Th noon-6pm, F 10am-4pm, Sa 10am-2pm. $3 per 15min.

Post Office: (☎8979 2727), at Jabiru Plaza, inside 2 Rivers News Agency. Open M-F 9am-5pm, Sa 9am-noon. **Postal Code:** 0886.

KAKADU REGIONS IN BRIEF

REGION	MAJOR SIGHTS	ACCOMMODATION	SERVICES
East Alligator	Ubirr, Guluyambi river cruise	East Alligator Kakadu Hostel	Food and fuel the Border Store
Jabiru	Bowali Visitors Centre	Kakadu Lodge and Caravan Park, Lakeview Park	Food and fuel in Jabiru
Jim Jim/Twin Falls	Jim Jim/Twin Falls	none	none
Mary River	Gunlom	Mary River Road House	Food and fuel at Mary River Road House
Nourlangie	Nourlangie	none	none
South Alligator	Mamukala Wetlands	Aurora Kakadu Resort	Food and fuel at Aurora Kakadu Resort
Yellow River	Gunlom Warradjan Aboriginal Cultural Centre, Yellow Water cruise	Gagudju Cooinda Lodge	Food and fuel at Cooinda

ACCOMMODATIONS & FOOD

Aside from camping, budget accommodations in Kakadu are sorely lacking. Budget dorms generally leave much to be desired and motel rooms are expensive. Large areas of the park lack any non-camping accommodations at all. Campsites tend to be situated in attractive spots with well-maintained, convenient facilities. However, sites with facilities tend to be crowded in the Dry and the proximity to water that often makes the sites attractive also means that they are rife with mosquitoes. Primitive camping areas with pit toilets are numerous and less crowded (Jim Jim and Twin Falls are exceptions). Throughout the park, bring plenty of water and your own food.

JABIRU, NOURLANGIE, & YELLOW WATER REGIONS

The Jabiru, Nourlangie, and Yellow Water regions are just a short drive from each other. **Lakeview Park ❺**, in Jabiru off Lakeside Dr., has adorable, rustic "bush bungalows" with canvas roofs, as well as 2-bedroom cabins. (☎8979 3144; lakeviewkakadu@bigpond.com.au. Bungalows $85, in the Wet $70; doubles $110/$90; cabins $180/$150.) Also in Jabiru, **Kakadu Lodge and Caravan ❶** is friendly, well-kept, and brimming with comforts such as A/C, linen, towels, a pool, laundry, and bistro. Occasional slide shows by park rangers are a draw. (On the right on Jabiru Dr. before town. ☎8979 2422. Reception 7:30am-7:30pm. Sites $10 per person, powered for 2 $25; dorms $31; lodge rooms for up to 4 $121; cabins with kitchen and ensuite for 5 $192.) **Gagudju Lodge Cooinga (YHA) ❶**, down a 5km turn-off in the Yellow Water region, has pricey motel rooms and a campground, as well as budget rooms. (☎8979 0145. Sites for 2 $15, powered $28; 3-bed dorms $30.50; budget doubles $70; motel rooms from $210.)

The two standard-fee **campsites** in the area have good facilities but are plagued by mozzies after dark. **Muirella Park Campground ❶**, down a 6km gravel track from the Kakadu Hwy. 30km from Jabiru, is in Nourlangie. **Mardugal Campground ❶** is 2km south of the turn-off for Yellow Water. Here, you get shower and toilet facilities and some of the best stargazing in the park. **Free bush camping** is available at **Sandy Billabong ❶**, 5km of unsealed road past Muirella, **Jim Jim Billabong ❶**, on a

6km 4WD turn-off across from the Yellow Water turn-off, and **Malanjbanjdju ❶** and **Burdulba ❶,** both around 16km south of the junction of the Arnhem and Kakadu Hwy. The latter two give lovely views of Burdulba Billabong, but, as usual, flies and mozzies can be unbearable at times.

Supplies are available in Jabiru at the Jabiru Plaza. Take a left on Castenzoon St. from Jabiru Dr. The **supermarket** is well-stocked but pricey. (Open M-F 9am-5:30pm, Sa 9am-3pm, Su 10am-2pm.) The **Jabiru Cafe ❶,** also in the plaza, has tasty hot dishes for $6-15. (☎8979 2570. Open M-F 7am-8pm, Sa 8am-8pm, Su 8:30am-late.) Farther south, **Gagudju Lodge Cooinda ❷** has petrol and basic groceries, as well as filling buffet meals three times a day. (Meals $14. Open daily 6:30am-7pm.) Fuel is also available at various places in Jabiru and at Cooinda. Ranger stations can be found at **Bowali Visitors Centre** (☎8938 1120), 2km south of Jabiru, and **Jim Jim Ranger Station** (☎8979 2038), down a 2.5km turn-off from the Kakadu Hwy., 45km south of Bowali, near the Yellow Water turn-off.

SOUTH ALLIGATOR REGION

The impressive and well-run 🏅**Aurora Kakadu Resort ❶,** 40km west of Jabiru and 73km from the Northern Entry Station, has laundry facilities and a swimming pool. (☎8979 1666. Sites $7.50; dorms $20; budget twins $50; motel doubles $198, in the Wet $138.) Just past the Northern Entry Station, a 4WD track extends north into the park. For 80km, it bumps its way to **Van Diemen's Gulf.** Along this road are two free secluded campsites with refreshingly few campers. **Two Mile Hole ❶** and **Four Mile Hole ❶** are 8km and 38km from the Arnhem Hwy., respectively. They lack any facilities but offer peaceful camping along the Wildman River. Be prepared, however, for swarms of mozzies. **Food, fuel,** and **beer** can all be found at the Aurora Kakadu Resort. The **South Alligator Ranger Station** (☎8979 0194) is near the resort.

EAST ALLIGATOR REGION

There are two places to stay in East Alligator, both near Ubirr. The **East Alligator Kakadu Hostel ❷,** run out of the **Border Store,** 3km south of Ubirr and 36km north of Jabiru, is a decent option with A/C and an above-ground pool. (☎8979 2474. All beds $25 per person.) **Merl Campground** is 4km from Ubirr and has shady sites. Swarms of mozzies, however, make it inhospitable in the Dry. Alternatively, the more varied and cushy accommodations of Jabiru are a short half hour away.

The **Border Store ❶** has expensive **groceries and fuel,** although it's only a short drive to Jabiru and its wealth of supplies. Buffalo, beef, or croc burgers ($8.80) at the store are a good way to inject some protein into your diet. The **East Alligator Ranger Station,** 36km north of Bowali Visitors Centre, is near the store on Ubirr Rd. (☎8979 2291.)

JIM JIM/TWIN FALLS REGION

Accommodations in the region are limited to a few campsites with well-kept facilities. Perhaps the best camping spot in the park, due to the lack of mozzies, is an **unnamed campsite ❶** with a view of the looming escarpment, two-thirds of the way on the 4WD track to Jim Jim Falls. **Jim Jim Creek Campground ❶,** at the falls, is brilliantly located but is consequently often crowded. There are no services available along the 4WD track to the falls. The **Jim Jim Ranger Station** (☎8979 2038) is down a 2km road off of Kakadu Hwy. 10km south of the Jim Jim turn-off.

MARY RIVER REGION

The only non-camping option in the entire expanse of the Mary River region is actually just outside the park border. The **Wirnwirnmila Mary River Road House ❶** is on the Kakadu Hwy., 11km from the Southern Entry Station. Accommodation is fairly priced and uncrowded. (☎8975 4564. Reception 7:30am-11pm. Sites $6.50

per person, powered for 2 $17; bunks $15; budget singles $30; doubles $40; hotel rooms $90.) For bedding options farther afield, **Pine Creek** is 59km south of the park entrance. Along the Kakadu Hwy. lie a few campsites. **Maguk ❶** and **Gungural ❶** are roughly halfway from the southern entrance to Yellow Water. **Gunlom ❶** is next to the major attraction of the same name. **Yurmikmik ❶,** perhaps the pick of the bunch due to its slightly greater distance from water (and hence, fewer mozzies), is halfway down the track to Gunlom, 24km north of the park's southern entrance. **Fuel, meals,** and **groceries** are available at the road house. The **Mary River Ranger Station** (☎8975 4578) is at the Southern Entry Station.

👁 📖 SIGHTS & HIKES

> ❗ **HIKING SAFETY TIPS.** Self-sufficiency is the key to a safe adventure in Kakadu, as help is often hours away.
>
> **Bring:** Lots of **water** (at least 1L per hour of walking), insect repellent, sunscreen, and sturdy shoes.
>
> **Beware:** These areas are full of **snakes** and **spiders;** long trousers and thick socks help protect against bites. **Salties** are also common, so keep a generous distance from the edges of bodies of water and don't swim.
>
> **Call:** There are **emergency call boxes** at the carparks of some of the more remote hikes, such as Jim Jim.

In planning your visit, consider two pieces of advice. First, don't let the subdivision of the park or Kakadu's vastness fool you: the most striking readily accessible attractions (with the exception of Jim Jim and Twin Falls) are actually relatively close to each other. A route starting at Mamukala in the west and reaching Ubirr, the Bowali Visitors Centre and Nourlangie, and finishing at Yellow Water, traverses only 170km, all on easy sealed roads. Don't let arbitrary subdivisions dissuade you from visiting several different regions. Second, much of Kakadu's majesty lies in its diversity—in culture, ecosystems, and geography. Make sure to sample the variety that Kakadu contains.

Walks and hikes range in difficulty levels to suit all visitors. The main sights are viewed from short, relatively tame walking trails; a few are wheelchair-accessible. The climbs to the lookout points at Ubirr and Nourlangie are steeper. A number of excellent, longer walks reward the fit and adventurous who choose to venture farther out into the bush.

All sights and walks are open during the Dry; many are subject to closure during the Wet. *Kakadu By Foot* ($3.30), available at the Bowali Visitors Centre, gives detailed descriptions of the walks. For experienced hikers, unmarked and **overnight bushwalks** are the most genuine way to see Kakadu without the crowds. These routes generally follow the creek lines and gorges along the escarpment. Routes and campsites on unmarked walks must be approved. For overnight camping permits and route plan approval, contact the Bowali Visitors Centre (see **Practical Information,** p. 276). Permits are free but require one week for processing.

SOUTH ALLIGATOR REGION

Squawks and whistles of flocks of birds from hundreds of species greet you as you walk the 100m **wheelchair-accessible path** to the viewing platform at **Mamukala Wetlands,** on Arnhem Hwy., 29km west of Jabiru. In the Dry, the horizons of the floodplains surrounding Mamukala are thickly clustered with birds, from darting, diving rainbow bee-eaters to deliberate, plodding Jabiru storks. The variety and abundance of birds here is truly overwhelming. A 3km **walk** branches off from the path to wind along the edge of the wetlands. Located only 10km to the west, the 3.6km **Gu-ngarre walk** is a pleasant if nondescript jaunt through monsoonal woodlands near the fringes of a billabong.

EAST ALLIGATOR REGION

The gem of this region is **Ubirr**. Here, in the stone country of northeastern Kakadu, hundreds of generations of Aboriginal artists created some of the world's most intricate and extensive rock painting in one of the Top End's most striking geological regions. A short **wheelchair-accessible circuit** walk (1km; 30min.) passes the major galleries. Countless paintings in the natural rock shelters around the sandstone monolith known as Ubirr document successful hunts, age-old ceremonies, and creation stories. They include depictions of long-extinct animals as well as more recent images such as two silhouettes of early bushmen with hands in pockets smoking pipes. A short but steep **climb** (250m; 15min.) leads to the top of Ubirr, with a spectacular view of the distant stone escarpment and the emerald floodplains. ■**Sunsets** on top of Ubirr are magical, but be prepared to share the experience with a crowd of tourists. (Open daily Apr.-Nov. 8:30am-sunset, Dec.-Mar. 2pm-sunset.) Four free art site talks are given daily during the Dry; check at Bowali for the schedule.

The **Guluyambi River Cruise** concentrates on educating guests about Aboriginal life. While drifting by the salties on the banks of the East Alligator River, Aboriginal guides explain local practices and demonstrate use of traditional tools and preparation of Aboriginal foods. (☎ 1800 089 113. 1¾hr. Departs daily Apr.-Nov. 9, 11am, 1, and 3pm. Call for schedules Dec.-May. $33, children $16.) The **Bardedjilidji Sandstone Walk** (2.5km; 40min.) highlights the intriguing weathered sandstone pillars, arches and caves of the stone country. The trailhead is near the upstream boat ramp on a turn-off 1km south of the Border Store. The flat **Manngarre Monsoon Rainforest Walk** (1.5km; 30min.) ambles through a lush rainforest on a flat and easy trail to a viewing platform. Beautiful and tropical, the walk features occasional croc sightings along the East Alligator River.

JABIRU REGION

The **Bowali Visitors Centre** provides an overview of the biology, geology, and cultural traditions of the park. A 25-minute nature film follows a smattering of wildlife through the yearly cycles (every hour on the half hour). A 9-screen slide show with soundtrack shows hundreds of vibrant photographs of the park, progressing from the Wet season through the Dry (every hour on the hour). While at Bowali, make sure to visit the desk and let the friendly rangers help you organize your stay. Also, pick up the schedule of events, called "What's On," and peruse the various informative park literature. (Film every hour on the half hour. Slide show every hour on the hour. See **Practical Information,** p. 276.)

The **Iligadjarr Walk** (3.8km; 2hr.) leaves from the Burdulba or Malabanjbanjdju campsites, crosses floodplains, and skirts the edge of Burdulba Billabong. Located east of Jabiru town, the opencut **Ranger Uranium Mine** has tours departing from the Jabiru Airport. (☎ 1800 089 113. Tours depart 10:30am. 1½hr. $20, children $10. Reservations essential.)

NOURLANGIE REGION

The principal draw of this part of the park is **Nourlangie** itself, a huge rock outlier used as a shelter and art studio by earlier Aborigines. A winding **wheelchair-accessible track** connects the major art sites (1.5km; 1hr.). Have a good look at the trail map on the sign at the trailhead before heading out—some of the galleries are on side loops which can be a bit confusing. Among the most engaging sites is the **Main Gallery,** with an extensive collection of layered work, and the **Anbangbang rock shel-**

ter, a shady overhang beneath a large boulder which has been frequented by native people since at least the last ice age. On the walls are found the images of many spirits, including that of *Nalbulwinj-bulwinj*, a dangerous spirit who eats females after striking them with a yam. The furthest point on the loop is **Gunwarrdehwarrde Lookout**, a craggy climb to a view of the escarpment, where Lightning Man *Namarrgon* is said to live. Three art site talks are given in the Dry for free.

The stunning **Barrk Sandstone Bushwalk** (12km; 4-5hr.), one of the longest and most dramatic established walks in the park, branches off from the walk around Nourlangie. Strictly for the fit and sure-footed, it heads straight up Nourlangie's steep sides to spine-tingling vistas of the surround region. Snaking across the flat plateau of Nourlangie, it passes through sandstone formations that evoke lost cities. A quick descent and a lengthy level path lead back to the rock art walk. Along the way back you'll pass the **Nanguluwur Art Gallery.** This walk is not to be taken lightly—be forewarned that the trail is difficult to follow at times. Move slowly and keep your eyes peeled for the orange trail markers. Sturdy footwear and upwards of 3L of water are essential.

Some of the shorter walks in the region afford views of Nourlangie from afar. The **Nawurlandja Lookout** (600m; 20min.) and **Mirrai Lookout** (1.8km; 30min.) are short steep climbs with photogenic views. **Anbangbang Billabong** (2.5km; 30min.) is easy and popular, circling the water lily-filled waters alongside jagged cliffs (accessible only in the Dry).

JIM JIM/TWIN FALLS REGION

The opening day of the 4WD-only access road in the Dry, eagerly awaited by tourists and tour guides alike, is frustratingly uncertain. Up a tough 60km road, **Jim Jim Falls** cascades 150m down into a deep, clear green pool. Jim Jim is not visible for much of the year, but in the Wet, the falls rush with roaring intensity. However, the same rain that causes the awesome spectacle also prevents road access to it; the only way to see the falls during the Wet is by air. There is a **lookout** 200m from the carpark. A boulder-laden **walk** (1km; 30min.) leads to the plunge pool, which remains quite cold for much of the Dry due to lack of direct sunlight. For experienced hikers, the stunning **Barrk Marlam walk** (3km; 4hr.) branches off the path at the lookout, climbing the escarpment to expansive views of the gorge.

The long journey to **Twin Falls** begins at the Jim Jim Campground. The first challenge is a formidable river crossing, for which a good 4WD is required and a snorkel recommended. A 10km rumble through the woods ends at the beginning of the trail. An easy 400m stretch leads to a sandy beach where many swim. The next step is a 500m swim up river between the sheer sides of the gorge. After this Herculean set of tests, you reach the sensational falls themselves. The double falls cascade over sandstone steps to a plunge pool with a pristine sandy beach.

Both Jim Jim and Twin Falls are home to freshies, which tend to leave people alone, and the very occasional saltie. The park takes all precautions to keep them out, and the risk is low, but *swimming is at your own risk*. For the 4WD-less, a few tour companies depart daily from both Jabiru and Cooinda. Try **Katch Kakadu Tours** (☎8979 3315; $127, children $99), **Lord's Kakadu** (☎8979 2970; $125, children $100, YHA discount $5), or **Kakadu Gorge and Waterfall Tours** (☎8979 0111; $130, children $110).

YELLOW WATER REGION

Yellow Water, part of Jim Jim Creek, teems with bird life and saltwater crocs. There are two ways to view the area. A **wheelchair-accessible path,** leaving from Yellow Water carpark, leads to a platform with views of a small part of the wetlands flanking the river and its abundant wildlife. As the area is difficult to access on foot, a better option is on a ▓cruise with the Aboriginal-owned **Yellow Water company.**

NORTHERN TERRITORY

Knowledgeable guides help to identify and explain the hordes of wildlife you'll see along the way, as well as answer questions you might have. (☎8979 0111. Book at the Gagadju Lodge Cooinda. 2hr. tours in the Dry at 6:45, 9am, and 4:30pm; $40. 1½hr. tours at 11:30am, 1:15, and 2:45pm; $33. The sunrise tour is best for viewing birdlife. The 9am is best for crocs.)

Also enlightening is the **Warrandjan Aboriginal Cultural Centre,** 1km from the Cooinda Lodge. The exhibits show the variety and complexity of local Aboriginal culture and do a good job of placing into context the otherwise disjointed bits of information found throughout the park. Built in the shape of a *warradjan* (turtle), the Centre contains wonderful displays on bushtucker, hunting techniques, Aboriginal arts, and the struggle to keep the culture alive. (☎8979 0051. Open daily July-Aug. 7:30am-6pm; Sept.-June 9am-5pm. Free.)

A pair of laid-back walks depart the Mardugal campground. The **Gun-garden walk** is a 2km circuit through woodlands, while the **Mardugal Billabong walk** is a 1km stroll past the billabong with views of the resident birdlife.

MARY RIVER REGION

Mary River, the region most recently incorporated into Kakadu National Park, lies to the far southwest corner of Kakadu, just inside the Southern Entry Station. Mary River boasts a collection of several enjoyable walks as well as peaceful Gunlom, the only 2WD-accessible escarpment waterfall in the entire park. For those with a limited amount of time in the park, Mary River often understandably gets short shrift—it is far from the major sights of the north and its attractions take a bit more effort to access.

Popular **Gunlom Falls** is the biggest draw in the Mary River region. A short **wheelchair-accessible path** leads to a plunge pool surrounded by sheer rocky walls situated just beneath the falls. A steep **trail** (1km; 30min.) travels to the top of the falls with beautiful views of the surrounding area.

The secondary sights in the region are more challenging for both your car and your legs. **Maguk,** or **Barramundi Falls,** is a smaller cascade; the 4WD turn-off is 32km north of the Gunlom turn-off on the Kakadu Hwy. It flows during both seasons and is reached via a 12km road and then a rocky **hike** (2km; 1hr.) through monsoon forest. The **Yurmikmik Walking Tracks** pass Wet season waterfalls. The trailhead is 21km down Gunlom Rd. off the Kakadu Hwy. There are three different circular day tracks (2km, 45min.; 5km, 2hr.; 7.5km, 4hr.) and two longer tracks that require overnight permits. The 11km walk features a series of waterfalls and the 13.5km walk features plunge pools during the Wet. Both of these longer walks are difficult, unmarked, and require good navigation and preparation. Near the Yurmikmik walks is **Jarrangbarnmi,** one of the *djang andjamun* areas that bring catastrophic consequences if entered. This series of pools on **Koolpin Creek** is home to *Bula* and *Bolung*, two Creation Ancestors. Visitor numbers are restricted, and no one can enter the area without a permit and entry key organized by the Southern Entry Station (☎8975 4859).

LITCHFIELD NATIONAL PARK

At Litchfield National Park, dusty roads wind through lush forest and mesmerizing termite mounds. A series of generally tame walks yield stunning vistas en route to inviting aqua pools tucked into the bases of tumbling, roaring waterfalls. While its proximity to Darwin can render solitude hard to find at the major sights, visiting Litchfield with a 4WD and staying for more than a day allows you to escape the crowds and explore the park's more hidden gems. Even without 4WD, however, many of the park's wonders are easily accessible, making Litchfield a rewarding daytrip from Darwin.

LITCHFIELD NATIONAL PARK AT A GLANCE	
AREA: 1460 sq. km.	**GATEWAYS:** Batchelor, Darwin (p. 263).
CLIMATE: Monsoonal, with distinct Wet (Nov.-Apr.) and Dry (May-Oct.) seasons.	**CAMPING:** Buley Rockhole, Florence Falls, Surprise Creek Falls, Tjaynera (Sandy Creek) Falls (4WD only), Wangi Falls, and Walker Creek.
HIGHLIGHTS: Spectacular waterfalls, tranquil walks, 4WD tracks, and towering termite mounds.	
	FEES: Entry free.

▐█ ▐▄ TRANSPORTATION & ORIENTATION

Two routes run from Darwin to the park, 118km southwest of the state capital. Some 90km down the Stuart Hwy., **Litchfield Park Road** juts west, passing 18km, through Batchelor, on its way to the eastern border of the park. On the other side of the park, it connects to an unsealed but passable road that leads back to Darwin (115km). Most sights lie along Litchfield Park Rd. **Tjaynera Falls** and **Surprise Creek** lie along a 4WD track just west of Greenant Creek. Though park maps still show a 4WD track connecting Lost City to this track, it is long since closed and overgrown. Litchfield Park Rd. is generally open to all vehicles in all seasons. 4WD tracks close in the Wet.

Tours from Darwin, some of which include Kakadu, abound. The cheapest is run by **McCafferty's/Greyhound**, a bus daytrip taking in the major sites accessible by sealed roads. (☎ 8941 5872. $75.) **Darwin Day Tours** runs a similar tour. (☎ 8924 1124. $104, children $75; lunch included.)

▐ PRACTICAL INFORMATION

There is no ranger station, but information is available through the **Parks and Wildlife Commission of the Northern Territory** (☎ 8999 5511) in Darwin, and detailed maps are available for free at the Batchelor Store. Park entry is free. Call ☎ 8976 0282 for **road conditions,** especially during the Wet. The nearest **post office** is in Batchelor. (☎ 8976 0020. Open M-F 9am-5pm, Sa 9am-noon.) **Petrol** is available next door at the Batchelor Store.

▐▀▐ CAMPING & ACCOMMODATIONS

Spending a night in Litchfield is highly recommended, if only for the superb stargazing. **Camping ❶** in the park generally costs $6.60 per person for basic unpowered sites with showers and toilets. Payment is made upon entering the campsites at unmanned drop boxes. The **Wangi Falls ❶** campground fills up early in the day and can be uncomfortably crowded; more serene options lie near **Florence Falls ❶** and **Buley Rockhole ❶.** Visitors with a 4WD have extra choices at Florence Falls and **Tjaynera (Sandy Creek) Falls ❶. Surprise Creek Falls ❶** and **Walker Creek ❶** have toilets and are half the cost of other sites. Be prepared for ravenous packs of mosquitos. Caravan camping is allowed only at Wangi Falls and Surprise Creek, and generators are not permitted anywhere in the park.

Litchfield Tourist & Van Park ❶ is 4km from the park border, on the way to Batchelor and fishing on the banks of the Finnis River. (☎ 8976 0070. Sites $7 per person, powered for 2 $16.50, families $25; overnight vans for 4 $50; cabins for 2 $60.) Just down the road is the family-run **Banyan Tree Caravan Park ❶.** (☎ 8976 0030. Sites $6 per person, powered for 2 $17.) The well-manicured **Jungle Drum Bungalows ❷,** next door to the Butterfly Farm in Batchelor, have Balinese decor and a relaxing atmosphere. (☎ 8976 0555. Dorms $25; cabin singles $68, doubles $92.)

NORTHERN TERRITORY

◐ FOOD

There is a food kiosk at **Wangi Falls.** (Open daily 9am-5pm.) In Batchelor, the **Butterfly Cafe Restaurant ❶** has hearty home-cooked meals; check out the **Bird and Butterfly Sanctuary** on the premises. (☎8976 0199. Cafe open daily 8:30am-4pm and 6-10pm. Sanctuary open daily 9am-4pm. $6, children $3.) Basic **groceries,** as well as LP fuel for stoves, are available at the **Batchelor Store.** (☎8976 0045. Open M-F 7am-7pm, Sa-Su 7am-5pm.)

⊙ ◢ SIGHTS & ACTIVITIES

WANGI. Converging streams cascade into a pool of clear water at bottom of Wangi (WONG-gye) Falls. Come early to avoid the throng of tourists. Snorkeling and swimming are relatively safe, but heed the warning and closure signs—salties sometimes like to swim here too. A walking trail (1km; 45min.) passes through the forest atop the falls, but affords no view of the falls themselves.

▨FLORENCE FALLS. The most impressive falls in the park are reached by a 15min. walk along the creek. Even in the Dry, copious volumes of water tumble 100m into a clear, calm pool. Nearby **Buley Rockhole** is not a single hole but a series of small pools and makes a great place for a swim. A short drive or a 3.2km walk through verdant monsoonal forest connects the two sights.

TOLMER FALLS. Only a short distance southwest from Florence Falls on the main road, a mild 1.2km walking loop winds past a natural stone arch, a lookout deck offering a commanding view of the falls, and a stretch of peaceful creek. Swimming is prohibited to protect the fragile ecosystem, which is home to several species of bats.

MAGNETIC TERMITE MOUNDS. Throughout Litchfield, majestic termite mounds approaching 7m high dominate the flat, open landscape. They are the handywork of two species of termites. Cathedral termites build towering conical mounds while magnetic termites construct flat, gravestone-like homes. The magnetic mounds are all aligned with their broad faces pointing east and west for temperature regulation—they soak up the softer light of morning and evening while escaping the harsh midday glare. A haunting field of magnetic mounds, along with information boards explaining termite life, can be found at the Magnetic Termite Mounds site near the eastern edge of the park. Mounds can also be viewed on the 4WD track to Surprise Creek.

LOST CITY. A 10km 4WD track leads to a collection of eroded rock outcroppings. A maze of short trails wind among the twists and turns, arches, and turrets of the formations, allowing endless exploration. In the early morning, a shroud of hazy mist heightens the towers' mystery.

TJAYNERA FALLS (SANDY CREEK FALLS). About 7km off Litchfield Park Rd. on a 4WD-track, a mild 1.7km path leads to a tranquil falls. The scene is excellent and the solitude is welcome after the crowds of Wangi.

▨SURPRISE CREEK FALLS. A farther 20km along the Tjaynera track, a series of pools connected by attractive falls create a refreshing oasis. A pond and two small bowl-shaped pools make for peaceful swimming. Thrillseekers jump from the top pool into the bottom. Typically deserted, the falls make for one of the best spots in the Top End.

STUART HIGHWAY: DARWIN TO KATHERINE

The lonely Stuart Hwy. connects Darwin to Adelaide, SA, slicing the continent down the middle. The first stretch runs 314km from Darwin to Katherine with a handful of diversions along the way.

About 25km south of Darwin is the turn-off for **Howard Springs Nature Park.** Once a WWII rest and recreation military camp, the springs offer swimming with barramundi and turtles and a 30min. nature hike. (☎8983 1001. Open daily 8am-8pm. Free.) About 10km farther down the Stuart Hwy., **Cox Peninsula Road** runs 11km west to **Territory Wildlife Park.** Paths transect 400 hectares of various recreated habitats. A nocturnal house, reptile pavilion, and host of pens feature a wide range of native fauna. The Birds of Prey presentation and enclosed tunnel aquarium are highlights. (☎8988 7200. Open daily 8:30am-6pm, last admission 4pm. $18, concessions $9, families $40.) **Darwin Day Tours** runs a half-day tour to the park. (☎8924 1124. Daily 7:30am-1:30pm. $47, concessions $43, children $42; includes entrance fee.) After animal gazing, relax 1km down the road at **Berry Springs Nature Park,** with picnic spots and lukewarm soaking grounds. (Open daily 8am-6:30pm. Free.)

Eighty kilometers south of Darwin and 7km down an access road lies **Lake Bennett Resort ❶,** an upscale lodge next to a fetching lake. Swim, canoe ($15 per hr., $40 per day), fish, or play golf before watching the sunset. Guest rooms include fridge, A/C, and TV, with shared bath and kitchen facilities. The staff will meet bus travelers at the Stuart Hwy. (☎8976 0960. Sites $10 per person; caravan sites $20, powered $25; dorms $25; twins $170; triples $195. NOMADS.) The turn-off for **Batchelor** and **Litchfield National Park** (see p. 282) is 6km south of the resort.

Between the fuel stops at Adelaide River and Hayes Creek, and 200km from Darwin, **Tjuwaliyn (Douglas) Hot Springs** is a worthwhile stop. The last 7km of the access road to the springs is gravel but tame enough for all cars in the Dry. At some places, the springs are exceedingly fiery; head downstream for cooler currents. **Camping ❶** is available ($3.50, children $1, families $8). **Pine Creek** is the final stop on the route, 50km north of Katherine.

PINE CREEK   ☎08

Tiny, friendly Pine Creek (pop. 650), slumbers at the junction of the Stuart and Kakadu Hwy. with a few places to stay and a decent pub. On the main street (named Main Terr.), the **Diggers Rest Motel ❺** has well-kept ensuite cabins with kitchen, TV, and A/C, and doubles as a **tourist center.** (☎8976 1442. Reception 8am-8pm. Singles $75; doubles and triples $85; rooms for 4-5 people $95.) Next door is **Ah Toys,** the general store that doubles as a **bus depot.** (☎8976 1202. Open M-F 9am-6:30pm, Sa and Su 9am-1pm.) **Greyhound/McCafferty's** runs to Darwin (3hr., 3 per day, $41) and Katherine (1hr., 3 per day, $18). Around the corner on Moule St., the **post office** doubles as a **bank.** (☎8976 1220. Open M-F 9am-noon and 1-5pm.) The adjacent **Mayse's Cafe ❶** serves good meals for $6-9 and pizzas for $13-18. (☎8976 1241. Open daily 7am-7pm.) Next door, the **Pine Creek Hotel ❺,** 40 Moule St. has nice motel rooms. Their **restaurant ❷** serves counter means for $12-20. (☎8976 1288. Motel rooms $100.) The **Pine Creek Service Station ❶** across the street has very basic but cheap accommodation. They also occasionally cook up good value meals for guests. (☎8976 1217. Sites $10, powered $14; singles $25; doubles $35; family rooms $35, extra child $5.) The casual and congenial **Kakadu Gateway Caravan Park ❶** has a range of accommodations, as well as BBQ, kitchen, TV room, and free laundry. (☎8976 1166. Sites can be booked at Ah Toys, or at the reception off Buchanan St. after 3:30pm. Sites $10; ensuite powered sites $22; singles $40; budget doubles $42; doubles $57; twins $67; family rooms $72; swag room with no beds $8 per person.) A sluggish **Internet** connection is available at the **public library** ($5.50 per hr.; open M-F 11am-5pm, Sa 11am-1pm). About 20km south of town on the Stuart Hwy., a turn-off leads to **Umbrawarra Gorge.** A fairly easy walk (1km; 30min.) leads to the river at the foot of the gorge. From here, it's possible to explore the length of the gorge along the river.

KATHERINE   ☎ 08

The only stoplight along the 1500km of the Stuart Hwy. between Darwin and Alice Springs is found in the rough-and-tumble town of Katherine (pop. 11,000), gateway to Nitmiluk. The town is edgy; noisy, often drunken conflict along the main streets in Katherine is not unusual. However, groceries and Internet access in Katherine are just as cheap as in Darwin, and it might hold the last fairly-priced pharmacy, travel agent, book store, or cinema that you'll find for a while.

ORIENTATION & TRANSPORTATION

Katherine marks the intersection of three main roads. The **Stuart Highway** becomes **Katherine Terrace** in town; most shops and services are here. The **Victoria Highway** leaves from the northern side of town, passing the hot springs and heading eventually to the Kimberley. Finally, **Giles Street** heads east from the middle of town, reaching **Nitmiluk National Park** (29km). The Transit Centre is on the southern end of Katherine Terr., near **Lindsay Street.**

Greyhound/McCafferty's buses (☎1800 089 103) stop at the **Transit Centre** on Katherine Terr. and run to: Darwin (4hr., 4 per day, $52); Alice Springs (15hr., 2 per day, $179); Broome (19hr., 1 per day, $226); and Townsville (29½hr., 1 per day, $290). Local car rental agencies are **Territory Rent-a-Car,** 6 Katherine Terr. (☎8971 3183), in the Transit Centre; **Hertz,** 392 Katherine Terr. (☎8971 1111), which has some 4WDs; and **Delta** (☎13 13 90), at Knotts Crossing Resort.

PRACTICAL INFORMATION

Tourist Office: Katherine Region Tourist Association (☎8972 2650), on the corner of Lindsay St. and Katherine Terr., across from the Transit Centre. Open Apr.-Oct. M-F 8:30am-6pm, Sa-Su 10am-3pm; Nov.-Mar. M-F 9am-5pm, Sa-Su 10am-3pm.

Bank: Several **banks** and 24hr. **ATMs** are on Katherine Terr. (All banks open M-Th 9:30am-4pm, F 9:30am-5pm.)

Work Opportunities: Working at hostels in exchange for accommodations is popular in Katherine, but call ahead. **Employment National,** 17 First St. (☎1300 720 126), produces a *Harvest Workers Guide* and can connect with local mango farms during picking season (Sept.-Nov.). Most work is piece-rate.

Police: (☎8972 0111), 2.5km south of town on the Stuart Hwy.

Internet: Didj Shop Internet Cafe (☎8972 2485), on Giles St. a block west of Katherine Terr. $8 per hr. Also has Aboriginal art. Open Apr.-Oct. M-F 10am-10pm, Sa 11am-7pm, Su 10am-3pm; Nov.-Mar. M-F 10am-7pm, Sa 11am-7pm, Su 10am-3pm.

Post Office: on the corner of Katherine Terr. and Giles St. Open M-F 9am-5pm. **Postal Code:** 0850.

ACCOMMODATIONS

▨ **Kookaburra Backpackers** (☎8971 0257; kookaburra@nt-tech.com.au), on the corner of Lindsay and 3rd St. Non-traditional backpackers arrangement with a few common spaces and self-contained units with kitchenette and bathroom shared between 4-8 guests. Free transport to and from the Transit Centre, pool, and organized BBQs. Runs 3-day camping tour through Kakadu from Katherine to Darwin ($380, includes meals and camping equipment). Laundry $3. Key deposit $10. Reception 7:30am-2pm and 4:30-7:30pm. Book ahead in the Dry. Dorms $16; twins with TV and fridge $44; light but tasty brekkie included. ISIC/NOMADS/VIP/YHA. ❷

Palm Court Backpackers YHA (☎8972 2722 or 1800 626 722), on the corner of 3rd and Giles St. Free pancake batter in the morning encourages friendly atmosphere in this converted motel. Pool, BBQ, and Internet ($2 per 20min.). All rooms have ensuite and desk. Free pick-up and drop-off. Laundry $3. Key deposit $10. Bikes $10 per day. Reception 6:30am-2:30pm and 4:30-7pm. Dorms $16; twins $46; doubles $48. NOMADS/VIP/YHA. ❷

Coco's Backpackers, 21 1st St. (☎8971 2889). Behind the didgeridoo shop, a ragtag mixture of Aboriginal artists, musicians, cyclists, and international travelers mill about amid the cluttered yard of Coco's. The rooms are simple and bare, but for those tired of the typical party-hostel fare, it might just be the perfect fit. Call ahead; the owners are only there sporadically and there is no formal reception area. Sites $9 per person; dorms $16; double $38.

Paraway Motel (☎8972 2644; paraway@nt-tech.com.au), on the corner of O'Shea Terr. and 1st St. One of the nicer of Katherine's many motels, with wheelchair-accessible rooms, pool, spa, laundry, and the town's only security carpark. Reception 7am-8pm. Singles from $84; doubles from $94. ❺

Camping is available along the Victoria Hwy. The **Red Gum Caravan Park ❶** (☎8972 2239) is 1km from town (a 10min. walk), and has laundry, pool, and BBQ. (Sites $9, for 2 $18, powered for 2 $23; cabins $65, for more than 2 $80.) The **Riverview Caravan Park and Motel ❷**, at the hot springs, has a pool, spa, laundry, and BBQ. (☎8972 1011. Sites for 2 $17, powered $22; singles $20; doubles and twins $30; budget cabins for 2 $50.)

🍴 FOOD

A giant Woolworths **supermarket** is across from the Transit Centre, on Katherine Terr. (☎8972 3055. Open daily 7am-10pm.) For those about to head bush, visit **Town and Country Butchery,** on Katherine Terr. across from the junction with the Victoria Hwy. They have the best selection of meats in town, from croc to kangaroo, and they'll Cryovac it for you on the spot so it will last weeks with only refrigeration— no need to freeze. (☎8971 0353. Open M-Sa 7am-5:30pm.)

🍔 **Bucking Bull Burger Bar** (☎8972 1734), Shop 1 on Katherine Terr. You know a place is good when all the locals have a tab there. Mouthwatering burgers from beef to barra. Great mango smoothies $3.50. Breakfast specials start at $6. Open daily 5am-5pm. ❶

Starvin's Pizza and Cafe, 32 Katherine Terr. (☎8972 3633). Gourmet pizzas from $12. A laid-back cafe atmosphere with some of the best food in Katherine. BYO ($2.20 corking charge per person). Open M-Sa 9am-10pm, Su 11am-10pm.

Paraway Buchanan's Restaurant (☎8972 2644), at the Paraway Motel (see above). While the fancy main dishes like lamb curried prawn can be a bit pricey ($18-22), Buchanan's actually holds the town's best hidden deal. Their themed Thursday night all-you-can eat buffets, ranging from seafood to Chinese, are culinary feasts. Each has a different price, but they start at just $12.50 for pizza and pasta night. Open Su and W-Sa 6:30-late. ❸

👁 SIGHTS & ACTIVITIES

Two kilometers along the Victoria Hwy. from Katherine Terr., **hot springs** bubble along the Katherine River. Popular with tourists of all ages, the springs have swimming, toilets, and wheelchair access along Croker St. Free. **Coco's Place** (see

Accommodations, p. 287) is a didgeridoo shop run by experts, making it a far better place to learn about the instrument than the backpacker-targeted shops in Darwin. Make your own didgeridoo (and keep it) with **Whoop Whoop** overnight trips. (☎ 8972 2941. Depart F-Sa. $220.) From May to October, evening **river cruises** provide wildlife spotting and lively dinner around a campfire. **Far Out Adventures** cruises the Katherine River and has BBQ-style meals with BYO. (☎ 8972 2552. $50; includes pick-up.) **Travel North** runs a **crocodile night** along the Johnstone River that includes wine and stew. (☎ 1800 089 103. Nightly 6:30pm. $45; with pick-up $55.)

NITMILUK NATIONAL PARK (KATHERINE GORGE)

The series of thirteen gorges collectively known as Katherine Gorge together form the third-most touristed destination of the Top End. Chiseled from a sandstone plateau, the rocky cliffs which rise from the river's edge draw boatloads of admirers. The wildlife here is an additional draw, with 168 species of birds dwelling in the monsoon forests which fringe the gorge.

The 450 rock art galleries which dot the park, including a series of paintings in the gorges themselves, are reminders that shutter-snapping tourists are not the first visitors to the area. Since 1989, the park has been owned by the traditional residents, the Jawoyn people, who leased its management to the Norther Territory government for 99 years. The history and future of the Jawoyn people is a theme throughout the park, from the Dreamtime stories as relayed in the paintings to the sometimes sober meditations on the future of Aboriginal culture found in the exhibits of the Visitors Centre.

NITMILUK AT A GLANCE

AREA: 292,008 hectares.	**GATEWAYS:** Katherine (p. 286).
FEATURES: Katherine River and 13 gorges, Edith Falls, 17 Mile Creek.	**CAMPING:** Permanent campgrounds near the Visitors Centre and at Edith Falls, and registered overnight bush camping.
HIGHLIGHTS: Canoeing down the river, hiking up cliffs and through shady gorges.	**FEES:** Entry free.

ORIENTATION & PRACTICAL INFORMATION

The 13 gorges on the Katherine River form the centerpiece of Nitmiluk. The gorges are accessed by boat or by foot on the Southern Walks from the **Nitmiluk Visitor Centre**, at the end of the sealed Gorge Rd. 30km east of Katherine. A second entrance to the park lies 40km north of Katherine on the Stuart Hwy., where a 20km access road leads to Edith Falls, with a campground and a few short hikes. The long Jatbula Trail connects the two.

 WHEN TO GO. The climate is most comfortable in the gorge from May-Sept., after the seasonal storms but before the unbearable humidity. In the Wet, floods can limit activities in the park, though the greenery is at its most vivid.

Buses: Travel North (☎ 1800 089 103) runs buses from all accommodations in Katherine to the Visitors Centre. (25min., 4 per day, $18 return.) Book ahead.

Tourist Info: Nitmiluk Visitors Centre provides hiking information and camping permits. A tourist desk in the gift shop books canoes, helicopter and boat tours, and campground sites. Free exhibits present a broad introduction to the park from natural history to the culture of the local Jawoyn people. A licensed **bistro ❶** serves $6-7 burgers and

$10 Thai chicken salad. (Centre ☎8972 1886, bistro ☎8972 3150. Centre and gift shop open daily 7am-7pm. Bistro open daily 8am-8:30pm; Happy Hour 5-6:30pm.) Contact the **Parks and Wildlife Commission** in Katherine for more info on Katherine Gorge. (☎8972 1886; fax 8971 0702. P.O. Box 344, Katherine NT 0851.)

Tours: Nitmiluk Tours offers **helicopter flights**. 3 gorges $55, 8 gorges $82.50, 13 gorges $137.50. Book at the Visitors Centre. (☎8972 1253.)

▶ CAMPING

A shady, but often crowded **caravan park ❶** near the Visitors Centre has toilets, showers, laundry, phones, and BBQ facilities. At night, wallabies scavenge for food scraps—clean up after yourself. Register at the Visitors Centre. (Sites $8 per person, powered $12.) Unpowered sites are available at a second **campground ❶**, next to Edith Falls, with showers, BBQ, a food kiosk, and a picnic area. Nearby pools and falls make it a pleasant, cool spot. Beneath a waterfall, the crystal clear **lower pool** is just a short walk from the carpark.

Camping ❶ in the depths of the park is permitted; register at the Visitors Centre. ($3.30 per person per night; $50 deposit, $20 if only going as far as Crystal Falls from the Center.) Campsites with toilets and (usually) a water source are along the Jatbula Trail and at the 4th, 5th, and 8th gorges in the Southern Walks area. Fires are permitted along the Jatbula but not in Southern Walks.

▶ NITMILUK BY WATER

Getting out on the Katherine River has many advantages—you can see much more of the gorges than you can along the trails; it is often cooler on the water than on the searing trails. From May to September, quiet waters allow for canoeing and boat tours. **Nitmiluk Tours** (☎8972 1253) is the only option for canoe rental and cruises, which can be booked at most accommodations in Katherine or at the Visitors Centre. Boat tours offer commentary and interpretation of the gorge and its plants and animals. Canoeing, on the other hand, affords more solitude, though the throng of fellow paddlers and passing boat tours limits the serenity of the trip.

CANOEING. Nitmiluk Tours rents Canadian-style canoes, which are a cross between a canoe and a kayak. This design is chosen for safety, not speed, and is a bit awkward to operate. They can provide, however, a tranquil trip along the sheer walls of the gorge, and at your own chosen tempo. Consider taking a full-day trip, allowing you to get to the third gorge and away from the stream of fellow paddlers. No more than 75 canoes are permitted in the gorge at once; book ahead. (Single canoes half-day $30, full-day $41, overnight $82; doubles $44/$61/$122. Half and full-day canoes require $20 cash deposit. Overnight canoes require $3.50 permit and $60 cash deposit.)

CRUISES. Zoom along the gorges in flat, shaded motor vessels; at the end of each gorge, passengers transfer to a new boat on the next gorge. Be warned: the crowded arrangement makes it hard to enjoy the natural solitude of the area, and the hustling tours destroy any chance of moving at one's own pace. (Departs from the boat jetty; 2hr.; 4 per day in the Dry; $34, children $13.50.) Daily "adventure" and "safari" tours combine boating and hiking. (Departs 9am. 4hr. $49; 8hr. $85.)

SWIMMING. The scorching sun makes taking a dip a popular activity, but keep in mind that you may be sharing the bath with freshies and power boats, so be careful. Many people like to swim near the boathouse or at the plunge pools or gorge access points at the end of some hikes.

NORTHERN TERRITORY

🅝 NITMILUK BY LAND

While the walking trails in Nitmiluk cannot match the area's boating and canoeing trips in terms of ease of access, the tracks tend to be much less crowded, and the views of the gorge from the top are truly phenomenal. However, unrelenting sun can make the trails, which are often 10°C hotter than it is near the water, unpleasant for visitors.

Walking tracks in the park run the spectrum from strolls to struggles and range from 2.5km to 66km. The Southern Walks are usually open year round; the Jatbula Trail is open only in the Dry. *For all overnight walks, register with the rangers before setting out.* Semi-detailed topographic maps are $7.50 at the Visitors Centre. Smaller trail maps are available for free.

SOUTHERN WALKS

The main trail of the Southern Walks starts at the Visitors Centre and runs parallel to the rim of the gorge at a distance of 1.5km. Each individual side trail branches off and meanders diagonally towards the gorge. The main trail follows a Wet season riverbed past sizeable rock slabs and eucalyptus saplings. However, it is the side trails which provide the postcard vistas. Trails are listed in order of closest to the Visitors Centre to farthest.

Lookout Loop. (3.7km return, 2hr., moderate.) This steep but well-maintained climb up the side of the gorge offers excellent views of the river and **Seventeen Mile Valley.** After the climb, it widens to an easy and smooth walk. Signs along the way detail the park's mythological and geological history.

Windolf Walk. (8.4km, 3½hr., moderate.) The side trail of the Windolf Walk follows a Wet season river bed almost to the edge of the gorge, at which point it forks. The right trail leads to **Pat's Lookout** on the gorge rim while the right descends to the **Southern Rock Hole.** Pat's Lookout oversees a bend in the gorge with sandy beach at the foot of a menacing cliff on the opposite shore. Picking your way along the rim to the right, you can reach a point with good views up the gorge. The trail to the left passes a Wet season waterfall and plunge pool with tiny frogs before reaching an inlet to the base of the gorge. It's a tucked-away spot and a great place to swim or just sit. A very steep and narrow trail leads to the right beyond Pat's Lookout to the base of the gorge. From here, the brazen may swim across to the sandy beach opposite and then walk along the canyon wall to the right to reach an **Aboriginal rock art gallery.** The sure-footed can follow the bank up the river to the end of the first gorge; if the water is low enough, you can use extreme caution and cross the natural rock bridge. With slippery rocks and raging water underneath, this can be a harrowing experience. Once across, follow the footpaths to the galleries.

Butterfly Gorge Walk. (12km, 4½hr., difficult.) A good overview of the region, with woodlands and rock formations giving way to a dense, tranquil monsoon forest in a side gorge. The last few hundred meters take you into a fantasy world where clouds of butterflies float through the trees. After a short but strenuous traverse down the cliff face, the walk ends at a deep swimming spot.

Lily Ponds Trail. (20km, 6½hr., difficult.) A challenging scramble in sections which leads to a sheltered pool in the third gorge. Among this walk's assets is the pall of visitors due to its length and rigors.

Eighth Gorge and Jawoyn Valley. (30-40km, overnight, very difficult.) The longest of the Southern Walks, the Eighth Gorge and Jawoyn Valley walk requires a night in the bush with a return by midday. The terrain is fierce, however. Carry extra supplies. The Jawoyn loop passes a rock art gallery.

JATBULA TRAIL

The popular Jatbula Trail winds approximately 66km over 5 days from the Visitors Centre to Edith Falls. Split into eight segments, the trail threads through rainforest pockets and waterfalls and passes an Aboriginal amphitheater. The first section makes the only plausible day walk, departing the Visitors Centre and winding through a valley before reaching the Northern Rockhole and adjacent rock face (16km; 4hr.; moderate).

OTHER TRAILS

At the opposite end of the Jatbula Trail (below), two short walks leave from the Edith Falls carpark. The **Sweetwater Pool** walk (9km, 4hr., moderate) leads to a waterhole and good camping. The **Leliyn Trail** (5.2km, 3hr., easy) leads to the smaller but no less attractive upper pools.

◙ ABORIGINAL ART

The first gorge harbors a series of impressive rock art galleries, some of which date to over 10,000 years ago. Each gallery has layered images, with more recent paintings superimposed on older work.

Little is known about the paintings of the **West Gallery,** now faded to a faint red shadow. The mysterious **Central Gallery** depicts a hunt or ritual. Curiously, the figures are upside down, interpreted variously as denoting sleep, ceremonial preparation, initiation, or death. A second debate focuses on six circles which are either bush potatoes or crocodile eggs. The oldest and most layered **East Gallery** depicts a powerful non-human male figure, a woman in a headdress, and a black wallaroo with joey. The woman and the wallaroo hold a stick from which flying foxes dangle. At the figures' feet lie the remains of a large mammal, perhaps a now-extinct species. A crowd in the background looks on.

ARNHEM LAND

Take the expansive wilderness, serenity, and culture of Kakadu, multiply it by ten, and you still won't be able to do justice to Arnhem Land's grandeur. Sprawling across the entire northeastern region of the Top End, and several times the size of Kakadu, this Aboriginal homeland was established in 1931. Though most of Arnhem Land is uninhabited, it has two modest towns (Oenpelli and Nhulunbuy), as well as several smaller settlements and around 150 Aboriginal outstations. The area's inland borders are cut square, but the endless coastline takes an untamed, jagged path from the **Cobourg Peninsula** in the west (location of **Gurig National Park**) to the **Gove Peninsula** in the east. The natural and cultural treasures here are incredible, but be aware that while there are Aborigines who welcome tourism and its revenues, there are also those who would prefer to see their lands free from swarms of outsiders.

Venturing into Arnhem Land is a serious matter. There are very few roads (those that do exist are erratically navigable only in the Dry), and there are virtually no signs or services. Moreover, Arnhem Land is off-limits by law to non-Aborigines, so a permit is required to enter. **Permits** for entering Arnhem Land vary depending on where you want to go. The **Northern Land Council** in the Jabiru Shopping Centre, next to the library, can issue permits for three locations close to Kakadu. (☎8979 2410. Open M-F 8am-4pm.) A permit for **Injalak** (IN-yaluk; $13.20 per person for 1 day) can be issued on the spot but may take up to an hour to process. Permits for **Sandy Creek** and **Wunyu Beach** ($88 per vehicle for 5 days) take longer, so allow 10 days for processing. To venture to the secluded beaches and wildlife of **Gurig National Park** on the Cooburg Peninsula, contact the **Parks and Wildlife Commission of the Northern Territory.** (☎ 8979 0244. $211 per vehicle with 5 adults for 7 nights.) If you're venturing to Nhulunbuy on the Central Arnhem Highway, permits are available through the **Northern Land Council** in Katherine (see Central Arnhem Highway, p. 292). For permits to other sections of Arnhem Land, contact Darwin's Northern Land Council (☎ 8920 5100).

For those seeking experienced guides and drivers, tours might be the best way to reach Arnhem Land. Multi-day tours with flights from Darwin run several thousands of dollars; 4WD daytrips from Kakadu are cheaper. Departing from Jabiru and Cooinda are **Outback NT Touring** (☎ 1800 089 113; $175, children $130) and **Lord's Kakadu and Arnhemland Safaris.** (☎ 8979 2422. $175, children $110.)

OENPELLI
☎ 08

Oenpelli (Gunbalanya) is a short 16km dirt-road drive from Ubirr. The road into Arnhem Land from Ubirr crosses the tidal **East Alligator River** at **Cahills Crossing.** Check with the Northern Land Council about tidal information before driving lest you find your car capsized in the waters.

The community is home to the **Injalak Arts & Crafts Centre,** where artists craft pandanus baskets, limited edition bark and paper paintings, screen printed textiles, and didgeridoos. The works are distributed to art galleries around the world, but visitors can purchase pieces on-site at prices far below those charged for the same work in both Kakadu and Darwin. (☎ 8979 0190. Open M-F 8am-5pm, Sa 8am-noon.) Injalak also sponsors ▣**Aboriginal-guided tours** through a local rock art gallery, the breadth and isolation of which put Ubirr and Nourlangie to shame—there are no crowds or roped-off sections here. (Tours leave 8:30-10am. 2hr. tours $90 total for 1-6 people. Book ahead.)

NORTHERN COAST

Even remoter than Injalak are Sandy Creek and Wunyu Beach. **Sandy Creek,** on Arnhem's north shore, offers excellent barramundi, salmon, and tuna fishing. Ideally, anglers should have a boat, though people do fish from the shore. The drive to Sandy Creek (3hr.) is 4WD only. Also on the northern shore is **Wunyu Beach,** a long, virtually untouched, and often windy beach ideal for relaxing and strolling. Sunbathers and would-be swimmers beware—both Wunyu Beach's and Sandy Creek's water is teeming with **salties.** The drive to Wunyu takes at least 2½hr. on a 4WD road. Neither Sandy Creek nor Wunyu Beach have facilities; people camp at their own risk. Campers must bring their own water, food, and shelter. Stopping on the road to Sandy Creek and Wunyu is prohibited.

CENTRAL ARNHEM HIGHWAY

The Central Arnhem Highway begins south of Katherine and passes through central and eastern Arnhem Land to the Gove Peninsula. The road is no joke, but the reward at the end is well worth the effort. *Let's Go* recommends using a 4WD vehicle for the 706km journey from Katherine, though a high-clearance 2WD is adequate. Locals (as well as insane travelers) have been known to attempt the drive in low-clearance 2WD vehicles, but the risk of serious damage from rocks or engine flooding is high. If you do decide to tempt fate, consider plugging your engine's air intake with a cloth and waiting for a 4WD to tow you through the deeper stream crossings. Or, better yet, find some locals planning to make the drive and ask to follow them. The trickiest parts are the **Wilton** and **Goyder** rivers. When crossing any stream, be certain to walk through before driving through, lest you find yourself nose-deep in a hole. It is also a good idea to leave your engine running on the other side for as long as possible, since a flooded engine may not start again for quite some time. If you plan to visit Gove by road, your first phone call should be to the NT Road Conditions hotline (☎ 1800 246 199).

There are no services and only one reliable source of fuel along the Central Arnhem Highway. The first turn-off on the left, 16km from the Stuart Hwy. is a **police** station. The next two landmarks are the Barunga and Beswick communities; stopping at either one is prohibited. It is imperative to refuel at the **Mainoru Store** (☎ 8975 4390), about 200km from the Stuart Hwy. Mainoru also sells shelf food and basic supplies. The store is open daily during the Dry 9am-5pm; hours vary during the Wet. The **Bulman Store** (☎ 8975 4887), 57km past Mainoru just before the Wilton River crossing, also sells fuel but has nebulous hours and is often closed. Bulman will have more up-to-date information about the river crossings than the NT roads hotline, so give them a ring before you set out.

There are cars on the highway every day, so stay alert for road-weary oncoming drivers at crests or around turns and take frequent breaks. Travel time from Katherine to Nhulunbuy is at least ten hours, but you should really camp overnight and take it slowly rather than push your luck. Avoid driving at night (especially near dusk and dawn) due to increased animal activity. As with any bush drive, check that your vehicle is in full working order before setting out. Also see **Driving in the Outback**, p. 79.

Because the road passes through Aboriginal lands, you must have a permit from the **Northern Land Council** in Katherine (☎ 8972 2799) before you start the drive. The permit is free, but it can take 3-10 days to process, and the application is rather involved. You must be visiting a resident of the region or have a booking at an accommodation in Nhulunbuy before you apply.

NHULUNBUY   ☎ 08

Nhulunbuy, a rugged bauxite mining town of around 4000, is an outpost of civilization in the vast frontier that is far northeastern Arnhem Land. Nhulunbuy is the sort of place where the speedway and motocross track are the most visible icons on the way into town, and nearly every house seems to have a rough-and-tumble 4WD and a boat. The town is of interest to travelers as a base for exploring the stunning beaches, dunes, and pristine bushlands of the Gove Peninsula. Nhulunbuy is also a good place to learn about the rich culture of the Yolngu people. The Yolngu have lived in this part of the world for countless generations—perhaps as long as 60,000 years—and for the most part they have remained undisturbed by European influence. The didgeridoo is originally from northeastern Arnhem Land, and the Yolngu are its traditional custodians. They possess ancient knowledge about making and playing the instrument (called *yirdaki* in the local languages).

☰ TRANSPORTATION. The most hassle-free way to visit Nhulunbuy and the Gove Peninsula is by air, and tickets can be quite affordable with a few weeks of advance planning. **Qantas** (☎ 13 13 13) flies to Nhulunbuy from **Darwin** and **Cairns**. **Airnorth** (☎ 8920 4000) also flies from Darwin, though in a rather small turbo-prop aircraft. Flying to Nhulunbuy requires no permit.

Once you're there, the best way to see Gove is in your own 4WD vehicle. Failing that, a high-clearance 2WD is adequate for exploring the beaches closer to town. Most rentals in Gove are booked solid three or four months in advance, so plan ahead or consider renting from Darwin. **Manny's** (☎ 8987 2300) rents 4WDs ($100 per day) and 2WD utes ($65). The friendly proprietor, Max, is also a travel agent who can help you find a cheap flight to or from Nhulunbuy. **Gove Rentals** has 4WD vehicles, 2WD utes, and standard cars, but only rents to drivers over 25. (☎ 8987

1700. 4WD $147-158 per day, utes $75, cars $86.) **Kansas Pty. Ltd.** rents 2WD twin-cab utes. (☎8987 2872. $55-75 per day.) **Taxis** will take you just about anywhere in town, but they can quickly get quite expensive. Try the **Amir Bus Service** (☎8987 1144) or **Kansas Pty. Ltd.** (☎13 10 08). If you need a bush taxi for remote areas, call Leon Reynolds (☎8987 3524).

⊞ ORIENTATION. Heading towards town, the **Central Arnhem Highway** and the road from the airport become **Melville Bay Road** as they converge, which runs past the large Aboriginal community of **Yirrkala** and **Matthew Flinders Way** (the road to the center of town), to the harbor. On the way into town along Matthew Flinders Way, the first left is Arnhem Rd., the location of the **Captain Cook Shopping Centre.** In town, **Westall Street,** off Matthew Flinders Way, borders **Endeavor Square,** the center of town.

🛈 PRACTICAL INFORMATION. The **East Arnhem Land Tourist Association,** in Endeavour House off the Woolworths parking lot, is a good source of information and brochures about local services, food, and accommodations. They also have a free town map. (☎8987 2255. Open M-F 9am-5pm.) **Dhimurru Land Management,** in the Captain Cook Shopping Centre, is the Gove Peninsula's unofficial tourist office. An incorporated Aboriginal organization, it was established by Yolngu land-owners to manage non-Yolngu access to Yolngu land. To leave town legally, a two-month general visitor's recreation permit ($22) is required. Some areas, such as Cape Arnhem, Caves Beach, Oyster Beach, Wonga Creek, and Memorial Park, require advance booking and special permits. An invaluable resource for any visitor to Gove is 📖**A Visitor's Guide to Recreation Areas,** available at Dhimurru for $10. The booklet, which has detailed information about every beach, creek, and camp-site in the area (including photographs), is well worth the price. It also explains Yolngu history and has a fascinating description of the intricate Yolngu social system. (☎8987 3992. Open M-F 8:30am-4pm.) The **Northern Land Council,** in Endeavour Square off the Woolworths parking lot, processes permit applications for driving along the Central Arnhem Hwy. as well as permits for anywhere not covered by Dhimurru permits. (☎8987 2602. Open M-F 8am-5:30pm.)

The **library,** 73 Matthew Flinders Way, has free **Internet.** (☎8987 0860. Open M-W 10am-5pm, Th 10am-7pm, F 10am-5pm, Sa 10am-1pm.) **Nambara Arts & Crafts,** in the YBE complex between town and the harbor, sells a small but high-quality selection of paintings and *yirdaki*. (☎8987 2233. Open M-F 8am-4:30pm.) **YBE** is the largest Aboriginal-owned company in Australia in terms of both assets and revenue, providing civil engineering and mine-site rehabilitation services.

Other services include **police** (☎8987 1333), **hospital** (☎8987 0211) on Matthew Flinders Way, and **post office** on Westall St. across from the taxi stand. (☎8987 1333. Open M-F 9am-5pm.) **Postal Code:** 0881.

🍴 ACCOMMODATIONS & FOOD. Everything in Nhulunbuy is expensive, and there are no dorm beds in town. The least expensive place to stay is the **Gove Peninsula Motel ❺** on Matthew Flinders Way at Melville Bay Rd. (☎8987 0700; fax 8987 0770). All rooms have ensuites and kitchenettes. Singles $121; doubles $132. If you prefer rooms with an ocean view, try the **Walkabout Lodge ❺,** 12 Westall St. (☎8987 1777. Triple shares $61-70 per person, twin shares and doubles $92.50-105 per person, singles $210 per person.) For most visitors, **camping ❶** is the best option (see **beaches** below).

The least expensive place to buy **groceries** is Woolworths (☎8987 1714) in Endeavour Square, open daily 8am-8pm. There's also an IGA **supermarket** and Mitre 10 Hardware at the Captain Cook Shopping Centre. For tucker, the best value in Arnhem Land is at **Coco's Cafe ❶** in Captain Cook. Delicious hot plates of curry, Italian food, and noodles are $9.50, and homemade pies and muffins are $4. (☎8987 2406. Open M-F 9am-4pm.) The takeaway with the longest hours is **Fred's Food and Fun ❷** in Endeavor Square. They have good pizzas after 5pm for $11-17.50. (☎8987 2455. Open daily 9am-9pm.) For seafood, try the **Gove Yacht Club ❸.** Turn left at the sign on Melville Bay Rd. just after the ore conveyor belt but before the harbor. Barra burger and chips are $10 at lunchtime and dinner seafood plates are $15-30. (☎8987 3077. Open M-F noon-10pm, Sa 10am-10pm, Su 11:30am-10pm.)

◪ **BEACHES.** The beaches on the Gove Peninsula are simply perfect. Pristine, untouched, and overflowing with the rugged beauty of Arnhem Land, Gove's beaches alone are worth the trip. Gove also has some of the world's best **fishing,** especially among the hundreds of small islands that dot the Arafura Sea. For boat hire, call **Arnhem Boat Hire.** (☎8987 3181. Tinnies from $170-190 per day.) Many beaches have snorkel-friendly reefs teeming with life. Be aware that **saltwater crocodiles** inhabit all waters in the area, but they are much less of a danger than in Darwin or Kakadu. No beach is completely safe for swimming, but some are less risky than others. Never enter the water near an estuary, and keep a watchful eye out for crocodile landings (muddy slides at the water's edge). Also watch for **buffalo**—the large animals are dangerous and unpredictable.

Gove is so isolated that it has yet to be discovered by the average tourist. As a result, with only a little effort you can have a world-class beach all to yourself. The Dhimurru *Visitor's Guide* has photographs and descriptions of all the beaches, as well as driving directions and detailed information about permits and camping. In general, most beaches between the airport and the harbor are accessible in a high-clearance 2WD vehicle, though you may have to park and walk part of the way. In particular, the **Rainbow Cliffs** area between Nhulunbuy and Yirrkala is usually accessible in a high-clearance 2WD and has several good campsites. The cliffs themselves are a sacred site, so refrain from walking on them. Nearer town and accessible in any vehicle, **East Woody Beach,** off East Woody Rd. past the BMX track, is comprised of a large estuary and a peninsula-island with a large rocky face. To reach **Wallaby Beach,** turn right off Melville Bay Rd. just before the ore conveyor near the harbor. The beach is picturesque but lacks good shade for camping, and a 4WD is usually required.

The best beaches accessible on the general recreation permit are past the airport on the way out of town, accessible via the turn-off for Daliwuy Bay. The unsealed road is heavily corrugated but manageable in a 2WD vehicle. The first beach is **Daliwuy Bay,** which has a good shady campsite with a bench and a boat ramp. The next beach, 4WD only, is **Macassans,** noteworthy primarily because of a stone pictorial record of ages-old Yolngu trade relations with the Macassan people from what is now Indonesia. The road becomes impassable to 2WD vehicles just before ▨**Turtle Beach,** but you can get close enough to walk if you veer off to the right into the bush just before the main road turns sharply to the left. The beach itself is small but breathtaking, with good surf on windy days and a little reef. Turtle Beach is a superb place to camp. Only 1.5km farther up the road is one of the jewels of Gove, ▨**Little Bondi Beach.** The bay is a near-perfect semicircle, with a small rip running straight up the middle to take you quickly to the symmetrical breaks on the left and right. This is the best surf beach in Gove, and it is a relatively safe spot to snorkel. When facing the ocean, the best waves are usually on the right side, since the water is quite shallow over the reef on the left. At the end of the track, **Rocky Point** is an exposed shelf with superb cliff-top views of Daliwuy Bay. A walking trail runs from Daliwuy to Rocky Point, with stops at all the beaches, so consider spending a day exploring them on foot if you don't have a 4WD. The visitor's guide has a good map of the trail.

There are also several excellent freshwater **campsites ❶** on various creeks, rock-holes, and billabongs in the area. **Giddy River, Wonga Creek,** and **Memorial Park** are some of the better known, but the latter two require special permits from Dhimurru. There are **no facilities** at any campsites in Gove, so bring all your own supplies (including water). Camping fees are included in the price of your permit.

◪ SIGHTS. The free **Mine Tour** (☎ 8987 5345) is surprisingly thorough and engaging, and it offers a thoughtful and well-balanced view of the mine's impact on the land. The construction of the mine sparked outrage among local Yolngu people, and the legal battle over the land rights went all the way to the supreme court. Though the mine won the case, the controversy led to the formation of the Northern Land Council, the entity responsible for reclaiming Aboriginal land and giving legal force to the traditional ownership system. The mine tour departs from the taxi stand on Westall St. every Friday morning at 8:30am. Book at least one day in advance, and wear sturdy closed-toe shoes. The **Roy Marika Lookout** on Mt. Saunders off Wuyal Rd. (take Matthew Flinders Way to Arnhem Rd. and then Arnhem to Wuyal Rd.) has a decent view of the town and the surrounding coastline.

◪ FESTIVALS. The famous **Garma Festival** (fax 8941 1088; www.garma.telstra.com), organized by the Yothu Yindi foundation, takes place every year during the second week of August at a site near the Cape Arnhem turn-off. Yothu Yindi are largely responsible for the international popularization of the didgeridoo *(yirdaki)*, and as a result the festival involves lots and lots of *yirdaki* playing, making, and teaching. *Balanda* (non-Aboriginals) must pay a hefty $1600 to participate in the week-long event. All meals, camping fees, and permits for the drive from Katherine are included.

YIRRKALA COMMUNITY   ☎ 08

Yirrkala is a large Aboriginal community with a gorgeous ocean view. Visitors should head straight to the **Buku-Larrngay Mulka Arts and Crafts Centre and Museum.** Buku-Larrngay, a non-profit community co-operative, houses an excellent collection of Aboriginal artwork, burial poles, and bark painting, as well as two renowned church panels depicting the Yolngu creation legend. Each of the sixteen clans in the region is responsible for painting one section of the panels, each in a different style. Buku-Larrngay is also perhaps the best place in Australia to find a traditionally crafted instrument-quality *yirdaki* (didgeridoo). All *yirdaki* are made by local Yolngu artists. Prices range from roughly $350-900. (☎ 8987 1701; www.aboriginalart.org/buku. Open M-F 8am-4:30pm, Sa 9am-noon.) No permit is required to visit the Centre, but to go anywhere else in Yirrkala requires a permit from the **Dhanbul Community Association,** around the corner and up the hill. (☎ 8987 3433. Open M-F 9am-4pm.) Yirrkala's **Shady Beach** is breathtaking, but no camping is permitted. Facing the water, follow the trail up the hill on the left and through some bush to reach a stunningly beautiful surf beach secluded from the rest of the community. Be advised that **kava** is legal in Yirrkala, but hefty fines await anyone who attempts to transport it outside town.

CAPE ARNHEM

If you have the time, apply for an $11 special permit to visit ◪**Cape Arnhem,** a wonderland of marine life and divine coastline. Sea turtles and manta rays abound in its waters, and anywhere else on earth the cape would be multi-million-dollar real estate. Access is limited to ten vehicles at a time, so book ahead with Dhimurru Land Management (see p. 294). Drive out of town, past the airport and past the

Daliwuy turn-off, and turn left at the Dhimurru sign. The track traces the top of a large escarpment; collect firewood before you begin the descent to the coast. At the bottom, be sure to deflate your tires to 20psi before the track becomes sandy. You'll eventually exit the track onto the long, wide **Malupinu Beach,** with a view of **Moon Island** directly in front of you. Keep the water on your right as you drive up along the beaches of the cape. You'll pass two large rock formations called the **Twin Eagles;** they are sacred sites, so don't camp near them. About halfway to the end, you'll drive up onto a sand dune; from here the track meanders its way past pandanus trees, through bush that looks more like the Sahara than the tropics, and eventually onto a beach with a huge expanse of rock pools. The track ends at a fence. This area is one of the few places on the Cape with shaded campsites. Beyond the fence is a bauxite shelf, and on moonless nights **crayfish** (tropical rock lobster) sit in the pools as if demanding to become dinner. There's some decent snorkeling beyond the rock pools and along the bauxite shelf, but be cautious of rough currents and rip tides. The entire trip is around 40km and requires a 4WD and a bit of sand driving know-how.

DOWN THE TRACK

Heading south down the Stuart Hwy. away from the city of Darwin, the lush vegetation and cinnamon earth so characteristic of the Top End give way to stretches of land dotted with grasses and shrubs and everything around you colored a deep, barren red that stretches for miles in every direction, broken only by the occasional rock outcropping.

VICTORIA HIGHWAY: KATHERINE TO KUNUNURRA

From downtown Katherine, the "Vic" careens westward 512km to Kununurra, WA (see p. 741). There's precious little between the two places to distract you from the sometimes startling escarpments and mountain ridges that run parallel to the highway as you approach Kununurra and enter the Kimberley. Located two hundred kilometers west of Katherine, the **Victoria River Roadhouse ❶** has petrol, a restaurant, and quiet campsites with views of the nearby escarpment. (☎8975 0744. Sites for 2 $15, powered $20, extra person $7.50/$10; doubles $65; motel rooms from $95.) A few Victoria River **cruises** leave from the Roadhouse. (3hr.; daily 9am; min. 4 people, $45.) The boat can be chartered for fishing cruises for up to 6 people for $65 per hr. Scenic helicopter flights also depart the roadhouse. (10, 20, and 30min. flights; $50 per 10min.)

The highway passes through **Gregory National Park** (Timber Creek Ranger Station ☎8975 0888). The Territory's second-largest national park (after Kakadu) features 2WD-accessible bushwalks and lookouts over Victoria River Gorge, as well as rugged 4WD tracks through the isolated surroundings. **Timber Creek,** a rowdy roadside town, is another 90km west of Victoria River. The **Wayside Inn ❷** has a small restaurant and a large selection of accommodations. (☎8975 0722. Sites $6 per person, powered $9; budget singles $40, ensuite $86; caravans $45-55.) River cruises can be booked next door at **Max's Victoria River Boat Tours** (☎8975 0850. $55 per 3½hr.). At the 468km mark, **Keep River National Park** is home to Aboriginal rock art sites and a few bushwalks. Camping is permitted at two sites (15 and 28km down a gravel road). Finally, about 480km west of Katherine (but less than 40km from Kununurra) is the border crossing into WA. There are strict quarantines against fruits, veggies, honey, and plant material. Also, be aware that Western Australia clocks are 1½hr. behind the Territory's.

STUART HIGHWAY: KATHERINE TO TENNANT CREEK

There are 672 long kilometers between Katherine and Tennant Creek. Twenty-seven kilometers south of Katherine is the 200km turn-off to an unsung gem, **Cutta Cutta Caves Nature Park** (☎ 8972 1940). Meaning "starry starry," the name refers to the delicate calcite crystals that grow within the dark, temperate passages. The cave extends 720m through an underground labyrinth of limestone columns and jagged ceilings, although visitors can only venture through the first 250m (the depths get too cold and reach 99% humidity). **Tours,** the only way to see the cave, are led by fun, knowledgeable guides, and proceed through five chambers. (1hr. Tours depart daily 9, 10, 11am, 1, 2, and 3pm, except during floods in the Wet. $10.) "Cultural Adventures" are offered at the Aboriginal-owned and operated tours of **Manyallaluk,** 100km southeast of Katherine (50km on the Stuart Hwy. and 50km on an access road. ☎ 8975 4727 or 1800 644 727. Operates Mar.-Dec. On-site 1-day tours $99, children $61. From Katherine 1-day tours $132/$72; 2-day $450/$200.) Another 106km south on the Stuart Hwy. is the township of **Mataranka,** renowned for **Elsey National Park** and the thermal pool near Mataranka Homestead.

TENNANT CREEK   ☎ 08

Dusty Tennant Creek (pop. 35,000), the self-proclaimed "Golden Heart" of the Northern Territory, appears to most travelers as a welcome reprieve from the monotonous stretch of road that runs from Alice to Darwin. The product of Australia's last great gold rush in the 1930s, Tennant has remained small despite a $4 billion output of gold since the 1960s. For those who pause for longer than it takes to fill up on gas and tucker, the **Devil's Marbles** (see p. 299), mining history, and the regional artistic flavor of the Warumungu Aborigines all make Tenant Creek a worthwhile visit.

◘ TRANSPORTATION. All **buses** in and out of town stop at the **Transit Centre** on Paterson St., near the intersection with Stuart St., at the north end of town. (☎ 8962 1070. Open M-F 7:30am-5:30pm and 9-11pm, Sa 8am-12:30pm and 2:30am-4:30am.) **McCafferty's/Greyhound** (☎ 13 14 99) run to: Alice Springs (5-6hr., 2 per day, $106); Darwin (13hr., 2 per day, $130); Katherine (8-9hr., 2 per day, $87); Mt. Isa (7½hr., 1 per day, $107); Townsville (20hr., 1 per day, $214). **Bicycle rental is at Bridgestone Rental,** 52b Paterson St., on the corner of Davidson St. (☎ 8962 2361. Half-day $5, full-day $10. Open M-F 8am-5pm.)

◖◗ ORIENTATION & PRACTICAL INFORMATION. The Stuart Hwy., called **Paterson Street** in town, runs from north to south. Intersecting Paterson are, from the north, **Stuart Street** (not to be confused with the Stuart Hwy.) and **Davidson Street,** then **Peko Road** from the east, which becomes **Windley Street** west of Paterson. **Memorial Drive** comes in from the west.

The tourist office, **Tennant Creek Regional Tourist Association,** 1½km up Peko Rd., will book tours. (☎ 8962 3388. Open May-Sept. daily 9am-5pm; Oct.-Apr. M-F 9am-5pm, Sa 9am-noon.) There is an **ANZ bank** (☎ 13 13 14), on Paterson St. between Davidson and Stuart St., and a **Westpac bank,** 64 Peko Rd. (☎ 8962 2801), at the corner of Paterson St. Both are open M-Th 9:30am-4pm, F 9:30am-5pm, with 24hr. **ATMs. Police** (☎ 8962 4444) are on Paterson St. near Windley St. There is **Internet** at the **public library,** on Peko Rd. (☎ 8962 2401; $2.20 per 30min; open M-F 10am-6pm, Sa 10am-noon.) It is also available at **Switch,** on Paterson St., just north of the Transit Centre. (☎ 8962 3124; $6 per hr.; open M-F 8:30am-5pm, Sa 9am-1pm.). The **post office** is at the corner of Paterson St. and Memorial Dr. (☎ 8962 2196. Open M-F 9am-5pm.) **Postal Code:** 0861.

⌕ ACCOMMODATIONS. Outback Caravan Park ❷, 600m from Paterson St. on Peko Rd., offers shady sites, manicured grass, and a fantastic swimming pool. They have kitchen, BBQ, laundry, and friendly staff. (☎8962 2459. Sites $8, powered for 2 $22; deluxe ensuite cabins $55-78.) Reach **Tourist's Rest Hostel ❷,** on Leichardt St., by walking south on Paterson and turning right on Windley St. Friendly and spacious, this hostel boasts full facilities, including kitchen, pool, TV, laundry, and an aviary. (☎8962 2719. Daytrips to Devil's Marbles $55, including 1-night's stay $67. Reception 24hr. Dorms $18, ISIC $17, VIP/YHA $16; twins and doubles $40/$39/$38. NOMADS/VIP/YHA.) **Safari Backpackers YHA ❷,** 12 Davidson St., west of Paterson St., is small, clean, and comfortable. There is a kitchen, laundry, and lounge, but baths are shared. (☎8962 2207. Reception 7am-9pm across the street. Dorms $17; twins and doubles $40. YHA discount $2.)

⌕ FOOD. Paterson St. is lined with takeaway snack bars and eateries. **Rocky's ❷,** next door to the Transit Centre, provides tasty takeaway-only pizza in a no-frills setting. (☎8962 2049. Open daily 4-11pm. Large pizzas $10-18.) **Top of Town Cafe ❶,** just north of the Transit Centre, has veggie burgers and a sandwich bar, all around $5.50. (☎8962 1311. Open M-F 8am-6pm, Sa-Su 8am-2pm.) At **Margo Miles Steakhouse ❸,** across the street from the Transit Centre, you can get fancy Italian dishes and, of course, plenty of steak for around $18. (☎8962 1311. Open daily 6-9pm, also M-F noon-2pm.) **Mr. Perry's Ice Cream ❶,** on Patterson St. south of Memorial Dr., actually has an adjoining cafe that serves good Chinese takeaway. (☎8962 2995. Open M-Sa 8am-5:30pm, Su 10am-3pm.) Adjacent is the **Tennant Food Barn,** which offers cheap **groceries.** (☎8962 2296. Open M-W and F-Sa 8:30am-6pm, Th 8:30am-6:30pm, Su 9am-6pm.)

STUART HIGHWAY: TENNANT TO ALICE SPRINGS

Geologists invoke water erosion. Aboriginal legend credits the Rainbow Serpent. Whatever the cause, the boulders known as the ◪**Devil's Marbles** are beautiful and baffling. The nearly spherical 7m granite rocks balance precariously on one another, just off the Stuart Hwy., 80km from Tennant Creek. Two tours run from Tennant Creek and include a BBQ back in town. **Devil's Marbles Tours,** led by witty and well-informed guides, emphasize geological and cultural appreciation. (☎0418 891 711. Departs daily from Tourist's Rest Hostel at noon; $55. Sunrise tours (min. 2 people) depart M and F 5am; $65.) **Garyo's** occasionally runs more action-packed tours, staging numerous photo-ops. (☎8962 2024. 11am-5pm. $55.) **Camping ❶** at the Marbles is basic. (Pit toilets, BBQ, no water. $3.30, children $1.65.) The closest town to Devil's Marbles is **Wauchope,** 9km south, which has petrol, food, **accommodations ❶** (☎8964 1963. Sites $6 per person, powered $16; motel singles without bath $30; ensuite doubles $70.). Small towns farther along the highway have roadhouses that provide basic services including petrol, food, and accommodations: **Wycliffe Well** (☎8964 1966), rumored to receive frequent UFO visits and have the largest beer selection in all of Australia; **Barrow Creek** (☎8956 9753); **Ti Tree** (☎8956 9741); and **Aileron** (☎8956 9703).

NORTHERN TERRITORY

RED CENTRE

Though home to less than one-half of 1% of Australia's population, for many foreigners, the Red Centre is the essence of the continent, where the orange hues of the desert shimmer beneath the sweltering sun. Everything in the Centre seems to have a mythical, larger-than-life quality. The landscapes here are nothing if not arresting, from red moonscapes of the Centre's vast expanses to the plunging depths of **Watarrka** (Kings Canyon) and the proud monolith of **Uluru** (Ayers Rock),

Australia's most enduring symbol. In the enormous skies, panoramic watercolor sunsets give way to millions of stars every night. Alice Springs, cradled in the bluffs of the MacDonell Ranges, is the only sizeable town in any direction, serving as the region's unofficial capital and gateway for many travelers. However, be forewarned! Even Alice is a five-hour drive to Watarrka or Uluru, so if your time is limited, consider flying directly to Uluru.

ALICE SPRINGS   ☎ 08

Proximity to abundant natural wonder and to precious little else has rendered dusty little Alice Springs an important center for commerce and tourism. With 27,000 residents, it dwarfs every settlement for nearly 1500km in any direction and is the largest town between Adelaide on the Southern Ocean and tropical Darwin. This position endows Alice with a feel and a collection of resources which are surprising for its size: the shopping is decent and the abundance of tourists and the inevitable set of attendant businesses lends the town a certain cosmopolitan, if slightly overrun, atmosphere.

A comely setting amid the MacDonell ranges, sparkling stars, and sunsets in which the innumerable colors of the desert stretch across the outback sky, make Alice a destination in its own right. However, it is not without problems. There exists a strict divide between white and Aboriginal. While whites go about the daily routines of an outback town, Aboriginals congregate on the city's fringes in the Todd River bed or the Todd St. Mall, and the two groups seem only vaguely aware of each other's existence.

▆ TRANSPORTATION

Airplanes: Alice Springs Airport (☎8951 1211), 20km south of the city on the Stuart Hwy. Provides domestic service, tourist info, currency exchange, and car rental. **Qantas** (☎13 13 13) flies to: Adelaide (2hr., 2 per day); Brisbane (4½hr., 2 per day); Cairns (3½hr., 1 per day); Darwin (2hr., 3 per day); Melbourne (3hr., 2-4 per day); Perth (3½hr., 2 per day); Sydney (3½hr., 2 per day); and Yulara (45min., 3 per day).

Trains: Alice Railway Station is a 20min. walk from central Alice. From George St., take a left on Larapinta Dr., which turns into the Stuart Hwy. and runs to Alice. The *Ghan* runs to: Adelaide (20hr., M and Sa, $215); Melbourne (33hr., Tu, $274); and Sydney (46hr., F, $314). The tourist office makes reservations, or you can call the *Ghan* direct ☎13 21 47.

Buses: McCafferty's/Greyhound (☎8952 7888) **buses** run from the station at the corner of Gregory and Railway Terr. Service to: Adelaide (19-20hr., 1 per day, $177); Cairns (33hr., 1 per day, $371); Darwin (18-20hr., 2 per day, $194) via Tennant Creek (5-6hr., 2 per day, $106); Sydney (45hr., 1 per day, $304); and Townsville (28hr., 1 per day, $320). They also provide: 2-day Ayers Rock and Olgas tour ($250); and 3-day Ayers Rock, Olgas, and King's Canyon tour ($279).

Public Transportation: ASBus (☎8950 0500), the public bus system, runs infrequently to the outskirts of town. Runs M-F 8 or 9am-6pm, Sa only in the morning. $1.40-2.40.

Taxis: Alice Springs Taxis (☎8952 1877) queue on Gregory Terr. just east of Todd Mall.

Car Rental: Territory-Thrifty (☎8952 9999), on the corner of Hartley St. and Stott Terr., has cars from $66 with a $16 under-25 surcharge per day, 4WD from $110 per day (not available to under-25s). Open daily 8am-5:30pm. **Hertz,** 76 Hartley St. (☎8952 2644), near Stott Terr., rents from $65 per day. **Britz** (☎8952 8814), corner of Stuart Hwy. and Power St., is the best deal in town, renting 4WD and campervans with unlimited kilometers from $100 per day, and 2WD starting at $62 (no surcharge for under 25). Open daily 8am-5pm. Local rental companies include: **Advance,** 9 Railway Terr.

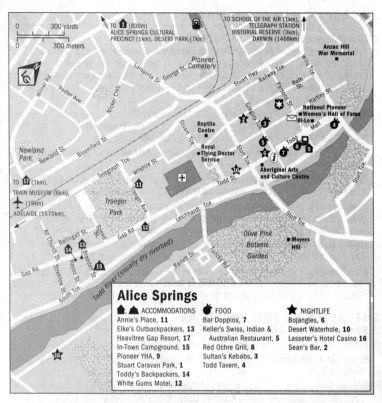

Alice Springs

▲, ▲ ACCOMMODATIONS
Annie's Place, **11**
Elke's Outbackpackers, **13**
Heavitree Gap Resort, **17**
In-Town Campground, **15**
Pioneer YHA, **9**
Stuart Caravan Park, **1**
Toddy's Backpackers, **14**
White Gums Motel, **12**

🍴 FOOD
Bar Doppios, **7**
Keller's Swiss, Indian &
   Australian Restaurant, **5**
Red Ochre Grill, **8**
Sultan's Kebabs, **3**
Todd Tavern, **4**

★ NIGHTLIFE
Bojangles, **6**
Desert Waterhole, **10**
Lasseter's Hotel Casino **16**
Sean's Bar, **2**

(☎8953 3700); **Boomerang Rental** (☎8955 5171); **Maui,** Stuart Hwy at Power St. corner (☎8952 8049) with 4WD and campervans; and **Outback Auto Rentals,** 78 Todd St. (☎8953 5333).

Roadside Assistance: AANT (24hr.☎8952 1087).

Road Conditions: 24hr.☎1800 246 199.

Bike Rental: Pioneer YHA (☎8952 8855), $5 per hr., $12 per half-day, $20 per day.

■ ORIENTATION

The Stuart Hwy. runs through Alice on its way from Darwin (1486km) to Adelaide (1570km). The dry **Todd River** bed provides a Western border to downtown; the **MacDonnell Ranges** form a natural border at the southern side of town. The break between the east-west ranges, called **Heavitree Gap,** allows both the Stuart Hwy. and the **Todd River** to pass through. Downtown, the major north-south streets are (from west to east) the Stuart Hwy., Railway Terr., Bath St., Hartley St., Todd St., and Leichhardt Terr.; the major east-west streets are (from north to south) Parsons St., Gregory Terr., and Stott Terr. The true commercial center of town is **Todd Mall,** a pedestrian-only stretch of Todd St. between Wills and Gregory Terr.; the two indoor malls are **Alice Plaza** (Todd Mall at Parsons St.) and **Yeperenye Plaza** (Hartley St. north of Gregory Terr.).

🗲 PRACTICAL INFORMATION

TOURIST & FINANCIAL SERVICES

Tourist Office: Central Australian Tourism Industry Association (☎8952 5800 or 1800 645 199; www.centralaustraliantourism.com), on Gregory Terr. at the end of Todd Mall. Books transportation, tours, and accommodations, sells road and Larapinta Trail maps, and has National Park info. Grab their free excellent city map. Open M-F 8:30am-5:30pm, Sa-Su 9am-4pm.

Budget Travel: Flight Centre (☎8953 4081), on Todd Mall, guarantees the lowest airfares. Open M-F 9am-5:30pm, Sa 9:30am-12:30pm. **Travelworld,** 40 Todd Mall (☎8952 7186), near Parsons St. Open M-F 8:30am-5pm, Sa 9am-noon.

Tours: Hostel-run tours often include accommodation. **McCafferty's/Greyhound** (☎8952 7888) buses to major Red Centre sights.

Currency Exchange: National Australia (☎8952 1611) and **ANZ** (☎8952 1144) are in Todd Mall, along with **ATMs.** Both open M-Th 9:30am-4pm, F 9:30am-5pm.

Work Opportunities: Alice has a year-round labor shortage that borders on crisis. Those with office or computer skills can get placement through **Work Zone** (☎8952 4300; www.workzone.org), on the corner of Gregory Terr. and Bath St., next to Video EZY.

Library: (☎8950 0555), on Gregory Terr. near Todd Mall next to the tourist office. Open M-Tu and Th 10am-6pm, W and F 10am-5pm, Sa 9am-1pm, Su 1-5pm.

Book Exchange: Helene's Books and Things, 113 Todd St. (☎8953 2465). Open M-F 9am-5:30pm, Sa 10am-2pm. **Boomerang Book Exchange,** Reg. Harris Ln. (☎8952 5843), off Todd Mall near Parsons St. Open M-F 9:30am-5pm, Sa 9:30am-1pm.

EMERGENCY & COMMUNICATIONS

Emergency: ☎000. **Crisis Line** ☎1800 019 116.

Police: (☎8951 8888), on Parsons St., at the corner of Bath St.

Hospital: Alice Springs Clinic, on Gap Rd. between Stuart Terr. and Traeger Ave. (☎8951 7777).

Internet Access: The best deal in town is **Todd Internet,** 82 Todd Mall. Knowledgeable staff and fast connections for $4 per hr. Open daily 9:30am-late.

Post Office: GPO (☎8952 1020), on Hartley St. south of Parsons St. Open M-F 8:15am-5pm. **Postal Code:** 0870.

🏠 🗲 ACCOMMODATIONS & CAMPING

The hostels of Alice Springs are pretty standard fare as far as Australian budget accommodations go: clean enough rooms full of bunkbeds, quirky common spaces, and pleasant, professional staff. All listings have A/C, a pool, and $2 laundry, all recommend booking in advance, most have bike hire from $12 per day, and *everybody* will be happy to book tours.

The closest **camping** option to town is at the aptly-named **In-Town Campground ❶,** on the corner of Breadon St. and South Terr., near Elke's. Grassy and caravan-free, it is spacious and friendly. (☎8952 6687. Sites $8.) The **Stuart Caravan Park ❶** is 2km west of town on Larapinth Dr. (☎8952 2547. Reception 8am-8pm. Sites $12, powered $20.) There's also camping at **Heavitree Gap Outback Resort** (see listing above).

🔲 **Heavitree Gap Resort,** on Palm Circuit. (☎8950 4444). Though a bit out of the city, the location couldn't be more fetching. The bluffs on either side of the resort are breathtaking. A walking trail climbs one, where blackfooted wallabies frolic on the hillside. Shuttle bus runs to town (though unfortunately only until around 4pm) and to the airport.

Motel doubles from $85. Budget doubles with ensuite $65 (the major difference being slightly older furnishings). Dorms $20. Camping $9 per person unpowered, $20 for a powered site for two. ❷

Pioneer YHA (☎8952 8855), on the corner of Parsons and Leichardt St., 1 block off Todd Mall. The most central location in Alice Springs. Good facilities include a pool, pool table, large kitchen and courtyard with chairs and cover from the sun. However, while the courtyard is a good place to hang out during the day, it is also popular among inconsiderate revelers at all hours, sometimes making it a bit noisy. 24hr. free safe and storage. Internet $6.50 per hr. Key deposit $20. Reception 7:30am-8:30pm. 6- to 16-bed dorms $22.50; 4-bed dorms $25.50. YHA discount $3.50. Wheelchair-accessible. ❷

Elke's Outbackpackers, 39 Gap Rd. (☎1800 633 354), at Baedem St., 1km south of Todd Mall. Elke's compensates for its distance from town by providing several free shuttles daily. A converted motel; ensuite dorm rooms have their own kitchenettes, TVs, and balconies. Reception 5am-8:30pm. 8-bed dorms $18; 4-bed $20; twins and doubles $50; motel rooms $75; free breakfast. VIP/YHA discount $2. ❷

Toddy's Backpackers, 41 Gap Rd. (☎8952 1322), next to Elke's. A good option if you don't mind being out of the town center. Bus (free from airport, $5 to airport) meets most flights and buses. Reception 6am-8:30pm. Dorms $12-18; singles, doubles, and twins with sink and fridge $44-58; budget motel rooms $44; ensuite motel doubles with TV and fridge $59 for 2, extra person $6; free breakfast. NOMADS. ❶

White Gums Motel, 17 Gap Rd. (☎8952 5144). Sparkling, comfortable rooms with personable service. Singles $70; doubles $80; $10 extra person. ❺

🍴 FOOD

If you've got the money to spare, there are a handful of overpriced outdoor cafes on Todd Mall near Gregory Terr. There is a Coles 24hr. **supermarket** located on Bath St. at Gregory Terr.

The Todd Tavern, 1 Todd Mall (☎8952 1255), near Wills Terr. Popular among tourists and locals alike, this half-pub-half-restaurant offers free salad bar with any meal. Hearty daily specials $9-10.50. Call ahead for a reservation. Open daily 10am-around 11:30pm. ❶

Bar Doppios (☎8952 6525), on Fan Arcade, at the Gregory Terr. end of Todd Mall. The town's most happening coffee shop serves extraordinary food at a good price. Australian, Middle Eastern, and Southeast Asian fare

THE HIDDEN DEAL

ANNIE'S PLACE

They say you can't please all the people all of the time...well clearly *they* haven't been to Annie's Place. Hidden among the forest of hostels on the streets of Alice Springs, this unassuming backpackers represents the best hidden deal in Alice.

The hostel itself holds some of the cheapest beds in town, despite the fact that its rooms are immaculate and the facilities are second to none. The fun and charming staff make this relaxed place a home-away-from-home for weary travelers.

Annie's **International Cafe** serves up delicious, hot dinners—both meat and veggie—for only $5 for backpackers. Annie's pub seems to be one of the most bustling bars in all of Alice Springs. The big screen TV broadcasts sporting events or whatever else happens to be on. They also boast the cheapest beer in town, with a pint costing a mere $3.50 and jugs a scant $8.

Annie's $10 daily sunset tours including dinner are a highlight. They also have tours to **Uluru, Kata Tjuta, and King's Canyon.**

4 Traegger Ave. (☎1800 359 089; www.anniesplace.com). Internet $6 per hr., $3 per hr. until 5pm. Reception daily 5:30am-8pm. 4- or 6-bed dorms with TV and ensuite $16; doubles $55. ❷ (mains $9-10). Don't miss their exceptional breakfasts served every day until 11am. Vegetarian and lactose-intolerant tolerant. BYO. Open M-Th and Sa 7:30am-5pm, F 7:30am-10pm. ❶

Red Ochre Grill (☎ 8952 9614), on Todd Mall near Parsons St. Sample what a top-notch chef can do with regional ingredients. Aboriginal artwork and didgeridoo music round out the atmosphere for a memorable but pricey meal. The Wallaby Mignon ($27) and smoked chicken with sun-dried tomatoes and pasta ($19) are delicious. Open daily 6:30am-10:30pm. ❹

Sultan's Kebabs, 52 Hartley St. (☎ 8953 3322). This fully-licensed Turkish restaurant is friendly and relaxed. Kebabs (with veggie options) from $6. Pizzas from $8. Sweet sut-lac (rice pudding) $4. Belly dancers F-Sa 8pm. Open M-Sa 11am-late, Su 5pm-late. ❶

Keller's Swiss, Indian, and Australian Restaurant (☎ 8952 3188), on Gregory Terr. east of Hartley St. Switzerland and India make an odd couple in many ways. Yet the unlikely pairing works splendidly at Keller's, with hearty and daring vegetarian-friendly fare. Beef vindaloo $19, Züricher Geschnetzeltes $23, or kangaroo filet stroganoff $23. Open daily 5:30pm-late. ❸

◉ SIGHTS

Many sights are near Todd Mall, but more distant sights are difficult to access without a vehicle. The **Alice Wanderer** shuttle service circles past the major sights in the greater Alice Springs area. It's a cheap way to get out to more distant attractions. However, the schedule requires that you spend an hour and ten minutes at each sight that you want to see, which is hard to fill at some stops. (☎ 8952 2211 or 1800 669 111. Runs 9am-4pm, departing from the southern end of Todd Mall. All-day ticket $30.)

CITY CENTER

ANZAC HILL. Though the aerial view of Alice is a trifle drab, Anzac Hill is a great place to watch a postcard sunset with the MacDonnells as a backdrop. *(Walk to Wills Terr. between Bath and Hartley St.; a metal arch marks the start of the easy 10min. "Lions Walk" from the base to the obelisk at the top. Vehicle access is around the corner on the Stuart Hwy.)*

REPTILE CENTRE. With an impressive collection of local lizards and snakes, some of which you can hold, the Reptile Center is a fun way to get to know the scaly residents of Australia. *(9 Stuart Terr., on the corner of Bath St. ☎ 8952 8900. Open daily 9:30am-5pm. Feedings 11am, 1, and 3pm. $8, children $4.)*

ABORIGINAL ARTS & CULTURE CENTRE. Owned and operated by the Arrernte peoples, the Centre incorporates a small art gallery, the one-hour "Didgeridoo University" course ($15) and a museum ($2 donation). The museum presents Aboriginal history including a summary of archaeological evidence for early inhabitation and technical innovation by Aborigines. The focus, however, is on recent history and the struggle for Aboriginal rights. Though not always even-handed, the collection is informative and eye-opening. *(86 Todd St. ☎ 8952 3408; www.aboriginalart.com.au. Open daily 9am-5pm.)*

NATIONAL PIONEER WOMEN'S HALL OF FAME. An enthusiastic and enjoyable tribute to over a hundred Australian women who broke ground in their field, from sports to medicine to politics. Includes an impressive quilt with the signatures of hundreds of pioneering Australian women. *(In the Old Courthouse on Parson St. at the corner of Hartley St. ☎ 8952 9006; www.pioneerwomen.com.au. Open Feb. to mid-Dec. daily 10am-5pm. $2.20.)*

OUTSIDE THE CITY CENTER

ALICE SPRINGS CULTURAL PRECINCT. This collection of art galleries and museums is a great way to spend a few hours learning about all aspects of the region. The **Araluen Centre and Galleries** has rotating exhibitions, the largest collection of work by renowned Aboriginal artist Albert Namatjira, and displays of local work. The **Museum of Central Australia** has a wonderful set of exhibits detailing the meteorology and biology of the region. The **Central Australian Aviation Museum** tells the story of Centralian aviation and the important role it played in the development of this remote region. The nearby cemetery contains the supposed remains of Lasseter as well as Namatjira's grave. *(1km out on Larapinta Dr.☎8952 5800. Open daily 10am-5pm. $8, children $5, families $20.)*

DESERT PARK. An impressive collection of local fauna and flora. The nocturnal house is an excellent place to view such reclusive and rare species as the bilby, dunnart, and mala. The nocturnal house and **Birds of Prey** show are highlights. *(8km west of town on Larapinta Dr. Desert Park transfers runs a shuttle every 1½hr. 7:30am-6pm from most accommodations to the park. Call for pick-up ☎8952 4667. $30, concessions $20; includes admission. Park ☎8951 8788. Open daily 7:30am-6pm. Birds of Prey show 10am and 3:30pm. $18, children $9, family $40.)*

SCHOOL OF THE AIR. Central Australia's answer to the daunting task of educating children on remote cattle stations, roadhouses, and Aboriginal lands. Using the Royal Flying Doctors' radio network, lessons are broadcast to 140 students over a network covering 1.3 million square kilometers. *(Coming from Alice, before the turn-off to the Reserve, a sign on the Stuart Hwy. points down Head St. ☎8951 6834. Open M-Sa 8:30am-4:30pm, Su 1:30-4:30pm. $4, concessions $3.)*

TELEGRAPH STATION HISTORICAL RESERVE. From its early days as a relay station for telegraphs between Darwin and Adelaide to a 10-year stint as a home for half-white-half-Aboriginal children to its use as a camp by Aboriginal people banned from Alice Springs after dark, the station has a long and intriguing history which is brought to life by tours and exhibits. *(Take the turn-off 3km north of the town center on the Stuart Highway. ☎8952 3993. $5.50, $3.50 children.)*

🎵 🎭 ENTERTAINMENT & NIGHTLIFE

The *Alice Spring News* (90¢) has a "Dive Into Live" section listing upcoming events. The 500-seat **Araluen Centre,** on Larapinta Dr., presents artsy, independent flicks every Sunday, as well as live theater and concerts. (☎8951 1122. Box office open daily 10am-5pm. $11, concessions $8.80.) The popular **Sounds of Starlight Theatre** is in the Todd St. Mall a few doors down from Parsons St. Led by a fine didgeridoo player, the performance has a natural beauty that unfortunately gets swept away by the overbearing synthesizer and cheap lighting tricks. (☎8952 0826. 1½hr. shows Apr.-Nov. Tu and F-Sa 7:30pm. $18, YHA $15.30.) For those with more cash, **Red Centre Dreaming** offers a combination traditional three-course NT dinner with an Aboriginal cultural display including an extensive performance by an Aboriginal dance troupe. (☎1800 089 616. Open daily 7-10pm. $85, children $49; includes pick-up and drop-off from any accommodation.)

Toasty taverns (and very tame dance clubs) are the staple of afterhours Alice. It all starts and ends at **Bojangles,** 80 Todd St., south of Gregory Terr., which is everything you could ask for in a saloon: a honky-tonk piano in the corner and a generous helping of tourists pretending to be cowboys. Be forewarned, however, that your late-night antics will be broadcast to the world over Bojangles' many

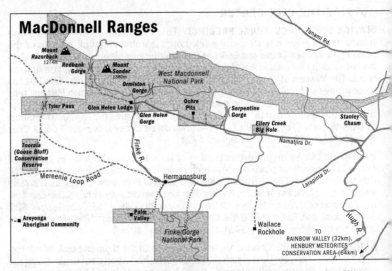

MacDonnell Ranges

web-cams scattered throughout the bar; check it out at www.boslivesa-loon.com.au. (☎8952 2873. Open daily 11:30am-3am. Live music daily. Blues Jam Su 3pm-late.) A few doors down at the Melanka Lodge, the dance floor of the **Desert Waterhole** typically draws the young backpackers. (☎8952 7131. Happy Hour 5-7pm, $7.50 jugs. M, W, F, and Su live music 8pm. Open daily 5pm-late.) **Sean's Bar,** 51 Bath St., is frequented mostly by locals and is your best bet for a pint ($6.50) of Guinness. (☎8952 1858. Open daily 6pm-late. Live music F-Sa 8pm, open jam session Su.) Across the Todd River and a $10 cab ride from town is **Lasseter's Hotel Casino,** the setting of the climax of *Priscilla, Queen of the Desert.* (☎8950 7777. Open Su-Th 10am-3am, F-Sa 10am-4am.)

◗ FESTIVALS & EVENTS

Heritage Week (Apr. 2004) features various historical reenactments and displays all over town. Around the same time Alice plays host to a month-long horse racing festival, the lavish **Alice Springs Cup Carnival** (April 17-May 3, 2004), which enter-tains at the town's Pioneer Race Park and culminates with the **Bangtail Muster** parade (May 3, 2004). On the Queen's Birthday Weekend, the plucky cars and motorcycles of the **Finke Desert Race** (Jun. 2004) traverse 240km of roadless dusty desert from Alice to the town of Finke in the south. The first Saturday in July hosts the more traditional, agriculture-focused **Alice Springs Show** (July 2-3, 2004). The not-so-traditional **Camel Cup Carnival** race (July 10, 2004; www.camelcup.com.au), including a Miss Camel Cup Competition, is held the following weekend. The **Alice Springs Rodeo** and the **Harts Range Annual Races** are both popular events held every year in Alice in August.

However, the definitive Alice Springs festival is the **Henley-on-Todd Regatta** (late Sept. 2004; www.henleyontodd.com.au). A good-natured mock celebration cen-tered on the dry river, the "regatta" race is done in bottomless "boats" propelled Flintstones-style—by swift feet. The **Corkwood Festival** (November 28, 2004) is a traditional folk event featuring craft booths during the day and energetic bush dancing at night.

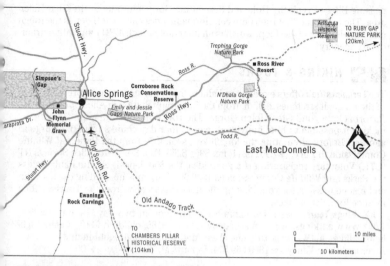

MACDONNELL RANGES

To the north of the Uluru-Kata Tjuta and Watarrka area, immediately outside Alice Springs, lie central Australia's mountains. The MacDonnell Ranges roll west to east across the horizon, as far as the eye can see, creating pockets of geological formations and wildlife that break up the flatness of the desert surroundings. From a distance, the green shrubbery that covers its ridges appears a soft blanket of grass, but up close, the landscape is identifiably Central Australian, with rusty orange earth and rock, prickly ground-cover, and glowing white ghost gums. The MacDonnell Ranges' myriad pastel colors have inspired painters and photographers throughout the ages, and numerous walking tracks through the area invite visitors to take a closer look.

MACDONNELL RANGES AT A GLANCE

LENGTH: 460km.

FEATURES: West MacDonnell National Park along Namatjira Dr., Finke Gorge Nat'l Park off Larapinta Dr., and several nature parks to the east.

GATEWAYS: Alice Springs (p. 300).

HIGHLIGHTS: Camping, walking, swimming, and scenery.

CAMPING: Throughout; they are described under each sight listing.

FEES: A small fee is charged only at Stanley Chasm (p. 308) and the Hermannsburg Historical Precinct (p. 308).

WEST MACDONNELLS

■ ORIENTATION

Larapinta Dr. heads straight out of town passing turn-offs to **Simpson's Gap** and **Stanley Chasm.** About 25km out of town, the road forks into two branches, with Larapinta Dr. continuing on to Hermannsburg and Finke Gorge and Namatjira Dr.

NORTHERN TERRITORY

passing Ellery Creek Big Hole and Serpentine Gorge en route to the Glen Helen area. The only road that runs between Hermannsburg and Glen Helen is the rough and tumble Tylers Pass loop, which is an incredibly rough 4WD loop with extraordinary scenery.

HIKING & TOURS

The **Larapinta Trail** offers experienced hikers the opportunity to reach remote areas of the range. It stretches 220km, from the Telegraph Station in Alice Springs to Mt. Razorback, beyond Glen Helen Gorge. The trail connects the main attractions, making it possible to hike individual two- to four-day chunks from one gorge to another. Before attempting the long hikes, seek info from the Park and Wildlife Commission in Alice. (☎8951 8211; fax 8951 8258. P.O. Box 1046, Alice Springs NT 0871.) Voluntary registration is a good idea; the $50 deposit is refundable unless the Parks and Wildlife Commission (☎1300 650 730) ends up sending out a search and rescue mission for you. Pick up the flyer *Bushwalks* from the Tourist Office in Alice for a list of hikes.

AAT Kings Tours does a Larapinta-Namatjira loop in two days by bus. (☎8952 1700; www.aatkings.com. Departs daily 7:30am. $180, children $140.) **Centre Highlights** makes a 4WD trek to some West MacDonnell highlights including Finke River and Palm Valley. (☎1800 659 574. Departs M, W, F 7:30am. $105.)

SIGHTS

The West MacDonnells' sights lie along two paved roads heading out from the town of Alice Springs. The distance from Alice is listed after the description of each sight in parentheses.

LARAPINTA DRIVE

JOHN FLYNN MEMORIAL GRAVE. Just off the road is the grave of the minister who created the Royal Flying Doctor Service. Sentiment that his gravestone should be something uniquely symbolic of the outback led to the selection of a massive boulder taken from the Devil's Marbles (see p. 299), near Tennant Creek—but the stone became the center of a 20-year battle between the caretaker of Flynn's grave and Aborigines, for whom the Devil's Marbles are sacred. The dispute was settled in 1999 with the substitution of a stone from the East MacDonnells and the return of the Devil's Marble to its original locale. *(7km.)*

SIMPSON'S GAP. Down a paved 8km turn-off, Simpson's Gap offers some nice hikes and views of jagged red rocks. The **Gap Walk** is an easy 20min. jaunt from the carpark. The **Cassia Hill Walk** is an equally docile 1.8km (30min.) climb to a lookout of the Gap. *(18km. Open daily 5am-8pm. Free.)*

STANLEY CHASM. Down a mostly flat 30min. path along a creek bed between rock walls, crowds gather to marvel at the glowing orange walls when the sun shines directly into this 80m-high fissure at midday. Past a shallow waterhole and up the rocky slide at the far end, you can enjoy a less crowded second chasm and an overhead view of the first. *(50km. ☎8956 7440. Open daily 8am-6pm. $6, concessions $5. Food and drinks available.)*

HERMANNSBURG HISTORICAL PRECINCT. Old homes from the early Lutheran mission are here, along with a gallery saluting Aboriginal artist Albert Namatjira. The service station sells the **Mereenie Tour Pass** for the 4WD track to Kings Canyon (see p. 312), and **petrol** and **groceries**. *(126km. ☎8956 7402. Open daily Mar.-Nov. 9am-4pm, Dec.-Feb. 10am-4pm. $4.50, children $3. Gallery $3.50.)*

■**FINKE GORGE NATIONAL PARK.** This 460km² park contains the Finke River, reputedly the oldest river on the planet; some stretches date back 350 million years. The park's main attraction is **No Palm Valley,** home to the rare Red Cabbage Palm. Two worthwhile walks are the **Mpulungkinya Walk** (5km; 2hr.), which traverses the thickest growth of palms, and the **Arankaia Walk** (2km; 1hr.), which turns back halfway and climbs the valley rim. Keep to the trail when on these walks to avoid further damage to the delicate palm seedlings. Near the full-facilities **campground ❶** (16km into the park), the **Kalaranga Lookout** (1.5km; 45min.) quickly surmounts some steep crags to bring 360° vistas of the park. *(146km. The park is accessed through the 21km 4WD-only road that follows the path of the mostly dry Finke River, off Larapinta Dr. Sites $6.60, children $3.30, families $15.40.)*

NAMATJIRA DRIVE

ELLERY CREEK BIG HOLE. Down a rough 2km access road (2WD-accessible), and a 100m wheelchair-accessible path, is this big (water) hole in Ellery Creek. Even in summer, it makes for a very nippy dip; don't even think about it in winter. The nearby **Dolemite Walk** (3km; 1hr.) traverses lush forest through spinifex. **Camping ❶** with basic facilities including wood BBQ. Caravans permitted. *(96km. Sites $3.30, children $1.65, families $7.70.)*

SERPENTINE GORGE. An easy walk along a service road (1hr.) leads to a serene gorge. The true highlight of Serpentine is the ■**lookout walk,** a short, steep climb starting near the gorge and ascending to one of the most picturesque overlooks in the entire West MacDonnells. *(102km.)*

SERPENTINE CHALET. Down a rough 3km road, the ruins of the Chalet are unremarkable, but it's a great spot for **bushcamping ❶**. *(105km. No facilities. There are 9 campsites, 4 of which can reached with a 2WD.)*

OCHRE PITS. The exposed cliffs here are an important source of the different hues of ochre used in Aboriginal art and decoration. A short wheelchair-accessible path leads to a platform overlooking the pits. From there, it's possible to walk along the riverbed to study the banded rock walls. *(108km.)*

■**ORMISTON GORGE.** A 10min. walk leads to some of the gorge's pools (some 14m deep). The excellent **Ghost Gum Walk** (1hr.) climbs the side of the gorge to an impressive lookout, then ends at the far end of the gorge, allowing a wander along the creek amid boulders stained silver, blue, and purple. During late afternoon, the orange walls glow in the sinking sun and wallabies come out to play. The **Pound Walk** (7km; 3-4hr.) is more peaceful, offering some great vistas of the surrounding hills before approaching the gorge from the back. **Camping ❶** available with showers. Caravans permitted. *(130km. Sites $6.60, children $3.30, families $15.40.)*

GLEN HELEN GORGE. At the end of the paved road, the **Glen Helen Lodge ❶** sits at the foot of Glen Helen gorge, illuminated at night with spotlights. It's the only place to fill up on gas and nutrition this side of Alice. *(134km. ☎8956 7489. Sites $10 per person, powered $11.50; dorms from $20, with linens $30; motel rooms $150. Helicopter flights of the region $35-190. Book ahead.)*

REDBANK GORGE. The narrow slit through the mountains shades a series of pools too chilly for swimming. There are two **campgrounds ❶** with basic facilities. *(156km. $3.30, children $1.65, families $7.70.)*

GOSSE BLUFF. You can view the site of the ancient crater up close from the 11km 4WD track, or take in the whole picture from the **West MacDonnell Lookout,** a turn-off near the north end of Tyler Pass. *(187km.)*

NORTHERN TERRITORY

EAST MACDONNELLS

■ ⬛ 🔁 ORIENTATION & TOURS

Just beyond **Heavitree Gap** south of Alice, **Ross Highway** branches off the Stuart Hwy. and heads eastward into the East MacDonnells. The road narrows to a single lane at times, and the area is filled with wandering **wild camels** which frequently travel down the center of the road. More varied, less crowded, and equally as fetching as their more lauded western neighbors, the East MacDonnells offer good 4WDing and rewarding hikes. Two tours offer daytrips to the area from Alice: **Discovery Ecotours** (☎ 1800 803 174; 6hr.; departs 6am; $92) and **Emu Run** (☎ 8953 7057; 9½hr.; departs 8am; $99). All **camping ❶** in this area costs $3.30, children $1.65, families $7.70.

🔁 SIGHTS

The distance from Alice along Ross Hwy. to the turn-off is listed after the description of each sight in parentheses.

EMILY GAP. Bold and unassuming, Emily Gap is an important site in the local Arrernte people's three-caterpillar Dreaming. The gorge holds a gallery of Aboriginal rock paintings marking the spot where *Intwailuka*, an ancestral hero, cooked and ate caterpillars on his Dreamtime journey. The paintings' vertical lines of alternating colors represent the caterpillars. Icy pools often obstruct the path into the gap and to the gallery. If the water appears low enough, leave your shoes behind and cross in the center of the pool where the water is shallowest. *(17km.)*

JESSIE GAP. Off to the right in this imposing gap is a painting reminiscent of those at Emily Gap. *(25km.)*

CORROBOREE ROCK CONSERVATION RESERVE. This fragment of rock ridge, still used in Arrernte ceremonies, stands out in the otherwise empty valley. An easy 15min. walk leaves from the carpark at the rock's base. *(51km.)*

ARLTUNGA HISTORIC RESERVE. A left turn-off of Ross Hwy. leads to the site of Central Australia's first town. Originally a ruby mine, the town seemed doomed when the "rubies" were determined to be useless garnets. Gold was discovered the same year; however, even gold mining was eventually abandoned as the lack of water for sifting and extraordinary distance from anywhere else rendered the mining unprofitable. The trip up to the reserve provides a welcome change from most Central Australian sights—the 33km gravel road leading to the reserve climbs through the hills, a relief if the surrounding flatness has you uncomfortably earthbound, and the collection of old buildings and contraptions offers a respite from the overall youth of the region's European settlements. Bring your flashlight for exploring the old mines. The visitors center is excellent and should not be missed. Camping with toilets and shower is $8 per person or $4 for children. *(72km.)*

RUBY GAP NATURE PARK. Along a 4WD track 39km beyond Arltunga lie the stunning gorge and excellent free **bush camping** (no water) of **Ruby Gap Nature Park.** Register with the ranger station at Arltunga before heading out. *(72km.)*

▨TREPHINA GORGE NATURE PARK. A partly paved 8km access road leads to the carpark for the **main campground ❶**. The **Trephina Gorge Walk** (2km; 45min.) follows the gorge rim before descending to the sandy riverbed—pay careful attention, as signs become less obvious as the walk wears on. The **Panorama** loop (3km; 1½hr.) climbs to an excellent lookout over the whole park. At the **John Hayes Rockhole,** 4km down a 4WD only track, there is **more camping ❶** and the **Chain Ponds walk** (4km; 1½hr.), a sojourn past a great lookout and through a picture-perfect series of pools. The **Hayes Trephina Bluff walk** is a six-hour one-way hike that highlights both regions of the park. Both campsites have pit toilets and BBQs. *(75km.)*

N'DHALA GORGE. An intermittently-marked 11km 4WD track leads through a thigh-deep creek before transecting a series of drier creek beds on its way to N'Dhala gorge. An otherwise unspectacular walking track (1.5km; 1hr.) weaves through the gorge, passing a couple Aboriginal rock carvings, some of which may be 10,000 years old. **Camping ❶** (without water) is available. *(82km.)*

ROSS RIVER RESORT. This laid-back **country inn ❶** caters to an older crowd looking for a more peaceful "outback experience." Check out their collection of historic visitor books, or take a leisurely bushwalk. The highlight of a stay here is their whip-cracking and boomerang lesson, complete with tea and damper. *(83km. ☎8956 9711. Lessons daily 10:30am; $7. Sites $10 per person, powered $15; 2-bed tents $22; 4-bed bunkhouse rooms $22 per person, with linens $33; single and double hotel rooms $125. Make sure to call ahead.)*

SIMPSON DESERT

South of Alice, the Stuart Hwy. passes Heavitree Gap and Palm Circuit. Past the Stuart's turn toward the south, on the road to the airport, the unsealed and isolated **Old South Road** veers right toward the **Simpson Desert.** It's rough country out here. Charles Sturt first explored this part of the Simpson in 1845, so bent on conquering the outback that many of his men died from complications related to the desert's harsh conditions. Stock up on supplies before heading out. All **camping ❶** in the area costs: $3.30, children $1.65, families $7.70. Several tours go to the Desert from Alice Springs. **Emu Run** does an afternoon tour of Rainbow Valley, complete with bush BBQ dinner. (☎8953 7057; www.emurun.com.au. Will pick up at most accommodations. $95.)

The first worthwhile spot is the **Ewaninga Rock Carvings,** 39km south of Alice. The weathered petroglyphs are a sacred site for Aborigines. A walk passing a series of claypans is pleasant but nondescript. The Aboriginal community of **Maryvale Station,** 62km more along the Old South Rd., marks the 4WD-only turn to **Chambers Pillar Historical Reserve** (4hr. one-way). This sandstone formation was a landmark for early travelers and their carved initials (a practice now subject to high fines). The trek is more taxing than stupendous, but sunsets at the rock are masterpieces of color. (No water or facilities.)

◙**Rainbow Valley** is a jagged, U-shaped ridge of bleached sandstone capped by more iron-rich multi-colored stone. The valley is most famous for its winter sunsets, when the red-orange-yellow formation is illuminated at the ideal angle. A short walk leads to its base. It's a striking sight, but remember that there's 97km of nothing between here and Alice. (East of the Stuart Hwy. on a sandy 4WD track. Camping with toilets and BBQ, but no water.) Another 51km down the Stuart, the unsealed **Ernest Giles Road** veers west toward Watarrka; 11km past the turn-off and 4km north on an access road lie the **Henbury Meteorite Craters.** A 20min. trail leads around the rim of a visually plain circular indentation caused 4000 years ago by a meteorite impact.

Basic **camping ❶** (no water) is available. Heading farther south, all that lies along the Stuart Hwy. until Coober Pedy, SA, are overpriced roadhouses rising from endless miles of spiky spinifex shrub.

FROM THE ROAD

DEAD BATTERY

The car just wouldn't start. I pressed all the buttons I could find. I pleaded. I prayed. It just wouldn't start. I had apparently run down the battery of my car by leaving the lights on while I explored the hikes around Kings Canyon. I bounced around the parking lot at the base of the canyon, asking everyone I found for jumper cables, getting the same answer, over and over: "No, mate. Rental car. Nothing like that."

Next, I asked a tour guide bus driver, who was willing to rally his squad of 24 package travelers to "bump" start my car. They lined up on the back bumper. With me in the driver's seat this time, we rocked down the dusty road. I put the car in gear and popped the clutch. After a couple of tries, we got a sputter, but nothing more. Hey we almost had it there! Let's try it again," I coaxed, but the weary tourists were already on their way back to the bus.

I finally accepted a ride back to town to find a mechanic. Just as we were pulling out of the road, a camper-van parked down a dirt side-road caught my eye. I dashed down to the van and asked a German couple if they had jumper cables. After some wild waving of hands, they decided that they did! Saved at last. Having a dead battery sure is a good way to meet people. It's not so good for getting to Uluru by dusk, though.

—Scott Roy

WATARRKA NATIONAL PARK (KINGS CANYON)

The increasingly popular Watarrka National Park centers around Kings Canyon. The views are photogenic and the pockets of lush greenery cradled within the canyon's walls are a refreshing change from the region's arid climb.

TRANSPORTATION. There are three different ways to drive to Kings Canyon from Alice Springs. First, the fully-paved route—the **Stuart Highway**—runs 202km south to the roadhouse settlement of **Erldunda ❷**, at its junction with the Lasseter Hwy. Travelers changing buses here may end up spending the night. (☎8956 0984. Sites for 2 $16, powered $21; motel singles $72; doubles $86.) From the junction, take the Lasseter Hwy. west 110km and turn right on Luritja Rd., which goes north 163km to the Kings Canyon park entrance. Second, the "shortcut" along **Ernest Giles Rd.,** a 100km stretch of unpaved road that begins 132km south of Alice off the Stuart Hwy. Check conditions. During good times, this route may shave some time off the trip (it cuts out some 170km), but is strictly for the brave, the foolhardy, and those with 4WD. Ernest Giles meets Luritja Rd. 100km south of the park entrance. Third, it's also possible to reach Kings Canyon from Alice Springs via **Hermannsburg** in the West MacDonnells. Take Larapinta Dr. to the scenic but corrugated 4WD-only **Mereenie Loop Rd.** (200km), which passes through Aboriginal land. There are no accommodations or camping allowed on the Mereenie, so plan to do the drive within one day. A $2.20 pass is required and can be obtained in Hermannsburg at Larapinta Service Station or Glen Helen Lodge, at Kings Canyon Resort, or at the Visitors Center in Alice. Most **tours** to Kings Canyon are included in Uluru-Kata Tjuta multi-day packages coming out of Alice Springs. **Emu Run** runs 12hr.-long day tours from Alice. (☎8953 7057. $150, children $75.)

ACCOMMODATIONS & FOOD. The **Kings Canyon Resort ❸**, 7km up the road from the canyon turn-off, is pleasant enough, although pricey. The resort has the **Desert Oaks Cafe** (open 11am-2pm) and a **grocery store** in the **fuel station** (open daily 7am-7pm). **Outback BBQ ❸** (open daily 6-9pm) offers pizzas from $17 and steaks from $29. Rooms at the resort have A/C, heat, TV, fridge, shared bath, and kitchen. (☎8956 7442; reskcr@austarnet.com.au. Reception 6:30am-9:30pm. Book ahead. Sites for 2 $28, powered $32; 4-bed dorms a whopping $43, YHA

$38; twins $100; quads $168.) Camping is available at the well-maintained **Kings Creek Station ❶**, about 30km south of the turn-off to the park. It's a more low-key outpost with a friendly staff, and you just can't beat the prices at **Camel Safaris,** which start at $7 for a five-minute ride or $40 for a sunset trek. (☎8956 7474; www.kingscreekstation.com.au. Sites $11.20, children $6, families $34.40; powered extra $3; cabin singles $68, includes breakfast.) **No camping** is allowed inside the Watarrka National Park.

🔲 **HIKING.** The park has three well-marked paths. An easy walk (2.6km; 1hr.) follows **Kings Creek** along the bottom of the canyon. Ending at a pleasant shaded viewing platform, it provides great views up the sheer canyon walls. The challenging **Kings Canyon Walk** (6km; 3hr.) scales the rocky, steep slope around the top of the canyon to provide a complete view of the canyon and surrounding country. Along the eastern edge, you wander through a collection of eroded sandstone domes dubbed the **Lost City.** There are rewarding views, on clear days stretching as far as Uluru. Two side tracks, one to the North rim of the canyon and another to the **Garden of Eden,** a greenery-rich waterhole, each take 20min. and are worthwhile excursions. The trailhead is just beyond the parking lot and well marked. There's an outhouse, info display and drinking water fountain.

The wheelchair-accessible **Kathleen Springs Walk** (2.6km; 1½hr.) winds gently through sandstone valleys to a rockhole sacred to local Aborigines. The access road is 20km south of the Canyon turn-off. The **Sunset Viewing** picnic area with water, toilets, and BBQ, is 1km before the main parking lot but is not as good as the resort's **Sunset Viewing Boardwalk,** with views of the George Gill Range.

ULURU-KATA TJUTA NATIONAL PARK

Uluru-Kata Tjuta National Park contains two of the most majestic of Australia's natural wonders, including its most enduring symbol. Mammoth Uluru's brooding colors are transformed with each sunset and sunrise, melting from bright orange to crimson to deep maroon, while sunlight and shadows flicker in the ridges and cave-like pockets of its surface. The 36 domes of Kata Tjuta, with their grainy stone-and-mortar texture, scatter across the landscape, allowing endless exploration of the valleys between.

Both have been sacred Dreaming sites of the Anangu for over 20,000 years, a history recorded in the artwork around the base of Uluru. For European newcomers, the site has had special meaning as a landmark and destination since Ernest Giles happened upon it in 1872. Today the park is jointly managed by the National Park Service and Anangu residents in a sometimes fruitful but occasionally uneasy partnership. While many visits to the park consist only of the climb and a few snapshots before sunset, those who linger, exploring the basewalks at Uluru and the trails around and through Kata Tjuta, are rewarded by a powerful connection with one of the world's most magnificent geological and cultural areas.

NORTHERN TERRITORY

ULURU & KATA TJUTA AT A GLANCE

AREA: 1325km²	**HIGHLIGHTS:** The colors of Uluru at sunset and sundown, the Valley of the Winds, walks through Kata Tjuta.
ULURU: 348m in height, 3.1km in length, 1.9km in width, 9.4km around.	
KATA TJUTA: Mt. Olga, its tallest peak, is 546m.	**CAMPING:** No camping is allowed within the National Park. There is a commercial campground at Yulara.
GATEWAYS: Alice Springs and Yulara.	**FEES:** 3-day entry pass $16.25.

TRANSPORTATION. By road, take the Stuart Hwy. to **Erldunda,** 202km south of Alice Springs and 483km north of Coober Pedy, then drive 264km west on the **Lasseter Highway.** Long before Uluru, you'll see **Mt. Connor,** a mesa in the distance. Often mistaken for Ayers Rock, it has its own viewing area right off the highway.

PRACTICAL INFORMATION. The Uluru-Kata Tjuta National Park **entrance station** (☎ 8956 2252) lies 5km past the **Yulara** resort village, where all visitors must purchase a three-day pass ($16.25). Uluru is 14km ahead, and 4km farther is the turn-off to Kata Tjuta (42km). These roads are all paved. (Park open daily hour-before-sunrise to hour-after-sunset: approx. Dec.-Feb. 5am-9pm; Mar. 5:30am-8:30pm; Apr. 6am-8pm; May 6am-7:30pm; June-July 6:30am-7:30pm; Aug. 6am-7:30pm; Sept. 5:30am-7:30pm; Oct. 5am-8pm; Nov. 5am-8:30pm.) **No camping** is permitted within the park. There are toilet facilities at the Cultural Centre, at the main carpark at Uluru, and at the sunset-viewing area at Kata Tjuta. Picnic facilities are at the Cultural Centre and the Kata Tjuta sunset-viewing area. As in the rest of the Red Centre, the **bush flies** can be unbearable from December to April. Bring mesh netting to cover your face. In case of **emergency,** radio alarms located throughout the park can be used to contact a ranger; otherwise, call the ranger direct at ☎ 8956 3138 (daily 7am-5:30pm).

The fantastic ▨**Uluru-Kata Tjuta Cultural Centre,** 1km before Uluru, gives the Anangu perspective on the region. (☎ 8956 3138. Free. Open daily Nov.-Mar. 7am-6pm; Apr.-Oct. 7am-5:30pm.) Constructed in a shape representing the Rainbow Serpent, it is full of displays relating the Anangu stories of Uluru's origin. A video details the preparation of a seemingly endless number of bush foods, as thorough a catalog of Aboriginal ingenuity in the face of adversity as is to be found in tourist Australia. Also contains an information desk, a snack bar, the **Maruka Arts and Crafts** shop (☎ 8956 2558; open daily 8:30am-5:30pm), and the **Walkatjara Art Centre.** (☎ 8956 2537. Open M-F 9am-5:30pm, Sa-Su 9:30am-2pm.)

ULURU (AYERS ROCK)

Few places could live up to the hype that surrounds Uluru. In fact only the tip of an enormous slab or rock extending underground for some 5-6km, Uluru towers elegantly over the surrounding arid scrub. What seem from afar to be only cracks and dimples become gorges and caves in the enormity of Uluru up close.

The two highlights of a visit to the rock are a walk around the base and a sunset viewing. The seemingly infinite faces and features of the rock make a walk around the base a constant surprise, as caves, valleys, and gorges sculpt the sheer enormity of the rock in a continuously changing landscape. At sunset, best viewed from a well-marked parking area 5km away, Uluru displays a series of changing hues ranging from pastel pink to deep scarlet while the flickering light plays in the caverns and crevices. Sunrise is equally stunning and viewed from the opposite side of the rock.

Visit the **Cultural Centre** before heading to the rock to learn about issues surrounding visiting and especially climbing this natural wonder. Stay on the marked paths and do not approach or touch cultural sights marked off with railings. Also, understand that exploring Uluru will put you in contact with sights meant only for men or for women. Members of the opposite gender should avoid looking intently at these sights. Above all, recognize and always keep in mind that you are in a place of great spiritual significance for the Anangu people.

THE CLIMB UP. The Anangu prefer that people not climb because of the spiritual significance the rock represents as the Mala Dreaming track. The Cultural Centre will give you a better understanding of Anangu motivations before you decide one way or the other. Aside from respecting cultural traditions, realize that it is a difficult hike (a full 2-3hr.), even for the young and able-bodied (notice the plaques at the base that memorialize those who have died—33 total deaths in the past 20 years). Visitors should avoid climbing in the middle of the day or if they have medical conditions or loosely attached accessories—many of the deaths have resulted from individuals chasing after blowing hats or cameras. Due to the high level of risk, the climb is closed on excessively warm or windy days. A fixed chain helps with the lengthy and brutal initial uphill, the steepest part of the climb. Past the chain, including the section that extends beyond the portion visible from the ground, the path, marked by white blazes, meanders along the top of the rock for over 1km. The trail is rugged and requires the scaling of near vertical sections at times 2m tall. The climb requires at least 2-3 liters of water and rugged footwear with ankle support. On descending, use extreme care. Sliding down in a sitting position over the coarse rock is not recommended; grasp the chain firmly and take small steps, or walk carefully backwards, pulling on the chain for support.

⚑ **HIKES AROUND THE BOTTOM.** There are several far less adventurous, less dangerous hikes around the base of Uluru. Grab *An Insight into Uluru* ($1), available at the Cultural Centre, for an expanded self-guided tour of these walks.

■ **Circuit Walk** (9.4km; 3-4hrs.) Flat and level but long, this walk offers the best opportunity to study the innumerable dimples, grooves and caverns of the rock. The path, by turns skirting the rock or following the more distant road, is the only real chance to escape the throngs and contemplate the mighty rock in solitude. As it is a circuit, the path can be picked up at many places around the base of Uluru.

Mala Walk (2km; 45min.). Part of the circuit walk, this wheelchair-accessible walk leads from the main parking lot past Aboriginal art sites and a waved-shape cave on Uluru's wall to **Kantju Gorge,** which holds an ancient sacred Anangu waterhole. The free engaging ranger-guided walks along this path present an Aboriginal perspective on Uluru. Meet the ranger at the Mala Walk sign at the base of the climb. (1½hr. Daily Oct.-Apr. 8am; May-Sept. 10am. Free.)

Mutitjulu Walk (1km; 30min.). Served by a smaller parking lot to the right of the loop entrance, this flat, wheelchair accesible track leads to a waterhole that is home to *Wanampi*, an ancestral watersnake. Signs along the way detail the battle between ancestral spirits *Kuniya* and *Liru*, the events of which are recorded in the rock's features.

KATA TJUTA (THE OLGAS)

Many visitors' favorite feature in the park, the 36 domes of Kata Tjuta are scattered over an area several times the size of Uluru. Anangu for "many heads," Kata Tjuta's many faces and angles adopt new characters and moods as you circle them or walk through the valleys between them. They are a mysterious and magical site rising proudly from the surrounding flatness.

The 42km road to Kata Tjuta leaves the main road 4km after the park entrance. The **Dune Viewing Area,** 25km down the road, is at the end of a wheelchair-accessible walk (300m), allowing relaxing, all-encompassing views of Kata Tjuta. The **sunset-viewing area** (toilets available) is near the starting points for the two walks.

■ **Valley of the Winds walk** (7.4km; 3hr.). This amazing hike traces a majestic circuit through the outer wall of **domes** and into the inner sanctuary. It is broken into three sections, offering three different length walks. It is 1.1km from the carpark to the **Karu Lookout,** after which the trail splits, going both north and south in a loop. To the south, you head through a narrow gap, emerging at a long set of natural steps. At the top of these steps, around 1.5km from the first lookout, is the walk's highlight, the **Karingana**

lookout. A sweeping view into the gorge, this view is one of the best and least crowded in the entire park. From there, either follow the steps down to do the full loop, or retrace your steps to the carpark.

Olga Gorge walk (2.6km; 45min.). An easy path that heads straight between a pair of the most daunting domes. The dome on the right is **Mt. Olga** (546m), the highest peak in the range. The lookout at the end is often crowded and the view is no more spectacular than the views along the path.

YULARA (AYERS ROCK RESORT)   ☎08

Ayers Rock Resort (the municipal name of Yulara applies only because there is a small employee housing district) is a series of hotels and shops stretched along a side road just outside the national park. Capitalizing on Uluru's draw, Yulara is overpriced, and prices continue to skyrocket, as it maintains a monopoly on accommodations and most other services. Fortunately, the nearby attractions are so wonderful that even the crass commercialism of Yulara cannot fully ruin your outback experience.

■? TRANSPORTATION & PRACTICAL INFORMATION. Connellan Airport lies 5km north of town. **Airnorth** and **Qantas** (☎13 13 13) fly to Adelaide, Alice Springs, Brisbane, Cairns, Darwin, Melbourne, Perth, and Sydney. A free airport shuttle run by AAT Kings meets all flights and picks up from all accommodations. **McCafferty's/Greyhound** (☎13 14 99 or 13 20 30) **buses** depart for Alice Springs daily from the Outback Pioneer Hotel (6hr., 12:30pm, $74. $56 to Kings Canyon). Ayers Rock Resort runs a free village shuttle around the resort loop. (Every 15min., daily 10:30am-12:30am.) **Territory Rent-a-Car** (☎8956 2030), **Hertz** (☎8956 2244), and **Avis** (☎8956 2266) have offices at the airport or at the **Tourist Info Centre** in the resort shopping center (☎8957 7324). Prices for cars start at around $50-60 per day. Most backpackers come to Yulara on camping tours out of Alice Springs, which can be combined with various stops to other sites.

A handful of walks around town lead to six different lookout points, all with impressive views. The fit can reach the rocks through pedal power with a **bicycle** (from $20 per day) from Ayers Rock Campground. Otherwise, to get to Uluru and Kata Tjuta from the resort, you'll need a vehicle. **Uluru Express** (☎8956 2152) offers the most flexible transportation to Uluru ($30, children $15) and Kata Tjuta ($45, children $25). **Anangu Tours** is owned by Anangu; book through the Cultural Centre. (☎8956 2123. 2hr. tours $52, children $27, families $158.) **McCafferty's/Greyhound** does a sunset run to Uluru (4hr., departs 3pm, $62) and to Uluru and Kata Tjuta (5½hr., departs 6am, $40); book ahead. If you've got the money, you can get there on a **Harley-Davidson motorcycle.** (☎8955 5288. Passenger tours from $65; 5hr. self-drive from $335; deposit $2000.)

The **Tourist Info Centre,** in the shopping center, has general info, weather conditions, and tour agencies. (☎8957 7324. Internet 30¢ per min. Open daily 8am-8pm; service desks maintain shorter, variable hours.) The **Visitors Centre,** with a grand set of stairs rising from the road near the entrance to the village, has a gift shop and museum of desert animals as well as a detailed history of Uluru. (☎8957 7377. Open daily 9am-5:30pm.) **Petrol** is available at the Mobil station. (☎8956 2229. Open daily 7am-9pm.) Other services include: **police** (☎8956 2166); **ANZ bank** with 24hr. **ATM** in the shopping center (open M-Th 9:30am-4pm, F 9:30am-5pm); and a **post office.** (☎8956 2288. Open M-F 9am-6pm, Sa-Su 10am-2pm.) **Postal Code:** 0872.

▪▫ ACCOMMODATIONS & FOOD. For all lodge reservations, call ☎1300 139 889. The **Outback Pioneer Lodge ❸,** on Yulara Dr., has impersonal barracks-style dorms. (☎8957 7639. Free storage. Reception 4am-11pm. 20-bed dorms $32, YHA

$29; 4-bed $40/$37.) The **Resort Campground** ❶ corners the market on camping, since it is not allowed elsewhere in the park. Campers have access to a pool, kitchen, laundry, hot showers, and BBQ. (☎8956 2055. Sites $12.60 per person, children $5.80, families $36; powered for 2 $30/$5.80/$40.) The options at Yulara are "budget" doubles ($152/$172) at the **Outback Pioneer Hotel** ❺ or cabins at the Campground ($148 with shared bath for 1-6 people). The only other option is 100km away at **Curtain Springs,** meaning either missing the sunrise/set or driving in the dark, which is a pretty bad idea. (☎8956 2906. Free unpowered sites. Powered sites $11, showers $1; rooms from $35 single, $45 double; ensuite from $70 single, $80 double.) Most food in the area is overpriced. Sadly, the best place for a cheap meal may be fish 'n' chips at the gas station ($4.50), a ten-minute walk from the Outback. Another option is a burger ($6.50) at the **Takeaway** in the shopping center. The **Outback Pioneer Lodge** has a run-of-the-mill **snack bar** ❶ with $7 burgers. Their nightly BBQ with live entertainment (6-9pm) ranges from burgers to emu sausages ($14-24). It's also the only place to buy takeaway **liquor.** (Open daily 11:30am-9pm.)

QUEENSLAND

If the continent's natural attractions could be condensed into one state, the result would look something like Queensland, Australia's deliciously layered natural paradise. Queensland changes, east to west, from reef islands to sandy shores, from hinterland rainforest to glowing red Outback. At the base of this fantasyland sits the capital city of Brisbane, a diverse and manageable urban break from the surf and sun, located on the southeastern border of the state. Traveling north, Queensland's coast crawls with backpackers year-round; with the same faces popping up in every town, the journey often feels like a never-ending party. The downside for those on this heavily-touristed route is that real Aussie culture can be masked by the young crowd that floods its shores. Moving from one hot-spot to another can be mind-numbing as you wade through a neverending swamp of brochures, billboards, and tourist packages.

The enjoyment of a Queensland visit will multiply the more you step off this beaten track. Those willing to temporarily trade sandals for hiking boots can explore the rainforest-drenched far north and the jewel-bedecked Outback, where history, like tourism, proceeds at a koala's pace. Inland, you'll encounter charming country towns, pockets of thriving Aboriginal culture, and plenty of history—all without a hint of the rampant tourism of the coast. Across the entire state, opportunities abound for workers seeking to make money and camaraderie as part of the flourishing fruit-picking subculture. In Queensland, appreciating Oz at its extremes can be as simple as driving toward Cape Tribulation and watching the rainforest melt into the pounding surf.

QUEENSLAND HIGHLIGHTS

GREAT BARRIER REEF. Dive this natural wonder and frolic among shimmering schools of fish. (p. 319)

FRASER ISLAND. Fulfill your deepest, darkest 4WD fantasies on the island's massive sand dunes. (p. 378)

TOWN OF 1770. Rent a "tinny" or body board on 1770's prime (and largely untouristed) beaches. (p. 387)

EUNGELLA NATIONAL PARK. Hike through lush rainforest and misty valleys filled with giant ferns. (p. 399)

CAPE TRIBULATION. Drive the rough 'n' tumble Bloomfield Track or camp on a secluded rainforest beach. (p. 444)

▐ TRANSPORTATION

The Queensland coast as far north as Cairns, along with the far north and its interior, is comprehensively serviced by public transportation. Don't underestimate the distances involved; even within the state, many people choose to fly if they want to get from Brisbane to Cairns quickly. If you've got the time for a leisurely trip, though, taking a bus up the coast allows you to stop at innumerable spots along the way. The major bus lines is **McCafferty's/Greyhound** (☎ 13 20 30 or ☎ 13 14 99), and the train line is **Queensland Rail** (☎ 13 22 32). If you have a few friends to chip in for costs or if you're traveling with a family, **renting a car** provides the most convenience and freedom to wander off the beaten track. All the major car rental establishments are here, plus dozens of cheaper local ones. To tackle the area from Cooktown north through Cape York as well as some of the desert roads, you'll need **4WD**. This is pricey; it's also tough to find an automatic transmission 4WD (try **Allcar Rentals** in Port Douglas, ☎ 4099 4123). Roads in the tropics are especially harrowing, and often impassible, during and immediately following the **Wet season** (Nov.-Apr.). It's best to call ahead for **road conditions** (☎ 3361 2406).

The central office of the **Royal Automobile Club of Queensland (RACQ)** is at 300 St. Paul's Terr., Fortitude Valley, Brisbane. With affiliations worldwide, RACQ has excellent maps, car buying or selling information, and technical services. (☎ 3361 2444, statewide roadside service ☎ 13 11 11. Open M-F 8:30am-5:30pm. 1-year membership $67, overseas transfer free.) For more info, see **On the Road**, p. 55.

⌕ GREAT BARRIER REEF

WHEN TO DIVE: July to December; November spawntime. Avoid diving from January to March, a day or two after a storm, south of a recent cyclone, or if the wind speed is above 20 knots.

WHERE TO DIVE: Cairns (see p. 425), Port Douglas (see p. 439), Cape Tribulation (see p. 444), Beaver Cay (in Mission Beach; see p. 421), Magnetic Island (see p. 415), *S.S. Yongala* wreck (see p. 413), and the Whitsundays (see p. 406) from Airlie Beach (see p. 401).

The Great Barrier Reef stretches 2300km, from just offshore of Bundaberg to Papua New Guinea, encompassing hundreds of islands and cays and thousands of smaller reefs. This marine wonderland is easily accessible from the Queensland coast. It's a good idea to first familiarize yourself with the types of reefs and wildlife you'll see (for an overview, see p. 74). *Let's Go* describes diving and snorkeling sites and operators throughout the book, but shop around and get a sense of what you're looking for before you decide on a dive.

WHAT YOU'LL NEED
Queensland requires a **certification card** for all dives. **Hervey Bay** (see p. 373) and **Bundaberg** (see p. 384) have the cheapest PADI certification courses in the entire state. But before you begin a course or set out on an extended trip, you might want to try an **introductory** or **"resort" dive** with a trained guide to see what diving's all about. If you decide to do a PADI course, try to get boat dives instead of shore dives simply because the diving's usually better off shore. A PADI Open Water certification is the minimum qualification to dive without an instructor, but more advanced levels are available for dive enthusiasts. Medical exams are required for all dive courses and can easily be arranged with dive centers and area medical centers for about $50.

ALTERNATIVES TO DIVING
Diving is the ideal way to get an up-close view of the reef, but it requires significant amounts of time and money. Snorkeling is a convenient alternative for swimmers; renting a mask and fins can be as cheap as $10 per day, though day-long snorkeling trips on the reef run anywhere from $50 to 130. Gear is sometimes free with sailing trips or even hostel stays. Good snorkeling is often available just off the shore of islands or beaches. When wearing fins, *be extremely aware of where you are kicking*—you may destroy coral growth hundreds of years in the making. If you don't want to get wet at all, view the reef through one of the glass-bottom boats cruising from islands or beach towns.

QUEENSLAND

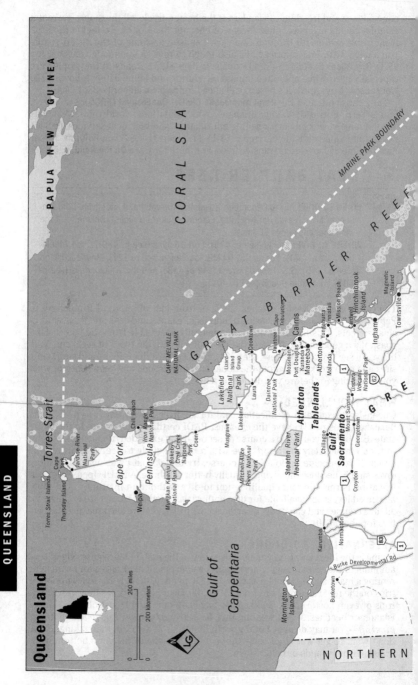

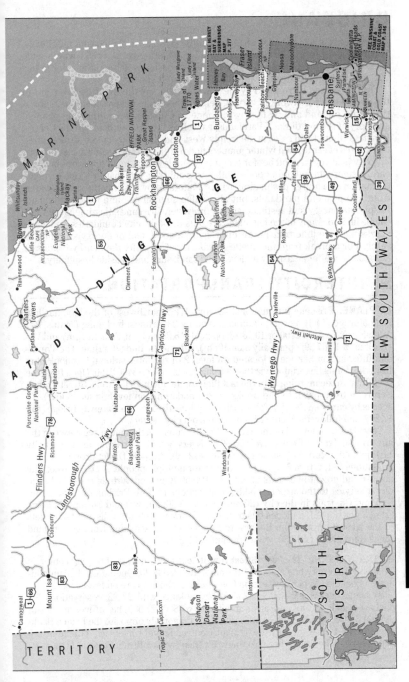

BRISBANE

☎ 07

Commonly unexplored (and unappreciated) by those on the coastal pilgrimage, Brisbane (pop. 1,580,000) spreads around its twisting central river with a wide spectrum of interests and attractions. Brisbane today is neither glitzy nor industrial, but instead practical, clean, and full of youthful energy.

The city center, surrounded by the graceful waters of the Brisbane River, sits in the middle of a patchwork of varying neighborhoods. Excellent public transportation, both on land and on the river, connects Chinatown and the well-planned greenery of the South Bank Parklands, as well as investment banks in the Central Business District and cafes in the trendy West End. The mild climate attracts artistic emigrés eager to shed winter jumpers and rev up the city's cultural institutions. The city is always a good bet for temporary employment, including work in childcare, restaurants and promotions. Still, it was only recently that Brisbane earned a reputation as a tourist destination, where visitors enjoy not only the serene waterfront and peaceful parklands, but also cafes, nightclubs, and live local music. Despite its energy and aesthetic appeal, however, Brisbane's daytime attractions can be limited. Many of the highlights are outside of the city boundaries, and while accessible by public transportation, require a good deal of energy and time to reach. For a break from the hustle and bustle of city life, the nearby islands of Moreton Bay offer amazingly undeveloped sand, surf, and seaside hospitality.

✈ INTERCITY TRANSPORTATION

BY PLANE. Brisbane International Airport, 17km northwest of the city, has luggage storage ($4-10 per day) and is served by 23 airlines, including Qantas, 247 Adelaide St. (☎ 3238 2700 or 13 13 13; open M-F 8:30am-5pm, Sa 9am-1pm) and Virgin Blue (☎ 13 67 89; open daily 5am-10pm), a domestic budget airline. The Travellers Information Service is located on level 2 of the international terminal, 3km from the domestic terminal via the $3 Coachtrans bus. (☎ 3406 3190. Open from the first flight in the morning until the last flight of the night.) The Roma Street Transit Centre in town has info and books accommodations on level 3 (see below). To access by car from the city, follow Highway 1 north, over the Gateway Bridge (toll $2.20), and follow the signs (25min. drive from city center).

CoachTrans, on level 3 of the Transit Centre, runs a daily **shuttle bus** between the airport and Transit Centre. (☎ 3860 6999. Every 30min. 8am-9pm; last bus to city 11:10pm. $9, return $15, same-day return $12, children $5. Direct drop at accommodations $11, return $17, and is cheaper for multiple people. A **taxi** between the airport and downtown costs about $27. Privately owned, **Airtrain** recently began direct service to the airport, making connections to both Brisbane's Queensland Rail and Citytrain in the city (25min., every 15-30min., $9) and Surfers Paradise (2hr.; 2 per hr.; $21, includes bus transfers). Many hostels offer discounted tickets to the airport on Airtrain. Be sure to ask. Timetable available from Queensland Rail's **Transinfo** (☎ 13 12 30; www.transinfo.qld.gov.au).

BY TRAIN & BUS. The **Roma Street Transit Centre,** 500m west of the city center, is Brisbane's intercity bus and train terminal. (☎ 3236 2020. Open daily 4:30am-midnight.) Lockers ($5 per day) are on level 1 and 3; showers are on level 2.

By train, **Queensland Rail** (☎ 3235 2222; bookings ☎ 13 22 32; reservations for packages, including air and accommodations ☎ 1800 627 655) has offices at Central Station on the corner of Ann and Edward St., diagonally opposite the Palace Backpackers, and on level 1 of the Transit Centre. Travel times vary considerably depending on the train. The snazzy new **Tilt Train** (www.tilttrain.com.au) is the fast-

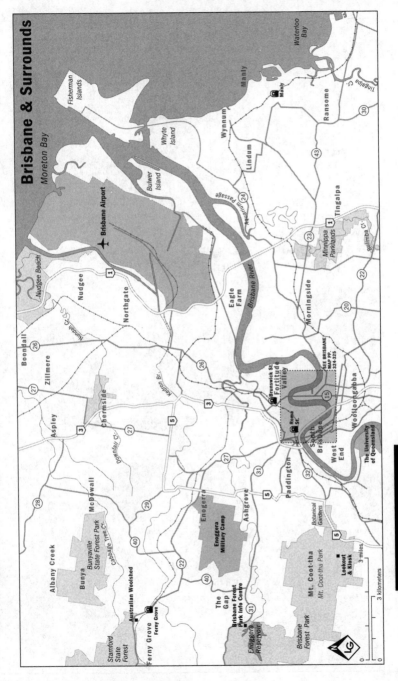

Brisbane & Surrounds

Moreton Bay

SEE BRISBANE MAP PP. 324-325

QUEENSLAND

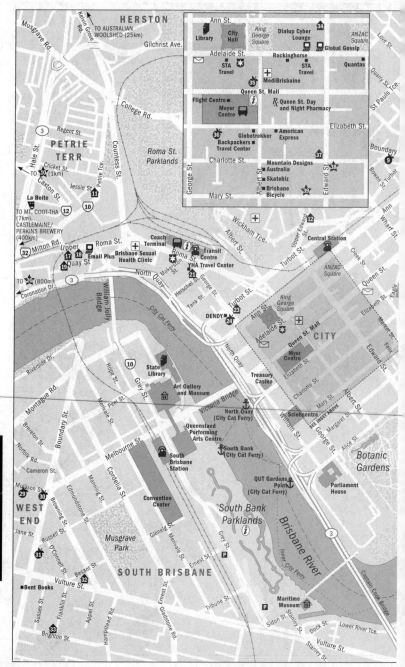

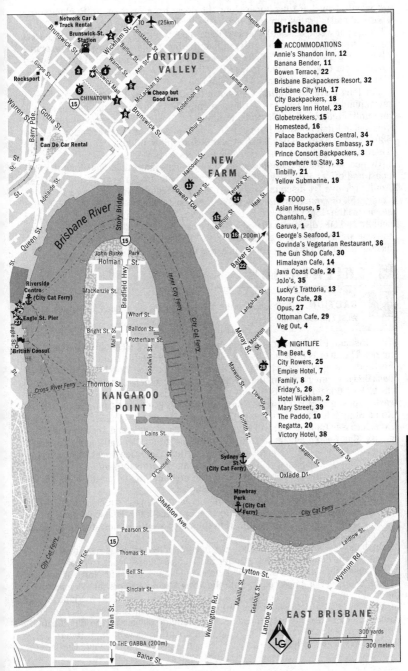

Brisbane

ACCOMMODATIONS
Annie's Shandon Inn, **12**
Banana Bender, **11**
Bowen Terrace, **22**
Brisbane Backpackers Resort, **32**
Brisbane City YHA, **17**
City Backpackers, **18**
Explorers Inn Hotel, **23**
Globetrekkers, **15**
Homestead, **16**
Palace Backpackers Central, **34**
Palace Backpackers Embassy, **37**
Prince Consort Backpackers, **3**
Somewhere to Stay, **33**
Tinbilly, **21**
Yellow Submarine, **19**

FOOD
Asian House, **5**
Chantahn, **9**
Garuva, **1**
George's Seafood, **31**
Govinda's Vegetarian Restaurant, **36**
The Gun Shop Cafe, **30**
Himalayan Cafe, **14**
Java Coast Cafe, **24**
JoJo's, **35**
Lucky's Trattoria, **13**
Moray Cafe, **28**
Opus, **27**
Ottoman Cafe, **29**
Veg Out, **4**

NIGHTLIFE
The Beat, **6**
City Rowers, **25**
Empire Hotel, **7**
Family, **8**
Friday's, **26**
Hotel Wickham, **2**
Mary Street, **39**
The Paddo, **10**
Regatta, **20**
Victory Hotel, **38**

QUEENSLAND

est way to travel; it runs north along the coast from Brisbane to Rockhampton (book ahead). Trains run to: **Bundaberg** (4¼-7½hr., 2-3 per day, $89.10); **Cairns** (32hr., 4 per week, $280.50); **Mackay** (18hr., 6 per week, $206.80); **Maryborough West** (3½-6¼hr.; 2 per day; $76, with connecting bus to **Hervey Bay** $54); **Proserpine** (19½hr., 6 per week, $216.70); **Rockhampton** (7-11½hr., 1-3 per day, $140.80); **Sydney** (16hr., 2 per day, $141); and **Townsville** (24hr., 6 per week, $244.20). Students with ID and children under 16 travel for half-price.

For long travel itineraries, Queensland Rail's **Sunshine Rail Pass** is good for a given number of travel days within a six-month span on any Queensland service and unlimited travel on **Citytrain,** the intracity network. Passes available at the Queensland Rail booth at Roma Street Transit Centre or Central Station. (14-day $307, 21-day $346, 30-day $432; students and children half-price. Book ahead.) There are many other passes available to overseas travelers.

By bus, **McCafferty's/Greyhound** (☎13 14 99) covers destinations along the east coast and offers 10% ISIC/VIP/YHA discounts and 20% for seniors and children. Adults receive 5% discounts on return fares. **Premier Coach Service** (☎13 34 10) grants 15% discounts for all concessions. **Kirklands Coaches** (☎1300 367 077), with service to the Gold Coast and Byron Bay, gives 25% discounts to YHA holders and seniors and 50% discounts to children. **Suncoast Pacific** (☎3236 1901) also services the Queensland coast and offers ISIC/YHA/VIP holders 20% discounts, seniors 10% discounts, and children 30% discounts. See table, p. 328.

✈ ORIENTATION

> ❗ **CAUTION.** Use caution in the areas surrounding Fortitude Valley and the West End, especially at night.

The Brisbane River meanders through the city, creating easily identifiable landmarks. The river is breached by four different bridges in the main part of the city: Fortitude Valley and Kangaroo Point are connected by the **Story Bridge;** the **Captain Cook Bridge** connects the southern edge of the city center to southbound highways; the **Victoria Bridge,** connects the city to South Bank; and the **William Jolly Bridge,** the easternmost and oldest bridge to span the waters. The **Transit Centre** is located on Roma St.; a left turn out of the building and a five-minute walk southeast down Roma crosses **Turbot Street** and leads to the corner of **Albert** and **Ann Street** and the grassy **King George Square** (a front lawn for the grand **City Hall**). **Adelaide Street** forms the far side of the square. One block farther, the **Queen Street Mall** runs parallel; it's a popular pedestrian thoroughfare lined with shops and cafes and the center of Brisbane proper. Underneath the mall and the adjoining **Myer Centre** shopping complex is the **Queen Street Bus Station.**

Continuing south from Queen St., the parallel east-west streets are **Elizabeth, Charlotte, Mary, Margaret,** and **Alice Street;** Alice borders the **Botanic Gardens.** Intersecting these streets north-south, from the river, are the major streets, **William, George, Albert, Edward,** and **Creek Street.**

Brisbane's neighborhoods radiate out from the city center. A right turn out of Roma St. (the commonly used term for the Transit Centre) leads to **Petrie Terrace** and **Paddington,** with close accommodations and mellow nightlife. North of Boundary St. is **Spring Hill,** bordered by both the **Roma Street Parklands** and **Victoria Park,** and a 15min. walk from the Queen St. Mall up steep Edward St. A 15min. walk down Ann St., the nightclub-heavy **Fortitude Valley** offers an alternative scene. Fortitude Valley is also home to the small but authentic **Chinatown,** the film location for several Jackie Chan flicks. Turning right down Brunswick St., a 10min. walk leads to **New Farm,** with its free art galleries and cafes. Near the Botanic Gardens at the city center's southern tip the Victoria Bridge footpath turns into Melbourne St. and heads into **South Brisbane,** crossing Boundary St. six blocks later in the heart of the **West End. South Bank** is to the east of the southern end of the bridge; farther along the riverside, **Kangaroo Point** forms a peninsula into the River.

⨲ LOCAL TRANSPORTATION

BY TRAIN. Citytrain, (Transinfo ☎ 13 12 30; www.transinfo.qld.gov.au), Queensland Rail's intracity train network, has three major stations and numerous stops throughout the city. The main transit center is at **Roma Street; Central Station** is at Ann and Edward St.; the final station is at **Brunswick Street** Citytrain also connects to **Airtrain,** with service to the airport (see above). One-zone journeys in the city cost $1.80, three zones $3.80. One-day unlimited travel is $8.60, three zones $21.60. Travel M-F 9am-3:30pm and after 7pm, as well as all day on weekends, is off-peak, meaning fares are half-price. (Trains run every 15-30min. M-Th 5am-11:30pm, F 5am-2am, Sa 6am-1am, Su 6am-11pm; times are variable for different destinations.

BY BUS. Citybus is the "all-stops" major service. Most buses depart from the **Queen Street Bus Station,** a huge terminal beneath the Myer Center and the Queen St. Mall. Platforms are named after Australian animals, while central city stops are numbered. Schedules organized by suburb and bus number are available at the very helpful **Queen Street Bus Station Info Centre,** located on the ground floor of the Myer Centre. (Open M-Th 8:30am-5:30pm, F 8:30am-8pm, Sa 9am-4pm, Su 10am-4pm.) Most bus stops also post times and a map for that particular route; otherwise contact Transinfo (☎ 13 12 30; www.transinfo.qld.gov.au) for timetables. Fares range from $1.80 to $3.80 (day rover pass allows access to all buses, ferries, and CityCats $8.40, concessions $4.20). The blue and white **City Circle bus** #333 runs a frequent city center circuit (M-F), convenient for sight-seeing (90¢). The white and yellow striped **Cityxpress** runs from the suburbs to the city approximately every 30min. Red buses operate on the free **Downtown Loop,** a circular service in the city center (M-F 7am-5:50pm). Buses #190 and #191 offer convenient routes from West End to New Farm.

BY CAR & TAXI. Network Car and Truck Rentals, 298 St. Paul's Terr., (☎ 3252 1599) in Fortitude Valley, rents from $39 a day. No age surcharge for those under 25, but reduced insurance coverage. (Open daily 8am-5:30pm.) **Can Do Car Rentals,** (☎ 3832 3666) at Wickham St. and Warren St., rents from $22 a day. $12 dollar age surcharge if under 25. (Open daily 9am-6pm.) For a **taxi,** try **Yellow Cab Company** (☎ 13 19 24) or **Black and White** (☎ 13 10 08); both operate 24hr.

BY FERRY. Brisbane's excellent ferry system makes good use of the Brisbane River, providing practical transport and cheap sightseeing tours. The sleek **CityCat** runs upstream to the University of Queensland and downstream to Bretts Wharf (CityCats run daily every 20-30min., 5:50am-10:30pm; blue sign at ferry stops). The central city stop is North Quay, near the Treasury Casino. The **City Ferry** operates around the city center and includes more stops than the CityCat (city ferries run daily at least every 20-30min. 6am-10:30pm; red sign at ferry stops). The **Crossriver** runs four routes connecting Brisbane's two banks, including downtown from the Holman St. and Edward St. stops (daily every 15min. 5:30am-10:30pm; green sign at ferry stop). The convenient **day rover pass** allows all-day travel on CityCats, ferries, and council buses ($8.40). Schedules are posted at every dock and stop, or call Transinfo (☎ 13 12 30; www.transinfo.qld.gov.au) for timetables. Fares for all ferries are $1.80-3.80 depending on distance.

QUEENSLAND

BUSES FROM BRISBANE TO:

DESTINATION	COMPANY	DURATION	PER DAY	PRICE
Adelaide	McCafferty's	40+ hr.	8	$206-230
Airlie Beach	McCafferty's	19hr.	5	$137
	Premier	18¼hr.	1	$123
Bundaberg	McCafferty's	6-7½hr.	4	$55
	Premier	7½hr.	1	$43
Byron Bay	Kirkland's	3hr.	4 M-F, 2 Sa-Su	$22.50
	McCafferty's	3¼hr.	7	$33
	Premier	3½hr.	3	$26
Cairns	McCafferty's	27-30hr.	7	$182
	Premier	28hr.	1	$175
Coolangatta & Tweed Heads	Kirkland's	2hr.	4 M-F, 2 Sa-Su	$15
	McCafferty's	2¼hr.	7	$16-17
	Premier	2¼hr.	3	$14
Hervey Bay	McCafferty's	7hr.	8	$41
	Premier	6hr.	1	$32
Lismore	Kirkland's	4½hr.	4 M-F, 2 Sa-Su	$33
	McCafferty's	5½hr.	1	$37
	Premier	5½hr.	1	$34
Mackay	McCafferty's	15-16hr.	6	$121
	Premier	16hr.	1	$109
Maroochydore	McCafferty's	2hr.	4	$20
	Premier	2hr.	1	$18
	Suncoast	2hr.	8 Su-F, 6 Sa	$22.50
Melbourne	McCafferty's	23¼-24hr.	1	$173
Mission Beach	McCafferty's	26¼hr.	4	$178
	Premier	26¼hr.	1	$168
Mooloolooba	Suncoast	2hr.	8 Su-F, 6 Sa	$22.50
Mt. Isa	McCafferty's	24hr.	1	$143
Noosa/Noosa Heads	McCafferty's	2½hr.	5	$20
	Premier	2½hr.	1	$18
	Suncoast	2-3hr.	7 Su-F, 5 Sa	$26
Rockhampton	McCafferty's	11½hr.	6	$79
	Premier	12hr.	1	$76
Surfers Paradise	Kirkland's	1¼-1½hr.	4 M-F, 2 Sa-Su	$15
	McCafferty's	1¼-1½hr.	7	$16
	Premier	1¼-1½hr.	3	$14
Sydney	McCafferty's	16-19hr.	6	$88
	Premier	16-19hr.	3	$84
Toowoomba	McCafferty's	2hr.	14	$20

⁊ PRACTICAL INFORMATION

TOURIST & FINANCIAL SERVICES

Tourist Office: The very busy **Brisbane Marketing Information Booth** (☎3006 6290) is in the middle of the Queen St. Mall, provides lots of info, but only on companies that are part of its association. Open M-Th 9am-5:30pm, F 9am-8pm, Sa 9am-5pm, Su 9:30am-4:30am. Touchscreen available 24hr. The free *Brisbane Visitors* guide is available at most tourist booths. The **Information Centre** (☎3236 2020), on the 3rd fl. of the Transit Centre, provides information on accommodations and attractions. Open M-F 7:30am-5:30pm, Sa-Su 8am-4pm.

Budget Travel Offices: Flight Centre (☎ 3229 6600 or 13 16 00) has 11 offices in the city and a guarantee to beat any quoted current price. Myer Centre office, on the basement level in front of Coles, open M-F 9am-5:30pm, Sa 9am-4pm, Su 10:30am-4pm. **STA Travel,** 111 and 57 Adelaide St. (☎ 3221 3722 or 13 17 76; www.statravel.com.au). Both offices open M-F 9am-5:30pm; 111 Adelaide open Sa 9am-3pm, 57 Adelaide open Sa 10am-4pm. **Backpackers Travel Centre,** 138 Albert St. (☎ 3221 2225). Open M-F 9am-6pm, Sa 10am-4pm. **YHA Travel Centre,** 154 Roma St. (☎ 3236 1680), across from the Transit Centre. Open M-Tu and Th-F 8:30am-5pm, W 9am-5pm, Sa 9am-3pm.

Consulates: British Consul, L26, 1 Eagle St. (☎ 3223 3200).

Banks: Banks on Boundary St. in South Brisbane, Brunswick St. in the Valley, and Queen St. in the city. Most are open M-Th 9:30am-4pm, F 9:30am-5pm. Typically $5 charge for traveler's checks and cash exchange. **ATMs** are located throughout the city. **American Express,** 131 Elizabeth St. (☎ 3229 2140), is open M-F 9am-5pm, Sa 9am-noon.

LOCAL SERVICES

Backpacking and Camping Equipment: Equipment stores line Albert St. between Elizabeth and Mary St. as well as in Fortitude Valley on Wickham St. between Gotha St. and Gipps St. **Globetrekker,** 142 Albert St. (☎ 3221 4476; www.globetrekker.com). Open M-Th 9am-6pm, F 9am-8pm, Sa 9am-4:30pm, Su 10:30am-4:30pm. **Mountain Designs Australia,** 105 Albert St. (☎ 3221 6756). Open M-Th 9am-5:30pm, F 9am-8pm, Sa 9am-4:30pm, Su 10am-4pm. YHA and student discounts.

Bookstores: The Queen St. Mall area has many bookstores. **Bent Books,** 205a Boundary St. (☎ 3846 5004; www.bentbooks.com.au), in the West End, has a broad collection of secondhand books available to purchase or trade. Open daily 10am-5:30pm.

Library: The **State Library** (☎ 3840 7666; www.slq.qld.gov.au), in South Bank, part of the Cultural Centre. Open M-Th 10am-8pm, F-Su 10am-5pm. Call ☎ 3840 7785 to book free 1hr. **Internet** access. The **John Oxley Library** (☎ 3840 7880), on level 4, is devoted to Queensland research and history and holds historical exhibitions. Open Su-F 10am-5pm. The **Central City Library** (☎ 3403 4166), on the corner of Ann and George St. on the bottom level of the City Plaza, allows book borrowing and free 30min. **Internet** access; book ahead in person. Open M-F 9am-6pm, Sa-Su 10am-3pm.

Public Markets: The Valley Markets (☎ 3854 0860), on Brunswick St. Mall, Fortitude Valley, is a hippie scene of second-hand items, clothes, and toys. Open Sa-Su 8am-4pm. The **Riverside Market** (☎ 0414 888 041), operates along the riverfront on Eagle St. between the Riverside Complex and Eagle St. Pier. Open Su 8am-4pm. For fresh produce, the **Farmers Market** takes place the 2nd and 4th Saturday of every month (7am-11:30am) at the Powerhouse Museum in New Farm. (☎ 3268 3889). The **South Bank Craft Village Market** (☎ 3867 2051; see **South Bank Parklands,** p. 335) offers a wide array of local talent. Open F 5pm-late, Sa 11am-5pm, Su 9am-5pm.

Used Cars: Cheap but Good Cars, 41 McLachlan St. (☎ 3252 7322), Fortitude Valley, with cars from $1000-3000. Open M-Sa 8am-6pm.

EMERGENCY & COMMUNICATIONS

Emergency: ☎ 000.

Police: Headquarters, 200 Roma St. ☎ 3364 6464. Other locations include City, 316 Adelaide (☎ 3258 2582); Fortitude Valley, in the Brunswick St. Mall near Wickham St. (☎ 3364 6237).

Crisis Lines: Statewide Sexual Assault Helpline ☎ 1800 010 120 or 3636 5206. **Suicide Prevention Medical Specialist** ☎ 1300 360 980. 24hr. **Drug and Alcohol Counselling** ☎ 3236 2414. **Pregnancy Counselling Australia** ☎ 1800 650 840.

QUEENSLAND

> ## MEDIA & PUBLICATIONS
> **Newspaper:** *The Courier-Mail* ($1), or pick up a free *Quest* community paper.
> **Nightlife:** *Time Off, Scene,* and *Rave* magazines (free). For info on gay and lesbian nightlife, check out *qp.*
> **Radio:** Rock, Triple M 104.5FM, B105FM, or Triple J 107.7FM; News, 936AM; Tourist Info, 88FM.

Pharmacy: Queen St. Mall Day and Night Pharmacy, 141 Queen St. (☎3221 4585), on the mall. Open M-Sa 7am-9pm, Su 8:30am-5:30pm.

Hospital: Holy Spirit Hospital, 759 Wickham Terr., Spring Hill (☎3834 6111). **MediCentre Brisbane** offers **Travellers Medical Service** and dive physicals, 245 Albert St. (☎1300 369 359 or 3211 3611). Open M-F 7:30am-7pm, Sa 8:30am-5pm, Su 9:30am-4pm.

Internet: State Library and **Central City Library** (see above). Internet cafes abound in Brisbane, especially in the downtown area. Most are similarly priced around $4-5 per hr. Try **Dialup Cyber Lounge,** 126 Adelaide St. (☎3211 9095). $4.40 per hr. Open daily 9am-7pm. **Global Gossip,** 288 Edward St. (☎3229 4033), next to Palace Backpackers Central, offers fax and copy services in addition to Internet. $5 per hr. Open daily 8am-midnight. Near Petrie Terr., try **Email Plus,** 328 Upper Roma St. (☎3236 0433). $4 per hr., $1 per 10min. Open daily 9am-2am.

Post Office: General Post Office, 261 Queen St. (☎3405 1434; Poste Restante ☎3405 1448). Half a block from the end of the mall. Open M-F 9am-6pm. Poste Restante open 9am-5pm. For weekend mail, try the Post at Wintergarden Centre Level 2 (☎3405 1380). Open M-Th 8:30am-5:30pm, F 8:30am-7pm, Sa 9am-4pm.

Postal Code: 4000 (city); 4001 (GPO).

⌐ ACCOMMODATIONS

Accommodations cluster in four main areas of the city: the pricey and convenient city center; South Brisbane and West End, near the riverside parklands, Cultural Centre, and Boundary St.; Fortitude Valley and New Farm, with cafes, galleries, festivals, and a funky night pulse; and the Petrie Terrace area, less aesthetically pleasing but close to the Transit Centre and Caxton St. party scene. Most of the accommodations listed have pick-up and drop-off, usually at the Roma St. Transit Centre. Call ahead to check times. Unless otherwise noted, check-out is 10am and key deposit $10. Linen and cutlery are usually free with a deposit.

CITY CENTER

Palace Backpackers Central, 308 Edward St. (☎3211 2433 or 1800 676 340; www.palacebackpackers.com.au), on the corner of Ann St. Filling in peak times to its 350-person capacity, this 7-level building is a backpacker landmark. Near-nightly after-hour parties make for noisy halls. 3-story veranda, big kitchen, rockin' backpackers pub (see **Nightlife,** p. 338), Internet, laundry, roof deck, and cafe. The $25 job club gives members a near guarantee of finding work. Reception 24hr. 8- to 9-bed dorms $20, weekly $126; 5- to 7-bed dorms $21/$137; 3-4 bed dorms $23/$147; twins $26/$168; singles $36/$238; doubles $48/$308. VIP. ❷

Palace Backpackers Embassy (☎1800 676 340; www.palacebackpackers.com.au), at the corner of Edward and Elizabeth St. Because its older sibling was so popular, Palace Backpackers recently opened up shop at a second, smaller location. Rooms are modern and clean, though the atmosphere is less wild than at Palace Central. Kitchen, Internet, roof deck, laundry, and a comfy common area with TV. Dorms $20-23, weekly from $126. Doubles $48, weekly $332. VIP. ❷

Explorers Inn Hotel, 63 Turbot St. (☎3211 3488 or 1800 623 288; www.pow-erup.com.au/~explorer), near the corner of George St. Pleasant budget hotel with an affordable restaurant (meals from $11). Compact rooms have private bath, fridge, and TV. Internet. Laundry. No smoking. Reception M-F 6:30am-10:30pm, Sa-Su 7am-10pm; late-night check-ins with advance notice. Singles from $75, doubles from $79. ❺

Annie's Shandon Inn, 405 Upper Edward St. (☎3831 8684), Spring Hill. Like Grandma's house, with family snapshots, cozy beds, and pastels. The perfect retreat after too many impersonal hostel dorms. Cold breakfast included. Kitchenette. Laundry. Reception 7am-9pm; late-night check-in with advance notice. Check-out 9am. Singles $50, ensuite $60; twins and doubles $60/$70; extra person $10. ❹

FORTITUDE VALLEY & NEW FARM

Prince Consort Backpackers, 230 Wickham St. (☎1800 225 005 or 3257 2252), Fortitude Valley. The newest hostel in the Fortitude Valley scene offers clean, comfortable rooms, a large Internet cafe, and homey TV area. Kitchen, free breakfast, laundry, organized pub crawls and trivia nights, friendly staff, and a hopping pub downstairs. Free drink on check-in. Dorms from $16, doubles $50. ❷

Homestead, 57 Annie St. (☎ 3358 3538), New Farm. Giant murals and rooms with names like "Popeye and Olive" (the honeymoon suite) and "Blue Mountains" (for nature lovers). Social atmosphere on a quiet street; extremely popular among backpackers. Su BBQ and soccer match. Free bus to airport, Transit Centre, and city. Internet ($1 per 16min.), laundry, TV lounge, kitchen, garden, tons of free hostel outings, and free bike use. Help with job placement and long term stays. Reception 7am-7pm. Dorms $16-18, weekly $80-95; twins and doubles $44/$245. VIP/YHA. ❷

Globetrekkers, 35 Balfour St. (☎3358 1251; www.globetrekkers.net), New Farm, between Brunswick St. and Bowen Terr. Small 1890s house with beautiful hardwood floors and furniture. Swimming pool. Unlimited Internet $2. Laundry. Women's dorm. Park your campervan in back and enjoy access to the facilities for $10 per person. Dorms $19, weekly $98; singles $33, ensuite $38; twins and doubles $44/$48; family rooms $50. Reception 9am-9pm. Book ahead. VIP/YHA. Cash only. ❷

Bowen Terrace, 365 Bowen Terr. (☎3254 1575 or 3254 0458), New Farm, on the corner of Barker St. Warm colonial house with a mellow, hippie feel. Bedrooms vary; ask for the lovely double with the bathtub and fireplace. Lounge, kitchen, and deck; doubles have TV and fridge. Singles $34; twins $40; doubles $48, ensuite $58. Cash only. ❸

PETRIE TERRACE

City Backpackers, 380 Upper Roma St. (☎3211 3221 or 1800 062 572). The big orange building 400m from the Transit Centre. A larger hostel with a social atmosphere and personable staff. Rooms were recently renovated: all are clean, comfortable, and with TV. Enormous kitchen, rooftop dining (staff cooks up cheap dinners multiple times a week) with city views, Internet, laundry, and an awesome pool with see-through windows on the deck below. The Irish pub downstairs, **The Fiddler's Elbow,** has live music Tu and Sa and a happening crowd every night. 4-, 6-, or 8-bed dorms $16-21; twins and doubles $48-63. VIP/YHA. ❷

TinBilly, 462 George St. (☎1800 446 646; www.tinbilly.com), at the corner of Herschel St. Clean, bright rooms can be found in one of the newest purpose-built hostels in Brisbane. All rooms ensuite, with TVs and lockers. Kitchen, laundry, $8 fitness club pass, and downstairs pub. Dorms $20-26, doubles $74. VIP. ❷

Yellow Submarine, 66 Quay St. (☎3211 3424). Painted bright yellow inside and out, this little house has a lot of character and community. Most guests stay on more of a long-term basis: the hostel staff offers job placement assistance. Outdoor TV lounge and a new pool. Laundry and kitchen. Courtesy van. Shared bath. No smoking. Book ahead. Reception 7am-10pm. Singles $22, weekly $125; doubles and twins $48, weekly $270. Cash only. ❷

Banana Bender, 118 Petrie Terr. (☎3367 1157), on the corner of Jessie St. One of the city's original small hostels, with a quiet, relaxed feel. Eating area with city view, Internet, laundry, kitchen, and TV lounge. The hostel has a liquor license, but only alcohol bought through Banana Bender may be consumed on property. Reception 7am-10pm. 4-bed dorms $20; 3-bed dorms $21; twins and doubles $48. VIP. Cash only. ❷

Brisbane City YHA, 392 Upper Roma St. (☎3236 1004). Private, clean, and low-key, with a friendly staff. Perfect for couples or friends, not for socialites. Kitchen, cafe, and reading loft. Lockers, laundry, and Internet. Dorms $24-26, twin $51, double $55, ensuite double $55. YHA discount $3.50 per person. ❷

SOUTH BRISBANE

▨ **Somewhere to Stay,** 45 Brighton Rd. (☎3844 6093 or 1800 812 398; reception@somewheretostay.com.au), entrance on Franklin St. A small, homey hostel in a beautiful old Victorian house. Large rooms with bath; some have city views. Lush greenery and swimming pool, big kitchen, tourist office, and free bus to city. Laundry. Internet $5 per hr. Reception 7am-10pm. Check-out 9:30am. Dorms $16-24, weekly from $100; doubles $42-60, weekly from $255. Wheelchair-accessible. NOMADS/VIP/YHA. ❷

Brisbane Backpackers Resort, 110 Vulture St. (☎3844 9956 or 1800 626 452), near the corner of Boundary St. Rooms feel sterile and impersonal, but amenities are worth it. Rooms have bath, TV, fridge, and lockers; many have balconies. Free bus to city and transit center. Tennis court, swimming pool, spa, game room, two kitchens, laundry, Internet, travel desk, bar, and **cafe** ❶ (brekkie $4-5; dinner $5). Reception 24hr. Check-out 9:30am. Key, linen and cutlery deposit each $10. 8-bed dorms $16; 6-bed $19; 4-bed $20; singles $52; twins and doubles $104. Weekly rates include the 7th night free. ISIC/VIP/YHA. ❷

◧ FOOD

The West End specializes in ethnic food and small sidewalk cafes, particularly along Boundary St. and Hardgrave Rd. Chinatown in Fortitude Valley has cheap Asian food, while trendier New Farm and the city center have more expensive eateries. Woolworths **supermarket** is located downstairs at McArthur Centre in the Queen St. Mall (open M-F 8am-9pm, Sa 8am-5:30pm, and Su 9am-6pm). For ice cream, try ▨**Cold Rock** on Grey St. in the South Bank Parklands.

CITY CENTER

▨ **JoJo's** (☎3221 2113), on the corner of Queen St. Mall and Albert St. Perched between the chaotic mall and majestic skyscrapers, JoJo's attracts travelers, students, and yuppie businessmen to its grill, Thai, and Italian counters. Reminiscent of a high class food court. Try their excellent pizzas ($8.50) or grilled sirloin($16). Daily specials. Open M-Th 9:30am-11pm, F 9:30am-midnight, Sa 11am-midnight, Su 11:30am-10pm. ❹

Java Coast Cafe, 340 George St. (☎3211 3040), near the corner of Ann St. The jungle-like courtyard dining area is an inner-city sanctuary. Top pick among the city's hundreds of coffee shops. Open M-F 7:30am-4:30pm. ❶

Govinda's Vegetarian Restaurant, upstairs at 99 Elizabeth St. (☎3210 0255; www.brisbanesgovindas.com). The Hare Krishna owners only serve one type of meal—an $8 all-you-can-eat extravaganza. The weekday cafeteria-style setting lacks atmosphere, but the Su $3 feast includes higher-quality meals, as well as chanting and dancing. Open M-Sa 11:30am-2:30pm, also F-Sa 5:30-8:30pm, Su 5-8:30pm. ❶

Opus (☎3229 9915), Eagle Street Pier, along the river. Brisbane's upper crust and business class enjoy a meal in one of the classy venues along the waterfront. Kangaroo fillet with beet and spinach $24. Open M-F 7am-midnight, Su 7am-4pm. ❸

WEST END & SOUTH BANK

▨ **George's Seafood,** 150 Boundary St. (☎3844 4100). A tiny seafood shop that will grill, batter, or crumb any fresh fillet for $1 extra. Unbeatable deal: crumbed cod and chips $4.50. Note that George's is takeaway only. Open M-F 9:30am-7:30pm, Sa 8:30am-7:30pm, Su 10:30am-7:30pm. ❶

The Gun Shop Cafe, 53 Mollison St. (☎3844 2241), at the corner of Boundary St. A gun shop for 60 years, the corner cafe now hits the bulls-eye with trendy, backpacker-friendly fare. Try the sesame tuna ($16) or lemongrass blackpepper beef ($14.50). Open Su and W-Sa 7am-midnight. ❷

Ottoman Cafe, 37 Mollison St. (☎3846 3555), a block west of the Boundary St. corner. The amazing Turkish cuisine, authentic decorations, and genuine service make for one of the best dining experiences in Brisbane. Mains start at $16. BYO. Open Su and W-Sa 5pm-late, also F noon-3pm. ❸

Chantahn, 150 Boundary St. (☎3844 8808). This small cafe offers Greek dishes and bargain vegetarian options. Try the chunky chickpea casserole or stir-fry veggies with ginger and chili ($5). Early bird dinner under $10 until 7pm. Belly dancing and plate smashing F-Sa nights. BYO. Open daily 8am-2pm and 5pm-late. ❷

NEW FARM

▨ **Himalayan Cafe,** 640-642 Brunswick St. (☎3358 4015). Tibetan and Nepalese delicacies in a warm atmosphere. The back room seats patrons on cushions; a great setting, though service is slow. Diced goat, lightly spiced, cooked with pumpkin and potato $14. Veggie options. Open Tu-Su 5:30-10:30pm. Book ahead. ❷

▨ **Lucky's Trattoria**, at the corner of Brunswick St. and Martin St. (☎3252 2353), between Fortitude Valley and New Farm. Excellent Italian favorites in a festive setting. Try the gnocchi with blue vein cheese sauce ($12.30) or the Capriciosa Pizza ($9.50). BYO. Open M-Th 6pm-10:30pm, F-Sa 6pm-midnight, Su 6-10pm. ❷

▨ **Moray Cafe** (☎3254 1342), on the corner of Moray and Merthyr Rd. Set in a residential location near the river, Moray Cafe is anything but quiet. It's as if a small corner of Hollywood found its way into Australia; crowds of hip twenty somethings with attitude crowd around the small tables. Best Caesar salad in Queensland, hands-down ($14). Licensed. Open daily 8:30am-late; kitchen closes 10pm. ❸

FORTITUDE VALLEY

▨ **Garuva,** 324 Wickham St. (☎3216 0124), on the corner of Constance St., in the black door near the Brisbane Saab dealership. Seductive and intimate. Sit on a cushioned rug as a white curtain is drawn around your table to ensure the utmost privacy. Meals from seven nations; sweet potato and bean curry to shark, all around $14. Book ahead. Open daily 6pm-late. ❷

Asian House, 165 Wickham St. (☎3852 1291). Within the multitudes of Asian restaurants that the area in and around Chinatown has to offer, Asian House comes out on top with its excellent dishes, friendly service, and casual dining. Try the chicken fillet and sweet ginger ($9.90) or mixed chinese vegetables in curry ($8.90). Open daily 11:30am-2pm and 5-10:30pm. ❷

Veg Out, 292 Wickham St. (☎3852 2668), near the Brunswick St. mall. Mix and match veggie meals. Or, get a coffee and check your email at the Internet cafe. Licensed. Open M-Th 8am-6pm, F 8am-10pm, Sa 8:30am-10pm, Su 10am-5pm. Cash only. ❷

◎ SIGHTS

CITY SIGHTS

CITY TOURS. City Sights is a 1½hr. bus tour of cultural and historical attractions. Jump on and off the circuit bus and get unlimited access on public bus and ferry networks. Buy tickets on the bus, from any customer service center, or at most tourist offices. *(Tours leave from City Hall, at the corner of Albert and Adelaide St., but you can start it at any of the 18 stops. Call Transinfo ☎ 13 12 30 for timetables. Daily every 45min. 9:06am-3:51pm. $20, concessions $15.)* For a tour of the Brisbane River, the large **Kookaburra River Queen** paddlewheel boat departs daily from the Eagle St. Pier, with commentary on passing sights and live accordion music. *(☎ 3221 1300. 1½hr. tea cruise $24, with lunch buffet $38, seafood buffet $58. 2½-3hr. buffet dinner cruise $52-68. Departs daily noon and 7pm.)* **Tours and Detours** *(☎ 1300 300 242)* offers a number of different city and river trips, including a half-day highlight tour *($44, concessions $40, children $28; leaves Brisbane 9:30am, returns 1pm)*, an afternoon float to Lone Pine Koala Sanctuary and Mt. Coot-tha *($48, concessions $46, children $30; leaves Brisbane 2:30pm, returns 6pm)*, or a night tour of Brisbane *($40, concessions $38, children $26; departs 7pm, returns 9:30pm)*. Those on foot can pick up a guide to the **Brisbane Heritage Trail.** The 3km path winds its way around the city, passing historical and cultural sights. *(☎ 3403 8888. Starts in King George Sq. Free maps and guides available at City Hall and the Brisbane City Council.)*

CASTLEMAINE/PERKINS BREWERY. XXXX, which proudly proclaims itself as "Queensland's beer," is brewed five minutes from Caxton St. on Milton Rd., adjacent to the Milton train stop. The 45min. walking tour ends with you, an hour, and four tall ones. Meet at the Castlemaine Sports Club, which is accessible by walking down Milton Rd., taking the first right after the Suncorp Stadium, and the first left onto Heussler Terr. *(☎ 3361 7597. Tours M-W and sometimes Th 11am, 1:30, and 4pm; occasionally also W 6:30pm. $8.50, W 6:30pm with BBQ $18.50. Book ahead.)*

CARLTON BREWHOUSE. Thirty minutes south of Brisbane are the brewers of VB, Foster's, and Carlton. The tour through the largest and most modern brewery in Queensland may be slightly dry, but the four beers at the end sure aren't. *(In Yatala. ☎ 3826 5858. By car, follow the Pacific Hwy. 41km south of the city, and exit at Yatala South. The brewery is inland from the highway. No public transportation to the brewery; brewery buses leave Tu and Th 11am or on demand. Tours M-F 10am, noon, and 2pm. $15, seniors $10, children $7.50. Transport from Brisbane, tour, light lunch, and 4 drinks $30. Book ahead.)*

CITY HALL. Opened in 1930, it earned the epithet "Million Pound Town Hall" for its outrageous building cost. 1hr. **tours** of the interior are given by local historians. The recently restored **clock tower,** a landmark of the city skyline, is 92m high and has an **observation deck,** which looks out onto buildings unfortunately much taller than it. The **Museum of Brisbane** hosts three rotating exhibits; one display is usually by a local artist. *(Tours ☎ 3225 4890 M-F at 1 and 2pm. $6, pensioners $4.50. Observation deck. Open Su-Tu 10am-5pm, Sa 10am-2:30pm. $2, concessions $1. Museum ☎ 3403 8888. Open daily 10am-5pm. Free.)*

QUEENSLAND CULTURAL CENTRE. On the south side of the Victoria Bridge, the Cultural Centre coordinates many of Brisbane's artistic venues, including the art gallery, museum, performing arts complex (see p. 337), state library (see p. 329), and theater company. The **Queensland Art Gallery** has over 10,000 works, primarily Australian, Aboriginal, and contemporary Asian. *(☎ 3840 7303. Open M-F 10am-5pm, Sa-Su 9am-5pm. Free guided tours M-F at 11am, 1, and 2pm, Sa-Su 11am, 1, and 3pm. Free; special exhibitions $8-15.)* The **Queensland Museum** is home to a wide range of Australian artifacts of cultural and natural interest, including such objects as dinosaur skeletons, stuffed birds, bugs, and mammals, and cars and planes from the early 20th century. (☎3840 7555; www.qmuseum.qld.gov.au. Open daily 9:30am-5pm. Free; special exhibitions $10-15.)

PARKS & GARDENS

SOUTH BANK PARKLANDS. Built on the former site of the 1988 World Expo, South Bank offers views of the river, a tree-lined and cafe-dotted boardwalk, and weekly markets. The **man-made lagoon**, surrounded by a real sand beach, fills with sun-seekers during both summer and winter months. (Lifeguard on duty 9am-5pm.) The Parklands also contains a **Maritime Museum,** with wrecks and models. (At the old South Brisbane Dry Dock, south end of the parklands. ☎3844 5361. Open daily 9:30am-4:30pm; last entry 3:45pm. $5.50, concessions $4.40, children $2.80, families $13.80.) On weekends, the park's central thoroughfares are lined with a **crafts village,** featuring crafts, jewelry, psychics, clothing, and massages. (Open F 5-10pm by lantern-light, Sa 11am-5pm, Su 9am-5pm.) The South Bank also organizes free events, including car shows, fireworks, and weightlifting championships, which are often held in the Suncorp Piazza. Obtain an event calendar and map from the **Visitor Information Centre,** in the center of the park at the Stanley St. Plaza. (Accessible by foot, by bus to South Bank or Cultural Centre stops, by CityTrain to South Brisbane station, or by ferry to terminal stop at South Bank. Info Centre ☎3867 2051; www.south-bank.net.au. Open Su-Th and Sa 9am-6pm, F 9am-9pm. Although there are no official gates, the Parklands are "open" daily 5am-midnight.)

BOTANIC GARDENS. Stroll among palm groves, camellia gardens, and lily ponds. If you search hard, you can see large goanna lizards strolling the ground as well. (A 10min. walk from the city center on Albert St., at the intersection with Alice St. ☎3403 0666. Open 24hr. Free tours depart the rotunda near the Albert St. entrance M-Sa 11am and 1pm.)

MT. COOT-THA. Mt. Coot-tha is split into two main sections: the botanical gardens and the Summit. Bus number #471 services both sections from town hall. (20min. to gardens, 25min. to the summit. 1 per hr. Last bus to city leaves gardens at M-F 4:10pm, Sa-Su 5:10pm.) The park is also accessible by car: drive down Milton Rd. and follow the signs. Queensland's premier subtropical garden, the Botanical Garden includes a Japanese Garden, botanical library, tropical dome, and plenty of picnicking green. (☎3403 2531. Gardens open 8am-5:30pm. Closed to vehicles M-F at 4:30pm and on weekends. Free tours M-Sa 11am and 1pm from the info center.) It also houses Queensland's first **Planetarium,** the Cosmic Sky Dome. (☎3403 2578. 45min. programs W-F 3:15pm, Sa 1:30, 3:15, and 7:30pm, Su 1:30pm and 3:15pm. $10, concessions $8.50, children $6, families $28; free exhibit in the foyer.) The **Mount Coot-tha Summit** offers a view of greater Brisbane that is spectacular at night. The casual **Kuta Cafe ❷** (meals under $12) and the fancier **Mount Coot-tha Summit Restaurant ❺** (mains $25) both have panoramic views. (Kuta Cafe ☎3368 2117; Summit Restaurant ☎3369 9922. Kuta open Su-Th 7am-11pm, F-Sa 7am-midnight; Summit open M-Sa 11:30am-midnight, Su 8-10:30am.) To walk between the two sections to the gardens, take the **JC Slaughter Falls track** (2km) from the summit, with an optional **Aboriginal Art loop.** At the bottom of the trail, exit the carpark to the right, and follow the busy main road for ten minutes to the garden entrance.

BRISBANE FOREST PARK. Picnic, camp, birdwatch, cycle, ride horses, and hike on over 29,000 hectares of eucalypt forest, but only if you have a car to take you there. The park headquarters offers bushwalking maps and contains the **Walkabout Creek Wildlife Centre,** a small sanctuary for wallabies, native birds, and various water creatures. Bushcamping is permitted throughout the park. Obtain a permit from the Brisbane Forest Park Headquarters before leaving ($4 per person per night). (60 Mt. Nebo Rd. Drive on Musgrave Rd. out of the city; it turns into Waterworks Rd., then Mt. Nebo Rd. 14km from city center. The #385 bus from Albert St. will get you to park headquar-

QUEENSLAND

ters, but trails and camps are accessible by private transport only. Rob's Rainforest Day Tours (see p. 337) brings daytrips M. Info Centre ☎ 3300 4855. Open M-F 8:30am-4:30pm, Sa-Su 9am-4:30pm. Wildlife Centre $3.50, concessions $2.50.)

ROMA STREET PARKLANDS. Below Wickham Terr. and above the Transit Centre, these parklands were recently created for public enjoyment. The $72 million renovation gave the park the official title of the largest subtropical garden in a city center. Enjoy free performances in the amphitheater, a walk though the recreated ecosystems, or a ride on the miniature train. *(☎ 3006 4545; www.romastreetparkland.com.au. Train runs M-F 10am-2pm, Sa-Su 10am-4pm. $3, children $2.)*

WILDLIFE

AUSTRALIA ZOO. The crocs get fed every day in the summer at noon and 1:30pm—a spectacle you won't forget, especially if Crocodile Hunter Steve Irwin is there. Cuddle a python, ogle the world's ten most venomous snake species, feed a kangaroo, and patiently follow Harriet, the world's oldest Galapagos tortoise. *(In Beerwah, 75km north of Brisbane. By car, take the Beerwah exit (Glass Mountains Tourist Route) off of the Pacific Hwy. and follow the signs. By public transportation, catch the "Crocodile Train" from the Transit Centre. Trains depart for Beerwah from city center every day ($16.50 return, $8.30 on weekends. Call ☎ 13 12 30 for time tables. ☎ 5494 1134 or 5436 2000; www.crocodilehunter.com. $23, concessions $19, children $14, families $65. Open daily 8:30am-4pm.)*

ALMA PARK ZOO. The hands-on zoo has walkthrough kangaroo and deer enclosures, koalas, monkeys, and water buffalo, and allows feeding of some of the friendlier animals. Twenty acres of beautiful tropical gardens with BBQs make it an ideal picnic spot. *(Alma Rd., Dakabin. By car, the zoo is 28km north of Brisbane on Bruce Hwy., at the Boundary Rd. exit. By public transportation, take the Caboolture train to Dakabin and snag a taxi at the Dakabin station. ☎ 3204 6566; www.almaparkzoo.com.au. Open daily 9am-5pm. Last entry 4pm. Pet koalas daily noon and 2:30pm. $20, concessions and children $10.)*

LONE PINE KOALA SANCTUARY. As the world's largest koala sanctuary, Lone Pine offers over 130 koalas to get up close and personal with. Be sure to check out the mums and babies section to see the adorable little ones. If you come around feeding time (usually around 2pm), you have an chance of seeing the usually lethargic animals moving around. Check out the wall of fame in the restaurant, where numerous entertainers have been photographed with one of the Pine's koalas. *(By car, follow Milton Rd. to the Western Freeway (number 32) and follow the signs. From public transportation, take bus #430 from the Koala platform in the Myer Centre (1 per hr.), or bus #445 from Adelaide St. opposite City Hall (1 per hr.). Or take the Mirimar Wildlife Cruise 19km upstream on the Brisbane River. Cruise ☎ 3221 0300 or 0412 749 426. Departs North Quay at 10am; free pick-up from city accommodations. Return $25, concessions $20, children $15. Sanctuary ☎ 3378 1366; www.koala.net. Open daily 8am-5pm. $15, students $13, children and pensioners $10, families $38.)*

AUSTRALIAN WOOLSHED. The Australian Woolshed attempts to give visitors a taste of the "real" Australian outback just 20min. from downtown Brisbane. With plenty of different activities, all priced separately, the grounds are a perfect place for families and small children. The highlight is the sheep shearing, where the clever sheep dogs steal the show. *(Samford Rd., Ferny Hills. 800m from the Ferny Grove Citytrain station, 30min. northeast of Brisbane. By car, head away from the city on Kelvin Grove Rd. in Petrie Terr. Kelvin Grove Rd. will turn into Samford Rd. After 23km, the woolshed is located on the left. 148 Samford Rd., in Ferny Hills. ☎ 3872 1100; www.auswoolshed.com.au. Open daily 8:30am-4:30pm. Shows and animal farm $16.50, concessions $12, children $11. Billy Tea and Damper (by request) $6.50, children $4.10. Waterslide $6.50 per hr. Mini Golf $5.50. Bungy Trampoline $5 per 5min.)*

☒ ACTIVITIES

ROCK CLIMBING & SKYDIVING. Join **Outdoor Pursuit** at Kangaroo Cliffs, past South Bank, for **rock climbing** or **abseiling** every other Sunday at 8:30am. They also journey outside of the city for canyoning trips. (☎3391 8776. $42, canyoning $105. Book ahead.) If you need practice, try **indoor climbing** with **Rock Sports.** (224 Barry Pde., Fortitude Valley. ☎3216 0492. Open M-F 10am-9:30pm, Sa-Su 10am-6pm. $14 for unlimited climbing. $11 harness, shoes and chalk rental. Bringing a partner is recommended.) A little higher up, **Brisbane Skydiving Centre** will show you the city at 200km per hour from 12,500 ft. (☎1800 061 555. $230; free pick-up.) Or, enjoy a more leisurely flight on a hot air balloon ride over the city with **Fly Me to the Moon.** (☎3423 0400; www.flymetothemoon.com. Weekdays $228, weekends $248. Both include five-star breakfast and pick-up.)

WATER ACTIVITIES. Brisbane has many waterways that are perfect for **canoeing.** Written guides to the popular **Oxley Creek** and **Boondall Wetlands** are available from libraries or the City Council Customer Services counter, in the City Plaza, on the corner of Ann and George St. For rentals, try **Goodtime Surf and Sail.** (29 Ipswich Rd., Woolloongabba. ☎3391 8588. Open M-F 8:30am-5pm, Sa 8:30am-4pm, Su 10am-3pm. Canoes from $28 per day; kayaks from $20. Includes paddles. Deposit $55.) **ProDive** goes to the area's reefs and wrecks. (☎3368 3766. Open M-F 9am-6pm, Sa-Su 9am-5pm. Daytrip 2 dives $125, gear $49; pick-up included.)

BUSHWALKING. Rob's Rainforest Explorer Day Tours takes you through Mt. Glorious and Samford Valley in Brisbane Forest Park (see p. 335) on Mondays, Glasshouse Mountains and Kondalilla Falls (see p. 373) on Tuesdays and Thursdays, the Green Mountains of Lamington National Park (see p. 356) on Wednesdays and Fridays, or Springbrook National Park (see p. 357) on Saturdays. (☎3357 7061 or 0409 496 607; www.powerup.com.au/~frogbus7. $55; includes pick-up and transport.)

♫ ENTERTAINMENT & FESTIVALS

Brisbane hosts seemingly continuous festivals, as well as diverse theatrical, artistic, and musical performances. Call the **Queensland Cultural Centre** (☎3840 7444) for a current schedule and info on discounts. For theater tickets, call QTIX (☎13 62 46; www.qtix.com.au).

QUEENSLAND PERFORMING ARTS CENTRE (QPAC). The Centre, just across Victoria Bridge in South Bank, is composed of four theaters: the **Concert Hall** hosts symphony and chamber orchestras; the 2000-seat **Lyric Theatre** sponsors drama, musicals, ballet, and opera; the 850-seat **Optus Playhouse** shows dramatic performances; and the 315-seat **Cremorne Theatre** stages smaller, more intimate productions. (☎3840 7444 or 13 62 46. Tours from the ticket sales foyer M-F noon. $5. Book ahead.)

OTHER FINE ARTS. The **Queensland Conservatorium** (☎3875 6222) presents university-affiliated and professional concerts. **Opera Queensland** (☎3875 3030) produces three operas and one choral concert annually. For contemporary Australian theater, **La Boite,** 57 Hale St., Petrie Terr. (☎3010 2600), on the corner of Sexton St., offers six plays per year. The **Queensland Ballet** (☎3846 5266), the oldest professional dance group in Australia, performs an annual program of contemporary classical works and audience favorites. (Tickets start around $30.) The **Queensland Theatre Company** offers eight shows annually. (☎3010 7600. $20-45.) The **Powerhouse Centre for Live Arts,** 119 Lamington St., adjacent to New Farm Park, is an alternative arts venue, housing performances in two separate theaters, dining, and galleries. (☎ 3358 8600; www.brisbanepowerhouse.org. Box office open M-F 9am-5pm, Sa noon-close.)

MUSIC, MOOLAH, MOVIES. Escape the mainstream and enjoy some top-notch jazz. **The Jazz and Blues Bar,** located below the Roma St. Transit Centre on Roma St., has live jazz and blues acts in a low key setting. (☎ 3238 2222. Open W-Sa 5pm-late). On Sunday nights starting at 5pm, try **Bin 220,** a tapas and wine bar that doubles as a live music venue. (☎ 3239 1459, at the corner of Boundary St. and Browning St. Open Tu-F 11:30am-2:30pm and Su and Tu-Sa 5pm-late). A Brisbane landmark, the enormous **Treasury Casino** contains five restaurants, seven bars, over 100 gaming tables, and more than 1000 gaming machines. (At the junction of Queen, Elizabeth, and George St. ☎ 3306 8751; www.treasurycasino.com.au. Open 24hr.) For movies, the huge **Hoyts Regent,** at 167 Queen St. in the Queen St. Mall, shows all the new releases. (☎ 3229 5544. $13, students $10, children $9.) Alternative films play at **DENDY.** (346 George St. ☎ 3211 3244; www.dendy.com.au. Open daily 11am-9:30pm. $13, students $10, children $8; M all films $8.)

SPORTS. The **Entertainment Centre,** on Melaleuca Dr. in Boondall, is Brisbane's largest indoor complex for sports, concerts, and events. (By Citytrain, take the Shorncliffe line to Boondall Station; 30min., departs at least every 30min. ☎ 3265 8111, tickets ☎ 13 19 31 or 3403 6700.) The **"Gabba"** is Queensland's major cricket stadium. (At Vulture and Stanley St., Woolloongabba. Take the bus to the station on the corner of Main and Stanley St. ($2.60) or the train to Vulture St. ☎ 3435 2222, cricket 3292 3100. Buy tickets from Ticketmaster ☎ 13 61 22.) The new **Suncorp Stadium** is now home to all football matches, including those played by the AFL's Brisbane Lions. (At the intersection of Hale St. and Milton St. accessible by foot from the city center or Citytrain's Milton Stop. ☎ 3335 1777 or Ticketmaster ☎ 13 61 22)

FESTIVALS. The **Brisbane River Festival** (☎ 3846 7444) celebrates spring the first week of September with fireworks, concerts, and river feasts on the William Jolly Bridge. The **Brisbane International Film Festival** (☎ 3007 3007; www.biff.com.au) is held annually in mid-July; the festival features alternative and retrospective film releases. The **Valley Fiesta** (☎ 3252 5999; www.valleyfiesta.com), also in mid-July, heats up Fortitude Valley with street festivals, local bands, and dance performances. On the first weekend of July, the **Jazz and Blues Festival** (☎ 1300 655 885; www.jazzandbluesfestival.com.au) showcases a number of jazz artists at Kangaroo Point for a $25 entry. Most exciting of all, the **Australia Day Cockroach Races** will be run on January 26, 2004, at the Storybridge Hotel, 196 Main St., Kangaroo Point (☎ 3391 2266). Buy your own racing roach, or root from the sidelines.

▧ NIGHTLIFE

Brisbane nights roll by in sweaty nightclubs, noisy pubs, and smoky jazz lounges. Fortitude Valley is home to Brisbane's most exciting nighttime scene, with alternative bars and huge dance clubs, live music, and several gay establishments. Be aware that most of the bigger dance clubs have dress codes, though the rules are loosely defined: classy streetwear or "valley fashion" is the best way to describe it. Weekends are huge and weeknights sparse on Caxton St. in Petrie Terr., with a decidedly more mainstream set. The city center is a big draw for backpackers, with its many Irish pubs, drink specials, and rocking Thursday nights.

Be glad you don't have to keep track of the myriad live performances in Brisbane—the Wednesday or Saturday editions of the *Courier-Mail*, as well as free entertainment guides such as *Rave*, *Time Off*, *Scene*, and *qp* (a guide to gay and lesbian entertainment and clubs), take care of this task. They are all at the record store, **Rocking Horse,** 101 Adelaide St. *(☎3229 5360; open M-Th 8:30am-6pm, F 8:30am-9pm, Sa 9am-5:30pm, Su 10:30am-5pm),* and many local nightclubs.

CITY CENTER & RIVERSIDE

▨ **Friday's,** 123 Eagle St. (☎3832 2122; www.fridays.com.au), Riverside Centre. A young crowd gets classy at this giant riverfront hangout. The maze of rooms offers various entertainment—dance music, modern tunes, and live music. Th-Sa live bands; Th university night $1.50 drinks 8pm-midnight. $8 cover on Th and Sa. Open Su-M 10:30am-late, Tu-Sa 10am-5am.

Mary Street, 138 Mary St. (☎3221 1511). User-friendly but packed. Squeeze your way past a young crowd to the nightclub, grunge stage, pool room, acoustic den, or beer garden. Live music W-F. Cover $7 after 9pm, 3-for-1 drinks Th. Open W-Sa 7pm-5am.

Victory Hotel, 127 Edward St. (☎3221 0444), on the corner of Charlotte St. This classic Aussie pub, with a beer garden, heaps of bars, and a nightclub, might be the busiest in all Queensland. Su and W-Sa live bands. Th jug specials. Happy Hour Su and W-Sa 7-9pm. Open M 10am-2am, W-Sa 10am-3am, Su 11am-1am. Nightclub open M-F 8am-5am, Sa-Su 6pm-5am.

City Rowers, 1 Eagle St. Pier (☎ 3221 2888). With a DJ spinning every night and a large dance floor, Rowers is the best place to dance in the city center. A younger crowd comes to unwind, especially on 2-for-1 Th nights. Open Su and W-Sa 11am-late.

FORTITUDE VALLEY

▨ **Family,** 8 Mclachlan St. (☎3852 1216). If you do one thing only in Brisbane—in fact, if you do one thing in all of Queensland—go to the Family. Recently voted "Best Club in all of Australia" by Bartender Magazine, the five floors of the Family are purely astounding. Fantastic house and trance music by some of the world's best DJs. An eclectic group of ravers, students, valley punks, and techno lovers mingles among sleek furnishings. Strict dress code. Cover usually $8-15, but varies with DJs. Open F-Su 9pm-5am.

▨ **Empire Hotel,** 339 Brunswick St. (☎3852 1216), at the corner of Ann St. A mix of different crowds and moods. Downstairs, the **Corner Bar** and **Press Club** cater to a more casual crowd. (Corner Bar open Su-Th 11am-midnight, F-Sa 11am-2am; Press Club open M-Th 5pm-1am, F-Sa 5pm-5am. No cover for either.) The upstairs nightclub, consisting of the **Middle Bar** and **Moon Bar,** satisfies a late-nighter of any breed. To the right, comfy couches and alternative tunes; to the left, fresh and funky chemical beats. Cover $5-15. Open F-Sa 9pm-5am.

The Beat, 677 Ann St. (☎3852 2661). And the Beat goes on, turning 25 this year. 5 rooms, 3 beer gardens, and a predominantly gay and lesbian crowd. The techno beat is straightforward; the scene is anything but. Th $1 drinks until midnight. Shows daily 11:30pm and 1:30am. Cover M-F $6, Sa-Su $8. Open daily 8pm-5am.

Hotel Wickham, 308 Wickham St. (☎3852 1301). A gay and lesbian pub that becomes an outrageous dance party on weekend nights. Costumes, cabarets—here, anything goes. Shows Su and Tu-Sa. Cover charge on occasion $5. Open Su-M 10am-midnight, Tu-Th 10am-3am, F-Sa 10am-5am.

PETRIE TERRACE

The Paddo, 186 Given Terr. (☎3369 0044). Restaurant **Fibber McGees** has fantastic deals. M $6 steaks; Tu $7 jugs; F live bands. **Saloon Bar** has daily live cover music and tons of specials. AFL players from nearby Suncorp Stadium have been known to stop by after games. Downstairs, **The Sitdown Comedy Club** has a different lineup every week. (☎3369 4466; www.standup.com.au. Shows $22-25.) Open daily 10am-3am.

Regatta, 542 Coronation Drive (☎3871 9595; www.regattahotel.com.au), in Toowoong. A favorite among university students, this sleek pub offers live music on Su, gaming, a dance floor, and cheap drinks. Open daily from 11am-3am. Accessible by the CityCat Ferry "Regatta" stop.

MORETON BAY & ISLANDS

With the Gold Coast to the south and the Sunshine Coast to the north, one would expect Moreton Bay to be filled with travelers. Instead, Brisbane's inland location draws journeyers *away* from one of Queensland's most spectacular areas. Don't let this happen to you. At Manly, at the mouth of the Brisbane River, a comfortable culture thrives in perpetual slow-motion. Across the bay, North Stradbroke Island offers diving, surfing, whale watching, and swimming, while Moreton Island invites adventure travel. Although this area lacks pre-packaged fun, the natural beauty of Moreton Bay is worth self-motivating.

MANLY   ☎07

At the friendly harborside village of Manly, there seem to be more boats than people. A quick trip from Brisbane and near most ferry services, the town serves as the perfect accommodations base for exploring nearby islands, as well as a quiet space to return to after a day spent fishing, sailing, or scuba diving. Lazy Wednesday afternoons bring sailing races, in which visitors can participate at no cost.

From Brisbane, take Citytrain to the Manly stop on the Cleveland line (35-40min. from Roma St., daily at least every 30min., $2.60). With your back to the train station, take the 2nd left-hand turn at the "Boat Harbour" sign to reach **Cambridge Parade,** the main thoroughfare. Cambridge Pde. heads towards the harbor and the **Esplanade,** which runs along the water. The **Tourist Information Centre,** 43A Cambridge Pde., is across from the Manly Hotel. (☎3348 3524. Open M-F 9am-5pm, Sa-Su 10am-3pm.) There is **Internet** at **Manly Video,** 11 Cambridge Pde. (☎3396 0554. $6 per hr. Open daily 10am-9pm.) There is a **Bank of Queensland** located in the shopping center on the corner of Cambridge Pde. and the Esplanade (open M-Th 9:30am-4pm, F 9:30am-5pm; 24hr. **ATM**). The **post office,** 222 Stratton Terr., also in the shopping center, changes American Express traveler's checks. (☎3396 2735. Open M-F 9am-5pm, Sa 9am-noon.) **Postal Code:** 4179.

■ **Moreton Bay Lodge ❷,** 45 Cambridge Pde., is a quiet, friendly spot, with spacious rooms, kitchen, TV lounge, and helpful owners. (☎3396 3020. Airport and train pick-up. Key deposit $20. Dorms $19, weekly $120; singles $35, ensuite $40; doubles $50/$60; triples $66/$76. VIP.) Across the stairway from the hostel is the casual but lovely **Moreton Bay Steakhouse ❸,** where hostel guests get a 10% discount. (Mains from $16, steaks start at $19. Food served daily noon-9pm.) **Manly Hotel ❹,** 54 Cambridge Pde., is a newly remodeled favorite of businessmen. The hotel has several bars and a **restaurant ❸** that serves three meals daily. (☎3249 5999. Th and Sa karaoke, F-Su live music. Restaurant open daily 7am-9pm; bars open M-Sa 10am-late, Su 11am-late. Singles $39-77; doubles $50-88.) **Fish Cafe Takeaway,** 461 The Esplanade, at the intersection with Cambridge Pde., is an excellent choice for quick, cheap seafood. The cod and chips ($6.65) and the fish cake panini burger ($5.75) are both excellent. (☎3893 0195. Open M-Sa 10am-late, Su 8am-late.) The **Manly Supermarket** is in the Shopping Centre. (☎3396 1980. Open M-Sa 7am-7:30pm, Su 7am-7pm.)

A brisk 30min. walk north along the Esplanade from the harbor leads to the center of a nearby town, **Wynnum by the Bay.** Along the way, you'll pass a huge **tidal wading pool,** perfect for a dip. Parks with changing rooms and BBQs run along the Esplanade. From Wynnum, continue walking another 40min. past the end of the

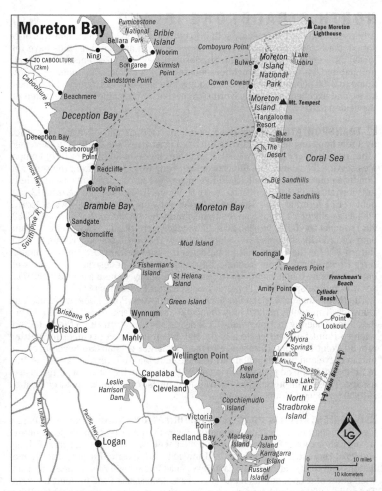

harborwalk and through the soccer and cricket fields to the **Wynnum Mangrove Boardwalk,** a 1km return walk guided by informative signs. The mangroves grow in dense concentration, and their roots protrude like small periscopes from the muck, which allows the trees to breathe. For a more sedate ride, **Manly Eco Cruises** offers family-oriented daytrips and 50min. weekend tours around Moreton Bay from Manly. (☎3396 9400. Daytrips M and F 9:30am-3pm. 50 min. tours depart hourly Sa-Su. Daytrips, including tea, boomnet rides, short canoe rides, and tropic lunch $89, children $40; 50min. tours $13, concessions $11, children $6.50. Book ahead.) For free sailing, show up at the **Royal Queensland Yacht Squadron (RQ)** for the friendly ◪**WAGS** races (WAGS stands for Wednesday Afternoon Gentleman's Sailing). Yacht owners are always looking for temporary crew members; if you are a beginner, they may teach you. The winning boat gets a bottle of rum. (☎3396 8666. A 10min. walk right down the Esplanade from Cambridge Pde. W noon. Women are welcome.)

QUEENSLAND

NORTH STRADBROKE ISLAND   ☎ 07

A fierce cyclone in 1896 cleanly split into two pieces the land mass that was once called just Stradbroke Island; since then, the north and south islands have followed different paths. While South Stradbroke (see p. 355) has remained relatively uninhabited, its northern neighbor, separated by a mere 200m channel, is now home to 2700 people. With miles of sandy white surf beaches, famous blue inland lakes, and excellent dive sites, North Stradbroke, or "Straddie" is an ideal step off the beaten path.

▛ TRANSPORTATION. Despite its isolation, North Stradbroke can be reached by a few hops on public transportation from Brisbane. Take **Citytrain** to Cleveland (1hr., usually every 30min., $3.70). From Cleveland, three different ferry companies service the island. The **Stradbroke Flyer Ferry** is accessible from the train station by a courtesy bus. Their "Gold Kat" passenger ferries arrive at One Mile Jetty in Dunwich. (☎3821 3821. 30min.; every 30-90min. 5:30am-6:30pm; return $12, students $10.) Alternatively, **Stradbroke Ferries** runs both a passenger **Water Taxi** as well as a vehicular ferry. From the train station, take a National Bus (☎3245 3333, 90¢) to meet the ferry. (☎3286 2666. Passenger ferry, 30min.; 10-12 per day, 6am-6pm; return $12, students $10. Vehicular ferry, 1hr., 10-15 per day 5:30am-6:30pm. Return $84 for the car and all its passengers.) **Islands Transport** runs a vehicular ferry to Stradbroke from Redland Bay, and although pedestrians are also welcome, be aware that it is difficult to reach Redland Bay without a car. (☎3488 9777; www.islandtransport.com. 11 per day. $88 per car. Pedestrians $11.)

The **North Stradbroke Island Bus Service** runs between Point Lookout, Amity, and Dunwich. Timetables make it easy to meet the various ferries. (☎3409 7151. 14 per day, less frequently to Amity; daily 6:35am-7pm; $4.80, return $9.) A **taxi** from Dunwich to Point Lookout costs a hefty $30, but it can be convenient for getting around Point Lookout. (**Stradbroke Island Cab Service** ☎ 19 36 85.) Several companies in Cleveland provide **rental cars** to the island, but 4WD rental is available only in Brisbane. If you do plan on driving a 4WD vehicle on the island, a permit is necessary. These can be purchased from the tourist office or at most campsites ($10.30 for 48hr., $15.40 per week.)

▚▟ ORIENTATION & PRACTICAL INFORMATION. North Stradbroke Island has three distinct townships: residential **Dunwich,** the ferry drop-off point on the western shore; **Amity Point,** north of Dunwich, with calm beaches and great fishing; and **Point Lookout,** 22km northeast of Dunwich, with most of the area's accommodations and tourist attractions. **East Coast Road** is the main road connecting Dunwich and Point Lookout; its name changes to **Mooloomba Road** in Point Lookout. The middle of the island consists of various lakes, swamps, national park land, and habitat reserves, while sand mines occupy a significant portion of the northern and southern ends of the island.

The **tourist office** is the yellow building on Junner St., at the base of the Dunwich football green near the Stradbroke Ferry Water Taxi. It's worth a stop for info, and also books tours and campground sites. (☎3409 9555; www.stradbroketourism.com. Open M-F 8:30am-5pm, Sa-Su 8:30am-3pm.) Although there's **no bank** on the island, Dunwich has an **ATM** in **Straddie Cellers** at the intersection of Junner and Ballow St. (☎3409 9761. Open M-Sa 9:30am-5:30pm, Su noon-5:30pm.) Other services include **police** (☎3409 9020), across from the tourist office in Dunwich, and **Stradbroke Island Medical Centre** (☎3409 8660), at Meegera Pl., off Endeavor St., Point Lookout. (Open M 8:30am-noon and 2-6pm, Tu-F 8:30am-1pm and 2-5pm, Sa 9-11am, Su 10-11am.) The **post offices** in Dunwich and Point Lookout also provide some banking services for visitors to North Stadbroke. **Dunwich Post** is located at 3

Welsby St. (☎3409 9010; open M-W, and F 8am-5pm, Th 7am-5pm, Sa 8-11am) and **Point Lookout Post** is at Meegera Pl., off Endeavor St. (☎3409 8210. Open M-F 9am-5pm.) **Postal Code:** 4183.

ff ACCOMMODATIONS. There's plenty of budget accommodations: two hostels and a caravan park in Point Lookout, as well as seven **campsites**—two in Dunwich, two in Amity, and three in Point Lookout. **Camping ❶** is also permitted on all of Flinders Beach and on Main Beach, at least 10km south of the paved causeway, both accessible only by 4WD. (Unpowered sites at designated campsites $6.40, powered sites $10.10, foreshore camping $4, all per person.) Make bookings through the tourist office or by calling NPWS (☎3409 9555).

The Straddie Hostel ❷, 76 Mooloomba Rd., is in the middle of Pt. Lookout, on the left side when coming in from Dunwich, just past Endeavor Rd. Six-bed dorms have separate baths and kitchens and there's free use of snorkeling gear, fishing rods, and boogie boards. (☎3409 8679; straddiehostel@hotmail.com. Reception 9am-11pm. Dorms $17, weekly $98; doubles $40/$245. Cash only.) **Stradbroke Island Guesthouse ❷,** on the left side of Mooloomba Rd., at the entrance to Point Lookout and close to Home Beach, has $8 transportation from the Roma St. Transit Centre in Brisbane on request (in summer M, W, F; in winter M and F) and an attached dive center. Rooms are sparse but clean. (☎3409 8888. Reception in summer 7am-late; in winter 8am-4pm. Key deposit $10. Dorms $22; doubles $50. VIP/YHA.) **Stradbroke Island Tourist Park ❶,** on Mooloomba Rd. in Point Lookout on the right, has simple cabins and campsites as well as a kitchen, laundry, pool, and BBQ area. (☎3409 8127; ladbrooke@ecn.net.au. Reception M-Sa 8am-5pm, Su 8am-2pm. Prices rise considerably during peak season. Sites for two $13.20, powered $17.60; cabins for two $55, ensuite $57.20; ensuite cabins for four $70.40.)

[] FOOD. Most restaurants are in Point Lookout, along Mooloomba Rd. On the left at the top of the hill towards Point Lookout, still on the outskirts of town, **Straddie Hotel Pub ❷** has a brasserie with mains for $14-20, but the dinner specials are the best value. (☎3409 8188. Open M-Th 7:30am-10pm, F-Sa 7:30am-midnight, Su 7:30am-8:30pm. Food served daily 7:30-9:30am, noon-2pm, and 6-8pm.) **La Focaccia ❸,** at Meegera Pl. off Endeavor St., serves $15 pastas and pizzas in an open-air setting. (☎3409 8778. Open daily 6pm-9pm.) A cheap, quick meal can be found at **Fish N' Fries ❶** in Megera Pl. Burgers ($4.50) and fish 'n' chips ($3.50) are part of the takeaway only menu. (☎3409 8080. Open Su-Th 11am-7:30pm, F 11am-8:30pm, Sa 11am-8pm.) For **groceries,** try Bob's 727 Foodmarket, Meegera Pl., Point Lookout. (☎3409 8271. Open 7am-9pm.)

G⊿ SIGHTS & ACTIVITIES. The island is known for its **scuba diving** and amazing marine animal life. **Stradbroke Island Scuba Centre,** below the Guesthouse, has 15 dive sites and daily trips. (☎3409 8888; www.stradbrokeislandscuba.com.au. Single dive $85 including equipment; double $120 including equipment; 4-day PADI $350, with accommodation $420; snorkeling $50, including boat trip and gear.) **Stradbroke Island Tours** (☎3409 8051 or 0438 098 059) will show you the island highlights by 4WD in half a day for only $30, children $15, with pick-up from accommodations. **Straddie Adventures** offers popular adventure tours. (☎3409 8414 or 0417 741 963; www.straddieadventures.com.au. Sandboarding 2-4pm $25; sea kayaking and snorkeling 9:30am-12:30pm $35; half-day 4WD tour $55. VIP.)

Miles of unspoiled beaches and seemingly unexplored bush can keep a spirited traveler busy for days. Heading toward the end of Point Lookout on Mooloomba Dr. is a "Beach Access" sign on the left for **Frenchman's Beach,** a convenient starting point for any beach walk and a popular surfing spot. About 400m further down Mooloomba Rd. lies the entrance to the ■**Gorge Walk,** a 15min. stroll past rocky headlands and gorges, white sand beaches, and blue waters. This walk is famous for **whale watching** from June to November and dolphins, turtles, and manta rays can be glimpsed year-round. The Gorge Walk also passes the **Blowhole,** where crashing waves are channeled up a narrow gorge and transformed into fountains of spray. **Main Beach** stretches 32km down the eastern edge of the island, luring **surfers** with some of Queensland's best waves during early summer's northerly winds. The swimming **lagoon,** 4.5km down Main Beach, is a lovely dayhike or picnic spot. **Cylinder Beach,** which runs in front of the Stradbroke Hotel on the north side of the island, is more swimmer- and family-oriented, but good surfing breaks can be found, especially during the winter months. **Deadman's Beach,** just before the Point, is a popular snorkeling spot.

MORETON ISLAND ☎ 07

While its southern neighbors fell prey to sand mining and logging, Moreton Island's status as a national park has left it in pristine condition. Remarkably untouristed, Moreton is a haven for adventurous souls. Just 35km from Brisbane, visitors can snorkel among shipwrecks, hike or toboggan down sand dunes, spot whales and dolphins, or just take in the sun on 40km of unbroken beach. Hiking trails weave among the dunes and to the top of **Mt. Tempest,** which at 280m stands as the world's highest coastal sand mountain. **The Desert** and the **Big Sandhills** are popular sandboarding and tobogganing spots. Wash the grit from your eyes in the **Blue Lagoon,** a clear freshwater lake with abundant wildlife. Around the northern headland is a walking track that leads to the **Cape Moreton lighthouse,** built in 1857, and a panoramic view of the bay, with great opportunities for whale watching in season. On the eastern coastline, **Ocean Beach** stretches the full 38km length of the island, while the view from the western side is dramatically broken by the **Tangalooma Wrecks,** 14 old dredges sunk between 1964 and 1984.

Five designated **campsites ❶** with toilets and showers are located on Moreton ($4 per person per night), and free camping is allowed on the majority of the island. Pick up a map and pay camp and 4WD fees ($30.80 per visit) at the ferry site on the mainland in Brisbane. Questions can be answered by the national park office at ☎3408 2710. Besides camping, accommodation on the island is steep. The massive **Tangalooma Resort** promises that all guests can hand feed dolphins, but at $200 for singles and $220 for doubles, you can decide whose dinner is more important. While the majority of the island is designated a national park, the resort and three small townships are located on the western side and fuel, food, and basic supplies are available at **Bulwer.**

The best way to get around the island is by 4WD; either rent on the mainland or take a guided tour. For the former group, there's a number of ferry options. **Moreton Island Ferries** leave from Howard Smith Dr. on Fisherman's Island for the Tangalooma Wrecks on Moreton; take Citytrain from Brisbane to Wynnum. With advance notice, the ferry will arrange pick-up from the train station. Otherwise, a taxi can also get you there. (☎3895 1000; www.moretonventure.com.au. 2hr.; 1 per day M and W-Th, 2 per day F-Su; return $25. Vehicle transport return $130.) Alternatively, take the **Combie Trader Ferry,** which leaves from Thurecht Pde., Scarborough Harbor, north of Redcliffe and Brisbane and arrives at Bulwer. (☎3203 6399; www.moreton-island.com. 2hr.; 2 per day M and Sa, 1 per day W-Th, 3 per day Su and F. Return $27, children $16. Vehicle transport return $125.) Guests at the **Tangalooma Resort** can also travel by the resort launch transfers. (☎3268 6333. 1½hr.; includes pick-up from Brisbane accommodations. Return $56, children $28.)

Tours to Moreton Island can be the easiest and most economical way of seeing the highlights of the island. **Moreton Bay Escapes** (☎1300 559 355; www.moretonbayescapes.com.au), offers excellent adventure-oriented trips to the island. The one-day tour from Manly includes sand tobogganing and sailing to the island on *Solo*, a famous Australia racing yacht, but two- to three-day tours are best to get a feel for the island. (Daytrip $99. Su, Tu, Th, Sa at 7am; 2-day 4WD with snorkeling, sandboarding, hiking, and fishing $199 plus $20 ferry. Leaves M, W, Sa at 7am.) **Dolphin Wild Island Cruises** also sends a power catamaran from the mainland for an eco-daytrip full of wrecks, dolphins, and sand tobogganing. (☎ 3880 4444; www.dolphinwild.com.au. Tours 9:30am-5pm. Depart from the Redcliffe Jetty in Redcliffe, north of Brisbane. $89, students and seniors $80, children $44. Transportation from hotels in Brisbane $15.) Charter the 10-person **Moreton Island Taxi Service** 4WD, or join them for a full-day tour of the island's highlights. (☎ 3408 2661. Tours M and F-Su; $160.) **Get Wet Sports**, located at the Tangalooma Resort, rents out kayaks and dinghies and offers guided snorkeling and diving. (☎ 3410 6927. Single kayaks $9 per hr., doubles $12; dinghies $18 per hr.; 1½hr. snorkeling at the wrecks $20, children $16; 3hr. intro dives $70, experienced divers $48.)

OTHER ISLANDS IN MORETON BAY

The 125km stretch of Moreton Bay is dotted with more than 300 islands perfect for daytripping. Cheap accommodation other than camping is sparse, but a day is enough to sample the islands' offerings: pristine beaches, snorkeling, and the occasional whale sighting.

COOCHIEMUDLO ISLAND. A popular getaway for locals, Coochiemudlo entices visitors with walkable beaches, restaurants, and occasional craft markets featuring local artists. **Coochiemudlo Island Ferry Service** runs a vehicular ferry from Victoria Point Jetty. While pedestrians are also welcome, the jetty is inaccessible by public transportation from Brisbane. (☎ 3820 7227. 12 per day. Return $33, pedestrians $2.) **Bay Islands Taxi Service** services Coochie from Victoria Point. (☎ 3409 1145. Every 30min.; M-F 5am-11pm, Sa-Su 6am-11pm; $2.40, children $1.20.) The **Coochie Bus Service** offers a 30min. tour. (☎ 0427 113 686. $5.50, children $2.50.)

BRIBIE ISLAND. At the northern end of Moreton Bay, Bribie is the only island accessible directly by car. From Brisbane, go 45km north to Caboolture then 19km east. Or take Citytrain from Brisbane to Caboolture, where a bus service runs to Bribie. The **tourist office** is just over the bridge from the mainland. (☎ 3408 9026. Open M-F 9am-4pm, Sa 9am-noon, Su 9:30am-1pm.) Bribie is separated from the mainland by **Pumicestone Passage,** a marine park teeming with sea cows, turtles, dolphins, and over 350 species of birds. Vehicles allow easy access to great fishing on the mainland side of the channel and surfing on the eastern side.

ST. HELENA ISLAND. In its glory days, St. Helena was the first prison in Queensland and the only commercially viable prison in the world. Today, St. Helena limits onshore visitors in order to preserve its National Parkgrounds. The only way to visit the island is by the **St. Helena Island Cat-o'-Nine-Tails** vessel, which offers environmental day tours and exciting night tours to the island in which actors role-play St. Helena's colorful past. Cruises run from **Manly.** (☎ 3396 3994. Both tours $48. Evening "ghost tour" is not primarily for children. Book ahead.)

GOLD COAST

Gorgeous beaches, thumping nightclubs, excellent theme parks, and plenty of accommodations make the Gold Coast Australia's premier holiday destination. The region's permanent population of 390,000 triples to 1.2 million every summer as Australian and foreign tourists flock to the sun, sand, and parties.

QUEENSLAND

Sunshine Coast & Gold Coast

COOLANGATTA & TWEED HEADS ☎07

The name Surfers Paradise might already be taken, but the outstanding point breaks off the twin towns of Coolangatta, QLD, and Tweed Heads, NSW, have created some of the best surfing in all of Australia, if not the world. With less neon, fewer skyscrapers, and better breaks and beaches, Coolie and Tweed Heads is the perfect place for a break on the up-tempo Gold Coast. The Tweed-Coolangatta border is only really marked by discrepancies in Daylight Savings time, most notably during New Year's Eve celebrations, when eager partygoers and champagne lovers run across the street and ring in the new year twice.

⌸ TRANSPORTATION

Buses: Coach Trans (☎3215 5000 or ☎13 12 30) runs to **Brisbane** (2¼hr., about every 30min., 6:29am-6:48pm, $14) and **Surfers Paradise** (1hr., every 15-60min., 24hr., $4.35). **McCafferty's/Greyhound** (☎5536 5177 or 13 14 99) stops in town on their way to **Brisbane** (2hr., 8 per day, $17) and **Sydney** (15hr., 4 per day, $93). **Suncoast Pacific's** (☎5531 6000) runs to **Noosa** (5hr., daily 2:45pm, $35) via **Maroochy** (4hr., $35). **Kirklands** (☎5536 1063) runs 2-4 buses per day to **Brisbane** (2hr., $15) and **Byron Bay** (1½hr., $17.50). **Surfside buslines** (☎3215 5000 or 13 12 30) runs the best **public transportation** within the Gold Coast. Routes 1 and 1A run from Kingscliff, NSW up to Paradise Point, including, of course, a stop at Surfers Paradise (45min., every 10-60min., 24hr., $4); 1-day unlimited pass $10. Sector tickets also available. Connections will get you to Gold Coast theme parks.

Taxi: Tweed Coolangatta Taxis (☎5536 1144), 24hr.

Car Rental: Economy Rental Cars, at the Gold Coast Airport (☎5536 8104 or 1800 803 374). Rentals from $29-160 per week including insurance.

✳❷ ORIENTATION & PRACTICAL INFORMATION

Entering the twin towns from the Pacific Highway, head southeast on **Marine Palisade**, which runs parallel to the beach and through **Kirra, Coolangatta,** and **Tweed Heads. Griffith Street,** the main drag of Coolangatta, runs parallel to Marine Pde. one block farther from the coast. At the **Twin Towns Service Club,** turn right from Griffith onto **Wharf Street,** the main throughway of Tweed Heads; continuing straight from this intersection, Griffith turns into **Boundary Street,** which divides the peninsula, terminating at the infamous **Point Danger,** whose cliffs were responsible for Captain Cook's shipwreck. It is now marked by the world's first laser lighthouse and a 270° view of the ocean.

Tourist Office: Gold Coast Tourism Bureau (☎5536 7765), at the corner of Griffith and Warner St., has discounts on theme parks and attractions and provides a wealth of information. Open M-F 8am-5pm, Sa 8am-4pm, Su 9am-1pm. **Tweed and Coolangatta Tourism Inc.** has a desk inside the Tweed Mall. Open M-Sa 9am-5pm, Su 10am-3pm.

Banks: Find 24hr. **ATMs** at **National Bank,** 84-88 Griffith St., at the corner of Warner St., and at **Commonwealth Bank** in the Tweed Mall. Both open M-Th 9:30am-4pm, F 9:30am-5pm.

Backpacking Supplies: Sherry's Camping, 53 Wharf St. (☎5536 4066), offers a wide range of backpacking and camping gear at reasonable prices. Open M-F 8:30am-5:30pm, Sa 8:30am-5pm, Su 10am-4pm.

Bookstore: The Bookshop, 26 Griffith St. (☎5536 7715), sells second-hand books. Open daily 8:30am-5:30pm. **Billabong Books,** near the corner of Griffith St. and Dixon St. (☎5536 9986), also has a selection of used books. Hours vary, but usually open M, W-Su 10:30am-4pm.

Pharmacy: Medicine Shoppe Pharmacy, 32 Griffith St. (☎5536 1013), across from Pipedreams. Open M-F 8am-5pm, Sa 8am-1pm; during holidays Su 9am-1pm.

Internet Access: PB's Oz Internet Cafe, 152 Griffith St. (☎5599 4536), offers a quick connection for $2 per 15 min. Also offers fax service and a wide range of phone cards. Open daily 8:30am-7pm. **Coolangatta Internet Cafe** (☎5599 2001) is in the complex on the corner of Griffith and Warner St., bottom level. Open M-F 9am-7pm, Sa 9am-6pm, Su noon-4pm. $2 per 10 min.

Post Office: 2 Griffith St., at McLean St. Open M-F 8:30am-5pm. **Postal Code:** 2485.

▟ ACCOMMODATIONS

There are plenty of beds, but budget digs are limited; book ahead in high season.

▧ **Sunset Strip Budget Resort,** 199 Boundary St. (☎5599 5517; www.sunsetstrip.com.au). Close to town and the best breaks, the Sunset Strip has excellent facilities, including an enormous kitchen and pool, as well as recreation and lounge areas. Guests of all ages mingle happily. Large, yet cozy and personal. Key deposit $10. Reception 7am-11pm. Singles $35; twins and doubles $55; triples $82.50; quads $90; rates lower for multiple night stays. 2 weeks maximum stay. ❸

Kirra Beach Hotel (☎5536 3311; www.kirrabeachhotel.com.au), on the corner of Miles St. and Marine Pde. It may be around Kirra Point from Coolangatta, but its clean, bright rooms (with private bath, fridge and TV) are a stone's throw from some of the world's most perfect barrel waves. Singles $50; doubles $60-75, depending on the view. Prices can double during peak season. ❸

Coolangatta YHA, 230 Coolangatta Rd. (☎5536 7644), Billinga, near the airport, 3km north of Coolie; look for the huge murals. Sandwiched between the airport and the Coolangatta road, rooms can be noisy. Features kitchen, laundry, game room, BBQ, TV lounge, pool, Internet access ($2 per 20min.), bikes with surfboard racks, daily drop-off and pick-up at the town center, and the best waves. Courtesy pick-up from bus stop with advance notice. Breakfast included. Lockers. Dorms $23, $130 per week including 5 dinners; singles $35; doubles $50. YHA discount $3 for dorms, $6 for doubles. ❷

Kirra Beach Tourist Park (☎5581 7744; www.gctp.com.au/kirra), on Charlotte St., Kirra. From the corner of Coolangatta Rd. and Musgrave St., follow Coolangatta Rd. back towards Coolangatta. At the first street, take a right on to Charlotte St.; the park will be at the end of the road. Great facilities: laundry, pool, TV room, and jungle gym for the kids. Linen $5 per person. Office open 7am-7pm. Rooms for up to 3 people with shared bath $40, peak $50; tent and van sites for 2 $24/$26; powered $23/$26; spacious cabin for 4 $70/$115. ❷

QUEENSLAND

🗘 FOOD

Restaurants of every kind and clientele thrive on Griffith St. Coles **supermarket** is located inside Tweeds Mall on Wharf St. (open M-F 6am-midnight, Sa 6am-11pm, Su 8am-8pm) and there is a 24hr. **convenience store** on Griffith St.

Dee and Paul's Rainbow Cafe, 13 Ward St. (☎5536 4999), provides a selection of wholesome breakfasts ($3-8), sandwiches ($5-7) and smoothies ($4). Though mostly takeaway, small tables are also available. Open daily 7am-10pm. ❷

Portuguese Hot Chicks, 91 Griffith St. (☎5536 6597), near Warner St., has late-night chicken burgers ($5.50) and chips. No promise of hot Portuguese women, however. Open Tu-Th 10am-10pm, F-Sa 10am-midnight, Su 10am-10pm. ❶

Ocean Deck Restaurant, 2 Snapper Rocks (☎5536 6390), inside the **Rainbow Bay Surf Club,** has an incredible view of Rainbow Bay and the surfers below. Family-oriented and packed in summer, they serve lunch ($7-14), dinner ($15-20), and drinks. Open daily 11:30am-2pm, and 5:30-8pm. ❸

👁 🗘 SIGHTS & ACTIVITIES

Coolangatta and Tweed Heads' greatest attractions are the beaches that line their perimeter. The family-oriented **Rainbow Bay** and **Coolangatta Beach,** off Marine Pde., have the safest swimming on the Gold Coast, with lifeguards on duty every day of the year. **Flagstaff** and **Duranbah Beaches** lie on the southeast side of the peninsula; the latter is famous among surfers for its fast waves. The three point breaks, **Kirra, Snapper Rocks,** and **Greenmount,** are some of the best in the world.

The walkway that begins to the left of Point Danger, facing the ocean, and continues to Greenmount Beach, is beautiful with lush greenery on one side, and sand and sea on the other. You'll trip over kangaroos, koalas, and saltwater crocs at the **Currumbin Wildlife Sanctuary,** 7km north off the Pacific Hwy. on Tomewin St., a Surfside bus stop (take route 1, 1A, or 11 to stop 20). Help feed the lorikeets (daily 8am and 4pm); be sure to duck to avoid their diving beaks. (☎5534 1266; www.currumbin-sanctuary.org.au. Open daily 8:30am-5pm. $22, children $14.) For great views of the ocean and surrounding communities and hinterlands, make your way up to either of two lookouts. The first is a small hike from the city center (25min. on foot): follow Wharf St. inland from the Twin Towns Service Club and take a right on Flo-

> **MIND THE FLAGS.** Swimmers and surfers should obey all posted warnings. **Red flags** mean the water is unsafe; **yellow flags** ask that visitors exercise extreme caution. **Red and yellow flags** mean swimming is safe between the flags. **Green flags** are put up when the water is safe within flagged areas.

rence St. At the first roundabout, take a left on Charles St., and follow up to the top of the hill. Be sure to continue up the railed footpath for the best views. Once at the top, take in the subtropical greenery and fabulous views of Coolie, Tweed Heads, and Mt. Warning off in the hinterland. For the less ambitious, head up the hill at the corner of Marine Pde. and Mclean St. The lookout on top provides panoramic views of the entire Gold Coast.

Surfers are welcoming and surf shops are on every corner. **Kirra Surf Club,** located where Coolangatta Rd. meets Musgrave St., is an area landmark. You can find board rentals at **Pipedreams** on Griffith St., in the Showcase Shopping Centre. (☎5599 1164. Boards half-day $20, full-day $30, weekly $140. Bodyboards half-day $15, full-day $20, weekly $105. Wetsuit and flippers half-day $5, full-day $7, weekly $5 per day. Open M-Sa 9am-5pm, Su 10am-3pm.) For a surfing lesson with plenty of one-on-one feedback, call the personable Dennis at **Walkin' on Water.** He'll provide all equipment and get you standing in no time. (☎5534 1886; www.walkinonwater.com. Two-hour group lessons $35, 90min. one-on-one sessions $60.)

During the annual **Wintersun Festival** (first week in June), Australia's biggest rock and roll event, the twin cities celebrate Elvis and the rocking fifties with cars, dancing, music, artists, and entertainers (☎5536 9509; www.wintersun.org.au.)

🎵 NIGHTLIFE

Though the waves are hot, local nightlife leaves a little to be desired. For endless clubs and pubs, head to **Surfers Paradise,** nightlife hub of the Gold Coast, just a quick bus away on Surfside buslines (see **Transportation,** p. 346).

Twin Towns Service Club (☎5536 2277), at Griffith and Wharf St. It's Vegas without the glamour. This gigantic spaceship-like club caters to an older crowd, with tons of slot machines, cheap food, and booze in 6 different restaurants, live entertainment, and free movie on Mondays at 11am and 7pm.

Calypso Tavern, 97 Griffith St. (☎5599 2441), features a video wall, plush seating, younger crowd and lots of different promotions, including trivia nights, pool tournaments, and drink specials. Open daily 10am-midnight.

Balcony Beach Club, on Marine Pde., has a chic nightclub feel. Open W, Th 8pm-late, F 4:30pm-3am, Sa 8pm-3am, Su 9pm-late. Downstairs, the **Original Cooly Beach Bar** has live music Th-Su, with karaoke Su afternoons and cover bands the rest of the week. Open M-Th and Sa-Su 9am-midnight, F 9am-1am.

SURFERS PARADISE ☎07

Narrow urban strips, packed with storefronts, cafes, and other amusements, hug miles of gorgeous beachside. Though towering hotels shade the very beaches that caused their creation, Surfers Paradise is on nearly every backpacker's itinerary.

🚌 TRANSPORTATION

Buses: The **Transit Centre** is at the corner of Beach Rd. and Ferny Ave. (Open daily 7am-10pm.) **McCafferty's/Greyhound** (☎13 14 99 or 13 20 30) offers service to: Brisbane (1½-2hr., 7 per day 4:35am-9:40pm, $18); Byron Bay (2hr., 7 per day 8am-9:15pm,

$29); Cairns (30hr., 6 per day 4:30am-8pm, $192); and Sydney (14-15hr., 5 per day 8am-9:15pm, $93). **Premier Motor Service** (☎ 13 34 10) and **Kirklands** (☎ 1300 367 077; best for Byron Bay and NSW coast) offer similar service with slightly cheaper fares. Lockers are available 6am-8:30pm (12hr. $4-8).

Local Buses: Surfside (☎ 5571 6555 or 13 12 30), the local 24hr. bus company, runs to roadside stops along the **Gold Coast Highway,** as well as the **Pacific Fair Mall** (Bus 1, $2.20 one way), the **theme parks** (Bus 1X or 1A, $2.20-4.35), and **Southport** (Bus 1, 1A, 3, or 10; $2.20-3.30). Buses pick-up along the Gold Coast Hwy. and Ferny Ave.; grab a schedule at the Surfside information kiosk, at Cavill and Ferny Ave., near the river. **EZY Passes** provide unlimited use of all buses and can be purchased from any driver (1-day $10, child $5; 1-week $43/$22). **Gold Coast Tourist Shuttle** (☎ 5574 5111) offers transport to all theme parks with pick-up and drop-off from local accommodation and unlimited travel on Surfside's service (1-day Gold pass $15, concessions $8; 1-week $60/$30).

Taxis: Regent Taxis (☎ 5588 1234 or 13 10 08) or **Maxi Taxi** (☎ 13 19 24), which has a fleet of larger vans.

Car Rental: All Ages and Moped Hire, 3024 Gold Coast Hwy. (☎ 5527 6088 or 1800 671 361), just past Hamilton Ave. Offers cheap car rental, even to those under 23 ($29 per day, $19 per day for weekly rental, 150km limit. $16.50 per day surcharge for drivers under 23). Open daily 8am-5pm. **Thrifty** (☎ 5570 9960 or 1300 139 009), on the corner of Enderley Ave. and Gold Coast Hwy., rents from $40 (100km limit, under 25 surcharge $16.50 per day).

■ ORIENTATION

Maps of Surfers are long and thin, reflecting the fact that all the action is squeezed into a strip many kilometers long and just a few blocks wide, between the ocean and the **Nerang River.** Three main avenues run parallel to the shore: the **Esplanade,** which skirts the beach; the southbound **Gold Coast Highway,** a block over; and **Ferny Avenue,** the northbound Gold Coast Hwy., one more block inland. Surfers centers on **Cavill Mall,** perpendicular to the ocean. The mall is a pedestrian street lined with restaurants, cafes, bars, souvenir shops, and the Paradise Centre. The Esplanade continues north past **Main Beach** to the **Marina** and the **Spit,** the end of the peninsula just past Seaworld. **Southport** is located along the Gold Coast Hwy., past Main Beach and 3km northwest of the city center. To the south is **Broadbeach,** home of the enormous Conrad Hotel Jupiter Casino and the monolithic **Pacific Fair Mall.**

■ PRACTICAL INFORMATION

Tourist Offices: Gold Coast Tourism Bureau (☎ 5538 4419) is the main tourist office, in a kiosk on Cavill Mall. Open daily 8:30am-5:30pm. The **Backpackers Information Centre** (☎ 5592 2911 or 1800 359 830), in the transit center, offers information and arranges transport to the hostels in their association. Open daily 8am-4:30pm, during the summer until 5:30pm. After-hours, info and a direct phone to hostels are still available.

Banks: Westpac, on the corner of Cavill Ave. and Gold Coast Hwy., has a 24hr. **ATM,** as does **Commonwealth Bank,** right next door on the highway. Both banks open M-Th 9:30am-4pm, F 9:30am-5pm. ATMs are also located in most shopping centers.

Police: 68 Ferny Ave. (☎ 5570 7888), opposite the Cypress Ave. carpark. There's also a substation (☎ 5583 9733) on the corner of Cavill Mall and the Esplanade.

Medical Services: Gold Coast General Hospital, 108 Nerang St., Southport (☎ 5571 8211). **Gold Coast Medical Transport** (☎ 13 12 33). **Day Night Surgery** (☎ 5592 2299), in the Piazza Mall on the Gold Coast Hwy., for non-emergency care. Open daily 7am-10pm.

Internet: Email Centre, 51 Orchid Ave., near Shooters Nightclub on Ochid Ave., (☎5538 7500). $5 per hr. Open daily 9am-midnight. **Mercari Imaging** (☎5538 4937), 3189 Gold Coast Hwy. between Cavill and Elkhorn Ave., offers a cheap, fast connection ($1.10 for 15 min.). Open daily 9am-7:30pm.

Post Office: Main branch located inside the Paradise Centre, on Cavill Mall. Open M-F 9am-5:30pm, Sa 9am-noon. **Postal Code:** 4217.

ACCOMMODATIONS

In Surfers, hostel staff assume the role of camp counselors, providing backpackers with an endless supply of all sorts of activities. Summer and Easter are peak seasons—book ahead and expect prices around $5 higher than current listings. Unless listed otherwise, hostels have free pick-up, 10am check-out, $10 key deposit, laundry, lockers (either in room or in a common area), and TV rooms.

▨ **Trekkers,** 22 White St., Southport (☎5591 5616 or 1800 100 004; www.trekkersbackpackers.com.au), 3km north of city center; call for free pick-up. 15min. from beach. Though far from downtown, the trek out is well worth it. Guests feel they are a part of this comfortable, social hostel. Dorms are spotless and comfortable, some with ensuite; the doubles are even better: all have TV and plenty of character, some complete with waterbed. Free courtesy bus into town and nightly outings to the clubs. Saltwater pool, free board and bike use. Linens provided. W BBQ night. Reception 7am-noon; 3pm-8pm. Dorms $21; doubles $52. VIP/YHA $20/$50. ❷

Surfers Paradise Backpackers Resort, 2837 Gold Coast Hwy. (☎5592 4677 or 1800 282 800; www.surfersparadisebackpackers.com.au), a 25min. walk south along the highway from the transit center to the corner of Wharf Rd., but a free courtesy bus is available. Spotless, happy, and family-run, "The Resort" also has outstanding facilities:

Surfers Paradise

⌂ ACCOMMODATIONS
Aquarius, 2
Backpackers in Paradise, 8
Cheers, 6
Gold Coast International
  Backpackers Resort, 11
Silver Sands Motel, 12
Sleeping Inn Surfers, 9
Surf 'n' Sun, 5
Surfers Paradise
  Backpackers Resort, 13
Trekkers, 1

♥ FOOD
Al Fresco, 10
Izakaya Ta, 19
Lemongrass on Tedder, 3
Peter's Fish Café, 4
Rios, 7

★ NIGHTLIFE
Cocktails and Dreams/
  The Party, 15
The Drink, 16
Melba's, 18
O'Malley's, 21
Rose and Crown, 20
Shooters, 17
Sugar Shack, 14

a big kitchen bar, tennis court, pool, free laundry, a small gym, and dorms with private bath. Free board use included in room rate. Bicycle rental $5. Sauna ($4 per 45 min.). Internet $1.50 per 15min. Linens $1. Reception 7:30am-7pm. Dorms $22, doubles $52. VIP/YHA discount $1. ❷

Sleeping Inn Surfers, 26 Peninsular Dr. (☎5592 4455 or 1800 817 832; www.sleeping-inn.com.au), a 10min. walk from the Transit Centre across Ferny Ave. 15 self-contained units each have their own kitchens and living rooms and a variety of doubles, twins, and dorms. Expect a quiet, mellow, friendly atmosphere, with the facilities (pool, hot tub, game room) to match. Reception 7am-10pm (11pm in summer), with late night check-in bell. Dorms $21; doubles $50; apartments from $110, for up to 6 people. ISIC/VIP/YHA/student discount $1. ❷

Aquarius, 44 Queen St., Southport (☎5527 1300 or 1800 229 955; www.aquarius-backpackers.com.au). Call for courtesy bus or, from Surfers, follow the Gold Coast Hwy. over the bridge and take your first left on Queen St. Aquarius is on the left at Scarborough St. Clean rooms, glow worm trips, Internet, pool, and spa with garden. Reception 7:30am-10pm. Dorms $18; doubles $44. Weekly $110/$300. ISIC/VIP/YHA. ❷

Surf 'n' Sun, 3323 Gold Coast Hwy. (☎5592 2363 or 1800 678 194; www.surfnsungoldcoast.com), on the corner of Ocean Ave., close to beach. Surf 'n' Sun makes up for its simple rooms with its famous party atmosphere, friendly staff, and schedule full of activities. Private bathrooms, courtesy bus, pool, Internet, and a comfy common room with a wide selection of DVDs. Reception 7am-10:30pm. Dorms $22; doubles $52. Weekly $133/$336. $1 VIP discount. ❸

Backpackers In Paradise, 40 Peninsula Dr. (☎1800 268 621; www.backpackersinparadise.com), a 10min. walk from the transit center across Ferny Ave. Look for the murals. Close to town and the beach, with simple dorms and spacious doubles. Offers plenty of package deals. Singles $17; doubles $45. ❷

Cheers, 8 Pine Ave. (☎5531 6539 or 1800 636 539; www.cheersbackpackers.com.au), located just off Ferny Ave. This is the largest hostel in Surfers. Rooms are no-frills and impersonal, but the bar and beer garden are the best among the hostels. Pool, hot tub, free Internet, $6 BBQ, and lockers. Reception 8am-10:30pm. Dorms $19, doubles $48. VIP/YHA. ❷

Gold Coast International Backpackers Resort, 28 Hamilton Ave. (☎5592 5888 or 1800 801 230; www.goldcoastbackpackers.com.au), on the corner of the Gold Coast Highway 2min. from the beach. More modern and less party-oriented than many of its competitors, the Gold Coast International has small dorms with balcony, TV, and private bath. Bar and beer garden, game room, free board use, Internet, kitchen, and secure underground carpark. Job placement help available. Key deposit $20. Reception 8am-10pm. Dorms $22; doubles $54. ❷

Silver Sands Motel, 2985 Gold Coast Hwy. (☎5538 6041), corner of Markwell Ave. and Gold Coast Hwy. Perfect for couples or small groups seeking more privacy and less partying than offered by the hostels. Modern, beach house rooms have A/C, kitchenette, private bath, and TV. Pool and BBQ. Only 11 rooms; book ahead. Reception 7am-7pm. Doubles $60 during the week, between $79-89 on weekends, and up to $109 during the peak season. ❺

🗋 FOOD

Inexpensive bistros, 24hr. cafes, fast food joints, and Asian restaurants cluster around Cavill Mall. Tedder Ave. near Main Beach is lined with excellent bistros, bakeries, and classy cafes. Thomas Dr., on Cheveron Island, is also home to a number of excellent restaurants. For groceries, a Woolworths **supermarket** is located in the basement of the Paradise Centre (open daily 8am-9pm).

Al Fresco, 2991 Gold Coast Hwy. (☎5538 0395), just past Hamilton Ave. This mum 'n' dad Italian eatery will have you smiling the minute you walk in the door and win you over with their excellent pasta ($13.50-20.50), friendly service, and complimentary after dinner drink. BYO wine only. Open daily 5:30pm-late. ❸

Rios, 53 Thomas Dr. (☎5538 2122), on Cheveron Island. Head away from the beach on Elkhorn Ave. and cross over the Nerang River. Rios is on the right halfway through Cheveron village. Along with a hopping bar and live music, Rios has scrumptious lunch and dinner menus with a sampling of many different styles. Mains start around $12. Call ahead; occasionally there are 2-for-1 dinner specials. Open Su and Tu-Sa 11am-late. ❷

Lemongrass on Tedder, 6/26 Tedder Ave. (☎5528 0289), in Main Beach. Excellent authentic Thai food in a romantic setting. Huge menu, and equally large portions. Appetizers $8-9, main dishes $14-24. Open daily for dinner 5:30pm-10pm. ❸

Izakaya Ta, in the Cavill Mall above the Cavill Inn Motel (☎5527 5701). Grab a seat on the balcony of this Japanese/Korean restaurant to overlook the madness on Cavill Mall below. Both their teriyaki combos ($11) and a fresh sushi platter ($11) will fill you up before you join in the fun. Open daily 5:30-10pm. ❷

Peter's Fish Cafe, 120 Sea World Dr. (☎5531 0077), toward the Spit and near the British Arms YHA. Opt for the best fish 'n' chips in town (lunch $5.50, dinner $9), or try any of their other fresh seafood dishes ($9-19). Open Su, Tu-Sa noon-3pm and 5-10pm. ❶

◪ BEACHES, SURFING, & WATER SPORTS

White sand beaches stretch unbroken 25km from the quiet **Main Beach** on the Spit peninsula south to Coolangatta's Snapper Rocks. Surfers Paradise is a bit of a misnomer, however. The outstanding beach breaks are great for beginners, but the best surfing is to the south, near Coolangatta and Tweed Heads (see p. 346). Surfing conditions vary considerably, especially as sand shifts to alter the breaks; locals sometimes drive up and down the coast looking for the best waves. For more detailed info, go to www.coastalwatch.com or listen to 90.9 Sea FM's surf reports. Pay attention to flags, which designate areas patrolled by Surf Life Savers.

The most popular beach among boardless beachgoers is **Surfers North.** Near the end of Staghorn Ave. and just north of Surfers Paradise, it's the most central hangout off the Paradise Centre Mall and the beneficiary of blaring music from the local radio station during the summer. Farther south is **Broadbeach,** then **Kurrawa,** near the Pacific Fair Shopping Centre. **Burleigh Heads** has a popular surfing area, though it can be mobbed and often has dangerous breaks. Recently, surfing has become popular at **South Stradbroke Island** as well. The beaches there are unpatrolled, however, so use common sense and bring a friend who knows the waters.

For equipment, try the convenient **Surfers Beach Clubhouse** kiosk on the beach end of Cavill Mall. (☎5526 7077. Longboards $15 per hr., $25 per 3hr., $40 per day. Wetsuits $5 with a board. Short boards or body boards $10 per hr., $20 per 3hr., $30 per day. Bag storage free with rental, otherwise $5.) Their surf school will get you standing for $45, or $35 for students and backpackers. (Open in summer 8am-5pm; in winter 9am-5pm.) **Gold Coast Kayaking** runs excellent sea kayaking tours from the Spit to South Stradbroke Island, where you snorkel, have tea or brekkie, and go for a bushwalk to the surf beach. (☎0419 733 202. 3hr. trips 6:30am and 2:30pm. $35, including pick-up and drop-off.)

▌ THEME PARKS & THRILL RIDES

Packed with domestic tourists and kids on candy highs, Surfers' theme parks are distinctive only for their setting: the town spawns roller coasters as frequently as shopping centers. Tickets to all parks can be bought at slightly reduced prices from the tourist info booth on Cavill Mall. Surfside, Coachtrans, and Gold Coast Tourist Shuttle provide **transportation** to all parks; Surfside offers $3 return transport to the park with purchase of a theme park ticket from the driver. When going to Wet 'N' Wild, Dreamworld, or Movieworld, be sure to catch the Surfside 1X express bus from the main stop in Surfers or risk wasting an hour on the 1A, which stops every 30sec. on its way north. For Sea World, simply take the 2 from any stop in Surfers. Wet 'N' Wild, Dreamworld, and Movie World are all 20min. north on the Pacific Hwy.; Seaworld is north on Seaworld Dr., on the Spit. Be sure to call ahead and check hours, as they are prone to change with demand.

DREAMWORLD. The much-trumpeted "Tower of Terror" is the tallest and fastest ride in the world, rocketing from 0 to 160km per hour in only seven seconds. For those wanting to keep terror to a minimum, wander over to Tiger Island and watch as the trainers keep the beasts in line. (☎5588 1111 or 1800 073 300; www.dreamworld.com.au. Open daily 10am-5pm. $56, children and pensioners $36.)

WET 'N' WILD. On hot summer days, the whitewater flumes of this water park will cool you down; in the winter, the slides and pools are heated. (☎5573 2255; www.wetnwild.com.au. Open daily 10am-4pm. $35, children and pensioners $22. Lockers $6.)

SEAWORLD. Lots of fish, dolphins, sharks, seals, some sad-looking pigeons, a few rides, and a hilarious sea lion show are all on display. The polar bear exhibit brings the Arctic to Oz. (☎5588 2205; www.seaworld.com.au. Open daily 10am-5pm. $56, children $36. Swimming with dolphins $110, children $45. Arrive early to reserve.)

MOVIE WORLD. This Warner Brothers park features movie sets and interactive shows as well as the 6min. *Wild Wild West* ride, which climaxes in a 70kph, 20m drop into water. (☎5573 8485; www.movieworld.com.au. Open daily 10am-5pm. $56, children and pensioners $36.)

🎵 🎭 ENTERTAINMENT & NIGHTLIFE

Aside from partying and drinking, the main nighttime activity in Surfers seems to be getting the best deals on partying and drinking. Most of the hostels provide free cover and some drink passes for several clubs on a given night. The majority of hot spots are on Orchid Ave., known as the "Avenue," and are open until 5am. **Bring your passport,** as some clubs won't accept other forms of ID. The Gold Coast Backpackers Association organizes events every night; highlights are Tuesday "70s night" and the infamous **club crawl.** (☎1800 359 830. W and Sa 9:30pm. $20 tickets from participating hostels include entry to clubs, a free drink at the three clubs, a photo, and a promotional lanyard) Be sure to check on the nightly drink specials at each of the clubs; there are often great deals to be found. Be aware that cover charges jump during peak times. High rollers try their luck at **Conrad Jupiters Casino,** in nearby Broadbeach. (☎5592 1133, box office 1800 074 144. Open 24hr.) For details on nightly events in the area, go to www.emugigs.com.

Melba's, 46 Cavill Ave. (☎5538 7411). A restaurant that transforms into a classy nightclub after dark, Melba's avoids Orchid Ave.'s meat-market feel. Grooves to mainstream and techno. Happy Hour 4-10pm in the upstairs nightclub, 4-8pm in the downstairs restaurant/bar. Cover in club $8, includes free drink. Club M, Su, and W-Sa 7pm-5am. Restaurant daily 8am-3pm.

Cocktails and Dreams, (☎5592 1955) The Mark, Orchid Ave. Cruise to this constantly packed club, popular with backpackers and more. Organizes events with the hostels, such as Tu 70s night, W and Sa Club Crawl. Open Su, Tu, Th-Sa 10am-5am. Downstairs, **The Party** is one of the only rock clubs in Surfers, and is usually home to a huge, mostly alternative, crowd. Cover $5-7 gets you into both. Open Su and Th-Sa 8pm-5am.

The Drink, 4 Orchid Ave. (☎5570 6155). Grind all night long at Surfers' ultimate dance club. After a night of partying, be sure to watch the four flights of stairs on the way back down. Cover after 10pm $5-10. Open Su, Tu-Sa 8:30pm-5am.

Shooters, The Mark, Orchid Ave. (☎5592 1144). This country saloon and dance club, owned by the biggest promotional company in Queensland, attempts to fill the Western niche with style. Cover after 10pm $5-10. Open daily 8pm-5am.

O'Malley's, 1 Cavill Ave. (☎5570 4075). Packed pub with balcony view and live pop rock music every night. Open Su-Th noon-midnight, F-Sa noon-2am.

Sugar Shack, 20 Orchid Ave. (☎5538 7600). Fun, casual dance hall that grooves to varied classic hits. Live music Su and Th-Sa. Cover $3-5. Open daily 11:30am-5am.

Rose and Crown, (☎5531 5425), Raptis Plaza on Cavill Ave. Popular with a younger crowd. Dance and Top-40 play in one room, while talented live bands perform in the swanky Lounge (W and F). Cover $3-6. Open daily 8pm-5am.

▣ DAYTRIP FROM SURFERS: SOUTH STRADBROKE ISLAND

Separated from the Spit by a thin channel, South Straddie is one of Surfers' hidden gems. Largely undeveloped and home to friendly free-roaming wallabies, the long, narrow island (22km by 3km) is lined by quiet river beaches on the west side and both gorgeous and empty surf beaches and dunes on the east. **Surf Beach,** on the ocean side, is usually patrolled by lifeguards; check with the resort about hours.

Ferries, operated by the S. Stradbroke Island Resort, run from Gate C of the Runaway Bay Marina, 247 Bayview St., off the Gold Coast Hwy. past Southport. (☎5577 3311. 25min.; depart Runaway daily 7am and 10:30am, return 3:30pm and 5pm; ferry $25 return; with lunch, free pick-up from surfers, and access to some resort facilities, $49.) One-way Surfside bus fare from Surfers Paradise transit center to Runaway Bay is $3.20, and runs approximately every half hour.

The main activity center is the **South Stradbroke Island Resort ❺**, with pools, spas, sauna, watersports, tennis courts, restaurants, and a virtual monopoly on non-camping accommodation. Individual cabins have TV and fridge. (☎5577 3311 or 1800 074 125. Room only $99, cabin and all the resort facilities start at $140.)

The island also offers camping options with toilets, showers, and BBQ. **Tippler's camping area ❶** is just 300m from the resort. (☎5577 2849.) The island's other campgrounds are more private and difficult to reach. **Water taxis** (☎04 1875 9789) also leave from Gate C of the Runaway Bay to motor guests to **Currigee ❶** (☎5577 3932; $30 one-way taxi for up to 4 people) and **The Bedrooms ❶** campgrounds (☎5577 2849; $80 one-way; sites for 2 $12, peak $13).

GOLD COAST HINTERLAND

Within an hour or so from the bustling coast, you can bushwalk through subtropical rainforest, enjoy spectacular views, and stroll through laid-back towns. The Hinterland makes for a perfect escape from the glitz of the coast.

Travel by car offers the most flexible and wallet-friendly means to explore. An easy one-day drive south along **Pacific Highway 1** from the Gold Coast starts at **Nerang** and works its way down towards **Currmbin,** allowing time to take the smaller roads inland to the many national parks. Along the way, you will see turn-offs for Lamington National Park, Mt. Tamborine, Springbrook National Park, and Mt. Cougal National Park. Unfortunately, many of the roads inland are not connected; therefore, some backtracking is inevitable. However, the parks are close enough to one another that two or more can be combined into a multi-day trip. For more info, contact Queensland National Parks (☎13 13 04; www.qld.gov.au).

Alternatively, buses and tours can get you almost anywhere in the Hinterland. **Mountain Coach Company** has a bus tour to Mt. Tamborine and O'Reilly's Park in Lamington National Park from Coolangatta, Burleigh, and Surfers. (☎5524 4249. $45, children $22, families $117; includes pick-up and drop-off from accommodation.) **Scenic Hinterland Day Tours** picks up from Gold Coast resorts and offers a trip to Springbrook and the Natural Bridge, including Purlingbrook Falls, a thousand-year-old forest. (☎5531 5536. $38, concessions $35, under 12 $26, families $115.) **All State Scenic Tours** accesses O'Reilly's Park in Lamington from the transit center in Brisbane. (☎3003 0700. Departs Su-F 9:30am, returns 5:45pm. $47, ages 4-16 $33.) Be sure to ask ahead of time how much time is spent at each of the parks to ensure that you have ample time to complete the hikes that you want. Some hostels offer tours to Lamington National Park or to see the glowworms at the Natural Bridge.

LAMINGTON NATIONAL PARK

The 200km² of Lamington National Park are split into two accessible sections: **Green Mountains/O'Reilly's** and **Binna Burra.** The park's 160km of well-trod paths lead to spectacular waterfalls, clear springs, subtropical rainforests, and the NSW border ridge, with magnificent views of Mt. Warning's ancient volcanic crater. Trails appeal to both daytrippers and more serious bushwalkers, ranging in length from 1 to over 20km.

GREEN MOUNTAINS. Green Mountains (and within it, the privately owned **O'Reilly's Park**) can only be reached via Nerang and Canungra along a switchback road off the Pacific Hwy. (70km). After passing through Canungra, the last 25km of road is winding and often very narrow, and is unsuitable for caravans. The **Visitors Centre** is located 5km into the park; leave your car in the large parking lot below O'Reilly's, and the Visitors Centre is up the hill and across the street. It houses the Woonoongoora World Heritage Room, provides maps and info, books on-site camping, and issues bush camping permits. (☎5544 0634. Open M and W-Th 9-11am and 1-3:30pm, Tu and F 1-3:30pm. On-site camping offers toilets and hot showers, but campfires are not allowed. $4 per person per night. Bush camping ☎13 13 04 or www.qld.gov.au. Requires advanced reservation. No bush camping is allowed Dec. 1-Jan. 31. $4 per person, per night.) **O'Reilly's ❺**, a rainforest guest-house in O'Reilly's Park, charges high rates for their location. (☎5544 0644; www.oreillys.com.au. Singles start at $125; doubles $200, and includes planned activities from 6:45am-9pm.) Take a 15min. walk among the clouds on the **O'Reilly's Tree Top circuit,** a bridge suspended from the heights of some impressive booyong trees. From O'Reilly's, the popular **Toolona Creek circuit** (17km, 5-6hr. return) will take you past numerous waterfalls and stands of native Antarctic beech trees on its way to stunning panoramas. The tracks to **Morans Falls** (4.6km, 1½hr., return) and **Python Rock** (3.4km, 1hr. return) start about 800m downhill from the information center; if you're only at the park for half a day, these routes are your best option. The paved Morans Falls trail descends deep into the rainforest before opening onto views of the Morans waterfall and gorge and the Albert River. The Python Rock trail follows an easier grade to a lookout over the Albert River valley and across to the impressive Castle Cragg.

BINNA BURRA. To get to **Binna Burra,** follow the signs for Beechmont and Binna Burra from Nerang (37km). The **Visitors Centre** books **bush camping ❶** and provides maps of the different hiking circuits. (☎5533 3584. Open Sa-Su 9am-3:30pm. Informative signs and maps are available at all times. Register for a bush camping permit through the Green Mountains park service. Closed Dec. 1-Jan 31. ☎13 13 04; www.qld.gov.au. $4 per person, per night.) On-site camping is available at the **Binna Burra Mountain Campsite ❶**, on your left 1km past the Visitors Centre. (☎

5533 3622. Tent site $10, students $7, 2-bed safari tent $40, 4-bed safari tent $60. Call ahead. Reception open 8am-6pm.) The **Binna Burra Mountain Lodge ❶**, on your right 1km past the Visitors Center, offers a charming B&B, and a daily bus service to the coast. (☎ 5533 3758. Rooms start at $167 a night, minimum 2 night stay. Bus $44 return, children $22.) **Caves circuit** (5km, 1½hr. return) starts from the information center and winds past sweeping views of Darlington Range and Kweebani Cave. **Ship's Stern circuit** (19km return) passes stands of giant gum and cedar trees as it descends into the Kurraragin Valley; beyond the Lower Ballunjui Falls, eucalypt forests and wildflowers dominate.

SPRINGBROOK NATIONAL PARK

As the northernmost remnant of Mt. Warning's explosive past, Springbrook plateau dominates the skyscape west of the Gold Coast. Covering over 2900 hectares of land, the national park consists of three accessible sections: **Springbrook Plateau,** the **Natural Bridge,** and **Mt. Cougal.** Springbrook's most noteworthy attractions are its striking rock formations, waterfalls, and well-developed trail systems.

SPRINGBROOK PLATEAU. From Mudgeeraba on the Pacific Hwy., head toward the mountains on Springbrook Rd. (29km); the park can also be accessed via the Nerang-Murwillumbah Rd. and Springbrook-Nerang Rd. (18km). Follow signs to the unattended **Visitors Centre** in the old schoolhouse for maps of the park's walks, lookouts, and camping and picnic areas. (Ranger ☎ 5533 5147.) **Camping ❶** is available at the Gwongorella picnic area ($3.85 per person, per night; book in advance through the number above.) The first accommodation on the mountain to catch the sun, **Springbrook Mountain Lodge YHA ❸**, 317 Repeater Station Rd., is a small hostel near the Best of All Lookout that is perfect for a weekend getaway. (☎ 5533 5366. Book ahead. Rooms weekdays $34, weekends $44 per person, YHA discount $4; self-contained family cabin $88, weekend $132, min. 2 nights.) Steeper accommodations can be found at any of the numerous B&B atop Springbrook Plateau.

The plateau offers 7 designated lookout points to the western mountains as well as the Ocean and Gold Coast. On a clear day at the **Best of All Lookout,** at the southern end of Springbrook Rd., you'll see Coolangatta and Byron Bay along the coast. The 700m return walk out to the lookout passes by a grove of ancient Antarctic Birch Trees. The park's best walking tracks are accessible from the Canyon Lookout off of Springbrook Rd. Both the **Twin Falls Circuit** (4km, 1.5hr.; adding on the 15min. jaunt to the base of Rainbow Falls after descending into the valley near Twin Falls makes for a doubly impressive experience) and the popular day-long **Warrie Circuit** (17km, 5-6hr.) begin here. Both tracks lead through rock wedge caves and behind, around, and under many waterfalls.

NATURAL BRIDGE. The Natural Bridge is located on the Nerang-Murwillumbah Rd., 30km from Nerang. Unfortunately, there is no direct road from the main plateau to the Natural Bridge. From the plateau, follow the Springbrook-Nerang Rd. to the Nerang-Murwillumbah Rd. and take a left. The Natural Bridge is 12km down the road. Springbrook's most popular sight is on a 1km paved track, 3km north of the NSW border. The land arch developed as a cavern under a forceful waterfall; eventually, the water broke through the ceiling of the cave to create the arch. At night, the cavern comes alive with bats and glowworms. (Ranger ☎ 5533 5147.)

MT. COUGAL NATIONAL PARK. Again, there are no direct road accesses to Mt. Cougal from the plateau. Instead, from the Pacific Hwy., take the Stewarts Rd./ Currmbin Valley exit towards the mountains. The park is located 21km from the highway. A rugged part of Springbrook National Park, Mt. Cougal offers several views of Currumbin Creek as it plummets down a **natural water slide** and pools in

QUEENSLAND

deep holes. Follow the 1.6km paved path up the creek to a disused saw mill. (25min. return. ☎5576 0217.) On your way to Mt. Cougal, don't miss the **Currumbin Rock Pool,** a deep freshwater pool with short cliff dives and smaller pools for lounging (12km from the Pacific Highway). Only very daring folks attempt the slides and jumps at the rock pools; **use caution** and common sense at all of these risky attractions, and obey posted warnings.

SOUTHERN & DARLING DOWNS

West of the Great Dividing Range lie the hills and valleys of the Southern Downs and the towns of Toowoomba, Warwick, and Stanthorpe. Toowoomba's carefully crafted greenery is only beginning to draw tourists, but the rustic beauty and small-town feel of Stanthorpe and Warwick draw backpackers, particularly those in search of seasonal work. Stanthorpe is also the center of Queensland's only wine region, the Granite Belt. For those coming to the Downs with time to spare, Girraween and Sundown National Parks reward visitors with their wildflower displays (Sept.-Mar.), rock outcroppings, and spectacular views.

TOOWOOMBA   ☎07

With over 200 parks and gardens, many connected by bike and walking paths, Toowoomba (pop. 105,000) has long outgrown its name, which is derived from an Aboriginal word meaning "swamp." Using "Garden City" as a more appropriate alias, Toowoomba's formidable commercial center fades into suburbia, backed by breathtaking views of the Dividing Range.

McCafferty's (☎4690 9888) **buses** leave from 28-30 Neil St., running to: Brisbane (2hr.; Su-F 13 per day, Sa 11 per day; $21, round-trip $38); Melbourne (22hr., daily 5:20pm, $182); and Sydney (15hr., daily 8:50pm, $88). For northern destinations, connect in Brisbane. To get to the **Toowoomba Visitor Information Centre,** 86 James St. when coming from Brisbane on Margaret St., take a left on Mackenzie St. and a right on James St. The center will be on the left. When coming from Warwick, take a right off of Ruthven St. onto James St. The center will be on your right. (☎4639 3797 or 1800 331 155; www.toowoomba.qld.gov.au. Open daily 9am-5pm.) The **City Information Centre,** 476 Ruthven St., between Margaret St. and Herries St., is centrally located and offers **Internet** but has less convenient hours. (☎4638 7555. Tourist desk M-F 10am-1pm and 2-4pm; Internet and local history desk Tu-F 10am-5pm, Sa 10am-2pm. $4.40 per 30min., students $2.20 per 30min.) **Commonwealth Bank** is at the corner of Ruthven St. and Margaret St. (open M-Th 9:30am-4pm, F 9:30am-5pm) but other **banks** and **ATMs** are easy to find, especially on Ruthven St. Internet can be found at **Coffee On Line,** 150 Margaret St. ($2 per 10min., students and backpackers $2 per 15min. Open M-Sa 9am-9pm, Su 10am-7pm. www.coffeeon-line.com.au). **Garden City Taxis** can be reached at ☎4633 1924. **Postal Code:** 4350.

The B&B **Self Healing Centre ❷,** 331 Margaret St., provides all the comforts of home, including breakfast, kitchen access, free laundry and Internet, and friendly clutter. Call ahead to ensure that someone will be there to check you in. (☎4639 3611. Key deposit $10. Dorms and singles $20; doubles $40, less expensive during the winter.) There are also two budget motels. The **James St. Motor Inn ❸,** at the corner of James St. and Kitchner, has large rooms with TV, A/C, heat, mini-fridges, and TVs. (☎4639 0200, rooms from $55.) The **Downs Motel ❸,** 669 Ruthven St., offers similar accommodations. (☎4639 3811. Singles $54; doubles $58.)

The Garden City is home to **Ju Raku En,** Australia's most traditional and largest **Japanese Garden,** located on the University of Southern Queensland campus. To get there, take a left out of the Visitor Centre parking lot onto James St., then a left onto West St. Look for Wuth St. on the right after about 1km and follow the signs.

The expansive **Queen's Park Gardens,** on Margaret St. between Lindsay and Hume St., are another floral highlight, and **Laurel Bank Park,** one block south of Margaret St. on West St., features a scented garden for the visually impaired. All parks are free and open daily dawn to dusk; they're best visited when at full bloom during the spring and summer. (Sept.-Mar.) You can also pick up more extensive guides to the numerous parks and gardens at the visitors center. The **Carnival of Flowers** (☎ 4632 4877; www.carnivalofflowers.com.au) is Toowoomba's biggest draw. Held for a week in late September, the carnival features a parade, flower shows, and an exhibition of prize-winning private gardens. For spectacular views year-round, head up to **Picnic Point,** a city park with some short walking paths and excellent vistas. From the visitors center parking lot, exit right onto James St., and follow up to Tourist Rd. Signs direct you up to Picnic Point.

STANTHORPE ☎ 07

As the commercial center of the Granite Belt, Stanthorpe (pop. 5000) is a convenient escape from the big city. A crisp winter climate and location in the heart of Queensland's best wine country make it a prime vacation spot for many Brisbane residents, while abundant fruit-picking opportunities attract hordes of backpackers during the summer months. The town is an ideal base for visiting renowned local wineries and exploring the granite formations and wildflowers of surrounding national parks (Girraween, Sundown, Boonoo Boonoo, and Bald Rock).

▄▟ TRANSPORTATION & PRACTICAL INFORMATION

The **bus station,** at the corner of Maryland and Folkestone St. (☎ 4681 4577), is inside the Mobil petrol station. **Crisps** and **McCafferty's** each send **buses** to: Brisbane (3½hr. and 5hr., respectively; Su-Th 2 per day, F 3 per day, Sa 1 per day; $36/$43); Toowoomba (2hr., M-Th 2 per day, F 3 per day, Sa-Su 1 per day; $29/$37); and Warwick (45min., Su-Th 2 per day, F 3 per day, Sa 1 per day; $16/$31). Concessions available on all fares. To reach the **tourist office,** 28 Leslie Pde., turn left off Wallangarra Rd. just past the bridge at Quart Pot Creek. (☎ 4501 2057. Open daily 9am-5pm.) **Banks** and 24hr. **ATMs** line Maryland St. on the left after it turns south.

> **WORK IN STANTHORPE.** From September to May each year, the ripened fruit and vegetable fields of the Granite Belt demand **picking,** and thousands of backpackers rush to Stanthorpe to fill the need. September marks the start of the steamfitter harvest (plums, cherries, and peaches); December through May is largely tomato and vegetable picking; apples run from February through May. Minimum wage is currently $12 per hr., but the amount of cash you make is largely up to you. Some picking jobs are more rigorous than others, with longer hours and higher wages.

▗ ACCOMMODATIONS

Several hostels in and around the town of Stanthorpe help backpackers find picking jobs and drive them to and from work. Although town pub hotels do not offer placement services, their central locations, low prices, and private rooms attract workers and travelers alike.

▧ **Backpackers of Queensland,** 80 High St. (☎ 4681 0999), on the right as you enter town. Backpackers rave about this hostel, which offers seasonal job placement and transportation, in addition to excellent facilities and large nightly dinners ($5). Co-ed dorms house 5 per room; each has its own bath. Lockers and laundry. Key deposit $20. Check-in by 7:30pm or call ahead. Transportation provided to and from bus station. Reservations are not accepted, but during the picking season call a day ahead to see if a bed is available. Wheelchair-accessible. Dorms $25, weekly $130. ❷

Country Style Tourist Accommodation Park (☎ 4683 4358), in Glen Aplin, 9km south of Stanthorpe on the New England Hwy. Don't let the distance deter you; the owner drives backpackers to and from work and the bus station. Job placement. Each dorm includes kitchen, bath, and TV. Internet access. Key deposit $10. 4-bed dorms (open only during the picking season) $18, weekly $75, with a $25 key deposit; caravans $75 per week; tent sites $45 per week. ❷

Blue Topaz Caravan Park (☎ 4683 5279), 5km south of Stanthorpe on the New England Hwy. Though the owners don't offer direct job placement, a bulletin board with daily job postings is available during the picking season. Offers small, simple cabins with detached bath (2 people $50, each additional $10, weekly $300, linens $6) and campsites (1 person $8, 2 people $14, weekly $65/$90). ❶

Country Club Hotel/Motel, 26 Maryland St. (☎ 4681 4888). Stay either in the cheaper rooms above the pub (try to get one facing away from the street to reduce noise) or in one of the nicer rooms in the motel out back (ensuite, with TV, fridge, large beds and 70s decor). Hotel singles $20, doubles $30. Motel singles $40, doubles $50. Pub singles $20, ensuite $35; doubles $35/$50. ❷

◻ FOOD

A Woolworths **supermarket** is on the corner of High and Lock St. (Open M-F 8am-9pm, Sa 8am-5pm.) There is a corner **grocery,** on the right at the southward bend of Maryland St. (Open daily 8am-7pm.)

Applejacks, 136 High St. (☎ 4681 0356). Great breakfast and lunch specials, served in a homey, country atmosphere. Their mushroom omelet is a must ($4.70). Open M-Th 8:30am-5pm; F 8:30am-5:15pm, Sa-Su 8:30am-2pm. ❶

Boulevard Court Restaurant, 68 Maryland St. (☎ 4681 2828). Chinese dishes feature fresh veggies and meats in sauces blended from local produce. Try the boneless chicken in peach or plum sauce ($12) or a vegetarian option ($5-11). Open daily 11:30am-2pm and 5-9:30pm. ❶

Regal Cafe, 159 High St. (☎ 4681 1365). Quick, cheap meals for either sit-down or takeaway. The no-frills fried fish ($3) and the whole Italian-style chicken ($7) are a great bargain. Open M-Sa 8am-7:30pm. ❶

Anna's Restaurant (☎ 4681 1265; www.annas.com.au), on the corner of Wallangarra Rd. and O'Mara Terr. Locals praise the weekend Italian buffets (F $23, Sa $28; book ahead) as some of the best food in town. During the week, sample a wide variety of Italian faves ($15-23) with local wines. Service can be a bit slow. Bookings highly recommended. Open daily 6-8:30pm. ❺

◪ WINERIES

Over forty famous Granite Belt wineries line either side of the New England Hwy. just south (and a little north) of Stanthorpe. Most offer free wine tasting and some give tours. Unfortunately, the wineries cannot be reached by public transportation or by foot. Tours ensure a jolly day and an obligatory late-afternoon nap. The tourist office lists all the local winery tours, as well as providing an extensive map of the area detailing all of the local wineries for those driving themselves. The best of the tours is **Filippo's,** which imparts an endless stream of amusing local knowledge while covering eight of the best vineyards. Includes pick-up, drop-off, and homemade lunch (☎ 4683 5126; www.filippostours.com.au. Full-day $51, full-day from Brisbane, $68, half-day with lunch $45, half-day without lunch $35, minimum 2 people). **The Grape Escape** offers a similar full-day package. (☎ 1300 361 150 or 4681 4761; www.grapeescape.com.au. $60. Minimum 2 people.) If you're driving (and wishing you weren't), the way to the wineries is well-marked; most are close to the highway and accessible by car. **Ballandean Estate Wines** is Queensland's oldest family operated-winery, though the Catholic Church claims title to the oldest vineyard in the valley. Ballandean sponsors the **Opera in the Vineyard** festival, a black-tie wine-and-dine opera extravaganza; every July brings **Jazz in the Vineyard,** a more low-key event. (☎ 4684 1226; www.ballandean-estate.com.au. Open daily 8:30am-5pm. Free tours 11am, 1, and 3pm.)

NEAR STANTHORPE: NATIONAL PARKS

In addition to the parks listed below, two New South Wales national parks, **Bald Rock** and **Boonoo Boonoo** (☎ 02 6732 5133), are accessible from Stanthorpe. Unfortunately, none of the parks can be reached by public transportation.

GIRRAWEEN NATIONAL PARK. Girraween is a popular destination for bush-walkers, birdwatchers, campers, and picnickers. Massive granite boulders, which seem precariously balanced on top of each other, are interspersed among eucalypt trees teeming with lyre birds. This park is also home to Queensland's only common wombat population (though these are very shy and difficult to find). In the spring, wildflowers sprout from the bases of rocks; hence the park's name, Girraween, which means "place of flowers" in Aboriginal languages. To get to Girraween, drive 26km south on the New England Hwy. from Stanthorpe; turn left at the sign, then drive 9km on a sealed road. The **Visitors Centre** (☎ 4684 5157), on your left as you enter the park, is usually open seven days a week; the rangers daringly post the day's hours on an erasable board. Nearby, there are picnic, swimming, and rock climbing areas. Camping is available in two designated areas with hot showers, toilets, and BBQ. ($4 per person per night, families $16. Register in advance ☎ 13 13 04.) Girraween features a number of different well maintained walking tracks. A 1½hr. return hike takes you to the granite ■**Pyramid Rock,** which offers a panoramic view of the famous **Balancing Rock** and **Bald Rock,** Australia's second largest rock, situated just across the border in NSW. The last portion of the climb scales the steep granite face; be sure to wear appropriate shoes and *do not climb when wet.* The trail leaves from the picnic center near the Visitors Centre. The **Castle Rock trail** (2hr. return) is a moderate climb with a steep final ascent that yields an impressive 360° view. The trailhead is located in the Castle Rock Campground, across the street from the Visitors Centre. For a more mellow hike, follow the flat trail out to **Underground Creek** (1hr. return). During the Wet, watch as water swirls around and under the large granite boulders. The trailhead is located 4km down the road from the Visitors Centre; note that some of the road is unpaved, but suitable for passenger cars.

SUNDOWN NATIONAL PARK. Sundown offers rugged bush, chiseled gorges, high peaks, and panoramic views, as well as swimming, fishing, and canoeing in a relatively undeveloped area. The 16,000-hectare park has different geology than neighboring parks, with sedimentary and metamorphic rocks combining to produce sharp ridges. The **Severn River** cuts the park in two. To get to Sundown, drive west on Texas Rd. from Stanthorpe and turn left at the signs for Glenlyon (75km). Continue on this road until you reach the dirt road marked by a Sundown National Park sign. You'll reach the park entrance after 4km on the rough dirt track; take it slow to avoid bottoming out. At the entrance, take the left fork of the track and follow it to the camp headquarters. While the Bruxner Hwy. does lead to Sundown as well, it is much less convenient when approached from Stanthorpe. Sundown is also accessible strictly by 4WD from the east via the marked turn-off in Balland-ean. Bushwalkers can also enter the park from this turn-off; simply park your vehicle right inside of the park entrance. Call **Camp Headquarters** ❶ (☎02 6737 5235), on the southwestern edge of the park, to check road conditions. Camping is accessible by 2WD vehicles and hikers on the western side of the river, near camp headquarters. All sites have pit toilets, fireplaces, and BBQ. ($4 per person, families $16.) As there are no graded walking tracks, areas of interest can be reached by following the river and side creeks. Bring a compass and a park map (available at park headquarters and the tourist office), as trails are poorly defined and often difficult to follow. The **Permanent Waterhole** is a large waterhole on a major bend in the river where an occasional platypus is spotted. To get there, park at the end of the dirt road at the campground near the information kiosk. There is a path directly ahead of the road which follows cuts into the hills following the river (45min. return). The **Split-Rock** and **Double Falls** are well worth the 3- to 4-hour return hike up **McAllisters Creek.** Cross the river east into the creek, being careful not to get sidetracked by the old 4WD track. The climb up **Ooline Creek** (the first deep gully on the left at the permanent watering hole) also features numerous waterfalls and gorges.

SUNSHINE & FRASER COASTS

As tourists make their way up the east coast from Sydney, the beach just keeps on coming. See surf and sun, bikes and boards, surfers and sophisticates—or see no one at all. The Sunshine Coast is a slightly warmer and less hyped alternative to Surfers Paradise. Here, the sun shines for 300 days of the year, quiet beaches and national parks stretch for miles, and resort towns like Noosa Heads rise suddenly from the sand. Fraser Island, the largest island in Queensland's coastal waters, consists of sand, rainforest, and 4WD tracks. Its legendary dunes and freshwater lakes are frequented by a parade of package tours and independent travelers.

MAROOCHY   ☎07

Maroochy (pop. 30,000) refers to the 18km of the sunshine coast that encompasses the towns of **Maroochydore, Alexandra Headlands,** and **Mooloolaba** (north to south). Die-hard surfers fill the beaches and their stereotypically laid-back attitudes permeate the region, although the area is getting more popular with resort dwellers and wealthy couples on vacation. An urban center located at the mouth of the Maroochy River, Maroochydore is oriented towards small industry and is thriving commercially. About 1km southeast, Alexandra Heads is best known for its great surfing waves. Another 2km south, a cafe-packed esplanade lines Mooloolaba's safe family beach. Maroochy is a popular base for fruit-picking work, with lychee and ginger season from February to March, strawberries from June to October, and tomatoes from November to February. Fruit-picking pays around $12-13 per hour, and most hostels assist in the job search (see **Alternatives to Tourism,** p. 62, for more info on working holidays).

E TRANSPORTATION. Suncoast Pacific, Premier, and **McCafferty's/Greyhound** all stop at the Suncoast Pacific terminal in the Scotlyn Fair Shopping Centre on First Ave., off Aerodrome Rd., Maroochydore. **McCafferty's/Greyhound** (☎13 14 99) runs to: Airlie Beach (16hr., 1 per day, $138); (2hr., 4 per day, $18); Cairns (26hr., 1 per day, $188); Hervey Bay (3¾-4¼hr., 4 per day, $29); Mackay (14½hr., 1 per day, $124); Noosa (30min., 3-4 per day, $12); and Rockhampton (10hr., 1 per day, $81).

Premier (☎13 34 10) runs daily to similar destinations at considerably cheaper prices. **Suncoast Pacific** (☎5449 9966) goes to Brisbane (2hr., 8 per day, $23) and the Gold Coast (3hr., 1 per day, $35). The blue **Sunshine Coast Sunbus** (☎13 12 30) connects the three towns with hail-and-ride service. Service #1 and #1A run from the Sunshine Plaza down Cotton Tree Pde. and from the Alexandra Headlands to the Mooloolaba Esplanade. (Bus #1/1A run M-F every 15-30min, Sa-Su every 30-60min. Fares $1.80-4.40 depending on duration. Sunbus #1 also continues to Noosa on a less frequent basis. $5.60-7.80 depending on starting location.) Service #2 departs from the Sunshine Plaza for Nambour.

⊞ ▓ ORIENTATION & PRACTICAL INFORMATION. Aerodrome Road is the main commercial strip in Maroochydore. In Alexandra Headland, it changes its name to **Alexandra Promenade** as it curves around to parallel the ocean. Further south in Mooloolaba, it changes again to the **Mooloolaba Esplanade.** It eventually intersects with **Brisbane Road,** one of the main thoroughfares in Mooloolaba.

The **tourist office** (☎5479 1566) is on Sixth Ave. just off Aerodrome Rd. (Open M-F 9am-5pm, Sa-Su 9am-4pm. Touchscreen available 24hr.) A smaller **info center** kiosk is in Mooloolaba, at the corner of First Ave. and Brisbane Rd. (☎5478 2233. Open daily 9am-5pm.) There are **banks** and 24hr. **ATMs** at the intersection of Horton Pde. and Ocean St., Maroochydore. **Police** (☎5475 2444) are on Cornmeal Pde., and a **7 Day Medical Centre** (☎5443 2122; open M-Sa 8am-8pm, Su 8am-6pm) and **pharmacy** (☎5443 6033) are at 150 Horton Pde. Other services include: **taxi** (24hr. ☎13 10 08; about $10 from Maroochydore to Mooloolaba); **Internet** at **Mooloolaba Internet Cafe,** Shop 2/20-22 River Esp., near the Wharf. (☎5477 5695, $5 per hr., open daily 9am-6pm); and **post offices** at 22 King St., Cotton Tree; 1/32 Brisbane Rd., Mooloolaba, and inside the Sunshine Plaza, Maroochydore. (☎13 13 18. All open M-F 9am-5pm, Sunshine Plaza location also open Sa 9am-3:30pm, Su 10am-2:30pm.) **Postal Code:** 4557 (Mooloolaba), 4558 (Maroochydore, Cotton Tree).

▐ ACCOMMODATIONS. Most hostels in Maroochy arrange fruit-picking work. **Maroochydore YHA Backpackers ❷,** 24 Schirrmann Dr., is a hike from the center of town, but the friendliness and freebies will blow you away: ice cream, bikes, canoes, boogie boards, and surfboards are all on the house. Ask for extra blankets in the winter, as rooms can get quite chilly. Large kitchen and common areas, pool, and table tennis. Laundry $2. Reception 7:45am-1pm and 5-7pm. Call for free pick-up from the bus station. (☎5443 3151; www.yha.org.au. Trips to the hinterland $10. Dorms $18; singles $35; twins and doubles $42. YHA.) **Mooloolaba Beach Backpackers ❷,** 75 Brisbane Rd., a colorful modern building, is near the nightlife. The great pool and common area are perfect for partying. Bunk dorms have kitchens and TV lounges on each level. Ensuite dorms with TV and spacious doubles are in a separate, motel-like building. (☎5444 3399 or 1800 020 120. Cafe and bar on-site. Laundry and Internet. Bike and board hire $5. Reception 7am-10pm. Dorms $21, ensuite $24; ensuite doubles $52. VIP.) **Suncoast Backpackers Lodge ❷,** 50 Parker St., off of Aerodrome Dr., Maroochydore, is small, family-run and clean, with an outdoor common space, kitchen, pool table, and continuous tunes. They are also the most serious about fruit picking, offering min. 2 week jobs on one of two local farms. (☎5443 7544. Courtesy pick-up and drop-off in Mooloolaba. Reception 8:30am-1pm and 5-8pm. Dorms $18, weekly $108; twins and doubles $40/$120. VIP.)

▐ ▓ FOOD & NIGHTLIFE. Maroochy has many good Thai restaurants, but the best is **Som Tam Thai ❷,** on the corner of Fifth Ave. and Aerodrome Rd. (☎5479 1700. Open daily 5-9:30pm. Mains around $14.) **Krishna's Cafe ❶,** Shop 2/7 First Ave., Maroochydore, has all-you-can-eat vegetarian meals. (Lunch $7, dinner $8. Open M-F 11:30am-2:30pm, also Su and F 5:30-8pm. Cash only.) Pick out a pot and

QUEENSLAND

THE HIDDEN DEAL

SMOOTH SAILING

The exorbitant cost of water sports can cast a dark cloud over the sunshine coast. Fortunately, a local pastime can help tourists avoid such costs.

At Mooloolaba Yacht Club, visitors can take part in "funsail" races aboard privately owned sailboats. The afternoon races cross a course marked by buoys or islands and teeming with dolphins and other marine life. Best of all, the experience is virtually free. Simply show up to the yacht club on Wednesdays or Sundays a little before noon and sign up for the "funsail." If a skipper has room aboard his yacht, or needs deck hands, he will ask you to join crew. Races commence around 1:30pm and last a couple of hours, depending on winds. Be sure to bring appropriate wet-weather clothing and white soled, non-slip shoes.

Following tradition, bring along a six-pack of beer as "payment" to the skipper for your ride. And as is also tradition, you can expect that the skipper won't let you ride without first sharing a cold one.

Mooloolaba Yacht Club (☎5444 1355), near the end of Parkyn Parade, on the right side of the spit past Underwater World. Funsail races W, Su noon. Inexperienced sailors welcome, but crew spots aren't guaranteed.

paint it at **Hard Clay Cafe ❶,** Shop 2/20 Brisbane Rd., Mooloolaba. It also has great breakfast and gourmet sandwiches for under $5. (☎5444 2144. Open M-Sa 8:30am-5pm.) Coles **supermarket** (☎5443 4633. Open M-F 8am-9pm, Sa 8am-5:30pm, Su 9am-6pm) is in the massive **Sunshine Plaza Mall,** off Horton Pde., along with 150 different shops and 40 eateries.

Of the three towns in Maroochydore, it's Mooloolaba that comes alive after dark. **Club WT ❷** and **The Wharf Tavern ❷,** on the Wharf next to Underwaterworld, are both modern, but the weatherboard sheds from the bar retain some of that old coastal Queensland character. The huge complex features a nightclub, restaurants and 3 bars. (☎5444 8383. Club WT open Tu and F-Su 9pm-3am. $7 cover F-Sa, $5 cover Tu with student ID. Tu is university night, with $2 basics. Bars open daily 10am-3pm, with live music Su. Food served daily from 10am-late.) At **O'Malley's ❷,** on Venning St. in the Mooloolaba Outrigger building, there are no less than 17 beers on tap. (☎5452 6344. Open M-Th 10:30am-midnight, F-Sa 10:30am-3am, last entry 1:30am. Happy Hour M-F 5-7pm, $3 pints of local beers.)

⬛ ACTIVITIES. Being in Maroochy means spending time near the water. **Maroochydore Beach** offers good breaks for shortboard riders, while **Alexandra Headlands** can have rips, large swells, and big crowds. **Mooloolaba Beach,** especially near the spit, is the safest beach for swimming. **Bad Company,** 6-8 Aerodrome Rd., Maroochydore, rents out boards across the street from a good strip of beach. (☎5443 2457. Open M-F 9am-5pm, Sa-Su 8:30am-5pm. Short boards and body boards half-day $15, full-day $20; longboards $25/$40.) If you'd rather ride the pavement, **Skate Biz,** 150 Alexandra Pde., offers in-line skates, bikes, and skateboards. Try them out at the public skate park directly across the street. (☎5443 6111. Open daily 9am-5pm. All rentals $20 per hr., $30 per day. Includes basic safety gear.)

⬛Underwater World, on the Wharf, has many beautiful displays of sea creatures of all kinds; it's the largest oceanarium in the Southern Hemisphere. Glide along a moving walkway underneath a 2.2 million liter aquarium, while sharks and giant rays swim inches overhead. There are fourteen shows daily, including shark and ray feedings. Don't miss out on the interactions with seals. You can kiss one or swim with many. (☎5444 8488; www.underwaterworld.com.au. Kiss and photo 11am, 1, and 3:30pm, $25 for photo; swim 2, 2:15, and 2:30pm, $75 includes 15-20min. swim, photo, and admission. Bookings essential. Open daily 9am-6pm; last entry 5pm. $22.50, students $16, children $13.) If seals don't give you enough of an adrenaline rush, take a dive with the aquarium's sharks with **Scuba World**. (☎5444 8595; www.scubaworld.com.au. 30min. Certified divers $95, includes dive, gear, and discounted admission into Underwater world. Dive and discounted admission only $82.50. Non-certified including intro scuba lesson, gear, dive, and aquarium admission $125.) Crew in sailing races at the **Mooloolaba Yacht Club** (☎5444 1355), near the end of Parkyn Pde., at noon Wednesday and Sunday. Spots aren't guaranteed, but sign up for the "funsail" and bring a six-pack for the skipper. See **The Hidden Deal: Smooth Sailing**, at left.

NOOSA ☎07

Upperclass couples, pensioners, Australian families, and backpackers all come to Noosa in roughly equal numbers to enjoy the gorgeous beaches, glitzy shopping areas, outdoor dining, and lush greenery. Those who find Hasting St. and its surrounds to be a bit pretentious can take relief in the multitudes of adventure activities, including great beaches for novice surfers, or rustic inland towns in the nearby hinterlands. Cooloola National Park, just north of Noosa, is a wilderness area ripe for 4WD-ing, hiking, canoeing, and camping.

▐ TRANSPORTATION

Buses: Noosa has no bus terminal; coaches pick-up and drop-off at **Noosa Parade Bus Interchange**, on Noosa Pde. near Noosa Dr. Be sure to book your tickets ahead of time. **McCafferty's/Greyhound** (☎13 14 99) runs to: **Airlie Beach** (15hr., 2 per day, $137); **Brisbane** (3hr., 5 per day, $21); **Cairns** (25hr., 2 per day, $186); **Hervey Bay** (2¼-3½hr., 5 per day, $25); **Mackay** (13hr., 2 per day, $123); **Maroochydore** (30min., 4 per day, $9); and **Rockhampton** (8½-9½hr., 2 per day, $79). **Premier** (☎13 34 10) runs one service per day to the same destinations, at significantly cheaper prices. **Suncoast Pacific** (☎5443 1011) goes to: **Brisbane** (2hr., 7-10 per day, $26); **Gold Coast** (3hr., 1 per day, $35); **Hervey Bay** (4hr., 1 per day, $23.50); and **Tin Can Bay** and **Rainbow Beach** (2hr., 1 per day, $18).

Public Transportation: Sunshine Coast Sunbus (☎13 12 30 or 5450 7888) leaves from the bus interchange and offers frequent hail-and-ride service around Noosa. Service #1 goes to Maroochydore, Mooloolaba, and Caloundra. Fares range from $5.60-7.80; buses run approx. every 1-1½hr. Service #10 connects the neighborhoods of Noosa: service starts in Tewantin and continues though Noosaville, Noosa Heads, Noosa Junction, Sunshine Beach, terminating in Sunshine Beach. Fares $1.80-3.30, buses run every 30min. Service #12 goes to Eumundi and Cooroy. Fares $4.80-5.60, buses run every 60-90min. All buses run approximately 7am-7pm, later on weekends.

Taxis: Suncoast Cabs (☎13 10 08) provides 24hr. service.

Car Rental: Europcar, 13 Noosa Dr. (☎5447 3777), rents from $49 per day, with 500km. 4WD from $165 to explore the north shore, $225 to go to Fraser. Age surcharge for those under 25 $18 per day. **Thrifty** (☎13 61 39) offers cars from $39 per day, as well as pricey 4WDs for Fraser Island (from $220 per day; must be 25 to rent).

Bike Rental: Koala Bike Hire (☎5474 2733) delivers to your accommodation. Bikes $17 for 24hr.; tandems $34 each for 24hr. Open M-Sa 7am-4:30pm, Su 7am-3pm.

✷ ORIENTATION

The Noosa area can be a bit confusing to navigate because its distinguishing features all have remarkably similar names. The three main communities are: Noosa Heads, close to the beach, Noosa Junction, with more low-key cafes and shops, and Noosaville, a quieter neighborhood on the Noosa River; Noosa National Park is also a prime attraction. Most tourist activity revolves around the sidewalk-chic **Hastings Street** in Noosa Heads, one block north of the **Noosa Parade Bus Interchange.** Many trendy shops, restaurants, and upscale hotels line the street next to Main Beach; the entrance to **Noosa National Park** is at the eastern end of the strip.

A 15min. stroll away from the beach on Noosa Dr. leads to the heart of **Noosa Junction,** Noosa's business center. The **post office, supermarket,** and a string of **banks** are all within 5min. of each other. **Noosaville** is 3km from of Noosa Heads along the Noosa River, an hours walk down Noosa Pde. from the intersection with Noosa Dr. Its main street, **Gympie Terrace,** is filled with international restaurants, motels, and boat hires. The **Sunshine Beach** area is around the point from Noosa Heads on a beautiful stretch of beach. Both Sunshine Beach and nearby **Sunrise Beach** are popular spots, but the total 40km stretch of sand leaves ample room for sunbathers to spread out.

◪ PRACTICAL INFORMATION

Tourist Office: Tourism Noosa Information Centre (☎5447 4988; www.tourism-noosa.com.au), at the intersection of Noosa Dr. and Hastings St., is the only official tourism bureau in the city. Open daily 9am-5pm.

Currency Exchange: Banks and 24hr. **ATMs** are on Hastings St., Noosa Heads; Sunshine Beach Rd., Noosa Junction; and Gympie Terr., Noosaville. All banks open M-Th 9:30am-4pm, F 9:30am-5pm, ATMs 24hr.

Bookstore: Noosa Book Shop (☎5447 3066), in the Suntop Plaza, Noosa Junction. Buys, sells, and exchanges used books. Open M-F 9am-5:30pm, Sa-Su 9am-5pm.

Police: (☎5447 5888) Main office on Langura Court, Noosa Junction (24hr.); A smaller Police Beat at the corner of Hastings St. and Noosa Dr., Noosa Heads.

Medical Services: Noosa Hospital, 111 Goodchap St., Noosaville (24hr. ☎5455 9200).

Internet Access: Surf Energy Noosa, 77 Noosa Dr. (☎5474 8208), near the corner of Sunshine Beach Rd., has quick, cheap access. $3 per hr. Open daily 8am-9pm. **Travel Bugs,** Shope 3/9 Sunshine Beach Rd., Noosa Junction (☎5474 8530 or 1800 666 720; www.oztravelbugs.com), has significantly slower service, but the first 15min. are free. $2 per hr., $5 unlimited use. Open daily 8:30am-9pm.

Post Office: 91-93 Noosa Rd., Noosa Junction (☎13 13 18). Open M-F 9am-5pm, Sa 9am-12:30pm. **Postal Code:** 4567.

◪ ACCOMMODATIONS

Lodging in Noosa comes in three general categories: hostels, motels or hotels, and "holiday units," which are often private homes or rentals. Intense competition for budget travelers makes for low hostel prices and special perks such as cheap meals, courtesy shuttle services, surfboards, and even on-site bars. With Noosa's increasing popularity, there aren't always enough budget beds to go around, and during Christmas and school holidays, rates can double; be sure to book ahead. The best location is in Noosa Heads, near the beach and all the action. Families may find it more economical to rent units or homes—**Accom Noosa,** 49 Hasting St. (☎5447 3444 or 1800 072 078; www.accomnoosa.com.au) can help find affordable, longer-stay lodging.

NOOSA HEADS

Halse Lodge (YHA), 2 Halse Ln. (☎5447 3377 or 1800 242 567), up the hill across Noosa Dr. from the Noosa Pde. bus interchange. This picturesque colonial home, with its stately veranda and large common areas, attracts a mellow, friendly crowd. Close to

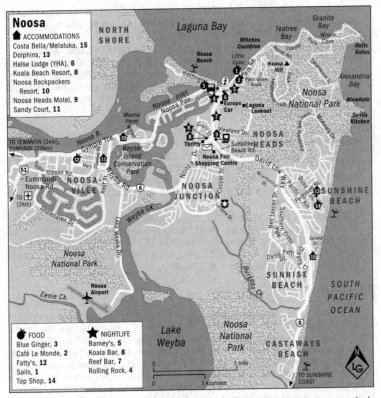

Noosa

■ ACCOMMODATIONS
Costa Bella/Melaluka, **15**
Dolphins, **13**
Halse Lodge (YHA), **6**
Koala Beach Resort, **8**
Noosa Backpackers
  Resort, **10**
Noosa Heads Motel, **9**
Sandy Court, **11**

🍴 FOOD
Blue Ginger, **3**
Café Le Monde, **2**
Fatty's, **12**
Sails, **1**
Top Shop, **14**

★ NIGHTLIFE
Barney's, **5**
Koala Bar, **8**
Reef Bar, **7**
Rolling Rock, **4**

the beach and Hastings St. A small bar is active until the 11pm common space lockdown (midnight F-Sa). Laundry $3. Reception 7am-8pm. Dorms $22, YHA $20; twins and doubles $50/$46. ❷

Koala Beach Resort, 44 Noosa Dr. (☎5447 3355 or 1800 357 457; www.koala-backpackers.com). A 10min. walk from the bus interchange; take a right onto Noosa Dr. and follow it over the hill. Popular with a young, hard-partying crowd. Sparse 5-bed ensuite dorms, courtesy bus, laundry, pool, volleyball court, tiny basement kitchen, and outdoor eating area. Internet $1 per 15min. Reception 7:30am-8pm. Dorms $20; walk-through twins and doubles $45. VIP. ❷

Noosa Heads Motel, 2 Viewland Dr. (☎5449 2873), corner of Noosa Dr., just up the hill from the Noosa Junction rotary. Just minutes away from the action, but a beautiful jungle-like lot makes it feel hidden in the wilderness. Perfect for families and couples; lovely self-contained units become better as the price gets dearer. Reception 9am-6pm. Downstairs units $70; upstairs units $80; best units $90; extra person $10, max. 4. ❺

SUNSHINE BEACH & SUNRISE BEACH

Costa Bella/Melaluka, 7 Selene St. (☎5447 3663 or 1800 003 663; www.melaluka.com.au). Take the highway to Sunrise Beach; turn left at Vernon St. and make 2 quick rights down the hill. It may lack a communal hostel atmosphere, but you'll have to pick your jaw off the floor after seeing the new, spacious, self-contained Costa Bella units with ocean views, kitchens, dining and TV areas, laundry, patios or balconies, and

QUEENSLAND

comfy beach house feel. 2 pools, BBQ, and Internet. Free pick-up from Noosa Heads. Reception 9am-6:30pm. Older units $40; twins and doubles $44. Costa Bella units shared by 2 couples; $60 per couple, entire unit $120. ❹

Dolphins Beach House, 14 Duke St. (☎5447 2100 or 1800 454 456; www.dolphins-beachresort.com). The comfortable, laid-back attitude is perfect for those coming to Noosa to get away from it all. The spacious outdoor common area is full of mellow hippie appeal. Self-contained units are available for big groups, while smaller doubles are perfect for couples. Internet, table tennis, and bike hire ($10). Reception 8am-9pm. Various sized units $23 per person, doubles $54. ❷

NOOSAVILLE

Noosa Backpackers Resort, 7-13 Williams St. (☎5449 8151 or 1800 626 673). Located on a side street 2min. from the river, 45min. from Main Beach. The happening Global Cafe makes up for distance from the center of town. Courtesy van, game room, beautiful swimming pool, and Internet. Dorm rooms have their own kitchen, doubles are located off the dorms. Reception 8am-9pm. 4- to 6-bed dorms $22; doubles and twins $50, ensuite $60. VIP. ❷

Sandy Court, 30 James St. (☎5449 7225). A half-hostel complex 2min. from the river. Units are motel rooms with bunks, which translates into spacious kitchens, TV lounges, and bathrooms. Parking, laundry, and Internet ($6 per hr.). Atmosphere is private and quiet. Free pick-up from Noosa Heads. Check-out 9:30am. Reception 8am-6pm. Dorms $20; doubles $55; motel doubles $65-75. ❷

⬛ FOOD

While there's over 140 restaurants in Noosa, it's all too easy never to venture beyond the hub of Hastings St. For better value eats, venture beyond the tourist strip. Cheaper meals can be found around Noosa Junction, and the surf clubs are a great place for a cheap meal or a sunset beer; try **Noosa Heads Surf Life Saving Club,** 69 Hastings St. (☎5447 3055. Open Su-F 11am-midnight, Sa 10am-midnight.) For the most part though, backpackers tend to eat at the hostels, many of which offer great meals for $8 or less. Coles **supermarket** is off Sunshine Beach Rd. on Lanyana Way, in the Noosa Fair Shopping Centre, Noosa Junction. (☎5447 4000. Open M-F 8am-9pm, Sa 8am-5:30pm, Su 9am-6pm.)

Café Le Monde, 52 Hastings St. (☎5449 2366), Noosa Heads. A local favorite and gathering place for surfer celebs. The express lunch baguettes are great, especially if you get them toasted (foot-long $9.20-11.90; available 11am-5pm). Most mains $18-27. Live music 4-5 nights a week. Open daily 6:30am-late. ❷

Top Shop, 36 Duke St. (☎5447 3913), Sunshine Beach. This small takeaway cafe features excellent sandwiches (from $3.10) and quintessentially Australian meat pies (from $4). Internet access available ($3.50 per 30min.). Open daily 7am-7pm. ❶

Blue Ginger, 30 Hastings St. (☎5447 3211), Noosa Heads. Bright and classy; serves gourmet Thai food (mains $17-28). Try the Stir-fried veggies and cashews ($20). BYO. Open daily 5-9:30pm. ❸

Fatty's, 4 Thomas St. (☎5474 4399), Noosaville. While the name suggests a grease-pit, Fatty's serves up gourmet pizzas and pastas ($17-19) in a modern, elegant setting. Licensed. Open Su and Tu-Sa 5pm-late. ❸

Sails (☎5447 4235), on the corner of Hastings St. and Park Rd., past the info center, on the beach. Candlelight, sexy music, and succulent seafood ($20-35) make for a blissful experience. Tables set for 2, with the sound of waves in the background. The excellent ambience is well worth the extra dollars. Try the Moreton Bay Bugs, a local specialty ($35). Open daily 8am-10pm. ❹

◎ ▣ SIGHTS & ACTIVITIES

NOOSA NATIONAL PARK

Just 1.4km from the city center, the Headlands Section of Noosa National Park is a 454-hectare area full of tropical vegetation, coastal walking paths, and rare wild-life. With 1.5 million visitors each year, the park bills itself as one of the three most visited parks in Australia. A short walk through the woods from the Noosa information booth on Hastings St. will land you at the entrance. The park is ideal for walking or jogging, and koalas perch in the trees; they are most often spotted at Tea Tree Bay and the foreshore area, and daily koala sightings are posted at the ranger station at the entrance to the park, which also provides maps of five inter-connected paths, ranging from 1 to 4.2km. (☎5447 3243. Open daily 9am-3pm.) Due to recent criminal activity, the rangers urge walkers to *never walk alone and stay on frequented paths*. Visitors should take special care around the Alexan-dria Bay area. The coastal track (5.4km return, 2hr.) offers elevated views of the ocean and ends at the exhilarating **Hell's Gates.** Many places to **surf** are available along the path; **Tea Tree Bay** and **Granite Bay** are popular among boogie boarders. A beautiful stretch of **beach** on the eastern side of the park at **Alexandria Bay** is acces-sible primarily from **Sunshine Beach.** Take the Alexandria Bay Track from McAnally drive (2km return; 45min.). Water and toilets are available, but camping is strictly prohibited.

SURFING

With warm water temperatures and a strong surfing community, the Sunshine Coast is a great place to surf. The best season is November to March, as winter waves tend to be fickle. Noosa is a wave mecca with five right-hand points, and the bonus of a beautiful backdrop. **First Point** is great for longboarders, while **Little Cove** suits beginners. Some of the best waves can be found at **National Park** and **Tea Tree,** where waves break over granite into long lines and barrel sections. Unfortu-nately, this is not a secret—in good conditions, both can get extremely crowded. To avoid the crowds, try **Double Island Point** to the north in Cooloola, but beware of strong rips and make sure to bring a friend. On the other side of Noosa National Park, try **Sunshine Beach;** conditions are erratic, but with so much surf, there's almost always a good break somewhere. With lessons taught by world champion Merrick Davis, **Learn to Surf** guarantees you'll be standing by the end of one lesson. (☎0418 787 577. Book ahead. $35 per 2hr. including wetsuit and board. 2 classes daily.) To rent your own board, try **Noosa Longboards,** Shop 4/64 Hastings St., Noosa Head, or 187 Gympie Terr., Noosaville. (☎5474 2828; www.noosalong-boards.com; body boards $15 per 4hr., $20 per day; shortboards $20/$30; long-boards $30/$45; open M-F 9:30am-5:30pm, Sa 9:30am-5pm, Su 10am-5pm); or **Surf Energy Noosa**, Shope 3/77 Noosa Dr. (☎5474 8208) across from Koalas. All boards half-day $20, full-day $30. Open daily 8:30am-9pm.

OTHER ACTIVITIES

Kitesurf lets you try out your water wings as kite and surfboard join forces in an exhilarating new sport. (☎5455 6677 or 0438 788 574; www.kite-surf.com.au. 2hr. lesson $95.) **Clip Clop Horse Treks** lets you trot through lakes and bush around Lake Weyba for a day. (☎5449 1254; www.clipcloptrecks.com.au. $165.) **Aussie Sea Kayak Company** runs sea kayaking tours in the waterways around the Sunshine Coast. (☎5477 5335. Daily 2hr. sunset tour with champagne $40, half-day $60; Tu and F-Sa full-day with lunch $105.) Tandem skydive over the coast with **Sunshine Coast Skydivers,** the cheapest operator on the east coast. (☎0500 522 533 or 0418 776 775; www.scskydivers.com. 12,000 ft. $240, backpackers $225; 14,000 ft. $290/$275. Free pick-up from Noosa.)

◙ NIGHTLIFE

With its unpretentious surfing mood and prime location, **Barney's,** on Noosa Dr. near Hastings St., is the perfect spot for a late afternoon beer. Enjoy a jug for $8.50. (☎5447 4544. Happy Hour 4-6pm. Live music Su and Th. Open 10am-late.) **The Koala Bar,** 44 Noosa Dr. (☎5447 3355), in the hostel, overflows with drunken, sun-kissed backpackers. Pool tables, Happy Hour 4:30-7pm, DJs, and nightly specials spice up the evening, which ends abruptly at the stroke of midnight. Wednesday night live bands are extremely popular; Monday theme night closed to non-guests. After Koala's closes, backpackers and trendsetters alike flock to **Rolling Rock,** Upper Level, Bay Village on Hastings St., the only nightclub serving a drop past midnight. Th guest DJs rock the house, while their New York Bar enjoys a quieter scene. (☎5447 2255. Cover M $6; Tu free; W and Su $5; Th-Sa $10. M $3 drinks. Open Su-Tu and F-Sa 8pm-3am, W 9pm-3am, but door closes at 1:30am. Cash only.) **Reef Bar,** near the crest of Noosa Dr., is a large, modern club with a big dance floor and lots of areas to chill. Be sure your shoes are up to dress code, meaning no flip flops or sneakers. (☎5447 4477. Cover F-Sa $5 from 10pm, free with passport. Open Su-Th 4pm-midnight, F-Sa 4pm-3am.)

COOLOOLA NATIONAL PARK

Extending 50km north of Noosa up to Rainbow Beach are the sandy, white coast and 56,600 hectares of Cooloola National Park. Together with Fraser Island, Cooloola forms the **Great Sandy Region,** the largest sand mass in the world. With twenty hiking tracks and navigable lakes and waterways, Cooloola beckons both experienced bushwalkers and Sunday strollers.

From the town of Noosa in the south, follow signs out of town to Boreen Pt. Instead of turning right to the point, continue straight out to Elanda Park. From Gympie in the north, take Tin Can Bay Rd. towards Rainbow Beach. After about 30km, turn right on Rainbow Beach Rd. which will take you into Rainbow Beach around 30km later. The rest of the access points to the park are 4WD only. The two-minute **Noosa Northshore Ferry** (☎5447 1321) transports 4WD vehicles from Moorindal St. in **Tewantin** to the northern shore of the Noosa River ($4.50 per vehicle, daily 6am-10:30pm, longer hours in summer). **Camping permits** are available from the **Great Sandy Information Centre** on Moorindal St. (☎5449 7792. $4 per person per night.) From the northern shore, 4WD vehicles can cut across to the beach, the park's primary 4WD vehicular thoroughfare. Be sure to check the tide times to avoid getting stranded on the beach, or worse, swept out to sea. **Rainbow 4WD Hire,** 9 Karoonda Crescent, Rainbow Beach (☎5486 3555), rents 4WDs from $150 per day; price goes up for those under 25 or for larger vehicles. **Cooloola Cruises and Safaris** picks up in Noosa for a full-day Everglades BBQ cruise. They also offer a two-in-one safari that includes a tour of Cooloola beach. (☎5449 9177 or 1800 657 666. Operates M and W-F. Everglades $82, children $45; 2-in-1 $133/$85.) **Polleys Coaches** travels to Tin Can Bay ($10) and Rainbow Beach ($13) from **Gympie.** (☎5482 9455. Departs Gympie M-F 6am and 1:30pm.) **Suncoast Pacific** also runs a daily service to Rainbow Beach from Noosa. (☎5449 9966. 2hr. Daily 9am. $18, concessions $15.)

Information and **maps** are available from a number of different locations. Try **Cooloola Shire Council,** 242 Mary St., Gympie (☎5482 1911; open M-F 8:30am-4:30pm); **Rainbow Beach Tourist Information Centre,** 8 Rainbow Beach Rd., Rainbow Beach (☎5486 3227; open daily 7am-6pm, longer in summer); **Queensland Parks and Wildlife Service** in Rainbow Beach, on the right as you enter town. (☎5486 3160; open daily 7am-4pm); and the **Great Sandy Information Centre,** on Moorindal St., in Tewantin (☎5449 7792, Open daily 7am-4pm).

The newest hostel on the scene is ■**Fraser's on Rainbow Beach YHA ❷**, 18 Spectrum Ave. The rooms are great: all dorms are spacious and ensuite, while motel-style doubles have TV and furniture. The bright common areas are even better: spacious room for Internet, huge lounge with projection TV, outdoor pool, game room with pool table, communal kitchen, laundry. (☎5486 8885 or 1800 100 170; www.frasersonrainbow.com. Dorms $18-22, doubles $60. YHA.) **The Rocks Backpackers Resort ❷**, 3 Spectrum Ave., Rainbow Beach, is a purpose-built hostel that organizes cheap Fraser 4WD trips for groups. Dorms have sink and fridge; some have bath. (☎5486 3711. Dorms $20, doubles $55. 3 day/2 night self-drive Fraser trip $135, plus 2 nights accommodation $150.)

Camping ❶ is permitted at a number of sites throughout the park, as well as in a 15km zone on Teewah Beach. Freshwater (accessible with 4WD via Rainbow Beach) is the only developed campground in the park, with treated water, toilets, hot pay showers, and a phone (☎13 13 04 to book ahead). The Upper Noosa River has 17 undeveloped campsites, all accessible by foot or canoe only. Book at Kinaba Info Centre. Poverty Point, accessible by 4WD, is undeveloped and beautiful. Self-register at campsite. The Cooloola Wilderness trail has four campsites: two are accessible by foot only, the others by 4WD. All campsites $4 per person, per night. Information on all campsites is available at both Kinaba and Tewantin.

The Cooloola National Park holds many natural wonders: rainforests growing from pure sand, meandering waterways shaded by mangroves, and massive sand blows surrounded by dense forest. Even the plants are unusual: endangered *boroniakeysii* (pink-flowered shrubs) mingle with thin, stubborn stalks of blackbutt, and melaluka "tea trees" dye the river a deep black. One of the best ways to enjoy the park is to **canoe** or motor up the **Noosa River,** around **Lake Cootharaba,** Queensland's largest natural lake, and through the **Everglades,** where the dark water creates mirror images of the dense riverbanks lined with sedges.

The beach in Cooloola is famous for its natural beauty. Extending from Rainbow Beach to Double Island Point are the 200m-high cliffs of the **Coloured Sands.** When the weathering of iron-rich minerals in the dune soils formed the cliffs, they became stained in a complex range of hues; rain intensifies the colors. Aboriginal legend speaks of Rainbow, a representative of the gods killed in an attempt to save a beautiful maiden: as he crashed to the ground, his colors permeated the sand.

Bushwalks are available throughout the park to see some of the more spectacular features. 2WD vehicles can access the path to the **Carlo Sandblow,** near Rainbow Beach. From Rainbow Beach Dr. as you head into town, turn right onto Double Island Dr. Then take a left onto Cooloola Dr. and follow until the end. An easy 600m walk will get you to the huge sand bowl of the Carlo Sandblow. Walk toward the ocean for spectacular views of the colored sands. Try to arrive during sunset, as the view from the other direction is particularly astounding. For serious bushwalkers, the Cooloola Wilderness Trail offers the ultimate challenge. The 46.2km trail connects East Mullen Carpark in the North to Elanda Point in the south. Pick up an information sheet and notify rangers of your itinerary before you set out.

SUNSHINE COAST HINTERLAND

Just inland of the Sunshine Coast lies a veritable smorgasbord of tourist delights: stunning national parks, roadside crafts markets, and kitschy but charming tourist traps. Most of the hinterland is inaccessible via public transportation and is best experienced by car. Several tour operators also offer trips to the region, but most involve more driving than hiking. **Storeyline Tours** offers several options, including a driving tour of Montville, the Blackall Range, and the Glasshouse Mountains, or a morning trip to the Eumundi Markets. (☎5474 1500; www.storylinetours.com.au. Montville-Glasshouse M half-day $36, concessions $34, children $18; full-day $52/

he remnants of 25 million year
old volcanoes, the Glass House
Mountains formed when lava
plugs at their center resisted erosion long after the sandstone surrounding them was carried away.
The Aborigines that once inhab-
ted this area developed a special
set of stories to explain these natural features. The legend goes
something like this:

The 10 major heights of the
Glass House Mountains compose
a family. The two largest peaks,
Tibrogargan and Beerwah, are the
father and mother, and the eight
mountains around them are their
children. Long ago, Tibrogargan
noticed that the seas were rising,
so he asked his eldest son to help
his mother gather the other children for protection. Since Beerwah was pregnant (notice her
enormous size), she was unable to
perform the task on her own.

The eldest, fearful of his
father's warning and oblivious to
his mother's condition, ran away,
claiming that since Beerwah was
the largest, she could gather the
rest of the children on her own.
Seeing what his son had done,
Tibrogargan became extremely
angry and struck him on his neck.
Thus, the eldest son became forever known as Coonowrin, or
Crookneck. Visitors can still see
the remnants of Tibrogargan's
rage: the mountain stands with its
back towards Coonowrin, forever
staring out to sea.

$48/$26. Markets W and Sa $12, children $7.) **Noosa Hinterland Tours** hits the same regions and also offers a trip to the Ginger Factory and Big Pineapple. While you're there, check out the Big Macadamia and be comforted to find that regardless of what certain authorities may say, you are definitely not the world's biggest nut. (☎5474 3366; www.noosa-tours.com.au. Montville-Glasshouse full-day daily $50, children $20; markets $12/$9; Ginger Factory and Big Pineapple $32/$15.) **Off Beat Rainforest Tours** accesses exclusive rainforest on eco-guided walks in Conondale National Park. 1hr. from Noosa. (☎5473 5135; www.offbeattours.com.au. $125, children $80; includes gourmet lunch.)

EUMUNDI MARKETS. Some hostels in Noosa pro-vide shuttle service ($10) to and from the famous **Eumundi Markets,** on Memorial Dr., with nearly 300 stalls of everything from sweets to sheets and soaps to boats. Get there early for the good stuff. Wednes-day markets are primarily fruits and veggies. (20km southwest of Noosa Heads, via Noosaville and Doonan; the blue Sunbus #12 or 12xs runs here from Noosa, every 1-1½hr., 7am-5pm. Parking can be diffi-cult to find; look in the dirt lots downhill from the market. For more info, contact the Eumundi Histori-cal Association ☎5442 8581. Open W 8am-1pm, Sa 6:30am-1:30pm.)

YANDINA. In the town of Yandina, just south of Eumundi, the **Ginger Factory,** 50 Pioneer Rd., churns out ginger for the zest on your sushi and the bite in your ale. The factory is the largest ginger processing plant in the Southern Hemisphere. (☎5446 7096. Open daily 9am-5pm. Free entry. Walking tour with tasting $10, students $9, children $7.) Across the street, **Nutworks** has free multi-flavored macadamia nut tastings and nut processing displays. (☎5446 3498; www.nutworks.com.au. Open daily 9am-5pm. Free.) Just off the Bruce Hwy. on the Nambour con-nection, a huge pineapple marks the entrance to the **Big Pineapple Plantation,** a working fruit and macad-amia nut farm. Though entry is free, taking all the tours costs a pretty penny. The best of them all is the pineapple train, which explains the working of the farms and animal nursery. (From Maroochydore, take bus #1a to Nambour. ☎5442 1333. Open daily 9am-5pm. Free entry. Access to all tours $24, conces-sion $21, child $19.)

MONTVILLE & BLACKALL RANGE. The sheer Blackall Range escarpment rises from the plains to cradle green pastures and rainforests, sprinkled with the old country villages of Mapleton, Flaxton,

Montville, and Maleny. Once known for its hippie appeal, Montville now thrives on several blocks of antiques, galleries, crafts, teahouses, a cuckoo clock shop, and domestic tourists. (From Noosa, follow the Bruce Hwy. south to Nambour and then turn toward the Blackall Range via Mapleton. The info center is on Main St., Montville. ☎5478 5544; www.montvillevillage.com.au. Open daily 10am-4pm.)

KONDALILLA & MAPLETON FALLS. Kondalilla and Mapleton Falls National Parks, both off the road north of Montville, have pleasant trails and picnic areas. The 80m Kondalilla Falls (Aboriginal for "rushing water") are especially gorgeous. Although the Picnic Creek walk (3.2km return, moderate climb, 45min.-1hr.) will get you to the lookout and rock pool, the best views of the rushing waters are sprinkled along the Kondalilla Falls circuit track (4.6km return from carpark, steep at places, 1½-2hr.) that begins at the lookout and drops down to below the falls. The Wompoo circuit (1.3km, easy grade, 30min.), at Mapleton Falls, just past Mapleton on the Obi Obi Rd., winds through rainforest to an excellent lookout, though the carpark lookout gives a better view of the falls. (Ranger ☎5494 3983. Station open M-F 7:30am-4pm.)

GLASS HOUSE MOUNTAINS. The Glass House Mountains rise abruptly from the rolling farmlands south of Landsborough. A couple of walking tracks are accessible to inexperienced bushwalkers; the rest of the hikes are limited to those with significant bushwalking experience. At **Mt. Tibrogargan,** take the 800m return **Mountain View** path up the base of the peak for views out to **Coonowrin, Beerwah, Tib-beroowuccum,** and **East** and **West Tunbubudla.** Experienced climbers can continue the 2.6km to the summit. Allow 3-4hr. for return. At **Mt. Beerwah,** the 2.6km return path to the summit is for experienced climbers only, but the inexperienced can hike the beginning 1km of the path. For those with limited experience but ample physical fitness, the best option is **Mt. Ngungun.** The 1.4km return path is shorter than the others, and the terrain is manageable. Nonetheless, caution is advised, and the path should not be attempted in wet weather. Camping is permissible only in Coochin Creek, 9km east of Beerwah. Sites are undeveloped. $4 per person per night is payable at the self-registration. (Ranger ☎5494 3983. All sections accessible from signs on the Glass Mountain Tourist Rd. To reach from the south, look for signs off the Bruce Hwy. just past Caboolture. From the north, exit the Bruce Hwy. at Landsborough.)

HERVEY BAY ☎07

For many travelers, Hervey Bay (HAR-vee; pop. 45,000) is little more than a rest on the way to Fraser Island, but since most backpackers stay here for at least a few nights either before or after their stay on Fraser, the hostel scene is one of the craziest on the coast.

⌐ TRANSPORTATION

Trains: A trainlink bus connects Hervey Bay to **Maryborough Coach Terminal,** on Lennox St., Maryborough (bus leaves 40min. before trains depart Maryborough). The **Tilt Train** (☎13 22 32) runs from Maryborough to: **Brisbane** (4½hr., 1-4 per day, $57.20); **Bund-aberg** (1hr., 1-2 per day, $27.10); and **Rockhampton** (4¾hr., 1-2 per day, $67.10).

Buses: Bay Central Coach Terminal, Bay Central Shopping Center, Pialba (☎4124 4000). Open M-F 6am-5:30pm, Sa 6am-1pm. Lockers available at $4 per day. **McCaf-ferty's/Greyhound** (☎13 14 99 or 13 20 30) and **Premier** (☎13 34 10) run to: **Airlie Beach** (13hr.; 5 per day; Premier $91, McCafferty's $129); **Brisbane** (5-6hr., 9 per day, $32/$43); **Bundaberg** (2hr., 4 per day, $12/$26); **Cairns** (23hr., 6 per day,

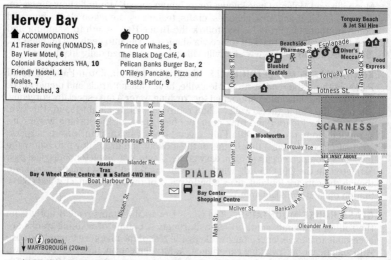

Hervey Bay

🏠 ACCOMMODATIONS
A1 Fraser Roving (NOMADS), **8**
Bay View Motel, **6**
Colonial Backpackers YHA, **10**
Friendly Hostel, **1**
Koalas, **7**
The Woolshed, **3**

🍎 FOOD
Prince of Whales, **5**
The Black Dog Café, **4**
Pelican Banks Burger Bar, **2**
O'Rileys Pancake, Pizza and
Pasta Parlor, **9**

$167/$177); **Mackay** (11hr., 6 per day, $77/$113); **Maroochydore** (4hr., 4 per day, $21/$29); **Noosa** (3½hr., 5 per day, $19/$25); and **Rockhampton** (6-6½hr., 6 per day, $43/$72). Premier runs once per day, usually later in the evening. **Wide Bay Transit** (☎4121 3719; www.widebaytransit.com.au) runs through Hervey Bay City and to Maryborough. Route #5 connects to the tilt train and passes by the Hervey Bay Visitor Information Centre. Route #14 goes to Pt. Vernon. Routes #16 and 18 connect Torquay and the Marina. Fares $1.80-4.80.

Taxi: Hervey Bay Taxi (☎13 10 08). 24hr.

Bicycle Hire: Rayz Pushbike Hire (☎0417 644 814) offers free delivery and pick-up. Half-day $10, full-day $20. Tandem bikes $28/$38. Open daily 7am-5pm.

✴ 🛈 ORIENTATION & PRACTICAL INFORMATION

Hervey Bay is actually a clump of suburbs facing north toward the Bay. From west to east, the suburbs are: **Port Vernon, Pialba, Scarness, Torquay,** and **Urangan.** Most action occurs along **The Esplanade** at the water's edge between Scarness and Urangan, which is lined with takeaway shops and tour booking agencies. The harbor extends down The Esplanade and around to Pulgul St., an excellent place to pick up cheap seafood fresh from the trawlers.

Tourist Office: The only accredited tourism bureau is the **Hervey Bay Visitor Information Centre** (☎4124 2912 or 1800 811 728; www.herveybaytourism.com.au), located on the Hervey Bay-Maryborough Rd., at the corner of Urraween, about 6km from the center of town. Open daily 9am-5pm. It is accessible by Wide Bay Transit Bus #5. In addition, there are countless booking agents on The Esplanade.

Currency Exchange: Banks and 24hr. **ATMs** are located at the bus terminal and on The Esplanade in Torquay. **National Bank,** 415 The Esplanade (☎13 22 65), has an **ATM.** Open M-Th 9:30am-4pm, F 9:30am-5pm.

Police: (emergency ☎000; 24hr. ☎4128 5333), corner of Queens and Torquay Rd.

Camping Gear: Torquay Disposals and Camping, 424 The Esplanade (☎4125 6511). Open M-F 8:30am-5pm, Sa 8:30am-4pm, Su 8:30am-noon.

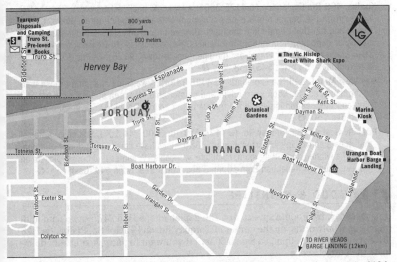

Internet Access: Available at **Bluebird Rentals,** 346 The Esplanade, Scarness (☎4124 2289). $3 per hr. Open M-Sa 8:30am-late, Su 9:30am-late.

Post Office: 414 The Esplanade, Torquay (☎4125 1101). Open M-F 8am-5:30pm. The office at **Bay Central Shopping Centre** (☎4125 9126), across from bus terminal in Pialba, has Sa hours. Open M-F 8:30am-5pm, Sa 8:30-11:30am. **Postal Code:** 4655.

Bookstore: Truro Street Pre-loved Books, 4 Truro St. (☎4125 2375), Torquay. Open M-F 9am-5pm, Sa 9am-1pm.

Pharmacy: Beachside Pharmacy, 365 The Esplanade (☎4128 1680), Scarness. Open M-F 8:30am-6pm, Sa-Su 8:30am-1pm.

ACCOMMODATIONS

Colonial Backpackers (☎4125 1844 or 1800 818 280; www.coloniallogcabins.com), on the corner of Pulgul and Boat Harbour Dr., Urangan. Rustic and sprawling, but removed from the center of town. Pool, spa, volleyball, basketball, tennis, parking, licensed restaurant, and picturesque pond. Perfect for families, couples, and those needing a break from the crowded hostel scene. Reliable Fraser safaris $135. Laundry. Key deposit $10. Reception 6:45am-9:30pm. Dorms $21-23, twins and doubles $52-62, log cabins for up to 5 $72, villas for 2 $92. YHA. ❷

The Woolshed, 181 Torquay Rd. (☎4124 0677), Scarness, 5min. from the beach and shops. A unique smaller hostel which features waterfalls, ponds, and gardens. Chickens and ducks have the run of the backyard, and cosy rooms have plenty of character. Co-ed bathrooms with great showers. Kitchen and BBQ area. Bike hire, Internet, and free breakfast. Laundry. Reception 7am-8:30am, 9:30am-7pm. Dorms $17; doubles and twins $40. ❷

A1 Fraser Roving, 412 The Esplanade (☎4125 3879 or 1800 989 811; www.fraserroving.com.au). A big, newer building right across from the beach. Though rooms are comfortable, the bar huge, the staff friendly, and the pool relaxing, Fraser Roving remains one of the quieter hostels. Game room, kitchen, Internet, and the most comfortable TV room on the coast. Key deposit $10. Reception 24hr. 8-bed dorm $15, 6-bed $18; ensuite $22. Doubles $44/$50. ❶

Koalas, 408 The Esplanade (☎4125 3601; www.koala-backpackers.com). Party hostel across from the beach offers a beautiful pool and a jungle-like atmosphere. Cheap meals and bar that pumps into the night. Beware of add-ons like linen hire $1.50 and heaps of deposits, from cutlery to blankets. Key deposit $10. Reception 7am-7pm. Their stand-by rates for Fraser are the cheapest in town ($125). Dorms $18, ensuite $20; doubles and twins $45/$58. VIP. ❷

Bay View Motel, 399 The Esplanade (☎4128 1134). A welcome change for those tired of the hostel scene. Rooms are bright and comfortable, common spaces are quiet and airy, and the location is right in the middle of the action. Doubles $50, ensuite with TV and fridge $60. ❸

Friendly Hostel, 182 Torquay Rd. (☎4124 4107 or 1800 244 107), Scarness. A hostel that does a convincing impersonation of a B&B. Units have small bright dorms and doubles off a kitchen and sitting room, complete with cable TV, games and books. pick-up on request. Laundry. Reception 8am-10pm. 3-bed dorms $19; twins $44. Cash only. ❷

🍴🍷 FOOD & NIGHTLIFE

For **groceries,** try **Food Express,** 414 The Esplanade (☎4125 2477; open 6am-midnight) or Woolworths, on the corner of Torquay Rd. and Taylor St., Pialba. (☎4128 3158. Open M-F 8am-9pm, Sa 8am-5:30pm.) If you want to party, hostel bars dominate the budget scene.

▨ **O'Rileys Pancake, Pizza and Pasta Parlour,** 446 The Esplanade (☎4125 3100). This family-owned pizzeria also serves excellent pasta ($9-14) and crepes ($8-12), as well as super-sweet creative pancake concoctions ($4-10). Don't miss their Tu night all you can eat pizza and pancake buffet ($12). Open M-F 7:30am-1:30pm, daily 5pm-late. ❶

The Black Dog Cafe, 381 The Esplanade (☎4124 3177). Trendy eatery serves sushi rolls ($5-6) and outstanding teriyaki burgers ($9.50) in a relaxed, comfortable setting. YHA/VIP discount 10%. Licensed. Open daily 5:30pm-late, also Th-Su 10:30am-2:30pm; kitchen closes at 9:30pm. ❶

Pelican Banks Burger Bar, 346 The Esplanade (☎4128 1777), at Queens Rd. If you're looking for something quick, delicious and cheap, this is one of your best options. Sandwiches $3-5, burgers from $5. Open daily 7am-7:30pm. ❶

Prince of Whales, 383 The Esplanade (☎4124 2466), Torquay. This traditional English pub—think dark wood panelling, fireplaces, tons of beers on tap and giant British flags—serves up such favorites as Ye Olde Steak, Kidney, and Guinness Pies ($13.75). Excellent service. Most mains $10-18. Open daily 4pm-late; food served until 9pm. ❷

▶ ACTIVITIES

WHALE-WATCHING

Weighing up to 40 tons—the equivalent of 11 elephants, or 600 people—the humpback whale stops in Hervey Bay on its southern migration after giving birth in the warmer waters up north. The whales assemble in Platypus Bay, 50km from Urangan Harbour, where sightings are undeniably dramatic. Whale-watching is big business from late July to November. Most boats offer guaranteed whale sightings during the season, or your next trip is free. All boats leave the Hervey Bay Marina in Urangan. The flagship vessel is the **Spirit of Hervey Bay,** built for whale-watching and underwater viewing, with a whale-listening hydrophone. (☎4125 5131 or 1800 642 544. Departs 8:30am and 1:30pm for a 4hr. half-day cruise. $72, children $44.) **Quick Cat II** offers a half-day, small-boat experience. (☎1800 671 977 or 4128 9611. Departs daily 8am and 1pm. $70, students $55, children $45.) If the whale season's

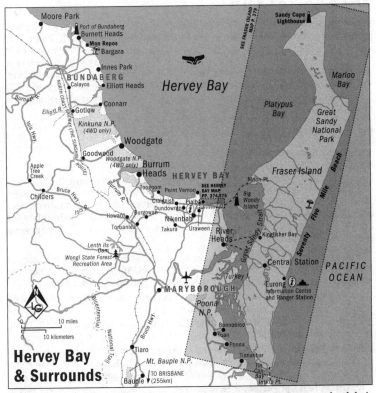

Hervey Bay & Surrounds

past and you're still itching for marine mammals, try **Whale Song,** a wheelchair-accessible vessel that guarantees dolphin sighting in the off-season. (☎1800 689 610 or 4125 6222. Half-day seasonal whale-watching daily 7:30am and 1pm. $76, children $42. Dolphin-watching 9am-2:30pm. $60, children $30.) Every year, the return of the humpback whales is celebrated with the **Blessing of the Fleet,** first weekend in August. The **Whales, Sails, and Fishing Tales Festival,** in November, features an **Electric Light Parade,** with glowing floats. (☎4125 4166.)

DIVING
Divers Mecca offers a fairly inexpensive PADI Open Water certification course. It includes four boat dives, not shore dives. (401 The Esplanade. ☎4124 7886 or 1800 351 626. Courtesy pick-ups. Open daily 9am-5pm; courses begin M and Th. Intro dive $110; PADI certification $209; advanced open water $252.)

OTHER ACTIVITIES
Torquay Beach Hire offers equipment for a wide array of beach activities and a 10% discount with presentation of *Let's Go.* (Across from 415 The Esplanade, on Torquay Beach. ☎4125 5528. Open daily 7am-5:30pm.) **Skydive Hervey Bay** includes a scenic flight over Fraser Island. (☎4124 8248. 10,000 ft. $219; 12,000 ft. $264; 14,000 ft. $308.) **Humpback Camel Safari** offers two-hour rides twice per day. (Toogoom, 15min. from Hervey Bay. ☎4128 0055; call ahead. Pick-up available. $44.)

QUEENSLAND

FRASER ISLAND
☎ 07

Fraser Island, the world's largest sand island and a World Heritage-listed national park, attracts 350,000 visitors each year. Backpackers up and down the coast can't stop talking about Fraser—an untrammeled wilderness scarred only by a 4WD track. An idyllic destination for bushwalkers, fishermen, and 4WDers, Fraser is manageable for less experienced outdoorsmen as well. Although a sand island, much of Fraser lies beneath a dense rainforest cover, punctuated by over 200 freshwater dune lakes, nearly half of the world's total. The winds perpetually resculpt the island's topography, but its unique natural beauty is a constant.

◪ TRANSPORTATION

BY BOAT

Most backpackers leave for Fraser from Hervey Bay, but Rainbow Beach, 1½hr. north of Noosa, is also becoming a popular departure point. If you're renting a 4WD, consider leaving from Rainbow Beach, as ferry costs are much lower. **Fraser Island Vehicular Ferry Services** runs ferries from several locations (return fare for Fraser Venture, Fraser Dawn, and Kingfisher: $18, vehicles $110 with three passengers, additional passengers $6.50):

Fraser Venture (☎ 4125 4444), the most convenient for independent 4WDers; leads to the best tracks. From Riverheads to Wanggoolba Creek. 30min.; daily 9, 10:15am, and 3:30pm, Sa also 7am. Returns daily 9:30am, 2:30, and 4pm. Sa also 7:30am.

Fraser Dawn (☎ 4125 4444), from Urangan Boat Harbor to Moon Point. 55min.; daily 8:30am and 3:30pm. Returns daily 9:30am and 4:30pm.

Kingfisher (☎ 1800 072 555), from Riverheads to Kingfisher. 50min.; daily 7:15, 11am, and 2:30pm. Returns daily 8:30am, 1:30, and 4pm.

Rainbow Venture (☎ 5486 3154), the southernmost access point to Fraser. From Inskip Point near Rainbow Beach (see **Cooloola National Park,** p. 370) to Hook Point. 15min.; continuously 7am-4:30pm. Vehicles $20, includes passengers; walk-ons free.

Kingfisher Fast Cat Passenger Ferry (☎ 4125 5511), the only pedestrian-only ferry in the area brings passengers from Urangan Boat Harbor to Kingfisher Bay Resort and the best walking tracks. 30min.; daily 8:45am, noon, 4pm, Su-Th also 6:30pm, F-Sa also 7 and 10:30pm. Returns daily 7:40am, 10:30am, 2, 5, 8pm, F-Sa also 11:30pm. $38, children $19.

BY PLANE

Air Fraser Island (☎ 4125 3600; www.airfraserisland.com.au) offers one-way or same-day trips ($60) and an overnight trip, including 4WD hire, return flight, and camping equipment ($205). They also offer a scenic flight over Fraser (30min.; $200).

GUIDED TOURS

Tours provide a structured, safe, and hassle-free way to see the island, though you'll have to forgo the freedom and excitement of a personal 4WD and outdoor camping. Many buses seat 30-40 people, all of whom must shuffle in and out at each stop before continuing on to the next lake. Be sure to inquire about group size before booking your tour; the smaller the group, the more personalized the experience. Also ask about accommodations and meals, so you'll know exactly what you're paying for. Tour options are plentiful; one-day tours are available, but two or three day tours are the best way to get a feel for the island. Prices are higher than the advertised hostel self-guided specials, but once you've factored in food, permits, and petrol, tours become somewhat comparable in cost.

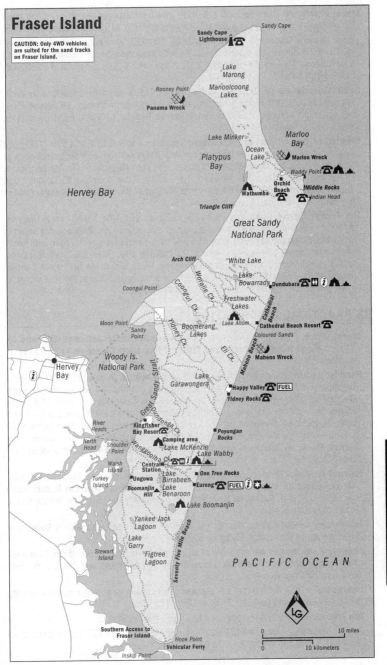

Fraser Island

CAUTION: Only 4WD vehicles are suited for the sand tracks on Fraser Island.

Sandy Cape

Sandy Cape Lighthouse

Lake Marong

Marloocoong Lakes

Rooney Point

Panama Wreck

Lake Minker

Marloo Bay

Ocean Lake

Platypus Bay

Marloo Wreck

Hervey Bay

Waddy Point

Orchid Beach

Wathumba

Middle Rocks

Indian Head

Triangle Cliff

Great Sandy National Park

Arch Cliff

White Lake

Lake Bowarrady

Dundubara

Coongul Point

Woralie Ck.

Coongul Ck.

Freshwater Lakes

Moon Point

Yidney Ck.

Sandy Point

Boomerang Lakes

Lake Allom

Cathedral Beach

Cathedral Beach Resort

Coloured Sands

Woody Is. National Park

Maheno Beach

Maheno Wreck

Eli Ck.

Great Sandy Strait

Lake Garawongera

Happy Valley

FUEL

River Heads

Dundonga Ck.

Wanggoolba Ck.

Yidney Rocks

Kingfisher Bay Resort

North Head

Shoulder Point

Poyungan Rocks

Walsh Island

Camping area

Lake McKenzie

Lake Wabby

Central Station

Turkey Island

Lake Birrabeen

One Tree Rocks

Ungowa

Eurong

FUEL

Boomanjin Hill

Lake Benaroon

Lake Boomanjin

Yankee Jack Lagoon

Lake Garry

Stewart Island

Figtree Lagoon

PACIFIC OCEAN

Seventy Five Mile Beach

Hervey Bay

Southern Access to Fraser Island

Hook Point

Vehicular Ferry

Inskip Point

N

LG

0   10 miles

0   10 kilometers

Fraser Experience Tours (☎ 1800 689 879; www.fraserexperience.com). Fun and informative tours with max. 14 in a group. 2-day departs M-W $195. 3-day departs F $295.

Fraser Venture Tours (☎ 4125 4444 or 1800 249 122; www.fraser-is.com). Their daytrips and 2-3 day safaris attract a younger set. Quad-share accommodation at Eurong Beach Resort. Daytour $99, children $55; 2-day safari $200; 3-day safari $260, with Indian Head $350.

Sand Island Safaris (☎ 1800 246 911 or 4124 6911; www.sandislandsafaris.com.au). More expensive outfit, running comprehensive 3-day tours with max. 16 people. Overnight accommodations at Eurong Beach Resort. Departs Tu-W and F-Sa; quad share $290, twin or double share $323.

Kingfisher Bay Wilderness Adventure Tours (☎ 4120 3333 or 1800 072 555; www.cooldingotour.com). The most expensive but very well-run, with accommodation at the spacious and beautiful Wilderness Lodge. 4WD bus holds up to 40. Age restriction: 18-35 yrs. only. 2-day overnight quad share $230; 3-day overnight $303; quad and twin share $270/$353. VIP/YHA discounts. Kingfisher Bay also runs a **Ranger Guided Day Tour,** 8:45am-5pm. $105, children $55.

The Fraser Island Company (☎ 4125 3933 or 1800 063 933; www.fraserislandco.com.au). A number of different tours to suit your needs. Their one-day safari is highly recommended ($99, children $55). Or try the exclusive one-day tour, with luxury meals and a plush 16-passenger van ($133, children $90). There are 2 different 2-day safaris to pick from: the wilderness safari (leaves Tu, Th, Sa) or the Northern Adventure (leaves M, W, F, Su) $185. The 3-day camping adventure sleeps at the tent village at Cathedral Beach. 16 passengers ($319, children $250).

▪ PRACTICAL INFORMATION

Tourist Office: For information, contact the **Hervey Bay Visitor Information Centre** (p. 373) or **Maryborough Fraser Island Visitor Information Centre** (☎ 4121 4111), in Maryborough.

Permits: If you're going over in a car, you'll need a **vehicle permit** ($31.80; valid for 1 month; includes map and island details). **Camping permits** ($4 per person per night) are good for all campgrounds except the privately-run Cathedral Beach Resort and Dilli Village, both on the east shore. With the permit comes a packet identifying allowed camping areas; all developed campgrounds have 9pm noise curfews. Both permits are available from the Riverheads Store, the Rainbow Beach Dept. of Environment, and **Marina Kiosk,** on Buccaneer Ave., Urangan, at the harbor (☎ 4128 9800; open daily 6am-6:30pm).

General supplies: Stock up at **Eurong Beach Resort** (open daily 8am-5pm), **Fraser Island Retreat** at Happy Valley (open daily 8am-6pm), **Kingfisher Bay Resort** (open daily 8am-6:30pm), **Cathedral Beach Resort** (open daily 8am-5pm), or **Orchid Beach** (open daily 8am-5pm).

Telephones: Central Station, Dundubara, Waddy Point, Indian Head, Sidney Rocks, and all of the above the resorts. Minimum $2 fee.

Showers: Cold showers are available at all campgrounds except Lake Allom. Coin-operated hot showers are available at Central Station, Waddy Point, and Dundubara. (50¢ for 3min.; 50¢-pieces only.)

Emergency: ☎ 000. Limited medical assistance also available at ranger stations and the Kingfisher Bay Resort (☎ 4120 3333 or 1800 872 555).

Tow Truck: ☎ 4127 9188 (Eurong) or 4127 9167 (Yidney Rocks).

Ranger Stations: Eurong (☎ 4127 9218), Central Stations (☎ 4127 9191), Dundubara (☎ 4127 9138) and Waddy Point (☎ 4127 9190). Hours vary.

ACCOMMODATIONS

Accommodation is included in the guided tour packages, but if you are arranging your trip independently, there are heaps of options. **Camping ❶** is the cheapest and most convenient island accommodation, enabling visitors to see different parts of the island without returning to the same location each night. There are seven main QPWS camping areas, all of which have a 9pm noise curfew, and camping is also allowed on designated beaches, including most of **Eastern Beach** (sites $4 per person per night; see **Practical Information,** above). Pay close attention to the signs on Eastern Beach which designate camping areas. Camping outside of these areas will result in a fine. Most campgrounds have taps, fire rings, and toilets. Some have hot water showers, BBQs, firewood, dingo fences and picnic tables.

    Cathedral Beach Resort and Camping Park ❶ has camping sites. (☎ 4127 9177. Sites for 2 $27, extra person $5.) **Eurong Beach Resort ❹** offers several budget options, as well as more expensive motel units. (☎ 4127 9122; www.fraser-is.com. Cabins $17 per bed, motel doubles $90, luxury 2-bedroom apartments $155-230.) **Fraser Island Retreat ❹** (☎ 4127 9144) in Happy Valley has individual lodges with kitchenette, TV, BBQ and pool for two ($120, peak $150) to five ($155/$190). **Yidney Rocks** (☎ 4127 9167; www.yidneyrocks.fi25.com) has family holiday units which sleep up to 8 people for $170. The upscale **Kingfisher Bay Resort ❺** (☎ 1800 072 555; www.kingfisherbay.com) is well-hidden in the bush on the western side of the island, offering luxury hotel rooms from $129 (min. 3 nights) and four-person self-contained cabins for $275.

SIGHTS & HIKING

INLAND
With unbelievably clear waters and white sandy bottoms, Fraser's freshwater lakes are one of its biggest draws. **Lake McKenzie** is the most popular, with two white sand beaches for bathers, shady pine trees, and water in various shades of perfect blue. **Lake Wabby** is at the eastern base of the steep **Hammerstone Sandblow,** which gradually encroaches on this barrage lake. Some visitors run down the dune and into the lake, but injuries and fatalities have occurred this way, so take caution. To get to Lake Wabby, follow the 1.4km track from the inland carpark, or take the 5km return circuit from eastern beach via the Hammerstone sandblow. Walking across the dunes feels like crossing a vast desert; in fact, Fraser and nearby **Cooloola National Park** (see p. 370) combined have more sand than the Sahara. The southernmost lake, **Boomanjin,** is, like many others, lined with fallen leaves from the overhanging swamp paperbarks and tea trees, which give it tea-colored water that softens the skin and hair. It's the largest lake on Fraser and the largest perched lake in the world. There are also a number of freshwater creeks good for swimming and wading, especially **Eli Creek,** accessible from Eastern Beach. **Wanggoolba Creek** is a silent beauty, muffled by its sandy bottom.

    D-I-N-G-O Don't confuse the **dingoes** roaming Fraser Island with domesticated dogs; keep your distance, and never pet or feed dingoes. The 160 dingoes that roam Fraser Island are some of the purest breed around; they have rarely interbred with domesticated dogs. By feeding the dingoes, however, visitors to Fraser have made them more aggressive and less fearful of humans. Now, dingoes routinely steal food from campsites. If you do happen upon a dingo, *don't run*. Instead, cross your arms over your chest and walk slowly backward, always maintaining eye contact with the dog.

EASTERN BEACH

There is a *lot* of beach on Fraser Island, and most of it looks the same, bordered by raging surf and low-lying trees announcing the tentative start of island vegetation. Eastern Beach is perfect for 4WDing, but be careful (see **Driving on Fraser,** p. 382). The drive from Hook Point north to Indian Head takes around 1¾hr., or longer when it has been raining and the streams are full. *Do not swim in the ocean,* as tiger sharks and riptides are real dangers. Heading north from Eurong, patches of rocks decorate the beach, with short bypasses at **Poyungan Rocks** and **Yidney Rocks** and a longer route around the **Indian Head** promontory, where one can spot dolphins, sharks, ospreys, and whales (late July to early Nov. on calm days). Almost at the top of passable beachland, a collection of shallow tide pools on **Middle Rocks** called the **Champagne Pools** make prime swimming holes at low tide. Be careful at the pools, as the rocks are slippery and incoming waves can cause serious injury by crashing over the rocks that dam the pools. Other attractions along the beach are **Rainbow Gorge,** the **Pinnacles,** and the **Cathedrals,** all impressive demonstrations of **Coloured Sands** (giant sand formations of countless shades), and the **Maheno shipwreck,** the remains of a massive cruise liner that washed ashore in a storm in the early part of the century. Do not walk on the shipwreck, as it is rusted and may cause injury or result in a fine.

HIKING

Hiking tracks riddle the interior of Fraser, connecting to some lakes that are inaccessible by 4WD. Walking is often cheaper and more rewarding than 4WDing and is the only safe way to access **Western Beach,** a soft white silica paradise. Again, *do not swim in the ocean;* even though there are no rips, tiger sharks are just as plentiful. Consider trying a smaller chunk of the island near Central Station (Ranger station ☎4127 9191; open daily 10am-noon), like **Lake McKenzie** and **Lake Wabby** before attempting a more ambitious itinerary off the beaten track. Pick up the Short Walks Pamphlet from any of the permit offices or ranger stations, which describes a number of 20min.-3hr. hikes. If hiking really interests you, try the Forest Lakes hiking trail, a 3- to 5-day hike that highlights a number of the inland lakes. If you plan on completing any or all of this hike, be sure to pick up the pamphlet and map, and notify rangers of your itinerary before starting.

 DRIVING ON FRASER

Driving on Fraser is only possible in a 4WD vehicle or a well-equipped motorcycle. Speed limits are established on the island: 80km per hr. on the Eastern Beach and 35km per hr. on inland roads, though 60km per hr. and 20km per hr. respectively is recommended. *Don't rush*—though there is a lot to see on the island, you'll spend

> **❗ CRASH COURSE: BEACH DRIVING.** Although beach driving can be a lot of fun, reckless driving can lead to disaster. The most serious danger is **creek cuts** in the beach; test the depth of a creek before attempting to cross. *Don't cross if the water is higher than your knees;* instead, wait for the tide to go down. Hitting washouts at high speed risks the vehicle rolling; it also can break the springs or cause front end damage, leading to expensive repair costs. Also, *don't drive at night,* when it is difficult to see and other drivers are more likely to be drunk and foolhardy. Location is important, as well; you're tempting fate by driving on the eastern beaches south of Dilli Village and Ungowa, north of the Ngkala Rocks, around Hook Point, or on the Western Beach.

more time getting yourself out of bad situations than you'll gain by speeding. The one-lane roads of the interior are pure, soft sand; getting stuck is not out of the ordinary (have shovels handy). Allow at least 30 minutes to travel 10km on inland roads. The beaches themselves are registered national highways—all normal traffic rules apply, and the roads are even patrolled by Breathalyzer and speedgun-wielding policemen. Larger vehicles will occasionally stay on the right, however; in any case, always use your blinker to indicate which side you'll be passing on. On the beach, drive only on hard, wet sand, and don't try to cross washouts that are above knee deep. Beware of the tides; the best times for beach driving are the three hours before and after low tide.

SELF-DRIVE WITH HOSTELS

Three-day and two-night unguided group 4WD tours are extremely popular among backpackers. Travelers bring back stories, dirty clothes, and lots of sand. Unlike in guided tours, guests camp out at night. Hostel self-drive safaris usually cost about $135 or so, plus the additional hidden costs of petrol (about $5-10 per person), insurance (around $15-20), and food. Packages include 4WD hire, ferry passes, camping permits, access fees, camping equipment, and full preparatory briefing. Usually, the hostel hosts an afternoon meeting on the day before departure, a 4WD briefing the morning of, and a pre-departure supermarket run. To drive, you must be over 21, but anyone can ride. Bear in mind that the entire group assumes responsibility for vehicle damage, regardless of fault, so it's best to keep an eye on whoever is driving.

When choosing a hostel with which to book your Fraser self-drive tour, there are a number of things that you should consider. First, look at the size of the tour group: most hostels designate groups of around 8 to 11. Try for a smaller group for more comfort while driving. You'll also want to ask where luggage and camping gear is stored while driving. Roof racks can make the vehicle unstable, but storing gear in the car makes for less room while traveling. Also, consider the total cost of the package. Be sure to add in insurance, bonds and sleeping bag hire (fuel, food and alcohol costs run the same across the board). The type of partying you'll get with a group is usually congruent to the atmosphere at the particular hostel: YHA attracts quieter groups and families, while Beaches, Koalas, and Fraser Escapes tend to party hard. Overall, most of the hostels offer very similar packages for similar costs. Often, travelers end up choosing the tour simply based on what hostel they book into.

RENT YOUR OWN 4WD

For folks who want the thrill of hurtling down a beach independently, several companies rent 4WDs at comparable costs: 2-seater $110, 4-seater $130-140; 5- to 6-seater $150-160, 8- 11-seater $160-170. **Aussie Trax** (see below), with new vehicles that are more expensive than standard 4WDs, also offers older model Land Rover ex-military vehicles (multi-day $120; seats 6). Hire companies lend out camping kits for $10-14 per person per day. Some good operators include: **Bay 4WD Centre,** 54 Boat Harbour Dr. (☎4128 2981 or 1800 687 178; www.bay4wd.com.au); **Aussie Trax,** 56 Boat Harbour Dr. (☎4124 4433 or 1800 062 275; www.aussietraxfraserisland.com); and **Safari,** 102 Boat Harbour Dr. (☎4124 4244 or 1800 689 819; www.safari4wdhire.com.au). Be sure to ask about permits for the island: most prices don't include them, but they can often be arranged. All of these companies pick-up locally. It's worth asking whether a rental agency belongs to the **Fraser Coast 4WD Hire Association,** the local watchdog. Some hostels, including The Woolshed in Hervey Bay and The Rocks Backpackers in Rainbow Beach, can also arrange cheap 4WD hire for groups.

BUNDABERG
☎07

Bundaberg (pop. 44,500) is not high on the list of Australia's choice idling spots; most visitors get coffee at the bus terminal, stretch their legs, and hop back on board. It is, however, a backpacker locus for vegetable-picking year-round, as well as a great, cheap place to learn to dive. In the fields, backpackers seeking to beef up bank accounts mix with seasoned life-long workers. At the end of the day, it's all about kicking the dirt off your work boots, occasionally splurging on Bundaberg's famous rum, and saving energy for another day in the fields. Some last a day; others, months. Despite Bundy's dearth of activities—or perhaps because of it—the survivors enjoy some of the strongest camaraderie on the coast.

HOSTEL FIRE. Located 53km south of Bundaberg, **Childers** struggles to come to terms with the tragic **Palace Backpackers fire** that killed 15 international backpackers in June 2000. Though investigators suspected that arson was the cause of the fire, the tragedy has drawn attention to the need for official guidelines—especially strict fire regulations—over the hostel industry.

◤ TRANSPORTATION

Trains: Queensland Rail (☎13 22 32) is at the corner of Bourbong and McLean St. Ticket office open M-F 4-5am and 7:45am-5pm, Sa-Su 8:45am-1pm and 2-4:15pm. **Tilt Trains** depart for **Brisbane** (1-2 per day, $89.10); **Mackay** (1-3 per day, $140.80); **Rockhampton** (1-3 per day, $81.40); and **Maryborough** (1-2 per day, $33), with bus connections to **Hervey Bay** ($25.30). Children and ISIC holders 50% discount.

Buses: The Coach Terminal (☎4152 9700) is at 66 Targo St., between Crofton and Electra St. To get to town from the station, turn right and pass the roundabout and McDonald's. Bourbong St. runs perpendicular. **McCafferty's/Greyhound** (☎13 14 99 or 13 20 30) and **Premier** (☎13 34 10; cheaper, but only one service in the middle of the night) run to: **Airlie Beach** (11hr.; 4 per day; Premier $79, McCafferty's $116); **Brisbane** (7-7½hr., 5 per day, $43/$58); **Cairns** (19-20hr., 5 per day, $143/$155); **Hervey Bay** (1¾hr., 5 per day, $12/$26); **Mackay** (8½hr., 5 per day, $66/$98); **Maroochydore** (5½hr., 2 per day, $31/$52); **Noosa** (5hr., 2 per day, $30/$48); and **Rockhampton** (4-4¾hr., 5 per day, $32/$56).

Local Bus Transport: Duffy's City Buses, 28 Barolin St. (☎4151 4226) travel around town and to the Bundy Rum distillery. Buses M-F 7:15am-5pm. **Stewart & Sons,** 66 Targo St. (☎4153 2646) leaves daily from the IGA on Woongarra St. for Innes Park (3 per day, $4.40), Elliott Heads (3 per day, $4.60), and Moore Park (2 per day, $4.60).

Taxi: Bundy Cabs (☎4151 2345 or 13 10 08). 24hr.

◢ PRACTICAL INFORMATION

Most of Bundy's action takes place on **Bourbong Street,** which runs parallel to and one block south of the **Burnett River.** Crossing Bourbong from west to east are **McLean,** with the rail station, **Maryborough, Barolin,** and **Targo Street,** with the bus station and several restaurants.

Tourist Office: Bundaberg City Visitors Centre, 186 Bourbong St. (☎4153 9289). Open M-F 8:30am-4:45pm, Sa-Su 10am-1pm. **Bundaberg Regional Visitors Centre,** 271 Bourbong St. at Mulgrave St. (☎4153 8888 or 1800 388 888; www.bundabergregion.info). Open daily 9am-5pm.

Currency Exchange: ATMs line Bourbong St. between Targo and Maryborough St.

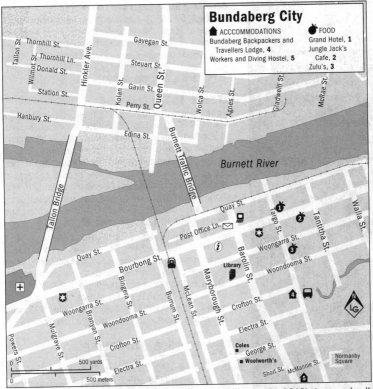

Bundaberg City

🏠 **ACCCOMMODATIONS**
Bundaberg Backpackers and Travellers Lodge, **4**
Workers and Diving Hostel, **5**

🍴 **FOOD**
Grand Hotel, **1**
Jungle Jack's Cafe, **2**
Zulu's, **3**

Bookstore: Boomerang Book Exchange, 26 Targo St. (☎4151 3812), buys and sells used books. Open M-F 8:30am-5pm, Sa 9am-1pm.

Police: 256-258 Bourbong St. (☎4153 9111), in the city center. 24hr.

Internet: The Cosy Corner, on Barolin St. at the corner of Bourbong, opposite the post office. $5 per hr. Open M-Th 7am-8pm, F 7am-7:30pm, Sa 8am-5pm, Su 11am-5pm.

Post Office: 157B Bourbong St. (☎4131 4451), on the corner of Barolin St. Open M-F 9am-5pm and Sa 8:30am-noon. **Postal Code:** 4670.

🏠 ACCOMMODATIONS

The better hostels help find jobs (usually within a day of beginning your search), provide free transport to and from work, and have strict alcohol and drug policies.

Workers and Diving Hostel, 64 Barolin St. (☎4151 6097). From the bus station call for a ride, or walk across the street, down Crofton St., and take a left onto Barolin St. (10min.). Despite the name, working is definitely the focus here. The most social and welcoming of the area's hostels, with a big outdoor common area, free pizza nights, a pool and a large common area with free movies. If you're planning a long stay, try to get into one of the units (as opposed to the house): with their own kitchens, TVs and baths, they feel just like home. Reception 8:30am-noon and 3:30-7:30pm. Dorms in house $19, weekly $115; in units $20/$120. Doubles $40/$240. NOMADS. ❷

HE HIDDEN DEAL

A TRUE DIVE

Australia hosts some of the best dive sites in the world, but to get to them, you'll first have to shell out the cash to get certified. One of the cheapest places in the world to take the required PADI course is Bundaberg, QLD. Located on the southern edge of the Great Barrier Reef, you can get certified before heading north to more popular locations such as Airlie Beach and Cairns.

Two of the best places to learn diving in Bundy are Salty's and Bundaberg Aqua Scuba; both offer $169 4-day Open Water certification courses. Courses include introductory pool lessons, as well as four dives on the coral covered shoreline. Expect to spend a bit more for additional fees; a $55 diving medical exam is a necessity for any course and students need to purchase or bring passport photos (around $4-5) and a log book ($8.75). At some dive centers, you will also need to purchase a dive manual ($45). Still, compared to the $300-400 you would spend to get certified elsewhere, this price is a definite steal.

If you need a place to stay while getting certified, keep in mind that most dive centers offer accommodation for around $14-15 per person per night. While rooms are nothing special, they are clean, quiet, and provide all necessities.

Bundaberg Backpackers and Travellers Lodge, 2 Crofton St. (☎4152 2080), across from the bus terminal at the corner of Targo. The Hilton of hostels, this is a no-nonsense, air-conditioned picker's haven, especially during the humid summers. Free pick-up at train station. Laundry, sterile TV room. Key deposit $20. Reception 7-11am and 2-7pm. Dorms $21, weekly $120. ❷

OUTSIDE TOWN

Iluka Forest Retreat, 127 Logan Rd., Innes Park (☎4159 3230 or 1800 657 005), on the oceanfront, 15km from Bundy. For those not working, another great budget option is close by, tucked between fields of sugar cane and the Woongarra Marine Park's reef. Spread-out cabins make for few people and lots of wildlife. Great for couples. Free snorkel gear and pick-up in Bundaberg. Shared amenities and kitchen; linen provided. Reception 7am-7pm. Dorms, doubles, and family rooms all $20 per person. ❷

Kelly's Beach Resort, 6 Trevor's Rd., Bargara (☎4154 7200 or 1800 246 141; www.kellysbeach-resort.com.au), on Baraga beach. Self-contained villas are more pricey, but the luxurious pool, tennis court, sauna and eco-tours all make up for it. 24hr. laundry, pick-up from Bundaberg for guests staying multiple nights. Key deposit $10. Twin share villas $92, with dinner and breakfast $117. 7th night free. ❷

🗎 🖪 FOOD & NIGHTLIFE

Both Coles (☎4152 5222; open M-Sa 8am-9pm) and Woolworths (☎4153 1055; open M-F 8am-9pm, Sa 8am-5pm) **supermarkets** are in the Hinkler Place Shopping Centre, on the corner of Maryborough and George St. After a long day picking, the takeaway branch of **Il Gambero ❶**, 57 Targo St., certainly hits the spot. The main restaurant serves the same food at a higher cost. (☎4152 5342. Pizza $8.50-14.50, Pasta $4-8. Open daily 5pm-late, also Th-F 11:30am-2pm.) **Zulu's ❷**, 61 Targo St., at the Queenslander Hotel, has a casual outdoor eating area, basic pub meals around $15, and $8 jugs of beer. (☎4152 4691. Open daily 10am-2am; food served 11:30am-2pm and 5:30-8:30pm.) If you're searching for a quick, healthy bite, try **Jungle Jack's Cafe ❶**, 56 Bourbong St. Lunches include quiches ($4-5), salads ($4-6), and smoothies for $3-5. (☎4152 8513. Open daily 7am-7:30pm.) **The Grand Hotel ❶**, 89 Bourbong St., on the corner of Targo, is the most popular joint in town for cheap meals and late-night beers. The scene can certainly get a little rowdy when the pickers have a day off. (☎4151 2441. Lunch and dinner specials $3-6. Open Su-W 10am-10pm, Th-Sa 10am-late; food served daily 11:30am-2pm and 6-8pm.)

👁 〰 SIGHTS & ACTIVITIES

Diving in Bundaberg is rock-bottom cheap. **Salty's,** 208 Bourbong St., offers an excellent four-day PADI course in an on-site heated saltwater pool, with four shore dives to the Coral Coast's volcanic rock reef. (☎4151 6422 or 1800 625 476; www.saltys.net; open M-Sa 8am-5pm, Su 1-5pm. 4-day classes start M and Th $169. Two boat dives on the artificial reef $100; two shore dives $45; two reef dives $215.) **Bundaberg Aqua Scuba,** 66 Targo St. (☎4153 5761; www.aquascuba.com. Open daily 9am-5pm), next to the bus terminal, offers two shore dives for $45, two artificial reef dives for $85, and a $169 PADI open water course that includes four shore dives; there is cheap accommodation ($14 a night) for those in courses. Call both places to organize dive trips to Lady Musgrave or Lady Elliot Islands.

Love it or hate it, Bundy **rum** is Australia's best-selling spirit. **Distillery tours** include a 10min. video, 45min. walking tour of the distillery including a look at the huge storage vats of thick, smelly molasses, and 2 drinks. Wear closed-toe shoes. Duffy's buses, routes #4 (to Bargara, 4 per day) and #5 (to Burnett Heads, 3 per day) stop near the distillery. (☎4153 5761; www.bundabergrum.aust.com. Tours every hr. M-F 10am-3pm, Sa-Su 10am-2pm. $9, concessions $7.70, children $4.40.)

Celebrating the start of the turtle nesting season, the week-long **Coral Coast Turtle Festival,** in November, features a carnival, markets, and parades. **Mon Repos** hosts the largest loggerhead turtle rookery in the South Pacific. During the season, night access to the beach is limited to guided tour groups. (15km from the city center; head east on Bargara Beach Rd. and follow signs to the rookery. ☎4159 1652. Open daily 7pm-2am. Nov.-Mar. 1hr. tours $5, children $2.50.)

TOWN OF 1770 & AGNES WATER   ☎07

Named for the year of Captain James Cook's second Australia landing, the area's natural beauty remains unmarred by two centuries of sleepy village life. Now, however, 1770 has been discovered a second time: backpackers on the coastal pilgrimage have begun to visit the town, drawn by its unspoiled beaches and two national parks. Although the mention of 1770 and Agnes Water still draws a blank for many tourists, it's a magical spot, and as the locals say, it's going to be big.

📟 **TRANSPORTATION.** Since the bitumen road heading into town is still relatively new, public transportation is still cumbersome and expensive. **McCafferty's/ Greyhound** (☎13 14 99 or 13 20 30) runs to Fingerboard Rd., 20km from Agnes Water. From there, hop on the smaller transfer bus into town. All fares listed include the price of this transfer. **Buses** arrive from: Brisbane (9hr., $85); Bundaberg (1½hr., $50); Hervey Bay (3hr., $51); Mackay (6hr., $109); and Rockhampton (3hr., $62). Northbound bus arrives at Fingerboard Rd. 8:35pm, southbound bus 6:50am. Alternatively, **Cool Bananas** (☎1800 227 660) offers free pick-up from Bundaberg Mondays and Fridays at 3pm.

🏧 📠 **ORIENTATION & PRACTICAL INFORMATION.** Agnes Water is located 123km north of Bundaberg. The town center lies at the intersection of **Round Hill Road,** the main access route into town, **Springs Road,** which runs south along the shoreline, and **Captain Cook Drive,** which rambles 6km north to the town of 1770. Most residences and attractions are located in 1770, while basic supplies and accommodations can be found in Agnes Water. There is no public transportation between the two towns.

Though privately owned, the **Discovery Centre,** in Endeavor Plaza, Agnes Water, offers friendly advice on all tours and accommodations in town. (☎4974 7002; www.discover1770.info. Open daily 9am-5pm.) The Westpac in Endeavor Plaza does not exchange currency, but there is an **ATM** in the Endeavor Plaza IGA. Other services include: **police** (☎4974 9708), in Agnes Water on Springs Rd. near Cool Bananas; **Internet** at Yok Attack, in Endeavor Plaza (☎4974 7454; open daily 6pm-late; $6 per hr.); **laundromat**, in Endeavor Plaza (☎ 4974 7107; open daily 7:30am-8pm; $3 wash, $1 per 10 min. dry.) and **post office** in Agnes Water Shopping Centre. (Open M-F 9am-1pm and 1:30-5:30pm.) **Postal Code:** 4677.

▪▫ ACCOMMODATIONS & FOOD. Backpackers in 1770 certainly can't go wrong with accommodations: both of the following hostels are some of the best you'll find on the coast. █**Cool Bananas ❷**, on Springs Rd., Agnes Water, comes out slightly ahead, with campfires, free eco-tours and M night BBQs, and courtesy pick-up and drop-off in Bundaberg (see above). Rooms are simple and clean, but it's really the pretty patio, hammocks, TV lounge, and atmosphere that will blow you away. (☎1800 227 660; www.coolbananas.biz.com. Bikes $8 per day. Internet $4.50 per hr. Reception 7am-2pm and 4-10:30pm; book in advance. Dorms $21 for the first 2 nights, then $20; weekly $120. NOMADS/YHA/VIP.) **Backpackers 1770 ❷**, Captain Cook Dr., Agnes Water, is quiet and clean, with a great kitchen, spacious ensuite dorms, and extremely helpful staff. (☎4974 9849 or 1800 121 770; www.backpackersqueensland.com. Reception 8am-9pm. 4-bed dorms $18; doubles $40. Cash only.) Four caravan parks are located around 1770. **Captain Cook Holiday Village ❶**, on Captain Cook Dr. between 1770 and Agnes Water, has six acres of land and an excellent restaurant. (☎4974 9142. Reception 8am-8pm. Sites for 2 $17, powered $20; self-contained cabins $44, ensuite $66.) If you're looking for some privacy right on the beach, try the **Mango Tree Motel ❸**, 7 Agnes St. 100m from Agnes Waters Beach. Rooms sleep up to 6 people and include TV, ensuite, and fridge. (☎4974 9132; www.mangotreemotel.com. Rooms from $70.)

Yok Attack ❷, Endeavor Plaza, serves authentic Thai mains for $12-18. Try the delightful chicken coconut cream for $15. (☎4974 7454. Open daily 6pm-late.) Cheaper eats are found at the pleasant **Palm's Cafe ❶**, at the Petrol station on the corner of Round Hill and Captain Cook Dr., where burgers are $4, pizzas start at $3.30, and a coffee is only $1.65. (☎4974 9166. Open daily 6am-9pm.) Crash the local pub scene at **1770 Foods and Liquors ❶**, past the Marina on Captain Cook Dr., where the food is delicious and an excellent value. (☎4974 9183. Open daily 10am-late; food served daily noon-2:30pm, 6pm-9:30pm.) **Groceries** can be purchased at the IGA, in Endeavor Plaza (☎4974 7991; open daily 6:45am-6pm), or at the Food Store in Agnes Water Shopping Centre. (☎4974 9911. Open daily 6:30am-7pm.)

◪◿ SIGHTS & ACTIVITIES. Located on the northernmost surf beach and surrounded by two national parks, 1770 is an unspoiled paradise. Around the rocky headland, a short **walking track** leads to panoramic views of blue water and crashing waves. Six kilometers of lonely beach separate the 1770 headland from the short, unmarked trails around Agnes Water, which begin behind the museum on Springs Rd. and lead to **Workman's Beach,** great for surfing and body boarding, as well as several lookout points. Past the picnic area, vehicular access changes to 4WD only; the track continues into **Deepwater National Park.**

To discover the depths of Deepwater (a land-locked series of lagoons), **1770 Adventure Tours** offers canoe tours. (☎4974 7068. Pick-up and drop-off available. Tours Tu, Th, Sa 8:30am-2pm. $49.) **LARCS** or **Lighter Amphibious Resupply Cargos,** enormous ex-military boats with wheels (now painted pacifist pink), rumble through Eurimbula Creek into **Eurimbula National Park.** (☎4974 9422 or 1800 177 011; www.1770holidays.com. Sunset cruise daily from 4:30-5:30pm $25; day tours on M, W, Sa from 9am-4pm $95, seniors and students $90.)

For a less conspicuous voyage through area waters, rent your own **tinny,** a powered aluminum boat. The cheapest rentals are at **1770 Camping Grounds**, on Cap-

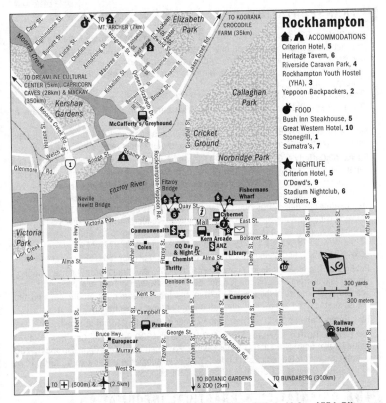

Rockhampton

🏨 🏠 ACCOMMODATIONS
Criterion Hotel, **5**
Heritage Tavern, **6**
Riverside Caravan Park, **4**
Rockhampton Youth Hostel
(YHA), **3**
Yeppoon Backpackers, **2**

🍎 FOOD
Bush Inn Steakhouse, **5**
Great Western Hotel, **10**
Stonegrill, **1**
Sumatra's, **7**

⭐ NIGHTLIFE
Criterion Hotel, **5**
O'Dowd's, **9**
Stadium Nightclub, **6**
Strutters, **8**

tain Cook Dr., at the beach. (☎4974 9286. Full-day $75, half-day $55.) **Bikes** are available at **Agnes Cycle and Sport,** in Endeavor Plaza. (☎4974 7550. Open M-F 9am-5pm, Sa 9am-1pm. $20 per day, $18 with copy of *Let's Go*.)

CAPRICORN COAST

Straddling the Tropic of Capricorn and stretching all the way from the Fraser Coast to the Whitsundays, this length of coastal tropics consists of one paradise right after another. The Bruce Hwy. winds its way north through this area, through sugar cane fields and along the shore, where seaside towns and secluded islands have become backpacker havens.

ROCKHAMPTON
☎07

Straddling the Tropic of Capricorn, the town makes for a refreshing break from the pre-packaged, stereotypical backpacker's route. Historical buildings loom over chain stores and shops on the town's meticulously plotted grid of streets. For the most part, Rockhampton is a serious, conservative town, with its share of hair salons and saddle shops. However, a few interesting cultural activities stir the country dust, providing a day's worth of entertainment.

QUEENSLAND

▮ TRANSPORTATION

Train Station: 320 Murray St. (☎ 4932 0234), at the end of the road. From the city center, head away from the river on any street, then turn left on Murray St. $6 day lockers available. The **Tilt Train** goes north and south along the coast, including stops at Brisbane (8hr., $93.50), Maryborough, with bus connection to Hervey Bay (4hr., $61.60), Mackay (5hr., $57.20), Proserpine, with bus connection to Airlie Beach (7hr., $73.70), Townsville (10hr., $107.80), and Cairns (17hr., $216.70). Northbound trains depart Tu, Th, Sa at 2:15am; Southbound trains depart M, Th, Sa at 1:35am and daily at 7:25am. The **Spirit of the Outback** also leaves Rocky on W and Su at 4:15am for Emerald (5hr., $51.70), Barcaldine (12hr., $85.80), and Longreach (14hr., $101.20). Children, QLD students or ones with ISIC cards, and pensioners receive half fares.

Buses: McCafferty's/Greyhound (☎ 4927 2844), on the corner of Linnet St. and Queen Elizabeth Dr. From the city center, follow Fitzroy St. over the river, where it becomes Queen Elizabeth Dr.; the terminal is 400m on the left. Lockers $6-11 for 24hr. **Premier** (☎ 13 34 10) picks up from the Mobil station, 91 George St., between Fitzroy and Archer St. Premier is cheaper but only sends one bus south (12:15pm) and one north (3:20pm). Both have service to: Airlie Beach (6½hr.; 6 per day; Premier $48, McCafferty's $73); Brisbane (12hr., 7 per day, $76/$83); Bundaberg (4hr., 5 per day, $32/$56); Cairns (17hr., 7 per day, $118/$128); Hervey Bay (6hr., 6 per day, $43/$72); Mackay (4hr., 7 per day, $33/$52); and Maroochydore via Noosa (10hr., 4 per day, $64/$81).

Public Bus: The blue **Capricorn Sunbus** (☎ 4936 1002; www.transport.qld.gov.au/public/index) leaves from Kern Arcade, on Bolsover St. between Denham and William St., and covers most corners of the city M-F 6:30am-5:45pm, Sa 8am-noon. Route maps posted at most stops and are available from the tourist office. Fares from $2-4.

Taxi: Rocky Cabs (☎ 13 10 08), or at the corner of Denham St. and the mall. 24hr.

Car Rental: Thrifty, 43 Fitzroy St. (☎ 4927 8755 or 1300 367 227). Cars from $31.90 with 100km limit. No rentals to those under 25. Open daily 7am-6pm. **Europcar,** 106 George St. with rates from $39. Under 21 $18 age surcharge per day. (☎ 4922 0044 or 13 13 90). Open M-F 7:30am-5:30pm, Sa 8am-1pm, Su 8am-11am.

▮ ▮ ORIENTATION & PRACTICAL INFORMATION

The Fitzroy River, the largest river in Queensland and second largest in Australia, is a defining landmark. On its south side, the city has a flawless grid design, with most of the action near the river's edge along Quay St. East St. runs parallel one street south from Quay and houses a pedestrian mall between Fitzroy and Denham St. On the north side of the Fitzroy Bridge, Fitzroy St. changes to Queen Elizabeth Dr., passes the transit station and continues on toward Yeppoon.

Tourist Office: Rockhampton Tourist Information Centre, 208 Quay St. (☎ 4922 5339; www.rockhamptoninfo.com). Open M-F 8:30am-4:30pm, Sa-Su 9am-4pm.

Currency Exchange: Banks and 24hr. **ATMs** are on the East St. pedestrian mall. **Commonwealth Bank,** 74 East St. (☎ 4922 1733), in the mall, and **ANZ,** 214 Bolsover St. (☎ 4931 7764), on the corner of William St., are both open M-Th 9:30am-4pm, F 9:30am-5pm.

Library: 69 William St. (☎ 4936 8265), on the corner of Alma St. Free **Internet** terminals; book ahead for a 30min. or 1hr. session. Open M-Tu and F 9:15am-5:30pm, W 1-8pm, Th 9:15am-8pm, Sa 9:15am-4:30pm.

Market: The **City Heart Market** (☎ 4926 6844), in the Kern Arcade **carpark** on Bolsover St., has crafts and a few veggie stalls. Open Su 8:30am-12:30pm.

Internet: Connect at **Cybernet,** 12 William St. (☎ 4927 3633; www.cybernet.com.au), for $5 per hr. Open M-F 10am-5:30pm.

Pharmacy: C.Q. Day and Night Chemist (☎ 4922 1621), on the corner of Denham and Alma St. Open M-Sa 8am-10pm, Su 9am-9pm.

Post Office: 150 East St. (☎ 13 13 18), between William and Derby St. Open M-F 8:30am-5:30pm. **Postal Code:** 4700.

▛ ACCOMMODATIONS

Yeppoon Backpackers, 30 Queen St. (☎ 4939 8080 or 1800 636 828; www.net-lynx.net/yeppoon), Yeppoon. A great gateway to explore Great Keppel, and a beachside treasure in itself. Pick-up from Rockhampton (daily 6pm), or take Young's bus from Rockhampton (6 per day, $7.50). One night in Yeppoon, one on Great Keppel, and all ferry and other transport fees $75. Hostel also runs trips to Cooberrie, Koorana, Fire Rocks (4WD), and "Serenade" boat trips. Pool, spa, kitchen, Internet, laundry, and big TV room. Reception 7:30am-8:30pm. 4-bed dorms $20; doubles $40. VIP/YHA. ❷

Rockhampton Youth Hostel, 60 MacFarlane St. (☎ 4927 5288). From the bus terminal, turn left on Queen Elizabeth Dr., walk 5min., and cross Musgrave St. MacFarlane is straight ahead. Rocky's youth hostel has a friendly but quiet crowd. Kitchen, laundry, TV room. Free pick-up from bus or train stations. Packages include 1 night in Rocky, 2 on Great Keppel, snorkel gear, return ferry ticket, and shuttle; dorms $129, twins/doubles $133 per person. Key deposit $10. Reception 7-11:30am and 3:30-9:30pm. Dorms $21; twins and doubles $50; Olympic cabins with ensuite $30 per person. YHA. ❷

Criterion Hotel, 150 Quay St. (☎ 4922 1225), just south of the Fitzroy bridge on the river. Grand and picturesque, with plenty of pictures displaying the building's colorful past. Two bars and a restaurant. Basic rooms have showers and A/C but no toilet; pricier rooms have toilets and TV, and some have fireplaces and balconies. Reception 7am-midnight. Singles $30-50; twins $46-55; doubles $40-55; triples $56-65. ❸

Heritage Tavern (☎ 4927 6996), on the corner of William and Quay St. A 107 yr. old heritage-listed hotel, the tavern has a great kitchen and common room for guests; perfect for backpackers. Laundry. Key deposit $5. Check-out 11am. Basic singles $25; doubles and twins $35. Singles with A/C, TV, fridge, and balcony $30; doubles and twins $40; quads $65. ❸

Riverside Caravan Park, 2 Reaney St. (☎ 4922 3779), along the river. The green park offers both sites and well-maintained cabins. BBQ and laundry facilities. Reception M-Sa 7am-7pm, Su 8am-7pm. Sites $7 per person, powered for 2 $18. Self-contained cabins sleep up to 7, $42 for 2, $7 per extra adult. ❶

▛ FOOD

Beef: it's what's for dinner. Buy your own at Coles **Supermarket,** City Centre Plaza, at Fitzroy and Bolsover St. (open M-F 8am-9pm, Sa 8am-5:30pm), and cook it on the free riverside BBQs. Competition among pub hotels keeps lunches cheap.

▓ **Stonegrill,** 117 Musgrave St. (☎ 4922 4719), at the Ascot Hotel. These are among the best steaks you'll ever have, hands down. The raw meat is brought out on extremely hot slabs of stone, which allows you to cook for yourself. The result is meat so tender and juicy that steak knifes aren't necessary: the only cutlery you'll need is an ordinary butter knife. Porterhouse steak $22. Open daily noon-2:30pm and 5:30-9pm. ❷

▓ **Great Western Hotel,** 39 Stanley St. (☎ 4922 1862). On event nights, the entire place is alive with the spirit of the outback. While the food (try the Rocky rump; $18) is excellent, it's the atmosphere that you come for. W practice rodeo rides 7:30pm; every second F bull rides. Weekly events include rodeos, meat-cutting, and indoor campdrafts. Cover $8-10 for rodeos; no cover W nights. Open Su-Th 11am-midnight, F-Sa 11am-3am. Food served daily noon-2pm and 6-9pm; no Su lunch. ❸

Sumatra's (☎ 4921 4900), on the corner of East and William St. A nice change from the steakhouse scene, Sumatra's offers trendy seating on the mall and veggie options. The staff is extremely friendly and their Th and Sa $12.95 all-you-can-eat themed dinners are exceptional value. Open M-Sa 10am-late. ❶

Bush Inn Steakhouse, 150 Quay St. (☎ 4922 1225), in the Criterion Hotel. Recommended by locals as a great place to chew some of Rocky's finest ($14-24). Food served daily noon-2pm and 6-9pm. ❸

👁 ⚠ SIGHTS & ACTIVITIES

BOTANIC GARDENS & ZOO. No need to choose; here you can sample native and exotic flora and fauna in one stroke. The zoo has an enormous geodesic dome aviary, chimpanzees, and the usual line-up of Aussie animals. Tours ($3.30) of the garden depart from the garden information center Tu, W, Th at 9:30am. *(15min. ride from the city on Sunbus route #4A; departs from the arcade carpark at least every hr. M-F 7:15am-5:35pm, Sa every hr. 8:15am-11:15pm. $1.90 one-way. ☎ 4936 8000 or 4936 8254. Feedings 3-3:15pm. Zoo open daily 8am-4:30pm; gardens open daily 6am-6pm. Both free. Tours of the garden depart from the garden information center Tu-Th at 9:30am. $3.30. Book ahead at ☎ 4922 1654.)* The **Kershaw Gardens,** stretching 1km along the Bruce Hwy. between Dowling and High St., recreate a natural Australian bush environment. *(☎ 4936 8254. Open daily 7am-6pm. Tours of the garden depart from the Knight St. Carpark Tu-Th at 1:30pm. $3.30. Book ahead ☎ 4922 1654.)*

DREAMTIME CULTURAL CENTRE. The Centre provides a modest but elegant portrayal of the indigenous peoples of Central Queensland and the Torres Strait Islands. It is set in a park with a meandering trail highlighting different medicinal plants of the area. Learn to throw a boomerang and hear a didgeridoo demonstration at the end of the tour. *(5min. north of Rockhampton by car, on the corner of Yeppoon Rd. and the Bruce Hwy. Sunbus #10 runs from the arcade carpark at least every hr. M-F 5:35pm, Sa 8:15-11:15. $2.70 one-way. ☎ 4936 1655. Open M-F 10am-3:30pm. 1½hr. tours are best for seeing the park; 10:30am and 1pm; $12.75, students $10.50, pensioners $9, children $6. Entry is free.)*

CAVING. The **Capricorn Caves** are ancient limestone caves that feature the **cathedral,** with incredible natural acoustics and a natural light spectacle during summer solstice (early Dec. to mid-Jan. on the 11am tour). One-hour tours cover the highlights of the extensive cave system. The caverns also host **Wild Caving Adventure Tours,** three hours of rock climbing, sardined in 12cm wide tunnels and squeezing through Fat Man's Misery. *(23km north of Rockhampton, in The Caves. ☎ 4934 2883; www.capricorncaves.com.au. Open daily 9am-4pm. Admission and basic 1hr. tour $14, children $7; with transport from Rockhampton M, W, F $33/$16; day tour with lunch, two other sites, and transport $64/$32; adventure tour $60, book at least 24hr. ahead.)*

ROCKHAMPTON HERITAGE VILLAGE. Experience Rockhampton from white settlement in 1854 through to the 1950s in the Heritage Village, an active township that recreates original homes and buildings from that era. Wander the town on your own, or book ahead for a guided tour that includes rides in a horse-drawn carriage and demonstrations of blacksmithing and woodcutting. *(On Boundary Rd., off the Bruce Hwy. #10 Sunbus from the arcade carpark at least every hr. M-F 7:15am-5:35pm, Sa 8:15-11:15am. $2.70 one-way. ☎ 4936 1026; heritagevillage@bigpond.com.au. Open M-F 9am-3pm, Sa-Su 10am-4pm. 2hr. self-guided tours $5.50, students $3.30, children $1.10.)*

HIKING. Looming 604m over Rockhampton, **Mt. Archer** offers amazing views of the city and surrounding countryside. Drive 5km from the base to the summit and walk several different tracks at the top. Hardy hikers can trek back to the base on the walking track (11km; 4-5hr.), but you'll need a friend to retrieve you at the bottom, as the walk into town is a long one. Pick up a brochure at the tourist office for more information. *(By car, head northeast towards the summit on Musgrave St. to Moores Creek Rd. Turn right on Norman Rd., and then left on Frenchville Rd, which winds up to the top. Open dawn-dusk. No camping.)*

FARM-STAY. Myella Farm-Stay ❺ offers an all-inclusive farm-stay with horse and motorbike riding, 4WD tours, cow milking, and, of course, campfires. *(125km southwest of Rockhampton. ☎ 4998 1290. 3-days, 2-nights $240; includes buffet meals, all activities, and return transport from Rocky.)* **Henderson Park Farm-stay** is a bit less activity oriented. You can join in with whatever the ranch is working on, but most guests simply relax and take in the stunning scenery. Two beautiful cabins, located on Hedlow Creek, include linen, laundry, cooking utensils, BBQ, campfire, and first morning breakfast basket. *(25km north of Rockhampton. ☎ 4934 2794. Cabins sleep up to 5 people. Two adults $100, each additional adult $10. Free pick-up from Rocky on request.)*

CARNARVON GORGE NATIONAL PARK. This rugged national park is rich with Aboriginal rock art, deep pools, and soaring sandstone cliffs. The gorges, however, are the main attraction. Cool temperatures make March through November the best time to visit, but be aware that night temperatures fall below freezing. The 35 national park camping sites are only available during Australian school holidays. *(500km southwest of Rockhampton and Gladstone on Bruce Hwy. For more info, pick up a map in the tourist office or contact the ranger ☎ 4984 4505. Book camping permits by calling ☎ 3227 8198.)* **Takarakka ❶,** 4km from the park, has sites and cabins. *(☎ 4984 4535; www.takarakka.com.au. Sites $8 per person, powered for 2 $22; cabins from $65. Linen $6.)* The luxurious **Wilderness Lodge ❺** *(☎ 4984 4503; www.carnarvon-gorge.com),* 3km from the park, offers self-contained units starting at $170.

📷🎵 NIGHTLIFE & ENTERTAINMENT

For a pint of Guinness ($6.20), live rock music (Th-Sa nights), and some Irish grub (mains $16-23), good laddies and lassies hit **O'Dowd's,** 100 Williams St. Every second Friday night, join the Guinness club and drink as much as you can for $25. (☎ 4927 0344; www.odowds.com.au. Open daily 8am-1am, or later when there's a crowd.) If you're looking for a more traditional nightclub, **Strutters,** on the corner of East St. and William St., is the place to go. On W and F, a $22 drink card will get you a whopping 20 basic drinks at the bar—be sure to bring plenty of friends. (☎ 4922 2882. $5 cover F, Sa. Open W-Th 8pm-3am, F-Sa 8pm-5am.) The sports-themed **Stadium Nightclub,** on the corner of Quay and William St. in the Heritage Tavern, has 20 TVs to ensure that you won't miss a moment of the action. It also bumps with Top-40 dancing late into the night. (☎ 4927 6996. Open Su and W-Sa 8pm-5am. Cover F-Sa after 11pm $5.) The **Criterion Hotel,** 150 Quay St., stands as an early meeting place and has three bars and live music Thursday through Saturday. (☎ 4922 1225. Open daily 10am-3am.)

GREAT KEPPEL ISLAND   ☎ 07

The most developed of the largely untouched Keppel Island Group, Great Keppel boasts unbelievably clear waters, 17 beaches with fine snorkeling right off-shore, and a brilliant night sky streaked by shooting stars. Spectacular coral reefs nearby make Keppel a favorite of divers as well. Budget accommodations abound, but the island's posh resort doesn't mind the odd backpacker crashing its nightlife or taking its catamaran out for a lazy afternoon. For many visitors, it's enough to just curl up on any of the beaches and seize a taste of paradise.

⌐ TRANSPORTATION

From Rockhampton, it only takes a bus transfer (40min.) and a ferry ride (30min.) to reach your own slice of heaven. Check with your accommodations to see if they can arrange these for you, otherwise, call the companies directly.

Young's Coaches (Route #20) runs to both ferries from the Kern Arcade, on Bolsover St. between Denham and William St., Rockhampton. (☎4922 3813. M-F 11 per day, Sa-Su 6 per day; $7.50 one-way.) **Rothery's Coaches** also leaves from Kern Arcade to meet both ferries. By booking ahead, you can arrange free pick-up at your accommodation. (☎4922 4320. Daily 8, 10:30am, and 1:30pm; $16.50 return, students $13.50, children $8.25.)

Freedom Flyer Ferry leaves from Keppel Bay Marina, Rosslyn Bay. (☎4933 6244. 9am, noon, 3pm. Return 10am, 2pm 4pm. $32 return, students $27, children $16.) They also run day cruises starting at $49. **Keppel Tourist Services** runs a ferry to the island from the Great Keppel Island Transit Centre, Rosslyn Bay. (☎4933 6744 or 1800 356 744; www.keppelbaymarina.com.au. Daily 7:30, 9:15, 11:30am, 3:30pm. Return 8:15am, 2, 4:30pm. $30 return, concessions $22, children $15.)

For drivers, follow the signs from Yeppon for the Rosslyn Bay Marina. Free parking is available at the Ferry terminal. **Great Keppel Island Security Carpark** (☎4933 6670), on the Scenic Hwy. just before the turn-off for Rosslyn Bay, offers a secured lot and a courtesy bus to the harbor ($6.50 per day, covered $8).

The ferries let passengers out on Fisherman's Beach, the main beach. Parallel to the beach is the island's main (and only) drag, the **Yellow Brick Road,** a pathway that runs the entire commercial strip of Great Keppel, a five-minute stroll.

⌐ ACCOMMODATIONS

When considering accommodations, look at the big picture—many accommodations on the island offer packages that include bus and ferry transfers and rooms on the mainland. Camping is not allowed on Great Keppel but is increasingly possible on nearby Keppel Group islands.

▨ **Great Keppel Island Holiday Village** (☎4939 8655 or 1800 180 235; www.gkiholidayvillage.com.au). A friendly, relaxed throwback to the way the island used to be. Co-ed dorm rooms are average, but stay includes free use of snorkel gear and 4WD drop-offs in the middle of the island every other day for hikers. Also organizes motorized canoe trips ($20) and camping packages on nearby Middle Island $30. Great kitchen and BBQ, laundry. Check-out 9am. Reception 8:30am-6:30pm. Quiet time 9:30pm, lights out by 10:30pm. Dorms $27; tents with a wooden double bed $60. Cabins for 2 with shower $100, each extra person up to 4 $15. ❷

Backpackers Village (☎4927 5288 or 4933 6416; yhagreatkeppelisland@bigpond.com). A huge new kitchen and common room, as well as bright, pleasant cabins, make for a well-run stay; perfect for families. A path-connected, plant-surrounded smattering of "safari tents" sits cozily out back. Reception 7am-1pm and 3-5pm; check-in at ferry on the mainland. Dorms $21.10; twins and doubles $47. Cabins $29.50-38.50 per person. YHA. ❷

Keppel Haven (☎4933 6744 or 1800 356 744). Army-style "safari tents" make a tent village, while bunkhouses and cabins provide more comfortable, expensive stays. The **Haven Bar** is one of two bars on the island (open daily 10am-9:30pm; Happy Hour 5:30-7pm). Very few showers and toilets in tent village. Laundry and BBQ. Key deposit $10. Reception 7:30am-5pm. Checkout 9am. Book through Keppel Tourist Services. Tents 3- or 4-share $18; singles $28; twins and doubles $40. Bunkhouses with linen doubles $80; quads $100. Self-contained cabins for 2 $120. ❷

🎭 🍴 FOOD AND NIGHTLIFE

Food is expensive; stock up prior to departure at **Woody's Supermarket,** 18 James St., Yeppoon. (Open daily 6am-9pm.) **Island Pizza ❸** serves tasty but pricey pizza. Small pizza from $14.90, large from $22.90. (☎4939 4699. Open Su and Sa 12:30-2pm and 6-9pm, Tu-F 6-9pm. Cash only.) For drinks, check out **Splash Bar,** in the Contiki Resort. The connected **Salt Nightclub** rages late into the night, especially during the warm summer months. (☎4939 5044. Live music F night and Su afternoon. Open daily noon-midnight, until 2am when nightclub is closed. Nightclub hours vary, check at the bar. Occasional $5 cover.)

🎿 ACTIVITIES

Seventeen beaches define the perimeter of Keppel; all of civilization is within an eight-minute stroll. The calm surf is perfect for swimming and snorkeling. **Shelving Beach,** a mere 30min. jaunt from the resort, heading away from the hostels, has the best and most accessible snorkeling. **Monkey Beach,** another 20min. further, also has great snorkeling, though the reef can be rough in southerly winds. Look for harmless shovelnose sharks against the rock wall. **Clam Bay,** on the island's south side, has the most vibrant coral, but the hike out is at least 4hr. return. With snorkeling, plan for an all day trek. **Long Beach,** a 35min. walk past the airstrip, exists in splendid isolation (1.8km one-way). Inland walks begin on the main track that leads from Contiki's watersports area. The difficult hike to 🏔**Mt. Wyndham** rewards with unparalleled panoramic views (2½hr., 7km return). Other walks go to the **Old Homestead** (1½hr.; 5.6km return) and the **lighthouse** (15.4km return). Trail junctures on inland tracks are not well posted, so keep your eyes peeled and bring a map. The *Souvenir Chart of Great Keppel Island* map is helpful for bush walks (available for 50¢ at the Keppel Tourist Services ferry terminal on the mainland; note that it costs $2 on the island).

The **Beach Shed** (☎4925 0624; open daily 10:15am-4pm), at Keppel Haven, has snorkel gear ($10 per day), and kayaks ($10 per hr.). The **Keppel Island Dive Centre** (☎4939 5022), up the beach from the Beach Shed, offers dive trips for the certified ($77, with own gear $55) and the uninitiated ($99); tag along and snorkel for $33.

The resort certainly offers plenty to do if lazing around in the sun isn't your cup of tea. To traverse the water with a bit of speed or sport, visit the friendly fellas at the **watersports area,** just before the resort. (☎4939 5044 ext. 4685. Open daily 10am-4pm.) They offer everything from high-speed banana rides ($12) to catamaran/windsurfer hire ($15 per hr.) to waterskiing or wakeboarding ($25 for 10min.) to parasailing ($70; open daily 9:30am-4:30pm). **Prodive** can get you under the crystal clear water. (Intro dive, $99, certified dive $99, 4 day open water course $395. Open daily 9am-5pm.)

For adventure seekers, activities include **Tandem Skydive,** with beach landings. (From $362; the higher the drop, the higher the price.) Also at Caps, the catamaran **Euphoria** runs a three-hour sail and snorkel trip as well as a sunset cruise (both $45). For a slower pace, hop on a dromedary and enjoy **camel riding** on the beach ($40 per 30min. or $60 for 1hr. sunset ride).

NEAR GREAT KEPPEL ISLAND: KEPPEL GROUP

The isolated and largely deserted islands in the Keppel Group invite exploration by adventuresome travelers. Coconut-infested **Pumpkin Island** offers beautiful vegetation, coral, and white beaches. A maximum of 28 people on the island choose from the five cabins at the **Pumpkin Island Eco Resort ❷** for up to five people; bring your own linen and food. (☎4939 4413 or 4939 2431. Cabins $154.) The island also has

QUEENSLAND

toilets, showers, BBQ, drinking water, and plenty of deserted beaches. For transport, call **Freedom Flyer Ferry Cats** (☎4933 6244) or a water-taxi (☎4933 6133). These are not cheap (ferry $175 for 2, taxi $260-300 return on a boat that can carry 6-10). **Middle Island, Humpy Island,** and **North Keppel** also offer camping. Permits are available at the QPWS in Rosslyn Bay, adjacent to the Tourist Services office.

WHITSUNDAY COAST

Stretching from Mackay to the small town of Bowen, situated right above Airlie Beach, the well-deserved claim to fame of this coastal stretch is undoubtedly the Whitsunday Islands. Experiencing the islands is a must for any passerby in this area: spend a few relaxing days sailing on the clear waters, explore the world underneath the water, and lounge on secluded patches of white sand marooned amid the tropical waters. Accessed by Airlie Beach, near Proserpine, the Whitsundays draw a crowd but still offer ample opportunities to enjoy the solitude so characteristic of northern Queensland.

MACKAY   ☎07

Emerging out of miles and miles of sugar cane, the town of Mackay (mick-EYE; pop. 70,000) serves as a convenient gateway to both the inland's rainforested national parks and the isolated islands offshore. Both within an hour's drive from the city, Eungella and Cape Hillsborough National Parks offer great hiking tracks and distinctive wildlife.

▐ TRANSPORTATION

Trains: The **train station** (☎4952 7418) is about 5km south of town on Connors Rd. There is no public transport from the station and a taxi costs about $10. Purchase tickets at the station (open M-F 9am-4:30pm) or in town. Trains run less frequently and take longer than buses. Lockers $2.

Buses: Mackay Bus Terminal, 141 Victoria St. (☎4944 2144). **Premier** and **McCafferty's/Greyhound** buses run to: Airlie Beach (1¾-2hr.; Premier 1 per day, McCafferty's/Greyhound 6 per day; Premier $19, McCafferty's $34); Brisbane (14hr., 1/7 per day, $109/$127); Bundaberg (8¼-9¾hr., 1/3 per day, $66/$98); Cairns (9½-12hr., 1/7 per day, $95/$102); Hervey Bay (10¾hr., 1/6 per day, $77/$113); Maroochydore via Noosa (12hr., 1/3 per day, $97/$124); and Rockhampton (4¼hr., 1/7 per day, $33/$52). Student and YHA discounts. Ticketing office open M-F 7:30am-5:30pm, Sa 9am-12:30pm; tickets can also be purchased at station coffee shop open 24hr.

Taxis: Mackay Taxi (24hr. ☎13 10 08).

Car Rental: Europcar, 6 Endeavor St. (☎4957 5606 or 1300 131 390), starts at $39 per day and offers courtesy pick-up. **Avis** (☎13 63 33 or 4951 1266) is located at the airport. **Thrifty** (☎4942 8755 or 1800 818 050), at the corner of Bruce Hwy. and Sands Rd., offers courtesy pick-up from airport.

⛨ ▐ ORIENTATION & PRACTICAL INFORMATION

Mackay's city center is oriented on the southern bank of the Pioneer River. **River Street** runs along the waterfront, and the town's main drag, **Victoria Street,** runs parallel one street away from the river. Nightlife and restaurants line **Sydney** and **Wood Street,** which run perpendicular to Victoria St. The **Bruce Highway** comes into the west side of town and exits to **Gordon Street,** the third street from the river, parallel

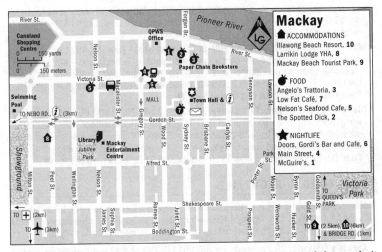

Mackay

▲ ACCOMMODATIONS
Illawong Beach Resort, **10**
Larrikin Lodge YHA, **8**
Mackay Beach Tourist Park, **9**

● FOOD
Angelo's Trattoria, **3**
Low Fat Café, **7**
Nelson's Seafood Cafe, **5**
The Spotted Dick, **2**

★ NIGHTLIFE
Doors, Gordi's Bar and Cafe, **6**
Main Street, **4**
McGuire's, **1**

to Victoria St. As the Bruce Hwy. enters town and curves toward the south, it changes its name to **Nebo Road** and continues onward to the major accommodations and the tourist office.

Tourist Office: Mackay Tourism Office, 320 Nebo Rd. (☎4952 2677; www.mackayregion.com), 3km southwest of the city center. Open M-F 8:30am-5pm, Sa-Su 9am-4pm. A small **Information Booth** (☎4951 4803) is located in the old Town Hall on Sydney St. Open M-F 8:30am-5pm.

Parks Office: Queensland Parks and Wildlife Service (☎4944 7800; www.epa.qld.gov.au), at River and Wood St. National park info, maps, and camping permits for the Cumberland Islands ($4 per person per night). Open M-F 8:30am-5pm.

Currency Exchange: Banks and 24hr. **ATMs** line Victoria St. between Gregory and Brisbane St. All offer traveler's check and cash exchange for a $5-7 fee and are open M-Th 9:30am-4pm, F 9:30am-5pm.

Internet: Hong Kong Importers, 128 Victoria St. (☎4953 3188). $5 per hr. Open M-F 8:45am-5:15pm, Sa-Su 9am-1pm.

Library: (☎4957 1787), behind the Civic Centre on Gordon St. Open M, W, F 9am-5pm, Tu 10am-6pm, Th 10am-8pm, Sa 9am-3pm.

Market: Victoria Street Markets feature arts and crafts. Open Su 8:30am-12:30pm.

Police: 57-59 Sydney St. (☎4968 3444), between Victoria and Gordon St. Open 24hr.

Post Office: 69 Sydney St. (☎13 13 18), between Victoria and Gordon St. Open M-F 8am-5:30pm. **Postal Code:** 4740.

▌ ACCOMMODATIONS

Because Mackay is not considered a prime backpacking destination, hostels are scarce. Budget motels line the streets of the city center and along Nebo Rd. Additionally, several caravan parks lie on the outskirts of town.

Larrikin Lodge YHA, 32 Peel St. (☎4951 3728; larrikin@mackay.net.au), located a quick 10min. walk from the city center. The small kitchen/TV area at Mackay's only hostel creates a friendly atmosphere. 10-person dorms remain unlocked here at all times, so learn to trust fellow travelers or grab a locker. Day tours to area national parks. Laundry $2. Internet $4 per hour. Reception 7-10am and 4:30-9pm. Dorms $20, YHA $17; twins $23/$17. YHA. ❷

Mackay Beach Tourist Park, 8 Petrie St., Illawong Beach (☎4957 4021 or 1800 645 111), 3km south of the city center, with the beach as a backyard. Great amenities, including pool, camp kitchen, small gym, games room, and wandering peacocks. Reception 7am-7pm. Sites for 2 $15.40, powered $21; cabins for 2 $75, ensuite $83; "camp-o-tels" with 2 beds and a table $22. ❷

Illawong Beach Resort, 77 Illawong Dr. (☎4957 8427 or 1800 656 944; www.illawong-beach.com.au), 6km south of the city center on the beachfront. Spacious, motel-style self-contained villas with 2 bedrooms, A/C, and TV for an upscale sojourn. Pool, lake, tennis courts, and licensed restaurant. Buffet breakfast included. Reception 7am-6pm. Doubles with garden view $110, ocean view $115; extra person $16. ❺

⬛🍴 FOOD & NIGHTLIFE

Woolworths **supermarket** is in the Caneland Shopping Centre, moving inland down Victoria St. (☎4951 2288. Open M-F 8am-9pm, Sa 8am-5pm.) A Coles **supermarket** is on Sydney St., opposite the post office. (Open M-F 8am-9pm, Sa 8am-5pm.)

Angelo's Trattoria, 29 Sydney St. (☎4953 5111). One of the most popular restaurants in town and serves excellent pasta ($14-18) as well as other Mediterranean fare for around $20-25. Open daily noon-2pm and 6pm-late. ❸

Nelson's Seafood Cafe, 171 Victoria St. (☎4953 5453). A favorite of locals and travelers alike for cheap fresh seafood to fillet at home or eat-in. Try the famous $5 fish 'n' chips. Open Su-Th 10am-7:30pm, F-Sa 10am-8pm. ❶

Low Fat Cafe: Pure and Natural Mackay ❶ (☎4957 6136), in the NAB Plaza across from the police station. Serves up tasty low fat and vegetarian options for breakfast and lunch and also has a variety of healthy snacks that lack calories, but not taste. Open M-F 7:30am-3:30pm, Sa 8am-2pm.

The Spotted Dick ❷, 2 Sydney St. (☎4957 2368). A unique eatery, with wacky decor and crazy cuisine. Meals run $9-19, and wood-fired pizzas are $11. W karaoke; Th-Sa house band. Happy Hour M-F 4:30-6:30pm. Open M-Sa 11am-late, Su 11am-8pm. Kitchen open daily noon-2pm and 6-9pm.

Main Street, 148 Victoria St. (☎4957 7737) One of the most popular nightspots. DJ-hosted party madness rages around pool tables and two bars. F-Sa cover $5. $2.50 basic spirits 10pm-midnight. Open W-Su 10pm-3am.

Doors, 85 Victoria St. (☎4951 2611). Drink specials, a big screen with not-so-subliminal messages like "take home someone ugly tonite," and a great dance pit make for a sweaty night of drunken fun. Downstairs, the more casual set at **Gordi's Bar and Cafe** spills out onto the street. Doors open Tu-Sa 8:30pm-3am; cover F-Sa $5. Gordi's open daily 9:30pm-3am; live entertainment nightly.

McGuire's, 17 Wood St. (☎4957 7464). Attracts a crowd of all ages for their cheap jugs of Toohey's New ($6) and live entertainment Wednesday through Sunday. Open M-W 9am-1am, Th-Sa 9am-2am, Su 10am-midnight.

👁🎯 SIGHTS & ACTIVITIES

While most of Mackay's attractions lie in its surroundings, the town does offer a few sights of interest. Pick up the tourist office's free guide, *A Heritage Walk in Mackay,* to direct you to the historical and cultural hotspots. Don't miss **Queen's Park,** on Goldsmith St. just north of Victoria Park, where the lovely **Orchid Gardens** overflow with delightful flowers. The **Mackay Entertainment Centre,** next door to the library on Gordon St., is your one-stop spot for drama, comedy, and concerts. (☎4957 1777 or 1800 646 574. Open M-F 9am-5pm, Sa 10am-1pm; also 1½hr. before shows.) The Centre also hosts the **Mackay Festival of Arts** (www.festival-mackay.org.au) in July, a two-week celebration with concerts, fashion parades, food fairs and comedy shows. **Farleigh Sugar Mill** offers two-hour tours during the sugar-crushing season that break down the history of the sugar industry. (No public transport; take the Bruce Hwy. 9km north from the city towards Proserpine, then turn right at Childlow St. ☎4963 2700. Tours late June-Nov. M-F 1pm. $15, children $8, families $35.) **Pro Dive Mackay,** 44 Evans Ave., leads diving and snorkeling trips around Keswick Island. (☎4951 1150. Snorkeling $139, children $114; PADI dive courses $235-395 depending on numbers of boat dives.)

NEAR MACKAY: BRAMPTON & CARLISLE ISLANDS

Like Heron Island to the south, Brampton Island is not that easily accessible to daytrippers, campers, or anyone loath to shell out $212 per person to stay a night at the luxury island resort. Eleven kilometers of National Park **walking tracks** over dunes, past rocky headlands, and through eucalypt forests rewards those who make the journey.

Although only resort accommodation is available on Brampton, nearby Carlisle Island has a **camping ❶** area with toilet, BBQ, and lots of shady trees but no walking trails. Pick up a trail map and arrange camping permits through the Parks office in Mackay ($4 per person per night). If the guests-only boat transfer to **Brampton Island Resort ❺** (☎4951 4499) is not full, you may be able to grab a spot ($54 return) and arrange a $10 return boat transfer to Carlisle. At low tide, Carlisle is accessible from Brampton via a sand bridge.

MACKAY TO EUNGELLA

To reach Eungella, follow along the Bruce Hwy (Nebo Rd.) heading south. Turn right onto Peak Downs Hwy. (Archibald Rd.) just past the tourist office and follow it until you reach a junction with Pioneer Valley Rd., where Eungella State Park is signposted. The road will stretch through acre upon acre of sugar cane fields before steeply winding up and over the Clarke Range to Eungella.

After passing the town of Marian on Eungella Rd., the **Illawong Sanctuary** is 4km past **Mirani**, 44km from Mackay. Hand-feed the 'roos and wonder at the peculiar ice cream-eating emu. (☎4959 1777. Open daily 9:30am-5pm. $12, children $6; also contact for tours to area national parks, 3 days starting at $145, or **accommodation ❹** at the sanctuary, $45 per person.) Farther along the Pioneer Valley Rd. is **The Pinnacle Hotel ❶,** an eatery where you can grab one of Wendy's famous homemade pies and a beer. (☎4958 5207. Pie $3.50. Open daily 10am-late.)

EUNGELLA NATIONAL PARK

Eighty kilometers west of Mackay on Pioneer Valley Rd. is the 52,000-hectare **Eungella National Park,** a range of steep rainforest-covered slopes and deep misty valleys. At Eungella, the "land where clouds lie low over the mountains," ten walking trails lead to spectacular hilltop and creekside views. The mountains—natural barriers between this park and other swaths of rainforest in Queensland—trap clouds, causing high precipitation. Red cedars, palms, and giant ferns coat many slopes, and platypi splash in the ravines. Over the years, Eungella has seen dramatic changes of focus—it has housed gold prospectors, sugar cane harvesters, loggers, and dairy cows, and in 1941, it was declared a National Park.

Walking tracks are in two sections of the park: the **Finch Hatton Gorge** and **Eungella/Broken River.** Trail maps are at the QPWS office in Mackay or the Ranger Station at Broken River (☎4958 4552). Although no public transportation runs to Eungella, the park is easily reached via car. Ambitious dayhikers can walk to the river and beyond, but be wary of the long trek back along the highway. Behind the Eungella Chalet, the 1.5km **Pine Grove Circuit** forks at 700m into the excellent **Cedar Grove Track** (3km; 30min.), which winds past stately red cedars to a roadside picnic area and short lookout track. Two hundred meters down the road from the picnic area is the Palm Grove trailhead (1.8km), which gives you the option of continuing on to Broken River via the **Clarke Range Track** (6.5km; 1¾hr.). Five kilometers on Eungella Rd. from the Chalet, you'll cross **Broken River,** with an excellent ▨**platypus-viewing platform,** a picnic area, a **campground ❶** with toilets and hot showers ($4 per person), as well as a ranger station. (☎4958 4552. Open M-F 8:30am-5pm.) Several additional trails lead from Broken River.

For an organized tour of the park, **Jungle Johno's Bush, Beach, and Beyond Tours** is led by farmer-cum-tour-guide Wayne, who is deeply knowledgeable in topics from horticulture to folklore. He'll take you to Finch Hatton Gorge and Broken River. (☎4959 1822 or 4951 3728. $75 full-day, $59 half-day.) Col Adamson's **Reeforest Adventure Tours** takes daytrips to Eungella and Cape Hillsborough. (☎4953 1000. $95; pensioners, VIP, and YHA $85; children $53.)

FINCH HATTON GORGE. After the Pinnacle Hotel is a well-marked turn-off to beautiful **Finch Hatton Gorge** (10km from Pioneer Valley Rd.), distinct from the other accessible regions of the park by its low elevation. Contact the Hatton Gorge ranger (☎4958 4552) or check with locals for the latest on road conditions in the area, as the narrow track dips through several creeks that are often too full to cross after heavy rains.

On the dirt road to Finch Hatton Gorge is the rustic ▨**Platypus Bush Camp ❶.** Open air huts, abundant wildlife, and adjacent creek (ideal for an afternoon dip) afford an authentic Aussie experience that you won't find at cookie-cutter resorts. There's also an outdoor kitchen, creekside hot tubs forged from river rocks, and a comfy enclosure surrounding a woodburning stove—the perfect venue for campsongs and traveler's tales. For those weary of sleeping outdoors, an old touring bus has been converted into sleeping quarters.

Finch Hatton's one hiking track leaves from the picnic area at the end of the Gorge Rd. The trail to **Wheel of Fire Falls** (4.2km; 1hr.) follows rapids as they cascade down the rocky riverbed; the last kilometer is a steep stair-climb. To see the rainforest from above, make a booking with **Forest Flying,** which suspends visitors from a self-propelling treetop cable. (pick-up from Gorge accommodation or kiosk. ☎4958 3359; www.forestflying.com. 2-3hr. depending on group size. $45, children $30.)

EUNGELLA TOWNSHIP. Continuing on Pioneer Valley Rd. 20km past the turn-off for Finch Hatton Gorge is **Eungella township.** Be careful on the road to Eungella, as it climbs 800m in just 3km; take the turns slowly. At the top of the hill in Eungella township is the historic **Eungella Chalet ❸.** Overlooking the vast Pioneer Valley, this mountaintop resort has a large restaurant, swimming pool, extensive gardens, and breathtaking views of the valley below. (☎4958 4509. Chalmer St., cabins $100-200.) Just past the chalet on the right is **The Hideaway Cafe ❶** provides a scenic backdrop for coffee and a strudel. (☎4958 4533. Open daily 8am-4pm.) **Kelly's Coach House and Gallery ❷,** across from the chalet, has comfortable dining around the woodstove and chatty hosts. (☎4958 4518. Breakfast 7:30-10am, lunch 11:30am, dinner 6:30pm.)

CAPE HILLSBOROUGH NATIONAL PARK

A coastal peninsula north of Mackay, Cape Hillsborough National Park contrasts sandy beaches with rugged pine- and eucalypt-covered hills. Rocky outcrops protrude from the tropical rainforest where kangaroos, lizards, and scrub turkeys roam. Although not as impressive as Eungella, the 816-hectare park makes for a good daytrip from Mackay. Take the Bruce Hwy. 20km northwest from the city to the right turn-off for Seaforth Rd.; turn right after another 20km on Seaforth Rd. to reach the Cape. The road to the Cape ends at the **Cape Hillsborough Tourist Resort ❶**, with beachfront access and a pool, BBQ, restaurant, and general store. (☎ 4959 0152; www.capehillsboroughresort.com.au. Reception 8am-10pm. Sites $12.50, powered $18; Rooms $39-79. Prices increase during holidays; book ahead.) Adjacent to Cape Hillsborough is the magnificent **Smalley's Beach** on a short unsealed road to Bali Bay. Its **campsite ❶** has toilets, water, and the beach as its front yard, but no showers. ($4 per person; self-register at the campsite.) Another camping option in the area is the pleasant **Haliday Hide-away ❶**, a budget caravan park at Haliday Bay. Follow the signs off the Cape Hillsborough road. (☎ 4959 0367. Sites $10, powered $12; budget cabins in summer $30, winter $25; self-contained cabins from $35. Cash only.)

Five short walking trails are concentrated on the eastern tip of the Cape. For more info on tracks, pick up a map at the parks office in Mackay, or peruse maps posted at the resort or the seldom-staffed ranger station (☎ 4959 0410), in the picnic area at the end of the cape. The **Diversity Boardwalk** (1.2km), at the park's entrance, is an aptly-named jaunt through mangrove of many varieties, an area of open woodland with grasstrees, and an Aboriginal midden heap (a massive pile of shells). After an initial steep ascent, the **Andrews Point Track** (2.6km one-way; 45min.) follows the ridge around the point, offering five spectacular lookouts and sea breezes. Return via the same track or along the beach, provided the tide is out. At low tide, the rocky beaches of **Wedge Island** become accessible to intrepid explorers, but there are no official tracks on the island. The **Beachcomber Cove Track** (1.6km) provides great views from the ridge before ending at the cove.

AIRLIE BEACH   ☎ 07

Airlie was nothing but mudflats until a developer's proposal was turned down by the Shire Council in nearby Bowen (see p. 406) and was moved to the oceanside. Equipped with truckloads of Bowen sand, he put the "Beach" in Airlie. The spot was an upscale tourist destination until a pilot strike in the 1980s stalled Queensland's tourist trade. In a bid for survival, the resorts turned budget, and enjoyed the ensuing business boom. Together with the variety of activities offered on the nearby waters of the Whitsunday Islands and the Great Barrier Reef, the town has become the biggest backpacker draw between Brisbane and Cairns.

▣ TRANSPORTATION

Trains: The rail station is in Proserpine. **Whitsunday Transit** (24hr. ☎ 4946 1800) picks up arriving train passengers and runs down Shute Harbour Rd., stopping in the center of Airlie and at some accommodations; timetables available all over town.

Buses: Travel offices and most hostel desks book transport. **McCafferty's/Greyhound** (☎ 13 14 99) drops off at the end of the Esplanade; accommodations offer courtesy pick-ups, but most hostels are in walking distance. Prices are listed as non-discounted, but ISIC/VIP/YHA will save you up to $15 on some tickets. **Buses** run daily to: Bowen (1¼hr., 5 per day, $26); Brisbane (18hr., 6 per day, $145); Bundaberg (12hr., 3 per day, $116); Cairns (10hr., 5 per day, $79); Gladstone (9hr., 5 per day, $102); Hervey

Bay (13hr., 4 per day, $130); Mackay (2hr., 6 per day, $35); Maroochydore (16hr., 3 per day, $130); Mission Beach (8hr., 3 per day, $83); Noosa (15hr., 3 per day, $137); Rockhampton (7hr., 6 per day, $70); and Townsville (4hr., 5 per day, $50).

Local Transportation: Whitsunday Transit (☎4946 1800) runs between Cannonvale and Shute Harbour at least every 30min. daily 6am-6:40pm, stopping in front of Oceania Dive. 10-trip ticket $19. Airlie Beach to Shute Harbour $4.10. Night service Th-Sa 7-11pm. **Whitsunday Taxi** (☎13 10 08) serves the whole area.

⚹ 🛈 ORIENTATION & PRACTICAL INFORMATION

The turn-off for Airlie Beach is at Proserpine, off the Bruce Hwy.; the road passes through Cannonvale and on to Airlie Beach (26km). The main road becomes **Shute Harbour Road,** running parallel to the water as it nears Airlie; it has most of the town's accommodations and restaurants. Upon entering the town from the Bruce Hwy. turn-off, you'll pass Abel Point Marina; at the opposite end, the road veers left to the **Esplanade** or continues straight towards Shute Harbour (8km). Picnic tables and BBQs line the beach area parallel to Shute Harbour Rd. Sunbathers laze on the newly created beach or on the grass around **Airlie Lagoon.**

Tourist Office: City Tourist Bureau, 348 Shute Harbour Rd. (☎4946 6673). Also serves as the Whitsunday Regional Tourist Bureau.

Budget Travel Office: One on every street corner. Some of the hostel tour bookings offer free rooms if you book sailing trips with them. The office at 259 Shute Harbour Rd. conducts tours and also offers **Internet** ($1 per hour).

Parks Office: National and Marine Parks Authority (☎4946 7022), on the corner of Mandalay St. and Shute Harbour Rd., 2km out of town toward Shute Harbour. Info on camping and national parks. Open M-F 9am-5pm, Sa 9am-1pm.

Currency Exchange: Commonwealth Bank (☎4946 7433) charges a flat $10 fee for traveler's checks and foreign exchange. Open M-Th 9:30am-4pm, F 9:30am-5pm. There's an **ATM** there, as well as at **ANZ Bank,** next to the post office.

Police: (☎4946 6445), on Altman St.

Medical Services: Whitsunday Medical Centre, 400 Shute Harbour Rd. (24hr. ☎4946 6275). Open M-F 7:30am-5:30pm, Sa 9am-1pm. Dive medicals $35. **Whitsunday Doctors Service** (☎4946 6241), on the corner of Shute Harbour Rd. and Broadwater Ave. Open M-F 8am-5pm, Sa 11am-1pm. Dive medicals $35.

Post Office: (☎4946 6515), in the Whitsunday Village Shopping Center on Shute Harbour Rd. Open M-F 9am-5pm, Sa 9am-11am. **Postal Code:** 4802.

🏠 ACCOMMODATIONS

Airlie's cornucopia of budget lodgings barely keep pace with backpacker demand, so book ahead. Ask about deals if booking tours through hostels; some offer free stays. The nearby Whitsundays have cheap **camping ❶**, but space is limited. Try **Koala Beach Resort ❶** (☎1800 800 421), on Shute Harbour Rd., or **Island Gateway Caravan Resort ❶** (☎4946 6228), 1km past town on Shute Harbour Rd.

🏅 Airlie Waterfront Backpackers (☎1800 089 000), on the Esplanade. Very clean with a quiet atmosphere. Multiple kitchens and large balconies that have great views of Airlie Bay. Internet $4 per hour. Reception 7am-8pm. Dorms $20; 3- and 4-bed $25 per person; doubles $55. ❷

Koala Beach Resort (☎4946 6001 or 1800 800 421; whitwand@whitsunday.net.au), on Shute Harbour Rd. Very different from other hostels in town, with rooms resembling resort cabins. This edition of the famed chain pulls in a varied crowd with their various

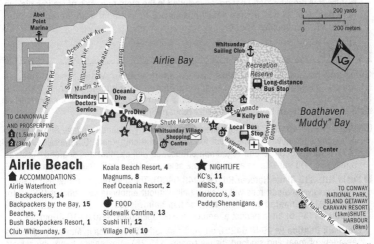

Airlie Beach

▲ ACCOMMODATIONS
Airlie Waterfront
  Backpackers, 14
Backpackers by the Bay, 15
  Beaches, 7
Bush Backpackers Resort, 1
Club Whitsunday, 5

Koala Beach Resort, 4
Magnums, 8
Reef Oceania Resort, 2

🍴 FOOD
Sidewalk Cantina, 13
Sushi Hi!, 12
Village Deli, 10

★ NIGHTLIFE
KC's, 11
M@SS, 9
Morocco's, 3
Paddy Shenanigans, 6

TO CONWAY
NATIONAL PARK,
ISLAND GETAWAY
CARAVAN RESORT
(1km)SHUTE
HARBOUR
(8km)

room options. 4-bed huts have a small kitchen, bath, and satellite TV. Pool, volleyball court, laundry, and Internet. Meal discounts next door at Morocco's. The only campsite in town. Reception 7am-8:30pm. Sites $10, extra person $5; dorms $16-20; twins and doubles $60; quads $80. VIP. ❷

Backpackers by the Bay, 12 Hermitage Dr. (☎4946 7267 or 1800 646 994), 650m from town toward Shute Harbour. 4-bed bunk-style rooms, chill atmosphere, and amenities galore. BBQ, laundry, pool, game room, Internet, free nightly activities, and a sweet view of the bay. Free pick-up and bus to town. Happy Hour daily 5:30-6:30pm (beers $2.50). Reception 7am-7:30pm. Dorms $20; twins and doubles $48. VIP/YHA. ❷

Club Whitsunday (☎4946 6182 or 1800 678 755), on Shute Harbour Rd. A friendly hostel where you don't have to compromise location for comfort. 4-bed dorm rooms with walk-through shared bathrooms. Fan, A/C, and TV. Free big breakfast daily 7-10am. Free luggage storage. Kitchen and laundry. Internet $4 per hr. Reception 7am-9pm. Dorms $21; doubles $50. ❷

Bush Village Backpackers Resort, 2 St. Martins Rd., Cannonvale (☎4946 6177 or 1800 809 256), 1½km out of town. The ultimate in cleanliness and warm hospitality. Cabins with kitchens and modern bath line a driveway that leads to the pool, porch, TV lounge, and videos. Continental breakfast included. Free shuttle to town 6:30am-11:30pm. Reception 7am-9pm. Dorms $22, members $20; doubles $48-68. ❷

Magnums (☎1800 624 634; www.magnums.com.au), on Shute Harbour Rd. in the center of Airlie Beach. Definitely the party hostel in town, with foam parties on F at attached nightclub, **M@ss** (see p. 404). All rooms are newly furnished and clean. Ask for a double for a more isolated, quiet atmosphere. Reception 7am-10pm. Dorms from $12; doubles $37. ❶

Beaches, 356-62 Shute Harbour Rd. (☎4946 6244 or 1800 636 630; www.beaches.com.au). One of the central party spots. Dorms in former motel rooms with balcony, kitchenette, bath, TV, and fan. Secured parking, laundry, game room, spacious kitchen, and Internet. Free night with overnight tour or dive course booking. Reception 7am-8pm. Dorms $22; doubles and twins $45-50. VIP. ❶

Reef Oceania Resort, a.k.a. **Reef O's,** 147 Shute Harbour Rd., Cannonvale (☎4946 6137 or 1800 800 795; info@reeforesort.com), located some 3km from town. Pool, volleyball court, free afternoon movies and popcorn, ping-pong, BBQ, bistro, live music

QUEENSLAND

nightly, free breakfast, and bar are all included in the room rate. Also offers free pick-up from bus stop, as well as free hourly bus service to and from town. Reception 24hr. Dorms $12-18; doubles $55. ❶

⬛ FOOD

Cafes and mid-range restaurants line the main drag in Airlie. Several hostels (Beaches, Magnum and Koala) also have affiliated bar/nightclub scenes that double as restaurants before 9pm. For simpler nourishment, there is a **supermarket** right in the middle of town. (Open daily 8:30am-8pm.)

▨ **Village Deli** (☎4946 5745), opposite the post office, Whitsunday Village Shopping Ctr. A healthy alternative to Airlie's fast food or fish and chip joints. Gourmet sandwiches ($7), a variety of pasta and vegetarian entrees, as well as meat and seafood. Also has a fully licensed bar with an extensive wine selection. Open daily 8am-9:30pm. ❶

▨ **Sushi Hi!,** 390 Shute Harbour Rd. (☎4948 0400). The only place for raw fish in town, their massive seafood rolls will fill your belly without emptying your pocket ($6.45 for half rolls). Marinated beef, chicken, or fish sandwiches are $7 per foot. Healthy smoothies ($4-6) are a perfect afternoon snack. Open daily 9:30am-10:30pm. ❶

Sidewalk Cantina (☎4946 6425), on the Esplanade. Specializes in Mexican, but offers a variety of meat and seafood dishes (mains $15-25). Also serves hearty breakfasts ($4-12). Open M, Th-Su 6pm-late. ❹

Beaches, 356-62 Shute Harbour Rd. (☎4946 6244). A perennially packed backpacker mecca. Dinner at long picnic tables. Mains $8-15. Get a free drink if you grab a coupon on the street and show up by about 5pm. Party games start daily around 9:30pm and are followed by dancing until midnight. ❷

⬛ NIGHTLIFE

M@ss, 366 Shute Harbour Rd. (☎4946 6266), part of Magnums' metropolis. Nights here get sticky, soapy, noisy, and naked. Live music outside daily 5pm; rowdy games and debauchery follows. Open Su-Th until late, F-Sa until morning.

Morocco's (☎4946 6446), next to Koala on Shute Harbour Rd. Slightly upscale decor with some outdoor tables and a huge TV screen inside. Games and prizes given away daily. Meals for $10-17, but you can usually pick up a $4 discount on the street, or at Koala's (p. 402) for guests. Open daily 7-10am and 3pm-2am.

Paddy Shenanigan's (☎4946 5055), near Beaches on Shute Harbour Rd. A popular place with Airlie dwellers and a great place to start the night off in style. Dance floor and good music. Open daily 5pm-2am.

KC's (☎4946 6320), on Shute Harbour Rd., on the right before the turn-off for the Esplanade. If you're looking for a big piece of steak and some great live music, this is the place. A truly relaxing and intimate pub environment. Open daily until late.

⬛ ⬛ SIGHTS & ACTIVITIES

While sailing the Whitsunday Islands and diving on the Great Barrier Reef are the two most popular reasons for travel to Airlie, here are some affordable alternatives to mainstream backpacker options.

BY LAND
Conway National Park is a few kilometers east of Airlie Beach. A self-guided walk lasts just over an hour and passes through a variety of Australian habitats. On the way, stop at the QPWS for a detailed leaflet. (QPWS ☎4746 7022. Open M-F 8am-

5pm, Sa 9am-1pm.) For those die-hard bush wranglers, try plowing through the bush on a four-wheeler with **Whitsunday Quad Bike.** (☎0418 745 444. Departs daily; half-day $100.) If you have a car, go to any local tourist office and ask for some self-drive suggestions, as the area has several other swimming holes and scenic picnic areas. If looking for a more up close and personal experience with local wildlife, try **Whitsunday Crocodile Safaris.** You'll cruise the Proserpine River in search of crocs, take an eco-tour in an open wagon, hike through the wetland environment and be treated to a BBQ lunch. (☎4946 5111. $85, children $49. Free transfers to and from Airlie.)

BY SEA

Reel it in with **M.V. Jillian;** troll for mackerel, cobia, and tuna, and then enjoy lunch on board. (☎4948 1301. Daytrips depart Abel Point 8:30am; return around 5:30pm. $111.) A more relaxing fishing excursion is aboard the **M.V. Moruya,** a local favorite. (☎4946 6665. Departs daily at 9am from Shute Harbour and returns around 5:30pm. Daytrip $100, concessions $90.) If you're looking for a longer fishing trip to the outer reef in pursuit of the lions of the fishing world, the beautiful **Marlin Blue** has a very experienced and knowledgeable captain. Come eye-to-eye with sea turtles and glide underneath the shadows of sea eagles as you explore the islands in a leisurely fashion. (☎4946 5044. 1-day trip $275.) One of the newest trends catching on in Airlie is sea kayaking. Join **Salty Dog Sea Kayaking** for a half-, full-, 2-, 3- or 6-day tours around the islands. Adventurers can bring their own food, or let the Salty Dog handle the catering. Sails offer a bit of help on windy days, and dormitory accommodation is available if you don't want to camp. (☎4946 1388 or 1800 635 334; www.saltydog.com.au. Half-day $50, full-day $90, 3-day $385, 6-day $120.) **Ocean Rafting** offers daytrips on a raft that tops 65km per hour. Trips include a chance to dive and tan on the beach, as well as either visit Aboriginal caves or take rainforest walks. (☎4946 6848; www.oceanrafting.com. $73, children $43; optional lunch $11.) If sea-kayaking doesn't float your boat, but you still want to see the islands, **FantaSea** offers catered ferry trips daily to nearby islands (☎4946 5111; www.fantasea.com.au. Hamilton $57, South Molle $44, Daydream $59, Whitehaven $72, 3 island Discovery $59.)

BY AIR

Cruise 300 ft. above Airlie with **Whitsunday Parasail.** Afterwards, you can enjoy the resort pool free of charge. (On the jetty near Coral Sea Resort. ☎4948 0000. $49. Jet ski hire $35 for 15min.) **Tandem Skydiving** will drop with you from 8000 ft. (At the Whitsunday Airport. ☎4946 9115; www.skydiveoz.com. $249.)

◢ DIVING

The scuba scene is hot in the Whitsunday area. Dolphins, whales (in the winter months), turtles, manta rays, and even small reef sharks are common visitors. The most popular site for overnight trips are on the outer reefs that lie just beyond the major island groups, including the **Bait, Hardy,** and **Hook Reefs.** Occasionally, boats will venture to the Black or Elizabeth Reefs. **Mantaray Bay** is the best spot nearby, and is also great for snorkeling. All trips incur an extra $5 per day Reef Tax.

FantaSea Cruises (☎4946 5111). Their *Reefworld* catamaran whisks you to the **Reefworld Pontoon** with its underwater observatory. Departs Shute Harbour and Hamilton Island daily. $152, students/seniors $130, children $81, families $355; 2 days, 1 night at Reefworld in dorm $325; twin-share $383.

Pro Dive, 344 Shute Harbour Rd. (☎4948 1888 or 1800 075 035; www.prodivewhitsundays.com). 3-day, 3-night all inclusive PADI course $499. Open daily 7:30am-7pm.

Oceania Dive, 257 Shute Harbour Rd. (☎4946 6032; www.oceaniadive.com.au). The new 27m boat *Oceania*, departs Tu and F for a 3-day, 3-night trip to Continental Shelf. The boat carries 30 passengers. Advanced courses available. 5-day PADI certification cruise $535. Open daily 7:30am-7pm.

Reef Dive and Sail (☎4946 6508; www.reefdive.com.au), in the Whitsunday Village Shopping Centre. Offers 2- to 3-day cruises on the *Romance* sailboat. 2-day $265; 3-day $420. Open daily 7am-7pm.

WHITSUNDAY ISLANDS

Over 90 islands constitute the Whitsunday group, a continental archipelago that was once a coastal mountain range until cut off from the mainland by rising sea levels at the end of the last ice age. The thousands of visitors who flock to this majestic area often come to sail, see the beaches, and coral reefs, or just relax at one of the luxury resorts. Whitsunday Island, home to the famous Whitehaven beach, is the largest and most appealing to campers and hikers. Other backpacker favorites include Hook Island, with its choice snorkeling spots and Aboriginal cave painting; Daydream Island; Long Island; and the Molle Island Group, of which South Molle is the best. At the posh resorts on Hayman, Hamilton, and Lindeman Islands, many guests arrive by private helicopter or plane, but the islands can make decent daytrips even for those who are strapped for cash.

◱ TRANSPORTATION

Choosing which island—or how many—to visit can seem quite overwhelming. The best way to really experience the island group is by taking a multi-day sailing trip, but it is possible to take ferries to different islands for just a day. Hamilton Island is very popular for daytrippers because it doubles as a small metropolis, though overnight stays can be quite expensive.

FantaSea, a.k.a. **Blues Ferries** (☎4946 5111). The only company to offer direct transfers between the islands and mainland departs daily from Shute Harbour. Schedules are available at almost any booking office or hostel. Multiple ferries leave the harbor daily to: Long Island ($25 return); South Molle ($22 return); Hamilton ($44 return). A **Discover Pass** will get you to all 3 in 1 day ($52). Child and family discounts available.

Island Camping Connections (☎4946 5255). Drops campers off at many of the island sites, and has camping, snorkeling and kayaking equipment for hire. Min. of 2 campers $45-150 person. A multiple-island daytrip is an option, though you'll spend more time on the 100-person boat than you will on the islands.

Whitsunday Island Adventure Cruises (☎4946 5255). Whisks you about the islands, stopping at Whitehaven, Long Island, and Hook Island Resort. A good way to get out on the water and do some snorkeling if you're pressed for time. Departs daily 9am, returns 5:30pm. $69, students $63, children $35; lunch $10.

Air Whitsunday Seaplanes (☎4946 9111). Flies over the islands. 3hr. reef sight-seeing and snorkeling $265; 6hr. snorkeling at the reef $295, dive $395; 1hr. reef and Whitehaven $175. Flight to Hayman Island to spend the entire day there $175.

Aviation Adventures (☎4946 9988). Scenic flights to the reef and beyond. 10min. $65, 15min. $95, 35min. $199, 2hr. $299. Other reef and island packages available.

⛺ ISLANDS

The Whitsundays Island group has a variety of cheap camping options; there are 21 campsites on 17 different islands. Before embarking on your trip, you must get a permit from **QPWS** at the **Marine Parks Authority,** on the corner of Shute Harbour and Mandalay Rd., Airlie Beach. (p. 402. ☎4946 7022. Open M-F 9am-5pm, Sa 9am-1pm. Permits $4 per night.) Walk-in applications are welcome, but you must book ahead to guarantee your spot.

WHITSUNDAY ISLAND. The most renowned destination in the Whitsundays is ◪**Whitehaven Beach,** a 6km-long slip of white along the western part of the island. Sand as pure as talcum powder swirls from one edge of the beach to the other; at low tide you can practically walk across the inlet to the longer portion of Whitehaven, where most day-tour companies moor and sail trips stop for sunbathing and swimming. Make sure you get to the **lookout;** from Tongue Bay, it's an easy 650m walk. Be aware: some tour companies will only take you to the portion of the beach that lies across the bay, but Whitehaven might seem a wasted trip unless you see it from above, so ask ahead and make sure the tour includes the lookout. The **campsite ❶** at Whitehaven Beach has toilets, picnic tables, and shelter (peak-season limit 60 people, off-peak limit 24). On the other side of the island is **Cid Harbour,** a common mooring site for the 2-night boat trips. Cid Harbor houses three **campgrounds.** The largest is **Dungong Beach ❶** (limit 36 people), which has toilets, drinking water, sheltered picnic areas, and a walking track (1km; 40min.) that leads to the second campground, **Sawmill Beach ❶** (limit 24 people). The same amenities are provided here. Bring a water supply if you're camping farther south at **Joe's Beach ❶** (limit 12 people). All campsites cost $4 per night. There is excellent **snorkeling** in the waters where stingrays and turtles are commonly spotted.

HOOK ISLAND. The beaches on Hook have beautiful stretches of coral just offshore, literally a stone's throw from **Chalkies Beach** and **Blue Pearl Bay.** On the south side of the island lies **Nara Inlet,** a popular spot for overnight boat trips. About 20min. up the grueling path is a cave shelter used by the sea-faring Ngalandji Aborigines, bordered on both sides by middens (piles of shells). The rare paintings inside date back to 1000 BC and may have given rise to the popular Australian myth that a boatload of exiled Egyptians washed ashore ages ago and left hieroglyphic-like traces in various corners of Queensland. Although the story is unsubstantiated, it is true that at least one glyph in the cave is a good match for "king" in Hieroglyphic Luwian, spoken in ancient Troy.

Maureens Cove (limit 36 people), on Hook's northern coast, is a popular anchorage and has **camping ❶** for $4 a night. Also on the island is **Steen's Beach campground ❶** (limit 12 people), a good sea-kayaking site. **Hook Island Wilderness Resort ❶,** just east of Matilda Bay, is a bargain resort with a range of activities from snorkeling (1-day $10) to fish and goanna feeding. Remember to bring a towel, kitchen utensils and sleeping bag or blanket. (☎4946 9380. Transfers $40. Camping $15 per person, children $7.50; hut-style dorms $24; beach-front cabins $79, $119 ensuite.) There is an underwater reef observatory (one of the oldest in the world) at the end of the jetty ($8); check with the resort for opening hours.

SOUTH MOLLE ISLAND. South Molle is a national park that offers some of the best **bushwalking** in Queensland. One of the best tracks is the hike to ◪**Spion Kop** (4.4km return, 1½ hrs.), a rock precipice on one of the island peaks. Adventurous hikers scramble up the rocks for an absolutely astounding 360° view of the Whitsundays. Nearby **Sandy Beach** (limit 36 people) has over 15km of hiking trails. Many two-night sailing excursions moor offshore, and guests come ashore to bushwalk or use the pool at the **South Molle Island Resort ❺,** located in Bauer Bay. (☎4946 9433 or 1800 075 080. Packages $125-419. Cheaper standby rates are often available.) Waterskiing ($35), catamarans ($10 per 30min.), jet skiing ($50 per 15min.) and dinghy hire ($25 per 30min.) are all offered at the island's water activities facility. (Open daily 8:30am-4:30pm.) The easiest and cheapest way to enjoy the resort is to buy an all-inclusive package (room, all meals, and all non-motorized water sports). All island walks are accessible from the resort, and reception can give you a map with descriptions of the different choices.

HAMILTON ISLAND. The mini-metropolis of the Whitsundays, the **Hamilton Island Resort ❺** has high-rise hotels and a main drag replete with an **ATM, general store,** and over a dozen restaurants. (☎ 4946 9999. Transfer included. Twin or double ensuite bungalows $104; 5-star Beach Club rooms $150 per person.) Golf buggies whisk well-heeled guests from beachfront to marina in minutes—surprisingly, they are the major form of transport on the island. (Buggy hire ☎ 4945 8095; $35 1hr, full-day $60). The pricey activities on the island will leave you breathless and spent. **Beach Sports,** conveniently located on the beach, rents catamarans ($30 per hr.), windsurfers ($20 per hr.), and snorkel gear ($12). Soar across a valley on the **Wire Flyer,** a hang glider attached to a 325m-long cable. Follow the signs posted around the island to find it. (☎ 4946 8780. $40, children $30.) **FantaSea** will take you to Hamilton for the day. (☎ 4946 5111. $44 return.)

LONG ISLAND. The closest island to the mainland, Long Island is perfect for snorkeling or hiking, as it has its own reef and 20km of walking trails through 1200 hectares of national park. There is also a campground at Sandy Bay (register at QPWS ☎ 4946 7022) and three resorts, including the comparatively budget **Club Crocodile ❺** (☎ 4946 9400 or 1800 075 125; garden room singles $209; doubles $398.)

OTHER ISLANDS. Though ferry service is limited to the islands above, private charters or one of the island camping companies will transport you to others for a fee. **Hayman Island** is known as one of the world's premier resorts; unless you have $500 for a night's stay, you're not going to visit for more than a day. **Camping ❶** remains one of the most rewarding ways to see the islands. On **North Molle Island** lies the mammoth Cockatoo Beach Campground (limit 48 people), fully equipped with facilities and seasonal water supply. Other fully equipped campsites include **Gloucester Island's** Bona Bay (limit 36 people), Northern Spit (limit 24 people, no water) on **Henning Island,** the secluded sites (limit 12 people) at **Thomas Island,** and **Armit Island** (limit 12 people). Basic grounds with simple bushcamping sites and a 12-person limit are Shute Harbour (views of Shute Harbour are actually concealed by **Repair Island**) on **Tancred Island,** Burning Point and Neck Bay on **Shaw Island,** **Saddleback Island,** Western Beach on **South Repulse Island,** and the four-person sites on **Olden Island, Planton Island,** and **Denmon Island.**

⚫ SAILING THE ISLANDS

Going to the Whitsundays without sailing the islands is like going to Paris without seeing the Eiffel Tower. A sailing safari is one of the most popular activities in Queensland. Some hostels offer a free night's stay if you book tours with them; while this may save you money, it might not get you on the best boat. Make sure you get the full details on every trip before booking. Ask how much time is actually spent on the trip. Many boats offer "three-day, two-night" trips that leave at midday and come back only 48hr. later.

There are four classes of boats at play: the uninspiring **motor-powered** variety, boats that have sails but nonetheless motor everywhere; the stately **tallships,** with the rigging of yesteryear but the elegance of age; the **cruising yachts,** which offer more comfort may give you the most sailing time with smaller numbers; and the proper **racing yachts,** called **maxis,** which are usually well past their racing prime, generally more expensive, and popular with partyers. During the low seasons (Oct.-Nov. and Feb.-Mar.), when discounts can be found, all sailing trips are usually booked solid a few days ahead of time, so book ahead.

■ **Southern Cross** (☎ 4946 4999 or 1800 675 790). *Siska*, 80 ft., is spacious and comfortable. *Southern Cross*, a former America's Cup finalist, holds 14 guests. *Boomerang* takes 26 guests and is said by some to be one of the best. (Each 3 days, 2 nights; $383). *Solway Lass*, a gorgeous 127 ft. built in 1902, holds 32 guests. (3 days, 3 nights; twins/doubles $429, 4-bed $409. 6 days and 6 nights; $785/$745.)

Prosail (☎ 4946 5433). Most Prosail 3-day, 2-night trips offer an additional day on *On the Edge* for 50% off. Choose between yachts, maxis or traditional boats. Fleet includes the *Matador*, the largest maxi ever built. 3-day, 2-night trips $429-469; 6-day, 6-night on a luxury catamaran $1395.

Aussie Adventure Sailing (☎ 1800 359 554; www.aussiesailing.com.au). With a wide range of sailboats, from maxis to tallships, they service a diverse group of customers. The *Ron of Argyll* offers an intimate 12-person experience. (Depart M, Th, Sa; 2-day, 2-nights $305.) *Dream Catcher* takes 10 people for the same amount of time and the same price (departs Su, W, and F 2pm.) *SV Whitehaven*, a tallship, carries both onboard passengers and beach front campers. (3-day, 2-night trip depart Tu, Th, and Su 1pm; $385.)

Queensland Yacht Charters (☎ 1800 075 013) hires fully equipped boats for those wishing to go it alone. Not including the hefty $700-1000 bond, rates start at $366 per night for yachts and $325 per night for powerboats plus fuel. When divided among a group, this often beats the cost of a cruise.

NORTH COAST OF QUEENSLAND

As the Queensland coast extends farther north, the sandy beaches stretch alongside some of the world's oldest tropical rainforests. To the west of the tropics, the earth becomes dry and the dirt turns red; much of this land sits on former volcanic shelves, its terrain rising high above sea level. Tall green fields, smoking mills, and Bundaberg rum all stand testament to the region's greatest agricultural asset: sugar cane. Just off the coast of tropical Townsville, the region's economic and residential center, sits Magnetic Island, a haven for both koalas and stressed city-goers. Between the island and Mission Beach, crystal clear water laps upon the beaches protected from rough seas by the Great Barrier Reef. The inland territory hides swaths of rainforest populated by birds, bugs, and bouncing 'roos.

BOWEN   ☎ 07

Despite being a regular bus stop on the coastal service, most travelers overlook Bowen for the non-stop party atmosphere of Airlie Beach 40 minutes to the south. Those who do stay are rewarded with tranquility afforded by the small population and the gorgeous, secluded beaches on the outskirts of town. Bowen is also a great place to earn some cash, as there are many fruit-picking and short-term work opportunities available April-November.

McCafferty's/Greyhound and Premier make daily stops in Bowen in front of **Bowen Travel,** 40 Williams St., where you can satisfy all your local and domestic travel needs. (☎ 4786 2835. Open M-F 9:30am-5:30pm; Sa 9:30am-1pm.) The cafe next door has **Internet** ($4 per hour).

Horseshoe Bay is the town's biggest attraction. To get there, follow Soldiers Rd. out of town, take a right onto Horseshoe Bay Rd., and follow it to the end. Although it is sometimes crowded, the clay water and coastal boulders create a picturesque setting in which to take a swim or catch the sun-rise. **Murray Bay** is a less frequented but equally beautiful beach. Turn right off Horseshoe Bay Rd. onto unsealed Murray Bay Rd. The road ends about a 10min. walk from the beach. Soldiers Rd. meets **Queens Bay** directly in the middle, along which there is ample park area for picnics. At the far right tip of Queens Bay is **Grays Bay,** with calm water and good **fishing. Bowen Bus Service** runs to the beaches from the library on the corner of Herbert and William St. (☎4786 4414. M-F 3 per day, Sa 2 per day. $2.)

Bowen Backpackers ❷ is a popular hostel on the corner of Dalrymple and Herbert St., on the opposite side of town from the bay. For travelers looking to earn some cash, owners Kate and Andy will set you up with temporary work in the area. Fully equipped kitchen, free bicycle use, and next door to a public pool and minutes from the beach. (☎4786 3433; www.users.bigpond.com/bowenbackpackers. Dorms $19.50; doubles $20.50.) One block down on the corner of Herbert and George St. is the **Central Hotel.** There you can grab a meal in the **Stunned Mullet Bistro ❷,** a beer at the bar, play the pokies, then head upstairs to bed. The rooms are reasonably sized, clean, and well-priced. (☎4786 1812. Rooms from $20.) At the other end of town is **Horseshoe Bay Resort ❸,** located at the end of Horseshoe Bay Rd., overlooking Horseshoe Bay. (☎4786 2564. Sites for two $16, powered $19.50. Cabins from $45. Suites from $62. Reception 8:30am-6pm.)

TOWNSVILLE ☎07

Townsville is a bustling city of over 100,000 that was established long before the backpacking subculture infiltrated North Queensland. The city, however, has done an excellent job of expanding to fulfil tourists' needs while fulfilling its responsibilities to the permanent populace. Shopping malls and office buildings jostle with hostels and museums in this evolving port city. Open air eateries, night markets, palm-lined promenades, and seemingly endless stretches of beach add the obligatory tropical flavor. Just outside of town (and off the mainland) is koala-filled Magnetic Island and the world-renowned dive site of the sunken *S.S. Yongala.* Travelers return from treasure-seeking expeditions to a sophisticated nightlife scene dominated by good wine and heaps of live music venues.

▌ TRANSPORTATION

Flights: The **airport** (☎4727 3211) is west of town. **Qantas** (☎4753 3311), at the Dimmey's entrance in Flinders Mall, flies direct to: Brisbane (1¾hr., 4 per day, $253); Cairns (1hr., 6 per day, $229); and Mackay (1hr., 3 per day, $253). An **airport shuttle bus** (☎4775 5544) runs to town daily 5:30am-9pm. Bookings to the airport must be made 30min. before scheduled pick-up time. One-way $7, return $11. To drive from the airport to town, take John Melton Black Dr., which becomes Bundock St. Bear right onto Warburton St. and again onto Eyre St., then go left on Denham St. to the town center.

Trains: The **train station** (☎4772 8288, reservations 13 22 32; www.qr.com.au) is at the corner of Flinders and Blackwood St. The *Inlander* train departs Su and W at 6pm for: Charters Towers (3hr., $21); Cloncurry (16hr., $85); Hughenden (8hr., $49); Mt. Isa (20½hr., $104); and Richmond (10¾hr., $61). The *Spirit of the Tropics* leaves Su and W at 4:10pm heading to: Brisbane (24hr., $153); Bowen (5½hr., $142); Mackay (7½hr., $130); and Rockhampton (13hr., $88). The **Queensland Rail Travel Centre** (☎4772 8358) is to the right of the station. Open M 7:15am-5pm, Tu and F 6am-5pm, W 7:15am-6pm, Th 8:30am-5pm, Sa 1-4:30pm, Su 7:15-10:45am.

Buses: The **Transit Centre** is on the corner of Palmer and Plume St., a 5min. walk from the city center. Open daily 6am-8:30pm. **McCafferty's/Greyhound** (☎13 14 99 or 13 20 30; open daily 5:30am-11pm) runs to: Airlie Beach (4hr., 6 per day, $49); Brisbane (20hr., 6 per day, $166); Cairns (4hr., 6 per day, $51); Cardwell (2¼hr., 6 per day, $33); Charters Towers (2hr., 2 per day, $27); Cloncurry (10hr., 2 per day, $107); Hughenden (4hr., 2 per day, $53); Ingham (1½hr., 6 per day, $26); Innisfail (4¼hr., 6 per day, $47); Mackay (5hr., 6 per day, $67); Mission Beach (3½hr., 4 per day, $47); Mt.

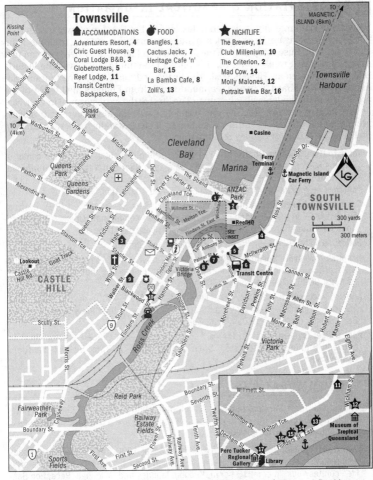

Townsville

⌂ ACCOMMODATIONS
Adventurers Resort, **4**
Civic Guest House, **9**
Coral Lodge B&B, **3**
Globetrotters, **5**
Reef Lodge, **11**
Transit Centre
Backpackers, **6**

🍴 FOOD
Bangles, **1**
Cactus Jacks, **7**
Heritage Cafe 'n'
Bar, **15**
La Bamba Cafe, **8**
Zolli's, **13**

★ NIGHTLIFE
The Brewery, **17**
Club Millenium, **10**
The Criterion, **2**
Mad Cow, **14**
Molly Malones, **12**
Portraits Wine Bar, **16**

Isa (12hr., 2 per day, $119); Richmond (5hr., 2 per day, $68); and Rockhampton (9hr., 6 per day, $103). **Premier** (☎ 13 34 10) stops in town twice a day: northbound at 1:35pm, southbound at 1pm.

Public Transportation: Sunbus (☎ 4725 8482; www.sunbus.com.au) has its main terminus in the center of Flinders Mall. Most tickets $3-4. 24hr. bus passes $10.

Car Rental: Local outfits don't allow cars beyond Charters Towers. **Townsville Car Rentals,** 12 Palmer St. (☎ 4772 1093). $44 per day, limit 100km. **Independent Rentals,** 25 Yeatman St., Hyde Park (☎ 4721 4766). 2-day minimum, $49 per day, 250km. Bigger companies allow unlimited kilometers. **Thrifty** (☎ 13 13 90), at the airport, rents from $49 per day.

Automobile Club: RACQ, 635 Sturt St. (24hr. ☎ 4721 4888). Open M-F 8am-5pm, Sa 8am-noon.

Taxis: Taxi Townsville (24hr. ☎ 4772 1555).

⚡🛈 ORIENTATION & PRACTICAL INFORMATION

Townsville is a large city with a complex layout, but the downtown area is relatively easy to navigate. Ross Creek separates the mall side of town from the Transit Centre side. Buses stop at the Transit Centre on Palmer St., where you can find several hostels. From Palmer St., it's only a ten-minute walk over the **Victoria Bridge** to the open-air **Flinders Mall.** The beach and many classy restaurants are lined along **The Strand,** a five to ten minute walk from Flinders Mall. Most of the cross streets to Flinders will take you to The Strand; the easiest way is to walk east down Flinders, towards ReefHQ, and turn left. **Castle Hill** looms in the city's background and is accessible both by road and by a steep walking trail; take Gregory St. from The Strand or Stanley St. from town.

Tourist office: Visitors Centre (☎4721 3660), the big circular kiosk in the center of Flinders Mall. Open M-F 9am-5pm, Sa-Su 9am-1pm. **Reef and National Park Information Centre,** Shop 12, Flinders Mall (☎4721 2399), opposite Hoges Cafe, has all the answers on marine life. Open M-F 9am-5pm, Sa-Su 10am-4pm.

Currency Exchange: Bank of Queensland, 16 Stokes St. (☎4772 1799), up from Flinders Mall on the left, often has the best rates. $7 commission. Open M-Th 9:30am-4pm, F 9:30am-5pm. Multiple **ATMs** in Flinders Mall and the city center.

Police: (☎4759 9777), on the corner of Stanley and Sturt St.

Hospital: Townsville Hospital, 100 Angus Smith Dr. (☎4796 1111). There's also a **doctor's office** across from the Holiday Inn, on the corner of Flinders and Stokes St. (☎4724 0026). Open M-F 8am-5:30pm, Sa 8am-noon.

Internet Access: Internet Den, 265 Flinders Mall (☎4721 4500), next to McDonald's. $5 per hr. Open M-F 9am-9pm, Sa-Su 10am-8pm. Free at the **library** across the mall. Book ahead. Open M-F 9:30am-5pm, Sa-Su 9am-noon.

Post Office: General Post Office (☎4760 2021), in Post Office Plaza, on Sturt St. between Stanley and Stokes St. Open M-Sa 8:30am-5:30pm, Su 9am-12:30pm. **Postal Code:** 4810.

🏠 ACCOMMODATIONS

Townsville is not a backpacker city, a welcome change from the late-night party atmosphere of some of the other coastal towns. There are a few pleasant places to stay, though they're a bit spreadout.

Civic Guest House, 262 Walker St. (☎4771 5381 or 1800 646 619; www.backpackersinn.com). Small, friendly, family-run service with free F night BBQs and wildlife expo. Free courtesy bus. Internet $5 per hr. Kitchen, laundry, and TV lounge. Reception 8am-8pm. 4- and 6-bed dorms $20; singles $39; doubles $42. Ensuites available. VIP. ❷

Coral Lodge B&B, 32 Hale St. (☎4771 5512 or 1800 614 613; www.coral-lodge.com.au). From Flinders Mall, follow Stokes St. for 4 blocks, turn left on Hale St., and it's on the left. Super friendly, clean, comfortable, family-run B&B. Great choice for those on a budget looking to avoid the hostel scene. All rooms have A/C, TV, and fridge. Singles $50, self-contained $65; twins and doubles $60/$75. ❹

Reef Lodge, 4 Wickham St. (☎4721 1112), off Flinders St. E. Newly renovated in 2003. Rooms are large and clean with new furniture. Attracts an interesting and diverse crowd. Free pick-up from Transit Centre. Laundry, BBQ, and kitchen. Reception 8am-10pm. Dorms $14; doubles $36; motel rooms $49. ❶

Globetrotters, 45 Palmer St. (☎4771 3242; globe@ultra.net.au), right next to the Transit Centre with amazing floral displays July-Sept. Laundry, pool, BBQ, TV, tropical garden. Reception 6am-9pm. Dorms $20; twins $46. VIP/YHA. ❷

Transit Centre Backpackers (☎4721 2322 or 1800 628 836; www.tcback-packer.com.au). Surprisingly quiet, given its bus terminal location, and impeccably clean. Free storage. Laundry, bar, kitchen (cutlery $5 deposit), and huge spa on the balcony. Reception 24hr. Dorms $20; singles $40; doubles $50. YHA. ❷

Adventurers Resort, 79 Palmer St. (☎4721 1522 or 1800 211 522). One of the biggest backpackers in town; feels more like an apartment building than a hostel. Huge, clean bathrooms, kitchen, large common areas, and secure parking. Linen deposit $5. Reception 8am-9pm. Dorms $20; singles $32; doubles $42. VIP/YHA. ❷

🍴 FOOD

Most of the city's restaurants are located on The Strand, Flinders St. E., or Palmer St. Woolworths **supermarket,** 126-150 Sturt St., is between Stanley and Stoke St. (Open M-F 8am-9pm, Sa 8am-5:30pm, Su 9am-6pm.)

🦐 **La Bamba Cafe,** 3 Palmer St. (☎4771 6322), near the corner of Dean St. Bright, colorful walls filled with local art. Australian-Mediterranean cuisine with a large selection of vegetarian options. A popular Southbank breakfast spot. Parisian croissants $4.50. Sandwich baguettes $8. Open daily 8am-2pm; also M-Sa 6pm-late, but hours vary. ❶

Heritage Cafe 'n' Bar, 137 Flinders St. East (☎4771 2799). Ultra-trendy scene with a large selection of Australian wines. Modern cuisine that includes pasta, seafood, and meat dishes up to $20. Th bucket of prawns and a XXXX beer or glass of wine for $10. Open daily 5pm-late for dinner, F 11am-3pm for lunch. ❷

Cactus Jacks, 21 Palmer St. (☎4721 1478). Wash down some spicy, sizzling Mexican fajitas ($18) with a wide selection of beers, from Negro Modelo to Moosehead. Cowboy boots and chaps optional. Open daily from 2pm-late. ❸

Zolli's, 113 Flinders St. (☎4721 2222). Listen to Italian music, imbibe red wine, and dine on authentic Sicilian cuisine. Many seafood and pasta choices (mussel pasta $9), as well as yummy pizzas ($6-16). Open daily 5pm-late. ❷

Bangles, 6 Wickham St. (☎4771 6710). Some of the cheapest, most authentic food in town. Enjoy Indian cuisine, like chicken masala or various curries, from $6. Open daily 11:30am-2:30pm, 5:30pm-late. No credit cards. ❶

🤿 DIVING

Kelso Reef, Townsville's most exceptional spot on the Great Barrier Reef, is home to over 400 kinds of coral and schools of tropical fish. **John Brewer, Loadstone, the Slashers,** and **Keeper Reefs** are other common dive sites. Townsville's best dive site isn't on the reef—in 1911, the 🚢**S. S. Yongala** went down in the tropical waters off the coast. The still-intact shipwreck is considered one of the world's best wreck sites, but it requires advanced certification or a professional guide.

Adrenalin Dive, 121 Flinders St. (☎4771 6527 or 1800 242 600). A small operation that offers the only daytrip to the Yongala wreck. The boat is nothing more than functional, but the company offers some of the best guided dives in Northern Queensland, along with daytrips to the reef. Yongala trip with gear $214.

ProDive, Reef HQ Complex Flinders St. (☎4721 1760), offers a 5-day open water course including dives to the Yongala ($615) and a 3-day, 3-night cruise to the Yongala aboard the *Pacific Adventure*. Open M-F 9am-5pm, Sa-Su 9am-4pm.

Sunferries (☎4771 3855), at the ferry terminal on Flinders St. Takes daytrips to John Brewer Reef. Departs daily 9am, returns 5:20pm. $129, students $99, children $54. Two certified dives extra $60; discover dive $60.

QUEENSLAND

Diving Dreams, 252 Walker St. (☎4721 2500). Offers dives on the reef, the Palm Islands, and Yongala. Live-aboard 5-day course that takes you to the Yongala $550.

🔵 SIGHTS

Townsville isn't known for its sights, but its sizeable population sustains a variety of cultural and historical attractions for a break from the beach. Each first Friday of the month, from May to December, the Strand **Night Markets** display food, crafts, rides, and entertainment (5-9:30pm).

REEFHQ. Re-opened in July 2002 after some serious renovations, ReefHQ is an aquarium and reef education center for all ages. The main attraction is a 2.5 million liter aquarium that mimics a reef ecosystem. Tours and shows occur almost every hour, including shark feeds and a visit to the sea turtle research facility. *(2-68 Flinders St. ☎4750 0800. Open daily 9am-5pm. $19.50, children $9.50, families $49.)*

MUSEUM OF TROPICAL QUEENSLAND. If you can't get to the Yongala, visit the next best thing: the relics of the *HMS Pandora*, displayed in this flashy new museum. Showcases Queensland's cultural and natural history. Don't miss the fascinating deep sea creatures exhibit. *(78-102 Flinders St., next to the ReefHQ complex. ☎4726 0606. Open daily 9am-5pm. $9, concessions $6.50, children $5, families $24.)*

BILLABONG SANCTUARY. Several daily presentations allow you to take a hot pic with your favorite Aussie animal. *(17km south of Townsville. ☎4478 8344; www.billabongsanctuary.com.au. Open daily 8am-5pm. Coach service available. $20, students and seniors $15, children $10, families $47.)*

🔵 ACTIVITIES

Sometimes Townsville can feel simply like a stopover for travelers, but there are plenty of activities to keep you busy during your stay. ◾**Castle Hill** has some challenging **walking paths** that lead to spectacular views of Townsville; the best times to go are sunrise and sunset. Bring water and hiking boots; the paths are steep, slippery, and long. There's also a road to the top for the less aerobically-inclined. **Right Training,** 53 Cheyne St., Pimlico (☎4725 4571), offers a three-hour abseiling and rock climbing combo for $87 on an outdoor cliff. They also have full-day training courses with certification ($175) or a beginner afternoon climb ($55). pick-up can be arranged. **Coral Sea Skydivers,** 14 Plume St., leads tandem jumps daily as well as two- and five-day certification courses for solo jumps. (☎4772 4889; www.coral seaskydivers.com.au. Book ahead. Tandem $290-390, depending on altitude.) **White Water Rafting: Raging Thunder Adventures** takes the rapids on Tuesdays, Thursdays, and Sundays. (☎1800 079 977; www.ragingthunder.com.au. Departs 5:25am, returns 6:45pm. $145.)

🔵 NIGHTLIFE

Remedy, a free monthly publication, will lead you to all the hottest shows and bars in town. ◾**Molly Malones,** on the corner of Flinders St. E and Wickham St., has live music nightly and Irish jam sessions on Sundays. They also have a great **restaurant ❷** with mains around $15 and burgers for $10. (☎4771 3428. Open daily 10am-late. No cover.) **Club Millennium,** 450 Flinders St. West., is always a good time. With live music, jam sessions, DJs, karaoke, and hardcore rave music, they cover it all. (☎4772 4488. Cover $10-15.) **Mad Cow,** 129 Flinders St. E., More tavern than nightclub features less drinking, live music downstairs Sunday, and an atypically lax dress code. Three pool tables contribute to the mellow atmosphere. (☎4771 5727.

W "Cowioki" nights. No cover. Open M-Th 8pm-3am, F-Su 8pm-5am.) A favorite hangout for young locals is **The Criterion,** on the corner of Wickham St. and The Strand, an old hotel pub that turns nightclub. Its sideshow beer garden, the Starter Bar, has your run-of-the-mill wet T-shirt contests and live music. (☎4721 5777. Open Tu-W 5pm-3am, Th-Sa 5pm-5am, Su 2pm-5am.) The newest hot-spot in town is **The Brewery,** on the corner of Denham and Flinders St. Award-winning brewer Brendan Flanagan concocts delicious home-brewed beers and a full dinner menu also pleases the crowds. (☎4724 0333. No cover. Open daily 11am-late.) Better your connoisseur skills at **Portraits Wine Bar,** 151 Flinders St. E, where wine-tasting occurs the first Tuesday of every month ($8). There are complimentary cheese platters from 5pm on Fridays. (☎4771 3335. Open nightly.)

MAGNETIC ISLAND ☎07

When Townsville natives need a vacation, they don't have to go very far; Magnetic Island is only a short ferry ride away. The island's beaches are wide and inviting, and its pockets of eucalypts are dotted with the largest concentration of wild koalas in Australia. The island's only inhabited area is a mere 20km of eastern coast—most of the island is made up of national park. On less crowded beaches, accessible by several walking tracks, people bathe in the buff. During the winter, the forests on the boulder-ridden hills glow at night from the seasonal fires, making the island appear volcanic.

▐ TRANSPORTATION

The only public transportation to the island is with **Sunferries Magnetic Island,** 168-192 Flinders St. E (☎4771 3855). **Ferries** leave from Flinders St. (30min.; M-F 12 per day, Sa-Su 9 per day; $17 return) and the Breakwater terminal on Sir Leslie Thieses Dr. by The Strand (20min.; M-F 12 per day, Sa-Su 9 per day; $17 return). The only way to get vehicles across the water is on Capricorn Barge Company's **Magnetic Island Car Ferry,** located down Palmer St. Six passengers and a car can travel for $123 return. (☎4772 5422. 1hr.; M-F 6 per day, Sa 3 per day, Su 4 per day.)

There are less than 20km of sealed roads on the island, and the bus system does a fine job of covering all of them. **Magnetic Island Buses** (☎4778 5130) run roughly every 50min.; stops are marked by blue signs. Tickets are sold on the bus ($2-5), and a one-day unlimited pass ($11) is available from the bus driver. Buses operate M-Th 5:25am-8:50pm, F-Sa 5:25am-11:50pm, and Su 6:50am-8:50pm. **Magnetic Island Taxis** (☎13 10 08) charges about $16 to cross the island.

Renting a "moke" (an open-air, golf-cart-like rig) is extremely popular. **Moke Magnetic,** in the Picnic Bay Mall, rents to 21 and over; rentals includes 60km and petrol costs ($65 per 24hr., under 25 $68). When split between a group of friends, this is quite inexpensive and a great way to enjoy some freedom. (☎4778 5377. Open daily 8am-5pm. $100 deposit or credit card imprint.) **Tropical Topless Car Rentals,** in Picnic Bay, has small open-roofed cars with unlimited kilometers. (☎4758 1111. $70 per 24hr.) Scooters can also be rented in Picnic Bay from **Road Runner Scooter Hire.** (☎4778 5222. Open daily 9am-5pm. $28 per day, $38 per 24hr. $100 deposit.)

▐ ORIENTATION

The island is roughly triangular in shape, and all accommodations, restaurants, and activities are spread out along the east coast. Eventually the main port on the island will be in **Nelly Bay.** Plans to build a new resort will follow completion of the marina. For now, most arrive via the ferry service in Picnic Bay. The sealed road from there only runs east, first passing Nelly Bay, which also has the island's main

QUEENSLAND

supermarket. Turning left and continuing north will take you to Arcadia, a 15min. bus ride from the ferry, which has several great beaches and a couple of nice restaurants. **Horseshoe Bay,** a 30min. bus ride from the ferry, is the island's northernmost populated area and includes the watersports center. From Picnic Bay you can also head west on an unsealed road (no mokes allowed) to **West Point,** a popular sunset spot. **Radical** and **Balding Bays,** near Horseshoe Bay, are only accessible by foot or 4WD; the walks are short and rewarding. **Florence** and **Arthur Bays** sit just a bit south and are closer to the main road.

🛈 PRACTICAL INFORMATION

Tourist Office: Information Centre (☎4778 5155), next to jetty in Picnic Bay. Books flights, buses, and other transport. Open M-F 8am-4:30pm, Sa-Su 8am-1pm.

Travel Office: Magnetic Travel, 55 Sooning St. (☎4778 5343), in the shopping plaza at Nelly Bay. Open M-F 8:30am-5:30pm.

Currency Exchange: The **post office** is the local agent for Commonwealth Bank. **ATMs** are in Picnic Bay, at **Express** Food Store in Horseshoe Bay, and at **Arkie's** in Arcadia.

Police: (24hr.☎4778 5270), on the corner of Granite and Picnic St., Picnic Bay. Open M 8:30am-noon, W and F 8:30am-2pm.

Medical Center: The **Magnetic Island Medical Centre,** 68 Sooning St., Nelly Bay (24hr. ☎4778 5614), does diving medical exams for $60. Open M-F 11:30am-5:30pm, Sa 9:30am-1:30pm, Su 11am-1:30pm.

Internet Access: Courtyard Mall Cyber Cafe, Shop 2 Courtyard Mall, The Esplanade, Picnic Bay (☎4778 5407). $6 per hr. Open daily 8:30am-5:30pm. Terminals are also available in most hostels and at the **Tourist Information Centre** for $5 per hr.

Post Office: Picnic Bay Arcade, The Esplanade (☎4778 5118). Open M-F 8:30am-5pm, Sa 9-11am. **Postal Code:** 4819.

🏠 ACCOMMODATIONS

Hostels are located in Picnic Bay, Arcadia, and Horseshoe Bay, providing accommodation in or around every inhabited area of the island. Many offer courtesy buses that cover the island, so you can prioritize quality over location.

Centaur Guest House, 27 Marine Pde., Alma Bay (☎4778 5668 or 1800 655 680; www.bpf.com.au). The best rooms on the island at what claims to be the world's first backpackers, est. 1947. Free activities include wine-and-cheese night (Sa) and pancake and ice cream night (Th). Internet $5 per hr. After-hours check-in available. Reception 7am-8pm. Dorms $18; singles $35; twins and doubles $42. 5th night free. ❷

Maggie's Beach House, 1 Pacific Dr., Horseshoe Bay (☎4778 5144 or 1800 001 544; www.maggiesbeachhouse.com.au), at the end of the beach road. Gecko's, its posh grill, offers great meals at reasonable prices (mains $8-19), and often has live music. Cafe, laundry, pool table, TV lounge, Internet. Reception 8am-7pm. Dorms $21; doubles $75. VIP. ❷

Sails on Horseshoe, 13-15 Pacific Dr. (☎4778 5117), 300m from Maggie's, on the bay. The newest of the luxury apartment complexes on the island, Sails is a great place for large groups. 1- and 2-bedroom suites with kitchen, spa, and TV. Reception 7am-6pm. $160-260 depending on length of stay, each sleeps several people. ❺

Dunoon (☎4778 5161), on the corner of The Esplanade and Granite St., Picnic Bay. A good deal for groups or families—sparkling beachfront cottages with kitchen, bath, dining area, and TV. Laundry, pool, BBQ, and children's area. Book ahead. Reception 7:30am-5:30pm. 1- and 2-bedroom cottages from $95. ❷

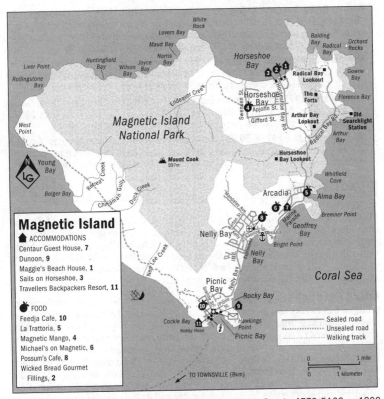

Magnetic Island

▲ ACCOMMODATIONS
Centaur Guest House, **7**
Dunoon, **9**
Maggie's Beach House, **1**
Sails on Horseshoe, **3**
Travellers Backpackers Resort, **11**

🍎 FOOD
Feedja Cafe, **10**
La Trattoria, **5**
Magnetic Mango, **4**
Michael's on Magnetic, **6**
Possum's Cafe, **8**
Wicked Bread Gourmet
  Fillings, **2**

Travellers Backpackers Resort, 1 The Esplanade, Picnic Bay (☎4778 5166 or 1800 000 290; travellers@ultra.net.au), right next to the pier. Nightly activities keep visitors going at this motel-turned-giant hostel. Complete with 4 bars and Magnetic's only public nightclub. Kitchen, pool, Internet, and 4m resident croc Rin Tin Tin. Reception 7:30am-midnight. Dorms $8-15; twins $46, doubles $50. VIP/YHA. ❶

🄵 🄵 FOOD & NIGHTLIFE

Magnetic Island's few restaurants are unique and reasonably priced. For the basics, go to the Magnetic Island **supermarket,** 55 Sooning St., Nelly Bay. (Open M-F 8:30am-7pm, Sa 8:30am-5:30pm, Su 9am-2pm.) If you want to go out for drinks, the crowds tend to huddle in Arcadia and at Horseshoe Bay, but be warned that the island bus service ends in early evening.

🥗 **La Trattoria** (☎4778 5757), on Alma Bay. Walk towards the beach at Alma Bay, stay left and follow the signs. Enjoy the Mediterranean-inspired menu from the restaurant bluff that overlooks the sparkling bay. Try their amazing dips ($9), huge salads ($12), or the pumpkin and garbanzo bake ($17). BYO. Open W-Su 11am-3pm and 6-10pm. ❷

Possum's Cafe, 55 Sooning St., Nelly Bay (☎4778 5409). In addition to great sandwiches ($3-4) and seafood boxes ($9), they have all-day breakfast ($6-11). Open daily 8am-8pm. ❶

Wicked Bread Gourmet Fillings, 6 Pacific Dr. (☎4778 5786), next to Maggie's on Pacific Dr. Enjoy a croissant or Danish straight from the oven every morning with a cup of coffee. They also sell gourmet cheeses with fresh loaves of bread and feature a large selection of sandwiches from $6.50. Open daily 8am-6pm. Cash only. ❶

Michael's On Magnetic, 5 Bright Ave., Arcadia (☎4778 5645). Thai and modern Australian cuisine that can be enjoyed in the tropical courtyard. Takeaway available. Pastas $8-15, mains $16-23, coffees $3. Open for dinner M-Tu and Th-Su 6pm-late. ❸

Feedja Cafe (☎4778 5833), on the Esplanade, Picnic Bay. Specializing in fresh, locally grown produce, they offer a variety of healthy, flavorful options. Focaccias from $6.50. Enjoy breakfast and read the paper on the bay. Open daily 8am-3pm. ❶

Magnetic Mango (☎4778 5018), at the end of Apjohn St., Horseshoe Bay. Any purchase from the kitchen gives you free access to attached mango plantation—complete with goats, gold mine, and mini-golf course. BYO. Open M-W and F-Su 10am-5pm. ❶

◪ ACTIVITIES

TOURS. Indulge the child within and career around Magnetic Island with ◪**Tropicana Tours,** 2/26 Picnic St. Guests tour the bush in a "luxurious" Queensland-style limo—a stretched Jeep Wrangler—observing wildlife, beaches, and beautiful sunsets. Pile into the 10-seat Jeep, cruise to loud music, feed lorikeets, see beaches, and finish with wine at sunset. (☎4758 1800; www.tropicanatours.com.au. 6hr. afternoon trip $88; full-day tour with lunch $125.)

GREAT OUTDOORS. Over 70% of Magnetic Island is national park, so there are multiple bushwalks and plenty of opportunities to enjoy the natural beauty of the island. Koala sightings are virtually guaranteed at the popular **Forts Walk** (4km; 1½hr.). It's best to go from 4-6pm, when the critters are just waking up and, in the winter, you can finish by watching the sunset atop the biggest fort. Another option is to take the island path (8km; 3hr.) that leads from Picnic Bay through wetlands and mangroves to **West Point.** For a list of the other walks on the island, go to the tourist office, ask the bus drivers, or grab a map at Maggie's. From Horseshoe Bay, two great and short walks lead to **Balding Bay** and **Radical Bay.** At dusk, dozens of rock wallabies come for a hand-fed snack to **Geoffrey Bay,** in Arcadia. **Bluey's Horseshoe Ranch,** 38 Gifford St., Horseshoe Bay, will take you riding bareback riding along the sand beach of Horseshoe Bay. (☎4778 5109. 2hr. $55; half-day $80.)

DIVING. Small and friendly dive shops on Maggie Island offer some of the most inexpensive dive opportunities in all of Queensland. A plethora of small wrecks and reefs provide endless exploration. Open water courses, daytrips and overnights are all available. **Pleasure Dives,** 10 Marine Pde., Arcadia, offers incredible deals on PADI certification classes from the shore (3-day course $220), and also has 4-day courses that include one day on the outer reef ($340). Other options include advanced courses to the Yongala wreck $369 and a PADI open water advanced Yongala package $575. (☎4778 5788 or 1800 797 797. Open daily 8:30am-5pm.) **Ocean Dive,** at the Coconuts resort in Nelly Bay, has occasional specials on PADI open water courses for as low as $199 and also does snorkeling daytrips to the reef for $129, $60 extra for certified divers (☎4758 1391. Open daily 9am-5pm.).

OTHER WATER ACTIVITIES. Magnetic Island Sea Kayaks, 93 Horseshoe Bay Rd., Horseshoe Bay, departs daily 8:15am and returns about noon. (☎4778 5424. $45; includes a light tropical breakfast.) Of course, you can always forego quiet contemplation and speed around the island on a roaring jet-ski with **Adrenalin Jet Ski Tours.** (☎4778 5533. 3hr. tour departs Horseshoe Bay at 10am, returns 1pm; $119.)

OTHER ACTIVITIES. At **Magnetic Island Mini Golf,** 27 Sooning St., Nelly Bay., 18 holes of putt-putt can be followed by pool, ping pong, air hockey, and more. (☎4758 1066. Open Su-F 9am-5pm, Sa 9am-late. Golf $4.50, children $3. Ask about package deals with other amusements.) **The Magnetic Island Country Club,** Hurst St., Picnic Bay, popular with Townsville and island residents, has a 9-hole course and a licensed bar and restaurant. (Open daily from 8am. $11, 18 holes $16.) Visit koalas, wombats, emus, and talking cockatoos at the **Koala Park Oasis,** Pacific Dr., Horseshoe Bay. (☎4778 5260. Open daily 9am-5pm. $10, children $4.)

CARDWELL ☎07

A small town between Mission Beach and Townsville, Cardwell brushes up against an appealing beach, perfect for admiring but not for a dip—salties from the bordering mangrove forests frequent the beach and boat launch. In the middle of several large farming communities, Cardwell is an ideal stop for work. National parks and Wet Tropics Heritage Areas surround the town, providing opportunities for great camping and hiking.

Cardwell Air Charters, 135 Bruce Hwy. (☎4066 8468), runs scenic flights ranging from local attractions only (20min., $49), and **Hinchinbrook Island** (40min., $80), to the "Grand Tour," which covers the Family Islands, Herbert River Gorge—the site of Survivor II—Wallaman Falls, and Brook Islands (75min., $149) and half-day **Undara Lava Tubes** trip ($255, includes lunch). Just 4km north of Cardwell along the coast is the entrance to **Edmund Kennedy National Park,** renowned for its diverse habitats, including eucalyptus forest, swamp and mangroves. No camping is permitted. For some safe and scenic swimming nearby, try **Five-Mile Swimming Hole,** a local favorite 8km south of town off the Bruce Hwy.

Most of the establishments in town are along Cardwell's patch of the Bruce Hwy., locally known as **Victoria Street.** The "Transit Centre" is basically a swath of bitumen in the center of town called Brasenose St. **McCafferty's/Greyhound** (☎13 14 99 or 13 20 30) **buses** run to Townsville (2hr., 7 per day, $32) and Cairns (3¼hr., 7 per day, $26). **Premier** (☎13 34 10) also stops here, going north at 4pm and south at 10:20pm.

The YHA-affiliated **Hinchinbrook Hostel and Kookaburra Holiday Park ❷,** 175 Victoria St., is by far the best hostel in town. Friendly and immaculate, it offers free pick-up from the bus stop (800m away), free bikes, free sporting and fishing equipment, kitchen, saltwater pool, and Internet. Camping gear is available for hire. (☎4066 8648; www.hinchinbrookholiday.com.au. Reception 8am-6pm. Sites for 2 $16.50; dorms $18; cabins for 4 $59.) For those seeking employment, the managers of **Cardwell Backpackers Hostel ❷,** 178 Bowen St., behind Muddie's restaurant, arrange **fruit-picking jobs** ($10-13 per hr.) for guests, and even bus them to work for $3. Privacy here is sacrificed in favor of a communal atmosphere; guests sleep in a 12-bed dorm enclosed by a partition. (☎4066 8014. Kitchen, TV room, and laundry. Dorms $15.40; cubicles $16.50; doubles $35.20.) ◼**Annie's Kitchen ❶,** 107 Victoria St., makes a mean burger for $4 and a huge milkshake for $3.50. (☎4066 8818. Open daily 6am-8pm.) The 5-Star **supermarket,** 198 Victoria St., offers a decent selection. (Open daily 6am-8pm.)

INGHAM & SURROUNDS

Best known for its association with the sugar-producing industry, the small town of Ingham is home to Victoria Sugar Mill, the largest in the southern hemisphere. For visitors, however, the most distinct feature isn't the cash crop, but rather the Mediterranean influence apparent everywhere. Over 60% of the population is of Italian descent, giving Ingham a culturally unique flavor among North Queensland

QUEENSLAND

townships. There is a **Visitors Centre** (☎4776 5211) on Townsville Rd. that provides information about traveling to the areas' spectacular rainforests and national parks. For camping permits, head to the **QWPS,** 49 Cassady St. (☎4776 1700). If staying the night, try the budget **Royal Hotel ❶,** 46 Lannercost St. (☎4776 2024), which offers beds for $14 a night, 2 to a room—no credit cards. The **Palm Tree Caravan Park ❶,** just 3km south of town on the Bruce Hwy., offers basic camping sites. (☎4776 2403. $15, powered $20.)

The region just west of Ingham and Cardwell has some of the most astounding natural attractions in Queensland. **Lumholtz National Park** (51km west of Ingham, 30km of unsealed road), is one of the world's oldest rainforests and home to **Wallaman Falls,** Australia's largest single-drop waterfall. The forest is home to several species of endangered plants and animals, as well as the amethystine python, Australia's largest snake. Camping permits are by self-registration ($4 per person). 24km south of Ingham and close to the Bruce Hwy is the cascading terrace of **Jourama Falls.** Freshwater swimming holes, turtle-spotting, and superb bird watching make this an idyllic daytrip destination. Another 20km south, the **Mt. Spec** section of **Paluma Range National Park** attracts visitors with crystal-clear streams that snake down the mountain under the canopy. Camping is permitted only at **Big Crystal Creek,** for which you will need a permit and a key from either Townsville (☎4722 5211) or Ingham (☎4777 3112) **QPWS.** Access can be difficult in the Wet.

HINCHINBROOK ISLAND   ☎07

Across the Hinchinbrook Channel, just 4km from Cardwell, is Hinchinbrook Island, Australia's largest island national park. The unspoiled wilderness of the area is breathtaking, with looming granite peaks, mangrove swamps, and a smattering of the endangered manatee-like dugong. There's plenty of snorkeling opportunities, as well as some superb bushwalks. The famous **Thorsborne Trail** (32km; 3-7 days) is the most popular hike on the island. The number of people allowed on the trail at one time is capped at 40, so it's best to obtain a permit several months in advance, allowing up to 12 months for the peak season of April-Sept.

Hinchinbrook Island Ferries, 131 Bruce Hwy., docks at the northern end of the island and offers day-tours, including walks to some of its pristine beaches. Oneway tickets are useful if you have a camping permit and want to walk the length of the island. (☎4066 8270 or 1800 777 021. $59, day-tour or return $90. Transfers available from Mission Beach and Cardwell.) **Hinchinbrook Wilderness Safaris** goes to the south end of the island. The small boat leaves from George Point and will bring you back to Lucinda, south of Cardwell. (☎4777 8307. $46.) **Hinchinbrook Marine Cove** (☎4777 8377) offers transfers from Townsville and day-tours for $57-99. Spot one of Australia's most elusive creatures with **Dugong Watching** tours; they also rent boats. (☎4066 8555. Departs daily 9:30am, returns 3:30pm. $70, children $40. Boat hire $240 per day.)

Daytrips to the island don't require bookings, but overnights, whether camping or staying in the resort, usually do. If camping, obtain a permit in advance and read up on various trail options to piece together a trip (camping permits $4 per night). Facilities at the campsite include picnic tables, gas BBQ, water, and toilet. Along the track, however, you'll find plenty of solitude. If you don't mind spending the money, the **Hinchinbrook Resort ❺** prides itself on being the ultimate eco-friendly destination, allowing only 50 guests at one time. (☎4066 8270 or 1800 777 021; www.hinchinbrookresort.com.au. Beach cabins $160, treehouse for several adults $250.) The folks at the QPWS, located at the **Rainforest and Reef Centre,** 14 Victoria St., Cardwell, on the north side of town near the jetty, are eager to help. The Centre has a free informational walk that details the science behind the rainforest and its inhabitants. (☎4066 8115. Open daily 8am-4:30pm.)

MISSION BEACH ☎ 07

Transformed virtually overnight into a major backpacker destination, this nearly continuous stretch of beach deserves all its hype. The town experiences heavy traveler traffic, though the expansive beach offers plenty of room for peace and quiet. The untouched corals and sand cays of the reefs off Mission Beach make it one of the best diving spots on the Great Barrier Reef. On land, the high concentration of cassowaries make for thrilling local rainforest walks.

▐ TRANSPORTATION

McCafferty's/Greyhound buses stop in Mission Beach several times per day, **Premier** twice per day. Greyhound runs to Cairns (2¼hr., 4 per day, $17) and Townsville (3¼hr., 4 per day, $46). Once you arrive in town, a hostel courtesy bus will take you to your accommodation. You can also use these buses during your stay, but at night you'll need the **Mission Beach Bus Service** (☎4068 7400), which runs about once per hour 9am-10pm except Monday and Tuesday, when service stops at 5:50pm ($1.50 per section, day-ticket $10). **Island Coast Travel,** in the Homestead Centre at Mission Beach, next to the post office, is a bus and rail ticket agent. (☎4068 7187. Open M-F 9am-5pm, Sa 9am-noon.)

▰ ▰ ORIENTATION & PRACTICAL INFORMATION

The region known as Mission Beach is actually a group of four communities lining a 14km-stretch of waterfront property. From north to south, these towns are: **Bigil Bay, Mission Beach, Wongaling Beach,** and **South Mission Beach.** The main streets are **Porter's Promenade,** which runs through Mission Beach proper, and **Cassowary Drive,** which runs through Wongaling. A popular landmark is the frighteningly large cassowary statue set in the center of Wongaling Beach, in front of the bus stop. Just off the coast are the **Family Islands,** including the daytrip destination **Dunk Island.**

The area tourist office is in the **Wet Tropics Information Centre,** on Porter's Promenade as you leave Mission Beach on the way to Bigil Bay. (☎4068 7099. Open M-Sa 9am-5pm, Su 9am-4pm.) Services include: the **police** (☎4068 8422), 500m past the large cassowary at the corner of Webb Rd. and Cassowary Dr. in Wongaling Beach; **Beverley's,** Shop 15, Hub Shopping Centre, where foreign currency and traveler's checks can be exchanged for no fee (☎4068 7365; open daily 9am-5pm); **ATMs** at the **supermarket** in Mission Beach and the Mission Beach Resort; **Internet** at **Traveljunkies,** next to the grocery store in Wongaling (☎4068 8699; open M-Sa 9am-6pm, Su 4-6pm), and at **Cybernet Club,** on the corner of Porter's and Campbell St. (☎4068 7789; open daily 9:30am-6pm); **pharmacy,** behind the bus stop in Wongaling (M-F 8:30am-5:30pm, Sa 9am-noon); and the **post office,** on Porter's Promenade, which doubles as a Commonwealth Bank. **Postal Code:** 4852.

▐ ACCOMMODATIONS

All hostels offer free pick-up at the bus station and courtesy buses around town at least four times daily, accept credit cards, and book tours. If you're camping or have a caravan, try **Hideaway Holiday Village ❶** (☎4068 7104), on Porter's Promenade, or go across the street to **Mission Beach Camping ❶,** where tent sites are cheaper (from $6 per person).

▧ **The Sanctuary** (☎4088 6064 or 1800 777 012; www.sanctuaryatmission.com), on Holt Rd., Bingil Bay. The most remote accommodation in Mission Beach is also its best. A beautiful hardwood treehouse overlooking the ocean is nestled in the rainforest, where the only thing between you and the resident cassowaries is the screen protecting you from the mozzies. Cafe serves superb dinners ($14-17). Internet, yoga classes, massages ($55), kitchen, pool, and 18 hectares of rainforest to explore. Doubles $60; deluxe double cabins $135. ❷

Scotty's Mission Beach House, 167 Reid Rd. (☎4068 8676; scottys@znet.net.au), located at the end Webb St., off Cassowary Dr. Young, hip staff are friendly and helpful. 24hr. kitchen and adjacent mini market. Every night's a party in Scotty's Bar (meals under $12), but it's far enough removed from rooms to assure a good night's sleep. Laundry, TV room with comfy chairs, kitchen, Internet, and drink vouchers. Reception 7:30am-7pm. 16-bed dorms $18; 4-bed ensuite dorms $21; twins and doubles $35, ensuite $45. VIP. ❷

Mission Beach Backpackers Lodge, 28 Wongaling Beach Rd. (☎4068 8317 or 1800 688 316; mblodge@znet.net.au). Behind the enormous cassowary in Wongaling. A 2-story house with recently refurbished rooms, pool, laundry, and Internet ($3 per hour). Reception 7:30am-7pm. Dorms $18; doubles from $40; triples $42. VIP. ❷

The Treehouse (☎4068 7137), on Bingil Bay Rd., Bingil Bay. Perched on a hill, not a tree. BBQ, pool, laundry, tiny grocery store, and comfy reading space. Team spirit is encouraged by communal showers (private ones also available) and rooms clustered around common area where music (guests' choice) plays until 11pm. Linen provided. F night all-you-can-eat BBQ $12. Reception 8am-8:30pm. Sites $12 per person; dorms $20; twins and doubles $46. YHA. ❶

🍴 FOOD

Several excellent restaurants are located on the Village Green in Mission Beach proper. For **supermarkets,** try Foodmarket, on Porter's Promenade, or Foodstore, in Wongaling Beach, behind the big cassowary. (Both open daily 8am-7pm.)

Toba, 37 Porter's Promenade (☎4068 7852), next to the Village Green. Serves a variety of Southeast Asian cuisine, including Indonesian, Vietnamese, and Japanese specialties. Chiang Mai salad $11. Mains $16-25. Open M and W-Su 6pm-late. ❹

Coconutz (☎4068 7397), next to the Village Green on Porter's Promenade. One of the few licensed bars in Mission Beach, it serves up delicious meals as well, specializing in Asian and Italian food. Mains $14-20. Inquire about budget backpacker meals. Also has a pool room and live music on weekends. Open 10am-midnight (low season), 8am-1:30am (high season). Exchanges travelers' checks free. ❸

Piccolo Paradise (☎4068 7008), on David St. in the Village Green. Piccolo Paradise is a popular cafe offers sandwiches on fresh baguettes, pasta, pizza, and a selection of espresso and juices ($3.30). Meals $5-10. Licensed bar after 6pm. Open Su and Tu-Sa 8:30am-9pm. ❶

👁️ 🄺 SIGHTS & ACTIVITIES

DIVING. Mission Beach is a unique spot on the reef, where coral drop-offs create long walls of underwater gardens. **Mission Beach Dive Charters** is the only PADI dive center in town. It arranges scuba courses and trips to the Lady Bowen, a 105-year-old shipwreck discovered in 1997. The center also makes outer reef daytrips, which include two dives with a maximum of 12 people. (☎4068 7277 or 1800 700 112. 4-day open water certification $440; shipwreck and outer reef $136; gear hire $30 extra. Daytrip with intro dive $180.) **QuickCat** also makes trips to the reef, both directly and via Dunk Island. (☎4068 7289 or 1800 654 242. $132, reef direct Su and W $80; 2 certified dives $85, 1 intro dive $80.)

HIKING. Several beautiful **walking tracks** are in the area. On the back of the Mission Beach street directory (free around town), you'll find a list of parks, forests, and walking tracks, all of which are readily accessible. There are several in **Licula State Forest,** including the **Rainforest Circuit Walk** (1.3km; 30min.), a jaunt under the canopy of Licuala Fan Palms. Start at the carpark of the Tully-Mission Beach Rd. **Licuala Walking Track** (7.8km; 3hr.) stretches north through coastal lowland rainforest to the El Arish-Mission Beach Rd. The **Cutten Brothers Walk** (1.5km; 30min.) snakes through mangroves between Alexander Dr. and Clump Point jetty. For longer walks, the **Bicton Hill Track** (4km; starts 3km past the Wet Tropics Info Centre) and the **Kennedy Track** (7km; 4hr.) feature mangrove, beach and rainforest.

OTHER ACTIVITIES. Jump the Beach offers tandem skydiving several times per day. (☎1800 638 005. Jumps from 8000 ft. $215, $48 for every additional 2000 ft.) **Raging Thunder River Rafting** takes groups on the grade 4 rapids of the Tully River daily. (☎4030 7990. Full-day rafting, lunch and transfers $135.)

⚡ DAYTRIP FROM MISSION BEACH: DUNK ISLAND

The close proximity of the **Family Islands** to Mission Beach make them ideal destinations to escape mainland life. **Dunk Island,** a.k.a. the "father island," is the most frequented. Its Aboriginal name is *Coonanglebah*, meaning "Island of Peace and Plenty." Dunk Island became famous through E.J. Banfield's *Confessions of a Beachcomber*, an account of his life on the island from 1897 to 1923. The largest of the islands' nuclear grouping, **Papa Dunk** is the only daytripper destination. Nearby **Bedarra,** also known as "the mother," is uninhabited, save for a hoity-toity resort. The "twins" are close together and slightly farther out. The smaller land masses at the fringe of the group are the brothers, sisters, and the triplets.

There are three boats that service Dunk Island. Those looking to maximize time on the island should opt for the **Dunk Island Express Water Taxi,** on Banfield Pde., near Scotty's in Wongaling Beach. (☎4068 8310. 10min., 5 per day, $22 return.) For those in no rush to get to Dunk, check out **Dunk Island Ferry & Cruises,** which departs from Clump Point Jetty, 1km north of the village green (also departs from Kurrimine Beach). They offer snorkeling (included on all trips), boom netting, and a BBQ lunch for an extra $10. (☎4068 7211. 30-45min; departs daily 8:45am and 10:30am; $21 return, under 10 free. Extra cruise to Bedarra, lunch and ferry $61.) **Quick Cat** also services the island for $19.50 return. (☎4068 7289. Departs daily 9:30am, returns 4:45pm. $29, children $14.50) **Coral Sea Kayaking** has daytrips to Dunk including small brekkie, lunch, environmental interpretation, and snorkeling gear. (☎4068 9154; www.coralseakayaking.com. Full-day $93, half-day $60.)

The **Dunk Island Resort ⑤** (☎4068 8199) monopolizes all island activities. Even though the room rates aren't prohibitive ($139 including breakfast and dinner), just steps from the jetty are some of the best-equipped **campsites ❶** in North Queensland (permits on site $4 per person per night), complete with hot showers. This isn't a well-kept secret, however—book well in advance. Daytrippers can purchase the **Resort Experience Pass** at the Watersports shed ($28), which entitles visitors to use of the resort facilities and a meal at BBs, or at EJ's in the resort. **Dunk Island Watersports** (☎4068 8199) issues **camping permits** and rents a slew of water toys: paddle skis ($15 per hr.), sailboards ($20 per hr.), snorkel gear ($15 per hr.), and catamarans ($25 per hr.). The only place to eat on the island, besides the resort's fancy restaurant, is **BB's on the Beach ❶,** next door to Watersports, which serves great burgers, pizza, grilled fish, and salads (☎4068 8199; open daily 11am-7pm). Still, it's cheaper to bring your own food. The main attractions on Dunk, aside from the postcard beaches, are the **walking tracks.** The local favorite is the 10km walk around the island (2-3hr.), which combines Dunk history with diverse

QUEENSLAND

landscapes and a trip to the island's highest point. An easier option is the coastal hike (1km; 15min.) up to **Muggy Muggy Beach** from the dock. Not only does Muggy Muggy hide itself in a pocket of 360 million year-old rocks, but it has some of the best snorkeling on the island. **Mount Kootaloo Lookout** (2hr.), the highest point on the island, can offer some of the best views and a good workout. The difficult walk around the island takes about three hours; carry water and wear sturdy shoes.

NEAR MISSION BEACH

PARONELLA PARK

Between Cairns and Mission Beach hides the Moorish castle of ⬛**Paronella Park** (☎ 4065 3225). Spaniard José Paronella built the main thoroughfare of Paronella in the 1930s as a gift for his bride-to-be. Uninhabited for many years, the buildings have degenerated into veritable ruins—testament to the intense north Queensland climate. The authenticity of the buildings and encroaching rainforest, however, make this a sight to be seen. Winner of Queensland's highest tourism award in 2001, the park has been discovered by the entertainment industry and has served as the backdrop for three movies, eight TV shows, a music video, and an international magazine photo shoot. Enthusiastic park guides give tours of the grounds ($17) and then leave you to explore on your own.

Though almost inaccessible via public transportation, it is not hard to find a day-tour from Cairns on Mission Beach (**Calypso Coaches**, ☎ 4068 9212 or **Dunk Island Cruises**, ☎ 4068 7211, offer such services). If you are driving, look for signs along the Bruce Hwy. for Paronella Park (the South Johnstone exit is the fastest); from the Tablelands, follow the signs to South Johnstone and you'll see the sign for the park. If you're not tying the knot or gawking at the exquisite architecture, take some time to stroll down Kauri Ave. or feed the fish and eels in the teeming waterfall pool in the ruins of the castle's grand staircase.

KURRIMINE BEACH

A short drive north of Mission Beach off the Bruce Hwy., Kurrimine Beach is one of the coast's most untouched stretches of sand. For a few days in July, the tides are just right to reach King Reef by foot. Ask at the local **Hub Cafe** for a tide chart and the best time to visit. Queenslanders are also drawn to this area for its great fishing and relaxing setting. The north end of the beach has a **caravan park ❷**; and at the southern end is **Kurrimine Beach Holiday Park ❹**, at the end of Jacob's Rd. (☎ 4065 6166. Camping $18, powered $20; cabins $44, ensuite $55. Book ahead.)

INNISFAIL

North of Mission Beach and enroute to Cairns is the town of Innisfail. Offering few tourist attractions, the Johnstone River and beautiful beaches make it a pleasant pit stop. Those who stay are drawn by its year-round demand for fruit-pickers. Just north of Innisfail, the road to the **Atherton Tablelands** (see p. 435) branches inland toward **Millaa Millaa**. The **railway station** is off the Bruce Hwy. west of town, and the **bus stop** is on Edith St. **McCafferty's/Greyhound buses** run daily to Cairns (1¼hr., 7 per day, $16) and Townsville (3½hr., 7 per day, $47). The **Information Centre**, at the corner of Bruce Hwy. and Lannercost St., books tours. (☎ 4061 7422. Open M-F 9am-5pm, Sa-Su 10am-3pm.) **The Codge Lodge ❷**, 63 Rankin St., near the corner of Grace St., is billed as a working hostel, but those not wanting to roll up their sleeves and head to the farms need not shy away. Close to the town center, the lodge is hands-down the best budget accommodation around, providing a kitchen and pool. (☎ 4061 8055. Reception often unattended so call ahead. Small 1-4 person dorms $15; singles $22. No credit cards.)

FAR NORTH QUEENSLAND

The northeast corner of the continent, from Cairns north into Australia's last great frontier, is nothing short of heaven for outdoor adventurers. The Great Barrier Reef snakes close to shore, luring divers to this spectacular underwater haven. Vast tropical rainforest presses up close to the Coral Sea by the green-covered mountains of the Great Dividing Range. The rich variety of wildlife and untouched landscape prove that the Far North's greatest attraction is its natural beauty.

Cairns now caters to travelers with city comforts, but the more remote parts of this land remain untamed wilderness. The Captain Cook Hwy. leads modern-day trailblazers north into the rainforest, which becomes incredibly dense around Cape Tribulation. Wilder yet is the Cape York peninsula, starting beyond Cooktown and stretching to the Torres Strait, which separates the Gulf of Carpentaria from the Coral Sea and Australia from Papua New Guinea. Travelers daring enough to make the journey should anticipate extremely basic unsealed roads.

CAIRNS ☎07

The last sizeable city at the corner of the great tropical outback, Cairns (CANS) is both the northern terminus of the backpacker route and the premier gateway to snorkeling and scuba diving on the Great Barrier Reef. Neon signs and tourist attractions bombard travelers with colors rivaled only by the flamboyant creatures of the underwater world off-shore. While tidal mudflats preclude traditional beach activities, bars, nightclubs, and cafes provide plenty of diversions for travelers between forays off the coast. The atmosphere of Cairns is friendly, laid-back, and very touristy. More of a big town than a small city, Cairns is also a perfect gateway for adventure activities of all kinds.

▐ TRANSPORTATION

INTERCITY TRANSPORTATION

Flights: The **airport** (☎ 4052 9744) is 6km north of Cairns on Captain Cook Hwy. Follow the signs. For the cheapest flights, try **Student Flights** (☎ 1800 069 063) or the major carriers to the region. **Qantas** (☎ 13 13 13; qantas.com) has daily flights to: Adelaide (5-8hr., 5-7 per day, $297); Brisbane (2hr., 11 per day, $165); Canberra (5hr., 10-13 per day, $318); Darwin (2-5hr., 6 per day, $291); Hobart (6-10hr., 6-7 per day, $362); Melbourne (5hr., 9 per day, $253); Perth (5-10hr., 6-9 per day, $425); and Sydney (3hr., 7-8 per day, $226). Smaller **Flight West Airlines** (☎ 13 23 92) has domestic flights and also flies to Papua New Guinea. **Virgin Blue** is a great domestic resource (☎ 13 67 89; www.virginblue.com.au). Many hostels run a free airport pick-up service; just call from the terminal. However, to get back to the airport, you'll have to book ahead and pay $7.50 for the **Airport Shuttle** (☎ 4048 8355). Buses also run to town from just outside the terminal ($4.50). **Taxis** to town, available 24hr., run about $13.

Trains: The train station is wedged between Bunda St. and the Cairns Central shopping mall. From The Esplanade, walk inland down Spence St. It's on the right, or straight through to the back of Cairns Central. Lockers $2 per day. **Travel Centre Office** (☎ 4036 9341, 24hr. bookings 13 22 32) sells tickets. YHA discount 10% for long-distance trips. Open M, T, Th 7:30am-5pm, W 9am-5pm, F 9:30am-5pm, Sa 7:30am-noon. The **East Coast Discover Pass** offers unlimited travel for up to 6 months and covers rail from Cairns to Brisbane ($205), to Sydney ($293), and to Melbourne ($374). Trains run to Brisbane (31-32hr.; M-Tu, Th, Sa 8:35am; $176). The scenic railway to Kuranda departs Su-F 8:30am and 9:30am, Sa 8:30am. (☎ 4036 9249 for bookings; $34, return $48, student, pensioner, and family discounts.)

Buses: The bus station is at Trinity Wharf, on Wharf St. Open daily 6:15am-1am. Leave luggage in lockers ($6-11 per day) or with Sun Palm Coaches ($2 per item; open daily 5:30am-6:30pm). **Sun Palm Coaches** (☎4099 4992) go to: Cape Tribulation (4hr., 2 per day, $45); Cooktown (inland: 5½hr., W and F-Sa 1 per day, $69; Coastal: 8hr.; June-Oct. Tu, Th, and Sa; $69); Karumba (11½hr., M and W-Th 1 per day, $150); Port (1¼hr., 8 per day, $25). **McCafferty's/Greyhound** (☎13 20 30) has 10% ISIC/VIP/YHA discounts and runs to: Airlie Beach (11hr., 6 per day, $75); Brisbane (28hr., 5 per day, $173); Cardwell (3hr., 5 per day, $25); Ingham (3½hr., 5 per day, $33); Innisfail (1½hr., 5 per day, $16); Mission Beach (2¼hr., 2 per day, $16); Rockhampton (15hr., 6 per day, $115); and Townsville (6hr., 5 per day, $47). **Premier Bus Service** (☎4031 6495 or 13 34 10) usually has less expensive rates and VIP/YHA discounts; however they have less frequent departure times.

Ferries: Quicksilver (☎4087 2100) departs from The Pier to Port Douglas (1½hr.; 1 per day; depart 8am, return 5:15pm; $24, round-trip $36).

LOCAL TRANSPORTATION

Buses: Sunbus (☎4057 7411; www.sunbus.com.au) on Lake St. in City Place. Fares $1-6; unlimited day pass $9.40, families $21; central Cairns-only pass $5. Buses go south into Cairns' suburbs and as far north as Palm Cove, but not to the airport.

Taxis: Black and White (24 hr. ☎13 10 08 or 4048 8333).

Car Rental: The bigger companies in Cairns charge those under 24 a surcharge or significantly raise the deductible, which can increase the rental price by up to $50.

National, 135 Abbott St., has weekly rates starting at $45 per day, 4WD $145 per day (☎13 10 45 or 1300 131 407; open M-F 7:30am-6pm, Sa-Su 8am-5pm).

Avis, 135 Lake St. (☎4051 5911), rents weekly starting at $49 per day, 4WD $160 per day.

A1 Car Rentals, 141 Lake St., has weekly rates from $39 and a great selection of higher-end vehicles (☎1300 301 175; open daily 7:30am-6pm).

Leisure Car Rentals, 314 Sheridan St. (☎4051 8988), is a bit far from the city center but has free pick-up and inexpensive rentals starting at $45 per day.

Travellers AutoBarn, 123-125 Bunda St., rents campervans with unlimited kilometers, local or one-way, from $65 per day. (☎4041 3722 or 1800 674 374; open M-F 9am-5pm, Sa 9am-1pm.)

Automobile Club: Royal Automobile Club of Queensland (RACQ), 138 McLeod St. (24hr. ☎4051 6543). Open daily 8am-5:15pm.

Bike Rental: SkyDive Cairns, 59 Sheridan St. (☎4031 5466). A great way to get around the long, flat streets of Cairns. $15 per day; credit card needed for imprint.

✳ ORIENTATION

Cairns is framed by rainforested hills to the west, a harbor to the east, and mangrove swamps to the north and south. In this modern city, the streets are straight and intersect at right angles, so navigation is easy. **The Esplanade,** with its many hostels and eateries, runs along the waterfront. At the street's southern end is the **The Pier,** with a man-made lagoon and pricey shopping at the heavily commercial Pier Marketplace. Farther south, the Esplanade becomes **Wharf Street** and runs past the **Trinity Wharf** and the **Transit Centre.**

Shields Street runs perpendicular to The Esplanade, crossing **Abbott Street** into **City Place,** a pedestrian mall with an open-air concert space. From this intersection, **Lake Street** runs parallel to the Esplanade. Continuing away from the water, Shields St. also intersects **Grafton Street** and **Sheridan Street** (called Cook Hwy. north of the city). The **Cairns Railway Station** is on **McLeod Street** in front of Cairns Central, the city's largest mall. Address numbers start low at the southeastern end of the Esplanade; cross street address numbers start low at the Esplanade end.

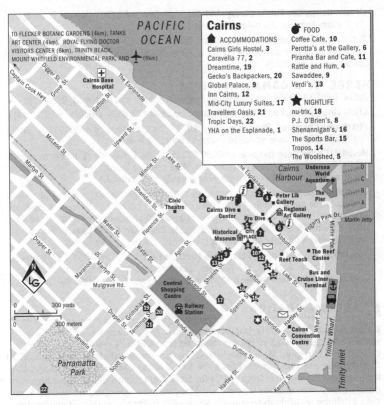

TO FLECKER BOTANIC GARDENS (4km), TANKS
ART CENTER (4km), ROYAL FLYING DOCTOR
VISITORS CENTER (6km), TRINITY BEACH,
MOUNT WHITFIELD ENVIRONMENTAL PARK, AND ✈ (6km)

PACIFIC OCEAN

Cairns

🏠 ACCOMMODATIONS
Cairns Girls Hostel, **3**
Caravella 77, **2**
Dreamtime, **19**
Gecko's Backpackers, **20**
Global Palace, **9**
Inn Cairns, **12**
Mid-City Luxury Suites, **17**
Travellers Oasis, **21**
Tropic Days, **22**
YHA on the Esplanade, **1**

🍴 FOOD
Coffee Cafe, **10**
Perotta's at the Gallery, **6**
Piranha Bar and Cafe, **11**
Rattle and Hum, **4**
Sawaddee, **9**
Verdi's, **13**

⭐ NIGHTLIFE
nu-trix, **18**
P.J. O'Brien's, **8**
Shenannigan's, **16**
The Sports Bar, **15**
Tropos, **14**
The Woolshed, **5**

🔢 PRACTICAL INFORMATION

TOURIST & FINANCIAL SERVICES

Tourist Offices: Traveller's Contact Point Cairns, 119 Abbott St. (☎4041 4677; cairns@travellers.com.au). Services include mail forwarding and job listings. **Internet** $1.50 per 30min., $2.50 per hr. Open daily 7:30am-midnight. **Tropical Tourism North Queensland,** 51 The Esplanade (☎4051 3588), near the Pier between Spence and Shields St., is the biggest agency in town. Open daily 8:30am-6:30pm. The **Visitors Info Bureau,** on the Esplanade, between Aplin and Florence St., is open 24hr. and has tons of information on accommodations, tours, bike hire, and the city itself.

National Parks Office: Queensland Parks and Wildlife Service (QPWS), 10 McLeod St. (☎4046 6600; fax 4046 6604). The *Australian Guide to National Parks* is helpful but pricey. Open M-F 8:30am-4:30pm.

Currency Exchange: Excellent rates are found at **Caravella's 77** hostel, 77 Esplanade (☎4051 2159; see p. 428). The **American Express Office,** 79-87 Abbott St., 2nd fl. (☎4031 0353), at Orchid Plaza, changes US travelers checks free of charge, but has an $8 minimum charge for currency exchange under AUS$800, 2% commission thereafter. Open M-F 8:30am-5pm, Sa 9am-noon. **Thomas Cook,** 59-63 Esplanade (☎4041 1000), exchanges currency for a $7 flat fee. Open daily 9am-8pm. Another branch at 71-73 Esplanade is open daily until 11pm.

Library: Cairns City Public Library, 151 Abbott St. (☎4044 3720). Open M 10am-6pm, Tu-F 10am-7pm, Sa 10am-4pm. **Internet** $3 per hr.

Ticket Agencies: TicketLink in the **Cairns Civic Theatre,** (☎4031 9555 or 4031 9933; www.ticketlink.com.au) at the corner of Florence and Sheridan St. (). Call for ticket prices and show listings.

EMERGENCY & COMMUNICATIONS

Police: (☎4030 7000), on Sheridan St., between Spence and Hartley St. Open 24hr.

Crisis Lines: Alcohol and Drug Information (☎1800 177 833). **Lifeline** (☎13 11 14).

Pharmacy: Chemmart Pharmacy, Shop 10, 85 the Esplanade (☎4051 9011). Open daily 9am-10pm. Gives advice to travelers continuing to Asia.

Hospital: Cairns Base Hospital (☎4050 6333), on the Esplanade at the opposite end of the Pier. 24hr. emergency department. More centrally located is the 24hr. **Medical Centre** (☎4052 1119), on the corner of Florence and Grafton St.

Internet Access: Internet access is everywhere in Cairns. **Mago Internet,** on Alpin St. between the Esplanade and Abbott St., has the cheapest rates ($1 per half hr.). **Internet Outpost,** on the corner of Shields and Abbott St., is good for anyone traveling throughout Australia and New Zealand, with a frequent buyer card and discounts. **Cairns City Public Library** (see above) and **Traveller's Contact Point Cairns** (see above) both charge $3 per hr.

Post Office: Cairns General Post Office (GPO), 13 Grafton St. (☎4031 4303), on the corner of Hartley St. Open M-F 8:30am-5pm. Smaller branch located in Orchid Plaza just south of City Place between Abbott and Lake Streets. **Postal Code:** 4870.

◤ ACCOMMODATIONS

Cairns may not be a big city, but its reputation as the gateway to Far North Queensland's ecological wonders have established it as a firm favorite for backpackers headed to this region. Most hostels in Cairns are clustered along the Esplanade, though there are also many others to be found in the center of town or near the train station. Prices range from $18-24 for most dorm rooms, though amenities and quality of accommodations vary greatly. Many include coin-operated laundry facilities, kitchens, and valuables storage. Some offer further incentives, including free airport pick-up, pools, and free or discounted meal rates at local restaurants. Cairns also provides opportunities to splurge for worn-out backpackers looking for a rejuvenating rest-stop. In any case, be sure to call ahead, as the best places tend to fill up quickly.

CENTRAL CAIRNS

Caravella's 77, 77 Esplanade (☎4051 2159; www.caravella.com.au), between Aplin and Shields St., 10min. from the bus station. Internet access, movies, and pool table. Tour bookings. Key deposit $10. About half of the rooms have baths and A/C; ask about them when you book. Flash your *Let's Go* and ask about a $5 discount on your 1st night's stay. Dorms $21; twins and doubles $43. VIP.❷

Cairns Girls Hostel, 147 Lake St. (☎4051 2767), between Florence and Aplin St. This clean, quiet **women-only hostel** has provided a safe haven for over 30 years. No noise after 9pm, but no curfew. 3 kitchens, 3 bathrooms, 2 lounges, and TV. Reception 7am-9:30pm. $16/night for a dorm, $100/week; $18/night for a twin, $110/week. ❷

Global Palace (☎4031 7921 or 1800 819 024), located at the corner of Lake and Shields St. Trendy decor and large open spaces. Rooftop pool, a cinema-screen TV, kitchen with balcony dining, pool tables, tour booking and Internet. Key and cutlery deposit both $20. 3-4 bed dorms with new mattresses (no bunks) $23; doubles and twins $50. VIP. ❷

YHA on the Esplanade, 93 the Esplanade (☎4031 1919; esplanade@yhaqld.org), near the corner of Aplin St., extremely close to nightclubs and cheap restaurants. A no-frills place to crash. Laundry, kitchen, TV, storage, linens, and Internet. Reception 7am-10pm. Dorms $20; twins and doubles $44-46. ❷

Mid-City Luxury Suites, 6 McLeod St. (☎4051 5050, www.midcity.com.au), right behind Cairns Central. A great stomping ground to rest and regroup. Rooms include living area, fully equipped kitchen, washer and dryer, bathroom, cable TV, Internet lines. Reception M-F 7am-7pm, Sa and Su 8am-5pm. Rooms $115-140. ❺

Inn Cairns, 71 Lake St. (☎4041 2350). A boutique hotel, providing holiday apartments complete with washer, dryer, kitchen, spa, community BBQ, and pool. Prices start at $120 and go up during the Dry. ❺

JUST OUTSIDE THE CITY CENTER

⊠ Dreamtime, 4 Terminus St. (☎4031 6753), just off Bunda St., behind Cairns Central and around the corner from Gecko's. Daily shuttles to Pier and bus station. Only 27 beds and 3-4 bed dorms. Pool, BBQ, kitchen. Book ahead. Reception 7:30am-noon and 4-8pm. Dorms $20; twins and doubles (some with fridge) $45. ❷

Tropic Days, 26-28 Bunting St., (☎4041 1521; www.tropicdays.com.au), behind the Showgrounds, north off Scott St.; a 20min. walk west from downtown. Jungle-themed paintings, a neatly tended tropical garden, and a sparkling pool. M BBQ. Free shuttle to city center. Bike hire and TV lounge. Sites $11; 3-bed dorms $18; doubles $42. ❶

Gecko's Backpackers, 187 Bunda St. (☎4031 1344 or 1800 011 334). Clean, bright rooms, all with comfortable mattresses. Friendly, helpful staff make this small backpackers seem like a second home. Internet $2 per 20min. Reception 7am-noon and 4-8pm. 3-4 bed dorms $18; twins and doubles $20, rooms with A/C more. ❷

Travellers Oasis, 8 Scott St. (☎4052 1377; travoasis@travoasis.com.au). 3 main houses around a courtyard, garden, free internet and pool. Management chose not to buy a TV; they'd rather have guests talking to each other. Coffee and tea included. Sa night BBQ. Reception 7am - 8 pm. 3- and 4-bed dorms $20; twins and doubles $44. ❷

⬛ FOOD

Cairns is overflowing with good eats, from all-night kebab and pizza stalls on the Esplanade to upscale restaurants specializing in seafood. Shields St. is known by the locals as "eat street"—wander around and do some menu shopping. Many restaurants offer up to 40% discounts if you are seated before a certain time, normally 7pm. Most of the hostels in town hand out meal vouchers to one of the local watering holes, though doing your own cooking is often the most economical dinner option. For basic **groceries,** try Woolworths, on Abbott St. between Shields and Spence St. (open M-F 8am-9pm, Sa 8am-5:30pm, Su 9am-6pm), or Bi-Lo Mega Fresh and Coles, in Cairns Central (open M-F 8am-9pm, Sa 8am-5:30pm, Su 9am-6pm).

Perrotta's at the Gallery (☎4031 5899), corner of Abbot and Shields St., next to the Cairns Art Gallery. This hyper-modern cafe was named Cairns Restaurant of the Year 2002. Stop in for pre-gallery brekkie ($4-10) or post-painting dinner ($20-25). Open daily 8:30am-10pm. ❹

Coffee Cafe, 87 Lake St. (☎4041 1899). Offers scones, jam, and a pot o' tea for $6, all within earshot of the open-air concert hall. Also serves up great lunches ($4-10), dinners ($10 and up), and gourmet dessert. Open M-Sa 7am-9pm, Su 8am-9pm. ❷

Piranha's, 64 Shields St. (☎4051 9459). Fairly new to Cairns, this Mexican grill and bar with ample outdoor seating caters to nacho-craving backpackers. Complimentary drinks with meal order during Happy Hour (daily 5-6pm). Open M-Sa for lunch (under $10) and dinner (under $17), Su for dinner only. ❸

Verdi's, 66 Shields St. (☎4052 1010). Italian restaurant serves up huge pastas ($15 and up) and fresh salads ($9-13). Open M-F from noon, Sa-Su from 6pm. ❸

Rattle and Hum (☎4031 3011), on the Esplanade. A very popular spot, where locals and travelers alike enjoy woodfired pizzas ($12-15) in the open air or a drink at the festive bar. Open daily 11:30am-midnight. ❷

Sawaddee, 62 Shields St. (☎4031 7993). Traditional Thai cuisine served among modern decor. Large variety of curries, stir fry, and vegetarian entrees for either eat-in or takeaway ($10-18). Open for lunch Th, F 12-2:30; for dinner daily 6pm-late. ❸

🔘 SIGHTS

■**TANKS ART CENTRE.** The center consists of a trio of WWII diesel tanks transformed into a massive art exhibition space. The best local art is on display here, with each show lasting three weeks. The last Sunday of every month from June to November, Tanks hosts **Market Day,** a free bazaar with live music and plenty of pottery, crafts, and herbs for sale. *(46 Collins Ave. Accessible from Sunbus #1B. ☎4032 2349. Open daily 11am-4pm. $2.)*

FLECKER BOTANIC GARDENS. Right next to Tanks, you can see a Gondwanan (evolutionary flora track) garden, a meandering boardwalk, fern and orchid houses, and a trail that crosses fresh and saltwater lakes. *(Take Sunbus #1B from City Place, $2.30, or drive north on Sheridan St. and take a left onto Collins Ave. ☎4044 3398. Guided walks M-F 1pm. Open M-F 7:30am-5:30pm, Sa-Su 8:30am-5:30pm. Free.)*

MOUNT WHITFIELD ENVIRONMENTAL PARK. The park is the last bit of rainforest in the Cairns area. The park's shorter Red Arrow circuit takes about one hour, while the more rugged Blue Arrow circuit is a five hour return trek up and around Mt. Whitfield. Don't stay after dark—finding a cab or a bus back into Cairns might be difficult. *(Wedged between the Tanks Art Centre and the Botanic Gardens on Collins Ave.)*

PETER LIK GALLERY. You've probably already bought at least 10 of his postcards—now see his pictures in life-size form. Recognized today as one of Australia's best photographers, Lik's popular prints of Australian wildlife are showcased in this modern gallery. *(4 Shields St. ☎4031 8177. Open daily 9am-10pm. Free.)*

KURANDA. The **Skyrail,** a gondola-like cableway, coasts for 7.5km above and through the rainforest to this popular mountain town. At the top, a boardwalk snakes through the trees; detailed information on the area is given one stop below. See p. 436 for more on Kuranda. *(Trains leave regularly from the station. If you are driving, go north on the Cook Hwy. and follow the signs. ☎4038 1555; www.skyrail.com.au. 1½hr. $32, children $16. Transfers cost extra.)*

UNDERSEA WORLD AQUARIUM. Houses a small but captivating presentation of the reef's brilliantly colored sea life. Make sure you have time for the shark feedings at 10am, noon, 1:30, and 3pm. Book ahead and you can even dive with the sharks for 30min.—after you sign the insurance waiver, of course. *(In the Pier Marketplace, near the wharves. ☎4041 1777. Open daily 8am-8pm. $12.50, children $7, families $30, 20% discount for students and pensioners. Shark diving 3:30-8pm. $85.)*

🔺 OUTDOOR ACTIVITIES

Cairns largely owes its tourist town status to its warm winters and proximity to the Great Barrier Reef. At night, travelers stay in town and drink at local pubs, but during the day they're often found outside the city limits enjoying racy thrills, bumps, and spills for reasonable prices. Activities can often be booked from hostels and most companies offer free pick-up and drop-off. Booking isn't necessary, however, to enjoy Cairns's outdoors lifestyle, evident everywhere from open-air markets to bountiful outdoor dining.

CYCLING. Ride with **Bandicoot Bicycle Tours** for an amazing day of cycling, wildlife-spotting, swimming, and relaxation in the tablelands above Cairns. Enjoy rides (3-7km) between trips to waterfalls, giant fig trees, and swimming holes. Lunch, morning and afternoon tea are included and feature a vegetarian-friendly BBQ and tropical fruit. (☎ 4055 0155; www.bandicootbikes.com. 10½ hr. Trips depart M, W, F 8am, return 6:30pm. $109.)

BUNGY JUMPING. AJ Hackett is a wild New Zealander—ask him about bungy jumping off the Eiffel Tower (and then getting arrested for it) and then sign up for one of his (legal) Australian jumps. Night bungy on request. (☎ 4057 7188 or 1800 622 888; bungy@austarnet.com.au. Open daily 9am-5:30pm. $109.)

FISHING. Cast for your own bait and then tow the line with **Fishing The Tropics.** They run their 6m boat in the Cairns estuary and Daintree River (☎ 4034 1500). **VIP Fishing & Game Boat Services** offers similar packages, along with others that feature fly and shark fishing, or hunting the black marlin from June to December. (☎ 4031 4355. Half-day trips cost around $75, full-day around $140.)

PARASAILING & SKYDIVING. Parasail 300 ft. above Trinity Inlet with **North Queensland WaterSports.** Jet skiing is also available. (☎ 4045 2735. $50, tandem $90.) Jump tandem with an instructor from 8000 ft., or learn to jump solo, with **Skydive Cairns.** (59 Sheridan St. ☎ 4031 5466. $235, upgrades $48 per 2000 ft.) For the only beach landing around, try **Skydive Mission Beach;** ask about combined rafting and kayaking packages. (☎ 1800 638 005. $235, includes transport.)

WHITEWATER RAFTING. Three companies offer basically the same deal—a wild day of rafting tame enough for beginners. **R' n' R Rafting** has several options including multi-day and family packages. The longer your trip, the rougher your rapids. (☎ 4051 7777. Half-day $88, full-day $145; 2-day helicopter in, raft out $630.) Or, check out **Raging Thunder Adventures** (24hr. reservations ☎ 4030 7990). **Foaming Fury** (☎ 4031 3460) has half-day rides and full-day rides that include rainforest walks.

BEACH. Cairns doesn't really have a beach—it has a mud flat. However, there is a new man-made (chlorinated) lagoon and park area that stretches for several hundred meters along the Esplanade. Twenty minutes by bus to the north will take you to **Palm Cove,** a beautiful beach lined with cafes and upscale resorts, offering respite from the burgeoning Cairns nightlife. (Sunbus #1, 1A, 1B, and 2X run to beaches from the depot in City Place. M-F every 30min., Sa-Su every hr.)

◢ DIVING & SNORKELING

The most popular way to see Cairns is through snorkel goggles. Every day, rain or shine, thousands of tourists and locals suit up with masks, fins, and snorkels to slide beneath the ocean surface and glimpse the Great Barrier Reef. ▧**Reef Teach,** 14 Spence St., has a 2hr. lecture by Paddy Colwell, a marine biologist who doubles as a comic. In his own passionate and entertaining way, Colwell teaches about the history of the reef and its biodiversity. (☎ 4031 7794; www.reefteach.com.au. Lectures M-Sa 6:15pm. $13; includes tea, coffee, and snack.)

As the main gateway to the reef, Cairns is studded with an overwhelming number of dive shops and snorkeling outfits. Knowing which one to choose can be tricky and even a little daunting when you're bombarded with brochures and

RECENT NEWS

RESCUING THE REEF

Stretching over 2000km along the northeastern coast of Australia, the Great Barrier Reef is the only natural wonder recognizable from space. Unfortunately, however, it's also threatened by increasing over-fishing, record high temperatures, tourism, and pollution.

To counteract eco-system deterioration, Australian authorities announced in June 2003 the implementation of a Reef Protection plan, increasing the protected regions, a.k.a. green zones, from just under 5% (16,000 sq.km.) to over 30%. (114,000 sq.km.) According to David Kemp, Federal Minister for the Environment and Heritage, this plan ensures the security of the Reef while also protecting the multi-billion dollar tourist industry that the Reef sustains.

But why limit the so-called green zones to 30%? Protected zones decrease the range of commercial and recreational fishing. However, protective measures will actually improve the variety of catches and size of fish seen in the unrestricted areas. This is because species that have traditionally been over-fished will benefit from the extra protection and will grow in size and numbers.

While the increased area of protection does nothing to combat the issue of global warming or the influx of polluted waters, it does promise to increase the Reef's resources for coping with other environmental hazards.

booking agents. Think about some questions in advance: how long do you want to dive—one day, or more than one day? How big a boat do you want? For personal dive instruction and a group atmosphere, smaller boats may be the way to go. Finally, are you going with other divers or with friends who may prefer other water activities? Unless you're all diving, you won't want a dive trip—maybe instead a cruise with diving options such as **Passions of Paradise.** The only place in the area that does snorkel-only sails is **Wavelength,** in Port Douglas (see p. 439).

In order to dive in Australia, you need an open-water certification, a driver's license for the water. The only way to get this certification is to spend about 4 days and at least $350 in scuba school, where you learn about scuba equipment and diving techniques. To enroll in dive classes, you need two passport-sized photos and a medical exam, which can be arranged with a local doctor for about $50.

Introductory dives offer a taste of scuba diving *without* scuba school. For those not planning to dive more than once, intro dives might be the way to go—you get an idea of what's down there without paying an arm and a leg (provided there aren't any sharks involved). Beware: some companies tack on payments as the day on the reef extends. Ask questions about how long the actual underwater experience will be before signing on. If your first taste of the undersea world leaves you hankering for more, many companies offer a second dive for an additional fee.

DIVING DAYTRIPS

Noah's Ark Too (☎4050 0677), located at the Pier. The motto at Noah's: "There are no rules." Relax on a boat that takes up to 28 people, sip a beer, have a laugh, and take the plunge on one of the 10 outer reef destinations chosen on the day of the trip. Departs daily 8:45am, returns 5pm. Certified dives $50, intro dives including a free 10-min. lesson underwater $80; additional dives $30.

The Falla, located in the Pier (☎4031 3488; www.fallacruises.com). A swanky, restored pearl lugger boat (a.k.a. sailboat) is chartered by a small crew, accommodating up to 35 passengers. The divemasters will take novices out for a day on Upolo Reef. Departs daily 9am, returns about 6pm. Base price $60, children $35, families $190; includes lunch. First intro dive $50, second $30. First certified dive $40, second $20.

Passions of Paradise (☎4050 0676) offers full-day cruises to Paradise Reef and Upolo Cay. This boat has a young, vibrant spirit; spontaneous conga dancing is not an unknown occurrence on the deck. Face-painting and chocolate cake keep the youngsters happy even at the end of the day. The high-speed catamaran can take between 60 and 70 passengers on the 10hr. trip. Departs 8am. Base price for snorkeling, lunch, and transport $70. Intro dive or 2 certified dives additional $55.

MULTI-DAY TRIPS & SCUBA SCHOOLS

☒ **Pro-Dive** (☎4031 5255; www.prodive-cairns.com.au), on the corner of Abbott and Shields St. Their most popular trip is the 5-day learn-to-dive course. Although the price tag may seem hefty at $650, it includes all diving, equipment, 2 nights accommodation, and 5 additional dives. If you're on a tight budget, they also offer a 3-day learn-to-dive trip on Fitzroy Island Dive for $325. This trip includes housing on the island and the camaraderie that comes with having 9-person classes. Open daily 8:30am-9pm.

Cairns Dive Centre, 121 Abbott St. (☎4051 0294 or 24hr. 1800 642 591; www.cairns-dive.com.au). Generally the least expensive trip to the outer reef, with a "floating hotel" catamaran for its flagship and a smaller boat for daytrips. 5-day live-aboard, learn-to-dive course $550; 4-day budget course $297. Open daily 7:30am-5pm.

Tusa Dive (☎4031 1248; www.tusadive.com), at Shields St. and the Esplanade. The first 2 days of their 4-day PADI courses ($572) are run in the classroom by ProDive instructors, but the 2 daytrips to the outer reef are on speedy new Tusa boats (maximum 28 passengers). A diver's dive company, Tusa is more expensive than others but ideal for those who want to get to the outer reef with experts and without the live-aboard experience. 2-day Nitrox certification courses $435. Open daily 7:30am-9:30pm.

Down Under Dive, 287 Draper St. (24 hr.☎4052 8300; www.downunderdive.com.au). A 2-masted clipper ship with a hot tub takes 2-day (or longer) trips, starting at $210 for snorkelers and $290 for certified divers. The company also offers diver training for those on a budget. A 4-day course starts at $280 for 2 days of pool training and 2 days on Hastings and Saxon Reefs. Open daily 7am-5pm.

◙ NIGHTLIFE

Despite its widespread and well-deserved reputation as a haven for backpackers, the Cairns nightclub scene is still a few paces behind that of other cities. Still, adrenaline-fueled days spent sky- and scuba-diving make for some explosive nightlife. Get your hand stamped before 10pm and the venues are all free. Hostels usually give out a free meal voucher for one of the clubs to draw in the young crowds. For the latest word on the street, editorials, and show listings, pick up a copy of *Barfly* (free), found all around town.

Ultimate Party is a Cairns pub crawl held every Saturday night. Pay $45 for entry into five bars and clubs, a shot in each one, two all-you-can eat meals, entertainment, transport, a photo, and a t-shirt. At the end of the night, pick up a book of vouchers for tattoos, adventure trips, and, of course, more alcohol. Sign up at the Tropical Arcade on the corner of Shields St. and Abbott St., or call ☎4041 0332.

The Woolshed, 24 Shields St. (☎4031 6304 for free shuttle bus until 9:30pm). A rowdy all-night party for travelers. Backpackers come here to dance on the tables, drink beer, and enter the M night Mr. and Ms. Backpacker contests. Practically every hostel in town offers meal vouchers ($4 off) for this place. M and W Happy Hour 9:30-11:30pm. $6 pitchers, $3 basics. Cover Su-Th $5, F $6, Sa free before 10pm. Open nightly 6-9:30pm for meals, club open until 5am. Downstairs is the **Bassment,** which plays dance music Th-Sa until 5am. Free until midnight.

Shenannigan's (☎4051 2490), on the corner of Sheridan and Spence St. This place boasts the best beer garden in Cairns; watch the latest sports matches on the 2 large screens, or listen to live music inside 4 nights a week. They also serve up huge meals. M jugs $6 until 1am, Tu Quiz night, F DJ night. Open daily 10am-2am.

P.J. O'Brien's (☎4031 5333), in City Place, at the corner of Shields and Lake St., always finds a reason to celebrate. With tables made from beer barrels, authentic Irish memorabilia, and quotes from Yeats in the murals, this place almost looks like an Emerald Isle museum. Pints of Guinness ($5.50) and tasty food (meals $12-18) make P.J.'s the next biggest hot spot in town. Live bands 6 nights a week, Happy Hour F 5-9pm (Guinness $4). Neat dress required.

Tropos (☎4031 2530), on the corner of Lake and Spence St. This techno club is everyone's last stop before bed at the end of the night. You can't miss it—the whirling spotlight can be seen across the street. W retro night. Cover $5.50, free before midnight. Open daily until 5am. Neat dress required.

The Sports Bar, 33 Spence St. (☎4041 2503), is rapidly rising in popularity with its vouchers for $1, heavily discounted meals, and 5-finger Tu. With billiards and multiple TV sets broadcasting all sports all the time, you can stay and enjoy your dinner, or your pint, without missing the big game. Open M-F 11am-5am, Sa-Su 6pm-5am.

nu-trix, 53 Spence St. (☎4051 8223), between Grafton and McLeod St. Hard to miss its rainbow-colored marquis. A gay bar and dance club with no dress code. Shows F and Sa nights; cover $5. Open Su and W-Th 9:30pm-late, F-Sa 9:30pm-5am.

◪ DAYTRIPS FROM CAIRNS

TJAPUKAI

Just north of Cairns and off the Cook Hwy. in **Smithfield** is the gem of Aboriginal cultural parks, **Tjapukai.** Pronounced "JAB-a-guy," this is the most wholly rewarding and culturally fair presentation of Aboriginal myths, customs, and history in all of Queensland. Learn how to throw boomerangs and spears, see a cultural dance show, view a film on Aboriginal history, and more. Set aside at least half a day for this experience. (☎4042 9999; www.tjapukai.com.au. Open daily 9am-5pm. $29, children $14.50. Packages and evening events also available. Transfers to and from Cairns and the Northern Beaches $18 round-trip.)

ZOOS

Hartley's Creek Crocodile Farm is unsurprisingly home to hundreds of crocs, as well as an array of kangaroos, koalas, and cassowaries. Keepers taunt a croc until it eats a hand-fed chicken in the heart-pounding "crocodile attack show," staged daily at the farm at 3pm. (On the Cook Hwy., 40km north of Cairns. ☎4055 3576; www.crocodileadventures.com. Open daily 8:30am-5pm. $24, children $12, families $60.) Transportation and tours to the farm are available from Cairns on **Hartley's Express** (☎4038 2992) and **All in a Day Tours** (☎4032 5050), as well as from the town of Port Douglas on **Wildlife Discovery Tours** (☎4099 6612). The larger **Wild World: The Tropical Zoo,** situated near Palm Cove on the Cook Hwy., 20min. north of Cairns, offers a unique hands-on approach, allowing you to get up close and personal with a variety of Australian wildlife. Daily shows and croc feedings add to the excitement. (☎4055 3669; www.wildworld.com.au. Open daily 8:30am-5pm. $24, children $12.)

CRYSTAL CASCADES

Only 30km from Cairns's center, this freshwater swimming and diving hole can fill up a few hours to make a hot, lazy day more exciting. The best part? It's completely free. Locals often frequent the spot for diving. Be careful on the slippery rocks in and around the cascades. There is also a short hiking trail in the surrounding area. (Drive north along Sheridan St., turn left on Aeroglen, head towards Redlynch and follow the signs.)

GREEN ISLAND   ☎07

Diminutive Green Island barely pushes above the water's surface; its perimeter can be walked in 15min. Though dominated by the resort in the island's center, a boardwalk through the rainforest and a beach path provide access to nature.

The cheapest and quickest way to the island is by ferry with **Great Adventures.** (☎4044 9944 or 1800 079 080. Departs Cairns daily 8:30, 10:30am, and 1pm; departs Green Island noon, 2:30, and 4:30pm. $46.) **Big Cat Green Island Reef Cruises** offers a day on the island and either a glass-bottom boat tour or snorkeling gear. (☎4051 0444. Departs Cairns daily 9am. $54, children $30, families $144.) Those looking for a more luxurious experience should skip the high-speed economy ferry and indulge in a leisurely sailing and snorkeling trip. **Ocean Free** sails to the island daily. On the way, you'll have lunch and stop at the reef for a couple of hours snorkeling. After a day on the island, the returning sunset sail includes wine, cheese, and desserts. (☎4041 1118. Departs Cairns daily 8:30am. $75, children $55.)

The main attraction on the island is **Marineland Melanesia,** a combination gallery, aquarium, and croc farm 250m left of the jetty. Come at 10:30am or 1:45pm to watch a live feeding of Cassius, the world's largest crocodile in captivity. You can also hold yearling crocodiles or tour the art collection. (☎4051 4032. Open daily 9:30am-4:15pm. $9.50, children $4.50.) Just off the end of the jetty is the **Marine Observatory,** from which you can observe bits of the coral reef from 1.5m below the surface ($3). **Green Island Resort ➒** (☎4031 3300) is a luxurious and expensive eco-tourist accommodation. A handful of boutiques and small cafes (open daily 9:30am-4pm) surround the pool by the entrance to the resort. Single suite packages start at $396 per night.

FITZROY ISLAND   ☎07

Fitzroy Island is much larger than Green Island and is generally a better choice for the budget traveler. There are affordable beds, though most people only go for a day. Its coral beaches and lush rainforest are pristine—only noise pollution disrupts the tropical scenery. **Sunlover Cruises** does the trip to the island or a combination of the island and Moore Reef. (☎4050 1333. Both cruises depart 9:30am, return 5pm. Fitzroy only $36, combo $50; children $18/$25, families $90/$126.) If a cruise sounds too easy, try traveling to Fitzroy Island via **sea kayak** with **Raging Thunder Adventures,** which now owns the resort on the island. A high-speed catamaran takes you most of the way, followed by three hours of reef kayaking, snorkeling, and lunch. An overnight package includes bunk accommodations at the Fitzroy Island Resort and two days of kayaking. (☎4030 7907. Daytrip $115, overnight $135.) You can also get to the island via the **Fitzroy Island Flyer,** which leaves from Cairns and the island. (3 times daily. $36, children $18, family $90.) Once there, you can rent kayaks ($15 per hr.) and fishing rods and tackle ($10 per day). **Fitzroy Island Resort ➌** has a variety of clean, bunkhouse-style accommodations. (Shared bunks $31; private bunks for 1-3 people $116; 4 people $124; doubles $58; cabins $250.) The resort has a **pool bar ➋** which serves meals ($5-15) daily 9am-5pm. The **Beach Bar ➌** serves dinner 6-8:30pm ($12-22). The **Flare Grill ➋** serves continental ($10) and cooked ($10-12) breakfast daily 8-10am.

The resort's **dive shop** offers introductory diving and snorkel gear at reasonable rates. (Open daily 9:30am-4pm. Intro dive $65, certified $50; snorkel gear $12.) Snorkel and dive trips leave at 10:30am, 12:30, and 2:30pm. The walk to the **lighthouse** (5km return) starts at a clearing adjacent to the **Reefarm,** a prawn breeding farm 1km north of the resort. There are a couple good 500m walks through the rainforest on the northern end of the island as well. Just past the restaurant, the **Secret Garden track** cuts west into the island, while **Nudey Beach track** continues

along the coast. The Secret Garden track is easy and has informative nature placards. The Nudey Beach track, a bit more challenging, is made of huge stone slabs
leading to boulders and the occasional nude sunbather at the shore.

ATHERTON TABLELANDS

Although much of northern Queensland is picturesque, nothing quite compares to
the Atherton Tablelands. Rolling hills meet unspoiled rainforest, creating a perfect
venue for spotting wildlife. Traveling northeast on the Kennedy Hwy., you'll find
the farming village of **Mareeba** and touristy **Kuranda**. The southern route via the
Gilles Hwy. passes through the residential township of **Atherton,** charming **Yungaburra,** and **Malanda.**

The mountainous lakeside roads give drivers both a mild challenge and rewarding panoramas. Although 4WD provides the fullest experience, the Tablelands are
accessible without a car. **White Car Coaches,** 8 McCowaghie St., Atherton, provides
service seven days a week from Cairns to the Tablelands, with stops in Kuranda,
Mareeba, Herberton, and Ravenshoe. (☎4091 1855; $22.) The **Skyrail Rainforest
Cableway,** a 7.5km gondola, lifts you up above the rainforest canopy into Kuranda
village. A 1½hr. round-trip originates in Carovonica Lakes, 10 min. northwest of
Cairns. (☎4041 0007 or 4038 1555. Open daily 8:30am-3:45pm. $49, children
$24.50.) The **Kuranda Scenic Railway** runs an antique train ride from downtown
Cairns to Kuranda. (☎4031 3636. From Cairns Su-F 8:30am and 9:30am, Sa 8:30am;
from Kuranda Su-F 2pm and 3:30pm, Sa 3:30pm. $33; concession discounts.)

KURANDA   ☎07

Many travelers get no farther than this mountain town, the gateway to the Tablelands. Its river cruises, street performers, and famous markets draw sightseers
from Cairns, though when the town shuts down after the last train leaves in the
afternoon, the intrepid traveler is left to wander its historical streets without the
crowds. In the morning, the hustle and bustle begins again when the **original markets** (open Su, W-Sa) and **Heritage Markets** (open daily 8:30am-3pm) transform the
cozy village into a bazaar of arts, crafts, and clothing.

Kuranda Backpacker's Hostel ❷ (a.k.a. "Mrs. Miller's"), 6 Arara St., is across the
street to the left of the train station on the corner of Arara and Barang St. With its
cast iron beds and pressed metal ceilings, you'll feel like you're taking a trip back
in time. In the mornings, the proprietor feeds over 50 rainbow lorikeets. Amenities
include a kitchen, pool, bike rental, tropical garden, laundry, and free pick-up from
Cairns. (☎4093 7355. Reception 8am-6pm. Dorms $18; twins and doubles $40.)
Kuranda Hotel Motel ❹, on the corner of Coondoo and Arara St., just across the
street from Skyrail, sports a garden bar restaurant, a pool, and tidy rooms with
bath, fridge, and TV. (☎4093 7206. Reception M-Sa 10am-10pm, Su 10am-4pm. Key
deposit $5. Singles $44; doubles $55; extra adult $11, extra child $5.50.)

Locals love **Frog's ❷,** 11 Coondoo St., with its spacious porch stretching out
back. (☎4093 7405. Sandwiches $8; gourmet pizzas $12 and up. Open daily 9:30am-
4pm.) Many places in town serve Devonshire tea, but only the ◪**Honey House ❷,** at
the entrance to the original **Kuranda Markets,** makes its sweets right on the premises. A hive of bees in the store produces sweet Kuranda honey, and the accompanying pumpkin scones are made fresh and from scratch. (☎4093 7261. Open
daily 8am-5pm.)

On the drive from Cairns, the road winds steeply through plush rainforest. Right
off the Kennedy Hwy., the award-winning **Rainforestation Nature Park** offers everything from Aboriginal tours and walks to a wildlife park. Hop on the amphibious
Army Duck, which crosses both land and water, to get a real taste of the region's

environment. Shuttles leave daily from Kuranda village headed for the Rainforestation Park. (☎4093 9033. Aboriginal culture tours $18, children $9; duck tours $14/$7; wildlife park $10/$6.)

Kuranda is also the gateway to the amazing **Barron Gorge National Park.** By car, follow the signs from the town's center; the gorge is about 2.5km from town. A good walk is also signposted from the center of town—the Kuranda Scenic Railway stops here and allows travelers to hop out for a quick view. A short boardwalk takes those on foot right through the dense rainforest to an incredible lookout above Barron Falls, one of the largest waterfalls in the Tablelands.

MAREEBA & ATHERTON   ☎07

While Mareeba and Atherton may lack the quaintness of Yungaburra or the scenic views of Kuranda, they illustrate the true rhythm of the Tropical Tablelands. Both towns claim to have "the best weather in the Tablelands," with over 300 days of sunshine a year. A short stop in Atherton will reveal much about the region's history and the town of Mareeba has begun to garner attention for its burgeoning industries—90% of Australia's coffee is produced here, as well as the regional specialty, mango wine.

The **Coffee Works,** 136 Mason St., in Mareeba, lures visitors with its aromatic home brews and coffee-tasting tours. (☎4092 4101 or 1800 355 526. Open daily 9am-4pm. Tours, $5.50, include free tasting of 12 coffees.) A short drive away, the **Golden Pride Winery,** on Bilwon Rd., is the world's only mango wine-producing factory and farm. Drive in and ring the bell for a free taste of any of their many divine dry, medium, and sweet wines. (☎4093 2524. Open daily 9am-10pm. Bottles from $22.) Another great attraction in town is the **Granite Gorge,** where locals come to swim and feed rock wallabies or hike the rocky walking trails. **Camping ❶** is permitted ($3 per person).

Atherton, located atop an extinct volcano, is a great base for Lake Tinaroo and other Tableland destinations. There is an **info center** (☎4091 1131) at the **Atherton Snack Bar ❶,** 104 Main St., which has budget meals and homemade cakes. An excellent place to stay, **Blue Gum B&B ❺,** 36 Twelfth Ave. (☎4091 5149), looks over the green hills of the Tablelands and has transfers from Cairns. For budget accommodation, try recently remodeled **Atherton Travellers Lodge ❷,** 37 Alive St. (☎4091 3552. Dorms $16; doubles $38.) To indulge your sweet tooth, drive down the Gillies Hwy. until you see the sign for **Shaylee's Strawberry Farm** (☎4091 2962), which sells strawberries from the field, homemade ice cream, and fresh jam (from $3.50).

LAKE TINAROO & CRATER LAKES NATIONAL PARK

Saturated with crater lakes and sprinkled with waterfalls, the volcanic soil of the central Tablelands of Australia sprouts lush forest that lines the shores of the **Tinaroo, Barrine,** and **Eacham Lakes.** Unsealed **Danbulla Forest Drive** circles only Lake Tinaroo. The free *Danbulla State Forest* visitor's guide, available from the **QPWS Forest Management,** 83 Main St., Atherton (☎4091 1844), lists sights along the 40min. loop. Contact the **QPWS Eacham District Office** (☎4095 3768) at Lake Eacham for information on walking paths around the picturesque lakes. The paved 31km **Lake Circuit track** around Lake Eacham in **Crater Lakes National Park** has muskrat-kangaroos and giant iguanas.

Coming from the gateway town of **Tolga,** off Hwy. 1, a barren road runs through farmland before reaching the forested area of Lake Tinaroo. At the entrance to the lake is the **Lake Tinaroo Holiday Park ❶,** which has a kiosk, fuel, and a game room. (☎4095 8232. Sites $15, powered $20; cabins $48; holiday units from $60.) The road also passes five **campsites ❶.** (Sites $4 per person; toilets available.)

Created by volcanic eruptions thousands of years ago, Lake Barrine and Lake Eacham exist today as prime spots to enjoy the beauty of the clear glassy waters reflecting the surrounding rainforest. The larger of the two, Lake Barrine is located just off the Gillies Hwy. on the way into Yungaburra. Tour the exotic gardens, dine at the **Lake Edge Teahouse Restaurant ❷** (open daily 9am-5pm) or cruise around the lake on a guided boat tour (departs daily from Teahouse 10:15, 11:30am, 1:30, 2:30, 3:30pm. $12, children $6).

To reach Lake Eacham, continue on Gillies Hwy. towards Yungaburra and turn left onto Lakes Dr. Lake Eacham is smaller and has no dining or boating options; however, a grassy beach and laffers into the water make it the better choice for swimming and sunbathing. Camping facilities are located nearby at the **Lake Eacham Caravan Park ❶**, with showers, laundry, a small general store, and a petting zoo. (☎4095 3730. Reception 7am-7pm. Sites for 2 $13, powered $16; cabins $54.)

YUNGABURRA   ☎07

Tiny Yungaburra (pop. 400) is at the heart of the Tablelands, with Lake Tinaroo and the Danbulla State Forest to the north, waterfalls to the south, Lakes Eacham and Barrine to the southeast, and the volcanic hills of the **Seven Sisters** to the west. The town is handsome and almost completely untouched by commercial tourism, yet still quite warm and welcoming to visitors. Yungaburra hosts the biggest **markets** in the north on the fourth Saturday of each month from 7am to noon where you can barter for homemade crafts, fresh produce, and even goats. From Cairns, take the Gillies Hwy. 60km west.

To the west of Yungaburra is the **Curtain Fig Tree,** a monstrous strangler fig forming an eerie curtain in the middle of the rainforest. Pick your gaping jaw off the ground and check out the 50m tall, 500-year-old **Cathedral Fig Tree** on the east stretch of Dunballa Forest Dr., accessed via the Gillies Hwy. en route to Cairns. The best place to spot a **platypus** is at the Atherton Shire Council Pumping Station. From Yungaburra, head past the bridge and turn right onto Picnic Crossing Rd. (the road sign is actually 10m ahead of the turn-off). Follow the second right-hand turn. You'll find a concrete picnic table and platypus families near the bend in the river. There is another platypus-viewing spot on the Gillies Hwy. at the Peterson Creek crossing, on the way out of town.

Yungaburra's sole hostel, ▓**On the Wallaby ❶**, is superb. On the Wallaby's common area feels like a mountain lodge, with its rustic furnishings and wood-burning stove. The bathrooms and showers of the hostel are sided with stone and wood, and the bunk rooms are clean and fresh. Enjoy the BBQ ($8), kitchen, garden, and laundry. Guests can also join the hostel-run tour activities (canoeing, biking, or making your own didgeridoo) on an individual basis. Platypus spotting trips run by the hostel are free. (☎4095 2031; www.onthewallaby.com. Bike hire half-day $10, full-day $15. Reception 8am-1pm and 4-8pm. Sites for 1 $10, for 2 $15; dorms $20; twins and doubles $45. Cairns transfers $20.) Another accommodations option is the pricier **Curtain Fig Motel ❺**, 16 Gillies Hwy., located in the center of town. Though the price is steep, the motel has sparkling rooms. (☎4095 3168. Reception 7:30am-8:30pm. Doubles $77, extra person $11.)

The coffee shop portion of the **Gem Gallery and Coffee Shop ❶**, 44 Eacham Rd., serves breakfast for under $2. The Gem Gallery portion specializes in a variety of inexpensive opals and free opal-cutting, as well as occasional gold-working demonstrations. (☎4095 3455. Open daily 8am-late.) Next door is **Flynn's ❶**, which has bigger meals than the Coffee Shop as well as affordable **Internet access.** (Open daily for breakfast 7:30-11:30am, lunch until 2:30pm, and dinner until 9pm.) **Yungaburra Market,** on Eacham St. serves as the local **supermarket.** (☎4095 2177. Open daily 6:30am-7pm.)

MALANDA ☎07

Only a short distance from Yungaburra, friendly and hospitable **Malanda** was founded in 1911 and grew around its timber industry. Nowadays, residents guard the remaining rainforest, magnificent waterfalls, and rare tree kangaroos. About 25km south of Malanda and beyond Millaa Millaa, the **waterfall circuit** leads past a series of spectacular swimming holes. From the north, a sign points to the falls. Catch the loop from the south by looking for the "Tourist Drive" sign. **Millaa Millaa Falls** is the perfect waterfall: a straight, even curtain with rocks at the bottom and a bit of green on either side. **Zillie Falls** starts off as a sedate creek at the top of the falls. A rocky, slippery-when-wet path through the adjacent rainforest leads to the roaring drop where the cascading **Ellinjaa Falls** spark their liquid fireworks. The last waterfall on the circuit is **Mungalli Falls**, which passes the **Mungalli Creek Dairy.** Owned and operated by the Watson family, this traditional dairy farm serves their products as fresh as the law allows. (☎4097 2232. Free cheese tastings. Open daily 10am-4pm.) For more information about the falls surrounding Malanda, the **Malanda Falls Visitor Centre** is just past **Malanda Falls** on the way out of town towards Atherton. (☎4096 6957. Open 10am-4pm daily. Tours $2.)

The best place to stay right near the falls is ☒**Travellers Rest ❹**, on Millaa Millaa Rd., just past Malanda. The owners, Mike and Tracy, have recently renovated this charming country cottage, complete with several acres of pasture where their miniature horses and several sheep graze. Weekend murder mysteries are also popular events for large groups, but reservations must be made about six months in advance. Visitors enjoy a night of role-playing and mystery, along with dinner and breakfast. (☎4096 6077. Double with breakfast $60.) The little-known **Platypus Forest Lodge ❹**, 12 Topaz Rd., 6km east of the town center off Lake Barrine Rd., is a stellar B&B perfect for nature buffs. The owners run an immaculate lodge complete with sauna, hot tub, canoes, wood-burning stove, and loads of hospitality. Out back, platypi, turtles, possums, and tree kangaroos inhabit a swath of rainforest. (☎/fax 4096 5926. Singles $45; doubles $55.) At night, check out the oldest movie theater in all of Australia, the attractive **Majestic Theatre,** located at Eachem Pl. (24hr. info line ☎4096 5726; www.majestictheatre.com.au. $8, children and pensioners $5.)

PORT DOUGLAS ☎07

Nestled between tropical rainforest and the Coral Sea, the considerable natural assets of Port Douglas support a burgeoning tourism industry. The cooler months of the Dry bring throngs of nature-lovers, marine enthusiasts, and short-term workers. Snorkel and scuba trips take travelers to the pristine outer reaches of the Great Barrier Reef and up the coast to the rainforests of Daintree National

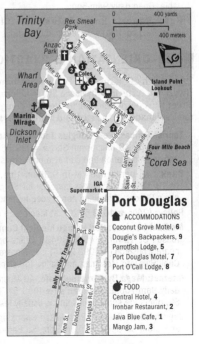

Port Douglas

⌂ ACCOMMODATIONS
Coconut Grove Motel, 6
Dougie's Backpackers, 9
Parrotfish Lodge, 5
Port Douglas Motel, 7
Port O'Call Lodge, 8

🍴 FOOD
Central Hotel, 4
Ironbar Restaurant, 2
Java Blue Cafe, 1
Mango Jam, 3

QUEENSLAND

Park. Others forgo these excursions to simply soak up the rays on Four Mile Beach. Waterbabies be warned, however: during the hotter months of the Wet, aquatic activities are hindered by the prolific jellyfish population.

▐ TRANSPORTATION

Buses: Sun Palm Coaches (☎4099 4992), at the Marina Mirage, runs daily to: the airport (1hr., 11 per day, $25); Cairns (1½hr.; 11 per day; $22, same day return $39, open return $39.50); Daintree Ferry (1hr; $15, return $30); Mossman (30min.; 12 per day; $8, return $14). Buses also run to Cooktown via the coast road (during the Dry Tu, Th, Sa 1 per day; $52) and via the inland road. (W, F, Su 1 per day; $58.) There is also a local shuttle which runs between the Rainforest Habitat and town, stopping at the major resorts and hostels on the way. ($3.50 one-way, $5 return.)

Ferries: Quicksilver (☎4099 5050) leaves for **Cairns** from the Marina Mirage daily at 5:15pm. Leaves Cairns for Port Douglas at 8:00am. (1½hr., $24, $36 return.)

Taxis: Port Douglas Taxis, 45 Warner St. (☎4099 5345). 24hr.

Car Rental: Thrifty Car Rental, #2 50 Macrossan St. (☎4099 5555), specializes in **4WD** (from $120 per day). **Allcar Rentals,** 21 Warner St. (☎4099 4123), start at $60 per day (less if rental lasts a week or more), 4WD from $95 a day. Both companies require 4WD drivers to be 25+. **Holiday Car Hire,** 54 Macrossan St. (☎4099 4999), rents compacts and small 4WDs, as well as beach-buggy "mokes", from $55.

Bike Rental: Check with the hostels before renting, as some have their own bikes or have arrangements with bike hires. Visit **Port Douglas Bike Hire** (☎4099 5799), on the corner of Wharf and Warner St. Half-day $10, full-day $14, weekly $59. All bikes are mountain bikes and rental includes locks and helmets. Child and tandem bikes available. Open daily 9am-5pm.

Road Report: Royal Automobile Club of Queensland (☎4033 6711; www.racq.com.au) gives all road conditions and closings.

✴ ▐ ORIENTATION & PRACTICAL INFORMATION

70km north of Cairns, Port Douglas Rd. branches right off of Hwy. 1 (Captain Cook Hwy.) and turns into **Davidson St.,** which runs to the main strip, **Macrossan St.** This street runs perpendicular to the Port Douglas peninsula, with **Four Mile Beach** (on the Esplanade) to the east and **Marina Mirage** (on Wharf St.) to the west.

Tourist Offices: Port Douglas Tourist Centre, 23 Macrossan St. (☎4099 5599) and **BTS Tours,** 49 Macrossan St. (☎ 4099 5665) both have all your necessary tour and activity information and can also book transport.

Banks: All banks open M-Th 9:30am-4pm, F 9:30am-5pm. **ANZ,** 36 Macrossan St. (☎13 13 14), exchanges currency for $5 commission. No fee for cashing AmEx Traveler's Checks. If heading north, keep in mind that ATMs may be few and far between.

Police: (24hr. ☎4099 5220), at Macrossan and Wharf St. Open M-Th 8am-2:30pm.

Medical Services: Port Village Medical Centre, Shop 17 in Port Village Centre on Macrossan St. (24hr. ☎4099 5043). Office open M-F 8am-6pm, Sa-Su 9am-noon. The nearest **hospital** (☎4098 2444) is in Mossman, on Hospital St. (Head north on Captain Cook Hwy into Mossman and follow the signs).

Internet: Mega Byte Internet Cafe, 48 Macrossan St. (☎4099 5568). $6 per hr. Open daily 9am-10pm. **Sheridan's** (☎4099 5770), on the corner of Wharf St. and Warner St., offers the same prices and is usually less crowded.

Supermarket: Coles in Port Village Shopping Centre on Macrossan St. between Wharf and Grant St. Open M-F 8am-9pm, Sa 8am-5:30pm, Su 9am-6pm.

Post Office: 5 Owen St. (☎4099 5210). On the corner of Macrossan and Owen St., half-way up the hill. Open M-F 9am-5pm, Sa 9am-noon. **Postal Code:** 4871.

ACCOMMODATIONS

Though there's no shortage of expensive beds in this bustling resort town, hostels abound in the Macrossan St. area. Hostels tend to be reasonably priced and well-equipped, with many boasting pools, bars, and restaurants.

Parrotfish Lodge, 37/39 Warner St. (☎4099 5011 or 1800 995 011; www.parrot-fishlodge.com). New in 2002, the Parrotfish is equipped with its own bar, restaurant, Internet lounge, billiard lounge and pool. Dubbed "budget accommodation with a touch of luxury," this mini-resort, complete with spacious decks, barbecue, and even satellite TV facilities, more than lives up to its breathless PR. All rooms have A/C. Reception 24 hr. 6-bed dorms $23-25, ensuite $26; double $75, ensuite $85. VIP. ❷

Dougie's Backpackers, 111 Davidson St. (☎4099 6200 or 1800 996 200; www.dou-gies.com.au). 15 min. walk from town center. Known as the party hostel around town, equipped with games, hammocks, and a bar (open 4pm-midnight). Sip champagne and watch for crocs on free steam train (every Su). Laundry, Internet, kitchen, pool, and bike rental ($1 per hour). Free bus to Cairns M, W, Sa 8:30am; free pick-up in Cairns at 10:30am same days. Sites $18; dorms $21; doubles $60. NOMADS/VIP/YHA. ❷

Port O'Call Lodge (YHA), 7 Craven Close (☎4099 5422 or 1800 892 800). Take a left off Port Douglas Rd. onto Port St. as you come into town. This incredibly comfortable, motel-like hostel has laundry, a pool, kitchen, bike rental, and Internet. Free shuttle bus to Cairns (departs M, W, and Sa 8:30am). The popular bistro serves large meals daily (mains $8-11; open 6-9pm) and swings during Happy Hour (5pm-7pm). Free lockers. Reception 7:30am-7:30pm. Check-out 9:30am. 4-bed dorm with bath $23, YHA $21.50; deluxe motel rooms $69-99. Cheaper during the Wet. VIP/ NOMADS. ❷

Port Douglas Motel, 9 Davidson St. (☎4099 5248). If you've got a few friends to share the cost, this place is a find. Just a 2min. walk to the beach. All rooms impeccably clean and equipped with kitchenettes, bathrooms, TV, A/C, and covered carpark. Prices range from $69-77 depending on the number of people. ❺

Coconut Grove Motel, 58 Macrossan St. (☎4099 5124). Well-maintained rooms are nestled in the trees. Restaurant, laundry, kitchen, BBQ, TV, and 2 pools. Reception 8am-7pm. 6-bed dorms with bath $20; motel rooms with TV, A/C, and fridge $85. ❷

FOOD & ENTERTAINMENT

If you know what you want to eat, chances are **Macrossan St.** will have it. Some of the new trendier restaurants setting up fort in Port Douglas might ask an arm, a leg, *and* your credit card for portion sizes that pale in comparison to some of the less expensive places. For meals overlooking the water, head to Marina Mirage, where several restaurants line the peaceful harbor.

Ironbar Restaurant, 5 Macrossan St. (☎4099 4776), is a family-friendly restaurant that caters to the resort crowd. The main attraction is the cane toad races, run by local entre-preneur Clancy, Sunday-Thursday at 8pm ($5, families $18) and 9:15pm (adults only). Choose your own finely dressed amphibian; the winner (human, not toad) gets a free drink. Offers a variety of Queensland delicacies such as kangaroo burgers, skewered croc, and barbecued prawns for $4-27. Open M-F 11am-2am, Sa-Su 8am-2am. ❸

Mango Jam, 24 Macrossan St. (☎4099 6611), with its lively terrace and good portions, is a great lunch option. Try their famous mango daiquiris or munch on one of their lesser-known but equally noteworthy pizzas. Meals $14-26. Open daily noon-2am. ❸

Java Blue Cafe, 2 Macrossan St., (☎4099 5814). Where Bill Clinton eats when he's in Port Douglas. Enjoy huge salads ($7-10), a full breakfast ($15), good veggie options, or a sandwich on one of several types of fresh bread. Open daily 7:30am-5pm. No credit cards accepted. ❷

Central Hotel, 9 Macrossan St. (☎4099 5271), in the center of town, serves a predominantly local crowd and has area bands Tu-F nights. The bar also broadcasts all national sporting events and hosts a small local jackpot every Monday night. If you find that drinking during a game works up an appetite, burgers and fish are available ($5-15). Open daily until midnight. ❶

◎ ◎ SIGHTS & ACTIVITIES

The Rainforest Habitat, located on Port Douglas Rd. coming into town, has eight acres, three enclosures, and over 1000 animals without cages or any discernible fear of people. This is a great place for those who want to mingle with cockatoos and parrots, tickle a fruit bat's tummy, or scratch a wallaroo behind the ears. Early risers can also enjoy "Breakfast with the Birds," a full buffet (with champagne) in the aviary. (8-11am. $38, children $19; includes entry fee.) There is also a restaurant and souvenir shop on premises. (☎4099 3235; www.rainforesthabitat.com.au. Open daily 8am-5:30pm; last entry 4:30pm. $24, children $12. 10% student discount. Wheelchair-accessible.)

Located at the east end of Macrossan St., **Four Mile Beach** is almost always quiet. This gorgeous stretch of sand attracts an array of locals, topless backpackers, and swanky resort-types. For safety reasons, swim between the flags (lifeguard on duty M-Sa 9:30am-5pm).

Extra Action Watersports (☎4099 3175 or 0412 346 303) is just north of Marina Mirage. Steve, the owner and self-defined "action man," can set you up with any number of heart-stopping adventures. **Parasailing** adventures last 20 minutes. (Solo $120, couple $85 each; 2hr. family packages $275.)

Visitors can **snorkel** independently or with several private outfits, most of which depart from Marina Mirage. **Sailaway-Low Isles,** 23 Macrossan St., fits snorkeling, riding in a glass-bottom boat, and "boom netting" into one day, but does not go out to the outer reef. (☎4099 5799; www.reefandrainforest.com.au. Departs daily 8:45am. 7hr. $105, children $60, families $285. Call for booking.) **Wavelength,** just north of the Marina Mirage, also offers daily snorkeling-only trips. Two boats depart daily at 8:30am for eight-hour ventures to the outer reef with a marine biologist on board. (☎4099 5031. $130, children $90.)

◎ DIVING

Haba Dive (☎4099 5254), in the Marina Mirage. Offers 2 dives on each daily trip. Small groups of 40 promise a more personal experience than some of the larger boats. Departs daily 8:30am with free pick-up and lunch. Snorkeling $130 (children $85), scuba $185 including gear.

Quicksilver Diver (☎4087 2100; www.quicksilver-cruises.com), in the Marina Mirage. The biggest operation in town, Quicksilver picks up divers at Cairns before continuing up to Port Douglas. Ride a high-speed catamaran to the outer reef and spend the day on a pontoon enjoying submersible rides, snorkeling, and lunch buffet. All equipment included. Catamaran departs daily 10am. $174-184 (no resort pick-up/drop-off), children $90. Special snorkeling tours with a marine biologist, additional $37. Quicksilver also offers a 4-day PADI course which leaves M, W, F, and by arrangement. (☎4099 5050; www.quicksilverdive.com.au. $535.)

Poseidon Outer Reef Cruises, 34 Macrossan St. (☎4099 4772; www.poseidon-cruises.com.au). This 1-boat operation offers dive courses in conjunction with Discover Dive at **The Links Health Club** (☎4099 5544; www.discoverdive.com.au), a five-star, PADI dive center specializing in small group training. $570 4-day open water course. Advanced, Rescue, and Divemaster courses are also available. Recreational snorkeling $135, scuba $175. Group sizes don't exceed 70; depart daily at 8:30am and return at 4pm. Office open daily from 9am-6pm.

🔳 DAYTRIP: MOSSMAN GORGE

For those looking to escape the nonstop activity of Port Douglas, Mossman Gorge provides unrivaled peace and quiet. Part of the **Daintree National Park,** the gorge has several hiking paths originating from the visitors' parking lot (follow the clearly posted signs). The shorter paths to the Mossman River and swimming holes are easy, but the 2.4km circuit track in the thick of the rainforest is slightly more challenging. On this track, be prepared to hop over small creeks (and an occasional small lizard) during the Wet. On any of the trails you'll feel engulfed by the magnificent green canopy.

Sun Palm Coaches runs to **Mossman** (30min.; 10 per day; $8, return $14). Some hostels also provide a few daily shuttles, though you might get stranded for longer than you desire until the next shuttle returns. If **driving,** take Hwy. 1 north from the junction to Port Douglas for about 20km. Follow the brown signs for Mossman Gorge and turn left across from the Mossman State High School. Drive about 4km to Kuku Yalanji and1km more to the carpark at the gorge.

Aboriginal tours can be arranged with **Kuku-Yalanji Dreamtime Walks,** which cover traditional medicines and bush tucker, and include tea and damper. The Aboriginal-owned operation also has a Visitors Centre and shop. (☎4098 2595. Open M-F 9am-4pm. Tours M-F 10am, noon, and 2pm. $16.50, children $8.25. Bookings essential. Mini-bus pick-up service for 10am walk from Port Douglas and Mossman $41, children $20.)

DAINTREE   ☎07

Daintree is a fitting gateway to the rougher frontier land of the north. Kingfishers, kookaburras, and friendly faces abound in this tiny forest village (pop. 120). The town's main economic assets are the estuarine crocodiles (or salties) that live in the Daintree River; boatloads of camera-toting croc-seekers pass through the village daily. Daintree Township is about 6km north of the turn-off for the Daintree Ferry on the Cook Hwy. Beware that this portion of the road can flood; call ☎4033 6711 or one of the local restaurants for road conditions.

You can book a river tour at the **Daintree General Store** (☎4098 6416), which also serves as the town watering hole and **post office.** Most river excursions are similar, varying primarily in length from 1-2½hr. Prices range from $17 to $30; children travel for less. Check out **Daintree Electric Boat Cruises** (☎1800 686 103) or **Daintree River and Reef Cruise Centre** (☎4098 6115). **Daintree Wildlife Safaris** (☎4098 6125) also cruise for crocs. **Chris Dahlberg** runs excellent morning bird-spotting tours from the Daintree jetty. (☎4098 7997. 2hr. $35. Bookings essential.)

A TV room, swimming pool, and BBQ are just some of the extras that convince many guests to stay longer than they originally planned at the 🔳**Red Mill House ❹.** Daily breakfast is made of fruit from the tropical garden in the backyard. The older part of the house has one single ($60), one double ($70), and one triple ($99) with bathroom facilities and a spa. The newer section offers four queen-size rooms with bath for $88. (☎4098 6233; www.redmillhouse.com.au.)

CAPE TRIBULATION   ☎07

About 15km north of the Daintree River, "Cape Trib" is in the heart of **Daintree National Park** and is really more of a landmark than a township. When locals talk about Cape Tribulation, they're usually referring to a large general area served by Cape Tribulation Rd., which runs north past Cow Bay, Alexandra Bay, Thornton Peak, and the Cape. Travelers continuing up the coast from Daintree will use the **Daintree Ferry,** which shuttles across the river from 6am-midnight. (Walk-on passengers $1, cars $8.) Access to Cape Tribulation from the south is Cape Tribulation Rd. Paved up until the carpark on the Cape, causeways and floodways crisscross it at multiple points. If traveling in the rainy season, be sure to call ahead for road conditions (☎4033 6711) and consider bringing a car with a snorkel. At Cape Tribulation, the rainforest crashes down onto the ocean surf and every inch of forest is teeming with wildlife.

▐▌ TRANSPORTATION & PRACTICAL INFORMATION

If driving, bear right after the ferry: this sealed road first passes the Alexandra Range Lookout, on the right. Just a few kilometers farther is the Environmental Centre, and the turn-off for Cow Bay, on Buchanan Creek Rd. A half hour drive farther north on Cape Tribulation Rd. passes Cooper Creek and finally Cape Tribulation. A 4WD-only road then continues on to Cooktown (see p. 447).

The distances between locales make getting around somewhat difficult without a car. However, many of the larger resorts provide shuttles to various sights and offer a number of adventures on their own premises. **Sun Palm Coaches** also has daily service from Cairns via Port Douglas at 7am and 3:30pm for $45 one-way that make stops upon request. There is no official information center in Cape Tribulation. The **Queensland Parks and Wildlife Service (QPWS) Ranger Station** has public info, but the hours are extremely limited. (☎4098 0052. Open M-F 9:30-11:30am.) Two other sources of info are the Daintree Rainforest Environmental Centre and the Bat House (see **Sights and Activities,** p. 442). **Rainforest Village,** a few kilometers before Cooper Creek, sells groceries and petrol and has a phone and a post box. (☎4098 9015. Open 7am-7pm.) The "last fuel" sign is slightly misleading; fuel is only a short distance away in Cape Tribulation (see **Wujal Wujal,** p. 447).

▐ ACCOMMODATIONS

Hostels here reflect the active beach and rainforest atmosphere that is Cape Trib. Each has a slightly different theme, either focusing on the beach, the rainforest, or a combination of the two, so choose according to your particular pleasure.

▨ **Crocodylus Village** (☎4098 9166; crocodylus@austarnet.com.au), on Buchanan Creek Rd., east off Cape Tribulation Rd. Take a right after the Daintree Environmental Centre if heading north from Daintree Ferry. This hostel is a backpacker oasis organically entwined with the rainforest, offering several open-air cabins scattered around a large wooden patio. Laundry, pool, horseback riding, sunrise paddle trek in a hybrid kayak/canoe, and guided bushwalks. Prices range from $30-179 depending on type and duration of trip. Complimentary bus to the beach four times per day. Reception 7:30am-11:15pm. Cabin rooms $20, YHA $18; ensuite cabin for 2 $75, each extra person $10, ages 5-15 $5, children under 5 free. ❷

Coconut Beach Rainforest Resort (☎4098 0033 or 1800 816 595; www.voyages.com), just past Cooper Creek on Cape Tribulation Rd. For those looking to splurge, this resort offers private cabins, fine dining, two inground pools and beach access. Private cabins and condominium style cabins from $300. ❺

Daintree Manor, 27 Forest Creek Rd. (☎4090 7041). Just north of the river, the Manor offers breathtaking views, encounters with friendly wildlife, beautiful handmade furniture, and a TV lounge with good reception. Owner also offers private river tours. Rooms from $99, breakfast included. ❺

Cape Trib Beach House (☎4098 0030). A rainforest camping ground converted into a rainforest cabin resort. Access is on the right after about a kilometer on the unsealed portion of Cape Tribulation Rd. Relax on their pristine beach with forest dragons and butterflies. Laundry, bar, restaurant, pool, Internet. 4 bed dorms $32; 5 bed dorms $25. Multiple private cabin sizes available, some beachfront, $70-125. ❸

PK's Jungle Village (☎4098 0400 or 1800 232 333). More appropriately called "PK's Jungle Party," this hostel is about 400m past the "Welcome to Cape Tribulation" sign on Cape Tribulation Rd. Volleyball, horseback riding, guided bushwalking, exotic fruit tasting, and bike rental (half-day $12, full-day $20). Laundry, kitchen, bar, and pool. Reception 7:30am-7pm. Check-out 9:30am. Dorms $25; doubles $75, with a bath $85, campsites $12 per person. VIP. ❷

More camping is available at **Rainforest Village** ❶ (☎4098 9015), a few kilometers before Cooper's Creek (sites $18; powered $20), or at **Noah's Beach Camping** ❶, just after Thornton Beach, on the right ($3.85, family $15.40).

🍴 FOOD

Fan Palm Cafe and Boardwalk ❷, on Cape Tribulation Rd., right after the Ice Cream factory, is a new restaurant catering to vegetarians and the backpacker set, cooking with all fresh fruit and veggies (☎4098 9119. Open in the Dry W-Su 10am-midnight, in the Wet Th-Su 10am-5pm. Mains $10-15, entrees $8-14. Lunch menu $5-14.) **Lync Haven** ❷ is perhaps the most unusual eating establishment with its wildlife sanctuary full of orphaned 'roos. Options include burgers ($5-7) and sandwiches ($4) plus a veggie-friendly dinner menu (everything under $12). They also have a wide range of accommodations. (See above. ☎4098 9155.) **The Waterhole Cafe** ❶, on Bailey's Creek Rd., specializes in Indonesian cuisine (meals $8.50), although they do serve burgers (including veggie) and all-day breakfast. The cafe shakes down with live music on the weekends. Because the population is so sparse and many travelers are without their own cars, most hostels and resorts also have their own bars and restaurants. The most hopping bar scene is at **PK's Jungle Village** ❶, where the bar is open from noon until midnight every day.

👁 🔆 SIGHTS & ACTIVITIES

All attractions on Cape Tribulation involve the wet tropics. **The Daintree Rainforest Environmental Centre,** just before Cow Bay off Cape Tribulation Rd., is a popular stop-off. The center is informative and unique, with a 23m canopy tower that allows visitors to view the rainforest from above the trees. The ticket price includes a guided walk on the rainforest boardwalk (40min.), wet tropic movies, and access to a reference library. (☎4098 9171; www.daintree-rec.com.au. Open daily 8:30am-5pm. $15, concession $12, families $35; concession rates for those lodging in the area.) A free walk around **Jindalba,** just 450m up the road from the Centre, has picnic facilities, bathroom, and sign-posted walks. The **Bathouse,** opposite PK's on the west side of the highway, is a less extensive source of forest info, but the all-volunteer staff will be happy to take your picture with their giant flying fox, Rex. (☎4098 0063; www.austrop.org.au. $2 donation.) Just down the road from the Bathouse is **Dubuji,** a visitor area with a spectacular 1.2km boardwalk through a variety of coastal forests and mangroves, a must for all visitors. Farther south is the **Marrdja** boardwalk through old growth rainforest and eerily beautiful

mangrove forest, home to many species of birds, including the threatened cassowary. On the **rainforest night walk**, led by a Daintree wildlife expert, you'll spot a variety of rainforest creepy crawlies, warm fuzzies, and slippery slimies (☎ 4098 0400. Departs daily at 7:30pm from PK's Jungle Village, reserve by 6pm. 3hr. $28).

Cape Tribulation Wilderness Cruises explores the mangroves of Cooper Creek in search of crocodiles. (☎ 4098 9052. Daily departure times vary. 1hr. $19. Bookings essential.) **Rum Runner** is one of the several tours based out of Cairns that runs daily trips to the reef off the Cape. (☎ 4098 9249 or 0500 509 249. Free bus to the beach from all Daintree/Cape Trib resorts, snorkeling equipment included. Snorkeling $104, introductory scuba dives minimum age 12.)

Tropical Sea Kayaks (☎ 4098 9166) offers a popular two-day, one-night trip to **Snapper Island** for $179 (available at the Crocodylus Village). This excursion features reef walking, snorkeling, and beach camping, including all equipment, as well as prepared meals. **Wundu Trail Rides,** between Lync Haven and the Rainforest Village, leads horseback tours of the coral coast. (☎ 4098 9176. Departs twice daily. 3hr. guided rides $55, 10% discount for groups of seven or more; min. age 10.)

ROUTES TO COOKTOWN

There are two routes from Cape Tribulation to Cooktown—one inland, one coastal. The Bloomfield Track is the coastal route, which beats through 150km of bush as it swerves and dips, carving through rugged coastal mountains. The Bloomfield Track in bad conditions is impassable. On a "good" day, however, the road is about as much fun as can be legally had in a 4WD. The rainforest and coastline views are amazing, and fording the rivers is tremendously exciting. The trek takes about five hours, with lots of veering, bumping, straying, and swerving—whatever is necessary—to avoid large potholes and fallen trees. Call ahead or check with locals for road conditions and bring lots of cash, as many places don't take credit. If you'd rather not be the one clutching the steering wheel, **Sun Palm Coaches** (☎ 4099 4992) departs from Port Douglas and Cairns several times a week.

The inland route to Cooktown is not quite the rugged adventure of the coastal track, as most of the road on this route is sealed. The stunning landscape will leave your jaw agape as you wind through thick rainforest and over mountainous terrain and green hills. In the late afternoon, drivers should look out for Brahma cattle.

BLOOMFIELD TRACK

Hold on to your hats! This track is a playground for those who want an intense 4WD experience. From Cape Tribulation, the road turns to dirt. A little over an hour later is **Wujal Wujal,** a tiny Aboriginal community with a **service station** and **general store** that stocks everything from food and drugs to camping supplies and clothes, as well as a **payphone.** (☎4060 8101. Store open daily 8am-5pm, payphone in front; service station open M-Th 9am-6pm, F 9-11:30am. Off the road, **Bloomfield Falls** is an isolated sight off the main road and is a terrific place to have a picnic lunch and relax after a rough ride, but watch out for feisty crocs.

Between Wujal Wujal and Cooktown, the mountains pull back from the coast and the dirt road winds through dry savannah. North of the bridge to Wujal Wujal, the road is easier. Along the way, there are occasional general stores and small-town hotels. About an hour north of Wujal Wujal in the town of **Ayton,** an **IGA Express** has basic **groceries,** supplies, a lunch **cafe,** a phone, and toilets around the corner. (Open M-F 8:30am-5:30pm, Sa-Su 8:30am-4pm.) **Bloomfield Cabins and Camping ❷** serves lunch and dinner ($5-15) and has rooms for two from $49. (☎4060 8207; www.bloomfieldscabins.com.) The final 1½hr. stretch of road before Cooktown runs past the **Lion's Den Hotel ❸.** (☎4060 3911. Open daily 10am-late. Beer $3.50, pub grub $12 per plate. Campsites $7 per person. **Payphone** in front.)

INLAND ROUTE

Traveling through the Far North, there are a handful of interesting stop-offs. One of the most scenic, **Mount Molloy,** is a 10min. drive (27km) southwest of Mossman on Peninsula Developmental Rd. The **Mount Molloy National Hotel ❷** is a large, grand building constructed in 1901. The rooms are a bit dusty, but homey, with comfy beds and a pub downstairs. (☎4094 1133. Reception at pub 10am-midnight. Meals $9-15, specials $6. Singles $25; doubles $40.) A **picnic area** with hiking info and public restrooms is 500m from the hotel. **Mount Carbine** sits 28km north of Mt. Malloy. Once a prosperous mining town, it now consists of three roadside buildings. The **Mount Carbine Roadhouse ❶** has petrol, food, backpacker lodging, and Brahma bulls outside. (☎4094 3043. Meals $5-7, milkshakes $3. Open daily 7am-7pm. Singles $15; doubles $25; extra person $5. EFTPOS.)

Continuing north, the road begins to literally cut through the hills, with walls of stone outcroppings flanking the pavement. The **Palmer River Roadhouse ❶,** 110km north of Mt. Molloy, is decorated with various murals tracing the area's mining history. Friendly service and a pool table make this a great place to regroup while filling up on petrol or diesel. (☎4060 2020. Open daily 7am-10pm. Sites $5.50; powered caravan sites $12. EFTPOS/V/MC.) Farther north (145km from Mt. Molloy), the bitumen gives way to a gravelly, snaky descent through the hills with beautiful views of the landscape.

COOKTOWN

☎07

In the winter, the south wind sweeps through Cooktown's dusty streets, bringing with it travelers who have abandoned the monotony of packaged tours and prepaid holidays. Many find themselves staying longer than they planned, captivated by the life in a town where the bars close when the last patron leaves and shoes are an infrequent sight. The history of Cooktown dates back to 1770 when Captain James Cook of England ran his ship, the *Endeavour,* onto the Great Barrier Reef. The 230 years since have witnessed settlement, abandonment, a gold rush, and a spotted history of devastating cyclones. Today, Cooktown (pop. 3000) is an eccentric community full of small-town Australian charm.

QUEENSLAND

⌐ TRANSPORTATION

Buses: Sun Palm Coaches (☎4099 4992) runs between Cooktown and Cairns. To Cairns by inland route (5hr.; Su, W, F 2:30pm; $69) via Lakeland (1¼hr.), Cape Tribulation (4¼hr.), Cow Bay (4¾hr.), Kuranda (4¾hr.), Mareeba (4¼hr.), Mossman (6hr.), Mt. Carbine (3¼hr.), Mt. Molloy (3½hr.), and Port Douglas (6½hr.); or by coastal route (7½hr.; Tu, Th, and Sa $69) via Lion's Den (30min.)

Car Rental: This far north, the aptly named **Cooktown Car Hire** (☎4069 5007) is one of the only options. **4WD** starts at $99.

Taxis: Cooktown Taxis (☎4069 5387). Service from 6:30am to when the pubs close.

Automobile Club: RACQ, Cape York Tyres (☎4069 5233), located at the corner of Charlotte St. and Furneaux St. Services include 24hr. towing. Open M-F 7am-7pm, Sa-Su 7:30am-6pm.

Service: AMPOL Station (☎4069 5354), at the corner of Hope and Howard St., has groceries. Open 24hr. EFTPOS. AmEx/V/MC.

⌐ ORIENTATION

Cooktown Development Rd. becomes **Hope Street** as you enter Cooktown proper and head toward **Grassy Hill.** Taking a left off that street and continuing two blocks will take you to **Charlotte Street,** which runs parallel to Hope St. and is home to a majority of Cooktown's shops and services. It's crossed by several streets, including Boundary, Howard, Hogg, and Walker St. Heading east on Walker St. leads to the Botanic Gardens and Finch Bay. At the northernmost end of town, Charlotte St. runs along the water, curves eastward, and becomes **Webber Esplanade** but is not a through road.

⌐ PRACTICAL INFORMATION

Tourist Office: The Croc Shop (☎4069 5880), on Charlotte St. next to Anzac Park. Visit local legend and author of Paradise Found Linda Rowe, for tips on trekking to the top. Open M-F 8:30am-5:30pm, Sa 8:30am-noon.

Banks: Westpac (☎4069 6960), on Charlotte St., between Green and Furneaux St., next door to the Post Office. **ATM** but no currency exchange. Open M-F 9am-4:30pm.

Police: (☎4069 5320) across from the wharf on Charlotte St. Staffed M-F 8am-4pm; after hours, use intercom at the office door.

Medical Center: Cooktown Hospital (☎4069 5433), on the corner of Ida St. and the Cooktown Developmental Rd., on the way out of town heading south.

Internet: Cooktown Computer Stuff (☎4069 6010), on Charlotte at Green St. Open daily 9am-5pm, $2 per 20min.

Post Office: (☎4069 5347) on Charlotte St., next to the bank and across from the Sovereign Hotel. Open M-F 9am-5pm. **Postal Code:** 4871.

ACCOMMODATIONS & FOOD

Pam's Place (☎4069 5166), at the corner of Charlotte and Boundary St., is the backpacker hub of Cooktown. Amenities include large kitchen, linens, laundry, bar, pool table, swimming pool, garden, and morning shuttles to the bus station and airport. Bike hire. Sites $8; dorms $19; singles $36; doubles $46. EFTPOS $1 per transaction. YHA. MC/V 3.5% surcharge. ❶

Seagren's Inn, 12 Charlotte St. (☎4069 5357). A historic building dating back to 1880, with a restaurant and accommodations. 6-bed dorms $20; doubles from $55. ❷

Hillcrest Bed and Breakfast (☎4069 5305; www.cooktowninfo.com), at the base of Grassy Hill on Hope St., is a friendly B&B with a sunny garden, veranda, pool, and restaurant. Laundry. Doubles $50, extra person $5-10; 3 motel units with TV, A/C, and bath $65. Continental breakfast 7-9am, $7. MC/V. ❸

Alamanda Inn (☎4069 5203), across from the Ampol station on the corner of Hope and Howard St., offers tidy guest house rooms amid beds of flowers. All rooms have A/C, fridge, TV, and sink. Singles $40; doubles $55; family units $75. MC/V. ❸

Cooktown Caravan Park (☎4069 5536; www.cooktowncaravanpark.com), on Hope St., at the end of Developmental Rd., is one of the nicest places to camp in Cooktown, featuring perhaps the best showers in all of Australia. Sites $16, powered $19. ❷

Groceries can be purchased at the **IGA Supermarket,** on the corner of Hogg and Helen St. (☎4069 5633. Open M-W, F and Sa 8am-6pm, Su 10am-3pm.)

SIGHTS

JAMES COOK HISTORICAL MUSEUM. The crown jewel of a town obsessed with the landing of Captain Cook, this former Catholic convent, built in 1889, has been expanded and renovated to house relics from Captain Cook's voyage, including the anchor and cannon he jettisoned here. A recent addition to the building is the Endeavour Gallery, which exhibits Cook's famous ship. (*On the corner of Helen St. and Furneaux St. ☎4069 5386. Open daily 9:30am-4pm. $7, discounts for children.*)

COOKTOWN CEMETERY. This cemetery, with its highly segregated plots divided into sections for Christians, Aboriginal, and Jewish residents, is the subject of many legends. The Chinese Shrine sits in the left-hand corner of the cemetery, where 30,000 migrants and their possessions were buried. Fact sheets about the cemetery can be found at any local accommodation. (*On McIvor River-Cooktown Rd.*)

OTHER SIGHTS. Twenty years ago, the city brought the **Botanic Gardens,** off Walker St., back to life after they were left to decay following the gold rush. Locals swim at **Finch Bay,** reached by following Walker St. to its end. The walking path leading to the bay branches into a trail to secluded **Cherry Tree Bay.** The trail from Cherry Tree Bay to the lookout is not well-marked at the beach and its challenging vertical inclines are unsuitable for small children. However, the lookout and lighthouse on **Grassy Hill** can also be accessed via car or foot from the end of Hope St. At the summit you'll have a 360° view and will be able to see the entirety of Cook-

QUEENSLAND

town, the surrounding rainforest and the Reef. During the Queen's Birthday weekend in June, the **Cooktown Discovery Festival** features truck-pulling and pie-eating competitions, reenactments of Captain Cook's landing, and other entertainment.

CAPE YORK

Cape York is one of the last great wilderness frontiers in Australia. Fortunately, it remains accessible via the **Peninsula Developmental Road** (unsealed), which is peppered every few hundred kilometers by small towns and roadhouses. If venturing out to the Cape, be sure to travel in a reliable 4WD that can handle the frequent and often unmarked potholes and abrupt dusty dips of the main route. The smaller roads and private tracks are even more of a challenge with river crossings, occasional fallen trees, and abundant wildlife. During the Wet season (Dec.-Apr.), most of the roads are completely inaccessible to travelers, and the only way to see the Cape is by flying over it or into one of the small airports on the coast. During the Dry, the one-week trip is still a challenge, but the reward is witnessing some of the most beautiful, diverse, and untouched landscape in all of Australia.

▐ TRANSPORTATION

During the Wet season, the unsealed roads are muddy, flooded, and often impassable. Barring any major tropical disturbances, the main roadways for the remainder of the year vary in quality, but are drivable. According to locals, a 4WD is not essential if staying on the Peninsula Developmental Rd., but if you're accustomed to driving on paved roads with well defined lanes, a 4WD with high ground clearance is recommended. If trekking off the main roads, the 4WD will prove even more useful, as river crossings, jagged rocks, and vegetation create plenty of driving hazards. Before tackling any new road, check with locals for advice.

Unless you own a car, you can't get to the northernmost point without spending some hard cash on a 4WD. **Leisure Wheels,** 314 Sheridan St., Cairns, has a minimum day limit on 4WDs taken to the Cape. (☎4051 8988. Large 4WDs start at $165 per day, with discounted rates for extended periods. Open daily.)

Aside from renting a 4WD, **tour packages** are often the only other option. Departing from Cairns, retired bombardiers air-drop mail over the Cape on **Cape York Air;** pilots will let passengers accompany them on their daily runs. (☎4035 9399. $236-472. Tu and Sa tours of the Cape $670.) If you can scramble up as far as the Jardine River, **John Charlton's Cape York Boat Adventure** will show you the rest for a very reasonable fare. (☎4069 3302. Full-day trips start at $125; self-drive $475.) **Billy Tea Bush Safaris,** an award-winning company, combines 4WD, flying, and boating in their trips to Cape York from Cairns. (☎4032 0077. Trips from $2100.)

BASE OF THE CAPE

Even if you haven't the time, money, or stamina for the full journey up the Cape, you can get an exciting sample of wilderness within a reasonable distance of Cooktown. A good 2- to 3-day trip runs southwest along the **Cooktown Development Road** to Lakeland and then northwest on the **Peninsula Developmental Road** to the outpost towns of Laura and Musgrave. From there, travel east into **Lakefield National Park,** where you'll see a variety of wildlife including kangaroos, wallabies, exotic birds, snakes, and perhaps even a croc. At the southern end of the park, turn east onto **Battle Camp Track** to complete the circuit. A large 4WD is highly recommended in this territory. Although the distance to Cooktown is not long, the rough terrain and river crossings will slow you down a fair bit.

In **Laura** (pop. 100), you'll find the **Laura Roadhouse ❶** that offers fuel, food, an ATM, and campsites (Peninsula Development Rd., upon entering town from the south, 24hr. emergency service ☎ 4060 3419.) Limited supplies are also available at the **Laura Store**. (☎ 4060 3238. Open daily 7:30am-6pm.) The **Ang-gnarra Visitors Centre**, across from the Laura Roadhouse, has a **Caravan Park ❶** with a pool and laundry. (☎ 4060 3214. $5, powered $6.) Laura's one must-see sight is **Split Rock**, a series of ancient Aboriginal art sites. (15min. self-guided walk $5; 3hr. walk $10.) Bring a hat, sunscreen, comfortable shoes, and water. The **Ang-gnarra Aboriginal Corporation** (☎ 4060 3200) offers tours of the sites. An hour southwest of Laura (50km, 4WD only), the Aboriginal-run **Jowalbinna Bush Camp ❶** also offers tours. (☎ 4060 3236. Sites $11 per person per night; cabins $69; permanent tents $80. Half-day tour of rock art sites $80, full-day $115; meals included.) Call them or the Cairns office (☎ 4051 4777) to book. The first pit stop north of Laura on Peninsula Developmental Rd. is the **Hann River Road House ❶**, 75km away. Pitch your tent here and fill up on gas or a tasty burger. (☎ 4060 3242. Sites $6; caravans $10; rooms $18.)

LAKEFIELD NATIONAL PARK REGION

Laura is the gateway to the south of the park, while **Musgrave,** 138km north of Laura on the Peninsula Developmental Rd., is the closest point of contact with the northern reaches. The only stop in town is the **Musgrave Roadhouse ❶**, which sports a restaurant, fuel services, and friendly staff. (☎ 4060 3229. Open daily 7:30am-10pm). There's also limited accommodation. (Sites $5; singles $40; doubles $50.)

To reach the heart of the park, travel back toward Cooktown along the **Battle Camp Track.** In the Wet, the track is submerged in water, but in the Dry, Lakefield is transformed into a bird sanctuary extravaganza. Crocodiles and feral pigs are also commonly spotted in this area. After entering the Battle Camp Track, travel east along the clearly-marked track past Lowlake. Bring emergency supplies and prepare for a long trip; it could take you seven hours or more to drive this route to the track. Be aware that locals avoid the route, so you may be alone for a while if something goes wrong.

Camping ❶ in these areas is by permit only ($3.85); these can be obtained through self-registration at any of the three stations (assuming spaces are available). The **ranger station** is in the middle of the park, 112km from Musgrave; register here for Kalpowar, Seven Mile, Melaleuca, Hanushs, and Midway sites. These are also boards with current road conditions. (☎/fax 4060 3271. Open daily 9am-5pm.) Camping in the southern half of the park requires a permit from the New Laura Ranger Station, while the Lakefield base requires a northern camping permit. There are also stations at Lakefield, Bizant, and at Hann Crossing.

Fishing and canoeing are the most popular activities in the park, with bird watching a close second. Barramundi and catfish are the most popular catches, but there are limits on the number you can keep, so be sure to consult a ranger or information board before fishing.

There is boat access to Princess Charlotte Bay but no vehicle access. The Bizant boat ramp, 20km from the Bizant ranger base in the north of the park, provides the best access to the bay. Many of the other small lakes are also suitable for small watercrafts, but you must bring your own boat. *The entire park is infested with estuarine crocodiles. Exercise extreme caution near any body of water. Never camp as close as 50m to water, don't swim in the park, and avoid contact with the water's edge.*

QUEENSLAND

COEN

North of Musgrave, the unexpected shifts in terrain and rapid directional changes of the Peninsula Developmental Rd. will test your reflexes. Fortunately, there aren't many other vehicles to contend with and the wide road allows for occasional spinouts and extreme maneuvering. After 109km on this "highway," you'll arrive in the tiny town of Coen (pop. 350).

Most services are on Regent St. **Ambrust General Store** offers groceries, petrol, a pay phone, and camping. (☎4060 1134. Store open daily 7:30am-6pm.) You can park your camper here or pitch a tent in the lot next door ($6.60). Many establishments close or operate minimally in the Wet. **QPWS** (www.epa.qld.gov.au), around the corner on Armbrust St., has info packets on nearby parks and campgrounds.

☒**Homestead Guest House** ❸ is filled with gold rush memorabilia. (☎4060 1157; fax 4060 1180. Laundry and kitchen. Reception 7am-9pm. Singles $40; Double $60; 5-person family $88. No credit cards.) The social center of Coen is the **Exchange Hotel** ❸. (☎4060 1133. Reception 10am-midnight. Singles $43; doubles $60.50, includes A/C). **Medical services** are available at Coen Clinic, Armbrust St. (☎4060 1166. Open M-F 8am-5pm, 24hr. emergency service).

NORTH OF COEN

Another 65km north along Peninsula Developmental Rd., a track of red earth and white sand filled with dips (miniature rivers) at every turn leads to the **Archer River Roadhouse** ❶. A popular spot for those coming to and from the Tip, the roadhouse is a welcome reminder that life does exist along these lonesome roads. The kitchen serves the usual beer, burgers, and full meals ($16). Limited accommodations are available. Stock up on supplies here, because it's nearly 200km to the next stop in Weipa. (☎/fax 4060 3266. Reception 7am-10pm.)

IRON RANGE NATIONAL PARK

Australia's largest lowland rainforest, Iron Range National Park is a tropical fantasy land of exotic creatures, isolated beaches, and stunning views. Access begins 20km north of the Archer River Roadhouse on the Peninsula Developmental Road. The terrain is tough and it will take about 4hr. to drive the 110km to the ranger station; then it's another 45min. through the heart of the rainforest to dead-end **Chili Beach,** an expansive, uninhabited strip.

There are both beach campsites and rainforest campsites between the ranger station and the beach; all require pre-registration and permits, available at the ranger station ($4 per person).

WEIPA

Beyond the Archer River, Peninsula Developmental Rd. bears west to the bauxite-mining town of **Weipa** (pop. 2000). The town is a great place to pick up supplies or get a good night's rest on the way to the Tip. If staying overnight, you can camp at **Weipa Camping Ground** ❶. The site also rents small fishing boats and cabins of various sizes, some with their own bathrooms and kitchens (☎4069 7871. Campsites $9 per adult, cabins $65-105; boats $110 per day, $70 per half-day). Those looking for a bit of luxury should check into **Heritage Resort** ❺. Clean rooms, a bar/restaurant, a pool with a rock waterfall and services including massage, babysitting, and a beauty salon offer many of the creature comforts you may be craving after days in the wilderness. (Behind the shopping center on Commercial Ave. ☎4069 8000. Double $110.)

Police (☎4069 9119) are across the street from the hospital on Northern Ave.; the **hospital** (☎4090 6222) is at the corner of Northern and Central Ave. Supplies can be purchased at the Nanum Shopping Centre on the corner of Commercial Ave. and Keer Point Dr., where you'll find a **pharmacy** (☎4069 7412), a **post office** (☎4069 7110, M-F 9am-5pm), a Woolworths **supermarket** (☎4069 7330; M, W, F 8am-7pm, Th 8am-9pm, Sa 8am-5pm), a bakery/cafe (M-Th 7am-6:30pm, F 7am-7pm, Sat 7am-noon, Su noon-7pm), and a Chinese restaurant.

WEIPA TO THE TIP

The trek north beyond Weipa is truly for the hardest-of-the-hardcore, born-for-the-bush traveler. First backtrack a short while along the Peninsula Developmental Rd. until you reach **Telegraph Road.** This road is well marked, though not in the best condition. Dusty, bumpy roads and river crossings will come to define much of the remaining journey to the Tip. North of the Archer River, the Cape's jungle becomes wilder, the heat hotter, tracks rougher, and Wet season wetter. Just before reaching the tip, you'll bypass the **Jardine River National Park,** which is wilderness at its most remote. Campsites are available at Captain Billy's Landing on the coast or at Eliot Falls, just off Telegraph Rd. Both sites require pre-registration, which can be obtained at the Heathlands ranger base south of Eliot Falls. The remainder of the trip to the Torres Strait, which separates Australia from Papua New Guinea, is not far from the park, though the Jardine River must be crossed. Doing so requires either a risky and highly inadvisable 4WD-only deep river crossing via the Telegraph Rd. or diverging onto the **Northern Bypass Road** and catching the **Jardine River Ferry.** About 30km past the crossing is the small community of Bamaga, where you'll be able to rest and refuel.

If you do make it all the way up, you'll probably have more company than you did for most of your trip. The small town of Seisia, 1hr. south of the Cape, offers accommodation to those on their way up and down. **Seisia Holiday Park ❷,** 6 Koraba Rd., (☎1800 653 243) rents villas, rooms and campsites. If the top of one continent isn't quite enough, you can catch a **Peddell's Ferry** (☎4069 1551) from Seisia to Thursday Island and explore the Torres Strait island culture. Tickets and tours range from $40 (student $30) one-way tickets to several hundred dollar tour packages that make multiple island and reef stops over the course of several days.

CENTRAL & WESTERN QUEENSLAND

Across Queensland's interior, roads are long, flat, and straight, crossing immense distances dotted with shrubby spinifex. In the towns, which are few and far between, the harsh, hot environment has led to a way of life entirely different from that on the coast—the pace is slower, the tourist activities less structured, and locals are more guarded. These distinctions mean that no Queensland experience is complete without a trip to the interior. Driving in this region is an endeavor in itself. Some of the highways are unsealed in patches. In general, the east-west routes are nicer to your tires than those heading north-south. The major ones are: the **Warrego Highway (Hwy. 54)** west from Brisbane eventually reaching the Mitchell Hwy.; the **Capricorn and Landsborough Highway (Hwy. 66),** from Rockhampton to the Gemfields, Barcaldine, and Mt. Isa; the **Flinders Highway (Hwy. 78),** from Townsville through Charters Towers and Hughenden to Mt. Isa; and the **Gulf Development Road (Hwy. 1),** including part of the **Kennedy Highway,** from the Atherton Tablelands outside Cairns through the Gulf Savannah to Normanton. Connecting them all, the so-called **Matilda Highway,** the major north-south road, actually encompasses various fragments of the Mitchell, Landsborough, and Capricorn Hwy. and the Burke Developmental Rd.

CAPRICORN & LANDSBOROUGH HWY.

The road west from Rockhampton cuts a diagonal through Queensland's Gemfields. **Route 66** is called the **Capricorn Highway** until its junction with the Matilda Hwy. in Barcaldine when it becomes the **Landsborough Highway,** which passes through Longreach and Winton and meets the Flinders Hwy. 2hr. east of Mt. Isa.

GEMFIELDS

Wanna be a millionaire? You might try digging in the dirt of Queensland's Gemfields. Fossicking in this area draws thousands of tourists each year. The income is hardly steady, but it can be lucrative.

Affluent **Emerald** (pop. 10,000), where no emerald has ever been found, is a major agricultural center for grain, cotton, and Mandarin oranges. A convenient stop on **McCafferty's/Greyhound** (☎4982 2755) route to Mt. Isa, the town is a jumping-off point for the Gemfields. Stop at the **Central Highlands Visitor Information Centre,** in the center of town on Clermont St., before venturing into the Gemfields. (☎4982 4142. Open M-Sa 9am-5pm, Su 10am-2pm.) The new **Central Inn ❸,** 90 Clermont St., has clean rooms with TV and fridge, as well a communal kitchen and lounge area. (☎4982 0800. Breakfast included. Singles $39; doubles $49.) There's a Coles **supermarket** on the corner of Clermont and Opal St. in the Market Plaza. (☎4982 3622. Open M-F 8am-9pm, Sa 8am-5pm.) The **Emerald Public Library,** 44 Borilla St., has free **Internet.** (☎4982 8347. Open M noon-5:30pm, Tu and Th 10am-5:30pm, W 10am-8pm, F 10am-5pm, Sa 9am-noon.) The open-face sandwiches at **KT's Coffee Lounge,** 14 Egerton St., cost $8-10 and are excellent. (☎4982 3384. Open M-F 8am-5pm, Sa-Su 8am-3pm.)

Forty kilometers west of Emerald, **Anakie** lies in the prime fossicking region. This village holds the last **petrol** station for 125km, and **The Big Sapphire Info Centre,** 1 Anakie Rd. The Info Centre also books fossicking tours that guarantee a jewelry-quality sapphire. (☎4985 4525; www.bigsapphire.com.au. Tag-along tours, with supplies, instructions and permits, $75 for 2 people. With transport, $120 per person. Tours run Apr.-Oct. 8:30am-3pm, Nov.-Mar. 6:30am-1pm. Open daily 8am-6pm.) Most tourists drive 10-18km farther north to **Sapphire** or **Rubyvale,** where you can stop along the road to sort through pre-dug buckets of dirt (around $5.50 per bucket). If you find a jewelry quality stone, most places can facet it for you for around $20. The **Rubyvale Caravan Park ❶,** on Main St. has a small heated pool. (☎4985 4118. Reception 8am-6pm. Sites $12, powered $17; cabins for 2 $45.)

LONGREACH

The micropolis of Longreach (pop. 4500) is the largest town in the Central West. With its own Pastoral College and School of Distance Education, Longreach acts as the public service and educational center for the area.

The town's biggest attractions are on the outskirts of town when approaching from Rockhampton. The **Australian Stockman's Hall of Fame and Outback Heritage Centre** is a massive multimedia museum off the Landsborough Hwy. (☎4658 2166; www.outbackheritage.com.au. Open daily 9am-5pm. $20, concessions $16.50, ages 8-16 $10, under 8 free.) Across the street, the **Qantas Outback Founder Heritage Museum** showcases the role airplanes have had on outback life. (☎4658 3737; www.qfom.com.au. $15, Open daily 9am-5pm.)

McCafferty's/Greyhound buses depart from **Longreach Outback Travel**, 115A Eagle St., (☎4658 1776, www.lotc.com.au; open M-F 9am-5pm, Sa 9am-noon and 3:30-4pm, Su 10-11am and 3:30-4pm), with service to Brisbane (daily at 3:55pm; $112) and Mt. Isa (daily at 10:50am; $81). The **Information Centre** is at Qantas Park on Eagle St. (☎4658 3555; www.longreach.qld.gov.au. Open M-F 9am-12:30pm and 1:30-5pm, Sa-Su 9am-1pm.) Free **Internet** is at the **library**, 96 Eagle St. (☎4658 4104. Open Tu and Th 9:30am-1pm, W and F 12:30-4:30pm, Sa 9am-noon.) The **post office** is next door. (☎13 13 18. Open M-F 9am-5pm.)

The cheapest place to stay is the **Royal Hotel ❶**, 111 Eagle St., but keep in mind that the pub downstairs hosts a disco 9pm-2am every Friday and Saturday. (☎4658 2118. Reception Su-Th 10am-11pm, F-Sa 10am-2am. Dorms $11; singles $22; self-contained single units $55; doubles $66.) The **Longreach Caravan Park ❶**, 180 Ibis St. at the corner of Owl St., is a bit quieter. (☎4658 1770. Reception 7am-10:30pm. Sites $14.30, powered for 2 $16.50; self-contained cabins for 2 $50, with shared toilets $28.) The IGA Cornett **supermarket** is on the corner of Eagle and Swan St. (☎4658 1260. Open M-W 8am-6:30pm, Th-F 8am-8pm, Sa 8am-4pm.)

FLINDERS HIGHWAY

A long, lonely route, Flinders Highway is primarily a straight shot from Townsville to Mt. Isa, but it passes through several small outback towns along the way. Ravenswood and Charters Towers are only a daytrip away from the coast, yet remote enough to offer a taste of the outback. As you head farther west, towns get smaller, marked by lower speed limits, a general store, and petrol pump. Most traffic heads straight to Mt. Isa, the largest city in the world in area (at 41,000 sq. km, it is larger than all of Switzerland) and a true mining outpost that serves as a gateway to the Northern Territory.

CHARTERS TOWERS   ☎07

South of the Atherton Tablelands, the land dries out and old outback towns begin to punctuate a barren landscape. Once nicknamed "The World" for its cosmopolitan flair, Charters Towers, 1½hr. (128km) west of Townsville, was the hub of Queensland. Nowadays, the vestiges of its glory days as a gold mine center remain only in the enthusiasm of locals who proudly call this town home.

▐▐ TRANSPORTATION & PRACTICAL INFORMATION. The **Queensland Rail Station** (☎13 22 32) is on Enterprise Rd. on the east side of town. From the Flinders Hwy., turn on Millchester Rd. towards town, and take a right onto Enterprise Rd. **Trains** go to Townsville (3hr., Tu and Sa 10:02am, $19.80) and Mt. Isa (17hr., Su and W 9:03pm, $98). **McCafferty's/Greyhound** and **Douglas buses** depart from the corner of Gill and Church St. to Townsville. (1¾hr., McCafferty's leaves at 4:55pm daily, $27; Douglas leaves M-F 8am, $20.) Book tickets at **Travel Experience**, 13 Gill St. (☎4787 2622. Open M-F 8am-5:30pm, Sa 9am-noon.)

The center of Charters Towers is created by the simple T-intersection of **Mosman** and **Gill Street**, known as the **Historic City Centre**. Government offices and "The World" theater run along Mosman St., while most shops, restaurants, and banks descend down Gill St. The **Information Centre**, 74 Mosman St., is at the top of Gill St., to the left of City Hall. (☎4752 0314; www.charterstowers.qld.gov.au. Open daily 9am-5pm.) There are several **banks** with **ATMs** strung along Gill St. The **library** is in the Old Bank, 34 Gill St. (☎4752 0338. Open M, W, F 10am-1pm and 1:45-4:45pm, Tu and Th 1:45-4:45pm, Sa 9:30am-noon.) **Internet** is at Charters Towers Computers, 59 Gill St. (☎4787 2988. Open M-F 9am-5pm and Sa 9am-noon; $6 per hr.) and at the library ($5 per hr.).

QUEENSLAND

◢◨◧ ACCOMMODATIONS, FOOD, & NIGHTLIFE. The **York Street Bed and Breakfast ❸**, 58 York St., is a friendly place to stay but a 15min. walk from the center of town. Rooms, especially in the main house, are comfortable and clean. (☎4787 1028. Lodge rooms share amenities and a kitchen; dorms $17, singles $25, doubles and twins $45. Rooms in the main house are self-contained and come with a full cooked breakfast; single $65, double $80.) For something cheaper, try the **Waverly Hotel ❷**, 19 Mosman St. Rooms have TV, fridge, and sink. Laundry, secure carpark, and tea and coffee are also available. (☎4787 2591. Twins $30.) Most hotels in town serve typical pub meals from $5. For something different, the **Golden Mine Chinese Restaurant ❶**, 64 Mosman St., features a 24-dish all-you-can-eat smorgasbord (☎4787 7609. Open for lunch M-F 11:30am-2pm, for dinner daily 5-9:30pm. Lunch $7.40, dinner $9.20.) Woolworths, on Gill St. at Deane St., has **groceries.** (☎4787 3411. Open M-F 8am-9pm, Sa 8am-5pm.) Nightlife in Charters Towers is confined to **Pegasus Night Club**, 33 Gill St., in the White Horse Tavern, where the DJ plays a Top 40 mix. (☎4787 1064. Open F-Sa 10pm-3am.)

◧◪ SIGHTS & ACTIVITIES. Once the center of a huge gold rush, Charters Towers has some interesting history. Check it all out at the **Venus Gold Battery,** the largest surviving gold battery relic in Australia. (☎4752 0314. Guided tours $11, children $5. Open daily 9am-3pm.) **Ravenswood,** one hour east of Charters Towers off the Flinders Hwy., is an old gold mining town that has resisted development. Check out old mines and city structures, but only if you have a car. Pick up a brochure at the information center that points out important buildings. **Geoff's City and Bush Safari** will keep you laughing and informed. (☎4787 2118. Departs daily 8am and 4pm. $20, children $10. Free pick-up and return.) See the entire city and its sights in a 60min. **walking tour,** with Sue's City Sites. (☎4787 7697. Departs from the Information Centre, M-Th and Sa-Su at 10am and 11:30am. $9, pensioners $8.80, children $4.40.) The **Zara Clarke Museum,** at the corner of Gill and Mary St., has an authoritative display of Charters Towers memorabilia including an old fire wagon and an iron lung. (Open daily 10am-3pm. $4.40.) Two cattle stations nearby offer "City Slicker" holiday packages: **Bluff Downs ❷** is a rough-and-ready real working cattle station—mud, blood, and billabongs included. This one is for those seeking the authentic outback experience. (☎4770 4084; rhonda@bluffdowns.com.au. Sites for 2 $18, powered $20; dorms $20, with meals $55. No credit cards.) For the tenderfoot, **Plain Creek ❷** is probably better suited. (☎4983 5228; www.plaincrkc-qhinet.ne.au. Camp and caravan sites $17; full board, including bed, meals, and all activities $165.)

FROM PENTLAND TO RICHMOND

PENTLAND

About halfway between Charters Towers and Hughendon is the town of Pentland (120km away, pop. 300). Pentland is a good place to stay if the sun is setting and the 'roos are on the road, as it has basic services and some accommodations. There is a **general store** with **post office** (☎4788 1130; open M-F 9am-1pm and 2pm-7pm, Sa 10am-noon, Su 5-7pm), a **Shell Service Station** (☎4788 1254; open M-F 7am-7pm, Sa-Su 7am-6pm), and cheap accommodations.

The **Pentland Caravan Park ❶** has several campsites, an inviting pool, and a convenience store. (☎4788 1148. Reception open 6:30am-10pm. Sites $13, powered caravan sites $15; singles $38.50; doubles $48.50.) The **Pentland Hotel Motel ❹** serves food, and their spotless rooms have TV, fridge, and bath. (☎4788 1106. Singles $50; twins and doubles $60.)

HUGHENDEN

Hughenden (HEW-en-den; pop. 1500) marks the eastern edge of Queensland's marine dinosaur territory: stop at the **Visitor Information Centre,** 37 Gray St., to see the **Muttaburrasaurus skeleton.** Gold-mining memorabilia is on display. (☎4741 1021; www.hughenden.sunzine.net. Open daily 9am-5pm. $2.) Budget accommodations are limited to the **Grand Hotel ❶,** 25 Gray St. (☎4741 1588; dorms $15, singles $25), and the **Allan Terry Caravan Park ❶,** 2 Resolution St. The caravan site is neatly kept, with swimming pool, laundry, and kitchen. (☎4741 1190. Reception M-F 6am-9pm. Sites for 2 $10, powered $14; units with shared amenities $40, ensuite cabins $60.) Opposite the Grand Hotel, new and immaculate rooms are a bit more expensive at **Wright's Motel ❹,** 20 Gray St. They have a fully licensed restaurant available for room service. All rooms have phones, A/C, TV, tea and coffee, and fridge. (☎4741 1677. Singles $42; doubles and twins $50, deluxe queens $68.)

   Porcupine Gorge, a pretty natural valley sometimes referred to as "Australia's Little Grand Canyon," is 63km north of town. Follow the signs in town, but be warned that the bitumen road turns to well-kept dirt 15.8km out of town. Camping is available at the Pyramid Lookout Campground, with self-registration ($4 per person per night), pit toilets and shelter shed. Be sure to bring your own water. If you brave the mountains on your own, make sure to get the free **required registration** at the **NPWS office** in town (☎4741 1113) or in Charters Towers (☎4787 3388).

RICHMOND

West of Hughenden along the Flinders Hwy., Richmond packs an impressive biological punch. **Kronosaurus Korner,** 93 Goldring St., is both the regional **Visitor Information Centre** and the **Richmond Marine Fossil Museum,** housing the bones of many local Cretaceous creatures. (☎4741 3429. Open daily 8:30am-4:45pm. $9.) Heading towards Mt. Isa on the Flinders Hwy., you'll see the **BP Roadhouse,** which has a big menu, the last petrol for 145km, showers, and toilets. (☎4741 3316. Open daily 6am-9pm.) Free **Internet** is at the **library,** 78 Goldring St. (open M-Tu and Th-F noon-4pm, W 9am-1pm); there is also a pay kiosk at the Visitors Centre. The brand-new **Moon Rock Cafe ❶,** in the Visitors Centre, cooks up a few more veggie-friendly options than the typical roadhouse ($3-4). The **Richmond Caravan Park ❶,** on your way into town from Hughenden before the Visitors Centre, is an exceptional value, with newly refurnished facilities that have A/C, shared bathrooms, and communal kitchen. (☎4741 3772. Key deposit $10. Sites $11, powered $14; twin-share bunk house $20 per person; ensuite cabins $50.) The **Mud Hut Motel ❹,** 72 Goldring St., has above-average pub rooms with A/C and TV. (☎/fax 4741 3223. Singles $44; doubles $55.) There is a BuyRite **supermarket** on Goldring St. (Open M-F 7:30am-5pm, Sa 7:30am-12:30pm, Su 7:30am-noon.)

MOUNT ISA   ☎07

Years ago, Mount Isa (pop. 22,200) was where hitchhikers heading to the Northern Territory broke down and bought a bus ticket. These days, with the area's impressive road improvement, travelers can make the long, sometimes bleak trip without many hassles. The Mount Isa Mines annually produce 11 million tons of ore. Before you leave, stock up on supplies and make sure your car is full of fuel.

🖥 **TRANSPORTATION** The **train station** (☎4744 1203) is on Station St.; from the town center, go over the Isa St. bridge and take a right. (Open M and F 11:15am-6pm, Tu-Th 8am-3:30pm.) The *Inlander* train departs 4:30pm Monday and Friday to: Charters Towers (16hr.); Hughenden (11¼hr.); Richmond (9¼hr.); Townsville (19hr.). **McCafferty's/Greyhound** is at **Underground@Isa,** 19 Marian St. (☎4749 1555 or 1300 659 660. Open daily 9am-5pm.) **Buses** run to: Alice Springs ($203); Brisbane

($143); Cairns ($161); Charters Towers ($106); Darwin ($232); Richmond ($56); Rockhampton ($211); and Townsville ($113). Call **United Cab** 24hr. ☎4743 2333.

ORIENTATION & PRACTICAL INFORMATION The city center is a manageable four-by-four grid, bounded by **Isa Street** to the north, **West Street** to the west, **Mary Street** to the south, and **Simpson Street** to the east. The **Barkly Highway** enters from Northern Territory and runs parallel to the **Leichhardt River** until the **Grace Street Bridge** turns left over the water into the city center, becoming **Grace Street**. From Cloncurry in the east, the Flinders Hwy. becomes **Marian Street**.

The **Outback@Isa** complex, 19 Marian St., serves as the center for travelers. It includes the information center, the bus station, and Internet cafe as well as two of the area's prime attractions: underground tours and the Riversleigh Fossil Centre. (☎1300 659 660 or 4749 1555. Open daily 9am-5pm). Other services include: **Commonwealth Bank,** 23 Miles St. (☎4743 5033; open M-Th 9:30am-4pm, F 9:30am-5pm); **police,** 7 Isa St., at the corner of Miles St. (☎4744 1111; open 24hr.); **Internet** at the **library,** 23 West St. (☎4744 4256; $5.80 per hr.; open M-Th 10am-6pm, F 10am-5pm, Sa 9am-4pm); **post office** on the corner of Camooweal and Isa St. (☎4743 2454; open M-F 8:30am-5pm) and also in Mt. Isa Square opposite K-Mart Place (☎13 13 18; open M-F 8:45am-5:15pm, Sa 9am-11:45am). **Postal Code:** 4825.

ACCOMMODATIONS & FOOD. The **Artisans Block and Sleeper ❷,** 62 Marian St., feels like home after a long roadtrip. Enjoy a cozy atmosphere and the new back yard BBQ, wok, and beds underneath the stars. (☎0412 962 069. Dorms $22; singles $55; doubles $60.50; all include continental breakfast.) You'll get the best value for money at the newly renovated **Central Point Motel ❺,** 6 Marian St. All rooms have A/C, TV, ensuite, fridge, and comfy beds. (☎4743 0666. Saltwater pool. Singles $70; doubles $70.) **Traveller's Haven ❷,** at Pamela and Spence St., has free pick-up and a nice pool. (☎4743 0313. Linen $1 per item. Key deposit $5. Reception 6:30am-1pm and 5-7pm. Dorms $20; singles $36; twins and doubles $46. VIP.) **Mt. Isa Van Park ❶,** 112 Marian St., is clean and well-tended, with lots of long-term residents. (☎4743 3252. Reception 7:30am-6:30pm. Sites $15, powered $18; cabins with shared amenities $45; ensuite self-contained villa for 2 with TV, A/C, and kitchen $60, extra adult $5.50, extra child $2.50.) The **Buffalo Club ❶,** on the corner of Grace and Simpson St., offers a $10 all-you-can-eat lunch buffet. (☎4743 2365; www.buffs.com.au. Open daily 8am-2am.) The **Irish Club ❶,** on the corner of Buckley and 19th Ave., has several bars, many food options, and lots of pokies. Coles **supermarket** is in K-Mart Centre, on Marian St. (☎4743 6007. Open M-Sa 8am-9pm.)

SIGHTS. The **Outback@Isa** center offers 1½hr. "working" mine tours for an example of what really goes on underground. The center is also home to the **Riversleigh Fossil Centre,** which allows visitors to peer into a working laboratory. (☎1300 659 660 or 4749 1555. Underground tour $40, concessions $36, children $26. Fossil Centre $10/$8/$6.50. Open daily 9am-5pm.) **Campbell's Tours** offers 2hr. surface tours at the mine and four-day safaris to **Lawn Hill National Park,** 220km north of Mt. Isa. (☎1800 242 329; 4743 2006; www.campbellstravel.com.au. Surface tours ($22) depart May.-Sept. M-F 9am and 1pm, Sa 11am; Oct.-Apr. M-F 1pm. Safaris ($495) depart Apr.-Oct. on Tu and F.) Australia's biggest **rodeo** comes to Mt. Isa in August, as do the world's greatest rodeo legends. (☎4743 2706; www.isarodeo.com.au.) **Lake Moondarra** is just 15min. west on the Barkly Hwy.; **Lake Julius** is another 90km farther and a great fishing spot. At night, view the lit-up desert from the town's **lookout** on Shacketon St., off Marian St. The **Mt. Isa Market,** in the library parking lot on West St., offers fruits, veggies, and crafts (☎4744 4206. Open Sa 6am-noon).

GULF SAVANNAH

The region between Atherton Tablelands and Gulf of Carpentaria, along the **Gulf Developmental Road,** revels in remoteness. This is the outback's Outback, an escapist's fantasy and urbanite's nightmare. Attractions include historic "nowhere-to-nowhere" trains, gorges, and lava tubes. Reach the sea by Karumba Point Rd. off Gulf Developmental Rd., 4km from **Karumba** (pop. 600) and 72km from **Normanton.** Visit in the Dry (Apr.-Oct.), though even then road conditions can be bad. The most common route is the Gulf Developmental Rd., from Cairns to Normanton, where it joins the north-south **Burke Developmental Road.** In the Dry, 2WDs are fine on most roads, but caravans should avoid unsealed roads. 4WD is essential for the Wet. The **Undara Volcano,** 40min. from Mt. Surprise, erupted 190,000 years ago, creating 69 **lava tubes** in the middle of dense rainforest, with caverns averaging 10m high and 15m wide. **Undara Experience** visits nine of them. (☎4097 1411. 2hr. tour daily 8:30am, 1pm, $33, children $16; half-day tours daily 8am $63/$31.) **Camp ❶** at Undara ($6 per person) or stay in the **tent village ❷** ($18 per person; linen $6), **Wilderness Lodge ❷** ($24), or **Lava Lodge ❺** ($75).

SOUTH AUSTRALIA

With coastal fishing towns, huge expanses of desert outback, grape-filled valleys churning out some of the world's best wine, and a capital that enjoys the good life, South Australia is more than meets the eye. South Australia's coastline offers everything: sheltered bays for swimming; surfing beaches exposed to the great Southern Ocean; the largest tuna fleet in the southern hemisphere; large populations of seals, sea lions, and steel-blue fairy penguins; and a breezy respite from the oft-raging inferno farther inland.

Step away from the coast and South Australia goes bush remarkably quickly. Town populations dwindle and the harsh dry landscape of the outback takes over. Highway 87 stretches from Port Augusta in the south and makes a pit stop in Coober Pedy before heading up to Alice Springs in the Northern Territory. Pilgrims on this outback trek will discover their true tolerance for wide open spaces. The endless sky cracks open above the endless stretches of dusty ground and at night the stars shine down in a stunning multitude. Farther into the void, the Flinders Ranges, a portfolio of spectacular sculpting by five billion years of geological processes, are a desert trekker's paradise. From the long stretch of road across the dreaded Nullarbor to the famed wildlife of Kangaroo Island to the exquisite restaurants and entertainment in Adelaide, South Australia deserves to be explored. Just don't get lost.

SOUTH AUSTRALIA HIGHLIGHTS

EYRE PENINSULA. Find yourself on the deserted, cliff-fringed beaches of the Eyre Peninsula (p. 509) or lose yourself in the nearby Outback (p. 509).

ADELAIDE. Relax and enjoy good food, festivals, culture, and calm in South Australia's capital, the city of churches (p. 462).

FLINDERS RANGES. Gain a new perspective on time and space in the ancient, gently folding mountains of the Flinders Ranges (p. 501).

KANGAROO ISLAND. Sleep under the tranquil Australian stars in the company of such unique native animals as echidnas, fur seals, goannas, kangaroos, koalas, wallabies, and sea lions (p. 481).

BAROSSA VALLEY. Enjoy the fruits of South Australia's premier wine region (p. 488).

COOBER PEDY. Chill out in the underground hostels of Coober Pedy (p. 511).

⌐ TRANSPORTATION

If you don't have a car, the best way to see South Australia is by bus. **McCafferty's/ Greyhound** (☎ 13 14 99 or 13 20 30) runs between Adelaide and Melbourne, Sydney, Alice Springs, and Perth, stopping over at a few destinations in between. **Premier Stateliner** (☎ 8415 5555) services smaller towns throughout South Australia. Three major train lines run through South Australia: the **Overland** to Melbourne, the *Indian Pacific* to Perth, and the legendary *Ghan* to Alice Springs. For more train information, see **By Train**, p. 462. Major **car rental** companies with branches in SA

SOUTH AUSTRALIA

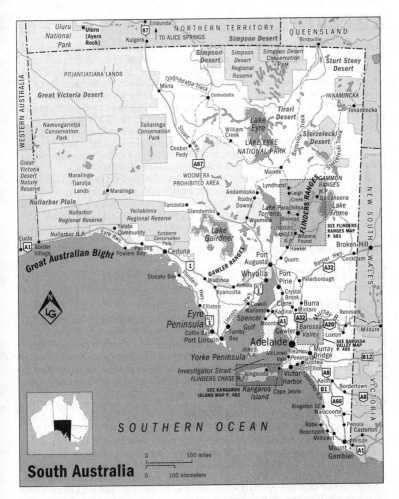

South Australia

0   100 miles

0   100 kilometers

include **Hertz** (☎ 13 30 39), **Avis** (☎ 13 63 33), and **Thrifty** (☎ 1300 367 227). Local out-fits, often with lower prices, are listed throughout this chapter. A conventional vehicle is fine for wine and beach country, but 4WD is strongly recommended for forays into the outback.

Another good option—an option often more practical for those traveling alone or going to more remote places—is to book a **tour.** Many choose the jump-on, jump-off flexibility of backpacker buses like the youthful **Oz Experience** (☎ 1300 30 00 28) or the twenty-something favorite, **Wayward Bus** (☎ 8410 8833 or 1800 882 823); plenty of local organizations also run excellent trips, and they are listed in the **Practical Information** section of most towns in this chapter. Most hostels give tour advice and book for guests, often at a discount. Still, the greatest way to see the state is to buy a used car or 4WD and sell it when leaving the country—this provides the ultimate in freedom and flexibility.

ADELAIDE ☎ 08

Spend any time in Australia and you're bound to hear someone describe South Australia's stately capital as boring. And it's true, Adelaide has no glitz and glam, no flashing neon or huge skyscrapers. But the city is far from boring, and those who take the time to explore will be richly rewarded. South Australians are proud of Adelaide, and visitors will find themselves smitten by its parklands and museums, its proximity to beaches and wineries, and its devotion to nightlife, music, and culture. The first completely planned city in Australia is centered around a one-mile-square grid and separated from the suburbs, where the majority of the population lives by vast green parklands. The city is pervaded by a youth culture refreshingly mindful of its heritage; residents take pride in the graceful colonial buildings and flourishing arts scene while enjoying a big-city lifestyle.

Life's finer pleasures are far less expensive in Adelaide than in its east coast counterparts. With more restaurants per capita than any other Australian city, Adelaide can satisfy any palate at any budget with the aid of some of the world's best wines. The city's cultural attractions, headed by the Adelaide Festival of Arts, include a symphony, small experimental theaters, and world-class galleries and museums. And lest you think there is nowhere to cut loose, the nightclubs along Hindley St., the pubs in the city center, and the cafes on Rundle St. do the trick.

◪ INTERCITY TRANSPORTATION

BY PLANE

The **Adelaide Airport** is 7km west of the city center. Most hostels in the city or Glenelg offer free pick-up with advance booking. Failing that, the cheapest way is the **Skylink Airport Shuttle,** which runs to both the airport and Keswick Railway Station and picks up and drops off in front of the Central Bus Station on Franklin St. as well as the many hotels in town. You must pre-book by phone to go from the city to the airport, but at the airport you can catch the bus at the domestic terminal directly in front of the currency exchange, or to the left as you exit the international terminal. (☎8332 0528; bookings 7am-10pm. Daily, every 30min. or 1hr., 5:45am-9:45pm; $7, return $12.) For two or more people, a **taxi** will end up being cheaper and more convenient than the Skylink bus. **Taxis** to the city run $11-15.

International travelers can get huge discounts on domestic one-way fares. **Regional Express** (aka Rex, ☎13 17 13; www.regionalexpress.com.au) is the biggest local carrier, with flights to 35 South Australian cities, including Coober Pedy, Kangaroo Island, Mt. Gambier, and Port Lincoln. **Airlines of South Australia** (**ASA;** ☎8682 5688 or 1800 018 234; www.airlinesofsa.com.au) services Port Lincoln and Port Augusta. **O'Connor** (www.oconnor-airlines.com.au) services Mt. Gambier and Mildura. **Emu Airways** (☎8234 3711 or 1800 182 343) services Kangaroo Island. **Virgin Blue** (☎13 67 89; www.virginblue.com.au) and **Qantas** (☎13 13 13; www.qantas.com.au) also offer competitive fares, and local backpackers travel agencies can often get you discounts.

BY TRAIN

All interstate and long-distance country trains use the **Keswick Interstate Rail Passenger Terminal** (☎13 21 47), which is just off the southwest corner of the central city grid, about 1km west of West Terr. The Skylink Airport Shuttle stops at Keswick and drops off at the central bus station and several points downtown. (☎8332 0528. Daily 5am-9pm; $3.50, return $6. Book ahead.) Taxis from the city run about $6. The Keswick terminal has parking. Only suburban commuter trains use the Adelaide Railway Station (☎8218 2277), on North Terr.

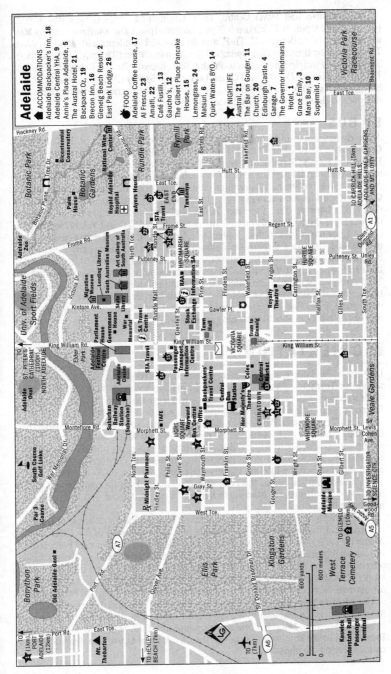

Adelaide

▲ ACCOMMODATIONS
Adelaide Backpacker's Inn, **18**
Adelaide Central YHA, **9**
Annie's Place Adelaide, **5**
The Austral Hotel, **21**
Backpack Oz, **19**
Brecon Inn, **16**
Glenelg Beach Resort, **2**
East Park Lodge, **26**

♦ FOOD
Adelaide Coffee House, **17**
Al Fresco, **23**
Amalfi, **22**
Café Fusilli, **13**
Gaucho's, **12**
The Gilbert Place Pancake
House, **15**
Lemongrass, **24**
Matsuri, **6**
Quiet Waters BYO, **14**

★ NIGHTLIFE
Austral, **21**
The Bar on Gouger, **11**
Church, **20**
Edinburgh Castle, **4**
Garage, **7**
The Governor Hindmarsh
Hotel, **1**
Grace Emily, **3**
Mars Bar, **10**
Supermild, **8**

SOUTH AUSTRALIA

The **Australian Rail Travel Centre,** 18-20 Grenfell St., sells tickets downtown. (☎8231 4366. Open M-F 8:30am-5:30pm, Sa 9am-1pm.) The **Overland** runs to **Melbourne** (12-13½hr.; departs M, Th-F, and Su 9am; $57, students $40, children $33). The *Ghan* runs trains to **Alice Springs** (19hr., departs M and Th 3pm, $197/$99/$89). The *Indian Pacific* runs trains to **Perth** (39hr., departs Tu and F 6pm, $283/$142/ $128). The *Indian Pacific* and *Ghan* both run to **Sydney** (24-25hr.; departs W and Su 7:45am, Sa 10am; $176/$88/$79). All three of the above train carriers offer a 10% discount to those who are YHA members.

BY BUS

Adelaide has two central bus stations, both located on Franklin St. **McCafferty's/ Greyhound** (☎13 14 99 or 13 20 30) has a station at 101 Franklin St., while **V/Line, Firefly,** and **Premier Stateliner** buses pull in to 111 Franklin St. National bus companies provide regular service to and from Adelaide at fares that generally beat rail and air travel; unfortunately, savings come at the price of comfort. **McCafferty's/ Greyhound** runs to: **Alice Springs** (20hr., 1 per day, $177); **Brisbane** (29hr., every other day, $232); **Darwin** (34hr., 1 per day, $371); **Melbourne** (10hr., 2 per day, $59); **Perth** (34hr., 1 per day, $264); **Sydney** (22hr., 1 per day, $127); and **Yulara/Ayers Rock** (20hr., 1 per day, $147). A new, budget-minded carrier, **Firefly Express** (☎8231 1488 or 1800 631 134) runs directly to Melbourne (10-11hr.; departs daily 7:30am and 8:30pm; $50), where you can connect to a bus heading onward to Sydney (Adelaide to Sydney $100). **V/Line** (☎8231 7260) runs a daily coach/rail combination to Melbourne via Bendigo (12hr.; $58, students and children $29). Within South Australia, **Premier Stateliner** (☎8415 5555) is the main carrier, serving over 200 destinations state-wide. The free *State Guide,* available at the tourist office and many hostels, is indispensable for planning area travel.

▣ ORIENTATION

Downtown Adelaide is a mere square mile in size, bordered by North, East, South, and West Terraces. The city is bisected north to south by **King William Street;** streets running east to west change names when crossing King William St. **Rundle Street,** home to chic sidewalk cafes, top-notch eateries, and vibrant nightlife, runs from East Terr. west to Pulteney St. in the city's northeast quadrant (known as the **East End**). From there, it becomes the pedestrian-only **Rundle Mall,** the city's main shopping area, west to King William St. before changing names yet again to become Hindley St. Many of the backpacker hostels are clustered in the western quadrant of the city, while the glittery upscale hotels can be found lining North Terr. **Victoria Square** lies at the center of the city grid, while **Light Square** in the northwest quadrant and **Hindmarsh Square** in the northeast quadrant are also important landmarks.

Keswick, which includes the railway station, is about 2km southwest of the central grid, and the beach suburb of **Glenelg** is 12km southwest of the CBD via the Anzac Hwy. (A5) or the Glenelg Tram. **North Adelaide,** a smaller grid centered on the trendy bistros and shopping of upscale **O'Connell Street,** sits a couple kilometers north of the CBD in the middle of the parklands that extend north from the banks of the River Torrens. Morphett St. and King William St. connect it to the center of town. Northwest of the CBD, on the Port River, is the suburb of **Port Adelaide.**

The **Adelaide Hills,** including Cleland Conservation Park and the scenic Mt. Lofty lookout, are visible just east of the city. Although the city of Adelaide in general is relatively peaceful, *the parklands are unsafe at night,* especially near the **River Torrens** and in the southwest corner of the city. **Hindley Street** also demands extra caution during the nighttime.

◨ LOCAL TRANSPORTATION

BY PUBLIC TRANSPORTATION

Adelaide is serviced by a web of public buses and trains that make up an integrated public transport system called the **Adelaide Metro** (www.adelaidemetro.com.au), which also runs two free bus services around the city: **Beeline** and **City Loop.** These yellow buses are easily identified and wheelchair-accessible. Beeline runs in the city center, from the railway station on North Terr. and down King William St. to Victoria Sq. and back. (Every 5min. M-Th 7:40am-6pm, every 5min. F 7:40am-9pm; every 15min. Sa 8:30am-5:20pm.) City Loop, true to its name, runs both directions around a loop that covers the north half of the city, with stops at North, East, and West Terr. as well as most major tourist attractions, Central Market, and near the bus station. (Every 15min. M-Th 8:30am-6pm and F 8:30am-9pm, every 30min. Sa 8:30am-5pm.) For those staying in the Adelaide Hills, there's a **Wandering Star** weekend service that runs from the city and drops passengers off at their door. Service runs from midnight to 4am and the city bus stops are conveniently located in heavily trafficked club areas. (☎8210 1000. $6.)

To roam farther, there are bus and train routes that comprise TransAdelaide's suburban system. The **Passenger Transport Information Centre,** at the corner of King William and Currie St., has route schedules and an info line. (☎8210 1000. Open M-Sa 8am-6pm, Su 10:30am-5:30pm.) **Single tickets** are good on any service (return included) for two hours and can be purchased from drivers and vending machines. (Single trip M-F 9am-3pm $1.90; all other times $3.) Daytrip tickets ($5.70) allow one day of unlimited travel on any service and can be purchased when boarding buses or trams, but must be bought beforehand for trains. An option for those staying longer is the **multitrip ticket,** which must be purchased prior to boarding. (10 trips $20, off-peak $11.)

The best way to get to **Glenelg** and the beach is by the trams ($3; M-F 9am-3pm $1.90) which run every 15-20min. from Victoria Sq. to Moseley Sq. (30min.; M-F 6am-midnight, Sa 7:30am-midnight, Su 8:50am-midnight.) For a guided tour of the area, **Adelaide Explorer** does a city-to-Glenelg hop-on, hop-off three-hour tour. Catch the small bus anywhere on the route or join at 38 King William St. Pay onboard. (☎8231 7172. Daily 9, 10:30am, noon, 1:30, and 3pm. $30 per day, ages 6-14 $15, families $70; 2nd day $7.) **CitySightseeing Adelaide** (☎8261 0588) offers a hop-on, hop-off tour on London-style red double-decker buses and comes by each stop on its route every 30min. ($25, backpackers $20 if booked through hostel.)

BY CAR

Hertz, 233 Morphett St. (☎13 30 39); **Budget** (☎13 27 27 or 8223 1400), on the corner of North Terr. and Frome St.; **Avis,** 136 North Terr. (☎8410 5727); and **Europcar,** 142 North Terr. (☎13 13 90; the cheapest, from $42 per day, with no one-way fees), have counters at the airport and in town. **Thrifty,** 296 Hindley St. (☎8211 8788 or 1300 367 227), offers 2WD from $55 and 4WD from $154 per day. The best outfit for 4WD rentals is the expensive **Complete Ute and 4WD Hire,** in the suburb of Findon, with free drop-off and pick-up anywhere in the city. (☎8244 5333. 4WD with 200km from $120. Min. age 21.)

With the exception of Thrifty, most of the national companies will not rent 4WD vehicles to drivers under 25 and charge a daily fee for 2WD vehicles. Those under 25 can get better deals on all types of cars from smaller agencies. These companies are scattered around the suburbs, but most pick-up and drop-off in town. Friendly **Koala Car Rentals** (☎8352 7299), part of the Cutprice Car Rental enterprise, on Sir Donald Bradman Dr., has cars from $22 per day and good deals on 4WD. The rental is cheaper if paid in cash instead of credit. The Adelaide-based **Smile Rent-a-Car,**

163 Richmond Rd., has no surcharge for drivers under 25, unlimited kilometers, and friendly service, but no 4WD. (☎8234 0655 or 1800 624 424. From $27.50-130; insurance $11 per day.) **No Frills Car Rental,** 235 Waymouth St., has no age limit and hires cars from $22 per day. No 4WD. (☎8212 8333 or 1800 999 978. $11 flat-rate insurance required.)

For campervans or motor homes, **Britz,** 376 Burbridge Rd. (☎8234 4701 or 1800 331 454), in Brooklyn Park, has two- to six-berth vans (from $126 per day) and one-way rental with unlimited kilometers. Ask about **relocation deals,** where you pay as little as $1 per day plus petrol costs to take a car or camper from Adelaide to another city in a set amount of time (3 days for the 10hr. drive to Melbourne). **Skippy Camper Rentals,** 1505 South Rd., Darlington (☎8296 2999), has regular campervan rentals (min. 5 days, one-way available, starting at $80) as well as some used campervans and 4WDs for sale with buy-back options.

BY TAXI

Des's (☎13 10 08), **Diamond** (☎13 24 48), **Yellow** (☎13 22 27), and **Access Cabs** (☎1300 360 940; wheelchair-accessible) all provide service.

BY BICYCLE

Adelaide is small enough to be easily biked. Many city streets have designated cycling lanes. The **Linear Park Bike and Walking Track** (40km one way) runs along the River Torrens from the ocean to the Adelaide Hills. **Flinders Camping,** 187 Rundle St. (☎8223 1913), is the best place to rent a bike. (Open M-Th 9am-5:30pm, F 9am-9pm, Sa 9am-5pm, Su 11am-4:30pm. Half-day $15, first day $17.50, extra day $10.) Other rental options include **Linear Park Mountain Bike Hire,** behind the Festival Centre on the south bank of the Torrens (☎8223 6271 or 0400 596 065; open M-F 9:15am-5pm, Sa-Su 9:15am-6pm; $5 per half hour; $20 per day, delivery, pick-up, and weekly/family rates available.), and some hostels (see Accommodations, p. 467). Keep your helmet on at all times; police are happy to give tickets to negligent bikers.

◪ PRACTICAL INFORMATION

TOURIST & FINANCIAL SERVICES

Tourist Office: South Australian Travel Centre, 18 King William St. (☎1300 655 276; www.southaustralia.com), is the city's main info center. Open M-F 8:30am-5pm, Sa-Su 9am-2pm. **Glenelg Tourist Information Centre,** Foreshore (by the jetty), Glenelg (☎8294 5833). Open M-F 9am-5pm, Sa-Su 10am-4pm. **Information SA,** 77 Grenfell St. (☎8204 1900), has Internet and information. Open M-F 9am-5pm.

National Parks Information: Department for Environment and Heritage Information Centre, 77 Grenfell St. (☎8204 1910; fax 8204 1919). Open M-F 9am-5pm.

Travel Agencies: YHA Travel, 135 Waymouth St. (☎8414 3000). Open M-F 9am-6pm, Sa-Su 10am-1pm. **Backpackers' Travel Centre,** 117 Waymouth St. (☎8212 8188), follows suit. Open M-F 9am-6pm, Sa 10am-4pm. **STA Travel** (☎8211 6600) is at 235 Rundle St. (open M-F 9:30am-5:30pm, Sa 10am-3pm) and also 38a Hindley St. (open M-F 10am-6pm Sa 10am-3pm). The **Wayward Bus Central Office,** 119 Waymouth St. (☎8410 8833), is open daily 9am-6pm.

Work Opportunities: Centrelink, 55 Currie St. (☎13 10 21) Open M-F 8:30am-4:30pm. They also have an office at 156-158 Jetty Rd., Glenelg, open M-F 9am-5pm. *Advertiser* has classifieds on W and Sa. Most hostels also have employment notice boards.

Consulates: U.K. Consulate (☎8212 7280; www.uk.end.gov.au), on Grenfell St. Open M-F 9am-12:30pm and 1:30-4pm.

Currency Exchange: Almost any time, if you're dressed nicely, at **Adelaide Casino,** at North Terr. and Railway Terr., in the same building as the train station. Passport or driver's license required. Open Su-Th 10am-4am, F-Sa 10am-6am. **American Express,** Shop 32, Rundle Mall (☎9271 8255). Open M-F 9am-5pm, Sa 9am-noon. **Thomas Cook,** 4 Rundle Mall (☎8231 6977). Open M-Th 9am-5pm, F 9am-7pm, Sa 10am-4pm, Su 10am-2pm.

LOCAL SERVICES

Bookstores: Borders Books, 97 Rundle Mall (☎8223 3333; open daily 9am-9pm), has one of the best selections of books in the city.

Library: State Library of South Australia (☎8207 7248; www.slsa.sa.gov.au), on North Terr. at the corner of Kintore Ave. Book ahead for free 30min. **Internet,** or wait for free 15min. slots. Open M-W and F 9:30-8pm, Th 9:30am-6pm, Sa-Su noon-5pm.

Ticket Agency: Most cultural and sporting events (especially football matches) are booked through **BASS** (☎13 12 46; www.bass.sa.net.au; open M-Sa 9am-8pm; $2.75 service charge per ticket), at a booth at the Visitors Centre on King William St. **VenueTix** (☎8223 7788) is the place to go for cricket and basketball tickets.

RAA: State Headquarters, 41 Hindmarsh Sq. (touring info ☎8202 4600 or 13 11 11). Open M-F 8:30am-5pm, Sa 9am-noon. Maps are free for members of RAA, AAA, or other affiliated organizations.

MEDIA & PUBLICATIONS

Newspapers: *The Advertiser* ($1).

All-purpose: *The Hip Guide,* a small book geared toward budget travelers with great suggestions on things to do, eat, and buy in Adelaide.

Nightlife: "The Guide" in the Thursday *Advertiser. Rip it Up* and *dB* on the nightlife and alternative club scene (free). For gay nightlife, try *Blaze* or *Gay Times* (free).

Radio: Commercial-free alternative rock, Triple J 105.5FM, Rock, 104.7FM; Pop, 107.1FM and 102.3FM; News, ABC 831AM; Tourist Info, 88.1FM.

EMERGENCY & COMMUNICATIONS

Emergency: ☎000.

Pharmacy: Midnight Pharmacy, 11 West Terr. (☎8231 6333). Open M-Sa 7am-midnight, Su 9am-midnight.

Medical Assistance: Royal Adelaide Hospital (☎8222 4000), on North Terr.

Internet Access: See **libraries,** p. 467. Most hostels have kiosks.

Post Office: General Post Office, 141 King William St. (☎8216 2222), at the corner of King William and Franklin St. Open M-F 8am-6pm, Sa 8:30am-noon. Poste Restante can be picked up M-F 7am-5:30pm, Su 9am-1pm. **Postal Code:** 5000.

▐ ACCOMMODATIONS

Hostels are scattered all over the city and are especially congregated within a few blocks of Light Square. Several classy highrise hotels lord over North Terr. near the museums. Adelaide hostels are rarely full in winter, but book a day or two ahead in summer and a week ahead during festivals. Those looking to escape the city should consider staying in the beach suburb of Glenelg (see p. 475) or in the Adelaide Hills to the east of town (see p. 475).

▨ **Brecon Inn,** 11 Gilbert St. (☎8211 8985 or 0418 896 931). This quiet 42-bed hostel may be a little removed from the action, but it draws a good crowd. Modern and clean rooms equipped with a fridge and lockers, daily *Simpsons* viewings, access to live-in owner Adam's extensive DVD collection, laundry, free pick-ups, employment info, comfy beds, Internet access ($1 per 15min.), and, best of all, 10% off at the Moores' Brecknock pub next door. Singles and doubles are in the hotel. Photo ID required for check-in. 4-bed dorms $23. NOMADS. Wheelchair-accessible. ❷

▨ **Glenelg Beach Resort,** 1-7 Moseley St. (☎8376 0007 or 1800 066 422; www.glenelgbeachresort.com.au), Glenelg, 1 block parallel to the shore and 20min. by tram from Victoria Sq. This award-winning 120-bed complex offers a full range of rooms. Licensed, with a lively bar, pool tables, small karaoke stage (W and F-Sa nights), common area with videos, and game room. Quiet time after 10pm, but downstairs in the bar theme nights range from toga party to the "bar Olympics." Clean rooms are high-ceilinged and the beds were christened by olympians in the Sydney Olympics. Bike hire half-day $10, full-day $15. Free wine tours Th, free Adelaide tours Tu. Free pick-up and drop-off. Internet $1 per 15min. Carpark $11 per night. Dorms in winter $18-20, summer $23-25; singles $44/$58; doubles $55/$68; 4-person apartment $88/$120. VIP/ISIC. ❷

▨ **Backpack Oz,** 144 Wakefield St. (☎8223 3551 or 1800 633 307; www.backpackoz.com.au), on the corner of Pulteney St. Close to Rundle St., feels like a college dormitory. Young backpackers chill out with a beer on the couches, shoot pool in the common room, and check their email in the sunny office. The annex across the street has a nicer kitchen and cable TV. Rooms have A/C and sweets on the pillows. Free pick-up, employment info, TV/video lounge, and tour bookings. Free breakfast and W night BBQ. Internet $4 per hr. Reception 6am-10pm. Dorms $20, $120 a week; singles $45; twins and doubles $52. ❷

Adelaide Central YHA, 135 Waymouth St. (☎8414 3010). The most popular backpackers in town, this 250-bed complex is clean and modern but lacks character, with A/C and individual reading lights by all the beds. Friendly staff, kitchen, TV, pool tables, smoking room, and a message board with current movies, lectures, and concerts. Internet $1 per 15min. Bike hire $10 per day. No lockout or curfew, but after 11pm you have to call the guard to let you in. Check-out 9:30am. Dorms $27; doubles $60.50, ensuite $75.50. YHA. ❷

Annie's Place Adelaide, 239 Franklin St. (☎8212 2668), a few blocks east of the bus station. Purchased in 2003 by Mulga, the owner of the immensely popular Annie's Place in Alice Springs, this historic old building is getting a new spin. Like its sister up north, Annie's draws a friendly crowd of lively backpackers for ensuite dorm rooms, basic but free brekkie, and Trevor's Famous BBQ W and Su evenings in the leafy courtyard. Dorms $20; twins and doubles $60. ❷

East Park Lodge, 341 Angas St. (☎8223 1228 or 1800 643 606; www.eastparklodge.com.au). Travelers who would rather be in a quiet neighborhood than the bustling city enjoy this quirky old 3-story building set on a quiet side street 20min. from Rundle St. The lodge has the only pool in town, a pool table, TV lounge, kitchen, free breakfast, and a multilingual staff. Free 30min. of Internet. Make your own didgeridoo for $80. Bike hire (half-day $7, full-day $10) and limited car and motorbike hire. Reception 6:30am-9pm. Check-out 9:30am. Dorms from $24; singles and doubles $60. VIP. ❷

Adelaide Backpacker's Inn, 112 Carrington St. (☎8223 6635 or 1800 247 725; abackinn@tne.net.au), a 10min. walk from Victoria Sq. Free nightly apple-pie-and-ice-cream desserts that are never rationed (4000 pies baked yearly) and $4 all-you-can-eat breakfasts make this a popular stop for malnourished backpackers. Free pick-up and drop-off, and free videos in the lounge. Internet $1 per 15min. Reception 6am-7:30pm. Dorms $23; singles $44; twins and doubles from $52. ❷

The Austral Hotel, 205 Rundle St. (☎8223 4660). If you want to be the life of the party, stay in the hotel that never sleeps. Weekdays are less noisy and travelers love the fantastic location in the swankiest part of town. Key deposit $10. Singles $35; twins and doubles $55; triples $70; quads $80. ❸

◘ FOOD

Adelaide is a gourmand's dream—every kind of food served in every kind of atmosphere. It's hard to walk without tripping over a restaurant in this city. **Gouger Street,** in the city center near Victoria Sq., offers a wide range of good, inexpensive ethnic cuisine and houses the ▨**Central Market,** a food lover's fantasy with stalls overflowing with colorful fruits and vegetables, various cheeses, and freshly risen breads. (Open Tu and Th 7am-5:30pm, F 7am-9pm, and Sa 7am-3pm.) **Rundle Street,** in the northeast section of the city, caters to the young hipster set. Clusters of restaurants can also be found on the upscale **Hutt Street** in southeast Adelaide and North Adelaide's equally upscale **O'Connell Street.** The flashy but cheap **Hindley Street,** across King William St. from **Rundle Street,** is the best spot for 24hr. eats. **Jetty Road,** in the beachside suburb of Glenelg, also bursts with cafes and ice cream shops. **Supermarkets** dot the city, particularly on Rundle Mall, Hindley St., and Victoria Sq. Coles, next to Central Market on Grote St., is very close to Victoria Sq. (Open M-Th noon-6pm, F noon-9pm, Sa noon-5pm, Su 11am-5pm.)

GOUGER STREET

Matsuri, 167 Gouger St. (☎8231 3494). Meaning "festival" in Japanese, Adelaide's best sushi restaurant features a rock garden and shoes-off policy. 6-piece packs $3-10. Noodle dishes $9-14. Open daily 5:30pm-late and F noon-2pm as well. Mention *Let's Go* and get a 10% discount. ❷

Cafe Fusilli, 68-72 Gouger St. (☎8221 6884). Masquerading as a standard Italian cafe by night, by day, Fusilli is a budget traveler's dream. Daily lunch specials, complete with melt-in-your-mouth garlic bread, cost just $6.50 from 11:30am-4pm ($12 for dinner). Open daily 9am-10pm, except Monday, when they close at 3pm. ❷

Gaucho's, 91 Gouger St. (☎8231 2299). Outstanding Argentinian food in a convivial setting. For a true splurge, order the traditional Argentinian specialty, the *parillada*, $60 for 2 people. Open M-F 11:30am-2pm and 5:30-10:30pm, Sa-Su 5:30-10:30pm. ❸

RUNDLE STREET

Lemongrass, 289 Rundle St. (☎8223 6627). This popular and pleasant restaurant has the best Thai food in town. The creative menu includes Aussie twists on Thai standards (kangaroo pad thai, croc curry) and good quality daily lunch specials for $6.50. Mains range from $10-18, while appetizers start at about $5 (spring rolls 3 for $6.50). Open M-F 11:30am-3pm and daily 5pm-late. ❷

▨**Amalfi,** 29 Frome St. (☎8223 1948), between Rundle St. and North Terr. This popular and packed "Pizzeria Ristorante" sneaks onto upscale gourmet dining lists with relatively budget prices. The *con pollo*, rigatoni with mushroom and apricots in a pepper cream sauce, is mouthwateringly good. Meat mains $14-19. Open M-Th noon-2:30pm and 5:30-10:30pm, F 11:30am-3pm and 5:30pm-11:30pm, Sa 5:30pm-midnight. ❷

Al Fresco, 260 Rundle St. (☎8223 4589). This people-watching landmark serves a tempting range of Italian cakes, focaccia, dynamite coffee, and the best gelato in the city (small $2.75). They also have sandwiches, salads, pasta dishes ($6-12), and a full breakfast menu ($5-8). Pick up a light meal in minutes or linger over a latte for hours. Open daily 6:30am-late. ❶

BEST OF THE REST

The Gilbert Place Pancake House (☎8211 7912), in an alley off King William St., between Currie and Hindley St. In a city that shuts down early, a sign reading "this door will never close" is a welcome sight for hungry eyes. Menu highlights include the fanciful $7-9 pancake creations (Jamaican banana, Bavarian apple) and Tu all-you-can-eat specials ($5). Also serves giant oversized sundaes ($7) and all manner of your standard breakfast fare ($5-10). The Pancake House may not be gourmet, but at 4am, who's keeping track? Open 24hr. ❶

Quiet Waters BYO, 75 Hindley St., (☎8231 3637). This downstairs Lebanese restaurant offers a wide range of vegetarian dishes. Mains from $7. Belly dancing every Saturday night. *Let's Go* readers get a 10% discount. Open daily noon-2pm and 5:30-9pm. ❶

Adelaide Coffee House, 73 Grenfell St., (☎8227 2001). Stepping into this small cafe is like stepping into the 1940s. There's art on the walls, jazz on the stereo, and an Italian-style coffee bar. Wine is served by the glass and there is a range of snacks. Espresso $2.30. Open M-F 7am-5pm. ❶

◎ SIGHTS

▨ **SOUTH AUSTRALIAN MUSEUM.** This gracious building is the brilliant center-piece of the North Terr. cultural district. It holds huge whale skeletons, native Australian animal displays, rocks and minerals, and an Egyptian mummy. The real highlight of the museum is the **Australian Aboriginal Cultures Gallery,** which has the largest collection of Aboriginal artifacts in the world and is one of the few museums in the country not to gloss over the less savory aspects of white and Aboriginal interaction. *(Next to the State Library, on North Terr.* ☎*8207 7500, tour info 8207 7370. Open daily 10am-5pm. Museum tours M-F 11am; Sa-Su 11am, 2, and 3pm. Free. Aboriginal Cultures tours W-Su 11:30am, and 1:30pm. $10, concessions $7. Wheelchair-accessible.)*

▨ **MIGRATION MUSEUM.** Combining history and oral tradition to explain patterns of immigration and exclusion that have shaped South Australian society, the museum's graphic stories and photographs make for an excellent, if sobering, visit. The museum, housed in the former buildings of Adelaide's Destitute Asylum, is particularly relevant now, as immigration policy has become one of the nation's most hotly contested political issues. Refreshingly, the museum does not shy away from controversy. Comment sheets from visitors illustrate the complex feelings Australians and visitors alike have towards immigration. *(82 Kintore Ave., off North Terr., behind the state library.* ☎*8207 7580. Open M-F 10am-5pm, Sa-Su 1-5pm. Free, $2.)*

▨ **ART GALLERY OF SOUTH AUSTRALIA.** This huge quiet gallery showcases Australian, Asian, and European prints, paintings, decorative arts, and Southeast Asian ceramics. The eclectic modern sculpture displays are surprising and entertaining. *(North Terr. near Pulteney St.* ☎*8207 7000, info desk 8207 7075; www.artgallery.sa.gov.au. Open daily 10am-5pm. Free. 1hr. tours M-F 11am and 2pm, Sa-Su 11am and 3pm. Free. Wheelchair-accessible.)*

▨ **TANDANYA—NATIONAL ABORIGINAL CULTURAL INSTITUTE.** The first major Aboriginal multi-arts complex in Australia hosts continually rotating exhibitions of indigenous artwork from around the country. Focusing on both contemporary and traditional expressions of Aboriginal culture, it is nothing short of fascinating. *(253 Grenfell St., at the corner of East Terr. on the City Loop bus route.* ☎*8224 3200; www.tandanya.com.au. Open daily 10am-5pm. $4, concessions $3. Book ahead for guided tours and talks. Didgeridoo performances M-Th and Sa-Su noon; Torres Strait Islander dance F noon.)*

NATIONAL WINE CENTRE. Constructed of materials used in wine production, the brand new Wine Centre beckons wine pilgrims heading to South Australia for the terrific vineyards. The highlight is the Wine Discovery Journey, which leads through four intriguingly styled rooms, teaching about grape types, holding virtual conversations with famous winemakers, inviting visitors to take various smell tests for cork rot and other more pleasant aspects of the winemaking process, and culminating in a quadruple tasting. The Centre includes a restaurant, wine bar and shop, and art gallery. *(On the corner of Hackney and North Terr., next to the Botanic Gardens.* ☎*8222 9222; www.wineaustralia.com.au. Restaurant open W-Su noon-3:30pm, additional hours F 5-9pm. Wine Discovery Journey open daily 10am-6pm; $8, concessions $6.)*

ADELAIDE BOTANIC GARDENS. Acres of landscaped grounds surround heritage buildings, a small lake with black swans, and meandering walkways. The lush and peaceful grounds contain the **Australian Arboretum, Yarrabee Art Gallery,** and a beautiful rose garden. The **Bicentennial Conservatory,** the largest glasshouse in the Southern Hemisphere, is the only section of the garden that is not free. Inside, the computer-controlled atmosphere simulates a tropical rainforest, complete with misty rain. *(On North Terr. ☎8222 9311; www.botanicgardens.sa.gov.au. Gardens open M-F 8am-dusk, Sa-Su 9am-dusk. Conservatory open daily 10am-4pm; $3.30, concessions $1.65. Free 1½hr. garden tours leave from restaurant-kiosk M-Tu, F, Su 10:30am.)*

ADELAIDE ZOO. Carved out of the Botanic Gardens, the Adelaide Zoo is home to more than 1300 animals. There are several daily feedings, including hippos, pelicans, and the popular big cats. The zoo runs **Monarto Zoological Park,** a 1000-hectare open range park 45min. away near Murray Bridge. A shuttle bus can pick-up and drop-off at the central bus station in Adelaide. Once there, several tours and walks lead visitors through the various habitats. *(Zoo on Frome Rd., less than 2km north of the city and a 15min. walk from North Terr. through the Botanic Gardens or down Frome Rd. Take bus #272 or 273 from Grenfell St. Popeye boats from the Festival Centre also run to and from the zoo in summer. ☎8267 3255. Open daily 9:30am-5pm. $14.50, concessions $11.50, children $8. Guided tours daily 11am and 2pm. Monarto. Take the Monarto exit off the South Eastern Freeway to the Princes Highway and follow the signs. ☎8534 4100; www.monartozp.com.au. Open daily for tours 10:30am-3:30pm. $15.50, concessions $12.50, kids $10.)*

HAIGH'S CHOCOLATES VISITORS CENTRE. Australia's oldest chocolate maker, Haigh's has been churning since 1915. At the Visitors Centre and factory, windows open onto the work areas, where workers in their white outfits and hairnets inspire memories of "Charlie and the Chocolate Factory." Free tastings and complimentary tea and coffee make this a nice place for a daytime caffeine booster. *(154 Greenhill Rd., 1 block parallel to South Terr. between Pulteney Rd. and Hutt Rd. ☎8372 7070; www.haighschocolate.com. Open M-F 8:30am-5:30pm, Sa 9am-5pm. Free guided tours with tastings M-Sa 1 and 2pm. Book ahead. Self tours anytime.)*

ADELAIDE GAOL. The old Adelaide Gaol was used for 147 years and executed 45 inmates, whose corpses are buried within the walls. Slightly creepy, the gaol now traps only tourists. *(18 Gaol Rd., Thebarton. From the corner of North and West Terr., take Port Rd. and turn right on Gaol Rd. A moderate walk northeast of the city or 5min. ride to Stop 1 on bus #151, 153, 286, or 287 from North Terr. ☎8231 4062. Open M-F 11am-4pm. $7, concessions $5.50, children $4.50. Guided tours Su 11am-3:30pm.)*

⚠ ACTIVITIES

Beach bums content to laze the day away should head to the suburb of **Glenelg** for plenty of fun in the sun. Those looking for a bit more action should visit the outdoor goods stores on Rundle St., most of which can point you towards the city's best purveyors of outdoor activities.

MOUNTAIN BIKING. Rolling On Mountain Bike Tours offers guided tours around Adelaide, its forests and vineyards, and the Barossa Valley, ranging one day to two weeks in length. A good choice even for those without much riding experience— trails are fairly flat and there's a backup vehicle if you get tired. *(☎8358 2401. Day-tours from $79-99, 2-week "Wine and Wildlife" tour $1400, and countless options in between. Bike hire. Also see **By Bicycle,** p. 466.)*

SNOW AND ICE. At **Mt. Thebarton,** 23 East Terr., Thebarton, you can ski, snowboard, sled, or skate year-round on South Australia's only "permasnow." Take bus #151, 153, 286, or 287 to stop 2 from North Terr. (5min.), or walk 15min. from the northwest of the city. (☎8352 7977. "Fresh 'n' Funky" F-Sa with DJs and lights. Open M noon-4pm, Tu and Th 10am-4pm, W and F 10am-4pm and 7:30-10pm, Sa-Su 12:30-4pm and 7:30-10pm. Skiing or boarding $15 for the first hour, $5 each additional hour; equipment $5.50-10. Skating $11.50, including rental.)

EARTH & SKY. Rock Solid Adventure offers abseiling, rock climbing, and a two-night caving trip to Naracoorte Conservation Park. (☎8322 8975; www.rock-solid-adventure.com. Abseiling and rock climbing $64 per 4hr., $79 per 5hr.; spelunking $259.) **SA Skydiving** is pleased to assist in your free-fall fantasies. They also offer a full-day solo jump course. (☎8272 7888; www.saskydiving.com.au. Tandem from $330, solo from $465, video $85.)

SURF, SCUBA, & SWIM. Surf Break Surf Classes offers lessons with pro-surfer Rebecca Osborne. (☎0210 8166 or 8327 2369. From $20 per hr.) **Red Sun Safaris** provides day-long Victor Harbor surf lessons. (☎0838 8456 or 8276 3620; www.red-sunsafaris.com.au; $65, including transfers, lunch, and all equipment.) **Glenelg Scuba Diving** runs daily boat dives to Adelaide's wrecks and reefs and a four-day PADI certification class. (☎8294 7744; www.glenelgscuba.com.au. Dives from $66; equipment hire available. 4-5 day PADI class $295-345.) The **Adelaide Aquatic Centre,** on Jeffcott Rd., North Adelaide, is a huge indoor complex with a 50m pool, diving and water polo area, and aqua-aerobics classes. (☎8344 4411. Pools open in summer daily 5am-10pm; in winter M-Sa 5am-10pm, Su 7am-8pm. Gym open M-F 6am-10pm, Sa 6am-6pm, Su 9am-5pm. Pool $5.10, concessions $3.80; gym $8.50 in peak hours, $6 off peak.)

SPECTATOR SPORTS. Australian Rules Football (mostly Sa) is played in the suburb of West Lakes (Adelaide Crows) and in Port Adelaide (Port Power). **Cricket** (Oct.-Mar.) is played at the **Adelaide Oval,** north of the city along King William St. There is a 2½hr. tour of the Oval that focuses on "Cricket's Greatest Batsman," the late Sir Donald Bradman. (☎8300 3800. Tours Tu and Th 10am; Su 2pm, except on match days. $5. Museum open Tu and Th 10am-1pm. $2. Tickets and schedules available at BASS ☎13 12 46 or VenueTix ☎8223 7788.)

🎭 ENTERTAINMENT

A two-minute walk north on King William St. from its intersection with North Terr. at Parliament House brings you to the huge **Adelaide Festival Centre** (☎8216 8600), the focus of Adelaide's formal cultural life. Pick up a calendar of events from inside the Festival Centre complex, access the schedule online at www.southaustralia.com, or call BASS (☎13 12 46). The **State Opera of South Australia** (☎8226 4790; www.saopera.sa.gov.au), the **Adelaide Symphony Orchestra** (☎8343 4111), and the **State Theatre Company of South Australia** (☎8231 5151; www.statetheatre.sa.com.au) all perform at the Festival Centre; it's also the place for big-name traveling musicals and theater performances. **Elder Hall,** on North Terr., part of the University of Adelaide, has concerts and some chamber performances by the Adelaide Symphony. (☎8303 5925. Lunch concerts F 1:10-2pm; $2.)

Adelaide's most accessible **alternative cinemas,** both on Rundle St., are the **Palace Eastend** (☎8232 3434) and **NOVA** (☎8223 6333). **Mercury Cinema,** 13 Morphett St., off Hindley St., has more artsy fare. (☎8410 0979; www.mrc.org.au. $10-13.) Tuesday is usually discount night at Australian theaters. December through February brings outdoor screenings of classics at **Cinema in the Botanic Gardens.** (Tickets at gate or through BASS ☎13 12 46. $13, concessions $10, children $8.50.)

◼ FESTIVALS

Adelaide has dubbed itself the "Festival City": check *The Guide*, *dB*, or *Rip it Up* for listings. **Arts Project Australia** runs a three-day show in Botanic Park, with dozens of acts and workshops on six stages, while a "global village" sells international food and crafts. Make sure to book lodging well in advance. (☎8271 9905. Weekend tickets $115, students and concessions $95; daily ticket prices from $45.) **Feast** (☎8231 2155) takes place for three weeks from late Oct. to mid-Nov. and is Adelaide's annual lesbian and gay festival, complete with masquerades, parties, and concerts. Occurring February 17 to March 14, 2004, the **Adelaide Festival of Arts** (☎8216 4444; www.adelaidefestival.org.au) is considered one of the world's best arts festivals. Overlapping with the Adelaide Festival, the **Adelaide Fringe Festival** (☎8100 2000) is considered by many Adelaide residents to be the hallmark of their city's identity: progressive, entertaining, and resolutely doing its own thing.

◼ NIGHTLIFE

The **East End**, which includes Rundle St. east of the mall, Pulteney St., and Pirie St., is the center of Adelaide's "pretty" scene and teems with University students and twenty-something professionals on the weekends. Bouncers here and at most of the city's dance clubs are very mindful of **dress code**. This usually means no sneakers, no T-shirts, no tank-tops, no flip-flops, and no hats, but can also be extended to include no jeans. The cafe scene dominates this area, as uni students and others drink schooners and smoke on the sidewalk. Rundle Mall morphs into **Hindley Street**, in the **West End**, home to many X-rated venues and numerous fly-by-night dance clubs butting up against stylish bars and bistros. Rundle Mall itself, next to Hindley St., is quiet at night except for the columns of semi-inebriated partygoers marching from the pubs of Rundle St. to the clubs of Hindley St. and Light Sq. The **Light Square** area is encircled by popular clubs.

PUBS

▨ **The Governor Hindmarsh Hotel**, 59 Port Rd. (☎8340 0744, gig info line 1300 666 GOV; www.thegov.com.au). Right across from the Adelaide Festival Centre, "The Gov," to those in the know, is the city's best small venue for good music. When the place isn't grooving, the bar is still a great place to hang out. Its pizza bar is excellent and the front bar, with wood paneling, backlit bottles, and wide windows, is a relaxing spot for a beer. Burgers are $4.50. Restaurant open daily noon-2pm and 6-9:30pm, bar open late.

▨ **Grace Emily**, 232 Waymouth St. (☎8231 5500). The chillest bar in Adelaide, crushed velvet curtains drape the stage and a pool table and outdoor courtyard complete the atmosphere. Live music almost every night. Monday nights are Billy Bob's Backyard BBQ Jam. No cover. Open daily 4pm-late.

The Bar on Gouger, 123 Gouger St. (☎8410 0042). The best place to meet up on food-filled Gouger St., the Bar has the most comfortable couches in Adelaide and a full range of drinks and "talk food." There's something going on most nights, including big screen viewings of Buffy the Vampire Slayer on Tuesdays. Open spaces, small photos on the wall, and deep colors lull Happy Hour drinkers into a relaxed state of happiness. Open daily 4pm to late.

Austral, 205 Rundle St. (☎8223 4660). Unmistakable, this Rundle St. landmark draws a young crowd. Live bands in the beer garden F-Sa, DJs Su-Th. If nothing's happening here, there's probably nothing happening in town. Open daily until late.

Edinburgh Castle, 233 Currie St. (☎8410 1211; www.geocities.com/theedcastle/). Owned by a gay couple with a mainly male clientele, the Ed is the best gay bar in town. The front bar and the courtyard "outback bar" are good places to relax with a friend, while on the dance floor the drag queen shows liven the atmosphere. All meals are under $10. Happy Hour W-Sa 9-10pm. DJs Th-Su nights. Shows Sa-Su nights. Bar open M-Sa 11am-late, Su 2pm-4am.

NIGHTCLUBS

Church (☎8223 4233), on Synagogue Pl., a little alley just off Rundle St. Cramming as many paradoxes into one space as it can, Church occupies a former synagogue and hosts a popular Friday night "Greed," an 80s-themed party that attracts the young, sleek Rundle St. crowd. Techno downstairs, hip-hop upstairs. "Greed" runs F 9pm-1am. Cover $8-10, entry often free before midnight (look for the spotlight).

Supermild, 182 Hindley St. (☎8212 9699), in the family of good clubs on Hindley's west end. Smart, laid-back atmosphere that lives up to its name. Live music on Su. Good DJs and an intimate, relaxed feel make this a popular late-night place. Open Su-Th 9pm-late, F-Sa 9pm-5am.

Garage, 163 Waymouth St. (☎8212 9577), on Light Sq. This isn't your dad's garage. Beautiful high ceilings and brick walls, coupled with spare decor proclaim this bar as "serious." If it isn't packed and beautiful, you're in the wrong place. Open M 9:30am-midnight, Tu-W 9:30am-7:30pm, Th 9:30am-2am, F 9:30am-5am, Sa 9pm-5am, Su 11am-10pm. Restaurant open for lunch M-F, dinner M, and brunch Su.

Mars Bar, 120 Gouger St. (☎8231 9639). Adelaide's best gay club, Mars is mellow enough to make clubbers of any persuasion feel comfortable. In addition to the familiar pulsing lights and pulsing beats of the downstairs dance floor, there is a small courtyard outside called the chill-out area. Clientele is about 70% male, 30% female. Floor shows Th-Sa nights, 2 dance floors F-Sa. Open W-Th 10:30pm-late, F-Sa 10:30pm-5am.

⚡ DAYTRIPS FROM ADELAIDE

PORT ADELAIDE. Port Adelaide features an historic port and lighthouse, a unique market, several antiques shops and art galleries, self-guided walking tours of landmark buildings, and several museums, in short, a perfect quiet day away from the city. The **Visitors Centre** (☎8447 4788; open daily 9am-5pm), on Commercial Rd. at the corner of Vincent St., has information and maps. The **Lighthouse,** on the wharf in front of the market, gives a great view of the area. (Open M-F 10am-2pm, Su 10am-5pm. $1, free with a ticket to the Maritime Museum.) **Fisherman's Wharf** (☎8341 2040), Lighthouse Sq., on Commercial Rd., is the place to be Sundays and public holidays 8am-5pm, selling everything from CDs to seafood to used books. Several companies operate **river cruises** (1¾hr.) on the Port Adelaide River that offer occasional dolphin sightings. (Departs daily at midday in summer, Sundays the rest of the year. $2.50-6. Book at wharf-side kiosks.) If you find yourself cursing your hostel bunkbeds, be sure to check out the third class berth in the **Maritime Museum's** recreation of an early immigrant ship. The museum is one block east of the lighthouse on 126 Lipson St. (☎8207 6255. Open daily 10am-5pm. $8.50, concessions $6.50, kids $3.50.) The **National Railroad Museum,** just up the street away from the wharf, houses mammoth old locomotives from Australia's early days, some of them refurbished and outfitted with creepy mannequins. But the highlight for the smaller set comes every July during the school holiday when the museum hosts a weeklong "Friends of Thomas the Tank Engine" festival. (☎8341 1690; www.natrailmuseum.org.au. Open daily 10am-5pm. $10, concessions $7, kids $4.50.) The longest-running cafe in the historic district is also the hippest. Conversation bounces off the brick walls at the ▧**Lipson Cafe,** 117 Lipson St., and its accompanying drygoods store **Teamaker.** Bright, rambunctious, and fun, this is the place to go for a burger or pad thai. Mains around $10, sandwiches $7. (☎8241 2442. Open Sa-Su, M-Tu 7am-5pm, and W-F 6-9pm.)

SOUTHERN BEACHES. Closest to Adelaide, Christies Beach has a park and many small shops along Beach Rd. For snorkelers or divers, the **Port Noarlunga Aquatic Reserve** is a shallow reef accessible from the end of the jetty. South again, Seaford has a walking and biking track along the cliffs.

NEAR ADELAIDE: ADELAIDE HILLS

A 20min. drive rewards those who venture from the confines of Adelaide's downtown with huge expanses of native forest, burgeoning vineyards, and traditional Germanic villages. Despite their seclusion, the various points of interest in the Hills are easy to get to. Much of the Adelaide Hills is a 15-40min. drive east from the Adelaide city center, along Hwy. A1 (known as Glen Osmond Rd. and leaving from the CBD grid's southeast corner). The **Adelaide Hills Visitors Centre** is at 41 Main St., Hahndorf. (☎8388 1185; www.visitadelaidehills.com. Internet access $2 per 20min. Open M-F 9am-5pm, Sa-Su 10am-4pm.)

MOUNT LOFTY SUMMIT & CLELAND PARK. Just 15km from the hustle and bustle of the big city are winding trails through rare eucalypt forests and parks full of hopping 'roos. Mt. Lofty, visited by 500,000 people annually, is part of the Cleland Conservation Park and one of the most popular and easily accessible attractions in the Adelaide Hills. From the 710m ▓**Mt. Lofty Summit,** the city glitters all the way to the coast. On a clear day the view stretches to far away Kangaroo Island. The complex at the summit includes a **cafe** and an **Info Centre** with brochures and advice about hikes in the park. (☎8370 1054. Info Centre open daily 9am-5pm. Cafe open M-Tu 9am-5pm and W-Su 9am-late.) Several trails wind around Mt. Lofty and the 1200km Heysen Trail connects the summit with the Clelend Wildlife Park. Just south of the summit, the **Mt. Lofty Botanic Gardens** are a great place for a picnic or a leisurely stroll. (☎8228 2311. Open M-F 9am-4pm, Sa-Su 10am-5pm.) The limited-access **Mt. Lofty YHA ❶,** 20km from Adelaide, is an easy choice for groups seeking an overnight in the Adelaide Hills. The stone cottage is rented out as a whole to groups of 2-16. (Book and pick up keys through Adelaide Central YHA, ☎8414 3000; $70 for YHA members, $80 for nonmembers. No linen.) The 1000-hectare **Cleland Conservation Park** is a native forest sanctuary that allows visitors to roam among the wildlife and pet the koalas at the **Wildlife Park.** (☎8339 2444. Open daily 9:30am-5pm, last entry at 4:30pm, $12, concessions $9, children $8.) **Aboriginal Cultural Guided Tours** (☎8341 2777) are given on Yurridla Trail.

▓**WARRAWONG SANCTUARY.** The Adelaide Hills area has recently become famous for its conservation efforts, thanks largely the Warrawong Sanctuary, on Stock Rd. in Mylor. All manner of native Australian species, some virtually extinct elsewhere, flourish here: bilbies, wallabies, short-nosed bandicoots, platypuses, and innumerable native bird species all call this place home. Admission is by guided walk only and the compound provides accommodation and a fancy restaurant for longer visits. The Warrawong Bilby Bus (☎8376 8999. $30 return) picks up and drops off in Adelaide on Friday nights from February-May. (☎8370 9197; www.warrawong.com. Dusk and dawn walks $22, children $17.50. Wetlands walks daily 11am and 3pm; $15. Book ahead. Overnight accommodation packages include 2 meals, 2 tours, and lodging; $150, children $70.)

ALDGATE. Tiny Aldgate is a good base for exploring the Hills, as it is also close to Warrawong Sanctuary and easily accessible. The best deal in town by far is ▓**Geoff and Hazel's ❹,** 19 Kingsland Rd., a "backpackers for couples." It features a balcony, cozy lounge room, and hammocks. From Adelaide, take Glen Osmond Rd. out of the city, to M1, the South Eastern Fwy. and exit at Stirling/Aldgate. At the town's main intersection turn right on Kingsland Rd. The hostel is 100m up the hill on the right. (☎8339 8360; www.geoffandhazels.com.au. Book ahead. Doubles $50, triple $70.) From there it's a quick pop down to **Cheers Cafe ❷**, on Main St. Delicious open-faced grilled sandwiches are about $8. (Open M-F 10am-5pm, Sa-Su 9am-5pm. Kitchen closes at 3:30pm.) Next door to Geoff and Hazel's, the community center shows double features for $6 on Tu, F, and Sa nights.

▓**HAHNDORF.** Originally settled by Prussian and East German immigrants in 1839, the most touristed village in Adelaide Hills is a charming town playing its heritage to the hilt. The avenues are tree-lined, the shops all sell bratwurst, and at least one brewhaus is playing "Roll Out the Barrel" at all times. But Hahndorf somehow manages to pull off what could have been unbearably cheesy. Beyond the German fare are restaurants of all stripes and colors, galleries featuring interesting local artists, and a growing number of wineries. Most businesses and shops in town are on Main St., including the area's **Visitors Centre**, (☎8388 1185. Open M-F 9am-5pm, Sa-Su 10am-4pm; packets available after hours at the local service stations on either end of town) several **ATMs**, and the **post office,** 73 Main St. **Hillstowe Wines,** 101 Main St., offers a tasting opportunity at its cellar door on the west end of Main St; be sure to try the shiraz. (☎8388 1400. Open daily 10am-5pm.) The **Beerenberg Strawberry Farm,** on the eastern edge of town, allows visitors to pick strawberries daily during the strawberry season, from October to May. (☎8388 7272. Entry $1, strawberries $6 per kg.)

FLEURIEU PENINSULA

The Fleurieu Peninsula (FLOOR-ee-oh) stretches southeast from Adelaide, encompassing the luscious vineyards of McLaren Vale, miles of coastline, and several charming seaside towns. The region's proximity to Adelaide has made it a popular weekend getaway, but there are affordable accommodations to be found and the Fleurieu's popularity rarely translates into crowding. Beautiful country drives weave past quiet pastures dotted with sheep and sloping vineyards to tranquil beaches and jaw-dropping views.

◆ TOURS OF THE FLEURIEU

Enjoy Adelaide operates a popular tour from Adelaide, with stops at two wineries in McLaren Vale, a train ride, and an evening Granite Island Little Penguin tour. (☎8332 1401. M, Th, Sa-Su. $55, children $36.) **Camel Winery Tours,** based at the Camel Farm between Kangarilla and McLaren Flat, offers a one-day winery safari on camelback with up to six winery visits and lunch included. (☎8383 0488. Starts at 10:30am. $80.) For a whopping fee, **Just Cruisin Chauffeur Car** provides the opportunity to tour the peninsula in a 1962 Cadillac, highlighting wineries, nature, galleries, and the region's history. (☎8383 0529 or 0414 807 891. From $450 per day.) The ▓**Glenelg Beach Resort** (see p. 468) has fun tours from Adelaide to McLaren Vale.

MCLAREN VALE   ☎08

Just 45min. (37km) south of Adelaide, the idyllic, sleepy set of vineyards near the small town of McLaren Vale (pop. 2000) sit in the grassy inland knolls of the Fleurieu Peninsula. The McLaren Vale wine region, which centers around the town of McLaren Vale and nearby Willunga and McLaren Flat, has nearly 70 vineyards, most of which process world-class wines and operate cellar-door sales and tastings. The area also boasts an outstanding stretch of beaches surrounding the small town of Aldinga, just west of McLaren Vale.

TRANSPORTATION & PRACTICAL INFORMATION

Premier Stateliner (☎8415 5555 or 1800 182 160) comes through town from the Adelaide central **bus station** (1hr.; M-F 4 per day, Sa 2 per day, Su 1 per day; $7) and loops around through Goolwa, Middleton, and Port Elliot. The best way to get to McLaren Vale is with a group of friends, a car, and a *designated driver*; it is not uncommon to find Random Breath Testing Units on main roads to and from wine regions. The **McLaren Vale and Fleurieu Visitors Centre,** on the left, offers a map of the wineries and handles B&B bookings. (☎8323 9944. Open daily 9am-5pm.) The road from the Visitors Centre south to Willunga has wineries at every turn. **McLaren Flat,** on Kangarilla Rd., 3km east of McLaren Vale is also surrounded by wineries. Main Rd. in McLaren Vale has a **supermarket,** a **post office,** and **ATMs.**

ACCOMMODATIONS & FOOD

The majority of accommodations are old-world B&Bs, but most travelers make the area a daytrip from Adelaide. The best B&B bargain is the **Southern Vales Bed and Breakfast ❺,** 13 Chalk Hill Rd. off the main street after the Visitors Centre. Very nice ensuite rooms look out over vineyards, and the chatty owner Allan is an attentive host. Ask to try his own Blackdog wine. (☎8323 8144. Rooms $115.) The only budget rooms around are in nearby **Willunga,** down Willunga or Victor Harbor Rd. from McLaren Vale, at the **Willunga Hotel ❸,** on High St. Their pub-hotel rooms are above-average and they offer generous counter **meals ❷** from $10. Try the Aussie Cider on tap. (☎8556 2135. Breakfast included. $30.) The **McLaren Vale Lakeside Caravan Park ❶,** on Field St., is conveniently located for wine-tasting trips and has tennis, swimming pool, and volleyball. (☎8323 9255. Sites $16, powered $19; vans with bath from $42; cabins from $62.) The Marienberg Limeburner's Centre, on the corner of Main St. and Chalk Hill Rd., houses the award-winning **Limeburner's Restaurant ❸,** which features delicious and well-presented meals at reasonable prices (mains around $20), and offers regional wine suggestions with every meal. (☎8323 8599. Open daily 10am-10pm.) In the heart of town on Main St. next to Hardy's Tintara, a converted railway car has become **The Almond Train ❶,** where nut lovers can try olives and almonds in every style known to man. (☎8323 8112. Open daily 10am-4:30pm. Attached cafe closed Tu-W.) The **supermarket,** at the corner of Main Rd. and Kangarilla Rd., is open daily 9am-9pm.

WINERIES

McLaren Vale is the best-known wine area in South Australia after the Barossa Valley. The majority of the nearly 70 vineyards and wineries in the region, 45 of which offer cellar-door tastings and sales, are small and family-owned; notable exceptions include **Hardy's, Middlebrook,** and **Rosemount.** Most cellar doors are open from 10am to 4:30 or 5pm daily; the Visitors Centre has maps and a complete list of hours for all vineyards.

Wirra Wirra Vineyards (☎8323 8414), on McMurtrie Rd.; follow signs from Willunga Rd. Read the labels on Wirra Wirra's bottles carefully—their humor is as dry as their wine. Their red was recently named one of South Australia's top 10 bottles. Open M-Sa 10am-5pm, Su 11am-5pm.

Hugh Hamilton Wines (☎8323 8689), on McMurtrie Rd. before Wirra Wirra. The beautiful tasting area has a 360 degree view of the Mt. Lofty ranges. Hugh's wines win the prize for the most entertaining names. "Menage a trois" and the sparkling "Moulin Rouge" are standouts. Open M-F 10am-5:30pm, Sa-Su 11am-5:30pm.

Hamilton Fine Wines (☎8556 2222), on Main Rd. The airy cellar door is set among the vines on the road toward Willunga. But the most interesting aspect of this vineyard is its rivalry between owner Richard Hamilton and his brother Hugh, who occupies a small vineyard perched a few kilometers away. Open M-F 10am-5pm, Sa-Su 11am-5pm.

Sarafino Wines (☎8323 0517), off Kangarilla Rd. before Dennis, is a new vineyard and its wines are complemented by an on-site chocolate factory, David Medlow Chocolates. There is also a hotel, picnic area, and restaurant in the complex. Open M-F 10am-5pm, Sa-Su 10am-4:30pm.

Dennis of McLaren Vale (☎8323 8665), on Kangarilla Rd. Discerning and well-educated drinkers would be remiss to leave the Vale without sampling Dennis's version of hot spiced mead. Made from fermented honey and scented with cloves, the drink is served warm to bring out the aromas. Open M-F 10am-5pm, Sa-Su noon-5pm.

Marienberg Wines, 2 Chalk Hill Rd. (☎8323 9666), just 100m from the info center, same building as Limeburner's Restaurant. Founded in 1966 by Australia's first female winemaker. Try their unique red "Sparkling Nicole." Open daily 10am-5pm.

◖ BEACHES

Just a few kilometers west of McLaren Vale, the beaches near Aldinga are among the finest you'll find on the Fleurieu. A beautiful and popular stretch of beaches line Aldinga Bay and include, from the south, **Sellick's Beach, Silver Sands Beach, Aldinga Beach, Port Willunga,** and **Maslin's Beach.** There is car access to the beach at Sellick's and Aldinga, and you can drive on the sand from one end to the other even in a 2WD, although you should be careful to stay out of the deep sand ($4.50 per car for beach access). **Maslin's Beach,** 5km north of Aldinga, is perhaps the best stretch. There is history here, as well: it was the first official "unclad bathing" beach in Australia and each January, the beach hosts a one-day "nude Olympics." The nude portion starts 500m south of the carpark, so fully clad bathers can also enjoy this spectacular expanse of sand.

VICTOR HARBOR   ☎08

Sheltered from the Southern Ocean by the sands of Encounter Bay, Victor Harbor (pop. 4600) has been popular with Adelaide weekenders since it was used as the summer residence of South Australia's colonial governors. The touristy town offers much to do: penguins, parasailing, museums, and whales all call Victor home. The town also boasts a summer temperature as much as 10°C cooler than steamy Adelaide.

▐ **TRANSPORTATION. Premier Stateliner buses** (☎8415 5555) run from Adelaide to Stuart St. in Victor Harbor (1½-2hr.; M-F 5 per day, Sa 2 per day, Su 1 per day; $14, continuing to Port Elliot, Middleton, and Goolwa. Buy tickets at **Travelworld** (☎8552 1200), in the Harbor Mall on Ocean St. To get to Kangaroo Island, book at the **Sealink Bookings Office** in the same building as the Visitors Centre for a **Sealink** bus to Cape Jervis or ferry tickets to the island. (☎1800 088 552 or 8552 7000. 1 bus per day to Cape Jervis; $11. For ferry prices see Cape Jervis section. Open daily 9am-5pm.) Other services include: **taxis** (☎131 008); **RAA** (☎13 11 11 or 0427 527 033); and **Victor Rent-a-Car,** 66 Ocean St. (☎8552 1033; 25+; from $66 per day).

▐▐ **ORIENTATION & PRACTICAL INFORMATION.** Victor Harbor is 85km south of Adelaide on the Main South Rd. Flinders Pde. runs along the ocean beneath the shade of massive fir trees. The main commercial drag, one-way Ocean St., runs parallel a block up, becoming Hindmarsh St. The main street on the western side of the city is Victoria St., which leads to the highway toward Cape Jervis. The **Tourist Information Centre**, near the causeway to Granite Island, is at the foot of Flinders Pde. and has a great map of town with shops and services listed on the back. (☎8552 5738 or 8552 7000; www.tourismvictorharbor.com.au. Open daily 9am-5pm.) Other services include: **ATMs** on Ocean St.; **police**, 30 Torrens St. (☎8552 2088); **library**, 14 Coral St., just off Ocean St., with free **Internet** (☎8552 3009; open Tu-Th 10am-5:30pm, F 10am-6pm, Sa 10am-1pm); and a **post office**, 54 Ocean St. (M-F 9am-5pm). **Postal Code:** 5211.

⚑◘ ACCOMMODATIONS & FOOD. The Anchorage ❸, 21 Flinters Pde., offers waterfront lodging at budget prices, along with a pricey restaurant and ship-shaped cafe/bar. (☎8552 5970; victor@anchorage.mtx.net. Key deposit $10. 4- to 6-bed family rooms $25 per person; hotel rooms come with continental breakfast; singles $65; doubles $70-85. Spa rooms $150.) The 100-year-old **Grosvenor Junction Hotel ❷**, 40 Ocean St., has simple rooms and a balcony with great views. (☎8552 1011. TV lounge and fridge, but no kitchen. Continental breakfast. Backpackers $25; singles $30; doubles $60.) **Victor Harbor Beach Front Caravan Park ❷**, 114 Victoria St., has beautiful sea views on the west side of the city. (☎8552 1111. Key deposit $10. Book ahead in summer. Sites for 2 from $22; cabins from $52.)

For a sit-down meal, the **Anchorage Bar and Restaurant ❶**, on Flinders Pde., has mains from about $15. (☎8552 5970. Breakfasts and lunches from $8. Open daily 8am-late). The **Original Victor Harbor Fish Shop ❶**, 20 Ocean St., is the real deal and offers fish 'n chips ($5-13) and burgers for $6-9. (☎8552 1273. Open Su-Th 10:30am-7:30pm, F-Sa 10:30am-8:30pm.) **Blenders**, on the tip of Ocean St. near the park, is a great little juice bar. (Open Su-Th 10am-5pm, F-Sa 10am-late.) Woolworths **supermarket** is in the Victor Central Mall on Torrens St. (Open daily 7am-10pm.)

◙◪ SIGHTS & ACTIVITIES. Little penguins win top billing on **Granite Island**, although the island is also home to a **walking trail** (45min. loop), a cafe, and a brilliant **lookout** with views back to the town and over expansive **Encounter Bay**. Entry is free if you take the ten-minute stroll across the causeway, but you can also cross on a Clydesdale-drawn **tram**. (Tram runs daily every 40 min. 10am-4pm; extended hours during holidays. $6 return, children $4.) The **little penguins** can only be seen at dusk; access to the island is limited to those on the guided tour to ensure penguin safety. The **Penguin Interpretive Centre** is open 30min. before the guided penguin walks, which start on the island side of the bridge. (☎8552 7555. $10, concessions $9, children $7. Daily in winter 5:30pm, in summer 8:30pm.)

The neighboring towns of Port Elliot, Middleton, and Goolwa (see below) are accessible by a **coastal drive**, the **Encounter Bikeway,** and the Goolwa to Victor Harbor **Cockle Train**. Rent a bike at **Victor Harbor Cycle and Skate**, 73 Victoria St. (☎8552 1417; half-day $14, full-day $20; open M-F 9am-5:30pm; Sa 9am-noon) and in Goolwa at the Goolwa Caravan Park at Laffin Pt. on the eastern edge of town (☎8555 2737; half-day $15, full-day $20). Pick up a route guide at the Visitors Centre in either town. The Cockle Train runs along Australia's first steel railway, laid between Goolwa and Victor in 1854. The train takes 30min., with trips nearly every day during January, April, July, and October, but just once a week in the off season. Check with the information centers in Goolwa or Victor to see when it's running (one-way $15, return $22; children $12).

PORT ELLIOT
☎08

Surrounded by towns swarming with tourists, Port Elliot has somehow remained a perfect little beach-town. There is a real community feel to the place, with old-fashioned dances in the church every Wednesday night, flyers everywhere, and cafes in every local shop. The Fleurieu Hwy. passes along the north side of town, assuming the name North Terr., while The Strand, the town's other significant street, heads south from North Terr. opposite the Royal Family Hotel to overlook the ocean. A small IGA **supermarket** (open daily 8am-7pm) is next to the hotel on North Terr., and The Strand is lined with an assortment of antiques and second-hand shops. ■**Arnella by the Sea (YHA)** ❷, 28 North Terr., occupies the oldest building in the town, with beautiful colonial-style rooms, a spacious kitchen, and leafy back patio. The wide choice of accommodations will suit any budget. The owners also arrange bike hire and tours. (☎8554 3611 or 1800 066 297; narnu@bigpond.com. Reception 8am-noon and 2-8pm, 6pm in winter. 3-bed dorms $22, YHA $20; singles $33/$30; twins and doubles $55/$50; family rooms $66/$60.) Just west of the main part of town is the **Port Elliot Caravan and Tourist Park** ❷ (☎8554 2134; sites $16, powered $20; cabins from $55), fronting beautiful (and appropriately shaped) **Horseshoe Bay**, the town's main beach. Up at the ocean end of the Strand sits **The Strand Inn** ❺, with bright open spaces and some sea views. (☎8554 2067; www.strandinn.com.au. Downstairs rooms $90, upstairs $100. Prices go down in winter.) The **Royal Family Hotel** ❸, just west of the Arnella on North Terr., offers standard pub accommodation and the only bar in town (☎8554 2219. Singles $30, doubles $40). For a delicious picnic on the beach, get supplies at the **Port Elliot Fruit & Veg & Gourmet Foods**, on North Terr. They have the freshest produce, exquisite cheeses, and mouth-watering smoothies. (☎8554 2025. Open daily 9am-5pm.) Good pizza and pasta for reasonable prices are at **Paradiso** ❶, 12 The Strand. (☎8554 2144. Pizzas $9, pasta around $14. Open Su, W-Sa 5pm-late.) Try the garden-fronted **Pie in the Sky Cafe** ❷, 40 North Terr., for breakfast or sandwiches. (☎8554 3755. Open M-Sa 10am-5pm, Su 9am-5pm.) **Middleton**, just 5km east of Port Elliot, is little more than a petrol station, a general store, and a caravan park, but is reputed to have the Fleurieu's best **surfing** at its spectacular beach.

GOOLWA

☎08

The town's main street is the road from Adelaide, which becomes Cadell St. in town and leads to the waterfront before making a westward turn and becoming Victor Harbor Rd. The **Signal Point Interpretive Centre**, at the end of Cadell St. on the waterfront, books local tours and excursions. (☎8555 3488. Open daily 9am-5pm.) The **police** can be reached at ☎8555 2018. **ATMs**, the **post office**, and restaurants can all be found on Cadell St., as can the **library** (☎8555 2030; open M-F 10am-5pm, Sa 9:30am-12:30pm; **Internet** free). The Foodland **supermarket** is on the Victor Harbor Rd. in the Goolwa Village Shopping Centre (open M-Sa 8am-7pm, Su 9am-6pm).

The **PS Murray River Queen** ❷, a floating motel permanently docked at the Goolwa wharf, has unbeatable views, though budget travelers will have to settle for below-deck accommodation with a small porthole for a window. (☎8555 1733. Budget singles $20, doubles $38; upper-deck staterooms $80.) Camping and cabins are available at the **Goolwa Caravan Park** ❶, on Noble Ave. at the far eastern end of town, where you can also rent bikes or canoes. (☎8555 2737. Bike hire $15 per half-day, $20 per full-day; canoes $10 per hr. Sites $15, powered $18; cabins for 2 from $53.) The **Woks 2 Eat** ❷ noodle bar on the corner of Cadell and Dawson in the center of town, offers fine Asian eat-in or takeaway. Specials are just $7. (☎8555 1491. Curries $11. Open daily noon-10pm.)

The ■**Signal Point (River Murray) Interpretive Centre**, on the Wharf in Goolwa, provides a fascinating education in the role of the Murray-Darling River, the fourth largest river system in the world. (☎8555 3488. $5.50, concessions $4.40, children $2.75. Open daily 9am-5pm; last entrance 4pm.) The recently completed **bridge** to **Hindmarsh Island**, across the Murray River from Goolwa, enables the visitor to drive right out to the Murray's mouth and see the **pelicans** that feed there regularly.

The **Encounter Bikeway** and **Cockle Train** link Goolwa to Victor Harbor. **Boat** excursions into the northern reaches of **Coorong National Park** or out to the Murray's mouth are popular, as well, with several tours operating from Goolwa's wharf. The free **Wellington Ferry,** east of town at the small hamlet of Wellington, crosses the Murray River, taking about eight cars across on each pass (open 24hr.). **Jet skis** can be hired at **Goolwa Jet Ski Hire** (☎8555 2573) and **canoes** and **bikes** are available from the Goolwa Caravan Park.

CAPE JERVIS   ☎08

Cape Jervis serves mostly as the jumping-off point for the **Kangaroo Island ferry.** Most simply shoot through en route to or from the ferry without stopping to appreciate the quiet solitude or the unique ▨**Cape Jervis Station ❷**, where options range from four-and-a-half star rooms in the homestead ($100) to the decked-out train car called the *Railway Cottage* (doubles $80) to the backpacker set-up in the cottage-like Shearers' Quarters ($20 per person). The Sealink bus picks up and drops off at the gate, and guests are entitled to free ferry transfers. (☎8598 0288 or 1800 805 288; www.capejervisstation.com.au. Sites $14, powered $17; dorms $20; singles from $50; doubles from $65, both with breakfast.) The rest of the "town" consists of the **pub/gas station/general store** complex between the Station and the Ferry. There is a **Sealink** office at the ferry dock, but book well in advance.

The **Deep Creek Conservation Park ❶**, 13km from Cape Jervis on the road to Victor Harbor, contains 4500 hectares of coastal bush land and features seacoast views of the Backstairs Passage and Kangaroo Island, as well as bushwalking and relative solitude. The **Park Headquarters** (☎8598 0263), by the entrance to the park, is infrequently staffed but stocked with maps and info. Self-register here for day passes ($5 per car) and camping permits. ($15.50 per car per night for the Stringybark area, near the ranger station, the only one with toilets and showers, or $6.50 per car per night for any of the 3 more remote bush camping sites. **The Eagle Waterhole** is accessible only by hiking and, along with the other campgrounds, is $4.)

KANGAROO ISLAND   ☎08

The crux of South Australian tourism, Kangaroo Island (pop. 4100) attracts throngs of travelers. For the most part, the hype is deserved—KI has 21 national and local conservation parks, including the magnificent Flinders Chase National Park. All of these offer good opportunities to see the abundant wildlife and to climb over and through awesome geological formations. Budget travelers be forewarned, however: getting to KI is an expensive proposition, and once there, it's necessary to join an organized tour or rent a car. Still, this spot is worth the dollars, offering bountiful flora, fauna, and fun.

✈ INTERCITY TRANSPORTATION

BY FERRY & COACH
Kangaroo Island Sealink ferry has the monopoly on transport to Cape Jervis and Kangaroo Island; consequently, prices are steep and discounts are hard to come by. Sealink has offices in Victor Harbor and at the ferry dock in Cape Jervis but it is advisable to book far in advance to avoid being turned away. Ferries take about an hour to cross the Backstairs Passage between Cape Jervis and Penneshaw and depart four times daily, with additional sailings during peak times. (☎13 13 01 or 8202 8688; www.sealink.com.au, Bookings for the ferry are mandatory. Daily 7:30am-10pm. $64 return, children $32; cars $138 return.) Sealink offers connect-

ing **coach** service between Adelaide and the Cape Jervis ferry dock from Adelaide's central bus station, 101 Franklin St. (Book ahead. 2hr.; 2 per day; one-way $16, return including ferry $96.)

BY AIR

Two airlines depart from Adelaide's airport, each two to four times per day, and land at **Kingscote Airport,** 13km from the town of Kingscote at Cygnet River. **Regional Express (Rex)** occasionally has good deals on airfares, especially during the fall and winter. (☎ 13 17 13; www.regionalexpress.com.au) **Emu Airlines** is not as earthbound as its flightless namesake and the Adelaide to Kingscote run its only regular route. (☎8234 3711 or 1800 182 353. From $114.50 one-way with a 2-week advance purchase.) The **airport shuttle** service that runs to Kingscote must be pre-booked. (☎8553 2390. $12 per person.)

█ LOCAL TRANSPORTATION

There is no public transportation on the island and many mainland car rental companies do not insure rentals for use on KI, so check ahead before bringing a car over on the ferry. The limited **Sealink coach service** runs between Kingscote and the ferry terminal in Penneshaw (1hr.), stopping in American River (30min.).

BY CAR

Most of the primary tourist thoroughfares are paved and unsealed roads leading to major sights are generally in good condition, so a 4WD is helpful but not necessary. Rental companies offer free shuttles between the airport and Kingscote and a ferry pick-up option. **Budget** has offices in Penneshaw next to the Sealink office and in Kingscote at 57a Dauncey St. They rent to those over 21, though you must be at least 25 to rent a 4WD. (☎8553 3133 or 0408 815 737.) Hertz-affiliate **Kangaroo Island Rental Cars** is on the corner of Franklin St. and Telegraph Rd., Kingscote. (☎8553 2390 or 1800 088 296.) **Penneshaw Car Rentals** rents late model cars with A/C to those over 21. (☎8593 0023 or 1800 686 620.)

TOURS

Most tours are led by friendly, knowledgeable guides and hit the "must-see" sights. One-day tours can be grueling, with most lasting 10-12hrs. Tours that allow at least one night on the island are a better way to go.

CampWild Adventures (☎ 1800 444 321; www.campwild.com.au) offers a 3-day 4WD camping trip that hits all the big sights at a relaxed pace. Fun activities include sandboarding, ATV rides, and sleeping under the stars. Departs in summer daily; in winter Tu, Th, and Sa. $350, ISIC/YHA $320. Price includes pick-up in Adelaide, private ferry with dolphin watching, meals, accommodation, and park entrance. Max. 10 people.

Adventure Tours Australia (☎ 1300 654 604) offers a good 2-day tour, along with a 3-day 4WD tour that hits more remote areas. Less of a boozing and partying crowd. 2-day leaves M, W, and Sa 7am; $320. 3-day departs M, Th, and Sa 7am; $495.

Wayward Bus (☎8410 8833) runs a popular 2-day tour from Adelaide's Central Bus Terminal, covering all the big sights along the south coast the first day and Flinders Chase and the north coast the 2nd day. Departs M, W, Th, and Sa 6:30am; additional departures Oct.-Apr. $350. Price includes all transport, meals, park entry fees, and accommodation at the KI Wilderness Resort.

Sealink (☎ 13 13 01) covers the big sights from Adelaide, Cape Jervis, or Victor Harbor. Standby-rates are 15% off and must be booked a day ahead; availability is limited in peak season. Departs Adelaide 6:45am, returns 10:30pm. From Adelaide $179, flight $341; from Cape Jervis $149; from Victor Harbor $171; from Penneshaw $99.

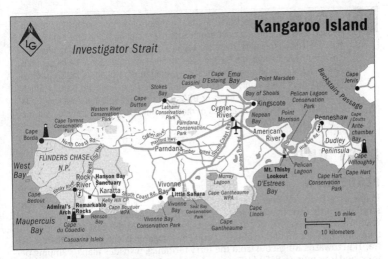

BY BIKE & OTHER MEANS

Penneshaw Youth Hostel and **Kangaroo Island Central Backpackers,** in Kingscote, both hire bikes (full-day around $20). **Bob's Bikes,** 1 Commercial St., Kingscote, rents single and tandem bikes. (☎8553 2349. $6.50 per hr., $16.50 per day; tandems $9/ $27.50). Be warned, however, that you're not going to see much of anything by bike unless you're a serious cycler with time to spare—the island is simply too big. For an aerial view of the island's sights, sign up for a breathtaking flight with **Kangaroo Island Wilderness Flights** in Parndana. (☎8559 4254. $65 per person per 30min., $120 per hr.) **KI Outdoor Action** offers day or evening ATV tours. (☎8559 4296. Surfboards, kayaks, and snorkeling gear also available for rent.)

■🛈 ORIENTATION & PRACTICAL INFORMATION

Kangaroo Island's 4500km² area make it Australia's third-largest island. The ferry lands in Penneshaw, on the top of Dudley Peninsula. **Hog Bay Road** heads southwest out of town to the narrow strip of land connecting the peninsula to the mainland and then curves northwest towards American River and Kingscote. **Playford Highway** heads west from Kingscote through the middle of the island, passing Parndana before ending at Cape Borda at the island's northwestern tip. The **South Coast Road** diverges from the Playford Hwy. 15km west of Kingscote and swings through most of the attractions on the south coast, leading to the main entrance to Flinders Chase National Park, which spans most of KI's west end. **The West End Highway** runs north through Flinders Chase and connects the South Coast Road to the Playford Hwy. All the main roads are sealed, but access roads to many sights along the way are unsealed. The unsealed **North Coast Road** is accessible via the Playford Hwy. and leads to the north coast's tranquil beaches.

The **Gateway Visitors Information Centre** is outside Penneshaw, on the road to Kingscote. (☎8553 1185. Open M-F 9am-5pm, Sa-Su 10am-4pm.) Aside from Kingscote and Penneshaw, **petrol** and **general stores** can be found at American River, Vivonne Bay, the KI Wilderness Resort, Island Beach, and Parndana. The **Island Parks Pass** allows unlimited access to Seal Bay, Kelly Hill Caves, Flinders Chase, and the Cape Borda and Cape Willoughby lighthouse tours. (Valid for 1 year. Available at Visitors Centre and park entrances. $32, children $23, families $84.)

> **WILDFIRE** Kangaroo Island treats the threat of wildfire seriously. Fire Ban Season lasts from the start of December to the end of April, the driest months of the year. During this time, there are a series of restrictions on camping fires: the fire must be contained in a BBQ, cooker, or fireplace, and cannot be bigger than one square meter in area. You must stay with the fire while it is lit. On particularly dry days the Country Fire Service might call for a Total Fire Ban, in which case only gas or electric stoves or BBQs can be used and many walking trails are closed. Never toss cigarettes or matches from cars. For more info, call the CFS hotline (☎1300 362 361).

EAST END

PENNESHAW
☎08

Penneshaw (pop. 250) is the arrival point for the ferry from Cape Jervis. A quick stroll up North Terr. from the jetty leads to the pub, **petrol station,** and a few small restaurants. Tiny Nat Turner St. connects North Terr. to the **post office** (open M-F 9am-5pm, Sa 9-11am) and to Middle Terr. The **Kangaroo Island Gateway Visitors Centre,** 1km towards Kingscote from the ferry terminus, provides maps, camping permits, and tour info. (☎8553 1185. Open M-F 9am-5pm, Sa-Su 10am-4pm.)

Although most of Penneshaw's visitors take the ferry, a group of regulars swim in with the tide. Each night after sunset, clans of little **fairy penguins** waddle from the sea to their burrows along the coastline. The **Penguin Interpretive Centre** is just east of the ferry dock, off Middle Terr. The lighted wooden boardwalk is closed to the public after dusk, making guided tours the only way to really see the penguins. (☎8553 1103 or 8553 1016. Tours including Penguin Centre admission daily at 8:30pm and 9:30pm; in winter 7:30pm and 8:30pm. $6.50, concessions $5.) February and March are bad months for penguin viewing—after molting, the birds spend weeks out at sea, leaving the burrows empty until autumn.

Penneshaw Youth Hostel ❷, 43 North Terr., has accommodations, with kitchen, TV lounge, and a small courtyard. (☎8553 1284. Reception 7:45am-7:30pm. 8-bed dorms $19; singles $25; twins and doubles $42/$45. Cutlery deposit $10. Internet $3 per 30min.) **Kangaroo Island YHA ❷,** 33 Middle Terr., offers six-bed rooms with stove, refrigerator, and bath, as well as motel-style doubles and triples. (☎8553 1233. Reception M-F 9am-5pm, Sa-Su 9am-noon. Dorms $22; twins and doubles $72. YHA $19/$66.) The most upscale option in Penneshaw is the **Kangaroo Island Seafront ❺,** 49 North Terr. The hotel caters to your every need with a pool, tennis courts, and glassed-in restaurant. (☎8553 1028. Doubles $120-195. Breakfast included.) The **Penguin Stop Cafe ❷,** just up from the ferry on Nat Turner St., offers sandwiches and high quality meals with a view. (☎8553 1211. Open for lunch Su and W-Sa and dinner Su and Th-Sa.) The IGA Welcome-Mart, on Middle Terr., has **groceries.** (Open M-F 8:30am-6pm, Sa-Su 8:30am-4pm.)

KINGSCOTE
☎08

Kingscote (pop. 1500), KI's largest town, can be a welcome stop for civilization-starved visitors returning from the western end of the island. Most of the shops and services are one block parallel to the beach on **Dauncey Street.** Services include: **tourist info** at the **Kingscote Gift Shop,** 78 Dauncey St. (☎8553 2165, after-hours call 8553 2826; open M-F 9am-6pm, Sa-Su 9am-5:30pm; camping permits and Island Parks Pass available); the **Sealink** office, next to the Newsagent on Dauncey St. (☎13 13 01; open M-F 9am-5pm, Sa 9am-noon); an **ATM** at Bank SA, on Dauncey

St.; **police** (☎8553 2018); **RAA** (☎8553 2162); the island's only **hospital** (☎8553 4200; call 000 for an ambulance); free **Internet** at the **library,** 41 Dauncey St., opposite Bank SA (☎8553 4516; open M 1-5pm, Tu-Sa 9:30am-5pm); and a **post office** on Dauncey St. (☎8553 2122. Open M-F 9am-5pm, Sa 9am-noon.) **Postal Code:** 5223.

The **KI Marine Centre,** on the wharf, has a small but interesting aquarium complete with sea dragons and cuttlefish. Tours of the local **penguin burrows** depart from the Centre at dusk, and **pelicans** get up close and personal at their 5pm feedings behind the center. (☎8553 2381. Aquarium $4. Penguin tours in summer 8:30pm and 9:30pm; in winter 7:30pm and 8:30pm. $10, children $5, families $20. Pelican feedings $2.)

Ellson's Seaview ❹, on Chapman Terr. on the south side of town, has large rooms equipped with TV, fridge, and tea and coffee. Rooms in the guest house share a clean bathroom and are cheaper than those in the main motel. Ask for a sea view. (☎8553 2030. Reception 8am-8:30pm. Motel singles from $115, doubles from $125; guesthouse singles $60; twins and doubles $70, extra person $10.) **Roger's Deli and Cafe ❶,** 76 Dauncey St., offers pies and burgers for $2-5 as well as Asian cuisine for $10-15. (☎8553 2053. Open M-Th 8am-6pm, F-Sa 8am-9pm, Su 8:30-6pm.) At the **Ozone Hotel ❶,** on the corner of Chapman Terr. and Commercial St., local prawns are $20; sandwiches run from $7-9. (☎8553 2381. Bar open daily 11am-midnight, lunch noon-2pm, dinner 6-8:30pm.) A Foodland **supermarket** is on the corner of Commercial and Osmond St. (open M-F 9am-5:30pm, Sa 9am-12:30pm) and an IGA supermarket is on Dauncey St. (Open M-F 9am-5:30pm, Sa 9am-noon.)

SOUTH COAST

Many of KI's most noteworthy sights line the south coast and are accessible via the recently paved South Coast Rd., which heads to Flinders Chase. Early morning is a good time to escape the heat and crowds.

■ **SEAL BAY CONSERVATION PARK.** Arguably Kangaroo Island's finest natural attraction, Seal Bay Conservation Park allows visitors to stroll through one of the few remaining colonies of **Australian sea lions.** A hike along the boardwalk brings you within viewing of the sea lions, but to get onto the beach, guided **tours** (45min.) are the only option. Pricier **sunset tours** reveal what happens in a seal colony when the sun goes down. (60km along the South Coast Rd. from Kingscote; allow 45min. to drive. ☎8559 4207. Tours depart daily every 30-45min. 9am-4:15pm; Dec.-Jan. 9am-7:45pm. Tour and boardwalk access $10.50, concessions $7.50, families $28. Boardwalk only $7/$5.50/$20. Sunset tours 2hrs Dec.-Jan. only $20/$12/$55.)

LITTLE SAHARA. A short drive west of Seal Bay, Little Sahara's surprisingly large dunes are here for the climbing. A 20min. walk leads to the top of a high sand ridge, where you'll have great views of the surrounding dunes and a fun tumble back down toward your car. In the summer, try to avoid midday—this is the Sahara, after all. (About 7km west of Seal Bay on South Coast Rd. watch for signs and turn left. The road into the carpark is about a 5min. drive along an unsealed road; use extra caution.)

VIVONNE BAY. Vivonne Bay, just west of Seal Bay and Little Sahara on the South Coast Rd., hides a stunning curve of sandy **beach** that is home to the island's lobster fleet and is ideal for picnics and surfing. The beach was recently voted one of the cleanest in Australia. Swimming at Vivonne Bay should only be attempted near the boat jetty or in the mouth of the Harriet River—the rest of the beach has a strong undertow. The **Kangaroo Island Outdoor Education Field Study Centre** organizes lessons on local wildlife.

SOUTH AUSTRALIA

The Bay is also a good place on the island to fill up on fuel and supplies at the general store. (☎8559 4291. Open daily 8am-8pm.) **Camping** near the beach can be arranged at the store. (From the general store, it is 3km down an unsealed road to the beach. Outdoor Ed. Centre is just off the South Coast Rd., behind the store. ☎8559 4232. Classes from 2 days to 3 weeks; accommodation provided. Call ahead. Camping $4 onsite.)

KELLY HILL. The **Kelly Hill Caves,** on South Coast Rd. about halfway between Vivonne Bay and the Flinders Chase Visitors Centre, are the main attraction of **Kelly Hill Conservation Park.** Adventure **caving tours** require advance booking and cover some of the smaller, more delicate caves. There is a picnic area near the car-park, as well as several walking trails through surrounding bushland. (25km west of Vivonne Bay, 20km east of Flinders Chase. ☎8559 7231. Tours daily 10, 11am, noon, 12:45, 1:30, 2:30, 3:30pm. $7, concessions $6, families $22. Adventure tours daily 2pm; book ahead. $23-34, concessions $5, families $59-87.)

HANSON BAY SANCTUARY. This privately owned wildlife sanctuary, 10km west of Kelly Caves and 4km west of the turn-off for Hanson Bay, is one of the island's prime koala-viewing spots. (☎8559 7344. $2 adults, children free, payment is on the honor system at the entrance to the walk. Money goes to improving the koala environment.)

SURFING. Kangaroo Island also provides ample opportunities to hit the **surf.** Visit the Kangaroo Island Gateway Visitors Centre in Penneshaw for the *Surfing Guide,* which details the breaks along the south coast at **Hanson Bay, Vivonne Bay, D'Estrees Bay,** and **Pennington Bay** and at **Stokes Bay** on the North Coast. The most convenient of these are Vivonne and Pennington Bays, both accessible via good roads and suitable for all levels of surfers. Full-length wetsuits are the rule, as the water is cool year-round.

WEST END

The West End of the island is where the wild things are. You will find few shops and restaurants out here, so bring food along. The serene and secluded **Flinders Chase Farm ❶** is the perfect place to stargaze. On a 2000-acre sheep and cattle farm just 15min. north of the park entrance on the West End Hwy., the friendly owners offer self-contained cabins and spotless dorms with full kitchen, BBQ, and bathrooms. (☎8559 7223 or 0427 722 778; chillers@kin.net.au. Linen provided. Dorms $15; cabins for 1 or 2 $50.) The **Western KI Caravan Park ❶** is 4km east of the Flinders Chase entrance on the South Coast Rd. (☎8559 7201; beckwith@kin.net.au. Sites $15, powered $18; tent hire from $20; cabins for 2 from $80 plus $20 for 1 night bookings, linen $5.50.) The **KI Wilderness Resort ❸,** on South Coast Rd. just before the entrance to Flinders Chase, offers accommodation ranging from dorms to a luxury suite with private spa. (☎8559 7275; www.austdreaming.com.au. 4-bed dorms $40; ensuite doubles $100; luxury motel $135 single, $180 double; spa suite $330.) The resort also has **petrol** and a **general store,** as well as a **pub ❶** (takeaway lunch served 11:30am-3pm; dinner served 6:30-8pm; counter meals from $10), a relatively upscale **restaurant ❹** (mains from $15 to $35), and **Internet** access (coin-operated, $2 per 10min.)

FLINDERS CHASE NATIONAL PARK

Visitors who bypass western KI's Flinders Chase National Park are missing out on the best of what the island has to offer. Animals coast, hop, and slither through the bush, and surreal rock formations crop up along the coastline. The most popular sights are clustered 15-20km south of Rocky River along a sealed road. Just over 100km from Kingscote, the **Visitors Centre** is at Rocky River, along the South Coast Rd., and has information, maps, limited supplies, and sells day-passes and camping permits. (☎8559 7235; fax 8559 7268. Open daily 9am-5pm. One-day park entry $6.50, children $3.60, families $16.)

The aptly named **Remarkable Rocks,** precariously perched on a 75m coastal clifftop, are huge hunks of granite sculpted into bizarre shapes by 750 million years of lichens and erosion by ice, wind, and water. The hooked beak of Eagle Rock is a perfect spot for a picture to send home. Be careful on this rocky playground; it's a long fall to the crashing waves below. 5km west of Remarkable Rocks, **Cape du Couedic** houses a red-capped sandstone lighthouse and a couple of short clifftop hikes. Just south of the lighthouse, a footpath winds to the edge of Cape du Couedic and then to the limestone cave of **Admiral's Arch.** A few thousand New Zealand **fur seals** call this area home and can be seen sunning themselves on the rocks and playing in the surf.

Flinders Chase National Park has **four camping sites ❶,** all non-powered and with toilet facilities. The **Rocky River site,** near the Visitors Centre, offers convenience and the only showers in the park; however, the sites are in a dirt clearing. Nine cheaper sites are 13km into the park at **Snake Lagoon,** where wildlife is much more plentiful. The campground at **West Bay,** 20km west of Rocky River along an unsealed road, is beautifully remote and just 200m from the beach. The campground at **Harvey's Return** is on the north coast. Permits are available for all sites at Rocky River Visitors Centre. (Book ahead ☎8559 7235. Caravans allowed only at Rocky River and Snake Lagoon. Rocky River site $18.50; all other sites $6.50. Prices do not include day fees. Rustic **cabins ❷** can be rented at Flinders Chase's three lighthouse stations. (Book ahead ☎8859 7235. Linen $12.50 per person. $40 per person, children $6.50. Min. charge: Cape du Couedic $120, Cape Borda $50.40, and Cape Willoughby $75.)

Numerous short **hikes** and excellent 2- to 7-day coastline treks are available for bushwalkers in Flinders Chase. Hikers should pick up the *Bushwalking in Kangaroo Island Parks* brochure from any Visitors Centre.

NORTH COAST

Thanks largely to the fact that it is accessed only by unsealed roads and bypassed by most tours, the north coast is still a tranquil place. Though most of the roads are in good condition and can be handled by a 2WD, 4WD vehicles will have an easier go of it. The remote lighthouse at **Cape Borda,** on the island's northwest tip, is open for tours and has a daily cannon firing. (☎8559 3257. 4-6 tours daily, depending on the season. 11am-3pm. $7, children $5.50, families $20.) Just north, **Scott's Cove** allows views east to the towering cliffs at Cape Torrens and Cape Forbin.

There is camping at the **Harvey's Return ❶** site, one of the Flinders Chase campgrounds (see above). ▓**Western River Cove,** at the mouth of the Western River, holds perhaps the prettiest and most secluded of all the beaches located on the north coast. The turn-off is on the Playford Hwy., 8km east of its junction with the West End Hwy., and the unsealed road leads to a carpark next to the river. **Snelling Beach,** about 15km east of Western River Cove, is a larger beach, with a long sweep of empty sand and gentle waves suited to swimming. From the west, the descent down Constitution Hill offers stunning views of the beach framed by surrounding cliffs and hills. From Snelling, North Coast Rd. continues 15km east to **Stokes Bay,** your best bet for surfing. Eighteen kilometers northwest of Kingscote is the 4km-long beach at **Emu Bay,** which has **campsites ❶** (☎8553 2015; site $3.85, powered $11; pay on site).

CENTRAL WINE REGIONS

The center of South Australia's wine universe is 70km northeast of Adelaide, in the well-known Barossa Valley. Grapes from the Barossa and its more rural neighbor, the Eden Valley, produce some of Australia's best wines, particularly the shiraz. The Clare Valley, 45min. north of Barossa and also strong contender, is filled with smaller, more specialized wineries. For the budget traveler, wine tasting is both a free buzz and a cultural endeavor.

BAROSSA VALLEY
☎08

Perhaps Australia's most well-known wine region, the Barossa Valley got an early corner on the market. Johann Gramp, a German settler, produced the first crop in 1850 on the banks of Jacob's Creek; in the century and a half since, the Barossa's output has been prolific. Most of Australia's largest wine companies are based here, along with plenty of renowned family operations. Though the vineyards are a fine sight in any season, those visiting during the vintage, from mid-February to late April or early May, will get to see them laden with fruit and might even be able to taste-test the different types of grapes, watch the harvest and pressing, or land themselves a picking job in the process.

▐ TRANSPORTATION

Renting a car in Adelaide is strongly recommended for those bent on doing a serious wine tour, as many wineries are out of the way. Follow Scenic Rte. 4 for a breathtaking drive as it makes a large loop through the region, passing the main towns and the bulk of the wineries. Driving parties should keep a **designated driver** absolutely alcohol-free. Barossa Valley's police are diligent and unforgiving when it comes to **drunk driving.**

Buses: Barossa Adelaide Passenger Service (☎8564 3022; after hours 8564 0325) runs to and from Adelaide (1-3 each way per day) stopping at: Angaston ($14.70); Nuriootpa ($13.40); and Tanunda ($12.40). Departs from the main bus terminal on Franklin St. in Adelaide.

Train: The **Barossa Wine Train** (☎8212 7888) runs restored 1950s passenger trains from Adelaide's central rail terminal to Tanunda. Ultimate Day Tour includes round-trip rail fare, wine and food tastings, and a full lunch. (Departs Th, and Sa-Su. $75 return. Ultimate Day Tour $139.)

Taxi: Barossa Valley Taxi, 7 Albert St. in Tanunda, (☎1800 28 8294 or 8563 3600). Book early. About $13 from Nuriootpa to Tanunda. 24hr. service.

Automobile Clubs: Royal Automobile Association, in Gawler (☎8522 2478) and Tanunda (☎8563 2123). For 24hr. service call ☎0500 832 123.

Bike Rental: Mountain bikes at **Barossa Bunkhaus Traveller's Hostel** (☎8562 2260), Nuriootpa ($10, $14, or $18 per day; $2 less for guests), or **Tanunda Caravan and Tourist Park.** (☎8563 2784. $6 per hr., $10 per half-day, $15 per day.)

✦ ▐ ORIENTATION & PRACTICAL INFORMATION

The Barossa Valley's main reference points are its three small towns: Tanunda, Nuriootpa, and Angaston. Most of the wineries and tiny hamlets are clustered around them. From Adelaide, take King William St. north to Main North Rd. (A1), and branch off to A20, the **Sturt Highway** B19 enters the Barossa from the north at Nuriootpa. For a more scenic drive, exit earlier at **Gawler,** where B19, the **Barossa**

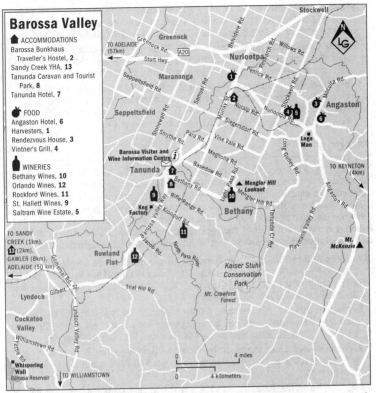

Barossa Valley

🏠 ACCOMMODATIONS
Barossa Bunkhaus
  Traveller's Hostel, **2**
Sandy Creek YHA, **13**
Tanunda Caravan and Tourist
  Park, **8**
Tanunda Hotel, **7**

🍴 FOOD
Angaston Hotel, **6**
Harvesters, **1**
Rendezvous House, **3**
Vintner's Grill, **4**

🍷 WINERIES
Bethany Wines, **10**
Orlando Wines, **12**
Rockford Wines, **11**
St. Hallett Wines, **9**
Saltram Wine Estate, **5**

Valley Way passes through **Lyndoch** (pop. 1000) and **Rowland Flat** before entering the main town of **Tanunda** (pop. 4000), 70km northeast of Adelaide. There, the highway's name changes to **Murray Street** as it continues on to **Nuriootpa** (noor-ee-OOT-pah; pop. 3500), called "Nuri" by the locals. From there, **Nuriootpa Road** leads east to **Angaston** (pop. 2700). The **Barossa Visitors Centre,** 66-68 Murray St., Tanunda, handles B&B bookings and provides maps. (☎ 1300 852 982 or 8563 0600; www.barossa-region.org. Open M-F 9am-5pm, Sa-Su 10am-4pm.) The banks in the valley all have **ATMs.** The **post office** on Murray St. in Tanunda is near the Visitors Centre. (Open M-F 9am-5pm.) The Nuriootpa Library, on Murray St. on the south edge of town, has free **Internet** access (☎ 8562 1107; open M-W and F 9am-5pm, Th 9am-6pm, Sa 9am-noon), as does the Tanunda **Library,** also on Murray St., across from the Visitors Centre. (☎ 8563 2729. Open M-F 9am-5pm, Sa 9am-noon.)

▌ ACCOMMODATIONS

Lodging in Tanunda tends to be more expensive than in Nuriootpa or Angaston. That said, there are plenty of affordable places to stay in the area, but for those looking for something more upscale, there are nearly 90 B&Bs in the region to choose from. For the cheapest pub accommodation, head to Angaston.

🛏 **Barossa Bunkhaus Traveller's Hostel** (☎ 8562 2260), on Nuraip Rd. Offers clean, high-ceilinged rooms with free continental breakfast. Singles $35; doubles $55. ❸

Tanunda Hotel, 51 Murray St. (☎8563 2030) Tanuda, within easy walking distance of shops and restaurants. Its bar is also a popular spot on the weekends. Clean singles with shared facilities $50; doubles $60. Ensuite singles $60; doubles $70. ❹

Tanunda Caravan and Tourist Park (☎8563 2784), just south of Tanunda on Barossa Valley Way. Convenient location. BBQ, kiosk, and laundry. Sites $14, powered $18; basic on-site vans for 2 from $35; cabins for 2 $45-110. ❶

Sandy Creek YHA, in Sandy Creek Conservation Park, 2km from Lyndoch. Groups should look into this restored stone farmhouse. The limited-access hostel sleeps up to 16. Book ahead and pick up key with the YHA Travel Centre, 135 Waymouth St., Adelaide (☎8414 3000). Cabin $80, YHA $70. Linen not provided. ❷

🗋 FOOD

Food runs a close second to wine as a regional priority, and the main streets of Tanunda, Nuriootpa, and Angaston are littered with yuppie joints from casual luncheries to elegant dinner spots. Weekly and daily specials abound, and bakeries and tea-rooms often offer a taste of the region's food at good prices. Many of the wineries have upscale lunch rooms or **bistros,** notably St. Hallett (see p. 492). **Bakeries** have shelves full of traditional German breads, cakes, and pastries, as well as heartier meals and sandwiches. All three towns have **supermarkets.**

▨ **Vintner's Grill** (☎8564 2488), on Nuriootpa Rd. between Nuri and Angaston. A little out of the way, but definitely worth it. The daily fish special is out of this world and goes well with a bottle of the chef's own white wine. Mains around $24. Lunches around $15. Open daily noon-2:30pm and 6:30-9pm.

Harvesters, 29 Murray St., (☎8562 1348), in Nuri, is a classy, if trendy, bistro on the main street. For a savory treat try the goat cheese and tomato basil tartlet ($9). Mains $16-18. Open W 10:30am-6pm, Th-Sa 10:30am-late, Su 12:30-6:30pm. ❹

Rendezvous House, 22 Murray St. (☎8564 3533), in Angaston, is an organic haven, with local produce and creative choices. Tapas are $10-13, wraps $10. Open M, W-Su 8am-6pm. ❸

Angaston Hotel, 59 Murray St., (☎8564 2428) Angaston. Daily lunch specials from $5; dinners starting at $8. Open daily noon-2pm and 6-8pm. Closed Su evening.❶

⚡ WINERIES OF THE BAROSSA VALLEY

The complete tour of the more than 50 wineries that offer cellar door tastings requires Bacchanalian spirit, Herculean effort, and Olympian ability to hold your liquor. Each winery has free tastings, with no obligation to purchase. The **vintage,** when grapes are harvested, lasts from late February into April or early May and is also the time to find **picking jobs.** (Check at cellar doors, or try calling the SA Student and Youth Council Job Prospects line at ☎8552 7455.) Most wineries in Barossa are open daily from 10am to 4 or 5pm.

WINE TRAVELING TIPS. Don't be tempted to buy a wine just because it's won an award. The efficient tourism industry has created so many competitions that virtually every winery has been recognized for some "outstanding" achievement or another. Find your own taste. Many a so-called expert's sobriquet is mere snobbery. Let your own palate be your guide. Finally, narrow roads, high-speed traffic, random police search points, and breathalyzers don't mix well with wine. Be smart: choose a designated driver, or hop on an inexpensive, informative day tour.

BEHIND THE SCENES

If you don't understand what all the fuss over wine is about (and even if you do), start your Barossa visit with an hour at **The Barossa Wine Centre**, 66-68 Murray St., Tanunda, in the same building as the tourist office. The exhibits make the craft of wine-making and the etiquette of wine-tasting accessible to novices. (☎8563 0600. Open daily 10am-3:30pm. $2.50.) Two wineries offer tours of their vineyards and buildings, focusing on the wine-making process and traditional methods: **Seppelt Winery** on Tourist Rte. 4 in Seppeltsfield (☎8568 6212; tours M-F 11am, 1, 2, and 3pm, Sa-Su 11:30am, 1:30 and 2:30pm. $7, children $2) and **Yaldara**, Gomersal Rd., Lyndoch. (☎8524 0225. Half hour tours daily 10:15am, 1:30, 2:30, 3:30pm. $5.50.) **Wolf Blass Wines**, 97 Sturt Hwy., on the north side of Nuriootpa, also has a small but informative wine heritage museum near its tasting rooms. (☎8568 7311. Open M-F 9:15am-5pm, Sa-Su 10am-5pm. Free.)

BY FOOT

If you're exploring on foot, four wineries just north of Tanunda are connected by the **Para Road Wine Path** (foot or cycle only). On the left side of Barossa Valley Way as you head north out of Tanunda, you'll find the first, the small **Stanley Brothers Winery**. (☎8563 3375. Open M-F 9:30am-5pm, Sa-Su 10:45am-5pm.) Not far away on Para Rd., **Richmond Grove Winery**, on the banks of the small Para River, specializes in Rieslings and has picnic areas among the gum trees. (☎8563 7303. Open daily 10:30am-4:30pm.) Down the Wine Path, **Peter Lehmann Wines** buys grapes from about 200 growers and crushes more than 10,000 tons of grapes every year. (☎8563 2500. Open M-F 9am-5pm, Sa-Su 10:30am-4:30pm.) The last winery on the wine trail, **Langmeil Winery** has a good tasting range in a cellar door dating from the 1840s. (☎8563 2595. Open daily 10:30am-4:30pm.)

TOURS

Most Barossa tours are full-day round-trip outings departing daily from Adelaide in small buses (about 20 people). **Groovy Grape Getaways** is the most popular backpackers tour to the Barossa, visiting 4 wineries, the Whispering Wall, and the world's largest rocking horse along the way. (☎1800 661 177 or 8371 4000. $65. BBQ lunch included. Free pick-up.) If you're less than thrilled about spending a day drinking with 22-year-olds, **Prime Mini Tours** runs two small tours. One hits the major non-wine sights as well as 4 wineries, while the more expensive one concentrates on 5 wineries and a delectable lunch. (☎8293 4900. $59 or $65. Free pick-up.) **Enjoy Adelaide** has been running tours

THE BIG SPLURGE

WINE ON THE MOVE

If you've got some serious cash to burn, check out these splurge options, guaranteed to provide a moving, even uplifting, perspective on South Australia's beloved wine region.

The **Barossa Wine Train** offers upmarket day and overnight tours that connect with train service, enabling visitors to go from train to coach to winery without breaking a sweat. (☎8212 7888. Ultimate Day Tour $139 per person, overnight packages from $325 per person.) Remember: the train can chug, but a wine drinker must *sip*.

Prefer to get high instead? A number of more exotic aerial tours have sprung up recently as well. **Barossa Helicopters** bills its trips as a "photographer's utopia." (☎8524 4209. From $396 per 30min. for up to 4 passengers; no drinking.) **Barossa Balloon Adventures** offers a one-hour flight with "memories that will last a lifetime." (☎8389 3195. $231 per person, children $165; includes champagne breakfast.) **Air Tours South Australia** (☎0419 806 262) can take you from the coast to the Barossa to the outback, starting from $250 per person. Whoever said wine and adventure travel had to be mutually exclusive?

for 16 years. (☎8332 1401. $65, children $38.) If you're staying in the Barossa Valley, **Valley Tours** has a full-day winery and sights tour. (☎8563 3587. $47 including lunch, pick-up and return to Barossa Valley accommodations. Full-day without lunch $39; half-day $28.)

BY CAR WITH A DESIGNATED DRIVER

For those not confined to walking distance, the options seem endless. While you're more likely to see familiar wines at the bigger producers, the small wineries offer a more intimate setting and a better chance to learn about wines from the people who actually make them.

▨ **Rockford Wines** (☎8563 2720), on Krondorf Rd. east of Tanunda. Rockford is a small winery that strongly emphasizes the winemaking history of the region (and beyond) as well as the traditional methods of the Barossa. It is housed in stone cottages that enclose a courtyard where grapes are pressed with traditional barrel-presses. Described as a cult classic, the premium here is on craftsmanship and quality, and Rockford's dedication has led to its ranking as one of the top 10 South Australian Cellar Doors of 2002. Open M-Sa 11am-5pm.

▨ **St. Hallett Wines** (☎8563 7070; www.sthallett.com.au), on St. Hallett Rd., just south of Tanunda. Since 1944, St. Hallett has made every drop of their wine exclusively from Barossa or Eden Valley fruit. Premium red table wines are the specialty; try the flagship Old Block Shiraz, a smoky, full-bodied mouthful. Open daily 10am-5pm.

▨ **Bethany Wines** (☎8563 2086), on Bethany Rd., just east of Tanunda. In a former quarry high above the rest of the valley, the Schrapel family and friendly cellar door staff will make you feel right at home while you sample their acclaimed Shiraz and Riesling. Their sparkling Pinot Noir is deliciously affordable. At vintage time, watch as grapes are dumped into the clifftop gravity-fed crusher that sends the juice to holding tanks below. Open M-Sa 10am-5pm, Su 1-5pm.

Orlando Wines (☎8521 3140), just past Rowland Flat on the road from Gawler to Tanunda, sits on the banks of Jacob's Creek itself and produces Australia's largest wine export brand. Gallery and cellar open daily 10am-5pm. Cafe open daily 11:30am-2:30pm for lunch.

Saltram Wine Estate (☎8564 3344), on the Nuriootpa-Angaston Rd., just outside Angaston. Smooth, fruity, and fabulously decadent, Saltram's Semillon is the stuff of wine dreams. This acclaimed winery has been working on their fantastic reds, whites, and ports since back in 1859; they recently opened the popular gourmet eatery **Salters Bistro** ❺ on-site. Open M-F 9am-5pm, Sa-Su 10am-5pm. Bistro open daily 11:30am-3pm, also F-Sa for dinner.

👁 🎵 SIGHTS & ENTERTAINMENT

Designated drivers, take heart: not every attraction in the Barossa requires drinking. **Mengler Hill Lookout,** on Mengler Hill Rd. east of Tanunda, near Bethany on Tourist Rte. 4, gives a crow's eye view of all those grapes you've been tasting. On the road linking Williamstown and Sandy Creek the **Barossa Reservoir** retains over 4500 Olympic-size swimming pools' worth of water. But its most interesting feature is its famous curved **Whispering Wall,** where sweet nothings can be heard 140 meters away. (Open daily 8am-6pm.)

As if you needed an excuse to drink, festivals abound. Foremost among these is the biannual **Barossa Vintage Festival** (April 2004), a celebration of all things viticultural, including the long-lost barefoot stomping of grapes. The **Barossa Jazz Weekend** occurs annually in August (August 2004) and adheres to a surefire recipe for festival success: wine, food, and good tunes. Every October, the **Barossa International Music Festival** (☎8564 2577) celebrates the arrival of spring.

CLARE VALLEY ☎08

Between Adelaide and the South Australian Outback, the Clare Valley is the final oasis before the earthy tones of the Flinders Ranges take command of the landscape. The valley runs north from Auburn up to Clare along the Main North Rd. and hosts some 30-odd vineyards. The higher altitude gives a respite from some of the lowland heat associated with the Yorke Peninsula, providing the perfect climate for the valley's farmhouse reislings.

🖫 PRACTICAL INFORMATION. Main North Rd. shoots straight through Clare Valley's small center on its north/south trajectory through the region. Running parallel to the Main North Rd. is Old North Rd., one block eastward; the Old North contains some businesses of interest not on the main road. At the north end of town, Farrell Flat Rd. heads east through the hills towards Burra. The **Clare Valley Tourist Information Centre**, 229 Main North Rd., in the town hall, has maps and the *Clare Valley Secrets* booklet. (☎8842 2131. Open M-Sa 9am-5pm, Su 10am-4pm.) Services include a **police station** (☎8842 2711) on Main North Rd. and free **Internet** at the **Clare Library**, 33 Old North Rd., one block east of the post office. (☎8842 3817. Open Tu, W, F 10am-6pm, Th 10am-8pm, Sa 10am-noon.) All the banks along Main North Rd. in town have **ATMs**. The **post office**, 253 Main North Rd., is open M-F 9am-5pm. **Postal Code:** 5453.

🛏🍴 ACCOMMODATIONS & FOOD. Built in 1848, the historic **Clare Hotel ❷**, 244 Main North Rd., may be pricey, but it's also the only pub accommodation in town. Shared rooms are a better deal than the ensuite. (☎8842 2816. Pub rooms with shared bath $22 per person; ensuite motel singles with TV $50; ensuite doubles $55.) The award-winning **Clare Caravan Park ❶**, 3km south of town on Main North Rd., has a lake, pool, and laundry, and is well-located for winery tours. (☎8842 2724. Reception 8am-7pm. Sites $15 per person, powered $20; self-contained cabins for 2 $42-67.50; on-site vans from $35.)

   Price's Traditional Bakery ❶, 269 Main North Rd., has been churning out pies, pastries, and sausage rolls for over a century. (☎8842 2473. Open M-F 8am-5pm, Sa 9am-1:30pm.) The staff of the friendly **Chaff Mill Country Kitchen ❸**, 308 Main North Rd., cooks breakfast, lunch ($6-16), and dinner ($16-22) of the steak and pasta persuasion. (☎8842 3055. Open M and W-Su 10am-9pm. Closed M lunch.) The **Clare Hotel ❶**, 244 Main North Rd. (☎8842 2816), offers $7 daily lunch specials. Clare has two **supermarkets: Foodland,** 47 Old North Rd. (open M-Sa 8am-7pm, Su 9am-7pm) and **IGA,** across from the post office on Main North Rd. (Open daily 8am-8pm.)

🍷 WINERIES OF CLARE VALLEY. The granddad of Clare wines is the famous **Riesling,** though nearly every other grape and wine variety has now gained a foothold. An old railway line, parallel to Main North Rd., has been converted into the 27km scenic **Riesling Trail.** The trail runs between Clare and Auburn and is suitable for walking and biking (2hr. by bike one-way). Convenient carparks in Clare, Sevenhill, Watervale, and Auburn allow walkers to take shorter journeys. The trail passes farms and vineyards, as well a few wineries, including historic Sevenhill Cellars. Bikes can be hired in Clare from **Clare Valley Cycle Hire,** 32 Victoria Rd., in a private house opposite the primary school (☎8842 2782 or 0418 802 077; half-day $16.50, full-day $22), or from Sevenhill Cellars (See below. 4hr. $15, full-day $30.) The tourist office also has info on many mini-bus and private tours, including **Clare Valley Experiences** (☎8843 4169, $120 for 2 hours in a Jaguar or Mercedes and $55 each additional hour) and **Clare Valley Tours** (☎0418 832 812, $40 per person for 4hr.); these tend to be comprehensive but pricey. The tourist office also leads half-day tours on Saturdays that include six wineries ($45).

▨ **Sevenhill Cellars** (☎8843 4222), on College Rd., Sevenhill, 6km south of Clare. Since 1851, the Jesuits at Sevenhill have produced wine for religious consumption, but even atheists will enjoy the impressive range of fine reds, whites, and fortified wines which comprise 75% of the output. There is also a small historical museum and a church with Australia's only crypt. Open M-F 9am-5pm, Sa 10am-4pm.

Leasingham Wines, 7 Dominic St. (☎8842 2785), Clare, just south of the town center. A perennial medal-winner and venerable Clare institution, the winery is graced with a lovely setting, friendly service, and small wine-making museum. Riesling was developed here; their Bastion is crisp, light, and fruity, while the aged Classic Clare is dry and smooth. Open M-F 8:30am-5pm, Sa-Su 10am-4pm.

Taylors Wines (☎8849 2008; www.taylorswines.com.au), on Taylors Rd. just north of Auburn, 25km south of Clare. The largest winery in the Clare Valley and the largest estate on one site in Australia, this winery is housed in an enormous castle look-alike. All wines are made from grapes grown on the estate, and all are bottled onsite. Open M-F 9am-5pm, Sa 10am-5pm, Su 10am-4pm.

BURRA
☎08

Once Australia's largest inland settlement, Burra hosted over 5000 miners and their families and boasted one of the largest copper mines in the world. Today, Burra has resigned itself to living in the past. The town was declared a State Heritage area in 1993 and the old buildings and historical focus lend it a ghostly feel.

Burra is 150km (2hr.) north of Adelaide and 40km (30min.) northeast of Clare on the main route to Sydney via Broken Hill. The highway leads to **Market Square,** at the intersection of Market and Commercial St.; the town is centered around a creek. The **Visitors Centre,** 2 Market Sq., books mining and Clare Valley winery tours. (☎8892 2154. Open daily 9am-5pm.) The Bank SA on Market Square has an **ATM.** There is free **Internet** access at the **library** in the school at the end of Bridge Terr., north of the creek. (Open M, W, F 9am-5pm, Tu and Th 9am-8pm.) The **post office** is on Market Sq., next to the IGA supermarket. **Postal Code:** 5417.

In Burra's early days, many miners lived in extremely modest mud dugouts along the banks of Burra Creek. In the 1840s, to alleviate the problem of occasional floods and improve quality of life for miners and their families, the South Australian Mining Association built the ▨**Paxton Square Cottages ❸,** on Kingston St., on the east side of town. The 32 restored cottages have stone floors, kitchens, fireplaces, and bath. (☎8892 2622. Doubles from $65.) The 154-year-old **Burra Hotel ❷** is in the town center and offers basic pub rooms with an exceptional balcony overlooking the square. (☎8892 2389. Singles $25; doubles $45.) The **Burra Hotel ❶** has lunch specials from $6 and dinners from $8. (☎8892 2389. Open M-Sa noon-2pm and 6-8pm.) Market Square has an IGA **supermarket.** (Open M-F 8:45am-5:30pm, Sa 8:45-11:30am, Su 10am-2pm.)

Burra's premier tourist attraction is the **Burra Passport,** an informative booklet and key that opens eight locked sites and allows visitors as much time as they need to complete the tour. The 11km tourist drive leaves from the town center and passes by all of the attractions. (Base passport $15; full passport with entrance to all 4 area museums $24.) The locked sights are eerily empty and some of them, including the old **Redruth Gaol** (the first South Australian jail built outside of Adelaide and used in the movie *Breaker Morant* in 1979) are downright spooky. Other sights on the tour include the **Unicorn Brewery Cellars,** the old **Burra Smelting Works, Hampton Village** (archaeological remains of an old township), and old **dugout homes** where the first European miners lived.

On the tourist trail out of town, the large open cut of the **Burra Mine,** also known as the **Monster Mine,** illustrates the importance of copper to Burra's history. The mine was one of the world's largest and was last used in the 1970s. The first weekend in March heralds **Jazz in the Monster Mine,** an annual performance held in the mine crater. **Morphett's Enginehouse Museum,** on the site of Burra Mine, details the mechanical aspects of the mine. Be sure to go through the miners' underground tunnel—at a mere 5 feet high, it was just tall enough for the short miners to scamper through en route to work. (Open M, W, F 11am-1pm; Sa-Su 11am-2pm. $4.50, concessions $3.50.) The **Bon Accord Mining Museum** focuses on the social history of the area's mines by telling the stories of individual miners who used to work here. (Open Tu-Th 1-3pm, Sa-Su 1-4pm. $3.50.)

LIMESTONE COAST REGION

Offering much more than limestone, this region boasts two national parks, many smaller conservation parks, a number of quiet seaside towns, and a significant amount of—you guessed it—limestone. The coast has also annexed some inland towns and attractions, such as the area's largest city, Mt. Gambier, and one of the area's star attractions, the caves at Naracoorte.

Though it is best seen by car, **Premier Stateliner buses** (☎8415 5500) pass through the region daily on the Adelaide to Mt. Gambier run. The best place to start any Limestone Coast adventure is at one of the helpful information offices that bookend the region: **The Signal Point Interpretative Centre** in Goolwa in the north (☎8555 3488; open daily 9am-5pm) and the **Visitors Centre** in Millicent in the south (☎8733 3205; open M-F 9am-5pm, Sa-Su 9:30am-4:30pm). Both offer the *Limestone Coast Secrets* information booklet and *The Tattler*, the essential publication covering the Coorong and other area parks.

COORONG NATIONAL PARK

The Coorong is an alluring stretch of white-sand dunes, dry salt lakes, and glittering lagoons. Virtually the only way to access the National Park's northern reaches is by **boat,** which is best attempted from the town of **Goolwa** (see p. 480), at the mouth of the Murray River on the Fleurieu Peninsula. Several tours highlighting the area's bird life operate out of the town of Goolwa, including the popular **Coorong Cruises.** (☎8555 1133. Departs Tu, Th, and Su 9am; returns 5pm. $75, children $45.) **The Spirit of the Coorong** is a boat tour with a more ecologically minded focus. Half-day tours on *The Spirit* depart every week M and Th at noon, while full-day tours depart at 10am W-Su (☎8555 2203 or 1800 442 203. Half-day $67, children $54; full-day $80/$50.)

The sealed **Princes Highway** skirts much of Coorong National Park and passes scenic lookouts all along the way, as well as a number of campgrounds, historic sites, and walking trails; all these are detailed in *The Tattler*. About 5km south of where the Loop Rd. rejoins the Princes Hwy., a marked turn-off for the **■42 Mile Crossing** leads down an unsealed road past the spectral outlines of several lakes 3km to a campsite, from where a 4WD track through the dunes leads to the beach. For those without a 4WD vehicle, this point provides the most convenient **walking access to the beach.**

Campsites ❶ are available at Pranka Point, the 42 Mile Crossing, and along the Loop Rd. and the Old Coorong Rd. The sites at Pranka Point and the 42 Mile Crossing are among the few in the area that have both water and toilets. **Permits** ($6 per car per night) are required for camping and can be obtained via self-registration at most sites or at the Signal Point Interpretive Centre in Goolwa (see p. 480), the Parks Office in Meningie (see below), or the Big Lobster in Kingston S. E. (also see below). For a budget snack, dig into the soft sand at the ocean's edge to find **cockles,** which can be eaten raw.

SOUTH FROM FLEURIEU PENINSULA: PRINCES HIGHWAY

The road from Tailem Bend south toward Mount Gambier runs along the Coorong, providing excellent access to both the wetlands of the coast and the beaches farther south. **Meningie** is the gateway to Coorong National Park (see p. 495) and is a nice place for a quick swim. The **National Parks and Wildlife Service** has an office at 34 Princes Hwy. (☎8575 1200) where you can pick up *The Tattler*, which covers southeastern coastal parks from Goolwa to the Victoria border. **Kingston SE,** Meningie's southern counterpart and self-declared rock lobster capital, is the more interesting of the Coorong's gateways. The town's most famous resident, **Larry the Lobster ①,** is a huge metal and fiberglass hulk towering over a snack bar and **Information Centre** (open daily 9am-5pm) on the roadside at the northern edge of town. **Robe,** 41km farther south and surrounded by water on three sides, is a sleepy little beach town with Victorian buildings and good surf. There is **tourist information** and **Internet** at the **Robe Institute and Library,** on Mundy Terr. (☎8768 2465. Open M-F 9am-5pm, Sa-Su 10am-4pm.) The **Robe Hotel ④,** facing the ocean on Main street, has perfectly decent ensuite and hotel rooms, and the bathrooms are reminiscent of submarines. (☎8768 2002. Hotel rooms $60, ensuite rooms $90.) For a great meal try the smoked chicken pizza with goat cheese, spinach, and garlic ($14.50) at the **Wild Mulberry Cafe ③,** on the main road across from the Robe Garage.

Beachport (pop. 440), 44km south of Robe, is a great place to relax. Buses leave from Rivoli's Deli next to the Bompas Hotel and head to Adelaide (5hr.; M-F at 9am, Sa at 12:49pm, Su at 3:49pm; $45) and to Mt. Gambier (M-F at 1:30pm; Su at 7:58pm; $13). The **Beachport Visitors Centre** is on the western side of town, along Millicent Rd. as you enter. (☎8735 8029. **Internet** $3 per 30min. Open M-F 9am-5pm, in summers also open Sa-Su 10am-4pm.) The friendly **Bompas Hotel ②** faces the water near the jetty in a nicely restored historic building dating from 1876. Ensuite doubles open onto a wraparound balcony with views of the jetty. The backpacker rooms don't have the view but are airy and bright. The **cafe/restaurant** serves good inexpensive meals. (☎8735 8128. Backpackers $20; ensuite doubles $80.) The **Beachport Caravan Park ①,** on the each road past the visitors center, has laundry, a playground, and beach views. (☎8735 8128. Unpowered sites $15, powered $17. Onsite caravan $38.50 in peak season, $33 low season. Cabins $60/$50. No linen provided.) Near the jetty on Main Street, **The Green Room** serves as a video store, surf rental, and takeaway joint. (Gyros $5.50. Open daily 8:30am-8pm.) Beachport's sister city **Southend** (pop. 296) is the gateway to the oft-neglected **Canunda National Park,** which encompasses 9300 hectares of coastal habitat and nearly 50km of coast between Southend and Cape Banks to the south. The park's main attraction in the Southend region is Cape Buffon, from where the **Cape Buffon Loop** traverses the cliff tops and provides some outstanding lookouts (1hr., 2½km). The longer **Seaview Walk** covers the cliffs to the south of Cape Buffon (2.5hr. return, 6km). The **Bevilaqua Ford site ①** has both water and toilets. You can get a permit ($6 per car) by self-registering at the site or at the **Parks Office** (☎8735 6053) in Southend, on Rainbow Rocks Rd. as it heads toward the park. The **Visitors Centre** in **Millicent** is 20km farther south from Southend. (☎8733 3205. Open M-F 9am-5pm, Sa-Su 9:30am-4:30pm.)

MOUNT GAMBIER   ☎08

Mt. Gambier (pop. 21,000) rests on the side of a volcano. Above the city lies the mysterious Blue Lake, a mile-deep lake that sits in the volcano's crater and shimmers with an intense shade of blue through the warmer months of the year, before returning to a bland winter gray hue around March. Beyond its lakes and caves, Mt. Gambier's size makes it a good base for exploring the nearby wineries of the Coonawarra region and the caves of Naracoorte.

▐▌ TRANSPORTATION & PRACTICAL INFORMATION. V/Line buses stop at the Shell Blue Lake service station, 100 Commercial St. W, and run to **Adelaide** daily (☎8725 5037; 6hr., $48.30) via the coastal towns of **Robe, Beachport,** and **Kingston** or via the inland towns of **Naracoorte, Tailem Bend,** and **Murray Bridge;** and Melbourne (7hr.; M-Sa 2 per day, Su 1 per day; $57.40) via the Victorian cities of **Portland, Port Fairy, Warrnambool,** and **Geelong.** Book at the Shell station.

The **Visitors Centre,** in the **Lady Nelson Centre,** has a huge land-locked ship on its front lawn. (☎1800 087 187. Open daily 9am-5pm.) The **library,** in the Civic Centre, has free **Internet** (☎8721 2540; open M, W, F 9am-6pm; Tu 9am-5pm; Th 9am-8pm; Sa 9-11:30am). Internet is also available at the terrific **Jonties Cafe and Cave Internet Lounge,** 15 Commercial St. E. ($5 per hour; open daily 8am-midnight) The **police** are on Bay Rd. (☎8735 1020). The **post office** is at 30 Helen St. (Open M-F 9am-5pm.) **Postal Code:** 5290.

▐ ACCOMMODATIONS. The Jail ❷, off Margaret St., promises to scare wayward visitors straight with a short, voluntary prison sentence. This recently converted prison was "decriminalized" in 1995. The bars on the windows remain, but the atmosphere is far more hospitable now. (☎8723 0032 or 1800 626 844. Dorms $20, 4-share rooms $22 per person, single $33, double $50. Breakfast included.) **Blue Lake City Caravan Park ❷,** on Bay Rd. just south of the lake, is spotless, with a pool, tennis and basketball courts, an 18-hole golf course, and outdoor cooking facilities. It's a 2km downhill walk to the CBD from the caravan park. (☎8725 9856. Sites $18, powered $21; caravans from $63.) The rooms at the **South Australian Hotel ❷,** 78 Commercial Ave. E., on the corner with Compton, are small but clean and the showers are big. (☎8725 2404. singles $20, doubles $40.) The nicest hotel accommodations are at the big old **Mt. Gambier Hotel ❺,** on the corner of Commercial St. and Penola. (☎8725 0611. Double $80; extra person $10.)

▐▌ FOOD & NIGHTLIFE. The Central Business District is packed with chip shops and takeaway joints, supermarkets and greengrocers. A cybercafe with flair, **Jonties ❷,** 15 Commercial St. E., is a great place to catch up on email and grab a great meal. Mains are $11-20. (☎8723 9499. Daily 8am-midnight, dinner stops at 9pm.) For a quality meal that won't break the bank, **Cafe Belgiorno ❷,** on the corner of Percy and Mitchell St., next to the Oatmill complex, is a local favorite. Its wood-fired pizzas ($10) have been annually voted among Australia's best. (☎8725 4455. Open Su-Th 11am-9:30pm, F-Sa 11am-11pm.) **Plants on Sturt ❶,** fittingly on 34 Sturt St., a few blocks off Bay Rd. is a plant nursery that doubles as a coffee shop. (☎8725 2236. Open W-M 10am-4pm.)

Many a drunken stumble has started at **Flanagan's Irish Pub,** on Ferrers St. just south of Commercial St. E., with live music and a lively singles scene Thursday through Saturday nights (open until 1:30am; pints $5). The **Mount Gambier Hotel,** 2 Commercial St. W., has high ceilings, pool tables, and occasional live music and dancing (open until 3am). **Blueberry's,** next to Baltimore's in the Oatmill complex, draws a younger crowd with a dance floor and the pool-hall. (Open until 3am.)

◙ SIGHTS. Bay Rd. goes south through town and meets up with John Watson Dr. to encircle **Blue Lake.** The lake itself fills the crater of a volcano that erupted 4000-5000 years ago and holds nine million gallons of water, which are used as the town's supply. You can only get to the lake's surface by a 45min. tour that goes down to the pumping station in a glass lift. (☎8723 1199. Daily tours hourly Nov.-Jan. 9am-5pm, Feb.-May 9am-2pm, June-Aug. 9am-noon, Sept.-Oct. 9am-2pm. $5.50, children $2.) Just south of the Blue Lake, by the entrance to the Blue Lake City Caravan Park, a road marked "Wildlife Reserve" leads down to a network of

SOUTH AUSTRALIA

walking tracks that access **Mt. Gambier,** the **Devil's Punchbowl,** the now-dry **Leg of Mutton Lake,** and **Valley Lake,** fed by a different source than Blue Lake. The 2.3km walk to the top of the mountain is best attempted in the morning. Those looking for similar views but a shorter hike can follow the signs to the **Centenary Tower** carpark, from where a 20min. walk leads to the tower and sweeping views of the lakes, the city, and the surrounding landscape all the way to the coast ($2; open when flag is flying from the tower).

While the nearby caves at Naracoorte (see below) get all the attention, there are a couple interesting holes in the ground right in the town center. The **Cave Gardens,** at Bay Rd. and Watson Terr., surround the town's original water source and are the centerpiece of the picturesque town square park, which is full of roses and trickling waterfalls (always open, lit at night, free).

About 20km north of Mt. Gambier, just past Panola on the road to Naracoorte, lies the **Coonawarra wine region,** a small stretch of vineyards that suddenly come out of the arid landscape. Twenty wineries in the region, the oldest dating from 1890, offer cellar-door sales and tastings, with a complete listing in the Food and Wine Guide available at the Lady Nelson Centre.

NARACOORTE   ☎ 08

Naracoorte's primary draw is the magnificent network of underground caves that lie 12km south of town. The famed Naracoorte Caves have been named a World Heritage site for their extensive deposits of 500,000-year-old megafauna fossils.

Almost everything is on one of two streets, **Ormerod (Commercial)** and **Smith Street,** running parallel on either side of the village green. From the south, the Riddoch Hwy. from Mt. Gambier leads into town, becoming **Gordon Street** before hitting the Village Green. **Premier Stateliner buses** on the inland Mt. Gambier to Adelaide route pass through town once a day in each direction. Tickets can be bought on the corner of Smith St. and Jones St. at Naracoorte Batteries. (☎8762 2466; 1hr. to Mt. Gambier, 5hr. to Adelaide.) There is a **Visitors Centre** at the Sheepsback Museum, on MacDonnell St. 1km out of town (☎8762 1518 or 1800 244 421; daily 10am-4pm) but all of the brochures can also be found at **Billy Mac's** pub in the Naracoorte Hotel. Services include: **ATMs** and banks in CBD; **library** with free Internet, across from the Naracoorte Hotel (open M 10am-5pm, Tu-W and F 9:30am-5pm, Th 10am-8pm, Sa 8:30am-noon); **police,** 56 Smith St. (☎8762 0466, after hours 131 444; office open M-F 8:30am-5pm); and **post office,** 23 Ormerod St. (open M-F 9am-5pm). **Postal Code:** 5271.

Naracoorte Backpackers ❷, 4 Jones St., a few blocks up the hill from the Village Green, doubles as a workers' hostel; however, the backpackers' standard dorm beds are just as good for those making a brief stopover. (☎8762 3835, or 0408 823 835. Internet $4 per hr. Dorms $22, YHA $20.) The **Naracoorte Hotel-Motel ❸,** 73 Ormerod St., across from the village green, offers your standard-issue hotel rooms with sinks and a nice balcony. (☎8762 2400. Hotel singles $27, doubles $47; motel-style singles $55, doubles $66.) **Bool Lagoon ❷** provides toilets, but no showers, and permits are via on-site self-registration ($15 per car, $7 per motorbike). To camp in the new **campground at the caves ❷,** which come with toilets, showers, and BBQ area, you'll need to get **permits** at the Conservation Park ticket office in the Wonambi Fossil Centre. (☎8762 2340. Open daily 9am-5pm; $18.50 per carload, $10.50 for bikes or motorcycles.)

Maddie's Cafe ❶, on Smith St., is a narrow understated cafe with tasty inexpensive sandwiches ($3-5) and large coffees. The apple and almond slice ($2.50) is divine. In the Naracoorte Hotel, **Billy Mac's ❸** serves typical pub fare and local wines. (Mains $15-20. Open daily for food noon-2pm and 6-8:30pm, later for drinks.) The Foodland **supermarket,** on Ormerod St., is the place to go to make your own meals while in Naracoorte, or to stock up on supplies for camping. (Open M-F 8:30am-8pm, Sa 8:30am-5pm, Su 9:30am-5pm.)

South of town (12km) is the **Naracoorte Caves Conservation Park,** a well-marked 4km west off the Riddoch Hwy. (Rt. 66). Along with the Riversleigh site 2000km away in northwest Queensland, the caves here are one of only two fossil sites in Australia awarded World Heritage protection. The **Wonambi Fossil Centre,** next to the carpark, is the place to buy tickets for cave tours and camping permits. (☎8762 2340. Open daily 9am-5pm.) The **Wet Cave** is the only self-guided cave tour. The most famous of the caves, **Victoria Fossil Cave,** was discovered in 1969, when two cavers wriggled through a tiny passage and emerged in the large chamber where the remains of nearly 100 different species of Pleistocene fauna from 10,000 to two million years ago now rest. **Tours** are available daily 9:30am-4pm on various routes through the area. (Tickets from the Wonambi Fossil Centre. 1 tour $10, concessions $8, children $6; 2 tours $18/$14/$11; 3 tours $24/$19/$14; 4 tours $28/$22/$16.)

YORKE PENINSULA

On boot-shaped Yorke, sandy flats punctuate rolling farmland, and sheer cliffs looming over the hinterland storm into the sea. The northern cuff is defined by a history of copper-mining. Sometimes called the "golden plains," the peninsula's extraordinary fertility has made it one of South Australia's leading grain-producing areas, raking in over $290 million annually. Native scrub still claims the bottom of the penninsula in rugged Innes National Park, where rare birds take refuge from the sweeping wind.

COPPER TRIANGLE ☎08

Known as the Copper Triangle, the northern towns of **Kadina, Wallaroo,** and **Moonta** sprang up as a result of discoveries of large copper deposits in the 1860s. Today, the towns revolve around the seasonal influx of Adelaide weekenders at holidays. Wallaroo (whose name, incidentally, is an approximation of the Aboriginal word for "wallaby urine") is on the ocean, Kadina is the largest and most cosmopolitan, and Moonta plays its Cornish and mining heritage to the hilt.

⊞ ⁊ ORIENTATION & PRACTICAL INFORMATION. Kadina, 50km northwest of Port Wakefield, is the farthest inland. Wallaroo is another 9km west of Kadina on the coast. Forming the bottom of the triangle, Moonta is 17km southwest of Kadina and 16km south of Wallaroo. **Premier Stateliner** runs **buses** from Adelaide via Port Wakefield to all three towns. (☎8415 5555. Buses depart from Adelaide M-F 2 per day, Sa-Su 1 per day. An extra bus returns to Adelaide Friday evenings. $21, concessions $13.) The **Moonta Station Visitors Centre,** on Kadina Rd. in the old railway station, serves the whole Copper Triangle and stocks two helpful tourist guides: the locally produced *Cousin Jack's Guide to the Copper Coast* and the glossier *Yorke Peninsula Secrets.* (☎8825 1891. Open daily 9am-5pm.) The newly opened **Kadina Visitors Centre** has info on the whole Peninsula. (☎8821 2333. Open M-F 9am-5pm, Sa-Su 10am-4pm.) A 2min. walk from the center of Kadina, the beautiful new **Kadina Community Library,** 1a Doswell Terr., offers free **Internet.** (☎8821 0444. Open M 9am-1:30pm, Tu-W and F 9am-5:30pm, Th 9am-8pm, Sa 9:30am-11:30am.) Only Kadina has **ATMs,** the area's **RAA** services (☎8821 1111 or 0418 859 070), and a **police** station (☎8828 1100). There is a **post office** in each town (all open M-F 9am-5pm).

ⁿ⁰ ACCOMMODATIONS & FOOD. For freedom from pubs, refuge can be found at the beautiful █Sonbern Lodge Motel ❸, 18 John Terr., Wallaroo. (☎8823 2291. Singles $28, ensuite $46; doubles $44/$63. Most have balcony. Deluxe motel singles $70; doubles $86.) In Kadina, pub rooms and cheap meals (from $5) can be found at the **Wombat Hotel ❷**, 19 Taylor St. (☎8821 1108. Singles $25; doubles $40; includes light breakfast.) Or try the **Kadina Hotel ❹**, 29 Taylor St., which has very nice rooms and a few exercise machines in the hallway for working off those greasy pub meals. (☎8821 1008. Shared singles $50, doubles $55; ensuite rooms $65/$70. Breakfast included.) In Moonta, the **Cornwall Hotel ❷**, 18 Ryan St. has cheap counter meals and nice rooms. (☎8825 2304. Singles $29; doubles $49; less for longer stays. Meal specials from $6.50.) Caravan parks abound on Yorke, and the Copper Coast has its fair share. There is a park on the beach at Moonta Bay and three along Wallaroo's waterfront, the best of the bunch being the **North Beach Caravan Park ❶**, right on the beach. (☎8223 2531. Office open M-Th 8:30am-6pm, F-Sa 8:30am-7pm, Su 8:30am-5:30pm. No bookings after 10pm. Sites $13, powered $18; self-contained cabins for 2 from $66.)

The entire Yorke Peninsula is famous for its Cornish cuisine, especially the pasty (about $2.50), but only Moonta is bold enough to claim the moniker "Australia's Little Cornwall." **Skinner's Jetty Fish Cafe ❷**, on Jetty Rd., Wallaroo, is a local favorite with fresh seafood and wood-oven pizza—mains start around $10. (☎8823 3455. Takeaway counter open daily 10am-9pm. Dining room open F 6-9pm, Sa 7:30-10am and 6pm-pm, Su 7:30-10am.) Moonta's impeccably kept **Cornish Kitchen ❶**, 8 Ellen St., serves up Little Cornwall's best pasties ($2.20) and other light meals for $3-5. (☎8825 3030. Open daily 8:30am-4pm.) Next door, **La Cantina Cafe ❷**, a combination Italian/Argentinian restaurant, serves pasta and steak. Mains around $15. (☎8825 3253. Open Tu-F 10am-late, Sa 3pm-late, Su 3-9pm.) For **groceries,** try the Woolworths along the Wallaroo Rd. in Kadina (open daily 7am-9pm).

◪ SIGHTS. The award-winning █Banking and Currency Museum, 3 Graves St., in Kadina, is probably the most secure museum in the world, complete with safes, vaults, and alarm systems. From Victoria Sq., walk west on Graves until it ends at Railway Terr. The museum is on the corner. (☎8821 2906. Open Su-Th 10am-4:30pm; closed June. $4, children $1.) Of the area's beaches, **North Beach** in Wallaroo is the best. The beach is just north of the jetty, with signs directing drivers toward the car-accessible beach entrance.

INNES NATIONAL PARK

█Innes National Park is the real attraction of the Yorke. A fantastic spot for surfing, the park is also known as a prime place to spot birds, particularly the Western Whipbird, which was rediscovered in the area in 1962 and is responsible for the area's designation as a national park. Buses go no farther than **Warooka**, west of Yorketown, and Stenhouse Bay is more than 50km farther, requiring a car for any measure of flexibility in exploring the park. A **day-pass** costs $6.50 per vehicle or $4 per motorcycle (fee waived if camping) and can be purchased from the **Visitors Centre** or from the self-registration station near the entrance to the park.

The **National Park Visitors Centre** (☎8854 3200. Open M-F 9am-4:30pm, Sa and Su 10am-3:00pm), at Stenhouse Bay, sells day-passes and camping permits and has guides for walking, driving, fishing, and surfing in the park. The **Innes Park Trading Post,** just inside the park entrance, includes a **general store** and **petrol station,** can refill scuba tanks, and has up-to-the-minute info on fishing and surfing. The attached **Rhino Tavern ❷** has nice views and mains from $12. (☎8854 4066. Store open daily 8am-9m, tavern serves meals daily noon-2pm and 6-8pm, open for drinks 11am-10pm.) Innes spreads its several **campsites ❶** around prime locations in the park. No bookings are required for sites in the park; register at the Visitors Centre or at one of the self-registration bays. Sites at **Pondalowie Bay** and **Casuarina** have water and toilets (Pondalowie $10.50 per vehicle, Casuarina $15.50). All other camping areas cost $6.50 per vehicle. There is also a **caravan park ❶** in Marion Bay just before the park entrance. Several **lodges** and **huts** are available in the historic ghost village of **Inneston;** contact the Visitors Centre for bookings. Near the park entrance, the **Stenhouse Bay Lodge ❶** is a cheaper option for single travelers. Book across the road at the Trading Post. (☎8854 4066. $10 per person.)

There are seven well-marked walking trails in the park ranging from 10min. to 2hr. in duration (pick up the *Innes Walking Trails* brochure at the Visitors Centre). Highlights include the layered limestone cliffs and spectacular views at **The Gap,** views of the Althorpe Islands from **Chinaman's Hat,** and the sunset views from **West Cape,** which overlooks Pondalowie Bay. **Snorkelers** should head to Cable Bay. The **Stenhouse Bay Fishing Charter** can be hired for 3-5 people for a full-day fishing trip (☎8854 4052, $120).

FLINDERS RANGES

The Flinders Ranges may not be as well-known as the Himalayas or the Andes, but these ancient peaks belong in the pantheon of awe-inspiring ranges. The main road (Hwy. 47) drifts between kangaroo-filled flatlands and sagebrush-covered hills. Dirt-tracks (4WD-only) lead through beautiful gorges. The Flinders are most popular from April to October, when the nights are chilly and the days sunny. It's hot in summer, but for drivers with A/C or hardcore hikers, it's worth the trip. The Ranges begin at the northern end of the Gulf of St. Vincent and continue 400km into South Australia's northern Outback, ending near Mt. Hopeless.

◥ TOURS

Many tours heading from Adelaide to Alice Springs stop in the Flinders Ranges. **Wallaby Tracks Adventure Tours,** run by the Andu Lodge in Quorn, picks up in Port Augusta or Adelaide and leads tours into central Flinders, including bushcamping and stops at Wilpena Pound, Aboriginal art sites, and Bunyeroo Gorge. (☎8648 6655 or 1800 639 933. 2-3 days $199-299.) **Quorn Flinders Ranges Eco-Tours,** 2 Railway Terr. (☎8648 6016), offers 4WD tours into **Dutchman Stern Conservation Park** (half-day $58) and northern Flinders tours (5 days). Self-drive tours are also available; inquire at Quorn's **Mill Motel,** 2 Railway Terr. (☎8648 6016), or at the Visitors Centre. **Adelaide Sightseeing** offers a one-night jaunt to Wilpena Pound. (☎8231 4144. $352.) **Wayward Bus,** 237 Hutt St., Adelaide, has an eight-day tour covering the Flinders and Coober Pedy. Travelers bus to Coober Pedy, then travel to the William Creek Pub and back south through the Flinders and the wine valleys. (☎8232 6646. $858, including meals and accommodation.) **Outback 'n' Coastal 4WD Adventures** has three-day Flinders camping trips. (☎0417 856 712. $330, max. 7 people.)

PORT AUGUSTA ☎08

Located at the intersection of Hwy. 1 and Hwy. 87, Port Augusta (pop. 14,800) is a common stop for travelers from Adelaide heading west toward the Nullarbor, or north to Coober Pedy and Alice Springs.

The **bus station** is opposite the library on Mackay St. Most action is on **Commercial Road,** with **post office, banks,** and **ATMs.** Services include: **Tourist Information Office,** 41 Flinders Terr., in the Wadlata Outback Centre building (☎8641 0793; open M-F 9am-5:30pm, Sa-Su 10am-4pm); **RAA** (☎8641 1044) **National Parks and**

SOUTH AUSTRALIA

Wildlife Service, 9 Mackay St. (☎8548 5300); and the **library,** on the corner of Mackay and Marryatt St., with free **Internet.** (☎8641 9151. Open M and F 9am-6pm, Tu-W 9am-8pm, Th 9am-9pm, Sa 10am-1pm, and Su 2-5pm.)

The **Bluefox Lodge ❷,** at the corner of Trent Rd. and Hwy 1., offers free pick-up from the bus station and a lounge with a pool table and videos. Owners also arrange car and 4WD hire, buy, sell, and rent quality camping gear at very reasonable prices (tent and stove $10 per day; used tents sold for $90), and book Outback tours. (☎8641 2960. Dorms $17; doubles and twins $42.) **Port Augusta International Backpackers ❶,** 17 Trent Rd., though not fancy, is ridiculously cheap, with free pick-up, laundry, bicycle use, and breakfast. There's also a bread machine for baking. (☎8641 1063. Dorms $11.) Coles **supermarket** is on the corner of Jervis and Maryatt St. (☎8641 1700. Open daily 6am-9pm.)

Visitors with any time to spare should check out the ■Wadlata **Outback Centre,** 41 Flinders Terr. Their excellent hands-on display of the stories, culture, and land of the Outback deserves a thorough exploration. (☎8642 4511. Open M-F 9am-5:30pm, Sa-Su 10am-4pm. $9, concessions $5.50, families $20.) The **School of the Air,** 39 Power Crescent, on the east edge of town, is an amazing foray into distance learning that began in 1958. (☎8642 2077; www.oac.sa.edu.au. Half hour tours M-F 10am. Donation $2.) Another highlight is the fascinating **Arid Lands Botanic Gardens,** 400m north of town off the Stuart Hwy., which has bushwalking trails with labeled plants. (☎8641 1049. Open M-F 9am-5pm, Sa-Su 10am-4pm. Free.)

SOUTHERN FLINDERS

MT. REMARKABLE NATIONAL PARK

Near the industrial town of **Port Pirie,** Mt. Remarkable National Park (15,632 hectares) is the pride of the southern Flinders. Here the arid north meets the wetter south and the flora and fauna blend together. The area is perfect for laid-back bushwalking, camping, and animal watching, not to mention a couple of winding drives that serve as a gentle introduction to the Flinders Ranges. The summit of **Mt. Remarkable** can be approached from the east on a 4hr. return hike from a trail starting 3km north of **Melrose,** along Main North Rd. The **Alligator Gorge trail** (1.2km; 1hr. return) has the best scenery on the eastern side of the park. **Alligator Gorge** is accessible at Wilmington, on Main North Rd. between Clare and Port Augusta, or by the **cross-park trail** (26km; 10hr.) from Mambray Creek.

The **park headquarters** is on the western side of the park at Mambray Creek, 45km north of Port Pirie, directly off Hwy. 1 on a road lined with magnificent eucalypts. There is a pay station with trail maps, a 54-site **campground ❶** with water, toilets, BBQ, picnic areas, and access to bushwalks through canyons or over ridges. There is a simple **cabin** for 4 at Mambray Creek that can be rented through the park service. Bring your own bedding and food, and book ahead. The rangers quarters at Alligator Gorge can also be rented. Call the park service for rates and bookings. (☎8634 7068. Park fees $6.50 per vehicle, $15.50 per vehicle to camp in high season, $10.50 off peak, motorcycles $7.50/$5.50; bushcamping $4 per person.) Bushcamping is prohibited during the fire ban season, from Nov. 1 to Apr. 30. **National Parks and Wildlife** (☎8634 7068), in Port Augusta, has more details.

Infused with the delicious menthol scent of eucalypt forests, the hamlet of **Melrose,** on the eastern side of the park 20km south of Wilmington, is the oldest town in the Flinders and sits peacefully in the shadow of Mt. Remarkable, making a good base for hikes in the park. **Bluey Blundstone's Blacksmith Shop ❺,** 30-32 Stuart St., is a blacksmith shop from 1865, but most customers are drawn more for the coffee shop and barn-turned-B&B, all centered on a flowery courtyard. (☎8666 2173. Cafe open M and W-F 11am-4pm, Sa-Su 10am-5pm. Singles $77; doubles $95,

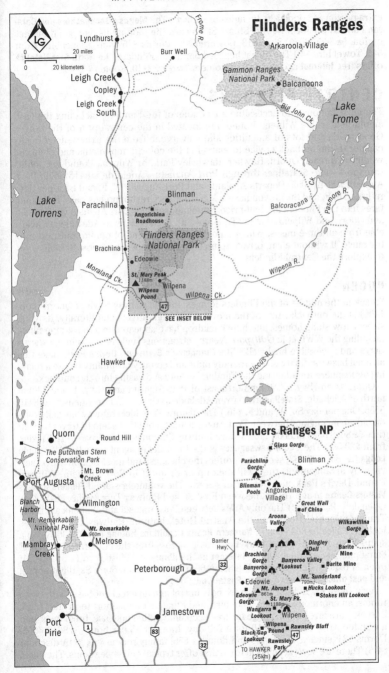

Flinders Ranges

Lyndhurst

Burr Well

Arkaroola Village

Leigh Creek

Copley

Leigh Creek South

Gammon Ranges National Park

Balcanoona

Big John Ck.

Lake Frome

Lake Torrens

Parachilna

Blinman

Angorichina Roadhouse

Balcorcana Ck.

Pasmore R.

Frome R.

Brachina

Flinders Ranges National Park

Edeowie

St. Mary Peak 1188m

Wilpena

Wilpena Pound

Wilpena Ck.

Wilpena R.

47

SEE INSET BELOW

Moralana Ck.

Hawker

Siccus R.

47

Quorn

Round Hill

The Dutchman Stern Conservation Park

Port Augusta

Mt. Brown Creek

Blanch Harbor

Wilmington

1

Mt. Remarkable National Park

Mt. Remarkable 960m

Mambray Creek

Melrose

Barrier Hwy.

Peterborough

32

Jamestown

Port Pirie

1

83

32

Flinders Ranges NP

Glass Gorge

Parachilna Gorge

Blinman

Blinman Pools

Angorichina Village

Great Wall of China

Aroona Valley

Wilkawillina Gorge

Dingley Dell

Barite Mine

Brachina Gorge

Bunyeroo Valley

Barite Mine

Bunyeroo Gorge

Bunyeroo Lookout

Edeowie

Mt. Sunderland 790m

Mt. Abrupt 861m

Hucks Lookout

Stokes Hill Lookout

Edeowie Gorge

St. Mary Pk. 1188m

Wangarra Lookout

Wilpena

Wilpena Pound

Rawnsley Bluff

Black Gap Lookout

Rawnsley Park

47

TO HAWKER (25km)

SOUTH AUSTRALIA

extra person $42; kids $20. Includes breakfast.) The **Melrose Backpackers and Cara-van Park ❶,** on Joe's Rd. off Stuart St. toward the mountains, is a good budget option. (☎8666 2060. Sites $13, powered $16; dorms $15; vans $35; cabins from $45. Towel hire $4.) The oldest licensed bar in the Flinders, the **North Star Hotel ❹** offers free **Internet** access to all customers. (☎8666 2110. Rooms $45-60.)

CENTRAL FLINDERS

The most famous and accessible attractions of the Flinders, including the vast amphitheater-like Wilpena Pound, are located in the central part of the range. Good roads and lots of amenities allow everyone from the experienced bush-camper to the outback novice to marvel at the colorful mountains and plentiful wildlife. To reach Quorn, Hawker, Rawnsley Park, or Wilpena Pound via public transport, take **Stateliner** through Port Augusta. (Adelaide ☎8415 5555; Port Augusta ☎8642 5055. Departs Adelaide and Port Augusta W, F, and Su 1 per day; returns Th, F, and Su.) If you have a McCafferty's/Greyhound bus pass, Stateliner fares into the Flinders are half-price. Stateliner services Port Augusta via Hawker and Quorn and Wilpena Pound (Th-F and Su). Connections to Adelaide are available from all three buses. Wilpena Pound marks the end of public transport into the range. If without a car, private tours offer the cheapest and most flexible ways to explore the Central Flinders.

QUORN   ☎08

Smack in the middle of the Flinders Ranges, the old railway town of Quorn (pop. 1400) is the outback town of the movies, both figuratively and literally. Its wide streets, low-slung homes, and hilly backdrop have appeared in at least nine films, including the WWII epic *Gallipoli.* Nearby attractions such as the stunning **Warren Gorge** and accessible bushwalks like **Dutchman's Stern** and **Devil's Peak** make this an ideal base for daytrips. The friendly pubs and country hospitality create a relaxing atmosphere for admiring the Flinders' beauty and easing into the outback.

Quorn is on Hwy. 47, 40km northeast of Port Augusta and Hwy. 1, and 340km north of Adelaide. **Stateliner** runs from Adelaide to Quorn via Port Augusta. (☎8415 5555. One per day Su, W, and F. $46.) The historic **Pichi Richi** railway has daily runs on old steam engines between Port Augusta and Quorn that seem to travel back in time (☎8648 6598 or 8658 1109. Quorn Railway Station is on Railroad Terr. Tickets from $29-58.) The **Quorn Newsagency** is the local ticket agent (☎8648 6042). **Andu Lodge** (☎1800 639 933; see below) offers the cheapest and most flexible travel service; by arrangement, they will pick-up or drop-off in Port Augusta, Wilpena Pound, Devil's Peak, and Dutchman's Stern. The volunteer-staffed **Flinders Ranges Visitors Centre** is at 3 7th St., between First St. and Railway Terr. (☎/fax 8648 6419. Open daily 9am-5pm.) The only **ATMs** between Port Augusta and Wilpena are in the Transcontinental Hotel and the Austral Hotel, both on Railway Terr. Services include: **Police** (☎8648 6060); **Northern Roads Conditions Hotline** (☎1300 361 033); a sparsely-stocked IGA **supermarket** on 7th St., across from the info office (open M-F 8am-6pm, Sa-Su 9am-4:30pm); **Internet** at the **library,** on West Terr. (☎8648 6101; open M 8:30am-4pm, Tu and F 8:30am-6pm, W-Th 8:30am-5pm, Sa 10am-noon); and **post office,** 21 Railway Terr. **Postal Code:** 5433.

Andu Lodge ❷, 12 First St., is a friendly hostel and an excellent base, with clean rooms, an enormous kitchen, bike hire, and Flinders tours. Short-term staff (min. 2 weeks) are hired in exchange for free accommodation, bike use, breakfasts, and a Flinders trip. Bike hire $10 for a full-day, Internet $5 per hour. (☎8648 6655. Dorms $24; singles $34; twins and doubles $55; family rooms $80; YHA discount $4-5) There are several **hotels** in town that offer typical pub-style rooms. The **Quorn**

Caravan Park ❶, at the east end of Silo Rd., offers caravan park basics plus some sad-looking caged kangaroos at the entrance. (☎8648 6206. Sites $15, powered $18.50; vans $36; cabins from $59.) There are also unpowered **camping ❶** sites in **Warren Gorge,** a beautiful spot 14km northwest of town off the Arden Vale Rd.; check with the Visitors Centre.

The **Quandong Cafe and Bakery ❶,** 31 First St., offers home-cooked food in a pleasant little dining room that doubles as a gallery for local artists. (☎8648 6155. Open Tu 9:30am-3pm, W-Su 9:30am-4pm. Breakfast $8, sandwiches and salads from $5.) The town houses a tasty Thai takeaway (meals $5-9) inside the **Buckaringa Better Buy Market ❶,** also on 1st St., an emporium for everything from beach toys (not much use here) to computer joysticks (circa 1989). The market also offers high priced Internet. (☎8648 6381. Open M and W-Sa 9am-7pm. Internet $7.70 per hour.) For sit-down meals, the **Criterion Hotel ❶,** Railway Terr., offers the cheapest specials in town ($6) with all-you-can-eat salad bar (open daily noon-1:45pm and 6-7:30pm), and $2 schooners; the other **pubs ❶** around town also offer quality meal specials from about $7.

With the trail base only 9km from town, Quorn has one of the most rewarding easy hikes in the area: **Devil's Peak** (2hr. return) affords stunning 360° views across the Flinders region. Hikers who climb **Dutchman's Stern,** a bluff 10km north of Quorn, are rewarded with views of **Spencer Gulf.** Two main walks include a ridge-top hike (8.2km; 4hr. return) and a loop walk (10½km; 5hr.). Another 10km north of Dutchman's, the stunning **Warren Gorge** is home to a number of short hikes and scrambles but is best known as a prime spot to view yellow-footed **rock wallabies. Mt. Brown Conservation Park,** 16km south of town on Richmond Valley Rd., contains the usually dry **Waukerie Falls** and **Mt. Brown.** Allow at least seven hours for the roundtrip to the summit and back. (Open Apr.-Nov.)

WILPENA POUND & FLINDERS RANGES N.P.

Wilpena Pound, in the Flinders Ranges National Park, is the stuff of legends—this is some of the best scenery in South Australia. The Pound looks like a huge crater, but is actually a hilly syncline (geological downfold) outlined in jagged quartzite faces, a remnant valley surrounded by much higher mountains. The surrounding national park offers spectacular views and challenging hikes.

Most of the tours through the Flinders stop by Wilpena Pound. You can also take the **Stateliner bus** (☎8415 5555) to the Pound from Adelaide (7hr.; Su, W, and F 1 per day; $65) or Port Augusta (departs Su, W, and F 1 per day; returns Th, Su, and F 1 per day; $32). In an **emergency,** contact the Visitors Centre (see below) or the **Wilpena Pound Resort** (☎8648 0004; open 24hr.) to be connected to emergency services. The helpful **Wilpena Visitor Centre** is the park's headquarters, offering general park and hiking info, day-passes ($6.50), camping permits (day and camping passes can also be done via self-registration stations at the park entrances), and bookings for scenic flights, 4WD tours, and horse tours. (☎8648 0048. Open daily 8am-6pm. Flights start at $75 for 20min.) There's a **general store** just behind the Centre with a limited supply of camping essentials, slightly pricey **petrol,** an **ATM,** and **Internet** access. (Open daily 8am-6pm. Internet $6 per 30min.) Visitors should leave **pets** at home: the park is full of fox traps laced with a chemical produced by Australian plants that is harmless to native animals but lethal to foxes and dogs.

Camping ❶ is available in the park and can be paid for at the Visitors Centre or via self-registration stations (sites $10.50 per vehicle). A few sites have toilets and water. For a shower, hit the refurbished **Wilpena Campground ❶,** next to the Visitors Centre. (Check-in at the Visitors Centre. Sites for two $16, powered $22, extra person $4.) The **Wilpena Pound Resort ❷** operates a restaurant, bar, pool, campground, and upscale motel down the road from the Visitors Centre. The resort has rooms with A/C and TVs, even in their backpacker accommodation. Bar meals are tasty and cheaper ($9-15) than the restaurant ones. (☎8648 0004 or 1800 805 802. Restaurant open daily 7:30-9am, noon-2pm, and 5:30-8:30; bar open 5pm-late. Linen $5. Dorms $22; doubles from $95.)

To explore **Wilpena Pound,** you must sweat or spend a bit, since no cars are allowed into the Pound itself. No worries, it's less than 1½hr. to the viewing platforms, from where the 8km long by 4km wide floor stretches below. For any walk, advise someone of where you're going and for how long; also make sure to sign the logbook at trailhead info boards. The brochure, *Bushwalking in the Flinders Ranges National Park*, is available at the Visitors Centre. Almost all the hikes leave from the Visitors Centre and follow the same path for the first 2km. After the trail climbs a bit, it crosses a creek and then leads to **Hill's Homestead,** a cabin with toilets. A short, steep walk up **Wangarra Hill,** behind the homestead, leads to the lower (10min.) and upper (20min.) lookouts over the Pound. A shuttle **bus service** from the Visitors Centre cuts 2km off the trip each way, leaving you about 1km from Hill's Homestead (1.6km from lookout) and making it a 90min. excursion up to Wangarra and back (4-6 buses per day; $4 return). The view from the lookouts provide a good sense of the immensity of the Pound but for a better view, the rocky trail to **St. Mary's Peak** (15km return, 6hr.; longer loop 20km return, 8hr.), a high-intensity climb for serious hikers, will yield the most spectacular views.

The Pound is not the park's only attraction. Seventeen trails branch off throughout the area, each more stunning than the last. Pick up a walking guide from the Visitors Centre and explore on your own. Many visitors take the 50km 🚗**drive** through the park's gorges, with their sheer, colored walls and harsh geological ramparts, more beautiful than the walk into the Pound itself, with the stretch through **Bunyeroo Gorge** and **Brachina Gorge** as its highlight. For those heading north to Parachilna, Leigh Creek, or the Oodnadatta Track, this is the most fun way to get back to the paved Hwy. 47, which you will rejoin 20km south of Parachilna, at the outlet of Brachina Gorge. The turn-off for the gorges is 4km north of the Wilpena junction on the road toward Blinman.

NEAR FLINDERS RANGES NATIONAL PARK

RAWNSLEY PARK STATION. Rawnsley Park Station (☎8648 0030), south of the park off the road between Wilpena and Hawker, is an outdoor enthusiasts paradise, offering horseback riding (min. 2 people; $45 per hr.; $60 per 2hr.; half-day $100), scenic flights (min. 2 people; 20min. from $65; 45min. from $100), 4WD tours (half-day $80; full-day $115 includes lunch), mountain bike hire ($10 per hr., half-day $30, full-day $50), and sheep shearing on school holidays, ($10.) The station also has a licensed restaurant and a full range of **accommodations ❷.** (Sites $16, powered $23; on-site vans for two $45; cabins for two $65. Ensuite from $80 for two, $100 with linen.) Swimming pool, camp kitchen. **Internet** access is available at the remote outpost as well. ($2 per 10min.)

PARACHILNA. The best way to get to Parachilna, just north of the park, is to drive the 4WD track out the back of the park via Brachina Gorge, joining Hwy. 83 just south of town, but it's also possible to get there on paved Hwy. 47. The 🏨**Prairie Hotel ❺**, pretty much the sole attraction in town, is impressive despite it's self-consciously touristy feel. Those without the cash to dish out for a spacious bi-level room (some christened by Harvey Keitel or Cate Blanchett) can rest assured that they'll still catch all the perks at the **Parachilna Overflow ❷,** the backpacker accommodation across the street. Backpackers enjoy the sparkling pool, a newly renovated kitchen, bar area with Internet, and rooms with A/C, though the large moths in the bathrooms can be somewhat unsettling. (☎8648 4814. Sites from $10; dorms $25; cabin singles $35, doubles $65. Deluxe rooms in the hotel, singles from $130, doubles from $145-260.) The hotel owners lead several tours of the area, from scenic flights ($45 for 15min.) to quad bike tours through shifting sand dunes (starting at $55 per person.)

BLINMAN POOLS. The 32km drive from Parachilna to Blinman is an unsealed, rocky road that passes through the spectacular **Parachilna Gorge** and past stunning scenery (4WD preferable; cars with low clearance will have a rough trip). The hostel at **Angorichina ❶**, halfway between Parachilna and Blinman, was created as a refuge for returned soldiers suffering from tuberculosis. It has a general store with **petrol** and tire repair, as well as bike hire. (☎8648 4842. Store open M-Sa 8:30am-6:30pm, Su 9:30am-6:30pm. Sites for $7 per person, powered $8; dorms $10-22; cabins $30-65; linen $6. Bike hire $25 for half a day, $40 full-day.) From the carpark, a rough hike to the spring-fed ▓**Blinman Pools** (6km return; 5hr.) follows Blinman Creek as it winds its way back towards two separate waterfalls. Better trail markings were in the works early in 2003, so the trail may be quite improved. Pick up a walking guide from the shop.

BLINMAN. At the crossroads where the road from Parachilna meets the road from Flinders National Park, Blinman is one of the few outcroppings of civilization in the Flinders that actually deserves the categorization of "town." The **Blinman Hotel** has lovely ensuite rooms with TV and A/C and touts a luxurious heated indoor pool. Those more interested in roughing it can opt for the campsites or bushcamping. Their **restaurant** has reasonable prices and good food; the native pepper leaf roo fillet goes for $18. They also book flights and 4WD tours. (☎8648 4867. Doubles $90, extra person $20. Powered sites $10, bushcamping around $5. 40min. flight $120 per person, price goes down for more than 2 people.) The town also has fuel, a general store, and lovely little **tea rooms** open from April to November in the town's old schoolhouse. The historic **old mine** site is reachable by a 1hr. trail just outside of town.

NORTHERN FLINDERS

If you've made it here you're one of the rare few who have reached the proverbial pot of gold at the end of the rainbow. Sage green shrubs dot the foreground while orange hills fade to red, blue, and purple mountains in the distance. And if you happen upon this

THE BIG SPLURGE

PRAIRIE HOTEL

Though you may at first think it merely a hallucination of your desert-addled mind, the **Prairie Hotel** in Parachilna is a true outback oasis that offers both budget and luxury accommodation, as well as innovative cuisine that's surely the best for hundreds of miles in any direction. The hotel's rustic elegance is the perfect treat after a day of churning up dust on Outback roads. The hotel itself features the original pub-hotel building, completely renovated, plus a spacious and beautifully modern new wing, as well as a landscaped courtyard and fantastic restaurant. Film crews shooting movies or 4WD commercials (the Flinders provide the perfect terrain for showing off that cornering power) often stay in the luxury section. The friendly folks at the hotel can also book 4WD and Camel tours for you, as well as set you up with accommodations on a working cattle station.

The hotel's scrumptious and multi-award winning **restaurant** does wonderful things with outback meat, offering a delicious emu burger ($15), a meat-lovers pizza ($13), and a feral mixed grill ('roo, camel, emu, goat $24). The scene in the bar can get rambunctious, and it stays open until the crowd decides to leave.

☎8648 4844; info@prairiehotel.com.au. Food served noon-8:30pm. Luxury singles from $120.

rugged landscape after a rare rainfall, thousands of yellow flowers blanket the normally dry ground. This is where the vastness of the Australian Outback hits home, as the mountains grow ever larger, the gorges ever deeper, and human company ever scarcer. Summer months can be stiflingly hot, but spring and winter are marked by warm days and cool desert evenings. To cover the couple hundred kilometers between **Flinders Range National Park** and **Gammon Ranges National Park**, drivers can either come up through **Wilpena** (see p. 505) and **Blinman** (see p. 507) or stick to the highway from Hawker and follow the paved road as far as Copley. The stops described here are along that highway, though the dirt-road route to Gammon will show you what the back of beyond is really about.

Travelers looking to head north of Gammon and Arkaroola will require a **Desert Parks Pass**. For info, call the Desert Parks Pass Hotline (☎ 1800 816 078) or talk to the rangers at Balcanoona in Gammon Ranges Park or at the Parks Office in Port Augusta (☎ 8648 5300). The pass costs $80, is good for a full year, and allows unlimited access to the Simpson Desert, Innamincka, Lake Eyre, and Dalhousie areas, among others. It comes with a packet of brochures and great regional maps. Call the **Road Conditions Hotline** (☎ 1300 361 033) before setting out.

LEIGH CREEK   ☎ 08

After Coober Pedy, Leigh Creek is the largest town in the state north of Port Augusta. The town, 22km south of the coalfield, was entirely planned and built by the **Electricity Trust of South Australia (ETSA)** between 1979 and 1984, and it shows. Bizarrely sterile, the town consists of gently curving residential streets lined gravel "lawns," all clustered around one central shopping center.

The **Visitors Centre** is near the supermarket in the central mall. (☎ 8675 2723. Open M-F 9am-5pm, Sa-Su 10am-2pm.) The landscaped downtown area has a **pub** and a well-stocked **supermarket** (open M-F 9am-5:30pm, Sa 9am-12:30pm). **Leigh Creek South Motors** has **petrol**, tires, showers, and toilets. (☎ 8675 2016. Open M-Sa 8am-8pm, Su 9am-8pm. Showers $3.30.) The **Leigh Creek Hotel ❺** in town isn't cheap, but all rooms are ensuite, with TVs, telephones, and fridges. (☎ 8675 2025. Singles $75; doubles $85.) The **Caravan Park ❶** is towards the highway on the outskirts of town. (Sites $11, powered $17; cabins from $70.) Leigh Creek is near the Oodnadatta Track (see p. 515). There's also a 50m community pool in town. (☎ 8675 2147. Open daily noon-9pm. $3, kids $1.50.) The **coalfield,** providing much of the economy for the dwindling town, is still in operation to the north and is open for tours. Book at the Visitors Centre.

GAMMON RANGES NATIONAL PARK

This is where central Australia gets serious. The 128,228 hectares of the Gammons are even more craggy, exotic, stunning, and isolated than the southern Flinders. The local Aboriginals, who co-manage the park with the National Park Service, call the area Arrkunha, or "place of red ochre," which describes the deep colors of the mountains. While there are hiking trails and some short 2WD-accessible roads in the Gammons, the park is best explored on unsealed 4WD tracks. Wilderness experience is a must, and you should be sure to bring enough food, water, and emergency supplies to remain self-sufficient during your stay. The ▨**4WD Loop Road** (70km; 4-5hr.) is a great introduction to off-roading and the easiest way to see the park's scenery. Keep an eye out for rare animals, like the yellow-footed rock wallaby and the wedge-tailed eagle, as well as more common ones, such as kangaroos, emus, and feral donkeys. Check in at the **NPWS** headquarters in **Balcanoona,** where the rangers have info on bushcamping and bushwalking, along with maps, brochures, and the **Desert Parks Pass** (see p. 508). There are also public **toilets,** rainwater-fed **showers,** and a **pay phone** in Balcanoona. It is important to plan ahead, as the Ranger Station is not always staffed. (Park office ☎8648 4829. Office usually open daily 8-9am.) For **emergencies** contact the Leigh Creek Police (☎8675 2004), Hawker Police (☎8648 4028), or the Wilpena Parks Office (☎8648 0049, mobile 0429 690 382). Less experienced nature-lovers can camp at **Italowie Camp** or **Weetootla Gorge,** both accessible via 2WD and connect with shorter trails (2km-16km) at the park's fringe. **Cabins** are operated by the parks service: the **Balcanoona Shearer's Quarters ❶,** at the ranger station in Balcanoona, can sleep up to 19 people in rustic but comfortable rooms centered on a communal kitchen and lounge. (Dorms $12; no linen.) **Grindell's Hut ❶,** on the 4WD loop and accessible only via 4WD, is a beautiful self-contained cabin in the middle of the park. (Cabin for eight $75.) **Nudlamutana Hut ❶** is on the park's north side. (Cabin for four $53.) For all the huts, make reservations through the Parks Office in Hawker (☎8648 4244) and pick up keys at the Balcanoona office. **Lake Frome,** 38km east of Balcanoona (4WD only), features sprawling lake-beds covered in glistening salt. No access is allowed after 3pm, when the area becomes a designated Aboriginal hunting ground.

ARKAROOLA

A 610 square-kilometer private conservation park, Arkaroola abuts the northern boundary of Gammon Ranges National Park and is reachable only through the park. The **Arkaroola Wildlife Sanctuary** is an amazing example of land reclamation and showcases stunning terrain. Founders Reg and Griselda Sprigg turned an abused-sheep station overrun with non-native flora and fauna into an almost entirely reclaimed refuge for native plants and animals. The **ridgetop tour** ($66) is a highlight of the Flinders—experience a geology lesson on the go as you climb impossibly steep roads in a specially constructed open top 4WD vehicle, stopping periodically to take in the view of the ancient granite mountains. ($65. Runs twice daily for 2 or more people.) There are several **self-drive 4WD tracks** in the preserve as well as **scenic flights** (from $88 per person). **Arkaroola Village ❶,** a mountain-oasis just 32km north of Balcanoona, has a tourist office, campsites, and a motel. (☎1800 676 042 or 8648 4848; www.arkaroola.on.net. Reception open daily 7:30am-6:30pm. Sites $15, powered $15; caravan park cabins $30 include no linen, furnished lodges for 2 from $65 to $145.) There is also a general store, with an eclectic assortment of goods from smoked oysters to motor oil, a **petrol** station, and the only **restaurant ❷** for many miles (mains from $12).

OUTBACK SOUTH AUSTRALIA

North and west of the Flinders, the Australian Outback surpasses legend and becomes dirt real. If you've ever wanted to go off the grid, this would be the ideal place to do it. The epitome of "Big Sky Country," here in the outback unsealed roads stretch out endlessly, crossing baked earth that your car will tease into a maddening cloud of dust. Intimidating signs read "Next gas: 454km" or "Danger: extreme conditions ahead," and the only living creatures along the way are the wandering cattle and soaring eagles. This is a land of rare oases and abandoned railroad tracks. It takes a tough (or slightly crazy) kind of person to live in this kind of place, someone who's not afraid of being alone. For most, a drive through from one end to the other is enough, but take your time and the dust will start to get under your skin. Prime tourist season in the Outback is from April to October, with peak season in the winter months, particularly July; summers are hot, with temperatures reaching 45°C (113°F) in the shade, and swarms of bush flies a constant presence. Two pamphlets are available for drivers planning a trip: *Driving*

Safely in the Outback, put out by the Tourism Board of South Australia offers vague hints in many languages and is available in major tourist centers. More helpful but harder to come by is *Remote Travel Hints for 4x4 Tourists*, put out by Four Wheel Drive Australia, offering simple tips for novice drivers. Also see **The Great Outdoors** (p. 72) for safety tips.

STUART HIGHWAY: ADELAIDE TO COOBER PEDY

As the Stuart Hwy. winds its way north and west toward the opal capital of the world, there is little to see other than the harsh red, arid terrain. This is pasture land, most of which is unfenced, so look out for free-roaming sheep and cattle. In the more remote areas north of Port Augusta, fuel prices will increase the farther you venture into the Outback, so it's a good idea to stop off in **Port Augusta** or **Pimba** before heading on into the baked red unknown. Throw a jerry can full of fuel into your trunk while you're at it—besides saving a few bucks, it can be a long way to a gas station if you run out.

WOOMERA

Originally designated a "secret" town by the Australian and British militaries, Woomera was created in 1947 as the unofficial capital of the **Woomera Prohibited Area**, a long-range weapons testing area that once covered nearly 270,000km²; the site is still the largest land-locked military test site in the entire world. The pre-planned village of Woomera, 7km north of Pimba, sits at the edge of the Area, known affectionately as "the range" by the locals. Joint European and Australian forces created the village, the location of which wasn't revealed on maps until the 1960s, and from 1970 to 1999, the American military was the primary partner in the Joint Defence Facility-Nurrangar, a satellite and missile tracking center. Reassuringly, the base is currently geared more toward satellite launching than bomb testing.

With a history like this, it's not surprising that the **Woomera Heritage Centre,** on Dewrang Ave. in the middle of town, professionally details the nuclear bombs, radio astronomy, and families of Woomera's unusual past. In an interesting juxtaposition, the centre is also home to a ten-pin bowling alley. (☎ 8673 7042. Open daily 9am-5pm. $3.)

The town itself has a hotel, **caravan park ❶**, big **supermarket,** and a **petrol** station. In another example of strategic (and some point out, unfortunate) positioning, the Woomera Refugee Detention Centre, opened in 1999, holds families of potential immigrants for months or even years as they await approval or deportation. Many find the Detention Centre nothing more than a misnamed jail. The immigration museum in Adelaide details some of the hardships faced by this new wave of immigrants.

GLENDAMBO

Glendambo, located 250km southeast of Coober Pedy, is the last stop and final **petrol** station before the famed mining town. The multi-purpose BP service station here runs both the **motel ❺**, the lone backpacker accommodation, and the **campsites ❶**. (☎ 8672 1030 for the motel, 8672 1035 for bunkhouse info. Caravan park sites $14.50, powered $18.50, shower $2.50; dorms $16; $10 key deposit, linen and pillows not supplied; motel singles $82.40; doubles $84.60.) About 100km north of Glendambo, the highway doubles as an emergency landing strip for the Royal Flying Doctor Service.

COOBER PEDY   ☎ 08

Supporting 80% of the world's opal industry, Coober Pedy, the "Opal Capital of the World," is like nowhere else on earth, making for an interesting (and popular) stop on the long, dry haul between Alice Springs and Adelaide. Over half of the 3500 residents live underground in homes almost invisible from the outside. To escape the extreme temperatures, which can reach 50°C (122°F) in the summer and plunge on winter nights, homes, churches, and businesses are carved out of the earth. The town owes its name to Aboriginal observation of this abnormal behavior: "coober" means "white man," while "pedy" means "hole in the ground." Nearly everyone in town is connected to the opal trade, which creates an unusual state of affairs. Disputes between miners are rarely resolved by the police. Instead a suspected opal thief may awake to find his car or home blown up. Despite its somewhat wild feel, the town is a remarkable example of diversity. Over 47 nationalities are represented in the area school and race relations are surprisingly smooth. Nowhere else in the world can you sit underground with a philosophizing jackeroo, surrounded by glinting opals. In short, Coober Pedy is not to be missed.

> **DON'T WALK BACKWARD.** Outside town boundaries, 1.5 million **abandoned mine shafts** make the danger of carelessly stepping backward and plummeting to your death very real. Signs around town, though co-opted by the tourist industry, are no joke; do not explore opal fields by yourself. Techniques of mining make it difficult to fill in the holes, so they are left open and uncovered.

TRANSPORTATION. McCafferty's/Greyhound (☎13 14 99 or 13 20 30) makes daily runs to Coober Pedy from Adelaide and Alice Springs. Virtually every tour between Adelaide and Alice stops off in Coober Pedy. The Stuart Hwy., running north-south across the country, goes straight through Coober Pedy. **Budget** (☎8672 5333; 4WD from $99 per day) and **Thrifty** (☎8672 5688; 2WD $99 per day), at the Desert Cave Hotel, rent cars. **Taxis** (☎0408 893 473) are also available.

ORIENTATION & PRACTICAL INFORMATION. Coober Pedy is 685km (6-8hr.) south of Alice Springs, 730km southeast of Uluru, 166km west of William Creek and the Oodnadatta Track, 538km north of Port Augusta, and 846km (8-10hr.) north of Adelaide. The turn-off from the Stuart Hwy. leads into **Hutchison Street**, the main street and location of virtually every establishment. The roundabout at the top of the hill in town makes a good landmark. The helpful **Tourist Information Centre** (☎8672 5298 or 1800 637 076; open M-F 8:30am-5pm) is at the south end of Hutchison St., across from the bus depot, but most people start at the unofficial tourist office, **Underground Books**, on Post Office Hill Rd. just off Hutchison St., which serves as the booking agent for tours. (☎8672 5558. Open M-Sa 8:30am-5:30pm, Su 10am-4pm.) Other services include: **ATM** at Westpac Bank and at the Opal Inn Hotel; **police**, on Malliotis Blvd. (☎8672 5056); **RAA** (☎8672 5230), at Desert Traders; **pharmacy** on Hutchinson St. across from the Umoona Mine (☎8672 3333; open M-F 9am-6pm, Sa 9am-2pm); IGA **supermarket** on Hutchison St. (Open M-Sa 8:30am-7pm, Su 9am-7pm.); and a **post office** (☎8672 5062) in the miners' store. **Postal Code:** 5723.

ACCOMMODATIONS & FOOD. **Radeka's Backpacker's Inn ❷**, at Hutchison and Oliver St., at the base of the hill after the roundabout, is a clean, comfortable maze of underground "caves" 6½m below ground. There are no doors, but the underground rooms are cool in the summertime and also infuse your Coober Pedy experience with authenticity. (☎8672 5223 or 1800 633 891. Kitchen, pool table,

THE HIDDEN DEAL

FORE!

Budget travelers, take heart: *Let's Go* has found a golf course within your price range. And this is no ordinary course: players never have to worry about replacing divots, they never hit trees, they needn't drive little carts, they never land in the rough, and water hazards are nowhere in sight.

Impossible? Nope. Welcome to golf in the Outback, where land is cheap, water precious, and grass nonexistent. The desolate plain may be hard, flat, almost treeless, and bone-dry, but that hasn't stopped Coober Pedy from installing an 18-hole course. There's not a scrap of fairway or tinge of bright green in sight, and so the greens fee is quite literal: $10 gets you a small square of green astroturf. Carry it around and set it down whenever it's time to take a whack at the ball. Regular cars are allowed on the course, though golfers must give right-of-way to cars when the fairway doubles as the road. Smart golfers use fluorescent orange golf balls both for visibility and because bearded dragons on the course mistake the white balls for their own eggs and steal them. Plaid pants still remain optional.

Just west of Coober Pedy on Seventeen Mile Rd. Green hire $10; club hire $10.

Internet $2 per 10min., TV room, bus pick-up and drop-off, and the cheapest bar in town. Linen $2. Dorms $24; doubles $55. Motel singles $80, doubles $90. VIP/YHA/NOMADS take off $2.) **Riba's Underground Camping ❶** is on William Creek Rd., outside of town. Coming from Port Augusta, turn off 4km before Hutchison St. (☎8672 5614. Above-ground sites $6, subterranean sites $9, powered sites $14.) The swankiest spot in town is the **Desert Cave Hotel ❺**, opposite Radeka's on Hutchison St. Equipped dugout rooms (TV, couch, phone, wine) are accompanied by a swimming pool, gym, and cafe/restaurant/bar. (☎8672 5688. Doubles $182.)

Run by an immigrant Sicilian family, **John's Pizza Bar ❶**, located in the strip mall on Hutchison St., serves great pizza for $6-10. (☎8672 5561. Open daily 10am-10pm.) **Traces ❶**, on the roundabout, serves terrific Greek food and has a nightly backpacker special for $10. (☎8672 5147. Open daily 4pm-late, with occasional music in the evenings.) The **Temptation Cafe ❷**, in the same complex as Underground Books (see above), has everything from curry ($11.50) to nachos ($8) in a relaxed environment. (☎8672 5871. Open Tu-Su 8:30am-5pm.)

🔲 **TOURS. Radeka's Desert Breakaways Tours** is popular with backpackers. The tour includes many stops around town and the opal fields, a trip out to the Breakaways, and a chance to noodle for your own opals. (☎8672 5223. Daily at 1pm. 4½hr.; $30.) The **Desert Cave Hotel's Tour** offers a similar trip for more money. (1800 088 521. Daily at 2pm.) **Riba's Evening Mine Tours** takes guests into a mine for a 1½hr. tour. (☎8672 5614. Daily 7:30pm. $14.) **Martin Smith's Night Sky** tours take advantage of the crystal clear night skies around Coober Pedy for some astronomy lessons and star gazing. (Book at Radeka's ☎8672 5223 or any accommodation. www.martinsmithsnightsky.com.au. 1½hr. $22, kids $11. For those who want to see a little more of the Outback, a scenic flight booked through **Wrightsair** might be the answer. (☎8670 7962. Local flights $45; Lake Eyre flights $135. Book at Underground Books.) **Dave Burge's Lunch at the Lake Day Tour** is a full-day tour that covers some 500km, including Lake Eyre, guided by a 35-year Coober Pedy resident. (☎8672 5900; www.backofbeyondtours.com. Departs daily 8am. $130, includes lunch and snacks.) For an unforgettable look at the Outback, join the mail carrier on the 12hr. 🔲**Mail Run** that covers a triangular route stopping at points of interest while delivering mail to cattle stations along the route. (☎1800 069 911 or at Underground Books ☎8672 5558. Departs M and Th 9am. $110. Book ahead.)

DON'T FENCE ME IN Meryl Streep's woeful cries of "the dingoes ate my baby!" in the 1988 film *A Cry in the Dark* (based on an infamous Australian child murder case in the late 80s) would have been cut short if only she had lived south of the longest fence in the world, located just outside Coober Pedy. Stretching for 5600km from Queensland through the northwest corner of New South Wales and over to Penong, SA at the start of the Nullabor Plain, the structure known as the **Great Dog Fence** delineates "dingo country," keeping the wild dogs firmly in the north. The fence, completed in 1940, is mostly 6-foot-high wire matting but around bigger cities is electrified. "Sheep country," to the south, is separated from "cattle country," to the north.

Though more than twice as long as the Great Wall of China, each part of the Great Dog Fence is regularly maintained and repaired by full-time dog fencers dotted along the route. Occasionally, though, the dingoes break through the fence, panicked cries of "the fence is down" ring through the local towns, and soon mangled sheep carcasses are found dotting the landscape.

◘ SIGHTS. The **Omoona Opal Mine and Museum**, is a not-to-be-missed landmark located on Hutchinson St. The complex is actually an award-winning multi-focused museum with displays on local Aboriginal culture, town history, and, of course, opals. The underground complex includes a full-sized underground home contrasting early and modern dugout styles. Check out the display dedicated to Eric the Plesiosaur, a sea-dwelling dinosaur whose fossilized skeleton (as well as the remains of his last supper) turned to opal. Eric himself is on display at the Australian Museum in Sydney. The mine tours next door allow visitors to go fossicking for their own opals. (☎8672 5288; www.omoonaopalmine.com.au. Mine and museum open daily 8am-7pm.)

The town's **underground churches** are usually open to visitors. The oldest of these churches is the **Saints Peter and Paul Catholic Church**, next to Radeka's. Another sort of underground shrine is **Crocodile Harry's Crocodile's Nest**, the lair of the legendary womanizer, adventurer, and crocodile-slayer who was the model for the character Crocodile Dundee. About 6km west of town on Seventeen Mile Rd., the walls of Harry's home are covered with underwear, graffiti, and photos of a much younger Harry wrestling crocodiles the size of dinosaurs. ($2 entry.) Outside town, **The Breakaways** are a set of flat-topped mesas. The track on **Moon Plain** (70km return; 2hr.), a post-apocalyptic lunar landscape of glinting rocks and the occasional browned piece of vegetation, is fun to explore. You can still see tracks where the cars from the film *Mad Max III* raced, as well as drive along the road where Priscilla the campervan traveled with a drag queen on the roof in the movie *Priscilla, Queen of the Desert*. The famous **Great Dog Fence** is about 15km outside of Coober Pedy (see **Don't Fence Me In**, above).

❒ OPAL SHOPPING. Coober Pedy is glinting with opal pushers and their wares, but not all are quality. Decent opals will give off multiple colors beyond the base color as you turn it in the light. The greater the intensity of these secondary colors, the better the opal. Doublets are the cheapest way to buy opal. Triplet stones are doublets with a protective cap of quartz. Solid opal is the priciest and highest quality. As all men know, size doesn't necessarily matter, and smaller opals are often of better quality. When buying, choose an opal store that's particularly well-lit; dim stores may be hiding flaws. Educating yourself about the stones before rushing off to buy is also a good idea. The **Umoona Opal Mine**, on Hutchison St., has informative displays and offers tours of a decommissioned opal mine (☎8672 5288. Open daily 8am-7pm. Four tours per day. $8, children $4.)

OFF THE STUART HIGHWAY: OODNADATTA TRACK

The ◪**Oodnadatta Track**, one of the most famous outback tracks in Australia, runs 619km from Marree, north of Leigh Creek in the Flinders, through William Creek and Oodnadatta to Marla, 235km north of Coober Pedy on the Stuart Hwy. Without a doubt a great way to see the heart of the outback, the track reminds visitors of the harsh realities of life in the center. The horizon shimmers like a mirage in the heat, and carcasses of cars that didn't make it home join animals met a similar fate. After rare rain the entire track can close, cutting residents off from the rest of civilization. Mostly follows the route of the *Old Ghan* train line that used to connect Alice Springs with points south, the trail passes the vast salt-beds of **Lake Eyre,** immense stretches of baked red nothing, ruins of ancient farm homes, and the legendary Dog Fence. The unsealed road can usually be driven (carefully) in a 2WD vehicle, though most do it in a 4WD; ask about road conditions in Marla or Marree before taking off, or call the **Northern Road Conditions Hotline** (☎1300 361 063). Regardless of your vehicle, the best advice is to slow down: the faster you go, the higher the likelihood of multiple flat tires.

MARREE. A mostly unsealed 120km northwest of Leigh Creek, **Marree** is the official starting point of both the **Oodnadatta** and **Birdsville Tracks.** The former heads northwest to the Stuart Hwy., while the latter slicing through the **Sturt Stony Desert** and parts of the **Strzelecki Desert** to the northeast en route to far western Queensland. The town possesses a surfeit of outback charm: locomotives from the *Old Ghan* dominate the town center, children play on the dusty football/cricket grounds, where not a single blade of grass is to be found, and the Afghan section of the town cemetery and the reconstructed ruins of a mosque uphold the memory of early Muslim cameleers. The Camel sundial made from old railway sleepers on the edge of town records the lumbering hours.

The **Marree Hotel ❸** is a friendly repository of outback history and was itself built in 1883. (☎8675 8344. Dinner from $12. Singles $40; doubles $65, families $90.) The **Drover's Rest Tourist Park ❷,** on the south side of town, perfectly fits the stereotype of a dusty outback caravan park, complete with a dusty old man on the front stoop and a dusty old dog chasing cars. (☎8675 8371. Sites $10, powered $20; budget rooms from $18, plus $5 for linen; on site vans $35; cabins for 2 from $60.) The old telegraph station next door to the hotel is now the **Oasis Cafe,** providing Internet access, tire repair, the cheapest **petrol** in town, and maps of the area. (☎8675 8352. Internet $2 per 10min. Open daily 7:30am-7pm.) The **Marree General Store,** which doubles as the **post office.** (☎8675 8360. Store open daily 8am-8pm; post office open M-F 9am-4pm.) **Postal Code:** 5733.

LAKE EYRE. Lake Eyre, 90km northwest from Marree contains Australia's lowest point at 39 feet below sea level. As Australia's largest salt lake, it acts as the drainage for an area approximately the size of Western Europe. Usually dry, it's especially impressive after a heavy rain. The Oodnadatta Track brushes up against the southern edge of **Lake Eyre South,** the smaller of the Lake's two parts, and a brief detour lets you drive right up to its salty edge. The two access roads to the larger **Lake Eyre North** are 4WD only, and depart from Marree (94km to the lake) and from a turn-off on the track 7km south of William Creek (64km to the lake). **Campsites ❶** are available near the lake on both access roads; passes are available at the Marree General Store or at the self-registration stations at the Lake Eyre National Park entrances (day-pass $10; overnight pass $18; free with Desert Parks Pass). The **NPWS info line** (☎1800 816 178) provides lake conditions. Take the weather into account before going, as temperatures up to 50°C (122°F) in the summer can make it unwise and unpleasant to visit.

WILLIAM CREEK. The next watering hole is 204km northwest of Marree at **William Creek** (technically on Anna Creek cattle station, which is the world's largest at nearly half the size of Tasmania), where airplanes can land and taxi right to the town's only substantial building, the ▧**William Creek Pub ❶**. Covered with signs and bedecked with visitors' bras, boxers, driver's licenses, foreign currency, and various other curiosities, this is the idiosyncratic Outback pub you've been looking for. (☎8670 7880. Linen $5. Sites $3.50; bunks $14; ensuite singles $35, doubles $60, kids are half price.) The pub also has **fuel** and tire repair. The new **Dingo Cafe and Caravan Park** sits nearby and has a coveted espresso machine (☎8670 7746 or 8670 7963). Drivers can head east to Coober Pedy directly from William Creek (164km east). **Explore the Outback Camel Safari** (☎8672 3968 or 1800 064 244; www.aust-camel.com.au/explore.htm) lets you spend 4 days seeing the Outback from the back of an ornery camel.

OODNADATTA. Oodna is yet another tiny outback settlement 203km northwest of William Creek, but it has precious amenities, including **car repair** facilities and the unmistakable **Pink Roadhouse ❶**, which offers valuable info on the area, **fuel**, groceries, and emergency supplies. Longtime owners Adam and Lynnie are happy to help each and every traveler who passes through. Check road and weather conditions with Pink's or with the **police** (☎8670 7805). The roadhouse also has a **post office** and accommodations. (☎1800 802 074 or 8670 7822. Open daily 8am-6pm. Sites for 2 $14.50, powered $20; ensuite cabins for 2 $80; hotel-style doubles $45; backpackers "shack" $10 per person.) They can also arrange car repairs and vehicle recovery. From here, you can either continue northwest on the track to its end at Marla (210km) or head southwest to Coober Pedy (195km). Oodna is also a good base to the beautiful oasis at **Dalhousie Springs** (190km north) and the expansive **Simpson Desert**, both popular destinations (**Desert Parks Pass** required for both; see p. 507). Pink's puts out a thorough ▧**mudmap** guide to the Oodnadatta Track which includes every detour and detail a traveler could desire. Try to pick it up before you go (if you call their tollfree hotline they will mail one to you), but if that's not possible be sure to check their website (www.biziworks.com.au/pink).

MARLA. Marla, where the Oodnadatta Track rejoins the known world, is an overgrown highway rest area that sits approximately halfway between Adelaide and Alice Springs. The **Traveller's Rest Roadhouse ❸** has **petrol**, a small **supermarket** (both open 24hr.), a bar, a restaurant, and pricey accommodations (☎8670 7001. Camping $5 per person, powered sights $12 per person; backpacker accommodations $20 and $30, budget cabin singles $30, doubles $40; TV-less motel singles $70, doubles $75, with TV add $10). For those heading north towards Uluru and Alice, get fuel here: your next petrol station will be **Kulgera,** 180km north just over the Northern Territory border.

EYRE PENINSULA

Stretching the definition of the word "peninsula" the region encompasses the long plain of the Nullarbor as far as Border Village in the west, but the real Eyre is the triangle from Ceduna to Port Lincoln to Whyalla. Tourists are cajoled into a 295km detour from the dull Eyre Highway with promises of a "Breath of Fresh Eyre."

The region's economy is dependent on the sea; Port Lincoln's fishing fleet is the largest in the Southern Hemisphere. Pick up the free "Seafood and Aquaculture Trail" guide, which maps out 12 tours highlighting the importance of the sea to the local economy—from learning to fillet King George whiting in Port Lincoln to abalone tours in Streaky Bay.

⬛ TRANSPORTATION

Premier Stateliner (Adelaide ☎ 8415 5555, Ceduna ☎ 8625 2279, Port Lincoln ☎ 8682 1734, Whyalla ☎ 8645 9911) is the only public **bus** carrier on the Eyre with frequent service, though Greyhound stops in Ceduna on the way to Perth. Stateliner runs between Adelaide and Whyalla (M-Th and Sa-Su 5 per day, F 6 per day; $41). Buses also leave Adelaide bound for Port Lincoln, stopping in towns along the eastern coast (depart Adelaide M-F 2 per day, Su 1 per day; depart Port Lincoln daily 2 per day; $72). Stateliner runs an overnight bus from Adelaide to Ceduna via Streaky Bay (depart Adelaide Su-F 1 per day; depart Ceduna daily 1 per day; $84). **By car,** traversing the Eyre Peninsula means diverging from the inland Eyre Hwy. (Hwy. 1), which runs 468km across the top of the peninsula from Whyalla to Ceduna. The highlights of the Eyre are on a triangular coastal route via the Lincoln Hwy. and Flinders Hwy. (Alt. Hwy. 1), which takes 763km to connect the same two towns.

WHYALLA   ☎ 08

It's easy to be ambivalent about Whyalla, the main eastern city of the Eyre Peninsula. Even its name is unsure of itself. Some brochures say Whyalla is Aboriginal for "place of the water," but others have it meaning "I don't know." That about sums it up. The town was once a thriving city of nearly 35,000, but since the 70s shipbuilding, steelworks, and heavy industry have declined—and so has the population. The town is working hard to cultivate the industry of tourism and Whyalla is now the self-styled Cuttlefish Capital of the World. The **Whyalla Tourist Centre** is on the east side of the Lincoln Hwy., next to the enormous ship that houses the Maritime Museum. (☎ 8645 7900. Open M-F 9am-5pm, Sa 9am-4pm, Su 10am-4pm.) The **Westland Shopping Centre,** on the corner of McDouall Stuart Ave. and Nicholson Ave., has two **supermarkets** and a food court. **ATMs** abound on Forsyth St. in the city center. The **library,** in the Civic Centre on Patterson St., just off Darling Terr., has **Internet.** (☎ 8645 7891; www.whyalla.sa.gov.au. Open Tu-W and F 10am-6pm, Th 10am-8pm, Sa 9am-noon.) **RAA** is at 33 Forsyth St. (☎ 8645 4404 and 0418 827 698.) Monarch ChemMart, in the Westland Shopping Centre on Nicolson Ave., offers **pharmacy** services. (☎ 8645 5045. Open daily 9am-9pm.) The **post office** is on Darling Terr. (☎ 13 13 18. Open M-F 9am-5pm.)

Friendly **Hotel Spencer ❸,** on the corner of Forsyth St. and Darling Terr., has pleasant ensuite rooms with TV, fridge, and A/C. (☎ 8645 8411. Singles $28-33; doubles $44.) The **Whyalla Foreshore Caravan Park ❶,** on Broadbent Terr., is 2km from the post office and close to the beach. (☎ 8645 7474. Sites $12, powered $16; on-site vans for 2 $28; cabins for two $44-53.) Tours of the Onesteel **Whyalla Steelworks** takes visitors to the heart of Whyalla, passing the blast furnace, coke ovens, and rolling mill on the way. (Two hour tours M, W, and F at 1:30pm. Book at the Visitors Centre, ☎ 8645 7900.) From May to August hundreds of thousands of the bizarre **Giant Cuttlefish** spawn near Whyalla. The cuttlefish belongs to the same family as squid and octopus but has the ingenious ability to change shape, texture, and color in seconds to blend in with its surroundings. Whyalla has seized upon this unlikely creature as its mascot and offers visitors the unique opportunity to see hundreds of them in easy shallow eco-dives. (Check out the website www.cuttlefishcapital.com.au.)

FLINDERS HIGHWAY: WHYALLA TO PORT LINCOLN

As Alt. Hwy. 1 speeds along the west coast, the road hosts a few dots of civilization tucked away in seaside breaks from the leisurely rolling plains. The quiet, friendly towns of **Cowell, Arno Bay, Port Neill,** and **Tumby Bay** are good places to stop and rest.

All four have **pub hotels ❸** (singles around $30; twins and doubles $40), **caravan parks ❶**, small **supermarkets, petrol stations,** and **post offices. Cowell,** 111km south of Whyalla, offers one of the safest and best fishing areas in South Australia at its **Franklin Harbour,** as well as a thriving oyster industry and the nation's only commercial jade mining. Tourist information is available at the **Town Council Office** on Main St. The **Franklin Harbor Hotel ❸**, 1 Main St., has clean rooms and a balcony overlooking the harbor. (☎8629 2015. Singles $30; doubles $40. Continental breakfast included.) The **Commercial Hotel ❸**, 24 Main St., offers similar accommodations. (☎8629 2181. Singles $30; doubles $40.) The tiny fishing town of **Tumby Bay,** 50km north, offers the cheapest option in the region, the **Seabreeze Hotel ❶**. (☎8688 2362. Singles $15, with ensuite $40; doubles $30/$50.)

PORT LINCOLN   ☎08

At the southern tip of the Eyre Peninsula, breezy and busy Port Lincoln (pop. 13,000) lords over **Boston Bay,** the second-largest natural harbor in the world. Port Lincoln was to be the state capital, but inadequate fresh water destined today's politicians for Adelaide instead. The town has done just fine, though, building itself into Australia's premier aquaculture center as well as the exporter of the largest tonnage of commercial fish in the country, worth more than $40 million dollars a year. Tuna is especially important to the city, evidenced by its annual Tunarama Festival over the Australia Day weekend, which sees the crowning of the Tunarama Ambassador.

Premier Stateliner buses depart from their booking office, across from the Pier Hotel on 24 Lewis St., a half-block south of Tasman Terr. (☎8682 1288; open M-F 8am-6:45pm, Sa 8:30-11:30am) and run to Adelaide via Port Augusta (Su-F 2 per day, Sa 1 per day. $50 to Port Augusta, $72 to Adelaide. Book ahead). For a **taxi,** call ☎131 008 or 8682 1222. The spacious **Visitors Centre,** 3 Adelaide Pl., across from the Post Office, offers local info as well as hotel bookings and permits for nearby parks. (☎8683 3544 or 1800 629 3544; www.visitportlincoln.net. Open daily 9am-5pm.) The **library,** in the Spencer Institute of TAFE building, just off Tasman Terr., has free 1hr. **Internet** sessions. (☎8688 3622. Open M-Tu and Th-F 8:30am-5pm, W 8:30am-8pm, Su 1-5pm.) The Port Lincoln **Hospital** is on Oxford Terr. (☎8683 2200, emergency after hours 8682 2273.) Sampson & Schultz **Pharmacy** is at 43 Tasman Terr. (Open M-F 9am-5:30pm, Sa 9am-noon and 7-8pm, Su 10am-12:30pm and 7-8pm.) **Banks** and **ATMs** can be found on Tasman Terr. and Liverpool St. Other services include **police** (☎8688 3020), **RAA** (☎8682 3501), and a **post office** at 68 Tasman Terr. (Open M-F 9am-5pm.) **Postal Code:** 5606.

The Pier Hotel ❷, at the center of Tasman Terr., offers adequate rooms, some with bay views, and the stumble-home convenience of having the raucous epicenter of Port Lincoln nightlife downstairs. (☎8682 1322. Singles $25, ensuite with TV $35; doubles $30/$45. Live music Th-Sa until late.) Though not quite as central, the **Hotel Boston ❷**, on King St. near the silos at the west end of Tasman Terr., features slightly nicer rooms. Queen Elizabeth II stayed here when she visited in 1954. (☎8682 1311. Singles $25, ensuite with TV $35; doubles $35/$60.) The glitzy **Grand Tasman Hotel ❹**, on the corner of Bligh St. and Tasman Terr., has ensuite rooms with TVs at inflated prices. (☎8682 2133. Singles $50; doubles $65.) **Kirton Point Caravan Park ❶**, at the end of London St., has a waterfront setting 3km from the town center. (☎8682 2537. Sites $8 per person; powered sites $19; cabins from $29.) The "doorstop" sandwiches on thick crusty bread ($8) are excellent at **Cafe Chino ❶**, 42 Tasman Terr. (☎8682 5509. Open M-F 9am-5pm and Sa 9am-2pm.) The **Cafe del Giorno ❷**, 80 Tasman Terr., offers light Italian meals and scrumptious pizza for $8-12. (☎8683 0577. Open daily 9am-10pm.) Many **pubs ❶** offer dinner specials from $6. Coles **supermarket** is on Liverpool St. (Open M-Sa 6am-6pm.)

Port Lincoln is home to the one-of-a-kind **Tunarama Festival,** a four-day extravaganza of fireworks, sand castles, and seafood held annually on the Australia Day long weekend in late January. The festival also features live music, a rodeo, and a highly competitive tuna-tossing contest. (☎ 1800 629 911.) The **Mediterraneo Festival,** held annually over the Easter long weekend, focuses on the fresh seafood and fine wines of the region, with cooking expositions and live music. For a truly unique experience, take the popular tour of the **Port Lincoln Seahorse Farm,** 5 Mallee Crescent, Australia's only sea horse breeding facility. (☎ 8683 4866, bookings 8683 3544; www.saseahorse.com. Tours 30min., daily 3pm. Book through the Visitors Centre. $5, children $4.) To get the insider's view of Port Lincoln's lifeblood, try the **Fishing Industry and Aquaculture Tour** at the marina. The tour includes viewing live rock lobsters and exploring a working prawn trawler. (☎ 8683 5100, bookings 8683 3544. 90min. tours M, W, F, Sa 10:30am. Begins at the Port Lincoln Leisure Centre. $6, concessions $4, families $15.)

COFFIN BAY   ☎ 08

A mere 47km from Port Lincoln toward Ceduna, you'll find the lazy town of **Coffin Bay,** gateway to the magnificent **Coffin Bay National Park,** 17km west of the main highway. This peninsular park is a remote beach heaven; surfers, picnickers, and pelicans coexist peacefully among the dunes, estuaries, and bays. **Yangie Bay** (15km from the entrance), **Almonta Beach** (16km from entrance), and **Point Avoid** (18km from entrance) are all accessible with 2WD, while 4WD vehicles can drive onto **Gunyah Beach** via a road through the dunes and reach the more remote areas of the park, such as **Black Springs** (28km from entrance), **Sensation Beach** (50km), and **Point Sir Isaac,** the westernmost point in the park (55km). **Bushcamping ❶** is allowed only at designated sites, all of which have toilets and limited rainwater supply. Camping permits and maps are available at the park entrance. (Entry $6 per car; camping $6 per car.) Tourist info is available from **Beachcomber Agencies** on the Esplanade in Coffin Bay. (☎ 8685 4057. Open daily in summer 8am-7:30pm; in winter 8am-6:30pm.) **National Parks and Wildlife Service** (☎ 8688 3111), in Port Lincoln, has further info, as does the Port Lincoln Visitors Centre.

The **Coffin Bay Caravan Park ❶** is on the Esplanade in Coffin Bay. (☎ 8685 4170. Sites $15, powered $19; on-site vans for 2 from $28; cabins for 2 from $45.) The **Coffin Bay Hotel/Motel ❺,** just south of town on the road toward the park, is a bit pricey, but it's the only hotel option in town and it has one of the town's few **ATMs.** (☎ 8685 4111. Singles $65; doubles $75.)

The ▨**Mount Dutton Bay Woolshed ❶** is 52km northwest of Port Lincoln and 22km southeast of a tiny town called **Coulta.** The historic building, with backpacker accommodations in the back and a museum in the front, is right on a beautiful waterfront. (From the direction of Port Lincoln take Farm Beach Rd. from Flinders Hwy.; from Ceduna, take Brookaburra Rd. ☎/fax 8685 4031. Museum open M-Sa 10am-5pm; $3. Sites $12; dorms $17. B&B doubles from $110.)

CEDUNA   ☎ 08

Ceduna (pop. 3800) is civilization's last watering hole before the arid westward trek across the Nullarbor Plain toward Perth. The **ATMs** in town are the last ones for 1300km heading west, although **EFTPOS** services are available at most roadhouses along the way. Ceduna provides basic beds, board, and booze, plus a few relaxing beaches. The long weekend in October is marked in Ceduna by the annual Oysterfest. The champion oyster speed opener goes to the national finals in Brisbane. **Decres Bay,** 12km from town in the **Wittelbee Conservation Park,** is a good swimming beach; a little farther on is **Laura Bay,** with more of the same. **Ceduna**

Gateway Visitors Centre, 58 Poynton St., is laden with info on fishing and outback tours. It is also your best source of info on the Nullarbor crossing (be sure to pick up a copy of *The Nullarbor: Australia's Great Road Journey* and the extremely thorough *Ceduna: from Smoky Bay to the Nullarbor Whales*). It also has **Internet** access and booking for buses. (☎8625 2780 or 1800 639 413; www.ceduna.net. Open M-F 9am-5:30pm, Sa-Su 9am-5pm. Internet $5 per 30min.) The town has **police** (☎8626 2020) and **taxis** (☎2825 3791). **Postal code:** 5690.

Ceduna Greenacres Backpackers ❷, 12 Kuhlmann St., on the right fork as you come into town from the east, is marked with a red sign. It has muraled concrete walls, metal bunks in small rooms, an airy courtyard, and free continental breakfast. Friendly owner Vaughn often hosts field trips to go crabbing or fishing, or to the spectacular (and not widely known) natural rock pool at the ▧**Point Brown Swimming Hole**—location divulged on a need-to-know basis only. (☎/fax 8625 3811 or 0427 811 241. Dorms $16.50.) Heading out towards the bay, the best of the 5 caravan parks in the area is the **Shelly Beach Caravan Park ❶,** 3km east of town on the Decres Bay Rd., right on a beautiful beach. (☎8625 2012. Sites $15, powered $17; 2 person cabins from $55; backpacker cabins $25 per person.) Standard motel accommodation for no-fuss stopovers is at the **Highway One Motel ❺,** at the edge of town on the Eyre Highway. (☎8625 2208. Singles from $70, doubles from $75.) On the way west out of town, don't miss **Ceduna Oyster Bar ❸,** where a half-dozen oysters on the half-shell will give you the energy to make the long trek across the Nullarbor. (☎8626 9086. Open M-Sa 9:30am-6pm, Su 1-6pm.) **Bill's Chicken Shop ❶,** on Poynton St., serves the town's best fried chicken, fresh fish 'n' chips ($8), and deli sides. (☎8625 2880. Open daily 9am-9pm.) The well-stocked Foodland **supermarket** is on the corner of Kuhlmann and Poynton St. (☎8625 3212. Open M-W and Sa 8am-6pm, Th-F 8am-7pm, Su 9am-4pm.)

EYRE HIGHWAY: CEDUNA TO PORT AUGUSTA

For those coming from the Nullarbor, the scrub-covered stretch of Hwy. 1 running from Ceduna to Port Augusta will seem like a tropical rainforest. Along the way, **Wirrulla** (92km from Ceduna), **Poochera** (140km), **Minnipa** (170km), **Wudinna** (209km), and **Kimba** (310km) are all very small towns; most have **petrol**, a small **supermarket** or general store, and accommodation. There are petrol stations every 100km or so across this stretch of road, with high prices. Accommodations on this stretch of road are limited. Wudinna has an **Internet** cafe on the west side of town in the **Wudinna Telecentre.** (Open M-F 9am-5pm. $5 per 30min.) Kimba's **Cafe@54 ❶,** on the town's main street, also has Internet ($2.75 per 30min.), along with cappuccinos ($2), sandwiches ($5), and burgers. (☎8627 2822. Open M-F 10am-5pm.)

At one of two area tourist information centers in **Kimba,** a strange creature looms in front. Cemented on top of its little hill, the ▧**Big Galah,** a huge, pink bird, motionlessly celebrates the halfway point across Australia and keeps a watchful eye on all the traversers of the Eyre Hwy. The **tourist center** (☎8627 2766) is open daily 8am-5pm, although the Big Galah never sleeps.

CROSSING THE NULLARBOR

Explorer Edward John Eyre minced no words describing the Nullarbor Plain, calling it "a hideous anomaly, a blot on the face of Nature, the sort of place one gets into in bad dreams." The place is shunned by the Aborigines as the waterless home of *Dijarra*, an immense legendary serpent. Welcome to the Nullarbor—a treeless plain that could contain England, the Netherlands, Belgium, and Switzerland, with 7000km^2 to spare. Despite, or perhaps because of, its miserable reputation, it remains one of the major treks to be ticked off by round-Australia travelers.

The largest single block of limestone in the world, the Plain encompasses over 250,000km² in total and formed around the same time as Australia broke away from Antarctica—about 50 million years ago. Although the ocean now lies far below the rugged cliffs, the plain was originally a vast seabed. Most travelers stick to the straight white line of the Eyre Hwy., but the plain extends from the plunging cliffs of the Great Australian Bight 320km north to the Great Victorian Desert. Intrepid explorers can veer off the highway on a number of unsealed roads.

The first car crossing of the Nullarbor was completed in 1912 by adventurer Francis Birtles. It had taken him 44 days to cross from Perth to Sydney by bike in 1909, and he presumably wanted to find a quicker route. Even by car it still took him 28 days. The old track is visible near Penong—look for abandoned vehicles that didn't quite make it. Travelers can now speed along the smooth black bitumen of the Eyre Hwy., finally completed in 1976 after construction began during World War II. The **Ninety Mile Straight** (147km) from **Caiguna, WA** to **Balladonia, WA** is the longest straight stretch of highway in the country. The road is traveled fairly heavily compared with the empty roads up north; it's rarely more than 100km between roadhouses with fuel, but repair facilities are few and far between. This is a road train route, so all drivers should brace for the turbulence from passing 25m trucks. Bring along bottled water, warm clothing, and blankets and equip cars with a jack, spares, coolant, and oil. Before setting off, have a mechanic check your vehicle. The **RAA** (☎ 13 11 11) has more info. Also see **Driving in the Outback** (p. 79).

Each of the **roadhouses** along the way has **EFTPOS** and major credit card facilities; almost all have a caravan park and camping sites, and most have cheap accommodations. **Yalata Medical Service** (☎ 8625 6237) is the best bet for medical assistance on the Nullarbor, although for emergencies, the Royal Flying Doctor services the barren plain. **Police** are located at **Penong** (☎ 8625 1006) and **Ceduna** (☎ 8628 7020); the Penong police can refer you to medical services as well. There are **quarantine checkpoints** at Norseman for westbound travelers and Ceduna for eastbound travelers. For details on roadhouses and scenic detours, pick up the free brochure, *The Nullarbor: Australia's Great Road Journey*, at the tourist office on either end. **Commemorative crossing certificates** are free at either office after completing the journey. **McCafferty's/Greyhound** (☎ 12 20 30) **buses** make this grueling desert haul to Perth from Ceduna (23hr., $264) or Adelaide (36hr., $264). The highly regarded **Nullarbor Traveller** is a backpacker-oriented camping trip that runs from Perth to Adelaide. Travelers snorkel, whale watch, explore caves, and camp under the stars. For those with the cash and the time, this is the way to cross in style. (☎ 8364 0407. 9-day Adelaide to Perth $945; 7-day Perth to Adelaide $735.)

EYRE HIGHWAY: CEDUNA TO BORDER VILLAGE

Penong had been dubbed the "town of 100 windmills," and while you might not dispute the windmill part, "town" is a little harder to swallow—there are probably more windmills than people. Visitors hypnotized by the swishing blades can spend the night at the **hotel ❸**. (☎ 8625 1050. Singles $33; doubles $44.) At **Cactus Beach,** 21km south of Penong along a well-maintained gravel road, you can watch territorial, top-notch surfers maneuver along famous breaks at one of Australia's best surfing beaches. Beginners enjoy the sandy bottom at **Shelly Beach,** east of Point Sinclair. Back on the main road, 78km west of Penong, accommodation is available at the all-encompassing **Nundroo Hotel Motel Inn ❶**. (☎ 8625 6120. Reception open 8am-8pm. Sites $13.50, powered $17.50. Backpacker rooms $18 per person; motel singles $71, doubles $82.) **Yalata Roadhouse ❶**, 52km west of **Nundroo**, is a decent camping spot and contains an Aboriginal museum and handicrafts for sale. (☎ 8625 6986. Open daily 8am-9pm. Sites $5 per person, powered $10; motel singles $50; linen $10.) A permit is required to enter the township of **Yalata** itself, home to an Anangu Aboriginal community (pop. 500), 200km north of Hwy. 1. Keep an eye out for the southern edge of the **Great Dog Fence** 7km east of Yalata. (See **Don't Fence Me In**, p. 513, for more on the fence.)

The **Head of Bight,** 78km west of Yalata and 16km east of Nullarbor, has stunning views of blue ocean, with sand dunes to the right and sheer cliffs to the left. Between May and October, 60 to 100 **southern right whales** breed, calve, and nurse here before returning to sub-Antarctic waters for the summer. Whale watching permits ($8) are required and available from Yalata Roadhouse or the **White Well Ranger Station** on the road south to Head of Bight from mid-July to October. (☎8625 6201. Call ahead for hours.) A sense of isolation takes over by the time you reach **Nullarbor,** 94km west of Yalata. There's accommodation at the **Nullarbor Hotel Motel ❷.** (☎8625 6271. Reception 7am-11pm. Singles $20; doubles $30.)

Just a few hundred meters off the main road, gorgeous coastal lookouts line the Nullarbor. The **Bunda Cliffs** (50km) plummet 90m straight down into the Southern Ocean, beginning at Twin Rocks and extending 200km to just east of Border Village. There's cheap accommodation and several food options at **Border Village ❷,** 188km west of Nullarbor, as well as a huge fiberglass kangaroo named Rooey II. (☎9039 3474. Budget singles $25; doubles $45; motel singles $79; doubles $89.) This is also the **agricultural roadblock** before entering Western Australia (at Ceduna if you're going east), where any fruit, vegetables, honey, and plant material will be confiscated to stop the spread of the fruit fly. (In WA ☎9311 5333, in SA ☎8269 4500.) As you enter Western Australia, it's still 710km from Border Village to **Norseman** (see p. 715), the official end of the Nullarbor Plain.

TASMANIA

Only 3% of the visitors to Australia make it to this little island, but Tassie is well worth the time and money spent getting there. A third of the state is under government conservation, mostly under the name Tasmanian Wilderness World Heritage Area, which includes one of the last great temperate rainforests on the globe. Bushwalkers from around the planet come to Tasmania's mountainous interior to explore the Overland Track, one of the premier hiking trails in the Southern Hemisphere. The uninhabited west coast bears the brunt of the Southern Ocean's fury, but the storms rarely push past the mountains, so the east coast and midlands are pleasant year-round. Tiny holiday villages filled with prosperous fishing fleets and vacationing families speckle the shore. In the southeast, the capital city of Hobart, Australia's second-oldest city, welcomes yachts from Sydney every December in a glorious and internationally famous turnout. Rolling farmland stretches north from Hobart to Launceston, Tasmania's second city and northern hub.

But perhaps the most spectacular thing about this magical island is its amazing natural diversity, its uncanny ability to house so many different species and environments in such a small space. In fact, some of Tassie's best known species can be found only within its borders, such as the slow-growing Huon pine, which can live for millennia, and the Tasmanian devil, a mysterious, scavenging marsupial. Many travelers try to see the island in just a few days, but once they lose themselves in the wilderness and history of Australia's secret stowaway, they might never get enough of Tasmania.

TASMANIA HIGHLIGHTS

SALAMANCA MARKET. Score a bargain and enjoy street performances in Hobart's eclectic shopping district (p. 530).

TASMAN PENINSULA. Tour the ruins of convict-built buildings at Tasmania's biggest tourist attraction (p. 533).

OVERLAND TRACK. Get into the bush on the world-famous Overland Track (p. 544).

FLINDERS ISLAND. Camp in utter remoteness or scope the other 54 Furneaux Islands from the peaks of Strzelecki National Park (p. 559).

▛ TRANSPORTATION

Tasmania has three principal gateways: Hobart's airport, Devonport's port via the *Spirit of Tasmania* overnight ferry, and Launceston's airport or its George Town port by *DevilCat* ferry. Getting around on a budget is a bit of a challenge. There is no rail network, and the main **bus** lines—**Redline** and **TWT's TassieLink**—are expensive, limited, and infrequent. TassieLink offers **Explorer Passes,** which are worth the investment when using their buses as a touring service (valid 7 days within any 10-day period $160, 21 days within 30-days $260). YHA members can purchase Explorer Passes that come with YHA accommodation vouchers (7-day pass $320, 14-day pass $520). On the bright side, many hostel managers offer reasonably priced shuttles and tours on a call-and-request basis. Seek local recommendations and check out hostel information boards.

Renting a **car** here is quite popular. The gateway cities have the major national chains and many small companies offering cheaper, older cars, but they are often

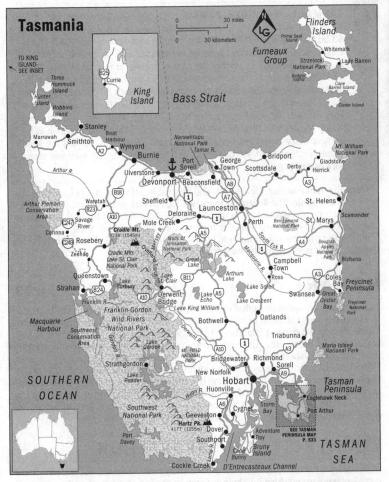

fully booked for weeks during the summer. Visitors unaccustomed to Tassie's narrow, winding roads should drive with added caution. Check with the rental company on their policy regarding unsealed roads; some prohibit driving on them altogether, while others increase the liability excess. 4WD vehicles, necessary for a portion of Tassie's backroads, come with better insurance policies on unsealed roads. Be aware that speed cameras are hidden along many roads and that petrol is rare outside of towns or cities.

Biking is a satisfying alternative in Tasmania, especially on the more accessible east coast of the island. The guide *Bicycling Tasmania*, by Terry and Beedham, is a helpful resource. The three major gateway cities have bike rental outfits catering to cycle touring, but gear will rarely be found outside of these major city outfitters. If you're planning on extensive bushwalking on the island, pick up a copy of *100 Walks in Tasmania*, by Tyrone Thomas, which has detailed track descriptions and excellent maps.

TASMANIA NATIONAL PARKS

All of Tasmania's national parks charge an entrance fee. A **24hr. pass** costs $3.50 (vehicles $10). There's also a two-month pass available for $13.50 (vehicles $33.50) or an annual pass for vehicles for $46 (one park only $20). Passes are available at most of the park entrances, or from any of the **Parks and Wildlife Service** offices. Parks and Wildlife prints two helpful pamphlets on the National Parks within Tasmania: *Tasmania: A Visitor's Guide* has a brief summary of every national park in Tasmania, and *Tasmania's Great Short Walks* outlines 30 fantastic walks most under one hour (both free). They also publish a handy booklet to reduce your environmental impact called the *Essential Bushwalking Guide & Trip Planner* (free). For more information, contact the head office in Hobart, 134 Macquarie St. (☎6233 6191), or visit their website at www.parks.tas.gov.au.

Tours also make seeing Tassie easy and enjoyable, allowing travel to places otherwise inaccessible. The **Adventure Tours** (☎1300 654 604; www.ozhorizons.com.au/tas/hobart/adventure/tour.htm. 3-day $355-505, 7-day $705-1140) and **Down Under Tours** (☎1800 064 726; www.underdownunder.com.au. 5-day $430, 7-day $550) offer touring options which include bookings for accommodation and everything that you might need along the way, for a partying crowd.

HOBART   ☎03

Tasmania's cosmopolitan capital city rests in a picturesque setting by the mouth of the Derwent River at the foot of Mt. Wellington. Shielded from the great Southern Ocean by a smattering of islands and breakwaters, Hobart (pop. 192,500) is Australia's second-oldest city. Although the area was originally a penal colony, the city itself was established in part by a booming mining industry. Despite its success, Hobart has somehow averted the big-city fate of increasing congestion and sprawling development. Hobart today is largely defined by its strong-willed environmental activists and abundance of remarkably good food and drink. Almost all of Tassie's visitors make at least a short stop here for one last dose of urban life drenched in history before heading into the island's vast wilderness.

◪ INTERCITY TRANSPORTATION

Hobart Airport is the most common port of entry into Tasmania—at least for those travelers who are not ferrying their car over to the island. Several well-maintained roads lead into the city center, including Highway 1, connecting Burnie, Devenport, Launceston, and Hobart. While it's hardly L.A., rush hour does see traffic into and, later, out of the city.

BY PLANE

Hobart Airport is located 17km east of Hobart on Hwy. A3. International flights must make connections to the island on the mainland. **Virgin Blue** (☎13 67 89; www.virginblue.com.au) flies four times daily from Melbourne ($99-209) with no advance purchase requirement. **Qantas** (☎13 13 13; www.qantas.com.au) flies to Melbourne up to nine times per day ($110-150) and Sydney twice per day ($190). **TasAir** (☎03 6248 5088) charters flights around the island and has two regular flights per day to Burnie. **Redline Airporter Bus** shuttles between the airport and lodgings. (☎1938 2240. $8.80, return $16.)

BY BUS

Timetables for Redline and TWT's TassieLink services can be picked up from Hobart's main **bus depot,** 199 Collins St. and at many Tassie hostels. Summer schedules run November through April.

TassieLink (☎ 1300 300 520), departing from 64 Brisbane St., buses to the Suncoast, including Swansea (2¼hr., M, W 11:15am, F, Su 10:45am, $21); Bicheno (3hr., M, W 1pm, F, Su 3:10pm, $26); and St. Helens (4hr., F, Su 12:40pm, $37.60); also Dover (2hr., 6 per day, $16); Cockle Creek via Huonville (3½hr., M, W, F 9am, $51.60); Mt. Field National Park (1½hr., M-Sa 5:20pm, T, Th, Sa 8:40am, $23.50); Port Arthur (2¼hr., M-F 4pm, in summer also M, W, F 10am, $18.50); and Strahan (9hr., T, Th, Sa 7am, F 4pm, Su 2:30pm, $55). In summer, inquire about Overland Track service including Hobart, Lake St. Claire, Cradle Mountain, and return ($90).

Redline Coaches (☎ 1300 360 000, line open daily 6am-9pm) runs from Hobart to Launceston (2.5hr., 3-5 per day, $24.70), connecting there to Burnie (2¼hr., 3 per day, $23.20), Devonport (1¼hr., 4 per day, $17.30), Bicheno (2¾hr., 1 per day, $27.40), and St. Helens (2hr., Su-F, 1 per day, $24.40). Student/YHA discount 20%.

Hobart Coaches, 21 Murray St. (☎ 13 22 01), runs to Cygnet (1hr. M-F approx. 9am, 3:10pm, and 5:15pm, $8.60) and Kettering (45min., M-F approx. 5:10pm, 6:15pm with day service on Th, $6.90).

⚑ ORIENTATION

Most tourist attractions and services are condensed into the downtown area west of the Sullivan's Cove wharf area, which is contained by Macquarie and Bathurst St., and interesected by the Elizabeth Mall. South of the Cove, and packed with antique shops and cottages, **Battery Point** is one of the oldest sections of the city. The northern border of Battery Point is defined by **Salamanca Place,** a row of old Georgian warehouses that have been renovated as shops and restaurants. **Franklin Wharf,** adjacent to Salamanca Place, is the departure point for numerous harbor cruises. Hobart is backed by the **Wellington Range,** which affords fine views from the imposing **Mt. Wellington,** dominant on the western skyline, and the smaller **Mt. Nelson** to the south. The city proper can be easily navigated on foot, while public buses run to the outer reaches of the suburbs.

Beyond the **Queen's Domain** north of downtown, the **Tasman Bridge** spans the Derwent River. There, the Tasman Hwy. (A3) heads east and connects to A9 and the Tasman Peninsula. **Brooker Avenue** leads north up the Derwent Valley, becoming Hwy. 1 to Launceston, and connecting to A10 to the west. **Davey Street** leaves downtown as A6, heading southward toward the Huon Valley and Bruny Island.

⬛ LOCAL TRANSPORTATION

Buses: Metro **city buses** run through Hobart and the suburbs. (☎ 13 22 01. Daily 6am-midnight. Purchase tickets onboard. $1.40-3.20 depending on number of sections traveled.) "Day Rover" tickets ($3.60) allow unlimited travel all day after 9am. **The Metro Shop,** 9 Elizabeth St., in a corner of the post office (open M-F 8:30am-5:15pm), has a complete timetable for 50¢, or visit www.metrotas.com.au.

Taxis: City Cabs (24hr. ☎ 13 10 08 or 6234 3633). City to airport $35-40.

Ferries and Cruises: The best deal around is **Captain Fell's Historic Ferries,** which offers morning, lunch, afternoon, and dinner cruises that depart every day from Franklin Wharf. (☎6223 5893. 2½hr. Dinner cruise 6pm. $23-25.) **Roche O'May Ferries** sails from Hobart's Brooke St. Pier to the Wrest Point Casino and the Cadbury Chocolate Factory. (☎6223 1914. Daily 10:30am, noon, 1:30, 3pm. $13.) Departing from Elizabeth

St. Pier, the sailboat **Lady Nelson** is a replica of an old English convict ship that once ferried convicts to the continent. (☎6234 3348. 1½hr. Summer Sa-Su 11am, 1, 3pm; winter Sa-Su noon and 2pm. $6.)

Tours: Day tours organized by **Tigerline** (☎1300 653 633) or **Experience Tasmania** (☎6234 3336) are good if you're short on time. Both offer pick-up and combo tours highlighting Hobart and southeastern Tassie. Book through the tourist office (☎6230 8233), with a hostel reception, or direct with the company. Tours $34-110.

Car Rental: Car rental agencies are everywhere in Hobart, but advance booking is essential in summer. Off-season rates run as low as $17 per day. Listed companies rent to ages 21-24 with no surcharge. **Autorent Hertz,** 122 Harrington St. (☎6237 1111), $40-70 per day. For a YHA discount, call ☎13 30 39 and quote Discount Program number 317961. **Thrifty,** 11-17 Argyle St. (☎6234 1341, airport 6248 5678), from $59. **Selective Car Rentals,** 47 Bathurst St. (☎6234 3311 or 1800 300 102), from $25. **Range** and **RentABug,** 136 Harrington St. and 105 Murray St. (☎6231 0678), rent older cars from $35, including minibuses and campervans.

Automobile Club: RACT (☎6232 6300, 24hr. roadside help 13 11 11, insurance queries 13 27 22), corner of Murray and Patrick St. 1 year coverage $70. Open M-F 8am-5:30pm, Sa 8am-1pm.

Bikes: Derwent Bike Hire (☎6268 6161), just past the Cenotaph on the cycleway at the Regatta Ground, hires road and mountain bikes, tandems, and inline skates from $7 per hr., $20 per day, and $100 per week. Open Sept.-Dec. and Feb.-May Sa-Su 10am-5pm, Jan. daily 10am-5pm; closed June-Aug.

🔁 PRACTICAL INFORMATION

TOURIST & FINANCIAL SERVICES

Tourist Office: Hobart Tasmanian Travel and Information Centre, 20 Davey St. (☎6230 8233), at Elizabeth St., dispenses information and books accommodations and cars ($2.20 fee), as well as tours and walks (free). Open in summer M-F 8:30am-5:15pm, Sa-Su 9am-4pm (in winter, Su 9am-1pm).

Budget Travel Office: YHA's Tasmanian Headquarters, 28 Criterion St., 2nd fl. (☎6234 9617; yhatas@yhatas.org.au). Travel insurance, passport photos, tickets, and travel advice, in addition to YHA memberships and hostel bookings. Open M-F 9am-5pm.

Currency Exchange: Many banks, most with **ATMs,** crowd in and around Elizabeth St. Mall. Most banks have a $5-10 fee. **Thomas Cook,** 40 Murray St. (☎6234 2699), charges $7 or 2% of traveler's checks. Open M-F 9am-5pm.

Tasmanian Parks and Wildlife Service: Service Tasmania, 134 Macquarie St. (☎6233 6191), in the Service Tasmania Bldg. Open M-F 8:15am-5:30pm. **Forestry Tasmania,** 79 Melville St. (☎6233 8203). Open M-F 8:30am-5:30pm.

LOCAL SERVICES

Bookstores: Fullers Bookshop, 140 Collins St. (☎6224 2488). Classy selection and quaint upstairs cafe. Open M-F 9am-5:30pm, Sa 9am-5pm, Su 10am-4pm.

Library: 91 Murray St. (☎6233 7462; internet booking 6233 7529), at Bathurst St. Reference library open M-Th 9:30am-6pm, F 9:30am-8pm, Sa 9:30am-12:30pm. Internet free; email for non-Australian residents $5.50 for 30min.

Market: Salamanca Market at Salamanca Pl. Open Sa 8am-3pm. See **Sights,** p. 530.

Outdoor Equipment: Countless gear stores cluster along Elizabeth St. near Liverpool St. Note that these are the only places to rent gear outside of Launceston and Devonport. **Jolly Swagman's Camping World,** 107 Elizabeth St., sells gear as well as renting tents

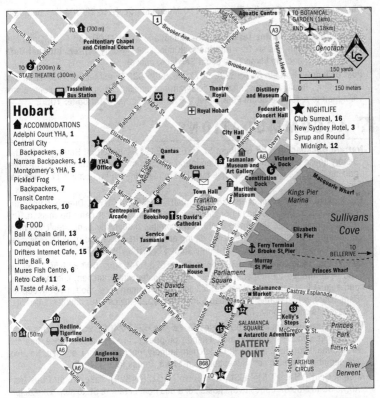

Hobart

ACCOMMODATIONS
Adelphi Court YHA, **1**
Central City
 Backpackers, **8**
Narrara Backpackers, **14**
Montgomery's YHA, **5**
Pickled Frog
 Backpackers, **7**
Transit Centre
 Backpackers, **10**

FOOD
Ball & Chain Grill, **13**
Cumquat on Criterion, **4**
Drifters Internet Cafe, **15**
Little Bali, **9**
Mures Fish Centre, **6**
Retro Cafe, **11**
A Taste of Asia, **2**

★ NIGHTLIFE
Club Surreal, **16**
New Sydney Hotel, **3**
Syrup and Round
Midnight, **12**

($50 per week, $300 bond), stoves ($25-100), packs ($30-200), and sleeping mats ($5-15). Open M-F 9am-6pm, Sa 9am-3:30pm. Service Tasmania has a list of all options to rent gear.

Fishing Equipment: Get info and fishing tackle (starting at $25 per day) at **Bridges Bros.,** 142 Elizabeth St. (☎6234 3791). Open M-Th 9am-5:30pm, F 9am-6pm, Sa 9am-1pm. *Angling Code for Inland Fisheries,* available at the tourist office, outlines all regulations.

MEDIA & PUBLICATIONS
Newspaper: *The Mercury.*
Entertainment: *The Mercury* includes *Gig Guide* on Thursday and *EG* on Friday.
Radio: Rock, Triple J 92.9FM; News, ABC 729AM; Tourist Info, 88FM.

EMERGENCY & COMMUNICATIONS
Emergency: ☎000.
Police: 37-43 Liverpool St. (☎6230 2111). **Lost and found** ☎6230 2277.
Crisis Lines: Crisis Watchline (24hr. ☎13 11 14). **AIDS Hotline** (☎1800 005 900). Staffed M-F 9am-5pm. **Alcohol and Drugs Hotline** (24hr. ☎1800 811 994).
Medical Services: Royal Hobart Hospital, 48 Liverpool St. (☎6222 8308). **City Doctors Travel Clinic,** 93 Collins St. (☎6231 3003). Open M-F 8:30am-5:30pm, Sa 10am-2pm.

Pharmacy: Corby's Everyday Pharmacy, 170 Macquarie St. (☎6223 3044). Open daily 8am-10pm.

Internet and Fax: Service Tasmania, 134 Macquarie St. (☎1300 135 513). Open M-F 8:15am-5:30pm. Has six **free terminals.** 30min. limit. Also try **Drifters Internet Cafe** (see p.529), and the **library** (see **Local Services,** above).

Post Office: 9 Elizabeth St. (☎6236 3577; fax 6234 9387), at Macquarie St. From this post office, Roald Amundsen sent a telegram announcing his accomplishment as the first man to reach the South Pole. Open M-F 8am-5:45pm. **Postal Code:** 7000.

ACCOMMODATIONS

Narrara Backpackers, 88 Goulburn St. (☎6231 3191). Turn left off Harrington St. This 3-story house offers spotless accommodation with a comfortable atmosphere. Off-street parking. Laundry. Free Internet. Bike hire. Reception 8am-10pm. Dorms $17; twins and doubles $44. ❷

The Pickled Frog Backpackers, 281 Liverpool St. (☎6234 7977). Directly behind the Transit Centre, the red facade of the newest addition to town can't be missed. The rooms are clean and the environment is welcoming, though the beds aren't the most comfortable. Off-street parking. Large dining area and free bike and pack storage. Free light breakfast. Internet $3 per hr. Dorms from $17. YHA/VIP. ❷

Central City Backpackers VIP, 138 Collins St. (☎6224 2404 or 1800 811 507), on the 2nd floor through the Imperial Arcade. A large hostel with a kitchen, common areas, and a great location. Sleepsheet $1, full linens $2. Laundry. Key deposit $5. Reception 8am-10pm. 8-bed dorms $18; 6-bed $20; 4-bed $22; singles $36; doubles $48. Cash or traveler's checks only. VIP. ❷

Transit Centre Backpackers, 199 Collins St. (☎/fax 6231 2400), above the bus terminal. Bright, spacious common area. Friendly proprietors live on-site. Fireplace, heaters, extra doonas for the winter chill, TV, kitchen, laundry, pool table. Free storage. No alcohol permitted on premises. Reception 8am-11pm. Dorms from $18. ❷

Adelphi Court YHA, 17 Stoke St., New Town (☎6228 4829). Take a Metro bus from Argyle St. to stop 8A opposite the hostel, or a bus from Elizabeth St. to stop 13. Adelphi is the pricey mothership of the Tasmania YHA fleet catering to a somewhat older crowd. Large common area with booking office, grocery kiosk, wash basins in rooms, laundry. Off-street parking. Continental breakfast $4.50; free with private rooms. Key deposit $10. Reception Dec. 16-Mar. 14 daily 7:30-10:30am and 4-9pm, Mar. 15-Dec. 15 8-10am and 4-7pm. Dorms $22, YHA $20; singles $51/$47; twins $58/$54. ❷

Montgomery's YHA and **Montgomery's Private Hotel,** 9 Argyle St. (☎6231 2600). Located downtown. Best-equipped of the Hobart hostels. Clean kitchen, common room with TV. Laundry. All rooms have phones; hotel rooms have towels, color TVs, and refrigerators. Storage, tour bookings. Reception 8am-10pm. Dorms $20-22; hotel twins and doubles $65-89; family rooms $105-119. ❷

FOOD

Hobart showcases a dizzying array of international cuisine: restaurants downtown serve meals from every region of Asia, while the pubs and grills of Salamanca Place serve lunch and dinner once brekkie is finished at the cafes. The best part of town for dining is Elizabeth St. in North Hobart, where a cluster of restaurants represent a great variety of cuisines—from Turkish to Mexican to Vietnamese. For a taste of traditional local fare, the ultimate Tassie tucker is abalone or salmon with a Cascade beer. **Purity,** 69 King St., Sandy Bay. (☎6211 6611) or 189 Campbell St.,

North Hobart (☎6234 8077), is an inexpensive bulk-buy **supermarket**. (Both open M-W and Sa 8am-6pm, Th-F 8am-9pm.) Get organic and bulk foods at Eumarrah Wholefoods, 45 Goulburn St., at the corner of Barrack St., or 15 Gregory St., Sandy Bay. (☎6234 3229. Open M-W 9am-6pm, Th-F 9am-7pm, Sa 9am-3pm.) The Saturday **Salamanca Market** has several takeaway vendors and deals on produce, sauces, spreads, honey, and cheese. (Open Sa 8am-3pm.)

Retro Cafe, 33 Salamanca Pl. (☎6223 3073), on the corner of Montpelier Retreat. Regulars enjoy fine food and excellent coffee. There's great people-watching at the Salamanca Market on Saturday. It can be hard to get a seat, but their all-day brekkie bagel with smoked salmon ($11) is worth the scramble. Open M-Sa 8am-6pm, Su 8:30am-6pm. Cash only. ❸

Cumquat on Criterion, 10 Criterion St. (☎6234 5858). Eclectic menu includes standard brekkie and Asian-inspired dishes ($8-16) including laksa, risotto, and good coffee. Vegetarian, vegan, and gluten-free options are clearly marked. Open M-F 7:30am-5:30pm. Cash only. ❷

Mures Fish Centre (☎6231 1999), Victoria Dock. A complete seafood complex, including a cheerful fishmonger (daily 7am-6pm). The sea-level **Bistro** serves up the town's best fish'n'chips ($8) in your choice of marinade. Separate, licensed beverage counter. Open daily 11am-9pm. The **Upper Deck** (☎6231 2121) has fine dining lunches (noon-2:30pm; $12-25) and specializes in char-grilled dinners (6-10pm; $20-47). To starboard, **Orizuru** (☎6231 1790) makes fresh sushi (lunches $13-14; entrees $7-12; mains $17-26). Open M-Sa noon-2:30pm and 6-9:30pm. **Polar Parlour** has ice cream and desserts. Open daily 8am-9pm. ❸

A Taste of Asia, 358 Elizabeth St., North Hobart (☎6236 9191). A favorite BYO with locals. Quirky Asian-inspired cuisine, from sushi to samosas. The large takeaway plates of Indian and Thai curries ($11) are a great deal. Open M-Th noon-8pm, F noon-9pm, Sa 4:30-9pm. ❷

Drifters Internet Cafe, Shop 9, 33 Salamanca Pl., The Galleria (☎6224 6286). Good homemade soups ($5), toasties ($4.50), and cappuccino ($2.50). Even better are the magazines, great music, and Internet access ($5 per hr.). Open M-Sa 10am-6pm, Su 11am-6pm. ❶

Ball and Chain Grill, 87 Salamanca Pl. (☎6223 2655). Wood tables filled with plates of char-grilled meats. Although slightly pricey (steaks $20-30), the meats are sizzled over real charcoal, and all mains come with a fantastic all-you-can-eat salad bar. Open noon-3pm and 6pm-late. ❹

Little Bali, 84a Harrington St. (☎6234 3426), near a cluster of small Asian eateries. Tiny orange dining room bright with wicker lampshades and flying animals. Tasty, quick Indonesian meals like satay with noodles (small $6, large $8.20; 50¢ table surcharge). Open M-F 11:30am-3pm and 5-9pm, Sa-Su 5-9pm. ❶

🔊 SIGHTS

Hobart is brimming with interesting convict history. The excellent free brochures *Hobart's Historic Places, Sullivan's Cove Walk,* and *Women's History Walk,* available from the tourist office, are a great place to start.

DOWNTOWN

TASMANIAN MUSEUM & ART GALLERY. The Tasmanian Museum's array of fine displays explore various aspect of the island, including its early convict history, unique ecology, and artistic heritage. The colonial-era art section is strong, while the mega-fauna models include a 10-foot kangaroo. Frequent exhibitions highlight the cultural and artistic history of the region. *(40 Macquarie St., near the corner of Argyle St. ☎6211 4177. Open daily 10am-5pm. Guided tours leave from the bookstore W-Su 2:30pm; tours can also be arranged. Free.)*

PENITENTIARY CHAPEL & CRIMINAL COURTS. One of the oldest, best-preserved buildings in Tasmania. Inside are the courtrooms and gallows of the grim 1830s, which were used until 1983. *(6 Brisbane St. Enter on Campbell St. ☎6223 5200. Open M-F 10am-2pm. Tours M-F 10, 11:30am, 1, and 2:30pm. $7.70, concessions $5.50. Ghost tours ☎0417 361 392. Daily 8pm. Book ahead. $7.)*

MARITIME MUSEUM. This facility highlights Tassie maritime heritage, with a focus on local shipping and whaling. Exhibits include thousands of photographs, paintings, ship models and replicas, and maritime equipment. Accounts of more recent catastrophic shipwrecks make for some riveting reading. *(16 Argyle St., in the Carnegie Building on the corner of Davey St. ☎6234 1427. Open daily 10am-5pm. $6.60.)*

CYCLEWAY. Along the western bank of the Derwent River is a north-south bicycle path with views of Mt. Wellington, the Regatta Grounds, the Tasman Bridge, Government House, the Queen's Domain, the Royal Botanical Gardens, and the shipyards in Hobart. *(Brochure with maps available from tourist office for $3.85.)*

OTHER SIGHTS DOWNTOWN. At Sullivan's Cove, the **Elizabeth, Brooke,** and **Murray St. Piers** harbor most of Hobart's large vessels. Look for the Antarctic Research Expedition's giant orange icebreaker, *Aurora Australis*, sometimes docked at Macquarie Wharf on the Cove's north side. **Constitution** and **Victoria Docks** are teeming with popular fishmongers and marine restaurants. Several companies run **harbor cruises** from this area (see **Ferries and Cruises,** p.525).

THE MOUNTAINS

MT. WELLINGTON. Several kilometers west of Hobart, Mt. Wellington (1270m) is a must-see. The top is extremely windy, cold, and often snowy. On a clear day, you can see the peaks of half the state, all clearly marked on signs in the observation shelter. The summit is also home to a huge telecommunications tower that can become crowded with vehicular visitors, but surrounding walking tracks are spectacular. The road to the top is occasionally closed due to snow and ice. **Fern Tree,** on the lower foothills of the mountain, is a picturesque picnic area with walking tracks up the slope. *(20min. from Hobart on B64 Huon Rd. By bus, take the #48 or 49 Fern Tree bus to stop 27, at the base of the mountain. Getting to the top without a car may involve shelling out some dough for a narrated van trip up the road. Mt. Wellington Shuttle Bus Service $25 return. Bookings ☎0417 341 804 (min. 2 people). Experience Tasmania (☎6234 3336) tours T, Th, Sa $35, concessions $32. Observation shelter open daily 8am-6pm. For track details, get the Mt. Wellington Walk Map ($4) from the tourist office.)*

MT. NELSON. South of central Hobart, the mountain offers views of Hobart and the Derwent estuary. A signal station at the top, part of the chain that connected Port Arthur to the capital, also has a restaurant. *(Take the #57 or 58 Mt. Nelson bus to its terminus. Road to the top open daily 9am-9pm. Restaurant open daily 9:30am-4:30pm. Tigerline ☎6272 6611, runs half-day tours of Mt. Nelson and city attractions on Sa for $30.)*

SALAMANCA PLACE & BATTERY POINT

SALAMANCA PLACE. This row of beautiful Georgian warehouses contains trendy galleries, restaurants, and the shops of the much-celebrated Salamanca Market. Busy all day, the outdoor market offers a wonderfully chaotic diversity of crafts, produce, food, performers, and good times. *(Open Sa 8am-3pm.)*

ANTARCTIC ADVENTURE. As one of the world's southernmost cities, the Hobart region has long served as a base for Antarctic exploration. This enjoyable discovery center and amusement park combines facts and fun, offering 20min. planetarium shows of the Southern Hemisphere's starry sky. The most popular exhibit, the Blizzard, simulates downhill speed skiing. (*2 Salamanca Sq. ☎ 6220 8220 or 1800 350 028. Open daily 10am-5pm. Planetarium show daily every hour 11am-4pm, subject to change. $22.50, concessions $17.50, under 14 $11.25, families $40; allows 1 year access.*)

BATTERY POINT. Adjacent to Salamanca Place is the lovely historic neighborhood of Battery Point, where many of Hobart's convict-era buildings have been preserved. The Battery Point National Trust leads tours through the village, including morning tea, or you can do a self-guided tour by referring to walking brochures available from the tourist office. (*☎ 6223 7570. Tours depart Franklin Sq. Wishing Well, at Macquarie and Elizabeth Sts. Sa 9:30am. 2½hr. $12, children $2.50.*)

PRINCES PARK. On the edge of Battery Point, just behind the Esplanade, this green space on a hill offers water-views through the trees. The park was once the site of Mulgrave Battery, Battery Point's oldest building, once a signal station relaying messages as far away as Port Arthur.

OUTLYING REGIONS

▦ CADBURY CHOCOLATE FACTORY. One of Hobart's most popular attractions, Cadbury provides tours showing all stages of the chocolate process, with free tastings every step of the way. Stock up on chocolate at the bargain sales shop at the end of the tour. (*In Claremont, north of Hobart and the Derwent River. Take the Claremont service #37, 38, or 39 to the factory. ☎ 6249 0333 or 1800 627 367. Tours M-F throughout the day 8am-3:30pm. Advance booking recommended. $12.50, concessions $9, children $6.50.*)

▦ CASCADE BREWERY. Fed by the clear waters of Mt. Wellington, the magnificent Old World-style Cascade Brewery was built in 1832 on designs by a convict in debtors' prison. Tours explore aspects of the brewing process, the brewery's history, and includes a stroll around the surrounding gardens. (*131 Cascade Rd. Take the Claremont service #43, 44, 46, or 49 to stop 17. ☎ 6221 8300. Tours M-F 9:30am and 1pm. 2hr. Bookings essential. Free beer at end. Long pants and flat shoes required. $11, concessions $7.50, children $4.50.*)

▦ BONORONG WILDLIFE PARK. See, hear, pet, and feed the beasts that roam the island's wilderness. Orphaned and injured Tasmanian devils, koalas, quolls, wombats, and birds live in enclosures. Every visitor gets a bag of kangaroo feed; also make sure to catch the devil feeding at 11:30am or 2pm. (*North of Hobart in Brighton. Metro bus X1 from Hobart to Glenorchy Interchange connects with #125 or 126 to Brighton, 1½hr. From Brighton, it's a 30min. walk. By car, it's a 25min. drive north on Hwy.1; follow the signs in Brighton. ☎ 6268 1184. Open daily 9am-5pm. $10, children $5.*)

HISTORIC FEMALE FACTORY & ISLAND PRODUCE TASMANIA FUDGE FACTORY. Once the Hobart jail and a factory for women and children in the 1820s, the site is now home to various building ruins, memorial gardens, and several fine confectioners. The poignant tours split their time rather incongruously between the historic site and today's small, handmade production of fudge and truffles. (*16 Degraves St., South Hobart, near Cascade Brewery. Take bus #43, 44, 46, 47, or 49 from Franklin Sq. to stop 16, cross onto McRobies Rd., and walk right onto Degraves St. ☎ 6223 1559. Shop and gardens open M-F 8am-4pm, in summer also Sa-Su 9am-noon. Tours M-F 9:30am, in summer also M-F 2pm and Sa-Su 9:30am. 1¼hr. $9, concessions $7, children $4.50, families $25. Free samples. Tours must be booked a day ahead.*)

ROYAL TASMANIAN BOTANICAL GARDENS. With 13 hectares and 6000 species, the Royal Tasmanian Botanical Gardens are the largest public collection of Tasmanian plants in the world and the largest collection of mature conifers in the Southern Hemisphere. The wildly popular Al Fresco Theatre runs an outdoor play in January and "Shakespeare in the Garden" in February. Tai chi comes to the gardens Monday, Wednesday, and Friday at 7:30am in January. *(North of the city, near the Tasman Bridge. Take any bus, including the MetroCity Explorer, headed to the eastern shore to stop 4 before the bridge; or take the X3-G express to Bridgewater, which stops at the main gate. Or walk 25min. from the city to Queen's Domain past Government House. ☎ 6234 6299. Open daily Oct.-Mar. 8am-6:30pm, Apr. 8am-5:30pm, May-Aug. 8am-5pm, Sept. 8am-5:30pm. Cafe open daily 10am-4pm. Free; donations encouraged. Book theater tickets through Centertainment (☎ 6234 5998). Outdoor Theatre $22, concessions $11.)*

🎵 ENTERTAINMENT

Check out the entertainment listings in the *EG* insert of Friday's *Mercury* newspaper. Tasmania's only independent movie theater is the **State Cinema,** 375 Elizabeth St., in North Hobart, with indie films in glamorous facilities. (☎ 6234 6318; www.statecinema.com.au. $11, W $7, concessions $7.50.) The **Theatre Royal,** 29 Campbell St., the oldest theater in Australia, stages plays, musicals, song and dance shows, comedy festivals, and a variety of other crowd-pleasers. (☎ 6233 2299. Box office open M-F 9am-5pm, Sa 9am-1pm. $22-42.) The more experimental **Peacock Theatre,** 77 Salamanca Pl., is in the Salamanca Arts Centre. (☎ 6234 8414; booking also at www.tickets.com. $4-15.)

The august **Tasmanian Symphony Orchestra,** 1 Davey St., in the Federation Concert Hall at the Hotel Grand Chancellor, is over 50 years old and still holds performances every few weeks. (☎ 6235 3633 or 1800 001 190. Box office open M-F 9:30am-4:30pm, Sa concert days 10am-2pm, and all concert nights from 6pm. $35-49, concessions $20.)

The **Wrest Point Hotel,** 410 Sandy Bay Rd., at Nelson Rd., is the oldest casino in Australia. Many of the bars also have live bands or DJs, in addition to two live entertainment venues. (☎ 6225 0112. Tables open Su-Th 2pm-2am, F-Sa 2pm-4am; machines open Su-Th 1pm-2am, F-Sa 1pm-4am. Book shows through Centertainment ☎ 6234 5998.)

🎵 NIGHTLIFE

The New Sydney Hotel, 87 Bathurst St. (☎ 6234 4516). An extremely popular Irish pub where margaritas, counter-intuitively, are the most popular beverage ($10). Tu-Su live music, mainly cover bands. Cover Sa $3. Open M noon-10pm, Tu noon-midnight, W-F 11:30am-midnight, Sa 1pm-midnight, Su 4-9pm. Kitchen open M-Sa noon-2pm, 6-8pm, Su 6-8pm.

Syrup and **Round Midnight,** 39 Salamanca Pl. (☎ 6223 2491). Above and next to Knopwoods Pub, Round Midnight is packed late nights on weekends. **Syrup,** on the 1st floor, is a mellow lounge-bar with appetizers and DJs that morphs into a club at midnight. **Round Midnight,** on the 2nd floor, hosts live bands and guest DJs. F-Sa cover $4-7. Both open in summer 6pm to the wee hours; in winter W 9pm-2am, F 9pm-4am, Sa 9pm-7am or later.

Club Surreal, 86 Sandy Bay Rd. (☎ 6223 3655), at the corner of St. George's, upstairs from St. Ives Hotel. Surreal Saturday nights are jam-packed. Huge video screens, TVs on the floor, pool tables, and dance floors connected with a slippery slide. Open W 9am-late (happy hour 10-11pm), Th pool night 10:30pm-late, F-Sa 10pm-late (happy hour 11pm-midnight). Cover W-Th $4, F-Sa $8; free before 10:30pm F.

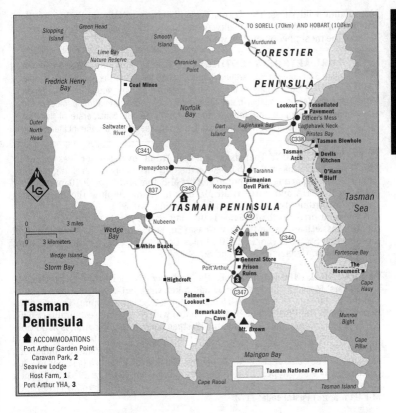

Tasman Peninsula

🏠 ACCOMMODATIONS
Port Arthur Garden Point
    Caravan Park, 2
Seaview Lodge
    Host Farm, 1
Port Arthur YHA, 3

THE SOUTH

Anchored by its capital city of Hobart, Australia's southern end is a wind-swept landscape dotted with picturesque towns. Ninety minutes east, the Tasman Peninsula and Port Arthur stand testament to Tassie's colonial history. To the west, the entrance to the vast Southwest National Park welcomes visitors to the Tasmanian Wilderness World Heritage Area. In between lie the hop vines of the Derwent Valley and the apple orchards of the D'Entrecasteaux Channel.

TASMAN PENINSULA & PORT ARTHUR

The narrow **Eaglehawk Neck** isthmus connects the Tasman Peninsula to the rest of Tasmania. Tourist buses now funnel through the very place where guard dogs once ravaged would-be escaped convicts. Initially known as the "Black Line," military units once dumped Aborigines and repeat offenders over the peninsula's steep cliffs and narrow neck into rumored shark-infested waters. From 1830 to 1877, 12,000 convicts were shipped to **Port Arthur** for offenses ranging from petty thievery to heinous murder. The ruins of the many convict-built sandstone buildings are Tasmania's most popular tourist attraction, drawing 250,000 visitors annually. If Port Arthur's commercialism is too much, escape the crowds in the surrounding wilderness. The Tasman coastline, now a National Park, is particularly astounding. Well-beaten walkways and open tracks along the coast provide some of the most phenomenal views in southern Tassie.

> **PORT ARTHUR SHOOTINGS.** On Sunday, April 28, 1996, a gunman killed 35 people in Port Arthur historic site and township. The shock to Tasmania and Australia still lingers; the violence triggered gun law reform. Information on the murders is available in any Tasmanian bookstore and in a free booklet of the court transcription available at the visitors' desk. Be considerate of the Port Arthur community by not asking staff and shopkeepers about the incident.

⌷ TRANSPORTATION. There is no real Port Arthur town, just services to the historical site. **TassieLink** (☎ 1300 300 520) is the only **bus** company servicing the tourist attraction, departing the depot in Hobart M-F 4pm and M, W, F 10am (summer only) for the YHA and Port Arthur Motor Inn. (2¼hr. Book at the YHA. Buses depart Port Arthur M-F 6am, Sa 1pm, holidays 7am. $18.50.)

A one-hour drive north, the **Sorell** is the main stop en route to the Suncoast (via the A3). **TassieLink** runs up the East Coast (Su, W, F mornings; in summer also M morning) to: Swansea (2hr., $21.10); Coles Bay (2½hr., $25.20); Bicheno (2½hr., $25.90); and St. Helens (3¾hr., F and Su, $37.60).

⃟ PRACTICAL INFORMATION. By the Eaglehawk Neck Historic Site on the A9, the **Officers' Mess** has basic **groceries** and takeaways. (☎ 6250 3722. Open in summer daily 8am-8pm; in winter Su-Th 9am-6:30pm, F-Sa 9am-7:30pm.) There is a **Visitors Centre** in the Port Arthur Historic Centre with a cafe and restaurant. (☎ 6251 2371. Open 8:30am-8pm.) In Sorell, the **Westpac bank,** with 24hr. **ATM,** is at 36 Cole St. at the junction of A3 and A9. (Open M-Th 9:30am-4pm, F 9:30am-5pm.) There is **Internet** ($3 per 15min., $8 per hr.) at the Arts and Crafts building on Andersons Rd., off A6. They also rent bikes ($8 per hr., $20 per day), canoes ($16 per hr., $65 per day), kayaks ($10 per hr., $45 per day), and some gear. (☎ 6250 3103. Open daily 7am-7pm.) There's a **post office** at 19 Gordon St., Sorell. (☎ 6265 2579. Open M-F 9am-5pm.) **Postal code:** 7172.

⌂⃟ ACCOMMODATIONS & CAMPING. The **Seaview Lodge Host Farm ❷**, 732 Nubeena Back Rd., Koonya, has a fairy-tale hilltop location, overlooking 90 acres of land. A variety of outdoor activities are run out of the farm, including kayaking (half-day $90), horseback riding ($15 per hr.), and rock climbing (half-day $60). Driving from A9 in Taranna, follow B37 9km to Nubeena Back Rd., and then head 1.5km up to the farm. TassieLink drops passengers off in Koonya 30min. before arriving in Port Arthur; free pick-up is available from Koonya or Port Arthur. (☎ 6250 2766. Linens $5. Laundry $2. Bike hire $15. Dorms $16; twins and doubles $35-40.) The quiet **Port Arthur YHA ❷**, on Champ St., the first left past the entrance to the historic site, sits mere meters from the ruins and houses a resident ghost named Alice. (☎ 6250 2311. Reception 8:30am-10am and 5-8pm. Dorms $25, YHA $19.) **Port Arthur Garden Point Caravan Park ❶** is a left off A9, 1km before the historic site. The 40-acre grounds hold 44 camp sites, 20 cabins, and large dorm accommodations. (☎ 6250 2340. Dorms $15; sites for 2 $16, powered $18; cabins $75-85.)

◑◩ SIGHTS & TOURS. The prison, lunatic asylum, hospital, and church of **Port Arthur Historic Site** are a visible reminder of Australia's convict heritage. From 1830 and 1877, over 12,000 re-offending male convicts were transferred to cold and desolate Port Arthur, many sentenced to years of timber hauling and rock-breaking. The downstairs museum area attempts to bring this turbulent story to life, allowing visitors to pick a convict and follow his history. The short **walking tours** of the grounds and the free **boat tours** (closed in August) provide further insight into convict life. A 20min. harbor cruise past the **Isle of the Dead,** the colony's cemetery, and **Point Puer,** the convict boys' colony, is included in the price of admission; book at the visitor complex. Cruises that actually land on the Isle of the Dead cost an extra $6.60 (children $5.50). The popular **Historic Ghost Tour** runs nightly, offering spooky stories, creepy shadows, and a bit of history. Admission tickets and Ghost Tour tickets can be purchased from the YHA or the visitor complex front desk. (☎ 1800 659 101. Open daily 9am-dusk, but most tours end and buildings close at 5pm; allow 4hr. to explore. Two-day admission $22, concessions $17.50, children $10; after 4:30pm $10. Ghost Tour 90min.; times vary; $14, children $8.60.)

AROUND THE TASMAN PENINSULA

Much of the Peninsula's coastline makes up **Tasman National Park,** which is lined by cliff-top **hiking trails.** Peter and Shirley Storey's handy *Tasman Tracks,* available at tourist shops on the peninsula, details about 50 walks and has good maps. The **Tasman National Park Tours** offers custom tours for up to three adults, including talks on history, geography, and wildlife. (☎ 6250 3157. 2-3hr. First person $88, second $44, third $33, children $22.) Another new way to view the spectacular cliffs of the park is with **Port Arthur Cruises** on the **Tasman Island Wilderness Cruise.** This two-hour cruise views the highest sea cliffs in Australia and is the only way to get close to Tasman Island. (☎ 6231 2655. Book 24hr. in advance. Departs Jan.-Apr. M-Th 8am; May-Dec., excluding Aug. M 8am. $49, children $35.)

One of the region's most intriguing sights is the **Tessellated Pavement,** located just before Eaglehawk Neck. This natural platform of sedimentary rock has grooves and splits across its surface, etched by the salt crystals left behind as sea water evaporates. The crystals dried up in the tiny cracks of the rock and then expanded, cutting open the rock and giving it the appearance of well-arranged bathroom tile. The carpark is 500m up Pirates Bay Dr., an easy 15min. return walk to the beach.

Continuing on A9 just past Eaglehawk Neck is C338, which leads to the **Devils Kitchen** and **Tasman Arch** carparks. Both remarkable cliffside sights were etched by centuries of wave action, and are easy 10-15min. return walks. Continue along the moderate gravel track to **Patersons Arch** (15min.) and **Waterfall Bay** (45min.), where it links up with the steep **Tasman Trail** (1¼hr.) to the falls and **Waterfall Bluff** (1½hr.). Walking from Devils Kitchen to **Fortescue Bay** can be a breathtaking 6-8hr. or overnight walk. Basic **camping ❶** is available with drinking water, showers, and toilets. (Sites $5.50, double occupancy $11. Park fees apply.) The Fortescue **ranger** (☎ 6250 2433) has details. To get to Waterfall Bay by car, take the first right off C338 and follow 4km to the cul-de-sac; for Fortescue Bay, follow a 12km sign-posted, unsealed road east off A9, south of the B37 Taranna junction.

From Fortescue Bay, the Tasman Trail leads to the rock formations at **Cape Hauy** (4hr.). Starting with a deep descent from the campground, this very difficult trek passes by spectacular the dolorite spires of **The Candlestick, The Needle,** and **The Lanterns,** popular among ambitious rock climbers. The three-day return trip to **Cape Pillar** is something to write home about. **Camping ❶** is available at **Lime Bay.** (Pit toilets, water. $3.30, children $1.60.) Check with the park office for updates and summer ranger activities. **Parks and Wildlife** (☎ 6250 3497) is on A9 before the Rescue Centre.

The **Tasmanian Devil Park Wildlife Rescue Centre,** in Taranna, houses devils, 'roos, and wallabies, all feedable and touchable—well, except the devils. They also have the only free flight show on Tasmania and devil feedings daily at 10, 11am, and 1:30pm. (☎ 6250 3230. Open daily 9am-5pm. $15, children $7.50, families $40.)

D'ENTRECASTEAUX CHANNEL

The channels, islands, and caves south of Hobart were first charted by Frenchman Bruni d'Entrecasteaux in 1792, more than a decade before the first English settlement in the area. The valley's cool climate and fertile soil, nourished by the Huon River, make the area perfect for growing berries, pears, and apples. The town of Cygnet provides services to the area, and antique shops and vineyards pepper the pastoral land between the river and the D'Entrecasteaux Channel. Bruny Island offers a tranquil escape into the wild, and a stop can be made in Geeveston before launching into the southwest.

CYGNET & HUON VALLEY   ☎ 03

Near the mouth of the Nicholls Rivulet on Port Cygnet and 60km southwest of Hobart, the artsy, tourist-friendly community of Cygnet hosts seasonal fruit pickers and year-round travelers en route to the Huon Valley. Testaments to the region's booming fruit trade lie on A6 to Huonville from Hobart. Twenty-five minutes south, **Doran's Jam Factory** is Australia's oldest maker of jams, churning out fruit preserves since 1834. Their spiced apple butter is the local favorite; savor it with scones in their tea room. (☎ 6266 4377; www.doransjams.com. Open daily 10am-4pm. Free self-guided tours and samplings.) Down the road, **The Huon Apple and Heritage Museum**, in Grove, explores the history of the "apple isle." A whopping 500 varieties of apples are on display from March to June. (☎ 6266 4345. Open daily Sept.-May 9am-5pm, June and Aug. 10am-4pm. $4.) History buffs will appreciate the **Cygnet Living History Museum**, at Uniting Church Hall, on Mary St. Preserved artifacts, photographs, and oral and written histories of the Huon Valley are on exhibit. (☎ 6295 1560. Open Th, F, Su 12:30-3pm, Sa 10am-3pm. Free.) Locally, this region of Tasmania is known for its cool-climate wines, many of which are available at the **Hartzview Vineyard and Wine Centre,** 10km east of Cygnet near Gardners Bay (via B68 and C626; keep an eye out for the grape sign). In addition to its own pinot noir and fruit wines, Hartzview provides products from the area's smaller vineyards. B&B accommodation available on-site. (☎ 6295 1623. Open daily 9am-5pm. Tastings $2, refunded on purchase. Singles and doubles from $130.) On the second weekend in January, Cygnet comes alive with the **Cygnet Folk Festival** (www.cygnetfolkfest.southcom.com.au), an open-air celebration of a variety of folk music and food.

Hobart Coaches leaves from 21 Murray St. in Hobart for the Cygnet carpark. (☎6233 4232. 1hr., M-F 9am, 3:10, 5:15pm, $8.60.) The █Balfes Hill Huon Valley NOMADS Backpackers ❸, 4 Sandhill Rd., Cradoc, 4½km north of Cygnet, caters to eager workers willing to pick berries or prune orchards November to May. The hostel managers will help find employment and provide transportation ($15 per week). The sizable compound houses comfortable bunks, clean bathrooms, kitchens, a video lounge, ping-pong, billiards, laundry, and a pay-phone. Call ahead for pick-up from the bus stop. (☎6295 1551. Reception 8:30-10am, 1:30-3pm, and 6-8pm. Twins $40, ensuite $55.) Set amid an apple orchard, Talune Host Farm ❺, at the intersection of B68 and C627, offers self-contained cabins for families. (☎6295 1775; wombat@talune.com.au. Cabin doubles $60, additional person $11.) █Red Velvet Lounge ❶, 87 Mary St., is part art gallery, part wholefoods store, and part cafe, serving good coffee and vego dishes. (☎6295 0466. Pizza with heaping portions of salad and macaroni salad $10. Open daily 9am-6pm.) Of the three supermarkets, Value-Plus, on Mary St., is open longest. (Open daily 7:30am-9pm.)

BRUNY ISLAND

Small, windswept Bruny Island is made of two chunks of land (North and South Bruny) joined by a narrow isthmus. Attracting walkers, animal and birdwatchers, and all manner of folk seeking seclusion, Bruny once bustled with a great whaling industry, but timber and agriculture reign today. The tamer North Bruny is home to 1000-year-old frayed-looking trees called "blackboys," while South Bruny houses most of the island's 500 locals and tourists, most drawn to its beautiful wilderness and diversity of wildlife. The island captivates its visitors with dramatic coastal scenery, remnants of an exploratory past, and plenty of space to bushwalk, bike, paddle, and swim.

▐▌ TRANSPORTATION & PRACTICAL INFORMATION. Ferries (☎6273 6725) run 10-11 times daily from 6:50am-6:30pm (8 times on Su) from Kettering to Bruny. Return fare for cars $21, peak hours $26, motorcycles $11/$15, bicycles $5, pedestrians free. Cash only.) Hobart Coaches leaves 21 Murray St. in Hobart for the ferry terminal. (☎6234 4077. 45min., M-F 8am, 2:40, 5:10, and 6:15pm, $6.90.) The island itself has no public transportation.

The Visitors Centre is across the channel in Kettering, by the ferry terminal. (☎6267 4494 or 1800 676 740. Open daily 9am-5pm.) The Adventure Bay General Store, 712 Adventure Bay Rd., has petrol, EFTPOS, and groceries. (Open daily 7:30am-8pm.) The Bruny Island Online Access Centre, at the Bruny Island District School in Alonnah, has Internet, scanning, and fax service. (☎6293 2036. Open Tu 2-5:30pm, W 9am-noon, 1-4pm, and 6-9pm, Th 1-4:30pm, F 1-4pm and 6-9pm, Sa 1-4pm. $5 per 30min.) There are no banks or ATMs on the island. The post office, at the Alonnah General Store, just off B66 in Alonnah, also has petrol. (Open daily 7:30am-7pm.) Postal Code: 7150.

▐▌ ACCOMMODATIONS & FOOD. The island's sole hostel, Adventure Bay Holiday Villages ❶, at the end of the road in Adventure Bay, is decorated with bleached whale bones. (☎6293 1270. After dark, ring bell to the right of door. Coin-op showers. Laundry. Sites for 2 $12, powered $14; on-site vans for 2 $32; cabins for 2 $50.) No longer a YHA, South Bruny's Lumeah ❺, on Main Rd. in Adventure Bay, offers spacious doubles, huge common areas, a brick fireplace, laundry, and BBQ. (☎6293 1265; lumeah@tassie.net.au. Linens $2. Closed June-Aug. Doubles $150.) If you are willing to splurge for some fantastic views, phenomenal landscapes, rooms with personality, and unique accoutrements, stay at one of the Morella Island Retreats ❺, on Simpsons Bay. (☎6293 1131; retreats@morella-island.com.au.

Breakfast $15. Self-contained houses $160-260.) At the start of the Penguin Island and Grass Point tracks, many of the island's protected lands offer free **camping ❶**. Within the National Park are Cloudy Bay and Jetty Beach, near the lighthouse, both requiring national park passes. These, along with Neck Beach, on the south end of the isthmus between North and South Bruny, offer sites with pit toilets, no water, and no firewood. Contact the ranger at the **Labillardiere State Reserve** (☎6298 3229) for more info. Within the Morella Island Retreats is the ▨**Hothouse Cafe ❸,** 46 Adventure Bay Rd., 6km north of Adventure Bay, a sheltered outdoor cafe with fantastic food and a beautiful garden, perfected by a panoramic view of the sea. The cafe's ambience more than makes up for its limited selection and slightly pricey meals; lasagna runs $20 and salmon $25. (☎6293 1131. Open daily in summer 10am-late, in winter 10am-5pm. Gardens and Gumtree maze $3.)

▨▨ **SIGHTS & OUTDOOR ACTIVITIES.** The ▨**Bligh Museum,** 880 Adventure Bay Rd., contains fascinating old maps, marine photos, and memorabilia relating to the explorers who landed here, including Cook, Bligh, Flinders, and d'Entrecasteaux. (☎6293 1117. Open Dec.-Apr. daily 10am-5pm, May-Nov. daily 10am-4pm. $4, concessions $3.) The **Bruny Island Charters** offer popular ecotours of the wild coastlines and adjacent waterways, including spectacular sightings of seals, penguins, dolphins, and other resident wildlife, departing from the Adventure Bay Jetty. (☎6234 3336; www.brunycharters.com. Operates Oct.-Apr. 3hr. tour daily 11am $70, full-day tour from Hobart Su-F 8:30am $130.) Book in advance. **Bruny Island Ventures** leads full-day land tours to the island, departing from Hobart daily at 8:30am and returning at 5:30pm. (☎6229 7475. Operates Oct.-Apr. $115.) The **Cape Bruny Lighthouse,** built by convicts between 1836 and 1838, is 30km southwest of Adventure Bay on an unsealed road. (☎6298 3114. Open daily 10am-4pm. Tours by arrangement $10, children $2.) Near the lighthouse, hike down the hills and through the coastal heath and coves of the **Labillardiere Reserve** (complete 7hr.; alternate circuit 1½hr.; moderate), but beware that trails are often poorly marked. From September to February, fairy penguins and muttonbirds roost on the Neck of the island. Parks and Wildlife runs free nightly **tours** from the Neck at dusk during the summer. The island is also a haven for rare white wallabies, diverse birdlife, dolphins, seals, and migrating southern right whales. **Cloudy Bay** has some of the best surf in Tasmania, while **Jetty Beach** offers more sheltered waters suitable for children. Some of the best views of the area can be had from the **Fluted Cape circuit** (3hr.), which starts at the end of the beach on the southeast end of Adventure Bay. Though only moderately challenging, the track includes the tops of some of the highest cliffs in Australia.

GEEVESTON & GATEWAYS TO WILDERNESS

Winding 25km south from Huonville along the d'Entrecasteaux Channel, A6 meets **Geeveston,** a town teetering on the edge of the southwest wilderness. A small community (pop. 800) with limited accommodations, the town serves travelers primarily as a gateway to the Hartz Mountains, Southwest National Parks (see p. 541) and nearby forest reserves. **TassieLink buses** (☎1300 300 520) run from Hobart to: Cockle Creek (3½hr.; M, W, and F 9am; $52); Dover (2hr.; $15); and Geeveston (1½hr., M-F; $11.20). For info on **flights** to the area, which run about $100 per person each way, contact **Par-Avion Wilderness Tours** (☎6248 5390) at the Cambridge Airport, 20km from Hobart, or **Tasair Wilderness Flights** (☎6248 5088).

The **Visitor Information** is in the **Forest and Heritage Centre** on Church St. (☎6297 1836. Open daily 9am-5pm. Museum $5. **Internet** $2 per 30min.) Church St. has several **supermarkets** (open Su-Th 8:30am-6:30pm, F 8:30am-7pm); a few **ATMs,** and a **post office.** (☎6297 1102. Open M-F 9am-5pm, Sa-Su 3-7pm.) **Postal code:** 7116.

The **Geeveston Forest House ❶**, at the end of Church St., has free laundry and basic dorm accommodation. (☎6297 1102. Singles and doubles $14. Book at the post office.) The region has many **camping** options, with free sites at the **Tahune Forest Reserve ❶**, 27km west of Geeveston, **Hastings Forest ❶**, 13km west of Dover, and **Cockle Creek ❶**, 25km south of Lune River. All are off of unsealed roads and offer pit toilets and drinking water. Cockle Creek also has a phone.

Even if you're not camping, follow the newly-sealed **Arve Road Forest Drive** from Geeveston to the Huon River and the Tahune Forest Reserve with its wildly popular **Airwalk**. The tree-top walkway passes over great patches of temperate eucalypt rainforest, the Huon and Picton Rivers, and gives a birds-eye view of strands of the native Huon pines (which take 500 years to mature and live up to 2500 years). At times close to 50m high and over half a kilometer in length, the Airwalk was an ambitious project by Forestry Tasmania that has paid off with a very positive reception. (☎6297 0068. Open daily 9am-5pm. $9, under 17 $6.) Nearby, the easy **Huon Pines Loop Trail** (20min.) meanders through these ancient pines. Take the Arve Loop Rd. to the **"Big Tree,"** an unbelievably wide 87m swamp gum. About 10km northwest of Lune River are the **Hastings Caves,** which house impressive dolomite formations, and the **Hastings Pool,** kept a constant 28°C by a thermal springs feed. (☎6298 3209. Tours every hr. Jan.-Feb. 10am-5pm, Mar.-Apr. 10am-4pm, May-Aug. 11am-4pm, Sept.-Dec. 10am-4pm. $14.50, concessions $11.50.) The Lune River area is also known for fresh and saltwater fishing. The carpark past the free camping area in **Cockle Creek** marks the end of Australia's most southerly road. An easy walk (4hr. return) from the campground goes to South Cape Bay, the closest you can get to **Australia's southernmost tip** and neighboring Antarctica. The area west of Cockle Creek is part of the **Southwest National Park** (see p. 541). Park passes are available from the Geeveston Forest and Heritage Centre.

DERWENT VALLEY & THE SOUTHWEST

Largely untouristed, the southwest affords a quiet wilderness experience that nevertheless keeps its visitors in awe. The agricultural Derwent Valley and the wild southwest are divided by the River Derwent, flowing from Lake St. Clair down to Storm Bay. Ridgeline after ridgeline of rocky peaks roll into the southern shores of this quiet Tassie valley. Stretching expansively toward the Southern Ocean, Southwest National Park includes the vast hydroelectric Lake Gordon and Lake Pedder, both the subject of heated environmental debate.

NEW NORFOLK ☎03

A misty valley enfolds the town of New Norfolk, 25km northwest of Hobart on the Derwent. For travelers, this is a good town to stop in on while heading west, with a few attractions that can warrant a longer stay. The climate is perfect for growing hops—regional cultivators harvest up to 45 tons per day. **Oast House,** on the Lyell Hwy. east of town, was once used to dry the harvest; now it's New Norfolk's most hopping tourist attraction, with a museum, gallery, and excellent cafe. (☎6261 1030. Open Sept.-Dec. W-Su 9:30am-5pm, Jan.-May daily 9:30am-5pm. $4.) A fine stretch of the Derwent River adjoins New Norfolk, attracting rafting, kayaking, fishing, and even swimming. Dating back to 1823, the **Anglican Church of St. Matthew,** on Bathurst St. across from Arthur Sq., is Australia's oldest church. The **Salmon Ponds** and **Museum of Trout Fishing**, situated 11km west of New Norfolk, constitute the oldest trout hatchery in the Southern Hemisphere. (☎6261 1076. Open daily 9am-5pm. $5.)

TassieLink (☎ 1300 300 520) runs **buses** to: Hobart (40min.; Tu, Th, Sa 6:20pm, F 8:40pm, Su 6:40pm; $5.90); Lake St. Clair (2½hr.; M, W 9:55am, Tu, Th, Sa 7:35am, F 4:50pm, Su 3:10pm; $33.60); and Queenstown (4½hr.; Tu, Th, Sa 7:35am, F 4:50pm, Su 3:10pm; $41.90). **Hobart Coaches** (☎ 6233 4232) runs from Hobart to Circle St. in New Norfolk (50min.; M-F 5 per day, Sa 3 per day; $5.40.) The **Derwent Valley Information Centre** is on Circle St. (☎ 6261 0700. Open daily 10am-4pm.) The **police station**, 14 Bathurst St., has free **Internet**. (Open M-F 9am-5pm.) The **Bush Inn Hotel ❸**, 49-51 Montagu St., north on the Lyell Hwy., is the oldest continually licensed hotel in Australia, and includes full breakfast. (☎ 6261 2256. Singles $33; twins and doubles $55.) The **New Norfolk Esplanade Caravan Park ❶**, on the riverbank, has coin-op showers and laundry. (☎ 6261 1268. Key deposit $5. Crowded sites for two $10, powered $15; cabins $50.) The Woolworths **supermarket** is on Charles St. (Open M-W and Sa 8am-6pm, Th-F 8am-9pm.)

MT. FIELD NATIONAL PARK

Summer visitors enjoy daywalks, short bushwalks and waterfalls, while winter visitors head for the slopes to downhill and cross-country ski in Tasmania's first national park convenient to Hobart. Bus companies do not service the park or its ski fields during the winter. **TassieLink** (☎ 1300 300 520) runs **buses** November through April from Hobart (1½hr., M, W 4pm, Tu, Th, Sa 7am, 4pm; return service M, W 7:15am, Tu, Th, Sa 1:05pm; $23.50). Some tour companies lead trips from Hobart: **Bottom Bits Bus** offers well-led, full-day tours during the summer. (☎ 1800 777 103. Departs Tu and Su 8:30am. $75.) Rangers lead free walks, slide shows, and nighttime wildlife-watching trips during the summer. Maps and park passes are available at the entrance station. Continue 100m up the road to the **park shop** (☎ 6288 1526) for more park info, takeaway food, and souvenirs. The **Mt. Field Information Line** (☎ 6288 1319) has a recording on ski and road conditions.

The National Park Office administers three basic six-person **cabins ❶** near Lake Dobson with mattresses, a wood heater, firewood, and cold water. (☎ 6288 1149. Book ahead. $11 per person, concessions $8.) The park shop also runs a self-register **campground ❶** near the park entrance with showers, bathrooms, BBQ, and laundry. Its grounds fill with pademelons, and the creek is home to platypuses. (Sites $6 per person, powered $8.50.) Past the park on B61 (Gordon River Rd.), **Mt. Field YHA ❷** provides basic beds in rooms without locks or lockers. (☎ 6288 1369. Book at pub across the road. Reception 8-10am, 5-8pm. Laundry. Linens $1. Dorms $19, doubles $38. YHA discount $3. Cash only.) Food options are scarce; Harry's mini-market, 12km west in Maydena, closes at 9pm.

The park can be divided into two distinct areas, the upper and lower slopes. The lower slopes near the park entrance have picnic and BBQ facilities, a park shop, easy walks to the tallest flowering plant in the world and a trio of waterfalls. **Russell Falls**, a paved walk (10min.) from the carpark through wet eucalypt forest, has long been a favorite destination. Continuing onward from here will lead to **Horseshoe Falls** and the **Tall Trees Walk** through the tall eucalypt. The worthwhile trek along the steep gravel road to **Lake Dobson** (16km) leads through eucalypts, mixed forest, sub-alpine woodland, and alpine mosaic. The upper slopes offer a network of extended bushwalks amid glassy highland lakes. The easy **Pandani Grove Nature Walk** (1hr.) circles Lake Dobson and introduces unusual vegetation, including pineapple grass, bright red scoparia, endemic conifers, and pencil King Billy pines.

Though snow cover varies, skiers travel up the slope by tow or by making their own tracks in the backcountry. Without 4WD, Lake Dobson Rd. can only be accessed with chains; the ski fields are a 40min. walk past the carpark. The ski kiosk rents skis and lift tickets.

SOUTHWEST N.P. & GORDON RIVER DAM

The largest of Tasmania's immense and wild national parks, **Southwest National Park** is mostly inaccessible by car, though Highway B61, better known as **Gordon River Road,** grants easy access to the awesome surrounds of Lakes Gordon and Pedder. From Maydena, B61 traverses 86km of mountainous terrain running through the settlement of **Strathgordon** (pop. 15) 12km before its abrupt end at the Gordon River Dam (about 1½hr.). **TassieLink** (☎ 1300 300 520) runs summer service between Hobart and Scotts Peak (4hr.; Tu, Th, and Sa 7am; $58.10) via Timbs Track (2hr., $55), Mt. Anne (2¾hr., $55), and Red Tape Track (3hr., $55). The construction of the Gordon River Dam and its two resultant lakes brought condemnation from international environmental activists, who argued that the dams would endanger the region's pristine wilderness. Regardless, the dams were built, and today the Gordon River Power Station is the largest in Tasmania, producing roughly a third of the state's energy—by itself, the station is capable of powering the entire city of Hobart.

Carved out of the Tasmanian Wilderness World Heritage Area, the man-made Lakes Gordon and Pedder are captivating. **Hydro's Visitor Centre,** on a ledge above the dam, has brochures on the dam's construction and history. Take 196 steps down to the top of the dam. (☎6280 1134. Open daily Nov.-Apr. 10am-5pm, May-Oct. 11am-3pm.) **Lake Pedder** can be viewed from both the main road and the entirely unsealed **Scotts Peak Road** This difficult road forks off the Gordon River Rd. 28km into the park at Frodshams Pass, ending 38km later at the Huon Campground. Just 2½km into Scotts Peak Rd. is the short and sweet **Creepy Crawly Nature Trail** (20min.). Longer walks go from Timbs Track to the **Florentine River** (4hr. easy rainforest walk), the **Eliza Plateau** (6hr.; difficult ridge climb to Mt. Eliza), and Lake Judd (8hr. unmarked track with difficult river crossings). Along Gordon River Rd., 13km from the Scotts Peaks Rd. junction, is the enjoyabe **Wedge Nature Walk** (30min.) through characteristic forest, and the trailhead to **Mt. Wedge** (5hr.), whose summit affords outstanding views of the park.

Picnic and free campsites at the **Huon Campground** ❶ grant easy access to the **Arthur Plains** and **Port Davey** walking tracks. Other sites are at **Edgar Dam** ❶, 8km before the end of Scotts Peak Rd., and **Teds Beach** ❶, east of Strathgordon. Strathgordon's **Lake Pedder Motor Inn** ❺ is the only other park accommodation. (☎6280 1166. Singles $60-95; twins and doubles $75-110.) **Trout fishing** is plentiful on Lake Gordon and Lake Pedder from August to April; boat launch sites can be found at Edgar Dam and Scotts Peak Dam, and along the road to Strathgordon. (License required.) For park info, contact the entrance station (☎6288 2258), or rangers at Mt. Field (☎6288 1141).

WESTERN WILDERNESS

From windy Strahan to the deep glaciers of Lake St. Clair and the slopes of Cradle Mountain, the scenic splendor of Tasmania's western wilderness sits amid highland pine forests. As one of the world's great temperate wildernesses, it also is one of its last. Most of the land in this region of Tasmania became protected in 1982 by the UNESCO Tasmanian Wilderness World Heritage Area, though logging and mining still threaten the areas just outside the official national park borders. While the area's well-trammeled trails justifiably attract plenty of visitors, most of the west is entirely unspoiled by human contact; lush rainforest, forbidding crags, windswept moors, and swirling rivers have been left almost as they were when explorers first came to the region.

CRADLE MOUNTAIN ☎03

Visited by thousands of wilderness lovers every year, Cradle Mountain rises majestically above Dove Lake. The surrounding area is a complex glacial fabric of deep creeks and crags that shelter the state's unique jewels: sweet-sapped cider-gum woodlands, rainforests of unique King Billy and celery-top pine, and lush carpets of cushion plants.

🚍 TRANSPORTATION. The town of Launceston serves at the urban hub for public transportation to Cradle Mountain, though it's also possible to make the long trip from Hobart by connecting in Queenstown. **TassieLink** (☎1300 300 520) runs daily from Launceston (3hr., daily 7am, $51.70) and Devonport (1½hr., daily 8:30am, $30), and on the West Coast from Strahan via Queenstown (3hr.; M, W, F 1pm Tu, Th, Sa, 11:15am; $30). **Maxwell's Coach and Taxi Service** (☎6492 1431) makes frequent, unscheduled runs between the campground, the Visitors Center ($3), and Dove Lake ($9), and offers 24hr. service to the northwest (see **Lake St. Clair,** p. 543; book ahead).

🛈 PRACTICAL INFORMATION. Cradle Mountain-Lake St. Clair National Park is the northernmost end of the **Tasmanian Wilderness World Heritage Area.** It is a 1½hr. drive south from Devonport on B19 and B14 and then west on C132 to the park entrance. From Launceston, it is a 2.5hr. drive on A1 to B13 and C156 through Sheffield. From the west, follow A10 for 2hr. to C132 into the park. There is no direct road through the park. Visitors will reach Lake St. Clair most easily via the Cradle Link Road (C132) and the Muchison and Lyell Highways (A10). Park fees apply ($10 daily fee per vehicle; up to 8 people). The **Visitors Centre,** just past the park entrance off of C132, features displays with helpful layouts of the walking tracks, registry for the Overland Track, and a public telephone. (☎6492 1133. Open daily in summer 8am-5:30pm, in winter 8am-5pm.) A 7½km gravel road runs south from the Visitors Center to **Waldheim** and **Dove Lake.**

🏠🍴 ACCOMMODATIONS & FOOD. In peak season, accommodations fill up fast, so book ahead. On the entrance road, 2km outside the park, the **Cradle Mountain Tourist Park ❶** provides tent sites, basic Alpine huts (intended for campers when it's raining), bunk rooms, self-contained cabins, and heaps of amenities. There's an unequipped cooking shelter with BBQ and a kitchen for hostelers. (☎6492 1395; cradle@cosycabins.com. Reception 8am-8pm. Sites $10-12 per person, powered $20-25; bunks $20-24; cabins for 2 $75-90, VIP/YHA.) The Visitors Center runs the eight **Waldheim Cabins ❺,** 5½km inside the park. The Overland Track begins right outside at the Ronny Carpark. Heating, basic kitchen, showers, composting toilets, and limited generated power for lighting are provided. (☎6492 1110. Bunk cabins $70 for two, extra adults $25.) Bring your own food—there is no produce at Cradle Mountain. The **Cradle Mountain Lodge General Store,** right outside the park, sells basic supplies, meals and petrol at inflated prices and has the only **Internet** ($2 per 15min.) and **payphone** with touch-tone service. (Open M-F 9am-5pm, Sa-Su noon-4pm; extended summer hours.) Grab some pancakes at **Moina Tearoom ❶,** at the intersection of Cradle Mountain Rd., only 20min. from Cradle Mountain. (☎6492 1318. Open daily 7:30am-5:30pm.)

🥾 HIKING. Cradle Valley is the northern trailhead for the **Overland Track** (see p. 544), Tasmania's most prominent walk, traversing the length of the Cradle Mountain-Lake St. Clair National Park. The Cradle Mountain area has a web of tracks to accommodate all degrees of fitness and ambition. The free park brochure map is useful only to those hiking the **Dove Lake Circuit** (2hr.), the most popular and environmentally friendly walk consisting of a beautiful, mostly boardwalked lakeside track through old-growth forest. Short tracks around the Visitors Center and the Cradle Mountain Lodge include a rainforest walk and **Pencil Pine Falls** (10min.). The map for sale at the Visitors Center ($4.20) is good for longer dayhikes. The first stage of the **Overland Track** and its side tracks offer more arduous climbs: the hike up to **Marions Lookout** (1223m) begins along the Dove Lake track, continuing steeply to the summit, and returning via **Wombat Pool** and **Lake Lilla** (2-3hr.); the ascent of **Cradle Mountain** (1545m) is a difficult hike from Waldheim or Dove Lake past Marions Lookout, involving some boulder-climbing toward the summit (6hr.). Registration is advised for any walks longer than two hours. It rains 275 days a year, is cloudless on only 32, and can snow at any time—dress accordingly. The lodge organizes bike hire (half-day $16, full-day $22, deposit $200) and a number of activities: walking tours (1-3½hr., $6-25), canoe trips (2½hr., $50), fly fishing (2½hr., $50), and horseback riding (1hr., $50).

LAKE ST. CLAIR   ☎03

Half of the headline act of the **Cradle Mountain-Lake St. Clair National Park,** Lake St. Clair is Australia's deepest lake and the source of the River Derwent. The lake anchors the southern end of the famous **Overland Track** (see p. 544), with Cradle Mountain at its northern terminus. One of the most popular attractions in Tasmania, a trip to Lake St. Clair and its surrounding forests makes for a fine day.

TassieLink (☎1300 300 520) **buses** run from Hobart (3hr., daily, $37.90), and Strahan via Queenstown (2½hr., Tu, Th-Su 1 per day, $30.20). From Launceston and Devonport, connect in Queenstown in winter (6hr., M-Sa 1 per day, $62.70) or, in summer, take the direct Wilderness shuttle (3hr., M, W, F, and Su 1 per day, $60). Overland Track specials including Lake St. Clair, Cradle Mt., and return to Hobart or Launceston available ($90-100; inquire with TassieLink). **Maxwell's Coach and Taxi Service** (☎6492 1431) operates a small 24hr. charter service in the Cradle Mountain-Lake St. Clair region to: Derwent Bridge (10min., $6); Frenchman's Cap (30min., $15); Hobart (3hr., $65); and Queenstown (1¾hr., $35).

The **Visitors Centre** at Cynthia Bay, at the southern end of the lake, is accessible via a 5km access road that leaves the Lyell Hwy. just west of Derwent Bridge. Register for any extended walks, especially the Overland Track. (☎6289 1172. Open daily Jan. 8am-7pm; Feb.-Dec. 8am-5pm.) Next door, **Lakeside St. Clair** is a tourist info center, restaurant, and booking agency. (☎6289 1137. Open daily in summer 9am-8pm, in winter 10am-4pm. Fishing gear $15 per day, canoes $30 per 2hr.)

The park has free camping ❶ sites within the entrance with walking access only and pit toilets. The closest camping is at Fergys Paddyock, a 10min. walk from Cynthia Bay toward Watersmeet; other sites are located at Shadow Lake, Echo Point, and Narcissus Bay. Lakeside St. Clair ❶ has several accommodations just outside the park entrance with coin-op showers, a pay phone, and a kitchen with a wood-fire stove. (Sites $12 per person, powered for two $15; doona $5; electrically-heated backpacker bunks $25.) Opposite the Lake St. Clair access road on the Lyell Hwy. is the barn-sized Derwent Bridge Wilderness Hotel ❸, which has petrol. Backpacker rooms are in the cramped, modular units detached from the main hotel building. (☎6289 1144. Singles and doubles $25.) The hotel serves meals ❷ at reasonable prices. (Open noon-2pm and 6-8pm.)

Lake cruises with commentary run the length of the lake from the Cynthia Bay jetty, on the southern end of the lake by the visitors center. (Daily at 9am, 12:30, and 3pm; in winter also 2pm. Echo Point $15, Narcissus Bay $20.) A return cruise to Narcussus Bay is also available (book ahead at the tourist office; 1½hr.; $25, children $20; minimum $80 in bookings for tour to operate). All walking tracks branch off from the **Watersmeet Track,** which starts at the carpark a few hundred

TASMANIA

meters to the west of the visitors center. At Watersmeet, the **Platypus Bay Trail** (1½-2hr.) makes an easy, enjoyable loop through the woods to the water. Longer hikes head west to the sub-alpine forests of **Forgotten and Shadow Lakes** (3-4hr.) alongside waratah (flowering Nov.-Dec.); over the ridge, you can tackle steep, weather-beaten **Mt. Rufus** (7hr. return). If you take the ferry out in the morning, the lakeside hike to **Cynthia Bay** from Narcissus Bay amid rainforest, tea-tree, and buttongrass takes 5hr.; it's 3hr. from Echo Point.

> **! COLD KILLS.** Many people come to Tasmania to hike the endless, untamed wilderness. Make no mistake: Tasmania's wilderness is still wild and dangerous. The greatest hazard in the wilderness is the unruly weather that can shift from zephyr to gale in a heartbeat. Even in the warmer months, carry heavy and waterproof clothing to prevent hypothermia, a lowering of the body's core temperature that can be fatal (it can snow, even blizzard, in summer). Dehydration is also a common cause of hypothermia, so take care to stay hydrated. The way to avoid hypothermia is preparation: plan your trip wisely. Do not attempt bushwalks without the proper equipment and experience. Ask about the expected conditions. Wear wool or fiber pile clothing, including gloves and a hat. Wet cotton, especially denim, is deadly. The Parks and Wildlife Service can advise on gear.

OVERLAND TRACK

Connecting **Cradle Mountain** and **Lake St. Clair** through 80km of World Heritage wilderness, the Overland Track is Australia's most famous trail. Every year, approximately 8000 adventurers attempt the track and most take five to eight days to complete it, depending on how many side trips they undertake. Purists contend that the track has become a congested highway, but its natural grandeur cannot be denied. The ascent of the state's tallest peak, **Mt. Ossa** (1617m), makes a good day-trip. The fickle weather will undoubtedly soak a portion of your journey.

The heavy traffic is having a disastrous impact on the path's fragile alpine ecosystems, so practicing minimum-impact bushwalking is crucial. Stay on the track, spread out when there is no track, walk on rocks, wear lightweight walking boots, rotate campsites, and use fuel stoves only. The *Essential Bushwalking Guide* is available at the normal brochure kiosks. The track huts fill easily, so hikers must carry **tents.** If you are planning to walk the track, read the walking notes online at www.dpiwe.tas.gov.au and write to request an information kit at the **Parks and Wildlife Service.** (☎6492 1133; fax 6492 1120. Cradle Mountain Visitor Centre, P.O. Box 20, Sheffield TAS 7306.) No special permit is required for the hike, but an extended national parks pass ($33.50 per vehicle for 2 months, or $13.50 for an individual) and a copy of the *Overland Track Map and Notes* ($10) are essential. The track itself can be undertaken from either Cradle Mountain (see p. 542) or Lake St. Clair (see p. 543); starting from Cradle Mountain is the most common route, as it gives a slight downhill advantage of heading toward Lake St. Clair and allows for a ferry trip if necessary.

STRAHAN ☎03

The only community of any size on the entire west coast, Strahan (STRAWN) is Tasmania's ecotourism capital, serving as a gateway to **Franklin-Gordon Wild Rivers National Park** and to all the glories of the southwest wilderness, including the World Heritage Area. Once home to the harshest of Tasmania's penal colonies, Strahan was little more than a sleepy fishing village until the 1980s, when Strahan vaulted into prominence when environmental protestors sailed from the town's wharf, situated on Macquarie Harbour, to successfully blockade the construction of dams on the Franklin and lower Gordon Rivers. Since then, environmentalism has been on the rise and tourists flock to experience the reverberations of a good cause. Strahan is now one of the state's most touristed cities, and it shows in the abundance of mid- to high-end tourist facilities in perpetually high demand.

🖥📠 TRANSPORTATION & PRACTICAL INFORMATION. TassieLink (☎1300 300 520) **buses** run through Queenstown (45min., $7) to: Devonport (5½-7hr., $37.10); Hobart (5¼-6½hr.; Tu, Th-Su; $55.30) via Lake St. Clair (4hr., $30.20); Launceston (7hr.; M-Sa, $70.20) via Cradle Mountain (3½-4½hr., $30). **West Coast Bike Hire** (☎6245 0680) hires bikes, and **Strahan and West Coast Taxis** provides taxis (☎0417 516 171). The **Strahan Visitors Centre,** on the Esplanade, is run by a theater company. The center also has the cheapest **Internet** in town at $3 per 30min. (☎6471 7622. Open daily Nov.-Apr. 10am-7pm; May-Oct. 10am-6pm.) The **Parks and Wildlife Office,** in the historic customs house on the Esplanade, sells passes to national parks. (☎6471 7122. Open M-F 9am-5pm.) **Azzas** (see below) has **petrol** and an **ATM** inside. The **police** (☎6471 8000) are on Beach St., and the **post office** is at the Customs House (open M-F 9am-5:30pm). **Postal Code:** 7468.

🛏🍴 ACCOMMODATIONS & FOOD. For a treat, the **Cape Horn ❺** cabins on Frazer St. have a fantastic view of the water and offer a pleasant stay without the outrageous prices that seem to plague the town. (☎6471 7169. Continental breakfast $5 per person; fully contained studio $65-85; self-contained cottage $75-105, extra adult $20, extra child $15.) The **Strahan YHA ❷,** 43 Harvey St., has kitchens, comfortable bunks, and a resident platypus. (☎6471 7255; strahancentral@trump.net.au. Reception 4-8pm; early arrivals go to Strahan Central (see below). Dorms $23, members $20; twins $51/$44; doubles $57/$50.) For a memorable experience, spend a night at **Franklin Manor,** on the Esplanade, an extraordinary old hillside estate. The 18-room hotel glows inside and out with uncommon charm and hospitality. (☎6471 7311. Doubles $200-280. Self-contained cottages $250. Full breakfast included.) **Strahan Central ❶** is a posh cafe and crafts store on the corner of Herald St. and the Esplanade. (☎6471 7612. Open M-F 9am-5:30pm, Sa-Su 10am-5:30pm. Meals $6.50-13.) The hotels also offer good counter meals. Azzas, near the campground, has **groceries.** (Open M-Sa 6:30am-9pm, Su 6:30am-8:30pm.)

👁📷 SIGHTS & ACTIVITIES. The **Sarah Island Historic Site** was once the penal colony reserved for "the worst description of convicts," subject to unspeakable hardships on this barren rock. Today, it is one of the stops on the Gordon River and World Heritage cruises (see below). Back in town, the local play *The Ship That Never Was* humorously explores the last great escape from Sarah Island's penal settlement. (Shows Jan. daily at 5:30 and 8:30pm, Feb.-Dec. 5:30pm. $12, concessions $9.) Also in the Visitors Centre is **West Coast Deflections,** an exhibit on Aboriginal and settler life which features artwork and reconstructions of their dwellings. (Open daily 10am-8pm. $3.50, concessions $2.50.) Newly opened, the steam **ABT Wilderness Railway,** is Australia's only rack-and-pinion railway. The train departs from the station at Regatta Point in the Esplanade for Queenstown, passing pristine rainforest and dozens of restored bridges along the way. (☎6471 1700. 4-5hr.; 2 per day; $65, return $95.)

The track to **Hogarth Falls** (40min. return), a few hundred meters from central Strahan, is rampant with wildlife. Accessed through **People's Park,** the track follows **Botanical Creek,** home to aquatic critters, including the elusive platypus. North of town at the end of Harvey Rd., **Ocean Beach** stretches from Macquarie Head to Trial Harbour over 30km north. The brooding surf and windy dunes at

Tasmania's longest beach makes swimming unsafe. In late September, thousands of **mutton-birds** descend on the beach after flying 15,000km from their Arctic summer homes and go about laying their one egg of the season. The fantastic **Henty Dunes** rise 30m high just 14km toward Zeehan. The dunes are sacred to the Aborigines, though 4WD tours explore the area and camping and dogs are allowed. Consider going by bike or taxi ($2 one-way) to avoid parking fees.

Strahan is at the northern end of the fully protected Macquarie Harbour, one of Australia's largest natural harbors at 100km². The placid, tannin-stained waters become choppy only at **Hell's Gates**—the narrow and dangerous strait where the harbor meets the Southern Ocean. The strait is the smallest in the world leading into a harbor and many ships have been wrecked on surrounding reefs and rocks.

▨**World Heritage Cruises,** on the Esplanade, runs the least expensive trips through the harbor and up the Gordon River (south of Sarah Island), including passage through Hell's Gates and into the tempestuous Southern Ocean, a 1hr. guided tour of Sarah Island, and 30min. at Heritage Landing up-river to admire a 2000-year-old Huon pine. (☎6471 7174. Smorgasbord $9. 5½hr.; departs daily 9am, in summer also 2-8pm; $55, children $25; half-day 9am-1:30pm in summer $50/$22. YHA discount 10%.) **Gordon River Cruises** offer similar trips with posher seating and dining arrangements. (☎1800 628 286; $55-118, lunch buffet $12 on lower decks.) **West Coast Yacht Charters,** on the Esplanade, offers sailing trips to **Sir John Falls, Heritage Landing,** and other sites. (☎6471 7422. 1 night $140, 2 nights $360.) The **Wild Rivers Jet** gives a faster and more violent tour of the King River. (☎6471 7174. $50.) **World Heritage Scenic Flights** (☎6471 7718) tours surrounding heritage areas and Cradle Mountain by plane or helicopter ($110-180). **Strahan Adventures** (☎6471 7776) offers **kayak tours** to search for platypi on the Henty (3hr., $80) or history tours around the harbor for $50.

QUEENSTOWN
☎03

In 1883, Mick and Bill McDonough (also known, for now-obscure reasons, as the Cooney Brothers) came across an ironstone outcropping that seemed the likely source of the gold traces in a nearby creek. They were right, and gold fever quickly flared up across the state. For a few years, prospectors cleared out immense chunks of hard rock, yielding only about two ounces per ton. As the fever began to cool, it became clearer that copper was the real bounty of that rock (after millions of pounds of it had already slipped away), and thus the **Mount Lyell Gold Mining Company** was formed in 1888, intent on exploiting copper, not gold. Though Queenstown's economy boomed, it was not without a cost: the smelter they built to process the copper ore wreaked environmental havoc. Nearly every large tree in the surrounding hills was felled to feed the smelter, while the young growth was killed by the thick yellow sulphur haze released during the pyritic processing. Additionally, the newly exposed topsoil was washed into the Queen River by heavy rainfall. The town (pop. 2200 and falling) currently resembles a lunar wasteland in the midst of dense vegetation.

The **Mt. Lyell Mine** still chugs along (as it is expected to do for at least another century), with tours exploring the working areas. All tours leave from the office at 1 Driffield St. Daily surface tours visit the old open-cut mines, the working copper mine, and other sites. (☎6471 2388. Book ahead. 1hr. Daily Sept.-May 9:15am and 4:30pm, June-Oct. 9:15am and 4pm. $15, children $7. Underground tours 2½hr., $55.) The old Iron Blow open-cut mine, just off the Lyell Hwy. near **Gomanston,** offers views of surrounding barren hills and of the water-filled crater. The **ABT Wilderness Railway** offers scenic stream train rides to and from Strahan; see the listing in Strahan for details. The thin road to Queenstown snakes above steep ravines (allow 45min. to Strahan). **TassieLink** (☎1300 300 520) runs to: Hobart (4¾hr.; Tu,

Th-Su; $47.80) via Lake St. Clair (2hr.; $22.70), Launceston (5-6hr.; M-Sa; $62.70) via Cradle Mt. (2½hr.; $22.50), and Devonport (4-5hr., $39.70) and Strahan (45min., Tu, Th-Su, $7.50). The **Mt. Lyell Mine Office** is the town information center. (☎6471 2388. Open daily in summer 8am-5pm, in winter 10am-4pm.) **Parks and Wildlife** (☎6471 2511) is represented by **Centrelink/Service Tasmania**, 34 Orr St., next to the post office. (☎1300 135 513. Open M-F 9am-5pm. Free **Internet**.) The **post office** (open M-F 9am-5pm) is at 32 Orr St. **Postal Code:** 7467.

The **Empire Hotel ❷**, 2 Orr St., retains some of the former glory of its heyday as a miners' pub. (☎6471 1699. Meals $10-20. Singles $25; twins and doubles $40, with bath $50.) **Queenstown Cabin and Tourist Park ❶**, 17 Grafton St., is across the river, 2km from town center. (☎6471 1332. Sites $9, for two $18; powered $10/$20; backpacker beds $20/$27; on-site caravans $40/$48; self-contained cabins for two $65).

FRANKLIN-GORDON WILD RIVERS NATIONAL PARK

Immense and pristine, Franklin-Gordon Wild Rivers is rightfully part of the Tasmanian Wilderness World Heritage Area. In 1983, a waterway blockade stopped the construction of a hydroelectic dam on the lower Gordon, preserving one the southern hemisphere's largest wildernesses. Seeing this extraordinary expanse can only be accomplished on foot or by air and rewards the determined with timeless glacial mountains, fast-flowing rivers, deep gorges, and endless rainforest.

On its way from Strahan to Hobart, the **Lyell Highway** (A10) runs between Queenstown and the Derwent Bridge through the park, which is otherwise roadless for kilometers to the north and south. To use any of the Park's facilities, purchase a National Parks Pass ($3.30 per person, $10 per vehicle per day up to 8 people), and *Wild Way*, which lists points of interest along the Lyell Hwy.

Three walks in particular stand out. The 10min. Nelson Falls Nature Trail, hidden in wet rainforest 25km east of Queenstown, leads to a lovely cataract. ⬛**Donaghys Hill Lookout** (40min. return), 50km east of Queenstown, should not be missed. Renowned for its sunsets, the track holds mind-blowing views of the Franklin River Valley and **Frenchman's Cap**, its principal peak (1443m, 3- to 5-day return hike to the top). The **Franklin River Nature Trail**, 60km east of Queenstown, is a well-maintained 20min. circuit through rainforest.

Between Queenstown and Nelson Falls, **Lake Burbury** has swimming, boating, trout fishing, and **camping ❶** surrounded by mountains. (No showers or laundry. Sites $5.) Between Nelson Falls and Donaghys Hill, the Collingwood River also has free basic **camping ❶** with fireplaces and picnic facilities. Roadside lookouts at **Surprise Valley** and **King William Saddle** (67km and 70km east of Queenstown, respectively) offer views of the eastern side of the wilderness area. The saddle marks a major divide of Tasmania, with the dry plains and highlands to the east; to the west, an annual rainfall of 2.5m flows into the Franklin-Gordon rivers, through wet rainforest, and out to Macquarie Harbour.

THE NORTHWEST

The ferry from the mainland brings most visitors to Tasmania to the Northwest first; after time on the northwest's Overland Track and the Franklin River, many have a hard time leaving. World Heritage wilderness is the big draw in the Northwest, punctuated by seaports on the northwest coast and mining towns on the western highways. As an Aboriginal homeland, a fierce wilderness, an ecotourism jackpot, a mining mother lode, and a land of colonial convict myth-memory, the Northwest sees the currents that dominate Tasmania's identity play out their drama in the starkest relief.

DEVONPORT

☎ 03

Lured by visions of an endless expanse of rainforest, ancient peaks, and wild rivers, travelers arriving in Devonport (pop. 25,000) may confront an unpleasant surprise. Its grim waterfront on the Mersey River, dominated by a cluster of huge gray silos, is an unremarkable gateway to Tasmania's wild charms. Though most visitors pass through quickly, a pleasant afternoon can be spent north of town walking around the point to explore the Aboriginal rock carvings and museum.

⌐ TRANSPORTATION. The **airport** is 8km east of the city center on the Bass Hwy. **QantasLink** (☎ 1800 688 118) flies four times a day from Melbourne (1¼hr., $110). **TasAir** (☎ 6427 9777) flies once a day to King Island (1¼hr., $170) and has on-demand charter flights. A shuttle transfers passengers between the airport and downtown twice daily (☎ 6424 6333; $10). **Taxis Combined** is a pricier but more reliable alternative. (☎ 6424 1431. One way to town $17-20.) Most popular with those transporting a car, the **ferry** *Spirit of Tasmania* departs from Melbourne. Breakfast, dinner, and accommodation are provided. (☎ 1800 634 906; www.spiritoftasmania.com.au. 10hr.; departs nightly from Melbourne and Devonport 9pm; Dec. 20-Jan. 19 also 9am. $100-370; cars extra $55, off-peak free; bikes extra $6, off-peak free.) The **Mersey River Ferry "Torquay"** transports from east Devonport back to the city center. With your back to the Spirit of Tasmania terminal, turn left at the road and head down the first street to reach the water; the shuttle ferry wharf is straight ahead. (Runs M-Sa 9am-5pm on demand; $1.70, children and students $1.20, bikes 50¢.) **MerseyLink** (☎ 6423 3231; www.merseylink.com.au) also buses around town M-Sa, including from the ferry to local accommodations ($1.40-2.30).

Redline Coaches, 9 Edward St. (☎ 1300 360 000; open daily 6am-9pm), runs daily buses to Launceston (1¼hr., 3 per day, $17.50), with connections to Hobart and the East Coast, and Burnie (1hr., 5 per day, $10). **TassieLink** (☎ 1300 300 520) buses leave the Visitors Center to Cradle Mountain Visitors Center (2¼hr., daily 8:30am, $30) and Strahan (7hr., $47.20) via Queenstown (4½hr.; M-Sa, in summer also Su; $39.70). Major car rental companies have counters at the airport and ferry terminals, including **Hertz** (☎ 6424 1013; open daily 8am-6pm; also at 26 Oldaker St.) and **Thrifty,** across from the ferry. (☎ 6427 9119. Open daily 6:30am-7pm. $42-69 per day; age 21-24 $15 per day surcharge.) Smaller firms are often cheaper but are less consistent in car quality; try **Advance,** at the airport and 11 Esplanade (☎ 6427 0888; open daily 9am-5pm) or **RentABug,** 5 Murray St. (☎ 6427 9034. Open M-F 8:30am-5:30pm, Sa 8:30am-noon.)

■◪ ORIENTATION & PRACTICAL INFORMATION. The port of Devonport is the mouth of the **Mersey River,** with the ferry terminal on its eastern bank. Devonport is bounded to the west by the **Don River** and to the south by the **Bass Highway** (Hwy. 1), which includes the only bridge across the Mersey. The city center lies on the western bank, with **Formby Street** at the river's edge and the **Rooke Street Mall** one block inland, both intersected by **Best Street** and **Stewart Street** running away from the river; most essentials lie within a block of these four streets. North of this square, Formby St. leads to **Mersey Bluff** and **Bluff Beach** at the western head of the river. The Bass Hwy. heads west to Burnie (46km) and southeast to Launceston (97km) and Hobart (300km). B14 leads through Spreyton and Sheffield to Cradle Mountain. **Tasmanian Travel and Visitor Information Centre,** 92 Formby Rd., around the corner from McDonald's, books accommodations and transport. (☎ 6424 8176. Open daily 9am-5pm; Travel Centre only M-F.) ▨**The Backpackers' Barn,** 10-12 Edward St., has all the info you need about environmentally friendly bushwalking throughout Tasmania, including the famed Overland Track. The building also offers a restroom, book exchange, showers, and a bulletin board for announcements. (☎6424 3628; www.tasweb.com.au/backpack. Open M-F 9am-6pm, Sa 9am-noon. Gear can be sent back by Redline Coaches for a fee. Lockers $1 per day, $5 per week, with optional free backpack storage for 1 day. Tents $10 per day, $40 for Overland Track; sleeping bags $5; packs $5; cook set $5; stove $5.) **Store 44,** next to the post office on Stewart St., has the cheapest **Internet.** ($4 per hr. Open M-F 7am-5:30pm, Sa 7am-2pm.)

⌂ ACCOMMODATIONS. Tasman House Backpackers ❶, 169 Steele St., is a large 102-bed, 11-acre complex with free city center pick-up, free storage, laundry, and Internet. (☎6423 2335. Reception 8am-10pm. Dorms $12; twins $14; doubles $38. VIP.) **Tasman Bush Tours** (www.tasadventures.com) operates out of the house, with daytrips from $53 and 6-day Overland Track trips from $980. **Formby Road Hostel ❶,** 16 Formby Rd., 500m south of the city center, is a brick Victorian house featuring quiet, roomy common spaces, a clean kitchen, laundry, and free bike use. (☎6423 6563. Linens $3. Laundry. Free bike use. Dorms $16; doubles $36. Cash only.) **Inner City Backpackers ❶,** 34 Best St., in Molly Malone's Irish Pub, is the only hostel remotely near the city center. Standard 4-bed dorms have sinks and heat. (☎6424 1898. Key deposit $10. 4-night max. stay. Check-in at the pub. Dorms $14; doubles $50.) **Abel Tasman Caravan Park ❶,** 6 Wright St., in East Devonport at the mouth of the Mersey, is at a nice waterfront location near the ferry dock. They have a laundry, playground, and BBQ. (☎6427 8794. Sites $13-16, powered $16-19; on site caravans $33-45; cabins $58-80.)

⫙⌴ FOOD & NIGHTLIFE. The **Rooke Street Mall** overflows with standard take-aways and fast food. The tastiest vegetarian meal in town may be found at ▨**Café Natur ❶,** next to the Backpackers Barn on Edward St. Grab a veggie burger ($5.50) and a fresh fruit smoothie for lunch. (☎6424 1917. Open M-F 9:30am-4:30pm, Sa 9:30am-2pm.) **The Cheesecake Shop ❶** bakes fantastic cakes daily and offers the **Movie Deal:** $16 gets you a drink, quiche, cake, and a movie ticket at the cinema next door. (Open Su-Th 10am-9pm, F-Sa 10am-11pm.) **Renusha's Indian Restaurant ❷,** 153 Rooke St., near the corner of Oldaker St., offers spicy meat and vegetarian curries. (☎6424 2293. Open M-Th 5:30-9:30pm, F-Sa 5:30-11pm, Su 5:30-8:30pm. Takeaway $11-14; eat-in $15-19 with $15 minimum charge.) Coles **supermarket** is on Formby Rd. and Best St. (Open M-W and Sa 8am-6pm, Th-F 8am-9pm.) **Spurs Saloon,** 18-22 King St., has a country-western theme, video games, and pool tables that attract a young crowd. (☎6424 7851. F-Sa live music. Open W-F 4pm-1:30am, Sa 5pm-1:30am.) **Warehouse,** next to Spurs, is actually a dance club. (Cover $5-6. Open F-Sa 10pm-3am.)

◧ SIGHTS. Tiagarra Aboriginal Cultural Centre and Museum, a 30min. walk from the city center to Mersey Bluff near the lighthouse, explores 40,000 years of Tasmanian Aboriginal history. Of all the people of the world, the Aboriginal Tasmanians are thought to have been the most isolated, having had no contact with other peoples until the 19th century. (☎6424 8250. Open daily 9am-5pm. $3.30, children and students $2.20.) A 15min. walk around the bluffs leads to historic **rock engravings.** The lighthouse provides a prime view of the shimmering blue Bass Strait. A pleasant bicycling and walking path leads all the way to the point from the city and rounds the edge towards the back beach. The fascinating **Devonport Maritime Museum,** 6 Gloucester Ave, once the harbor master's home, houses a collection of maritime articles, including an extensive photo library. (☎6424 7100. Open Su, Tu-Sa 10am-4pm, in summer Su, Tu-Sa 10am-4:30pm. $3, children $1.)

The **Leven Canyon Reserve,** about 60km southwest of the city near Nietta, has a lookout with stunning views of Leven Gorge. To get there, take the Bass Hwy. west, then B15 south to Nietta, then C128 to the Canyon. About 15km from Leven

Canyon, through Nietta and South Nietta, the 5hr. return walk to **Winterbook Falls** follows an old logger track to a three-tiered cascading waterfall. A bit to the north of Leven Canyon off C125, the **Gunns Plains Caves** feature underground wonders as well as a creek with platypuses, freshwater crayfish and lobsters. (☎6429 1335. Tours daily on the hour 10am-4pm. $9, children $4.)

Narawntapu National Park, formerly known as the Asbestos Range because of its rich asbestos reserves, is a small coastal heathland reserve about an hour from both Devonport and Launceston. With ample fishing and swimming opportunities at Bakers and Badger Beach, the reserve is also popular for its walking tracks and abundant wildlife. The park is accessible by car only via three gravel roads. From Devonport take C740, which heads north from B71 between Devonport and Exeter. Register to camp at **Springlawn,** just past the park entrance. Sites have flush toilets, BBQ, tables, water, and a public telephone. (☎6428 6277. Book ahead in summer. $4.40 per person.) Two more scenic **camping ❶** areas are 3km farther down the road on the beach near **Griffiths Point** and **Bakers Point,** and have pit toilets, fireplaces, tables, and water. (Firewood included. Sites $4.40 per person, families $11.) The easy **Springlawn Nature Walk** (45min.) passes through scrub and lagoons, offering a chance to see wallabies and pademelons (their smaller relatives). The moderate track continues up to **Archers Knob,** revealing a view of the surrounding hills and coastline. (2hr. return.) A 6-8hr. return daytrip from the bird hide on the Springlawn Walk follows a coastal track to **Badger Beach,** passing rocky Copper Cover on the way.

DELORAINE & SURROUNDS   ☎03

In the foothills of the Great Western Tiers, huddled in the agricultural Meander Valley between Devonport and Launceston, Deloraine functions as a perfect base for exploring the World Heritage wilderness to the southwest.

▐▊ TRANSPORTATION & PRACTICAL INFORMATION. Redline buses (☎1300 360 000) run out of Cashworks, 29 W Church St. (☎6362 2143), with daily service to: Burnie (2hr., 1-3 per day, $16); Devonport (1hr., 1-3 per day, $11); and Launceston (1hr., 3-5 per day, $8). **Deloraine Visitor Information Center,** 98 Emu Bay Rd., doubles as the folk museum. (☎6362 3471. Open M-F 9:30am-4pm, Sa 1-3:30pm, Su 2-4pm. Museum $2.) Services include: **ANZ** with **ATM** on the corner of Emu Bay Rd. (open M-Th 9:30am-4pm, F 9:30am-5pm); **police** on Westbury Pl. (☎6362 4004); a **pharmacy** at 62-64 Emu Bay Rd. (open M-F 8:45am-5:30pm, Sa 9am-noon); **Online Access Centre,** behind the library at 2 Emu Bay Rd., with **Internet** (☎6362 3537; open M 10am-5pm, Tu, Th 10am-4pm, W, F 10am-7pm, Su 2-4pm; $3 up to 30min., $5 per hr.); **post office** at 10 Emu Bay Rd. (☎6362 2156. Open M-F 9am-5pm.) **Postal Code:** 7304.

▐▊ ACCOMMODATIONS & FOOD. The **Deloraine Highview Lodge YHA ❷,** 8 Blake St., is the best hostel around, with views of Quamby Bluff and the Great Western Tiers, comfy bunks, and proprietors who can arrange tours. Go up Emu Bay Rd., turn right on Beefeater St., then left on Blake St. (☎6362 2996. Reception 8-10am and 5-10pm. Dorms $21.50, YHA $18.) Closer to town, **Deloraine Modern Backpackers,** 24 Old Bass Hwy., has simple shared dorms, laundry, and a kitchen. (☎6362 2250. Dorms $18, after one night $16.) The **Apex Caravan Park ❶,** on West Pde., parallel to Emu Bay Rd. off the roundabout, has river sites and showers for $4 per person. (☎6362 2345. Sites for 2 $12, powered $15.) For lunch, stop in at **Deloraine Deli ❷,** 36 Emu Bay Rd., and grab some homemade lasagna for $11. (☎6362 2127. Open M-F 9am-5pm, Sa 9am-2:30pm.) About 8km north of town on the Bass Hwy, **Christmas Hills Raspberry Farm Cafe,** serves fresh, delicious raspberry desserts ($4-7) and savory sandwiches and burgers ($7-13). (☎6362 2186. Open daily 9am-5pm.) The Woolworths **supermarket** is at 58 Emu Bay Rd. (Open M-W and Sa 8am-6pm, Th-F 8am-9pm.)

PARKS. A 1½hr. drive southwest from Deloraine will take you to the arterial walking track into the **Walls of Jerusalem National Park.** Less trafficked than Cradle Mountain, the park contains the same craggy bluffs, vales, and ridges, with lakes and stretches of green moss. The mostly duckboarded track begins from a carpark with a pit toilet off the Mersey Forest Rd. (C171) and continues to the dolerite walls in a moderate 3-4hr. one-way trek. The first hour is a steep walk to the park's border and to an old trapper's hut. From there, it's relatively level except for inclines through the gates of the Walls. A compass, a $9 park map, and overnight equipment are required, even for dayhikes, due to the highly variable weather and changing elevations. Despite the moderate inclines and boarding, the Walls are not to be taken lightly; rangers recommend it only to experienced hikers. (☎6363 5182. Call ahead. Park fees apply.)

About 35km west of Deloraine off B12, **Mole Creek Karst National Park** (☎6363 5182), is home to over 200 caves, with two spectacular ones open to the public. The enormous **Marakoopa Cave** features a glowworm chamber, while **King Solomon's Cave** is much smaller with fewer steps and more colorful formations. Temperatures in the caves can drop to a chilling 9° Celsius. Park fees do not apply, but NPWS runs tours for a fee. ($8.80, both caves $14; children $4.40; families $22.) A few pleasant walking tracks traverse the above-ground park. A half kilometer before Marakoopa Cave, **Fern Glade Walk** is a 20min. trail alongside the Marakoopa Creek. **Alum Cliffs,** from a turn-off 1km east of Mole Creek, is a 1hr. hike to a lookout over the cliffs.

About 25km south of Deloraine on A5 and then C513 awaits the fantastic **Liffey Forest Reserve.** If your car can handle the steep, potholed dirt road, it is well worth the visit, as it is less frequented by tourists and houses some of the lushest forests in Tasmania. Hike out to the great **Liffey Falls** (45min. return) on the well-maintained track and viewing blocks. Continuing on to Gulf Road picnic area makes for a longer (3hr. return) walk.

NORTHWEST COAST: ALONG THE A2

West of Devonport, Bass Hwy. 1 and A2 Hwy. trace the northern coast of Tasmania. Bass Hwy. passes through Ulverstone and Burnie before reaching the junction where A2 continues northwest and A10 branches south toward Queenstown, Zeehan, and Strahan. From Burnie, A2 continues past Wynyard (18km) and Rocky Cape National Park (30km) to Smithton (74km) and nearby Stanley (66km).

BURNIE. The area's major transport hub is Burnie, a relatively large and heavily industrialized paper mill town. **Redline,** 117 Wilson St. (☎1300 360 000), connects Burnie to Stanley (1hr., 2 per day, $12) via Boat Harbour (30min., $5) and Launceston (2½hr., 2 per day, $21.10) via Devonport (1hr., 2 per day $8.40) and Deloraine (1¾hr., $16). **TassieLink** (☎6272 7555), buses from the Information Centre in Civic Sq to Hobart (5hr.; M, W, F 7am; $50) via Devonport (45min., $8.80), and Launceston (2¼hr., $25.30). The **Tasmanian Travel and Information Centre** is in the Civic Centre complex. (☎6434 6111. Open M-F 9am-5pm, Sa-Su 1:30-4:30pm.) An **ANZ Bank** with an **ATM** is on the corner of Wilson and Cattley St. (Open M-Th 9:30am-4pm, F 9:30am-5pm.) The only budget accommodation is the friendly **Treasure Island Caravan Park ❶,** 253 Bass Hwy., 4km away in Cooee, with an indoor pool. (☎6431 1925. Sites $14, powered $16; dorms with kitchen $14; caravans $42; cabins $65.) Burnie's most savory sight is the **Lactos Cheese factory,** on Old Surrey Rd. (☎6431

2566. Open for free tastings M-F 9am-5pm, Sa-Su 10am-4pm.) The popular Burnie Rail **Market Train,** by Marine Terrace, chugs to Penguin and Ulverstone and back on the 2nd and last Sunday of the month in summer. The train stops at the Penguin Old School Market, featuring trinkets and food. (☎6437 2935. $6.50 per sector.)

ROCKY CAPE NATIONAL PARK. Rocky Cape National Park (☎6458 1100) features a mountainous coastline, rare flora, and **Aboriginal cave sites.** The two ends of the park are accessible by separate access roads. The 9km eastern access road turns off A2 12km west of Wynyard and leads to walking tracks and **Sisters Beach.** The 4km western access road, 18km further down A2, ends at a lighthouse and great views of Table Cape and the Nut. Aboriginal caves can be accessed from both entrances via short walking tracks; the **Coastal Route** track traverses the length of the park along the undeveloped coast (11km; 3hr.) while the **Inland Track** heads in the same direction with somewhat better views. There is no Visitors Center, but the shops near both entrances stock park brochures. The small park is geared toward day use; the low-growing vegetation is still recovering from a severe bushfire and offers little protection from the sun during extended walks. The **Nut,** a 152m volcanic plateau about 20km northeast of Rocky Cape in nearby **Stanley,** makes a good daytrip. Take a steep but short (10-15min.) plod up to the top of the Nut and then a leisurely walk (45min.) around. A **chairlift** goes up (open in summer daily 9:30am-5:30pm, in winter 10am-4pm; $7 return, children $5), and the **Nut buggy tour** carts people around the top ($5; closed in winter).

THE NORTHEAST

Tasmania's northeast is blessed with a sunny disposition. The pleasant coastline is dotted by quiet fishing and port towns that make suitable summer holiday spots for families with young children.

LAUNCESTON
☎03

Built where the North and South Esk rivers join to form the Tamar, Launceston (LON-seh-ston; pop 90,000) is Tasmania's second-largest city and Australia's third-oldest, founded in 1805. The intense historic rivalry between Hobart and Launceston manifests itself most clearly in beer loyalty: Boag's is the ale of choice in the north, Cascade in the south. Though this university town continues to grow, steeple-tops still dominate the sky-line above the town's many red and green roofs as steadfast guards of Launceston's old-world Victorian charm.

▐ TRANSPORTATION

Flights: Launceston Airport, south of Launceston on Hwy. 1 to B41. **VirginBlue** (☎13 67 89; www.virginblue.com.au) flies twice daily to Melbourne (1hr., $115-200) and once a day to Sydney (2hr., $185-300). **Qantas** (☎13 13 13) also flies to Melbourne (1hr., 5 per day, $150-235) and Sydney (1¾hr., 1 per day, $160-330). **Tasmanian Shuttle Bus Services,** 101 George St., provides airport **shuttles** that meet flights and will pick-up from accommodations but only run 8:45am-5pm. (☎6331 2009. $10.)

Buses: The **Redline Coaches** terminal is at the new bus terminal at Conrwall Sq. (☎6336 1444; reservations 1300 360 000 daily 6am-9pm; www.tasredline.com). Their buses run to: Burnie (2.25hr., 3 per day, $24.70); Devonport (1¼hr., 4 per day, $17.30); Bicheno/Swansea (2¾hr., 1 per day, $27.40); St. Helens (2¼hr., Su-F 1 per day, $24.40); and Scottsdale/Derby (2¼hr., Su-F 1 per day, $16.50). **TassieLink** buses (☎1300 300 520) run to: Hobart (2½hr., 1 per day, $24); Devonport (1¼hr., 1 per

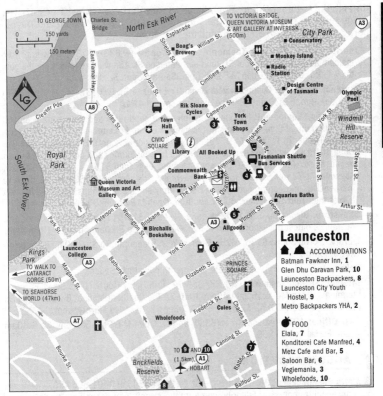

Launceston

🏠 ▲ ACCOMMODATIONS
Batman Fawkner Inn, **1**
Glen Dhu Caravan Park, **10**
Launceston Backpackers, **8**
Launceston City Youth
Hostel, **9**
Metro Backpackers YHA, **2**

🍎 FOOD
Elaia, **7**
Konditorei Cafe Manfred, **4**
Metz Cafe and Bar, **5**
Saloon Bar, **6**
Vegiemania, **3**
Wholefoods, **10**

day, $16.50); Cradle Mountain (3hr., in summer 1 per day, $51.70); Strahan (9hr., M-Sa 1 per day, $70.20) via Queenstown (6hr., M-Sa 1 per day, $62.70); and Bicheno (2½hr.; F-Sa 1 per day, in summer also M, W; $24.30).

Public Transportation: Metro (☎13 22 01) buses run daily 7am-7pm. Fares $1-3. The bright orange **City Go Round bus** (☎6336 3133) hits major tourist stops including the museums, brewery, and gorge. 24hr. $6, concessions $3, families $15; buy on board.

Taxis: Taxi Combined (☎6331 5555 or 13 10 08). Fare to airport $20-30.

Car Rental: Budget (☎6391 8566), at the airport, from $40 per day. Ages 21-24 $18 surcharge. **Economy,** 27 William St. (☎6334 3299), from $31, rents to ages 17+.

Automobile Club: RAC Tasmania (☎6335 5633, 24hr. 13 11 11), at the corner of York and George St. Open M-F 8:45am-5pm.

Bike Rental: Launceston City Youth Hostel, 36 Thistle St. W, (☎6344 9779), starts at $10 per day but usually rents on a weekly basis with all the gear for long trips (mountain bikes $110 per wk., touring bikes $70 per wk.).

◼🔢 ORIENTATION & PRACTICAL INFORMATION

The town is best explored by foot, since most attractions are within four blocks of the **Brisbane Street Mall** and all the streets are one-way. The city center is bounded on the north by the **North Esk River** and on the west by the **South Esk,** which flows through the Cataract Gorge. From here, A8 runs north to George Town; Hwy. 1 heads south to Hobart through the Midlands and west to Deloraine and Devonport; A3 snakes east to St. Helens and the east coast.

Tourist Office: Gateway Tasmania Travel Centre (☎6336 3133; www.gateway-tas.com.au), on the corner of St. John and Paterson St. 1hr. walking tours from the center M-F 9:45am, $11. Open M-F 9am-5pm, Sa 9am-3pm, Su 9am-noon.

Currency Exchange: Commonwealth Bank, 97 Brisbane St. (☎6337 4432). Open M-Th 9:30am-4pm, F 9:30am-5pm. The mall has several **ATMs.**

Bushwalking Equipment: For quality equipment at good rates and excellent advice and instruction on all things outdoors in Tasmania, head to ■ **Launceston City Youth Hostel,** 36 Thistle St. W (☎6344 9779; http://beh.fusionware.net). Experienced manager Doug Snare will be happy to help you prepare for your journey and outfit you right down to your socks. Tents from $20 per week, sleeping bags from $15, outdoorwear $10-20. **Allgoods,** 71-79 York St. (☎6331 3644; www.allgoods.com.au), at St. John St. Huge, is inexpensive, and comprehensive, and sells army surplus and maps. Basic equipment hire at their **Tent City** annex, 60 Elizabeth St. Open M-F 9am-5:30pm, Sa 9am-4pm.

Bookstore: Birchalls, 118-120 Brisbane St. (☎6331 3011; www.birchalls.com.au). Australia's oldest bookshop. Open M-F 8:30am-6pm, Sa 8:30am-5pm, Su 10am-4pm.

Library: 1 Civic Sq. (☎6336 2625). Open M-W 9:30am-6pm, Th-Sa 9:30am-9pm. **Internet** $2.50 per 15min.

Police: (☎6336 3701), on Cimitiere St. Enter through Civic Square.

Internet: Service Tasmania (☎1300 366 773), in Henty House, Civic Sq., has 3 free terminals. Open M-F 8:15am-4:45pm. **iCaf,** 22 The Quadrant Mall, at Brisbane and St. John St. (☎6334 6815). $2 per 15min. Coffee $2. See also **Library**, above.

Post Office: 107 Brisbane St. (☎6331 9477). Open M-F 9am-5:30pm, Sa 9:30am-1pm. **Postal Code:** 7250.

▛ ACCOMMODATIONS

■ **Metro Backpackers YHA,** 16 Brisbane St. (☎6334 4505 or 0401 666 436; www.back-packersmetro.com.au). Friendly, comfortable, swank, and convenient to downtown. Wall-to-wall carpeting, comfy lounge with satellite TV, large kitchen and balcony with BBQ, off-street parking, and laundry. Info center twice as good as the official one. Ask manager Mark about his flags. Internet $2 per 10min. Bike rental $15 per day. Reception 7:30am-10pm. Dorms in summer $23, YHA $20, in winter $19/$16; themed doubles and twins in summer $55/$50, in winter $45/$40; family rooms in summer $95/$90, in winter $85/$80. ❷

Launceston Backpackers, 103 Canning St. (☎6334 2327), across from Brickfields Reserve, off Bathurst St., a 7min. walk from the city center. Clean dorms await in this grand restored home. Large kitchen, free long-term storage, and laundry. Internet $2 per 10min. Key deposit in summer $10. Female-only dorms on request. Reception 8-11am and 1-10pm. 4- to 6-bed dorms $17; twins $38; doubles $40; singles $25, in summer $38. VIP. ❷

Batman Fawkner Inn, 35 Cameron St. (☎6331 7222), next to La Porchetta. If you don't need cooking facilities, hop on over to the Inn to get a clean bed, duvet, towel, ensuite, and TV all to your own. Complimentary tea and coffee in each room. Singles $25-45; twins $60; doubles $70; extra bed $10. ❷

Launceston City Youth Hostel, 36 Thistle St. W (☎/fax 6344 9779), opposite the Coats Patons building at Glen Dhu St. Turn right onto Howick from Wellington St., then left onto Glen Dhu St.; or take Metro #24 from Allgoods to stop 8; 15min. walk to town. Spacious and clean building with 100 beds. Dining room, common room, and kitchen.

Coin-op shower (10¢), free linens, security lockers, and midnight quiet time. No co-ed dorms. Bike and hiking equipment rental (see **Practical Information**). Dorms $15, 3 nights $39; singles $20; family rooms $40. VIP/YHA discount $2. ❶

Glen Dhu Treasure Island Caravan Park, 94 Glen Dhu St. (☎6344 2600), 2km south of downtown. Follow directions to City Youth Hostel. Lots of noise from neighboring Hwy. 1. BBQ, showers, laundry, outdoor campers' kitchen with kettle, hot plate, TV, and toaster-oven. Reception 8:30am-7pm. Sites for 2 $16, powered $18; caravans $40; cabins $65-72. ❷

▸ FOOD

Coles **supermarket** is at 198 Charles St. (☎6334 5744. Open M-W and Sa 8am-6pm, Th-F 8am-9pm.) Organic Wholefoods Launceston is at 54 Frederick St. (☎6331 7682. Open M-F 10am-6pm, Sa 9am-5pm, Su 11am-5pm.)

Konditorei Cafe Manfred, 106 George St. (☎6334 2490). Old-world patisserie serving excellent baked goods and light meals ($3-5). Tasty cafe meals for a pre-dessert munch. Open M-F 9am-5:30pm, Sa 8:30am-4pm. ❶

Elaia, 238-240 Charles St. (☎6331 3307), 2 blocks south of Princes Sq. Mediterranean decor and classy food. Great focaccia ($10.40). Eat indoors or out. Mains $11-20. Open M-Sa 9am-late, Su 10am-5pm. ❸

Veglemania, 64 George St. (☎6331 2535). Tasmania's first and only vegetarian and vegan restaurant. Thai, Chinese, and Indian-inspired dishes from $12. $6 lunch special noon-2pm. Open M-F noon-2pm and 5-10pm, Sa 5-10pm, Su 5-9pm. ❶

The Metz Cafe and Bar, 119 St. John St. (☎6331 7277; www.themetz.com.au), on the corner of York St. Upscale pizza pub and wine bar attract a mixed crowd of young business folk, couples, students, and travelers. Filling, innovative dishes and wood-fired pizzas $14-18. Open daily 8am-midnight. ❸

Saloon Bar, 191 Charles St. (☎6331 7355), in Hotel Tasmania. It's hard to find more for your money than at this faux-Western hangout. Heaping plates of roast or mixed veggies $5. Burgers $7, Porterhouse steak $12. Decent wine list. W and Sa live music; cover $5. Kitchen open daily noon-9pm; bar Su-Tu noon-midnight, W-Sa noon-3am. ❶

◉ ☠ SIGHTS & ACTIVITIES

The most spectacular sight in Launceston is the handiwork of the South Esk River. At the **Cataract Gorge Reserve,** see awesome sheer cliffs holding the river flow. A 20min. walk from Paterson St. toward Kings Bridge, it's not exactly pristine wilderness; the First Basin of the gorge has been popular since the town's settlement and now hosts peacocks, an exotic tree garden, a restaurant, and a free swimming pool. Walking tracks run on either side of the river from King's Bridge; the one on the north side is easy, while the one on the south climbs to the gorge's rim for excellent views of the cataracts. It is not advisable to walk around in this area after dark. A **chairlift** connects the two sides at the First Basin. (Open daily 9am-4:30pm. $6.) The **Band Rotunda,** on the First Basin's north side (cross the Basin on the swinging Alexandra Suspension Bridge), and the **Duck Reach Power Station,** at the far end of the gorge, provide info on the gorge. (☎6337 1288. Rotunda open M-F 9am-4pm, Sa-Su 9am-4:30pm. Power station open daily dawn-dusk.)

The **Queen Victoria Museum and Art Gallery** is split between the exhibits at **Royal Park** and at **Inveresk.** Royal Park, on the corner of Cameron and Wellington St., houses an impressive local and natural history display focusing on Tasmania's wildlife. The upstairs gallery offers a brief but sweet peek of Tasmanian sculpture, paintings, ceramics, and textile art. A highlight is the Chinese temple (Joss house) built by immigrant miners in a nearby town in the 19th century. The Planetarium is part of the complex. The **Inveresk Museum** (across the river on Tamar St.) houses a Tasmanian art gallery, exhibits on immigration to Tasmania, a railway exhibit, a blacksmith ship, artifacts from the Pacific, and a fantastic display of ⊠**Aboriginal shell necklaces.** Be sure to check out the Maireener shells and the rice shells. (☎6323 3777; www.qvmag.tased.edu.au. Open daily 10am-5pm. Both museums $10. Planetarium shows Tu-F 3pm, Sa 2 and 3pm. $5, children $3, families $12. No children under 5.)

A great way to enjoy the city and its fantastic surroundings is on a tour. ⊠**Devil's Playground Ecotours** (☎6458 2020) offers day tours with excellent guides, lunch, and all entry fees included. Among the most popular tours are Cradle Mountain (W and Su, $80), Waterfalls Caves (Th and Su, $65), and Wildlife (F, $80). For wild adventures, try **Tasmanian Expeditions,** 110 George St. (☎6334 3477 or 1800 030 230; www.tas-ex.com. Half-day rock climbing/abseiling $85; two-day cycling and canoeing $375; six-day Cradle Mountain and Walls of Jerusalem National Parks $995.) Finally, spend a day with informative guide Lee on **Tasmanian Wilderness Tours** (☎0418 520 391 or 6394 3212; www.tigerwilderness.com.au) either touring the wine region of the northeast on the Wine and Waterfall Tour (half-day $60, concessions/YHA $55) or exploring Cradle Mountain at the Marakoopa Glow Worm Cave and other stops along the way (M, W, Sa; full-day $95, concessions $90).

For more pampered relaxation, the **Aquarius Roman Baths,** 127-133 George St., has an indoor frigidarium (cold bath), tepidarium (warm bath), caldarium (hot bath), and rubarium (heat lamps) in the style of ancient Rome. (☎6331 2255; www.romanbath.com.au. Open daily 9am-9pm. $20, double-entry $33.) For an illuminating overview of the beer-brewing process followed by free samples, take the **Boag's Brewery** tour, 21 Shields St. (☎6331 9311; www.boags.com.au. Open M-Th 2:30pm. Tours 1-1½hr. Free.)

■ DAYTRIP FROM LAUNCESTON: GEORGE TOWN

North along A8 (50km), on the east side of the cove where the Tamar River meets the Bass Strait, lies George Town. Once considered the capital of the north, George Town now acts as an historical center and Launceston's port. It does, however, lay claim to the title of the oldest *town* in Australia and the third oldest settlement. Mellow and quiet, it affords visitors serene views across the river and—if you're lucky—glimpses of glorious pink sunsets over the western hills.

The town's seafaring history has been preserved in the **Pilot Station & Maritime Museum** in **Low Head,** 5km north of the town. Established in 1805, this convict-built estate is the oldest continuously operating facility of its kind in Australia, with displays featuring artifacts like beer bottles salvaged from shipwrecks. (☎6382 1143. Open daily 8am-8pm. $3, concessions $2.) The road ends at the **Low Head Lighthouse** (1888), with great views of the peninsula and the Tamar River (☎6382 1211. Gate to the lighthouse locked at 6pm.) Worth a visit, **The Grove,** 25 Cimitiere St., is a grand Georgian home dating to 1827. (☎6382 1336. Open M-F 10:30am-3pm, in summer daily 10am-5pm.) Enjoy impressive views from the lookout on **Mt. George,** also the home of a restored semaphore signal mast. **Fairy penguins** and seals use some of the beaches around George Town and Low Head as nesting places during the spring. **Fairy Penguin Twilight Tours** leads nightly tours one hour before sunset. (☎0418 361 860. No tours May-June. $12, children $7. Warm clothes recommended.) **Seal & Sea Adventure Tours** offers seal-watching tours of the Hebe Reef and Tenth Island. (☎6382 3452 or 0419 357 028; www.sealandsea.com. 3-4hr.; 2 or more people $121, 3 or more $94 each with $200 min. charge; families $280.)

Redline Coaches (☎1300 360 000), operating at Pinos Hardware, 21 Elizabeth St., buses to and from Launceston (45min., M-F 3 per day, $8.60). The **Visitors Center** is on the road entering town from the south. (☎6382 1700. Internet $2 per 30min. Open daily Aug.-Sept. 10am-2pm; Oct.-July 9am-5pm.) The **Online Access Centre,** next to the **library,** in Regent Sq., also has **Internet.** (☎6382 1356. Open M-F 9am-8pm, Sa-Su 1-5pm. $5 per 30min.) **Banks,** the **police station** (☎6382 4040), and the **post office** (open M-F 9am-5pm) cluster on Macquarie St. **Postal Code:** 7253.

George Town itself doesn't warrant more than a day's visit, but if you visit the delightful ⬛**Traveller's Lodge (YHA) ❶,** 4 Elizabeth St., you will definitely want to spend the night. Turn left at the third roundabout. The super-cozy cottage doubles as a National Heritage Landmark (ca. 1870) with the oldest tree in George Town in the backyard. (☎6382 3261. Sites $10; bunks $22, YHA $18; doubles $50.) There's a **supermarket** at 8 Bathurst St. (Open M-W, Sa 8am-6pm, Th-F 8am-9pm.)

A3 EAST: LAUNCESTON TO THE SUNCOAST

MT. VICTORIA FOREST RESERVE. The Reserve is 45min. past Scottsdale. From A3, follow signs south to Ringarooma and continue 15km on mostly unsealed roads to the carpark. The strikingly thin single-drop **Ralph Falls,** reckoned to be the tallest in Tassie, is a 10min. walk from the carpark, and Cashs Gorge lies 30min. beyond. The waterfall also happens to be the site of ⬛**Norm's Lookout,** which provides a fantastic view of the gorge below. The tough hike up Mt. Victoria passes a melange of ecosystems and a panorama of the whole Northeast.

DERBY. Derby is a historic tin-mining town, though its mines have been closed for over 50 years now. The quirky **Tourist Centre/butcher shop** (☎6354 2364; open daily 5am-5pm) and the **painted fish rock** are on the north side of A3 heading east, past the second bridge. Derby's big draw is the ⬛**Tin Mine Centre,** which boasts a tea room, museum, reconstructed mining village, and the opportunity to pan for miniscule gemstones. (☎6354 2262. Open daily Sept.-May 9am-5pm; June-Aug. 10am-4pm. $4.50, children $2.50, families $12.) The town comes alive in late October for the **Derby River Derby,** a mad and motley 5km river race.

CLOSER TO ST. HELENS. Blue Lake is in South Mt. Cameron on B82 as you approach **Gladstone** and **Mt. William National Park,** about 12km northeast off A3. An inadvertent product of mining, Blue Lake's unearthly shade of aquamarine is due to the mineral composition of the soil. The **Weldborough Pass Scenic Reserve,** just beyond Weldborough, offers a rainforest walk guided by "Grandma Myrtle" right by the highway. The 15min. circuit weaves beneath huge tree-ferns and myrtle beeches. About 30min. west of St. Helens, in the middle of a pasture in Pyengana just off A3, **Pub in the Paddock–St. Columba Falls Hotel ❸** recalls a time before pubs had to be Irish, Western, or serve pokies to attract customers. Slops, the beer-drinking pig, draws droves of fans. (☎6373 6121. Open daily 11am-late. Meals served noon-2pm and 6-8pm. Singles $35; doubles $45.) The sole producer of Pyengana Cheddar, the **Pyengana Cheese Factory,** St. Columba Falls Rd., is open daily for touring, snacking, and sales. (☎6373 6157. Open daily 10am-4pm, in summer 9am-6pm.) Nearby, the 90m cascading **St. Columba Falls** unleashes 42,000L per minute. Drive ten minutes beyond the pub on an unsealed road ending at a carpark, then walk ten minutes to the falls. Keep a close lookout for the supposedly extinct Tasmanian tiger while in the area; a ranger allegedly spotted one here in 1995.

BRIDPORT
☎03

A longtime holiday and weekend town for Launceston urbanites, Bridport lies along the sheltered beach of **Anderson's Bay** at the mouth of the **Brid River.** With few sights, Bridport lends itself to relaxing on the beach and enjoying the estuary: there are birds to spot, oysters to dig up, and beach cricket to play.

The **Redline** (☎ 1300 360 000) **bus** from Launceston to Scottsdale (1¼hr.; M-F 2 per day, Su 1 per day except Jan.; $11.10) connects with **Stan's Coach Service** to Bridport. (☎ 6356 1662. 30min., M-F 2 per day, $3.) Everything in town is on Main St., including the **Bridport 2000 Plus Visitor Centre** (☎ 6356 0280; open M-Sa 10am-4pm, Su 10am-1pm) and the **Service Tasmania,** which has free **Internet.** (☎ 1300 135 513. Open M-F 9am-5pm.) Bridport has no bank, but there is an **ATM** at the Bridport Ex-Service and Community Club. (Open M-Tu 11am-12:30pm and 3:30-8pm, W-Th 11am-12:30pm and 3-10pm, F-Sa 11am-11pm, Su 11am-7pm.) Tubby's **supermarket** has **EFTPOS** and a **post office** desk. (☎ 6356 1282. Open daily 7am-7pm; post office open M-F 9am-5pm.) **Postal code:** 7262.

The custom-built ▧**Bridport Seaside Lodge YHA ❷,** 47 Main St., is a budget traveler's dream. There's a large kitchen, tidy rooms, free canoes, tea and coffee, and a veranda with views of the estuary beach. (☎ 6356 1585. Reception 9am-8pm. Free canoe use. Dorms $19; doubles $46-51; twins $46-29; YHA discount $3.) **Bridport Caravan Park ❶,** on Bentley St., has close-quarter wooded sites along the beach, but fills up quickly during the high season. (☎ 6356 1227. Sites $11, powered $15, extra person $5.) Bridport has the standard takeaway joints, but the real find for cheap and tasty eats is **Springfield Fisheries ❶,** the fish slaughterhouse, on Main St. just before crossing the bridge into Bridport. Survive the spectacle of bloody fish guts to buy smoked trout. (☎ 6356 0556. Open F 8am-4pm. $8 per kg.)

A 30min. shoreline stroll north from the Main St. bridge past the old pier takes you to the **Mermaids Pool** swimming hole. Extend the walk past **wildflowers** in the spring by heading down Main St., turning right just past Walter St., and looping back around along the coast (2½hr.). Another walk to **East Sandy Point** (1½hr. return) grants great views and leads to huge dunes. To get to the start of the track, follow Main St., which turns into Sandy Points Rd., and park at the gateway where the road becomes a rough 4WD track.

MT. WILLIAM NATIONAL PARK

More of a hill than a mountain, Mt. William overlooks a quiet stretch of coast in the sunny northeast corner, east of Bridport. Travelers flock to Mt. William to relax and camp beside the park's extraordinary beaches—widely considered the best in the state—and to safari among marsupials. Wallabies are everywhere, and echidnas pop up in the daytime. At dusk, chest-high Forester kangaroos are in motion, as well as smaller pademelons, wombats, and chazzwazzers. After dark—with a good flashlight—spot brushtail possums, spotted-tail quolls, and Tasmanian devils. Eagle-eyed visitors might even glimpse the rare New Holland mouse.

Mt. William is a relatively isolated national park with no facilities. Bringing drinking water is essential; head to Gladstone for food or petrol. In an emergency, call the ranger (☎ 6357 2108) at the north entrance. The park is accessible via the north entrance, at the hamlet of Poole, following the signposts through the gateway of Gladstone (17km southwest), or from St. Helens to the southern entrance at Ansons Bay via C843 and C846. No buses run to the park, but Terry's Bus Service (☎ 6357 2193) meets Redline coaches in Derby and goes to Gladstone (1½hr., M-F 12:30pm, $2), about 20km southwest of the park entrance. From St. Helens, the drive to the southern entrance takes about 1½hr. The gravel access roads are a bumpy ride even at slow speeds. Both ends of the park offer ample free coastal **camping ❶** (only at designated sites), short walking tracks, and beach walks. Park fees apply. The northern access road leads to Forester Kangaroo Dr., past the turn-off for Stumpy's Bay and its camping areas, and on to the trailhead for the Mt. William walk (1½hr. return; moderate). Starting along the road to campsite 4, a short track passes through coastal heath to the extraordinary coastline at Cobbler Rocks (1½hr. return; moderate).

FLINDERS ISLAND ☎ 03

The largest of the Furneasux Group islands (pop. 800), approximately 60km north-east of Tasmania, Flinders Island is exceedingly remote, unpopulated, and blessed with a preponderance of natural beauty. Less beautiful, though, is the tiny island's long, grim human history. Though once home to a small, indigenous population of Aborigines (presumably living on the island when it broke from the mainland), this group died off ages ago, for reasons yet to be determined. After centuries of desolation, Tasmanian Aborigines found themselves on Flinders again; this time, as part of an ill-conceived plan by British settlers to "civilize" what remained of the decimated people. In this bleak and unfamiliar environment, most perished.

Today, Flinders Island caters to the enterprising, adventuresome outdoor enthusiast, though getting to the island can be challenging. **Island Airlines** runs flights out of Launceston. (☎ 1800 645 875. 40min.; M-F 2 per day, Sa-Su 1 per day; $279 return, $400 return to Melbourne.) **Sinclair Air Charter** will take up to 5 passengers from Bridport. (☎ 6359 3641. $280 one-way min. charge.) **Southern Shipping** can carry up to 12 passengers on their **cargo freight** from Bridport to Lady Barron. (☎ 6356 1753. From 8hr. up to 37hr. M evening; returns Tu, arriving Bridport W. $77 return, children $44. Vehicles $500-800. Book 1 month in advance and bring food.) The island's **Information Centre**, 7 Lagood Rd., in Whitemark, has everything you would want to know about the island. Pick up a *Critter Spotters Guide*, a *Walking Guide to Flinders Island*, and any and all info about accommodations and rental cars. (☎ 6359 2380. Open M-F 9am-5pm.) Even though Flinders is a Tasmanian municipality, rental companies generally forbid long ferry vehicle transport. **Bowman & Lees Car Hire** (☎ 6359 2388), **Flinders Island Car Rentals** (☎ 6359 2168), **Flinders Island Transport Services** (☎ 6359 2010), and **Flinders Island Lodge Furneaux Car Rentals** (☎ 6359 3521) rent cars on the island from $60 per day; most accommodations do as well. No bike hire is available on the island. Whitemark also has all basic amenities, including: **Walkers Supermarket,** which has **petrol** (☎ 6359 2010; open M-F 9am-5:30, Sa 9am-noon); a Westpac **bank** (open M-Th 11am-2:30pm, F 11am-2:30pm and 4-5pm); **Internet** at Service Tasmania (open M-F 10am-4pm); and a **post office** (open M-F 9am-5pm). **Postal Code:** 7255.

The island has fantastic **camping,** usually along the beaches; otherwise, budget stays are hard to come by. **Flinders Island Cabin Park ❶,** 1 Bluff Rd., near the airport, has numerous accommodations and hires cars for $55 per day. (☎ 6359 2188. Sites $5, powered $7; single cabins $30; cabins for 4 with outside amenities: $45 for 2, extra person $10; family cabins $65 for 2, extra person $10; double ensuite $75.) **Interstate Hotel ❷,** in Whitemark, has basic rooms, modern rooms, and ensuites. (☎ 6359 2114. Singles $35-58; twins and doubles $55-88.) The island is fully supplied with B&Bs and farmstays. Check www.flindersislandonline.com.au, which is constantly updated. For a real treat, **Flinders Island Local Food Hampers** (☎ 6359 2219) delivers gourmet picnics.

At 756m, Mt. Strzelecki in **Strzelecki National Park** (☎ 6359 2217) is the highest point on the island, from which you can see the other 54 Furneaux Islands, and, if you're lucky, Wilsons Promontory in Victoria. This moderately challenging walk (3km; 5hr.) traverses fern gullies and craggy outcrops. Be sure to bring plenty of water because much of the track is exposed to sun, and wear sturdy shoes, as the track goes over large rocks. Park fees apply. At the terminus of C806 is the peaceful **Trousers Point** beach, great for a picnic and dip. Camping is also available. Test your luck by digging for **Topaz diamonds** in Killiecrankie. Rent a shovel and bucket ($4) and a treasure map ($4) from the **general store.** (☎ 6359 8560. Open daily 9am-5pm.) The store also rents cars ($66 per day) and runs sealwatching tours ($55 per person). **Flinders Island Adventures** leads tailored day tours of the island for a minimum of two people. (☎ 6359 4507. $110 per person.)

TASMANIA

THE SUNCOAST

Tasmania's east coast is the island's softer side, where the weather and even the people are milder. With its mountainous interior, this side of Tassie is sheltered from the storms that pound the west. Agriculture and holiday tourism when summer travelers come for fishing, swimming, and loafing in the sun—sustain the towns. The drive along the coast can ease the weariest traveler.

SAINT HELENS   ☎03

St. Helens, located off the A3 just south of Mt. William National Park (see p. 558), is the largest and northernmost of the coast fishing and vacation villages of Tasmania's east coast. Peaceful and easygoing, the town serves as a perfect gateway to the nearby coastal attractions.

Getting to these treasures some 15km northeast of town requires a car and the ability to handle weaving gravel roads. **Humbug Point**, via Binalong Bay Rd., offers great walks and views, while **St. Helens Point**, via St. Helens Point Rd., has free camping with pit toilets, decent fishing, and good surf at **Beerbarrel Beach.** On St. Helen's Point, the **Peron Dunes** cover a large expanse of coast, attracting dune buggies and sand boarders. North of Humbug Point, the **Bay of Fires Coastal Reserve**, named for the red rocks that Capt. Tobias Furneaux mistook for fire, has long beaches and basic campsites. The access road ends at the privately owned **Gardens** and **Margery's Corner**. **Leda Falls** (1½hr. drive) is open to the public at Cerise Brook on Medea Cove Rd.

Redline (☎6376 1182) **buses** sell tickets at the newsagency at Quail and Cecilia St. Their buses run to: Hobart (4-5hr., Su-F 1 per day, $38.20); Launceston (2½hr., Su-F 1 per day, $24.40); and St. Mary's (40min., Su-F 1 per day, $6.20). **TassieLink** (☎1300 300 520) also operates in this area, running to: Hobart (4hr., Su and F 2pm, $37.60) via Bicheno (1hr., $10.10), the highway turn-off for Coles Bay (1¼hr., $11.60), and Swansea (1¾hr., $14.20). The **St. Helens Travel Centre,** 20 Cecilia St., makes TassieLink bookings. (☎6376 1533. Open M-F 9am-5pm, Sa 9am-noon.) **St. Helens History Room,** 59 Cecilia St., offers local history and **tourist information.** (☎6376 1744. Open M-F 9am-5pm, Sa 9am-2pm, in summer also Su 10am-2pm; history room $2, children $1.) A 24hr. **ATM** is available at **Trust Bank,** 18 Cecilia St. **Service Tasmania,** 23 Quail St., has free **Internet.** (☎6376 2431. Open M-F 8:30am-4:30pm. Max. 30min.) The **post office** is at 46 Cecilia St. (☎6376 5350. Open M-F 9am-5pm.) **Postal Code:** 7216.

The quiet **St. Helens YHA ❷,** 5 Cameron St., off Quail St., has all you might need in a fabulous 70s-esque setting. Hostel owners provide a helpful driving map of the nearby attractions. (☎6376 1661. Reception 8-10am and 5-10pm. Dorms $20, YHA $16; doubles $40/$36.) The standard but well-situated **St. Helens Caravan Park ❶** is 1.5km from the town center on Penelope St., just off the Tasman Hwy. on the southeast side of the bridge. (☎6376 1290. Sites for 2 $17, powered $22, ensuite $28; on-site caravans $40; cabins $68-80.) The ▨**Wok Stop ❶,** 57a Cecilia St., has South and East Asian dishes in all sizes plus fresh juices and ice cream. (☎6376 2665. Open M-Sa 11:30am-8:30pm, Su noon-8pm.) The ValuePlus **supermarket** is at 33 Cecilia St. (☎6376 1117. Open daily 7:30am-8pm.)

South of the Scamander Township on A3 between St. Helen's and Coles Bay awaits a fantastic little stop for lunch, the ▨**Eureka Farm ❷.** Full of fresh fruit and outstanding homemade ice cream, the Eureka Farm's small cafe (located within the farm) serves superb dishes from a recently expanded menu. Meals are quite affordable, ranging from $8 to $12, and include such highlights as fresh salmon and focaccias. (☎6372 5500. Open Nov.-May 10am-5pm. Cash only.)

BICHENO ☎03

The spectacular 75km drive south from St. Helens along A3 traces the coastline's sand dunes and granite peaks to the small town of Bicheno (BEE-shen-oh; pop. 750). With its mild climate, rocky seashore, neighborly community, and proximity to postcard fairy penguins and national parks (Freycinet and Douglas-Apsley), Bicheno is enchanting. It's hard to avoid beach activities while enjoying the 3km **Foreshore Footway** coastal track that begins at the bottom of Weily Ave., left off Burgess St. The walk leads past the blowhole, the marine reef around Governor Island, and numerous nooks for swimming, snorkeling, and diving.

Redline buses leave from the main bus stop at Four-Square Store on Burgess St. (open M-Sa 8am-6:30pm, Su 8am-6pm) and run to the Coles Bay turn-off (10min., M-F 1 per day, $5.50), continuing to Swansea (35min., $9), with connections to Hobart (5hr., $37.40) and Launceston (2¾hr., Su-F 1 per day, $27.40). **TassieLink** (☎ 1300 300 520) runs **buses** from the bus stop to: the Coles Bay turn-off (5min.; M, W, F, Su 1 per day; $2.50); Hobart (3hr.; M, W, F, Su 1 per day; $25.90); Launceston (2½hr.; F, Su, in summer also M, W 1 per day; $24.30); St. Helens (1hr., Su and F 1 per day, $10.10); and Swansea (40min.; M, W, F, and Su 1 per day; $5.50). **Bicheno Coach Service** (☎6257 0293) runs to Coles Bay (40min., M-Sa 1-4 per day, $9.50) and **Freycinet National Park** (50min., $8.80), making Redline and TassieLink connections from the Coles Bay turn-off. The **Tourist Information Centre** (☎6375 1333) is the surf shop in the town center. It books nightly **penguin-spotting** tours year-round (1hr.; $15, children $7), glass-bottom boat tours (45min., $15/$7), and 4WD tours (2½hr., $35), and sells surf gear and boogie boards. The **Online Access Centre** is on Burgess St. near the Primary School. (☎6375 1892. Open M 10am-1pm, and 2-5pm, Tu 10am-3:30pm, W, F, Sa 10am-1pm, Th 9am-noon. $5 per 30min.) The Value-Plus **supermarket** (open daily 7:30am-6pm) and the **post office** (with limited **banking;** ☎6375 1244; open M-F 9am-12:30pm and 1-5pm), are in the area of the A3 elbow in the town center. **Postal Code:** 7215.

As a popular holiday town, Bicheno is in no shortage of comfortable accommodations. For a fantastic view of the ocean, all the amenities of home, and the opportunity to pick your own fresh fruits and vegetables, stop in at the ▩**Bicheno Berrie Retreat ❺**, about 4km outside of town heading north on A3. Each unit has its own washer and dryer, VCR and videos, books, and free continental breakfast. The view from the balcony of Unit 1 (sleeps 6) cannot be beat. (☎6375 1481. Units $120, extra person $20.) The above-average **Bicheno Hostel ❶**, 11 Morrison St., lies off A3 behind a little white church near the post office. Guests get 10% off penguin tours, comfortable bunks, coastal views from the kitchen, and access to a free washer. (☎6375 1651. Dorms $15.) Both **pubs** in town have counter meals.

DOUGLAS-APSLEY NATIONAL PARK

Douglas-Apsley lacks the poster appeal of a mountain, rainforest, or windswept beach, but it's the last significant dry eucalypt forest in Tasmania, and with its wide rivers and wildflowers, it's a pleasant change of pace from your typical Tassie park. Its elevation to national park status in 1989 marked the greening of Tassie politics. No roads lead through the park.

From the southern carpark, a short track leads to the Aspley River Lookout (15min.), which doubles as a sign-posted nature trail. Signs along the **lookout walk** introduce the park's tree species, such as the blue gum, black wattle, and native cherry—springtime brings beautiful wildflowers. An unusual number of creatures lurk in the park, such as the endangered Tasmanian bettong and southern grayling fish. The **Apsley waterhole** is a deep pool in the middle of the slow Apsley River, 10min. from the southern carpark. The waterhole can be accessed from the carpark and from a shortcut near the lookout. A loop to the **Apsley River Gorge** (3hr.) follows a track from the north side of the waterhole uphill and back down into the gorge, returning on an undefined track downstream along the river. The return trip includes moderate climbing, sometimes tricky rock scrambling, and river crossings, so only the fit and agile should attempt it, when the river is low and the rocks are dry. The three-day **Leeaberra Track,** running from north to south to prevent the spread of root-rot fungus, goes the length of the park.

The popular southern end of the park (Apsley River and environs), is a 15min. drive from Bicheno (see p. 561), the nearest service center—the park has no telephones or drinking water. The obscure southern access road leaves A3 5km north of Bicheno, heading west along 7km of gravel road. The northern access road from St. Mary's, mostly along the MG logging road, is even harder to find. There is no bus service to the park, but the Bicheno Coach Service can charter a minibus. (☎6257 0293. To southern entrance: 2 people $30 return, $15 per extra person. To northern entrance: 1-4 people $50 return, 5-12 people $100 return.) There are free **campsites ❶** with pit toilets near the carparks; others are 50m from the Apsley waterhole. The nearest **rangers** (☎6375 1236) are in Bicheno. Park fees apply.

COLES BAY
☎03

The tiny township of Coles Bay (pop. 100) is the service and lodging center for **Freycinet National Park.** Its sunny shelter in the lap of **Great Oyster Bay** satisfies many summer vacationers, while its remote location (27km south on C302 off A3 between Bicheno and Swansea) ensures elevated prices. **TassieLink** (☎1300 300 520) and **Redline** (☎1300 360 000) **buses** run as close as the turn-off for Coles Bay on A3 south to Hobart (3-5hr., Su-F 1 per day, $25-30) and north to Launceston (2½hr., Su-F 1 per day, $22); from the turn-off, take **Bicheno Coaches** (☎6257 0293) to town (30min.; M-Sa 1-3 per day; $12) or the park (40min.; $7.50, return $14). **Freycinet Rentals,** 5 Garnet Ave. (☎6257 0320), rents Canadian canoes ($60 per day), dinghies ($25 per hr.), and 16 ft. runabouts ($80-140). They also rent camping gear and essentials for the area, like flippers and goggles. The **supermarket,** on Garnet Ave., offers limited **banking** and **petrol** and houses the **Visitors Centre,** a **coffee shop,** and the **post office.** (☎6257 0383. Open daily 8am-6:30pm.) Info on the park can be found at the **East Coast Interpretation Centre,** at the park's entrance. There is **Internet** at the **Freycinet Cafe and Bakery** on the Esplanade behind the YHA. (☎6257 0272. $6 per hr. Open daily in summer 8am-9pm; in winter 8am-5pm.)

The YHA-affiliated **Iluka Holiday Centre ❷** is a campground and backpackers at the western end of the Esplanade. The interior may be sparsely decorated, but it's just a hop, skip, and jump away from the beach. (☎6257 0115 or 1800 786 512; iluka@trump.net.au. Reception 8am-6pm. Sites $17, powered $20; dorms $22, YHA $19; twins and doubles $75-110; on-site vans for 2 $60.) For a rustic experience, the **Coles Bay Youth Hostel (YHA) ❸,** in the national park at Parsons Cove, has ten bunks with pit toilets and no running water. Reservations are essential, especially during summer. (☎6234 9617. Bunks $10, cabins $50.) **Freycinet Backpackers ❷** is part of the **Coles Bay Caravan Park ❶,** 3km north of town off the Coles Bay main road, or an easy 30min. walk along Muir's Beach. They offer a great kitchen, free laundry, and a return bus voucher to walking tracks. Bunks are in two-person dorms. (☎6257 0100. Book 3 months ahead during peak summer season and holidays. Linen $4.50. Reception 8am-9pm. Sites for 2 $13.20, powered $15.40; twins $33 1st night, $27 each extra night, 7th night free.)

Tours out of Coles Bay range from sea charters to kayak tours to scenic flights. **Freycinet Sea Charters** have two- to six-hour tours all along the coast, offering frequent sightings of dolphins, seals, and penguins. (☎6257 0355. Departs 10am and 3pm or by arrangement. $55-200.) **Freycinet Air** does scenic flights over the National

Park and Wineglass Bay. (☎6375 1694. From $75 for 2.) **Freycinet Adventures** does day tours with sea kayaking ($55-140), abseiling ($90), and 4-wheel motorbiking ($55-80). The also rent kayaks and mountain bikes. (☎6257 0500; www.freycinetadventures.com). **All4Adventures** (☎0438 509 022) also does 4WD tours of the park from $55 per person.

FREYCINET NATIONAL PARK

Freycinet National Park (FRAY-sin-nay) is rich with mountains, beaches, postcard sights, and diverse and abundant activities. Just a three-hour drive from Hobart or Launceston, the park is home to red-granite **Hazards** and photogenic **Wineglass Bay.**

  Bicheno Coaches stops in Coles Bay en route to the park's tracks. (☎6257 0293. Departs M-Sa morning; Su and return service by bookings only. $8.80, return $16.) They also offer service between Coles Bay, the Coles Bay turn-off (30min., $6.30) and Bicheno (40min., $7.50); at the turn-off, you can connect with TassieLink and Redline services to other destinations (see **Coles Bay,** p. 562). An hours walk away, Coles Bay is the service and lodging center for Freycinet, but for information on the park, stop at the **visitors kiosk** near the park entrance. Register and pay at the kiosk; park fees apply. (☎6357 0107. Hours vary.) **Campsites ❶** with wood, water, and basic toilets are available at Richardson's Beach (sites $5.50, powered $6.60), while free undeveloped campsites can be found at Friendly Beach.

  At an outdoor theater past the kiosk, rangers offer free programs, including nocturnal walks and primers on Aboriginal land use. (Dec.-Jan. Three per day.) Nearly all the short walks in the park are extraordinary. Just past the Freycinet Lodge, there's a turn-off on an unsealed road for Sleepy Bay (1.8km) and the ◪**Cape Tourville Lighthouse** (6.4km). It's an easy 20min. return walk to the Bay, which offers good swimming and snorkeling; the Lighthouse provides amazing views of the coast. Honeymoon Bay, popular for snorkeling, and Richardson's Beach, popular for swimming, are also on the main road. All major walking tracks begin at the carpark at the end of the road; a moderate 33km hike around the whole peninsula takes two to three days. Be sure to bring your own fresh water on dayhikes. The **Wineglass Bay Lookout walk** (1-2hr.) is a classic choice: the fairly steep trail climbs up through the red-granite Hazards and opens onto a fabulous view of the bay and Freycinet peninsular mountains. The four- to five-hour loop by Wineglass Bay and Hazards Beach (11km) is a pleasant alternative, though you might want to bring some bug spray, as the flies can get nasty in summer. Though the **Mt. Amos track** (3-4hr. return) is taxing, it has spectacular views. The white sands of Friendly Beaches, and its rare population of hooded plover, can be accessed via the 4.5km unsealed Friendly Beaches Rd., 18km north of Coles Bay. Free **campsites ❶** are available at **Isaacs Point** (with pit toilets) and **Ridge Camp;** neither has fresh water.

TRIABUNNA ☎03

On **Prosser Bay,** 50km southwest of Swansea and 87km northeast of Hobart, Triabunna (try-a-BUN-na; pop. 1200) is a tiny port town where you can stock up on food and spend the night before heading to Maria Island. **TassieLink** (☎0030 0520) runs to: Hobart (1½hr.; M-F 1 per day; $14.90); and Swansea (45min.; M-F 1 per day; $6.20). They also connect to the **Eastcoaster Island Ferry** in Orford (5min.). The **Tourist Information Centre,** at the Esplanade, has **Internet.** (☎6257 4090. Open daily 10am-4pm. $2 per 5min.) When managers Don and Fran renovated the 12-acre ◪**Udda Backpackers (YHA) ❷,** 12 Spencer St., they also incorporated hospitality and home-baked cookies. The solitude and comfort of this small, personal hostel may convince you to extend your stay. Follow Vicary St. toward the fire station, turn left after the bridge onto a gravel road, and then left onto Spencer St.; signs point the way. (☎6257 3439. Free Maria Island ferry pick-up. Dorms $16; twins and doubles $36.) **Triabunna Caravan Park ❶,** 6 Vicary St., is friendly and gets the job done. (☎6257 3575. Sites $12, powered $14; on-site vans for 2 $30-40.) Value-Plus **supermarket** is at Charles and Vicary St. (Open daily 8am-6pm.)

MARIA ISLAND NATIONAL PARK

Maria (muh-RYE-uh) Island has housed penal colonies, cement industries, whalers, and farmers. Today, the island national park is almost devoid of civilization, preserved for its historical and natural significance. The ruins of a settlement at **Darlington**—along with the area's abundant wildlife, natural beauty, and isolation—are the island's main attraction. Brochures about the park are available at the tourist office in Triabunna; the ferry has detailed descriptions of walking tracks. Walks wander through the **Darlington Township** ruins (1½hr.), over the textured sandstone of the **Painted Cliffs** (2hr., best at low tide; check schedule at Visitors Centre), and to the rock-scramble up **Bishop and Clerk** (4hr.).

To reach Maria, the **Eastcoaster Express catamaran** departs Eastcoaster Resort, 5km from both Triabunna and Orford. (☎6257 1589. 30min. Late Dec.-Apr. 9, 10:30am, 1, and 3:30pm. Daytrip $19, children $11; overnight $22/$14; bikes and kayaks $3.) Take the turn for Louisville Pt./Maria Island Ferry off A3. To get beyond the Darlington ferry wharf, walk or bring a mountain bike. On the island itself, there are no shops or facilities save a **Visitors Centre,** with maps and brochures, and a **ranger station** (☎6257 1420) with a telephone. The **Old Darlington Prison ❶** has been resurrected into six-bed units, each with a table, chairs, and fireplace. (Book ahead with ranger. Shared toilets, sinks, and hot showers. Beds $8.80, children $4, families $22.) The island has three **campsites ❶: Darlington,** with ample grassy space (sites $4.40, families $15); **French's Farm,** 11km south down the main gravel road, with an empty weatherproof farmhouse, pit toilet, and rainwater tanks; and **Encampment Cove,** 3km down a side road near French's Farm, with a small bunkhouse and pit toilet.

VICTORIA

Victoria may be mainland Australia's smallest state, but it's blessed with far more than its share of fantastic cultural, natural, and historical attractions. Its environment runs from the dry and empty western plains of the Mallee to the inviting wineries along the banks of the Murray River, from the Victorian Alps's ski resorts to the Gippsland coast's forested parks. Nowhere else in Australia is so much ecological diversity only a daytrip away. Meanwhile, the capital of the state and the cultural center of the nation, sleek and sophisticated Melbourne overflows with eclectic ethnic neighborhoods, public art spaces, back-alley bars, verdant gardens, and a vibrant, energetic atmosphere. It's no wonder that many Aussies claim that the best-kept secret about Australia is Melbourne.

Victoria's most distinctive attractions are found on the coast. West of Melbourne, the breathtaking Great Ocean Road winds its way along the roaring ocean. Hand-cut between 1919 and 1931 from the limestone cliffs, the road passes surfing beaches, coastal getaways, temperate rainforests, and geological wonders, including the Twelve Apostles rock formations, which poke precariously from the sea like jagged giant's fingers. East of the capital, the coastline unfolds past Phillip Island's penguin colony and the beach resorts on Mornington Peninsula, before heading into Gippsland. Here, crashing waves collide with granite outcroppings to form the sandy beaches at the edge of majestic Wilsons Promontory National Park. East Gippsland's beaches slowly give way to sandy tidal estuaries.

Most of Victoria's interior is remarkable less for its natural grandeur than for its historical significance. The mountainous exceptions are the ranges of the Grampians National Park, whose mammoth beauty evokes awe in inevitably humbled onlookers. North of the Grampians, the river-wrought lands of the Wimmera and the scraggly plains of the Mallee don't overwhelm at first sight, but the subtleties of the bush have their own delicate, subtle beauty. Victoria's historical heart beats to the drum of the mid-19th century gold rush, which flooded central Victoria with fortune-seekers. When the ore waned, a host of dusty country towns were left in its wake, today preserved by tourist-oriented nostalgia—the Goldfields and the Murray River towns in north and Central Victoria are defined by a fascinating past of mangled miners and rugged riverboats. The 20th century has brought extensive agricultural and commercial development, including massive hydroelectric public works projects that continue to impact the state's ecosystems. Still, Victoria's physical beauty remains, tempered by a refined sensibility and cosmopolitan flair.

VICTORIA HIGHLIGHTS

TWELVE APOSTLES. Play unabashed tourist at the spectacular Twelve Apostles rock formations in the Port Campbell National Park (p. 618).

THE LEDGE. Abseil 60m down The Ledge in Grampians National Park (p. 633).

RUTHERGLEN WINERIES. Pamper your palate with free tastings at Rutherglen Wineries (p. 656).

WILSONS PROM. Experience this UNESCO Biosphere Reserve's diversity of terrain on the Sealers Cove dayhike (p. 663).

SCENIC DRIVE. Take in the magnificent sights with a two-day scenic drive around Snowy River National Park (p.675).

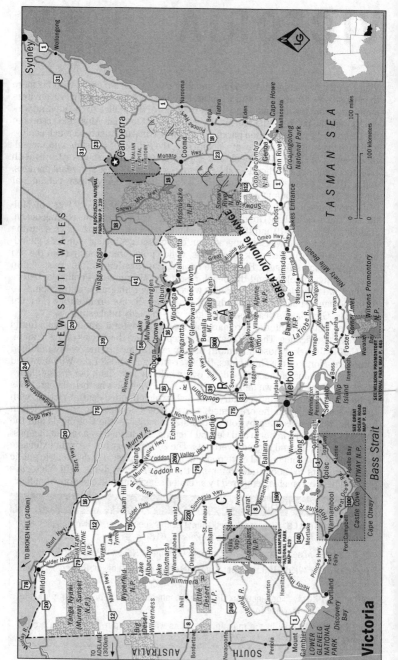

VICTORIA

Victoria

▛ TRANSPORTATION

Getting around Victoria is a breeze, thanks to the thorough, super-efficient system of intrastate trains and buses of **V/Line** (☎13 61 96; www.vlinepassenger.com.au), which runs an info center at its main terminal, Melbourne's Spencer Street Station. V/Line has interstate options, but **McCafferty's/Greyhound** (☎13 14 99 or 13 20 30; www.mccaffertys.com.au or www.greyhound.com.au) has much more complete national service. Renting a car allows more freedom, and Victoria's highway system is the country's most extensive and navigable. To cut down on occasionally prohibitive rental costs, check hostel ride-share boards. The **Royal Automobile Club of Victoria (RACV)**, 360 Bourke St., Melbourne (☎13 19 55 or 9703 6363; roadside assistance ☎13 11 11; www.racv.com.au), has great maps and sells short-term traveler's insurance. Members of other automobile clubs may already have reciprocal membership. To join in Victoria, the RACV Roadside Care package (including 4 free service calls annually and limited free towing) costs $50, plus a $30 first-time-joiner's fee for 21+. For more info on insurance, see **Insurance at a Glance**, p. 54.

MELBOURNE   ☎03

It all began rather inauspiciously in 1825 when John Batman sailed a skiff up the Yarra, got stuck on a sandbank, then justified his blunder by claiming he had found the ideal "place for a village." Then named Batmania, the small town underwent a phenomenal growth spurt at the onset of the Victorian Gold Rush three decades later. "Marvelous Melbourne" celebrated its coming-of-age in 1880 by hosting the World Exhibition, which attracted over a million people. When the Victorian economy crashed in the 1890s following bank failures, Melbourne's infrastructure collapsed and its fetid open sewers earned it the nickname "Marvelous Smellbourne." By the 20th century, though, things other than the sewage were up and running again, and Melbourne posed a legitimate challenge to Sydney for the honor of being Australia's capital. While the Canberra compromise deprived both of this status, Melbourne was happy to serve as the government's temporary home until the Parliament House was completed. The city's 20th-century apex was the 1956 Olympics, which brought the city's love for sport to an international audience.

The subsequent years have seen more population growth and an increasingly international flavor. Most recent immigrants hail from China, Southeast Asia, Italy, and Greece (Melbourne has the world's largest Greek population outside Greece). Melbourne's various neighborhoods—the frenetic Central City, bohemian Fitzroy, Italian Carlton, down-to-earth St. Kilda, chic South Yarra—invite exploration and are minutes from each other by tram. With picturesque waterfronts and parks, epic sporting events, raging nightlife, and world-class culture, Melbourne coaxes visitors to enjoy big city attractions with a refreshing absence of tourist hype.

MELBOURNE HIGHLIGHTS

AUSSIE RULES. Catch a game of Aussie Rules Football, Melbourne's sports obsession, at the historic Melbourne Cricket Ground. (p. 590)

QUEEN VICTORIA MARKET. Get great bargains in the Queen Victoria Market. (p. 591)

BOTANIC GARDENS. Forget the city by meandering through 36 acres of urban parkland. (p. 591)

BRUNSWICK ST. The main drag of this youthful, artsy and bohemian suburb has excellent cafes and even better shopping, most of it quite affordable.

SWANK BARS HIDDEN IN BACK ALLEYS. The CBD is full of them.

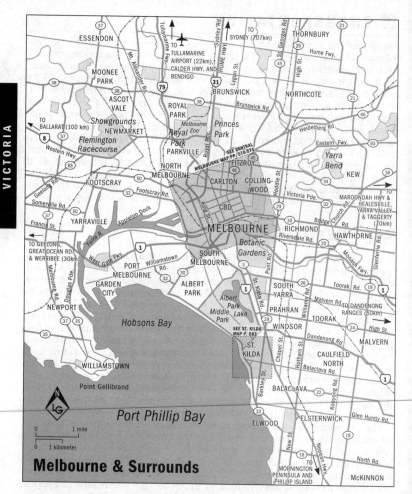

Melbourne & Surrounds

✈ INTERCITY TRANSPORTATION

BY PLANE

Boomerang-shaped **Tullamarine International Airport** is 25km northwest of Melbourne (30min. by car) and has three terminals. The international terminal houses several outfits and sits in the middle of the two domestic terminals, Qantas and Virgin Blue (formerly the now-defunct Ansett terminal). Visit www.melair.com.au for extensive information on all airport services.

Skybus (☎9335 2811) provides ground transport to Melbourne's Spencer St. Station in the city center, from where trains and buses depart. ($13, return $22; approx. every 15-25min. in either direction during the day and evening, every 30-

60min. at night). **Taxis** to the city center cost roughly $35 and take about 25 minutes. **Car rental** companies are clustered to the left, when exiting from the international arrival terminal (see **By Car**, p. 574).

International terminal: Houses 25 airlines and all international arrivals and departures. **Qantas international** (☎13 12 11) operates on the 1st fl. **Travelers Information** (☎9297 1805), in front of arriving international passengers as they exit, books same-day accommodations, and has maps, brochures, and a backpacker bulletin board.

Domestic terminals: Qantas (☎13 13 13; www.qantas.com.au) heads the left terminal and ◼**Virgin Blue** (☎13 67 89; www.virginblue.com.au) heads the right. Each flies to all Australian capitals at least once daily. Virgin Blue has last-minute specials that often rival the price of bus tickets.

BY BUS & TRAIN

Spencer Street Station, at the intersection of Spencer and Bourke St., is the main intercity bus and train station. (☎9619 2340. Open daily 6am-10pm.) **V/Line** (☎13 61 96; www.vlinepassenger.com.au) offers unlimited travel passes within Victoria for seven days ($75) to overseas tourists only. **Countrylink** (☎13 22 32; www.countrylink.nsw.gov.au) covers multiple-day passes to destinations in NSW, as well as Brisbane. **Great Southern** (☎13 21 47; www.gsr.com.au) has destinations across Australia. The **Melbourne Transit Centre**, 58 Franklin St. (☎9639 0634; open daily 6am-10:30pm), near Elizabeth St., is the hub of **McCafferty's/Greyhound** (☎13 14 99 or 13 20 30; www.mccaffertys.com.au or www.greyhound.com.au). They are listed in the chart below (see p. 569) as McCafferty's.

DESTINATION	COMPANY	DURATION	FREQUENCY	PRICE
Adelaide	McCafferty's V/Line	9-10hr. 10½hr.	3 per day 2 per day	$54 $58
Albury	V/Line	3½hr.	4-6 per day	$44
Alice Springs	McCafferty's Great Southern	28hr. 36hr.	1 per day 1 per week	$214 $294
Ararat	V/Line	3hr.	3-5 per day	$30.40
Ballarat	V/Line	1½hr.	7-12 per day	$15.60
Bendigo	V/Line	2hr.	5-11per day	$23.50
Bright	V/Line	4½hr.	1 per day	$44
Brisbane	McCafferty's Countrylink	27hr. 35hr.	3 per day 1 per day	$156 $178.50
Brisbane (via Sydney)	McCafferty's	30hr.	4 per day	$144
Cairns	McCafferty's Countrylink	56hr. 70hr.	2 per day 4 per week	$329 $342.10
Canberra	V/Line McCafferty's	8½hr. 8hr.	1 per day 1-3 per day	$56 $56
Castlemaine	V/Line	1½hr.	5-11 per day	$17.20
Darwin	McCafferty's	50hr.	1 per day	$389
Echuca	V/Line	3½-4hr.	2-9 per day	$30.40
Geelong	V/Line	1hr.	11-26 per day	$9.70
Mildura	V/Line	9½hr.	1 per week	$60.60
Perth	McCafferty's Great Southern	42½hr. 60hr.	1 per day 2 per week	$280 $342
Sydney	McCafferty's Countrylink	11-15hr. 11hr.	4 per day 2 per day	$59 $112
Yulara (Ayers Rock)	McCafferty's	25hr.	1 per day	$285

Central Melbourne

ACCOMMODATIONS

Chapman Gardens YHA Hostel, **1**
The Friendly Backpacker, **38**
The Greenhouse Backpacker, **44**
Hotel Bakpak, **27**
Hotel Lindrum, **47**
Hotel Y, **25**

The Melbourne Connection, **36**
The Nunnery, **21**
Queensbury Hill YHA, **6**
Stork Hotel, **24**
Toad Hall, **28**
Royal Derby Hotel & Backpackers, **2**

VICTORIA

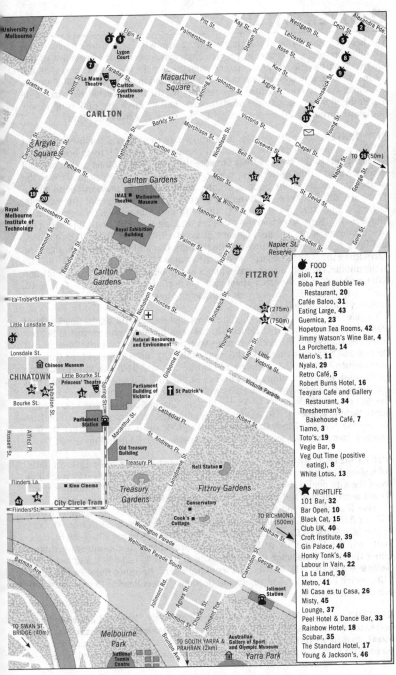

🍎 FOOD
aioli, 12
Boba Pearl Bubble Tea
  Restaurant, 20
Cafée Baloo, 31
Eating Large, 43
Guernica, 23
Hopetoun Tea Rooms, 42
Jimmy Watson's Wine Bar, 4
La Porchetta, 14
Mario's, 11
Nyala, 29
Retro Café, 5
Robert Burns Hotel, 16
Teayara Cafe and Gallery
  Restaurant, 34
Thresherman's
  Bakehouse Café, 7
Tiamo, 3
Toto's, 19
Vegie Bar, 9
Veg Out Time (positive
  eating), 8
White Lotus, 13

⭐ NIGHTLIFE
101 Bar, 32
Bar Open, 10
Black Cat, 15
Club UK, 40
Croft Institute, 39
Gin Palace, 40
Honky Tonk's, 48
Labour in Vain, 22
La La Land, 30
Metro, 41
Mi Casa es tu Casa, 26
Misty, 45
Lounge, 37
Peel Hotel & Dance Bar, 33
Rainbow Hotel, 18
Scubar, 35
The Standard Hotel, 17
Young & Jackson's, 46

✈ ORIENTATION

The heart of one of the world's largest urban sprawls, Melbourne's lively, dense core comprises a geometrically precise city center surrounded by a slew of distinctive suburbs. The city center alone could take up the whole of a short visit, but it's in the surrounding neighborhoods that you'll find the true spirit of Melbourne. For those keen to conquer the entire metropolis, the irreplaceable *Melway* guide has detailed street directories of Melbourne and its environs; pick it up in any bookstore (around $40), or photocopy the desired pages from the library.

CITY CENTER. The city center, also known as the Central Business District (CBD), is composed of a well-arranged rectangular grid of streets bordered by **Spencer Street** to the west, **La Trobe Street** to the north, **Spring Street** to the east, and **Flinders Street** to the south. Five major streets run east to west: La Trobe (the northernmost), Lonsdale, Bourke, Collins, and Flinders. To the north of all but La Trobe are "little" streets—roads named after their southern superior (for example, Little Collins St. is just north of Collins St., and Flinders Ln. is just north of Flinders St.). Nine streets cross this grid running north to south: Spencer (the westernmost), King, William, Queen, Elizabeth, Swanston, Russell, Exhibition, and Spring. **Spencer Street** runs by the primary bus and train depot, bridges the Yarra River to South Melbourne, and carries trams #12, 75, 95, 96, and 109. Directly in the middle, **Elizabeth Street** carries major northbound tram lines (#19, 57, 59, and 68). One block east, **Swanston Street** also has north-south trams (#1, 3, 5, 6, 8, 16, 22, 25, 64, 67, and 72). On the east end, **Spring Street** borders Parliament and the Treasury and Carlton Gardens.

The eastern half of the city contains most restaurants and sights. **Bourke Street Mall** (a pedestrian stretch of Bourke St. between Elizabeth and Swanston St., traversed by trams #86, 95, and 96) swarms with people every day; the intersection of Bourke and Swanston St. marks the heart of the city. Both **Hardware Lane** (running north-south between Lonsdale and Bourke St.) and **DeGraves Street** (running north-south between Collins and Flinders St.) are alley-like pedestrian walks that contain shops, restaurants, and cafes with outdoor seating. The area just north of the city center bordered by La Trobe, Queen, Elizabeth, and Victoria St. borders **Queen Victoria Market** (p. 591) and is a hive of budget accommodations, while East Melbourne contains **Fitzroy Gardens** (p. 589) and Victoria's sporting shrine, the **Melbourne Cricket Ground**. (See p. 590. Take tram #48, 70, or 75 from Flinders St.)

NORTH MELBOURNE. North Melbourne is a pleasant mix of bungalows, flats, refurbished residences, and neighborhood shops and eateries, all easily reachable from the city center. Forming its eastern edge, **Elizabeth Street** continues north from the city center and passes the **Queen Victoria Market** with its abundant, inexpensive food stocks and wares; travel west along Victoria St. (traversed by tram #57) to find loads of cool budget eateries. William St. heads north from the city center past **Flagstaff Gardens** and becomes **Peel Street**. Peel and Elizabeth St. intersect near the University of Melbourne, where Elizabeth continues northwest under the name **Flemington Road** (along which trams #55 and 59 continue) to the **Melbourne Zoo** (p. 591). At this intersection, Peel St. becomes **Royal Parade** (tram #19), which borders the University and becomes **Sydney Road** to the northern suburb of Brunswick.

CARLTON. Carlton, Melbourne's unofficial "Little Italy," begins at **Nicholson Street** and extends west past the Carlton Gardens to the **University of Melbourne**. On **Lygon Street**, its primary thoroughfare, upmarket Italian bistros, somewhat cheaper *gelaterias* and *pasticcerias*, and a smattering of ethnic and eclectic foods cater to a crowd of old Mediterranean types and college students. Public transportation does not go along Lygon St. in Carlton. To get to Carlton's Lygon St., either take a tram up Swanston St. (#1, 3, 5, 6, 8, 16, 22, 25, 64, 67, or 72) and then walk east along Queensberry or Faraday St., or take #96 from Bourke St. up Nicholson St. and walk west along Faraday St.

FITZROY. Fitzroy, Melbourne's bohemian district, is a shopping mecca for cutting-edge new or used clothing, music or books, and also hosts a bustling cafe culture. Fitzroy houses a healthy mix of "ferals" (Aussies' term for the nose-ring crowd), families, and everyone in between. The area is gentrifying rapidly as young urban hipsters start building loft-style apartments on prime real estate. Tram #11 runs the length of **Brunswick Street,** the main artery of Fitzroy. **Smith Street** marks the boundary between Fitzroy and its eastern neighbor, **Collingwood,** and is home to a number of fine eateries and factory outlet stores. Just east of Smith are a handful of **gay bars** (and a fair number of straight ones, too). The blocks of **Johnston Street** between Brunswick and Nicholson St. in Fitzroy form the smallish Latin Quarter, with stores, restaurants, tapas bars, and dance clubs.

SOUTH MELBOURNE. Melbourne south of the Yarra tends to be fancier than the more working-class suburbs to the north. South Melbourne, west of St. Kilda Rd. and stretching south from the West Gate Freeway to **Albert Park,** is an exception. More blue-collar than adjacent communities, this neighborhood has some quality restaurants and nightspots along its main drag, **Cecil Street.** It's also a quick walk to the **Royal Botanic Gardens** (p. 591), the city center, or the **beach** at Port Phillip Bay. Take tram #96 or 12 from Spencer St.

West of South Melbourne along Port Phillip Bay are three of Melbourne's quietest, most posh suburbs. **Station Pier** marks the division between **Port Melbourne,** the more commercial side of the area, and the more urbane **Albert Park,** an upscale residential neighborhood with stately seaside bungalows; ferries to **Tasmania** depart from Station Pier at the terminus of tram #109.

SOUTH YARRA & PRAHRAN. South Yarra, Prahran (per-RAN), and Windsor span the area enclosed by the Yarra to the north, St. Kilda Rd. to the west, Dandenong Rd. to the south, and William St. to the east. The focus of Melbourne's gay community, **Commercial Road** runs east-west, separating South Yarra from its southern neighbor Prahran. The border between Windsor and Prahran is a bit more blurred, and even locals confuse the two. The district's main street is **Chapel Street;** the section of the boulevard in South Yarra is the commercial face of the fancy suburbs south of the river. On sunny Sundays, the beautiful people come here to shop for Prada and Versace and snipe about catty salesgirls from sleek seats in pricey sidewalk bistros. Chapel St. becomes more down-to-earth south of Commercial Rd. in Prahran, closer in spirit to St. Kilda. **Greville Street** branches west from Chapel just below Commercial St. and is a den for second-hand clothing, record stores, and bizarre restaurants. Continuing south, the next major intersection is High St., set in an area full of sidewalk eateries, bars, and hair stylists. Trams #78 and 79 run along Chapel St. By tram from Flinders St. Station, #8 travels below the Botanic Gardens, then along Toorak Rd. to its intersection with Chapel St., while #5 and 64 head south along St. Kilda Rd., and then go east along Dandenong Rd. to Chapel. The quickest way to get to there from the central city, though, is to hop on a **Sandringham Line** train from Flinders St. Station to South Yarra, Prahran, or Windsor Stations—each lies only a few blocks west of Chapel St.

ST. KILDA. Though it's a bit removed to the southeast of the city center (and officially in the city of **Port Phillip**), St. Kilda is a budget hotspot with cheap accommodations and popular eateries. Trams #12 and 96 bring people to St. Kilda from

Spencer St. Station, while #16 runs from Flinders St. Station. Tram #16 travels along **St. Kilda Road** and passes Melbourne's two largest green spaces, the **Royal Botanic Gardens** via **Albert Park.** At **St. Kilda Junction,** St. Kilda Rd. and Fitzroy St. intersect; from here, Fitzroy curves south toward the waterfront, becoming the Esplanade. **Barkly Street** runs south from the junction on the other side, completing a triangle with Fitzroy St. and the Esplanade. Running between Fitzroy and Barkly St., **Grey Street** is the focus of St. Kilda's budget accommodations. The last street that branches south from Fitzroy St. before it turns into the Esplanade is **Acland Street,** the southern end of which is one of Melbourne's many excellent cafe districts, distinguished by its old-time cake shops.

⌐ LOCAL TRANSPORTATION

PUBLIC TRANSPORTATION

Melbourne's superb public transportation system, the Met, consists of light-rail trains, buses, and trams. (☎ 13 16 38; www.victrip.com.au. Open daily 7am-9pm for inquiries.) Tram routes criss-cross the metropolitan area and are the most useful means of navigating the city and its proximate outskirts. On weekdays, they run every 3-12min., nights and weekends every 20min. or more; services operate M-Sa 5am-midnight, Su 8am-11pm. You don't actually have to show your pass to ride trams, but if an inspector decides to make a spot check and you're without a valid ticket, expect a $100 fine.

The entire network comprises three Met zones, though you'll probably stay in Zone 1 unless you travel out to a distant suburb. Tickets are sold at stations, on board trams and buses (coins only), and at the **Met Shop,** 103 Elizabeth St., near Collins St. (Open M-F 8:30am-4:55pm, Sa 9am-1pm.) **Tickets** within Zone 1 can be used on any of the three types of transportation and are valid for unlimited travel for two hours ($2.60), a day ($5.10), a week ($22.20), a month ($83.30), or a year ($897). **Concession** rates are roughly half-price; you qualify if you are under 15 years old, have a valid Australian university ID (ISIC cards or international university IDs not accepted), or have a pensioner card. Only two-hour tickets can be purchased from coin-operated machines on trams and buses. If you're going to be in town for a while, the long-term passes save a lot of time, money, and hassle; buy them at a station machine or ticket counter. You must validate any ticket you purchase, including ones purchased on trams, by putting it in one of the electronic green ticket validation boxes; you can be fined for not doing this even if you have a ticket. For more info and route maps, grab the free *Met Fares and Travel Guide* from any station.

The burgundy-and-gold **City Circle Tram** circumnavigates the **Central Business District (CBD)** in both directions, provides running commentary on the city's sights and history, and is **free** (every 10min.; Su-W 10am-6pm, Th-Sa 10am-9:30pm). The bus and **light-rail train** systems are mostly for commuters going to residential areas or distant suburbs, and you can't board without a valid Metcard. There are train stops at **Melbourne Central, Flagstaff Gardens, Parliament,** and **Spencer Street,** though the main rail hub is the beautiful golden-colored **Flinders Street Station** at the southern end of Swanston St., identifiable by its big clock.

BY CAR

The usual national car-rental chains mostly have offices in the Melbourne city center and at the airport, but it's cheaper to rent in the city, as the airport offices generally include a 9% airport tax. They tend to rent only to people over age 25, though some accept renters aged 21-24 with a **surcharge.** Prices for all fluctuate frequently due to seasons and specials. National agencies include those listed below.

The **Royal Automobile Club of Victoria** (**RACV;** ☎ 13 13 29), on the corner of Little Collins and Queen St., with a second location at 360 Bourke St. (☎ 13 19 55), is a comprehensive driving resource with good maps for sale. Members receive emergency roadside assistance. Backpackers commonly join forces and buy or rent a used car. A good but out-of-the-way option for long-term rental is **Car Connection** near Castlemaine, 120km northwest of Melbourne. They offer a station wagon for up to six months for $1950 plus a $750 insurance charge and full camping equipment for two for $250. Being a bit out of town, they also provide free pick-up from Melbourne airport or any city hostel as well as free first-night lodging in Castlemaine. (☎ 5473 4469; www.carconnection.com.au. Open M-F 9am-5pm.)

In addition to the agencies below, there are a few **bargain agencies** that are only half-joking about their cars' quality. **Rent-a-Bomb** (☎ 13 15 53; www.rentabomb.com.au) has 11 offices in the Melbourne area; their main office is at 149 Clarendon St. (☎ 9696 3939). The deals can run as cheap as $36-41 per day for one-day rentals, $23-29 per day for weekly rentals, and $17-23 per day for monthly rentals. Still, we advise you to weigh the savings against the potential costs of breaking down in the middle of nowhere. For information on driving in Australia, see p. 79.

Atlas (☎ 9663 6233, airport 9335 1945; www.atlasrent.com.au). In Melbourne Transit Centre, 58 Franklin St., or at the airport. From $52 per day, $11 surcharge. Open M-F 7:30am-6pm, Sa-Su 7:30am-2:30pm.

Avis, 20-24 Franklin St. (☎ 9663 6366, airport 9338 1800). From $55 per day, $27.50 surcharge. Open M-Th 7:30am-6:30pm, F 7:30am-7pm, Sa-Su 8am-5pm.

Backpacker Car Rental, 103 Railway Ave., Werribee (☎ 9731 0700). Charges $137 per week for the Melbourne metro area; has an all-Victoria rate at $192.50 per week for Victoria, which includes unlimited kilometers, insurance, and RACV roadside assistance; drivers must be at least 23 years old. Open M-F 9am-6pm, Sa 9am-5pm.

Budget, 398 Elizabeth St. (☎ 13 27 27 or 9203 4846, airport 9241 6366), on the corner of A'Beckett St. From $55 per day, $16.50 surcharge. Open M-Th 8am-7pm, F 8am-6pm, Sa-Su 8am-5pm.

Delta Europcar, 89 Franklin St. (☎ 13 10 45 or 9600 9025; www.deltaeuropcar.com.au). From $55 per day, $13.20 surcharge. Open M-F 7:30am-6pm, Sa-Su 8am-5pm.

National (☎ 9348 9449; www.nationalcar.com), at Franklin and Elizabeth St. Same rates as **Delta,** its owner. Open M-Th 7:30am-6pm, F 7:30am-6:30pm, Sa 8am-5pm.

Hertz, 97 Franklin St. (☎ 9663 6244, airport 9338 4044). From $42, $16.50 surcharge. Open M-Th 7:30am-6pm, F 7:30am-7pm, Sa 7:30am-5pm, Su 8am-5pm.

Thrifty, 390 Elizabeth St. (☎ 8661 6000, airport 9242 6100). From $62, $15.50 surcharge. Open daily 8am-6pm.

BY TAXI

If you're out after the Met stops running at midnight, you'll have to take a taxi. Cabs can be hailed at any time of day on the street. All companies have a $2.80 base charge plus $1.31 per km. There's a $1 surcharge when you arrange cab pickup by phone, and if you ride between midnight and 6am. Both **Silver Top** (☎ 13 10 08) and **Yellow Cabs** (☎ 13 22 27) are yellow.

BY BICYCLE

An extensive **bike trail** runs along the Yarra River, and others loop through Albert Park and Middle Park, along the Port Phillip beaches, and around North Melbourne's gardens. Southern Melbourne's flat bayside roads make for low-impact, scenic cycling. **St. Kilda Cycles,** 11 Carlisle St., has good rates. (☎ 9534 3074. Open M-F 9am-6pm, Sa 9am-5pm, Su 10am-4pm. $15 per half-day, $20 per day, $80 per week, $200 per month.) Or try **Fitzroy Cycles Bike Hire**, 224 Swanston St. (☎9639 3511. Open M-F 9am-6pm, Sa 9:30am-5pm. $9 per hr., $35 per day.) Rates include helmet and lock. Many hostels rent bikes for little or no charge. **Bicycle Victoria (BV)**, level 10, 446 Collins St. at Williams St. (☎9328 3000 or 1800 639 634; www.bv.com.au), provides insurance for members (yearly membership $63, concessions $57, families $78-88) and free info for non-members on rules of the road and bike-related events.

❼ PRACTICAL INFORMATION

TOURIST & FINANCIAL SERVICES

Tourist Offices: ▧**Melbourne Visitor Information Centre** in Federation Square, across from Flinders St. Station at the corner of Flinders St. and St. Kilda Rd (☎9658 9924). The sprawling new center offers Internet and email, transport and entertainment ticket sales, ATM, the **Best of Victoria** accommodations and tour booking service (☎9663 0800), and the **Melbourne Greeter Service**, which gives free 2-4hr. tours of the city tailored to your personal interests. Tours are offered in many languages. Arrange by filling out a brief application at least 3 working days in advance (book online at www.melbourne.vic.gov.au). There is also an info booth at the **Bourke Street Mall**. Open M-F 9am-5pm, Sa 10am-4pm, Su 11am-4pm.

Disabled and Elderly Travelers Information: Travellers Aid, 169 Swanston St., 2nd Fl. (☎9654 2600), has a tearoom with old-fashioned fittings along with great services. Open M-F 8am-5pm. Also at Spencer St. Station (☎9670 2873). Open M-F 7:30am-7:30pm, Sa-Su 7:30am-11:30am. Will meet and assist elderly and disabled travelers on trains and buses M-F 7:30am-7:30pm, Sa-Su 7:30am-11:30am. Arrange ahead.

Outdoors Information: Natural Resources and Environment (NRE), 8 Nicholson St., at Victoria Pde., East Melbourne (☎9637 8325, hotline 13 61 86; www.nre.vic.gov.au). Maps, books, and info on licenses. Open M-F 8:30am-5:30pm. Also call **Parks Victoria** (☎13 19 63; www.parks.vic.gov.au) for all state and national park info.

Budget Travel: YHA Victoria, 83-85 Hardware Ln. (☎9670 9611; www.yha.com.au). Provides a full listing of YHA hostels and a booking service. YHA member international booking surcharge $6, domestic surcharge $2 after first 2 bookings. Non-YHA member domestic surcharge $2, no non-member international booking. Attached budget travel agency. Open M-F 9am-5:30pm, Sa 10am-1pm. **STA Travel Victorian Headquarters**, 260 Hoddle St., off Johnston St. in Abbotsford, just outside of Fitzroy (☎8417 6911) and *all* over Melbourne and its surrounds, including 208 Swanston St. (☎9639 0599). Open M-F 9am-6pm, Sa 10am-4pm. **Backpackers World**, 167 Franklin St. (☎9329 1990), in Hotel Bakpak. Open M-F 8am-7pm, Sa 9am-6pm, Su 10am-5pm. Also at 35 Elizabeth St. (☎9620 2300). Open M-F 9am-6pm, Sa 11am-5pm. **Backpackers Travel Centre**, Shop 1, 250 Flinders St. (☎9654 8477; www.backpackerstravel.net.au). Open M-F 9am-6pm, Sa 10am-4pm. Also at 377 Little Bourke St. (☎9642 1811). Open M-F 9am-5:30pm, Sa 10am-3pm.

Consulates: Great Britain, Level 17, 90 Collins St. (☎9652 1600). Open M-F 9am-4:30pm. **United States**, Level 6, 553 St. Kilda Rd. (☎9526 5900). Open M-F 8:30am-noon and 1-4:30pm.

Currency Exchange: 109 Collins St. (☎9654 2768). Open daily 8am-8:40pm. All banks exchange money during regular operating hours. Open M-Th 9:30am-4pm, F 9:30am-5pm. **American Express** (see below) exchanges all traveler's checks free of commission. **Thomas Cook Foreign Exchange**, 261 Bourke St. (☎9654 4222), near Swanston St., has a $7 commission on checks and cash. Open M-Sa 9am-5pm, Su 11am-3pm. Several banks have offices at the airport. 24hr. ATM outlets adorn the city.

VICTORIA

American Express Travel Services: 233 Collins St. (☎9633 6318). Buys all traveler's checks (no charge); min. $8 or 2% fee on cash exchanges. Poste Restante for AmEx card or traveler's check holders. Wire transfers. Open M-F 9am-5pm, Sa 9am-noon.

Work Opportunities: Most *Let's Go* accommodations listed have employment bulletin boards; some help find temp jobs free of charge. BRC, in the lobby of Hotel Bakpak (see Accommodations, p. 578, ☎9329 7525), can help find top jobs. Open M-F 1-5pm. Melbourne's biggest daily paper, *The Age*, has classifieds on Sa and can be accessed online at www.theage.com.au or picked up for free at the Melbourne Museum.

> **MEDIA & PUBLICATIONS**
>
> **Newspapers:** The main newspapers are *The Age* ($1.10) and *The Herald Sun* (99¢) for local coverage and *The Australian* ($1.10) for national news.
>
> **Nightlife:** *InPress* and *Beat* (www.beat.com.au), released on Wednesday (free). For gay news and nightlife, check out *MCV* (by subscription, but found in most gay establishments) and *B.News* (free, released every other Th).
>
> **Entertainment:** *Age's* Entertainment Guide and *Herald Sun's* Gig Guide, found in Friday's paper.
>
> **Radio:** Alternative, Triple R 102.7FM; Rock, Triple J 107.5FM and Triple M 105.1FM; News, 1026AM; Tourist Info, 88FM.

LOCAL SERVICES

Bookstores: Angus & Robertson Bookworld (☎9670 8861; www.angusrobertson.com.au), 360 Bourke St. at the corner of Elizabeth St., is huge and has frequent sales. Open M-Th 9am-6pm, F 9am-8pm, Sa 9am-6pm, Su 10am-5pm.

Library: State Library of Victoria, 328 Swanston St. (☎8664 7000), on the corner of La Trobe St. Open M-Th 10am-9pm, F-Su 10am-6pm.

Gay and Lesbian Information: The ALSO Foundation, 35 Cato St., Prahran (☎9827 4999; www.also.org.au). Gay and lesbian helpline (☎9827 8544 or 1800 631 493).

Ticket Agencies: Ticketek (☎13 28 49 or 1800 062 849; www.ticketek.com.au) and **Ticketmaster** (☎13 61 00; www.ticketmaster7.com.au) for sports, performances, and other events. Handling fee for phone booking. Both open daily 9am-9pm. **Halftix,** a booth on Bourke St. Mall opposite Myer Department Store, sells half-price tickets on performance day (Su performances sold Sa); often sells out by 2pm. Cash only; no phone orders. Open M 10am-2pm, Tu-Th 11am-6pm, F 11am-6:30pm, Sa 10am-2pm.

> **CYBER MELBOURNE**
>
> **www.visitvictoria.com** Comprehensive government web site with tons of info on food, nightlife, accommodations, and events in Melbourne and all of Victoria. Events searchable by type, town, and date.
>
> **http://melbourne.citysearch.com.au** An eating and drinking guide, up-to-date entertainment listings, and a comprehensive business directory.
>
> **www.mdg.com.au** A selection of the best restaurants in Melbourne, searchable by location and cuisine, with online reservation placement.

EMERGENCY & COMMUNICATIONS

Emergency: ☎000.

Police: 637 Flinders St. at Spencer St. (☎9247 6666), 226 Flinders Ln. between Swanston St. and Elizabeth St. (☎9650 7077), and 412 St. Kilda Rd. 200m south of Toorak Rd. (☎9865 2111).

Crisis Lines: Victims Referral and Assistance Hotline (☎9603 9797). **Centre Against Sexual Assault** (☎9344 2210). **Lifeline Counseling Service** (☎13 11 14). **Poison Information Service** (☎13 11 26). **Coast Guard Search and Rescue** (☎9598 7003). **Alcohol and Drug Counselling** (☎9416 1818).

Helpful numbers: Directory assistance ☎12 23, international ☎12 25; collect calls ☎1800 REVERSE or 1800 738 3773; translation and interpretation ☎13 14 50.

Pharmacy: Many along Elizabeth St., including **ChemWorld** (☎9670 3815), on the corner of Elizabeth and Little Collins St. Open M-W 7:30am-6pm, Th 7:30am-6:30pm, F 7:30am-8pm, Sa 9am-5pm, Su 11am-5pm.

Hospital: St. Vincent's Public Hospital, 41 Victoria Pde., Fitzroy (☎9288 2211). To get there, take any tram east along Bourke St. to stop #9. **Royal Melbourne Hospital,** on Grattan St. at Flemington St., Parkville (☎9342 7000). Take tram #19 from Elizabeth St. to stop #16.

Internet Access: There are 8 free terminals at the **State Library** (see p. 577); sign up in advance for 30min. sessions. The library's email terminals are for Australian citizens and residents only (including foreigners with a work visa or Australian student ID). In the city itself, prices tend to hover around 11-15¢ per minute. A major exception is **Traveler's Uni-Net Stop,** 78 Howard St. (☎9329 1338), in the Queensbury Hill YHA. Open daily 9am-midnight. Another good deal is **Backpacker's World,** 167 Franklin St. (☎9329 1990), in Hotel Bakpak (see Accommodations below). $6 per hr.; prepaid Happy Hours $3.50 per hr. Open M-F 8am-9pm, Sa-Su 9am-8pm. St. Kilda's backpacker trades keep competitive pricing of about 7¢ per minute; multitudes of Internet shops line Fitzroy St.

Post Office: GPO (☎9203 3076), located on the corner of Elizabeth and Bourke St. Mall. Fax and Poste Restante services. Open M-F 8:15am-5:30pm, Sa 10am-1pm. **Postal Code:** 3000 (CBD).

▐ ACCOMMODATIONS

Melbourne's tourist industry supports numerous budget accommodations to host its backpacker population. The two biggest hostel hives are **St. Kilda** and the area just **north of the city center** enclosed by La Trobe, Queen, Elizabeth, and Victoria St. The YHA-affiliated hostels in **North Melbourne** tend to be quieter and more sedate, popular with at least as many school groups and elderly travelers as 20-something backpackers, while the accommodations in the **city center** are as boisterous as they are conveniently located. **South Yarra** and **Prahran** lie farther afield but are preferred by those who enjoy the proximity to these districts' shopping and nightlife. The St. Kilda options generally make up for what they lack in cleanliness with an unquenchable thirst to party.

Availability drops during the **high season** (roughly Nov.-Feb.) and most accommodations raise their prices a tad ($2-4). The more popular hostels tend to be booked solid during these periods (and are also in demand during school holidays June-Aug.), so be sure to book far in advance. During summer holiday, you can usually find accommodation at universities. **Melbourne University** (Ormond College ☎9344 1121) offers B&B accommodations Jan. and Feb. and again in July. (Students $55 per night, non-students $60; longer than 4 days $49.50/$55.) **Monash University** (Halls of Residence ☎9905 6200; www.monash.edu.au/MRS) provides singles with shared bath from $117 per week from Dec. to late Jan.; these are not just for students. **Chisholm College** caters toward backpackers, be they students or not. (☎9479 2875. Singles $20; twins $15.40 per person. Weekly $129.50/$100. Blankets and sheets $6; available Nov. 24 to early Feb.) Take bus #350 (45min.) or #250 (1hr.) from Flinders St. Station.

Unless noted otherwise, all accommodations have a common room with TV, hall baths, 24hr. access, luggage storage, a guest kitchen, laundry machines ($2-3 wash, $1-2 dry), free linens, and no chore requirements.

CITY CENTER

▓ The Greenhouse Backpacker, 228 Flinders Ln. (☎9639 6400 or 1800 249 207; www.friendlygroup.com.au). Near Swanston St. Reception is on the 6th floor. Possibly the best hostel in town, the Greenhouse provides both a lively nightlife and a quiet day. Most rooms have 4 beds with spring mattresses, some have windows. Large lockers, sparkling bathrooms, cable TV room, large communal dining room, industrial-size kitchen, and an expansive roof garden. Helpful and tirelessly friendly staff offer regional tours, job advice, and travel services. Pub crawl every Th night, free weekly BBQ Tu, free pancakes Su, free Internet 30min. per day. Coffee, tea, and first-morning brekkie included. Dorms $26; singles $55; doubles $70. Weekly dorms $168 when paid in advance. Wheelchair-accessible. ❷

The Melbourne Connection, 205 King St. (☎9642 4464; www.melbourneconnection.com). Take the free city circle tram to Spencer and Lt. Bourke St. and walk one block up Lt. Bourke to King St. A small, clean, and friendly hostel, with good dorm accommodations, nicer twins and singles, and very nice doubles overlooking a busy street. Ask for a room on the first floor. Large lockers sit on wood floors in bright, airy rooms. Internet $0.06 per min. Book tours here. Reception 8am-12:30pm and 5:30-8:30pm. 12-bed dorms $21; 6-bed $23; 4-bed $24; 3-bed $25; singles $45; doubles $60. Weekly 12-bed $120; 6-bed $140; 4-bed $150; 3-bed $160; singles $280; doubles $375. Wheelchair-accessible. Credit cards 5% service charge for weekly rates, cash only for daily rates. 70 beds. ❷

The Friendly Backpacker, 197 King St. (☎9670 1111 or 1800 671 115; friendlybpacker@optusnet.com.au), 1 block east of Spencer St. Station at the corner of Little Bourke St. Smaller but friendlier than its brother the Greenhouse. Hallway lounges on each of 4 floors encourage interaction; cable TV and TV/VCR with movie collection encourage loafing. Weekly in-house and on-the-town activities. Heat and A/C, free Internet 30min. per day, coffee and tea, and first-morning brekkie included. Key deposit $10. Book 1 week in advance Oct.-May. Free pick-up from bus station, Tassie ferry, and around town. Oct.-Mar. dorms $24; Apr.-Sept. $21. Weekly Oct.-Mar. $154; Apr.-Sept. $133. Wheelchair-accessible. ❷

Hotel Lindrum, 26 Flinders St. (☎9668 1111; www.hotellindrum.com.au). A boutique to delight even the most jaded boutique connoisseur. Big old beds, antique furniture, a swank bar, and lots of hardwood. All rooms have A/C and heat, direct telephone and fax lines, dataports, TV, CD players, and a whole lot of style. Standard suite summer M-Th $300, F-Su $230; winter $210. Superior suite $315/$230/$225. Deluxe suite with great views of the city $330/$290/$254. Junior suites large enough for 3 $345/$260/$225. ❺

JUST NORTH OF THE CITY CENTER

Walk uphill on Elizabeth St. past La Trobe St. or take tram #19, 55, 57, or 59 to some of the nicest budget accommodations in town.

▓ Hotel Bakpak, 167 Franklin St. (☎9329 7525 or 1800 645 200; www.bakpak.com/franklin/index), between Elizabeth and Queen St. This cavernous 6-level facility can sleep up to 600 and has established itself as a pulsing, party-hearty nerve center for Melbourne's backpacker scene. Bathrooms can be a mystifying trek from far-away rooms, and paper-thin walls may compromise privacy (or sleep), but no one beats Bakpak's cornucopia of amenities, including a budget travel agency, free airport pick-up, employment service, basement "Roo Bar," cafe, Internet ($6 per hr.), small movie theater, and unique "Cabana style" showers. Roo Bar parties pave the way to friendship for many travelers with daily Happy Hours that offer amazingly cheap drinks. No smoking. Breakfast included. 10- to 16-bed barrack $19; smaller dorms $21-25; singles $50; twins and doubles $60. VIP. ❷

■ **Stork Hotel,** 504 Elizabeth St. (☎9663 6237; www.storkhotel.com), at the corner of Therry St., adjacent to the Queen Victoria Market. Brimming with character, the rooms in this historic building are full of 1920's-era art deco lamps and gorgeous antique bedsteads. Most have their own informative themes; ask for the Great Ocean Road room, the Foster's Lager room, or even the Ned Kelly room. Ground-floor pub attracts a quirky mix of locals and travelers, and hosts live music featuring area artists nightly (no cover). Sunny cafe attached makes cheap meals with fresh market produce. Towel and soap included. 5-bed dorms $25; singles $43; twins and doubles $58. ❷

Toad Hall, 441 Elizabeth St. (☎9600 9010; www.toadhall-hotel.com.au), between A'Beckett and Franklin St. A classier, more reserved place, several cuts above the frenetic backpacker scene, Toad Hall combines the intimacy of a B&B with the conveniences and attentive staff of a large inn. Airy kitchen, plant-filled patio, quiet reading room, and basement den with TV, VCR, and stereo. Shared bathrooms; larger dorms have bath. Cushy quilt included. Laundry facilities and off-street parking. Heat in private rooms and larger dorms. Key deposit $20. Reception 7am-10pm. Dorms $20-25; singles, twins $60; doubles $70; ensuite $90. Bookings advised. 134 beds. ❷

Hotel Y, 489 Elizabeth St. (☎9329 5188 or 1800 249 124; hotely@ywca.net), between Therry and Franklin St., less than a block from the Transit Center. The Y has the feel of a luxury hotel with stellar ensuite rooms, snazzy lobby, and the sleek Cafe Y. Internet $2 per 30min. Coffee, tea, TV, phone, soap, and shampoo in every room. The roof garden and hallway picture-windows offer high-rise views of the city below. Check-in 1pm. Budget singles $80, deluxe with A/C $99; twins and doubles $98/$120; triples $115/$131. YMCA/YWCA 10% discount. Book several weeks ahead; credit card to confirm booking. 60 rooms. ❺

NORTH MELBOURNE

The largely residential North Melbourne district is quieter and more relaxed than the busy city center. Though the area's accommodations are located quite a hike from downtown, North Melbourne is accessible by tram #57 and 59 from Elizabeth St. and tram #55 from William St.

Chapman Gardens YHA Hostel, 76 Chapman St. (☎9328 3595; www.yha.com.au). Take tram #57 north to stop 18 and turn right onto Chapman St.; the hostel is on the left. Small but cozy rooms in a quiet, residential neighborhood, with a gazebo out back. As a newly-designated eco-hostel, the C-Gardens uses solar heating, recycles everything from clothing to food waste, and raises their own worms to fertilize the backyard herb gardens. Free parking, bike hire, and passes to the City Baths. Luggage storage $2. Key deposit $5. Reception 7:30am-12:30pm and 2-10pm. 3-, 4-, and 5-bed dorms $27.50, YHA $24; dorm twins $28.50/$25; singles $51.50/$48; doubles $65/$58. 7th night free in winter. Book ahead. ❷

Queensberry Hill YHA, 78 Howard St. (☎9329 8599; queensberryhill@yhavic.org.au). Take tram #55 north from William St. to stop 11 on Queensberry St. From there, walk 2 blocks west to Howard St. Institutional but functional, the Queensberry Hill YHA is a 348-bed congregation of services beyond simple shelter from the storm. Free parking and bike hire, passes to city baths, rooftop patio with BBQ, licensed bistro, travel agency, huge kitchen, and pool tables. Internet ($4 per hr.); currency exchange $2. 2-week max. stay. Dorms $26.50, YHA $23; singles $61.50/$58; ensuite doubles $88/$81; family rooms $95/$88; apartments $120-127. Book ahead in summer. Wheelchair-accessible. ❸

FITZROY

If the backpacker-clogged St. Kilda scene isn't your style and you don't want to deal with the hustle and bustle of the city center or the uppity denizens of Prahran, Fitzroy may be just the ultra-suave suburb for you. With loads of excellent places to eat, drink, and shop, as well as some of the city's best live music venues, Fitzroy rivals any of Melbourne's satellite communities in both quality and character.

The Nunnery, 116 Nicholson St. (☎9419 8637 or 1800 032 635; www.bakpak.com/nunnery). Stop 13 on tram #96, at the northeast corner of Carlton Gardens. Housed in the former convent of the Daughters of Mercy, this heavenly hostel has dorms with high ceilings, halls snazzily decorated with an incongruous mix of religious paraphernalia and New Age psychedelia, a breezy wooden deck with BBQ, and rooms with balconies overlooking the Gardens. The attached guest house (122 King St.) is considerably quieter, with upscale boutique rooms featuring classy wicker furniture and fireplaces. Towel and soap included. Wine and cheese F night, fluffy pancakes Su brekkie. Internet $2 per $20min. Key deposit $20 or passport. Check-out 9:30am. Reception M-F 8am-8pm, Sa-Su 5-8pm. 10- to 12-bed dorms $23; 6- to 8-bed $25; 4-bed $27; singles $55; bunk twins $60; twins and doubles $70; triples $85; boutique doubles $85; family rooms $90. Weekly singles $151; bunk twins $155; twins and doubles $179. Guest house singles $65; doubles $85. VIP. ❷

Royal Derby Hotel and Backpackers, 446 Brunswick St. (☎9417 3231), at Alexandra Pde. The Royal Derby is a lively pub and nightspot that caters to travelers who care more about having a well-located place to crash than having a peaceful night's sleep. During the popular Sunday School, local DJs educate residents and locals alike, spinning everything from deep house to progressive breaks. M is Movie night, Tu pool competition, Th quiz night. $20. Weekly $120. 30 beds. Bar open Su-Th noon-midnight, F-Sa noon-3am. ❷

SOUTH YARRA & PRAHRAN

Chapel St. Backpackers (NOMADS), 22 Chapel St., Windsor (☎9533 6868 or 9533 6855; www.csbackpackers.com.au), just north of Dandenong Rd. across from Windsor train station, on tram routes #78 and 79. A great hostel just a stumble from Melbourne's best nightlife and St. Kilda. Staff is super-friendly and guests are social, often teaming up to hit the local hotspots. Dorms and doubles have refreshingly clean bathrooms. Heat and A/C. Breakfast included. Internet $5 per hr. Key deposit $20. Check-out 10:30am. 6-bed dorms $20; 4-bed $25; 3-bed $26; twins $29; doubles $70. Weekly 6-bed $133; 4-bed $168; doubles $483. Prices rise slightly in the summer. ❷

Claremont B&B (NOMADS), 189 Toorak Rd., South Yarra (☎9826 8000 or 1300 301 630; www.hotelclaremont.com), 1 block east of the South Yarra train station, on tram route #8. A beautifully refurbished 1886 building, it retains much of its Victorian charm while still providing all the modern amenities. Clean, bright rooms with hardwood floors, wrought-iron beds, heaters, ceiling fans, and TVs. Small but spotless hall baths. Breakfast and towels included. Internet $6 per hr. Singles $62; doubles and twins $72; additional person $15; $10 surcharge during special events, holidays, and festivals. Reservations essential. ❹

Lord's Lodge, 204 Punt Rd., Prahran (☎9510 5658). Take tram #3, 5, 6, 16, 64, or 67 south on St. Kilda Rd. to stop 26; from there it's a quick walk east 2 blocks along Moubray St. A bit removed from St. Kilda proper but just a short walk to Chapel St., several tram stops, Albert Park, and Commercial Rd. This reasonably clean and airy house attracts seasoned travelers of all types. All rooms have heaters, lockers, and fridges, except for the one tiny single dubbed the "dog's box." Three private bungalows out back have TVs and mini-fridges. Request the one with the black-and-white tiled floor. Coffee and tea included. One 6-bed all-female dorm. 9:30am checkout. Cheap Internet and fax. Reception M-Sa 8:30-11:30am and 5-6pm, Su 8:30-11:30am. 4- to 8-bed dorms $18. Weekly $115. Dog's box $25; doubles and bungalows $45, in summer $55. Camping $9 per person. ❷

The Hatton Hotel, 65 Park St. (☎9868 4800; www.hatton.com.au). A petite "boutique" with just 20 rooms, a silver spoon's throw from the Botanic Gardens. Flowery scents waft into elegantly appointed (and super-clean) chambers, where much care is given to color-coordination and preservation of the building's 19th-century eccentricities. All rooms ensuite, with A/C and heat, kitchenette with sink, microwave, fridge, TV, king- or queen-sized bed, hair dryer, and iron and board. Standard doubles and twins $185; "superior" $210; 1 very special double with antique Asian furniture $275. ❺

ST. KILDA

St. Kilda is **backpacker heaven,** with dirt-cheap and often unkempt, grungy hostels—but hey, you get what you pay for. The hostels, centered around Grey St., largely mirror the precinct's fun-loving, gritty flavor. Though removed from the city center, it's easily accessible by tram (stop 133 on lines #16 and 96). The beach, restaurants, and lively nightlife of St. Kilda are in easy reach. If you're coming in March, book way ahead to avoid the hassle of the Grand Prix crowd (see p. 597).

Olembia, 96 Barkly St. (☎9537 1412; www.olembia.com.au), tucked behind a small canopy near the intersection with Grey St. You'll never believe you're in a hostel. Gorgeous living room with sofas and fireplace, glass doors, and a loving feline named Alexander the Great. Ornate, high-ceilinged, heated rooms with comfy mattresses are impeccably clean, as are the bathrooms. Sincere and friendly staff will point you to all the best places in town. Free parking. Bike hire $12. One week max. stay. Key deposit $10. Reception 7am-1pm and 5-8pm. 3- to 4-bed dorms $24; singles $46; twins and doubles $73. Book ahead in summer. ❷

Jackson's Manor, 53 Jackson St. (☎9534 1877; www.jacksonsmanor.com.au). The one-time home of a rich English architect, this little yellow Edwardian gem attracts a quieter crowd. Well heated and impeccably clean throughout with comfortable rooms and a spacious living area featuring plants, stained glass windows, and a large oriental rug. Amenities include a furnished kitchen and ping pong and foosball room. Internet $4 per hr. Job and travel assistance. Free parking. 6- to 10-bed $20; 4-bed $25; singles $59; twins and doubles $61. Weekly 6- to 10-bed $130; 4-bed $151; singles $381; twins and doubles $381. ❷

Pint on Punt (NOMADS), 42 Punt Rd. (☎9510 4273 or 1800 737 378; admin@pinton-punt.com.au), just north of St. Kilda Junction, on the corner of Peel St. Take tram #3, 5, 16, 64, or 67 from Flinders St. Station. New and clean, the Pint has large rooms with new mattresses. Free continental breakfast and 30% discount offered on pub meals downstairs. Open mic W nights and live music Th-Su, but rooms generally stay quiet. Free pick-up from city or airport; arrange ahead. Internet $1 per 15min. Key deposit $10. Check-in at reception 7am-noon or at the bar until 1am. Bar open M-Sa noon-1am, Su noon-11pm. 4- to 6-bed dorms $17-22; singles $35; twins and doubles $50. 7th night free. NOMADS/VIP/YHA. ❷

Enfield House, 2 Enfield St. (☎1800 302 121; enfield@bakpakgroup.com). Take tram #16 or 96 to stop 30 by Fitzroy and Grey St. Walk half a block down Grey St., turn right on Jackson St., then left onto Enfield St. Another B&B-stylish gem. Same owners as **Hotel Bakpak** (see p. 579) downtown, but much more mellow. Front living room hosts M movie nights on a funky old-time projector. Circus-colored heated rooms and shared bathrooms are clean. Job assistance. Free continental breakfast M-F, BBQ Sa, pancakes Su. Reception M-F 8am-8pm, Sa-Su 8am-1pm and 5-8pm. 4-to 8-bed dorms $19-24; singles $45; twins and doubles $60; triples $80. 7th night free. Prices rise $2-3 in summer; book ahead. VIP. ❷

St. Kilda

🏠 ACCOMMODATIONS
Coffee Palace Backpackers
Hotel, **5**
Enfield House, **8**
Jackson's Manor, **7**
Olembia, **9**
Pint on Punt (NOMADS), **1**
The Ritz for Backpackers, **3**
Tolarno Boutique Hotel, **6**

🍴 FOOD
Blue Corn, **13**
Chinta Ria, **12**
Monarch Cake Shop, **11**
Wild Rice, **14**

⭐ NIGHTLIFE
The Elephant and
Wheelbarrow, **2**
Esplanade Hotel, **10**
The George Public Bar, **4**

Coffee Palace Backpackers Hotel, 24 Grey St. (☎9534 5283 or 1800 654 098; info@coffeepalace.com), 1 block off Fitzroy St. Really popular, especially with those who enjoy a party atmosphere. Plenty of amenities, including travel and employment services, a games room, and free bus or airport pick-up. Morning pancakes included. Hallway walls not notable for their soundproofing. Internet $5 per 80min. Key deposit passport. 6-bed dorms $18; 4-bed $19, ensuite $22; twins and doubles $44. Pay 2 nights stay in full on arrival in winter and get 3 free nights. Prices rise in summer. VIP. ❷

The Ritz for Backpackers, 169 Fitzroy St. (☎9525 3501 or 1800 670 364). Tram #16 lets off at stop 132 out front. Just above the **Elephant and Wheelbarrow** (see p. 601), the Ritz is friendly, active, and absolutely mad in summertime. Group activities inspire close bonds between staff and guests. Rooms are fairly sparse, but the 10-bed apartment suite upstairs has a couch, kitchen, and large windows with a view of Albert Park. Heaters available in winter. Cable TV room. Free morning pancakes. Key deposit passport or license. Internet $5 per hr. Reception 6am-10pm. Limited positions available to work in exchange for accommodation. Dorms $18-21; twins and doubles $44-52; apartment suite $22 per person. Prices rise in summer. VIP. ❷

Tolarno Boutique Hotel, 42 Fitzroy St. (☎9537 0200 or 1800 620 363; www.hoteltolarno.com.au). Tolarno is an upscale paradise of just 31 rooms with a bar/restaurant downstairs and fine attention to detail everywhere. Built in 1884 to be the mayor of Melbourne's mansion, the building underwent additions and renovations in the 1930s and '60s and emerged with an amalgam of styles: from Deco to rococo to retro, it's (as its owners say) "glowing inside and out." Suites $115-300, all with TV, heat, queen-sized bed, and coffee maker; balconies, kitchenettes, and Japanese baths available. Twin-shares for up to 3 $150. ❺

🄲 FOOD

Of the Australian cities known for great food, Melbourne has perhaps the most diversity, taking its cuisine from its multicultural makeup. Explore steamy China-town holes-in-the-wall, Fitzroy *café couture*, Carlton's Italian cuisine, South Yarra's sidewalk bistros, or St. Kilda's mix of backpacker-targeted and upscale eat-eries. Interesting hybrids arise, with Chinese restaurants serving french fries, sushi, and cappuccino. The city's restaurants constitute a scene in and of them-selves; on most nights, Melbournians pack into their favorite eateries until closing time (which is often whenever the proprietors feel like shutting the doors).

CITY CENTER

Amid the fast-paced urban jungle of Melbourne's CBD lurk what seem like a mil-lion fantastic eateries, hidden away in labyrinthine corridors or diminutive cran-nies between high-rise buildings. Many are Asian, representing Chinese, Japanese, Indian, Nepalese, Sri Lankan, Malaysian, Indonesian, and Vietnamese flavors. Neon-pulsing **Chinatown** fills the stretch of Little Bourke St., hemmed in by colorful red gates between Swanston and Exhibition St. Blink and you'll miss the **Greek Pre-cinct,** on Lonsdale St. between Swanston and Russell St. It's only a half dozen or so pricey Hellenic restaurants and taverns, but serves transcendent baklava. Many of the coolest cafes, most with a European air, lurk in narrow brick pathways (such as the **Block Arcade,** between Collins and Little Collins St. at Elizabeth St.) that snake through the city. For those do-it-yourself folks, a Coles 24-hr. **supermarket** hides amid the bustle of Elizabeth St. just north of Flinders St. Above all, the city center rewards the adventurous gourmet; wander around with only your nose and palate as a guide and you're sure to find a culinary treasure.

■ **Cafée Baloo,** 260 Russell St. (☎9663 3226), between Little Lonsdale and Lonsdale St. Mixes South Asian fare with pasta and sandwiches in an environment that attains just the right balance of trendy and friendly. Bowls of produce displayed out front go into heaping portions of tasty curry and pasta with or without meat, all around $8-10. 50¢ table charge per person. Licensed for beer ($5 stubbies) and wine only ($5 glass, $20-30 bottle). Open M-F noon-10pm, Sa-Su 5-10pm. ❶

Hopetoun Tea Rooms (☎9650 2777), in the Block Arcade off Elizabeth St., ground level. Enjoy very fine teas (from $5) in super-posh, evergreen surrounds. A nice spot to alight in the afternoon and impress friends with your good taste. Also serves light fare under $25. Open M-Th 9am-5pm, F 9am-6pm, Sa 10am-3pm. ❷

Teayara Cafe and Gallery Restaurant, 230 King St. (☎9600 2777), between Little Bourke and Londsdale St. Opened in May 2001, this classy eatery offers quality pastas ($6.50), 3-course lunch boxes ($15-25), coffee and cake specials ($4), integrated with Indonesian cuisine. Upstairs seating among authentic Indonesian paintings, masks, and furniture provides a romantic and exotic setting. Fully licensed and BYO. Open M-F 11:30am-3:30pm and 5:30pm-late, Sa 5:30pm-late. ❶

Eating Large, 227 Collins St. at Swanston St. (☎/fax 9654 5008). The optimal break-fast value in the Central Business District. The ■ **open plate** ($6) is perhaps the best breakfast in the city; a heaping mess of eggs, bacon, mushrooms, onion, and tomato served on two giant pieces of wholemeal toast. Also serves sandwiches and light fare. Open M-F 9:30am-4:30pm. ❶

NORTH MELBOURNE

The Queen Victoria Market (QVM; see p. 591) serves as the focal point of culinary North Melbourne. In fact, much of the city congregates here, where you can get all the fresh ingredients you need to cook up a fabulous and inexpensive dinner. The surrounding area is home to some fine eateries as well. From the city, take any tram north on William or Elizabeth St.

see p. 591

▨ **The White Lotus,** 185 Victoria St. (☎9326 6040). 1 block west of QVM. An entirely vegan menu at this glowing white restaurant attempts to guide the "way to heaven," following the Buddhist tenets of Tien Tao. All meals are delicious and prepared without meat, animal products, or even onions and garlic. Carnivores will be placated—nay, amazed—by the excellent imitation meat dishes, like mock abalone made from soy and wheat gluten or the spicy Mongolian "beef." Lunch specials $4.50-7. Dinner meals $8-14. Dine-in or takeaway. BYO wine only, $1 corkage fee. Open Su, Tu-W, Sa 5:30-10pm; Th-F 12-2:30pm and 5:30-10pm. ❷

Vic Marketplace (☎9320 5822), in the QVM. The covered arcade has excellent budget fare, mostly made from fresh goods sold next door. **Vic Fish** serves a $6.80 fish 'n' chips lunch packet. Cafe Verona serves pizza, pasta, and gelato ($3-7). The **Consciousness Cafe** has healthy salads and sandwiches ($4-6). Hours vary, but market usually open Tu and Th 6am-2pm, F 6am-6pm, Sa 6am-3pm, Su 9am-4pm. ❶

aioli, 229 Victoria St. (☎9328 1090), 2 blocks west of QVM. Bright green and red walls and a garden out back only enhance the atmosphere of this classy, healthy culinary establishment. A variety of wraps run $6, while the uniquely blended "aioli cleanser" drink goes for $3.50. Open Tu-Sa 7:30am-4:30pm, Su 10am-3pm. ❶

La Porchetta, 302-308 Victoria St. (☎9326 9884), across from the QVM. "The Pizza Institution." Tantalizing wood-fired pizzas (small $4.80, medium $6.10, large $7.20), in styles from Margarita to Mexican, all excellent and at unbeatable prices. Fully licensed and BYO wine only. Open M-Th 11am-midnight, F-Sa 11am-1am. ❶

CARLTON

The best known street in Carlton is **Lygon Street,** where tons of chic Italian pizzerias, cafes, and gelaterias compete with cheap but tasty Thai and Vietnamese joints along the five-block stretch between Queensberry St. to the south and Elgin St. to the north. The eclectic nature of the area draws in a diverse crowd; sadly, despite its attendant student traffic from the nearby University of Melbourne, most of the Italian eateries remain out of the budget traveler's range. There are, however, a fair number of affordable non-Italian places, and a few cafes where you can find cheap dishes. Hawkers outside all the major restaurants after nightfall ensure that not too much exploration is necessary to find a fine eatery.

▨ **Threshermans Bakehouse Café,** 221 Faraday St. (☎9349 2319). Long communal tables and brick floors transport you to a farm in the south of France and set you up for the best dining value in Carlton: $6 for up to three selections of pasta or Asian stir-fry, $3.80 for a focaccia pizza, $5 for soup and bread. With all the money you've saved on dinner, head over to the other counter for a delicious cannoli ($2.80) or an enormous slice of cake ($4.20). Fresh, creative fruit juices ($3.70) are squeezed before your very eyes. After 4pm, day-old pastries are just $1. Internet $2 per 20min. Open daily 6am-11pm; hot food served 11am-10pm. ❶

▨ **Jimmy Watson's Wine Bar,** 333 Lygon St. (☎9347 3985). With over 300 wines to choose from and courses on wine appreciation, Jimmy's, one of the oldest wine bars in Melbourne (since 1932), caters to an older local crowd for the most part. But your more discerning Uni students can definitely be found at the bar. Traditional restaurant serves meals that run $18-40+. Open M 11am-6:30pm, Tu-Sa 11am-11pm. ❺

Tiamo, 303 Lygon St. (☎9347 5759). Dishing up flavorful Italian cuisine, this pasta palace is of the same quality as its pricier neighbors across the way. Its next-door sequel, **Tiamo2** (☎9347 0911), serves a more sophisticated selection in a lighter, classier setting. Cooked-to-perfection pasta $10-12, creamy tiramisu $6, breakfast until noon $4-11. Licensed and BYO. Tiamo open M-Sa 7am-11pm, Su 8am-10pm; Tiamo2 open M-Sa 9:30am-10:30pm. ❷

Toto's, 101 Lygon St. (☎9437 1630). Big and busy, Toto's serves a range of meals (from pasta to sirloin to fish-of-the-day), but their pizza's the real sensation. 3 sizes and about a dozen combinations, all hot, chewy, and flavorful ($7-11). Breakfast $3.40-4.50; all-you-can-eat lunch $10 daily till 2:30pm. Licensed and BYO wine. Open M-Th 11:30am-10pm, F-Sa 8am-11:30pm, Su 11:30am-10pm. ❶

Boba Pearl Bubble Tea Restaurant, 122 Lygon St. (☎9663 0498). Serves excellent Chinese noodles and more ($7-9), but the real story here is the 62 varieties of tea and tea-related frozen drinks ($3.50) available. Put some lychee, peppermint, taro, or red bean into your day. Open daily 11am-late. ❶

FITZROY & COLLINGWOOD

The heart of Melbourne's bohemian scene and cafe society lies in the Fitzroy neighborhood, along **Brunswick St.** between Gertrude and Princes St. Particularly on sunny weekend days, hippies, post-hippies, ferals, and freaks of every ilk frequent the countless artsy coffeehouses and eateries, shadowed by the more mainstream and wannabe chic. The area gets progressively posher as you go south along Brunswick, closer to the city. The stretch of Johnston St. just west of Brunswick St. is Melbourne's Latin Quarter, with Latin dance clubs, Iberian grocers, and several great—but pricey—tapas bars. There are also dining options galore along **Smith Street** in Collingwood.

🔲 **Nyala,** 113 Brunswick St. (☎9419 9128). The best of East Africa, with some Gambia and Morocco thrown in for kicks. Nyala is all about flavor; meat and vegetable mains ($12.50-15) retain their natural savory goodness while enhanced by special combinations of season and spice. If you're strapped for cash, try one of the tasty dips, served with the delightfully satisfying thin Mahloul bread ($6.50). You'll have room for one of their rich desserts ($4-6) and still be able to reach the $10 per person minimum (only on F-Sa nights). Open Su, W-Sa 11:30am-3pm and 6-10:30pm, Tu 6-10:30pm. ❷

Guernica, 257 Brunswick St. (☎9416 0969). Award-winning nouveau-Aussie cuisine doesn't come cheap, and this place (with $30 mains) is no exception. Great fusion and seafood will win you over. Open daily 6-10:30pm, also Su-F noon-3pm. ❺

Mario's, 303 Brunswick St. (☎9417 3343). This cafe is hard to spot—look for the small neon sign—but it sports some of the best breakfast buys in town ($8-12), served all day. Those who spurn the first meal of the day can grab $10-17 pasta dishes or just pop in for a gourmet dessert ($6-8). Fully licensed. Open daily 7am-midnight. ❷

Veg Out Time (positive eating), 406 Brunswick St. (☎9416 4077). Also located at 63a Fitzroy St., in St. Kilda (☎9534 0077). Has cheap Indian and Thai delights ($6-9). Open daily 4-10pm. ❶

Vegie Bar, 380 Brunswick St. (☎9417 6935). A converted warehouse where Fitzroy's large meat-averse population gathers to chow guilt-free, single-g "vegie" meals. They promise "food for the body and soul" and serve it up in heaping portions. Mains all under $9.50. Quiet during the day, but evenings draw a crowd. Loads of vegan and wheat-free options. Fully licensed and BYO wine only. Open daily 11am-10pm. ❷

Robert Burns Hotel, 376 Smith St. (☎9417 2233). Just north of Johnston St on Smith St., which runs parallel to Brunswick St. a few blocks to the east. Behind the non-Iberian name hides great value Spanish fare. Eat in the large, simple restaurant, or for a cheaper meal, sit in the bright front bar. Beyond the standard tortilla, the Robbie Burns serves a range of steaks $12-24. Seafood galore from $10. Paella $15 per person, 2-person min. Tapas served from 2:30pm in the bar. Nightly live music. Bar open M-Sa 11am-midnight; kitchen open M-Sa noon-2:30pm and 6-10pm. ❸

Retro Café, 413 Brunswick St. (☎9419 9103; www.retro.net.au), on the corner of Westgarth St. If you think the bright yellow facade on the building is cool, check out the waterfall and TV-turned-aquarium inside. Meals run the gamut in both price and cuisine, from Dolmades (vine leaves stuffed with rice, $6.90) to Aussie kangaroo with roasted root veggies ($21.90). 2-course menu $28 per person; 3-course $33. Live music every Th 8:30pm; cover $5. Open daily 7am-late; breakfast served until 6pm. Bar open M-Sa until 1am, Su until 11pm. ❹

SOUTH YARRA & PRAHRAN

Preened, pricey South Yarra aggressively markets itself as the place to see and be seen in Melbourne, and its chic, mod-Oz bistros with sidewalk seating see their share of black-clad fashion mavens. There are some excellent budget options though, particularly south of Commercial St. in more down-to-earth Prahran. The ubiquitous coffee bars are a wallet-friendly way to sample the scene (cappuccino around $2.50). Check out the **Prahran Market,** on Commercial Rd. at Izett St., for cheap, fresh produce, meat, and ethnic foodstuffs. **Windsor Cellars,** 29 Chapel St., is just north of Dandenong Rd. and has a **24-hour bottle shop,** one of only two in the city (☎9501 4050).

▨ **Borsch Vodka and Tears,** 173 Chapel St. (☎9530 2694). A divine, warm little den of 60 vodkas ($6-8 per drink, traditionally served neat in a tall shot glass sunk in a bed of ice), dumplings, sausages, and of course that cool beet-y soup, borscht (soup $6-9, mains $16.50-18). The Spirytus is 160 proof fuel—you bring the rocket (and the tears). Open daily 10am-1am. ❸

▨ **Gurkha's Brasserie,** 190-192 Chapel St. (☎9510 3325; www.gurkhas.com.au). Delicious Nepalese cuisine comes at a reasonable price in an ornate restaurant bedecked with lanterns and awash in peaceful South Asian music. It might take you a while to figure out what to order, but a good bet is the *Dal Bhat Masu,* which comes with your choice of meat curry (the goat is wonderfully tender), soup, and rice or bread for only $14. Mains $11-19. Licensed and BYO wine ($1 corkage per person). Open daily 5:30-10:30pm. ❷

Sushi Bar Aka Tombo, 205 Greville St. (☎9510 0577). Around the corner from the bustle of Chapel St., this is perhaps the best sushi value in town. Two bites of the large sushi platter alone justify the $22 bill. Rolls $4.50, nigiri $2.50, lunch boxes $15-25. Fully licensed. Open Tu-Sa 12-2:30pm, 6:30-11pm. ❹

Cafe Gelato, Shop 3, 534 Chapel St. (☎9824 0099). Offering some of the least expensive meals in South Yarra, this colorful cafe is a good break from shopping or people-watching. Deli-style focaccia sandwiches, filled pastries, french crepes, and Sicilian-style pizzas from $4.90; homemade gelato ($3-6). Open daily 8:30am-late. ❶

ST. KILDA

As hip as South Yarra and Chapel St. but far less pretentious, St. Kilda offers diverse and exciting menus in quality affordable eateries interspersed with many decidedly non-budget options. The result is a delightful mix of value and vogue. You can't go wrong with the holes-in-the-wall or fancier bistros on Fitzroy St.; the Barkly St. end of Acland St.—legendary among locals for its divine cake shops—also has a menagerie of great cuisine of all ethnic stripes. Coles 24hr. **supermarket** is in the Acland Court shopping center near Barkly St.

▨ Chinta Ria, 94 Acland St. (☎9525 4666). The "soul" point of a local Malaysian restaurant triangle (its sister establishments are home to the "jazz," 176 Commercial Rd., Prahran; and "blues," 6 Acland St., St. Kilda). New York chic but still contemplative, Ria matches its delectable $15-19 mains with comparable quality. Fried rice and noodle selections $8-12. The changing dessert menu is sweet and sinful ($7-10). Open M-Sa noon-2:30pm and 6-10:30pm, Su noon-2:30pm. ❸

Monarch Cake Shop, 103 Acland St. (☎9534 2972). The oldest cake shop on Acland St.'s cake-shop row (est. 1934 in Carlton, moved to St. Kilda late-1930s) and still the best. Their famous plum cake is the most popular seller ($3 slice), but the chocolate *kugelhopf* is near bliss ($14-15). Open daily 7am-10pm. ❶

Wild Rice, 211 Barkly St. (☎9534 2849). Also at 159 Chapel St., South Yarra. Enter this dark store front to find an imaginative universe of vegan delicacies. Meals are based on the principle of "macrobiotics;" they use only seasonal produce in order to "balance the body's energy." Rice, veggie, and noodle mains $10-14, but pakhoras and tofu pockets fall under $7. Lush garden courtyard out back. Deluxe veggie brekkie served Su 9am-3pm. Open daily noon-10pm. ❷

Blue Corn, 205 Barkly St. (☎9534 5996).Blue Corn features very fresh gourmet Mexican fare at excellent prices. Try the array of dips with blue corn bread (guacamole, salsa, black turtle bean dip, and olive chipotle $14.50) or the lime and swordfish taco ($16.50). Open M-Su 6-10pm. ❷

◉ SIGHTS

CITY CENTER

▨ RIALTO TOWERS. Rising 253m above the city, the Rialto Towers is the tallest office building in the Southern Hemisphere. The 55th floor observation deck provides spectacular 360° views of the city and surrounds. The addictive "Zoom City" live-action video cameras allow you to zoom in and see people crossing the street all the way across town. **Rialtovision Theatre** plays a 20-minute film, *Melbourne, the Living City* that highlights tourist spots with cheesy music and dramatic, wide-angle shots. *(525 Collins St., 1 block east of Spencer St. Station, between King and William St. ☎9629 8222; www.melbournedeck.com.au. Open Su-Th 10am-10pm, F-Sa 10am-11pm. Film every 30min. Film and deck $11, concessions $9, children $6, families $30.)* To those on a tighter budget, **Hotel Sofitel,** at the opposite end of Collins St., at the intersection with Exhibition St., offers a similar view, free of charge. Take the elevator to the 35th floor bathroom and stare through the window into the abyss of the Melbourne skyline.

IMMIGRATION MUSEUM. Chronicling the 200 years of Australian immigration, the Immigration Museum combines various collected artifacts with a moving soundtrack, much of which is triggered by visitors' footsteps in the gallery. A mock ship in the main room shows typical living quarters aboard ocean-going ships from the 1840s to the 1950s. Recent exhibits focus on the Aboriginal struggle for continuity in a dominant foreign culture. Ground-floor resource center contains links to immigrant ship listings as well as a genealogy database. *(400 Flinders St., in the Old Customs House on the corner of William St. A City Circle Tram stop. ☎9927 2700. Open daily 10am-5pm. $7, concession and YHA $5.50, children $3.50, families $18; resource center free. Wheelchair-accessible.)*

ST. PAUL'S CATHEDRAL. The Anglican cathedral, completed in 1891, impresses not in its scale but in the intricacy of its detail. The beautifully stenciled pipes of the 19th-century Lewis organ are easy to miss; look up to the right of the altar. Evening song services echo throughout the hallowed hall Monday through Friday

5:10pm and Su 6pm. Restoration of the two main spires is scheduled for completion in early 2004. *(Presides over the corner of Flinders and Swanston St., diagonal to Flinders St. Station. Enter on Swanston St. Open daily 7am-6pm. Free.)*

STATE LIBRARY OF VICTORIA. A great space to read or work, with a variety of international newspapers, the State Library is worth a visit if just for the interior design. The whole place is undergoing a $200 million renovation (completion date set for January 2004) that will most notably reinstate glass to the roof of the Domed Reading Room, a spectacular octagonal space soaring 35m high. *(At La Trobe and Swanston St. ☎9669 9888; www.slv.vic.gov.au. Free tours M-F and every other Sa 2pm. Open M-Th 10am-9pm, F-Su 10am-6pm.)*

CHINATOWN. The pagoda gates at the corner of Swanston and Little Bourke St. indicate your arrival at a two-block stretch of Asian restaurants, groceries, and bars that was first settled by Chinese immigrants in the 1870s. A block and a half east, the back-alley **Chinese Museum** houses *Dai Loong* (Great Dragon), the **biggest imperial dragon in the world** (not the longest, which is in Bendigo; see p. 640) and a staple of Melbourne's Moomba festival (see p. 597)—so huge it has to be wound around two entire floors. *(22 Cohen Pl. ☎9662 2888. $6.50, concessions $4.50. Open daily 9am-5pm. Wheelchair-accessible.)*

PARLIAMENT OF VICTORIA & OLD TREASURY. Victoria's parliament is a stout, pillared 19th-century edifice every bit as stolid and imposing as a seat of government should be. Free tours detail the workings of the Victorian government and the architectural intricacies of the parliament chambers. *(On Spring St. north of Bourke St. A City Circle Tram stop. ☎9651 8568; www.parliament.vic.gov.au. Guided tours when Parliament is not in session 10, 11am, noon, 2, 3, and 3:45pm.)* Designed in Italian Palazzo style by a 19-year-old prodigy, the **Old Treasury Building** contains a museum chronicling Melbourne's past, including some great stories about the idiosyncrasies of the city's first years. The gold vaults in the basement were built to prevent a crime wave that plagued the Treasury during the Victorian Gold Rush; they now house a multimedia exhibit detailing daily life and events of Melbourne's gold-rush era. *(On Spring St., at Collins St. ☎9651 2233; www.oldtreasurymuseum.org.au. Open M-F 9am-5pm, Sa-Su 10am-4pm. $5, concessions $3, seniors $4, families $13.)*

FITZROY GARDENS. These gardens, originally planted in 1848 and laid out in the shape of the Union Jack, bloom year round. On the south end is Cook's Cottage, a small stone home constructed by Captain James Cook's family in England in 1755 and moved to Melbourne in 1934 to celebrate the city's centennial. Cook never actually reached the site and may not even have spent time in this house, but the information room has a concise history of his voyages. Next door, the colorfully stocked **Conservatory Greenhouse** has seasonal plants and flowers. Weekends in December through January often bring concerts and other summer events to the gardens. *(Gardens bordered by Lansdowne, Albert, and Clarendon St. and Wellington Pde. Tram #48 or 75 from Flinders St. www.fitzroygardens.com. Free garden tour W 11am, starting from the conservatory. Cook's Cottage: ☎9419 4677. $3.30, concessions $2.35. Conservatory: ☎9419 4118. Free tour W 12:30pm. Both open daily 9am-5pm.)*

ST. PATRICK'S CATHEDRAL. A beautiful product of Gothic revival, St. Patrick's Cathedral comes replete with grotesque gargoyles, elaborate stained glass, and a magnificent altar. Among the traditional Catholic relics in the cathedral, you'll also find an Aboriginal message stick and stone inlay, installed as a welcoming gesture to Aboriginal Catholics and a reconciliation for past wrongs committed against their people. The cathedral is most spectacular when seen at ■night, at which time its 106m spires are illuminated by floodlights. The well-manicured cathedral grounds are home to a bubbling fountain and make for a nice stroll. *(West of the*

Fitzroy Garden's northwest corner on Cathedral Pl. ☎ 9662 2332. Open 7:30am-6pm. Free guided tour M-F 10am-noon. No tourists during mass M-Sa 7-7:30am and 1-1:20pm, Sa 8-8:30am, Su 7am-12:30pm and 6-7:30pm.)

MELBOURNE CRICKET GROUND (MCG). First established in 1853 and expanded in 1956 for the Olympics and again in 1992 to seat 92,000, the MCG functions as the sanctum sanctorum of Melbourne's robust sporting life. It houses Australian Rules Football (AFL) every weekend in winter, including the Grand Final the last Saturday in September. There are also, of course, cricket contests (Oct.-Apr.), highlighted by test matches between Australia and South Africa, England, New Zealand, Pakistan, and the West Indies. The north side of the MCG contains the **Australian Gallery of Sport and Olympic Museum,** further celebrating Australia's love for sport. The venue houses the **Australian Cricket Hall of Fame** (which requires some understanding to appreciate), an AFL exhibition, a new feature on extreme sports, and the **Olympic Museum,** with a focus on Australian achievements and the 1956 Melbourne games. The best way to see the stadium and gallery is with a guided tour from the northern entrance, which offers unique insight into the MCG's history, allowing you to step inside the player's changing rooms, the **Melbourne Cricket Club Museum,** and onto the hallowed turf itself. Entertaining guides make the one-hour tour worth the price even if you don't have the slightest idea what a wicket, over, or googlie are. *(Take the Met to Jolimont. ☎ 9657 8888; www.mcg.org.au. Tours led by former presidents of the club run on all non-event days on the hour, and often every 30min., 10am-3pm. $18, concessions $13, families $44. Admission includes tour and access to galleries with audiocassette guide.)* **AFL games** at the MCG are also a must, allowing you to experience an essential aspect of Melbournian culture. To achieve, or at least mimic, authenticity, order a meat pie and beer, choose a favorite team, and blow out your vocal chords along with the passionate crowd. Make sure to stay for the winning team's song played after the game. *(The MCG is in Yarra Park, southeast of Fitzroy Gardens across Wellington Pde. Accessible via trams #48, 70, and 75. Tickets $15-22, concessions about half-price; prices vary by entrance gate, so search around.)*

MELBOURNE PARK (NATIONAL TENNIS CENTRE). To the west across the railroad tracks from the MCG and Yarra Park sits the ultramodern tennis facility of the **Melbourne Park.** The entire complex, which is composed of the domed Rod Laver Arena, the new and sleek Vodafone Arena, and numerous outer courts, hosts the **Australian Open** Grand Slam event every January. You can wander around and see the trophies and center court for free or take a 40min. guided tour. Though you can't play on the center court, the outer courts give proximity to greatness for a $16-24 hourly playing fee. During the Open, a $20 **ground pass** will get you into every court except center; go during the first week and you're likely to see many of the big names playing on the outer courts. *(Take tram #70 from Flinders St. Australian Open tickets ☎ 9286 1600. To hire a court, book at ☎ 9286 1244. Open M-F 9am-5pm. Tours $5, concession $2.50.)*

NORTH OF THE CITY CENTER

▨ **OLD MELBOURNE GAOL.** This prison was opened in 1845 and housed a total of 50,000 prisoners in its 84 years. The main structure has three levels of cells linked by iron catwalks. The tiny cells each house small displays about everything from the history and specifications of the jail to fascinating stories about **Ned Kelly's gang,** the creepiest displays feature the stories and death masks of the most notorious criminals executed here. Kelly, Australia's most infamous bushranger, was hanged in the jail in 1880, and a scruffy wax likeness stands on the original trap door and scaffold. Downstairs is the suit of armor that Kelly, or one of his cohorts, wore in the gang's final shoot-out with police. Wonderfully spooky evening tours led by professional actors provide a chillingly vivid sense of its horrible past. *(On Russell St. just north of La Trobe. ☎ 9663 7228; click on "properties" at www.nattrust.com.au. $12.50, concessions $9.50, children $7.50, families $33.50. Night tours W and F-Su 7:30pm. $20, children $13, families $48. Bookings essential for night tours; call Ticketmaster ☎ 13 28 49. Open daily 9:30am-4:30pm.)*

CARLTON GARDENS & MELBOURNE MUSEUM. Spanning three city blocks, the verdant gardens, criss-crossed with pathways and spectacular fountains, offer peaceful repose and potential possum sightings in the evening. Standing within the gardens is the grandiose **Royal Exhibition Building,** which was home to Australia's first parliament and now sometimes hosts major expositions, temporary exhibits, and, more often, rug and furniture blow-out sales. Behind the Exhibition Building stands the multimillion dollar **Melbourne Museum,** a new, stunning facility that contains a range of science-related galleries, including an IMAX theater (see **Cinema,** p. 595), a rainforest, an Aboriginal center, a children's museum, and a mind and body gallery. *(Bordered by Victoria, Rathdowne, Carlton, and Nicholson St. On the city circle tram, or take tram 96. Museum ☎ 8341 7777; www.melbourne.museum.vic.gov.au. $15, concessions $11, ages 3-16 $8, families $35. Museum and IMAX showing $20/$12/$15/$55. Open daily 10am-5pm. Free after 4:30pm. Public tours of Royal Exhibition Building daily 2pm; $5, with museum admission $3. Wheelchair-accessible.)*

QUEEN VICTORIA MARKET. The modernizing development that brought the rest of Melbourne into the 21st century somehow passed over the QV Market. It remains an old-fashioned, open-air market, abuzz with hundreds of vendors hawking their wares to the thousands of Melbournians who pack in for excellent bargains on produce, dairy products, and meat. Saturdays and Sundays see the market at its frenetic best. Don't be afraid to bargain with vendors; good deals can turn into amazing ones after noon, when sellers are anxious to empty their stock. Walking tours explore the market's history and cultural importance and include plenty to eat. From late November to early March, the market is also open at night (6-10pm), when the focus turns multicultural. *(On Victoria St. between Queen and Peel St. Open Tu and Th 6am-2pm, F 6am-6pm, Sa 6am-3pm, Su 9am-4pm. ☎ 9320 5822; www.qvm.com.au. Tours depart from 69 Victoria St., near Elizabeth St. Food tour Tu and Th-Sa 10am. $22. History tour 10:30am. $17. Book ahead ☎ 9320 5935.)*

MELBOURNE ZOO. Many sections of this world-class, 142-year-old zoo are expertly recreated native habitats that allow visitors to view animals much as they live in the wild. The African Rainforest—with pygmy hippos, arboreal monkeys, and gorillas—is first-rate, with a new and elaborate Asian elephant exhibit. Of course, you won't want to miss the Aussie fauna, which include echidnas, wombats, goannas, emus, flying squirrels, and red kangaroos with whom visitors can play—if the 'roos feel like it. From early January until early March, the zoo hosts twilight festivals Th, F, Sa, and Su evenings with a live band. On these nights, the zoo remains open until people leave. *(On Elliott Ave., north of the University of Melbourne. M-Sa take tram #55 from William St. to the Zoo stop; Su take tram #19 from Elizabeth St. ☎ 9285 9300; www.zoo.org.au. Free tours for the elderly and disabled M-F 10am-3pm, Sa-Su 10am-4pm. Open Mar.-Dec. daily 9am-5pm; Jan. M-W 9am-5pm, Th-Su 9am-9:30pm; Feb. M-Th 9am-5pm, F-Su 9am-9:30pm. $15.80, concessions $11.70, ages 4-15 $7.80, families $42.60.)*

SOUTH OF THE YARRA RIVER

▨ KING'S DOMAIN & ROYAL BOTANIC GARDENS. Over 50,000 plants fill the 36 acres stretching along St. Kilda Rd. east to the Yarra and south to Domain Rd. The gardens first opened in 1846, and the extensive array of mature species reflects a long history of care and development. Stately palms unique to Melbourne share the soil with twisting oaks, rainforest plants, possums, wallabies, and a pavilion of roses. A number of walking tracks highlight endemic flora. There's also a steamy **rainforest glasshouse** and lake where you can have tea and feed the ducks and geese. *(Open daily 10am-4:30pm.)* Special events, such as **outdoor film screenings,** take place on summer evenings (see **Cinema,** p. 595). The **Aboriginal Heritage Walk** explores the use of plant-life by local Aboriginal groups in ceremony, symbol, and food. *(Th 11am and alternate Su 10:30am. $15.40, concessions $11, ages 12-16 $6.60. Book ahead.)* Near the entrance closest to the Shrine of Remembrance are the **Visitors Center** and the **observatory.** The Visitors Center houses an upscale cafe, the Terrace Tearooms and Conference Center, and a garden shop. *(Open M-F 9am-5pm, Sa-Su 10am-5:30pm.)* The observatory includes an original 1874 telescope only accessible by day tours, which give a close-up look at the 'scopes; night tours allow visitors to use the instruments with the help of qualified astronomers. *(Tours W 2pm. $6.60, concession $4.40. Night tour Tu 7:30pm. $15.40, concessions $11, families $37.40. Book ahead.)* The small cottage by Gate F is the **La Trobe Cottage,** home of Victoria's first lieutenant governor, Charles Joseph La Trobe. *(Open M, W, and Sa-Su 11am-4pm. $2.20.)* Tours leave from the cottage to **Government House,** the Victorian Governor's official residence. *(4 Parliament Pl. ☎9654 4711; www.rbgmelb.org.au. Tours $11, concessions $9, children $5.50. Book ahead. Gardens ☎9252 2300. Open daily Nov.-Mar. 7:30am-8:30pm; Apr.-Oct. 7:30am-5:30pm. Free. Tours of the garden depart the Visitors Center Su-F 11am and 2pm. $4, concessions $2. Wheelchair-accessible.)*

NATIONAL GALLERY OF VICTORIA (NGV). The massive National Gallery of Victoria had to adopt the confusing post-phrase "of Victoria" when the Australian National Gallery was built in Canberra. Still considered to house the finest collection in the Southern Hemisphere, the NGV is undergoing a $136 million renovation and is scheduled to re-open as **NGV: International.** The postmodern facilities of the **Ian Potter Centre NGV: Australia,** in the new Federation Square building at Swanston and Flinders St., house three levels of Aboriginal, colonial, and contemporary Australian art. This new center, a strikingly original huddle of prisms of glass and steel, is the only entirely Australian collection of art anywhere in the world, and it will remain the focus of the Australian portion of the National Gallery collection even after NGV: International reopens. *(180 St. Kilda Rd. and Federation Sq. ☎9208 0222; www.ngv.vic.gov.au. Gallery open daily 10am-5pm. Free guided tours M and W-F 11am, 1, and 2pm; Tu 1 and 2pm; Sa 2pm; Su 11am and 2pm. Admission to permanent collection free. Wheelchair-accessible.)*

SHRINE OF REMEMBRANCE. A wide walkway lined with tall, conical Butan cypresses leads to this imposing temple, with columns and a ziggurat roof, that commemorates fallen soldiers from WWI. Crowning the central space are a stepped skylight and the **stone of remembrance,** which bears the inscription "Greater Love Hath No Man." The skylight is designed so that at 11am on November 11 (the moment of the WWI armistice), a ray of sunlight shines onto the word "Love" on the stone. Ascend to the shrine's balcony for spectacular views of the Melbourne skyline and the neighboring suburbs. Or, venture down into the crypt and view the colorful division flags and memorial statues. Outside, veterans of subsequent wars are honored with a memorial that includes the **perpetual flame,** burning continuously since Queen Elizabeth II lit it in 1954. *(On St. Kilda Rd. www.shrine.org.au. Open daily 10am-5pm. $2 donation requested.)*

SOUTHBANK. The riverside walk that begins across Clarendon St., Southbank, has an upmarket shopping and sidewalk-dining scene. It's most crowded on sunny Sundays, when an odd mix of skater kids, athletic health nuts, and the Armani-clad gather here to relax, show off, and conspicuously consume. The area extends along the Yarra for two very long city blocks. While you could easily squander your entire budget here within a day, you can window-shop, people-watch, and get some great views of Flinders St. Station and the city skyline for free. There are also a slew of expensive but enjoyable river ferry rides as well as interesting fountains, wacky sculptures, and endlessly imaginative sidewalk chalk drawings.

VICTORIAN ARTS CENTRE. This enormous complex is the central star of Melbourne's performing arts galaxy. The 162m white-and-gold latticed spire of the **Theatres Building** is a landmark in itself, and inside there's more room for performance than most cities can handle. Home to the **Melbourne Theatre Company, Opera Australia,** and the **Australian Ballet,** this eight-level facility holds three theaters (see **Performing Arts**, p. 594) that combined can seat over 3000. The Theatres Building also serves the visual arts, as the space that once belonged to the Performing Arts Museum is now used for free public gallery shows. Next door is the 2600-seat **Melbourne Concert Hall,** which hosts the renowned **Melbourne Symphony** and the **Australian Chamber Orchestra**; its chic **EQ Cafebar** (☎9645 0644) is a bit pricey but offers award-winning meals and great views of the Yarra. Finally, the third tier of the Victorian Arts conglomerate, the **Sidney Myer Music Bowl,** is across St. Kilda Rd. in King's Domain Park. After extensive renovations, the bowl will be the largest capacity outdoor amphitheater in the Southern Hemisphere, sheltering numerous free and not-so-free summer concerts. Its "Carols by Candlelight," in the weeks before Christmas, draws Victorians by the sleighloads. Sunday the Centre hosts a free arts & crafts market from 10am-5pm. *(100 St. Kilda Rd., at the east end of Southbank, just across the river from Flinders St. Station. ☎9281 8000; www.vicartscentre.com.au. Open M-F 7am-late, Sa 9am-late, Su 10am-after the last show. Free admission. Guided tours leave from concierge desk M-Sa noon and 2:30pm, though hours vary. $10, concessions $7.50. Special Su 12:15pm backstage tour $13.50.)*

MELBOURNE AQUARIUM. Focusing on species of the Southern Ocean, this high-class facility offers a unique look at Australia's lesser-known wildlife. Its three levels include an open-air billabong and a 2.2 million liter "Oceanarium," featuring a glass tunnel that allows visitors to walk beneath roaming sharks and giant rays. Don't miss the car-turned-aquarium dubbed "A fish called Honda." *(On King St. at the corner of Queenswarf Rd., across from the Crown Casino. ☎9923 5999; www.melbourneaquarium.com.au. Open daily Jan. 9:30am-9pm, Feb.-Dec. 9:30am-6pm; last admission 1hr. before close. $22, concessions $14, children $12, families $55. MC/V.)*

ST. KILDA

Bayside St. Kilda lies just far enough away from the city to be relaxed, but close enough to maintain a lively vibe during the day; at night, more of the same citywide scene of black-clad bar-hoppers appear. St. Kilda has recently undergone a departure from its former seedy image of drugs and prostitution; although remnants of the past still linger, a new attitude is coming to life. There aren't a lot of tourist sights *per se*, but the offbeat shops, gorgeous sandy shoreline, and comfortably mixed population of the weird and the ordinary are indeed a sight to behold. St. Kilda Beach is easily accessed by any number of trams (see **Orientation,** p. 572), and swarms with swimmers and sun-worshippers during summer. The **Esplanade,** along the length of the strand, is a great place for in-line skating and jogging. On Sundays, the Esplanade craft market sells art, toys, housewares, and everything else, all handmade.

LUNA PARK. The entrance gate of this St. Kilda icon is a grotesque, mammoth funhouse face. Venture through its mouth to find classic carnival rides all permanently protected by the historical commission, which is attempting to honor the park's near-century long existence. Built in 1912 by a triad of American entrepreneurs hoping to capitalize on the fame of Coney Island's successful Luna Park, Melbourne's Luna has the largest wooden roller-coaster in the world. *(On the Lower*

VICTORIA

> ## WHAT'S THAT ON THE SIDEWALK? One part of
> Melbourne's oft-cited liveability is the attention paid to public art. Deb Halpern's
> **Ophelia** on Southbank, is the fat-lipped, multi-colored, Y-shaped visage that has
> become one of the city's most prominent icons. On the pavement in front of Halpern's
> work, look for the ephemeral chalk drawings of Bev Isaac. North along Swanston St. in
> front of the State Library of Victoria, a stone cornice with part of the word **"library"** pro-
> truding from the pavement draws a crowd for its uniqueness and quirkiness. Perhaps
> the most popular of the sculptures is the group of **three businessmen** cast in bronze
> standing at the corner of Swanston and Bourke St. Their emaciated frames and wild-
> eyed expressions inspire amusement in most onlookers, but was originally underwritten
> by the government of Nauru to reflect the greed and spiritual impoverishment of the
> Australian businessmen who plundered the tiny Polynesian country's natural resources.

Esplanade. ☎ 9525 5033; www.lunapark.com.au. Free entry. Unlimited ride tickets $30, ages 4-12 $20; single rides $6.50, ages 4-12 $5, ages 1-3 $3. Open F 7-11pm, Sa 11am-11pm, Su 11am-dusk; public and school holidays M-Th 11am-5pm, F-Sa 11am-11pm, Su 11am-7pm.)

ALBERT PARK. Adjacent to Fitzroy St. on the north lies Albert Park, the southern extension of Melbourne's vast park system, with ample green space, free BBQs, tennis courts, and groups of kids playing footy. Visitors can drive on the Grand Prix course here, abiding by speed limits, of course (see **Recreation**, p. 596). The huge interior lake is great for sailing or paddleboating, but no swimming is allowed. (For info, call Parks Victoria ☎ 13 19 63.)

JEWISH MUSEUM OF AUSTRALIA. The Jewish Museum outlines both the history of the Jewish people as a whole and the 200-year experience of Australia's 90,000 Jews from the time of the First Fleet. A stunning hallway draws a timeline of Jewish history, complete with fascinating and state-of-the-art multimedia displays. The Belief and Ritual Gallery provides a thorough overview of Judaism's basic tenets, including a painfully detailed French woodcut of a circumcision ceremony. There are also rotating displays of art and Judaica, and an extensive reference library and archive, available for use upon request. (26 Alma Rd., east of St. Kilda Rd. by stop 32 on tram #3 or 67. ☎ 9534 0083; www.jewishmuseum.com.au. Museum open Tu-Th 10am-4pm, Su 11am-5pm. $7, students and children $4, families $16. Present a print-out of the front page of the web site and get a 50% discount on admission. 30-40min. tours of the adjacent synagogue Tu-Th 12:30pm, Su 12:30 and 3pm; free with admission. Wheelchair-accessible).

🎭 ENTERTAINMENT

Melbourne prides itself on its style and cultural savvy, and nowhere is this more evident than in its entertainment scene. The range of options can seem overwhelming: there are world-class performances at the Victorian Arts Centre, edgy experimental drama in Carlton and Fitzroy, popular dramas and musicals in opulent theaters, and a panoply of independent and avant-garde cinema. The definitive web site for performance events is www.melbourne.citysearch.com.au.

PERFORMING ARTS

Book for larger shows through **Ticketek** (☎ 13 28 49 or 1800 062 849; www.ticketek.com) or **Ticketmaster7** (☎ 1300 136 166; www.ticketmaster7.com), or try **Halftix** for half-price same-day tickets (see **Ticket Agencies**, p. 577); for smaller productions, call theater companies directly. The hard-to-miss **Victorian Arts Centre**, 100 St. Kilda Rd., sports an Eiffel-like spire right on the Yarra across from Flinders St. Station. It houses five venues: the **State Theatre** for major dramatic, operatic, and dance performances; the **Melbourne Concert Hall,** for symphonies; the **Playhouse,** largely used by the Melbourne Theatre Company for plays; the **George Fairfax Studio,** similar to the Playhouse but smaller; and the **Black Box,** for cutting-edge, low-budget shows targeted at an under-35 audience. (☎9281 8000, box office ☎1300 136 166; www.vicartscentre.com.au. Tickets range from free to $180; $6.90 transaction fee when not purchased at box office. Box office open M-Sa 9am-9pm.)

La Mama, 205 Faraday St., Carlton (☎9347 6948), about halfway up Lygon St. Head east on Faraday; it's very near the intersection, hidden down an alleyway and behind a parking lot. Serving up esoteric Australian drama in a diminutive, black-box space since 1967. M nights see fiction readings; poetry and plays read some Sa nights (when there's no performance). Similar cutting-edge work performed at the affiliated **Carlton Courthouse Theatre,** 349 Drummond St., just around the corner in the old courthouse building, across from the police station. Tickets $11-16. Free tea and coffee at performances. Wheelchair-accessible.

Last Laugh at the Comedy Club, Level 1, 380 Lygon St., Carlton (☎9348 1622), in Lygon Ct. Melbourne's biggest comedy-club scene, with big-name international jokesters. Ticket prices vary depending on the act. Show starts 8:30pm and usually end around 12:30am. Seats 360. Tickets $25-50, depending on whether or not dinner is included.

National Theatre (☎9534 0221; www.nationaltheatre.org.au), on the corner of Barkly and Carlisle St., St. Kilda. Offbeat, cosmopolitan fare, like modern dance, drama, opera, and "world music." Ticket prices depend on the show, but generally fall between $10-60.

Palais Theatre (☎9534 0651), on the Esplanade, St. Kilda. Holds the largest chandelier in the Southern Hemisphere. Seats 3000. Tickets $40-60.

Princess' Theatre, 163 Spring St. (☎9299 9850). Home to an annual line-up of cheesy, big-budget musicals. 1500-seat venue that has been around since 1885. Tickets $40-80. Book through Ticketek (☎13 28 49).

Regent Theatre, 191 Collins St. (☎9299 9500), just east of Swanston St. The dazzlingly ornate Regent Theatre was once a popular movie house founded in 1929 and dubbed the "Palace of Dreams"; it now hosts big-name touring musicals and international celebrity acts. Seats 2000. Tickets $50-80. 2hr. tours of Regent and Forum every Tu; $18, students $15. Book ahead.

The Forum, 150 Flinders St. (☎9299 9700). Looks like a combination of an Arabian palace and Florentine villa, with a few gargoyles thrown in for good measure. Big-budget dance and drama ($50-80), as well as periodic concerts ($20-30) and even occasional movies. Bookings through Princess' Theatre (see above).

CINEMA

Melbourne has long been the center of Australia's independent film scene, and there are heaps of old theaters throughout the city that screen artsy and experimental fare as well as old cinema classics. The arthouse crowd logs on to www.urbancinefile.com.au, which features flip reviews of the latest stuff.

The annual **Melbourne International Film Festival** (see **Festivals,** p. 597) showcases the year's international indie hits, and the **St. Kilda Film Festival** (see **Festivals**) highlights short films of all shapes and sizes. An especially select crew of home-grown flicks can be viewed in late July at the **Melbourne Underground Film Festival,** an occasionally bizarre showing from local students in Fitzroy. You'll have to have your eyes peeled to catch it; check for posters and pray.

Plenty of cinemas in the city center show mainstream first-run movies as well. **Movieline** (☎9685 7111) has a ticketing service and recorded info on showtimes and locations. At the theater, try a "choc-top," the chocolate-dipped ice-cream cone that's a staple of Australian movie-going ($2-3).

Australian Center for the Moving Image, Federation Square (at Swanston St. and Flinders St., ☎8663 2200, www.acmi.net.au). The ACMI screens an eclectic array of film and video works and displays installation pieces and multimedia exhibitions. Also houses the nation's largest public collection of film, video, and DVD titles, as well as the world's largest screen gallery (spanning the entire length of Federation square underground). Free. Open 10am-6pm.

Astor Theatre (☎9510 1414; www.astor-theatre.com), on the corner of Chapel St. and Dandenong Rd., St. Kilda. Spectacular Art Deco theater that still bears many of its original furnishings and all of its stately beauty. Mostly repertory and reissues. Seats 1100. Still runs along the same lines as it did when it opened in 1936, showing mostly double features ($12, concessions $11, children $10, book of 10 tickets $90).

Cinema Nova, 380 Lygon St., Carlton (☎9349 5201, www.cinemanova.com.au), in Lygon Ct. Indie and foreign films. Claims the oxymoronic title of "second-largest art-house megaplex in the world." $13.50, concessions $9.50, children $8. Special M $5 before 4pm, $7.50 after.

IMAX, Melbourne Museum, Carlton (☎9663 5454; www.imax.com.au), off Rathdowne St. in the Carlton Gardens (see p. 591). Daily screenings of 5 films every hr. $15, concessions $12, children $10, families $42; 3-D shows $1 extra ($4 for families). Su-Th 10am-10pm, F-Sa 10am-11pm. YHA and RACV discount 20%, NOMADS 10%.

Moonlight Cinema (☎9428 2203; www.moonlight.com.au), in the Royal Botanic Gardens. From mid-Dec. to early Mar., movies play on the central lawn, with a licensed bar and gourmet catering. Films start at sundown, approximately 8:45pm; tickets can be purchased at the gate from 7:30pm. $14, concessions $11, children $9.50.

The Kino, 45 Collins St. (☎9650 2100), downstairs in the Collins Place complex. Independent and foreign films. $13.50, concessions $10.50; M special $8.50.

SPORTS & RECREATION

Melbournians refer to themselves as "sports mad," but it's a good insanity—one that causes fans of footy (Australian Rules Football), cricket, tennis, and horse racing to skip work or school, get decked out in the costumery of their favorite side, and cheer themselves hoarse. Their hallowed haven is the **Melbourne Cricket Ground (MCG)**, adjacent to the world-class **Melbourne Park** tennis center (see p. 590). A new ward, **Colonial Stadium,** right behind Spencer St. Station, has begun to share footy-hosting responsibilities with the more venerable MCG and also hosts the majority of local rugby action. The lunacy peaks at various yearly events: the **Australian Open,** a Grand Slam tennis event in late January; the **Grand Prix** Formula-One car-racing extravaganza in March; the **AFL Grand Final** in late September; the **Melbourne Cup,** the "horse race that stops the nation" in early November; and cricket's **Boxing Day Test Match** on Dec. 26 (see **Festivals,** p. 597).

Melbourne's passion for sport is not limited to spectator events. City streets and parks are packed with joggers, skaters, and footy players. The newly refurbished, crushed gravel tan track that circles the Royal Botanic Gardens is best for **running;** stick to the track, as recreational activities are strictly prohibited in the Gardens proper. Other great routes include the pedestrian paths along the Yarra, the Port Phillip/St. Kilda shore, and the Albert Park Lake. All of these wide, flat spaces make for excellent **in-line skating** as well. **City Skate,** Wednesday at 9pm, draws local bladers together at the Victorian Arts Centre near the waterfall; folks convene and break into smaller groups based on preferred city route and skill level. You can rent equipment at the **Skate Warehouse,** 354 Lonsdale St. (☎9602 3633. $7.50 per hr., $12.50 per 3hr., $17.50 per day, $27.50 for F-M. Open M-Th 10am-6pm, F 10am-9pm, Sa 9am-5pm, Su 10am-5pm.)

The **beach** in St. Kilda, accessible by tram #16 and 96, is not Australia's finest, but it'll do for sun and swimming. **Albert Park** (see p. 594) has a lake good for sailing but not for swimming. Just inside its Clarendon St. entrance, **Jolly Roger** rents boats. (☎9690 5862; www.jollyrogersailing.com.au. Sailboats $40-65 per hr.; rowboats $32 per hr.; aquabikes $22 per half hour. Open Su, Tu-Sa 8:30am-4:30pm.) The **Melbourne City Baths,** 420 Swanston St., on the corner of Franklin St., offer two pools, sauna, spa, squash courts, and a gym in a restored Neoclassical building. (☎9663 5888. Open M-Th 6am-10pm, F 6am-8:30pm, Sa-Su 8am-6pm. Pool $3.80, 10-ticket pass $34.20; sauna and spa $8.20.)

GAMBLING

The Australian penchant for "having a flutter" (betting) reaches its neon-lit apotheosis at **Melbourne's Crown Casino,** 8 Whiteman St., at the western end of Southbank. A little slice of Las Vegas down under, this $1.6 billion complex houses the most gaming tables of any casino in the world, plus five-star accommodations, luxury shopping, Elvis impersonators, fog-filled, laser-lit jumping fountains, and three **nightclubs:** Heat, Club Odeon, and the Mercury Lounge. The evening pyrotechnic displays out front on the Yarra are not to be missed; every hour, starting at 7pm, you'll think it's some sort of independence day celebration. Minimum bets are around $5, though the more cautious can start at the less cut-throat "how to play" tables. (☎9292 8888. Open 24hr., and busy just about every one of those hours.)

■ FESTIVALS

Melbournians create excuses for city-wide street parties any time of the year. Below are the city's major events. For a complete guide, grab a free copy of *Melbourne Events* at any tourist office, or do an events search at www.visitmelbourne.com. All dates listed are for 2004.

Midsumma Gay and Lesbian Festival, Jan. 17-Feb. 8 (☎9415 9819; www.midsumma.org.au). Three weeks of hijinx all over the city ranging from the erotic (a "Mr. Leather Victoria" contest) to the educational (a Same-Sex Partners Rights workshop), with lots of parades, dance parties, and general pandemonium.

Australian Open, Jan. 9-Feb. 1 (tickets ☎9286 1175; www.ausopen.org). One of the world's elite four Grand Slam tennis events, held at Melbourne Park's hard courts.

Foster's Australian Grand Prix, early Mar., 2004 (tickets ☎13 16 41; www.grandprix.com.au). Albert Park, St. Kilda. Formula One frenzy holds the city hostage.

Moomba, Mar. 25-Apr. 18 (☎9650 9744; www.melbournemoombafestival.com.au). A non-stop four-day citywide fête amid food, performances, and events.

Melbourne Food and Wine Festival, Mar. 29-Apr. 14 (☎9412 4220; www.melbfoodwinefest.com.au), on Collins St. A free and delicious way to celebrate Melbourne as Australia's "culinary capital."

International Comedy Festival, Mar. 27-Apr. 20 (☎1900 937 200; www.comedyfestival.com.au). Huge 3-week international and Aussie laugh-fest, with over 1000 gut-busting performances.

International Flower and Garden Show, Mar. 31-Apr. 4 (☎9639 2333). Royal Exhibition Building and Carlton Gardens, Carlton.

Anzac Day Parade, Apr. 25 (☎9650 5050). ANZAC vets in the Commemoration March head down Swanston St. and St. Kilda Rd. to the Shrine of Remembrance.

St. Kilda Film Festival, late May-early June (☎9209 6711). Palais Theatre and George Cinemas, St. Kilda. Australia's best short films: documentary, experimental, and comedy.

ROM THE ROAD

A DAY AT THE RACES

wo days after arriving in Austra-
ia, I dragged myself out of bed
nd, dressed in my only collared
shirt and a borrowed tie, followed
a pack of eager travelers out the
hostel door. The city was flooded
with exquisitely-dressed Austra-
ians, all walking determinedly
owards the train station to see
he **Melbourne Cup**, a world-
famous horse race that captivates
he collective attention of the
entire nation.

I was totally unprepared for the
scene at Flemington Racecourse,
site of the Cup. Even with my tie, I
elt quite under-dressed in a sea
of dark three-piece suits and well-
polished dress shoes. Even more
mpressive were the women sport-
ng large, intricate hats of all
shapes and sizes. Almost as
hyped-up as the race itself was
he award show for best dressed
and best hat. I placed a $5 bet on
he race and sat on the Great
Lawn—meat pie and a VB in
hand—to observe the festivities.
After a day watching elegant Aus-
ralians consume mass quantities
of alcohol, shout and scream at
heir favorite horses and riders,
and bet large sums, I found that
my horse had come in third. That
hight, I discovered that Melbournian revelry never ceases, even
after an entire day of drinking in
he sun. Post-race after-parties
streamed out the doors of bars
and pubs everywhere, and the
beer flowed through the streets.

—Marc A. Wallenstein

International Film Festival, July 22-Aug. 9 (☎9417
2011; www.melbournefilmfestival.com.au). The cream
of the international cinematic crop, plus top-level local
work.

Royal Melbourne Show, Sept. 19-29 (☎9281 7420;
www.royalshow.com.au). At Ascot Vale. Sideshow
alleys, rides, entertainment, animal exhibitions for
judging.

Melbourne Fringe Festival, Sept. 28-Oct. 19 (☎9481
5111; www.melbourne fringe.org.au). Centered on
local artists. Opens with a parade on Brunswick St.,
Fitzroy. Performance and parties all across town.

Melbourne Festival, Oct. 7-23 (☎9662 4242; www.mel-
bournefestival.com.au). A 3-week celebration of the
arts, attracting world-famous actors, writers, and dancers for over 400 performances, workshops, and parties
in 30 different venues.

Spring Racing Carnival, late Oct.-early Nov. (☎9258
4666; www.racingvictoria.net.au). Flemington Racecourse. Australia's mad love for horse racing reaches
fever pitch.

🎌 **Melbourne Cup Day,** 1st Tu in Nov. On the first Tuesday
every November, Melbournians, along with the rest of
Australia, put life on pause to watch, listen, or talk
about the most hyped-up and fashionable horse race in
the country, if not the world. Ladies, gents, and Australia's elite come dressed to impress for a lovely (and
almost always drunken) day at the races. See **From the
Road: A Day at The Races,** at left, for more.

Melbourne Boxing Day Test Match, Dec. 26-30 (☎9653
9999; www.baggygreen.com.au). More than 100,000
cricket fans pack the MCG to root for the boys in green
and gold against top cricketers from around the world.

▣ NIGHTLIFE

Melbourne pulses with a world-class nightlife scene.
Only a handful of venues play the standard bass-
heavy club remixes of familiar mainstream dance
hits. Instead, most clubs feature DJs (some with
international followings) who spin funky selections
of various kinds of house (tech, deep, French, vocal),
trance (mostly psychedelic), drum 'n' bass and jungle, UK garage and two-step, and a range of break-
beats (funky, intelligent, nu skool), all eminently
danceable and with major followings throughout the
city. Tons of retro nights feature '70s and '80s faves,
with crowds in campy period wear. Covers are ubiquitous outside of Fitzroy and range up to $20, but you
get your money's worth—few clubs close earlier than
3am, and some rage nonstop from Thursday all the
way until Sunday night.

▼ **GAY MELBOURNE.** Melbourne is Australia's "second" gay city (after Sydney, of course). Melbourne has a warm and wonderful queer culture, especially in neighborhoods like Fitzroy, Carlton, Prahan, and St. Kilda, which particularly shine during the **Midsumma Festival** (see p. 597), a celebration of sport and art throughout the city in January and February, and the **Melbourne Queer Film and Video Festival,** which takes place in March. To see and be seen in the city year-round, check out free newspapers *Melbourne Star Observer* and *Brother Sister* for interesting venues. There are lots of good nightlife options, too: **Commercial Road** in Prahan is probably Melbourne's most infamous strip, and **Gipps Street,** near Fitzroy, also boasts a lively scene. More info can be culled by browsing www.out.com.au or www.also.org.au, or dialing the **Gay and Lesbian Switchboard Information Service** (☎0055 or 12504), a 24hr. line that gives out info on everything from support groups to nightlife.

There are three main areas for **nightclubs.** Downtown tends to be straighter (as in less gay and more mainstream), though you'll find a little bit of everything. South Yarra and Prahran have the trendiest venues and the best **gay scene** (see **Gay Melbourne,** p. 599). Though most clubs in the area are gay-friendly, predominantly gay places are concentrated along Commercial Rd. Melbournians take their nightlife seriously—the more you pay and the trendier the venue, the more attitude you get at the door. To keep up with the fast-changing scene, read the weekly listings in *In Press, Hr,* and *Beat* magazines; all are free and released every Wednesday. For music shows, the best coverage is in The Age's *Entertainment Guide (EG)* or the Herald-Sun's *Gig Guide,* in their respective Friday papers.

In Melbourne, the distinction between pubs, bars, and nightclubs is blurry at best. Pubs are generally loud, raucous places to sit and drink, and many have live music (and a $3-5 cover) on weekends. Bars are usually more classy, with stricter dress codes, trendier designs, and pricier drinks. Most bars are small and oscillate between lounge-style setup during the day and more dance-floor-oriented (usually with a cover) at night. Some bars, however, are purely for lounging. Nightclubs are more focused on dancing and always have a cover charge (usually $5-10, occasionally as high as $20 for larger venues on weekends or during big events).

BARS & PUBS

CITY CENTER

▨ **Croft Institute,** 21-25 Croft Alley, off Paynes Pl. off Lt. Bourke St. between Russell St. and Exhibition St (☎9671 4399). One of the best bars in Melbourne, the Croft epitomizes the classy, hard-to-find Melbournian back-alley bar while managing to maintain an open vibe (mostly) free of pretension. Themed around a science lab, the Croft is full of glass chemistry equipment, including a fully-operational vodka distillery across from the restrooms. The surface of the bar in the gym on the third floor is covered in (living) grass. Beer and drinks $7. Open M-Th 5pm-1am, F 5pm-3am, Sa 8pm-3am.

▨ **Gin Palace,** 190 Lt. Collins, entrance on Russell Pl. (☎9654 0533). No bar in Australia takes its alcohol more seriously. Many of the mixed drinks are made with fresh fruit mashed in the glass. The martinis are expensive ($14.50), but you get what you pay for (all ingredients in the Surrealist Martini, for example, are frozen for two days before serving). Large selection of Australian microbrew beers that you've never heard of and extensive collection of bourbon. Open daily 4pm-3am.

▨ **La La Land,** 391 Lt. Lonsdale, entrance on Hardware St. (☎9670 5011). This up-and-coming Central Business District nightspot rivals its older cousin of the same name, located on Chapel St., in both character and style. Couches and seats of various shapes and sizes litter the floor, all thickly padded with smotheringly soft cushions. Schooners $4, stubbies $6, longnecks $10, mixed drinks $7-9. No cover. Open M-F 5pm-late, Sa-Su 7pm-late.

Young & Jackson's, 1 Swanston St. at Flinders St. (☎9650 3884; fax 9662 1287; young.and.jackson@alhgroup.com.au). A Melbourne landmark since 1861, Young and Jackson's is often the first thing that visitors see after stepping onto the street from the Flinders St. Station. Three bars downstairs. Brasserie upstairs houses the world-famous *Chloe,* an 1875 oil painting by Joseph Lefebvre. Tu backpacker's night has $4.70 pints (usually $5.90) and a live 2-bass band. DJ F-Sa nights, Jazz music Sa-Su in the afternoon. Open M-W 10am-midnight, Th-F 10am-1am, Sa 9am-1am, Su 9am-midnight.

FITZROY & COLLINGWOOD

■ **Rainbow Hotel,** 27 St. David St, between Moor St. and Bell St. one block east of Brunswick St. (☎9419 4193). Some of the best live music in Melbourne. Su after 5pm, you get a stageful of blues and gospel you won't soon forget. Packed with locals of all ages. Open daily 3pm-1am.

■ **Black Cat,** 252 Brunswick St. (☎9419 6230). A small cafe-lounge with remarkably discerning musical taste. M-Tu open decks, W hiphop, Th breaks, F-Sa eclectic (jazzy funk, hiphop, breaks, drum n' bass), Su progressive house. Light lunch 11am-4pm ($4-7). Beergarden just outside on Greeves St. Open M-F 10:30am-1am, Sa-Su 11am-1am.

■ **The Standard Hotel,** 239 Fitzroy St., between Bell St. and Moor St. Hidden just around the corner from busy Brunswick St., The Standard is a homey local's local that few travelers ever find. One of the few bars in Fitzroy with a proper beergarden, The Standard serves superb pub food (mains $6-14) and $12 jugs. Open daily 3pm-1am.

Bar Open, 317 Brunswick St. (☎9415 9601). Portraits of the Queen Mum on thickly painted red walls oversee the youngish crowd in these intimate environs. W-Sa nights local jazz and funk talent. Beergarden, fireplace, and an atmosphere full of cameraderie. Open daily noon-2am.

Labour in Vain, 197 Brunswick St. (☎9417 5955). Four self-proclaimed beer lovers started this little joint on the site of an 1850s hotel that bore the same name. Today it hops with locals from every walk of life. Bar opens daily anytime between 1:30 and 3:30pm (whenever the staff recovers from the previous night) and closes M-Sa 1am, Su 11pm.

101 Bar, 99-101 Smith St. (☎9419 2687), near Gertrude St. Energy-filled Reggae and African beats encourage enthusiastic dancing. F is reggae and calypso-driven, Sa brings soca bands from the Congo and elsewhere. Cover Sa $5, on special nights $8. Open Su, Th-Sa 6pm-3am.

The Peel Hotel and Dance Bar (☎9419 4762), on the corner of Peel and Wellington St., An institution in Melbourne's gay nightlife, the Peel is more down-to-earth than its Commercial Rd. counterparts. The club pumps commercial house to an almost exclusively gay male crowd. The attached pub is more laid-back and straight-friendly, with cheap drinks (pots $1.40-3, spirits $3.50-5.50) and relaxed conversation. Club cover $5-7. Open Th-Su 11:30pm-8am; pub open M-Tu 5pm-3am, W-Sa 5pm-5am, Su 5pm-1am.

SOUTH YARRA & PRAHRAN

La La Land, 134 Chapel St. (☎9533 8972). A gallery, winebar, and retreat for weary space cadets. Plush recliners and a hip atmosphere. Wine by the glass $6.50-8, bottles from $30. Melting smorgasbord of dip-ables plus pot o' fondue $20. Beers $6-12. Open daily 5pm-late.

The Social, 116 Chapel St. (☎9521 3979). Upscale lounge/eatery catering to the well-dressed and those drooling momentarily upon their hemlines. Brunch daily until 6pm ($10-20 mains). Mixed drinks $6-8. Lines weekend nights. Open daily 11:30am-late.

Bridie O'Reilly's, 462 Chapel St. (☎9827 7788), with an additional location at 62 Little Collins St. (☎9650 0840), in the CBD. Live cover bands every night; Irish folk Su-Th, more contemporary covers F-Sa. No cover. Open Su-Th 11am-1am, F-Sa 11am-3am.

ST. KILDA

🏨 **Esplanade Hotel,** 11 Upper Esplanade (☎9534 0211; http://theesplinadeho-tel.com.au). Multifaceted seaside hotel known fondly as the "Espy." Down-to-earth Lounge Bar carries 3-4 live music acts Th-Su. The ornate Gershwin Room has bigger-name live music acts (usually rock and roll) Th-Sa and comedy acts Su (cover $5+). Beneath is the gritty Public Bar which has happy hour 5 days a week (pots $1.50 5-7pm). Public Bar open M-Sa 11am-1am, Su 11am-11:30pm. Lounge Bar and Gershwin Room open M-F noon-1am, Su noon-11:30pm.

The George Public Bar, 125 Fitzroy St. (☎9534 8822). Not to be confused with the **George Melbourne Wine Room** next door that carries over 500 wines ($18-500), the subterranean George Public bar is super-stylish in an understated kind of way, featuring old-fashioned fittings and a tall, room-length zinc bar. Try their "world-famous" chili mayo chips; only $5 for a big basket. Live music Sa 4-7pm and Su 6-9pm; trivia night M 7:30pm. Open Su-Th noon-1am, F-Sa noon-3am.

The Elephant and Wheelbarrow, 169 Fitzroy St. (☎9534 7888). Twin brother of the E&W on the corner of Bourke and Exhibition St., CBD. A very fun "traditional English pub" known mostly for its M "*Neighbors* Night," where cast members of this popular Aussie soap opera mingle with patrons and help with trivia games (cover $35). Live classic rock and oldies W-Su nights. No cover. Open daily 11am-3am.

NIGHTCLUBS

CITY CENTER

🏨 **Honky Tonk's,** on Duckboard Pl. (also accessible via Corporation Ln.), both of which are on the south side of Flinder's Ln. between Russell St. and Exhibition St. (☎9622 4555). W hiphop and breaks, Th funky beats and rare grooves, F funky house, Sa house, Su popular end-of-weekend party with an eclectic mix of genres, usually house, 2-step, or electro. Cover varies, usually $3-10 weekend nights (but sometimes free). Open W-Th 7pm-3am, F 5pm-5am, Sa-Su 9am-5pm.

🏨 **Scubar,** 389 Lonsdale St. (☎9670 2400). A small basement venue home to the friendly local broken beat scene. The kids at Scubar know how to throw a party, and things don't really get started until 2am. Bonuses include a fish tank in the ceiling, an animal-print pool table, a video projector (expect Japanese Anime or footage of nuclear weapons testing), and soft cushions and candles galore. W electro breaks, Th the most legit hip hop night in town, F hard dark breaks, Sa superb drum n' bass. Cover after 10pm W-F $5, Sa $7. Open W-F 4pm-5am, Sa 8pm-5am.

🏨 **Misty,** 3-5 Hoiser Ln. off Flinders Ln. between Swanston St. and Russell St. Another side alley hideout, Misty is a small and unpretentious bar with a whole heap of taste that often masquerades as a nightclub. W experimental electronica alongside analog synth and bass guitar, Th soulful funky 70's-influenced lounge music, F-Sa mixed house. Stub-bies $4.50, basic spirits $6.50. The house special "Misty Beach" (vodka and campari) is refined but playful. Open M-Th 4pm-1am, F-Sa 4pm-late.

Lounge, 243-5 Swanston St. (☎9663 2916), north of Bourke St. Ideally located above Melbourne's main drag, Lounge is a reliably good time any night of the week. Upstairs you'll find some solid beats and comfortable seats by day and a thumpin' dancefloor by night. Downstairs is a hip eatery and bar with a warm atmosphere and a distinctly Mel-bournian decor (mains $14-18, snacks $6-8). W tech house, Th drum n bass, F mixed breaks. Upstairs cover $5-10. Open daily 10:30am-late.

Mi Casa es tu Casa, 213 Franklin St. (☎9328 8072), at the bottom of the roundabout. This welcoming venue wants nothing more than to smooth your feathers after a long day in the city. An eclectic assortment of local art and dark mood lighting are filtered through a mix of styles of house music. Relaxed lounge by day, club by night, this is not your average CBD place: it's your house away from house. $5 cover weekends after dark. Open M-Sa 11am-3am.

Club UK, 169 Exhibition St. (☎9663 2075). Club UK quivers with ubiquitous Union Jacks, strikingly accurate Prince Charles cartoons, and pulsating Brit beats. Popular among uni students and backpackers, this club attracts outrageous dress and a young crowd. Three levels of Pommy madness: subterranean dance-pit, ground-level pub, and balcony. W draws a huge crowd for $2 pints. Cover $2 W after 9pm, $5 Th after 10pm. Open W-Th 4pm-3am, F-Sa 4pm-5am.

Metro, 20-30 Bourke St. (☎9663 4288; www.metronightclub.com). Unbelievably massive and commercial dance club; indeed, the Metro is the largest club in the Southern Hemisphere, feature seven bars and five full levels of dance action. Marble staircases, brass banisters, and Victorian ceilings spared since the building's theater days form an odd but idiosyncratic juxtaposition with Metro's space-age glitz. Th "Goo," alternative-grunge; F "BOOM BOOM BOOM," featuring remixed versions of all your soul, funk, and R&B favorites; Sa "Pop," mainstream dance hits. Call ahead for dress code and arrive before midnight if you want to get in. Cover $5-11. Open Th 9pm-5am, F 10pm-2:30am, Sa 9pm-6am. ATM inside.

SOUTH YARRA & PRAHRAN

🎱 **Revolver,** 1st fl., 229 Chapel St. (☎9521 5985, www.revolverupstairs.com.au). An excellent place to party any time of day or night. Strong Sa afternoon reggae, dub 'n' bass sessions. Lines can get long at night, but once you're in you can literally stay the entire weekend. Thai food available at the in-house restaurant. Cover $5-10 Th-Sa after 9pm. Open M-Th noon-3am, F noon-Su 3am.

The Market, 143 Commercial Rd. (☎9826 0933), attracts a mixed crowd—gay, lesbian, and straight. The Market's hard-working dance floor changes faces each night. Th alternates between drag and cabaret, while F is a self-titled "Meat Market," featuring beefy brawny male pole dancers. The weekend "straightens" out a bit, with two commercial DJs Sa and a funk-soul-R&B DJ for "Burning" Su. Cover $5 Th, $8 F-Sa, $10 Su after 10pm. Open Su, Th-Sa 9pm-late.

Dome, 19 Commercial Rd. (☎9529 8966). Melbourne's most popular and expensive nightclub is the place to be seen. The main arena is a vast, crowded, sweaty vortex of dance action, where box-dancing glowstick mavens groove to progressive house. Cover $15. Dress sharply. Open Sa 11pm-9am.

▶ DAYTRIPS FROM MELBOURNE

🏛 **HEALESVILLE SANCTUARY.** An open-air zoo, the Healesville Sanctuary lies in the Yarra Valley, located 65km from Melbourne, a place better known for its wineries than its wildlife. The sanctuary's minimum security and daily "Meet the Keeper" presentations allow visitors to interact with and ask questions about the native creatures; keeper talks start at 11am and occur roughly every 30min. The Sanctuary also has programs on Warundjeri Aborigines and Aboriginal culture. *(On Badger Creek Rd. From Melbourne, take the Met's light rail to Lilydale, then take McKenzie's tourist service bus #685. for about 35min. Only 2 buses go directly from the station weekdays at 9:40 and 11:35am. McKenzie's ☎5962 5088. Sanctuary ☎5957 2800; www.zoo.org.au/hs. Open daily 9am-5pm. $15.80, concessions $11.70, ages 4-15 $7.80, families of 6 $42.60. Free guided tours 10am-3pm; call ahead.)*

WERRIBEE PARK & OPEN RANGE ZOO. For a relaxing daytrip from Melbourne, the mansion at **Werribee Park** is a good bet, with serene sculptured gardens, an imposing billiards room, and an expansive nursery wing. From October to May, 5000 roses bloom in the state-pruned garden. *(On K Rd. 30min. west of Melbourne along the Princes Hwy., or take the Weribee line to Weribee, then bus #439. ☎ 9741 2444 or 13 19 63. Open daily 10am-5pm. $10.30, concessions $6.20, ages 3-14 $5.20, families $26.70. Wheelchair-accessible.)* You can go on safari among animals from the grasslands of Australia, Africa, and Asia at Victoria's **Open Range Zoo,** just behind the mansion on K Rd. To explore on your own, take the two 30min. walking trails; a tour of the 200-hectare park takes about three hours. *(☎ 9731 9600; www.zoo.org.au. Open daily 9am-5pm; entrance closes at 3:30pm. 50min. safaris daily 10:30am-3:40pm. $16.80, concessions $11.70, ages 3-15 $7.80, families $42.60. Wheelchair-accessible.)*

ORGAN PIPES NATIONAL PARK. Australia is all about unique geological formations, and the Melbourne area features one of its own: the Organ Pipes National Park. Although the 6m metamorphic landmarks look more like french fries than organ pipes, they're still a good daytrip or stop en route to the central Goldfields. Look for the **Rosette Rock,** which resembles a flowing stone frozen in time (400m past the Organ Pipes). The park is also a laboratory for environmental restoration and has been largely repopulated with native plants and trees since the early 1970s, when weeds concealed the pipes. The park has picnic and BBQ facilities and charges no entrance fee. *(Just off the Calder Hwy. (Hwy. 79), 20km northwest of Melbourne. Public transport from Melbourne is slightly tricky: take tram #59 from Elizabeth St. to Essendon Station, then switch to bus #483 to Sunbury. ☎ 9390 1082. Open daily for cars 8:30am-4:30pm, open anytime for visitors on foot; on weekends and public holidays during Daylight Savings 8:30am-6pm. Wheelchair-accessible.)*

HANGING ROCK RESERVE. The unique rock formations on this bit of crown land were featured in the famous 1975 film (first a novel by Joan Lindsay) *Picnic at Hanging Rock,* in which several young schoolgirls disappear during the course of a school outing in 1900. *(Calder Hwy., past Organ Pipes National Park; follow signs and enter at the south gate on South Rock Rd. Or, take V/Line from Spencer St. Station to Wood End and walk or take a cab 7km from the station. ☎ 5427 0295. Open daily 8am-6pm. $8 per car.)*

PUFFING BILLY STEAM RAILWAY. The train is a relaxing way to see the interior of northeast Victoria's Dandenong Ranges, as it travels through a verdant netherworld of lush rainforest terrain. Note: you will be sharing this choo-choo with many small children. *(40km east of Melbourne on the Burwood Hwy. to Belgrave. Or, take a 70min. Connex Hillside Train (☎ 13 16 38) from Flinders St. Station. ☎ 9754 6800; www.pbr.org.au. Train from Belgrave to Lakeside: 1hr.; 2-5 per day; $27.50 return, $16.50 one way; concessions 21.50/$13; children 4-16 $12.50/$7.50. From Belgrave to Gembrook: 1¾hr., 1-2 per day, adults $38/$24.50; concessions $30/$19.50; children $17/$11.)*

NEAR MELBOURNE

YARRA VALLEY WINERIES

The Yarra Valley produces some top-grade wines and attracts a large daytrip crowd from the Melbourne area. Located about 60km from Melbourne, the Yarra's vineyards were started in 1835 with 600 procured vine cuttings from the Hunter Valley. After a depression in the 1890s decimated wine demand, the Yarra basically shut down. Grapes were replanted in the 1960s, and today the Yarra has more than tripled its size from its peak in the 1800s. The Yarra's cool climate makes it ideal for growing Chardonnay, Pinot Noir, and Cabernet Sauvignon grapes; virtually

THE BIG SQUEEZE

After ten consecutive years of dramatic growth, a crisis looms for the Australian wine industry. In world rankings, Australia is currently eighth in volume of wine exports and has the fourth most profitable wine industry. Only ten years ago, production was less than half its present level. Last year, industry experts made estimates about global demand in tune with the pattern of growth over the previous nine years. As it turns out, these estimates were well off the mark; global demand could not keep up with fast-expanding domestic production. A rash of over-planting based on inflated projections of world demand would force many of the younger small producers out of the business. Drought conditions are easing the excess in the short term, as the 2003 grape harvest is expected to fall by 10-30% in key regions throughout the country.

The transition from glut to shortage, however, hasn't really solved the problem. Small producers who faced low sales last season now fear they will be unable to produce enough wine to meet demand this season. Large producers claim that the drought will streamline the Australian wine industry, but even the largest wine houses are worried about the falling grape harvest. It might help large producers this season, but if the drought continues, seasons to come may see the decline of the Australian wine industry.

every one of the over 30 wineries produces wines of these varieties. Quality sparkling wines abound, as Chardonnay and Pinot Noir are two of the principal grapes used for the bubbly.

Public transportation options to the wineries are limited; Lilydale, 10-20km outside the Yarra, is on the Met train line, but after that there's no way to get to the wineries without hiring a car; remember *Let's Go* does not recommend drinking and driving, and perhaps more importantly, neither do the police. Pick up a free *Wineries of the Yarra Valley* or *Wine Regions of Victoria* at the Melbourne tourist office, or check out www.yarravalleywineries.asn.au. For accommodation information in the area, call the Yarra Tourist Association in Healesville (☎ 5962 2600). There are several tour options from Melbourne, though by far the best and most affordable is ◪**Backpacker Winery Tours** (☎ 9877 8333; www.backpackerwinerytours.com.au). The $79 tour runs virtually every day and offers pick-up and drop-off at major hostels in the CBD and St. Kilda, free tastings at four wineries, and a gourmet lunch overlooking the valley, not to mention knowledgeable commentary and lessons on wine quality and tasting from extroverted and entertaining guides who have worked in the industry themselves. Tours usually last from 9:30am until 4:30pm.

You can't go wrong with any of the options offered here, especially at the normal price of $2 for a taste of their whole selection (tasting fee usually refundable upon purchase). Hours vary from place to place, but wineries are generally open daily 10am-5pm. Call directly to arrange a walkthrough with the winemaker. Here is only a selection of the many establishments in the valley.

◪ **Rochford Wines** (☎ 5962 2119; www.rochford-wines.com.au), on Maroondah Hwy and Hill Rd. in Coldstream. A gorgeous winery situated on a beautiful property with a bandshell and excellent gourmet **restaurant ❹** (mains $18-30). The 2001 Eyton Chardonnay is rich, full, and flavorful, with a thick, earthy nose. Certainly one of the most unique wines in the valley. Art gallery under construction, scheduled for completion by 2004. The winery also has a tower with superb views of the surrounding vineyards. Restauraunt open daily 10am-3pm, winery open daily 10am-5pm.

◪ **Domaine Chandon** (☎ 9739 1110; www.chandon.com.au), "Green Point," on Maroondah Hwy. One of seven global producers of Moët & Chandon sparkling wine, the Domaine is the most polished spot in the Yarra, with an in-depth walkthrough exhibit on production and breathtaking views of the valley from its restaurant. No free tastings—only $5.50 flutes with a free bread, cheese, and chutney plate, or $20-40 bottles to go. Free tours 11am, 1, 3pm, or guide yourself with the informative plaques. Open daily 10:30am-4:30pm.

Yering Station, 38 Melba Hwy. (☎9730 1107; www.yering.com). 1hr. east of the city. On the site of Yarra's 1st vineyard founded in 1838, Yering's tasting area has a delightful art gallery, and the multi-million dollar complex next door has a top-notch restaurant with a huge glass wall overlooking the Valley. Bottles $13-45. Open M-F 10am-5pm, Sa-Su 10am-6pm; restaurant open M-F 12-3pm, Sa-Su 12-4pm.

St. Huberts (☎9739 1118), on St. Huberts Rd. Founded in 1863. Small winery offering a very popular Cabernet, and is one of only four Australian wineries to produce Rhone River Valley Roussane, a unique flavor great for mixing. All its wines are exclusively sold in Australia. Bottles $19-30. Open M-F 9:30am-5pm, Sa-Su 10:30am-5:30pm.

PORT PHILLIP & WESTERNPORT BAYS

Two strips of land, the Bellarine Peninsula to the west and the Mornington Peninsula to the east, curve south from Melbourne around Port Phillip and Westernport Bays. Both areas have awesome scenery, sandy beaches, and excellent surfing.

PHILLIP ISLAND   ☎03

Phillip Island has become synonymous with the endearing Little Penguins that inhabit its southwest corner. A whopping 3.5 million visitors a year gather to witness the smallest of 16 species of penguin scamper back to their burrows nightly in a "Penguin Parade." A wide assortment of other wildlife abound, including koalas, wombats, seals, and hundreds of species of birds, all easily spotted on nature walks or at wildlife centers. Large breakers crashing against the island's southern shore create a surfers mecca in summer while families frolic in the calm water on the north shore. The Grand Prix motorcycle race draws bikers and their fervent followers in early October. Despite the crowds, the rolling hills and vibrant blue Bass Strait waters make Phillip Island a great place to relax for a few days.

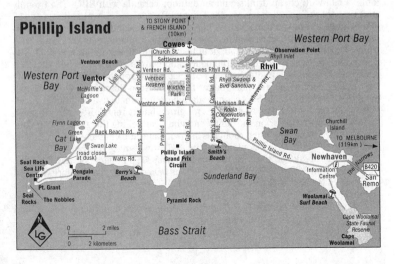

VICTORIA

TRANSPORTATION. Phillip Island lies across a narrow strait from **San Remo,** 145km southeast of Melbourne. Numerous backpacker-oriented tours take groups to the island. **Duck Truck Tours,** run by the folks at Amaroo Park Hostel (see below), includes Melbourne transfers, up to three nights at the hostel, a guided tour of the island, meals, and a half-day of bike use. (☎5952 2548. $135, VIP/YHA $125. Day and night tours from $70.) The Duck Truck will also shuttle you to and from the island for $15 each way. By car, Phillip Island is 2 hr. from Melbourne; take the South Eastern Arterial (M1) to the Cranbourne exit to the South Gippsland Hwy. (M420), then turn onto the Bass Hwy. (A420) and finally onto Phillip Island Tourist Rd. (B420) This road becomes Thompson Ave. when it reaches **Cowes,** which is the island's biggest township.

V/Line buses serve Cowes from Melbourne (3hr.; May-Nov. 1 per day, Dec.-Apr. Sa and F-Su 2 per day; $22-32). To purchase V/Line tickets in town, head to **Cowes Travel** (☎5952 2744; open M-F 8:30am-5:30pm, Sa 9am-11am) or **Going Places Travel** (☎5952 3700; open M-F 9am-5:30pm), both on Thompson Ave. For a scenic trip, there is a daily ferry service between Stony Point and Cowes via French Island on **Inter Island Ferries.** (☎9585 5730. 30min.; 2-4 per day; $9.)

PRACTICAL INFORMATION. Once on Phillip Island, you'll see the **Phillip Island Information Centre** on the right after the bridge. (☎5956 7447; www.phillipisland.net.au. Open daily 9am-5pm.) Buy tickets for the Penguin Parade here to avoid long queues. Other services include: **police** (☎5952 2037); **hospital** (☎5952 2345); **ATMs** on Thompson Ave.; **Internet** at **Waterfront Computers,** 130 Thompson Ave. (☎5952 3312; www.waterfront.net.au; $1.50 per 15min., hot drinks $1.50; open M-F 9am-5pm, Sa 10am-1pm); **post office,** 73 Thompson Ave. (Open M-F 9am-5pm.) **Postal Code:** 3922.

ACCOMMODATIONS & FOOD. True budget lodging on the island is scarce, though a hostel and several caravan parks meet the needs of most campers and backpackers; try the **Amaroo Park Hostel (YHA) ❶,** 97 Church St., Cowes. Head down Thompson Ave. and hang a left on Church St. Though mostly a trailer park, the backpacker accommodations are lovely, with nice wooden furniture, a pool table, a **pub** with cheap drinks, and an outdoor veranda with BBQ. The friendly staff runs tours (including ones to the Penguin Parade; see above) and serves a $7 dinner and a $6 cooked breakfast. (☎5952 2548; phillipisland@yhavic.org.au. Internet. Swimming pool. Call to inquire about pick-up in Melbourne. Book ahead. Sites from $11; dorms $23, YHA $19.50; doubles $57/$50.) **Cowes Caravan Park ❷,** 164 Church St., is ideally located by the beach and Cowes attractions. (☎5952 2211. Laundry, showers, camp kitchen. Sites $19; caravans from $60.) If you're looking for a splurge, it doesn't get much better than **Holmwood Guesthouse ❸,** on Chapel St. at the corner of Steele St. Accommodation options include a traditional guesthouse, cottages, and whole townhomes for group/family rental. Relax in the guest lounge with open fire or on the sunny veranda overlooking the garden with your home-cooked breakfast. Each room has its own name and character. (☎5952 3082. Guest rooms $150-160; self-contained units $175; townhomes for four $215.)

For all-day breakfast, head for the **One Stop Shop ❶,** 58 Chapel St. (☎5952 1439. Open daily 7am-8:30pm.) For udderly delicious baked goods and deli fare (around $9), steer to **MadCowes ❷,** #17 on the Esplanade. They also wrangle picnic baskets and takeaway meals. (☎5952 2560. Open M-F 7am-6pm, Sa-Sa 7am-9pm.) For more upmarket eats, **Café Terrazzo ❸,** 5 Thompson Ave., serves up a range of pasta and wood-fired pizza ($8-15) in a whimsical bistro. (☎5952 3773. Open daily 5-9pm, also in summer M and F-Su noon-3pm.) An IGA **supermarket** is at the corner of Thompson and Chapel St. (☎5952 2244. Open M-Sa 7:30am-8pm, Su 8:30am-6pm.)

ACTIVITIES & WILDLIFE. Phillip Island's tourist magnet is the **Little Penguin Parade,** at the Phillip Island Nature Park. Each night, up to 1000 mini penguins return to their burrows after lengthy fishing expeditions to rest or tend to their hungry chicks. These wobbly, dark blue little creatures are the world's smallest variety of penguin. People await the penguins from a large grandstand along the boardwalk at sunset; after a 30min. to 1hr. wait, the penguins emerge and their parade lasts nearly an hour. The **Information Centre** provides extensive information about the penguins, including interactive exhibits. (☎5951 2800; www.penguins.org.au. Open daily from 10am-10:30 or 11pm. $15, concession $10, children $7.50, families $37.50. Wheelchair-accessible. Book ahead.)

Although the penguins are the main draw, Australia's largest colony of **Australian fur seals** lives just offshore from the **Nobbies** volcanic rock formation. These are the largest fur seals in the world, and the male seals can exceed 350kg. A boardwalk approaches the Nobbies, enabling you to take in the beautiful eroded hills and crashing sea. (Open 7:30am-dusk.) The **Seal Rocks Sealife Centre** displays local marine life, a live video of the seals, and a boat ride past animated displays tracing the area's seal hunting and conservation history. (☎1300 367 325. Open 10am-dusk. $11, students $8.80, children $5.50, families $30.80.) The **Koala Conservation Centre,** south of Cowes on Phillip Island Rd., is a sanctuary housing 23 koalas in eucalypt canopies. The marsupials are most active at feeding time, 1½ hours before dusk. (☎5952 1307. Open daily 10am-5pm. $6, children $3, families $15.) The Bunurong Aborigines originally lived on **Churchill Island,** but it then became one of the first European settlements in Victoria. Enjoyable scenery predominates at this historic site. (☎5956 7214. $8, children $4, families $20. Open daily 10am-4:30pm.) The Information Centre offers a **Rediscover Nature Ticket,** which covers the Parade, the Koala Centre, and Churchill Island. ($24.80, children $12.40, families $68.)

Throughout the year, but particularly in summer, Phillip Island offers great outdoor recreation. Surfers swarm to the island's southern coast, particularly Woolamai and Smiths Beaches, and the Information Centre provides a *Surfing Guide to Phillip Island.* **Island Surfboards,** 147 Thompson Ave. and 65 Smith's Beach Rd., can set you up with a board and excellent instruction. (☎5952 3443. Boards from $30 per day. 2hr. lesson $40.) To fully enjoy the area, take a scenic flight with **Phillip Island Air** (☎5956 7316; $39-99) or view the area by boat on **Bay Connections,** departing from Cowes. (☎5952 3501. 2hr. seal watching cruise $45, students $41, children $30, families $130; 5hr. French Island tour $67/$63/$44/$200.) **Cape Woolamai,** on the southeast corner, has the island's highest point, numerous walking trails, and a patrolled beach for swimming between the flags. Bushwalking trails cover the island, ranging from casual to hard; the info center's pamphlet *Discover Phillip Island Nature Park* is a good resource to start planning bushwalks. Host to the late-October Motorcycle Grand Prix and several other fuel-injected frenzies, the **Phillip Island Grand Prix Circuit,** Back Beach Rd., Cowes, also hosts a year-round Visitors Centre, with racing displays and an opportunity to explore the circuit. (☎5952 9400. Open daily 9am-5pm.)

SORRENTO ☎03

Though slightly more pricey, Sorrento (pop. 1500) draws handfuls of summer visitors to its history-rich parklands and rocky cliffs for fine surfing and a relaxing getaway. Near the very tip of the Mornington Peninsula, the town is a pleasant stop on the fantastic drive along the coast from Melbourne.

From Melbourne, take a **train** to Frankston (1hr., $4.60), then **bus** #788 to stop 18 (1½hr.; M-F 12 per day, Sa 6 per day, Su 5 per day; $7.30, concessions $3.20). If you're coming from the Great Ocean Road, you can reach Sorrento via **ferry** from Queenscliff, on the Bellarine Peninsula (1hr.; every hr., on the hr. 7am-6pm; $8,

VICTORIA

concessions $7, children $6, cars from $42). The **Information Centre** is on St. Aubins Way, on the shore next to the boat launch. (☎5984 5678. Open daily 10am-4pm.) Along **Ocean Beach Road**, Sorrento's main street and a traffic nightmare, you'll find numerous **ATMs.** There is **Internet** at the **Sunny Side Up** next to the water on Point Nepean Rd. (☎5984 4255; open daily 8am-3pm; $1 per 10min.) and a **post office** on 16 Ocean Beach Rd. (Open M-F 9am-5pm.) **Postal Code:** 3943.

From the roundabout at the inland end of Ocean Beach Rd., follow the YHA signs up Ossett St. to the **Sorrento Backpackers YHA ❷,** 3 Miranda St., stop 18 on the Frankston bus. Only five minutes from Back Beach, this backpacker retreat has good facilities: an outdoor patio with BBQ, kitchen, open fireplace, and Internet ($2 per 15min.). The hostel operators will eagerly lead you to beautiful walking tracks and can secure discounts on everything from horse rides to swims with dolphins. (☎5984 4323. Book 1 week ahead in summer. Dorms $26, YHA $20.) Ocean Beach Rd. is lined with eateries. **Stringer's Cafe ❶,** 2-8 Ocean Beach Rd., offers made-to-order sandwiches and salads along with cafe fare. (☎5984 2010. Meals $3-8. Open daily 8am-5pm.) There's also a **supermarket** next door. (Open Su-F 8:30am-5:30pm, Sa 8:30am-6pm; in summer M-Th 8am-7pm, F-Sa 8am-7:30pm, Su 8am-6pm.) For Danish hot dogs ($4) and amazing ice cream, head for **The Little Mermaid ❶,** 70 Ocean Beach Rd. (Open daily in summer 11am-10pm; in winter Sa-Su 11am-10pm.) For an upscale yet casual experience, try the contemporary cuisine at the award-winning **NV Cafe ❷,** 13 West Coast Dr. Gourmet sandwiches ($7-8), pastas ($16-19), and hearty meals ($18-28) are complemented by fine wine and views.

The town's main attraction is its gorgeous blue bay at the bottom of Ocean Beach Rd. While the bay is popular for swimming and sailing in summer, exercise caution: the riptides here change rapidly. For an unforgettable experience, swim with dolphins and seals with **Polperro Dolphin Swims.** (☎5988 8437. 3-4hr. Sept.-Apr. 2 per day 8:30am-1:30pm. $90, observers $40, children $27.50.) The most popular area to hang out and **surf** is **Back Beach,** on the west of the peninsula. You can learn to surf with the **Sorrento Surf School,** on Ocean Beach Rd. (☎5988 6143. 2hr. lesson $30.) History buffs will find plenty of interest in town. The **Collins Settlement Historic Site,** just east of Sorrento on Pt. Nepean Rd., is the location of the first European settlement in Victoria, abandoned in less than a year for lack of fresh water. The display center is closed, but the graves of four settlers can be viewed. The **Nepean Historical Society Museum,** at the corner of Melbourne and Ocean Rd., houses over 2000 artifacts related to Aboriginal life and early European settlement. (☎5984 0255. Open Sa-Su 1-4:30pm. $3, 18 and under $2.)

MORNINGTON PENINSULA

Mornington Peninsula National Park is divided into different regions of coastline and bush country spanning over 40km across. The western tip of the peninsula is **Point Nepean.** The best way to see this part of the park is by bus from the **Visitors Centre,** at the end of Point Nepean Rd.; schedule 3hr. for the visit. (☎5984 4276. Open daily 9am-5pm. Buses depart daily 9:30am-3pm in summer every 30min.; in winter every hr. $12.40, concessions $7.50, families $32.50; park fees included.) Disembark at the first stop and walk to **Fort Nepean** (3.5km one-way), a former military base and quarantine station, and take the bus from there.

The scenic drive along the peninsula is also dotted with a number of **vineyards** and picnic stops. The **Dromana Estate Vineyards,** on Harrisons Rd. in Dromana, is open for tastings. (☎5987 3800. Open daily 11am-4pm. Tastings $3.) Pick-your-own fruit farms also abound; check out **Sunny Ridge,** on the corner of Mornington-Flinders and Shands Rd. (☎5989 6273. Open Nov.-Apr. daily 9am-5pm; May-Oct. Sa-Su 10am-4pm. $8 per kg of strawberries.) At the very southern end of the park, **Cape Schank** and its **lighthouse** are another key attraction. Several walking tracks depart from around here, including a short boardwalk to the astounding coast, and the **Bushrangers Bay Walk,** a 45min. walk by basalt cliffs with breathtaking vistas. The lighthouse, functioning since 1859, has a Visitors Centre and runs tours. (☎5988 6184. Open daily 10am-4:30pm. Tours and admission $10, children $8.)

QUEENSCLIFF ☎03

Rustic, relaxing, and maybe even a little romantic, tiny Queenscliff perches perilously on the easternmost tip of the **Bellarine Peninsula,** 120km southwest of Melbourne, overlooking one of the most dangerous stretches of water on the seven seas. These rip-roaring waters were the basis for the town's settlement, attracting a pilot boat industry that exists to this day. Growing eventually to include fishing, defense, and, in the Victorian era, a wildly popular tourism industry, the town has since settled into its role as an easygoing and historical getaway. With grand old architecture and a leisurely ambience well suited for beach-sitting and twilight strolls, many travelers choose Queenscliff to start, or end, their journey on the **Great Ocean Road** (see p. 611).

Take the **V/Line train** from Melbourne to Geelong (1hr.; M-F 27 per day, Sa 19 per day, Su 11 per day; $14), and then **McHarry's Buslines** (☎5223 2111; www.mcharrys.com.au. 1hr.; M-F 9 per day, Sa 7 per day, Su 4 per day; $6.40). **Ferries** run from the Sorrento Pier, just across the bay (☎5258 3244; www.searoad.com.au. 1hr.; 5-9 per day; $8, cars from $42). The **Visitor Information Centre** is at 55 Hesse St. and has **Internet** for $3 per 30 min. (☎5258 4843. Open daily 9am-5pm.) Services include ANZ **bank** at 71 Hesse St. (open M-Th 9:30am-4pm, F 9:30am-5pm) and **post office,** 47 Hesse St. (☎5258 4219. Open M-F 9am-5pm.) **Postal Code:** 3225.

A jewel in the crown of hosteling, the YHA-affiliated ⊠**Queenscliff Inn B&B ❷,** 59 Hesse St., offers an elegant but affordable taste of the town's luxury. A red brick 1906 Edwardian building, the Inn boasts a gorgeous drawing room with an open fire and a convenient kitchen. The delectable breakfast ranges from continental for $6 to full cooked meals for $13.50. (☎5258 3737. Linens $2.50. Dorms $20; singles/doubles $45.) If you can't get a bed here, some of the scuba diving outfits rent out bunkbeds. Try the **Queenscliff Dive Centre ❸,** 37 Learmonth St., opposite Town Hall. (☎5258 1188. Bunks from $30; private rooms from $57.) Queenscliff Dive Centre runs scuba certification classes and conducts snorkeling tours where you can swim with a colony of playful fur seals and dolphins. (☎1800 814 200. Book ahead. 2hr. tour from $40.) The **Marine Discovery Centre** also runs informative events during the summer. (☎5258 3344. Tours $3.50.)

For a light lunch starting at $4 or a $3 milkshake, rub elbows with locals at the **Promenade Cafe ❶,** 1 Symonds St. (☎5258 2911. Open daily 8am-5:30pm; in winter 10am-5pm.) **Mietta's ❷,** 16 Gellibrand St., offers delicious Italian fare, ranging from a delicate tomato bruschetta to a homemade basil ravioli. (☎5258 1066. Open daily 10am-8pm; in winter 10am-3pm. Meals $9.50-12.) For a proper meal, try **Queenscliff Fish and Chips ❷,** 77 Hesse St., where the fish is extra fresh. (☎55258 1312. Open daily 11am-8pm.) There's a **supermarket** at 73 Hesse St. (☎5258 1727. Open M-Th and Sa 9am-6pm, F 9am-7pm, Su 9am-5pm.)

GEELONG ☎03

The second largest city in Victoria, Geelong (pop. 200,000) is on the shore at the western end of Port Philip Bay, an hour southwest of Melbourne on the Princes Hwy. (Hwy. 1). Its oft-mispronounced name (it's juh-LONG) comes from the Aboriginal *Jillong,* "a place of the sea bird over the white cliffs." By the mid-1800s, sheep outnumbered the seagulls and Geelong flourished as the hub of Victoria's substantial wool trade. Though currently of interest to the traveler primarily as the

VICTORIA

departure point for buses and trains heading to the **Great Ocean Road** and other points west, Geelong is a pleasant place to stop for a day. The revamped waterfront and surprisingly interesting wool museum are highlights for visitors.

☐ TRANSPORTATION. The **V/Line Station** (☎13 61 96), on the western edge of the downtown area, remains Geelong's most important building for most travelers. V/Line runs **trains** to **Melbourne** (1hr., daily every hr., $10) and **Warrnambool** (2¼hr., 3 per day, $28). V/Line **buses** depart for the **Great Ocean Road** from the station, making numerous stops before arriving in **Apollo Bay** (2½ hr.; M-F 4 per day, Sa-Su 2 per day; $21). Buses also head to **Ballarat** (1½hr.; M-Sa 3 per day, Su 2 per day; $11). In summer, the town offers a **free shuttle bus** around town. Visitors can pick up the route map at any of the visitors centers.

◪ PRACTICAL INFORMATION. Geelong is situated on the northern side of the Bellarine Peninsula, and the ocean somewhat confusingly forms the northern border of the city. The Princes Hwy. (Latrobe Terr.) runs north-south along the western edge of town, while Moorabool St. heads from the waterfront. Its intersections with Malop and Little Malop St. host most of the town's action. The monolithic Market Square mall lies at the intersection of Moorabool and Malop and contains the **post office** (M-F 9am-5:30pm, Sa 9am-1pm), a Safeway **supermarket** (open M-Th 8:30am-6pm, F 8am-9pm, Sa 9am-5pm, and Su 11am-5pm), a drycleaners (open daily 9am-5pm), and a **Visitors Centre.** (☎5222 6126. Open daily 9am-5pm.) There is another excellent visitors center located in the Wool Museum (☎5222 2900; open daily 9am-5pm) and a third next to the carousel on the waterfront (open daily 10am-4pm). **Geelong Hospital** (☎5226 7111) is on Ryrie St. between Bellerine and Swanston. **Banks** with **ATMs** line Moorabool St., and free **Internet** access is available at the **city library**, 48 Little Malop St., on the south side of Johnston Park. (☎5222 1212. Open M-F 10am-8pm, Sa 9:30am-noon, Su 2-5pm; book ahead.) **Postal Code:** 3220.

☐ ACCOMMODATIONS. Though a bit of a hike from the waterfront, **Irish Murphy's ❷**, 30 Aberdeen St., has laundry, kitchen facilities, and a comfortable TV lounge. The pub below features beautiful wood finishing and great Guinness. To get there from the train station, take a right on Fenwick St., keeping Johnston Park to your left, then make a right on Ryrie St. and follow it for two blocks as it becomes Aberdeen St. (☎5221 4335. Pub open M-Th noon-midnight, F-Sa noon-1am, Su noon-11pm. Live music Th-Su nights. Bunks $19.) Closer to the action, the **National Hotel ❷**, 191 Moorabool St., has been converted into a backpackers' establishment. Basic but bright and convenient, it sits above an inexpensive noodle bar and a raucous pub that hosts most of the town's headline gigs. (☎5229 1211 or 0410 529 935. Pub open Tu-Su nights. Bunks $19.) The **Carlton Hotel ❸**, on Malop St. near the park between Gheringhap and Moorabool St., offers decent private rooms with shared baths above a pub with pool tables. (☎5229 1954. Singles $40, doubles $60. Breakfast included.)

☐ FOOD. Noodle bars cluster together on Malop St. while Little Malop St. features slightly more upscale cafes and restaurants. A variety of eating options line Moorabool St. as it approaches the bay. But the best spot for a bite is the relaxed **Wharf Shed Cafe ❷**, 15 East Beach Rd., right of the carousel when facing the water. It offers a wide-ranging menu (brick oven pizza $11-15, cajun chicken with couscous $16), a lively bar, and live music Friday nights. (☎5221 6645. Open M-F 10am-late, Sa-Su 9am-late.) **Le Parisien ❹**, in the same building, is about double the cost, but boasts over 300 wines and has live jazz and all day brunch on Sundays. (☎5229 3110.) The **Scottish Chief's Tavern Brewery ❸**, 99 Corio St. near the Bay City Plaza mall, is a great place for gourmet beer lovers; even the fish is battered in "amber ale." Sandwiches are about $7, dinner $15-18. Live bands Thursdays through Saturdays. (☎5223 1736. Open Su-W 11am-11pm, Th-Sa 11am-3am.) It may not be gourmet, but for budget-conscious travelers, **Smorgy's ❷** is all-you-can-eat buffet heaven. Its location 300m out into the bay, on the end of Cunningham Pier, affords exceptional views for diners not fixated on their food. (☎5222 6444. All-you-can-eat lunch daily 11:30am-2:15pm, $11. Dinner 5-9:15pm, $16, children $8.50.)

◙ ▣ SIGHTS & ENTERTAINMENT. Geelong's main tourist attraction is the informative and fascinating **Wool Museum,** housed in a handsome old stone wool trader's building at 26 Moorabol St., a block back from the waterfront. The entrance to the displays is graced by well-known Aussie sculptor Les Kossatz's "Hard Slide"—life-sized sheep falling from a chute in the ceiling to a chute in the floor. Live weaving demonstrations and interactive displays illustrate the important history of Geelong's wool industry. (☎5227 0701. Open daily 9:30am-5pm. $7.30, concessions $6, children $3.65.) The museum is a short walk from the **waterfront,** an attraction in itself, featuring **Cunningham Pier,** a swimming beach with a kiddie pool, and an 1892 **carousel** living out its days in a glass-enclosed pavilion at the end of Moorabool St. ($3, children $2.50.) Lining the waterfront all the way through town are 104 painted wooden sculptures created by Jan Mitchell from old timber and piles. Called the **Baywalk Bollards,** the tall figures illustrate various aspects of Geelong's history. Guides can be picked up at the visitors centers. **Johnston Park** is worth a look, with well-kept lawns and an overgrown and ornate gazebo greeting visitors as they emerge from the train station.

GREAT OCEAN ROAD

The ◪**Great Ocean Road** is one of the world's greatest driving experiences and one of Australia's proudest tourism showpieces. Tossed up by winds that blow unimpeded across thousands of miles from Antarctica, the turbulent waves of the Southern Ocean sculpted the coast's unearthly stone pillars and arches and sent many sailors to a watery death in the region's hundreds of shipwrecks. The 175km road winds around celebrated surf beaches, through forests clinging to the edge of cliff-tops, and across windswept coastal plains, passing in the meantime through idyllic hamlets, vibrant beach communities, and national parks teeming with plants and animals. This is the stuff that great roadtrips are made of.

Though the Road itself runs from Torquay to Warrnambool, the Great Ocean Road region encompasses the entire serene and spectacular southwestern coast of Victoria, from Geelong to Nelson. Heading west from Melbourne, the first part of the Road is called the **Surf Coast.** Stretching from Torquay to Lorne, this area hosts some of the country's best surfing and endless miles of beaches for wandering and swimming. The **Otway Ranges,** on the 73km stretch from Anglesea to Apollo Bay, has a cool, rainy climate that nurtures tree ferns, large pines, breathtaking waterfalls, and a range of fauna, culminating in the **Otway National Park,** just west of Apollo Bay. Rejoining the shoreline on the other side of the park, the aptly named **Shipwreck Coast** is home to the unrelenting winds and unpredictable offshore swells that made the region a graveyard for 19th-century vessels but also shaped the famous ◪**Twelve Apostles** rock formations. Moving west, discover whales off **Warrnambool,** mutton birds in **Port Fairy,** seal colonies at **Cape Bridgewater,** towering sand dunes in **Discovery Bay Coastal Park,** and estuary fishing in **Lower Glenelg National Park.** Though visitors have been known to complete the entire Road in just a day or two, it is worth as much time as you've got, and a week on the Great Ocean Road is a week well spent.

VICTORIA

⌐ TRANSPORTATION

PUBLIC TRANSPORT

The most satisfying way to see the Great Ocean Road is by **car**. Public transport along the road is infrequent and inconvenient and probably won't get you everywhere you want to go. **V/Line trains** (☎ 13 61 96) from Melbourne will get you as far as Geelong. **Buses** run both ways along the Great Ocean Road between Geelong and Apollo Bay, passing through Torquay, Anglesea, Lorne, and other towns along the way (M-F 4 per day each way, Sa-Su 2 per day). On Fridays year-round and also on Mondays from December to January, one special **"coast link" V/Line bus** runs each way between Apollo Bay and Warrnambool, making stops in Port Campbell and other towns along the way, with brief stops at tourist lookouts along the Shipwreck Coast; otherwise, it is difficult to progress farther west than Apollo Bay via public buses, which often run only once a week.

Breathtaking in more ways than one, **bicycling** along the highway is becoming popular, but the narrow, winding road (with no protective shoulder in most places) and the steeply hilly topography of some sections of the route combine to make it quite a difficult bike tour.

BUS TOURS

Bus tours along the Great Ocean Road offer more flexibility than public transport and are the best way for those without a car to see the area. Tours generally come in two varieties: those that make a loop starting and ending in Melbourne and those that run between Melbourne and Adelaide. Tours returning to Melbourne generally only go as far as Port Campbell before turning north and taking the inland Princes Hwy. back to the city, but they are the best way to see the Road for those not interested in heading to South Australia. For those heading west from Melbourne to Adelaide, there are a number of 3-day tours connecting the cities via the Great Ocean Road at prices rivaling air or rail travel between the two cities. Those short on time can choose to do the trip all at once, while some companies allow those with more time to take as many layovers as they want.

Otway Discovery (www.otwaydiscovery.primetap.com) is the most affordable and flexible of the loop tours. The friendly drivers run along the Road from Melbourne to Port Campbell and then back to Melbourne via the inland route, allowing free hopping on and off. There is no time limit, but you only get to do the loop once and the bus only travels west along the Road, so don't miss anything, as you can't go back. Departs daily 7am. $65.

Wildlife Tours (www.wildlifetours.com.au) runs a one-day highlight tour of the Great Ocean Road (Melbourne to Port Campbell), as well as structured 3-day return tours that include the Grampians and 2- or 3-day Melbourne-to-Adelaide trips. Stopovers may be allowed, provided the next bus has room for you. Highlights $59; return tours $139; Melbourne-Adelaide from $145. ISIC/NOMADS/VIP/YHA.

Groovy Grape Getaways (☎ 1800 661 177; getaways@groovygrape.com.au) runs a high quality backpacker-oriented all-inclusive 3-day trip in either direction between Melbourne and Adelaide, hitting all the main sights and providing all accommodation, meals, park entrance fees, and a knowledgeable guide. $285 per person. Departs Melbourne Tu and F 7am; departs Adelaide Tu and Sa 7am. No hop-on/hop-off allowed.

Oz Experience (☎ 1300 300 028; www.ozexperience.com) runs a popular 3-day journey along the Road in both directions between Melbourne and Adelaide, allowing you to hop on and off the ubiquitous big green bus for up to 6 months. Accommodation not included in the price. $194, ISIC/YHA $184.

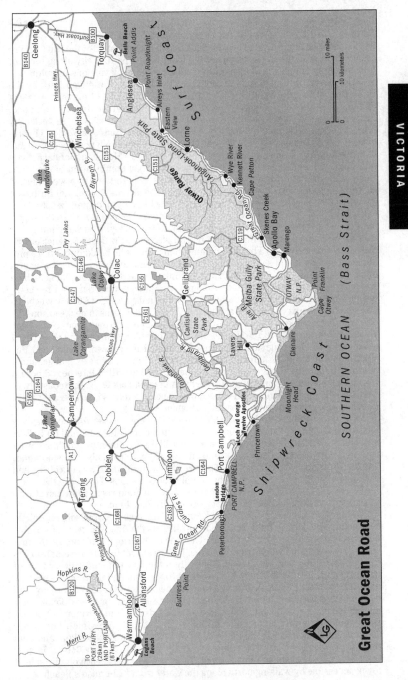

VICTORIA

Great Ocean Road

VICTORIA

TORQUAY ☎ 03

Torquay (tor-KEY) is a mecca for Victoria's surfers. Boarders from all over the world make the pilgrimage to nearby Bells Beach every Easter for the Rip Curl Pro Classic, and gear shops cluster along the main drag. The first city along the Surf Coast stretch, Torquay is a town infused with the laid-back vibe of surf culture.

V/Line buses (☎13 61 96) leave from outside the Bernell Caravan Park by the Bells Beach hostel on the Surf Coast Highway. Buses head north to **Geelong** (45min.; M-F 4 per day, Sa-Su 2 per day; $5.20) and west on the Great Ocean Road, making numerous stops, including **Lorne** (1hr., $10), before arriving in **Apollo Bay** (2hr.; M-F 4 per day, Sa-Su 2 per day; $17.70). **Bellarine Transit** (☎5223 2111) provides buses to **Geelong** (M-F 14 per day, Sa 6 per day, and Su 3 per day; $5.20) and to **Apollo Bay** (M-F 4 times a day, Sa-Su 2 per day; $17.70.) Most commercial activity takes place along the Surfcoast Hwy. (Geelong Rd.), a continuation of the Great Ocean Rd., or just off the highway on Gilbert St., where there is a well-marked shopping district with **ATMs** and food options. The **Visitors Centre**, 120 Surfcoast Hwy., is in the Surfworld Museum in the Surf City Plaza retail center. (☎5261 4219. Open daily 9am-5pm. **Internet** $7 per hr.) The **Torquay Pharmacy** is next to the supermarket on Gilbert St. (☎5261 2270. Open M-Sa 8:30am-6:30pm, Su 9am-6pm.)

Book well ahead for the Easter surfing competition. **Bells Beach Backpackers ❷**, 51-53 Surf Coast Hwy., is a brightly painted, bungalow-style bunkhouse with a pronounced surfing mood set by posters, magazines, and nearly constant screenings of surf documentaries. Bells Beach also has immaculate bathrooms, lockers, bike and surf equipment rentals, Internet ($5 per hr.), and good vibrations. Free courtesy bus to town and nearby beaches three times a day. (☎5261 7070; www.bellsbeachbackpackers.com.au. Key and linens deposit $10. Dorms in peak-season $23, off-peak $19; doubles $55/$45.) Close to Bells Beach but farther from town, **Pointbreak Backpackers ❷**, 185 Addiscott Rd., is about 8km southeast via the Great Ocean Rd. (watch for sign marking turn-off). Tucked away down a shady road, this quiet hostel has a full kitchen, BBQ, laundry facilities, a book exchange, and a courtesy bus to the town center and the beach. (☎5261 5105. Internet $6 per hr. Dorms in summer $20, in winter $18.) **Bernells Caravan Park ❸**, 55 Surfcoast Hwy., next to Bells Beach Backpackers, has a pool, spa, and tennis court. (☎5261 2493. Check-in 1:30-8pm. Powered sites $22-38; cabins $45-75.)

Hordes of surfers with the munchies provide a large market for the takeaway joints that dominate Torquay's food scene, centered on Gilbert St. and on Bell St. near the beach. The ◧**Bees Knees Cafe ❶**, 27 Gilbert St., downtown on the corner with Pearl St., has large and tasty sandwiches ($7) and heavenly fruit smoothies. (☎5261 4074. Open W-M 9am-6pm.) **Spooner's ❶**, 57 Surfcoast Hwy., is a cheap and friendly coffeehouse next door to the complex of surf shops. They have big wraps for $8. (☎5261 9949. Open daily 8am-5pm.) There's a Foodworks **supermarket** with a LiquorWorks attached on Gilbert St. (Open daily 7am-10pm.)

Peak **surfing** season is from March to August. The **Torquay Surf Beach,** off Bell St. a ten-minute walk from Bells Beach Backpackers, is the first in a string of surfable beaches that stretches down the coast. The king of them all is **Bells Beach,** the first surfing reserve in the world, where the reef breaks attract top professional surfers for the Easter **Rip Curl Pro Classic.** Bells offers the intrepid surfer every type of wave imaginable. It's a ten-minute drive from town, although the most scenic way to reach it is via the **Surf Coast Walk,** a trail that begins at the beach at Torquay. The trail, which is great for mountain biking, follows the coast for nearly 35km, passing **Jan Juc,** the second-best surfing site around (also safe for swimmers) before Bells, and continuing on to Point Addis, Anglesea, and Airey Inlet. For closer swimming beaches, cross the highway from Bells Beach Backpackers and continue down Zeally St. for ten minutes to Zeally Bay, where **Cozy Corner, Torquay Front Beach,** and **Fisherman's Beach** await. There is also a **nude beach** on that side of town, accessible by walking north along the water from Fisherman's Beach.

FROM TORQUAY TO LORNE

POINT ADDIS. The turn-off to **Point Addis** appears abruptly about 5km west of Torquay on the Great Ocean Road, or can be reached by traveling the short coastal road out of Torquay. The point offers outstanding views of Victoria's western coast, serrated by silty clay and gray cliffs. The path at the right side of the carpark leads to a long stretch of empty beach, while a trail to the left 200m before the carpark will take you to the **Pixie Caves,** a small cove beach on the east side of the point with small caves carved out of the sandstone. Between Point Addis and the highway is the beginning of the recently cleared **Koorie Cultural Walk** (2km; 1hr. return) which leads through the **Ironbark Basin Reserve.** Displays along the way elucidate the history of the Aborigines who once inhabited the area.

ANGLESEA. Most visitors stop just long enough to visit the **beach** at the mouth of the Anglesea River or the **golf course** on the northwestern edge of town, which has a reputation as a reliable place to spot kangaroos. Hitting a kangaroo is bad form, but there's no penalty for a golfer who hits a tourist, so stay off the fairways. Signs lead the way from the Great Ocean Rd. to both the beach and the golf course. Surfing lessons, including loan of boards and wetsuits, can be had at short notice through **Go Ride A Wave,** with one lesson at $45 ($40 if you pay a day ahead) or a four-lesson package for $140. No classes Sunday. (☎5263 2111; www.graw.com.au.) The company also operates out of Torquay and Lorne. For immaculate accommodation, try the beautiful **Anglesea Backpackers ❷,** 40 Noble St. (☎5263 2664. Dorms $23, off-peak $18, ensuite from $50, powered sites for RVs $70. Internet $10 per hour.)

LORNE   ☎03

As long ago as the 1890s, well before the advent of Great Ocean Road made it accessible to hordes of tourists, the government of Victoria declared Lorne (pop. 1100) a place of "natural beauty and special significance." Visitors stream in to the relaxing town to share in Lorne's surprising contradictions: the impressive mountains of Angahook-Lorne State park curve up from expansive beaches, backpackers set up in the shadow of million-dollar vacation homes, and trendy shops and bistros share space with surf shops.

The Great Ocean Rd. morphs into **Mountjoy Parade** as it passes through town. **Buses** depart four times daily during the week and twice daily on weekends from the Commonwealth Bank at 68 Mountjoy Pde. to **Apollo Bay** (1hr., $5.50), **Geelong** (1½hr., $13), and **Melbourne** (2½hr., $25). During January a free shuttle bus cruises up and down Mountjoy Pde from the Ridgeway's Supermarket to the **Lorne** pier. (Every half hour. Daily 10am-6pm.) The **Visitors Centre,** 144 Mountjoy Pde., a few blocks west of the V/Line stop, has excellent maps and information on activities, hiking, and camping in the area, and sometimes even offers massages. (☎5289 1152. Open daily 9am-5pm.) Behind the Visitors Centre there is a good **book exchange** (open daily 11am-4pm).

The very laid-back **Erskine River Backpackers ❷,** 4 Mountjoy Pde., is on the west bank of the river at the bend in the road on the Geelong side of town. Most rooms open onto a leafy courtyard, and the place has a decidedly homey feel. Doors are not locked, but ask the owner to store valuables. (☎5289 1496. Dorms $20, deluxe $25; doubles $60. Stay for a week, get the 8th night free; stay for 4 weeks get the 5th free.) **Great Ocean Backpackers (YHA) ❷,** on the east side of the Erskine River, is a colony of wooden cabins set amid the trees on the hillside behind the supermarket. (☎5289 1809. Book ahead. Dorms $23.50, YHA $20; twins and doubles $60/$50.) Free **camping ❶** without amenities is available inside the Angahook-Lorne State Park (☎5289 1732). Complete camping facilities are available 10km west of town at the beautiful **Cumberland River Camping Reserve ❷.** Several short walks lead from the area and there is a little swimming beach across the road. (☎5289 1790.

Sites from $15; cabins $60.) The Visitors Center has information on the numerous **B&Bs ❺** in the area, most starting around $100 per night. The hippest joint in town for drinks and a bite to eat is **Reifs Restaurant and Bar,** 84 Mountjoy Pde., next to the movie theater. (☎ 5289 2366. Open daily 9:30am-1am. Occasional live music on weekends.) Ridgeway's **supermarket,** 1 Great Ocean Rd., is on the Melbourne side of the river. (Open M-Th and Su 8am-7pm, F 8am-8pm, Sa 7am-8pm.)

ANGAHOOK-LORNE STATE PARK

The northern section of this 22,000 hectare reserve, accessible from Aireys Inlet, is characterized by dry coastal heathlands, but the more than 64km of walking trails in the Lorne area also meander through temperate rainforests, cool fern gullies, and past striking waterfalls. While it is helpful to have a car to access most of the trailheads, several walks take off from the town itself. The best of these is the hike up to **Erskine Falls** (7.5km; 4hr. one-way), which begins at the bridge over the Erskine River in Lorne and follows and criss-crosses the river through the temperate rainforests of the Park and past **Splitter Falls** and **Straw Falls** before arriving at Erskine Falls. These 38m falls are the most famous in the area and have attracted tourists since the trail was constructed in 1890, including a visit by Rudyard Kipling in 1891. The route from town to the falls is a long uphill battle. If no rides are available, those wishing to see the falls without spending the whole day can take a taxi up and walk back down into town. (Taxi approximately $19. Check at the visitors center for companies.) A much shorter walk from town will bring you to **Teddy's Lookout,** a high point at the southern edge of town that presents sweeping views of forested mountains abutting wide-open ocean. (30min. walk; go up Bay St. from the Great Ocean Rd. in Lorne and make a left on George St.) The **Allenvale Mill Site,** a 30min. walk or 10min. drive from town along Allenvale Rd., is a good jumping-off point for a beautiful trail that leads to **Phantom Falls, the Canyon,** where you squeeze through the 8m walls of a small canyon, and **Henderson** and **Won Wondah Falls** before winding up at the Sheoak Carpark. From there, walk back along the road to the Allenvale carpark. (9km, 4hr. return from Allenvale carpark).

The other main trailheads in the area, the **Blanket Leaf Picnic Area** and the **Sheoak Picnic Area,** are best reached with a car, though you can also walk to them. Various easy tracks begin at the Sheoak Picnic Area, a 1hr. walk or 15min. drive up Allenvale Rd. from Lorne. The walk to **Sheoak Falls** follows a gentle track by the creek and eventually reaches the ocean (1½hr.), while the **Lower Kalimna Falls Walk** (1hr.) leads beneath a waterfall, which can be seen from above on the **Upper Kalimna Falls Walk** (add an extra half hour). A fairly easy walk (1½hr. return) connects the **Blanket Leaf** carpark to **Cora Lynn Cascades.** Other hikes from Blanket Leaf head to Phantom Falls (3½hr.) and to Allenvale Rd. at the Allenvale Mill Site (4hr.).

Before heading off on any adventures in the area, a stop at the Lorne **Visitors Centre** is a good idea, as they will have the latest information on trail and campsite closures and conditions, as well as maps. There are a number of **free camping sites ❶** in Angahook-Lorne (the biggest is on Hammonds Rd. in Airey's Inlet to the east of Lorne); camping in picnic areas or carparks results in a fine. **Allenvale Mill,** a 200m walk-in from the carpark, has toilets (tents only). The **Wye River Rd.,** a 20min. drive west on the Great Ocean Rd., has 15 sites that are all accessible by car.

APOLLO BAY ☎ 03

Apollo Bay sits in an idyllic cove at the base of the rolling Otway mountains. Waves lap at the shore, sun-lovers gather at beachfront cafes, and glowworms light up the quiet nights. A placid setting, ample accommodations, and easy access to activities in Otway National Park make Apollo Bay a popular stop along the Great Ocean Road, and its annual music festival is among the biggest in Australia.

▐ ▌ TRANSPORTATION & PRACTICAL INFORMATION. The Great Ocean Rd. is the main street through town, with side streets running north off it. **Buses** leave from the front of the Visitors Centre (M-F 4 per day; Sa-Su 2 per day) going to: **Geelong** (2½hr., $20); **Lorne** (1hr., $5.40); and **Melbourne** (3½hr., $28). Buses to **Warrnambool** (3½hr., $24) and other points west along the Great Ocean Rd. leave Fridays only, except in December and January, when they operate once on Monday as well. Helpful volunteers will book accommodations and tours and advise on road closures and campsite availability in the Otways at the **Tourist Information Centre,** 157 Great Ocean Rd. (☎5237 6529. Open daily 9am-5pm.) A **beach wheelchair** is available at the Apollo Bay Surf Lifesaving Club on the foreshore. (Free. Sa 1-4pm, Su 9:30am-3pm.) The stretch of highway through town also has two 24hr. **ATMs. Internet** is available at **Nautigals Cafe,** 58 Great Ocean Rd. (Daily 8:30am-8pm. $6 per hr.) **Paradise Book Shop,** 4 Hardy St. next to the supermarket, is a funky little shop selling both new and used books. (Daily 10am-6pm.)

▐ ▐ ACCOMMODATIONS & FOOD. The newly expanded ▊**Surfside Backpackers ❶,** on the corner of the Great Ocean Rd. and Gambier St. at the west end heading out of town, has two kitchens and lounge areas, a record player instead of a TV, and ocean views from some rooms. Robyn, the owner, is one of the friendliest, most helpful people you're likely to meet. (☎5237 7263 or 1800 357 263. Internet $2 per 10min. Book ahead. Reception 8-10pm. Sites $10; dorms $18; doubles $40-55.) Billing itself as "the chilled out cottage by the sea," is the relaxed **Apollo Bay Backpackers ❷,** 47 Montrose Ave., a ten minute walk from the Great Ocean Road on a quiet residential street. (☎0419 340 362; backpack@vicnet.net.au. Dorms $20; singles and doubles $50. Breakfast included. Internet $5 per hour.)

Beautiful beach views come free with the meals at ▊**La Bimba ❷,** 125 Great Ocean Road. The upstairs cafe creates unique meals (pumpkin pancakes with avocado, tzatziki, and lemon aioli, $12.50) without charging exorbitant prices. Good salad options and nice breakfasts. (☎5237 7411. Open daily 8am-4pm, 6pm-late.) The cosmic center of Apollo Bay's hippie culture is **The Sandy Feet Cafe ❶,** 139 Great Ocean Rd., where you can get your very own astrological calendar for $7.50, along with a veggie burger for $5.50 or salad for $4-6. (Open daily 9am-5pm.) The **Panache Cafe and Creperie** next door has crepes for around $7, and there is also a focaccia bar. (☎5237 7110. Open daily 8:30am-4pm, later in summer.) There are two **supermarkets** on the Great Ocean Rd. as it goes through town, both open M-Sa 8am-8pm and Su 8am-6:30pm.

▐ ▌ SIGHTS & ENTERTAINMENT. While the Otways get all the attention, there are plenty of things to see right around town, starting with the gently curving bay itself, best viewed from the **Marriner's Lookout** (on Marriner's Lookout Rd., about 1.5km from Apollo Bay towards Lorne). Recreational **fishing** is a popular pastime in Apollo Bay, both from the beach and from chartered fishing boats; book at the Visitors Center. (4hr. tours $60 plus $5 for required fishing permit.) Apollo Bay's most illuminating feature are its **glowworms,** which are actually local flies in their larval stage. **Sunroad Tours,** 71 Costin St., picks tourgoers up just after dark for a 1½hr. daily tour (☎5237 6080 or 0429 002 296. $20, under 12 free.) Those looking for a bit of exercise might want to try a **mountain biking** tour with **Otway Expeditions.** (☎0419 007 586; from $30). Surfers should stop by **Hodgy's Surf Center,** 143 Great Ocean Rd., which offers daily lessons. (1½hr., $40. 2hr. sea kayaking trips $45.) The best surf beach in the area is **Johanna Beach,** reached by taking Johanna Rd. 5km before Laver's Hill. The **Apollo Bay Shell Museum,** on Noel St. at the western edge of town, is the quirkiest museum you're likely to find on the Great Ocean Road. (☎5237 6395. Open daily 9:30am-8pm. $2.50.) Each year in March, the town grooves to the folksy sounds of the **Apollo Bay Music Festival,**

which attracts acts from all over Australia as well as from around the world and a crowd that consumes every available bed and campsite available in town. (☎5237 6761; www.apollobaymusicfestival.com. All-weekend tickets $100, concessions $90.) On Saturday mornings the **Apollo Bay Market** sets up on the foreshore and sells local handicrafts.

OTWAYS RANGE

The Otway Range stretches 60km west of Apollo Bay and encompasses three major parks: **Otway National Park, Otway State Forest,** and **Melba Gully State Park.** Even on scorching hot days, the temperate rainforest stays cool. Myrtle beeches provide shade while tree ferns dominate the eye-level scenery, occasionally animated by wallabies, possums, and gray kangaroos. Waterfalls cascade down steep hillsides to form clear creeks. The **Mait's Rest trail** (30min. loop), named after the district's first forester Maitland Bryan, who apparently rested his horse in the general vicinity, is one of the best-known rainforest walks in Victoria, 17km west of Apollo Bay along the Great Ocean Rd. Check out the Myrtle beech whose roots sprang from 3 trees and grew together. Shortly after Mait's Rest is the turn-off for the **Cape Otway Lightstation.** (☎5237 9240. Open daily 9am-5pm. $8, concessions $5; daily guided tours $11/$5.) The walk through **Melba Gully** is short (30min. return), but promises a glimpse of a unique, fragile environment and a chance to view the mildly famous and suitably large "Big Tree," a 200-year-old Otway messmate. At night, glow worms line the tracks; take a flashlight if you venture out to find them. The turn-off for Melba Gully Rd. is about 5km past Lavers Hill, heading west on the Great Ocean Rd. from Apollo Bay. **Triplet Falls,** a quiet getaway near Laver's Hill (40km west of Apollo Bay on the Great Ocean Rd.), is a three-tiered waterfall reached by taking the Lavers Hill-Beech Forest Rd. from Lavers Hill, turning right onto Phillips Rd., then following signs on rough unsealed roads.

Maps for the Otways' well-marked walks are available at the **Apollo Bay Tourist Info Centre** (☎5237 6529). A 4WD can make the tracks much easier to navigate. For camping, check into the vast Bimbi Park (see **Accommodations,** p. 617), or use one of the five **camping ❶** areas in Otway National Park. In summer, pitch at **Blanket Bay;** follow Lighthouse Rd., then watch signs for a left turn. (All sites ☎5237 6889. Blanket Bay sites $10.20.) The area is safe for swimming. The **Aire River** camping areas are reached from the Great Ocean Rd., another 5km west by way of the Horden Vale turn-off. The Aire River is suitable for swimming and canoeing, and three walks diverge from the grounds. (Sites $10.20. Caravan sites on the west side.) Both **Parker Hill** and **Point Franklin** have small camping areas with few facilities. Parker Hill campers will have to park and walk in (Sites $4.20.) **Johanna Beach** has a basic campsite and the best **surfing** in the area, though the beach is not safe for swimming. Take Johanna Rd. from the Great Ocean Rd. (Sites $10.20.)

PORT CAMPBELL   ☎03

The Great Ocean Rd. becomes Lord St. in town and is the center of all the action. **Buses** leave once a week (F, Dec.-Jan. also M) from in front of Ocean House Backpackers and head to **Melbourne** ($31) and **Warrnambool** ($9), stopping at most towns along the way in either direction. The **Visitors Centre,** on the corner of Morris and Tregea St., one block south of Lord St., has a wealth of data for all things related to the Great Ocean Road. (☎5598 6089. Open daily 9am-5pm.) The **post office** is in the **Port Campbell General Store,** Lord St., which also has basic **groceries.** (☎5510 6255. Open daily 8am-7pm.) The Pharmacy on Lord St. doubles as a shipwreck museum. Check out the relics while stocking up on toothpaste. **Internet** at the Seafoam Cafe ($2 for 10min.). **Postal Code:** 3269.

Facing the beach on Cairns St., **Ocean House Backpackers ❷** is clean, simple, and friendly, with ocean-views from some rooms. The common area has board games and a fireplace (☎ 5598 6223; check in at the **Camping Park** (see below) if owner is not there. $20.) The **YHA Hostel ❸**, 18 Tregea St., one block south of Lord St., around the corner from the beach, has a huge kitchen and a helpful message board. (☎/fax 5598 6305. Key deposit $5. Towel $1. Internet $2 per 15min. Reception 8-10am and 4-9pm. Dorms $21.50, YHA $18; doubles $51/$44; cabins $67/$60.) The **Port Campbell National Park Cabin and Camping Park ❷**, next to the info center on Morris St., has BBQ, showers, and laundry. (☎ 5598 6492. Reception 8:30am-9pm. Powered sites for two $20; unpowered sites $16; ensuite cabins from $80, extra adult $11, extra child $5.50. Low-season rates lower.)

The throngs of tourists passing through Port Campbell have created a demand for all kinds of restaurants, from beachfront takeaways to pricey balcony restaurants. The best place to grab and go is at the **Koo Aah Shop ❶**, on Lord St., which serves up fish, lentil, and noodle dishes with an Asian influence, as well as beef burgers for $7 and sizable sandwiches for $5. (☎ 5598 6408. Open daily 10:30am-late.) Upstairs from the Koo Aah and run by the same people, **The Splash ❸** is the upmarket alternative. Mains run around $20 and include inventive dishes such as the raspberry salmon pasta for $19.50. (Open daily 6-9:30pm.) On the corner of Morris and Lord St., the **Cray Pot Bistro ❷** serves up filling meals for about $15. (☎ 5598 6320. Food served daily noon-2:30pm and 5-9pm, sometimes open for breakfast; drinks served weekdays until 11pm, weekends until 1am.)

The gentle Port Campbell **Discovery Walk** (2½km) begins at the cliff base at the western end of the beach or at the carpark west of the bay. While local surfers paddle out to the breaks off of the points on either side of Port Campbell's small bay, the small beach along Cairns St. is probably a better place to take a dip. **Port Campbell Boat Charters** offers crafts for diving, fishing, or sightseeing expeditions. (☎ 5598 6411 or ask at the Mobil Service Station; from $40 per person.) You can also see the Twelve Apostles in a small plane from **Peterborough Airfield**. (☎ 5598 5441. 20min. flight for up to 3 $80.)

FROM PORT CAMPBELL TO WARRNAMBOOL

TWELVE APOSTLES & LOCH ARD GORGE. The ▨**Twelve Apostles,** 12km east of Port Campbell on the Great Ocean Rd., are the most famous of the rock formations in the area, and for good reason. At sunset, when the stones blaze red before fading slowly to shadows in the waning light, the spectacular vista will be enough to forget the hordes of tourists jostling for a view. The **Interpretive Centre** is open daily 9am-5pm and has ample parking and a walkway under the highway leading to the viewpoints. PremiAIR helicopter flights take off behind the Centre. The flights give those with thicker wallets a breathtaking view of the jagged coastline. (☎ 5598 8266. Open daily 9am-dusk. 10min. flight over the Apostles $70. 15min. flights to London Bridge and back $90, 25min. flights all the way up to the Bay of Martyrs $175.) **Gibson Steps,** 2km east of the Twelve Apostles, allows a descent and a view of one of the Apostles from sea level, where you can better appreciate the monoliths' enormous scale. Another worthwhile stop-off, 3km west of the Twelve Apostles, towards Port Campbell, is **Loch Ard Gorge**, named for the clipper *Loch Ard* that wrecked there in 1878, killing 52. The park around the gorge offers lookout points and walks venturing to points of interest like **Thunder Cave**, the **Island Archway, Mutton Bird Island,** and the **Blowhole**, a churning and spitting sea water lake a few hundred feet inland, connected to the ocean by an underground tunnel. Allow an hour or so to walk around. Theater companies occasionally stage appropriately themed plays in the Gorge—Shakespeare's *The Tempest* was a recent production.

VICTORIA

BAY OF ISLANDS & BAY OF MARTYRS. To the west of Port Campbell, the **Bay of Islands Coastal Park** begins at little Peterborough and stretches 33km west along the coast. A number of scenic viewpoints allow views of other limestone oddities, from pillars to islands to arches, all shaped by the Southern Ocean and the unrelenting Antarctic winds that sweep in from 3000km away. Notable features include **The Arch, The Grotto,** and **London Bridge.** The **Bay of Martyrs** and **Bay of Islands** viewpoints (both turn-offs clearly labeled on the Great Ocean Rd.), perhaps the best along this stretch, offer stunning views and walks among smaller limestone formations on the beach.

WARRNAMBOOL   ☎03

The largest city on the Great Ocean Road, Warrnambool (pop. 30,000) is just built-up enough to support dance-until-3am nightlife and a host of amenities not found elsewhere along the coast, yet still small enough to retain a familial feel. It also has beautiful beaches and southern right whales in residence for half the year. The whales, sand, and surf make Warrnambool a popular holiday destination. Cargo ships preceded vacationers; in the 1880s, the Port of Warrnambool saw more action than Melbourne. And before that, there is rumor of a Portuguese vessel called the "Mahogany ship" that ran aground in the bay—a legend that, if proven true, would disrupt the well established history of coastal discovery.

⊏ TRANSPORTATION. The **West Coast Railway Station** (☎5561 4277) is on the south end of town, just north of Lake Pertobe on Merri St. **V/Line trains** run to **Melbourne** (3½hr.; M-F 4 per day, Sa-Su 3 per day; $40) and **Geelong** (2½hr.; M-F 4 per day, Sa-Su 3 per day; $29). V/Line **buses** run to: **Apollo Bay** (3hr.; F, Dec.-Jan. also M; $24.20); **Ballarat** (2½hr., M-F 1 per day, $21); **Mount Gambier** (2½hr., 1 per day, $31.40); **Port Fairy** (30min.; M-Sa 2 per day, Su 1 per day; $5); and **Portland** (1½hr.; M-Sa 2 per day, Su 1 per day; $14). In town, **Transit Southwest** runs seven bus routes across the city, with stops at each location roughly on the hour; pick up a timetable from the Visitors Centre or buy one at a newsstand for 20¢. (☎5562 1866. $1.20, concessions 80¢. Tickets good for 2hr. unlimited rides.) For a **taxi,** call ☎13 10 08.

◪◪ ORIENTATION & PRACTICAL INFORMATION. The Princes Hwy., which becomes **Raglan Parade** in town, runs along the top edge of the downtown area. The town's main streets run south towards the sea from Raglan Pde., with Banyan St., on the east side of downtown, turning into **Pertobe Road** to round the lake before heading down to the bay, the beach, and the breakwater. **Liebig Street,** the town's main drag, heads south from Raglan Pde. at the McDonald's, crossing Lava St., Koroit St., and Timor St. before winding up at Merri St. on the southern edge of downtown. It is lined with most of the restaurants, pubs, **banks,** and **ATMs.** The scenic **Visitors Centre,** in the Maritime Museum at Flagstaff Hill on Merri St. near Banyan, provides free maps of the area and has a good message board with current events. (☎5564 7837 or 1800 637 725. Open daily 9am-5pm.) Services include: **police,** 214 Koroit St. (☎5560 1179); **library,** at the south end of Liebig St., with free **Internet** (☎5562 2258; open M-Th 9:30am-5pm, F 9:30am-8pm, Sa 9:30am-noon); and two **post offices,** one on Koroit St. and the other on Timor St, both between Kepler and Liebig. (Open M-F 9am-5pm, Sa 9:30am-12:30pm.) Internet is also available at **Southern Right Computers,** 105 Liebig St. ($6 per hour. Open M-F 8:30am-5:30pm, Sa 11am-4pm.). **Postal Code:** 3280.

⋔ ACCOMMODATIONS. Book ahead November through March. ◪**Warrnambool Beach Backpackers ❷,** 17 Stanley St., offers clean and colorful rooms with close proximity to the beach. Owners John and Cheryl provide everything a backpacker could want, including Internet ($7 per hr.), a licensed bar with a tiki theme, TV with DVD, a pool table, a full kitchen, free use of mountain bikes and canoe, coin laundry, and good meals for $5-7. Cassie, the resident dog, is always up for a beach walk. The back bunkrooms are quiet and the mattresses are thick. (☎/fax 5562 4874; www.beachbackpackers.com. Key deposit $10. Reception 7:30am-10pm. Dorms $20; ensuite doubles $60. No credit cards, but there's an in-house ATM.) **Hotel Warrnambool ❸**, 185 Koroit St, on the corner with Kepler, is an old-fashioned hotel with a nice pub downstairs. Some rooms are nicer than others but all are clean and quiet. (☎5562 2377. $40 per night, with breakfast. Pub open 11am-late.) The **Stuffed Backpacker ❷**, 52 Kepler St., just south of Koroit St., next to the cinema, has clean, breezy rooms in a roomy old building. Check in with Leo, the friendly owner, in the candy shop below the hostel. (☎5562 2459. Key deposit $10. Reception 9am-midnight. Dorms $20; singles $30; doubles $45; prices sometimes go down in winter and Leo will extend discounts to NOMADS and YHA members.)

🍴🍺 FOOD & NIGHTLIFE. The bottom half of Liebig St. has a cluster of great restaurants and bars. **Bojangles ❷**, 61 Liebig St., serves inventive wood-fire pizzas for $13-16 (takeaway $10-12) piled high with delicious creative combinations. (☎5562 0666. Open daily 5pm-late.) Next door, hip **Fishtales ❶**, 63 Liebig St., specializes in fish, vegetarian pasta, and Asian food for under $10. (☎5561 2957. Open daily 8am-10pm.) At the other end of the street, the **Princess Alexandra ❸** sits on the corner of Liebig and Lava St. The prices are geared more towards kings than paupers, but the $20 lunch special is a steal with two courses, dessert, and two glasses of wine. The cheese and fruit board ($8 for 1 person, $15 for 2) features award-winning local cheeses. (☎5562 2271. Open daily 11:30am-late.) The 24hr. Coles **supermarket** is on Lava St. between Liebig and Kepler St. Everything is fresh at the seasonal **Grower's Market,** on the Civic Green at the bottom end of Liebig St. (☎5562 7030. 8am-noon on the 1st Saturday each month Dec.-May.)

The neighborhood around the bottom of Liebig St. is also where Warrnambool hits the pubs. The best place in town is the slick **Liquid Lounge,** 58 Liebig St. Loaf on the comfy couches and imbibe a few cocktails or inexpensive beers while peering through the blue waters of the fishtank. (☎5562 9753. Beers from $2.50. Open daily 4:30pm-1am). The **Seanchai Irish Pub,** next to the Liquid Lounge, looks like every other Irish pub in every other non-Irish city around the world. But here you can not only throw darts and pound pints of Guinness, but also check your e-mail. (☎5561 7900. Open daily 2pm-1am. Live music W-Su nights. Internet $6 per hour.) **The Whaler's Inn,** across from Seanchai, is a popular post-Seanchai destination (pints $4, cocktails from $5; Su-Tu open until 1am, W-Sa open until 3am) and is graced by three model whales suspended from the ceiling. **The Gallery Nightclub,** on the corner of Kepler and Timor St. is where the diehards head late-night and dance until the wee hours. (Open until 3am.) For **karaoke,** check out the **Victoria Hotel** on Friday nights (open until 1am).

📷 SIGHTS & ACTIVITIES. The most popular thing to do in Warrnambool from May to October is to watch whales. The info center has booklets on the continuously tracked **southern right whales.** Every winter in late May or June, a population of whales stops just off **Logans Beach,** to the east of the Bay, to give birth to their calves. They stay until September or October, when they return to the Antarctic to break their five-month fast. To watch the beautiful beasts roll, blow, and breach, tourists gather on viewing platforms built above the beach to protect the delicate dune vegetation. Guests at Warrnambool Beach Backpackers can borrow bikes and ride along the Promenade to get to the beach. Southern Right Charters and Diving leads **whale watches,** as well as fishing and diving tours. (☎5562 5044 or 0419 349 058; www.southernrightcharters.com.au. Whale watching from $35.)

VICTORIA

If your visit doesn't coincide with that of the whales, don't despair; the endlessly interesting ◾**Flagstaff Hill Maritime Museum,** overlooking Lady Bay on Merri St., is fascinating even for those not intrigued by nautical history. The 10-acre museum is an outdoor re-creation of a late 19th-century coastal village. The stunning mast-head **Loch Ard peacock,** taken from the wreck of the *Loch Ard* in 1878, is located in the Public Hall. Considering that only two people among hundreds survived the wreck, the fully intact peacock is something of a miracle. Those who want to see more of the Loch Ard than just the peacock can return at sunset for *Shipwrecked*, the museum's recently installed laser show. (☎5564 7841; www.flagstaffhill.info. Museum open daily 9am-5pm; last entrance 4pm. $12, concessions $9, children $5. *Shipwrecked* shows daily at sundown, $20. Book ahead.)

Boasting ample beach-space and parks, Warrnambool is a great spot for outdoor recreation. The 5.7km **Promenade** lining Warrnambool Bay is popular with cyclists, in-line skaters, and evening strollers. For the best sunset views, head to **Thunder Point,** just west of the Bay, where there is a lookout point and walking trails along the coast and inland along the Merri River. Step off the path to explore the rocks and find a secluded spot to watch the sun meet the sea. At low tide it is possible to cross the breakwater over to **Merri Island** where a colony of fairy penguins returns at dusk to roost. (Guests at nearby Warrnambool Beach Backpackers can borrow flashlights from the front desk.) Families will enjoy the new **Adventure Playground,** adjacent to Lake Pertobe. The park, built over 35 hectares of former swampland, features a maze, giant slides, and lots of children screaming in joy. Bowlers can head to **Pins and Play,** 153 Timor St. for ten-pin **bowling.** (☎5561 6877. Open daily 9am-late. First game and shoes $7.50, $13.50 for two games.) The protected bay has a beautiful, curving **beach,** great for swimming. For top-notch surf lessons at good prices, talk to Tristan at the **Easyrider Surf School.** (☎5560 5646 or 0418 328 747; www.easyridersurfschool.com.au. Daily 2hr. group lesson $35; private lesson $55; 3 lessons for $99; boards, wetsuits, and sunscreen provided. Book ahead.)

PORT FAIRY ☎03

Most of the town's action occurs on Banks St. and Sackvill St., which intersect a few blocks from the water. Historical details and a walking tour map are available from the **Tourist Information Centre,** on the south end of Bank St. (☎5568 2682. Open daily 9am-5pm.) **Buses** leave from the bus depot next to the Tourist Centre on Bank St. (☎5568 1355; office open M-F 9:10am-3pm) and head to **Hamilton** (M-Th at 4:05pm, F at 12:20pm) and to **Warrnambool** (M-F 6 per day, Sa 4 per day, Su 1 per day; $4.80). Services include: **police** (☎5568 1007); **RACV,** across from the YHA (☎5568 2700, after hours 5568 1017); **hospital** (☎5568 0100); and a **post office,** 25 Sackville St., which has **Internet.** (Open M-F 9am-5pm. $5 per hr.) **Postal Code:** 3284.

Although most of the town's accommodations are better suited for wealthy vacationers, budget travelers should head to the surprisingly nice **Emoh YHA Hostel** ❷, 8 Cox St. A lovely old house built by Port Fairy's first official settler, William Rutledge, the Emoh has TV, Internet, a pool table, a friendly lounge area, and a kitchen. Bikes and boogie boards are available. Some of the nice doubles in the back are in a renovated carriage house. (☎5568 2468; akzehir@austarnet.com.au. Book ahead for March. Internet $2 per 10min. Dorms $21.50, YHA $18; singles $38.50/$35; doubles $53/$46; family rooms $67/$60.) For a real splurge try out the 5-star **Victoria Hotel** ❺, 42 Banks St. The stunning suites have leather furniture, spa baths, and sparkling kitchens. Coupled with the quiet feel of the town, staying at the Vic makes for a perfect holiday getaway. (☎5568 2891; www.vichotel.com. Queen $160; spacious king $200.) The **Dublin House** ❺, 57 Bank St., has a beautiful garden and doubles of varying elegance. (☎5568 2022. Doubles $90-150.) **Eumarella Backpackers** ❷ is 17km west of Port Fairy in Yambuk, 200m south of Hwy. 1. The nice but remote hostel is a converted 19th-century schoolhouse, run by the Peek Whurrong people of the Framlingham Aboriginal Trust. It's next to the Deen Maar, Victoria's first Indigenous Protected Area. (☎5568 4204. Kitchen, laundry, and bike and canoe hire. Dorms $16.50.)

Ginger Nut's, on the corner of Banks and Sackville, is a restaurant, cafe, and bakery all in one. Their breads and pastries are delicious and their meals have an emphasis on fresh local produce. (☎5568 2326. Open daily 7am-10pm.) The **Victoria Hotel ❸,** 42 Banks St. has nice meals in its interestingly designed dining room for under $20, and on Tuesday-Saturday nights they have a gourmet four-course set menu for $55. (☎5568 2891. Open daily 9am-10pm.) The sticky date pudding at **Cobb's Port Fairy Bakery ❶,** 25 Bank St., will change your life for the better. (☎5568 1713. Open daily 8am-5pm.) The IGA Everyday on Sackville St. is both **grocery store** and bottle shop. (Open daily 8am-8pm.)

There's nothing much to do in Port Fairy, which is exactly its attraction. The **beach** is excellent for swimming (lifeguards on duty Sa-Su), and the **wharf** is a great place to watch the ships come in or get a fresh seafood meal. Maps of suggested **walking tours** covering the town's historical sights and buildings are available at the Visitors Centre. Visits can be arranged at the wharf to **Lady Julia Percy Island,** 19km out in the Bass Strait, home to seals, fairy penguins, and peregrine falcons. Contact the Visitors Center for information. **Port Fairy Boat Charter,** stationed at the harbor, goes to Lady Julia for $55 and does daily 30min. bay cruises ($11 per person). Childishness is encouraged at **Kitehouse,** on the corner of Bank and Grant St., where all kinds of kites, wind socks, and other high flying toys are for sale. Bikes are also available for rent. (☎5568 2782. Open daily 10am-5pm.)

Port Fairy has made a name for itself as the unlikely host for some of the world's best music. Almost every bed on the Shipwreck Coast is hired out in March during the **Port Fairy Folk Festival,** held over Australia's Labor Day weekend. The festival attracts folk, blues, and country music acts from all over Australia and the world. During the weekend, the population of the town jumps from 2600 to over 30,000. (☎5568 2227. Order tickets months in advance.) **Rhapsody in June** is an annual three-day event held over the Queen's Birthday long weekend and focuses on food, art, and concerts. In October the **Spring Music Festival** is held, and during December and January the town is transformed by the **Moyneyana Festival.**

PORTLAND ☎03

Portland was the first town settled in Victoria, and the weary industrial feel that permeates it betrays its age. This area was once a base for whalers, sealers, and escaped convicts, before the Henty brothers and their sheep enterprise permanently settled it in 1834. Its harbor is still quite active and maritime history buffs may take pleasure in Portland's storied past, but most travelers use the town more as a jumping off point for the Great South West Walk, Discovery Bay National Park, and Lower Glenelg National Park.

🖅🖪 TRANSPORTATION & PRACTICAL INFORMATION. V/Line buses depart from the north side of Henty St., just west of Percy St. One heads east through **Port Fairy** (1hr., $10) to **Warrnambool** (1½hr.; M-Sa 2 per day, Su 1 per day; $14), where connections can be made to Melbourne. One bus per day heads west to **Mount Gambier** (1½hr., $13). On Friday morning (Dec.-Jan. also M), a bus runs to **Apollo Bay** (4hr., $39), Lorne (5hr., $44), and **Port Campbell** (2½hr., $25). Tickets can be purchased at **Harvey World Travel,** 53 Julia St. near the corner with Percy. (☎5521 7895; www.harveyworld.com.au. Open M-F 9am-5:30pm and Sa 9am-noon.) The two main north-south streets in town are the waterfront **Bentinck Street,** with cafes, takeaway joints, and pubs, and **Percy Street,** one block up, which has the majority of the town's commercial activity. Percy is the continuation of the Henty Hwy., which enters the city from the north, where it is lined with chain motels. Percy and Bentinck St. are connected in the center of town by, from north to south, Henty, Julia, and Gawler St. At the town's southern end, Bentinck St. becomes Cape Nelson Rd. and heads southwest to Cape Nelson State Park. On Lee Breakwater St., down the hill between Bentinck St. and the bay, in a gray building north of the fishing jetty, is the **Portland Visitors Centre.** (☎5523 2671. Open daily 9am-5pm.) More information on the Lower Glenelg and Discovery Bay (as well as useful maps) can be obtained from the **Parks Victoria** office, 8-12 Julia St. (☎13 19 63. Open M-F 9am-4:30pm.) **Internet** access is available at the **library** on Bentinck St., just south of Gawler St. (☎5523 1497. Open M-Tu and Th-F 10am-5:30pm, Sa 10am-noon. $2 per 30min.; book ahead.) The **post office** is at 108 Percy St. **Postal Code:** 3305.

⌐⌐ ACCOMMODATIONS & FOOD. Close to the waterfront in town, the **Gordon Hotel ❷,** 63 Bentinck St., provides pub accommodation with a regal balcony and great harbor views. The kitchen is limited but continental breakfast is included. (☎5523 1121. Singles from $28; doubles from $35.) For those willing to venture farther afield, the opportunity to fraternize with sheep and wake up to the sounds of breaking waves awaits at the hard-to-find **Bellevue Backpackers ❷,** Sheoke Rd., on the way to Cape Nelson. Keep a hawk's eye out for the faded white sign on the left just before a sharp right curve in the road just before Yellow Rock. Accommodation consists of your own personal trailer complete with dining area, TV, kitchen, bunk and double beds. (☎5523 4038. Caravan $20.) The classiest downtown hotel is **Mac's Hotel Bentinck ❹,** on the corner of Gawler St. and Bentinck St., where the Victorian ensuite rooms will cost a pretty penny but the back motel rooms are a better bargain. (☎5523 2188. Hotel doubles $105, motel doubles $60.) **Portland Backpackers Inn ❷,** 14 Gawler St., is an old house but comfortable, with a nice picnic table in a leafy courtyard and the price is right. (☎5523 6390 or 0407 854 051. Dorms $15.)

Portland's rough industrial edges are soothed at **Sully's Cafe ❶,** 55 Bentinck St. The focaccia sandwiches ($8.50) are fantastic and they have a fully stocked bar in the back. Rumor has it Sully's is moving to a larger spot on the same street, so keep an eye open all along Bentinck. (☎5523 5355. Open M-F 11am-11pm, Sa-Su 10am-11pm.) Health food nuts can get tea or a lentil burger while browsing supplies of wheat germ and lemongrass at **Sunstream Wholefoods ❶,** 49 Julia St. Soy burger with lime coriander and yogurt sauce is only $5.50. (Food M-F 9am-3:30pm; store open until 5:30pm; Sa 10:30am-12:30pm.) **Port Of Call ❷,** 85 Bentinck St., has good coffee, great views, and a variety of fresh fish options for eat-in or takeaway. (☎5523 1335. Open daily 7:30am-11pm.) A large Safeway **supermarket** is on Percy St., across from the post office (open daily 7am-10pm).

◙◙ SIGHTS & HIKING. Though this stretch of waters is safer today, many ships in the Portland harbor area once became all-too-intimately acquainted with the ocean floor. The **Maritime Discovery Centre** memorializes some of those ships and celebrates the city's fishing and whaling history. The prized display is the reconstructed skeleton of a sperm whale beached in 1987, complete with a bench built under the rib cage, but word wizards can entertain friends with nautical definitions gleaned from the wall near the entrance. The museum shares space with the Visitors Centre and a cafe with great views. (☎5523 2671. Open daily 9am-5pm. $8, concession $5.50.) Behind the Maritime Centre, a restored 1885 **cable tram** will take you on a waterfront ride to several of Portland's tourist attractions. (Tickets bought onboard or at the Maritime Centre. $10, concessions $8, children $5.50.) The free **gardens,** on Cliff St. toward the commercial wharf from Bentinck St., are worth a look, and their dizzying array of plant life is on display all day, every day.

The waters off Portland are popular with both divers and fishermen. For the experienced **diver,** equipment rental and charters are available at the **Dive Shop,** on Townsend St. (☎ 5523 6392. Open M-F 9am-5:30pm, Sa 10am-2pm, Su 10am-2pm in summer. Gear rental from $55; 3-week diving classes from $290). **Fishing** charters and **harbor cruises** are available from **Southwest Charters.** (☎ 5523 3202 or 0418 306 714. Prices vary; call ahead.) **Bikes** can be rented from the Visitors Centre for coastal rides (half-day $12; full-day $20).

Starting and ending at Portland's information center, the looping, 250km **Great South West Walk** rambles along the coast through the Discovery Bay Coastal Park, then doubles back through the Lower Glenelg National Park. The walk traverses a variety of terrains and provides a grand introduction to the wildlands of southwest Victoria. There are four main sections of the walk, which is promoted as a "symphony in four movements": The Three Capes and Bays, Discovery Bay Beach and Mt. Richmond, the Glenelg River and Gorge, and the Cobboboonee Forest. Campsites are provided all along the trail for walkers, and detailed maps are available at the Portland Visitors Centre. The trail is clearly marked, occasionally with a black emu badge but more often with red metal arrows and signs pointing you in the right direction. Daytrip-access sections range from 8-20km in length, although shorter sections, the most accessible of which are in **Cape Nelson State Park** (see p. 625), can be walked as well. Most of those choosing to walk it in its entirety do so in about 12 days. If you want to walk a section and need pick-up or drop-off services, call the **Friends of the Great South West Walk.** (☎ 5523 5262; gbennett@datafast.net.au. Prices for this service vary depending on distances and time of year.) Register with the info center before setting off.

CAPE NELSON STATE PARK

Cape Nelson State Park, a 243-hectare reserve, lies just 11km southwest of Portland and plays host to some beautiful bushwalks, impressive coastal cliffs, a prime surf beach, and the **last manned lighthouse** in Victoria. The view from the lighthouse alone is worth a trip out here. (☎ 5523 5100. Entrance daily 10am-4pm. Admission $4, concessions $3; lighthouse tours $10/$8.) The best approach to the park is to head south out of Portland on Bentinck St., which becomes Cape Nelson Rd., and then make a left on Sheoke Rd., heading east. As Sheoke Rd. swings south, it becomes the Scenic Rd., and almost immediately you'll see the parking lot for **Yellow Rock,** the area's top surf spot, where a boardwalk leads down from the clifftops to the beach and provides several sitting areas to take in the view of the yellowish monolith for which the beach is named. For more info, consult with *Surfs Up in Portland* compiled by the Portland *Observer,* available at the Maritime Centre.

The **Great South West Walk** (see p. 624) intersects the park, affording the opportunity to walk short sections of it; one of the best is the **Enchanted Forest** walk (3km return), which winds through groves of short trees twisted into strange shapes by strong winds. The carpark is just off Sheoke Rd., about halfway to the lighthouse. The **Sea Cliff Nature Walk** (a 3km loop) begins at the Sea Cliff parking lot, at the intersection of the Scenic Rd. and Cape Nelson Rd., and includes displays explaining some of the rare plants and animals protected in the park. The **Lighthouse Walk** (6km, marked with blue arrows), which can be started from either the Sea Cliff carpark or the lighthouse, wanders through inland areas and joins with the Great South West Walk east of the lighthouse for spectacular clifftop views of the ocean.

There's no camping in the park itself, but the **lighthouse-keeper's cottage ❺** is perfectly secluded and offers stunning views. (☎ 5523 5100. Doubles $110, extra person $30; entire house for 8 people $400; book ahead.) Another option out this way is the small **Bellevue Backpackers ❷** (see p. 624), which sits on the northern edge of the park near Yellow Rock.

VICTORIA

DISCOVERY BAY COASTAL PARK

Discovery Bay Coastal Park stretches 55km from Portland to the South Australia border. Connecting the sea to freshwater lakes and swamps are mobile dunes up to 20m high; be sure to stay on the marked walking tracks. **Cape Bridgewater,** at the park's southern end, 18km west of Portland via the Bridgewater Rd. (from town, take Otway St. west until it becomes Bridgewater Rd.), holds a resident **seal colony,** excellent surfing and swimming, and three of the park's most well known attractions: the **Blowholes,** the **Petrified Forest,** and the **Springs.** Limited **tourist info** is available at the kiosk on the beach (open daily 9:30am-5pm). The carpark for the seal walk is just up the hill from the beach, on the left side of the road. From there, it's a 1hr. hike on a fairly steep and winding cliff trail to a **viewing platform** high above a rockshelf on which Australian fur seals sun themselves with abandon. A less strenuous but longer hike to the seals runs in the opposite direction, following the Great South West Walk from the blowholes carpark to the seal walk carpark, but requires that you find a way back to your car (9km, 3hr.). To avoid the hard work altogether, **Seals By Sea** runs 45min. tours from Cape Bridgewater, allowing you to get up close and personal with the seals. (☎5526 7247. $20, concessions $17, children $12. Book ahead). The **Cape Bridgewater Holiday Camp ❷** offers great views of the stunning bay and beach as well as a range of options, from backpacker-style bunks to the more refined (and possibly sacrilegious) accommodations offered in the town's original church, dating from 1870. (☎5526 7267. Dorms $15; doubles from $30; church doubles $50, extra persons $10.)

At the end of Bridgewater Rd., on the western side of Cape Bridgewater, is a parking lot with access to the Springs, the Blowholes, and the Petrified Forest. Straight up from the carpark, waves crash into the **Blowholes** at the foot of the sea cliffs. To the left is the **Petrified Forest,** eerie rock formations in cavities left when trees rotted away. Virtually indistinguishable from tidal pools, the **Springs** (1hr.) are in fact freshwater springs formed as rainwater seeps through limestone farther inland. From Cape Bridgewater, the Bridgewater Lakes Rd. will lead you back to the Nelson-Portland Rd., passing by the Amos Rd. turn-off, which leads to a nice surf break at **White's Beach** on the northern side of the Cape, and the freshwater **Bridgewater Lakes,** a popular swimming, boating, and picnicking area, on the way. Shortly after Bridgewater Lakes Rd. rejoins the main road, a well-marked turn-off heads into **Mt. Richmond National Park,** where an 8km sealed road will bring you to the summit of Mt. Richmond and views towards the towering dunes of Discovery Bay. Short, clearly marked hikes branch off from the picnic area at the top of the mount, with the **Ocean View Walk** (a 1hr. loop) leading to sweeping views of, well, the ocean. The park and its abundant bird life and wide variety of wildflowers are 18km west of Portland on the Portland-Nelson Rd. (C192).

LOWER GLENELG NATIONAL PARK

Lower Glenelg National Park protects a rich patch of dense forest surrounding the Glenelg River. The best way to see the interior of the park and commune with nature is via canoe. The Glenelg River meanders its way through virtually the entire length of the park and passes a succession of **campsites ❶,** many accessible only to boaters. Three or four days of paddling will bring the water-borne from Dartmoor, on the Princes Hwy., to the mouth of the river at Nelson. Several companies based in Nelson rent canoes ($25-30 per day) and will drop you off at the starting point on the northeast edge of the park. **Nelson Boat and Canoe Hire** has a variety of canoes and kayaks to choose from and has special group rates (☎08 8738 4048; from $33 per day). They run a daytrip that covers the stretch of river just above the Margaret Rose Caves and includes a stop at the caves and pick-up and drop-off in Nelson ($47.50 per person), and can arrange special multi-night trips. The **Nelson Visitors Centre and Parks Victoria Office,** on Leake St. in Nelson, provides camping permits and can answer questions about river conditions and canoe rental. (☎ 08 8738 4051. Open daily 9am-5pm.)

A 4WD is the next best way to see the park, as several tracks access its interior. Even without a 4WD, **Glenelg Drive** makes the park accessible to all. The 22km road winds through dense forest alive with the sounds of birds, passing occasional river views. Be aware that many of the tracks branching off of Glenelg Dr. are in considerably worse condition. To access the road from the east, turn right onto the Nelson-Winnap Rd. shortly after passing the Lake Monibeong turn-off and then make a left onto Glenelg Dr. about 12km after that. From the west, take the North Nelson Rd. north out of Nelson. Glenelg Dr. will appear on your right.

Limestone dominates the topography, and percolating rainwater or underground watercourses have formed many caves. The largest and most spectacular (and the only ones open to the public) are the **Princess Margaret Rose Caves,** 2km east of the South Australia border and 15km south of the Princes Hwy. (☎ 08 8738 4171. Tours daily 10, 11am, noon, 1:30, 2:30, 3:30, and 4:30pm. $7.50, concessions $6, children $4.) The tour illuminates the caves' varied features. This area also features a few nature walks, a large wooded picnic area with BBQ, and limited **camping ❶** facilities. Camping arrangements must be made before 5pm with the ranger at the **Caves Information Centre** (sites for 4 people $12; on-site cabins $45). From Nelson, the most convenient access to the caves is either by water (see canoe info above and boat info below) or by a 15km unsealed road that heads north from the highway a few kilometers west of Nelson. Those partial to sealed roads should plan to visit the caves from Mt. Gambier, where the road to the caves is sealed.

OUTBACK VICTORIA

Outback Victoria encompasses mountains, lakes, swamps, wildlife reserves, rich farmland, and rugged bushland. West of the Goldfields, inland Victoria rises among the rugged peaks of Grampians National Park before gradually settling into an immense plain that stretches west into South Australia and north into New South Wales. The **Wimmera** region draws its name from the river that begins in the Grampians and wanders north past the surprisingly lush Little Desert National Park. North of Little Desert and west of the Sunraysia Hwy., all the way up to Mildura, is the semi-arid expanse of the **Mallee,** named for the *mallee eucalypt*, a hardy water-hoarding tree that thrives in the rugged plains.

GRAMPIANS (GARIWERD) NATIONAL PARK

In 1836, Major Mitchell, in command of a British expedition, stumbled upon a range of mountains he designated as the Grampians, after a range in his home country of Scotland. Ensuing hordes of settlers steadily pushed the Koori Aborigines out of their ancestral home of Gariwerd. A visit to the park now promises an insight into both Aboriginal cultural history (80% of the Aboriginal rock art sites in Victoria can be found here) as well as access to breathtaking ranges, abundant wildlife, rare birds, and a springtime carpet of technicolor wildflowers.

■ ▐▀ ORIENTATION & TRANSPORTATION

The northern approach passes through **Horsham,** at the junction of Western and Henty Hwy., roughly 18km north of the park. From the south, the town of **Dunkeld,** on the Glenelg Hwy., provides access via Mt. Abrupt Rd. From the east, the closest

VICTORIA

GRAMPIANS NATIONAL PARK AT A GLANCE

AREA: 167,000 hectares.

WHERE: The end of the Great Dividing Range. 260km west of Melbourne.

FEATURES: Koori rock paintings, the Balconies (Jaws of Death), MacKenzie Falls, climbs in the Wonderland Range and Hollow Mountain.

GATEWAYS: Halls Gap (east); Horsham (north); Dunkeld (south).

CAMPING, HIKING, CLIMBING: 13 campgrounds, each with dozens of sites, 160km of walking track, and a variety of rock climbs.

FEES: Camping $11 for up to 6 people and one car. $5 per additional car.

town is **Stawell**, 26km away. The **most convenient point of entry** is on the eastern edge of the park at **Halls Gap.** This is the park's only town (and it's small), but it has the basic amenities and is within walking distance of many of the park's points of interest. When reading about the town's offerings, remember that, unless otherwise noted, everything is clustered together in a small strip on **Grampians Road,** also called Dunkeld Rd., Stawell Rd., and sometimes even Main Rd., which runs from Halls Gap to Dunkeld.

One **V/Line** bus per day leaves from across the newsagent bound for: Ararat (1hr., $12); Ballarat (2½hr., $25); Melbourne (4½hr., $40); and Stawell (30min., $8). Several private companies also run multi-day tours from Melbourne and Adelaide, often incorporating the Great Ocean Road along the way. One option is **EcoPlatypus Tours,** (☎1800 819 091) which runs a bus to Melbourne Su, Th, and F at 4:30pm for $30. During the school year (late Feb.-early Nov.) you can hitch a ride on the local **schoolbus** between Halls Gap and Stawell (20min., weekdays only, departs Halls Gap outside Post Office 7:55am and 4:38pm, departs Stawell visitors center 7:20am and 4pm, $8).

⚡ PRACTICAL INFORMATION

Brambuk, The National Park and Cultural Centre, 2.5km south of Halls Gap town center on Dunkeld Rd., is the best resource for would-be hikers and bush campers. The engaging displays provide excellent information on the Grampians' flora, fauna, and history. (☎5356 4381. Open daily 9am-5pm. Hiking maps $3.30; donations appreciated.) From outside Halls Gap, **Parks Victoria** (☎13 19 63; www.parkweb.vic.gov.au) is also an excellent resource. The Halls Gap **Visitors Center** in the town center has great info and can answer questions about the park. (☎5356 4616 or 1800 065 599. Open daily 9am-5pm.) The **newsagent** next door also has plenty of maps as well as an **Internet** kiosk. (Open daily 7am-7pm. $2 per 10min.) The Mobil **petrol** station has basic provisions, and an **ATM.** (☎5356 4206. Open daily in summer 7am-8:45pm, in winter 7am-7:45pm.) If you break down, **Stawell & Grampians Towing** (☎5358 4000) is open 24hr. The **post office** is hidden in the well-marked bottle shop. (Open M-F 9am-5pm.) The Halls Gap **Police Station** (☎5356 4411) is located just north of the town center, at the intersection of Grampians Rd. and Mt. Victory Rd. **Postal Code:** 3381.

🏠 ACCOMMODATIONS & CAMPING

The quality of the accommodations here is as high as the Grampians themselves. There are 13 major **camping ❶** areas in the park, all with toilets and fireplaces and most with water. All sites are on a first-come first-served basis; campers must pay $10.70 (up to 6 people and 1 vehicle, additional vehicles $4.70) for permits available at the National Park Centre. Rangers advise stopping at the Centre first for a

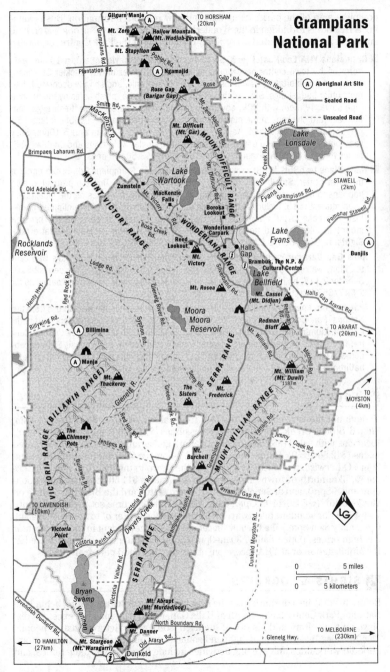

Grampians National Park

Legend:
- (A) Aboriginal Art Site
- Sealed Road
- --- Unsealed Road

TO HORSHAM (20km)

Western Hwy.

Gilgurn Manja

Mt. Zero

Hollow Mountain (Mt. Wudjub-guyun)

Mt. Stapylton

Grampians Rd.

Plantation Rd.

Pohler Rd.

Ngamadjid

Rose Gap (Barigar Gap)

Rose Gap Rd.

Smith Rd.

Mackenzie R.

Mt. Zero Halls Gap Rd.

Mt. Difficult (Mt. Gar)

MOUNT DIFFICULT RANGE

Ledcourt Rd.

Lake Lonsdale

Brimpaen Laharum Rd.

Lake Wartook

Old Adelaide Rd.

Zumstein

Mt. Victory Rd.

MacKenzie Falls

Boroka Lookout

Fyans Creek Rd.

Fyans Cr.

TO STAWELL (2km)

Grampians Rd.

Wonderland Carpark

WONDERLAND RANGE

Rose Creek Rd.

Reed Lookout

MOUNT VICTORY RANGE

Mt. Victory

Lake Fyans

Rocklands Reservoir

Lodge Rd.

Red Rock Rd.

Halls Gap

Brambuk, The N.P. & Cultural Centre

Lake Bellfield

Pomonal Stawell Rd.

Bunjils

Henty Hwy.

Glenelg River Rd.

Silverband Rd.

Mt. Rosea

Mt. Cassel (Mt. Didjun)

Halls Gap Ararat Rd.

Billywing Rd.

Moora Moora Reservoir

Redman Bluff

TO ARARAT (20km)

Billimina

Syphon Rd.

SERRA RANGE

Mt. William Rd.

Reeder Rd.

Manja

Glenelg R.

Red Hill Rd.

Serra Rd.

Mt. Thackeray

VICTORIA RANGE (BILLAWIN RANGE)

The Sisters

Green Creek Rd.

Mt. Frederick

Mitchell Rd.

Mt. William (Mt. Duwil) 1187m

MOUNT WILLIAM RANGE

TO MOYSTON (4km)

The Chimney Pots

Jensens Rd.

Billawin Rd.

Yarram Rd.

Jimmy Creek Rd.

TO CAVENDISH (10km)

Mt. Burchell

Victoria Valley Rd.

Grampians Tourist Rd.

Dwyers Creek

Grampians Rd.

Yarram Gap Rd.

Dunkeld Moyston Rd.

Victoria Point

Victoria Point Rd.

SERRA RANGE

N

0   5 miles

0   5 kilometers

Bryan Swamp

Victoria Valley Rd.

Wannon R.

Mt. Abrupt (Mt. Murdadjoog) 826m

Cavendish Dunkeld Rd.

Mt. Danner

North Boundary Rd.

Old Ararat Rd.

Glenelg Hwy.

TO MELBOURNE (230km)

TO HAMILTON (27km)

Mt. Sturgeon (Mt. Wuragarri)

Dunkeld

complete map of the park's campsites and new relevant information. Bush camping is free but is forbidden in the Wonderland Range, the Lake Wartook watershed, and other areas demarcated accordingly on maps. Visit the Park Centre for details.

Grampians YHA Eco-Hostel (☎5356 4544; grampians@yhavic.org.au), a 10min. walk north of the town center on Grampians Rd., at the corner of tiny Buckler St. Clean, classy, and comfortable, as well as more luxurious, scenic, and sharply decorated than most other budget digs. State-of-the-art kitchen, dining area, plush sofas by the antique pipe stove, TV room with VCR, adventure booking office, herb garden, fresh eggs from the backyard chickens in the morning, and laundry. Wheelchair-accessible. Internet $2 per 15min. Linens included. Key deposit $10. Reception 8-10am and 5-10pm. Busy year-round. Heated 4-bed dorms with lockers $25; singles $53; twins and doubles $55; family rooms $80. YHA discount summer $5, winter $3.50. 60 beds. ❷

Tim's Place (☎5356 4288; www.timsplace.com.au), on Grampians Rd., 500m north of the town center. Small, cozy, intimate, and centrally located. Tim, the proprietor, also happens to be president of the local golf club and arranges 9 holes on the local green upon request ($15, includes clubs). Free tea and french press coffee, unlimited breakfast, free cake in the afternoon, laundry, BBQ, and linens. Internet $3 per hr. Free mountain bike use and free tickets to the Brambuk Centre Dreaming Theatre (see **Sights**, p. 630). Dorms $22; singles $30-40; doubles $50. 22 beds. ❷

Halls Gap Caravan Park (☎5356 4251; hgcp@netconnect.com.au), in Halls Gap center. Many walking trails start just behind the campground. Linens $7. Key deposit $20. Sites for 2 $17, holidays $20; powered $21/$23, extra person $5. On-site caravans for 2 $47/$53. Discounts for longer stays. ❷

Brambuk Backpackers (☎5356 4250; www.brambuck.tourvic.com.au), across from the National Park Centre on Dunkeld Rd. Very clean rooms, with lockers, heaters, and bath. Kitchen, laundry, BBQ, Internet $2 per 10min. Affiliated with the Brambuk Cultural Centre; free tickets to the Dreaming Theatre. Breakfast included. Key deposit $10. Reception 8:30am-1pm and 5-8pm. Sites $15 per person, includes light breakfast and use of bathrooms; dorms $22; singles $22; doubles $55; ages 10-16 $13, under 10 $8. ❶

🍴 FOOD

Though not the very cheapest, the best food value in town is **Black Panther Cafe,** Shop 6, Stoney Creek Stores, which serves pizzas ($12-19.50), pasta ($11.50-14.50), focaccias with salad ($8.50, served until 5pm), and a range of exquisitely-prepared mains ($12.50-18.50). Happy hour ($1 pots) 4-6pm. (☎5356 4511. Open daily 8am-8pm.) Otherwise, the cheapest eats are at the bistro in the **Halls Gap Hotel and Tavern ❷,** 3km north of town on Grampians Rd. (mains $11.50-18, open daily noon-2pm and 6-8pm), and at **Suzie's Halls Gap Tavern ❷,** toward the Brambuk Centre on Dunkeld Rd. (☎5356 4416. Open daily 11am-11pm; 3-course set menu daily until 7pm $10.) For standard takeaway, try **Ralphy's,** in the center of town. (☎5356 4348. Open daily 8am-8pm.) **The Friendly Grocer** next to the newsagent in the town center has high prices. (Open daily 7:30am-9pm.) Some food items can be purchased at the Mobil station or at YHA reception; otherwise, buy food before arriving.

🔶 SIGHTS & LOOKOUTS

Before heading into the park, visit the **Brambuk Aboriginal Culture Centre,** behind the National Park Centre 2.5km south of Halls Gap, which has small but excellent displays on the culture and history of the **Koori,** southwest Victoria's native people. The **Dreaming Theatre's** 15min. light-and-sound show tells a traditional Koori story. Periodic workshops and evening activities include boomerangs, didgeridoos, and

Koori traditional dance. The Centre also offers a **guided rock-art tour.** (☎5356 4452. Open daily 9am-5pm. Entry free. Theatre $4.40, concessions $2.80, families $16.40. 2hr. tours Su-F 10am-noon. $15, concessions $11, children $8; book ahead.)

Unfortunately, most sights are a good distance from Halls Gap and require a car to reach. This does not deter many tourists—hikers report finding rides at the Park Centre or at their accommodations, though *Let's Go* does not recommend hitchhiking. The **Balconies** (Jaws of Death), the Grampians' predominant icon, lie about 1km up from the Reed Lookout carpark off Mt. Victory Rd. The mostly flat approach (20min.) ends in sweeping panoramas. The Balconies themselves, a pair of parallel slabs of sandstone, jut out over the steep sides of Mt. Victory and are a superb spot to watch the sunset. Those who brave the steep, slippery path to **MacKenzie Falls,** which begins at the carpark just off Lake Wartook Rd., are rewarded with one of Victoria's most spectacular waterfalls—an 11m wall of crashing water. A new wheelchair-accessible approach was recently opened. **Zumstein picnic area,** west of Lake Wartook on Mt. Victory Rd., is extremely popular because it crawls with kangaroos, but you can see herds of hopping 'roos just about everywhere in the park. Five **Aboriginal art sites** are open to the public but are considerably far apart. **Touring Downunder** runs a full-day **Aboriginal Culture and Art Sites Tour** from the Brambuk Centre that includes informational talks, the Dreamtime Theatre, a bush tucker lunch, afternoon tea, and visits to three art sites. (Book through Brambuk ☎5356 4452. Tours 9:30am-5:30pm. $69.)

▧ HIKING

Although rugged, the Grampians is very user-friendly; most of its highlights can be reached via relatively easy walking trails, without the need to drive to a trailhead or camp overnight in the bush. It is thus a favorite among families and nature lovers of the less-hardcore variety. At the same time, the park caters to more experienced hikers with difficult tracks in the northern and southern regions (most of which are hard to reach without a car). The **Wonderland Range** adjacent to Halls Gap in the park's eastern end holds a number of the main attractions. **Mt. Victory Road,** in particular, is loaded with phenomena to impress even the staunchest urbanite. The indispensable *Northern Walks, Southern Walks,* and *Wonderland Walks* maps (each $3.30) in the Park Centre give details on hiking and driving.

Some Wonderland walks lead to serene waterfalls and curious rock formations. To the south, **Victoria Valley** is carpeted with red gum woodlands and is home to emus and kangaroos. **Manja** and **Billimina,** at the park's western border, contain some of the Grampians' best **Aboriginal art sites.** Experienced hikers might want to tackle some of the steep trails on the Grampians' highest peak, **Mt. William** (1168m), at the park's extreme eastern end; the actual "trail" to the summit is disappointingly fully paved and well-traveled. The Wonderland hikes vary by difficulty and duration (from 30min. to 6hr. to several days). The trails below start near Halls Gap; all distances reflect return trips.

Wonderland Loop (9.6km; 5hr.). Starts in back of the town center carpark. Walk past the swimming pool and rear asphalt road and turn left before the Botanical Gardens. Of medium difficulty, this hike traverses many of the most touristed sites, though slightly more strenuous detours abound off the track. A perfect family outing, the half-day loop along well-formed tracks leads first to the **Venus Baths,** a series of rock pools popular for swimming in summer, and then to the photogenic **Splitters Falls.** The trail continues through the lush forest along a creek to the Wonderland carpark, then up the spectacular **Grand Canyon** and eventually to the narrow rock tunnel **Silent Street.** At the awe-inspiring **Pinnacle,** sweeping views of the valley reward breathless hikers. The quick descent through stringy-bark forests offers completely unobstructed ridge-line views of

Halls Gap and the surrounding countryside. The trail is extremely well-marked (and well-traveled), except for the bit just after Silent Street. To reach the pinnacle, follow the orange arrows that point up into the rock rather than the sign which directs you back to the Wonderland carpark.

Mt. Rosea Loop (12km; 4-5hr.). A more difficult hike that is best attempted with a copy of the **Wonderland Walks** map ($3.30), available from the Brambuk center. Starts at the Rosea Campground, located on Silverband Rd. off Mt. Victory Rd. The hike begins by crossing Stony Creek Rd. and then ascends through a forest to a sandstone plateau. The orange markers are somewhat difficult to follow in this area, so be careful not to lose the trail. After a bit of scrambling over rocky ledges, turn left at the sign for Mt. Rosea. The summit has one of the most spectacular vistas in the Grampians. Follow the trail back to the intersection and head left, away from the Rosea campground, through a forest and then onto a 4WD track, leading to the Burma Track. Keep left around the outlying portions of the Sierra Range. At Silverband Rd., turn right and walk for 200m to the Dellys Dell Track and then walk uphill for about 700m to the Rosea Campground.

Boronia Peak Trail (6.6km; 2-3hr.). Starts past the kangaroo fields next to the Brambuk Centre or alternatively from the narrow path by the bridge just north of Tim's Place. A little harder than the Wonderland Loop, but shorter. The dense trees add to the tranquil solitude of this much less touristed route without obscuring bird and other fauna watching. The mostly medium-grade terrain ends in a short unmarked rock scramble to the peak. With a large lake to the south, flat bush country to the east, and the jagged Wonderland range to the west, the view is worth the haul to the top.

Boroka Lookout Trail (12.4km; 4-5hr.). Same starting location as Wonderland Loop; turn right off the trail just before Splitters Falls. The toughest hike from Halls Gap. An unrelentingly steep ascent to this lookout in the **Mt. Difficult Range** rewards with spectacular views of the **Fyans Valley** and the **Mt. William** and **Wonderland Ranges,** the rough slopes of which have been aptly named the Elephant's Hide (also viewable from the nearby carpark).

Chatauqua Peak Loop (5.6km; 2-3hr.). Starts from behind the Recreation Oval on Mt. Victory Rd., 150m from the intersection with Grampians Rd. The hike opens with an up-close view of the tranquil **Clematis Falls,** best seen after rain. The final 400m boulder climb to the peak is long and strenuous, but the views of Halls Gap and the valley are perfect. The less mobile can skip the boulder hop; the main trail continues on through to **Bullaces Glen,** a lush fern gully, and ends in the botanical gardens in Halls Gap.

Mt. Stapylton Summit (4.6km; 2-3hr.). Located in the northern Grampians, Mt. Stapylton is a challenging hike that requires a bit of scrambling over elevated ledges and some basic navigational skills. Before setting off, purchase the **Northern Walks** map from the Brambuck Center ($3.30), and also ask them for a (free) photocopy of a topographical map of the area. Drive 40min. north on Mt. Victory Rd. and turn right on Plantation Rd. and the left on Winfield Rd, which is unsealed. The road to the Mt. Zero campground is well-marked and on the right. The hike begins with a long uphill walk over the unshaded **Flat Rock,** and then passes through a wooded area to the base of Mt. Stapylton. The hike to the summit is strenuous and should be attempted only by confident hikers. The view from the top includes many of the surrounding mountain ranges and plains. On the way back down, you have the option of returning to the Mt. Zero Picnic area directly or turning the outing into a half-day hike by tackling the entire **Mt. Stapylton Loop** (12.2km; 5-7hrs.) Follow the signs for the trail to the Stapylton Campground (4.4km), which passes through dense scrub. From the campground, signs mark the trail back to the Mt. Zero Picnic Area. The loop and summit can also be attempted by starting from and returning to the Stapylton Campground. This option may be preferable to starting at the Mt. Zero picnic area, since it puts the most strenuous hiking before the summit rather than after.

⚡ OTHER ADVENTURES

There are opportunities galore and plenty of companies around to book your next requisite adrenaline rush. All outfits provide free pick-up in Halls Gap and often cheaper group rates. The **Adventure Company** (☎ 5356 4540; www.adventurecompany.com.au), in the Grampians YHA, offers adventure in every length and level, including canoe trips (2-3hr. $45, full-day in central Grampians $95), 25km downhill bike rides ($55), and a range of full- and half-day rock climbing and abseiling courses ($65-95). One abseil drops you 60m over ◨**The Ledge** (no experience necessary; YHA discount 10%; open M-Tu, F-Sa 5:30-7:30pm). The above activities can be booked directly or through the **Grampians Central Booking Office,** in the Halls Gap newsagent. (☎ 5356 4654; www.grampianstours.com. Open daily 9am-5pm, but desk may be unattended during tours.)

The Booking Office also runs several other tours, including **Grampians Highlight Tours,** which offers a nighttime spotlight tour ($12, families $39), a full-day bush tour every day at 9am for $39, and a more extensive 4WD bush tour for $59. **Grampians Adventure Services,** in Shop 4 of the Stony Creek stores in Halls Gap center, runs a number of activities and tours and also rents mountain bikes. (☎ 5356 4556; www.grampians.org.au/gas. Open daily 10am-5pm. Climbing and abseiling $35-85; bike tours $30-40, night $30. Bike hire also available.)

LITTLE DESERT NATIONAL PARK

The Little Desert is not, in fact, a desert. So-christened because early settlers found the land ill-suited for farming, the Desert's 132,000 hectares are teeming with diverse vegetation and wildlife. In the late 1960s, the government announced that 80,000 hectares of the park would be subdivided and cleared for farmland, sparking one of Australia's first major preservation campaigns, which the environmentalists won. The harsh landscape won't wow you with sweeping vistas or spectacular wonders like the Grampians, but it beckons with subtle beauty—a delicately blooming wildflower here, a rare bird there.

⚡⚡ TRANSPORTATION & PRACTICAL INFORMATION. The Little Desert is best approached from Nhill (pop. 1900), north of the central parkland or from Dimboola (pop. 1500), on the Wimmera River to the east. Two V/Line (☎ 13 61 96) **buses** per day Sunday to Friday and one Saturday depart Nhill from the stop opposite Rintoule's Travel Service, with service to: Adelaide (4hr., $51.50); Ararat (2-4hr., $27); Ballarat (4-5hr., $42); Bendigo (4hr., $32); Dimboola (30min., $5.50); Horsham (1-2hr., $10); and Melbourne (5½-6½hr., $52). Dimboola's bus station is at Lochiel and Hindmarsh St.; the bus also stops at the Caltex Roadhouse on the corner of High and Horsham St. If arriving by car, be aware that the area between Horsham and the border with South Australia is an infamous speedtrap.

The **ranger station,** on Nursery Rd. in **Wail,** is 5km south of Dimboola on the Western Hwy. (☎ 5389 1204. Open M-F 8am-4:30pm.) **Parks Victoria** (☎ 13 19 63; www.parkweb.vic.gov.au) and the **Hindmarsh Info Centre** in Nhill, on Goldsworthy Park along Victoria St. (☎ 5391 3086; open daily 9am-5pm) have basic information about the area. **Rintoule's Travel Service** is at 37 Victoria St. in Nhill and can book tours of the park. (☎ 5391 1421. Open M-F 9am-5pm.) **Commonwealth Bank,** 14 Victoria St., Nhill, has a 24hr. **ATM.** Dimboola has no ATMs. **Nhill Online Solutions,** 121 Nelson St., has **Internet** access. (☎ 5391 1910. Open M-F 10am-5pm. $3 per hr., $1.50 min. charge.) The **post offices** are in Nhill, 98 Nelson St. (☎ 5391 1256; open M-F 9am-5pm; **Postal Code:** 3418), and Dimboola, 61 Lloyd St. (☎ 5389 1542; open M-F 9am-5pm; **Postal Code:** 3414).

VICTORIA

VICTORIA

ACCOMMODATIONS & FOOD. Get the complete experience at **Little Desert Nature Lodge ①**, set on over 600 acres of bush and owned and operated by Malleefowl expert Whimpey Reichelt and his wife Maureen. Take Nhill-Harrow Rd. 16km south of the Nhill town center; signs point the way. (☎5391 5232. Serves **dinners ④** when there's a full house ($20-25). Campsites for 2 $12.50, powered $15; bunks with no linens $24; singles with linens $48; twins and doubles $58. Book well ahead.) The lodge and aviary are also a nature-lover's mecca, full of unique flora and fauna of all sorts, but especially notable for their rare and diverse assortment of bird species (see **Sights and Activities,** p. 634). The informative film 'Whimpey's World' explains the history of the lodge and its role in wildlife conservation.

The **Farmers Arms Hotel ②**, 2 Victoria St., in Nhill, is a decent pubstay with clean, basic rooms, a TV lounge with refrigerator, and friendly staff. (☎5391 1955. Reception 10am-1am. Singles $20; doubles $30. Weekly $100/$150.) In Dimboola, along Horseshoe Bend Rd., 4km from the Dimboola post office, **Little Desert Log Cabins and Cottage ⑤** is right in the bush, near the park entrance, and offers self-contained cabins with the works. (☎5389 1122. Doubles from $75. Group discounts.)

There are two **camping areas ①**, one just south of **Kiata,** a hamlet on the Western Hwy. between Nhill and Dimboola, and the other at **Horseshoe Bend** and **Ackle Bend,** south of Dimboola. Both campgrounds have fireplaces, tables, and toilets. The fee covers six people and one vehicle ($11; additional vehicle $5; payable at any ranger station or in the pay receptacles at the campsites). Bush camping is allowed in the western and central blocks only and must be vehicle-based.

Nhill's restaurant pickings are slim. Get **groceries** at the IGA on Victoria St. (Open M-Th 8:30am-6:30pm, F 8:30am-7pm, Sa-8:30am-6pm, Su 9am-6pm.) Most pubs in both Nhill and Dimboola offer lunch and dinner.

SIGHTS & ACTIVITIES. Little Desert's unique ecology is best explored on foot, although 4WD drivers can usually use the rough, unpaved roads (often closed in winter) to reach remote corners. An excellent 30min. introductory walk leads to the lookout on **Pomponderoo Hill,** showing off typical area terrain. Go through the gate marked "Gateway to Little Desert" at Dimboola (not the official entrance), turn left after crossing the Wimmera River bridge, and go south, following the "National Park" signs; the trailhead is 1km past the entrance down a marked dirt road on the right. Other **walks** begin at the campground south of Kiata and at Gymbouen Rd., south of Nhill; large map boards at each campground show the trails. The hardcore can take on the 84km **Desert Discovery Walk,** a one- to four-day trek across the park's eastern section, doable in parts or at once. Detailed brochures on all the walks are available at ranger stations and tourist offices. The well-marked walk is best attempted in spring, when the weather is mild and the wildflowers are in bloom. Overnight campers should register at Wail's Park Office (☎5389 1204).

The **Little Desert Lodge** (☎5391 5232) has direct access to bushwalks, including the Lodge Loop (1hr.) and the Stringybark Loop (45min.). They also run 4WD tours, including a visit to Whimpey's **Malleefowl Sanctuary,** a stretch of protected land that attracts birdlovers. (Half-day tour $35; full-day $70. Min. 6 persons.) The **Malleefowl Aviary** at the Little Desert Lodge offers a closer view. (Open M-Sa 9:30am-4:30pm, Su 1:30-4:30pm, or by appointment. $5.50, children $3.)

GOLDFIELDS

In 1851, the first year of Victorian statehood and just two years after the California gold rush in the United States, this most precious of metals was discovered in the unassuming burg of Clunes. A year later, the *London Times* reported that 50,000 diggers had already converged upon Victoria's goldfields.

Gold proved the great equalizer of classes, as convicts hardened by years of manual labor—as well as rugged immigrants from all corners of the world—dug ore more efficiently than their effete bourgeois counterparts. Soon, the silk-clad landed gentry found themselves having to rub elbows with an unpedigreed nouveau riche. The established classes didn't willingly allow this social shake-up, and forced the Australian government to invoke mining taxes and grog prohibition, factors that ultimately led to the brief and bloody Eureka Rebellion of 1854. By the end of the 19th century, the mines were largely exhausted, and most of the boom towns withered away to ghost towns. A few, such as Ballarat and Bendigo, remain substantial cities.

BALLARAT ☎03

Victoria's second largest inland city (pop. 83,000), Ballarat is the self-appointed capital of the Goldfields and the birthplace of Australian democratic idealism: the site of the Eureka Rebellion. Although the gold is long gone, much of the 19th-century architecture has been preserved, and the city's golden past has been channeled into a bustling tourist trade that centers on **Sovereign Hill**, a replica of an old gold town, replete with townspeople dressed in period attire.

⌐ TRANSPORTATION

Trains and Buses: V/Line (☎13 61 96) services both buses and trains, depending on destination, from **Ballarat Station**, 202 Lydiard St. N., reached by bus #2 from Curtis St. Service to: Ararat (1¼hr., 6 per day, $13); Bendigo (2¼hr., 2 per day, $21); Castlemaine (1½hr., 1 per day, $14); Daylesford (40min., 1 per day, $10); Geelong (1¾hr., 3 per day, $11.40); Maryborough (1hr., 1 per day, $8.70); and Melbourne (1½hr., 12 per day, $16.40). Frequency varies Sa-Su.

Public Transportation: (☎5331 7777), most **bus** routes depart from behind Bridge Mall, on Curtis St. $1.55 ticket valid for 2 hours of unlimited use. Purchase from driver. Helpful transit guide (20¢) from tourist office or on bus. Services typically run every 35min. M-F 7am-6pm; Sa limited schedule. **Ballarat Taxis** (☎131 008) line up in the city center and run personal tours of Ballarat and nearby wineries.

Car Rental: Avis, 1113 Sturt St. between Talbort St. and Ascot St. (☎5332 8310). $39, limit 200km per day. **Budget,** 106 Market St. (☎5331 7788). $55 per 200km. Both agencies charge 27.5¢ per km above 200.

◪ ⊡ ORIENTATION & PRACTICAL INFORMATION

Ballarat straddles the Western Hwy., called **Sturt Street,** as it runs through town east to west. The **train station** is a few blocks north of Sturt on **Lydiard Street.** From the station, turn left on Lydiard and cross Mair St. to get to Sturt St. At its eastern end, Sturt becomes **Bridge Mall,** a pedestrian mall with shops, restaurants, and supermarkets. Following that, it becomes **Victoria Street,** which veers north, and **Main Road,** which veers south (not to be confused with Mair St., which runs parallel to Sturt St. one block north).

Tourist Office: 39 Sturt St. (☎5320 5741 or 1800 44 66 33 for accommodations bookings only; www.ballarat.com). From the V/Line station, walk left along Lydiard to Sturt St., turn left, and walk 1 block downhill to the corner of Albert St. Signs point the way. Free maps. Open daily 9am-5pm.

Banks: Banks and **ATMs** line Sturt St.

Laundromat: Ballarat Laundry, 711 Sturt St., near Raglan St. Open daily 6am-10pm.

Police: (☎5337 7222), on the corner of Dana and Albert St., behind the tourist center.

Internet Access: Free at the **library,** 178 Doveton St. N (☎5331 1211). Book ahead. Open M 1-6pm, Tu-Th 9:30am-6pm, F 9:30am-7pm, Sa 10am-1pm, Su 1:15-4pm. **Net-Connect Communications,** 33 Peel St. S (☎5332 2140). $5 per 30min. Open M-F 9am-5:30pm.

Post Office: (☎5336 5736), in the Central Sq. Marketplace. Fax services. Poste Restante. Open M-F 9am-5pm, Sa 9am-noon. **Postal Code:** 3350.

▐ ACCOMMODATIONS

Ballarat's accommodation market aims mostly at Melbourne families on weekend trips, but there are some budget options. Rooms tend to be in short supply because of the city's popularity with school groups, so book well in advance.

Sovereign Hill Lodge YHA (☎5333 3409; www.sovereignhill.com.au), on Magpie St. at Bourke St. Take bus #2 or #9 from Bridge Mall to Sovereign Hill or walk for about 20min. up a steep hill by following Peel St. south at the eastern end of Bridge Mall; take a left on Grant St. and then right on Magpie St. By car, follow signs to Sovereign Hill from Main Rd., then take Bradshaw St. to Magpie St. and turn left. Clean verging on sterile, but the beds may be the most comfortable hardwood bunks you'll ever find in a hostel. Laundry, kitchen, TV lounge, and bar. Heat, but no A/C. Linens included. Courteous staff issues discounted tickets for Sovereign Hill events. Reception Su-M 7am-10:30pm, Tu-Sa 24hr. book in advance due to hordes of school groups. Dorms $22, YHA $19; singles $28/$32. Limited wheelchair access. ❷

Irish Murphy's, 36 Sturt St. (☎5331 4091; ballarat@irishmurphys.com.au). A popular Aussie pub chain with live music Th-Su nights (F-Sa after 10pm cover $3). Clean doubles might be a tad loud for the light dozer. Communal unisex bathroom. Key deposit $10. Check-in after noon. Dorms $16, with linens and doona $19. ❷

Robin Hood Hotel, 33 Peel St. N (☎5331 3348). Fairly basic pub bunk accommodations with good location one block from Bridge Mall. Billiards bar and bistro downstairs (bistro open daily noon-2pm and 6-8:30pm). Book several days in advance on holidays and weekends. Bunks $25. ❷

Ballarat Goldfields Holiday Park, 108 Clayton St. (☎5332 7888 or 1800 632 237; www.ballaratgoldfields.com.au). Campsites and cabins 300m from Sovereign Hill. Kitchens, recreation rooms, playground, heated pool, and heated communal bathrooms. Internet $2 per 10min. Reception 8am-8pm. Book cabins in advance. Sites for 2 $19; powered $21, in summer $22; powered with bath $26/$28; 4- to 6-person ensuite heated cabins with A/C, kitchenette, and color TV from $65. ❶

▐ FOOD

Sturt St. is lined with fish 'n' chips shops, bakeries, and other takeaway places. The best cafes are up the hill, especially between Dawson and Doveton St. Lake Wendouree provides a serene view for numerous cafes as well. Coles 24hr. **supermarket,** a produce shop, and a bakery are at the far eastern end of Sturt St., behind the Bridge Mall at Peel St. Several inexpensive eateries sit just east of Sovereign Hill.

Restaurante Da Uday, 7 Wainwright St. (☎5331 6655), off the west side of the Main Rd. just north of Sovereign Hill. A quick hop away from Sovereign Hill, this two-room establishment serves Indian, Thai, and Italian cuisines ($9-20). It's not often that you can order gnocchi bolognaise with a side of garlic naan and a Thai iced tea all at the same restaurant. They also have a cheaper takeaway menu ($7.50-13.50). Reservations compulsory F-Su. Fully licensed or BYO (wine only). Open daily noon-2pm and 5:30-10:30pm. ❷

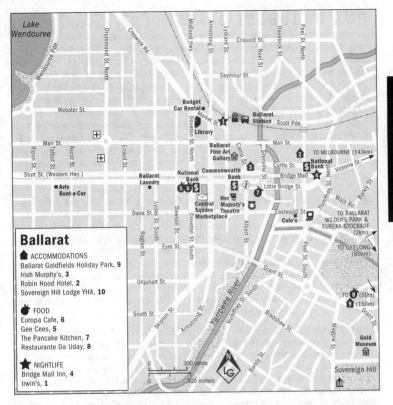

Ballarat

▲ ACCOMMODATIONS
Ballarat Goldfields Holiday Park, **9**
Irish Murphy's, **3**
Robin Hood Hotel, **2**
Sovereign Hill Lodge YHA, **10**

🍎 FOOD
Europa Cafe, **6**
Gee Cees, **5**
The Pancake Kitchen, **7**
Restaurante Da Uday, **8**

★ NIGHTLIFE
Bridge Mall Inn, **4**
Irwin's, **1**

VICTORIA

The Pancake Kitchen, 2 Grenville St. S (☎5331 6555). This restored 1870s building dishes out pancakes and crepes in assorted fruit or meat incarnations ($8-18). Daily specials and Tu half-priced drinks. Fully licensed or BYO. Open M 10am-10pm, Tu-Th 10am-late, F-Sa 7:30am-late, Su 7:30am-10pm. ❷

Europa Cafe, 411 Sturt St. (☎5331 2486). Mediterranean fare with an artsy New York feel. Chalkboard menu changes weekly. Mains $13.50-21, light fare $7.50-13.50. The large window counter is a great place to try one of their 79 Aussie wines. Fully licensed or BYO. Open Su-W 8:45am-6pm, Th-Sa 8:45am-late. ❶

Gee Cees, 427 Sturt St. (☎5331 6211; geecees@netconnect.com.au). Bright, big, and busy, Gee Cees serves gourmet food in an informal yet stylish setting. Order food (mains $15-20, pizzas $10-17) at the counter and drinks at the bar while a youthful waitstaff maintains fast service. Go early on weekends—it's crowded with locals and tourists. Food served daily 8am-late; bar open Su-Th until 11pm, F-Sa until midnight. ❷

🜨 SIGHTS

The Ballarat tourism network offers a *Welcome Pass* that includes two-day unlimited entry to Sovereign Hill, the Gold Museum, and the Eureka Stockade and Fine Art Gallery. ($32, concessions $22, children $15, families $82. Purchase from tourist office or at attractions.) Inquire at the Visitors Center about tours of Ballarat's

OUR PROUDEST DEFEAT The story of Ballarat's Eureka Rebellion, Australia's closest brush with civil war, is told *ad nauseum*. During the gold rush, the colonial government in Melbourne set up a system to milk the miners of their spoils. Miners had to pay a license fee whether or not they found gold—and the regular license hunts filled the governor's pockets. The "police" were ex-convicts drafted to "keep order" in the bustling gold towns. A digger found without a license was ordered to pay a fine of £10 or was chained to a log until he could (to keep the arrested man's hands in the cuffs, the police often smashed them with a mallet so they would bruise and swell). When Scottish miner James Scobie was murdered outside the hotel of a government supervisor, the already tense situation boiled over. The miners formed a reform league and shortly set up a stockade on the Eureka Lead. They burned their licenses, swore allegiance to the Southern Cross flag, and defended themselves valiantly—albeit briefly—when government forces attacked the next day. On December 3, 1854, 30 miners were killed and 114 taken prisoner. But the brutality outraged the rest of Australia, and reforms were soon passed abolishing the licenses and giving miners representation and voting rights. All those charged with High Treason were acquitted, and the miners' leader, Peter Lalor, later became Speaker of the House. Ballarat retains a stronghold on its past by billing itself "the birthplace of Australian democracy."

historic areas. The **Ballarat Begonia Festival** (Mar. 5-15, 2004) is an open-air arts and crafts fair. **Royal South Street** music, debate, and performance competitions attract top talent (late Aug.-mid Oct. 2004). The tree-lined pathways of **Victoria Park,** south of Lake Wendouree, make for a good view of the city, and a hike up to the **lookout** on Black Hill is a quiet spot for a nighttime stroll.

■**SOVEREIGN HILL.** While a reconstructed gold town built around a mine won't make you rich, Sovereign Hill will at least give you a taste of the area's wealthy past. Sovereign Hill staff, dressed in period attire, roam about town pretending to be miners and townfolk. The exhibits here include gold-pouring, candle-making, smelting, musket-firing, and a 40min. tour of the mine that reveals the harsh conditions of mining life. Pan for gold yourself or ride the horse-drawn carriage through the streets of this outdoor museum. *(Take bus #2, 9 or 10. Signs point the way.☎5331 1944. Open daily 10am-5pm. Combined admission with Gold Museum $27, concessions $20, children $13, families $70.)*

GOLD MUSEUM. Declaring that "the story of gold is firmly linked to the story of man," this Sovereign Hill appendage traces the importance of gold across time and cultures. It also houses an expensive collection of gold coins, ornaments, and replicas of the two largest gold nuggets ever found. If you somehow grow tired of gold, the museum also features some interesting but unrelated exhibits, including a section on the Chinese in Australia, an Aboriginal display with an assortment of boomerangs, and the Ballarat Sports Hall of Fame, containing the Sydney 2000 Olympic torch. *(Next to Sovereign Hill, on Bradshaw St. ☎5331 1944. Open daily in summer 9:30am-6pm; in winter 9:30am-5:20pm. $6.80, concessions $4.20, children $3.30.)*

■**BALLARAT WILDLIFE PARK.** The park's 14 acres of open bush are home to some of Australia's diverse fauna, including fearsome saltwater crocodiles and Tasmanian devils, and less imposing emus, goannas, wombats, koalas, and free-roaming 'roos that will eat right out of your hand. The weekend crocodile feed is a special thrill. *(On York St. at Fussel St. Take bus #8 or 9 or drive down Victoria St. to the stoplights at Fossell St. and turn right. The park is at the intersection of Fossell and York St. ☎5333 5933; wildlife@lin.cbl.com.au. Tours 11am. Open daily 9am-5:30pm. $14, students $12, children $8, families $39.)*

EUREKA STOCKADE. This sleek $4 million multimedia adventure commemorates the Eureka Rebellion on the site of the miners' stockade. If you've already seen **Blood on the Southern Cross** (see below), the 1hr. self-guided tour may be a little redundant. *(Eureka St. at Rodier St. Drive 2km out of town on Main Rd. and turn right at the Eureka St. roundabout; it's 1km up the road. Or, take bus #8.* ☎5333 1854; www.sovereign-hill.com.au/eureka.htm. Open daily 9am-5pm. $8, concessions $6, children $4, families $22.)*

🎵 🎭 ENTERTAINMENT & WINERIES

On weekends, the **Bridge Mall** at the east end of Sturt St. fills with pedestrians and street musicians. Numerous hotels and pubs serve as venues for live bands. The **Bridge Mall Inn**, 92 Bridge Mall, encourages up-and-coming musicians and draws university students from the area. (☎5331 3132. Open Tu-Sa 7pm-late.) The locals prefer the digs at **Irwin's**, 121 Lydiard St., across from the train station. Jugs $7 nightly 6-10pm. Sa chill to "techno funk-nasia." (☎5332 1660. Open daily 1pm-4am.) The historic **Her Majesty's Theatre**, 13 Lydiard St. (☎5333 5888; www.her-maj.com), presents live drama, with tickets ranging anywhere from $20-50. Call ahead for show information. **Blood for the Southern Cross**, a twice-nightly 80min. sound and light show under the open night sky at Sovereign Hill, is worth the price. It introduces diggers' lives on Sovereign Hill and recounts the bitter Eureka Rebellion. (☎5333 5777. M-Sa, also Su during holiday periods. $31, concessions $25, children $17, families $85. Book ahead.)

Most vineyards in the Ballarat region began production in the 1980s. With cool-climate Chardonnays becoming increasingly popular, the region is on the rise. Get the *Wine Regions of Victoria* booklet in local tourist offices. At 🏆**Dulcinea Vineyard**, owner Rod Stott urges visitors to roam his small cellar and vineyard, tasting his delectable blends as he answers questions on the way. Take the Midland Hwy. from Ballarat north 11km toward Creswick. (☎5334 6440; dulcinea@cbl.com.au. Open daily 9am-5pm. Bottles $10-18.) **St. Anne's Vineyards**, 22km east of Ballarat and 77km from Melbourne off the Western Hwy., has free tastings in a cool, blue stone cottage. A peppery red Shiraz and a fortified tawny port top the list. (☎5368 7209. Open M-Sa 9am-5pm, Su 10am-5pm.)

FROM BALLARAT TO BENDIGO

The Midland Hwy. goes north from Ballarat toward Bendigo, meeting the Calder Hwy. (from Melbourne) at Harcourt, 9km north of Castlemaine.

DAYLESFORD & HEPBURN SPRINGS. Daylesford is 107km northwest of Melbourne and 45km northeast of Ballarat. Visitors come here to soak in the waters of its neighbor, Hepburn Springs, which contains the largest concentration of **curative mineral springs** in Australia. Aborigines revered the springs even before European settlement, but many guest cottages and B&Bs have sprung up recently. New Age commercialism has infused these quiet communities replete with healing crystals, essences, oils, and aromatherapy. While most of the restaurants and services are in Daylesford, the spa complex is in Hepburn Springs, 4km north. **Buses** run between the towns (depart every 25-45min. from the main roundabout in the center of Daylesford), but it is a pleasant 40-minute walk if you're up for it. The **Hepburn Regional Park** lets you pump your own mineral water, but take care to avoid falling into abandoned mine shafts (maps at info center).

Most of the area's lovely guest cottages and B&Bs will set you back $80-100 per night. **Continental House ❷**, 9 Lone Pine Ave., described by some of its patrons as a living work of art (and by others as a hippie hideaway), is secluded behind an impressively dense 5m tall hedge just a few hundred meters from the spa. Refresh yourself at this vegetarian, relaxed guest house with tranquil common areas, a full kitchen, basic bunkrooms, and a health banquet Sa night. Prices vary depending on length of stay and, in the case of private rooms, number of people. (☎ 5348 2005. Linens $3. Bunks $25, concessions $18; singles $35/$30; doubles $27/$23.) The **Hepburn Spa Resort,** in Hepburn Springs, provides the works. Services range from the normal pool and spa (weekdays $10, weekends $14) to massages (45min., $58) to flotation tanks (30min., $42). Use of spring waters is free. (☎ 5348 2034; www.hepburnspa.com.au. Open M-Th 10am-7pm, F 10am-8pm, Sa 9am-10pm, Su 9am-7pm.)

CASTLEMAINE. Sleepy and provincial, this town 120km northwest of Melbourne in the central Goldfields has quiet charm and bears the unexpected moniker "Street Rod Capital of Australia." Sure enough, hotrods, three-wheelers, and even the occasional low rider gun down the main drag at regular intervals. If you've got money to spare, stay at the **Old Castlemaine Gaol ❹,** on Bowden St., overlooking the town atop the hill to the west of the railroad station. The 1861 jail held felons, lunatics, and juvenile offenders before its 1990 renovation into a well-heated and ventilated B&B. The dungeons, once the site of horrific torture, now house a wine bar and lounge. The Gaol won't take groups smaller than 20 unless a large group is already here, but even if you're not staying, it's worth taking a self-guided tour. (☎ 5470 5311; www.gaol.castlemaine.net.au. Tours $5, children $2.50, families $11. Call ahead. Bunk-style dorms $55; doubles $170.)

In case the jail thing just doesn't work out, nearby Maldon has the surprisingly nice **Central Service Centre Accommodations ❸,** at the merging of Main and High St. This garage-turned-hotel features heating and A/C, bathroom, TV, fridge, and coffee and tea in every room. (☎ 5475 2216. Reception 8am-5:30pm. Singles $30; doubles and twins $60.)

Only 4km east of Castlemaine on Hwy B180 towards Melbourne is the wild and popular ▨**Dingo Farm Australia.** Just past the "Welcome to Chewton" sign, turn right and drive 3km along what quickly becomes a dirt road. Bruce, the amiable one-of-a-kind caretaker, has been breeding these peculiar canines for nearly 24 years in an attempt to keep the purebred dingo from becoming extinct. Although dangerous in the wild, over 100 are domesticated and sheltered, right on the premises. (☎ 5470 5711; www.ins.net.au/dingofarm. $8, children $4. Large groups book in advance. Open daily 9am-5pm.)

BENDIGO ☎ 03

Like almost all the Victorian goldfields' towns, Bendigo (pop. 90,000) sprang into existence in the 1850s when scores of miners flooded in, lured by the promise of striking it rich. While many of its neighbors were tossed from prosperity to obscurity by the boom and bust cycle, Bendigo continued to prosper into the 20th century thanks to its seemingly endless supply of gold-rich alluvial quartz. (Though it stopped mining commercially in 1954, Bendigo still holds rank as the second-highest gold producer in the country.)

▌ TRANSPORTATION

Trains and Buses: Bendigo Station is behind the Discovery Centre at the south end of Mitchell St. **V/Line** (☎ 13 61 96) has **trains** and **buses,** depending on destination, to: Adelaide (8½hr., 1 per day, $62); Ballarat (2hr., 1 per day, $21); Daylesford (1¼hr., 1 per day, $12.50); Geelong (3¾hr., 1 per day, $35); Maldon (2hr., 2 per day, $9) via Castlemaine (22min., 11 per day, $6.20); Maryborough (1hr., 3 per day, $10); Mildura (5hr., 4 per day, $55); Melbourne (2hr., 11 per day, $22.50); and Swan Hill (3½hr., 2-3 per day, $28). Infrequent service Sa-Su. Round trips Tu-Th 10% off.

Public Transportation: Local **buses** depart from the corner of Hargreaves and Mitchell St. **Taxis** line up along Queen St. between Mitchell and Williamson St.

Car Rental: Hertz (☎5443 5088), at the corner of High and Thistle St. From $39 for 300km per day, 23¢ each additional kilometer. Open M-F 8:30am-5:30pm, Sa 8:30am-12:30pm, Su 9-11am. **Budget,** 150-152 High St. (☎5442 2766). $48 for 330km per day. Open M-F 8:30am-5:30pm, Sa 8:30am-12:30pm, Su 9-11am.

🔆 🔢 ORIENTATION & PRACTICAL INFORMATION

Bendigo is a combination of well-planned streets and winding gullies packed down by diggers' feet. Most points of interest are near the city center, bounded on the south and east by railroad tracks and on the north by Rosalind Park. The **Calder Highway (Hwy. 79)** from Melbourne runs into the city center, becoming High St., then Pall Mall (at Charing Cross), then McCrae St., and eventually **Midland Highway,** which leads to Elmore and Echuca. The popular pedestrian **Hargreaves Mall** runs one block along Hargreaves between Mitchell and Williamson St.

Tourist Office: 51-67 Pall Mall (☎/fax 5444 4445), in the Victorian post-office building. Mini-museum detailing Bendigo's history. Open daily 9am-5pm.

Currency Exchange: ANZ (☎5443 9399), on the corner of Queen and Mitchell St. Open M-Th 9:30am-4pm, F 9:30am-5pm. 24hr. **ATM.**

Bookstores: Book Now (☎5443 8587), on Farmers Ln. off Bridge St., carries a brilliant selection of cheap secondhand books that occasionally attracts shoppers from as far as Melbourne. Open daily 10am-5pm. **Bendigo Bookmark,** 29 High St. (☎5441 7866), will buy, sell, and exchange. Open M-F 9:30am-5:30pm, Sa 9:30am-1pm.

Public Library: 251-259 Hargreaves St. (☎5443 5100; www.ncgrl.vic.gov.au). **Internet** access. First 15min. free, each additional 30min. $3. Open M-F 10am-7pm, Sa 10am-1pm.

Police: (☎5440 2510), on Bull St. behind the law courts.

Internet Access: In the public library (see above). **Bendigo Web Central,** 36 High St. (☎5442 6411), has a fast connection and charges $5 per hr. Open M-F 9am-9pm, Sa-Su 10am-7pm.

Post Office: (☎13 13 18), on the corner of Hargreaves and Williamson St. Open M-F 9am-5pm, Sa 9:30am-12:30pm. Poste Restante. **Postal Code:** 3550.

🚩 ACCOMMODATIONS

The strip of Calder Hwy./High St. running south of town is loaded with cookie-cutter chain motels. Nicer motels and B&Bs ($50-90 per person per night) infused with historical charm line McCrae and Napier St. just northeast of the city center.

🏠 **NOMADS Ironbark Bush Cabins** (☎5448 3344; www.bwc.com.au/ironbark), on Watson St. Located 5km from the city center, the Ironbark is out of walking distance, but the owners will pick you up from Bendigo station. By car, head north on Pall Mall. Turn left onto Nolan St. and then right onto Bridge St. Follow the tram tracks until the train tracks, continuing onto Finn St. Watson St. is on the right, across from a yellow Ironbark sign. A refreshing and pleasant taste of the bush with 8 small, tidy cabins that sleep 4 to 9 people. A recently-built 5-room dorm features cozy 4-bed ensuite rooms. All cabins have heating, bathrooms, refrigerators, and coffee makers. Towels and linens included. BBQ (dinner $12) and bar (beer $2.50) in evenings around the campfire (when there's no fire ban), and a brand-new 🏊 **75m waterslide** to keep you cool in summer. On-site horseback riding $20 per 30min., $28 per hr. Gold panning and metal detector rentals (see **Bendigo Goldfields Experience,** p. 643). Special weekend package deals include horseback riding and meals. All beds $20. ❷

VICTORIA

Buzza's Bendigo Backpacker YHA, 33 Creek St. (☎/fax 5443 7680; buzza@ben-digo.net.au). A comfortable converted house in a quiet residential area close to the center of town. Three individual shower/bathrooms offer some privacy, while the large dining room and the reading room with open fireplace and TV allow guests to interact at their leisure. Linens and towels included. Laundry $2. Internet $2 per 30min. Free parking. Check-in 8:30-11:30am and 4:30-10pm. Dorms $21, YHA $17; singles $35/$31; doubles $52/$44. Family suite also available. Wheelchair-accessible. ❷

Marlborough House, 115 Wattle St. (☎5441 4142; http://home.primus.com.au/marlboroughhouse), on the corner of Rowan St. A gorgeous B&B that looks a bit like a palace and makes guests feel like royalty. The 130-year-old house overlooks the city and sits just a block from the Sacred Heart Cathedral. Guests are pampered with a courtyard garden, intimate library, drawing room, and TV room. Sunlit bedrooms are spacious and well-decorated, with all but one containing queen-sized beds (twins available) as well as delightful ensuites. Full breakfast included in room price; guests order from the house menu and are served in the dining room. Reception 24hr. Su-Th singles $90; doubles $145. F-Sa all rooms $145. ❺

Shamrock Hotel (☎5442 0333), on the corner of Pall Mall and Williamson St. A local landmark with a quintessentially Victorian aesthetic. The first floor drawing room and terrace over Williamson St. are a tour-de-force. All rooms are nicely furnished and have heat, fridge, minibar, TV, and free tea/coffee. "Traditional Rooms" (comfortable, with shared bath, can fit up to 4) $70; ensuite rooms $95; 2-room suites $180. Reception M-F 7:30am-8:30pm, Sa 7:30am-9:30pm, Su 8am-7:30pm. ❺

Central City Caravan Park, 362 High St. (☎/fax 5443 6937), at Beech St. Take bus #1 from Hargreaves Mall. The CCCP, a former YHA affiliate, is the cheapest place around, offering hostel accommodation with full kitchen, comrade. Sites for 2 $15, powered $20; dorms $15. Reception M-F 9-11am and 2-4pm, Sa-Su 9-11am. ❶

🍴 FOOD

Most popular restaurants are near the tourist office, especially on Bull St. and Pall Mall; Main St. also has several options. Budget-friendly restaurants are all around town. The **Hargreaves Mall** has a food court that bustles during lunch hours. Coles 24hr. **supermarket** (☎5004 436 311) is on the corner of Myers and Williamson St.

Cafe Kryptonite, 92 Pall Mall (☎5443 9777). Features meals ($9.90-21.50) almost as colorful as its interior design, as well as several veggie options and a braggable selection of wine and tea (from $3). Open daily 10am-late. ❷

Pugg Mahones (☎5443 4916), on the corner of Bull and Hargreaves St. Beautiful stained-glass windows and dark-wood bar. Pub-style mains $12.50-17.50. Open M-Sa noon-2:30pm; also M-W 6-9pm, Th-Sa 6-9:30pm. ❷

Gillie's Famous Pies (☎5443 4965), on the corner of Hargreaves Mall and Williamson St., features meat pies and sweet cakes ($2-3). Open M-Th 8:30am-6pm, F 8:30am-8pm, Sa 9am-5:30pm, Su 10am-5pm. ❶

Toi Shan, 65-67 Mitchell St. (☎5443 5811). All-you-can-eat smorgasbord meal Tu-F 11:30am-2:30pm ($9.30), F 5-9pm ($10.30) and convenient self-serve takeaway packs ($4-7). Open Tu-F 11:30am-2:30pm and 5-9pm, Sa noon-2:30pm and 5-9:30pm, Su noon-2:30pm and 5-9pm. ❶

👁 SIGHTS & OUTDOORS

CENTRAL DEBORAH MINE. 80min. tours take visitors 61m down the last mine to operate commercially in Bendigo. Explanations of mining history and techniques are interactive; volunteer and you may even get to show off your skill with the

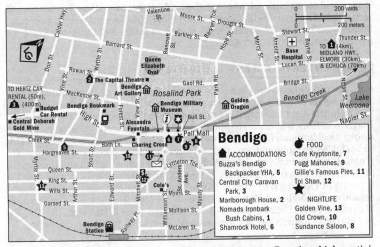

Bendigo

ACCOMMODATIONS
Buzza's Bendigo
  Backpacker YHA, **5**
Central City Caravan
  Park, **3**
Marlborough House, **2**
Nomads Ironbark
  Bush Cabins, **1**
Shamrock Hotel, **6**

FOOD
Cafe Kryptonite, **7**
Pugg Mahones, **9**
Gillie's Famous Pies, **11**
Toi Shan, **12**

NIGHTLIFE
Golden Vine, **13**
Old Crown, **10**
Sundance Saloon, **8**

drill. True thrill-seekers can try the **Underground Adventure Tour,** in which participants don miner's garb and go down one extra level to use real mine equipment for two hours. *(76 Violet St.☎ 5443 8322, group bookings 5443 8255; www.central-deborah.com. Open daily 9:30am-5pm. Regular tours 7 per day, every 70min. $17, concessions $15. Underground Adventure: with lunch $53, concessions $48, children $28, families $135; with morning/afternoon tea $45/$41/$23/$115.)*

BENDIGO GOLDFIELDS EXPERIENCE. Located at the NOMADS Ironbark (see **Accommodations,** p. 641), the Goldfields Experience could pay for your entire trip, if you're lucky. If not, at least you'll have bragging rights that you learned how to pan for gold. *(On Watson St., 5km outside of town.☎ 5448 4140; www.bendigogold.com.au. Metal detector rental $45.75 per day. Gold panning $10 per hour (includes 15min. lesson). Bike hire $20 per day. Open daily 8:30am-5pm.)*

LANDMARKS. Tours, complete with recorded commentary, cover the town using the restored turn-of-the-century tram system (1hr.; $12.90, concessions $11.50, children $9, families $46). Trams run hourly, picking up from the elaborate **Alexandra Fountain** near the tourist office or from the Central Deborah Mine. The late-Victorian feel of Bendigo's architecture is most pronounced along **Pall Mall.** Most impressive are the **old post office building** (which now houses the Visitors Center) and the adjacent Bendigo Law Courts, both with ornate facades on all four sides. The **Shamrock Hotel,** at the corner of Williamson St. and Pall Mall, began as a roaring entertainment hall in the golden 1850s. **Rosalind Park,** on the site of the old 1850s police barracks north of Alexandra Fountain, is a vast expanse of greenery scattered with winding pathways, trees, and statues—including a fairly unflattering likeness of Queen Victoria. If you brave the 124-step climb up its observation tower, the reward is a view of Bendigo and the surrounding gold country. The stunning **Sacred Heart Cathedral,** on High St. between Wattle St. and Short St., sends its spires soaring towards heaven from atop a hill overlooking town.

GOLDEN DRAGON MUSEUM. This collection provides an overview of both Chinese culture in Australia and its particular impact on Bendigo. Displays offer a look at the Chinese-Australian experience in the place they dubbed "Dai Gum San" (Big Gold Mountain), but do gloss a bit over the racism that Chinese-Australians often faced. The collection's highlight is the fantastically ornate Sun Loong, the longest and oldest imperial dragon in the world at just over 100m. The **tea room** ❷ serves light fare from $6-12. *(5-9 Bridge St. ☎5441 5044; www.goldendragonmusem.org. Open daily 9:30am-5pm. $7, concessions $5, children $4, families $20. Garden only $2.20, children 60¢. Tea room open 9:30am-4:30pm.)*

🎵 🎸 ENTERTAINMENT & NIGHTLIFE

Pubs are everywhere. Most are tame local hangouts that close around midnight, but weekends can be rowdier when tourists funnel into its small watering holes. The main late-night entertainment options are on the few blocks of Pall Mall and Hargreaves from Williamson to Mundy St. The **Old Crown,** 238 Hargreaves St., is a smoky neighborhood haunt filled with families by day and burly locals at night. (☎5441 6888. Karaoke and live music on weekends. Occasional cover $3. Open Th-F until 1-2am, Sa until 3am.) **Pugg Mahones,** on the corner of Bull and Hargreaves St., offers a selection of Irish beers on tap ($3.50 a pot) and live music (W-Sa) starting at 10pm. (No cover. Open until 1-2am.) There's more live music at the **Sundance Saloon,** on Pall Mall and Mundy St., which hosts Melbourne's top cover bands on Thursdays. (☎5441 8222. Open Th-Sa 8:30pm-late.) The **Golden Vine,** 135 King St. (☎5443 6063), attracts a young local crowd with its chill music and late nights.

MURRAY RIVER AREA

Australia's longest river, the Murray, rambles along the New South Wales-Victoria border for 2600km before meeting the sea in South Australia's Encounter Bay. The river became an essential artery in the late 19th century, its waters traveled by giant freight-toting paddlesteamers, but extensive rail and road networks rendered these boats obsolete by the end of the 1930s. Today the river feeds production of vegetables and fruits (including wine grapes) through a complex irrigation system. It's also a favorite spot for picnicking, water sports, and fishing, drawing travelers for a day or a week of relaxation along the banks of the grand old Murray.

ECHUCA   ☎03

As the closest point to Melbourne along the Murray, Echuca was once Australia's largest inland port and a clearinghouse for the wool and agricultural products of southern New South Wales. Old-time facades dominate its main streets, but despite its exterior, Echuca has the bustle of an entirely modern city and its tourist industry avoids the theme-park hokeyness of other historic river towns, making this the best place to immerse yourself in the Murray riverboat culture.

🚍 TRANSPORTATION

V/Line buses run from the **Visitors Centre** or the Ampol Road House on the Northern Hwy. to: Albury (3-4hr., 1-3 per day, $23-39); Bendigo (1¼hr., 1-3 per day, $7); Melbourne (3½-4hr., 4-6 per day, $31); Mildura (5½hr.; 1 per day M, W, Th, Sa; $38); Swan Hill (2hr., 1-2 per day, $21). A **steam locomotive** now runs from Melbourne Apr.-Nov. on the last Sunday of every month, Dec. on the weekend before Christmas. The train leaves Melbourne at 8:15am, arrives at the Echuca Station at noon, and then gives its riders 4hr. to tour Echuca before leaving for Melbourne at 4pm and arriving at 8pm. (☎5221 8966. Open M-F 9am-5pm. Economy non-A/C tickets $55, with guided tour $85; children $10/$25; concessions $35/$60; families $100/$148. Book ahead.)

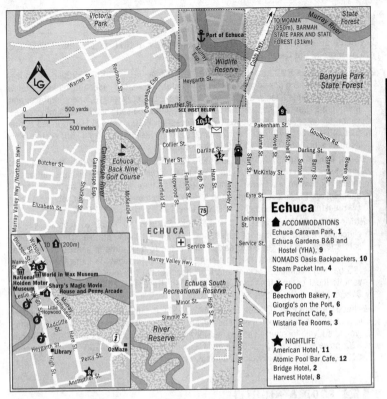

Echuca

▲ ACCOMMODATIONS
Echuca Caravan Park, 1
Echuca Gardens B&B and
    Hostel (YHA), 9
NOMADS Oasis Backpackers, 10
Steam Packet Inn, 4

🍴 FOOD
Beechworth Bakery, 7
Giorgio's on the Port, 6
Port Precinct Cafe, 5
Wistaria Tea Rooms, 3

★ NIGHTLIFE
American Hotel, 11
Atomic Pool Bar Cafe, 12
Bridge Hotel, 2
Harvest Hotel, 8

VICTORIA

✈ 🛈 ORIENTATION & PRACTICAL INFORMATION

Echuca, from the Aboriginal word meaning "meeting of the waters," lies about 200km north of Melbourne at the intersection of two rivers, the **Campaspe** (north-south) and the **Murray** (east-west), and of two highways, the **Murray Valley Highway** and **Northern Highway**. Echuca's main drags are **Hare** and **High Street,** parallel roads that run north-south from the Murray River to the Murray Valley Hwy. From the Visitors Centre, take the bridge across the Muray to the **Cobb Highway** in Echuca's twin city of **Moama** in New South Wales, notable predominantly for its diverse array of gambling clubs.

The **Visitor Information Centre,** 2 Heygarth St., is on the Echuca side of the Echuca-Moama bridge. (☎5480 7555 or 1800 804 446; www.echucamoama.com. Open daily 9am-5pm.) **ANZ, National,** and **Commonwealth banks** with 24hr. **ATMs** are side by side on Hare St., just south of Anstruther St. (All open M-Th 9:30am-4pm, F 9:30am-5pm.) The **library,** at the corner of Heygarth and High St. across the intersection from McDonald's, offers **Internet** access. (Research free, email $2.50 per 30min. Book ahead at ☎5482 1997. Open M-Tu and Th-F 10am-5:30pm, W noon-8pm, Sa 10am-1pm, Su 2-4:30pm.) The **police** station (☎5482 2255) is at 7-11 Dickenson St. and the **post office** is on the corner of Hare and Anstruther St. (Open M-F 9am-5pm, Sa 9am-noon.) **Postal Code:** 3564.

VICTORIA

🏠 ACCOMMODATIONS

Echuca's accommodation scene consists mostly of luxury riverside B&Bs and pricey motels, but there are a few budget options.

Echuca Gardens B&B and Hostel (YHA), 103 Mitchell St. (☎5480 6522; www.echuca-gardens.com), 8 blocks east from the city center. The second-oldest hostel in Australia. Beautiful gardens filled with fruit trees. Kitchen, BBQ, cozy lounge, open fireplace, and memorable German Shepherd named Baron. Sauna and spa encourage friendly conversation among guests. Key deposit $10. Reception 8-10am and 5-10pm. 4-bed dorms $21.50; doubles $49; ensuite B&B singles with TV Su-Th $80, F-Sa $100; ensuite B&B doubles with TV Su-Th from $120. YHA discount $3.50. ❷

Steam Packet Inn, 37 Murray Esplanade (☎5482 3411). A worthwhile extravagance. The Steam Packet is located on the port in one of the original port buildings and appropriately decorated in a typical 1860s style. Guests here are pampered by the new management with luxurious ensuite rooms, A/C, refrigerators, electric blankets, and color TV. Breakfast included. Singles $80; doubles Su-Th $90, F-Sa $130. ❺

NOMADS Oasis Backpackers, 410-422 High St. (☎5480 7866; www.backpackersechuca.com), on the corner of Pakenham. In town and well-kept, this NOMADS outpost caters largely to budget backpackers who come to pick fruits in season in the area. Courtesy bus transports guests to picking sites nearby. Kitchen, TV lounge, and Internet ($5 per hr.) available. Lockers and thick-beam beds. The room key gets discounts at various local establishments. Linens included. Reception 24hr. 4- to 12-bed dorms $18; doubles $46. Weekly $118/$300. ❷

Echuca Caravan Park, Crofton St. (☎5482 2157). Gigantic and sprawling, but nevertheless choked with campervans, especially during the holiday seasons, due to the campground's idyllic location right on the Murray River. No linens. Sites for 2 $22, off-peak $20; powered $24/$22; 5- or 6-person ensuite cabins $80-98/$65-78, extra persons $10, extra children $5. Book in advance. ❶

🍴 FOOD & NIGHTLIFE

The standard Australian assortment of chip shops, grub-serving pubs, and fast-food joints line High St., and the Murray Esplanade has more upmarket riverfront spots. If at the port, check out **Wistaria Tea Rooms** ❷, 51 Murray Esplanade, for a delicious meal in 19th-century style. (☎5482 4210. Open 8am through lunchtime.) Otherwise, have a focaccia ($6.80), a pie ($1.10-3.25), or a fresh snickerdoodle (love at first bite, $4.10) at the **Beechworth Bakery** ❶, 513-517 High St. (☎5480 6999. Open daily 6am-7pm.) **Port Precinct Cafe** ❶, 591 High St., serves breakfast all day ($5-11) and inexpensive gourmet burgers ($4-6) by an open fire. Their **Internet cafe** is unfortunately not as cheap. (☎5480 2163. $2 per 12min., $9 per hr. Open daily 8am-5pm or later.) For a splurge, visit **Giorgio's On the Port** ❸, 527 High St. (☎5482 6117), which is not actually on the port, but serves authentic Italian meals from $16 nevertheless. There is also a 24hr. Coles **supermarket** located on the corner of High and Darling St.

Numerous pubs on High and Hare St. are peopled by crowds of friendly locals. The most active watering holes in town are the **Harvest Hotel,** at the corner of Hare and Anstruther St., the **Bridge Hotel** on Murray Esplanade right by the port, and the **American Hotel** at Hare and Pakenham St. A younger crowd chills at the **Atomic Pool Bar Cafe,** 207 Darling St., which draws in customers with the offer of free pool all day Sa-Su. (☎5480 2227. Open Su noon-1pm; Tu-Th 5pm-1am, F 5pm-2am, Sa noon-2am. F-Sa cover $5 after 10pm.)

⚙ SIGHTS

Although most of Echuca's sights center around its storied paddlesteamer history, the small river-town atmosphere of the place provides some great day-strolls that are sure to enchant visitors.

HISTORIC PORT. The main attraction in Echuca is its port, consisting of the wharf and several historic buildings. The 1865 red-gum wharf has three levels to accommodate changing river conditions. Blacksmith and woodturning shops sell handmade wares, and a steam display explains the workings of the portentous invention that brought on the Industrial Revolution. (*Historic Port Area, along Murray Esplanade.* ☎5482 4248; www.portofechuca.org.au. Open daily 9am-5pm. $10.50, concessions $9, children $6.50, families $29.50.)

PORT PRECINCT. The port precinct, which is free for strolling, has several old hotels on display. The **Star Hotel** (☎5480 1181) is equipped with every fraternity brother's dream: a secret underground tunnel that allowed drinkers to escape police raids after the place was de-licensed in 1897. The **Bridge Hotel,** (☎5482 2247) Echuca's first, has a carefully preserved suite and gallery upstairs. At the other end is the old **Customs House,** which exacted tariffs from passing watercraft during Echuca's days as the commercial hub of the Murray. Today, the Customs House building is home to the **Murray Esplanade Cellars,** which exacts a tariff of zero dollars for sampling its excellent wines and spirits. (*2 Leslie St.* ☎5482 6058. Open daily 9:30am-5:30pm. Free entry.) An even tastier stop is **Iron House Coopers** (☎5480 6955), in the old Freeman's Foundry at 13-17 Murray Esplanade, where you can sample a myriad of intriguing port wines, including Jack Daniels and Jim Beam varieties. (*Open M-Sa 9am-5pm, Su 10am-5pm.*)

PADDLESTEAMERS. Several paddlesteamers still ply the waters off the old port and are now open to the public for leisurely cruises. The Port Authority runs one-hour cruises on *P.S. Pevensey, P.S. Alexander Arbuthnot,* and the **P.S. Adelaide,** the oldest wooden paddlesteamer in Australia. Buy tickets at 52 Murray Esplanade. (☎5482 4248. 5 per day. $16.50, concessions $13.30, children $7, families $40. Joint port and cruise: $22/$18/$12/$54.) A private company runs the paddlesteamers *Pride of the Murray* and *Emmylou;* the *Emmylou* is worth the slightly higher price, and if you really want to splurge, overnight **accommodation ❺** is available from $180 per person. (*Buy tickets at the Custom House Agents or at 57 Murray Esplanade.* ☎5480 2237 or 5482 5244. Pride of the Murray: 1hr.; 6 per day; $13.50, seniors $12, children $6.50, families $38. Emmylou: 5 per day; 1hr.; $16.50, children $8; 1½hr. $20, children $10.) The same company also runs 1hr. cruises on the steamer *P.S. Canberra.* ($15, seniors $13.50, children $7.50, families $40.)

WORLD IN WAX MUSEUM. Although not particularly relevant to the history of the Murray, the wax museum in front of the port could be the most fun place in town. Figures include dignitaries both foreign and domestic, arranged by era and disposition (amusingly, Stalin, Hitler, and Castro share a case with Churchill). Humorously informative notes line the walls. (*630 High St.* ☎/fax 5482 3630. Open daily 9am-5:30pm. $9, concessions $8, children $4.50. YHA discount $1.)

NATIONAL HOLDEN MOTOR MUSEUM. For car-lovers or those who want a fascinating perspective on an iconic slice of Australiana, the Holden Motor Museum is a must-see. It showcases over 50 years of "Australia's Own" automobile, with over 40 lovingly restored Holden models, including the only space-age 1969 experimental "Hurricane." The amusing video retrospective spotlights not only the car, but also Australia's love for Holden ads. (*7-11 Warren St.* ☎5480 2033. Open daily 9am-5pm. $6, concessions $4.50, children $3, families $14.)

SWAN HILL ☎ 03

Tranquil, rural Swan Hill, located on the Murray River about 340km northwest of Melbourne, is ideal for families, caravaners, and all who value peace over pace. The area has a smattering of nurseries, craft shops, tea rooms, and wineries. This part of the Murray has great fishing, and its relaxing rented-houseboat cruises are particularly popular.

TRANSPORTATION. V/Line trains leave daily for Melbourne (4½hr., $50.60) from the station on Curlewis St., between McCrae and Rutherford St., near the Giant Murray Cod. Bus service is available to: Adelaide (6hr., 1 per day, $31.20); Albury (5½-7hr., 1-2 per day, $40.40); Echuca (1½hr., 1-2 per day, $21); Kerang (40min., 2-3 per day, $7.10); and Mildura (2½hr., 2-3 per day, $34.20).

PRACTICAL INFORMATION. Swan Hill's civic activity centers on the manicured strip of Campbell St. (Murray Valley Hwy.) between Rutherford and McCallum St. The **Swan Hill Development and Information Centre,** 306 Campbell St., on the corner of Rutherford St., is one block west of the river. (☎5032 3033 or 1800 625 373; www.swanhillonline.com. Open daily 9am-5pm.) Heaps of banks with 24hr. **ATMs** are on Campbell St., especially near McCallum St. (All banks open M-Th 9:30am-4pm, F 9:30am-5pm.) The **library,** 53-67 Campbell St., offers free **Internet** access for research and email at $1 per hr. (☎5032 2404. Book ahead. Open M-Tu and Th-F 10am-5:30pm, W 10am-5:30pm and 7-8:30pm, Sa 10am-noon.) There's a **post office** on 164 Campbell St. (Open M-F 9am-5pm.) **Postal Code:** 3585.

ACCOMMODATIONS & FOOD. Budget accommodations are few; most of Campbell St.'s numerous motels run $40-110 per night. If you're driving, the **Commercial Hotel ❶,** 14km south at Lake Boga, on Marraboor St. off Station St. from the highway, may be your best option. The pub accommodation includes continental breakfast, kitchen, laundry, and electric blankets. (☎5037 2140. Singles $15; doubles $20; families $25. Hot breakfast $5, dinner $8.50-12.50.) Otherwise, the **Pioneer Settlement ❷,** on Horseshoe Bend, sometimes allows backpackers to stay in one of its three lodges, though frequent school groups have priority. There is a kitchen and TV lounge, but only two bedrooms have doors. (☎5036 2410. Linens $5.50. Book ahead. 4- to 6-bed dorms $16.50 first night, each extra night $11, weekly $70.) The **Riverside Caravan Park ❷,** 1 Monash Dr., on the river adjacent to the Pioneer Settlement, has a pool and spa, BBQ, kitchen, and small grocer. (☎5032 1494. Sites for 2 $20-22, powered $22-24; on-site caravans $45-65; cabins $59-127. Reception 8am-8pm.) **Cafe Allure ❷,** 147 Campbell St., serves up an eclectic mix of gourmet breakfasts ($5-12.50), smoothies ($3.50), rich, large focaccias ($7.60), and classy dinner fare. (☎5032 4422. Open M-Tu 9am-4:30pm, W-Su 9am-9pm.) For dinner, both the service and the Italian fare (dine-in pasta dishes $13.50-17, takeaway personal pizza $9.50-14.50) are superb at **Quo Vadis ❷,** 255-259 Campbell St. (☎5032 4408. Pizzeria open daily 5pm-late; more upscale restaurant open daily 6pm-late.)

SIGHTS. The **Horseshoe Bend Pioneer Settlement,** on Horseshoe Bend, is the oldest outdoor museum in Australia. Heading south on Campbell St., turn left on Gray St. and cross the railroad tracks. A full century (1830-1930) of the history of frontier agricultural settlement is represented by original buildings and antique equipment. Dressed in old-fashioned clothing, the employees perform uproarious slapstick street theater; paddlesteamers cruise the river along the banks of the settlement, and nighttime brings the **Sound and Light Show,** a family-friendly, if slightly hokey, cart-ride through history under the southern stars. (☎5036 2410. Open daily 9am-5pm. $16, children $9, families $41. Light Show $10, children $6, families $26.

Cruise on the paddlesteamer *Pyap* 1hr.; 2 per day; $12, concessions $8, children $7, families $31. Joint passes available.) Smaller than the Pioneer Settlement, but perhaps more engaging, is the **Swan Hill Regional Art Gallery,** housed in a modern mud-brick structure next door. Three rotating galleries showcase local work. There's also a permanent collection of contemporary Australian art, concerts, films, and lectures. Free guided tours are offered every Sunday at 1:30pm. (☎5036 2430. Open Tu-F 10am-5pm, Sa-Su 11am-5pm. Gold coin donation suggested.)

Swan Hill's pride in its fishing has resulted in the **Giant Murray Cod.** Towering over its living brethren, the statue is quite possibly the largest Murray Cod in the world. It measures 6m by 11m by 6m, and was originally built as a prop for the movie *Eight Ball.* The statue now guards the north end of the rail station on Cur-lewis St. The best fishing holes (mainly cod and carp) are 20min. away; ask for updates at the **Department of Primary Industries** office, 324 Campbell St. (☎5033 1290. Open M-F 9am-5pm.) The DPI also has info on the town's **required fishing license** ($5 for 48hr., $10 for 28 days, $20 for year.)

MILDURA ☎03

With its wide, palm-lined streets and bustling riverside wharf, Mildura is an oasis in dry Mallee country. The cleverly harnessed waters of the Murray support thriv-ing citrus groves and make Mildura one of Australia's most productive fruit-grow-ing areas; as such, it attracts hordes of backpackers seeking itinerant work (the best time of year is Feb.-Mar., but every month except May is good). It's also one of the sunniest parts of Australia, and were it not for the massive irrigation system, the landscape would be as arid as the Outback that stretches to the horizon. Enjoy it while you're here; Mildura is the last bastion of green for a long, long time.

▐ TRANSPORTATION. The train and bus station is on 7th St., across from the northern end of Langtree Ave. **V/Line** runs to: Albury (10hr.; 1 per day Su, Tu-W, F; $64.20); Echuca (5hr.; 1 per day Su, Tu-W, F; $39.90); and Melbourne (7-9hr., 2-3 per day, $62.40) via Bendigo (5-7hr., $54.70) and Swan Hill (3-4hr., $34.20). **Coun-trylink** runs to Sydney (15hr., daily 4am, $110). **Tom Evans** coaches (☎5022 1415) ser-vices Broken Hill (3½hr.; M, W, and F 9am; $49).

▐▐ ORIENTATION & PRACTICAL INFORMATION. Well-planned Mildura is laid out in a grid on the southern bank of the Murray. In the city center, 7th-10th St. run roughly east-west. They're encountered in numerical order, with 7th St. clos-est to the river. These cross the north-south avenues, from the westernmost Olive Ave. through Pine, Lime, Langtree, Deakin, and Madden Ave. The commercial cen-ter, the strip of Langtree Ave. from 7th to 10th St., includes a **pedestrian mall** from 8th to 9th where speakers blare endless elevator jazz. The **Mildura Visitor Informa-tion and Booking Centre,** 180-190 Deakin Ave., on the corner of 12th St., is housed in the brilliant Alfred Deakin Centre; look for the silver tornado sculpture out front. (☎5018 8380; www.milduratourism.com. Open M-F 9am-5:30pm, Sa-Su 9am-5pm.) For car rentals, **Avis** (☎5022 1818), **Budget** (☎5021 4442), **Hertz** (☎5022 1411), and **Thrifty** (☎5023 2989) are in the airport, 8km out of town on the Sturt Hwy., with rentals from $55-70 per day. Avis also has a branch at 7th St. and Madden St. (☎5023 1263). For **work opportunities,** ask for the thorough and free *Working Holi-day and Backpacker Information Sheet* from the Visitors Centre, or contact **MADEC Jobs Australia,** 95 Lime Ave. off 10th St. (☎5021 3359. Open M-F 8am-7pm). You can also check with the **Mildura Harvest Labour Office** on Deakin Ave. near 10th St., but they specialize in government-related aid programs (☎5021 1432. Open M-F 9am-5pm.) Work can often be found in the *Sunraysia Daily's* employment sec-tion. The **library** is in the Visitors Centre and has free **Internet** access for research;

Australia is the most arid country in the world and its water woes have been recently exacerbated by the worst drought in over a decade. Nearly 90% of the land in New South Wales faces drought conditions, and large tracts of Queensland, Victoria, and Western Australia are also experiencing shortages. Most of the stricken areas haven't seen rain in months, and some parts have been entirely dry for two years or more.

To combat the devastating economic consequences of the drought, which could be as high as AUS$7 billion this year alone, leaders of the largest businesses in the nation have donated nearly AUS$9 million to a private drought relief fund. Led by Kerry Packer, Australia's richest citizen, the group of businessmen hope to spur popular support for a large-scale governmental drought relief program. Chief among the group's goals if the creation of a system to bring water to dry inland areas in order to prevent repeated droughts in the future.

The drought has also had a noticeable effect on travel in Australia. Bottled water prices have increased to nearly $3 per liter, restaurants serve water only upon request, and nearly every accommodation has signs pleading with guests to limit the length of showers. Australians take the drought seriously, so conserve water to avoid coming across as uninformed or disrespectful.

$2 for 30min. email or chat. (☎5018 8350; book ahead.) **Police** are on Madden Ave. between 8th and 9th St. (☎5023 9555) and the **post office** is on the corner of 8th and Orange Ave., and in the Langtree Ave. Mall. Open M-F 9am-5pm. **Postal Code:** 3500.

▐ ACCOMMODATIONS. Most of Mildura's budget stays are backpackers designed with the migrant worker in mind. Basic rooms, work placement, and transport to work run about $20 per night ($100-110 per week). **Riverboat Bungalow ❷**, 27 Chaffey Ave., near 7th St., is a five-minute walk from the train station. This laid-back hostel is complete with a large aquarium and tropical decor throughout, bedrooms named after paddlesteamers, clean bathrooms, and a lounge area with free pool. Friendly guests bond in the evening by the backyard campfire and on weekend canoe trips along the Murray. A second bungalow is now at 206 8th St, offering the same amenities plus swimming pool. (☎5021 5315. Linens and cutlery included. Internet $2 per 30min. Dorms $20; doubles $44. Weekly dorms $120. VIP discount $1.) **NOMADS Mildura International Backpackers ❶**, 5 Cedar Ave., off 11th St., has two full kitchens and two lounge areas. (☎/fax 5021 0133. Dorms $20. Weekly $120.) **Northaven ❷**, 138 Deakin St. between 10th and 11th St. offers basic backpackers rooms all with TV, fridge, and bath. (☎5023 4499. 4- and 6-bed dorms $20; doubles and twins $130. Weekly dorms $120.)

◼◼ FOOD & NIGHTLIFE. Mildura's restaurants are surprisingly varied. The **Langtree Avenue Mall,** one block west of Deakin Ave. between 8th and 9th St., has cheap takeaways, while Langtree between 7th and 8th St. is a veritable international bazaar. **Fasta Pasta ❷**, 30 Langtree Ave., serves delicious gourmet-tasting pastas ($7-13), pizzas ($10-15), and vegetarian options at reasonable prices. (☎5022 0622. Open M-Sa 11:30am-3pm and 5-10pm, Su 11:30am-3pm and 5-9:30pm.) The best lunch deal is at the **Rendezvous Bistro ❶** at the Sunraysia Wine Center, 34 Langtree Ave. Just $8.90 gets you a gourmet main and an all-you-can-eat salad bar. (☎5023 1571. Open M-F 12-2:30 and 6pm-late, Sa 6pm-late.) **Siam Palace ❶**, 35 Langtree Ave., serves Chinese and Thai dishes. The steal is the lunch and dinner special ($6-7), which offers a choice of dishes with steamed rice. (☎5023 7737. Open Su-Th 5:30-10pm, F-Sa noon-2pm and 5:30-late.) There is a 24hr. Coles **supermarket** at 8th St. and Lime Ave. A few nightclubs are at 8th St. and Langtree Ave. **Sandbar** warms the chilliest winter nights with its tropical decor. (☎5021 2181. Happy Hour daily 5-8pm; W-Sa live bands 10:30pm. Open Tu noon-midnight, W-Sa noon-3am. Cover $5 F-Sa after 10pm.)

⬢ **SIGHTS.** Mildura is the base camp for nearby national parks and the outback. The **Visitors Centre** has info and books all the commercial tours. For nearly 30 years, Tom Evans has been running tours in the Mildura area, bringing his encyclopedic knowledge on his **Junction Tours** (☎5027 4309) to Mungo National Park (Su $70); local hotspots (Tu, Th, and Sa; $46-57); or Broken Hill (M, W, F, 8:45am-8pm $120). **Harry Nanya Tours** runs half- and full-day trips focusing on Aboriginal history and the Dreaming. (☎5027 2076 or 1800 630 864; www.harrynanyatours.com.au. Mungo: $75, concessions $60, families $200. Wentworth: 2 per day; half-day $35/ free/$120; full-day $75/$60/$200. Call about prices for multi-day camping canoe tours.) **Jumbunna**, runs trips to Mungo as well as a Mildura nature walk. These tours are guided by an Aboriginal guide and focus on tribal culture and the outback. (☎0412 581 699. Day-tour $60, concessions $56, children $29, families $166.)

As is often the case for the towns along the **Murray River,** the main summertime attraction is the local swimming hole. ⬛**Apex Park,** at a wide, slow-moving bend in the river, boasts a sandy beach shaded by ash trees. From town, take 8th St. past the train station and turn right on Chaffey Ave., which winds its way to the park. The 1881 paddlewheeler *Rothbury* cruises to Trentham Estate winery. (☎5023 2200. 5hr.; Th 10:30am; $46, children 5-14 $20. Evening cruise with dinner and live entertainment 3hr.; Th 7pm; $46. Short cruise upstream past Buronga and Gol Gol townships, $19.50; book ahead.) Of the seven local wineries in the immediate area, the most internationally famous is **Lindemans,** on Edey Road in Karadoc. To get there, you'll need a car; drive from Mildura down 15th St. (the Calder Hwy.) through Red Cliffs, then look for the signs. (☎5051 3285. Open daily 10am-4:30pm.)

HUME CORRIDOR

The Hume Hwy. links Melbourne and Sydney via 872km of relatively unspectacular scenery. Those intrepid travelers who venture an hour or two off the Hume are rewarded with beautiful mountain vistas and powdery ski slopes, world-class wineries, the legend of folk hero Ned Kelly come alive in Glenrowan, dusty hamlets, and inviting country towns. Farther west along the Murray Valley Hwy., Yarrawonga and Cobram's sun-drenched banks lend themselves to fishing, swimming, and snoozing. Across the river, the Hume continues north into New South Wales.

MARYSVILLE & LAKE MOUNTAIN   ☎03

A small town 1½ hours northeast of Melbourne, Marysville is best known as the closest town (22km) to cross-country ski mecca Lake Mountain. About twenty minutes outside of town when coming from Healesville or Melbourne, the road to Marysville passes through an awe-inspiring forest of giant ferns and massive ramrod-straight ash trees planted by locals after a devastating fire. **The Mystic Mountains Tourist Information Centre,** on Marysville's main drag, Murchison St., posts Lake Mountain snow reports and road conditions, and has accommodations info. (☎5963 4567; www.marysvilletourism.com.au. Open daily 9am-5pm.) For local **snow and road conditions,** contact the Official Victorian Snow Report. (☎1902 240 523; www.vicsnowreport.com.au. 24hr. 55¢ per min.) The police station (☎5963 3222) is next to the Tourist Centre.

The **Marysville Caravan Park ❷,** on Buxton Rd., is by the Steavenson River at the end of Murchison St. (☎5963 3443. Sites for 2 from $17, powered from $20.50; caravans from $54; cabins from $49; prices rise in-season.) For quick and cheap eats, check out the **Marysville Country Bakery ❶,** on the corner of Murchison St. and Pack Rd. (☎5963 3477. Open daily M-F 7am-5:30pm, Sa-Su 7am-6pm. Sandwiches $2-5.20, pies and pasties $3-4.)

The 31km of regularly groomed cross-country **ski trails** at Lake Mountain are packed in-season (entry fee $20; trail fee $10, children $5). Take the Maroondah Hwy. (Hwy. 34) to Woods Point Rd. (Hwy. 172). **Chains** are required for the drive up Lake Mountain during winter, though you can keep them in the trunk. Back in Marysville, local shops rent skis, skates, toboggans, chains, and outerwear; just about everything is under $30. One of Victoria's highest waterfalls is out in the bush near Marysville: **Steavenson Falls,** 4km down Falls Rd., is illuminated nightly by its own hydroelectric power. A 30min. ascent to the top of a nearby peak gives a great view of the falls and leads to a 40min. trail downhill through the town to Gallipoli Park, behind the Tourist Centre.

MANSFIELD ☎ 03

Mansfield's *raison d'être* is its proximity to Mt. Buller, allowing tourists to stop and rent skis and chains before making the 45km ascent to Victoria's most popular ski resort. The **Mansfield Passenger Terminal** is at 137 High St. **V/Line buses** (☎ 13 61 96) serve Melbourne (3hr., 2 per day, $30) and Mt. Buller (1hr., 7 per day, $34 round-trip) during ski season. For $104, V/Line will take you round-trip from Melbourne to Mt. Buller; this price includes snow fees. Law requires all vehicles heading to Mt. Buller to carry **snow chains** from the Queen's Birthday weekend until the end of the ski season. You can leave them in the trunk, but there are spot checks and hefty fines for not carrying them at all.

⚅ PRACTICAL INFORMATION. The **Mansfield Visitors Centre** is just out of town at 167 Maroondah Hwy. (☎ 5775 7000, bookings 1800 039 049; reservations@mansfield-mtbuller.com.au. Open daily 9am-5pm.) Heading east into town on **High St.,** the town's main drag, you'll find ski rental places and a few **ATMs.** The **library,** at the corner of High and Collopy St., has **Internet;** you must fill out a form, even for one-time use. (☎ 5775 2176. Open Tu 2-8pm, W 9:30am-1pm, Th-F 9:30am-5:30pm, Sa 9:30am-noon. $2 per 30min.) **Internet** is also available at **Cafe Connect,** 62 High St., for $3 per 30 min. (☎ 5779 1082. Open M-Th 10am-6pm, F-Sa 2-10pm.) The **post office** is at 90 High St. (☎ 5775 2248. Open M-F 9am-5pm.) **Postal Code:** 3722. The **police station** is next to the post office (☎ 5775 2555). **Ski Centre Mansfield,** 131 High St. (☎ 5775 2859 or 1800 647 754), and its nearby affiliate, **PJ's Ski Hire,** 149 High St. (☎ 5775 1624), rent chains (full-day $15) and a wide range of ski equipment and clothing. (Open June-Oct. Su-Th and Sa 6am-7pm, F 6am-midnight.) There are similar ski hire joints all along High St., all offering comparable deals (full-day skis, boots, and poles $25-30; snowboard and boots $45-50).

⌂⌂ ACCOMMODATIONS & FOOD. The best budget beds in town are at the ⬛**Mansfield Backpackers Inn ❷,** 116 High St., part of the Mansfield Travellers Lodge. The friendly owners keep the place clean and comfortable, and provide a kitchen, lockers, and TV. (☎ 5775 1800; travlodge@cnl.com.au. Book 1-2 weeks ahead. Reception 24hr. Dorms $23; singles $60; doubles $66-85; families $125-135.) The **Commercial Hotel ❸,** one of the pubs near the intersection of High and Highett St., offers simple lodging with shared bath. (☎ 5775 2046. Singles $30; doubles $50; includes continental breakfast.)

For cheap, good eats, try the **Ski Inn Cafe ❶,** 61 High St., which offers tasty chicken breast burgers ($5), a range of fish 'n' chips options, and pastries. (☎ 5775 2175. Open 6am-9pm.) For quality fresh produce, stop by the **Mansfield Fruit Palace,** 68 High St. (☎ 5775 2239. Open M-F 8:30am-6pm, Sa 8am-2pm.) There are two **supermarkets:** Foodworks, 12 Highett St. (☎ 5775 2255), and IGA, 47 High St. (☎ 5775 2014). Both are open daily 8am-8pm.

MOUNT BULLER ☎03

Victoria's largest ski resort, Mt. Buller is a three-hour drive from Melbourne, with arguably the best terrain in Victoria. Though it's not the Alps or Rockies, it's a mecca for Aussie skiers and snowboarders from mid-June through early October.

⌐ ⁊ TRANSPORTATION & PRACTICAL INFORMATION. Along with **V/Line** (see Mansfield), **Mansfield-Mount Buller Bus Lines** operates coach service to Mt. Buller from Mansfield. (☎5775 2606; www.mmbl.com.au. 1hr., 6-8 per day, $34.) **Snowcaper Tours** departs from Melbourne and offers tour packages that include return transport, entrance fees, and a full-day lift ticket. Participants leave Melbourne at 4am and return by 9:30pm. (☎5775 2367, reservations 1800 033 023. Midweek $110, Sa-Su $120.) All buses pull into the **Cow Camp Plaza**, in the center of Mt. Buller village. If going by car, bring **snow chains** (it's the law) and take Hwy. 164 (Buller Rd.) east to Mt. Buller. (Car admission $20 per day; overnight fee Su-Th $3.30 per night, F-Sa $6.60 per night.) Free parking is on the side of the mountain. To get to the village from the parking lot, visitors without luggage can take a free shuttle; those with luggage must take a taxi ($10). Beware: all these daily charges add up fast. Consider taking the bus, especially if you're staying on the mountain for a while.

The village is the hub of accommodation, food, and ski services. The Cow Camp Plaza houses lockers, ATMs, and **Cow Camp Alpine Ski Rentals.** (☎5777 6082. Skis, boots, and poles $28; snowboard and boots $40-45.) The **Information Centre**, opposite the plaza, has maps of the resort and slopes, as well as info on work and long-term accommodations options. (☎5777 7600, reservations 1800 039 049; reservations@mansfield-mtbuller.com.au. Open during ski season daily 8:30am-5pm; in summer, visit the post office.) The **lift ticket office** sits across the village center from the info tower. (☎5777 6800 or 5777 7877. Day pass $75, 48hr. $145.) For the latest **snow conditions,** call the Official Victorian Snow Report (☎1902 240 523; www.vicsnowreport.com.au. 24hr. 55¢ per min.) or tune into 93.7FM. La Trobe University has **Internet** at the Reception Office, Level 5, on New Summit Rd. (☎5733 7000. $4 per 30min.) The Resort Management Building in the village center has a **post office.** (☎5777 6013. Open daily 8:30am-5pm.) **Postal Code:** 3723.

⌐ ACCOMMODATIONS. The **Mount Buller YHA Hostel Lodge ❹** is the least expensive lodging on the mountain, and, in winter, you can literally ski to its front door. The dorms are well-heated. (☎5777 6181; mountbuller@yhavic.org.au. Book at least 3 weeks ahead July-Aug. Ski lockers available. Reception 8-10am and 5-10pm. Dorms $55, YHA $50. 20% discount during Winterfest in mid-June.) Next door to the YHA, the **Kooroora Hotel ❺** has more intimate four-person dorms with showers. There is a 15% guest discount for on-site ski hire. (☎5777 6050; kooroora@bigpond.com. Open only during ski season. Reservations require a 50% deposit. 18+ only. Dorms M-Th $70, F-Su $80.) In summer, the best (and potentially the only) accommodations on the mountain are at **Kandahar ❸,** office located at the Ivor Whittaker Memorial Lodge on Summit Rd. (☎6777 6024. Backpacker dorms $15; dorms at the nicer Kandahar lodge $30. Weekly $70/$180.)

⌐ ⌐ FOOD & NIGHTLIFE. ABOM ❶, on Summit St., couldn't be further from its full name (Abominable). Despite the menacing polar bear lurking next to the doorway, this European-style resort is the perfect refuge from the cold with affordable bistro fare. (☎5777 7899; www.mtbuller.com/abom. Pizza slice $5, toasted sandwich $4.) The **Cow Camp Plaza** houses **Skiosk ❶** (☎5777 6503), serving up fast food (hot dogs $5). Open from 8 or 9am until late; hours depend on crowds.

Kooroora's Pub is hands-down the place to go for nightlife; besides a great atmosphere, it's the only place on the mountain regularly open past midnight. Bands (Sa) and DJs (every other night) rage until 3am; its kitchen is open until 10pm. **Mooseheads Bar,** downstairs at the ABOM, caters to a more laid-back, couch-lounging crowd. With the cheapest spirits on the mountain ($5), the Happy Hour from 4-6pm might just be the happiest time to visit. (Open 5pm-2am.)

🎿 **SKIING.** Intermediate runs dominate, but several expert trails are sprinkled on the southern slopes. On the south face, **Fanny's Finish** and **Chute 1, 2, and 3** separate the skiers from the snowbunnies. First-time skiers have plenty of long runs to choose from, as well as numerous lesson packages. The lift capacity is excellent and lift lines are usually not long. Those ready for an aerobic challenge will find 75km of cross-country skiing trails (approx. half of which is groomed) and an entire mountain, **Mt. Stirling,** set aside for their use. (Resort management ☎0419 514 655; ticket office 5777 5625. Open during daylight. No overnight accommodations on the mountain except camping, which is free.) The **Information Centre** (next to the carparks) contains a public shelter with fireplace, ski and toboggan hire, and food. (Car entry $20; trail $8.80; cross-country ski hire $33; telemark $45.)

🥾🚵 **HIKING & MOUNTAIN BIKING.** Though Mt. Buller was once a prime mountain biking destination with miles of bike trails, the activity is now permitted on vehicle-access roads only. Though lifts to bike trails may operate during the end of December and January in 2004, they were closed during summer 2002 and 2003. Cheaper biking without a chairlift is possible, as are various free hikes. The **Summit Walk** (1½hr. return, moderate), beginning and ending at the clock tower, rewards hikers with views of the High Country below. The summit can also be reached by driving to the end of Summit Rd and following a marked unsealed road to the base of the final leg of the summit hike (approx. 200m). Popular with mountain bikers, a longer hike to **Mount Stirling** via **Corn Hill** and **Howqua Gap** (5-7hr. return, moderate) offers a grand perspective of Mt. Buller. The shortest of the hikes, the **Blind Creek Falls** walk (40min. return; hard) is accessible from Boggy Corner, 3.5km below the village. The path leads down a switchback to the Chalet Creek and then to the falls.

WANGARATTA   ☎03

Referred to endearingly as "Wang" by locals, Wangaratta (pop. 25,000) is a quiet town seated conveniently at the junction of the Hume Hwy. and the Great Alpine Road. Though it offers few tourist attractions save the Murray River, Wang can be a suitable base for exploring Victoria's alpine country and nearby vineyards.

📧📞 **TRANSPORTATION & PRACTICAL INFORMATION. V/Line** (☎13 61 96) runs from the station on Norton St. to: Melbourne (2½hr., 3 per day, $33.10); Albury (1hr., 3 per day, $11); Wodonga (1hr., 3 per day, $8.40); Bright (1½hr., 1 or 2 per day, $11.80); Beechworth (30min., 1 per day, $5.80); and Rutherglen (30min., 1 per day, $4.80). **Countrylink** runs to Sydney (9hr., 2 per day, $90.20).

The Hume Hwy. from Melbourne runs into town as Tone Rd., becoming Ryley St., then **Murphy Street** for the stretch through the city center. Murphy intersects Ford, Ely, Reid, and Faithfull St. as it runs northeast. **Ovens Street** runs parallel to and northwest of Murphy St. The **Visitors Centre** is on Tone Rd. 1km southwest of the city center and has a useful, free map of town. (☎5721 5711 or 1800 801 065. Open daily 9am-5pm.) The **library,** 62 Ovens St., has **Internet.** (☎5721 2366. Book ahead. Open M-Tu and Th-F 9:30am-6pm, W 9:30am-8pm, Sa 9am-noon. $2 per

30min. Max. 1hr.) The **post office** is across from the intersection of Murphy and Ely St. (Open M-F 9am-5pm.) **Postal Code:** 3677.

▐ ▐ ACCOMMODATIONS & FOOD. The **Billabong Motel ❸**, 12 Chisholm St., at the end of Reid and a block east from Murphy St., has basic heated rooms with linens and TV. (☎5721 2353. Singles from $30, ensuite $40-45; doubles $50-65.) The **Wangaratta North Family Motel ❷** is 5km north of town on the Old Hume Hwy., making them difficult to reach without car. (☎5721 2624. Dorms $22, linens included; singles from $49; doubles from $59.) Across the Ovens River on Pinkerton Cr., just north of Faithfull St., is **Painters Island Caravan Park ❶**, with a brand-new swimming pool. (☎5721 3380. Reception 8am-8pm. Sites $7.50 per person, powered for two $17.60; on-site caravans $33; cabins $44, ensuite $55.)

▐Scribbler's Cafe ❶, 66 Reid St., has cheap deluxe sandwiches ($7-9), veggie options, and cuisine from around the globe. (☎5721 3945. Open daily 8am-5:45pm. Kitchen closes around 5pm. BYO.) **Reid on Ovens ❸**, formerly Vespa's Cafe, at Reid and Ovens St., has a bar specializing in local wine, a delightfully eclectic menu, and themed event nights once a month. They also sell discount tickets to the first-run cinema next door. (☎5722 4392. Open Tu-Th 9:30am-10:30pm, F-Sa 9:30am-midnight. Entrees around $10, mains $19.) Safeway **supermarket** is on Ovens St. between Reid and Ford St. (open daily 7am-midnight), and Coles 24hr. supermarket is on Tone Rd., south of the city center.

▐ ▐ SIGHTS & WINERIES. The best daytrip is 15km southeast via Oxley Flats Rd. at the **Milawa Gourmet Region.** The classy **Brown Brothers Vineyard,** on Snow Rd., could sate a small nation with its five tasting bars. Every course at its Epicurean Centre restaurant includes its own accompanying wine. (☎5720 5500. Open daily 9am-5pm; restaurant open daily 11am-3pm.) Around the corner on Factory Rd., the ▐Milawa Cheese Factory has free samples of gourmet cheeses handmade from the milk of local goats, ewes, and cows, as well as a snazzy new **restaurant ❷** (mains $13-24) and a first-rate bakery that uses a stone-based oven and has a 9-year-old sourdough culture named George. (☎5727 3589. Open daily 9am-5pm. Open for lunch daily noon-3pm, dinner Th-Sa at 6:30pm; book ahead.)

Back in Wang, **Kaluna Park** (☎5751 1238) offers ample space for picnic and play just east of Murphy St. Visitors can bike, hike, or ride horses on the **"Murray to the Mountains Rail Trail."** The 94km paved trail follows historical railway lines and passes through **Bowser, Beechworth,** and **Myrtleford** all the way to **Bright.** The Murray **River** is deepest and most easily accessible for cooling off on a hot day near the footbridge off Pinkerton Ct. Wangaratta's renowned **jazz festival** (☎5722 1666 or 1800 803 944; www.wangaratta-jazz.org.au), the first weekend of November, ranks among Australia's best; accommodations can be booked up as early as June.

Just up the Hume Hwy. (Hwy. 31), nearby **Glenrowan** is where folk hero/notorious bushranger Ned Kelly was finally corralled. Its prime attraction is the $2.5 million animatronic **Ned Kelly's Last Stand,** a corny, cultish narrative presentation—entertaining to kids and at least appreciated by adults. (At the **Glenrowan Tourist Centre.** ☎5766 2367. Daily every 30min. 9:30am-4:30pm. $16, concessions $14, ages 5-15 $10, families $45.) Next door is the **Ned Kelly Memorial Museum and Homestead.** (☎5766 2448. $3.50, children $1.)

RUTHERGLEN   ☎02

At the heart of Victoria's most renowned wine region, Rutherglen is an excellent base for touring the surrounding wineries. The Murray Valley Hwy. (Hwy. 16), called Main St. in Rutherglen, runs from Yarrawonga (45km west) through Rutherglen to Albury (50km east). **V/Line buses** leave Rutherglen's BP service station for

Melbourne via Wangaratta (3½hr.; M, W, F 6:35am; $39). Purchase tickets from the news agency on Main St. **Webster** Bus Service shuttles to Albury at 9:30am on weekdays from the BP station west of the city center (☎6033 2459; $7). The new visitors center (officially called the **Rutherglen Wine Experience,** 55 Main St.) is located right on the town's central roundabout and is the place to go for winery literature and bicycle hire. The *Rutherglen Touring Guide* is an indispensable map of the region for anybody considering visiting any of the wineries. (☎6032 9166 or 1800 622 871. Open daily 9am-5pm. One-day bike rental including helmet, pump, and bottled water $22.) The **post office** is at 83 Main St. **Postal Code:** 3685.

The **Star Hotel ❸,** 105 Main St., has good self-contained motel units with TV, A/C, and continental breakfast. (☎6032 9625. Singles $35, doubles $60.) The **Victoria Hotel ❸,** 90 Main St., offers cozy budget rooms with electric blankets, linens, towels, and breakfast. (☎6032 8610. Singles and twins Su-Th $25, F-Sa $35 per person; doubles $45/$55; ensuite $55/$65. Third night free if you stay 2 nights Su-Th.) **Rutherglen Caravan Park ❶,** 72 Murray St., has tent space as well as luxurious cabins by the lake. (☎6032 8577; rutherglencvanpark@iprimus.com.au. Sites for two $13, powered $16.50; fully-furnished cabins $40-75. Wheelchair-accessible.) For **free camping,** or just a quick swim in a remote and beautiful setting, drive north towards Yarrawonga for 5km and turn right on Moodamere Rd., which becomes an unsealed road after 2km and eventually leads through a cattle grate down into **Stantons Bend,** a low-lying riverbed area. Drive slowly, especially in a 2WD vehicle. From the cattle grate, veer left at every turn towards **Moodamere Lake,** which is more of a wide eddy in the Murray River than a proper lake. Locals inhabit caravans near the lake and practice wakeboarding, and short-term camping is free. Be aware that the current is very, very strong; don't swim into the middle of the river.

For a real treat, eat at **Parker Pies ❶** (formerly the Rutherglen Tea Rooms), 86-88 Main St. Their chicken, cheese, ham, and mustard pie was voted best chicken pie in Australia in 2000, and they've been awarded 24 medals in the Great Aussie Pie Competition. The ultra-friendly staff deserves national recognition as well. (☎6032 9605. Pies $2.80-4.50.) The **Poachers Paradise Hotel,** 120 Main St. has $6 pub food lunches. (☎6032 9502. Open daily 8-9:30am, noon-2pm, and 6-8:30pm.) The IGA **supermarket,** 95 Main St., caters to all your budget needs. (☎6032 9232. Open M-W and Sa 7:30am-7pm, Th-F 7:30am-7:30pm, Su 8:30am-6pm.)

WINERIES NEAR RUTHERGLEN

Rutherglen's temperate climate allows vineyards to keep grapes on their vines longer, favoring full-bodied red wines and fortified varieties like Tokay and Muscat. Choosing from among the excellent local wineries can be quite difficult, especially since they all offer free tastings. For those traveling by car, the *Rutherglen Touring Guide,* available at the **Visitors Centre** and most wineries, is an indispensable free map. Or grab a free *Muscat Trail Map* for help navigating by bike. Horse-drawn stagecoach tours leave from **Poachers Paradise Hotel,** 120 Main St. (☎6032 9502. Daily 10am and 1pm. Three wineries in 2hr. $15 per person, under 7 free. Bookings essential.) **Grapevine Getaways** designs tours based on individual interests and requests. Groups of 20 or more can arrange pick-up from just about anywhere, including Melbourne and Sydney. (☎6032 9224 or 0407 577 241; www.grapevinegetaways.com.au. From $30; bookings essential.)

The Rutherglen vineyards sponsor several festivals throughout the year. The most popular is the carnival-like **Rutherglen Winery Walkabout** (on Queen's Birthday weekend) featuring food and entertainment at the estates and a street fair downtown. True connoisseurs would probably prefer to skip the big production and instead sample the impressive food and wine combinations during the **Tastes of Rutherglen** (Labor Day weekend in March).

■ **St. Leonards Vineyards** (☎6033 1004; wwww.stleonardswines.com) on St. Leonards Rd. just north of All Saints Rd. In a smart location next to a placid lagoon fed by the Murray River, St. Leonards Vineyards boasts an array of delectable wines, including a unique Orange Muscat (crisp, light, and sweet), and a smooth 2000 St. Leonards Shiraz (toasty and oakey, with a dark wooden finish). The winery is also home to **The Lazy Grape Cafe ❷**, an outdoor restaurant that specializes in cook-it-yourself gourmet BBQ (mouth-watering scotch fillet $18.50, Italian sausages $12.50). Lazy Grape kitchen open daily 12-3pm. Live jazz 1st and 3rd Su of the month. Cellar open for tasting daily 11am-5pm.

■ **Pfeifer Wines** (☎6033 2805), on Distillery Road. A small, unpretentious family-run winery that holds its own against the larger estates that surround it. Pfeifer Wines' 1997 Merlot is rich, full, and luscious, while their popular 2002 Reisling is crisp and floral in addition to being an amazing value. The crown jewel of the cellar, however, is the 1990 reserve chardonnay, which is uncharacteristically rich, smooth, buttery, and soft. If you need a break, consider taking advantage of the nearby picnic bridge over the Murray River. Open M-Sa 9am-5pm, Su 10am-5pm.

All Saints Estate (☎6035 2222; www.allsaintswine.com.au). Head northwest of Rutherglen via Corowa Rd., then north on All Saints Rd. The most polished, tourist-oriented winery in the area with towering elms lining the driveway, a red-brick castle tasting room, and a sculptured rose garden with central fountain. Marked self-guided tour past picture-perfect gardens, huge display casks, and a playground; pick up map from the cellar door. Peek into the **Chinese Dormitory and Gardens** on the grounds for a sense of early laborers' living conditions. Located just behind the castle is the **Rutherglen Keg Factory,** which manufactures wine kegs and offers a number of hand-hewn kegs and wine racks for show and for purchase. The winery offers free delivery to Rutherglen for cyclists interested in buying some of their wine. Winery open M-Sa 9am-5:30pm, Su 10am-5pm. Restaurant open Su-F 10am-5:30pm, Sa 10am-7pm; book ahead on weekends. Keg factory open M-Sa 9am-5pm, Su 10am-5pm.

Morris Vineyards (☎6026 7303), off Mia Mia Rd. from the Murray Valley Hwy. A non-irrigated, family-run vineyard with a full-bodied, intense 1999 Durif. Open M-Sa 9am-5pm, Su 10am-5pm.

Cofield Wines (☎6033 3798), northwest of Rutherglen on Distillery Rd., just off Corowa Rd. Cofield Wines is quite small relative to nearby vineyards, and completely family-run. The winery's signature press is a fantastic sparkling shiraz; also popular is the superb 2000 Quartz Vein Shiraz, with its rich and dark overtones with just a touch of cherry, a floral nose, and a round-bottomed finish. The **Pickled Sisters Cafe** located next door is enormously popular as well. Cellar door open M-Sa 9am-5pm, Su 10am-5pm; cafe open M and W-Su 10am-4pm.

Chambers Rosewood Winery (☎6032 8641). An easy-to-miss building on Barkley St., 1km from the tourist office. Simple, unpretentious, relaxed tasting area gives no hint of the international praise lavished on its rare Tokays and Muscats. Open M-Sa 9am-5pm, Su 11am-5pm.

Gehrig Estate (☎6026 7296), 22km east of town on the Murray Valley Hwy. Gehrig Estate is Victoria's oldest winery, established in 1858. Produces a wide range including excellent shiraz and durif, as well as a fresh, zesty cherin blanc. Open M-Sa 9am-5pm, Su 10am-5pm.

Fairfield Vineyard (☎6032 9381). To get to the Fairfield Vineyard, head due east from Rutherglen on the Murray Valley Hwy. The vineyard is housed in an idyllic old cellar building that is even better than their choice selection of wines. Open M-F 10am-4pm, Sa 10am-5pm.

VICTORIA

HIGH COUNTRY

Victoria's High Country, tucked between the Murray River and Gippsland's thick coastal forest, is a contrast to Australian sights like Surfers Paradise or the Red Centre. Ancient forests display dazzling autumn leaves, and rambling valleys nurture spring flowers in colors that only the rare sunset can capture. In winter, Mt. Hotham and Falls Creek offer the continent's best skiing. In summer, abseilers, climbers, and mountain bikers tackle the steep slopes and cliffs of Mt. Buffalo.

BEECHWORTH   ☎03

Beechworth, Victoria's best-preserved gold town, lies off the Owens Hwy. to the northeast. Traces of gold were discovered here in February 1852; miners swarmed to the area. By 1866, over 4.1 million ounces had been found. Today, visitors flock to Beechworth for museums, a "conversation" with Ned Kelly in the courthouse where he stood trial, or a treat from regionally renowned Beechworth Bakery.

The bus stop is on Camp St., just west of Ford St. **V/Line buses** (☎13 61 96) run to: Bright (1hr., 1-2 per day, $5.20); Melbourne (3-4hr., 1-4 per day, $40.20); and Wangaratta (35min., 1-6 per day, $5.80). **Wangaratta Coachlines** (☎5722 1843) runs on weekdays to Albury (1hr., 2 per day, $7.10), making stops in Yackandandah (15min., 2 per day, $3.50), Baranduda (30min., 2 per day, $7.10), and Wodonga (45min., 2 per day, $7.10). There are also **taxis** (☎5728 1485); the **police** office (☎5728 1032) is located next to the Visitors Centre on Ford St. Free **Internet** at Zwar Library, at the bottom of Camp St. across from the bowling green. (☎5728 3092. Open M 3-5:30pm, W 3:30-5:30 and 7-8:30pm, F 10am-noon and 3:30-5:30pm, Sa 10-11:30am.) The **Visitors Centre** (☎1300 366 321 or 5728 3233) is in Shire Hall on **Ford Street,** Beechworth's main north-south street.

Beechworth overflows with B&Bs. The info center can help you select an accommodation based on price, theme, or amenities. Centrally located **Tanswells Commercial Hotel ❸,** 30 Ford St., offers basic rooms with shared bath and a common lounge. (☎5728 1480. Singles $40; doubles $60.) **Lake Sambell Caravan Park ❶** is 1.5km outside of town. Take Ford St. north, veer right on Junction St., and follow the signs. (☎5728 1421. Laundry, BBQ. Sites $16, powered $18.50; caravans for four $35; cabins for four $60.)

No one who prizes leavened treats should miss the award-winning ▨**Beechworth Bakery ❶,** 27 Camp St. Tasty focaccias ($6.80), loaves (San Francisco sourdough $3.60), and mouth-watering desserts (fresh raspberry snickerdoodles $2.45) keep the crowds coming back. (☎5728 1132. Open daily 6am-7pm.) For a splurge, try **The Bank Restaurant ❺,** 86 Ford St. Situated in the old Bank of Australasia building (built in the 1850s), the dining rooms have 18-foot ceilings and beautiful period decor. Mains like lamb loin with caramelized onion, artichoke, and a pencil leek tart in a red wine reduction ($27.90) can be complemented by a variety of regional wines. (☎5728 2223. Open daily from 6:30pm, Su lunch from noon.)

Inquire at the info center about local **bike rentals** and 1½hr. **walking tours** of historic Beechworth. (Half-day bike rental $19. Tours daily 11am and 2pm; $10, concessions $8, children $5.) Behind the Visitors Centre, on Loch St., the **Burke Museum** displays gold-rush era artifacts, the oldest and most comprehensive known collection of Southwest Victorian Aboriginal weapons, and stuffed animal and bird specimens including the Thylacine, a now-extinct Tasmanian marsupial. (☎5728 1420. Open daily 9am-5pm. $5.50, concessions $3.50, children $3.) At the Beechworth **cemetery,** north of the town center on Cemetery Rd., you'll find the **Chinese Burning Towers** and rows of simple headstones—reminders of the Chinese presence in gold-rush Beechworth. Chinese miners once outnumbered whites five to one, but their tight-packed graves testify to the discrimination they faced. Inside the **Beechworth Historic Court House,** 94 Ford St., the courtroom has been preserved in its 19th-century condition, right down to the dock where bushranger Ned Kelly stood during his trials and the cells in which he and his mother were (at separate times) detained. A soundscape system recreates the trial as you walk through. Watch out at the cells—Ned and his mother aren't too shy to speak to visitors. (☎5728 2721. Open daily 9am-5pm. $4, concessions $2.50, families $10.)

MOUNT BUFFALO NATIONAL PARK

Mt. Buffalo rises imposingly alongside the Great Alpine Rd., signaling the site of a rich sub-alpine ecosystem with plenty of outdoor adventure opportunities throughout the year. Founded in 1898, Mt. Buffalo is one of Australia's oldest national parks, and though its craggy walls may intimidate from afar, the gentle, heavily family-oriented ski slopes are mainly for beginner and intermediate skiers.

The **park entrance gate** (☎5756 2328) serves as the primary information source on site, though the actual **Parks Victoria Office** is 20km beyond the entry. (☎5755 1466, 24hr. 13 19 63; fax 5755 1802. Open daily 8am-4pm; usually staffed M-F early mornings and late afternoons.) The entrance, 5km north of Bright (see p. 660), is just off the Great Alpine Rd. roundabout by Porepunkah. (Entrance fee $12.50, off-season $9; concessions half-price; guests of mountaintop lodging free.)

The clean, simple lines of the main lounge and bistro at the **Mt. Buffalo Lodge ❶,** 7km along the main road from the **Visitors Centre,** overlook the slopes. (Mains $4-10.) Inside, a ski shop serves both cross-country and downhill skiers. The rates are comparable to those in Bright (downhill package $29; 1½hr. ski lesson, lift pass, and equipment $72). Guests have access to laundry, a games room, a small bouldering wall, and a TV lounge. There is a **family unit ❺** with 16 beds, a kitchen, and shared facilities. (☎5755 1988 or 1800 037 038. Twin lodge units $90 per adult; family unit $750; less in off-season.) Great **campsites ❶** lie beside Lake Catani, 2km beyond the park office. Some are caravan-accessible, and there are toilets, water, hot showers, and a laundry basin. (Open Nov.-Apr. Unpowered sites for 4 $12.70-17.40, extra person $3.70, additional vehicle $4.70. Six person maximum.)

Lift passes are available for the **Cresta Valley site** adjacent to the Mt. Buffalo Lodge. (Half-day $45; 2-day $92; ages 8-15 $34 per day. Lift ticket and lesson package $72, under 16 $55.) In the park, 11km of groomed (and two more ungroomed) cross-country ski trails lie across the road from the Mt. Buffalo Lodge parking lot at Cresta Valley. There is no fee levied for cross-country skiing; just be sure to ask for the information sheet at the entrance gate. (On-site rental of cross-country skis and boots $16 per day.)

Mt. Buffalo is also an excellent choice for hikers. The dramatic mountain road up the flanks of Mt. Buffalo winds through dense eucalypt forests, obscuring whatever surprises lurk around the next hairpin turn. Rare views of **waterfalls** plunging over sheer cliffs into deep gorges punctuate the drive. Within the park are some spectacular lookouts as well as numerous walking tracks. The most challenging hike is **The Big Walk** (11.3km; 4-5hr. from Park Entrance to the Gorge Day Visitor Area). It ascends over 1000m in only 9km as it climbs the plateau. The **Eurobin Falls** track (1.5km; 45min. return) is much shorter, with a trailhead approximately 2km past the park entrance. Beginning with an amble and ending in a steep clamber, the walk features spectacular views of the falls careening down the bare rock. At the top of the mountain, adjacent to the Mt. Buffalo Chalet, **Bent's Lookout** dazzles with a panoramic sweep across the Buckland Valley. On clear days, **Mount Kosciuzsko** is visible. Driving past the park office toward the Mt. Buffalo Lodge, you'll see numerous marked walking trails. The steep but relatively short **Monolith Track,** across from the park office, leads to a precariously balanced granite monolith and is definitely worth the effort (1.8km; 1hr. circuit).

Mt. Buffalo's other warm-weather activities are as popular as its winter ones. Abseilers go over the edge near Bent's Lookout year-round. The **Mount Buffalo Chalet Activities Centre** (☎0419 280 614 or 5755 1500; www.mtbuffalochalet.com.au) runs rock climbing, caving, and rugged mountaineering expeditions. The climbing on the north wall of the Gorge is world-renowned. The site of the 1986 World Championships, Mt. Buffalo's has superb hang gliding. Lake Catani is a small man-made lake perfect for swimming, fishing, and canoeing; its surroundings also provide good bushwalking.

BRIGHT   ☎03

Both a popular summer hiking and adventure sports destination and a base for winter skiing at Mt. Hotham, Falls Creek, and Mt. Buffalo, Bright is an apt name for this town of radiant natural beauty and glowing hospitality. Excellent budget accommodations and proximity to mountain trails, snowfields, wineries, and larger towns make Bright a great base for outdoor extravaganzas.

ORIENTATION & PRACTICAL INFORMATION. Bright is located 79km southeast of Wangaratta along the **Great Alpine Road** (renamed **Gavan Street** and then **Delaney Avenue** while within town limits). The town center lies hidden off the highway behind a roundabout with an Art Deco clock tower. Both **Barnard** and **Anderson Streets** link the main drag, **Ireland Street,** with Gavan St. The **Bright Visitors Centre** is at 119 Gavan St. (☎5755 2275 or 1800 500 117; bright@dragnet.com.au. Open daily 8:30am-5pm.) Public transportation in and out of Bright is limited and expensive, so having a car helps. However, **V/Line** (☎13 61 96) serves Melbourne (4½hr., 1-2 per day, $45.50) and Wangaratta (1½hr., 1-2 per day, $11.80). The **post office** is located at the bottom of Ireland St. just above the roundabout at Cobden St. **Postal code:** 3741.

ACCOMMODATIONS. Bright's centrally located backpacker accommodation is the ▓**Bright Hikers Backpackers Hostel (VIP)** ❷, 4 Ireland St. on the second floor, across from the post office. Guests of the hostel are welcome to borrow a limited selection of snow chains and skiing gear. Kitchen, dorms, and bathrooms are sparklingly clean. (☎5750 1244; backpackers@brighthikers.com.au. Linens $3. Non-suspension mountain bikes $10 per 2hr., $1 per additional hr. Internet $2.50 per 10min. Reception 9am-10pm. Dorms $19; doubles $40. Weekly from $105/$270.) The **Bright & Alpine Backpackers** ❶, 106 Coronation Ave., is five minutes outside town; follow the Great Alpine Way east past the info center, turn sharply right onto Hawthorne St. then left onto Coronation St. The backpackers is on the right, just before the small bridge. The facility is filled with a sense of nostalgia but does show its age. Free pick-up from town if arriving by public transportation. (☎/fax 5755 1154. Kitchen, laundry. Linens $5. Reception 24hr. Sites $8, powered $9; singles $16; doubles $30.)

SKIING. Gear shops and businesses in Bright cater to adrenaline junkies. At the center of town, a handful of ski-hire establishments will outfit you with a full range of skiing and snowboarding equipment, snow chains, and clothing. **Adina Ski Hire,** 15 Ireland St., offers both new and used budget skis for rent. (www.adina.com.au. Open Su-Th and Sa 7am-7pm, F 7am-late. Downhill skis, boots and poles $39 per day, $115 per week; budget $29/$86; snowboard and boots $50/$125. Deposit required. 20% YHA discount.) **Bright Ski Centre,** 22 Ireland St. (☎5755 1093), and **JD's for Skis** (☎5755 1557), on the corner of Burke and Anderson St., offer similar services and hours.

⚑ OTHER OUTDOOR ACTIVITIES. Warm thermal air currents make the valleys surrounding the town of Bright ideal for hang gliding and paragliding—the area was home to the 1986 World Championships. **Alpine Paragliding,** 100 Gavan St. across from the Visitors Centre, offers intro flights as well as advanced options and licensing courses. (☎5755 1753. Tandem flight, $130, 2-day licensing course $180 per day) **Bright Microlights** (☎5750 1555) offers a 15min. introductory "Bright Flight" ($95). Their 20min. "Mt. Buffalo Flight" takes you over the gorge and then glides back to earth ($125).

The local ranges are perfect for mountain biking during warm, dry weather. **CyclePath Adventures,** 74 Gavan St. (☎5750 1442 or 0427 501 442; www.cyclepath.com.au), has customized and fully supported one- to five-day high-country, singletrack, and food and wine gourmet bike tours. **Adventure Guides Australia** (☎5728 1804 or 0419 280 614; www.adventureguidesaustralia.com.au) conducts full-day abseiling from $150, full- and half-day caving trips ($160/$88), full-day rock climbing from $150, and bushwalking and camping excursions. All but rock climbing are year-round, though they're all subject to weather.

MOUNT HOTHAM

With Victoria's highest average snowfall, 13 lifts, and a partnership with nearby Falls Creek (see p. 662), Mount Hotham is Victoria's intermediate and advanced skiing and snowboarding headquarters. Mt. Hotham is considered the hottest place in Victoria for all thrill-seekers, but it is held in especially high regard by **snowboarders.** The slopes are more challenging than in the rest of Australia, with short but steep double black diamonds cutting through the trees in the **"Extreme Skiing Zone."** Beginner skiing is limited, though lessons are available. With a constant stream of uni groups filling club lodges in the ski season, the mountain is a little younger and a little more hip than nearby Falls Creek, though *après*-ski offerings are more or less on par with its rival. In the summer, Hotham is relatively quiet, with nature trails and a few shops and lodgings open for visitors.

From the north, Mt. Hotham is accessible in the winter by a sealed road. Entrance from Omeo to the south is safer and more reliable, but inconvenient for those in Melbourne or Sydney. To get to Mt. Hotham by **bus,** depart from Melbourne's Spencer St. Station (6¼hr., 1 per day, $118.50 return); Wangaratta Railway Station (3¼hr., 1 per day, $81.80 return); or Bright's Alpine Hotel (1½hr., 2 per day, $36.50 return). There is an extra bus each Friday. Contact **Trekset Tours** (☎9370 9055 or 1800 659 009; www.mthothambus.com.au) to book.

There's a fee to enter the resort, payable at the tollbooth 1½hr. from Bright on the Great Alpine Rd., though it is waived if you're just driving through without stopping. (Cars 3hr. $12; 24hr. $25; 48hr. $50; season pass $250; lift tickets not included.) From mid-October to the Queen's Birthday in June, resort admission is free. Drivers heading from Bright can rent mandatory **snow chains** from **Hoy's A-Frame Ski Centre,** on the right just after the school bridge in Harrietville. (☎5759 2658. $27, deposit $50.) These can be returned to the BP **petrol station** in Omeo, on the south side of Mt. Hotham.

The resort is constructed around the Great Alpine Rd., which climbs the mountain. The lodges cluster to the south, with ski lifts and services farther north. Village buses transport folks for free around the resort. The **Visitors Centre** (☎5759 3550; www.mthotham.com.au) is on the first floor of the Resort Management building, just above the Corral carpark. Directly across the street, Hotham Central houses the **Snowsports School office** (☎5759 4444), ski rental places (downhill package $27; snowboard and boots $55), a small **grocery store,** and a **lift ticket** office, which sells passes valid both here and at Falls Creek. (Full-day ticket $69, children $35-40; lift and lesson packages from $89.) Tickets for round-trip **helicopter rides** to

Falls Creek are $89 with a valid lift ticket or $99 without. Trips must be booked in person on the day of travel. The Big D lift hosts night skiing from late June to October. (Open W and Sa 6:30-9:30pm. With lift ticket $6, without $11.)

Lodging on Mt. Hotham is pricey, and Bright's excellent hostels offer an inexpensive alternative. **Mount Hotham Accommodation Service** (☎5759 3636) can sometimes place you in a club lodge cheaply. The **Summit bar ❶**, in the Snowbird Inn, features outstanding views, live bands (Th and Sa), happening crowds, and five-drink jugs for $7.50 from 4:30-6:30pm. (☎5759 3503. Open daily 3:30pm-2am.)

FALLS CREEK   ☎03

An hour's drive from Bright along roads with sweeping views of the Victorian Alpine country, **Falls Creek Ski Resort** takes guests as high as 1842m. **Lift ticket** prices are comparable to other resorts. (☎5758 3733; www.skifallscreek.com.au. $65-78 per day, children $37-41, students $55-66; lifts plus lesson $92-113/$65-77/ $68-83.) The ample snowfall, both natural and man-made, is a selling point, and the spread of trails means that bad weather conditions from one direction leave good skiing elsewhere on the mountain. Few trails are very long and most are intermediate-level runs. Advanced skiers can expect to spend more time on the chairlifts than on the slopes. An area of black diamond trails known as **The Maze** and a snowboarding terrain park with a **half-pipe** are opened as snowfall permits. A Kat service transports skiers in heated Kassbohrers up the back-country slopes of **Mt. McKay** (1842m) for thrilling black and double-black diamond bowl runs ($69 with lift pass). Falls's ambience is more family-oriented than nearby Mt. Hotham's (see p. 661), though their partnership gives multi-day skiers the chance to try both (lift tickets are priced the same and allow access to both resorts).

Driving to the slopes from June to October requires carrying **snow chains** (24hr. rental in Tawonga and Mt. Beauty $18-22) and paying a hefty entrance fee (day visit $18-23, overnight $30-38; $12-15 each additional night). It is more practical to stay in Bright and use public transport to reach the resort for the day. **Pyle's Falls Creek Coach Services** (☎5754 4024) runs a ski-season service from Melbourne (6hr., 1-2 per day, $115 return), Albury (3½hr., 1-2 per day, $63 return), and Mt. Beauty (50min., 5-8 per day, $33 return). All prices include entrance fee.

Activity is concentrated at the edges of the village. The **Falls Creek Information Centre** is at the bottom of town, opposite the day parking lot, and has info on lessons, packages, and lodgings. (☎5758 3490; fallsinfo@fallscreek.albury.net.au. Open daily 9am-5pm.) Staying on the mountain lets you sleep longer, party later, and make snow angels outside, but the privilege does not come cheap. A horde of small, independent lodges offers varying styles of accommodation; the folks at **Central Reservations** (☎5758 3733 or 1800 033 079) can direct you.

Quiet stays in the delightfully swanky ▨**Alpha Lodge ❸**, 5 Parallel St., are available year-round. It has an excellent kitchen, roomy common area, drying room, laundry, BBQ, and sauna. (☎5758 3488; manager@alphaskilodge.com.au. 4-bed dorms $24-91; 2- to 3-bed dorms with ensuite $30-103.) The **Frying Pan Inn ❹**, 4 Village Bowl Cir., at the base of the Summit and Eagle chairlifts, is the place to be on weekends, when there are live bands, dance parties, and drink specials to fuel the debauchery. (☎5758 3390. Pub open daily 5pm-late; bistro open daily 8am-8pm.) **The Man,** 20 Slalom St., is the heart of the nightlife, with food, beer, live bands, multiple bars, pool tables, foosball, and **Internet**. (☎5758 3362. Open daily in winter noon-late; in summer 5pm-late. Internet $5.50 per 30min.)

An active summer resort as well, Falls Creek has bushwalking, horseback riding, tennis, and water activities from October to June. A smaller number of lodges offer housing during the summer (call Central Reservations ☎5758 3733 or 1800 033 079 for current openings), but prices are lower.

GIPPSLAND

Southeast of Melbourne, the Princes Hwy. snakes toward the border of New South Wales, loosely following the contours of the Victoria coast through verdant, rolling wilderness interspersed with extensive lake systems and small towns.

FOSTER   ☎ 03

While gold-hungry miners flocked to Foster (pop. 1000) in search of supplies and a warm bed, most of today's visitors are headed to the Prom; Foster is just 30km north of the entrance to Wilson's Promontory National Park. To drive from Melbourne (170km), take the South Eastern Arterial (M1) to the South Gippsland Hwy. (M420), following signs to Phillip Island, then to Korumburra (where the highway becomes A440), and finally to Foster. **V/Line** (☎ 13 61 96) **buses** run from Melbourne (2¾hr.; M-Su 4:30pm, F 6pm; returns M-Sa 7:49am, Su 3:25pm; $32), requiring that you spend the night in Foster before shuttling to the Prom with the **Foster-Tidal River Bus Service** (see below). **Tourist information** is inside the Stockyard Gallery at the end of Main St. toward the park. (☎ 5682 1125. Open Su and Th-Sa 10am-4pm.) **Parks Victoria** staffs an office in the same building. (☎ 5682 2133. Open M-F 8am-4:30pm.)

Cozy **Foster Backpackers Hostel** ❷, 17 Pioneer St., is the most affordable option, with shared kitchen and outdoor BBQ. Ask the owners about their **farm hostel** ❷. From the S. Gippsland Hwy., turn right onto Main St., then left on Bridge St.; Pioneer St. is on the right and the hostel on the right side. (☎ 5682 2614. Checkout 10am. Main hostel dorms $20; fully contained doubles $50. Farm hostel $25/$50.) Margaret from the Visitors Centre also rents out the **"Rose Cabin"** ❸ behind her house. Surrounded by grapefruit groves and blueberry bushes, it includes a solar-powered shower. (☎ 5682 2628. Each person $35, max. 2.) Foodway, on the corner of Main St. and Station Rd., sells **groceries**. (Open M-Sa 7am-7pm, Su 8am-6pm.)

WILSONS PROMONTORY NATIONAL PARK

The southernmost jutting tip of the Australian continent, **the Prom** is both wildly popular, attracting 400,000 visitors a year, and virtually unspoiled, thanks to generations of passionate conservation.

Preserved as a national park back in 1898 and now a UNESCO World Biosphere Reserve, the Wilsons Promontory National Park has long been off- limits to settlement and most transportation. The area is characterized by its prominent granite peaks, flanked by tidal flats and marshland, meeting clusters of heath, towering gum forests, and rich fern gullies. The diverse flora creates habitats for scores of native marsupials, reptiles, birds, insects, and sea creatures. For more **information** on Wilsons Promontory, call ☎ 1800 350 552, or visit the Parks Victoria website (www.parkweb.vic.gov.au).

THE PROM AT A GLANCE	
AREA: 490km² of parkland; 83km² of marine parks.	**GATEWAYS:** Foster and Yanakie.
FEATURES: A UNESCO World Biosphere; home to Mt. Oberon and Sealers Cove.	**CAMPING:** Must register with the ranger. Fees vary through the park.
HIGHLIGHTS: Easy to challenging hikes and walks, from day to overnight routes.	**FEES:** $9 per vehicle. Fishing permits are required; all payments and inquiries at Tidal River.

VICTORIA

📳 TRANSPORTATION & PRACTICAL INFORMATION

From Foster, turn left at the end of Main St. onto the **Foster Promontory Road,** which snakes 30km to the park entrance, nearly 10km past Yanakie (entry $9 per car, 2-day pass $14, 5-day $27; motorcyles $2.50). Without a car or motorcycle, the only transport into the park is by the **Foster-Tidal River Bus Service,** run by Anne at the Foster Backpackers Hostel (see above), delivering passengers from Foster to Tidal River. (☎5682 6614. By request. One-way $15 with min. 2 people; entrance fee included.) Some touring companies offer daytrips into the park; try **Duck Truck Tours,** which carts people over from Phillip Island. (☎5952 2548. $85, YHA $75.)

From the entrance station, the park's only sealed road, **Wilsons Promontory Road,** winds 30km along the Prom's western extremity, providing many opportunities to turn off for picnics and hikes. The road ends at **Tidal River,** a township with basic facilities, camping, and lodging. Many visitors take overnight hikes or daytrips from this area. During its busiest periods, the park runs a **free shuttle bus** between the Norman Bay carpark, at the far end of Tidal River, and the Mt. Oberon carpark. (From Norman Bay every 30min. in summer 8am-7pm; in winter 8am-4:45pm. From Mt. Oberon every 30 min. in summer 8:15am-7:15pm; in winter 8:15am-5pm.)

Visitors who wish to stay overnight, obtain a fishing license, or get weather updates should go to the **Tidal River Information Centre** at the end of the main road. Visitors must **register** bushwalking and camping plans with park officials here. (☎5680 9555. Open daily 8am-4:45pm.) A 24hr. **Blue Box** phone for contacting a ranger is outside the info center. Tidal River also has a free storage room for superfluous gear, along with the last toilets, pay phones, and food available before the bush. During the summer and Easter holiday period, Tidal River's amenities include an **open-air cinema,** with a 9:15pm nightly screening of a recent release. Purchase tickets at the cinema 45min. before showtime. ($10, children $7.)

🏠 ACCOMMODATIONS & CAMPING

While campsites within the park are held on a first-come-first-serve (non-booking) basis for most of the year, bookings are both available and essential on and around Christmas, Easter, Labour Day, Australia Day, and Melbourne Cup Day. Bookings are also recommended in January. The parks service often reserves a few first-come sites during the holidays, but only for out-of-state visitors, and these usually go fast. (☎5680 9555. Nov.-Apr. $19 for up to 3 people, additional adult $4.10; off-peak $15.50/$4.10.) For outstation **camping ❶,** there's usually no need to book in advance, but you must obtain a permit and pay nightly fees ($6.20, children $3.10). All sites have a one-night maximum stay, except **Roaring Meg** campsite and northern sites (2-night max.). Toilets in outstation sites have no toilet paper, and no sites are powered.

Lodging is considerably more difficult to come by and always requires an advance booking. Options in Tidal River range from basic cold-water huts to ensuite cabins with microwaves. Try to reserve three to six months in advance, and even earlier for summer weekends. Bookings operate under a ballot system for the Christmas holiday, and ballots are only accepted in May. **Cabins ❺,** all over the park, have bath, kitchen, and living room and include towels and linen. (Singles and twins Sept.-Apr. $140, additional person $18.50, off-peak $127.50/$18.50; bunk-style units from $101, off-peak $63; 4-6 bed huts from $51/$77.) Book through the Tidal River Info Centre (☎5680 9555; or write The Parks Office, Wilsons Promontory National Park, Tidal River 3960).

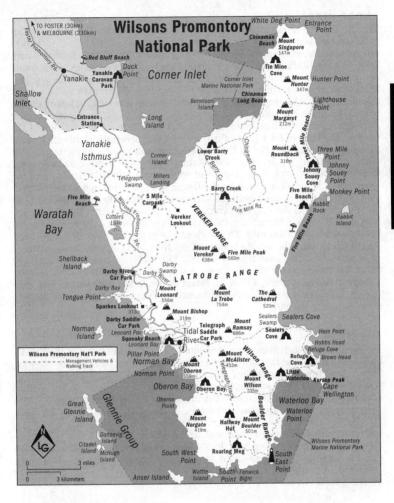

Wilsons Promontory National Park

HIKING

To best experience the Prom, tackle a few bushwalking tracks and take a dip in its crystal-clear water. Although most visitors sample the Prom in a day, you should allow 3-5 days to really take on the entire park. A terrific assortment of tracks enable walkers of all abilities to explore the park's diverse landscape. The Visitors Centre's *Discovering the Prom* ($15) details the over 100km of trails that criss-cross the park, and *Down Under at the Prom* ($19) points to dive sites for scuba and snorkeling. One of the most popular swimming beaches is at **Norman Bay,** past Tidal River.

VICTORIA

SHORT HIKES

Past the Yanakie entrance to the park, the first left leads to the **Five Mile Track Carpark,** allowing access to the northern reaches traversed mostly by overnight hikers. A short detour along the Five Mile Track leads to the **Miller's Landing Nature Walk.** The easy walk (5km; 1½hr.) leads through banksia woodlands to the dwarf mangroves and mudflats of Corner Inlet. A short brochure serves as a guide. Somewhat more challenging, a track about 200m from the carpark leads to some excellent views at **Vereker Outlook** (6km, 2.5hr.) Several short walks (1-2km) depart from Tidal River, including: **Whale Rock** (1km; 20-35min.), a loop track winding gradually uphill through tea-tree, banksias, and sheoaks to a delightful view of Mt. Oberon; and **Loo-errn Track** (2km; 1hr.), a wheelchair accesible boardwalk leading through swamp paperbark and fishing stations to an overlook. For a longer walk with good views, try **Squeaky Beach Nature Walk** (5km; 1½hr.), which passes through dunes, coastal scrub, and granite outcroppings to Pillar Point. Look for wombats in the scrub, and once on the beach, slide your feet to hear the remarkably uniform white-grained quartz sand squeak. **Lilly Pilly Gully Nature Walk** (4.7km; 2hr.), starting from the Lilly Pilly carpark 2km up the road from Tidal River, follows a slight incline through coastal woodlands of paperback thickets and eucalypt forest into the rainforest. This walk can be extended by leaving from Tidal River (6.7km; 4hr.); the section between Tidal River and Lilly Pilly Gully is wheelchair-accessible. The upper track of the Lilly Pilly walk also connects with a track to the **Mt. Bishop** summit (319m). About 5km up the main road is a turn-off for the Telegraph Saddle carpark, where the **Mount Oberon Nature Walk** begins. The walk (6.8km; 2-3hr.) climbs steadily up to the summit (558m), leading to one of the best sunrise spots in the park.

DAYHIKES

For more ambitious hikers, three incredible dayhikes cover some of the Prom's most beloved spots. In the park's southern half, **Tongue Point Track** (5.6km one-way; 2½hr.) starts from Darby Saddle (6.7km north of Tidal River) and proceeds, sometimes steeply, past two sweeping lookouts to a small granite peninsula with a stunning view of the coast. The return trip can be shortened by returning to Darby River carpark (3.5km, 1hr.) and getting a ride from there. The **Oberon Bay Track** (12.4km; 5hr.) leaves from Tidal River and follows Norman Bay Beach, whose yellow sands mirror the scenic coastline along the western bays to Oberon Bay. In the opposite direction, departing from the Mt. Oberon carpark, the **⬛Sealers Cove Track** (20.4km; 5-6hr.) almost traverses the peninsula, and takes you across nearly every environment in the Prom (for more details, see below). Outstation camping is available at the cove.

OVERNIGHT HIKES

The overnight hikes in the south are absolutely worth the time and extra preparation, as they allow hikers to relish the multitude of terrains and spectacular secluded spots. The less-traveled northern part of Wilson's Prom has a circuit but lacks toilets. The most popular 2- to 3-day hike sweeps 36km around the eastern coastal areas along well-maintained trails to Sealers Cove (10.2km), Refuge Cove (6.4km), and Waterloo Bay (7km). An extra 2 or 3 days will offer the Prom's full beauty, with a hike down to the lighthouse and the southeast point. Overnight camp areas are near walking tracks; make sure to carry a gas or fuel stove, as fires are not allowed at any time. All overnight sites have water, but it's taken directly from the creek, and probably best boiled or treated. The following outlines the legs of the southern overnight hike leading to sites.

Telegraph Saddle Carpark to Sealers Cove (9.6km, 2½hr; moderate). This track leads through a stretch of stunning rainforest filled with brown stringy bark and banksia, then into a Messmate forest of austral mulberry and musk daisy-bush before arriving at Windy Saddle, between Mts. Latrobe and Wilson. The forest gets darker and the terrain muddier as the trail heads into Sealers Swamp. Keep an eye out for colorful fungi. The track switches to a boardwalk before opening out to the magnificent cove.

Sealers Cove to Refuge Cove (6.5km; 2hr.; easy-moderate). The beautiful coastal views offered by this track will hopefully distract from its slight rolling. It can get muddy as you head inland, but eventually the coast merges into lush forest. Climbing a few large granite rocks rewards you with a stunning view. The track is poorly marked at this point, so stay on the high side of the first rock; directly ahead, at the top of another large rock, is the pebble track. A short route along the coast heads inland again into stringy bark, then a fern-filled rainforest. A short decline leads you to the beach before heading briefly back into forest, taking you to a campground with water and a flushable toilet.

From Refuge Cove to Waterloo Bay (7km; 3-4hr; moderate-difficult). The track ascends steeply in some parts through stringy bark woodland, dipping briefly into a small gully before heading up again to reach the Kersops Peak lookout. Leave your pack at the signpost to catch a glimpse of the approaching bay by the detour (600m, 10min. return); look out for snakes, as the track has many overhanging plants. Also, keep your eyes peeled for humpback whales. The track then heads steeply down to the beach and traces the coast on an extremely narrow track with raised roots and large rocks. After a quick bend around the coast, the track inclines before heading back into the forest briefly. The beach, directly in front of the Little Waterloo Campground, is a perfect spot for a quick dip. From here, you can follow the lower part of the circuit to join up with Telegraph Track (5.8km, 2hr.), which will take you north to return to the carpark (6.1km, 2hr.), south to Roaring Meg camp (4.8km, 2hr.) and from there an easier route to the lighthouse (7.2km, 2hr.), or farther west to Oberon Bay (3.4km, 1hr.; see **Dayhikes**, above). The fit and ambitious can continue directly to the lighthouse from Little Waterloo camp.

Waterloo Bay to Lighthouse (10.9km; 4-5hr; difficult.) The longest straight incline on the hike leads above Waterloo Point. This uphill stretch is exposed to the sun, has sword-grass, and is quite rocky. Heading inland, the track opens onto a large faced rock with an amazing view, then passes through a stretch of cut forest, enters a eucalyptus forest, and heads down into rainforest. The track rolls through fern forests to the branching for the lighthouse. If you can get a bed there, it's doubly worthwhile to make the steep trek. (Bookings through Tidal River. Bunks from $40, Sa from $65. Lounge, full kitchen and bath.) Otherwise, leave your pack to make the detour (2km return).

The Lighthouse to Roaring Meg (3.7km, 1-1½hr; moderate-difficult). Though short, this portion of the track is a rollercoaster of ups and downs. The track is mostly in the moist rainforest, so be wary of mud and leeches. Turn right when the track empties onto the Telegraph Track and follow the road 700m until it splits to offer the walking track to Roaring Meg (2.3km farther) on your left. Deceptively flat to start with, the track returns to extreme ups followed directly by downs, finally ending at the bridge over the creek (the campsite's water supply). The campsite also offers a short hike (7.4km; 2½hr. return) out to the **southeasternmost point** in mainland Australia.

Roaring Meg to Halfway Hut (via walking track) and Oberon Bay (3.3km; 1¼hr.; easy-moderate). Though the road is shorter, the walking track has better scenery. After a short steep incline, the track remains relatively flat before opening into a short growth forest. A left at Telegraph Track will lead you downhill along the road to the Halfway Hut. This campground has a composting toilet, water, and a small stone hut. The flat track leading to Oberon Beach crosses dry and shaggy forest. Walk along the beach to the right and cross over a small tidal pool to see the track to Tidal River.

Oberon Bay to Tidal River (6.2km; 1½-2½hr.; moderate). Climbing the length of the point, the track flattens out at the rounding of the peninsula. Head down the beach (do not walk up on the grassy dunes) and inland to the next trailhead to round Norman Point. This final peninsula requires a steady climb but offers fantastic views of Little Oberon Bay and its many islands. Rock steps make the track slightly easier, and as the last point is rounded, Norman Bay comes into view and the track leads steadily down to the sand. For the best views, walk the length of Norman Beach, heading inland at the final fence markings to reach a wooden track leading directly into the campground.

YARRAM ☎03

Yarram (pop. 2000) is a small rural service town, most of whose out-of-state visitors are on their way to the **Tarra-Bulga National Park.** A 15km turn-off in Toora, about a third of the way between Foster and Yarram, will lead you to **Agnes Falls,** the highest single-span waterfall in Victoria, dropping 59m into the Agnes River. In the other direction, about 30km east of Yarram, you can access the southern portion of **Ninety Mile Beach,** an unusually long and quite exceptional stretch of white-sanded coastline extending past Lakes Entrance. To reach **Woodside Beach,** popular for **swimming** and **surfing,** follow the S. Gippsland Hwy. to Woodside and turn right onto Woodside Beach Rd.

Yarram is 50km east of Foster on the S. Gippsland Hwy., which becomes Commercial Rd. as it passes through town. The **Harvey World Travel** office on Commerical Rd. sells **V/Line bus** tickets to Melbourne via Foster. (☎5182 6322. 3½hr., departs M-Sa 7am, Su 2:35pm; $31.40. Office open M-F 9am-5pm, Sa 9am-noon.) The **Tourist Information Centre,** in the old Court House at Commercial Rd. and Rodgers St., has lots of helpful info. (☎5182 6553. Open M-F 10am-4pm, Sa-Su hours vary.) The **library,** 156 Grant St., has **free Internet.** (☎5182 5135. Open M and Th-F 10am-6pm, Tu-W 2-6pm, Sa 10am-noon.) **Banks, ATMs, pharmacies,** and a **post office** (open M-F 9am-5pm) are on the main street. **Postal Code:** 3971.

Yarram has a few motels and caravan parks within budget range. **Tarra Motel ❹**, 387 Commercial Rd., is a family-run establishment with good amenities. (☎5182 5444. Doubles from $52, deluxe rooms from $63.) If you are willing to spend a few extra bucks, head next door to the **Ship Inn Motel ❺** (☎5182 5588. Singles from $55; doubles from $65, deluxe from $75.). For food, the **Federal Coffee Palace ❸**, 305 Commercial Rd., housed in Yarram's oldest building, is definitely the hippest place in town, with cushioned chairs, books, board games, and $3 lattes. Try their $16 chicken filet with apricots and camembert. (☎5182 6464. Open Su 9am-4pm, Tu 11am-5pm, W-Th 10am-10pm, F-Sa 11am-late.) IGA **supermarket** is in the Yarram Plaza. (☎5182 6033. Open M-F 8am-6pm, Sa 8am-1pm.)

TARRA-BULGA NATIONAL PARK

The Tarra-Bulga National Park, a section of the **Strzelecki Ranges,** features breath-taking cool temperate rainforests filled with Myrtle Beech, Mountain Ash stands, fern trees, and lyrebirds. The vegetation here is not unlike that found throughout much of Tasmania, and represents what once covered the Stzelecki Ranges before European settlement.

The park can be approached from either the **Tarra Valley Road** through the Tarra Valley or the unsealed **Balook Yarram Road** through the Bulga Forest. Not far from **Yarram** (follow the signs), they connect perpendicularly to **Grand Ridge Road,** forming a loop through the forest. The ascent through the **Tarra Valley,** along a narrow and windy 25km stretch of sealed road, passes through lush fern, eucalypts, and occasional patches of yellow wildflowers. Don't take any unmarked roads without 4WD, as it rains a lot and the area is rarely patrolled. About 20km up the road lies the superb **Tarra Falls.** Another kilometer up, at the Tarra Valley picnic area, follow the easy **Tarra Valley Rainforest Walk** (1.2km; 30min. return) through the rainforest all the way to **Cyathea Falls.**

At the junction of Grand Ridge Rd. and Balook Yarram Rd. is the **Tarra Bulga Visitors Centre,** with maps and info on day-walks and driving tracks. (☎5196 6166. Open Sa-Su and holidays 10am-4pm.) From here you can follow the **Lyrebird Ridge Track** (2.4km) to the **Ash Track** (1km) to access the **Fern Gully Nature Walk** (500m). This short walk is the site of the **Suspension Bridge,** which stretches high above a breathtaking fern gully that houses birds, wallabies, bats, and bush rats. To reach the Fern Gully Walk, head down Grand Ridge Rd. about 1km past the Visitors Centre to the Bulga carpark. The **Forest Track** (4.3km; 1½hr. return) is a slightly longer but moderate walk through the park, leaving from the Visitors Centre.

The park is primarily geared toward day visitors, and hence there is no bush camping within the park itself, though there are two **caravan parks** inside the forest along Tarra Valley Rd. Coming into the park from Yarram, the first one you'll hit is the **Nangeela Tourist Park ❶,** 1369 Tarra Valley Rd. (☎5186 1216. Sites for 2 $15; powered $20; cabins for 2 $55, for families $61-79.) About 2km further up the road, the **Tarra Valley Caravan Park ❶,** 1385 Tarra Valley Rd., serves meals ($23) on Friday and Saturday nights. (☎5186 1283. Sites for 2 $15; powered $18; cabins for 2 from $42-72, extra adult $8.) Both parks have bathrooms, showers, laundry, game room, and a small selection of groceries in the office. Originally lodging for saw mill workers, the **Tarra-Bulga Guest House ❺,** Grand Ridge Rd., by the park entrance, serves as the local indoor option, with 11 B&B-style rooms. (☎5196 6141. Doubles from $90, including breakfast.)

BAIRNSDALE   ☎03

Bairnsdale is a useful place to refuel before venturing into **Mitchell River National Park** or the **Australian Alps.** The town boasts the magnificent **St. Mary's Church.** Completed in 1937, the church showcases spectacular murals by Italian artist Frank Floreani. (Open daily 9am-5pm; service daily at 9am.) The **Krowathunkoolong Keeping Place,** 37-53 Dalmahoy Rd., houses an excellent collection of local Aboriginal artifacts. (☎5152 1891. Open M-F 9am-5pm. $3.50, children $2.50.)

About 275km east of Melbourne and 35km west of Lakes Entrance, Bairnsdale is accessible by the Princes Hwy. (A1), called **Main Street** in town. Bairnsdale is the starting point of the **Great Alpine Road,** a 300km drive that takes you through the **Australian Alps,** near the **Falls Creek Ski Resort,** to **Wangaratta.** You can also walk in the Alps on the **Australian Alps Walking Track,** which begins in **Walhalla** (approximately 50km from Bairnsdale) and goes all the way to Mt. Tennent (655km), outside Canberra. This epic bushwalk over many of the area's highest mountains can be completed in ten weeks. For more info, contact **Parks Victoria.** (☎13 19 63.)

Bairnsdale has a train station with no trains, but there are plenty of **V/Line buses** on MacLeod St. (☎5152 5592), across from the tourist office and down Pyke St. Buses run to Melbourne (4hr.; M-F 3 per day, Sa-Su 2 per day; $55.80) via Sale, where you switch to a train (1hr., $43.80), and to Lakes Entrance (30min.; M-F 4 per day, Sa-Su 1 per day; $11). **Bairnsdale Visitors Centre,** 240 Main St., between McDonald's and the church, has a knowledgeable staff. (☎5152 3444. Open daily 9am-5pm.) The library around the next block on Service St. has **free Internet.** (Open M 10am-5pm, Tu 10am-1pm, W and F 9am-6pm, Th 9am-7pm, Sa 9:30am-noon.)

The accommodations in Bairnsdale are limited. Try camping in **Mitchell River National Park** (see below) or stay at the **Espas Arts Resort** on Raymond Island (see below). If you are driving out to Bairnsdale from Yarram, there is a spotlessly clean caravan park halfway in the award-winning **Stratford Top Tourist Park ❶.** There is a kitchen, BBQ area, one dorm for backpackers, musical bathrooms, and it's near a swimming pool. (☎5145 6588. Sites for 2 $16-17.50, powered $18.19.50; dorms $18; vans $35-45; cabins $40-60.) For motel-style lodging, try the **Bairnsdale Main Motel**, 544 Main St., with its swimming pool, BBQ, and free laundry. (☎5152 5000. Singles $59-69; doubles $69-79.) Safeway **supermarket** is behind McDonald's. (Open M-Th 8am-7pm, F-Sa 8am-8pm, Su 9am-6pm.)

NEAR BAIRNSDALE

RAYMOND ISLAND. Raymond Island is a great daytrip for wildlife spotting, especially on weekends. **Buses** run from Bairnsdale to nearby Paynesville (30min.; M-F 4-5 per day, Sa 1 per day; $7.10); from there, you can take a 2min. **ferry** to the island. (☎0418 517 959. Ferry runs M-F 7am-10:30pm, Sa 7am-midnight, Su 8am-10:30pm. Cars $5, pedestrians free.) The tiny island has a huge population of **wild koalas,** which are most easily spotted off Centre Rd. and the walking tracks that branch off of it toward the south. For those looking to koala-watch in style, **First Bumper Carriage Co.** provides Clydesdale-drawn carriages. (☎5634 8267. Weekends and holidays 10:30am-2:45pm. 25min. tours $8.50, children $5, families $25.) The island is dotted with cozy bed and breakfasts, and the **Espas Arts Resort ❸** is a sparkling but pricey facility near the ferry and right on the water. The complex also has a cafe with an equally steep menu. (☎5156 7275. Call ahead. Cafe open F-Sa 10am-late, Su 10am-5pm. Doubles $80, extra person $10.)

EAGLE POINT. Just south of Bairnsdale, off C604, and right next to Paynesville, Eagle Point is best known for its gigantic **mud silts**, second in size only to those on the Mississippi River in the United States. The silt jetties stretch out for kilometers, with the Rivermouth Road traveling their length. **Eagle Point lookout** provides the best views of the silt jetties. Aside from a few potholes, the road is suitable for a 2WD. Grab some fishing gear and head out for one of the many prime spots along the jetty. Two caravan parks line the waters in town and offer a quiet night's rest. **Lake King Waterfront Caravan Park ❶** has a games room, pool, laundry, and campsites. (☎5156 6387. Sites $13-18, powered $16-24; onsite caravans $42-52; ensuite units $48-70.) Slightly larger and with permanent residents, **Eagle Point Caravan Park ❶** is the first park as you enter town on Bay Rd. (☎0409 382 542. Sites $12, powered $15; ensuite cabins $45-90. $5 key deposit.) Both have petrol.

MITCHELL RIVER NATIONAL PARK

Flowing from the alpine high country down to the Gippsland Lakes, the Mitchell River bisects the 12,200 hectares of warm temperate rainforest and rugged gorge land that comprise the park. Canoeing, rafting, and hiking through the **Mitchell River Gorge** are the best ways to see the park's splendors. To reach the park from Bairnsdale (45km), turn right about 3km west of town onto Lindenow Rd., which becomes Dargo Rd.; a number of well-labeled right-hand turns lead from here. Most roads through the park are unsealed and are navigated most safely in a 4WD.

Beside the gorges and high cliffs looming over the river, most daytrippers venture into the park to pay respect to the **Den of Nargun.** Gunnai/Kurnai legend describes Nargun as a giant stone female creature who destroyed intruders by reflecting their spears and abducted children who strayed from camp. The **Den of Nargun Circuit** (1hr.) loops around **Bluff Lookout,** sweeping down to the **Mitchell River** and the Den of Nargun before heading back up to the carpark. Wear appropriate clothes—much of the walk is in chilly rainforest, and many steps are made of rocks, which are slippery when wet. You can sit by the water's edge to absorb this site's mystical energy, but the cave's fragile stalagmites make it both prohibited and **unsafe to enter**. The more ambitious will appreciate the 2-day **Mitchell River**

Walking Track, which traces the river from Angusvale 17km downstream to the Den of Nargun, taking in some awesome riparian scenery along the way.

There are two places to **camp** in the park. **Angusvale ❶** can be reached by turning right off Dargo Rd. onto the unsealed Mitchell Dam Rd. (River water only; pit toilets. Free.) The other, at **Billy Goat Bend ❶**, is accessible only by foot: turn right off Dargo Rd. onto Billy Goat Bend Rd., follow to picnic area, and then hike in about 1km. (Free.) There's also a natural amphitheater at the Bend that yields some spectacular views of the Mitchell River gorge. **Bairnsdale Parks Victoria** (☎5152 0400) has more information.

LAKES ENTRANCE ☎03

Lakes Entrance is the unofficial capital of the Gippsland Lakes region, the largest inland waterway in the Southern Hemisphere. With expansive beaches, excellent fishing, numerous boating opportunities, caravan parks, and mini-golf courses, it comes as no surprise that Lakes Entrance is heavily touristed by families and retirees during the summer.

◢◪ TRANSPORTATION & PRACTICAL INFORMATION. V/Line buses leave near the post office and head to Narooma, NSW (5½hr., 1 per day, $55) and Melbourne (5hr.; M-F 2 per day, Sa-Su 1 per day; $40-80) via Bairnsdale (30min.; M-F 4 per day, Sa-Su 1 per day; $9.) **McCafferty's/Greyhound** also stops here on its Sydney-Melbourne route. (Daily eastbound 1:15pm, westbound 1am. $62.) For reservations, call **Esplanade Travel**, 309 Esplanade. (☎5155 2404. Open M-F 9am-5pm.)

The Princes Hwy., called the **Esplanade** in town, becomes a waterfront strip lined with largely unimpressive shops. The **Lakes Entrance Visitors Centre,** on the western end of the Esplanade, has plenty of regional information. (☎5155 1966. Open daily 9am-5pm.) Most **banks** and **ATMs** are a few blocks east of the Visitors Centre. The **library,** 55 Palmers Rd., up the hill at the east end of town, offers free **Internet** access. (☎5150 9100. Open M-F 8:30am-5pm.) The **post office** is at 287 Esplanade. (☎5155 1809. Open M-F 9am-5pm.) **Postal Code:** 3909.

⬛ ACCOMMODATIONS. Tempting as it may be, beach camping is illegal and the area is frequently patrolled—luckily, reasonably priced alternatives are everywhere and easy to find. **Riviera Backpackers (YHA) ❷,** 5 Clarkes Rd., off the eastern end of the Esplanade, has spacious rooms right on the lake. Ask the bus to stop at the hostel bus stop. This excellent motel-style YHA earns high marks for its clean facilities and has a large lounge with TV, a solar-heated pool, billiards, bike rental ($1 per hr., $5 per day), laundry, kitchen, Internet ($2 per 15min.), and storage. (☎5155 2444; riviera@net-tech.com.au. Reception 8am-10pm. Dorms $17.50, doubles $18.50 per person; doubles with ensuite $50. Book a few weeks ahead for Dec.-Jan.) **Echo Beach Tourist Park ❷,** 33 Roadknight St., 1 block from the Esplanade, is a 4-star park with kitchen, BBQ, laundry, pool, playground for the kids, private spa, TV, and billiards. (☎5155 2238. Reception 8am-10pm. Powered sites $19, peak season $32; self-contained flats $65-100/$135-200, self-contained ensuite cabins $55-65/$115-130.)

⬛ FOOD. The Esplanade brims with takeaway food shops, and the hotels in town tend to have good bistros in the mid-price range. **Pinocchio Inn Restaurant ❷,** 569 Esplanade, usually has a special such as all-you-can-eat pasta or two large pizzas for $22, along with a full menu of tasty Italian fare. (☎5155 2565. 10% YHA discount. Open daily 5pm-late; in summer noon-3am.) For a light meal for minimal dough, the **Lakes Entrance Bakery ❶,** 537 on the Esplanade, rises above the average meat pie vendor. (☎5155 2864. Open daily 6am-5pm.) **▨Riviera Ice Cream Parlour ❶,**

opposite the footbridge on the Esplanade, sells an award-winning farm-produced ice cream ($2-6) in 35 flavors and generous portions. (☎5155 2972. Open daily 9am-5pm; in summer 9am-11pm.) Get **groceries** at Foodworks, 30-34 Myer St. (☎5155 1354. Open daily 8am-7:30pm.) For **bulk foods** or a quick bite from the take-away menu, try Lakes Health Bar, 10 Myer St. (Open M-F 8am-5pm, Sa 9am-noon.)

SIGHTS & ACTIVITIES. Jemmy's Point Lookout, about 2km west of town, affords a perfect view of the patchwork Gippsland Lakes. **Ninety Mile Beach,** a long and thin stretch of sand that encloses the region's lakes and swampland, is the town's biggest attraction. To get there, cross the footbridge opposite Myer St. From the snack bar and toilet area, a walking track (1hr.) follows the coast to the man-made boat entrance to the deep, blue waters of the Bass Strait. You can also paddle out from the far end of the footbridge by renting a canoe at **Lakes Entrance Paddleboats.** (☎0419 552 753. Canoes $8 for 30min.) Most visitors hire boats from one of the jetties along Marine Pde. Try **Victor Hire Boats,** on the north arm of Marine Pde. (☎5155 3988. 8-passenger cabins $25 per hr., each extra hour $15; half-day $70.) **Barrier Landing** is the western strip of land created by the entrance. Only accessible by boat, the landing has great fishing and rests by both a lake beach and a surf beach. Contact **Mulloway,** on the Marine Pde., for a three-hour all-inclusive **fishing trip.** (☎5155 3304. Trips 9am-noon and 1-4pm. $40.) To find out where to fish, pick up the *East Gippsland Fishing Map* ($8) at the Visitors Centre.

BUCHAN   ☎03

Loads of people visit the town of Buchan (BUCK-in; pop. 200), 58km north of Lakes Entrance and 50km northeast of Bruthen, either on the Snowy River scenic drive or to tour the spectacular limestone Buchan Caves. Buchan is surrounded by rolling hills at the base of the Snowy River Valley and is a base for some serene bushwalks within Snowy River National Park.

No public transport serves Buchan, so most backpackers drive or arrive on touring buses to Melbourne or Sydney. From Lakes Entrance, take the Princes Hwy. 23km east to Nowa Nowa, turn left onto C620 and right onto C608, following signs to Buchan. From Orbost or starting the Snowy River National Park Scenic Drive (this takes longer but offers better views), turn left off Princes Hwy. to veer under the overpass, then right at the T; then look for the next right onto Buchan Rd.

Just south of the Buchan Caves, the small town center contains a **general store** with basic food and **tourist information.** (Open M-F 8:30am-5:30pm, Sa 8:30am-12:30pm, Su 9am-1pm; holidays 8:30am-5pm.) The **Parks Victoria office** right before the caves has the most info on camping and the national parks area, as well as tickets for the caves and reservations for the 100 closely-packed campsites in the area. (☎5155 9264. Sites $11-14.50, powered $15.50-19; extra person $3.30, cabins $50.50-60.) The **Buchan Outreach Resource Centre,** 6 Davidson St., over the bridge onto Orbost Rd. then right onto Davidson St., has **Internet** access. (☎5155 9294. Open daily 9am-4:30pm. $3 per hr.) The **post office** is across from the general store. (Open M-F 9am-5pm.) **Postal Code:** 3885.

The ▨**Buchan Lodge ❷,** left after the bridge on Saleyard Rd. just north of the town center, provides outstanding budget accommodation in a beautifully constructed wooden building. The grand main room houses a lounge, dining area, wheelchair facilities, and a well-decked kitchen. The lodge is a short walk either to town or the caves. (☎5155 9421. All-you-can-eat breakfast included; complimentary tea and coffee all day. Bunks $20.) **Willow Cafe ❷,** the muraled house a few doors down from the post office, has tasty meals. (☎5155 9387. Open daily 9am through dinner.) Afterward, amble across the street to the **pub** at the **Caves Hotel.** (☎5155 9203. Open M-Sa 11am to 10pm-1am, Su noon-8pm.)

The history of the 260-hectare **Buchan Caves Reserve,** begins at least 300 million years ago, when the skeletal remains of ancient coral and shellfish formed a layer of limestone on what was then ocean floor. Around 25 million years ago, underground rivers began to carve out the vast cave system, while mineral-enriched rain seepage began forming the caves' stalactites and stalagmites. Today, over 300 caves are known to exist in the region, with some reaching down to depths of over 50m. The two big caves in the area, **Fairy Cave** and **Royal Cave,** open alternately for guided tours. (1hr. Oct.-Mar. 10, 11:15am, 1, 2:15, 3:30pm; Apr.-Sept.-11am, 1, 3pm. $11.30, children $5.60, families $28.70.) For more of a challenge without all the railings and floodlights, book a group tour of Federal Cave through the Buchan Lodge. (Min. 5 people. $15.)

The Buchan Caves Reserve has a few pleasant bushwalks, none longer than 2½hr. The **Spring Creek Walk** (1½hr., 3km) travels the tea-tree track past limestone and old volcanic rock; leading to Spring Creek Falls and returning by the lower Kannoka Track, you will pass through a fern-filled forest. Keep an eye out for lyrebirds. The Parks Office (above) has more information on other short walks.

SNOWY RIVER NATIONAL PARK

With some of the starkest and most unspoilt wilderness in Australia, the Snowy River National Park surrounds the Snowy River with jagged hills dressed in grey gum, alpine ash, and native pine. It was the untamed beauty of this landscape that inspired Banjo Paterson to pen his bush ballad *The Man From Snowy River,* which glorifies those who choose to take on the harshness of bush life.

▐ TRANSPORTATION. The gorgeous scenic drive around the park can be completed in six hours. The park road is mostly unsealed, becoming increasingly windy and narrow as it heads north. Its suitability for 2WD vehicles depends on the weather, road conditions, and your confidence as a driver. The road is closed to all vehicles during winter. Call **Parks Victoria** in Orbost (☎5161 1222) or Buchan (☎5155 9264) for up-to-date driving reports. If you are driving from Buchan, you can take either the **Buchan-Gelantipy Road** (C608) through the countryside or the unsealed **Tulloch Ard Road** through the forest, both of which end in Gelantipy. To reach Tulloch Ard Rd., head north out of Buchan and take a right on Orbost Rd. Continue straight on Basin Rd. and turn left onto Tulloch Ard. The Buchan-Gelantipy Rd. leads through **Wulgulmerang,** the last place to get petrol and supplies until you reach Bonang east of the park. Fill up before entering the park, as the stations keep odd hours. About 1km down the road, take the right fork onto Bonang-Gelantipy Rd., which follows a steep descent to **MacKillop Bridge** and continues east until its intersection with **Bonang Main Road.** You can either take this all the way to Orbost or turn right onto **Yalmy Road** to reach the eastern sections of the park.

▐▟ ACCOMMODATIONS & ACTIVITIES. The █**Karoonda Park YHA ❷,** 1½hr. from the Princes Hwy. and 40km north of Buchan on the Buchan-Gelantipy Rd. (C608), is a functioning sheep and cattle farm and ranch with a swimming pool, ping-pong, billiards, darts, tennis, bar, wheelchair facilities, and Internet access. An extra few dollars buys you a bountiful evening feast, and after two nights as a paying guest, useful hands can stay longer as farm workers in exchange for room and board. Onsite, **Snowy River Expeditions** has many adventure options: overnight rafting trips (seasonal; $120, backpackers $80); overnight horseback trips ($120, backpackers $80); abseiling (intro $10, full 40m $25); and indoor rock climbing ($5). Oz Experience stops here; call ahead for pick-up from Lake's Entrance. (☎5155 0220. Dorms $24, YHA $20; with board $39/$36, motel singles $26, with ensuite $30; doubles $52; cottages $90.) About 30km farther north along the dirt track en route to Suggan Buggan and Jindabyne, NSW (see p. 234), is the tranquil mountain retreat of **Candlebark Cottage ❸**. This secluded cottage sleeps eight, with a double bed, six loft bunks, and a kitchen. Popular with cyclists and families, the cottage is ideal for bushwalking, trout fishing, or winter expeditions. (☎5155 0263. $95 for two, each extra person $6. Book ahead.) The most popular **campsites** in the park are **MacKillop Bridge, Raymond Falls,** and **Hicks Campsite.** Raymond Falls and Hicks Campsite can be reached off Yalmy Rd. on dirt tracks suitable for 2WD. All have pit toilets; only MacKillop Bridge has a $9 fee. The area around MacKillop Bridge, the only portion of the river accessible by conventional vehicles, is the starting point for many of the park's most popular activities. A canoe launch sets rivergoers downstream to explore rocky gorges, the trailheads to dayhikes and the 18km Silver Mine Trail originate here, and just upstream, sandy river beaches invite swimming and splashing. West of MacKillop Bridge, a signed turn-off from Bonang Rd. leads to the track to a lookout of Victoria's deepest gorge, **Little River Gorge,** a breathtaking sight.

ORBOST   ☎03

Orbost, a logging and service town 60km northeast of Lakes Entrance, serves locals as a commercial hub and visitors mostly as a pit stop on the way to nearby beaches and national parks. The town is the start and finish of the Snowy River National Park Scenic Drive, and two worthy but seldom visited sights lie about an hour away, inaccessible by public transportation. To the north, **Errinundra National Park** is home to Victoria's largest stretch of rainforest. To the south, **Cape Conran** offers beautiful beaches away from the tourist hubbub.

V/Line buses on the Capital Link between Melbourne and Canberra or between Melbourne and Sale run to Orbost from: Bairnsdale (1½hr., 1-2 per day, $22); Canberra (5hr., 2 per week, $54); Melbourne (5hr., 1-2 per day, $54). Buy tickets at **Orbost Travel Centre,** 86 Nicholson St. (☎5154 1481. Open M-F 9am-5:30pm, Sa 9am-noon.) By car, Orbost is just off the Princes Hwy. via Lochiel or Salisbury St.; both exits intersect with Nicholson St.

The **Snowy River Orbost Visitors Centre,** on Lochiel St. just off the Princes Hwy., has info on East Gippsland's national parks and two outdoor paths that snake through manicured rainforest, and a relocated slab hut made to demonstrate an early settler's hovel. (☎5154 2424; open daily 9am-5pm.) In town, there are **ATMs;** the Business Centre **library,** just off Nicholson on Ruskin St., with free **Internet** (☎5150 9100. Open M-F 8:30am-5pm); and a **post office,** on the corner of Nicholson and McLeod St. (Open M-F 9am-5pm.) **Postal Code:** 3888.

Snowy River Orbost Camp Park ❶, 2-6 Lochie St. at Nicholson, is a standardish park near a supermarket and trail along the Snowy River. (5154 1097. Tent sites $12, powered $15; caravans from $30.) The **Orbost Club Hotel ❷,** 63 Nicholson St., is an average budget accommodation with standard Australian-Chinese menu options. (☎5154 1003. Singles $25; doubles $30; twins $35; triples $50.) The **Snowy River Kingfruit Shopping Complex,** 28 Salisbury St., is the best option for food and supplies. (☎5154 1577. Open M-Sa 8:30am-5:30pm.)

ERRINUNDRA NATIONAL PARK

Normally, cool rainforests like the Errinundra are dominated by ancient myrtle beeches, as in the Otway Ranges of southwestern Victoria. Here, however, black olive berry and cinnamon-scented sassafras cover the forest floor, while a tall, wet eucalypt overstory extends through much of the Errinundra Plateau. Errinundra is primarily a daytrip destination for nature walks and forest drives, although soggy camping is available. Approach the forest either by the winding **Bonang Road** from

SCENIC DRIVE. The scenic drive is a great way to experience the area's highlights. Be sure to grab the *Snowy River Country Trail* brochure in Orbost before you head toward Buchan.

1. BUCHAN TO SELDOM SEEN. From Buchan along Tulloch Arc Rd., start your journey at Ash Saddle, halfway to Gelantipy. From here, the Betts Creek Track (1-2km; 30min.) begins an easy loop through a magnificent stretch of massive, old-growth mountain ash. Follow the Betts Creek 4WD track and look to your left for a narrow trail leading through a break in the trees. Continuing farther north, the Seldom Seen Track is a left-hand turn 15km north of Gelantipy. Suitable only for 4WD vehicles or walkers, this 7km uphill track leads to the Mt. Seldom Seen Fire Tower.

2. HANGING ROCK. On the way into the park, **Bonang-Gelantipy Road** offers outstanding views, but the road becomes increasingly windy and narrow, veering perilously close to the edge. Take care: drive slowly and prepare to meet oncoming traffic at each turn. The first sight is **Little River Falls,** with a 400m walking track leading to a viewing platform. Back on the main road, a sign for **Alpine National Park** leads left to a steep unsealed road. This road goes to **Hanging Rock,** or World's End, one of the park's best but least-known lookouts. To reach Hanging Rock, turn left after the bridge (Milky Creek Track), left at Rocky River Ridge Track, and left again at Hanging Rock Track (5km, 4WD vehicles only). The rock is a 10min. ascent with a view of the countryside.

3. HIKE IT UP. Back on the main road, 1km farther into the park, lies the 400-million-year-old **Little River Gorge,** the steepest gorge in Victoria (500m). A 400m trail leads down to the gorge from the carpark. **MacKillop Bridge,** spanning the Snowy at the north of the park, is the starting point of the busiest walking track in the park. The **Silver Mine Walking Track** (15.5km; 3½-5hr.) passes by old silver mines, offering spectacular views of the river and mountains to the west. Unfortunately, this track is poorly maintained and often difficult to see, especially along the river—a compass and map are necessities. The track starts along the 4WD **Deddick Track,** passes through native pines, rises steadily to some fantastic lookouts, then drops down to a poorly marked walkers-only track. Stick close to the river and eventually you will approach an overnight hiker campsite. The walk ascends again to an amazing lookout before heading back down toward the bridge. For the less ambitious, the **Snowy River Track** (1.5km, 30min.), leaving from MacKillop Bridge, is a self-guided nature walk along the Snowy.

4. THE FINAL LEG. MacKillop Bridge soars 30m above luxuriously warm and clear waters. The scenic drive continues around the park toward Bonang, the only source of petrol near the park after Gelantipy. The road from Goongerah onwards is sealed and slightly less windy, traveling through dense forest before returning to Orbost.

VICTORIA

Snowy River in the north or by Princes Hwy. from the south. About 11km south of Bonang and 54km east of Orbost, these roads intersect with the two ends of Errinundra Rd., which leads into the park.

The signs and markers within the park are notably inconsistent—be sure to get a map beforehand and have adequate petrol and enough daylight time to get out. Most of the roads in the park are unsealed but navigable in a 2WD vehicle on a good day; on rainy days, which are not uncommon, call the **Parks Victoria** office in Orbost to check for closures. (☎5161 1222. Open M-F 8am-5pm.) There are a few operators in the town of Orbost that offer tours to Errinundra National Park, but they tend to be pricey. **Eastour** leads trips upon request, including an Errinundra 4WD day tour. (☎5154 2969. $130.)

To tackle the park on your own, get a map and the *Guide to Walks and Tours* (available at the info center in Orbost) and ask which tracks are in good condition. Most visitors make their first stop at **Errinundra Saddle**, where scenic Errinundra Rd. passes through the plateau. Here, a 1km **nature walk** brings folks close to an interpreted patch of the spectacular rainforest. For an uphill challenge, climb to the top of **Mt. Ellery**, over 1km above sea level, for a grand view of the forest (2.5km return). To get there, take Errinundra Rd. to Big River Rd. at the Mt. Morris picnic area, and follow signs to Mt. Ellery. The **Coastal Range track** (25km; 6hr.) is an easy to moderate daytrip along an old 4WD track that showcases the forest's unique features. Farther down the road, you'll hit the **Goonmirk Rocks track** (1km; 30min.), which leads through mountain plum pines, silver wattle, and in springtime, the red flowers of the Gippsland waratah. The most popular place to **camp** near the park is **Ada River**, on the southern section of Errinundra Rd. **Frosty Hollow** is a remote camping area in the park's eastern reaches; take Bonang Rd. to Gap Rd. to Gunmark Rd. to Goonmirk Rocks Rd. to Hensleigh Creek Rd. Both are **free**, with pit toilets and a water source, though there are also other campsites within the park. Check with Parks Victoria for current camping regulations. This area is the rainiest in eastern Gippsland, so most visitors flee for permanent shelter at nightfall.

CAPE CONRAN

Cape Conran and its Coastal Park are just 35km southeast of Orbost via Marlo, offering sandy beaches, serene coastal walks, rich wildlife viewing, and plenty of opportunities for watersports. The cape's geography is a solitary and rugged melange of dunes, heath, wetlands, swamps, and woods. From Orbost, go south down Nicholson St. to Marlo-Cape Conran Rd. and follow it to the end. From farther east, turn left off Princes Hwy. onto Cabbage Tree Rd., 30km east of Orbost, and avoid the right fork to Marlo. The road ends at Marlo-Cape Conran Rd.

Coming from Orbost, there are some serene spots on the road past **Marlo.** One of the best is **French's Narrows,** where the Snowy River meets the sea, about 5km east of Marlo. Two thin strips of land divide the murky river's end from its shallow estuary and the breaks of the Bass Strait. Five kilometers farther down the road is **Point Ricardo,** a secluded beach popular for fishing. From here, it's 7km to the West Beach, which can also make for a 3hr. walk. A short jaunt from the park's accommodations is the main East Cape Beach. The two primary walking options both begin at the carpark on the beach at the end of the road, where there is a map. The mainly coastal **Dock Inlet Walk** (28km; 5-6hr.) is for the physically fit and ambitious. The track leads to the Dock Inlet, a still body of fresh water, separated from the sea by dune barriers, and continues to Pearl Point, known for its rock formations. The **Cape Conran Nature Trail** goes inland (2.5km; 1hr.) and has a map and information sheet for all the markings along the way. Because of occasional flooding, check with rangers (☎5154 8438) before setting out. The trail connects with an interpreted **boardwalk,** also originating at East Cape beach, which explores the history of area settlement. The Yeerung River is popular for **fishing** and **swimming.** The best places to swim in the area are Sailors Grave (East Cape Beach) and Salmon Rocks (near West Cape Beach).

If you plan to spend the night on the Cape itself, the only options are the **Parks Victoria cabins ❸** or camping at Banksia Bluff, left off Cape Conran Rd. onto Yeerung River Rd., just before East Cape Beach. The eight wooden self-contained cabins, one of which is wheelchair-accessible, are comfortable, right next to the beach, and feature toilets, hot showers, laundry, and outdoor barbecues. Bring sleeping gear, towels, and food, though the Marlo supermarket drops by daily around 11:30am with groceries. (☎5154 8438. Book well in advance. Cabins for four $93, peak season $115.) **Campsites ❷,** though more plentiful, are also in demand. (Sites for four $14, peak season $18.40.) If local sites are all booked up, standard accommodation options are available in Marlo.

CROAJINGOLONG NATIONAL PARK

Tracing Victoria's eastern coastline from the New South Wales border to Sydenham Inlet is the phenomenal Croajingolong (crow-a-JING-a-long) National Park. Recognized by UNESCO as a World Biosphere Reserve, it extends nearly 100km and covers 87,500 hectares, encompassing a remarkable diversity of landscapes.

█ ORIENTATION. Croajingolong National Park is located 450km east of Melbourne and 500km south of Sydney. Gateway towns Cann River and Mallacoota serve as good bases for those unprepared to camp. The Princes Hwy. passes through Cann River and Genoa before crossing the border into New South Wales. At Cann River, the highway connects with Tamboon Rd., leading south into the park. The 45km drive down unsealed roads (the Tamboon Rd. and then left on Pt. Hicks Rd.) leads to the **Thurra** and **Mueller Inlet,** ending at a trail to the Point Hicks Lighthouse. At Genoa, further east along the Princes Hwy., the Mallacoota-Genoa Rd. forks south toward Mallacoota.

◪ PRACTICAL INFORMATION. Cann River and Mallacoota both provide services for the park. In Cann River, the **Parks Victoria Information Centre,** on Princes Hwy. near the east end of town, has info on the park's road and trail conditions and area accommodations. (☎5158 6351. Open daily 9am-5pm; in winter M-F 9am-4pm.) Cann also provides a **supermarket** across from the Cann River Hotel (open M-F 8am-6pm, Sa 8am-1pm, Su 9am-1pm) and a stop for **buses** heading to Melbourne at Princes Hwy. and Cox St. (6½hr., 1 per day, $58) or Canberra (4hr., M and Th 1 per day, $47). Mallacoota's services include: a **Parks Victoria Office** on the corner of Buckland and Allan Dr. with info on local walks (☎5158 0219; open M-F 9:30am-noon and 1-3:30pm), and two **supermarkets** at the top of Maurice Ave. (Both open daily 8:30am-6:30pm.)

█ ACCOMMODATIONS. There are four main camping areas within the park, as well as several in the immediate surrounds. The campgrounds at **Thurra** (46 sites) and **Mueller Inlet** (8 sites) ❶ are now run by the folks at Point Hicks Lighthouse, so Parks Victoria has no info on availability ($13.50 per night). Both have fireplaces, pit toilets, and river water. Thurra is more popular because of its private sites, small caravan access, and overnight parking. It's also located near a few trailheads. Between Cann River and Genoa is a turn-off for the park's most attractive 24 sites at **Wingan Inlet ❶,** with popular bushwalking as well as fireplaces, pit toilets, a water source, and fishing. (Inquire at Parks Office for permit. Sites $12-15.) There is also the 600-site **Mallacoota Camp Park ❷,** on Allan Dr. in Mallacoota, with tremendous waterfront lookouts at the Howe Range. The park caters to park visitors, caravaners, and anglers alike. (☎5158 0300. Sites $15-19, powered $17-25.50; non-camper showers $2.)

▨ HIKING. The **Heathland Walk** (2km return; 30min.), leaving from the Shipwreck Creek Day Visitor Area, affords gorgeous views of Little Rame Head to the east and the Howe Range to the west. **Wingan Inlet Nature Trail** (3km return; 45min.) leaves from the Wingan Day Visitor Area and leads past a tidal estuary populated by flocks of waterfowl and ends with a sweeping view of the coast. The **Genoa Peak**

trail (3km, 2hr.) is a moderately challenging track that summits the 490m peak, yielding extraordinary views of Eastern Gippsland and a vast stretch of coast. The ascent is rocky and includes a steel ladder climb toward the end. Starting near campsite 14 in Thurra River, the **Dunes Walk** (4km; 2hr.) leads through tea-tree forest to 150m-high dunes. The **Elusive Lake Walk** (6km; 2hr.) leaves from a carpark on W. Wingan Rd., 3km from the campground, and leads to the lake through fields of wildflowers. The still, deep lake has no above-ground feeds; its fresh water reserves are fed by underground seepage and rainfall. The **Wilderness Coast Walk** is a 70km multi-day trek that takes you along a beautiful, sandy shoreline punctuated by grassy outcroppings and massive algae-coated boulders at the water's edge. There are 10 campsites ($5 each) along the walk, starting with Shipwreck Creek and terminating at Bemm River. Trekkers can access the track at a number of points, though Thurra River is the most popular and convenient. To minimize impact on the environment, all overnight hikers must receive a free permit from the Parks Victoria office in Cann River or Mallacoota before hitting the trail.

WESTERN AUSTRALIA

Western Australia is distinct from the rest of the country in numerous ways and can seem overwhelming at first. The state covers about a third of Australia, and visitors soon realize that simply getting from place to place is often an adventure in itself. Tiny pieces of the map translate into full days on empty roads, affording plenty of time to reflect on the surrounding natural wonders. The upside of WA's immensity is a collection of landscapes and activities that no other area in Australia can rival. Yet, most visitors—like most Australians—don't bother to explore the West, intimidated by its mammoth proportions. Even native West Aussies usually only see a fraction of their state. Of WA's 1.8 million people, 1.4 million live in the Perth area, and most of the rest cling to the coast, along the vineyards of the south or the surf-pounded capes of the north. The hardy tourists that do make it out west are met with a friendly, relaxed welcome, and with good reason: tourism has become one of the state's economic mainstays, and a lot of effort has gone into making WA a tourist-friendly destination.

From diminutive quokkas in the south to outsized camels and salties in the north, a host of Australian animals call WA home. The flora is equally distinctive: WA's interior is a vast, untouched bushland of spinifex grass and red plains beneath an endless expanse of clear blue sky. Between August and November, the land comes alive as carpets of wildflowers burst into being along the coast south from Exmouth into the Great Southern. The Southwest is the domain of ancient forests, hauntingly beautiful as they rise from mist-shrouded roots into the sun-drenched heavens. Here, the majestic Karri, one of the world's largest trees, stretches to heights of 80m. In the north, the desert gives way to the rugged tropical vegetation of the Kimberley. A few rough roads carve through the huge expanses of rainforest, around unearthly rock formations, and past waterfalls that cascade into the Indian Ocean.

WESTERN AUSTRALIA HIGHLIGHTS

ROTTNEST ISLAND. Get up close and personal with quokkas (rat-like wallabies) at the only place they exist on earth. (p. 694)

BUNBURY. Frolic with Flipper in the Southwest's dolphin mecca. (p. 697)

NINGALOO REEF. Swim with whale sharks along 250km of coral reef. (p.722)

CABLE BEACH. The sunset camel rides in Broome never fail to impress. (p. 730)

GIBB RIVER ROAD. Stumble upon a tropical gorge and other surreal wonders along this untouched desert track. (p. 736)

▛ TRANSPORTATION

Because of the distances between attractions and the dearth of long-haul transportation, many travelers—even those on a budget—**buy a car** for long visits (see **Buying and Selling Used Cars**, p. 54). A thriving market exists for used cars, 4WDs, and campervans, fueled by message boards and the *West Australian* classifieds. **Used car dealerships** line Beaufort St. in and around Mt. Lawley, north of Northbridge.

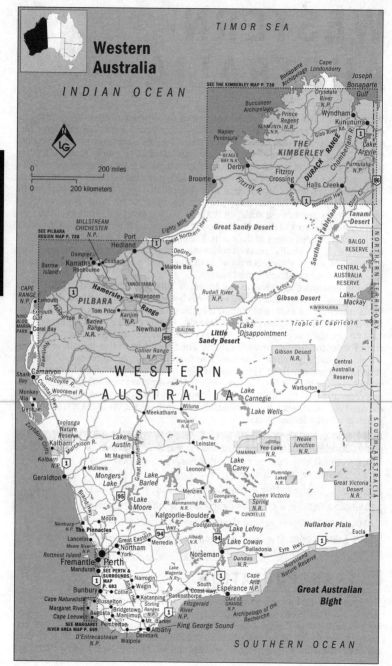

Before paying, have the car checked by a mechanic. Some car dealers prey on backpackers and don't honor warranties. The **Royal Automobile Club (RAC),** 228 Adelaide Terr., Perth, at the corner of Hill St., offers inspections for members and provides roadside assistance. (☎ 13 17 04, roadside assistance 13 11 11. One-year membership $86.90; inspections from $100.) For more info, see **On the Road,** p. 55.

By far the most popular means of getting around WA as a backpacker is **Easyrider** bus tours, which offer "jump on, jump off" service to virtually all towns worth visiting. Drivers are usually young and act as de facto tour guides; they also work well with local hostels to arrange convenient pick-up and drop-off times. With the exception of the Kalgoorlie to Perth route, serviced by the *Indian Pacific* and Transwa Prospector trains, and a commuter train from Perth to Bunbury, passenger **rail** service is essentially nonexistent. **South West Coach Lines** and **Transwa** operate **bus** services southwest of Perth. **Integrity** Buslines services towns between Perth and Broome and tends to be a good deal; **McCafferty's/Greyhound** runs buses throughout the state, but be aware that they do not run directly to Kalbarri, Monkey Mia, Coral Bay, or Exmouth. It will be necessary to catch a shuttle from the North West Coastal Highway to each of these locales; the shuttles run only every third day, so plan on staying for that long. If you plan on a lot of bus travel, cheaper passes are available. For more info, see **By Bus,** p. 682.

Portions of Western Australia can be toured by **bicycle,** but you must carry significant amounts of water. In northern WA, it's not advisable to bike in the hotter, wetter months. Advise regional police and the **Royal Flying Doctor Service** of your itinerary. The **Ministry of Sport and Recreation** (☎ 9387 9700) has more info.

⚠ WESTERN AUSTRALIA NATIONAL PARKS

Access to national parks in Western Australia requires a pass, available from CALM offices and most visitor centers.

Individual Parks: Day Pass $9 per vehicle; Annual $17.50.

All Parks in Western Australia: Holiday Pass (4 weeks) $22.50 per vehicle; Annual Pass $51.

PERTH ☎ 08

Perth is quickly becoming a city of bustling business and booming tourism, but it remains the city of "no worries." Proximity to Asia and an increasing role as a tourist gateway have given Perth a cosmopolitan population and a bustling feel. Single blocks offer cuisine from every continent, 19th-century churches look surprisingly comfortable nestled between glass skyscrapers, and tours leaving for a thousand destinations are advertised in shop windows everywhere. In such an energetic metropolis, it's easy to forget that Perth is the world's most isolated capital city, but a short trip outside the city limits will quickly remind you that the surrounding areas are a different story. Indeed, 90% of the state lives within these few square kilometers. For those less enamoured with the new Perth, nearby historic Fremantle (known as "Freo") is a link to the slower-paced past.

⊠ INTERCITY TRANSPORTATION

BY PLANE

Flights arrive at and depart from Perth Airport, east of the city. The international terminal is 8km away from domestic terminals; keep this in mind if you're planning a connection. **Qantas,** 55 William St. (☎ 13 13 13; www.qantas.com.au), flies daily to: Adelaide (2¾hr.), Brisbane (4½hr.), Darwin (3½hr.), Melbourne (3¼hr.), and Sydney (4hr.). For trips within the state, try **Qantas, Virgin Blue** (☎13 67 89; www.virginblue.com.au), or regional carrier **SkyWest** (☎13 13 00; www.skywest.com.au). Most major towns in WA are serviced by one or all of these airlines. There are a few transport options between the city and airport. **TransPerth buses** #36, 37, and 39 run between the domestic terminal and the city, leaving from the north side of St. Georges Terr., stop 39 (35min., every 30min., $3). An **Airport City Shuttle** (☎9475 2999) runs frequently between most city hotels and hostels in Perth and both the domestic ($11) and international ($13) terminals. The **Fremantle Airport Shuttle** goes to both terminals, departing daily from the Fremantle Railway Station regularly until midnight; pick-up at Fremantle accommodations is available 24hr. when booked in advance. (☎9383 4115. $15.) A **taxi** to the city center costs around $25 from domestic terminals and $25-30 from the international terminal and takes 20 or 30min., respectively.

BY TRAIN

All eastbound trains depart from the **East Perth Terminal,** on Summer St. off Lord St., a 25min. walk northeast of the city center. **TransPerth trains** run between the station and the city center every 15min. on weekdays and every 30min. on weekends. **Transwa** (☎1300 6622 05; www.transwa.wa.gov.au) serves Bunbury and Kalgoorlie. The *Indian Pacific* runs east to: **Adelaide** (43hr., $283); **Melbourne** (56hr., $340); **Sydney** (65hr., $459).

BY BUS

Easyrider (☎9226 0307; www.easyridertours.com.au) has a number of routes to the major sights and towns throughout the state and picks up at your hostel. **Transwa** (☎1300 6622 05; www.transwa.wa.gov.au) runs buses from the East Perth Terminal. The more expensive **McCafferty's/Greyhound** (☎13 14 99 or 13 20 30) departs from Perth Station in the city center, as does **Integrity** Buslines (☎1800 226 339), which allows unlimited stopovers on its Perth to Broome ($234) and Perth to Exmouth ($149) lines. **Southwest Coach Lines** (☎9324 2333) leaves from the Perth City Bus Port, Mounts Bay Rd. See the table on p. 684.

BY CAR

There are over a hundred rental companies in greater Perth. Some quote dirt-cheap daily rates, but read the fine print—many have 100km driving limits, voiding your insurance if you drive north of a certain limit. As in most industries in Perth, there are often backpacker specials. All companies listed rent to drivers over 20, usually with an extra charge of $10-15 per day for those under 25. **Bayswater,** 160 Adelaide Terr. (☎9325 1000), or 13 Queen Victoria Ave., Fremantle (☎9430 5300), allows trips as far north as Carnarvon or to Port Hedland for an extra $100 total. **Europcar,** 266 Great Eastern Hwy. (☎1300 13 13 90), allows its cars to go further north for no extra charge, so long as you inform them beforehand. **Atlas Rent-a-Car,** 36 Miligan St. (☎9481 8866 or 1800 659 999), also allows travel to Exmouth. Costs vary depending on distance and vehicle, but rates in the city are reasonable: $40-50 per day for 500km per day; weekly rates are cheaper. Though there are sometimes exceptions, **4WD vehicles** are generally the only way to explore unsealed areas; 4WDs start at $100 per day, often with extra charges for unlimited kilometers and drivers under 25. **ATC,** 145-151 Adelaide Terr. (☎9325 1833), and **South Perth 4WD Rentals,** 80 Canning Hwy., Victoria Park (☎9362 5444; enquire@sp4wd.com.au), rent 4WDs. **Wicked Campervans** (☎1800 2468 69; www.wickedcampers.com.au) rents campers with cooking facilities to backpackers from $38 per day. **Backpackers Travel Centre,** 223 William St., helps backpackers with rentals and insurance.

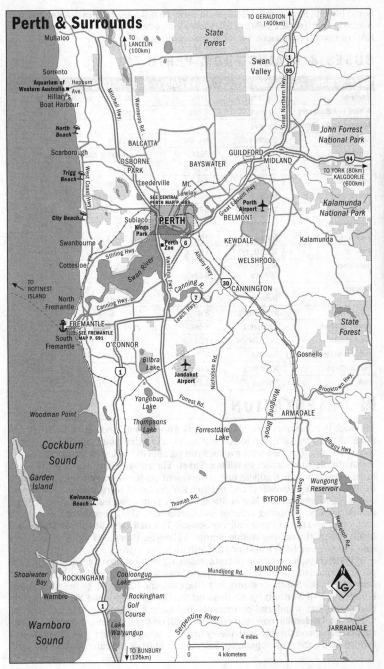

Perth & Surrounds

Some hostels have special deals with local companies. **The Royal Auto Club,** 228 Adelaide Terr. (☎9421 4400), offers roadside assistance (☎13 11 11) to members of RAC or several overseas automobile associations.

BUSES & TRAINS FROM PERTH TO:

DESTINATION	COMPANY	DURATION	FREQUENCY	PRICE
Adelaide	McCafferty's	36hr.	M-W, F, Su 1 per day	$238
Albany (via Bunbury)	Transwa	6-8hr.	1 per day	$41
Albany (via Mt. Barker)	Transwa	6hr.	1-2 per day	$41
Augusta	Southwest	5-5½hr.	2 per day	$30
Broome	McCafferty's	32hr.	1 per day (F and Su 2)	$266
Bunbury	Southwest	2½hr.	3 per day	$19
Busselton	Southwest	4hr.	3 per day	$22
Carnarvon	McCafferty's	12hr.	1 per day (Su, W, F 3)	$103
Darwin	McCafferty's	56hr.	1 per day	$496
Dunsborough	Southwest	4½hr.	1 per day	$24
Esperance	Transwa	10hr.	Su, W, F 2 per day	$62
Exmouth	McCafferty's	16½hr.	1 per day	$159
Geraldton	McCafferty's Transwa	6hr. 6-8hr.	1 per day (Su, W, F 3) 1-2 per day	$35 $43
Kalbarri	McCafferty's Transwa	8hr. 8hr.	1 per day (Su, W, F 2) 1-2 per day	$74 $54
Kalgoorlie	McCafferty's	8hr.	M-W, F, Su 1 per day	$106
Margaret River	Southwest	4½hr.	2 per day	$27
Monkey Mia	McCafferty's	12-14hr.	1 per day (W, F, Su 3)	$122
Pemberton (via Bunbury)	Transwa	5½hr.	1-2 per day Su-Th	$38
Port Hedland	McCafferty's	24hr.	1-2 per day	$185
York	Transwa	1½hr.	1-2 per day Su-F	$12

■ ORIENTATION

Although Perth's streets are not quite aligned north-south and east-west, it helps to think of them as such, and locals will understand what you mean if you refer to them that way. The east-west avenues run parallel to **Wellington Street.** The north-south streets run parallel to **William Street.** The railway cuts east-west through town, separating the business and government center of downtown to the south from the cultural, culinary, and backpacker center of Northbridge. Downtown, east-west streets **Hay** and **Murray Street** become pedestrian malls between William and Barrack St. Shopping arcades and overhead walkways connect the malls to each other and to the Perth Railway Station. The **Wellington Street Bus Station** is a block west of the railway station, across William St. Downtown Perth is relatively safe, but not well lit. *It's best not to walk alone at night.*

In **Northbridge,** a multitude of restaurants, nightclubs, travel agencies, and budget accommodations cluster in the square bounded by Newcastle St. to the north, James St. to the South, Beaufort St. to the east, and Russel Sq. to the west. A few blocks north of Northbridge on Beaufort St., the up-and-coming **Mt. Lawley** neighborhood offers wonderful restaurants and more sophisticated nightlife. In the northwest, **Leederville,** one stop north of Perth on the Currambine line, is a pleasant place to spend the day, with plenty of pubs, cafes, and funky shops centered on Oxford St. To the west, upmarket **Subiaco** is a hotspot for cafes and cuisine, and has weekend market stalls on either side of the Subiaco train stop on the Fremantle line. The great, green expanse of **Kings Park** rises just southwest of downtown, overlooking the city and the Swan River. Although technically its own city and 30min. away, **Fremantle (Freo)** is effectively part of greater Perth. While Perth has the central business district, Freo is a laid-back fishing port and arts hotbed. **TransPerth** buses and trains run regularly between the two (15min.). The Fremantle train also passes through the lively beach suburbs of **Swanbourne** and **Cottesloe**.

◘ LOCAL TRANSPORTATION

Like all cities of a million-plus people, Perth takes up a bit of space. However, downtown and Northbridge are compact and easy to navigate on foot. The free **CAT bus services** whisk passengers around downtown Perth and Fremantle. The **blue CAT** runs a north-south loop from the Swan River to Northbridge; the **red CAT** runs east-west from West Perth to East Perth. The new **Fremantle CAT** runs a skinny loop along the harbor. (☎ 13 62 13. Blue CAT every 7min., weekends every 15min.; M-Th 6:50am-6:20pm, F-Sa 6:50am-1am, Su 10am-5pm. Red CAT every 5min., weekends every 35min.; M-F 6:50am-6:20pm, Sa-Su 10am-6:15pm. Freo CAT every 10min.; M-F 7:30am-6:30pm, Sa-Su 10am-6:30pm.)

The **TransPerth** network of **buses, trains**, and **ferries** is divided into eight **fare zones** connecting to outlying areas; a two-zone ride costs $3 and will get you from the city center to the airport, Fremantle, or the beach. Save your **ticket stub**—it allows transfer between bus, train, and ferry services. Tickets are generally valid for two hours. **All-day passes** ($7.50) and **multi-ride cards** are available at TransPerth Info-Centre machines and newsagents. It's tempting to ride without paying, but $50 penalties await freeloaders who get caught, and there's no shortage of ticket-checking officers on trains. Maps, timetables, and additional info are available by phone (☎ 13 62 13. www.transperth.wa.gov.au) or at the four TransPerth InfoCentres: Plaza Arcade, Wellington St. Bus Station, City Busport, and the train station.

It's also easy to get around by **taxi**; a ride between the international airport terminal and Northbridge costs between $25 and $30. **Swan Taxi**, 1008 Wellington St. (☎ 13 13 30), or **Black and White Taxi** (☎ 13 13 08) can be hailed around the city, especially along Wellington St. or William St. The tourist office has maps of **bike** routes. The **Bicycle Transportation Alliance**, 2 Delhi St. (☎ 9420 7210), has info, maps, and advice on bike routes. Bikes can be rented at Kings Park or stands around the city.

◪ PRACTICAL INFORMATION

TOURIST & FINANCIAL SERVICES

Tourist Offices: Perth Visitors Centre (☎ 1300 361 351; fax 9481 0190), on the corner of Wellington and Forrest Pl. Open M-Th 8:30am-6pm, F 8:30am-7pm, Sa 8:30am-12:30pm; May-July M-Th 8:30am-5:30pm, F 8:30am-6pm, Sa 8:30am-12:30pm. **Fremantle Tourist Bureau** (☎ 9431 7878), on the corner of High St. and William St., Kings Sq. Open M-F 9am-5pm, Sa 9am-4pm, Su noon-5pm.

Outdoors Info: CALM, 17 Dick Perry Ave. (☎ 9334 0333; www.naturebase.net), near the corner of Hayman Rd. and Kent St., Kensington. Take bus #33 east to stop 19. Open M-F 8am-4:30pm.

Budget Travel: YHA Western Australia, 236 William St., (☎ 9227 5122; enquiries@yhawa.com.au), Northbridge, and Raine Sq. on William St. downtown, arranges YHA discounted travel and sells memberships. **STA Travel,** 100 James St., Northbridge (☎ 9227 7569). Open M-F 9am-5pm, Sa 10am-3pm. Branch at 53 Market St., Fremantle (☎ 9430 5553). Open M-F 9am-5pm, Sa 10am-3pm, Su 11am-3:30pm.

Consulates: Canada, 267 St. Georges Terr. (☎9322 7930); **Ireland,** 10 Lilika Rd., City Beach (☎9385 8247); **Great Britain,** 77 St. Georges Terr. (☎9221 5400); **United States,** 16 St. Georges Terr. (☎9231 9400).

Currency Exchange: Thomas Cook (☎9481 7900), at the Piccadilly Arcade on Hay St. Open M-F 8:45am-4:45pm, Sa 10am-2pm. **American Express,** 645 Hay St. Mall (☎9221 0777), London Court. Foreign exchange open M-F 9am-5pm, Sa 9am-noon. **ATMs** and **banks** everywhere, especially on William St. in Northbridge and on Hay St. in the mall area between Barrack and William St.

Work Opportunities: Most hostels, particularly bigger ones, maintain notice boards with job openings. A great resource, particularly for work in the WA countryside, is **Workstay,** 158 William St., 1st fl. (☎9226 0970. Open M-F noon-4pm.). Workstay maintains a network of farms and other horticultural businesses that need temporary labor. They are well-coordinated with area hostels and have a burgeoning network in Perth. They also have a growing network of pubs outside Perth that are looking for service staff. As of Aug. 2002, a **membership** costs $25 per year and pub work $50 per year, though prices are due to rise. Employment agencies in Perth are generally uninterested in back-packers staying less than a couple of months. **Hays Personnel Services,** 172 St. Georges Terr. (☎9322 5198), may be a bit more traveler-friendly. **Adecco,** 37 St. Georges Terr. (☎9461 4800), is another option. **Free Spirit,** 18-20 Howard St. (☎9485 0788), off St. Georges Terr. near William St., is a good resource for traveling office workers. A **job center** with a searchable database is on the corner of Wellington and Milligan St., though most of its resources are reserved for Australian residents. (Open 8:30am-4:30pm.)

LOCAL SERVICES

Public Markets: Subiaco, at the Pavilion at Rokeby and Roberts Rd. Open Th-F 10am-9pm, Sa-Su 10am-5pm. **Fremantle:** 84 South Terr. Open F 9am-9pm, Sa-Su 10am-5pm.

Library: The **Alexander Library Building** (☎9427 3111), at the north end of the Perth Cultural Centre. **Internet** for research only. Open M-Th 9am-8pm, F 9am-5:30pm, Sa-Su 10am-5:30pm. Wheelchair-accessible. The **Fremantle City Library** is on the corner of William St. and Newman Ct., in the Town Hall Centre (☎9432 9766). Open M-F 9:30am-8pm; Sa 9am-12:30pm.

Ticket Agencies: For sporting events, try **Ticketmaster** (☎13 61 00; www.ticketmaster7.com), at Perth Entertainment Centre at Wellington and Milligan St., and in the underground at 713 Hay St. Mall. Open M-F 9am-5:30pm, Sa 9am-1pm. For theatrical and musical events throughout the city, reach **BOCS Tickets,** Perth Concert Hall, 5 St. George's Terr. (☎9484 1133; fax 9221 2241). Open M-F 8:30am-5:30pm.

MEDIA & PUBLICATIONS

Newspapers: *The West Australian* (88¢).
Nightlife: *XPress* and *Hype* come out weekly (free). For gay nightlife, try the weekly *Out in Perth* (free). *Women Out West* is a lesbian monthly ($4.50).
Radio: Rock, 96FM and 92.9FM; News, ABC 720AM; Tourist Info, 88FM.

EMERGENCY & COMMUNICATIONS

Emergency: ☎000.

Police: ☎9222 1111; Fremantle ☎9430 1222.

Hotlines: Sexual Assault (24hr. ☎1800 199 888). **AIDS/STD Line** (☎9429 9944). **Suicide Emergency Service** (☎9381 5555). **Poisons Information Centre** (☎13 11 26).

Hospital: Royal Perth Hospital (☎9224 2244), on Wellington St. near Lord St. **Fremantle Hospital** (☎9431 3333), corner of Alma St. and South Terrace.

Internet Access: Student Uni Travel, 513 Wellington St. (☎9321 8330), offers 15-20min. free email. Open M-F 8am-6pm, Sa 11am-3pm. The going rate in Northbridge is $3 per hr. Fast connections include: **Internet Go Go,** 150 William St., Northbridge (☎9226 3282), at $3 per hr., and **net.CHAT,** shop 14, Wesley Way Arcade, Market St., Freo (☎9433 2011). 10¢ per min., $4 per hr. Open daily 8-11am and 9-11pm.

Post Office: 3 Forrest Pl. (☎9237 5460). Poste Restante M-F only. Open M-F 8am-5:30pm, Sa 9am-12:30pm, Su noon-4pm. **Fremantle GPO,** 13 Market St. (☎9335 1611). Open M-F 8:30am-5pm. **Postal Code:** 6000 (Perth); 6160 (Fremantle).

◤ ACCOMMODATIONS

Perth has many luxury hotels and a slew of hostels, with little in between. Hostels downtown and in Northbridge tend to be large and institutional party places. North of Northbridge, converted houses offer more privacy and space. All hostels listed book or help out with tours, will generally pick up, and offer luggage storage, on-site laundry facilities, and kitchens. Call ahead if arriving late.

CITY PROPER

▨ **The Witch's Hat,** 148 Palmerston St., Northbridge (☎9228 4228; witchs_hat@hotmail.com). This beautiful pointed building was built in 1837 by the architect of the Horseshoe Bridge, which takes William St. over the train station. Hardwood floors, grand front hall, and a brick courtyard in a quiet neighborhood just north of Northbridge. Most dorms have 4 or 6 beds. Internet $5 per hr. Dorms $19; twins $49; doubles $54. ❷

▨ **Underground Backpackers (NOMADS),** 268 Newcastle St. (☎9228 3755; fax 9228 3744). Enough beds and amenities to accommodate an army in style. 6- to 10-bed dorms with big windows and high ceilings. Licensed bar, pool, and brick basement lounge—complete with big-screen TV—in a superb location close enough to the heart of Northbridge to be convenient but still removed enough to allow for some quiet. Some doubles come equipped with televisions and DVD players. Internet $5 per hr. Dorms $19; 4-bed dorms $22; twins and doubles $58. ❷

Billabong Resort Backpackers (NOMADS), 381 Beaufort St. (☎9328 7720). A new, swanky megaplex. An old college dormitory renovated into a state-of-the-art, 180-bed hostel with exercise room, game room, library, and pool. Internet $4 per hr. 4-bed dorms $20; 6-bed $19; 8-bed $18; singles, doubles, and family rooms $55. ❷

Britannia International YHA, 253 William St., Northbridge (☎9427 5122; britannia@yhawa.com.au). A massive place right in the middle of Northbridge, with dining space. Internet $4 per hr. Reception 24hr. 6- to 8-bed dorms $21.50, YHA $18; 3- to 4-bed $23.50/$20; singles $31.50/$28; doubles $62/$55; family $72/$65. ❷

Townsend Lodge, 240 Adelaide Terr., East Perth (☎9325 4143; www.townsend.wa.edu.au). A great deal for clean singles in a convenient downtown location amid the skyscrapers. Popular with students, so book ahead. Internet $5 per hr. $50 room/key deposit. Singles $35, 3+ nights $26, students $22; doubles $45. ❸

Cheviot Lodge, 30 Bulwer St. (☎9227 6817; www.cheviotlodge.com), close to the East Perth train station. This homey, attractive former college residence has lots of desks and furniture, as well as either partitions or curtains between beds to provide guests some more privacy. Holds fairly regular art workshops. Free Internet. Dorms $16-18; twins $40; doubles $44. ❷

The Coolibah Lodge, 194 Brisbane St., (☎9328 9958), Northbridge. A maze of lounges, dorms, and kitchens in a remodeled colonial home. Will help guests find work in Perth or the country through Workstay. Mostly 4-bed dorms, two 6-beds. Free pick-up. Internet $2 per 20min. Dorms $20; singles $36; doubles $50-52. VIP. ❷

Perth City Hotel, 200 Hay St. (☎9220 7000; info@perthcityhotel.com.au). Nice motel-style rooms in a basic hotel. One of Perth's cheaper hotels. Doubles $83; triples $94; quads $105. ❺

FREMANTLE

▨ **Old Firestation Backpackers,** 18 Phillimore St. (☎9430 5454; fax 9335 6828), at Henry St. Unlimited Internet, videos, digital jukebox, and Playstation make it difficult to leave this hostel. Separate girls wing with own kitchen and lounge. Most rooms have TVs. Cheap curries from the connected restaurant ($4-7). Dorms $17; twins and doubles $44. Weekly $105/$250. ❷

▨ **Sundancer Backpackers Resort,** 80 High St. (☎1800 061 144). This brand-new hostel is a restored turn-of-the-century hotel, with one of the most interesting, elegant hostel lobbies around. Futuristic artwork, a heated spa, and an in-house bar. Dorms $16-20; singles $40; doubles $50, ensuite $70; family rooms $70. ❷

YHA Backpackers Inn Freo, 11 Pakenham St. (☎9431 7065; fax 9336 7106). From the train station, turn right onto Phillimore St., then left onto Pakenham. Attractive, spacious renovated warehouse space. Relaxed and quiet. Free videos. Reception 7am-11:30pm; 24hr. check-in available. Bike hire $10 per day. Dorms $18; singles $35; doubles $48; family rooms $60. NOMADS/VIP/YHA. ❷

Cheviot Marina Backpackers, 4 Beach St. (☎9344 2055; fax 9433 2066). Turn left down Elder St. from train station (becomes Beach St.). A big, sunny place with a friendly lounge upstairs and discounted drinks at the bar next door. Internet $1 per 20min. Dorms $14; singles $27; twins and doubles $35. VIP/YHA. ❶

His Majesty's Hotels (☎9335 9516), on the corner of Mouat and Phillimore St. Huge, somewhat bare doubles and smaller singles in a historic hotel with a classy bar downstairs. Singles $35; doubles $70, ensuite $110. ❸

◖ FOOD

Perth's cuisine offerings are tremendously varied. Northbridge has a horde of delicious Italian restaurants and noodle houses. Culinary diversity peaks in Mt. Lawley, where a dozen nationalities are represented in two blocks. Subiaco is elegant (and pricey), while in Fremantle, sophisticates loll about in cafes.

Grab meats and produce at **City Fresh Fruit Company,** 375 William St. (open M-Sa 7am-8pm, Su 7am-7pm), or hike to the more comprehensive **Foodland,** 556 Hay St. (open M-Th 8am-6:30pm, F 8am-8pm, Sa 9am-6pm, Su 10:30am-6pm). For cheap, quality imported bulk pasta, cereals, and deli foods, elbow through the crowds into **Kakulas Brothers Wholesale Importers,** 185 William St. (Open M-F 8am-5:30pm, Sa 8am-noon.) On the corner of Market and Leake St. in Fremantle, **Kakulas Sister** emulates her Perth sibs. (Open M-F 9am-5:30pm, Sa 9am-5pm, Su noon-5pm.)

A number of pubs and clubs cater specifically to the backpacker set (vegetarian-friendly), enlivening the crowds with free meals and drink specials. The determined can find free food almost every night. M: **The Deen,** 84 Aberdeen St. (☎9227 9361); Tu and Th: **Hip-E-Club** (☎9227 8899), on Newcastle and Oxford St. in Leederville; W: **The Post Office** (☎9228 0077), on Aberdeen and Parker St.

CITY PROPER

▨ **Il Padrino,** 198 William St. (☎9227 9065). Perth's best pizza ($15-25). Tu dinner half-price pizza and $10 pasta. Open Tu-F 11am-3pm and 5pm-late, Sa-Su 5pm-late. ❶

Chef Han's Cafe, 245 William St. (☎9328 8122), also 546 Hay St. With a few locations around Perth, Chef Han is the emperor of local budget cuisine. Delicious, fast heaps of vegetarian-friendly noodle and stir-fry for $6-8. Open daily 11am-10pm. ❶

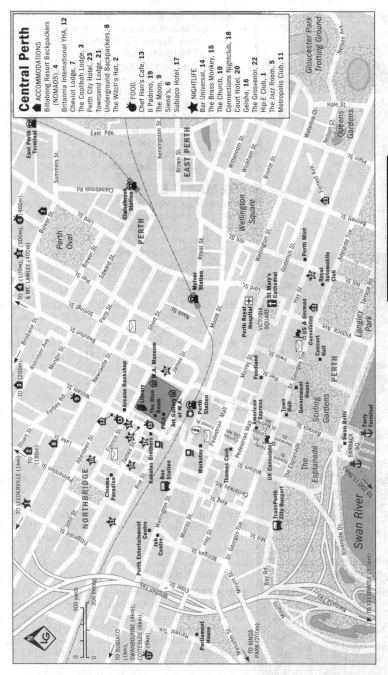

Central Perth

▲ ACCOMMODATIONS
Billabong Resort Backpackers
(NOMADS), 4
Britannia International YHA, 12
Cheviot Lodge, 7
The Coolibah Lodge, 3
Perth City Hotel, 23
Townsend Lodge, 21
Underground Backpackers, 8
The Witch's Hat, 2

🍴 FOOD
Chef Han's Cafe, 13
Il Padrino, 19
The Moon, 9
Siena's, 6
Subiaco Hotel, 17

★ NIGHTLIFE
Bar Universal, 14
The Brass Monkey, 15
The Church, 10
Connections Nightclub, 18
Court Hotel, 20
Geisha, 16
The Grosvenor, 22
Hip-E Club, 1
The Jazz Room, 5
Metropolis Club, 11

WESTERN
AUSTRALIA

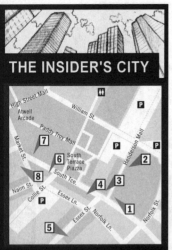

THE INSIDER'S CITY

VERY FREO

*Fremantle's "Cappuccino Strip"
offers a cosmopolitan oasis where
you can sip lattes while casting
withering glances over wire-rimmed
glasses or digging through stacks of
literary treasures.*

1 Browse the famous **Fremantle Markets** for anything and everything you could imagine.

2 Find that out-of-print literary gem at musty **Magpie Books** (☎9335 1131).

3 **The Mill Bakehouse** is a great place to grab a pastry and coffee (☎9430 4252).

4 Look sophisticated while sitting at a sidewalk table with your latte at **Dome** (☎9336 3040).

5 Indulge your cultural side by catching an artsy independent flick at the **Luna** theater (☎9430 5999).

6 Stop for a cake or a cocktail at **Gino's** (☎9336 1461).

7 Peruse the extensive selection at **Elizabeth's Secondhand Bookstore** (☎9433 1310).

The Moon, 323 William St. (☎9328 7474). A space-age-retro diner filled late at night by young, black-clad trend-setters. Several veggie options. Pasta, seafood, burgers $10-18. Open daily 5pm-late. ❷

Subiaco Hotel (☎9381 3069), located on the corner of Hay and Rokeby St. Award-winning nouveau cuisine—everything from risotto to lamb and rabbit—in an elegant setting ($17-25). ❸

Siena's, 500 Beaufort St., Mt. Lawley (☎9227 6991), and also 115 Oxford St., Leederville (☎9444 8844). One of countless great restaurants in Mt. Lawley. Delicious cakes, pizzas, and pasta $12-20. Open noon-11pm; sometimes closed in the afternoon. ❸

FREMANTLE

☒ Cicerello's, 44 Mews Rd. (☎9335 1911). One of Western Australia's classic fish 'n' chips joints. Hang out with the hundreds of multicolored fish in the 15m fish tank while you munch on their well-fried brethren ($5-10). Open daily 10am-8:30pm. ❶

Fiorelli, 19C Essex St. (☎9430 6119). Friendly staff and satisfying Italian food ($12-16). The pizzas are especially tasty and filling. Open daily 11am-late. ❷

Hara Cafe, 33 High St. (☎9335 6118). Good, cheap vegetarian meals. Thalis $6-9, teas $3.50 a pot. Open M-Tu 11am-4pm, W-F 11am-9pm, Sa-Su noon-9pm. ❶

Roma, 9-13 High St. (☎9335 3664). Good Italian food served in a relaxing atmosphere ($11-18). Try the ravioli ($8) or spaghetti ($7). Open M-Sa noon-2pm and 5pm-late. ❷

⊙ SIGHTS

CITY PROPER

SWAN BELLS. Perth's most recognizable landmark is a glass spire bell tower vaguely reminiscent of a swan. Perched on the shores of the Swan River, with Perth's modern skyline as a backdrop, the tower houses twelve bells originally cast in 14th century England and given to the city on Australia's bicentenary in 1988. The bells are rung periodically; check the website for dates and times. *(Barrack Square, at the river end of Barrack St. Take the blue CAT to stop 19. ☎9218 8183; www.swanbells.com.au. Open daily 10am-4pm. $6; concessions $5; children $3.)*

PERTH ZOO. The Australian section has frilled lizards, crocodiles, echidnas, and wallabies, while the African Savannah has lions, meerkats, and rhinos. Get up close and personal with the kangaroos and observe the koalas in hopes they wake up long enough to yawn. If you can dodge all the strollers, it's

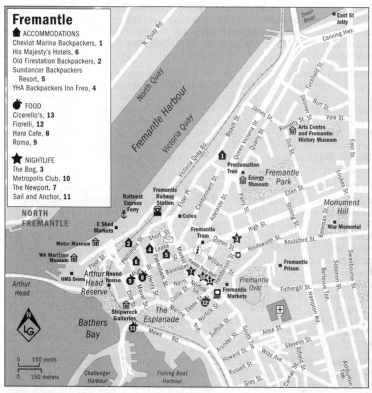

Fremantle

ACCOMMODATIONS
Cheviot Marina Backpackers, **1**
His Majesty's Hotels, **6**
Old Firestation Backpackers, **2**
Sundancer Backpackers
Resort, **5**
YHA Backpackers Inn Freo, **4**

FOOD
Cicerello's, **13**
Fiorelli, **12**
Hara Cafe, **8**
Roma, **9**

NIGHTLIFE
The Bog, **3**
Metropolis Club, **10**
The Newport, **7**
Sail and Anchor, **11**

a fun day. (On Labouchere Rd. in South Perth. Take the blue CAT to the jetty and then ferry across the river for $1.20, or take bus #35 from the City Bus Port. 24hr. infoline ☎ 9474 3551. Open daily 8am-5:30pm. $14, children $7, under 4 free.)

AQUARIUM OF WESTERN AUSTRALIA. Leafy sea dragons, saltwater crocodiles, and four kinds of sharks make AQWA their home. Walk through a tunnel surrounded by fish and watch divers feed the sharks by hand (twice per day). Touch squid and stingrays in the discovery pools. Adults can book ahead to dive with the sharks, turtles, and stingrays off the coast or go whale-watching, each for $90. (North of Perth along the West Coast Hwy. at Hillary's Harbour, off the Hepburn Ave. exit. Take the Joondalup train to Warwick, then the #423 bus to Hillary's. $3. ☎ 9447 7500; www.aqwa.com.au. Open daily 10am-5pm; Dec.-Apr. Wed 10am-9pm. $20, concessions $16.50, children $12.50, families $58, under 4 free. 10% YHA/VIP discount.)

PERTH MINT. Several million dollars worth of gold is just beyond your fingertips at this historic mint, built in 1899 as a means of parlaying the burgeoning gold rush into an economic boom for all of Western Australia. (310 Hay Street, East Perth. Take the red CAT to stop 3 or 11. ☎ 9421 7223. Open M-F 9am-4pm, Sa-Su 9am-1pm. Gold pour on the hour. $6.60, concessions $5.50, children $3.30, families $16.50. Student discount.)

KINGS PARK. A spectacular view of Perth and the Swan River can be seen from Kings Park, perched atop Mt. Eliza just west of the city. Larger than New York's Central Park, its **Botanic Gardens,** next to the **War Memorial,** are home to 1700 native species; free walks depart from the karri log opposite the Memorial daily at 10am and 2pm. A unique and well-hidden walk begins at the base of the riverside edge of the park, just next to the old brewery. *(A 20min. walk by foot west from the city center up St. Georges Terr., or take the red CAT to stop #25. Free parking. Info center ☎ 9480 3600. Gardens open daily 9am-4pm.)*

BEACHES. The Perth beach experience is calm and carefree, with numerous clusters of shops and cafes. Families flock to **Cottesloe Beach,** on the Fremantle train line, for swimming and mild surf, while **Swanbourne Beach** is a favorite spot for nude sunbathers. *(Bus #71, 72, or 75, or a 2km walk from the Swanbourne stop on the Fremantle train.)* **City Beach** is a great swimming spot. *(Bus #81, 84, or 85 from the stop in front of Hobnobs on Wellington St.)* **Scarborough** has bigger surfing waves and crowds of twenty-somethings. *(Bus #400 from Wellington St. Station.)* Surfers rip through the tubes at **Trigg Beach,** just north of Scarborough; the waves here can get a bit rough for swimming. *(Joondalup train to Warwick, then bus #423.)*

EARTH, SEA, AND SKY. Captain Cook Cruises, Pier 3 Barrack Square, has a selection of tours, including cruises to the Zoo and Aboriginal Heritage Tours. *(☎ 9336 3311; www.captaincookcruises.com.au. $15-80.)* Rent catamarans and windsurfs on the south bank off Mill Point Rd., opposite the city center. **Malibu City Dive** has diving tours to Rottnest Island (see p. 694), noted for its unique corals and fish, and also offers scuba certification classes. *(126 Barrack St. ☎ 9225 7555. Rottnest trips including equipment start at $135, without equipment $80.)* **Planet Perth** has several tour options, from a short night tour of a wildlife park with kangaroos, koalas, and Tasmanian devils to trips farther afield to many WA destinations. *(☎ 9225 6622; www.planet-tours.com.au. Tours start at $40.)* For Pinnacles tours (see **Nambung NP,** p. 717), popular options are **West Coast Explorer** *(☎ 9418 8835),* **Redback Safaris** *(☎ 9275 6204; www.redbacksafaris.com.au),* and **Travelabout Outback Adventures** *(☎ 9244 1200; tours from $90).* **W.A. Skydiving Academy** offers tandem jumps. *(199 William St., Northbridge. ☎ 9227 6066 or 1800 245 066. From $220.)*

CULTURAL CENTRE. The Perth Cultural Centre, abutting William St. in Northbridge, packs several good museums and performance centers as well as the city library into one city block. **The Art Gallery of Western Australia** has large collections of modern and classical Australian art including some Aboriginal carvings and paintings, and also hosts traveling international exhibits. *(☎ 9492 6600. Open daily 10am-5pm. Free guided tours Su and Tu-Th 1pm, F 12:30pm. Free, except for special exhibitions.)* **The Perth Institute of the Contemporary Arts (PICA)** has contemporary and student art and hosts evening performances. Pick up a booklet of events or call for schedules. *(☎ 9227 6144. Open Tu-Su 11am-7pm. Gallery free, performance prices vary.)* **The Western Australian Museum** showcases WA's natural history and culture. Don't miss the blue whale skeleton and the Aboriginal exhibit. *(☎ 9427 2700. Open daily 9:30am-5pm. Free.)* **The Blue Room** provides an energetic venue for local theater. Productions are chosen by application and range from classics to experimental pieces by local playwrights. *(☎ 9227 7005; www.blueroom.net.au. Cover charges $10-20.)*

FREMANTLE

■**WA MARITIME MUSEUM & SUBMARINE** *OVENS.* Freo's brand-new maritime museum is housed in an architecturally arresting building at the mouth of the Swan River. Exhibits on sail-boat racing, shipping, warships, and fishing practices from Aboriginal times to today. Don't miss the superb tours, some led by former sub captains, inside the Oberon-class submarine *Ovens,* in active service until 1997. *('A' Shed Victoria Quay. ☎ 9431 8444; www.mm.wa.gov.au. Open daily 9:30am-5pm. Sub tours every half hour but fill early in the day. Museum only $10, children $3, concessions $5, families $22; sub only $8/$3/$5/$22; both museum and sub $15/$5/$8/$35.)*

FREMANTLE MOTOR MUSEUM. Home to one of only six pre-WWI Rolls Royce limos in the world today. The massive collection of vintage luxury automobiles, race cars, and motorbikes will leave you yearning for the halcyon days of yore when petrol prices were low and cars were built like tanks. *('B' Shed Victoria Quay. ☎9336 5222. Open daily 9:30am-5pm. $9, children $5, families $23.)*

FREMANTLE PRISON. Get a thorough look at a maximum-security prison without committing a felony. The prison was closed only 13 years ago following a riot. *(1 The Terrace. ☎9336 9200; info@fremantleprison.com.au. Tours every 30min.; last tour 5pm. Spooky candlelight tours W and F; book ahead. Open daily 10am-6pm. $14.30, concessions $11, children $7.15, families $48.50.)*

FREMANTLE MARKETS. One can find just about anything in the markets, from clothing to massages. Fresh veggies abound; produce prices hit rock bottom around closing time on Sunday. *(On the corner of South Terr. and Henderson St. ☎9335 2515. Open F 9am-9pm, Sa 9am-5pm, Su 10am-5pm.)*

🖪 NIGHTLIFE

There's no shortage of good pubs, clubs, or cafes with amiable, relaxed crowds. The budget scene in Northbridge rages deep into the night on weekends. Mt. Lawley and Subiaco have more upscale, subdued scenes. Pick up the free weeklies *XPress* and *Hype* at hostels, news agencies, or record stores or visit the website www.perthtribe.com to find out what's on. Covers and dress codes are rare, but jeans may get the occasional scowl and most places require closed-toed shoes.

Perth is reasonably **gay- and lesbian-friendly;** for event info, listen to *Sheer Queer*, a gay and lesbian radio program on 92.1FM (Th 11pm-1am) or check out the free *Out in Perth*, a gay and lesbian newspaper. The lesbian publication *WOW* comes out monthly ($4.50). The best resource may be the 🖪**Arcane Bookshop,** 212 William St., which is full of info on Perth's gay and arts scenes. *(☎9328 5073; arcane@info-structure.com.au. Open M-F 10am-6pm, Sa 10am-4pm, Su noon-5pm.)*

NORTHBRIDGE & CITY PROPER

🖪 **The Brass Monkey,** 209 William St., (☎9227 9596), Northbridge. A big, fun place; serves local microbrews. Pool tables, indoor courtyard and a second floor veranda overlooking the Horseshoe Bridge. Connected to suave wine bar and brasserie. Open M-Th 11am-midnight, F-Sa 11am-2am, Su noon-10pm.

The Church, 69 Lake St. (☎9328 1065). A former church now turned a glitzy club featuring trance and, on Saturday, disco mixes. Bring your own whistles and glow sticks. Open F-Sa 9pm-6am.

The Grosvenor, 339 Hay St. (☎9325 3799). Relaxed pub with occasional live events in spaces ranging from small and intimate to big and loud. Open M-F noon-9pm; Sa-Su noon-2:30pm and 5-9pm.

Bar Universal, 221 William St., (☎9227 9596), Northbridge. Live jazz, sake, and a slightly older, sophisticated crowd. Dress code. Open M-Tu 4pm-midnight, W-Th 4pm-1am, F-Sa 4pm-2am, Su 4-10pm.

Connections Nightclub, 81 James St., Northbridge (☎9328 1870). A popular gay-owned club with DJ-spun house and techno beats. Theme nights like "Lesbian Mud Wrestling." Shows F and Su. Cover $3-10. Open W, F and Sa 10pm-6am, Su 9pm-late.

The Court Hotel, 50 Beaufort St., Northbridge (☎9328 5292), on the corner of James St. The scene here varies from drag queens and theme nights like "bears' night"—for big hairy men and their fans—to a standard dance pub. In summer, live bands play outside in the beer garden. Open M-Sa 11am-midnight, Su 3-10pm.

Metropolis Club, 146 Roe St. (☎9228 0500). Trendy multi-level dance club like its sister location in Freo (see **Fremantle,** below). Cover $10 F after 10pm, Sa after 10pm. Open F 9pm-5am, Sa 9pm-6am.

Geisha, 135a James St. (☎9328 9808). Pulsates with various genres of dance music, sometimes from celebrity guest DJs, including Heath Ledger and Toni Collette. Sign at the door tells male patrons to "turn off your engines" as it is a female-friendly establishment. Open F-Sa 11pm-6am, Su 9:30pm-late.

The Jazz Room, 677 Beaufort St., (☎9271 1792), Mount Lawley. Along with nearby Luxe, one of the centers of the calmer, sophisticated Mt. Lawley scene, with full bar and leather couches. DJs spin downtempo W and F-Sa. No cover. Live bands Th nights; cover $5-10. Open W-Th 9pm-1am, F-Sa 9pm-5am.

Hip-E Club (☎9227 8899), on the corner of Newcastle and Oxford St., Leederville. Groovy 60s and 70s club, with 80s Su. Free entry until 10 or 11pm. Tu and Th backpacker nights with free BBQ. Open 8pm-1am.

FREMANTLE

The Bog, 189 High St. (☎9336 7751). There's almost always something going on here. Tu free food and $6 jugs of beer. Open M 6pm-4am, Tu-Sa 6pm-6am, Su 8pm-1am.

Sail and Anchor, 64 South Terr. (☎9335 8433). British pub with a wide variety of drinks. More locals, fewer backpackers. Freo is the home of Redback beer; this is a good place to hoist one. Open M-Th 11am-midnight, F-Sa 11am-1am, Su 11am-10pm.

The Newport, 2 South Terr. (☎9335 2428). Pool room, outdoor space, and a dark smoky area at the heart of Freo's late-night sector. Good place to see local bands. Cover varies. Open M-Th 11am-midnight, F-Sa 11am-1am, Su noon-10pm.

Metropolis Club, 58 South Terr. (☎9228 0500). Glitzy, multi-level dance club abounding in black-clad youth. Cover $10 F after 10pm, Sa after 10pm. Open Th 9pm-6am, F 9pm-5am, Sa 9pm-6am.

NEAR PERTH: ROTTNEST ISLAND   ☎08

Dubbed a "rat's nest" by Dutch explorers who mistook the island's quokkas (wallabies) for giant rats, Rottnest Island is an 11km-long hunk of limestone off the Fremantle coast (30min. by ferry, 90min. from Perth). Pristine white beaches meet rolling green hills broken only by the occasional stony outcropping, clear, blue interior lakes, and two lighthouses. The island was settled by farmers in 1830 but became an Aboriginal prison in 1838. Today, tourists and locals flock to this nature reserve to cycle, swim, snorkel, and surf.

■■ **TRANSPORTATION & PRACTICAL INFORMATION.** Several companies offer similarly priced **ferry service** to Rottnest from Perth, Fremantle, and Hillary's Harbour. **Oceanic Cruises** (☎9325 1191) departs from Pier 4 of the Barrack St. Jetty (daily 8:45 and 10am; $58, children $19) and from the East St. Jetty or B Shed on Victoria Quay, Fremantle (daily 10am and 11:30am; same-day return $43, children $15; extended-stay $5 extra). They offer free pick-up from Perth hotels and the Fremantle train station. **Rottnest Express** (☎9335 6406) has several daily departures from Victoria Quay, C Shed, Fremantle (daily 7:30, 9:30 and 11:30am; same-day return $43, children $15; extended stay $5 extra.) Both ferries offer $5 VIP/YHA discounts. Courtesy buses depart from the main jetty roughly every hour and head to the accommodations in Geordie Bay, Kingstown, and the airport. The **Bayseeker Bus** is a good way to get around the island (45min. loop around the island; every hr. 8:30am-4:30pm; day-ticket $7, children $3.50). The best way to see Rottnest is by bike—the island is only 11km by 4½km—though be prepared for some hilly terrain. **Rottnest Island Bike Hire,** 300m left of the jetty, has a wide selection that includes bike buses (4 people; all pedal, one steers) for family groups. (☎9292 5105. 1-speed $15 per day, 18-speed $20; $25 deposit. Locks and required helmets included. Open daily 8:30am-5pm.)

The **Visitors Centre** is 150m to the left of the jetty at Thomsons Bay. (☎9372 9752; fax 9372 9775. Open daily 8am-5pm.) To the right of the jetty is a pedestrian mall with an **ATM,** the **post office,** the bakery, and the grocery store. North of the mall 400m is the **nursing post** where medical attention can be obtained. (☎9292 5030. Open daily 8:30am-4:30pm.)

▛▙ ACCOMMODATIONS & FOOD. The **YHA Kingstown Barracks Youth Hostel ❷** is in Kingstown, a 15-minute walk or a quick bike ride from the Visitors Center (left from jetty, 1.8km). A free shuttle bus runs from Thomsons Bay every 30min., 8am-9pm. The hostel is inside an old army barracks with simple, spacious rooms. (☎9372 9780; fax 9292 5141. Reception 8am-5pm. Dorms $21, YHA $18; family rooms $50/$43.) Though there are meals available in the barracks complex ($7), it's a good idea to bring food. Back in Thomsons Bay settlement, immediately to the left of the Visitors Center, **Dôme Cafe ❶** (☎9292 5026) serves up Anzac biscuits or Biscotti ($2), gourmet coffee ($5) and various soups and salads ($8-10). Fish 'n' chips ($6) and milkshakes ($4) can be found at **Rottnest Tearooms Family Cafe ❶** next door. Both afford splendid views of the Bay.

▟ ACTIVITIES. Rottnest Island's beaches get emptier as you head away from settled areas—go far enough and you may have a cove all to yourself. **Narrow Neck** and **Salmon Bay** offer good **fishing,** and **The Basin, Pinky Beach,** and **Parakeet** are among the many good swimming spots near the settlement. **Little Salmon Bay** and **Parker Point** have good snorkeling, and **Strickland Bay** has good surfing. Whales and dolphins are often seen from the windy cliffs at **West End**, where 10-foot-high waves crash upon the limestone, ending their long journey across the Indian Ocean. Ask at the Visitors Centre for a booklet of "snorkel trails" ($5.50). **Rottnest Malibu Dive** is the only dive shop on the island and is located below Dôme Cafe. (☎9292 5111. Snorkel gear $16.50; 1 dive $60, 2 dives $110.) A break from the sun and surf can be found at the **Museum** (☎9372 9753; adults $2.20, children $1.10), recounting Rottnest's history.

SOUTHWEST

The Southwest coast of Australia is experiencing a boom in both tourism and residency. It's not hard to see why—Mother Nature has indeed been kind to the Southwest. The adventurous can hike in the Stirling and Porongup ranges or dive with dolphins and surf in the warm coastal waters. Solace-seekers can sample award-winning local vintages, peruse local art studios, gaze at the springtime wildflowers, watch for whales, or drive down forest-lined roads.

▐ TRANSPORTATION

The easiest way to see the Southwest is by car; many sights are well off the bus routes, and public transportation in many of the towns is either inadequate or non-existent. Once you get completely out of Perth, the 3hr. drive south toward Margaret River takes you past shoreline, forests, farms, cattle stations, and the occasional limestone quarry. Several options exist for the auto-less. The **Easy Rider Backpackers** bus offers a three-month pass ($215) that covers bus service between

HE HIDDEN DEAL

DOLPHIN DISCOVERY

raveled across the barren Nullarbor or over the vast expanse of the ndian Ocean to see Western Australia's dolphins? Well, don't be ed to believe they're only to be ound in touristy and pricey Monkey Mia, some 750km north of Perth. Just to the south of the state capital, 180km along the South West Highway, is Bunbury's non-profit **Dolphin Discovery Centre.** For $2, adults can view the Centre's interesting collection of sealife specimens and interactive exhibits on the biology of the region, while children do so for a mere $1 and families for $5. The Centre's real treasures, however, are the approximately 100 wild bottlenose dolphins which have made Koombana Bay their home. Included in admission is access to he beach where they come to isit daily. Trained dolphin experts are on hand to guide you in how to approach and touch these intelligent and spirited creatures.

The dolphins are not fed and come of their own free will, usually n the late morning. For the less patient, eco-cruises ($27) and eight-person swim tours ($99) are also available, taking you to meet he dolphins out in the bay itself.

Koombana Drive, Bunbury. 1.5km rom Bunbury city center. ☎ 9791 3088. Open daily Oct.-Apr. 8am-5pm; May-Sept. 9am-3pm.

most regional hostels. (☎ 9226 0307. Dec.-Feb. 6 per week; Sept.-Nov. and Mar.-May 4 per week; June-Aug. 2 per week. 24hr. notice required for pick-up.) **Westrail's** (☎ 13 10 53) handy 28-day Southern Discovery Pass ($140) allows for travel to most southern and eastern destinations in the region including Albany, Esperance, and Kalgoorlie.

PERTH TO BUNBURY

The drive south from Perth to Bunbury features wineries and forests perfect for those who may not make it farther south. There are about 20 wineries, some of which offer tours and wine tastings, along the 100km of Hwy. 1 between Perth and **Yalgorup National Park.** The park itself features nature reserves, miles of dunes, stromatolites, and a forest of tuart and jarrah trees with peppermint undergrowth. Drive carefully; kangaroos in the road are frequent, as are emus, wallabies, and several species of trans-hemisphere migrating birds. Yalgorup is the Noongar word meaning "place of lakes" and the park's 10 lakes are indeed its centerpiece.

To see the interesting stromatolites on the shores of Lake Clifton, turn right off Hwy. 1 onto Mt. John Rd. and continue 3km to the observation platform. Further south, the two best ways to see the park are at **Clifton Beach** (turn onto Clifton Downs Rd. 2km north of the Lake Clifton Tavern) and **Preston Beach** (turn left on Preston Beach Rd. marked by the Yalgorup National Park sign, just south of the turn-offs for Pinjarra and Warnoona).

There is camping at the **Martin's Tank campsite ❶,** 7km from the turn-off then 2km down an unsealed road. (Pit toilets; no running water. Sites for 2 $10, extra person $5.50, payable to the ranger.) From there, take one of several trails to the beautiful clear lakes. Powerboats are allowed on some, while on others only sailboards and canoes are permitted. **Preston Beach Caravan Park ❶,** 3km beyond the turn-off for the campsite, is a good source of park info and accommodations. (☎ 9739 1111. Caravan sites for 2 $7, powered $21; cabins for 4-6 $60-90, low-season $40-60; extra person $5.)

Watch for the **wrecked truck** hanging 10m up in a tree on the south-bound site of Hwy. 1—it should serve as an effective deterrent against speeding. This stretch of highway also offers various scenic detours into the surrounding regions, the southernmost of which takes you through **Australind** right along the beach. In Australind, the 500m long boardwalked outcropping into the estuary is an excellent opportunity for bird watching.

BUNBURY ☎08

Two hours (180km) south of Perth, Bunbury (pop. 28,000) is a unique combination of cosmopolitan and sleepy. Over 100 sociable dolphins have made the shores of Bunbury their home for decades, and recently more and more Westralians have decided to do the same. Though there is no shortage of dolphin-admiring visitors, Bunbury has escaped the tourist deluge that plagues Monkey Mia.

◪ TRANSPORTATION. Downtown Bunbury is located 3km from Wollaston on the southern end of Western Australia's **train** network. Present your ticket stub on the bus for a free lift downtown. **South West Coachlines,** in the Old Railway Station at Carmody Pl. and Haley St. (☎9791 1955; open daily 8am-6pm), runs to Perth (2½hr.; 3 per day: 8:45am, 2pm, 6:45pm; $20.20, students $10.10) and Augusta via Busselton and Margaret River (2½hr.; daily 4:20pm; $17.20). 10% YHA discount. Local **buses** circle the city. (M-W and F 7am-6pm, Th 7am-9pm, Sa 7am-1:15pm; $1.80, $2.70 for outlying areas.)

◪ PRACTICAL INFORMATION. The Old Railway station houses the **Bunbury Visitors Centre** (☎9721 7922; open M-Sa 9am-5pm, Su 9:30am-4:30pm), the bus station, and the **Bunbury Internet Cafe.** (☎9791 1254. $4 per hr. Open M-Sa 8am-4:30pm.) Services include: several **banks** along Victoria St.; **police** (☎9791 2422), on the corner of Wittenoom St. at Stephen St.; and a **post office** in the Bunbury Plaza Shopping Centre on Spencer St. just south of downtown. (☎9721 3551. Open M-F 9am-5pm, Sa 9-11am.) **Postal Code:** 6230.

◪ ACCOMMODATIONS. The **Wander Inn YHA,** 16 Clifton St., near Wittenoom St., has ping-pong and pool tables, BBQ, and clean, brightly colored rooms. The hostel provides snorkel gear, rents bikes and body boards, and can book dolphin tours, bushwalking, mountain-biking, and kayaking. (☎9721 3242. Internet $5 per hr. Dorms $23, $20 with VIP/YHA; singles $35/$32; doubles $56/$50; family rooms $76/$72.) For a change of pace, the tranquil **Castlehead Bed and Breakfast ❸,** 44 Elinor Bell Rd., 10km north of town, offers clean, beautiful rooms with estuary views. Take the scenic drive off of Old Coast Rd. in Australind and turn inland onto Elinor Bell Rd. (☎9797 0272. Singles $40, ensuite $50; doubles $65/$75.)

◪ FOOD. The main strip, on Victoria St. between Wellington and Clifton St., has many pricey restaurants. For the more frugal, try **Orka Kebabs and Turkish Bakery ❶,** 57-59 Victoria St. (☎9791 2440), or **V Cafe ❶,** 57 Victoria St., next door. Coles **supermarket** is in the Centrepoint Shopping Center, behind the tourist office. (Open M-W and F 8am-6pm, Th 8am-9pm, Sa 8am-5pm.)

◪ SIGHTS. Dolphins are the main draw for most tourists in Bunbury. Dolphin-sighting tours are run by **Naturaliste Charters** from the jetty on Koombana Dr. (☎9755 2276. 1½hr. Tours daily 11am and 2pm. $25, students $22, children $18.) Across from the Dolphin Discovery Centre on Koombana Dr., the **Mangrove Boardwalk** weaves through the southernmost mangrove ecosystem in Western Australia. The **Big Swamp Estuary** on Prince Philip Dr. has over 70 species of birds, and the **Big Swamp Wildlife Park,** also on Prince Philip Dr., has white kangaroos, tawny frogmouths, and many birds. From Ocean Dr., turn onto Hayward St. and look for the sign at the next roundabout. (☎9721 8380. Open daily 10am-5pm. $5, seniors $4, ages 2-12 $3.) The **Marlston Hill Lookout,** near the oceanside end of Koombana Dr., provides panoramic views of the area. There are beautiful beaches along Ocean Dr., including the popular **Back Beach.**

MARGARET RIVER AREA
☎ 08

Around Margaret River, dramatic rock and coral formations rise from the pounding surf, vast cave systems weave through the subterranean depths, celebrated vineyards cover the countryside, and artisans of every medium draw inspiration from it all. With so much to do, visitors invariably many will find themselves lingering longer than they planned on the area's westernmost tip.

✳ 🚍 ORIENTATION & TRANSPORTATION

Margaret River lies 100km south of Bunbury on the **Bussell Highway** (Hwy. 10). The scenic **Caves Road** branches from the Bussell Hwy. at **Busselton,** 52km from Bunbury, and winds its way to Margaret River through wineries and beaches, as well as the towns of **Yallingup** and **Dunsborough.** About 45km south of Margaret River, the Blackwood River meets the ocean at **Augusta.**

The size of the region and lack of centralized attractions means transportation is often a hassle. The best way to get around is by car. **Avis,** 91 Bussell Hwy. (☎ 1800 679 880), **Hertz** (☎ 9758 8331), and **Budget** (☎ 9757 2453) all have offices in Margaret River. You can also rent bikes at various places in town. **South West Coachlines** stops at Charles West St., two blocks from the Bussell Hwy., Margaret River, and goes to Perth (4½hr.; 2 per day; $27.70, YHA discount $24.95). **Westrail** (☎ 13 10 53) uses **Harvey World Travel,** 109 Bussell Hwy., as its Margaret River agent. (☎ 9757 2171. Open M-F 9am-5pm, Sa 9am-noon.)

🛈 PRACTICAL INFORMATION

Tourist Offices: Augusta Visitor Centre (☎ 9758 0166), on the corner of Bussell Hwy. and Ellis Street. Books economical package deals featuring several local sights. River cruise, Jewel Cave, and lighthouse $35; whale watch cruise, Jewel Cave, lighthouse $60. Open M-F 9am-5pm, Sa-Su 9am-1pm. **Busselton Tourist Bureau** (☎ 9752 1288), 38 Peel Terrace. Open M-F 8:30am-5pm, Sa 9am-4pm, Su 10am-4pm; May-Sept. same except Su 10am-2pm. **CALM,** Busselton office, 14 Queen St. (☎ 9752 1677); Margaret River office (☎ 9757 2322), on the Bussell Hwy. north of town. National Park hiking and camping info. Open M-F 8am-5pm. **Caves Park Store** (☎/fax 9755 2042), on Yallingup Beach Rd. near Caves Rd. Yallingup info. **Dunsborough Tourist Bureau** (☎ 9755 3299), in the shopping center on Seymour Blvd., Dunsborough. Books tours and accommodations. M-F 9am-5pm, Sa 9am-3pm, Su 10am-2pm. **Margaret River Visitor Centre** (☎ 9757 2911; www.margaretriverwa.com), on the corner of Bussell Hwy. and Tunnbridge St. Maps, brochures, and a wine showroom. Open daily 9am-5pm.

Work Opportunity: Manpower, 157 Bussell Hwy. (☎ 9757 3911; www.manpower.com.au), is an employment agency for people looking for short-term work. Work is easier to find in winter; in summer the area is flooded by eager job-seekers.

Police: 42 Willmott Ave. (☎ 9757 2222), Margaret River.

Internet Access: Cybercorner Cafe, 72 Willmott Ave., Margaret River (☎ 9757 9388). $6 per hr. Open summer M-Sa 8am-8pm, Su 1-5pm; winter M-Sa 9am-6pm, Su 1-5pm.

Post office: 53 Townview Terr. (☎ 9757 2250), 1 block up Willmott Ave. from Bussell Hwy., Margaret River. Open M-F 9am-5pm. **Postal Code:** 6285.

🛏 ACCOMMODATIONS

There are several well-located hostels in the area. For those looking to splurge, contact the Margaret River Visitors Centre (☎ 9757 2911) to book one of the many wonderful B&Bs. Rooms fill up quickly from October to March; be sure to book in advance for summer weekends. From June to August, bargains abound. Contact **CALM** (see p. 698) if you want to camp in Leeuwin-Naturaliste National Park.

MARGARET RIVER

Margaret River Lodge YHA, 220 Railway Terr. (☎9757 9532), 1.5km southwest of the Bussell Hwy. off Wallcliffe Rd. This YHA offers standard hostel rooms close to wineries in a relaxed and easy-going atmosphere. Manager Steve offers free pick-up from bus station along with free bikes. Pool and organic vegetable garden. Internet $5 per hr. Sites $12; dorms $22-26; doubles $58, ensuite $68. YHA discount $3.50. ❶

Surfpoint Resort (☎9757 1777), on Riedle Dr. south of Prevelley, just north of Gnarabup Beach and within walking distance of the Rivermouth area. Clean and spacious. Bike and boogie board rental, BBQ, Internet $5 per 30min. Book ahead in summer. Dorms $23; doubles $56, ensuite $85; discounts in low-season. ❷

Inne Town Backpackers, 93 Bussell Hwy. (☎9757 3698 or 1800 244 115). The only backpackers in town. Clean, friendly, and lively. Book ahead year-round. Laundry. Internet $2 per 30min. Dorms $19; doubles $50. No credit cards. ❷

Matan's Lodge (☎/fax 9757 2936), on Caves Rd., just north of the intersection with Wallcliffe Rd. Houses emus, 'roos, and an art gallery/studio where guests can make their own stone mosaic. Features basic rooms but spacious common spaces for relaxation. 3-bed rooms $85; occasional winter backpacker specials $18; significant discounts for long-stay artists. ❸

Prevelly Park Beach Resort (☎9757 2374), on the way into Prevelly Park if you're taking Wallcliffe Rd. west out of Margaret River. Sites $11-15; basic on-site vans $90, low-season $50; 5-person cabins with cook facilities $95/$60. ❶

WESTERN AUSTRALIA

Margaret River Area

BUSSELTON, DUNSBOROUGH, & YALLINGUP

Dunsborough Beach House YHA, 201-205 Geographe Bay Rd. (☎9755 3107). Excellent location on the beach. Manager Adrian is level-headed, knowledgeable, and ever-amiable. Free bread and sticky buns donated by local bakery. Books tours. Internet $6 per hr. Dorms $24, YHA $20; doubles $54/$50. ❷

Busselton Backpackers, 14 Peel Terr., Busselton (☎9754 2763). Basic rooms. Laundry. Dorms $20; doubles $40. No credit cards. ❷

Hideaway Holiday Homes, 24 Elsegood Ave., Yallingup (☎9755 2145). Big ensuite cabins. Simple, with several bathrooms and a kitchen but no linen. Doubles from $45; 6-bed rooms from $85. ❹

Yallingup Holiday Park, 1 Valley Rd. (☎1800 220 002), as you enter Yallingup proper. Great location near the biggest surf break in the area. Sites for 2 $34, low-season $18; cabins $135/$50, ensuite $170-205/$85-100. ❸

Dunsborough Lakes Caravan Park, 2-48 Commanage Rd. (☎9756 8300), off the Bussell Hwy. just north of Dunsborough. Miniature golf, tennis courts, pool. 1-3 bed cabins $85-140, low-season $55-85. ❺

AUGUSTA

Baywatch Manor Resort YHA, 88 Blackwood Ave. (☎9758 1290). Relaxed atmosphere, superb facilities, spacious, and well-maintained. Native jarrah wood dining tables and the antique furniture in the bedrooms. Owners arrange tours and whale-watching at 10% discount. Rents bikes $12 per day, $8 half-day. Internet $6 per hr. Dorms $20 (with free lockers); doubles $58, low-season $50; ensuite $78/$70. ❷

Doonbanks Caravan Park, (☎9758 1517; www.netserv.net.au/doonbank), just north of town on Blackwood Ave. Camp kitchen, BBQ. Sites $16, low-season $14, powered $18/$16; cabins $60/$40, ensuite cabins $70/$50. ❷

▮▮ FOOD & NIGHTLIFE

Margaret River's restaurants are good but pricey. Dewson's **supermarket,** next to the tourist office on the Bussell Hwy. in Margaret River, sells **groceries** (daily 7:30am-8pm). Small restaurants line **Dunn Bay Road,** which runs through Dunsborough. Many area wineries also have restaurants. In Augusta, there is a **fruit market** and **grocery store** on Blackwood Ave., north of the tourist office.

MARGARET RIVER

Goodfellas Cafe Woodfire Pizza, 97 Bussell Hwy. (☎9757 3184). Huge bowls of pasta and exotic pizzas in a candlelit setting. Meals $14-18. Open daily 5:30-9pm. ❷

The Green Room, 113b Bussell Hwy. (☎9757 3644). Locals rave about the burgers ($6-8) and specials. Open daily 11am-6pm, Th-Sa later. ❶

Puravita, 113a Bussel Hwy. (☎9757 2622). Inexpensive Italian food; free tastings of various breads and meats. Open daily 11am-9pm. ❷

Settler's Tavern, 114 Bussell Hwy. (☎9757 2398). Live bands play this popular watering hole 4 nights per week. Pool tables and big screen TV. Cover varies. Open M-Th noon-midnight, F noon-2am, Sa 10am-1am, Su noon-10pm. ❷

BUSSELTON, DUNSBOROUGH, & YALLINGUP

Caves House Bistro (☎9755 2131), first building upon entering Yallingup. Art deco furnishings and a hardwood bar, complete with brass accoutrements, gives this historic local favorite a classy feel. The seafood chowder and the chicken salad are popular ($13). Open daily 6-8:30pm. ❷

Evviva (☎9755 3811), corner of Cyrillean Way and Dunn Bay Rd., Dunsborough. Sit on the terrace and watch the town come alive in the morning while enjoying a warm fruit compote, topped with yogurt and nuts, and cinnamon strips ($9). Also serves lunch. Open daily 7am-3pm. ❶

Shakes Diner, 34 Dunn Bay Rd. (☎9755 3599), Dunsborough. This shiny, open-air retro diner serves up chicken salad or leg ham sandwiches ($5). Also try the double-decker Big BLT ($11). Open daily 8am-5pm; closes 3pm in winter. ❷

Ripenup, 237 Naturaliste Terr. (☎9755 3563), Dunsborough. Excellent farm-style market with a wide selection of organic fruits and vegetables grown locally and around the world. Open daily 9am-6pm. ❶

AUGUSTA

Augusta Bakery and Cafe, 121 Blackwood Ave (☎9758 1664). Bakery with superb pastries and meat pies ($2). Gigantic, topping-laden pizzas are offered Friday nights ($7-9). Open M-Th 8am-5pm, F 8am-8:30pm, Sa-Su 8am-3pm. ❶

Colourpatch Cafe (☎9758 1295), on Albany Terr., just south of town. Specializes in fish 'n' chips ($8). Open daily 8am-8pm. ❶

🜚 SIGHTS

The area boasts over 70 wineries, dozens of art galleries, and numerous farms that offer food tastings, demonstrations, and farmstays. A large number of activities are clustered close enough to Margaret River to make them accessible in a daytrip, but not everything is within walking distance.

The 2km-long **Busselton Jetty** is a thin plank jutting way out into the Indian Ocean. It's a good hike to the end of the jetty, and waters below are a popular seasonal diving area. *(At the end of Queen St. in Busselton. $2.50, children $1.50; trolley to the end $7.50, children $2.50, departs on the hour 10am-4pm.)* The **Eagles Heritage Raptor Wildlife Centre,** on Boodjidup Rd. near Margaret River, houses Australia's largest collection of birds of prey and is dedicated to education, rehabilitation of injured birds, and breeding projects. Have a bird of prey sit on your arm during the flight demonstrations led by Philip Pain, a strident advocate of raptor protection on the state and national level. *(☎9757 2960. Open daily 10am-5pm. Flight displays daily 11am and 1:30pm. $9, seniors $7, children $4.50, families $23. Wheelchair-accessible.)* **The Wardan Aboriginal Centre,** run by the native Wardandi People, offers a glimpse of Aboriginal culture and is the only facility of its kind in Western Australia. Cultural interchanges with tribes elsewhere in the nation are frequent. *(Head 6km south on Caves Rd. from Yallingup, turn right on Wyadup Rd. and then left on Injidup Springs Rd. ☎9756 6566. Open M, W-Su 10am-4pm.)*

🜚 WINERIES, WINE TOURS, & WINE EDUCATION

WINERIES

Most wineries are clustered in the area bordered by Caves Rd. and Johnson Rd. between Yallingup and Margaret River. For an enjoyable tour, mix older vintners, such as **Cullen** or **Vasse Felix,** which are usually more personable, with the many newcomers, such as **Howard Park** *(☎9756 5200; www.howardparkwines.com.au; 10am-5pm),* which have gorgeous estates and great views. **Woody Nook** is an intimate, long-established option with several award-winners, including its flagship Gallagher's Choice Cabernet Sauvignon. *(☎9755 7547. Metricup Rd., north of Cowaramup. Open daily 10am-4:30pm.)* **Settler's Ridge** provides the region's only fully organic wines. *(54b Bussell Highway, Cowaramup.☎9755 5883. Open daily 10am-5pm.)*

Those walking from Margaret River can reach at least two wineries on foot. **Chateau Xanadu** features an award-winning chardonnay and an elegant but welcoming setup. *(Walkers and bikers may use the gravel service road. Take Railway Terr. 3km south to Terry St. Drivers should take the smoother main entrance off Boodijup Rd.☎9757 3066. Open daily 10am-5pm.)* The **Cape Mentelle** winery was one of the first in the area; it remains a relaxed, friendly place. *(Just off Wallcliffe Rd. south of town. ☎ 9757 3066. Open daily 10am-4:30pm.)* A longer walk could include the beautiful gardens and wines of **Voyager.** *(☎9757 6354. Open daily 10am-5pm.)* Bikers have the additional option of taking a tour of the production facilities at **Leeuwin Estate Winery.** *(Off Gnarawy Rd. ☎9759 0000. 1hr. tours daily 11am, noon, and 3pm; $8. Open daily 10am-5pm.)*

WINE TOURS & WINE EDUCATION

While hiring a car makes area wineries more accessible, driving and drinking don't mix. A popular option for wine-tasters is a wine tour, which generally costs about $50 for a half-day and $90 for a full-day. The widely acclaimed **Great Wine, Food, Forest Bushtucker Tour** packs in a drive through a karri forest, a gourmet lunch, and six vineyards. *(☎9757 1084. 5hr. tours daily at noon. $55.)* **Taste the South** will cater the tour to your interests, picking up and dropping off at your accommodation. *(☎0438 210 373; tastethesouth@netserv.net.au.)* A more economical option is the wine mini-tour run by **Margaret River Vintage Wine Tours,** which visits Voyager, Leeuwin, Redgate, and Xanadu for $35. *(☎9757 1008; winetours@swisp.net.au. Tours daily 2:30pm.)* The **Margaret River School of Wine** offers a basic one hour wine tasting and etiquette class for $25, and for $125, a more comprehensive full-day course called "Mastering Wine Appreciation." *(☎9753 1007; www.margaretriverwine.com.au.)*

▧ OUTDOOR ACTIVITIES

The beaches and surf along the coast are stunning. **Caves Road** south of Margaret is one of the area's most spectacular drives, running through karri forests and past hundreds of hidden caves, seven of which are open to the public. **Biking** is a good way to get around, and there are many rewarding bike trails. **Down South Camping,** 144 Bussell Hwy., in Margaret River, rents bikes. *(☎9757 2155. $30 per 24hr. period, $20 same-day return. Mountain bike guided day tours $50.)* There are also a number of **walking tracks** and **canoeing** opportunities in the region. One of the best hiking trails is the 15km (roundtrip) walk to **10 Mile Brook Dam** along the Margaret River. (Trailhead at intersection of the river with Bussell Hwy.)

▨ LEEUWIN-NATURALISTE NATIONAL PARK

Spanning much of the coast from Cape Naturaliste to Cape Leeuwin, Leeuwin-Naturaliste National Park encompasses wild forests, untouched beaches with jagged rock formations rising from the water, caves with fossils of extinct megafauna, remote campsites, excellent whale-watching spots, lighthouses, and many walking trails. The CALM offices in Dunsborough and Margaret River service the park. **Canto's Spring** is a basic campsite where thundering waves crash on enormous boulders rising from the sea. From the site, you can walk north along ocean cliffs or south through the majestic Boranup forest. (At the Lake Cave turn-off from Caves Rd. south of Margaret River. Pit toilets. Sites $6, children $2; pay upon entry.) Whales can be seen from **Cape Naturaliste, Gracetown, Canal Rocks,** and **Injidup Beach.** Beware, however, when standing on the rocks near breaking surf—locals warn about "King Waves" coming in unexpectedly from the Indian Ocean and washing sightseers and rock fishermen to a watery grave. There are bushwalks all along the coast and near Margaret River. Cape Naturaliste's walks wind past the lighthouse to cliff lookouts. **Boranup Campground**, at the southern end of the Boranup Forest scenic drive, provides secluded sites. ($6, children $2; payable to ranger.) The best hiking in the region is the **Cape to Cape Walk** from Cape Leeuwin in the south to Cape Naturaliste in the north. The trail includes everything from soaring forests to towering cliffs to isolated beaches. All told, the 130km walk takes five to seven days and is accessible throughout the year, though be prepared for the occasional rainstorm in winter and hot afternoons in summer. For a shorter glimpse of one of the more spectacular segments of the total walk, go to **Prevelly Beach** and hike due north along the Cape Walk, following it across the Margaret Rive Mouth for 3km.

CAVES

A network of caves runs through Margaret River, containing fossils of extinct species, as well as evidence of Aboriginal occupation dating back some 32,000 years. Though the most historically interesting caves are inaccessible to the public, the seven open caves are nonetheless amazing. The two southernmost caves, **Jewel Cave** (the most magnificent) and **Lake Cave,** are both lighted and offer guided tours. **Mammoth,** nearest to Margaret, has tape-guided tours of its lighted caves. (☎9757 5714. Jewel and Lake tours daily every hour on the half hour, 9:30am-4:30pm. Mammoth open daily 9am-4pm. Each cave $15, children $6.50. All 3 $36/$15.50.) **Moondyne** is not lit but offers guided flashlight tours. (☎9757 5714. Open daily 11am-2pm, bookings advised. $20, children $10.) **Calgardup** (open daily 9am-4:15pm) and **Giants** are less impressive but provide the solace of plunging underground unguided. Giants is the more strenuous of the two. (Open 9:30am-3:30pm on school holidays and long weekend. ☎9757 7422. $10, children $5.; no children under 6.) Near Yallingup, **Ngilgi Cave** (☎9755 2152), named after an Aboriginal female water spirit (a good spirit) believed to have taken over the cave, provides both guided, lighted tours (daily every 30min. 9:30am-3:30pm; $15, children $5, families $40) and guided flashlight "adventure" tours. (Daily, given on demand; 3hr. $50; limited to ages 16 and older.)

SURFING

Packs of grommets (young surfers) learn the ropes in the relatively tame surf at **Rivermouth** and **Redgate** near Margaret River; more experienced surfers delight in the breaks off **Surfer's Point,** or head farther north to **Gracetown** and **Injidup Point.** There are tons of other surf spots nearby; stop at **Beach Life Surf Shop,** 117 Bussell Hwy., near the tourist office, for info, advice, or to set up a surfing lesson. (☎9757 2888, 24hr. surf report 1900 922 995. Group lessons $40 per person.)

Farther north, **Yallingup Beach** was one of the first breaks surfed in Western Australia (in the 1950s). The best time for surfing is October through April, though it gets very crowded, especially in December and January. The two best spots in the Yallingup area are Yallingup Beach itself, right in front of Yallingup's Surf Shop at the bottom of Yallingup Beach Rd., and **Smith's Beach,** just to the south. In Dunsborough, surfboards can be rented at **Yahoo Surfboards,** at the corner of Clark St. and Naturaliste Terr. (☎9756 8336. Full-day $30, half-day $20.)

DIVING & SNORKELING

In Dunsborough, Eagle and Meelup Bays both have great beaches for snorkeling and surfing; turn-offs are well marked on Cape Naturaliste Rd., north of town. **Bay Dive and Adventures,** 26 Dunn Bay Rd., Dunsborough, offers diving classes and diving and snorkeling trips (☎800 199 029). **Cape Dive,** 222 Naturaliste Terr., Dunsborough, also runs diving trips to the wreck of the HMS Swan off Cape Naturaliste. (☎9756 8778. Two dives $160, one dive $100.) The Swan's descent was a planned sinking executed in 1997 in order to provide a diving site for the region. **Hamelin**

Bay, near Augusta, is another good dive and snorkel spot. Indeed, the bay may be beautiful to the point of distraction—the area has seen some 11 shipwrecks since 1882. You can scuba dive or go snorkeling at the four visible wrecks, but you have to swim from shore to get there. Check with someone before diving; the wrecks are old and shift around a bit.

Swimming here is sheltered, and fishing in the area is superb. Stingrays often feed below the boat ramp. **Augusta Hardware and Scuba Supplies,** on Blackwood Ave. across from the post office, has diving info and gear. (☎9758 1770. Open M-F 8:30am-5:30pm, Sa 8:30am-4:30pm, Su 9am-1pm.)

OUTDOOR TOURS

Several companies organize half- or full-day adventure tours of the area, most of which can be booked through tourist bureaus. ◪**Naturaliste Charters** runs **whale-watching** tours that bring sightseers to the Humpback whales off Augusta (see p. 700) in the winter (June-Aug.) and Dunsborough in the spring (Sept.-Dec.). Southern Right whales frequent the area in August and Blue whales in December. (☎9755 2276; www.whales-australia.com. Departs daily from Boat Ramp on Geographe Bay Rd. in Dunsborough or Davies Rd. in Augusta. 3hr. $45, children $25, under 4 free; 10% YHA discount.) **Augusta Eco Cruises** has deep sea fishing expeditions, along with river cruises and seal and dolphin observation trips. (☎9758 4003. $30 for 2-3hr. river cruise.) The popular **South-West Fishing Adventures** offers tailor-made fishing on the Blackwood River and Hardy Inlet by way of 4WD or boat. (☎9758 1950. Daytrips $150.) **Bushtucker River Tours** gives guided canoe trips up the Margaret River to historical sights and a lunch featuring local produce, with native flora and fauna identified along the way. (☎9757 1084. Departs from the Margaret Rivermouth, off Wallcliffe Road in Prevelly Beach; tour lasts from 9:45am-2pm. Adults $40, children $20.)

GREAT SOUTHERN

Sprawling karri and tingle forests, rugged mountain ranges, and the vast nothingness of the Nullarbor Plain are all part of the beautiful region known as the Great Southern. The South Western Hwy. links the region's many parts and Albany functions as an urban hub for the sparsely populated southern coast, but by the time you reach Esperance, Perth's cosmopolitanism seems a world away.

WALPOLE & WALPOLE-NORNALUP NATIONAL PARK   ☎08

Tiny, congenial Walpole is nestled in the middle of the national park and makes an excellent home base. **Transwa buses** (☎1300 6622 05. www.transwa.wa.gov.au) run once a day to Albany and Bunbury. The volunteer-staffed **Walpole-Nornalup Visitors Centre,** on the highway, is a great source of information on the many nearby natural wonders and can book tours. (☎9840 1111. Open M-F 9am-5pm, Sa-Su 9am-4pm.) Nockolds St. holds a **post office** (☎9840 1048; open M-F 9am-5pm). **Walpole Backpackers ❸,** corner Pier St. and Park Ave., has well-maintained rooms. (☎/fax 9840 1244; walpolebackpackers@bigpond.com. Dorms $22; twins and doubles $54; family rooms $72.) **Tingle All Over YHA ❷,** 60 Nockolds St., has a BBQ, kitchen, laundry, and a beautiful outdoor chess set with two-foot pieces made from red gum and jarrah woods. (☎9840 1041; tingleallover2000@yahoo.com.au. Dorms $21; singles $37; twins and doubles $50. YHA discount $1.) The **Rest Point Holiday Village ❷** is right on the water west of town, at the end of Rest Point Rd. (☎9840 1032. Sites for 2 $22; ensuite cabins for 2 $95, extra person $28.)

Walpole-Nornalup National Park incorporates forests of giant tingle trees, inlets from the ocean, sand dunes, pristine beaches, and the wildlife-rich Franklin River. The ◙**Tree Top Walk**, 13km east of town, is a 600m state-of-the-art metal catwalk through the canopy of tingle trees. The views are incredible, but those scared of heights be forewarned—the swaying walkways reach heights of 40m. (☎9840 8263. Open daily 9am-5pm, last entry 4:15pm. $6, children $2.50, families $14.) The **Ancient Empire** boardwalk, a short, pleasant walk, departs from the Tree Top Walk info center and passes through a grove of red tingle trees. The park's beautiful drives include the gravel **Hilltop Road,** which passes the Giant Tingle and Circular Pool, the **Valley of the Giants Road** through towering forests, and the **Knoll Drive,** which passes dunes and dramatic views of the inlets. The **Nuyts Wilderness Peninsula** portion of the park is accessible by way of the superb ◙**Wow Wilderness Cruises,** offering a 2½hr. cruise through the double inlets, punctuated by a short hike across the peninsula and a traditional tea. Gary, the captain and guide, is energetic and a veritable encyclopedia of local history, lore, and facts concerning native flora and fauna. (☎9840 1036. Daily at 10am. $25; under 14 $12, under 5 free. Book at tourist bureau in Walpole. Departs from Jones St. jetty in Walpole.)

STIRLING RANGE & PORONGURUP

These two national park ranges, separated by a mere 30km, have very different histories and geologies. The Porongorups date back over a billion years, making them one of the most ancient volcanic formations on the planet. The Stirlings were formed more recently. Giant eucalypts are found up the sides of the Porongorups, while in the higher Stirling Range the vegetation is hardier scrub. Both offer hiking and, in spring, the bloom of over 1600 species of wildflowers. The town of **Mt. Barker** is a convenient gateway to both parks.

█⚐ **TRANSPORTATION & PRACTICAL INFORMATION.** From Albany, the Porongurups are 30km north on the **Chester Pass Road.** The Stirling Range is another 30km further along the road. **Porongurup Road** is a sealed road running west through the park to Mt. Barker, 15km from the park. **Stirling Range Drive** is a pretty but corrugated road running west through the Stirlings from Chester Pass.

Transwa buses (☎1300 6622 05; www.transwa.wa.gov.au) run to Mt. Barker from Albany or Perth once per day. The helpful Mt. Barker **tourist office,** in the train station on Albany Hwy., has information about the parks and the town. (☎9851 1163. Open M-F 9am-5pm, Sa 9am-3pm, Su 10am-3pm.) It is possible to walk from the Porongurup Shop and Tearooms to the Porongup trails. However, the best way to see the parks is by car. Rental is easily arranged in Albany (p. 706). There are **ranger stations** in Stirling Range National Park at Moingup Spring (☎9827 9320) and Bluff Knoll (☎9827 9278). The nearest **hospital** (☎9826 1003) is in Gnowangerup.

█▢ **ACCOMMODATIONS & FOOD.** The **Porongurup Shop and Tearooms ❷,** on Porongurup Rd. at the main entrance to Porongurup National Park, has an easy-going, down-to-earth feel. They offer Internet access ($5 per hr.) and good meals incorporating vegetables fresh from the garden ($10-15). Upon request, the owners will try to arrange a pick-up from Mt. Barker or Albany, making a stay here the best option for those without a vehicle. (☎9853 1110. Dorms $20; ensuite cabin with kitchen and room for 3 $50.) In the Stirling Range National Park, the **Stirling Range Retreat ❶** is just beyond the turn-off for Bluff Knoll. The owners have slide shows ($3) and guided orchid and bird walks ($15-20) in season. (☎9827 9229. Sites $9 per person; powered for two $22, extra person $9; dorms for two $38, extra person $19; cabins for two $45-125.) In Mt. Barker, **Chill Out Backpackers ❷,** 79 Hassell St., off the start of Porongurup Rd., is intimate and homey with immaculate rooms in a beautiful A-frame building. (☎9851 2798. Dorms $20; singles $25; doubles $40.) At the north end of Mt. Barker is the **Mt. Barker Caravan Park ❷**. (☎9851 1691. Singles $17.50; powered sites $16.50; ensuite cabins for 2 with kitchens $49, off-season $44.) Food options in town are limited, but there is a roadhouse in the BP gas station that has good breakfasts. **The Enchanted Tree Frog ❷**, 34 Albany Hwy., serves salads, pastas, and main dishes of fish, lamb, or chicken for $13-20. (☎9851 1728. Open Su and Tu-Sa 11:30am-2:30pm and 6pm-late.) **Wing Hing Chinese Restaurant ❷**, 26 Albany Hwy, has takeaway lunch specials for $7 and dinners for $11-15. (☎9851 1168. Open Su and Tu-Sa 5pm-9:30, W-F also noon-2pm.) Supavalu, on Lowood Rd., sells **groceries.**

🔋 **HIKING.** There are three major hikes in the Porongurups. The **Tree in the Rock circuit** (6km; 3hr.) originates at a picnic area at the end of Bolganup Rd., clearly marked off Porongurup Rd. After passing a sizeable eucalypt sprouting from a crack in a boulder, the track continues to Hayward Peak for panoramic views of the surrounding country, then along a ridge of Nancy Peak and Morgan's Views. A **side trail** (2hr. return from picnic area) off of the Tree in the Rock circuit winds up the sometimes slippery rock of the Devil's Slide to a summit of stark rock faces and towering granite. The equally challenging **Castle Rock trail** is a 45min. jaunt to the side of a massive granite boulder perched on the mountaintop. The last 30m include a scramble through a crevice, a short ladder, and a catwalk affording tremendous views.

Within the Stirlings, geologically younger than the Porongurups and more rugged, there are a variety of walks. The most popular is 🔋**Bluff Knoll** (1094m). The Aboriginal name of *Bullah Meual* ("Great Many Face Hill") reflects its multi-faceted shape. The trail that climbs its sides (5km; 3-4hr. return) is well-maintained, complete with stairs, but it is steep at points on the southwestern face and the wind can be quite brisk. The views of the surrounding formations from the top are exhilarating, and the contrast with the flat, vast surrounding farmlands is impressive. **Toolbrunup Peak,** the second-highest in the park (1052m), is a challenging 3hr. scramble over rocks of varying sizes. It is less popular than Bluff Knoll, in spite of its unobstructed 360° views from the top, and thus might afford some well-earned solitude. A shorter hike (2km; 2hr. return) is **Mount Trio** (856m). From the saddle, you can choose the East or North Peak. Two others are **Mount Hassell** (847m; 2km; 1½hr. return) and **Mount Talyuberlup** (783m; 3km; 2½hr. return).

Both parks require a $9 per car entry fee, which is good in both parks for one day. All of the trails listed here, save Hassell and Talyuberlup, are accessible by smooth gravel roads shorter than 10km. The others require longer drives along the corrugated Stirling Range Dr.

ALBANY
☎08

Established in 1826, Albany was the first colonial settlement of Western Australia, beating out Perth by a year. From colonial outpost to whaling village to regional center, Albany remains the preeminent city of the Great Southern.

📧🚆 **TRANSPORTATION & PRACTICAL INFORMATION. Transwa buses** (☎1300 6622 05; www.transwa.wa.gov.au) depart from in front of the tourist office to: Bunbury (6hr.; M and Th 8:35am, Tu-W and F-Su 8am; $40) via Walpole, Pemberton, Augusta, and Margaret River; Esperance (6hr.; M and Th 11:45am; $47); and Perth (6hr.; M-Sa 9am and Su 3pm, extra buses F 5:30pm and Sa 11am; $42). The two hostels in town have a steady stream of travelers sharing rides; hitchhikers usually wait by the "Big Roundabout" on the Albany Hwy., 2km west of the north end of York St., though *Let's Go* does not recommend hitchhiking. **Love's Bus**

Service provides city transport for $2 a trip (☎9841 1211. Open M-Sa). Car rental is easily arranged in Albany: try **King Sound Vehicle Hire,** 145 Albany Hwy. (☎9841 8466); **Budget,** 386 Albany Hwy. (☎9842 2833); or **Albany Car Rentals,** 386 Albany Hwy. (☎9841 7077). Prices range from $45-55 per day.

York Street runs north-south through the center of town. The **tourist office** is in the Old Railway Station, just east of the southern end of York St. near Stirling Terr. (☎800 644 088. Open daily 9am-5pm.) There is **Internet** access at Rainbow Coast Souvenirs, 191a York St. (☎9842 3570. Open daily 9am-5pm. $2.50 per 15min.) York St. also hosts the **post office** and **ATM.**

🏠🍴 ACCOMMODATIONS & FOOD. Albany has no shortage of budget accommodations. The very lively **Albany Backpackers ❷** is on the corner of Stirling Terr. and Spencer St., one block east of York St. It has elaborately painted rooms with themes ranging from underwater life to the Pinnacles, free continental breakfast, and a variety of evening dinners and get-togethers each week. (☎9841 8848; abp@albanybackpackers.com.au. Internet $5 per hr., first 10min. free. Bike hire $15 full-day, $10 half. Dorms $22.50, $20 with discount; singles $39/$36; twins and doubles $58/$55. ISIC/NOMADS/VIP/YHA.) The **Albany Bayview YHA ❷,** 49 Duke St., two blocks west of York St., is another good option with a nice view of the bay and free movies. Visitors can rent bikes ($15 full-day, $10 half) while boogie boards and fishing gear are free. (☎/fax 9842 3388; albany@yhawa.com.au. Internet $6 per hr., first 10min. free. Dorms $21.50; twins and doubles $51.50; family rooms $75. YHA discount $2.50.) The **🏠Cruize-Inn ❸,** 122 Middleton Rd., is one step up from hosteling, with beautiful, homestyle accommodations complete with kitchen, TV lounge and a superb stereo system. (☎9842 9599; narelle@cruizeinn.com. Singles $35; twins $55; doubles $60; triples $80.) **Middleton Beach Holiday Park ❷,** at the end of Middleton Rd., is farther from the center of town, but right on the beach. (☎9841 3593. Sites $25, $22 off-season, powered $27/$23; ensuite sites $34/$30.)

The Earl of Spencer ❷, on the corner of Earl and Spencer St., is a favorite pub among the locals, serving up the hearty "Earls Famous Pie and Pint" for $13 and the "Drunken Chicken" for $15. (☎9841 1322. Open M-Sa noon-midnight, Su 2pm-10pm.) **Dylan's on the Terrace ❶,** 82 Stirling Terr., has top-notch food and atmosphere, serving sandwiches and burgers ($6-8) and breakfast all day ($7-9). Try the BBQ beef kebabs. (☎9841 8720. Open daily 7am-late.) Next door, **Harvest Moon ❶** has huge vegetarian sandwiches, salads, and curries ($7-11), along with fresh-made juice drinks for $4. (☎9841 8833. Open M-W 10am-5pm, Th-F 10am-8pm, Su 11am-4:30pm.) **Tango's ❸,** 135 York St., has a vegetarian stir-fry for $15 and chicken caesar salad for $17. (☎9841 4626. Open daily 5:30pm-late.) **Giardini's Delicatessen,** 189 York St., has **groceries,** including high-quality gourmet cheeses, meats, and rolls. (Open daily 6:30am-10pm.)

🔲 SIGHTS. Albany has the distinction of being home to the world's largest whaling museum. **Whaleworld,** on Frenchman Bay Rd. past the Gap and Blowholes, is on the site of Australia's last whaling station, which closed in 1978. There are blubber vats, a whaling boat, and loads of other paraphernalia. (☎9844 4021. Open daily 9am-5pm. 30min. tours every hr. 10am-4pm. $15, concessions $11, ages 12-16 $11, ages 5-12 $7, families $37.) You can see the whales live with **Southern Ocean Charters,** a.k.a. **Big Day Out.** (☎0409 107 180. Departs May-Oct. daily 9:30am, also 1pm depending on weather. $45, children $25, families $125.) Within town, there are a number of fascinating historical sights. **Mt. Clarence,** at the end of Apex Dr., has a lookout with stunning views of Princess Royal and Oyster Harbors. Near the top, a deeply-moving monument to the ANZAC (Australia New Zealand Army Corps) troops who died in WWI should not be missed. As Albany was the staging point for the convoys heading to Gallipoli, Mt. Clarence was, for many of the soldiers, the last glimpse of home soil they would ever see. Nearby, on Ports Rd. is the **Princess Royal Fortress,** built in 1893 as a coastal defense and later used by the American submarine garrison in WWII. Inside is a large collection of military paraphernalia, including gear from the WWI 10th Lighthorse Division. (Open daily 7:30-5:30pm. $4, children $2, families $9.)

⚡ OUTDOOR ACTIVITIES. Albany's most impressive sights are in **Torndirrup National Park,** 20km south of town on Frenchman Bay Rd. The **Natural Bridge** is a rock formation that spans 24m above crashing waves. The **Gap** has dramatic waves pounding into a 30m inlet. At the **blowholes,** spray from the ocean below shoots out 10m high through a crack, though only in rough weather. *Do not go beyond the blowholes; people have died trying to get a good photo.* Albany also boasts a recent shipwreck, the intentionally submerged *Perth,* a decommissioned navy vessel with the distinction of being the only Royal Australian Navy ship hit by enemy fire in the past 50 years. It serves as an artificial reef for divers. The **Middleton Bay Scenic Path** runs from **Middleton Beach,** just outside of town, to Emu Point. **West Cape Howe National Park** (about 30km west of Albany) has a treacherous 4WD track through pristine bush and beach. Those in 2WD can head to **Shelley** and **Cosy Corner** beaches or to **Two Peoples Bay Reserve,** 35km east of town.

Adventure activities in the area include scenic flights over Albany and the coastline with **Great Southern Aviation.** (☎0427 206 210. $70 per seat for 30min. flight. Free pick-up from wharf or town.) Deep-sea fishing, with all gear included, is offered by **Spinners Charters** (☎9841 7151. Half-day $100, full-day $132. Departs Emu Point.) Horseback riding along a 4km scenic trail is available at **Willowie Horse Riding Centre.** (☎9846 4365. Riding $20, lessons $12.50. 20km east of Albany along Nanarup Rd., Two Peoples Bay turn-off.) **Albany Motorcycle Touring Co.** (☎9841 8034) can set you up with your own bike and offers a variety of "joy rides" from $5 around town to $50 for a ride to the Gap and Natural Bridge. Deep-water diving to the *Perth* is available through **Albanydive.com.** (☎0429 664 874. Departure times every two hours 6:30am-2:30pm and at 6:30pm. $85 with full gear hire, $50 with own gear; double dives for $135/$85.)

EPIC HIKE. The popular Bibbulmun track runs 964km from Kalamunda, outside Perth, to Albany, passing through North Bannister, Dwellingup, Collie, Ballingup, Bridgetown, Manjimup, Pemberton, Northcliffe, Walpole, and Denmark. The trail passes campsites, shelters with bunks, and towns with hostels and B&Bs that pick up hikers from the trails. The track can be easily divided into sections or even used for short dayhikes. Contact any local Conservation and Land Management (CALM) office for details (www.calm.wa.gov.au).

FITZGERALD RIVER NATIONAL PARK

Halfway between Albany and Esperance lies the enormous **Fitzgerald River National Park.** Named a "Biosphere Reserve" for the abundance and diversity of its wildlife, the park hosts rare creatures like the malleefowl, the chuditch (a carnivorous marsupial) and the dibbler (a marsupial once thought to be extinct). **Whales** can be seen from the tower at Point Ann, near the western edge of the reserve. The park is also home to thousands of species of plants, including dazzling spring wildflowers from September to November.

Accessing the park can be difficult. All roads are unsealed, and most are unpleasant or downright impassible by 2WD; caravans shouldn't bother trying. Ocean kayaking along the coast is dangerous and should only be undertaken by experts. The park has two main access points: **Bremer Bay** on the western end and

Hopetoun on the eastern end. A few unsealed roads run south from the South Coast Hwy. to the park. To get to Bremer Bay from the South Coast Hwy., turn right onto Bremer Bay Rd. about 120km east of Albany, then travel 65km east. Hopetoun is 50km south of Ravensthorpe on Ravensthorpe Hopetoun Rd. Hammersley Rd. cuts through the park from the highway to Hopetoun.

The area features good rock climbing, abseiling, diving, and hiking for all skill levels. The **East Mount Barren Walk** (3hr.), starting about 12km west of the Hopetoun entrance, is of medium difficulty and features great views of the beach; try also the **Horrie and Dorri Walk** (1-2hr.) or the **West Mount Barren Walk** (1-2hr.), or take a three- to five-day walk along the coast from Bremer Bay to Hopetoun. Plan ahead—the area lacks the readily accessible information and spate of tour companies that one finds elsewhere. Bob Wilson of **Great Southern Adventure Tours** (☎9837 4067), in Bremer Bay, is an adventuring jack-of-all-trades who can design itineraries that include activities from canoeing to bushwalking to abseiling and rock climbing. He also has maps for the primitive coastal walk.

Passes for the park are available at **CALM** offices in Albany (☎9842 4500) or Esperance (☎9071 3733) and the tourist bureau in Ravensthorpe. Deposit day passes in an honor box at the entrance ($9 per vehicle). **Four Mile Beach** (just west of Hopetoun) and **Saint Mary Inlet** (at Point Ann) are the easiest **campsites ❶** to access by car. (Sites for two $12, extra person $6, children $4.) To reach **Point Ann,** a particularly good whale-watching spot, take Pabelup Dr. from the north or Devils Creek Rd. from the west. Fires are not allowed, but gas BBQs are available for free at Mylies, Point Ann, Quoin Head, and Fitzgerald Inlet.

There are no reliable sources of water in the park, so be sure to bring enough for the duration of your stay. **Mt. Madden, Mt. Short,** and **Mt. Desmond** are not in the park itself but are all near Ravensthorpe and offer excellent views of the area. **Cheynes Beach** in **Waychinicup National Park** is also highly recommended. There are **ranger stations** in the park at East Mt. Barren (☎9838 3060) and on Murray Rd. (☎9837 1022), toward Bremer Bay.

ESPERANCE ☎08

Esperance (pop. 13,500) may be rather remote—it's 400km from the nearest stoplight—but it has magnificent surroundings and some of the best beaches and diving in all of Australia. The town's coastline is unsurpassed and nearby Cape Le Grand National Park is one of the southwest's true jewels. Summer tourists flock to the area to swim, fish, dive, and explore nearby parks.

⬛ TRANSPORTATION. All **Transwa buses** (☎1300 6622 05; www.transwa.wa.gov.au) to town stop near the tourist office and run to: Albany (6-10hr.; Tu-W and F-Sa 8am; $48); Kalgoorlie (5hr.; W and F 8:35am, Su 2pm; $40); and Perth (10hr., M-Sa 8am, $63). Two major **car rental** companies have offices in town and both offer airport pick-up: **Budget,** corner of Sims St. and Harbour Rd. (☎9071 2775; esperance@budgetwa.com.au), and **Avis,** 63 The Esplanade (☎9071 3998; avisesperance@wn.com.au).

⬛ PRACTICAL INFORMATION. The **South Coast Highway** (Monjingup Rd.) intersects Harbour Rd., which runs south into town. The **Esplanade** flanks the bay, and **Dempster Street** snakes along roughly parallel to it. The **tourist office** is near the center of town, on the corner of Dempster and Kemp St. (☎9071 2330; fax 9071 4543. Open Sept.-Apr. daily 9am-5pm; May-Aug. M-Sa 9am-5pm, Su 10am-4pm.) **Internet** access is at **Computer Alley,** 69c Dempster St. (☎9072 1293. Open M-F 9am-5pm, Sa 9am-noon.) **Police** (☎9071 1900) are located at 100 Dempster St.

WESTERN AUSTRALIA

WESTERN AUSTRALIA

▶️🍴 ACCOMMODATIONS & FOOD. The **Blue Waters Lodge YHA ❷**, 299 Gold-fields Rd., near the intersection of Dempster and Norseman St., is across the street from the ocean. Formerly an Australian Army Corps building in Kalgoorlie, it was transported to Esperance, reassembled, and spruced up. The hostel is a 15min. walk from the city center along the harbor bike path. Perks include pool table, ping pong, Internet ($6 per hr.), and book exchange. (☎/fax 9071 1040; yhaesperance@hotmail.com. Free bus station pick-up and drop-off. Dorms $19, YHA $18; singles $31/$30; twins $50/$48; families $76/$72.) **Esperance Backpackers ❷**, 14 Emily St., in the heart of town, runs reasonably priced half-day 4WD fishing tours to Cape Le Grande for $45. (☎9071 4724. Internet $4 per 30min. Free pick-up from the bus stop. Dorms $20, with discount $18; twins and doubles $50/$48. NOMADS/VIP/YHA.) **NOMADS Shoestring Stays ❷**, 23 Daphne St., also runs tours. (☎9071 3396. Internet, free bike hire, lockers, and breakfasts, and free pick-up and drop-off. Dorms $18; doubles $42. NOMADS/VIP/YHA.) The **Esperance B&B By the Sea ❺**, Lot 30, Stewart St., is a striking new house with comfortable rooms featuring views of Blue Haven Bay. (☎9071 5640; www.esperancebb.com. Singles $70; doubles $90.) The **Esperance Seafront Caravan Park ❷** is next to the YHA at the base of Goldfields Rd. (☎9071 1251; www.esperanceseafront.com. Sites for two $19, powered $22, extra person $5; caravans for two $60; ensuite holiday units $96.) There is good **camping ❶** in Cape Le Grand National Park, 60km east of town ($9 per car; sites for two $12.50, extra person $5.50), and on **Woody Island** (see below).

Good meals and spectacular views of Esperance Bay are to be found at virtually any hour of the day at **Taylor Street Tearooms ❷**, at the Taylor St. jetty, just off The Esplanade, which serves breakfasts for $7-9 and dinners for $10-17. (☎9071 4317. Open daily 7am-10pm.) **Ocean Blues Cafe ❶**, 19 The Esplanade, affords unparalleled beach access and is a good place to grab a bite after a few hours fun in the sun, with meals from $6-11. (☎9071 7107. Open Tu-Su 9am-2:30pm, 5:30pm-8pm.) There are a couple of pubs on Andrew St., with **Esperance Motor Inn ❶** featuring good-sized bar meals $7 at lunch. (Open daily 10am-2pm, 6pm-8pm.) Duncan's SupaValu **supermarket** is at the corner of Andrews and Dempster St. (Open M-W and F 8am-6pm, Th 8am-8pm, Sa 8am-5pm.)

🎬🥾 SIGHTS & OUTDOOR ACTIVITIES. Drivers or bikers with strong legs should try the 38km loop along the **◢Great Ocean Drive**, which snakes along the coast and by the (sometimes) **Pink Lake**. The tourist office has maps and the road is clearly marked. Take care if biking: the road is narrow and curvy, and with such stunning coastal views drivers may have a hard time keeping their eyes on the road. The drive begins at the southern end of Dempster St. and turns right onto Twilight Beach Rd., passing great beaches including **Blue Haven** and **Twilight**. The rotary lookout at the beginning of the scenic drive on Wireless Hill is a great place to watch the sunset.

Diving around Esperance is quite good. *Sanko Harvest*, the second-largest **wreck dive** in the world, is popular among experienced divers. **Esperance Diving and Fishing**, 72 The Esplanade, guides dives and charter fishing trips. (☎9071 5111; www.esperancedivingandfishing.com.au. Diving from $80. Fishing charters from $145.) **Peak Charles National Park,** an hour and a half north of Esperance along the Coolgardie-Esperance Hwy., has **rock climbing;** inquire at the **CALM** office, 92 Dempster St. (☎9071 3733. Open M-F 8:30am-4:30pm.) **Mackenzie's Island Cruises,** 71 The Esplanade, runs daily cruises to **Woody Island** in the Recherche Archipelago. (☎9071 5757. $53, concession $49, under 16 $20, family $128. Departs 9am, weather permitting, from Taylor St. Jetty.) Woody Island is fully equipped with hot showers, BBQ areas, camp kitchen, and fresh water. Safari huts with beds and private decks and tents with mattresses are available, as is camping with your own tent. (Sept.-Apr. Huts for two $68, with linen $78; tents for two $37, for one $20; own tent $9 per person.) The 4WDing along the beach and among the sand dunes north of town is incredible, but beware of patches of quicksand. **Esperance Eco-Discovery Tours** runs popular 4WD trips to Cape Le Grand and Cape Arid; these include meals and park fees. (☎0407 737 261; www.esperancetours.com.au. Half-day $75, children $50, families $190; full-day $135/$95/$395. Tag-along also possible with your own 4WD.) Experience the sights nearer to town on a motor-bike with **Esperance Harley Tours,** 117 Dempster St. (☎9072 1611. 20min. for $30, 40min. for $45, pick-up and drop-off included.) Finally, the **Esperance Museum,** corner of James St. and The Esplanade, has a massive collection of local historical artifacts, including remnants of NASA's "Skylab" space station, which broke up over the town on July 12th, 1979. (☎9071 1579. Open daily 1:30pm-4:30pm.)

CAPE LE GRAND NATIONAL PARK

Nature has outdone herself at ◨**Cape Le Grand National Park.** Hiking trails of all durations and difficulties pass cavernous granite formations dating back 2.5 billion years, affording breathtaking views of the coast and weaving through an astoundingly diverse array of plants that becomes even more striking in the orchid-filled spring. The reds, oranges, and golds of the rock mingle with the many greens of the plants and the blues of the lichens. Take Goldfields Rd. north to Fisheries Rd., turn right onto Marivale Rd., and right again onto Cape Le Grand Rd.; signs point the way. For transport to the park, ask at Esperance Backpackers or Shoestring Stays about tours.

A 15km coastal track connects the park's five stunning bays. From west to east, these are: Le Grand Beach, Hellfire Bay, Thistle Cove, Lucky Bay, and Rossiter Bay. The bays themselves are wonderful, with white sand, green and blue waters, and very friendly 'roos, but the scenes along the tracks between them are even more impressive. The stretch from **Le Grand Beach to Hellfire** (3hr.) is a hard walk through sandy coastal plains and along the slopes of the lichen-encrusted **Mt. Le Grand.** The track from **Hellfire to Thistle** (2½hr.) is challenging, weaving through low scrub and snowy banksia flowers. The track from **Thistle to Lucky** is the easiest of the four legs but is still a challenge, with heart-stopping views of caves, waves, and stunning granite forms. The moderate hike from **Lucky to Rossiter** features more granite outcrops, where plants cling to windswept dunes. Those attempting the 15km walk should register with the ranger. Another track ascends **Frenchman Peak** to magnificent views of coast and sea. In summer, there is good snorkeling, but beware of riptides. **Hellfire Gallery,** on Tyrrell Rd., off Merivale Rd., 30km east of Esperance, has several dozen fine art pieces scattered through its gallery and lush garden. There is a lovely **cafe ❶** attached, serving drinks, cakes, and muffins for $2-5. (☎9075 9042. Open M and Th-Su 10am-5pm.)

At the far eastern end of the park, overlooking Duke of Orleans Bay, the small town of **Wharton** caters to those willing to make the 83km trek from Esperance seeking equally beautiful but less crowded beaches. **Orleans Bay Caravan Park** has sites for $15, powered $18; park homes for six $35; ensuite chalets $60. (Take Fisheries Rd. east and turn south on Orleans Bay Rd. at Condingup. ☎9075 0033; orleansbay@wn.com.au.) Based in the caravan park, **Duke Charters & Scenic Tours** offers whale and dolphin sight-seeing cruises and fishing charters for tuna, snapper, gnanagi, and harlequin. (☎9075 0033. Rates vary.)

On Fisheries Rd., 120km east of Esperance, lies the remote **Cape Arid National Park,** where more surf-pounded granite headlands and pristine white beaches can be enjoyed in one of the most isolated coastlines on the Southern Ocean. Camping here is free and there are BBQ facilities and pit toilets, but bring your own water as none is available in the park.

> **PRETTY IN PINK** Why are many lakes in Western Australia pink? The *Dunaliella salina* algae and a bacteria called *Halobacterium cutirubrum* thrive along the salt crusts at the bottom of lakes, living in water with salinity as high as 35% sodium chloride—over 10 times the salinity of seawater. When salinity, temperature, and sunlight are at high levels, the bacteria produce beta carotene to protect themselves, breaking out into natural pink hues. The algae is even farmed in some places to make food coloring or dietary supplements.

GOLDFIELDS

Hundreds of kilometers east of Perth and nearly an equal distance north of Esperance, a handful of towns cling to existence in Western Australia's harsh interior. Two things keep these towns from disappearing altogether: water, piped in from the coast, and gold. In 1893, a group of Irish prospectors stumbled onto an area that would become the Golden Mile, the most gold-rich square mile in the world, and the city of Kalgoorlie was born. For the traveler, Kal offers a drastic contrast to the rest of the beach-mad southwest, but it's a long trip to get there and a long trip back, with nothing in between but 'roos and road trains. Unless particularly interested in gold mining, those heading west to Perth from Eyre should consider taking the South Coast Hwy., which allows a much more relaxing and varied trip.

GREAT EASTERN HIGHWAY

Long (600km) and mind-numbing, the drive from Perth to Kalgoorlie along the Great Eastern Highway is good training for a Nullarbor crossing. The traffic in Perth's eastern suburbs can be frustrating, but the tension melts away as you drive through the verdant fields and wildflower-filled forests of the Darling Range. By the time you reach the towns of **Merredin** and **Southern Cross,** the only traffic is swaggering road trains bearing farm equipment and even buildings. This part of the highway is not as well maintained, so fuel up whenever possible.

Merredin (pop. 3700), which contests Kalgoorlie's claim to the world's longest road train (Merredin's is over 600m), is the largest town on the Great Eastern Hwy. between Coolgardie and Perth. The **tourist office, post office, bank, and supermarket** are all within one block of each other on Barrack St., which is just one block north of the highway. There are several hotels in town, including **Commercial Hotel ❸,** on Barrack St. (☎9041 1052. Singles $27.50; doubles $49.50.) The **Merredin Caravan Park ❶,** 2 Oats St., has sites and backpacker rooms. (☎9041 1535. Sites $12, powered $15; singles $22; doubles $33; motel-style villas $65-70.) The comfortable **Hay Loft Coffee Lounge ❶,** on Bates St., one block north of the tourist office, is one of several nice eateries in town, with cakes for $4.50 and meals for $7-10.

Coolgardie is a dusty frontier town that serves mainly as a residential satellite for families of Kalgoorlie miners. The main street, Hwy. 94 (Bayley St. in town), houses a **tourist office.** (☎9026 6090. Open daily 9am-5pm.) There are no **ATMs** in town, but most roadhouses have **EFTPOS,** and the post office does banking. The **Caltex Roadhouse ❹,** on Bayley St., rents simple, clean rooms. (☎9026 6049; fax 9026 6756. Singles $50; doubles $60.)

KALGOORLIE-BOULDER ☎08

The twin towns of Kalgoorlie and Boulder (total pop. 30,500) claim an impressive catalog of odd superlatives—the largest hole in the southern hemisphere, the richest mile of gold mine on the planet, and Australia's longest roadtrain. The streets of downtown Kai are lined with impressive old Victorian hotels. Today, however, with the romance of prospecting long gone, mammoth mining interests run the show. It's a dusty, grimy place, where dump trucks, dynamite, and drills toil away all day long. Still, pay can be high, and workers flood the area's hostels, creating an atmosphere that backpackers may find a bit gritty.

TRANSPORTATION

The **airport** is south of Boulder off Gatacre St. **Qantaslink, Skywest,** and **Virgin Blue** offer daily service to Perth (1-3 times per day; times and prices vary). The **bus stop** is between the tourist office and the post office on Hannan St. **McCafferty's/Grey-hound** (☎ 13 14 99 or 13 20 30) runs to Perth (8hr., Su 12:20am, $118; book at tourist office). Leaving from the tourist office, **Goldfields Express** runs to Perth (8hr.; M 11am; Su, Tu, Th, F 2:45pm; W and F 11pm; $83, YHA $75). **Prospector trains** (☎ 13 10 53) depart from the station, on the corner of Forrest and Wilson St., for Perth (8hr.; M-Sa 6:55am, M, F 2pm, Su 1:25pm; $56, YHA $50).

ORIENTATION & PRACTICAL INFORMATION

The **Great Eastern Highway** (Hwy. 94 from Coolgardie) becomes **Hannan Street,** the main drag, running northeast through town. One block northwest is **Hay Street,** the **red light district,** where the town's hostels occupy former brothels. Lionel St., Wilson St., and Boulder Rd. are all major roads running perpendicular to Hannan and Hay St. To reach Boulder from downtown Kalgoorlie, turn right on Boulder Rd. at the north end of Hannan St. and follow it into Lane St.

The **tourist office** is at 250 Hannan St. (☎ 9021 1966. Open M-F 8:30am-5pm, Sa-Su 9am-5pm.) **Internet** is available at **NetZone,** to the left of the tourist office. (☎ 9091 4178. Open M-F 10am-7pm, Sa-Su 10am-5pm. $1 per 10min.) The **post office** is on Hannan St., south of city center. (Open M-F 8:30am-5pm.) **Postal Code:** 6430.

The police maintain that no areas of Kalgoorlie-Boulder are particularly unsafe, although they do warn to *be careful of deep mining holes* when bushwalking. Much of the city is poorly lit, and it is a good idea to exercise caution after dark. The center of Kal's red-light district, Hay St., with neon-adorned tin shacks advertising sauna and spa services, is home to three working brothels. *Women may not want to walk alone in this area after dark.*

> **WORKING IN KAL.** The main reason people come to Kal is to work, but finding a job in mining is not as easy as one might expect. Many mining companies will only hire employees who have previous experience and pass a drug test. They also require safety training and certification, which takes time and costs money. It can be done, but it isn't a breeze—non-mining jobs may be easier to come by. The service industry offers a fairly good number of jobs, though job openings in this sector reportedly come and go with no particular pattern. **Gold Dust Backpackers** (see p. 714) is a good place to start your search.

ACCOMMODATIONS

At the turn of the 19th century, Kal boasted 93 hotels, more than any other town its size in the world. There are still a heap of nice places to stay in town, though they tend to be pricey. On the other end, most budget accommodations are geared toward long-term workers. This leaves Kal's two backpacker hostels smack in the middle of the red light district. The **caravan parks** on the way out of town toward Coolgardie are a good alternative.

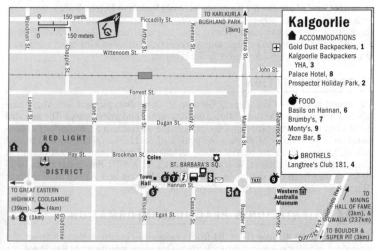

Kalgoorlie

🏠 ACCOMMODATIONS
Gold Dust Backpackers, **1**
Kalgoorlie Backpackers
 YHA, **3**
Palace Hotel, **8**
Prospector Holiday Park, **2**

🍴FOOD
Basils on Hannan, **6**
Brumby's, **7**
Monty's, **9**
Zeze Bar, **5**

🛏 BROTHELS
Langtree's Club 181, **4**

Kalgoorlie Backpackers YHA, 166 Hay St. (☎9091 1482 or 0412 110 001; backpackers@kalgoorlie.com), near the intersection with Lionel St. The one cheap place in town more oriented towards travelers than long term workers. Shared kitchen, laundry, lounge, A/C, and swimming pool. There's a notice board for work opportunities. Dorms $20, with discount $18; singles $26/$24; doubles $52/$48; weekly rates available. ISIC/NOMADS/VIP. ❷

Gold Dust Backpackers, 192 Hay St. (☎/fax 9091 3737; golddust@aurum.net.au). Clean, with kitchen and nice lounge spaces. Offers transport around the city for a fee. Internet $6 per hr. and A/C. Dorms $18, with discount $17; singles $30; twins and doubles $40. ISIC/NOMADS/VIP/YHA. ❷

Prospector Holiday Park (☎9021 2524; prospector@acclaimparks.com.au), on the corner of the Great Eastern Hwy. and Ochiltree St., has Internet and swimming pool. Sites $21, powered $23; cabins $65; ensuite cabins $79. ❷

The Palace Hotel (☎9021 1788; admin@palacehotel.com.au), on the corner of Hannan and Maritana St. Nice rooms and an in-house movie channel in a heritage-listed building. Note the mirror downstairs given to a barmaid, along with a poem, by the young Herbert Hoover, who would later become President of the United States. Singles $62; doubles $84; family $109. ❺

🔲🔳 FOOD & NIGHTLIFE

Monty's ❸ (☎9022 8288), at the corner of Hannan and Porter St., is open 24hr. and has $9 pasta on Tuesdays and mains from $17-25 in an elegant setting, complete with comfy leather and wicker chairs. The **Zeze Bar** ❸, at the corner of Hannan and Wilson St., makes excellent woodfire pizzas from $14-20. (☎9021 3046. Open daily noon-2:30pm and 6-9pm.) **Cafes** line Hannan St.; many open early and close late. Vegetarian sandwiches can be found for $7-9 at **Basils on Hannan** ❶, just beside the tourist office, while next door is **Brumby's** ❶, a fantastic little bread bakery.

Tiny Kal boasts nearly 30 **pubs;** many are clustered at the corner of Hannan and Maritana St. The Coles **supermarket** is located at the corner of Wilson and Brookman St. (Open M-W and F 8am-6pm, Th 8am-9pm, Sa 8am-5pm.)

◉ SIGHTS

The best place to learn about mining is the extensive ▨**Mining Hall of Fame,** located at **Hannans North Historic Mining Reserve,** a right turn off Goldfields Hwy., 3km north of Hannan St. It features biographies of mining legends, demonstrations of gold pouring and panning, and a tour of an underground mine. (☎9091 4074. Open daily 9am-4:30pm. $20, without underground tour $12; concessions $15/$10, children $10/$6, families up to six $50/$35.) The **Super Pit,** an immense open-pit working mine, is the largest hole in the Southern Hemisphere at 3km long, 1.4km wide and 330m deep. For an added treat, the miners often set off explosions once a day; check with the tourist office for the time of the day's blast. The lookout is just outside town; head toward Boulder on the Goldfield's Hwy., then turn left at the sign for the pit. (Open daily 6am-7pm, except when closed for blasting. Free.) The **WA Museum of Kalgoorlie,** 17 Hannan St., houses an old fire truck, huge banners from the heyday of the labor unions, and a vault full of valuable gold pieces. (☎9021 8533. Open daily 10am-4:30pm.) Find out about the **Royal Flying Doctor Service,** which began medical service to isolated outback communities in 1928 and continues to do so to this day, at their visitors center, located at the airport on Hart Kerspien Dr. (☎9093 7595. Open M-F 10am-3pm. Tours on the hour. Admission by donation.) The recently refurbished **Langtree's Club 181,** 181 Hay St., may be the world's only working brothel that offers tours. (☎9026 2111. 18+. Tours daily 11am, 3 and 6pm; $25.)

NORSEMAN ☎08

About 100 years ago, "Hardy Norseman" was tethered here overnight as his rider slept. The restless horse pawed at the dusty ground, uncovering a chunk of gold. Prospectors rushed to the area, and the town of Norseman was born. Today, most visitors are on their way elsewhere. For those heading north from Esperance, Norseman is the first encounter with the Goldfields. For those heading east across the desolate Nullarbor Plain, it is the last taste of civilization for over 1000km.

The **tourist office,** on Robert St., one block east on the highway between Sinclair and Richardson St., has information about Norseman and traveling the Eyre Hwy. They also offer free showers, a dream come true for Nullarbor survivors. Permits to go fossicking for gemstones at a site 12km north of town are available for $5.50. (☎9039 1071. Open daily 9am-5pm.) The people of Norseman were shocked when ANZ bank recently installed an **ATM.** There is **Internet** at the **Telecentre** on Robert St. (☎9039 0538. Open M-F 9am-4pm. $2.50 per 15min.)

The family-run **Lodge 101 ❷** on Prinsep St. (the Coolgardie-Esperance Hwy.) offers comfortable accommodations. Backpackers can use a small kitchen and an outdoor sheltered lounge area. Free local bus pick-up. (☎9039 1541. Dorms $19; singles $32; doubles $50; family $70. Continental breakfast $5.50.) Budget accommodation is also available at the **Norseman Hotel ❸,** 90 Roberts St. (☎9039 1023. Singles $33; twins $49; doubles $55; family $60.) There is also the **Gateway Caravan Park,** corner of the highway and McIvor St. (☎9039 1500. Sites $16, powered $20; cabins $55; ensuite cabins $75.)

Norseman's various hotels and motels have restaurants, but these tend to be pricey. One budget option popular with the big appetites of hard-working local miners is **Topic Caterer ❷,** with an all-you-can-eat buffet for $11. (☎9039 9899. Open daily 5pm-7:30pm. Take Ramsay Rd. south off Prinsep St., turn left onto Battery Rd. and then right on Phoenix Rd.) Another option is the newly-reopened **Dromedary Cafe ❶,** on the corner of Ramsay St. and Prinsep St., which serves breakfasts for $5-7 and meals for $7-12. (Open daily 6am-8:30pm.) The **SupaValu,** 89 Robert St., has groceries. (Open M-F 8:30am-6pm, Sa 8:30am-5pm, Su 9:30am-1pm.) The **BP 24-hour Travelstop,** north of town at the exit for the Eyre Hwy., has a diner, convenience store, and **petrol.**

CROSSING THE NULLARBOR

The **Eyre Highway,** running between Norseman and Adelaide across the **Nullarbor Plain** (see p. 519), is a grueling desert haul by car or bus; on a Greyhound **bus,** it's a mind-boggling 27hr. trek. ($230, with YHA discount $203. Departs Norseman BP Th 2:20am.) The one noteworthy sight is the pink **Lake McDonald** near Penong. **Ninety Mile Straight,** the longest completely straight stretch of highway in Australia, begins just west of Cocklebiddy. For questions on what is allowed across the border into SA, call the **agriculture department.** (☎9039 3227 in WA, ☎8625 2108 in SA; www.agric.wa.gov.au.) The **tourist office** in Norseman has helpful info and handles bus bookings. When you reach **Ceduna** at the eastern corner of SA's **Eyre Peninsula,** pick up a Nullarbor certificate of completion at the tourist office or, if you're headed the other direction, get your certificate at the Norseman tourist office. See **Crossing the Nullarbor,** p. 519, in the South Australia chapter, for more information.

BATAVIA COAST & MIDLANDS

The region just north and east of Perth represents different things for different people. For windsurfers, Lancelin and Geraldton offer world-class gusts. Fishermen reap the bountiful harvest of the Batavia Coast's treacherous waters. For many backpackers, the region is little more than the long and straight Brand Hwy., running 600km north from Perth to the jagged gorges of Kalbarri and beyond with a stop at the ghostly Pinnacles. But those willing to do some exploring along the way will be treated to a beautiful coastal road with views of the sea, thrilling water sports, a glorious wildflower season (June-Nov.), and pristine coastal dunes.

LANCELIN ☎08

Lancelin (pop. 800), 126km north of Perth, is often regarded as the windsurfing capital of Australia. The Aborigines called the area *Wangaree,* meaning "Good Fishing Place," and this small fishing village still thrives upon the ocean's bounty, working the seas from September to June. But Lancelin is equally a place of good winds, and thrillseekers flock here from October through March to ride its air currents. The famed Ledge Point Sailboard Classic is held in the second week in January, but even in the off-season, there's almost always a good breeze.

There is no public transportation to Lancelin, but **Coastal Coachlines** runs **buses** from Perth to nearby Regans Ford. (☎9652 1036. 2hr., departs Perth train station M-F 4:30pm, $14. Book ahead.) Alternatively, the YHA will pick up from Perth for $25. The easiest way to reach Lancelin is by car; from Perth, take Bulwer St. to Charles St., which becomes Hwy. 60 (Wanneroo Rd.). The **Tourist Info Centre** is at 102 Gingin Rd. (☎9655 1100. Open daily 9am-6pm.)

The sparkling, well-run ⚑**Lancelin Lodge YHA ❶,** 10 Hopkins St., has two comfy lounges, free bikes, boogie boards, fishing rods, a lovely kitchen, and a new pool. It's only a short walk to Lancelin's beautiful beach, and the people couldn't be nicer. (☎9655 2020; www.lancelinlodge.com.au. Internet $6 per hr. Dorms $20, with YHA $18; twins/doubles $50/$48; family rooms $60/$58.) The other budget alternative is the **Lancelin Caravan Park ❶,** just down Hopkins St. from the YHA. (☎9655 1056. Sites $9 per person, powered $11; on-site vans $22.) **Lancelin Holiday Accommodation ❺,** 102 Gingin Rd., has motel-style apartments. (☎9655 1100. Apartments $65-75. Weekly $320-480.) Food options are limited. **El Tropo Restaurant ❷**, 119 Gingin Rd., is popular with the locals and offers a number of seafood dishes, with mains $13-23. (☎9655 1448. Open Th-Sa 6-8pm.) **Endeavor Tavern ❷**, corner of Cray St. and Gingin Rd., offers standard pub fare in an adjoining restaurant for $9-14. (Open daily noon-2pm, 6:30pm-8pm.) A **supermarket** is on Gingin Rd. (☎9655 1172. Open daily 7am-7pm.)

Windsurfing lessons and equipment are available at **Werner's Hotspot** (☎9655 1553). Another Lancelin attraction is its sand dunes, accessible by car, which extend for miles to the north and east of town. The dunes are a 4WD playground as well as a practice area for the Australian **military;** check with the info center, as practice bombing may close some portions of the beach and national park to the north. **Desert Storm Adventures** offers a one-hour veritable rollercoaster ride over the dunes in a schoolbus with monster truck tires and an equally monster stereo. You don't crush any cars, but it's a fun trip all the same. (☎9655 2550; www.desert-storm.com.au. $35, concessions $30, children $25, families $10 discount, YHA $2 discount.) **Lancelin Off Road Motor Bike Hire** lets you jump on a dirt bike and explore the open country on your own. (☎0417 919 550. Quad-wheels $70 per hr., 2-wheels $65 per hr.) The Tourist Centre and hostels provide maps of several coastal **nature walks** in the area, including an 11km, 3hr. return trek to Ledge Point that affords splendid views of the reef and coast. Lancelin's coral reefs are unusually close to shore, which makes for good snorkeling and diving. The lagoon on the far side of **Lancelin Island**, a bird sanctuary within swimmable distance, is one of the best spots. Very experienced divers enjoy the **Key Biscayne Dive** around an old drilling rig, 19km northwest of Ledge Point. Other nearby dive sites include the **Grace Darling,** a 1914 wooden schooner wrecked in 1914 just off the Lancelin coast, and the **Gilt Dragon,** a Dutch East India Company ship wrecked in 1656 south of Ledge Point. **Lancelin Surf and Dive,** 127 Gingin Rd., rents scuba, snorkeling, sandboarding, and surfing gear. (☎9655 1441. Dive gear $55 per day; sandboards, surfboards, and snorkels $11 for 2hr., $22 per day. Open daily 8am-4pm; later in summer.)

NAMBUNG NATIONAL PARK: THE PINNACLES

Between Lancelin and Geraldton, the **Pinnacles Desert**, in **Nambung National Park,** is a popular destination for day-tours from Perth. The barren, jagged landscape isn't really a desert at all but an expanse of sand dunes with thousands of wind-eroded limestone pillars up to 4m tall. Dutch sailors sighting the rocks from the sea mistook them for the ruins of an ancient city. The park has a ghost town-like feel, and the forms of the worn rocks are intriguing. Climb the **Pinnacles Lookout** at the northernmost edge of the vehicle loop for splendid views of the contrasting Red Desert to the east and the White Desert to the west.

The park is a good 250km north of Perth, near the small town of **Cervantes. McCafferty's/Greyhound** (☎13 14 99 or 13 20 30) drops off right in town (2hr., 1 per day, $25). Perth day-tours range from $80-100, though there are cheaper deals in winter. **West Coast Explorers** (☎9418 8835), which arrives at sunset, and **Redback Safari** (☎9275 6204) are popular, as is **Western Geographic** (☎9336 4992; www.westerngeographic.com.au. $120, concessions $115, children $85. Departs Fremantle 7am, Perth 7:30am; returns 7:30pm.) In Cervantes, **HappyDay Tours** (☎9652 7244) gives three-hour walking tours ($25) and **Turquoise Coast Enviro Tours** gives two-hour driving tours of the Pinnacles. (☎9652 7047; miken@wn.com.au. $25. Departs 8am and 3pm; full-day $110.) However, there aren't many advantages to a guided tour over an independent walk around the Pinnacles—the walk is easy and no 4WD is necessary. Hiring a car is the cheapest and most flexible way to see the park. Allow one hour west from the left turn off the Brand Hwy.; turn left into the park just before Cervantes. Once inside the park, the **Kangaroo Point** and **Hangover Bay** turn-offs afford beach access. **Lake Thetis,** between the park turn and Cervantes, is home to ancient stromatolites.

GERALDTON   ☎ 08

Geraldton (pop. 24,000) is the gateway to the beautiful **Abrolhos Islands,** where the diving is superb. Windsurfers eager to test their skill in the strong southerly winds also flock to Geraldton every summer.

⌨🚻 TRANSPORTATION & PRACTICAL INFORMATION. From the Brand Hwy., head straight through the rotary up Cathedral Ave. to get to the town center. The town's main drag, **Chapman Road,** and the shop-lined **Marine Terrace** both run parallel to the coast and intersect Cathedral Ave. **McCafferty's/Greyhound** (☎ 13 14 99 or 13 20 30), **Transwa** (☎ 1300 66 22 05; www.transwa.wa.gov.au), and **Integrity** (☎ 1800 22 63 39) run buses to Perth (6hr.; 2-3 per day; $37, YHA/VIP $33). McCafferty's runs to Broome ($295/$266) via Carnarvon ($66/$59) and Exmouth ($159/$145). Integrity hits the same destinations for considerably cheaper: Broome $260, concession $234; Carnarvon $60/$54; Exmouth $140/$126. The **Tourist Office** is inside the Bill Sewall Complex at the corner of Bayly St. and Chapman Rd., about 1km north of Cathedral Ave. (☎9921 3999; fax 9964 2445. Open M-F 8:30am-5pm, Sa 9am-4:30pm, Su 9:30am-4:30pm.)

🛏🍴 ACCOMMODATIONS & FOOD. The convenient **Batavia Backpackers ❷,** next to the tourist office, has oceanfront balconies and private dorms. (☎9964 3001. Dorms $18; singles $23; twins $35. ISIC/VIP/YHA.) **Geraldton YHA Foreshore Backpackers ❷,** 172 Marine Terr., a block southwest of Cathedral Ave., has a rustic flavor and ample space. Some of the rooms have patios overlooking the ocean. (☎9921 3275; fax 9921 3233. Free pick-up and drop-off. Internet $7 per hr. Dorms $18; singles $27; twins and doubles $42; family rooms for 2 $40, children $5 each. ISIC/NOMADS/VIP/YHA.) The **Belair Caravan Park ❷** is across from Pages Beach on Willcock Dr. in the West End. (☎9921 1997. Sites $15.50, powered $18.50; cabins from $30; chalets from $58.) The **Ocean Centre Hotel ❸,** on the corner of Foreshore Dr. and Cathedral Ave., has rooms with all the comforts desired. (☎9921 7777. Singles $90, ocean view $110.) Woolworths **supermarket,** on Sanford and Durlacher St., has cheap **groceries.** (Open M-W and F 8am-6pm, Th 8am-9pm, Sa 8am-5pm.) **Planet Bean ❶,** in the Marine Terr. mall, has good, inexpensive breakfasts and lunches for $7-11. (☎9965 2233. Open M-F 6:30am-2:30pm, Sa 8am-1:30pm.) **Tanti's Restaurant ❷** serves up Thai options, many of which are vegetarian, for $10-13. (☎9965 2964. Open M-Sa 5:30pm-10pm.) There is no shortage of great restaurants in town, however; the tourist office has a helpful guide to Geraldton's cuisine.

🌅🎯 SIGHTS & ACTIVITIES. Most people come to Geraldton for one reason: **windsurfing.** The best conditions are October to November and March to April, though it is good year-round. Bring your own gear or rent at **Sailwest,** at the Point Moore Lighthouse on Willcock Rd. west of town. (☎9964 1722. Windsurfing gear $90 per day, surfboards $30, lessons $25 per hr. Open M-F 9am until the wind reaches 20 knots, Sa-Su 10am until 20 knots.) The best windsurfing in the area is at **Point Moore,** the windiest spot around. **St. George's Beach** has tamer winds, but also a shallow reef that can be dangerous. Surfers prefer **Greys Beach, Sunset Beach,** and **Back Beach.** The **Abrolhos Islands,** an archipelago comprising over 120 islands, about 60km off of Geraldton, were the site (and cause) of the *Batavia* wreck. The islands are rich in marine life, making for incredible diving. With a fast boat, **Abrol-**

hos **Odyssey Charters** (☎ 0428 382 505; abrolhosodyssey@westnet.com.au) runs day-trips to the islands, and both the Odyssey and **Eco Abrolhos Tours** (☎ 9964 7887) offer extended tours from $200. **Shine Aviation Services** (☎ 9923 3600; sas@wn.com.au) takes visitors on sightseeing flights from $165.

KALBARRI NATIONAL PARK

Kalbarri National Park encompasses miles of sandstone sculptures, carved by the elements over millions of years. The rugged red-and-white landscape is further enhanced in the late winter and early spring by countless wildflowers.

▋ PRACTICAL INFORMATION. The township of **Kalbarri,** located in the heart of the national park at the mouth of the **Murchison River,** is the primary starting point for exploring this natural wonderland. Most services lie on or near **Grey Street,** which follows the river and turns into the south-bound **Red Bluff Road** and north-east-bound **Ajana-Kalbarri Road** at either end of town. The former leads to Geraldton via a newly sealed road that makes for a great coastal drive; the latter goes to the NW Coastal Hwy. The **Visitors Centre** is on Grey St. to the left of Woods St. when facing the ocean. (☎ 9937 1104; www.kalbarriwa.info. Open daily 9am-5pm.) The **Department of Conservation and Land Management (CALM)** office (☎ 9937 1140) is on the Ajana-Kalbarri Rd., 1km east of town. The **Health Centre** (☎ 9937 0100) is on Kaiber St. Transportation in town or to the coastal cliffs and inland gorges is available through **Kalbarri Taxi** (☎ 9937 1888).

▐ ▌ ACCOMMODATIONS & FOOD. Kalbarri Backpackers ❷, 52 Mortimer St., offers decent rooms, a pool, cozy lounges, BBQ, bike rental ($10 per day), 4WD rental ($77 per day; ages 25+), and free use of snorkel gear and boogie boards. From the Visitors Centre, turn right on Grey St., then right on Woods St. (☎ 9937 1430; fax 9937 1563. Dorms $19; doubles $46. 7th night free. VIP/YHA.) **Kalbarri Anchorage Caravan Park ❷,** across from the jetty at the north end of Grey St., is in a pretty location with great views and has an enclosed kitchen. (☎ 9937 1181; fax 9937 1806. Sites for 2 $20, on-site vans $40; extra person $5.)

▨Finlay's Fresh Fish BBQ ❷, on Magee Crescent, serves up tasty seafood with a folksy flare ($10-22). To get there from Grey St., turn left at Porter St., right on Walker St., then right onto Magee Crescent. (☎ 9937 1260. Open Su and Tu-Sa 5:30-8:30pm.) **Duncan Good ❶,** Shop 2 in the small shopping center on Grey and Porter St., has Chinese and Mexican takeaway fare for $6-16. (☎ 9937 2898. Tu-Sa 11am-2pm, 5pm-8pm.) Kalbarri **supermarket,** also in the shopping center, is family-owned and has an extensive fruit and veggie section, as well as an **ATM.** (☎ 9937 1100. Open daily 6:30am-6:30pm.)

◪ ▐ SIGHTS & HIKING. The park has two main sections: the coastal cliffs and the river gorges. Along the 10km of the coastal road just south of the town of Kalbarri, numerous sideroads lead out to soaring cliffs overhanging the Indian Ocean. The **Natural Bridge** was created by waves that eroded part of a cliff, leaving a rock slab bridging a gap filled with crashing white caps. Nearby, **Island Rock** rises 20m from the surf. Other impressive formations include **Red Bluff Lookout, Eagle Gorge,** and **Rainbow Valley.** The eye-popping **cliffside hike** (10km one-way; 4hr.) takes in the whole series of cliffs, running from Eagle Gorge to the Natural Bridge. A shuttle drops hikers off at the Natural Bridge for the hike back into town. (☎ 9937 1161. Departs daily 9:30am. $9.) The river gorges section of the park, carved by the waters of the Murchison River, features top-down views of the gorges and hikes along the jagged ledges of the river bank. **Nature's Window** is a red rock arch that frames a river landscape behind it. It is found near the beginning of the **Loop trail**

(8km; 4hr.), a challenging but rewarding climb that runs along clifftops, down to the river bed, and then along the river level ledges before climbing up again to the top of the gorge. Keep the river on your right and stay close to water level, even if it seems like you're not on the trail. To experience those gorges inaccessible by road, the intensive 38km **hike** from the **Ross Graham Lookout** farther west past the **Hawks Head Lookout** to the Loop trail runs along the path of the river. Allow four days and hike in groups (CALM recommends parties of five or more). For any overnight hiking, alert CALM (☎9937 1140) beforehand. Access to the River Gorges area costs $9 per vehicle. Bring exact change in case no one is on duty. The park's unsealed roads are generally in good 2WD condition, but the 25km to the Loop and Z Bend can be very corrugated at times and caravans should be left behind. It's always a good idea to check with CALM to obtain current reports.

OUTBACK COAST & GASCOYNE

The Outback Coast is an unfathomable expanse of bushland, broken up only by termite mounds and the occasional befuddled emu crossing the road. Although the distances between towns are daunting, the desolate landscape holds its own sense of wonder. The dazzling ocean that abuts this semi-desert counters its sparseness with a lush flowering of marine life, from the dolphins and dugongs of Shark Bay to the whale sharks and coral of the Ningaloo Marine Park. Winter is peak season, when Perthites park themselves along the sunny coast.

SHARK BAY

Shark Bay, Western Australia's much-touted World Heritage area, was the site of the earliest recorded European landing in Australia. In 1616, Dutch Explorer Dirk Hartog came ashore at Cape Inscription on the island that now bears his name. Today, Shark Bay is known mainly for the dolphins at Monkey Mia, tranquil shell beaches, and the "living fossils" (stromatolites) at Hamelin Pool. The best way to see the area is by car or on a tour; buses are infrequent.

MONKEY MIA. At Monkey Mia, the Indian bottlenose dolphins of Shark Bay swim right up to the shore to be fed by herds of tourists. Only a handful, mostly children, get to feed the creatures, so flash the ranger a winning smile and catch his or her eye. The dolphins have been visiting Monkey Mia since the time it was nothing but a sheep-farming area, but in the past ten years, the playful creatures have become an international sensation. Some think Monkey Mia provides an unparalleled opportunity to interact with intelligent, sociable animals; others find it a contrived and exploitative show. One-day access to the site is $6, a family pass costs $12, and four-week passes are $9, although it only takes an hour or two to "do" the Monkey Mia dolphin bit. Generally there are three feedings between 8am and 1pm each day; it's best to get there early in the morning. The reserve is home to an **info center** and the **CALM office,** which has displays, videos, and talks. (☎9948 1366. Open daily 8am-4pm.) If you've just missed a dolphin-feeding, there is an easy **walk trail** (2km; 1½hr. return) that starts from the carpark and proceeds along the coast and up a low ridge. The **YHA Monkey Mia Dolphin Resort ❶,** right next to the dolphin interaction site, has backpacker beds in cramped, aging campervans, and sites. (☎9948 1320; fax 9948 1034. Sites $10; dorms $18; vans from $38.) Bring food to Monkey Mia; the restaurants and mini-mart food shop (open 7am-6pm) are expensive. The road to Monkey Mia from Denham is well-marked and departs from the western tip of Knight Terr. Those without cars can take the Denham YHA's **shuttle.** (Guests free; others $5. Departs daily 7:45am, returns 4:30pm.)

DENHAM. The westernmost town in Australia is perhaps the best base for exploring Shark Bay. The main street, **Knight Terrace,** runs parallel to the beach. The **Greyhound bus** departs for the Overlander Roadhouse on the North West Costal Hwy. from the Caltex station on Knight Terr. (M, Th, and Sa 5am and 6pm). The area is best seen by car; **Shark Bay Car Hire** (☎ 9948 1247), on Knight Terr., rents cars. The **tourist bureau,** 71 Knight Terr., a few doors down from the Shell station, is very helpful and has **Internet.** (☎ 9948 1253; fax 9948 1065. Internet $5 per 30min. Open daily 9am-5pm.) Internet can also be found at the **Telecentre,** a few doors down. (Tu and W 12:30-3:30pm, Th 12:30-3pm, F 12:30-2pm. $8 per hr.) Next door, the **CALM** office, 67 Knight Terr., provides information and sells National Park passes. (☎ 9948 1208. Open M-F 8am-5pm.) The **post office** is on Knight Terr. (Open M-F 8am-4:30pm.) **Postal Code:** 6537. The facilities at the **YHA Denham Bay Lodge ❷,** 95 Knight Terr., 100m south of the bus stop, are a real treat—dorms are shared ensuite units with a kitchen. The managers will book all tours and are very helpful in arranging transportation to and from Denham. (☎ 1800 812 780; fax 9948 1031. Free bus to Monkey Mia daily 7:45am, returns 4:30pm. Dorms $22.50; twins and doubles $52.50. VIP/YHA.) The **Denham Seaside Tourist Village ❷,** at the western end of Knight Terr., is another budget option. (☎ 9948 1242. Sites $17, powered $20, with bath $23; cabins from $45, extra person $7.) Tradewinds **Supermarket** is at the BP Station, 1 Knight Terr. (Open daily 7am-7pm.)

CARNARVON   ☎ 08

Carnarvon (pop. 7000) is a good place to catch your breath between destinations on the west coast, but most people come here looking for work at the 170 local fruit plantations, which supply nearly 70% of the state's tropical fruits and vegetables, or to see the 30m high blowholes north of town. **McCafferty's/Greyhound** (☎ 13 14 99 or 13 20 30) runs daily to: Broome ($254), Coral Bay ($68), Darwin ($509), Exmouth ($68), and Perth ($103). **Integrity** (☎ 1800 226 339) goes to Exmouth (M and W 8:30am, $68) via Coral Bay ($60) and Perth (M, W, F; $108). A big yellow plastic banana welcomes visitors as they head into town along Robinson St. from the North West Coastal Hwy. The center of Carnarvon is **Robinson Street,** between **Babbage Island Road** and **Olivia Terrace,** which passes along the water. The **Visitors Centre** is at 11 Robinson St., in the Carnarvon Civic Centre at the corner of Stuart St., and has an extensive guide to the town's history and services. (☎ 9941 1146; cvontourist@wn.com.au. Open M-F 8:30am-5pm, Sa 9am-noon.) The **police** (☎ 9941 1444) are next door in the Civic Centre, while the **post office** is just across Camel Ln. The **hospital** (☎ 9941 0555) is on Cleaver St.; turn left on Fancis St. at the Visitors Centre, then left on Cleaver.

WORKING IN CARNARVON. There are really only two consistently successful ways to find work in Carnarvon. Those with their own mode of transport can visit the **plantations** that line the north and south sides of the Gascoyne River and inquire about work. Those without transportation are dependent on the **Carnarvon Backpackers,** who find work for guests (the process generally takes 3-5 days) and provide transportation to work sites. They keep a list of guests looking for work and pass out available jobs to those waiting the longest.

Carnarvon Backpackers ❷, 9790 Olivia Terr., south of Robinson St., has small, self-contained units that were built for American scientists on the Apollo and Gemini missions. With a large contingent of working travelers, the management has heaps of info on jobs. There's BBQ, off-street parking, A/C, fans, and canoe use. (☎/fax 9941 1095. Internet $1 per 10min. Dorms $18-20; doubles $47. Weekly

$114/$270.) The **Carnarvon Tourist Centre Caravan Park ❷**, 108 Robinson St., is five blocks down Robinson St. from the Visitors Centre. (☎9941 1438. Sites $17, powered $19.50; clean cabins with TV and A/C for 2 $55, extra person $5.)

The **Dragon Pearl ❶**, corner of Johnston and Francis St., serves up Chinese fare for $6-11. (☎9941 1941. Open Su and W-Sa 6-9pm.) **River Gums Cafe ❶** is a popular local hangout with mains from $8-13 and delicious mango smoothies for $5; turn at the big banana onto Boundary Rd. and follow the signs. (☎9941 8281. Open daily 10am-5pm.) Woolworths **supermarket,** in the shopping center on Robinson St., has cheap **groceries.** (☎9941 2477. Open M-W and F-Su 8am-8pm, Th 8am-9pm.)

Babbage Island Rd. runs along the coast to **Pelican Point** and makes for a pleasant bike ride among mangroves. Along the way, the mile-long jetty has good fishing and crabbing. A drive or bike ride east of town, on the back roads just north of the North West Coastal Hwy., passes many banana and mango **plantations.** Fresh fruit and veggies are plentiful and cheap; ask if you can collect the fruits deemed not for sale lying on the ground. **Carnarvon Bus Charter** visits the plantations as well as the prawn factory, boat harbor, salt mine, blowholes, jetty, and the OTC—the out-of-use NASA communications center on the outskirts of town. (☎9941 1146. Town tour $28, children $17; saltmine and blowholes $50/$39.) ◪**The Blowholes,** on a 50km dirt road off a turn-off 24km north of town, are natural wave-driven water jets that spurt 30m in choppy weather. Together with the eroded moonscape surrounding them, they make a wondrous site that shouldn't be missed. A lovely beach is 1km south. Carnarvon is a popular base for trips to **Mt. Augustus,** the largest rock in Australia at twice the size of Ayers Rock, with a summit at 1105m. The trip is 460km by car on Gascoyne Junction, a 2WD unsealed road that can get rough; check road conditions at the Visitors Centre before leaving.

CORAL BAY   ☎08

Coral Bay is one of two gateways (Exmouth is the other) to the splendid Ningaloo Marine Park. The Ningaloo Reef, over 250km long, starts south of Coral Bay and stretches north around the Northwest Cape and back into Exmouth Gulf. The town itself is a street crowded with a resort, caravan park, and dive shops. The beach is good for snorkeling and swimming.

McCafferty's/Greyhound (☎13 14 99 or 13 20 30) and **Integrity** (☎1800 226 339) **buses** head to Perth (Su and Th, $200) and Exmouth (M, $60). **The Mermaid's Cave,** in the shopping arcade on the right side of the road as you enter Coral Bay, is a good resource for tourist info and books tours for Coral Bay Adventures. (☎9942 5955. Open M-Sa 9am-1pm and 2-5pm, Su 9am-1pm.) The **nursing post,** in the shopping center, treats injuries. (☎9942 5828 or 0429 425 844 after hours. Open M-F 8:30am-12:30pm, 1pm-5pm.) Also in the center, Coral Bay News and Gifts serves as the local **post office.** (☎9942 5995. Open M-F 8:30am-5pm.) **Postal Code:** 6701.

The monolithic **Ningaloo Club ❷**, opened in late summer 2002, has an amazing pool, spotless kitchens, BBQ, Internet ($5 per hr.), and a stonework patio—the facilities can't be beat. The brightly lit rooms have lockers. Even though it's huge, it fills up fast, so book well in advance. (☎9948 5100; www.ningalooclub.com. 10-bed dorms $18, with A/C $20; 4-bed dorms $23/$25; twins and doubles $60/$65; ensuite doubles $80/$85. VIP.) Just across the street is **Bayview Coral Bay Holiday Village ❷**, an extensive caravan park with grassy sites. (☎9942 5932. Sites $17, powered $22; cabins for four with kitchens and A/C $72.)

In the People's Park Caravan Village, the ◪**Fins Cafe ❸** is popular for seafood and **Internet.** ($6 per hr. Open 7:30am-10pm.) Immediately on the left when entering town is **Reef Cafe ❷**, serving salads, pizzas and seafood for $12-20. (☎9942 5882. Open daily 5:30-late.) In the shopping center, there is a small **supermarket.** (Open daily 7:30am-7pm.)

Divers flock to Ningaloo in droves, and while they'll find more options in Exmouth, Coral Bay proves a quieter alternative destination. **Ningaloo Reef Dive Centre** (☎9942 5824), in the shopping arcade, offers two-dive trips from $150 and a 4-5 day certification course for $425 (starts Sa). **Power Dive** offers intro dives; an air-hose connects you to the surface and you can go down to 6m. (☎9942 5889. $50.) Some of the best snorkeling in Australia is just a 150m swim off the beach. Rent gear at one of the many shops for $10 a day and walk down the beach to the south. Enter the water in the shallows and swim out until you hit the live reef, as some of the colonies nearer to shore were destroyed in 2002 by natural disaster. Watch out for the occasional boat and let the gentle northerly current carry you back into the bay. Another option is to rent a canoe and go out a bit farther before snorkeling. In general, the farther from shore, the more spectacular the reef. **Coastal Adventure Tours** takes you to the outer reef for a different perspective and provides all gear and meals. (☎9948 5190. Located in the shopping center. Half-day $65, children $35; full-day $85/$45.) If you've always dreamt of swimming with the giant and majestic manta rays, **Ningaloo Experience** will make it happen in small groups of 12 people, snorkeling gear and meals included. (☎9942 5877. Daytrip 9am-2pm. $120, children $90. Book ahead in winter.) Those who prefer to stay dry should stick with **Sub-Sea Explorer;** they have one-hour cruises in which the reef can be seen through underwater windows. (☎9942 5955. $30.) Cap off the perfect day with a sunset cruise with **Coral Coast Dive,** opposite the tourist bureau. (☎9949 1004. Open 4:30-7pm. $44.)

EXMOUTH ☎08

The scuba diving epicenter of the west coast, Exmouth (pop. 3500) is the place to swim with easygoing whale sharks and manta rays. The colorful Ningaloo Reef is complemented on land by the beautiful Cape Range National Park. The main township area is inland and not much to look at, but as a diving and fishing destination, Exmouth can't be beat.

TRANSPORTATION & PRACTICAL INFORMATION. Most action takes place around **Maidstone Crescent,** which intersects **Murat Road** at both ends. **McCafferty's/Greyhound** (☎13 20 30) **buses** run to Perth (1-2 per day, $220) and Broome (1 per day, $260). **Integrity** (☎1800 226 339) also runs to Perth ($220). The Exmouth Tourist Village provides **car rental.** (☎9949 1101. Ages 21+. $42 per day, three-day minimum; 4WD ages 25+ from $110 per day.) **What Scooters,** corner of Pellew St. and Murat Rd., have scooters that come with snorkel gear. (☎9949 4748. $33 per day.) The **tourist bureau** is on Murat Rd. (☎9949 1176; fax 9949 1441. Open M-Sa 8:30am-5pm.) The shopping center just off Maidstone houses a **pharmacy** (open M-F 9am-5:30pm, Sa 9am-12:30pm) and a SupaValu **supermarket** (open M-W and Sa-Su 7am-7pm, Th-F 7am-7:30pm). The **hospital,** the only full-scale medical facility for 500km, is two blocks west, on Lyon St. near Fyfe St. (☎9949 1011. Dive medicals $60 cash; call ahead.) **Internet** is available at **Blue's Net Cafe,** in the back of the shopping center. (☎9949 1119. $3 per 30min. Open daily 9am-7pm.) **Challenge Bank,** on Learmouth St., is home to Exmouth's only **ATM.** Across the street is the **police station** (☎9949 2444) and the **post office** (open M-F 9am-5pm). **Postal Code:** 6707.

ACCOMMODATIONS. Most of the backpacker joints in Exmouth are part of sprawling tourist villages, which have their own dive shops and tours in addition to sites, cabins, or in some cases, hotel rooms. Many people stay wherever they're doing their diving course—some places even offer package deals. Competition among Exmouth's tourist parks has led them to offer guests lots of freebies, including free bike use, BBQ, swimming pools, and A/C. ▓**Exmouth Cape Tourist Vil-**

lage ❶, immediately on the right upon entering town, has spotless rooms and backpacker beds in comfortable cabins with A/C, as well as camping sites. It offers a host of services including free beach bus runs to Bundegi Beach every other day, free bikes, and diving and snorkeling gear at low prices. (☎9949 1101; exmouthvillage@nwc.net.au. Sites $19, powered $22; dorms $18; singles $24; doubles $48. YHA.) **Excape Backpackers ❷**, within the Potshot Resort on Murat Rd., has spacious brand new dorms. Reception is at the resort bar. (☎1800 655 156. Key deposit $10. Dorms $19, with a scuba package $14; twins $55. VIP/YHA.) The **Winston's Backpackers ❸**, in the Ningaloo Caravan and Holiday Resort on Murat Rd., along with Coral Coast Dive, has tiny rooms in a well-kept building with a kitchen, pool table, and boat hire. (☎9949 2377. Dorms $18.) Although slightly out of the way, the **Sea Breeze Resort ❺**, next to the naval base north of town, offers spotless, classy hotel rooms, as well as kitchens and access to the base's pool and gym. The **restaurant ❺** boasts a renowned chef and prices to match. (☎9949 1800. Hotel rooms from $90-130, with frequent special discounts.)

Camping ❶ is permitted in designated sites within Cape Range National Park (sites for 2 $10, extra person $5.50; vehicle entry fee not included). However, you cannot camp elsewhere—rangers do patrol the area. Fires are prohibited and there is no water in the park, so come prepared.

⬭ FOOD. The **Rock Cod Cafe ❷**, just after the Ampol station on Maidstone Crescent, has seafood specials, pasta, and burgers for $7-19. (☎9949 1249. Open daily 9:30am-9:30pm.) Behind the shopping center, **Whaler's Restaurant ❸** does delicious gourmet food ($10-20) in an upscale setting. (☎9949 2416. Open M 8:30am-3pm, Tu-Su 8:30am-3pm and 6:30pm-late.) Another popular choice is the **Golden Orchid Chinese Restaurant ❸**, in the shopping complex, with an $18 all-you-can-eat buffet. (☎9949 1740. Open daily 5pm-10pm. Buffet Th 5:30-9pm.)

⬭ NIGHTLIFE. There are two nightlife options in town. **Grace's Tavern**, on Murat Rd. across from the Exmouth Tourist Village, is a pleasant hangout with indoor and outdoor areas. (Open M-Sa 10am-midnight, Su 10am-10pm.) The **Potshot Resort**, on Murat Rd., has a complex of nightspots with an elegant main bar, the Bamboo Room (called "the bimbo bar" by locals), and the more crowded Vance's Bar. Friday is the big night, when beer flows until the wee hours. (☎9949 1200. Open M-Th 10am-midnight, F 10am-1:30am, Sa 9:30am-1:30am, Su 10am-10pm.)

NINGALOO MARINE PARK

Most people come to Exmouth and Coral Bay to see the impressive **Ningaloo Reef,** and the town is full of dive shops catering to all experience levels. Introductory PADI courses are good value at $300-330; they take four or five days and include four ocean dives. Arrange a diving medical in advance, or put up $60 in cash at the local clinic. Shop around before choosing a dive shop; all have certified instructors, good equipment, and a specified instruction regime, but class size and quality of instruction vary. For veteran divers, there are many great dives in the area, including **Lighthouse Bay, Navy Pier, Muiron Islands,** and the **Hole-in-the-Wall,** on the outside of the reef near the North Mandu campsite.

The cheapest PADI course in town is run by **Coral Coast Dive,** near Winston's Backpackers in the Ningaloo Caravan Resort, with training facilities at the naval base; it has computer-oriented PADI classes with a maximum class size of six. (☎9949 1004; ccd@bigpond.com. Dives from $90; classes $300.) **Diving Ventures** is a big, Perth-based operation with four-day PADI courses and two reef dives. (☎9949 2300. PADI M and Th $350; 2 dives $120.) **Village Dive** has resort pier dives and well-organized PADI classes. (☎9949 1101. Pier dive $70; PADI $330.) **Exmouth Dive Centre** (☎9949 1201) has a sleek boat, upper-level classes, and pier and island dives from $150. **Whale shark snorkeling** is inordinately expensive (about $290, 1 dive $50 extra) but also a unique experience you won't get any other way. The Ningaloo is one of the few areas in the world where the world's biggest fish visit consistently; they appear most frequently between March and June. A number of the dive shops listed above do whale shark tours. The best surfing is found at **Surfers Beach** at Vlamingh Head, at the northern end of the cape.

CAPE RANGE NATIONAL PARK

The rugged limestone cliffs and long stretches of sandy white beaches of **Cape Range National Park** lie to the west of Exmouth on Yardie Rd., providing a haven for bungarras, emus, and Stuart's desert peas. The solar- and wind-powered **Milyering Visitors Centre,** 52km from Exmouth, hands out maps and info on the parks and has some interesting displays on local geography. (☎9949 2808. Open daily 10am-3:30pm.) The sealed main road into the park leads to the north to the tip of the cape and then south along the west coast of the cape to Yardie Creek, which makes it a relatively long trip. Keep a sharp eye for kangaroos on the road, especially at night. There are a couple of unsealed roads (Shothole Canyon Rd. and Charles Knife Rd.) that run across the cape from Minilya-Exmouth Rd. into the eastern section of the park, but they can be quite rough going—check with CALM (☎9949 1676) before heading into the park this way. If you don't have a car, you can use the Cape's excellent shuttle service, **Ningaloo Reef Bus,** which stops at the lighthouse, Yardie Creek, Turquoise Bay, Reef Retreat, the Milyering Visitor Centre, and Tantabiddi Reef. (☎9949 1776. M-W and F-Su $22 to Turquoise Bay, children $11; includes park entry.)

The park has several short walking trails, revealing nice ocean views while offering visitors plenty of quality time with the jagged sandstone characteristic of the area. The best of the walking trails is the **Mandu Mandu Gorge Walk** (3km; 1hr.), which treks along the gorge ridge to a nice lookout, then descends to return through the gorge itself. The shorter **Yardie Creek Walk** (1.5km; 1½hr.) lets visitors explore a limestone ledge overlooking a clear blue creek. The significantly longer **Bajirrajirra Walk** (8km; 5hr.) is not worth the effort, but the **Shothole Canyon Walk** (250m; 30min.) is a rewarding, if slightly steep, climb that rises quickly to a great lookout over the entire cape.

WESTERN AUSTRALIA

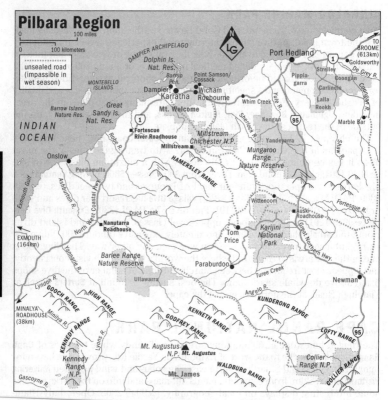

Pilbara Region

0 — 100 miles
0 — 100 kilometers

unsealed road (impassible in wet season)

DAMPIER ARCHIPELAGO

Dolphin Is. Nat. Res.
Barrow Pen.
Point Samson/Cossack

MONTEBELLO ISLANDS

Dampier
Karratha
Wickham
Roebourne

Port Hedland

TO BROOME (613km)
Goldsworthy
Strelley
De Grey R.
Coongan R.
Pippingarra
Carlingle

Barrow Island Nature Res.
Great Sandy Is. Nat. Res.

Mt. Welcome

Whim Creek
Yule R.
Kangan

Lalla Rookh
Marble Bar

INDIAN OCEAN

Fortescue River Roadhouse
Millstream

Millstream Chichester N.P.
Sherlock R.
Yandearra

95

Onslow
Peedamulla

Mungaroo Range Nature Reserve

Shaw R.

Rope R.

HAMERSLEY RANGE

Wittenoom

AUSKI Roadhouse

Fortescue R.

Great Northern Hwy.

EXMOUTH (164km)
Ashburton R.
North West Coastal Hwy.

Duck Creek

Nanutarra Roadhouse

Tom Price

Karijini National Park

Yannarie R.
Bariee Range Nature Reserve
Paraburdoo

Ullawarra

Turee Creek

Newman

Lyndon R.

GOOCH RANGE

HIGH RANGE

Angelo R.

KUNDERONG RANGE

MINALYA ROADHOUSE (38km)
Minilya R.

Lyons R.

KENNEDY RANGE

GODFREY RANGE

KENNETH RANGE

LOFTY RANGE

95

Kennedy Range N.P.
Mt. Augustus N.P. Mt. Augustus

Mt. James

WALDBURG RANGE

Collier Range N.P.

COLLIER RANGE

Gascoyne R.

WESTERN AUSTRALIA

Swimming and snorkeling are very popular along the pristine tropical coast of the park. However, the ceaseless rip tides here—caused by the nearby stretch of coral reef—can make swimming very dangerous outside of the various sheltered coves in the area. The coves of Turquoise Bay, Sandy Bar, and Mesa Bay are the best swimming spots, although their fine sands and sharp windy weather means sunbathing at these spots can be more like a sand-blasting. *Extreme care should be taken in the water.*

PILBARA REGION

The Pilbara is a harsh land. Hundreds of kilometers of arid, undeveloped Outback separate the region's small, industrial towns, bumpy dirt roads weave through its mountainous, mineral-rich interior, and the searing temperatures of summer hold dangers for those who don't come prepared.

KARRATHA   ☎ 08

Karratha is the region's administrative center and is a good resupply point for exploration of Karajini National Park. It is also home to the largest mall outside of Perth, containing an ATM, pharmacy, and two **supermarkets** (both open until midnight). The mall, police, and hospital are clustered between Warambie and Welcome Rd. off Balmoral Rd., which intersects Dampier Rd. at both the east and west ends of town. The fairly plain **Tourist Bureau** is on Karratha Road 1km south of town and offers one of the town's few **Internet** hookups. (☎9144 4600. $5 per 30min. Open M-F 8am-5:30pm, Sa-Su 9am-4pm.) The **library**, in the TAFE complex, immediately south off Dampier Rd., also has Internet. ($4 per 30min. Open M, W, F 8:30am-5pm; Tu, Th 8:30am-8:30pm.)

Karratha Backpackers ❸, 110 Wellard Way, off Searipple Rd., has dorms as well as spacious doubles and twins. (☎9144 4904. Dorms $20; doubles and twins $50.) There are no other strictly budget options in Karratha, but **Pilbara Holiday Park ❷** has pleasant, shaded sites and the most inexpensive motel-style accommodation in town. To get there, turn left off Dampier Rd. onto Rosemary Rd., west of the town center on the way to the town of Dampier. (☎9185 1855. Sites $20, powered $23; motel unit $89.) **Karratha Caravan Park ❶**, located south of town on Karratha Rd., in the light industrial sector, has several cheap sites available. (☎9185 1012. Sites $8 per person, powered $21.80.)

Within the shopping center is **Karratha Chinese Garden Restaurant ❷**, Shop 63, which serves up tasty Asian fare in a slightly upscale setting. Mains are quite affordable, averaging $11-22. (☎9185 2469. Open M-Sa 11:30am-2pm, 5pm-10pm; Su 5pm-10pm.) On the corner of Balmoral Rd. and Morse Ct. is the busy **Karratha Pizza Bar ❷**, which has hearty takeaway vegetarian and meat pizzas for $12-18. (☎9185 2780. Open daily 5pm-9pm.)

Dampier is 16km northwest of Karratha, along Dampier Rd. A pleasant coastal location makes for an ideal place to refresh yourself after long, dusty treks into the Pilbara interior. Dampier is also the gateway to the **Dampier Archipelago**, a string of 42 untouched granite and basalt islands, most of which are now nature reserves. More accessible is **Burrup Peninsula**, immediately to the east of town, the home of nearly 10,000 Aboriginal rock engravings. The town is booming with the expansion of the immense North West Shelf Natural Gas Plant, also on the Burrup Peninsula.

In Dampier, superb views of the harbor, along with budget singles, ensuite motel-style rooms, a swimming pool, and a gym, are to be found at **Peninsula Palm Resort ❹**, a right turn on The Esplanade from Central Ave., the town's main artery. (☎9183 1888. Singles $47.15; motel doubles $96.) Next door, and also on The Esplanade is the **Dampier Transit Caravan Park ❶**, which has basic sites. (☎9183 1109. Sites $13.50, powered $17.50.)

KARIJINI NATIONAL PARK

Karijini is a rugged and magnificent wonderland in the heart of the Pilbara. Homeland to the Banjima, Innawonga, and Kurrama Aboriginal people, the park takes its name from their traditional word for this land. Aboriginal legend has it that the gorges of Karijini were formed by *Thurru*, giant serpents that once snaked through the rocks and now reside within the glistening waters of Karijini. While in recent years the short and very basic walks in the park have started to draw tour buses, the park's true glory is only found deep within the gorges and remains guarded from crowds by challenging and sometimes dangerous passageways.

KARIJINI NATIONAL PARK AT A GLANCE

AREA: 100,000km².

FEATURES: Junction Pool, Dales Gorge, Kalmina Gorge, the Hancock and Weano Gorges, and Fortescue Falls.

GATEWAY: Tom Price.

HIGHLIGHTS: Hiking the expansive gorges. Swimming in the rock pools.

CAMPING: Sites for 2 $10.

FEES: $9 per vehicle entry fee. See national park fee info box.

WESTERN AUSTRALIA

TRANSPORTATION

It will take a car or a tour to conquer Karijini. The park's northern entrances, through Yampire Gorge and Wittenoom, are closed. Both are contaminated by asbestos, inhalation of which can cause cancer or death. **Banjima Drive** is the main thoroughfare, a right turn 30km from the Great Northern Hwy., winding through the park to the other entrance 40km further west. From there, Tom Price is another 50km. Banjima is largely unsealed and moderately corrugated at times, but navigable with care in a 2WD during the Dry. Check road conditions before heading to the park (☎1800 013 314). A 4WD is safer, however; rental is $90-100 per day and is available in Karratha through **Avis** (☎9144 4122), on Warambie Rd., or **Thrifty** (9143 1711), on Bayly Ave.

There are several tour groups that go into Karijini, offering a tame look around the park. **Snappy Gum Safaris,** based in Karratha, has more adventurous options, including a three-day trip that includes a scale of the perilous 25m waterfall in the Weano Gorge area. (☎9185 2141. $390.) Out of Tom Price, **Lestok Tours** runs day-trips to the major gorges. (☎9188 1441. $98.) For getting around in Tom Price, a **taxi** service (☎9189 2015) runs till midnight.

PRACTICAL INFORMATION

Karijini is a big place with fairly basic infrastructure, so come prepared. The one-day park entrance fee is $9 per car. Untreated **water** is available in the park at a turn-off near the Visitors Centre and on Banjima Dr. near the turn-off for Weano gorge, but it's best to carry a lot when you arrive. **Petrol** and supplies are available west of the park in **Tom Price** and at the **Auski Roadhouse** (see below) to the north-east. Maps, updates on road conditions, and weather forecasts can be found at the **Tom Price Tourist Bureau** (☎9188 1112; open M-F 8:30am-5:30pm, Sa-Su 9am-noon.) as well as at Karijini's **Visitors Centre,** near Fortescue Falls.

The impressive, multi-million-dollar new Visitors Centre has exhibits on local flora and fauna, geology, and Aboriginal and colonial history, but little practical information. It also has showers. (☎9189 8121. Showers $2 per 20min. Open daily 9am-4pm.) For more practical info, ask attendants at park entrances and camp-sites, or contact the **CALM ranger station** (☎9189 8157, after-hours emergency 9189 8102). There is an **emergency radio** in the Weano gorge day-use area, and the good people of Tom Price provide the nearest medical and rescue services. The **hospital** is a left turn off Mine Rd., immediately before entering Tom Price. (☎9189 1199.)

ACCOMMODATIONS & FOOD

Camping ❶ is permitted in the rocky, designated areas near Weano Gorge and Fortescue Falls. (Pit toilets. Sites for 2 $10.) For more comfy quarters, head to the **Tom Price Tourist Park ❶**, 3km outside of town, which has showers, a camp kitchen, and telephones. (☎9189 1515. Sites $7.70 per person, powered $19.80 per site; 4-bed dorms $20; cabins for 2 $83.) Even more luxurious still is the **Tom Price Hotel Motel ❺**, on Central St., the town's main drag. (☎9189 1101. Doubles $117.) On the northeastern corner of Karijini, just before the dusty turn-off to Wittenoom, the basic rooms at the **Auski Roadhouse ❹** are clean and well-kept. (☎9176 6988. Budget singles $45; doubles $50; motel doubles $110.) There is a well-stocked Coles **supermarket** in Tom Price, on Central St. (Open daily 8am-8pm.) The **Bistro ❷** at the Hotel Motel has mains for $11-20 and pizzas for $10-16. (Open M-Sa noon-1:30pm and 6pm-8:30pm, Su 6pm-8pm.) Next to Coles, the **Millstream Cafe ❶** serves tasty breakfasts, made to order, for $8-11. (☎9189 1271. Open daily 8:30am-9pm.)

⬛ HIKING

⬛**DALES GORGE.** One of the more moist and lush gorges, Dales is 20km into the park from the east. A great day-use area here has gas BBQs and shade; camping is within walking distance. There is a trek down to **Fortescue Falls** (800m; 30min. return), a spring-fed watercourse that runs year round, cascading into a deep blue-green pool, the ideal spot to take a dip. Follow the stream down the gorge 750m as it gurgles over roots and stones until reaching Circular Pool, a diminutive amphitheater where emerald moss trails down the rock walls. Hike back up a steep stairway to the **Rim Trail,** following it past stunning views back into the gorge.

KALAMINA FALLS. This little gorge, 25km west of the Visitors Centre, is a good introduction to the park. A walk (3km; 2hr. return) leads past a small waterfall and along a creek to Rock Arch Pool, which sits beneath a natural archway. The sure-footed can climb up the gorge wall right through the doorway of the arch itself, aided by a sturdy tree that clings miraculously to the hard rock.

JOFFRE FALLS & KNOX GORGE. A farther 10km west on Banjima Dr., turn right to discover the tallest waterfall in the park. Though the water flow is often not immense, the falls are picturesque as they cascade dozens of feet downwards. The **walk** (3km; 3hr. return.) down to the pool at the base of the falls is a steep descent. Farther up the road, Knox Gorge is one of the deeper gorges in the park, and a trek (2km; 3hr. return) to its base will reveal its wonders.

WEANO GORGE. This gorge is certainly the deepest in the park, plunging into shadowy depths touched by the sweltering hot bush sun only at high noon. The views from the lookout are quite stunning and stretch all the way to Hancock Gorge and Red Gorge. A **walk** (1.5km, 3hr. return) will take you to the base of Hancock and to Kermit's Pool.

MT. BRUCE. The turn-off is 3km east of the western entrance to the park. The **walk** (9km, 5hr. return) to the summit (1235m) should be started in the morning. There are several excellent vantage points along the way if you haven't the time or the energy for the full ascent. That said, the views from the top are breathtaking and well worth the effort.

PORT HEDLAND   ☎08

Port Hedand, located about 200km from Karratha and over 600km from Broome, is little more than a port, a huge mountain of salt, and an iron ore plant that operates around the clock; it is an industrial town and nothing but a waystation to much more interesting places.

At the west tip of the peninsula, Wedge St. holds the **Port Hedland Visitors Centre** (☎9173 1711; Internet $5 per 30min; open M-F 8:30am-5pm, Sa 8:30am-4pm, Su 10am-2pm), a 24hr. **ATM,** and the **post office** (open M-F 9am-5pm). **Postal Code:** 6721.

Dingos Oasis Backpackers ❷, on Kingsmill St., has a unisex bunk house and a sprawling ocean view. (☎9173 1000. Dorms $20; twins and doubles $50.) For a cozier feel, try the family-run and well-kept **Harbour Backpackers ❷,** on Edgar St. (☎9173 4455. Free bus pick-up. Dorms $17; doubles $40.) The **Port Hedland Caravan Park ❶** is on Great Northern Hwy., just opposite the airport. (☎9172 2525. Sites $7.50 per person, powered $22; doubles $69.)

The shopping center at the south edge of town, on the corner of Wilson St. and Cooke Point Dr., has an Action **Supermarket.** (Open M-W and F 8am-8pm, Th 8am-9pm, Sa-Su 8am-5pm.)

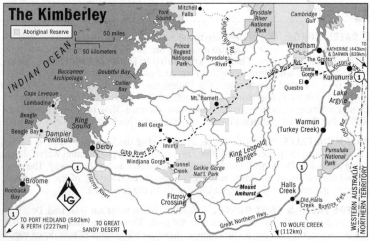

The Kimberley

Aboriginal Reserve

0   50 miles

0   50 kilometers

INDIAN OCEAN

York Sound

Mitchell Falls

Drysdale River National Park

Cambridge Gulf

Prince Regent National Park

Drysdale River

Wyndham

KATHERINE (443km) TO & DARWIN (839km)

The Grotto

Emma Gorge

El Questro

Kununurra

Buccaneer Archipelago

Doubtful Bay

Collier Bay

Mt. Barnett

Lake Argyle

Cape Leveque

Lombadina

Beagle Bay

Beagle Bay

King Sound

Bell Gorge

Dampier Peninsula

Derby

Imintji

Gibb River Rd.

Windjana Gorge

Tunnel Creek

Geikie Gorge Nat'l Park

King Leopold Ranges

Warmun (Turkey Creek)

Purnululu National Park

Broome

Roebuck Bay

Fitzroy River

Fitzroy Crossing

Mount Amhurst

Halls Creek

Old Halls Creek

Bungle Bungle Rd.

TO PORT HEDLAND (592km) & PERTH (2227km)

TO GREAT SANDY DESERT

Great Northern Hwy.

TO WOLFE CREEK (112km)

WESTERN AUSTRALIA / NORTHERN TERRITORY

From Port Hedland, the Great Northern Hwy. winds 600km along the coast to **Broome** (see p. 730). Roadhouses can be up to 300km apart, so fuel up whenever you get the chance and take your time, as kangaroos, cows, sheep, and wild camels populate the barren scrubland along the way.

THE KIMBERLEY

Pressed between the Indian Ocean and the Great Sandy Desert, entire sections of the vast open Kimberley have remained completely uncharted and untouched until recent decades. The highway splits 177km east of Broome into the two major routes running through the Kimberley. To the south, the Great Northern Highway runs through tiny Fitzroy Crossing and Halls Creek on the way to Kununurra and finally Wyndham. To the north, the Derby Hwy. runs north to Derby, where the 4WD-only Gibb River Rd. starts, running east through the heart of the Kimberley, ending between Wyndham and Kununurra. There are few buildings along this route, let alone towns. The Great Northern is the quicker of the two and the only option in the Wet. The Gibb is the adventurer's domain, with countless remote gorges and rutted tracks.

Rainfall levels change drastically between the Kimberley's two seasons. Flooded rivers during the Wet (Nov.-Mar.) often close roads, while during the Dry (Apr.-Oct.), the parched land bakes endlessly under cloudless skies, and even a brief, refreshing shower is a rarity.

BROOME   ☎ 08

Sprawling gracefully between the ocean and the mangroves, the city of Broome (pop. 14,000) has an immaculate shoreline and a carefree aura, in abrupt contrast to the harsh territory stretching in every direction around it. This seaside mecca's fame grew as a result of a thriving pearling industry that flourished here in the 1880s. Today, it attracts vacationers seeking to sink their toes into the cool sands of its many excellent, pristine beaches. Many a visitor to Broome has issued a weary sigh when leaving town in order to return to the harsher realities of the seemingly endless outback.

◼ TRANSPORTATION

Airport: Broome International Airport (☎9193 5455). A 10min. walk from downtown. Follow the signs from Coghlan St. in the city center to McPherson St. **Qantas** flies direct to: Perth (3hr.); Darwin (2hr.); Alice Springs (2½hr.); Uluru (2hr.).

Buses: Bus station next door to Tourist Bureau. **Greyhound** (☎9192 1561) has service to **Perth** (32½hr., daily 8:30am, $295) and **Darwin** (27hr., daily 7:15pm, $255), via **Kununurra** ($173). **Integrity** (☎9226 1339) departs from **Terri's Travel,** 31 Carnavoran St., and offers a scenic bus to **Perth** (35hr., M and W 8am, $260).

Public Transportation: Town Bus (☎9193 6585) connects **Chinatown, Cable Beach,** and several hotels. (1 per hr. 7:10am-6:30pm, every 30min. 10am-3pm.) First bus of the day departs town at 7:10am and reaches **Gantheaume Point** with no return service (prepare for the 5km walk to Cable Beach). $2.70, concessions $0.80, children $1.

Taxis: Broome Taxis (☎9192 1133). **Roebuck Taxis** (☎1800 880 330). 24hr. service. **Chinatown Taxis** (☎1800 811 772). **Pearl Town Taxi** (☎1800 622 433).

Car Rental: Budget (☎9193 5355 or 1800 649 800; jbusby@budgetwa.com.au), at the airport; **Hertz,** 69 Frederick St. (☎9192 1428 or 1800 655 972; hertz.brm@bigpond.com); and **Broome Broome** (☎9192 2210), corner of Hamersley St. and Frederick St., each offer one-way rental options from $400. Broome Broome also has a YHA discount of $5 per day. **Broome Discount Car Hire** (☎9192 3100), 100m from the airport on McPherson St., has no one-way option. If you're considering trying some of the Kimberley's 4WD tracks, try **Britz** (☎9192 2647; www.britz.com) on Clementson St., with campervans starting at $196 per day. All of the above prefer drivers 25+; all except Hertz will rent to 21+ for an additional fee. Book ahead in the high season from Apr.-Oct. **Note:** Car rentals vary drastically in prices, availability, and model due to weather concerns and road closures, especially during the Wet.

◼ ORIENTATION

Broome occupies a peninsula. The business area is tucked on Roebuck Bay to the east. The beach stretches along the Indian Ocean to the west. **The Great Northern (Broome) Highway** runs into town from the north along the eastern coast and into **Chinatown,** becoming **Hamersley Street** as it crosses **Napier Terrace.** Most shops and restaurants in town cluster one street to the east on a couple of blocks of **Carnarvon Street.** A block south of Napier Terr., Frederick St. heads west; going that way, a right on Cable Beach Rd. E., a right on Gubinge Rd., and then a left on Cable Beach Rd. W. will lead to **Cable Beach** on the other side of the peninsula. East of Broome, the Great Northern Hwy. enters Kimberley proper and commences its grueling haul toward the Northern Territory.

◼ PRACTICAL INFORMATION

Tourist Office: Broome Tourist Bureau (☎9192 2222; www.ebroome.com/tourism). Well-marked on the corner of Broome Rd. and Bagot St. Open Apr.-Sept. M-F 8am-5pm, Sa-Su 9am-4pm; Oct.-Mar. M-F 9am-5pm, Sa-Su 9am-1pm.

Budget Travel: Harvey World Travel (☎9193 5599), Paspaley Shopping Centre in Chinatown. Serves as the broker for Qantas and other carriers. Open M-F 8:30am-5:30pm, Sa 9am-1pm. **Traveland,** 9 Johnny Chi Ln. (☎9193 7233), off Carnarvon St. across from the movie theater. Open M-F 9am-5pm, Sa 9am-noon.

Currency Exchange: ANZ Bank, 16 Carnarvon St. (☎13 13 14). Open M-Th 9:30am-4pm, F 9:30am-5pm. **Commonwealth Bank** (☎9192 1103), on Hamersley and Barker St. Open M-Th 9:30am-4pm, F 9:30am-5pm. Both have a $7 charge for currency exchange.

Work Opportunities: Typically plenty of temporary food-service work in the Dry season; check the message boards at hostels for postings and requests.

Police: (☎9192 1212), at the corner of Frederick and Carnarvon St.

Internet Access: Internet access available at most institutions from souvenir shops to travel agents along Carnarvon St. and at hostels. The going rate is $6 per hr.

Post Office: (☎9192 1020), in Paspaley Shopping Ctr. on Carnarvon St. Open M-F 9am-5pm. Poste Restante. **Postal Code:** 6725.

ACCOMMODATIONS & CAMPING

During the Dry (Apr.-Oct.), it is essential to book in advance if coming to Broome, even if you're on planning on staying at campgrounds. Most of Broome's back-packers have their own in-house bars, which means that BYO is strictly prohibited. All of Broome's hostels seem to have a tropical resort feel to them. The big decision when choosing a place to stay is whether you want to be close to the amazing Cable Beach or the shops and nightlife of Chinatown. Cheaper rates are often available during the Wet.

Camping is a popular option around Cable Beach. The most frequented campsite in this area is the four-star **Cable Beach Caravan Park ❶**, on Millington Rd., where good location compensates for the seemingly endless crowds. The camp also offers amenities such as laundry facilities, a pool, and a handy kitchen. (☎9192 2066; fax 9192 1997. 12min. to the beach. Sites $7.50-8.50 per person, powered sites for 2 $20-24. Disabled facilities available.) **Tarangau Caravan Park ❶**, 16 Millington Rd., at the corner of Millington Rd. and Lullfitz Dr., is quieter and much less crowded, but a good 20min. walk from Cable Beach. (☎9193 5084; fax 9193 7551. Sites for 2 $15.40, powered $22.)

▨ **Kimberley Klub** (☎9192 3233; www.kimberleyklub.com), on Frederick St. between Robinson and Herbert St., a 5min. walk from Chinatown. Backpackers lounge at the tables in the courtyard and bar from early morning until late evening. Very luxurious by backpackers standards with an enormous lagoon-shaped pool, full bar and snack counter, ping-pong, billiards, TV lounge, and volleyball court. Kitchen, laundry, coin-operated A/C for some rooms, Internet, and tour booking desk. $10 deposit each for cutlery and linen. Reception 6:30am-8pm. Free pick-up from Greyhound depot. Dorms $23; 5-bed $25; twins and doubles $75. NOMADS $1 discount or seventh night free. ❷

▨ **Cable Beach Backpackers,** 12 Sanctuary Rd. (☎9193 5511 or 1800 655 022; meyo@tpg.com.au). An ideal location for beach lovers, the isolation from town is eased by a free shuttle to Chinatown, Greyhound, and the airport. Intimate and lively with friendly staff. Kitchen, bar with fabulous Happy Hour, laundry, pool, billiards, Internet, and scooter rentals. 7-bed dorms $19; 4-bed dorms $22; twins and doubles $62. VIP/YHA $1 discount. ❷

Roebuck Bay Backpackers (☎9192 1183; fax 9192 2390), on Napier Terr. This busy hostel sits at the border of Chinatown near Broome's nightlife with 5 bars and a liquor store on premises. Luggage storage, kitchen, laundry, pool, and BBQ. Reception 7am-4pm and 5-8pm. 12-bed dorms $15; 8-bed with A/C $16; 4-bed with A/C and ensuite $18; doubles $65. Wet prices $2 cheaper for beds, double $55. ❶

Broome Motel, 34 Frederick St. (☎9192 7775; www.broomemotel.com.au), opposite the junction with Robinson St. Just outside of Chinatown, total convenience with none of the late-night ruckus. Spacious ensuite rooms, all with A/C, are arranged bungalow-style around the parking lot, pool, BBQ, and laundry facilities. Reception 7am-8pm. Standard motel rooms $99; self-catering from $120. Discounts for multi-night stays and during the Wet. Wheelchair-accessible rooms available. ❺

Broome

ACCOMMODATIONS
Broome Motel, **1**
Cable Beach Backpackers, **7**
Cable Beach Caravan Park, **5**
Kimberley Klub, **2**
Roebuck Bay
  Backpackers, **13**
Tarangau Caravan Park, **3**

FOOD
Blooms Cafe & Restaurant, **12**
Broome Fish and
  Chips, **14**
Cable Beach Sandbar
  and Grill, **6**
Fong Sam's Cafe, **9**
Shady Lane Cafe, **11**

NIGHTLIFE
Divers Camp Tavern, **8**
Nippon Inn, **10**
Sunset Bar, **4**

FOOD

Food offerings in Chinatown are varied and enticing, though notably un-Chinese. Coles **supermarket** is in the Paspaley Shopping Centre. (☎9192 6299. Open daily 6am-midnight.) Action Supermarket is in the Boulevard Shopping Centre. (☎9192 1611. Open daily 8am-8pm.)

　Broome Fish and Chips (☎9192 1280), at Frederick and Hamersley St. No frills. No nonsense. Just heaps of great fish. Open daily 10:30am-2:30pm, 4:30pm-8:30pm. ❶

　Cable Beach Sandbar and Grill (☎9193 5090), on Cable Beach Rd. W., adjacent to pedestrian access to the beach. The sandy and sunburned patrons of Cable Beach come crawling in from the sand for this super-snackbar. Featuring everything from tasty nachos ($10) to beef bourguignonne pie ($15), the extensive menu includes light and

HE LOCAL STORY

OLD MACDONALD
HAD A CROC

*3rent Thoms is a career fireman vho spends his holidays as a croc feeder at **Malcolm Douglas 3roome Crocodile Park**.*

LG: What do you do here?

3T: I prepare the food for the farm crocodiles. We feed the crocs at the farm and clean up after them. Me and three other guys do the tours here at the park in Broome.

LG: Ever been bitten?

3T: No, I don't put myself in a situation I think is dangerous. Out at the farm we're dealing in groups of probably 100 crocs, but they're all under 2 meters long. They're not really dangerous unless you provoke them. Keep a stick in your hand, and that'll fend one off just by hitting them on the nose.

LG: What role do farms play in the preservation of crocodiles?

3T: They educate the public, but they also provide us a breeding stock for the sustainable farming operation. While you got commercial farms around, you've got a big stock of crocodiles. If some viral disease was going through the natural waterways to kill off the natural crocs, you've got a source of crocodiles that you can start stocking back up the waterways.

LG: What parts are usable?

3T: Pretty much every part. The skin is the main thing—belly skin— that's the big thing of value, but every part of the skin is used. The teeth are sold as things to put in

(Continued on next page)

hearty meals from around the world, vegetarian and otherwise, along with a kids menu. Grab a frozen mango daiquiri ($10) from the full bar and enjoy the eatery's stunning ocean view. Open daily 7am-9pm. ❷

Fong Sam's Cafe (☎9192 1030), on Carnarvon St. across from the cinema. Delicious baked goods, large portions, and reasonable prices. Pasties from $0.90. Fresh quiche and salad $11. Try a side of their amazing sautéed mushrooms ($2). Open daily 6:30am-5pm. ❶

Blooms Cafe and Restaurant, 31 Carnarvon St. (☎9193 6366). Choose from huge portions of pasta, pizza, and Thai curry from $12-25. Lots of vegetarian options. BYO. Open 7am-9:30pm. ❷

Shady Lane Cafe (☎9192 2060), on Johnny Chi Ln. off Carnarvon St. Hidden away on a pedestrian alley. Grinning patrons munch filling flapjacks ($7.50), toasted focaccia ($10.50), and smoothies ($4.50). Open daily 7am-2:30pm. ❶

👁 🔖 SIGHTS & ACTIVITIES

▨**CABLE BEACH.** At this small slice of paradise, 22km of clear Indian Ocean lap against the glowing, pearly-white sand. Go for some fun in the sun, take a camel, sailing, or hovercraft tour, or just head to the clothing-optional portion of beach, past the rocks to the north. Whatever you do, be sure to stick around for the sunset.

WATER ACTIVITIES. Surfboard rental *($8 per hr.)* is available on Cable Beach. Parasailing, jet skiing, and tubing operators work out of the vans that cruise the sand to rent out equipment. Would-be mer-people visit **Workline Dive & Tackle** *(☎9192 2233)* on Short St. in Chinatown for all there is to know about scuba diving in Broome.

REPTILES. Get up close and personal with the aggressive 5m saltwater crocodiles that populate this part of Australia at **Malcolm Douglas Broome Crocodile Park.** See the sidebar **Old MacDonald Had a Croc,** at left, for an insider's perspective on the park. *(200m from the beach access on Cable Beach Rd. ☎9192 1489. In the Dry: Feedings W-Su 3pm. Guided tours M-Tu 11am and 3pm. Open M-F 10am-5pm, Sa-Su 2-5pm. In the Wet, call for times. $15, concessions $12, children $8, families $38.)*

▨**Gantheaume Point** is home to a set of **dinosaur footprints** preserved for eons among the rocks. Found on the far western tip of the Broome Peninsula, located about 5km from Cable Beach, the 120-million-year-old prints surface only during very low ocean tides. *(To get to the prints, take a left onto Gubinge Rd., where Cable Beach Rd. turns to the right.)*

OTHER BEACHES. Town Beach is farther south on the Roebuck Bay shore, at the end of Robinson St. For three days each month from March to October (check at the tourist bureau for exact dates), Broome's massive 10m tide is so low that the exposed mudflats stretch for kilometers, reflecting the light of the full moon in a staircase pattern. The city celebrates with the **Staircase to the Moon Market** at Town Beach. At the lowest tides, the waters off the beach recede to uncover skeletons of sunken WWII boats. The **Mangrove Walk,** on the east coast between Chinatown and the Historical Society, weaves its way through a forest of mangroves.

TOURS. Ride camels down Cable Beach at sunset, threading your way up the dunes to reach the hilltop at twilight. **Ships of the Desert** has morning, sunset, and twilight camel tours. (☎9192 6383. $30 per hr., full-day $75.) Also try **Red Sun Camel Safaris.** (☎1800 184 488 or 9193 7423. 1hr. sunset rides $35. 40min. morning rides $25.) Without a strong 4WD, **land tours** may be your only way to see the rugged Kimberley or northern shoreline. **Discover the Kimberley Tours** runs daytrips to the pristine beaches of the Dampier Coast, north of Broome. (☎1800 636 802. 8hr. tours depart W and F. $180, with Pearl Farm tour $215.) **Over the Top Adventures** offers several tours that run to the Dampier Peninsula and the Gibb River Rd. (☎9192 5211. Dampier 1-day $220, 2-day $380; Windjana Gorge and Tunnel Creek 2-day $395; 5-day trip along the Gibb River Rd. $890.) **Scenic flights,** some of which travel all the way to Mitchell Falls and the Buccaneer Archipelago are another option. **Broome Aviation** (☎1300 136 629), **Seair Broome** (☎9192 6208), and **King Leopold Air** (☎1800 637 155) start at $300 for 2½hr.

FESTIVALS. The **Easter Dragon Boat Regatta** is featured Saturday of Easter weekend at the Town Beach. Horse racing is big throughout July when the town starts hopping for the **Broome Cup.** The **Shinju Matsuri Pearl Festival** runs for 10 days in early September. The **Mango Festival** (last weekend in November) marks the harvest with a Mardi Gras celebration and "Great Chefs of Broome Mango Cook Off."

🔲 NIGHTLIFE

No visit to Broome is complete without catching a feature at the world's oldest operating outdoor movie theater. ◪**Sun Pictures Outdoor Cinema,** on Carnarvon St., spun its first reel in 1916. Curl up on the canvas chairs. (☎9192 1077. Films nightly. $13, concessions $11.) Broome boasts a handful of decent bars and a sole nightclub. **"The Roey,"** in the Roebuck Hotel on Carnarvon St., aims to lure oglers and listeners with

(Continued from previous page(

your hat for people who want to look like Crocodile Dundee. The meat is packaged up and sent to Asia. But there's starting to become quite a local market for the meat. You can go down to a Pizza Hut here and order a crocodile pizza.

LG: After working with crocs for so long, what do you think about them?
BT: They're not a very intelligent reptile, and reptiles are mainly instinctive. Their brain's the size of a golf ball. So there's not a lot to work with. But they are man eating. Anything that's over 3 meters long is quite capable of taking you and pulling you down and making you into his meal. It's quite easy to read what they're going to do, just by the way they're pulling their front legs back, ready to run at you. You're just watching that, that's really telegraphing their movements to you. And what they're looking on...they really do focus. But they're quite predictable as well. When you're in a working environment with them, you sort of know they're going to be aggressive.

LG: What do you see as the biggest public misconception about crocs?
BT: I think up this way people tend to get a little bit blasé. They come up here probably as a tourist and think that a lot of the warning signs are just there for show. But once they've started to go 'round the park here, they realize just what they [crocs] are and what they look like. I think it freaks people out to think these guys are inhabiting the waterways and estuaries right next door.

scantily-clad waitstaff and live music nightly. (☎9192 1221. Open M-W 10am-midnight, Th-Sa 10am-1am, Su noon-10:30pm.) The **Nippon Inn**, on Dampier Terr. near Short St., is Broome's only nightclub. As Broome's bars shut, "the club" is just winding up with techno beats and purple walls. (☎9192 1941. Open M, W, F-Sa 9pm-4am.) At Cable Beach, locals and campers gather around the pool tables at **Divers Camp Tavern,** on Cable Beach Rd. (☎9193 6066. Open M-Sa 10am-midnight, Su 10am-10pm. Beers from $2.20.) At the relaxed **Sunset Bar** at the Cable Beach Resort on the beach, nurse a cocktail ($12) or beer ($4.50) while soaking up the view. (☎9192 0400. Open daily 4pm-midnight.) The Cable Beach area clears out after sunset when great herds of campers and backpackers migrate to Chinatown for the late-night scene. The beach bars often close early on slow nights.

GREAT NORTHERN HIGHWAY

There's no use pretending: this road is unlikely to win awards for charisma. It's flat, repetitive, and long. There are two towns along the way, Fitzroy Crossing and Halls Creek, but don't be fooled by the big map lettering; they're no more than pit stops. **Geikie Gorge,** 18km north of **Fitzroy Crossing,** offers a 1-3hr. walk through the gorge or a **boat tour** from the gorge parking lot. (1hr.; June-Sept. 3 per day, Apr.-May and Oct.-Nov. 1-2 per day.) There is a **supermarket** on Forrest Rd. (Open M-F 8:30am-5:30pm, Sa-Su 8am-1pm.) Another 287km down the highway is **Halls Creek.** The remains of **Old Halls Creek** mark the site of the original gold rush in Western Australia. (16km down the unsealed Duncan Hwy.) The **grocery store** (☎9168 6186; open M-F 8am-6pm, Sa 8am-noon, Su 9am-noon) and the **Shell Station** (☎9168 6060; open daily 6am-10pm) are the only other diversions. From Halls Creek it's 107km to the Purnululu turn-off and another 235km to Kununurra.

DERBY   ☎08

A west to east voyage along the Gibb starts at Derby. Check in at the **tourist office** at the end of Clarendon St. for the latest road conditions information. (☎9191 1426. Open Apr.-Sept. M-F 8:30am-4:30pm, Sa-Su 9am-1pm; Oct.-Mar. M-F 8:30am-4:30pm, Sa-Su 9am-4pm.) The **West Kimberley Lodge ②**, at the corner of Sutherland and Stanwell St., has quiet rooms with A/C and fridge. (☎9191 1031. Twins $65; doubles $78; rooms for 3-4 $130.) The grassy **Kimberley Entrance Caravan Park ①** on Rowan St., around the curve from the tourist office, overlooks mudflats. (☎9193 1055. Sites $9; powered $15, for 2 $22.) Be sure to register with the **Derby police** (☎9191 1444), on Loch St. near the Old Derby Gaol, before starting on the road. Get petrol on your way out of town at the **BP station,** on Loch St. (Open M-Sa 5:30am-7:30pm, Su 6am-7pm.) Across the road is Woolworths **supermarket.** (Open M-W and F 8am-6pm, Th 8am-8pm, Sa 8am-5pm, Su 10am-4pm.)

GIBB RIVER ROAD

The Gibb River Road is one of Australia's last frontiers, though with every passing year more and more voyagers are opening up even this most secluded pocket of the great Outback. Cleared in the middle part of last century for the purpose of transport between the cattle stations which dot the area and the ports of Wyndham and Broome, the road still remains a rough gravel track.

The road offers unexcelled access to the famed beauty of the Kimberley's towering rock faces and round waterfall carved pools. From popular sign-posted tracks to chasms only known to locals and vast gorges so remote they are only known from aerial photographs, the twists and turns of the Kimberley landscape afford endless opportunities for exploration.

GIBB RIVER ROAD AT A GLANCE

LENGTH: 647km.

FEATURES: Windjana Gorge, Tunnel Creek Nat'l Park, King Leopold Range.

HIGHLIGHTS: Dips into pristine, saltie-free gorges, unpopulated walks, and cliff jumping for the super-foolhardy.

GATEWAYS: Derby (p. 736) and Kununurra (p. 741).

DURATION: In good conditions the road can take as little as 2 days, but it will take 4-5 days to enjoy the primary gorges and longer to tackle the more remote turn-offs.

ORIENTATION & PRACTICAL INFORMATION

The Gibb River Road begins 6km south of **Derby** off the **Derby Highway** and ends at the **Great Northern Highway,** which is half-way between **Wyndham** (48km from end) and **Kununurra** (45km from end). The most commonly visited gorges are concentrated anywhere from 120 to 220km east of Derby, as well as in the privately-run **El Questro,** 35-45km of the road's eastern end. Gorges along the 400km between these two regions are less readily accessed, meaning that if you have limited time on the Gibb, you may want to drive straight through this section. Those with more leisure could consider a detour on the **Kalumburu Road,** which intersects the Gibb 406km east of Derby (241km west of Kununurra) and continues on northward to **Drysdale National Park** and **Mitchell Falls.**

Services along the way are very limited. Roadhouses and stations with accommodations tend to have a very few groceries and the odd camping supply, but don't count on buying anything along the road. Bring enough cash—only Mt. Barnet, El Questro and, along the Kalumburu Rd., Drysdale, take credit cards and they are either very unenthusiastic or unwilling to give cash out. The Broome, Derby, and Kununurra tourist offices are good places to pick up advice on preparation and itineraries. Camping supplies are available in Kununurra and Broome, as well as a smaller selection in Derby.

Guides: Tourist offices in Kununurra, Derby and Fitzroy Crossing sell the *Traveller's Guide to the Gibb River and Kalumburu Roads,* with limited information on distances and services along the roads. The *Guide* can also be purchased from the **Derby Tourist Bureau.** (☎9191 1426; www.derbytourism.com.au. Guide $3. Write to Derby Tourist Bureau, PO Box 48, Derby WA 6728.) A map of the Kimberley ($7.95), put out by HEMA and widely available, is essential. It includes brief summaries of the major sites on the back.

Auto repairs: Neville Heron's Over the Range Repairs (☎9191 7887), next to the Imintji store (222km) is the only mechanical repair service that operates along the road and is the only place to get used tires. A limited supply of new tires is available at Mt. Barnet and sometimes at Home Valley.

Gas: Petrol is available at Iminitji (diesel only), Mt. Barnet Roadhouse (306km), and El Questro (614km). On the Kalumburu Rd., it is available at Drysdale (59km from the junction with the Gibb) and at the tippity-top of the road at Kalumburu (267km from the Gibb). It's expensive everywhere. Don't risk not making it to the next place in hope of saving a few dollars.

Tours: Many people do the Gibb River Rd. via small private group tours, which can be cheaper than renting a 4WD and going it yourself. **Kimberley Adventure Tours** (☎1800 805 101; www.kimberleyadventure.com) offers a 5-day Gibb trek ($750) and a 13-day tour that runs between Darwin and Broome ($2190). **Kimberley Wilderness Adventures** (☎1800 804 005; www.kimberleywilderness.com.au) has 5-day ($1200) and 7-day ($1900) Gibb tours.

WESTERN AUSTRALIA

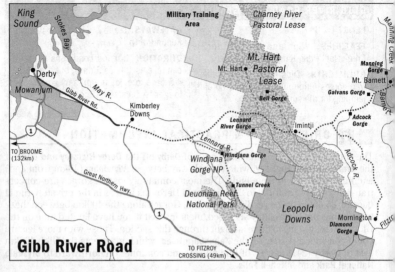

Gibb River Road

ACCOMMODATIONS

The distance along the Gibb River Road (coming from Derby) is listed after each accommodation in parentheses.

WESTERN REGION (DERBY TO IMINTJI: 0-221KM)

There's **camping** ❶ at Windjana (119km) and Bell Gorge (214km) for $9 (children $2) with flush toilets and cold showers. Bell has private, secluded first-come-first-served camps near the gorge, with standard camping available when these are full.

Mt. Hart Wilderness Lodge (184km; ☎9191 4645), down a 50km access road. An upscale lodge with gardens, a waterhole, and self-guided bushwalks. Rooms $150 per person, children $75. Bookings essential. ❺

Yuwa Station Camp (123km; ☎1800 804 005), between Windjana Gorge and Tunnel Creek. Aboriginal-owned twin-share tents. Closed from 9am-3pm. Rooms $99 per person, children $66; includes dinner and breakfast. ❺

CENTRAL REGION (IMINTJI TO HOME VALLEY: 221-581KM)

Camping ❶ is available at a few free no-facilities sites along the way. An especially nice one is on the **Barnet River** (329km). Camping with facilities is available at Manning Gorge, behind the **Mt. Barnet Roadhouse** ❶ (306km). The area right next to the river can be crowded; more tranquility can often be found down the road to the right. Warm showers and flush toilets from 5:30am-5:30pm. Outside of those hours, only pit toilets are available. (☎9191 7007. Sites $9, children $2.)

■ **Ellenbrae** (476km; ☎9691 4325). Quite possibly the best place to stay on the Gibb. Canvas-and-rammed-earth cabins cluster around an open-air homestead. As close to sleeping outdoors as you can get without the accompanying inconveniences. ❸

Mount Elizabeth Station (338km; ☎9191 4644), down a 30km access road. A similar station format to others along the road. Sites $11, children $2; rooms $140 per person, children $88. Bookings essential. ❶

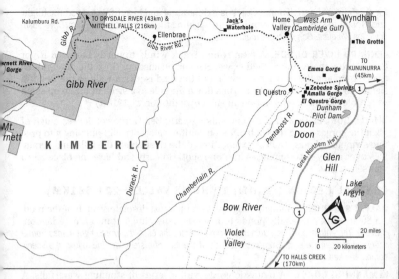

EASTERN REGION (HOME VALLEY TO GREAT NORTHERN HIGHWAY: 581-647KM)

Home Valley Station (581km; ☎9161 4322). A friendly place with very basic rooms. Sites $9, children $3; singles $40; doubles $60, with dinner and breakfast $120.

El Questro (614km; ☎9161 4318), down a 16km access road which passes Zebedee Springs and El Questro Gorge. Lodge accommodations and private campsites overlooking the river. Sites $12.50 per person; bungalows with A/C for 1-4 people $198.

Emma Gorge Resort (624km; ☎9161 4388). Also part of El Questro, offering tented cabins. Cabins for 1-2 people $133, with ensuite $182; deluxe cabins with ensuite for 1-4 people $198.

◉ 🏔 SIGHTS & GORGES

The distance along the Gibb River Road (coming from Derby) is listed after the description of each sight below, in parentheses.

WESTERN REGION (DERBY TO IMINTJI: 0-221KM)

🏔**WINDJANA GORGE.** Some 360 million years ago, when the area to the north and west were underwater, this area was the coast, and a huge fringing coral reef thrived here. Erosion of surrounding areas has unearthed the harder coral skeletons. Purple and terracotta, they now loom hundreds of meters above the Lennard River and its sandy banks. Aside from the beguiling landscapes, the 7km round trip hike through the gorge offers the best readily-accessible opportunities in the Kimberley to observe freshwater crocodiles. *(119km. Off a 21km access road.)*

TUNNEL CREEK. So you've always wanted to be Indiana Jones? Training starts here. The walk through this 850m cave is in total darkness, with carnivorous ghost bats flapping overhead as you wade through thigh-deep water—inhabited by freshwater crocodiles, no less. Then, when you reach the blessed clearing at the end, turn around and go back through, because there's no other way around. Not for the faint of heart, Tunnel Creek is exhilarating and beautiful. A good flashlight and closed-toe shoes are essential for navigating the rocky floor. *(119km. Drive 55km down the Windjana Gorge access road.)*

LENNARD RIVER GORGE. A 6km rough track winds towards Lennard River Gorge. From there, one can either walk (recommended) or drive the ditch-ridden track stretching the next 2km. The end of the road is a 1km walk to the rim of a slender 8km gorge. A steep track runs down the side to a swim in the steep-sided waterhole or further exploration up and down the gorge. *(191km.)*

■ **BELL GORGE.** Down a flat 1km walking path, Bell Gorge condenses much of what the gorges along the Gibb offer—beautiful waterfalls, cliff-jumping into pristine swimming holes, endless exploration of the river above the falls, and scrambles over rocky outcroppings—into one spot. Go early and have the place all to yourself. *(213km.)*

CENTRAL REGION (IMINTJI TO HOME VALLEY: 221-581KM)

GALVANS GORGE. A hidden refuge just off the most desolate stretch of the road. An 800m walk passes lily-ponds to a serene falls plunging into a blue lagoon. *(286km. The entrance is in an unmarked carpark. From the east, it's on the right across from a scenic photo camera sign. From the west, it's at the foot of a steep decline following a scenic camera-marked overlook.)*

■ **MANNING GORGE.** A fantastic gorge with a series of stunning waterfalls. A 2km trail leads from the campsite to the top of the first waterfall. From there, a trail leads over the river and then runs along the rim for another 2km past a second small waterfall and a third as wondrous as the first. It's a great place to relax and explore aside the tumbling falls. *(306km. The road to the falls begins from behind the Mt. Barnet Roadhouse.)*

EASTERN REGION (HOME VALLEY TO GREAT NORTHERN HIGHWAY: 581-647KM)

All listings are part of the million-acre El Questro cattle station/park, down a side road 33km from the eastern end of the Gibb River Rd. (614km from Derby). Admission costs $12.50 per person for a week at the park or $5.50 per person for a day at Emma Gorge only, accessed by a separate entrance 10km east of the main entrance. Detailed maps are available at the Emma Gorge Resort and at the Station Township in the main part of the park. Organized tours are available, but with your own 4WD, a tremendous amount of El Questro is accessible on your own.

■ **AMALIA GORGE.** The park's most rewarding walk requires thought and careful foot placement to negotiate the boulders and rock slabs along the way. The waterfall-fed pool at the end is a contemplative spot. Amalia gets more sunlight and is hotter than most gorges, so early morning or late afternoon is the best time to hike it. *(7km along the main El Questro road.)*

EL QUESTRO GORGE. A 3.6km return path leads over fairly easy terrain to a thigh-deep pool. Wade across that pool and climb a short ladder to Middle Pool, a pleasant swimming spot. Beyond this, the trail rapidly gets more challenging. A climb over a field of large boulders leads to a narrow gorge with a small droplet waterfall. The full walk is 7.4km; 3-5hr. return. *(11km along the main El Questro road then down a 1km side road.)*

EXPLOSION GORGE. 4WD fanatics will enjoy this rough track which runs to three overlook points on the rim of Explosion Gorge. It bumps along for 10km beside the attractive Elgee Cliffs, passing a turn-off for Branco's Lookout, with a vista of the area. *(Past El Questro Station Township. Follow the signs.)*

EMMA GORGE. A 3.6km trail leaves from the Emma Resort carpark. Winding through the gorge among lush greenery, the shady track leads to a chilly swimming hole and then along a short path modestly labeled "waterfall" to the real highlight. Overhanging cliffs carpeted with ferns surround a round pool fed by a trickling waterfall.

WYNDHAM ☎ 08

A 20m long crocodile statue welcomes you to Wyndham (pop. 800), the northernmost point on the Great Northern Hwy. Here the pioneer spirit thrives against the dramatic backdrop of the Bastion Range and the Cambridge Gulf. Wyndham is neatly divided into two clusters. Most shops and services (and the big croc) are found in the southern section (vaguely referred to as "town"), including the **tourist office** in the Mobil station (☎9161 1281; open daily 6am-6pm) and **Internet** access at **BEC/Telecentre,** 6 O'Donnell St., opposite the Boab gallery. (☎9161 1161. Open M-Sa 9am-5pm.) The cheerful staff at the **Wyndham Caravan Park ❶,** near the Mobil station, will be more than glad to show you the town's most impressive sight, the giant 2000-year-old boab tree at the back of the park. (☎9161 1064. Sites $9, powered $12; budget doubles $40.) ▧**Gulf Breeze Guest House ❷** is cozy, personable, and relaxed. Reserve and pay for a room at the Wyndham Caravan Park. (☎9161 1401. Singles $25; twins $20; doubles $50; families $60.)

Follow the signs east from the highway for the ▧**Five River Lookout,** 7km up a steep road with popular sunset views of mudflats and the Ord, Forrest, King, Durack, and Pentecost Rivers emptying into the gulf. At the **Wyndham Zoological Gardens and Crocodile Park,** just north of the wharf, a series of enthusiastic placards applaud the mating successes of males in the captive breeding program. (☎9161 1124. Open in the Dry daily 8:30am-4pm; feedings at 11am. Call ahead in the Wet. $14.) Thirty kilometers along the road to Kununurra, a 1km gravel road leads to **The Grotto.** Nearly 200 stone steps descend to a pretty but often crowded pool and waterfall. The scene is more impressive and less crowded in the Wet.

KUNUNURRA ☎ 08

Five-hundred kilometers west of Katherine, NT, the little pocket of civilization known as Kununurra (kuh-nah-NUR-ah; pop. 5000) sleeps beneath the sandstone formations of the eastern Kimberley. The name, meaning "big waters," is appropriate for a town that grew during the effort to reroute the Ord River for irrigation in the 1960s and 70s. Most travelers use Kununurra as a base to explore the dramatic attractions in the eastern Kimberley region, including Purnululu (Bungle Bungle) National Park, Lake Argyle, and the Gibb River Rd.

⊏ TRANSPORTATION. The **airport** is 5km down the Victoria Hwy. toward Wyndham. **Air North** (☎ 1800 627 474) flies twice daily to Broome ($312) and Darwin ($220). **Buses** arrive at the tourist bureau at the corner of Coolibah Dr. and White Gum St. **McCafferty's/Greyhound** (☎ 13 20 30) departs for Broome (13½hr., daily 5:45pm, $173); Katherine (5½hr., daily 9:20am, $75); Darwin (13hr., daily 9:20am, $129). There are several car rental companies in town: **Budget,** 947 Mango St. (☎9168 2033), also at the airport; **Avis,** 12 Coolibah Dr. (☎9169 1258), also at the airport; **Thrifty Territory Rent-a-Car,** 596 Bandicoot Dr. (☎9169 1911), at the BP service station; **Handy Rentals** (☎9169 1188), at the corner of Messmate Way and Bandicoot Dr.; and **Hertz** (☎9169 1424), on Coolibah Dr. **Kimberley Outback Hire** (☎9168 1657), 20 Mango St., rents 4WDs, trailers and camping equipment. Two **taxi** companies operate: **Spuds Taxis** (☎9168 2553 or 0408 938 888) and **Alex Taxi** (☎ 13 10 08).

⚡ PRACTICAL INFORMATION. Messmate Way turns off the Victoria Hwy. at a petrol station and heads into town, where it crosses **Konkerberry Drive** and ends at **Coolibah Drive.** The **Kimberley Tourism House** is on Coolibah Dr. (☎9168 1177. Open in the Dry M-F 8am-5pm, Sa 8am-3pm, Su 9am-1pm; in the Wet M-F 9am-4pm.) The **Commonwealth Bank,** on the corner of Coolibah Dr. and Cotton Tree Ave. near the tourism office, has a 24hr. **ATM.** (☎13 22 21. Open M-Th 9:30am-4pm, F 9:30am-5pm.) **Police** are located at the corner of Coolibah Dr. and Banksia St. (☎9166 4530. Open M-F 8am-4pm.) **Internet** is available at **Harvey World,** on Konkerberry near the traffic circle. (Open daily 8:30am-8pm. $6 per hr.) **Telecentre,** in the same building as the tourist office, around the back, also has Internet. (☎9169 1868. Open M-F 9:30am-5pm, Sa 1:30pm-4pm. $6 per hr.) The **post office** is across from the police station. (☎9168 1395. Open M-F 9am-5pm.) **Postal Code:** 6743.

⚡⚡ ACCOMMODATIONS & FOOD. All accommodations in town fill to over-flowing during the Dry; book ahead. **Kununurra Backpackers Adventure Centre ❸,** 24 Nutwood Crescent, is a 10min. walk from the tourist office; follow Konkerberry away from the highway, then turn right on Nutwood. With new stoves, a bubbling fountain, pool, and small VCR-equipped theater furnished with airplane seats, the Centre has great facilities. They also have free pick-up and drop-off. (☎9169 1998. Key deposit $10. Dorms $21; twins and doubles $50.) **Desert Inn Kimberley Croc Back-packers ❷,** two blocks from the shopping center on Tristania St. near Konkerberry St., has a pool, patio, lounge areas, spacious kitchen, and laundry, as well as free pick-up and drop-off. (☎9168 2702. Dorms $19; doubles $48; triples and quads $20 per person. 7-night max. stay. VIP/YHA $1 discount.) The **Red Gum Caravan Park ❶** is a 10min. walk from town. (☎8972 2239. Laundry, pool, and BBQ. Sites $9, for 2 $18, powered $22; cabins $80, each extra person $7.) Food options in Kununurra are limited. **Coles** in the shopping center has **groceries.** (☎9168 2711. Open daily 5am-midnight.) The main pub in town is **Gulliver's Tavern ❷,** on Konkerberry Dr. at Cotton Tree Ave. Fish 'n' chips is the cheapest thing on the menu at $12.80. (☎9168 1666. Open M-Th noon-11pm, F noon-midnight, Sa noon-11pm, Su 1-9pm.)

⚡ SIGHTS. Kelly's Knob overlooks the stunning terrain of Kununurra. Take Konkerberry Dr. to its end; turn left on Ironwood, right on Speargrass, and right again at the large stone tablet. **Mirima (Hidden Valley) National Park,** 2km east of town, looks like a miniature Purnululu range, without the 6hr. drive. Three paths wind past the 350-million-year-old formations. The **Derdebe-Gerring Banan Lookout Trail** (400m) ascends a steep hill for a view of the Ord Valley and nearby sandstone ranges. The **Demboong Banan Gap Trail** (250m) heads through a gap in the range, then through a small valley, to a lookout over Kununurra. Ranger-led walks meet at the carpark at the end of Hidden Valley Rd. and at the lovely secluded retreat of Lily Pool in Hidden Valley. However, Lily Pool, along with the area that extends away from it down Lily Creek, are sacred men's places for the Miriwoong people—female travelers should respectfully avoid this part of the park. **Wild Adventure Tours** (☎0945 6643) offers travelers a more interactive and ecologically friendly take on the Kununurra area, with abseiling tours and instruction at local sites, including Kelly's Knob ($60) and the Grotto ($110).

LAKE ARGYLE

Nestled between ancient orange sandstone hills and dotted with 90 islands, at 850 sq. km., Lake Argyle is the biggest freshwater body of water in the Southern Hemisphere, with a capacity 18 times that of Sydney Harbour. The lake was created in the early 1970s as part of the ambitious Ord River Irrigation Project. Much of the land flooded by the rerouting was home to the Miriwoong people who were in no way consulted about the project. Their sacred sights now lay at the bottom of the lake. Drive 35km south of Kununurra on the Victoria Hwy. and turn onto the access road. Another 35km leads to the **Lake Argyle Tourist Village.**

Cruises are a popular way to see a fraction of the lake. **Lake Argyle Cruises** has a booking office at the Lake Argyle Tourist Village. (☎9168 7361. Tours May-Sept. daily, Oct.-Apr. by demand. 2hr. wildlife morning cruise $38; 2½hr. sunset cruise $48; 6hr. best of Lake Argyle cruise $99. Children 40-50% cheaper. pick-up in Kununurra $15.) **Ord Tours** explores other parts of the waterways heading to the Lower Ord River, famous for its salties and many species of birds. (☎9169 1165. 5hr. Tours Su, Tu, Th, Sa 7am and 1pm. $45.) **Lower Ord Tours** offers a slightly more luxurious tour complete with afternoon tea and local fruits and vegetables. (☎9168 2144 or 0408 919 280. Full-day $95, children $45.) **Triple J Tours** has 6hr. cruises of the lake and the Ord River. (☎9168 2682. From $95 including pick-up.) **Kimberley Canoeing** offers a three-day self guided tour. (☎1300 663 369. $145, includes drop-off, pick-up, canoe and camping gear; min. 2 persons.) The **Lake Argyle Tourist Village ❶** has accommodations. The **caravan park ❶** has showers and laundry. (☎9167 1050. Sites $7, powered $11.50.) The **motel ❺** next door has a pool and restaurant. (☎9167 7360. Singles $70; doubles $80.)

PURNULULU (BUNGLE BUNGLE) NATIONAL PARK

Purnululu, a national park since only 1986 and unknown to the outside world before 1983, is famous for its towering orange-and-black eroded dome structures, often compared to beehives. While an oft-repeated sentiment holds that the domes' grandeur can only be appreciated from the air, the views from the bottom are equally heart-stopping. The awkward name "Bungle Bungle" is thought to be either a corruption of the Kija word *purnululu*, meaning "sandstone," or a misspelling of a commonly found grass in the area, *Bundle Bundle*.

PURNULULU AT A GLANCE

AREA: 209,000 hectares.

FEATURES: Bungle Bungle Range, Ord River.

HIGHLIGHTS: Scenic helicopter flights, walks through gorges.

GATEWAYS: Kununurra (p. 741), Halls Creek (p. 744), Warmun (below).

CAMPING: At Walardi and Kurrajong campsites, or registered overnight bush camping ($9 per night per person).

FEES: Entry $9 per vehicle.

▣ ◪ TRANSPORTATION & PRACTICAL INFORMATION

There are two ways into Purnululu: by road or by air. While the drive in is grueling, it also offers wonderful scenery, and having your car in the park gives you independence. Alternatively, a flight-tour option offers the famous views of the park from above, but it doesn't come cheap. To drive to Purnululu, you need a high clearance 4WD. The **Spring Creek Track,** leaves the Great Northern Hwy. 250km south of Kununurra and 109km north of Halls Creek. For 53km, the track rumbles, splashes, bumps, and grinds its way to the Visitors Centre. Allow five hours driving time from Kununurra or four hours from Halls Creek to reach the park; the Spring Creek Track alone takes from 1½ to 3hr. depending on conditions and traffic. The vehicle **entry fee** is $9; fees are payable 24hr. at the **Visitors Centre** near the entrance to the park.

Vehicular access to the park is closed during the Wet (Jan. until the track is passable, usually Mar.), but temporary closure due to rain is possible at other times. Call the **Department of Conservation and Land Management** (☎9168 4200) for conditions. **Camping ❶** is $9 per person. The park has toilets and untreated water, but no food or fuel.

⛺ CAMPING

The only two legal campsites available within the park have untreated water, toilets, and firewood. A left at the T after the Visitors Centre leads after 7km to **Kurrajong campsite ❶**, in the region of the park near Echidna Chasm and Froghole Gorge. After a right at the T, it's 13km to the quieter **Walardi campsite ❶**, closer to the domes. (All sites $9.)

🥾 HIKING

BUNGLE BUNGLE RANGE
This range is composed of fragile sandstone; to protect this natural wonder, people are not allowed to climb to the top. Fantastic walking trails wind around and through the formations. They can occasionally be difficult to follow, but nearly all follow dry stream beds—when off the stream bed, stay on marked and well worn trails, as moving off the trail can damage plant life. Bring enough water. Three walks depart from Piccanninny Gorge carpark, 25km south of the Visitors Centre.

Domes Walk (1km). The only trail to actually feature the famous domes, a relaxed circuit links up with the Cathedral Gorge Walk.

Cathedral Gorge Walk (3km return; allow 1½hr.). This easy trail follows a river bed up the gorge to the immense Wet-only waterfall at the end. The hollowed-out pool and surrounding amphitheater are of a humbling scale and beauty. The Domes Walk loops into the Cathedral Gorge Walk; the two are best done in conjunction.

Piccanninny Creek and Gorge Trail (30km return). The longest walk; hiking the entire length requires spending the night on the trail (register with the ranger station before departing). The first 7km is a smooth trail over bedrock and makes a nice dayhike. From there, the trail turns into the range and becomes rocky and much more difficult.

WESTERN HIKES
The western section of the park features an imposing conglomerate escarpment. Though none of the famous and domes are to be found here, the walks through the gorges here just as awe-inspiring as their eastern counterparts.

Echidna Chasm (2km return). A flat gravel path threads the improbably narrow crevice cut in the towering red rock by millions of Wet season downpours. The passage squeezes past a pair of boulders fallen from the rock walls and leads up a short steel ladder to a modest chamber at the end of the crack. At midday, the sense of wonder is heightened by the sun's rays probing the tops of the walls along the path.

Froghole Gorge (1.4km return). A challenging and rewarding scramble and squeeze among a field of fallen boulders leads through a palm-filled valley to a small pool filled with hundreds of tiny rockhole frogs. **Walanginjdji Lookout** (500m return), a short, sandy side trail to a peaceful spot, gives a great view of the range's western cliffs.

Mini Palms Gorge (5km return). The park's most difficult day trail follows rocky river beds to a steep and boulder-strewn final ascent to a series of levels, the last of which is an observation platform. The view from atop is less captivating, looking as much back over the trail as forward into an area of palms.

APPENDIX

AUSSIE BEVERAGE GUIDE

TERMS OF EMBEERMENT

Nothing's more Australian than **beer,** and accordingly, the language used for it has an Aussie twist too. Because of the hot climate, Australian pubs generally eschew the British pint in favor of smaller portions, which stay cold until you're done. Thus, size is a major variable in the argot of ale. If you're too drunk to think of the proper terms, ordering by size, in ounces, usually works. On the mainland, try a "5," "7," "10," or "15." In Tasmania, order using the numbers "6," "8," "10," or "20." Most importantly, don't forget to **shout** your new-found mates a round—that is, to buy them all a drink.

REGION	BRING ME A...	STATE BEER
New South Wales	Pony 140mL (5 oz.), Beer / Glass 200mL (7 oz.), Middy 285mL (10 oz.), Schooner 425mL (15 oz.)	Tooheys
Northern Territory	Darwin Stubbie 1.25L (40 oz.) bottle	"None"
Queensland	Beer / Glass 200mL (7 oz.), Pot 285mL (10 oz.), Schooner 425mL (15 oz.)	XXXX
South Australia	Butcher 200mL (7 oz.), Middy / Schooner 285mL (10 oz.), Pint 425mL (15 oz., smaller than the British or American pint), Real Pint 560mL (20 oz.)	Coopers
Tasmania	Real Pint 560mL (20 oz.)	Cascade, Boag's
Victoria	Beer / Glass 200mL (7 oz.), Pot 285mL (10 oz.)	VB
Western Australia	Bobby / Beer 200mL (7 oz.), Middy 285mL (10 oz.), Pot 425mL (15 oz.)	Emu Bitter
Australia	Handle 285mL (10 oz.) glass with handle, Long Neck 750mL (25 oz.) bottle, Stubbie 375mL (12 oz.) bottle, Tinny 375mL (12 oz.) can, Slab case of 24 beers	

COOL BEANS

Australians love **coffee** and have plenty of ways to prepare it. Any of these drinks can be made weak, medium, or strong. Coffee drinks are all made with espresso, as opposed to automatic-drip style brewing machines, so black coffee is generally a bit stronger in Australia. Whole milk is always used unless you specify lowfat ("skim"). The American milk variety of "cream" is not used.

WHAT TO ORDER...	...AND WHAT YOU'LL GET.
short black	60mL of espresso
long black	120-200mL of espresso
flat white	espresso with cold milk
cafe latte	espresso, hot milk, and froth
cappuccino	espresso, hot milk, and heaps of froth
macchiato	espresso with a bit of froth
vienna coffee	espresso, whipped cream, and powdered chocolate

GLOSSARY OF 'STRINE

'Strine is 'stralian for "Australian." The main thing to remember when speaking Australian slang is to abbreviate everything: **Oz** for Australia, **brekkie** for breakfast, **cuppa** for cup of tea, **uni** for university. Australian **pronunciation** is harder to learn than the lingo—with Aboriginal words especially, but even with English-derived proper nouns, it's difficult to pin down any definite "rules." One quirk to note: when Australians spell a word out or pronounce a number, they always use the expression "double," as in "double-seven" (77).

ablution block: shower/toilet block at a campground
abseil: rappel
ace: awesome
aggro: aggravated
ANZAC biscuits: honey-oat cookies
arvo: afternoon
Aussie: Australian (pronounced Ozzie—thus, "Australia" is "Oz")
backpackers: hostel
bagged: criticized
barbie: barbecue
bathers: bathing suit
beaut: as in "You beaut!", positive exclamation
beetroot: beet, a common hamburger filling
belt bag: fanny pack (don't say "fanny" in Oz: it's a crude word for a part of the female anatomy)
billabong: a water hole
biro: pen
biscuit: cookie
bitumen: a rough black asphalt used to pave roads
bloke: guy, man (familiar)
bludger: malingerer
bluey: someone with red hair (seriously)
bonnet: hood of a car
boofhead: fool
book: make reservations
boot: trunk of a car
bottle shop: liquor store
brekkie: breakfast
Brizzy: Brisbane, QLD
bugger: damn
Bundy: Bundaberg, QLD, as in the rum
bush: scrubby countryside
bush tucker: traditional Aboriginal wild foods
bushwalking: hiking
busk: to play music on the street for money
BYO: bring your own alcohol
campervan: mobile home, RV
capsicum: bell peppers
caravan: a trailer; term for any sort of cabless campervan
carpark: parking lot

chap: guy, man; see "bloke"
chemist: pharmacy
chips: thick french fries, often served with vinegar and salt
chock-a-block: crowded
chook: chicken
chunder: vomit
coldie: a cold beer
concession: discount; usually applies to students, seniors, or children, sometimes only to Australian students and pensioners
cordial: concentrated fruit juice
cossie: swimsuit
crook: sick
crow eater: South Australian (a tad disparaging)
D&M: deep and meaningful conversation
dag: one who is daggy (usage is common, often benevolent)
daggy: unfashionable, goofy
damper: a term for traditionally unleavened bread
dear: expensive
dill: silly person (affectionate).
dobber: tattle-tale
dodgy: sketchy
doona, duvet: comforter, feather blanket
dramas: problems. "no dramas" = "no worries"
drink driving: driving under the influence of alcohol
drongo: idiot
dunny: toilet, often outdoors.
ensuite: with bath
entree: appetizer ("main" is a main dish)
esky: a cooler
excess: deductible (as in car insurance)
fair dinkum: genuine
fair go: equal opportunity
fairy floss: cotton candy
fancy: to like; as in "would you fancy...?"
feral: wild, punky, grungy
flash: fancy, snazzy
free call: toll-free call
full on: intense
furphy: tall tale, exaggerated rumor (as in, "tell a furphy")

g'day: hello
give it a go: to try
good onya: good for you
glasshouse: greenhouse
grommet: young surfer
ground floor: American first floor ("first floor" is second floor, etc.)
grog: booze
hire: to rent
hitching: hitchhiking
holiday: vacation
hoon: loud-mouth, show-off
icy-pole: popsicle (any sweet frozen treat on a stick)
jackaroo: stationhand-in-training
jersey: sweater, sweatshirt
jillaroo: female jackaroo
journo: journalist
jumper: see "jersey"
keen: term of respect ("a keen surfer")
Kiwi: New Zealander
knackered: really tired
lad: guy, man; see "chap"
licensed: serves alcohol
like hen's teeth: rare
lollies: candies
magic: really wonderful, special
mate: friend, buddy (used broadly)
milk bar: convenience store
Milo: chocolate product in bar and drink varieties
mobile: cell phone
moke: an open-air, golf-cart-esque vehicle
mozzie: mosquito
nappy: diaper
narky: annoyed
newsagent: newsstand/convenience store
nibblies: snacks
no worries: sure, fine, or "you're welcome"
ocker: hick, Crocodile Dundee-type
ordinary: bad; an "ordinary" road is full of potholes.
Owyergoin'?: How are you?
Oz: Australia
pavlova: a creamy meringue dessert garnished with fruit
pensioner: senior citizen
perve: a pervert, also used as a verb, "to perve"
petrol: gasoline
piss: beer (usually)
pissed: drunk (usually)
pokies: gambling machines
polly: politician
Pom: person from England
powerpoint: power outlet
prawn: jumbo shrimp

pub: bar
raging: partying
ratbag: corrupt, unethical person
rego: car registratrion papers
return: round-trip
'roo: as in kanga-
roobar: bumper protecting your car from 'roo damage
roundabout: traffic rotary
rubber: eraser
sauce: usually tomato sauce; closest equivalent to ketchup
serviette: napkin
sheila: slang for a woman
shout: buy a drink or round of drinks for others; also a noun, as in an evening's worth of everyone buying rounds for each other
side: team
singlet: tank top or undershirt
skivvie: turtleneck sweater
sook: crybaby; see "winge"
spider: ice cream float or nasty arachnid (use context clues here)
squiz: a look, as in, "to take a squiz at something"
sticky beak: nosy person
'strine: Aussie dialect (from Australian)
'straya: Australia
swimmers: swimsuit
sunnies: sunglasses
suss: figure out, sort out
ta: short for thank you—usually muttered under breath
ta ta: goodbye
TAB: shop to place bets, sometimes in pubs
takeaway: food to go, takeout
Tassie: Tasmania (TAZ-zie)
tea: evening meal
thongs: flip-flops
throw a wobbly: get angry
Tim Tams: chocolate- covered cookie
torch: flashlight
touch wood: knock on wood
trackies: sweatpants
track suit: sweat suit, jogging suit
uni: university (YOU-nee)
unsealed: unpaved roads, usually gravel, sometimes dirt
ute (yute): utility vehicle, pickup truck
upmarket: upscale, expensive
Vegemite: yeast-extract spread for toast and sammies
veggo: vegetarian
wanker: jerk (rude term)
winge: to whine or complain
yakka: hard work
yobbo: slobby, unthinking person
zed: Z (American "zee")

TEMPERATURES

CELSIUS–FARENHEIT CONVERSION

To convert from °C to °F, multiply by 1.8 and add 32. For a rough approximation, double the Celsius and add 25. To convert from °F to °C, subtract 32 and multiply by 0.55. For a rough approximation, subtract 25 and cut it in half.

°CELSIUS	-5	0	5	10	15	20	25	30	35	40
°FAHRENHEIT	23	32	41	50	59	68	77	86	95	104

AVERAGE TEMPERATURES

LO/HI PRECIPITATION	JANUARY			APRIL			JULY			OCTOBER		
	°C	°F	mm	°C	°F	mm	°C	°F	mm	°C	°F	mm
Adelaide, SA	16/28	61/82	19	12/22	54/72	43	7/15	45/59	65	10/21	50/70	43
Alice Springs, NT	21/36	70/97	40	13/28	55/82	17	4/19	39/66	12	15/31	59/88	20
Brisbane, QLD	21/29	70/84	161	17/26	63/79	89	10/20	50/68	57	16/26	61/79	77
Cairns, QLD	24/31	75/88	407	22/29	72/84	200	17/26	63/79	27	20/29	68/84	38
Canberra, ACT	13/28	55/82	58	7/20	45/68	53	0/11	32/52	40	6/19	43/66	67
Darwin, NT	25/32	77/90	393	24/33	75/91	103	20/31	68/88	1	25/34	77/93	52
Hobart, TAS	12/22	54/72	48	9/17	48/63	52	4/12	39/54	54	8/17	46/63	64
Melbourne, VIC	14/26	57/79	48	11/20	52/68	58	6/13	43/55	49	9/20	48/68	68
Perth, WA	18/30	64/86	9	14/25	57/77	46	9/18	48/64	173	12/22	54/72	55
Sydney, NSW	18/26	64/79	98	14/23	59/72	129	8/16	46/61	100	13/22	55/72	79

APPENDIX

INDEX

A

AAA. See Australian
  Automobile Association.
Aboriginal
  art 18, 94, 98, 133, 149,
    150, 161, 225, 254, 258,
    269, 290, 291, 292, 296,
    297, 304, 308, 310, 311,
    315, 334, 335, 393, 406,
    451, 501, 549, 552, 627,
    631, 692, 727
  cultural centers 218, 274,
    282, 304, 392, 434, 470,
    549, 630, 701
  Dreaming 9, 16
  history 9
  sacred sites 9
  Stolen Generations 12
  tours 158, 252, 281, 292,
    298, 305, 436, 443, 451,
    475, 631, 651, 692
Abrolhos Islands, WA 718
abseiling 85
acacia 72
accommodations 37–41
  bed and breakfasts 40
  campers and RVs 41
  camping 41, 76–79
  hostels 37
  hotels 39
  university dorms 40
adaptors 35
Adelaide Hills, SA 475
Adelaide Wetlands, NT 272
Adelaide, SA 462–475
  accommodations 467–
    468
  daytrips 474
  emergency and
    communications 467
  entertainment 472
  festivals 473
  food 469–470
  local services 467
  media and publications
    467
  nightlife 473–474
  orientation 464
  practical information
    466–467
  sights 470–471
  tourist and financial

services 466
transportation, intercity
  462–464
transportation, local
  465–466
adventure activities
  land 85
  organized trips 85
  water 84
aerogrammes 41
Agnes Water, QLD 387
AIDS 34
Airlie Beach, QLD 401–406
airplanes. See flights.
Albany, WA 706
Albury, NSW 242–244
alcohol 31
Aldgate, SA 475
Alexandra Heads, QLD 362
Alice Springs, NT 300–306
Alternatives to Tourism
  62–71
American Express 27, 28,
  29, 35, 53
American Red Cross 32
Anakie, QLD 454
Angahook-Lorne State
  Park, VIC 616
Anglesea, VIC 615
animals 73–76
  dangerous 75
Anzac Day 11
Apollo Bay, VIC 616
Arkaroola, SA 509
Armidale, NSW 217
Arnhem Land, NT 291–297
Arno Bay, SA 516
arts
  film 18
  literature 16
  music 17
  visual arts 18
Asbestos Range National
  Park, TAS. See
  Narawntapu National
  Park.
Ashes, the 15
Atherton Tablelands, QLD
  436–439
Atherton, QLD 437
ATM cards 28
Augusta, WA 698
Austinmer, NSW 226

Australia and New Zealand
  Army Corps (ANZAC) 11
Australia Post 41
Australian Alps, VIC 669
Australian Automobile
  Association (AAA) 55
**Australian Capital
  Territory** 86–99
Australian Football League
  (AFL) 15
  Adelaide, SA 472
  Brisbane, QLD 338
  Darwin, NT 271
  Melbourne, VIC 590, 596
  Sydney, NSW 135, 140
Australian Open 16, 590,
  597
Australian Quarantine and
  Inspections Service 25
Australian Tourist
  Commission 23
Australind, WA 696
automobile assistance 55
Ayers Rock Resort, NT. See
  Yulara.
Ayers Rock, NT. See Uluru.

B

B&Bs 40
backpacks 77
Bairnsdale, VIC 669
Balancing Rock, QLD 361
Bald Rock National Park,
  NSW 216, 361
Balladonia, WA 520
Ballarat, VIC 635–639
Ballina, NSW 198
bandicoot 73
Bangalow, NSW 201
banksia 73
Barossa Valley, SA 488–
  492
Barron Gorge National
  Park, QLD 437
Batavia Coast, WA 716–
  720
Batemans Bay, NSW 231
Bathurst, NSW 246
Battery Point, TAS 531
Bay of Fires Coastal
  Reserve, TAS 560
Bay of Islands Coastal

MAP INDEX

MAP LEGEND

- Point of Interest
- Accommodations
- Camping
- Food
- Nightlife
- Shopping
- Winery
- Adult Entertainment
- Airport
- Bank
- Beach
- Bus Station

- Cave
- Church
- Consulate
- Ferry Landing
- Garden
- Golf Course
- Hospital
- Internet Café
- Library
- Lighthouse
- Mountain
- Museum

- Pharmacy
- Police
- Post Office
- Ranger Station
- Restrooms
- Shipwreck
- Synagogue
- Telephone Office
- Theater
- Tourist Office
- Train Station
- Waterfall

- Beach
- Building
- Park
- Water
- 4WD Road
- Ferry Line
- Pedestrian Zone
- Railroad
- State Boundary
- Unsealed Road
- Walking Trail

The Let's Go compass
always points NORTH.